THE AMERICAN PRESIDENT

FALL RIVER PRESS

New York

An Imprint of Sterling Publishing
387 Park Avenue South
New York, NY 10016

FALL RIVER PRESS and the distinctive Fall River Press logo are registered trademarks of Barnes & Noble, Inc.

Interior design by Christine Heun

ISBN 978-1-4351-4602-0 (print format)
ISBN 978-1-4351-4067-7 (ebook)

Distributed in Canada by Sterling Publishing
c/o Canadian Manda Group, 165 Dufferin Street
Toronto, Ontario, Canada M6K 3H6
Distributed in the United Kingdom by GMC Distribution Services
Castle Place, 166 High Street, Lewes, East Sussex, England BN7 1XU
Distributed in Australia by Capricorn Link (Australia) Pty. Ltd.
P.O. Box 704, Windsor, NSW 2756, Australia

For information about custom editions, special sales, and premium and corporate purchases, please contact Sterling Special Sales at 800-805-5489 or specialsales@sterlingpublishing.com.

Manufactured in the United States of America

2 4 6 8 10 9 7 5 3 1

www.sterlingpublishing.com

Disclaimer: Every effort has been made to verify the facts presented in this book. Historians, however, sometimes disagree about certain pieces of information—popular vote tallies, for instance—so prevailing opinion has been presented herein.

PAGE II–III: HERBERT HOOVER'S INAUGURATION AT THE CAPITOL ON MARCH 4, 1929. DESPITE LIGHT RAIN, A LARGE CROWD GATHERED TO HEAR PRESIDENT HOOVER SPEAK.

PAGE X–1: PRESIDENT WILLIAM MCKINLEY TAKES THE OATH OF OFFICE FOR HIS SECOND TERM ON A COVERED PLATFORM IN FRONT OF THE EAST PORTICO OF THE CAPITOL ON MARCH 4, 1901. THEODORE ROOSEVELT IS MCKINLEY'S NEW VICE PRESIDENT.

★ ★ ★ ACKNOWLEDGMENTS ★ ★ ★

This book, as with many projects, took longer than anticipated. I owe an enormous debt of gratitude to my family, friends, and colleagues whose encouragement never wavered (although my spirits sometimes did!). Thanks to the staff at Barnes & Noble for their support and help throughout the extensive publication process.

I am especially grateful to my mother Barbara Moore who instilled in me a love of history and a desire to learn more about the fascinating people behind it. My husband D.M. Giangreco has provided invaluable assistance at every step by discussing content and making editing suggestions. Most of all, my thanks to our sons Michael and Steven for their abundance of patience with me while my evenings, weekends, and holidays were usually spent writing.

Soon after I signed the contract for *The American President*, my father died following a short illness. This book is dedicated to Jack Moore and his steady support for all that I did. You are greatly missed, Dad.

CONTENTS

GEORGE WASHINGTON

JAMES MADISON

MARTIN VAN BUREN

ABRAHAM LINCOLN

GROVER CLEVELAND

Woodrow Wilson

Franklin D. Roosevelt

John F. Kennedy

Ronald Reagan

Barack H. Obama

Introduction

"I am heartily rejoiced that my term is so near its close. I will soon cease to be a servant and will become a sovereign," wrote eleventh president James K. Polk. Nearly identical sentiments revealing an enormous sense of relief surface repeatedly as America's chief executives prepare to leave behind the responsibilities of the presidency. Although many had fought furiously to reach the pinnacle of power, most were glad to hand over its reins to their successors.

This book is an attempt to provide not only an objective account of each presidency and an appreciation of each man's character and abilities, but perhaps equally important, describe events and people shaping the lives of those who have taken the presidential oath of office. By and large, each man had the intellect and ability to hold the post, sometimes rising to meet the challenges of his time. Each was also human, complex, and contradictory, with flaws and foibles that often resulted in his being revered or dismissed. Historians often attempt to discern commonalities among this small group of men in the hope of determining what attributes best prepare a person for the presidency. The following illustrates some of these shared characteristics.

> *"It isn't how long you are president that counts, but what you accomplish as president. I've had my chance; I did fairly well with it. I made some kind of a place in history for myself. Someone else might have done better than I did, but I could not; for I did my best."*
>
> —*Theodore Roosevelt*

Most of the presidents were middle-born, with the greatest of that number being the second child of the family. Episcopalian has been the predominant religious affiliation (eleven), with Presbyterian having the second highest number (six). While being an attorney is the primary occupation, many presidents could also list academic or military experience on a résumé. Most had served in some type of elected office before moving to the nation's highest. Fourteen had previously served as vice presidents; five were US senators; and nineteen had been elected to the House of Representatives. (John Quincy Adams's tenure in the House was after his presidential term.)

When running as a presidential candidate, most winners have been Republicans (eighteen). Fourteen have been Democrats; and the rest represented earlier political parties. Most were in their fifties at the time of their inauguration, but Theodore Roosevelt still holds the record as the youngest president, at age forty-two (John F. Kennedy was the youngest elected president, at forty-three), and Ronald Reagan was the oldest when he was sworn in, at age sixty-nine.

Much about the presidency has evolved and grown over the lifetime of the institution. George Washington had five cabinet members and a handful of staff to run the executive branch. His salary was set at $25,000 (although he refused it) and that salary would not increase for nearly one hundred years. The current White House office staff numbers over four hundred, but each cabinet member rules a sizeable bureaucracy. Presidents now earn $400,000 yearly and, beginning with Truman, are also paid a pension.

Not only has the office of the presidency changed over the last two centuries, but the theory of democracy continues to evolve, inspiring discussion and passion along recurring political themes. Debate marches on about the need for more or less government in the lives of its citizens, especially in terms of regulating, taxing, and supporting the masses. Should power reside with the federal or state governments, the executive, legislative, or judicial branch, or should we attempt a balance, and how? Should we be isolationists or the world's superpower and police? These questions continue to divide the nation and have often influenced and shaped an administration.

President James K. Polk, 1846

President James K. Polk, 1849

The upward climb to the presidency often reveals itself to be much easier than undertaking the tasks and responsibilities of the office. Enemies abound and their actions have resulted in the deaths of four presidents and multiple attempts on the lives of others. Another four died of natural causes during their term. Unquestionably, the job of running the country—whether a century ago or today—takes its toll on a person. One merely needs to examine photographs taken "before" and "after" presidential terms to discern the shocking change exacted by the time spent in the nation's highest office. (The two official portraits of President Polk shown here, painted by the same artist, are a dramatic example. The first was painted at the beginning of his term, in 1846, and the second at the end of his term in 1849.)

Finally, every president is concerned with how he will be viewed by future generations. With the fate of his country and more recently, the world, upon his shoulders, each occupant has contemplated how he would be remembered, hoping that his decisions would be greeted positively by posterity.

Historian Arthur Schlesinger Sr. introduced the practice of rating presidents in 1948, and other surveys have been conducted since that time. The majority of chief executives are typically ranked in the average category, with the "great" including Washington, Abraham Lincoln, and Franklin D. Roosevelt. Those often in the bottom ranking include Andrew Johnson, Franklin Pierce, Warren G. Harding, and James Buchanan. Such lists, however, should be treated with caution, I believe. How does one compare the presidency of a Franklin Roosevelt dealing with the nation's worst fiscal depression and then World War II with, say, a Calvin Coolidge who was president during the booming 1920s? Those who served in the nation's highest office would probably concur with fellow president Theodore Roosevelt: "It isn't how long you are president that counts, but what you accomplish as president. I've had my chance; I did fairly well with it. I made some kind of a place in history for myself. Someone else might have done better than I did, but I could not; for I did my best."

GEORGE WASHINGTON

★ ★ ★ FIRST PRESIDENT ★ ★ ★

LIFE SPAN
- Born: February 22, 1732, in Westmoreland County, Virginia
- Died: December 14, 1799, at Mount Vernon, Virginia

NICKNAME
- Father of his Country

RELIGION
- Episcopalian

HIGHER EDUCATION
- None

PROFESSION
- Land surveyor, politician, farmer

MILITARY SERVICE
- Lieutenant Colonel in French and Indian War
- Led Continental Army to victory against the British in Revolutionary War

FAMILY
- Father: **Augustine Washington** (1694–1743)
- Mother: **Mary Ball Washington** (1708–1789)
- Wife: **Martha Dandridge Custis Washington** (1731–1802; a widow with two small children); wed January 6, 1759, at New Kent County, Virginia
- Stepchildren: **John "Jacky" Parke Custis** (1754–1781); **Martha "Patsy" Parke Custis** (1756–1773)

POLITICAL LIFE
- Virginia House of Burgesses (1758)
- Justice of the Peace, Fairfax County (1770)
- Delegate to the Williamsburg Convention (1771)
- Delegate to the First Continental Congress (1774)
- Delegate to the Second Continental Congress (1775)
- Delegate and president of the Constitutional Convention (1787)

PRESIDENCY
- Two terms: April 30, 1789–March 4, 1797
- No political party (opposed formation of political parties)
- Reason for leaving office: set precedent of two-term presidency
- Vice president: **John Adams** (1789–1797)

ELECTION OF 1789
- Electoral vote: unanimously elected by newly formed Electoral College (the only person ever to be elected president unanimously)
- Popular vote: none

ELECTION OF 1792
- Electoral vote: unanimously elected by newly formed Electoral College
- Popular vote: none

CABINET

SECRETARY OF STATE
Thomas Jefferson (1789–1793)
Edmund Randolph (1794–1795)
Timothy Pickering (1795–1797)

SECRETARY OF THE TREASURY
Alexander Hamilton (1789–1795)
Oliver Wolcott Jr. (1795–1797)

SECRETARY OF WAR
Henry Knox (1789–1794)
Timothy Pickering (1795–1796)
James McHenry (1796–1797)

ATTORNEY GENERAL
Edmund Randolph (1789–1793)
William Bradford (1794–1795)
Charles Lee (1795–1797)

POSTMASTER GENERAL
Samuel Osgood (1789–1791)
Timothy Pickering (1791–1795)
Joseph Habersham (1795–1797)

Towering above the city bearing his name is an obelisk rising more than 555 feet (169m) high. It is fitting that the Washington Monument soars higher than any other monument in the city, for during his lifetime George Washington's presence acted as a beacon of hope to all, as Americans endured war and took their first shaky steps as a new nation.

EARLY LIFE

Born February 22, 1732, at Pope's Creek in Westmoreland County, Virginia, George Washington was the first son of Augustine "Gus" Washington and his second wife, Mary Ball. Augustine had two sons, Lawrence and Augustine, by his first wife, who died in 1729. He remarried over a year later. George was later joined by three brothers and one sister who lived to adulthood.

George Washington's early education apparently only included the basics taught by tutors at home and in nearby schoolhouses. Mathematics became his favorite subject. When he was only eleven years old, he lost his father. The two had never been particularly close—Gus, a slave-owning planter, was often away acquiring and overseeing land in other parts of Virginia, and had business in England, as well. Consequently, George's older half-brother Lawrence stepped in and became his surrogate father.

Lawrence had served at sea under British admiral Edward Vernon, and younger brother George looked to a life at sea as a respectable vocation. Mary Ball Washington strongly disagreed. Unable to follow his dream, George left his mother and moved in to Lawrence's estate, Mount Vernon. He also taught himself how to survey—a first step toward earning a living while waiting to inherit land from his father's estate, which would occur when he turned twenty-one.

Lawrence had married neighbor Ann Fairfax of the wealthy and powerful family at Belvoir plantation. This new familial connection enabled young George to broaden his world. Always graceful in the saddle, as well as on the dance floor, he became a favorite for parties at the Belvoir estate. At six feet three inches, he easily stood above anyone in a room and caught the eye of many a young lady.

Washington continued his education by reading classics from the family library and enjoying musical entertainments, although he refrained from singing or playing an instrument. Most importantly, Washington joined the circle of men who discussed the economy, the price of tobacco, and the issues concerning Virginia, as well as its mother country. Lord Fairfax and his friends were impressed by the young man and decided to offer him a job that would take him deep into the frontier that he would later defend.

GOING WEST

By 1748, Virginians greedily eyed lands to the west in the Shenandoah Valley. Speculators snapped up titles, but disputes over land grants abounded; consequently, accurate surveys were desperately needed. Lord Fairfax employed a local surveyor for the task but also asked sixteen-year-old George Washington to be the assistant. Eager for the chance, George agreed; however, he still needed his mother's permission. Mary Washington only acquiesced when she was told her son would be paid. The next month Washington was viewing a world of endless economic potential, in his words "[spending] the best part of the day in admiring the trees and richness of the land."[1] The surveying team traveled by horseback through rugged terrain and swollen rivers, paddling canoes when necessary. They met German settlers, and even

NATIONAL EVENTS

FEB 4: Presidential electors cast votes for first time

MAR 4: First Congress convenes in New York City

APR 30: Washington sworn in at first presidential inauguration, New York City

JUL 4: Congress passes first tax

JUL 27: Congress creates the Department of Foreign Affairs (renamed Department of State on SEP 15)

AUG 7: War Department established

SEP 2: Department of the Treasury established

1789

WORLD EVENTS

JAN 17: Antoine Lavoisier writes first modern chemistry book, *Traité Élémentaire de Chimie (Elementary Treatise of Chemistry)*

APR: Ottoman sultan Abdul Hamid I succeeded by Selim III

APR 28: Sailors aboard the HMS *Bounty* mutiny

MAY 5: Estates-General convenes in France for the first time in 175 years

JUN 14: HMS *Bounty* mutiny survivors reach Timor after 4,000-mile journey

Native Americans "coming from war with only one scalp,"[2] who performed a war dance for them. They battled heavy rain and floods. Nevertheless, the teenager performed his tasks and all that was required with aplomb and skill. Lord Fairfax's choice had served well.

When the job was completed, Washington returned to Belvoir for a festive occasion—young George William Fairfax had recently married and brought home his bride, Sally Cary. Nearly two years his senior, Sally instantly captivated Washington with her beauty, wit, and charm. He became smitten and cherished any time he spent in the lady's company.

After acquiring his surveyor's license, Washington frequently trekked out to the frontier for other surveying jobs. He now had the title of Culpeper County surveyor, and continued as well in the employ of Lord Fairfax. He earned a healthy income, sometimes being paid in cash, other times in land, which allowed him to begin to plan for the future.

Plans were put on hold, however, when his brother Lawrence asked George to accompany him on a voyage to Barbados. After enduring years of illness and now tuberculosis, traveling to the Leeward Islands seemed the only remedy for Lawrence. Unfortunately, he did not improve, and George developed smallpox. With such a strong constitution, Washington survived the attack, but Lawrence died six months later.

Knowing that Lawrence's estate was to go to his infant daughter, George decided to request the unthinkable and asked Robert Dinwiddie, lieutenant governor of colonial Virginia, for Lawrence's adjutant general's position. Without military experience or powerful family connections, the thought of acquiring such a well-placed title seemed ludicrous. The governor, though, believed that the young man was deserving, and Washington was granted one of four military districts, albeit the smallest. George Washington was now Major Washington, a remarkable achievement for a man who had just turned twenty-one.

MAJOR WASHINGTON

After learning of a broadening French presence in the upper Ohio Valley—with the aim of controlling the many rivers there for transporting furs to Europe—Governor Dinwiddie wrote to King George II for instructions. His Majesty agreed that the French must be told to remove themselves from the region. The governor needed an emissary who could endure the travails of such a wilderness journey in winter—George Washington eagerly volunteered.

Washington and six other men, including a guide and an interpreter, began the nearly six-week journey to reach Fort Le Bouef near Lake Erie. Washington successfully delivered the ultimatum and gathered intelligence regarding the strength of the French. The French boasted over wine that "it was their absolute design to take possession of the Ohio, and by G-- they would do it, for though they were sensible that the English could raise two men for their one, yet they knew their [the English colonies'] motions were too slow and dilatory to prevent any undertaking of theirs."[3]

Washington survived numerous threats to his life during his journey back to the Virginia capital in Williamsburg, including being shot at by an Indian, falling into the icy Allegheny River, and sleeping in buckskins that froze to his body. These would not be the last instances when George Washington would narrowly escape death.

SUPREME COURT APPOINTMENTS

★★★★★★★★★★

John Jay, Chief Justice, 1789

James Wilson, 1789

John Rutledge, 1790

William Cushing, 1790

John Blair, 1790

James Iredell, 1790

Thomas Johnson, 1792

William Paterson, 1793

John Rutledge, 1795 (an associate justice 1790-1795)

Samuel Chase, 1796

Oliver Ellsworth, Chief Justice, 1796

SEP 24: Congress passes Federal Judiciary Act creating Supreme Court of six justices

SEP 25: Congress proposes 12 constitutional amendments

SEP 29: US Army established

OCT 15: Washington tours New England

OCT 19: John Jay appointed first chief justice of the Supreme Court

NOV 26: First Thanksgiving Day established

JUL: Scottish-Canadian explorer Alexander Mackenzie discovers Arctic Ocean

JUL 14: French Revolution begins with fall of the Bastille

AUG 26: French Assembly adopts *Declaration of the Rights of Man*

SEP 11: 100,000 Turks defeated by Russia in Battle of Rymnik

NOV 8: First bourbon whiskey distilled, quickly becomes popular

STATE OF THE UNION
★★★★★★★★★★

US POPULATION IN 1790
3,929,214

PRESIDENT'S SALARY
$25,000/year (he declined it)

STATES ADMITTED TO UNION
North Carolina, November 21, 1789 by ratification of the Constitution

Rhode Island, May 29, 1790 by ratification of the Constitution

Vermont, May 4, 1791

Kentucky, June 1, 1792

Tennessee, June 1, 1796

THE FRENCH AND INDIAN WAR

At Governor Dinwiddie's request, Washington wrote his report of the journey for publication, the account appearing not only in the colonies, but in London, as well. The governor subsequently promoted his emissary to lieutenant colonel and ordered him to recruit a hundred men from northeastern Virginia in response to the reported intentions of the French. In the spring of 1754, worried that the French might reach the new fort constructed by Virginians on the forks of the Ohio River (present-day Pittsburgh), Washington was ordered to defend the fort.

En route, Washington learned that the French had indeed seized the fort and constructed their own larger one on the same site and named it Fort Duquesne. Washington ordered a stockade, which was named Fort Necessity, to be built approximately fifty miles east in an open clearing known as the Great Meadows. One night, under cover of darkness, he, his fellow Virginians, and fifteen Iroquois attacked the French. Stunned by the surprise attack, the French barely retaliated. Their commander, Ensign Joseph Coulon de Jumonville, was killed by the Iroquois chief—war had begun.

On July 3, the French, led by Jumonville's brother, attacked Fort Necessity—"that little thing in the meadow,"[4] in the words of a Seneca chief. Washington's force was greatly outnumbered by the French, and Fort Necessity, being simply a depression in an open field, was at a severe disadvantage. Rain pounded and French sharpshooters picked off the Virginians. The French suggested surrender, a proposal that Washington was slow to accept. Finally, he sent an interpreter to open negotiations. For three hours, Lieutenant Colonel Washington considered his next action. Ultimately, he signed a surrender, unwittingly admitting to the "assassination" of Jumonville. The French would later use Washington's admission as "proof" that this was a war initiated and commenced by the British. The Battle of the Great Meadows, or the Battle of Fort Necessity, marked the beginning of the French and Indian War, and would be George Washington's only military surrender.

The disheartened officer returned to Virginia, assuming that his military career was at an end. His brother Lawrence's daughter had died, and his widow remarried. Washington resided at Mount Vernon, which his sister-in-law had now leased to him. Still, Washington longed to join the British military presence building up in Virginia preparing to march on the French Fort Duquesne.

King George and Parliament concluded that British regulars were more experienced and reliable than colonial militia so, in 1755, the British army was sent in force to win this war against its longtime foe. General Edward Braddock—who was more comfortable behind a desk pushing papers than sitting on a horse commanding men in battle—took charge in Virginia. Washington negotiated with Braddock for a position equal in rank to British officers; both agreed that Washington would serve as a volunteer and aide-de-camp to the general.

Washington fought dysentery and was dangerously ill for days while the army advanced toward its destination, Fort Duquesne. Wanting to participate in the upcoming victory, he managed to rejoin the army in its final march. On July 9, 1755, with only eleven miles to go, the French force of nine hundred men, mainly Native Americans, attacked British and colonial troops. Although superior in numbers, the British were

NATIONAL EVENTS

JAN 8: First State of the Union address

APR 17: Benjamin Franklin dies at age 84

APR 21: Franklin's funeral draws more than 20,000 mourners

MAY 31: Copyright Act is passed, mainly owing to Noah Webster's efforts

JUL–AUG: Pierre Charles L'Enfant chosen to design new capital city in District of Columbia

AUG 1: First census shows America's population at slightly less than four million

1790

WORLD EVENTS

FEB 20: Holy Roman Emperor Josef II dies in Vienna

MAR: Belgians revolt against new emperor Leopold

MAY 13: Russia defeats Sweden in Battle of Reval

JUL 9: Second Battle of Svensksund, Swedish navy captures one third of Russian fleet

AUG: Treaty of Värälä ends Russo-Swedish War

unable to recover from the shock of the screaming attackers who were snatching scalps with lightning speed. Washington watched the panic-stricken regulars run about and recalled, "Nothing but confusion and disobedience of orders prevailed among them."[5] The memory of that sight, as well as Braddock's stubborn insistence to fight in the open, would linger with Washington. He ended the day with two horses shot from under him, one musket ball hole in his hat and four through his coat. General Braddock, on the other hand, did not escape serious injury. He was shot in the lung and lingered for three days while Washington and other surviving officers supervised the retreat.

Upon his return to Virginia, Washington found himself a hero, as well as the sole officer of his colony to survive the battle without being wounded. He quickly wrote to family members assuring them he was alive, since word had circulated to the contrary. Twenty-three-year-old Washington used his newfound fame to bargain a plum assignment from Governor Dinwiddie. Now he would serve as a full colonel and commander in chief of the Virginia Regiment, with the power to appoint his own officers; be paid well and reimbursed for expenses; take responsibility for his own budget; and fashion a new uniform of his own design. Soon Washington was riding about the countryside exhorting militia to be vigilant against Native American attacks and correcting their lax discipline. He also recommended sites of new fortifications and improvements for existing ones. Being on frontier outposts and far from friends, family, and home gave him time to contemplate his future, and he decided to make a few changes.

After a whirlwind courtship, George and the wealthiest widow of Virginia, Martha Dandridge Custis, became engaged. On January 6, 1759, they were wed, and he soon resigned his military commission. Martha had two children, Jack and Patsy, both toddlers, from her first marriage to Daniel Parke Custis, and now George was content to retire to Mount Vernon with his new family. He also took his first steps in a political career and was elected to a seat in the Virginia House of Burgesses. George Washington was truly leading the life of a southern gentleman.

FRENCH AND INDIAN WAR (1754–1763) ★ The French and Indian War was actually the fourth installment in a series of wars between longtime rivals Great Britain and France. The first war, King William's War (1690–1697), did not settle the battle over the colonies. Another war, Queen Anne's War (1702–1713), continued the same bloody conflict on colonial frontiers, as French Canadians and their Indian allies attacked settlements in New England, and British colonists retaliated in kind. The Treaty of Utrecht ceded lands including Hudson Bay, Acadia, and Newfoundland to the British, but ill feelings remained between neighbors. A third war, King George's War (1744–1748), once again saw fighting on the frontier, but the status quo was returned with the Treaty of Aix-la-Chappelle. Seven years later, the ongoing tensions between France and Great Britain heightened yet again, with France controlling the lion's share of territory and attempting expansion. When the British pushed back (partly owing to the efforts of a very young Major George Washington), war ensued. This time, there was a major prize at the end—the winner took northern and eastern North America.

OCT 20–22: General Josiah Harmar is defeated near present-day Fort Wayne, Indiana, by Native Americans led by Little Turtle

DEC: National government moves to Philadelphia while Washington, D.C., is built

MAR: Congress passes a tax on whiskey

MAR 4: Vermont becomes 14th state

APR–MAY: President Washington tours southern states

1791

SEP 4: Amateur Swiss scientist Jacob Schweppe produces carbonated beverage in London

DEC 11: Russians storm Izmail, kill 26,000 Turks in Russo-Turkish War

MAR: Thomas Paine wanted for treason in Great Britain after publication of *The Rights of Man*, which calls for end of British monarchy; he flees to France

JUN: French royal family attempts to flee the country, but is recaptured

BATTLE OF THE MONONGAHELA, (July 9, 1755) ★ British General Edward Braddock and his force of fifteen hundred British and American colonial troops were ambushed approximately ten miles east of Fort Duquesne (present-day Pittsburgh). French troops and approximately six hundred Indian allies overwhelmed their enemy and imposed devastating casualties upon them in a bloody battle of hand-to-hand combat. Braddock was fatally wounded, and Washington was his only officer to escape from the conflict unscathed. The young Virginian took control and led the British and militia troops out of the area to safety.

CALM BEFORE THE STORM

While living at Mount Vernon, George Washington experimented with new farming techniques, including crop rotation, and switched from soil-destructive tobacco to wheat as his cash crop. He watched Martha's children grow and treated them as his own, but the couple never had any children of their own. Patsy suffered with epilepsy, and despite her parents' efforts to find medical treatment that would cure her, the fits continued until one killed her when she was a teenager.

As British trade policies gained a stranglehold on colonial affairs, Washington pushed for the colonies to take action. He supported boycotts of some imports, but resisted forbidding all British trade. In 1770, he undertook a task of special significance, inspecting lands of the Ohio country, which were compensation for the men who had served in the French and Indian War. Proudly he later wrote of this effort, "If it had not been for my unmerited attention to every favorable circumstance, not a single acre of land would ever have been obtained."[6]

Washington traveled to Philadelphia in 1774 as part of the Virginia delegation to the First Continental Congress. There he met other concerned colonists, including the Adams cousins—John and Samuel. They agreed to boycott British goods, as well as to meet again in May 1775.

The meeting in May occurred in a decidedly different atmosphere. Weeks before, British regulars and colonial militia had clashed at Lexington and Concord. Now the question of what action to take next needed to be addressed. The Second Continental Congress appointed Washington to head committees on military matters, hoping a southerner would be able to broaden support for the revolt beyond New England. His military service was a matter of record, and his uniform, which he wore daily to Congress, was a steady reminder of his pride of service.

On June 14, 1775, John Adams nominated Washington to become commander in chief of the newly created Continental army. The nominee immediately stepped out of the chamber so his fellow delegates could debate his qualifications. The following day he was unanimously elected general. He began writing letters to various friends, but most importantly to his wife Martha. He wrote, "Far from seeking this appointment, I have used every endeavor in my power to avoid it . . . It has been a kind of destiny, that has thrown me upon this service, I shall hope that my undertaking it is designed to answer some good purpose."[7]

GENERAL WASHINGTON

The new commander arrived in Cambridge, Massachusetts, on July 2, 1775. The army was still reeling from its loss at Bunker Hill weeks before, and New England officers greeted Washington with resentment. Lack of discipline and organization plagued

NATIONAL EVENTS

DEC 15: Bill of Rights ratified

FEB 20: Presidential Succession Act passed

APR: US Mint is created in Philadelphia

MAY: Captain Robert Gray finds and names Columbia River

MAY 17: New York Stock Exchange opens

JUN 1: Kentucky becomes 15th state

1792

WORLD EVENTS

AUG: Lafayette declared a traitor by French government; flees to Austria, where he is imprisoned

AUG 6: Berlin's Brandenburg Gate completed

SEP: Mozart premieres *The Magic Flute*; he dies in December

JAN: *A Vindication of the Rights of Women* is published in England by Mary Wollstonecraft and read widely in America

JAN 9: Treaty of Jassy ends Russo-Turkish War

MAR 16: King Gustav III of Sweden shot in the back at a midnight masquerade at the Royal Opera

the fledgling army. General Washington repeatedly begged Congress for more men and supplies while also pleading for a reorganization of the army and the development of a navy. These problems would dog Washington for the entire war.

An overwhelming defeat on New Year's eve of American forces attempting to invade Quebec dampened spirits as the year 1776 began, but Washington thrilled Bostonians when cannons miraculously hauled from Fort Ticonderoga at Lake Champlain in New York were installed, forcing the British from the city. Buoyed by this victory and the issuance of the Declaration of Independence, people looked forward to a quick end to the war. All hopes vanished, however, during the fighting in New York as the British soundly beat Washington time and again during the summer and fall. Faced with being outnumbered and, as John Adams said, "outgeneraled," Washington came within a hair of losing at least half his forces. Fortunately the British moved slowly and allowed Washington the opportunity to retreat. This he did, and continued to do so across New York and New Jersey, all the way across the Delaware River to Pennsylvania.

Determined not to give up—but fearing his men would when their enlistments expired at year's end—Washington planned a daring move. He would mount a surprise attack on Hessian troops garrisoned at Trenton, New Jersey, on Christmas night. The gamble worked, and he followed up this victory with another a fortnight later at Princeton. There he narrowly pulled victory from the jaws of defeat by slipping around the British at night and attacking them from the rear the following day. Washington led his men in the fighting, and a Pennsylvania militiaman wrote, "I saw him brave all the dangers of the field and his important life hanging as it were a single hair with a thousand deaths flying around him."[8]

> ***"A government is like fire, a handy servant, but a dangerous master."***
>
> *—George Washington, in Congress on his appointment as commander in chief, 1775*

Although 1777 began victoriously, Washington and the Continental army lost at Brandywine and Germantown, as well as at Philadelphia, forcing the Continental Congress to flee one step ahead of the British. Only the great victory of American troops at Saratoga, New York, in October provided any encouragement for the war-weary Americans. By now, Washington's staff had been joined by a French nobleman—Marquis de Lafayette. The nineteen-year-old quickly won over Washington with his sheer determination and desire to aid America in its quest for freedom. The two men shared a mutual regard for each other that lasted the rest of their lives.

Meanwhile, rumblings in Congress grew ever more vocal to replace Washington with Horatio Gates, the senior commander of the battle of Saratoga. Lacking a stellar record in the current conflict, detractors thought Washington incapable of winning the war and worked to remove him. Fortunately, despite their behind-the-scenes machinations, Washington remained in command.

Then in December, the army went into winter quarters, thus beginning the most depressing chapter yet of the Revolution—the encampment at Valley Forge. Washington watched his

SEP 18: President Washington lays cornerstone of the capitol in Washington, D.C.

OCT 12: Columbus Day celebrated for the first time, in New York City

OCT 13: *Farmer's Almanac* is published for the first time

NOV 7: Washington reelected president

APR: Citizen Genet arrives from France, works to initiate expeditions against the British, angering Washington and his government

1793

MAR 23: King Gustav III of Sweden dies; succeeded by his son Gustav IV Adolf

APR: France declares war against Prussia and Austria

AUG 10: Tuileries Palace stormed in French Revolution; Louis XVI arrested

SEP 2: September Massacres of the French Revolution

SEP 22: Republic of France proclaimed

JAN 21: French King Louis XVI is beheaded at the guillotine; his wife, Queen Marie Antoinette, is executed nine months later

AMERICAN REVOLUTION (1775–1783)

During this period of the second half of the eighteenth century, broad social shifts were occurring in American society and new republican ideals were being championed. When Britain determined the colonies should pay for their own defense and imposed a series of taxes to that end, the colonists protested against being taxed without representation. Fighting broke out in 1775, and in 1776, representatives of the thirteen colonies voted unanimously to adopt a Declaration of Independence. An alliance with France in 1778 allowed the newly formed United States of America to approach the strength of the British military. After British armies were captured at Saratoga in 1777 and Yorktown in 1781, the Treaty of Paris was signed in 1783, recognizing the United States as an independent nation bordered by British Canada on the north, Spanish Florida on the south, and the Mississippi River on the west. These are the battles George Washington was involved in.

NEW YORK CAMPAIGN (1776) ★ The campaign was a series of battles fought in August and September 1776. The first was the Battle of Long Island, where Washington's men were outnumbered two to one and hit from in front by Hessians and successfully cut off from behind by British general Sir William Howe's men. Although disheartened, Washington managed to save his remaining army by ferrying them across the East River to Manhattan at night. More battles and defeats ensued for the beleaguered Continental army as they retreated northward, and by the end of October, they were pushed out of New York to New Jersey.

BATTLE OF TRENTON, NEW JERSEY (December 25, 1776) ★ Knowing that enlistments were over as of December 31, 1776, and that the men's spirits were at an all-time low following their loss of New York, Washington crafted a plan to surprise Hessians camped at Trenton, New Jersey, on Christmas night. His plan worked and his twenty-four hundred men only suffered four deaths while capturing more than one thousand Hessians.

BATTLE OF BRANDYWINE, PENNSYLVANIA (September 11, 1777) ★ Hoping to prevent the British from taking Philadelphia, Washington fought them on the Brandywine River on September 11, 1777. Outmaneuvered by General Howe, and fighting against fog and confusion, the Americans lost the battle, and Philadelphia was taken two weeks later without a shot.

NATIONAL EVENTS

APR 22: Washington issues Proclamation of Neutrality, hoping to avoid war with Britain and France

DEC 31: Thomas Jefferson resigns as secretary of state

United States agrees to pay tribute to Barbary pirates of North Africa

MAR 14: Eli Whitney patents the cotton gin

MAR 27: Permanent US Navy established

1794

WORLD EVENTS

FEB 1: France declares war on Great Britain, thus making war against Britain, Holland, Spain, and the Holy Roman Empire

NOV 8: The Louvre palace opens as an art museum

DEC 22: Napoleon Bonaparte promoted to brigadier general at age 24

MAY 6: Haitian revolt against France begins

MAY 8: French scientist Antoine Lavoisier is guillotined

BATTLE OF GERMANTOWN, PENNSYLVANIA (October 4, 1777) ★ On October 4, 1777, five miles north of Philadelphia, Washington planned to surprise Howe's encampment as he had successfully done against the Hessians the year before. His efforts, however, failed this time when American forces encountered considerable resistance and were forced to retreat. More than a thousand men were killed or wounded; British losses were half that number.

BATTLE OF MONMOUTH, NEW JERSEY (June 28, 1778) ★ The struggle was the first battle for American troops following training by General Friedrich von Steuben at Valley Forge. Ten thousand Americans fought an equal force under the command of Lieutenant General Sir Henry Clinton in the drenching heat of June 1778, near Monmouth Courthouse, New Jersey. The beginning of the battle, however, started poorly for the Americans when General Charles Lee ordered his men to retreat, causing Washington to become quite upset and swear profusely at Lee, directing him to leave the field. The battle is considered a draw.

SIEGE OF YORKTOWN, VIRGINIA (September 28–October 17, 1781) ★ In the spring of 1781, Washington met with French leader Comte de Rochambeau at Newport, Rhode Island, to plan a joint military effort against the British. They determined that their best hope was to attack Lord Cornwallis's forces in Virginia. In July, Washington once again managed to pull a sleight of hand by fooling British commander General Clinton into believing that the Americans were planning to remain in the New York area and attack him. Leaving behind a small force for the charade, the rest of the continental troops marched southward and by September were in Williamsburg, Virginia.

Cornwallis was awaiting British support at Yorktown, but the French fleet cut off his plans and his hopes of escape. At the Battle of the Virgina Capes on September 5, the French under Admiral de Grasse successfully forced the British navy to retreat to New York, leaving Cornwallis to face his fate against Washington and the French. On October 9, the siege began as allied cannons pounded the British position continuously. Within the week, the British had pulled back, and the Americans and French moved in closer. When efforts to retreat across the York River failed on the night of October 16, Cornwallis determined he must ask for terms. Then on October 19, Cornwallis's men, numbering more than eight thousand, surrendered to the Americans and French, whose combined forces totaled more than seventeen thousand.

AUG: Whiskey Rebellion in southern Pennsylvania by poor farmers protesting whiskey tax

AUG 20: General "Mad" Anthony Wayne wins major victory over northwestern Indians at Battle of Fallen Timbers

NOV 19: Jay's Treaty concluded between United States and Great Britain

JUL 13: France defeats Prussian and Austrian forces at Battle of the Vosges

JUL 28: Maximilien Robespierre is guillotined

1795

JAN: Yazoo Land Act passed in Georgia, transferring millions of acres of present-day Mississippi and Alabama lands to land companies; ultimately, land claims will cost American taxpayers $8 million

Persian invaders led by Agha Mohammad Khan sack the Georgian capital Tiflis (Tblisi)

José Maria Guadalupe Cuervo receives the first license to produce tequila in New Spain

ragtag army of 11,000 men dwindle daily—some deserted, but more often the cause was death from disease, starvation, and the bitter cold. He lost nearly one-third of his men that winter. The remaining soldiers were drilled into a fighting force with the arrival of Prussian officer Baron Frederich von Steuben. Finally, in June 1778, the previously demoralized troops marched out of Valley Forge, heads high, for they now looked and acted like a disciplined army. Their endurance through that horrible winter symbolized the heroism shown by American patriots during "the times that try men's souls,"[9] as Thomas Paine wrote.

By 1778, French support began arriving. Washington led his troops to a tactical draw at the battle of Monmouth, New Jersey. Here they displayed their newfound discipline and looked and acted as one army.

Unable to win the war in New England or the middle states, the British next took the war to the south. The British sent General Charles Cornwallis, and Washington dispatched General Nathanael Greene. Fighting began in South Carolina and continued north to Virginia. In the meantime, Washington met with French General Comte de Rochambeau to plan how the French could work jointly to win a decisive victory over the British. The French disagreed with Washington on how best to achieve this goal and left him fearful about the future.

During this period, the traitorous actions of the American general Benedict Arnold to cede West Point to the British came to light, causing Washington, who had long been his champion, no small degree of discomfort. Further, mutinous activities by unpaid Pennsylvania soldiers began on the first day of 1781. General Washington subdued the uprising and ordered executions for two New Jersey ringleaders. Concerned that the French would not remain in the fight much longer, and wearying of the ongoing difficulties in keeping Americans fighting, he wrote that his country was on the "verge of ruin."[10] Fortunately, the tide turned and by the end of 1781, prospects for victory appeared more favorable.

Moving northward to Virginia, British general Cornwallis provided an opportunity for Washington's troops and the French to trap the British forces at Yorktown, Virginia. In September 1781, the French navy defeated the British in the battle of the Chesapeake, also known as the Battle of the Virginia Capes. It was the only major defeat for the Royal Navy in the eighteenth and nineteenth centuries. Next, the Franco-American troops arrived and tightened the noose around the British defensive works. Digging in, they laid siege to the British lines. For nearly three weeks, Cornwallis attempted to avoid the inevitable, but by mid-October he could delay no further.

On October 19, 1781, the British army surrendered, although General Cornwallis begged leave and sent his second in command to actually perform the painful duty. Washington refused to accept the snub and instead referred the officer to his own second in command. Although ecstatic about this surrender, Washington's spirits were dampened by the death of his stepson Jack Custis, who had served with him at Yorktown until he fell ill.

The last two years of the American Revolution were scenes of infrequent skirmishes but no large-scale battles. Washington returned to New York to keep British general Henry Clinton in check, but American officers grew restless from lack of pay. Some apparently contemplated dismantling Congress and replacing it with military authority—namely George Washington. Washington

NATIONAL EVENTS	**JAN 29:** Naturalization Act passed requiring five years residency	**JAN 31:** Alexander Hamilton resigns as secretary of the treasury	**FEB 7:** Eleventh Amendment ratified	**MAY 8:** First US life insurance policy issued by Insurance Company of North America (later Cigna)	**AUG 3:** Treaty of Greenville signed by General Wayne and 12 Ohio Indian tribes; cedes large tracts of their land to the United States
WORLD EVENTS	**APR 7:** France becomes first nation to adopt the metric system	**JUN 7:** Duchy of Luxembourg surrenders to French after 82 years of Austrian rule	**JUN 8:** Louis XVIII becomes titular king of France (becomes actual king APR 6, 1814)	**JUL 22:** Spain cedes its half of Hispaniola to France	**SEP 16:** British begin seizing Dutch colonies, beginning with the Cape of Good Hope

addressed the dissatisfied men with a speech that moved them to forego their scheme; instead, they signed a letter pledging their loyalty to Congress.

In 1783, the Treaty of Paris was finally signed, officially ending the American Revolutionary War between the Kingdom of Great Britain and the United States of America, and British troops packed and left American shores. In December, General Washington took leave of his staff and traveled home to Mount Vernon. The weary warrior had served his country and now only hoped for a peaceful retirement.

RETIREMENT, BUT NOT FOR LONG

Anxious to continue improvements at Mount Vernon, Washington immediately busied himself with enlarging and remodeling the house, as well as improving the plantation's productivity through better farming practices. Attempting to likewise raise his financial productivity, he renewed his longtime interest in land speculation. In 1784, he toured his western lands in the Shenandoah Valley, where he found, to his disgust, squatters who had moved onto his lands and now considered them their own. Washington disagreed. The squatters were not swayed, and a two-year legal wrangle ensued. Washington emerged victorious, but his reputation was damaged by the image of the absentee landlord mercilessly throwing peasants off his land.

Looking to the future, Washington struggled with his reliance on slavery. Officers, including Lafayette, had urged him to support emancipation with the successful conclusion of the Revolution. Conflicted by the understanding of the immorality of being a slave owner but foreseeing the complexity of such an emancipation, Washington considered whether he should free his slaves. Ultimately, he compromised by granting their emancipation in his will, but only after Martha's death.

Washington grew increasingly distressed by the ineffective means of government provided by the Articles of Confederation. In 1785, he wrote to fellow Virginian James Madison, "We are either a United people, or we are not. If the former, let us, in all matters of general concern act as a nation . . . If we are not, let us no longer act a farce by pretending to it."[11] This unicameral government lacked both executive and judicial branches, as well as basic powers, including taxation. States held the key authority and their individual interests at times threatened the whole. Leaders from various states sounded out the former commander in chief about the possibility of his attending a convention to discuss the Confederation's shortcomings. Henry Knox, one of Washington's former generals, offered a military analogy, saying that Washington should only attend (go into battle) knowing the outcome would be victorious;[12] he discouraged Washington from lending his name or presence unless this convention would produce something meaningful. Madison and others worked to convince Washington that he should attend the Philadelphia convention beginning in May 1787.

THE CONSTITUTIONAL CONVENTION

Once the convention began, electing a president to chair it was a relatively easy decision. Unanimously they put their trust in the man who had led them through the dark days of war. As their leader, Washington seldom participated in any debates, but in private discussions with delegates it was apparent that he favored a strong federal government as a replacement for the weak confederation. During a ten-day break in the proceedings, Washington journeyed to two places of importance to him

DID YOU KNOW?

Washington was descended from King Edward III (1312–1377) of England through his paternal grandmother.

Washington was a second cousin seven times removed of Queen Elizabeth II (1926–).

OCT 27: Pinkney's Treaty signed with Spain allowing American use of New Orleans

1796

FEB 29: Jay's Treaty proclaimed

APR 13: First elephant arrives in US from India

MAY 18: Congress passes Public Land Act to allow distribution of western lands in minimum tracts of 640 acres each and no less than $2 per acre

FEB: British seize Ceylon from the Dutch

MAR 9: Napoleon Bonaparte marries Josephine; weeks later successfully invades Italy and then defeats Austrians

APR 12: Napoleon's first victory as an army commander at the Battle of Montenotte

MAY: English physician Edward Jenner begins experimentation with smallpox vaccine

during the war—Trenton and Valley Forge, finding the latter "overgrown with weeds."[13]

He returned to the convention, which finished its business on September 17, 1787.

Washington watched from the sidelines while supporters and opponents fought for and against the ratification of the Constitution. Washington allowed his name to be mentioned as a key supporter but wrote no speeches or essays, such as those penned by Madison, Jay, and Hamilton in *The Federalist Papers*. He did not attend any conventions in Virginia or elsewhere, but stayed close to Mount Vernon. In June, word arrived that the necessary majority of states had approved the Constitution. Now a president needed to be elected. News of his unanimous electoral election reached Washington on April 14, 1789. Then, in New York City on April 30, George Washington was inaugurated as the first American president.

THE PRESIDENTIAL OATH OF OFFICE ★

Each president recites the following oath, in accordance with Article II, Section I of the US Constitution: "I do solemnly swear (or affirm) that I will faithfully execute the office of President of the United States, and will to the best of my ability, preserve, protect, and defend the Constitution of the United States."

DID YOU KNOW?

Washington was the only president inaugurated in two cities: New York, 1789, and Philadelphia, 1793.

PRESIDENT WASHINGTON

As America's first president, Washington embarked on a journey without a map, or as he said, "I walk upon untrodden ground."[14] Apprehensive about taking a misstep, he tread cautiously. He rented a fine house in New York and set up housekeeping alone, no doubt impatient for Martha to make the trek from Mount Vernon.

Anxious to adhere to his interpretation of the chief executive's duties as detailed in the Constitution, Washington had precious little work to do in his opening months. Congress made the laws, and the president sat back to determine whether he should sign the bills into law. He believed that he should consult the Senate for its "advice and consent" before negotiating a treaty with the Creek Indians, and appeared personally to discuss the issue. To Washington's dismay, his request set off a vigorous debate, which the president felt had been a waste of time. A precedent was set. All future treaties would be negotiated by the executive branch *and then* submitted to the Senate for approval.

Other precedents established in those first months included determining the proper way to address the president. Some preferred a highly formal title, such as "His Excellency," but many considered it too monarchial. President of the United States or Mister President were finally agreed upon as the accepted manners of address for the leader of the new republic. Washington also decided that he would hold two weekly receptions open to the public; otherwise, he was available by appointment only. The president originally began his term in office intending to resign before its expiration in favor of John Adams, thereby serving only a partial term. He changed his mind, however, and fulfilled his first term, as well as a second one. Stepping down after the second term itself became a precedent followed by all others except Franklin D. Roosevelt.

FIRST TERM

Fully aware of his limitations, Washington set out to surround himself with cabinet members he could trust and who would represent the country geographically. He asked his old friend Henry Knox

NATIONAL EVENTS

- **JUN 1:** Tennessee becomes 16th state
- **JUL 8:** US State Department issues first American passport
- **SEP 17:** President Washington issues his Farewell Address
- **NOV 4:** Treaty of Tripoli signed between US and Tripoli
- **NOV:** First American ship, the *Otter*, arrives at Monterey Bay, California, opening New England–California trade route

WORLD EVENTS

- **MAY 10:** Napoleon defeats Austria at the Battle of Lodi
- **MAY 15:** Napoleon's troops take Milan
- **MAY 15:** France and Sardinia sign Peace Treaty of Paris
- **SEP 8:** French troops defeat Austrian forces at the Battle of Bassano
- **OCT 5:** Spain declares war on England

to lead the War Department and trusted aide Alexander Hamilton to become secretary of the treasury. Fellow Virginian Edmund Randolph was appointed attorney general, but the secretary of state's position remained open for a year. Ultimately he named another Virginian, Thomas Jefferson, to the post. Little did Washington realize that the appointment would permanently impact America's national politics. Ideological differences between Jefferson and Hamilton would form the outline of the nation's first party system: Federalists, under Hamilton, who supported expansive federal power, and Democratic-Republicans, under Jefferson, who supported states' rights and limited federal power. By assembling a talented cabinet, he felt confident in their opinions and advice. Cabinet meetings, though, were a rarity. Instead, Washington would send a messenger to a cabinet secretary with files and expected a verbal response within four hours. The commander in chief was not interested in wasting time; he wanted matters addressed in a timely manner.

Financial concerns facing the country were uppermost for both Washington and Secretary of the Treasury Hamilton. Hamilton fashioned a series of proposals to gradually pay America's multi-million-dollar debt, as well as to secure a sound foundation for its future finances. As the proposals were unveiled, Secretary of State Jefferson objected to them one by one, arguing that each overstepped the authority of the federal government. Likewise, James Madison attacked the measures as they came before the House of Representatives. Nevertheless, Hamilton's proposals passed, and, to Jefferson's dismay, each was also signed into law by President Washington. Both Jefferson and Hamilton sought the president's ear, and he in turn examined their arguments closely. But understanding the need for a stable economy, he leaned toward Hamilton.

FRENCH REVOLUTION (January 21, 1793) ★

Beginning on July 14, 1789, with a mob in Paris storming the Bastille (an old French prison), the French Revolution began. Former American general Marquis de Lafayette served as one of the leaders in this effort to emulate the liberty sought successfully by Americans. Within three years, efforts to establish a constitutional monarchy under King Louis XVI and his wife Marie Antoinette failed, as did those to create a republic. The world heard with horrified shock the news of the king's beheading by the new French invention, the guillotine, on January 21, 1793. European powers, including Great Britain, determined not to allow the infectious spirit of revolt to spread and attacked France. This ongoing conflict threatened to embroil the new American nation, as well, and so Washington issued the Neutrality Proclamation.

During Washington's first term, he traveled to every state because he believed it was imperative that he see the nation and that he, as representative of the federal government, be seen by the people. First he visited New England, where he was snubbed by Massachusetts governor John Hancock, who thought the president should call on him. Washington disagreed, knowing that the subordinate calls on the superior in such social situations and that if he called on Hancock, it would be understood that the federal government was subordinate to the state governments. Hancock relented and paid the president a call, thus establishing that the president outranked any governor in any state.

The Industrial Revolution was in its infancy, and the president toured a textile facility that was using child labor. He also visited Harvard College,

NOV: John Adams elected America's second president; Thomas Jefferson is vice president

NOV: Andrew Jackson elected as first delegate to Congress from Tennessee

DEC: American portrait artist Gilbert Stuart completes two paintings of George Washington

NOV 17: France defeats Austria in Italy at the Battle of Arcole

NOV 17: Catherine the Great of Russia dies at age 67

NEUTRALITY PROCLAMATION ★ Fearful of being dragged into a war that America could ill-afford to fight, President Washington issued a Neutrality Proclamation on April 22, 1793, against the advice of his secretary of state, Thomas Jefferson, who felt it violated America's earlier treaties with its ally France. The issuance of the proclamation launched a pamphlet war between Hamilton (writing for the Federalists) and Madison (writing for the Jeffersonians/Republicans).

continued on to Maine, and then returned through the "amazingly crooked"[15] roads of Massachusetts. He refrained from traveling on Sunday since the people of Connecticut disapproved.

In May 1790, people of New York and elsewhere fretted over news that the president lay dangerously ill from pneumonia. Within a week, though, he was out in public again and celebrating the news of Rhode Island's ratification of the Constitution. Now all thirteen states were one nation. That nation, however, faced a crisis on its frontier from its former foe, the British. Neglecting to obey the Treaty of Paris, British forces remained in their forts and outposts along the Great Lakes. Using these as bases to aide their Indian allies, they launched attacks into the American frontier. Washington sent troops to fend off these assaults, but the inexperienced soldiers were handed devastating defeats. Attempting to find a competent officer to crush the enemy would not be an easy task. Eventually the president appointed General "Mad" Anthony Wayne, one of his former Revolutionary War officers, who employed skilled tactics to defeat the Native Americans at the Battle of Fallen Timbers. The president understood that even with military victories, the underlying problem remained—the continual stream of settlers onto native lands—and he wrote, "Scarcely any thing short of a Chinese wall will restrain Land jobbers and the encroachment of settlers upon the Indian country."[16]

In 1791, Washington traveled by coach to the southern states. This excursion took him nearly two thousand miles, where he was greeted and feted in town after town. The hero rode one of his personal mounts, a white stallion named Prescott (complete with leopard-skin cloth and gold-rimmed saddle), into the major towns. Washington gave speeches tying the Revolution to the new nation's first steps and visited battlefields from the war. Meanwhile his cabinet continued to battle itself.

Hamilton and Jefferson debated Hamilton's financial plans for the young nation's future, including a tax system, an independent central bank, and a dollar tied to gold. They eventually signed, along with James Madison, the Compromise of 1790, which would move the capital from New York to Philadelphia for ten years, then permanently move it to Washington, D.C. Packing, moving, and finding new schools and tutors for President and Mrs. Washington's adopted grandchildren caused the First Lady considerable additional effort and she looked with great anticipation to the end of her husband's term. To her surprise and dismay, her husband served a second term, but she dutifully remained beside him. Washington himself was not happy at the prospect of serving a second term, but his cabinet begged him to do so, insisting that the country depended on his leadership.

SECOND TERM

By 1793, war between Great Britain and France had ignited once again. Both nations wanted America's help, but Washington understood only too well that it was not in his country's best interests to be dragged into war by either side; consequently, he issued a Neutrality Proclamation. While some Americans were relieved, others, especially French supporters, saw it as a slap to America's former ally. France's representative, Edmund Genet, was dispatched to the United States and did his best to stir the pot of anti-British feelings, which proved embarrassing to Secretary of State Jefferson. Not surprisingly, President Washington demanded the French recall their diplomat.

Closer to home, rebellion threatened. Another ingredient of Hamilton's financial plan was the levying of an excise tax on whiskey. Western Pennsylvania farmers who distilled their grain into whiskey for easier transportation angrily refused to pay a tax. Understanding the need as chief executive to enforce laws, however unpopular they may be, Washington took action. He and Hamilton donned their old uniforms and led 15,000 militia to the area to quell the Whiskey Rebellion. Rather than fight, the lawbreakers backed down, and another precedent was set, crushing this first real challenge to federal authority.

Weary of the continual quarreling and political backbiting, Jefferson resigned in 1793 as secretary of state. By now the difference in vision between Jefferson and Hamilton had created political parties. Democratic-Republicans followed Jefferson and Hamilton led the Federalists. Washington watched with mounting concern the growing tensions between factions and cautioned of its danger. In 1795, Hamilton also resigned, but the damage was done.

In 1795, Washington applauded the Treaty of Greeneville, which ceded more Native American lands in the Northwest Territory to the US. This capped a nearly four-year war between US forces and Native Americans.

Also that year, the Senate ratified two other important treaties. Pinckney's Treaty with Spain met with greater approval since it opened the port of New Orleans and improved relations with that country. Jay's Treaty with Great Britain required the British to finally vacate their forts in the Great Lakes, as ordered in the Treaty of Paris in 1783, which had ended the Revolutionary War a decade earlier. Strong disapproval, however, greeted Jay's Treaty because it failed to address two key issues: British boarding of American ships and inspecting them for contraband, and the British practice of "impressment" by which they could seize sailors from American ships and force them into service of the Royal Navy by claiming the Americans were still Englishmen.

> ***"Promote then, as an object of primary importance, institutions for the general diffusion of knowledge. In proportion as the structure of a government gives force to public opinion, it is essential that public opinion should be enlightened."***
>
> *—George Washington, Farewell Address, 1796*

Finally, George Washington could look toward his second retirement. Absolute in his refusal to serve a third term, he now only desired to spend what time he had remaining at Mount Vernon with his family. Ending his presidency provided the opportunity to say goodbye to a grateful nation. In his Farewell Address, mainly crafted by Hamilton, Washington cautioned the nation of the "baneful effects of the spirit of party" and their willingness to exploit the differences of geographical regions for political gains. He warned against incurring a large national debt "upon posterity the burden which we ourselves ought to bear." Regarding foreign relations, he advised, "The great rule of conduct for us in regard to foreign nations is, in extending our commercial relations to have with them as little political connection as possible." Copies of his Farewell Address were reprinted throughout the country (it was never delivered orally), and by mid-March 1797, George Washington was once again a private citizen, residing at Mount Vernon.

FINAL RETIREMENT

A number of household repairs required Washington's immediate attention upon his return home. He and Martha also played host to a steady stream of visitors. In 1798, with a war looming against France, President John Adams asked Washington to once again assume control of the army. George Washington agreed, but only on the condition that he would not be required to actually take command in person.

By now, the man who once embodied strength and vitality required glasses and was hard of hearing. Washington's teeth were now nearly all gone,

DID YOU KNOW?

★★★★★★★★★★★

Washington refused a third term.

Washington declared the first official Thanksgiving in 1789, "A Day of Publick Thanksgiving and Prayer."

US currency: Washington is on the quarter and the one dollar bill.

DID YOU KNOW?

Washington introduced the mule to American agriculture. The king of Spain gave Washington a donkey, named Royal Gift, which Washington sent on a thousand-mile tour of southern states to sire strong and hardy mules.

replaced by hippopotamus ivory, and his hair was white. During his presidency, he had endured the removal of a cancerous growth on his leg and a bout of pneumonia. He was slow to recuperate from both.

On December 12, 1799, planter Washington took his customary ride over his lands for nearly five hours. As he rode, temperatures dropped and snow began to fall, which later turned to sleet. By late afternoon, he rode back to the house but failed to change from his cold wet clothes, as he had guests and correspondence that required his attention. The following day he developed a sore throat that by the middle of the next night left him gasping for air. Martha wanted to send for a doctor, but he refused, saying that they could wait until morning. During the next day, three physicians arrived, and they bled the patient four times, but Washington's breathing only grew more labored and he could no longer swallow. Adding insult to injury, the doctors purged their patient with laxatives, which only increased his discomfort. By now, his windpipe was nearly closed; the man who had stared down death countless times was now being choked to death by his own body.

By the evening of December 14, Washington told them to stop. He said, "Doctor, I die hard, but I am not afraid to go."[17] A little after 10:30 p.m., George Washington breathed his last after telling his secretary Tobias Lear, "Have me decently buried and do not let my body be put into a vault in less than two days after I am dead." He asked Lear if he understood; Lear replied he did. Washington's last words were "'Tis well."[18]

Washington was buried on December 18, 1799. The funeral included soldiers, patriotic music, and a group of Masons from Washington's lodge in Alexandria. His will freed one slave and allowed the rest to be emancipated upon Martha's death. She died three years later, on May 22, 1802, and was laid to rest beside her husband of nearly forty-one years in the family vault at Mount Vernon.

HIS LEGACY

During his lifetime, George Washington had been a man bound by duty—first for his colony and then for his country. He had forsaken pay to win a war and serve as his nation's first president. In that office, he had established numerous precedents involving the chief executive, his role, and how he is perceived by the people. Washington was loved by Americans then and is admired today. Former Revolutionary War cavalry commander General "Lighthorse" Harry Lee summed up the legacy of the first president best when he said: "First in war, first in peace, and first in the hearts of his countrymen."

> ***"...that the free Constitution, which is the work of your hands, may be sacredly maintained; that its administration in every department may be stamped with wisdom and virtue; that, in fine, the happiness of the people of these States, under the auspices of liberty, may be made complete by so careful a preservation and so prudent a use of this blessing as will acquire to them the glory of recommending it to the applause, the affection, and adoption of every nation which is yet a stranger to it."***
>
> —*George Washington, Farewell Address, 1796*

ENDNOTES

1 Willard Sterne Randall, *George Washington, A Life*, New York: Henry Holt and Co., 1997, p. 48.

2 George Washington diary, March 23, 1748.

3 Ibid, p. 78.

4 John E. Ferling, *The First of Men, A Life of George Washington*, Knoxville: University of Tennessee Press, 1988, p. 29.

5 Randall, p. 137.

6 James T. Flexner, *George Washington: A Biography*, Boston: Little Brown & Company, vol. I, p. 301.

7 Ralph K. Andrist, editor, *George Washington, A Biography in His Own Words*, New York: Newsweek, 1972, p. 102.

8 Ferling, p. 191.

9 Thomas Paine, *The Crisis*, December 23, 1776.

10 Ibid, p. 289.

11 Joseph Ellis, *His Excellency, George Washington*, New York: Alfred A. Knopf, 2004, p. 170.

12 Ibid, p. 174.

13 Ferling, p. 360.

14 Randall, p. 445.

15 Andrist, p. 309.

16 Ellis, p. 214.

17 Ibid, p. 269.

18 Richard Norton Smith, *Patriarch: George Washington and the New American Nation*, Boston: Houghton Mifflin, 1993, p. 355.

John Adams

JOHN ADAMS

★ ★ ★ SECOND PRESIDENT ★ ★ ★

LIFE SPAN

- Born: October 30, 1735, in Braintree (now Quincy), Massachusetts
- Died: July 4, 1826, in Quincy, Massachusetts

NICKNAMES

- Atlas of Independence, Architect of the Revolution, Colossus of Debate, Colossus of Independence, His Rotundity, Duke of Braintree

RELIGION

- Unitarian

HIGHER EDUCATION

- Harvard College, 1755

PROFESSION

- Schoolmaster, lawyer, farmer

MILITARY SERVICE

- None; considered founder of US Navy

FAMILY

- Father: **John Adams** (1691–1761)
- Mother: **Susanna Boylston Adams** (1709–1797)
- Wife: **Abigail Smith Adams** (1744–1818); wed October 25, 1764, in Weymouth, Massachusetts
- Children: **Abigail Amelia "Nabby"** (1765–1813); **John Quincy** (1767–1848) sixth president; **Susanna** (1768–1770); **Charles** (1770–1800); **Thomas Boylston** (1772–1832)

POLITICAL LIFE

- Massachusetts delegate to the Continental Congress (1774–1777)
- Commissioner to France (1778)
- Minister to the Netherlands (1780)
- Minister to England (1785)
- Vice president (1789–1797)

PRESIDENCY

- One term: March 4, 1797–March 4, 1801
- Federalist
- Reason for leaving office: lost to **Thomas Jefferson** in 1800 election
- Vice president: **Thomas Jefferson** (1797–1801)

ELECTION OF 1796

- Electoral vote: **Adams** 71; **Jefferson** 68
- Popular vote: none

CABINET
★★★★★★★★★★

SECRETARY OF STATE
Timothy Pickering (1797–1800)

John Marshall (1800–1801)

SECRETARY OF THE TREASURY
Oliver Wolcott Jr. (1797–1800)

Samuel Dexter (1801)

SECRETARY OF WAR
James McHenry (1797–1800)

Samuel Dexter (1800–1801)

ATTORNEY GENERAL
Charles Lee (1797–1801)

SECRETARY OF THE NAVY
Benjamin Stoddert (1798–1801)

POSTMASTER GENERAL
Joseph Habersham (1797–1801)

On July 4, 1826, John Adams finally succumbed to the ravages of age—he was ninety. Brought to bed by pneumonia and a weak heart, he was unable to participate in the country's festivities celebrating the fiftieth anniversary of the Declaration of Independence. The events of that day fifty years earlier still weighed on his mind. His final words were, "Thomas Jefferson still survives." Little did he know that his old friend and sometime rival had preceded him in death by only a few hours. Within days, news of this amazing coincidence traveled throughout the nation. Many considered the deaths of these leaders on such a historic occasion a divine message acknowledging that the country was flourishing and strong enough to survive the loss of two of its founders.

EARLY LIFE

On October 30, 1735, John Adams was born to John and Susanna Boylston Adams in the family's saltbox home in Braintree, Massachusetts. His father worked as a farmer and performed various civic roles including tax collector, constable, selectman, and deacon in the town's Congregationalist church. His father tutored him when he was a child, and later John attended nearby schools. Not always mindful of his studies, the boy often hunted and fished instead with his two younger brothers.

STAMP ACT (March 1765) ★ Parliament passed the stamp tax as a way to raise revenue for offsetting the expense of sending British troops to guard America's frontier borders. Although its cost was trivial, colonists believed its concept was monumental. Protests began and the words "No taxation without representation!" rang through the colonies.

Farming did not require such diligent application, he reasoned. His father, however, wanted his son to attend Harvard College, possibly with an eye toward becoming a minister.

John Adams entered Harvard in 1751 and a new world of knowledge, reading, and debating opened before him. He joined a literary society and found he had a special flair for public speaking. His thoughts turned from the ministry to the law. Adams graduated in 1755 and immediately went to Worcester to teach in a local school during the day and read law at night. He passed the bar in 1758 and returned home to Braintree to begin his legal career.

RESPECTED CITIZEN

The young attorney built a solid law practice, but it required him to travel often, throughout Massachusetts, including the area now known as Maine. Still, he found time to court various young women, and he nearly proposed to one, Hannah Quincy. Two of Adams's friends arrived as he was about to pop the question, and Hannah ended up marrying someone else. Consequently, a few years later he was free to win the heart of young Abigail Smith, daughter of a local parson. Although Abigail was never able to attend school, her parents made sure that she was well read and trained in housewifery skills. Against her mother's wishes, who fretted over her daughter marrying the country lawyer son of farmers, Abigail and John became engaged and were wed on October 25, 1764. The following year they welcomed their first child, a daughter, and later, three boys who survived to adulthood, including future president John Quincy Adams.

During the early years of his marriage, John Adams embarked on a political career. The Stamp Act prompted him to write, "We have always

NATIONAL EVENTS	**MAR 4:** Adams inaugurated as second president	**MAY 10:** First ship of new US Navy is launched—USS *United States*	**JUN 7:** Senate ratifies treaty with the Bey of Tripoli	**JUL 8:** William Blount of Tennessee first US senator to be expelled	**SUMMER:** Three peace commissioners dispatched to France
1797					
WORLD EVENTS	**FEB 26:** Great Britain issues first £1 bank notes and copper pennies	**MAY 12:** Napoleon I of France conquers Venice (ending 1,070 years of independence); the last doge steps down	**JUL 9:** France proclaims Cisalpine Republic (of Milan, Modena, Ferrara, Bologna, Romagna)	**OCT 17:** Peace of Campo Formio ends Austrian opposition to France; Austria cedes	

understood . . . that no freeman should be subject to any tax to which he has not given his own consent."[1] His remarks were reprinted throughout the colony, and he was asked to join others protesting British actions. The ardent young lawyer attended political meetings at the invitation of his cousin Samuel Adams and friend James Otis.

Eager to expand his business prospects, John Adams abandoned the country life, opening his law office in Boston, in 1768, and renting a house for his family. One of his clients was the wealthy John Hancock, whom Adams defended successfully against a smuggling charge. In another case, he defended four American sailors charged with killing a British naval officer. Their case was self-defense, Adams argued, for the British had tried to force these men into service in the British navy. This would not be the last time Adams would challenge the British practice of impressment.

Unquestionably the most famous case of John Adams's legal career was his defense of the British soldiers tried for the Boston Massacre in 1770. British soldiers had killed five colonists and the people of Boston demanded blood payment. Adams believed the soldiers deserved a fair trial and accepted the case, which no one else was willing to pursue. One of his first requests was a postponement to allow the city's temper to cool. He then gained an acquittal for the officer, Captain Preston. By ensuring the jury was composed of rural men rather than city folk of Boston, he eventually won acquittals for five soldiers and manslaughter convictions for the other two.

The same year, 1770, John Adams was elected to the Massachusetts legislature, where he served for the next four years. Boston, meanwhile, continued to be troublesome for the British king and Parliament. In December 1773, members of the Sons of Liberty stealthily climbed aboard tea ships at anchor and dumped their contents into the harbor. British retaliation was swift, and Boston harbor was closed as of June 1, 1774. That autumn, the first meeting of the Continental Congress was held in Philadelphia, and John Adams was selected to be one of the five delegates from Massachusetts. A non-importation agreement was drafted as well as an agreement to organize local committees for enforcement. In preparation for the unwelcome event of war, the Congress also called for more militia training throughout the colonies. The decision was made to reassemble the following spring if there was no improvement in the colonies' relations with Great Britain.

BOSTON MASSACRE ★ Growing tensions in Boston between its citizens and British troops quartered there erupted into bloodshed on March 5, 1770. Confronted by an angry mob, British soldiers fired into the crowd, mortally wounding five citizens. Later, the officer in charge, Captain Thomas Preston, was arrested, along with eight of his soldiers, and they were charged with murder. John Adams agreed to defend the men at trial. Preston and five of his men were acquitted; the remaining two were convicted of manslaughter.

REVOLUTIONARY

When John Adams returned to Philadelphia in May 1775, circumstances had changed drastically over the five ensuing years. Blood had been shed in Lexington and Concord; war seemed more imminent. Toward this end, Adams was keenly aware of the need to unite the country. At the time, the struggle seemed to be a concern only for New

DID YOU KNOW?

Adams was the first president to attend Harvard College.

Adams was the first president to live in the White House (then called the Executive Mansion).

Eli Whitney develops concept of interchangeable parts, enabling mass production; awarded contract to produce 10,000 muskets in 28 months

APR: Report of French attempt to bribe American commissioners, known as XYZ Affair

APR 7: Mississippi Territory (later Alabama and Mississippi) is created

APR 30: Department of the Navy is created, independent of the War Department

JUL 7: Quasi-War with France begins when US revokes its treaties because of XYZ Affair

1798

French Council of 500 introduces idea of sitting "right" or "left" of center depending on political ideology

Samuel Coleridge publishes poem "The Rime of the Ancient Mariner"

Silk hats introduced, eventually replacing beaver in fashion

Thomas Robert Malthus writes "An Essay on the Principles of Population," arguing that since population grows at a faster rate than food production, the world will eventually reach a food crisis

SONS OF LIBERTY ★ Several groups known as the Sons of Liberty formed in the colonies originally to protest the Stamp Act in 1765. Members organized protests against British policy that, while peaceful at first, sometimes degenerated into more violent demonstrations. Leaders of the Boston Sons of Liberty included Sam Adams and Paul Revere.

England; something had to be done to demonstrate a broader support base. Adams nominated Virginian George Washington, instead of his friend and fellow delegate John Hancock, to be commander in chief of the newly created Continental army.

The months that followed were agonizing for John Adams, as he waited impatiently for other delegates to agree that the time had come to part company with their mother country. Adams likened the colonies to a fleet at sea that could only sail as fast as the slowest vessel. He served on various committees, including chairing the War and Ordnance Board, but the committee assignment that brought him the most fame was his appointment with Thomas Jefferson and Benjamin Franklin to draft the Declaration of Independence.

In Thomas Jefferson, whom he met on the Virginian's arrival in Congress the previous year, John Adams believed that he had found a soul mate. He also considered Jefferson a better writer, so when the committee met, the decision was quickly made to make Jefferson the declaration's author. Once it was completed, Adams and Franklin looked the document over, made a few suggestions and changes, and then submitted it to Congress.

DID YOU KNOW?

Adams was one of three presidents who died on the Fourth of July, along with Jefferson and Monroe (in 1831).

On July 1, debate began over Virginia's Resolutions for Independence, approved weeks before by their House of Burgesses, which stated, "All political connection between them [the colonies] and the state of Great Britain is, and ought to be, totally dissolved." Leading the charge in opposition was John Dickinson of Pennsylvania, who feared that his colleagues were acting too rashly and not permitting enough opportunity for compromise with their mother country. Standing to answer "with a power of thought and expression that moved us from our seats,"[2] Jefferson later wrote, was John Adams. No notes remain of Adams's speech, but the following day, the Second Continental Congress approved independence and began debating the Declaration. Again it was John Adams rallying to its defense, since Jefferson was a notoriously poor speaker. The Declaration of Independence was adopted on July 4 and the official copy signed on August 2.

John Adams continued working as a key delegate and, with others on his war committee, worked fifteen-hour days attempting to do what was needed to ensure America kept troops in the field. Toiling on the Articles of Confederation also demanded much of his attention. He wrote Abigail, "Never in my life, had I so many cares upon my mind at once."[3]

DIPLOMAT

In 1778, Congress appointed John Adams as representative to France to negotiate an alliance. Deciding it was a marvelous educational opportunity for his eldest son, John took eleven-year-old John Quincy. They stayed a year, but Adams felt uncomfortable serving with the wildly popular Benjamin Franklin. Moreover, the more sexually open French culture offended the Puritan in him, and he longed to rejoin his family in Braintree.

During the years of her husband's absence to Philadelphia and then to France, Abigail had

NATIONAL EVENTS	**JUL 11:** US Marine Corps created	**JUL 14:** Alien and Sedition Acts passed	**NOV 10:** Legislature adopts Kentucky Resolutions—Thomas Jefferson's response to the illegality of the Alien and Sedition Acts	**DEC 24:** Virginia ratifies similar resolutions drafted by James Madison	**MAR 2:** US standardizes weights and measures
					1799
WORLD EVENTS	**MAY 24:** Irish rebellion begins, lasts five months **JUL 1:** Napoleon's troops land in Egypt	**JUL 24:** Napoleon occupies Cairo	**JUL 24:** Great Britain enacts legislation outlawing trade unions	**AUG 1:** British Admiral Horatio Nelson defeats French fleet at the Battle of the Nile	Humphry Davy, English chemist, discovers anesthetic quality of nitrous oxide (laughing gas)

managed the farm and family, taught their children, and wrote her husband daily. Finally father and son returned. Very quickly, though, Massachusetts required her husband's services. More than three hundred delegates attended a convention to write the state's constitution. John Adams soon joined them, and they happily handed over to him the duty of drafting the document, into which he inserted a section detailing the importance of education, as well as a Declaration of Rights.

John Adams had hardly settled back into the domestic routine of his household and law practice when he received news that Congress required his services yet again. Appointed as peace commissioner, Adams was being sent to Europe on the all-important mission of securing a treaty with Great Britain, as well as loans from Dutch bankers. Ultimately he was successful on all counts. Adams relished the experience more this time because his family accompanied him. Soon, to his delight, Thomas Jefferson arrived to replace Franklin as American minister to France. There, the two old friends enjoyed the opportunity to become reacquainted while tending to commerce and diplomatic matters for the United States at the court of Versailles, where King Louis XVI and his wife Marie Antoinette presided.

Then in 1785, he was ordered to Great Britain as America's first ambassador to that nation. He and his family found this assignment quite pleasant. King George III granted Adams an audience and when the king asked John Adams if he was partial to France, Adams answered, "I have no attachment but to my own country." The king replied, "An honest man will never have any other."[4] While there, Adams wrote a multi-volume treatise on political philosophy, but by 1787, he was eager to pack up his family and return home.

BOSTON TEA PARTY ★ On December 16, 1773, members of the Sons of Liberty stealthily boarded British tea ships anchored in Boston harbor. Angry that the British were attempting to undercut the price of smuggled tea by removing the middleman and selling the tea wholesale with the tea tax, Sons of Liberty, dressed as Indians, boarded three ships and tossed forty-five tons of tea into the harbor rather than see it unloaded and sold.

MR. VICE PRESIDENT

After numerous communications with Congress and making arrangements for their move, John and Abigail finally reached America in 1788. The country's new Constitution had been ratified, and in his absence, he had been elected to the first House of Representatives. Others believed a higher office would be more suitable—namely, the vice presidency. Theodore Sedgwick, speaker of the Massachusetts House of Representatives, wrote to Alexander Hamilton praising Adams "as a man of unconquerable intrepidity & of incorruptible integrity."[5]

Without a doubt, more thought was given to the vice presidential candidate than the presidential. George Washington would be the first president. But the vice president, a heartbeat from the presidency, engendered more discussion. John Adams was attractive to some because he was from New England and would balance the Virginian Washington; moreover, he had proven himself in important political and diplomatic positions. Ironically, his time spent in Europe in the service of the new republic almost resulted in near disaster for him during his first days as vice president.

SUPREME COURT APPOINTMENTS

★★★★★★★★★★

Bushrod Washington, 1799

Alfred Moore, 1800

John Marshall, Chief Justice, 1801

MAR 30: Adams appoints second negotiating team to go to France

SEP 1: Bank of the Manhattan Company opens on Wall Street (forerunner of Chase Manhattan)

DEC 14: George Washington dies at age 67 at Mount Vernon

Royal Military Academy at Sandhurst opens its doors as officer-training school

Frenchman Baron Cuvier introduces the term phylum to indicate a more general category than classes

JAN 9: British Parliament passes the world's first income tax

JUL 15: Rosetta stone found in Egypt by French troops

DEC: Napoleon named first consul of France

STATE OF THE UNION
★★★★★★★★★★

US POPULATION IN 1797
5,308,483

NATIONAL DEBT IN 1797
$82,064,479.33

PRESIDENT'S SALARY
$25,000/year

STATES ADMITTED TO UNION
None

On the issue of how the president was to be addressed, Adams posed the question to the Senate and suggested, "His Highness, the President of the United States and Protector of their Liberties." Senators and newspapers derided him behind his back, and John Adams himself gained a new title, "His Rotundity." This episode taught him to distance himself from Senate debates and to consider as his primary purpose keeping order and voting if a tie occurred. Still, the damage was done, and some insisted the views found in his books displayed a monarchial bent. John Adams continued to attend the Senate sessions and, with deference and acceptance, stated: "My country has in its wisdom contrived for me the most insignificant office that ever the invention of man contrived or his imagination conceived."[6]

President George Washington did not consult his vice president on matters of importance. They saw each other and other members of the government at social functions, but that was the extent of their official contact. As needed, John Adams cast tie-breaking votes in accordance with the president's opinions. He shared Washington's concern regarding the growing factions caused by Hamilton and Jefferson. Both men feared that no good would come from creating political parties. By this point, Adams and Jefferson were scarcely on speaking terms.

With Washington's announcement that he would retire after two terms, many assumed Adams would run for the office against his rival of the newly created Democratic-Republican Party, Thomas Jefferson. Although Adams was a Federalist, he and its founder Alexander Hamilton disagreed strongly on many major issues that would only become more apparent once John Adams became president. George Washington endorsed Adams, and very likely ensured his election.

ARTICLES OF CONFEDERATION ★ The Articles of Confederation was America's first governing document, but its weaknesses threatened the stability of the newly formed nation. Ratified in 1781, lack of central government authority (no executive or judicial branches) and emphasis on state power created considerable obstacles when the thirteen states failed to work together. Its failure led to the drafting of the US Constitution in 1787.

PRESIDENT ADAMS

In 1796, the Electoral College cast seventy-one votes for John Adams and sixty-eight votes for Thomas Jefferson. According to the Constitution, the candidate in second place became vice president; consequently, for the one and only time in American history, men of opposing political parties held the top two positions in the government.

The commanding presence of George Washington was replaced by a shorter, rounder, more outspoken president with even less patience for the nuances of his position than his predecessor. Writing years earlier, John Adams said, "Thanks to God that he gave me stubbornness when I know I am right."[7] This trait would help ensure peace for the country throughout his administration.

Within weeks of Adams's inauguration, the country's division grew more pronounced when word arrived that France had attacked American ships. France's actions were a result of Jay's Treaty (p. 17) between the United States and Great Britain, which the French perceived as an alliance against them; in response, France severed

NATIONAL EVENTS

Candidates for presidential election decided: Federalists—John Adams and Charles C. Pinkney; Democratic-Republicans—Thomas Jefferson and Aaron Burr

APR 24: Library of Congress founded

MAY 7: Congress creates Indiana territory

AUG: Planned slave insurrection fails in Virginia; leaders are hanged

1800

WORLD EVENTS

Italian physicist Alessandro Volta develops electric storage battery

Mason Locke ("Parson Weems") publishes *Life of Washington*, a popular but largely fictional biography of George Washington

MAR 21: Pope Pius VII ordained

MAY 15: Napoleon crosses the Alps and invades Italy

JUN 14: Battle of Marengo: Napoleon defeats Austrian forces in Italy

diplomatic relations with America. Learning of France's unlawful actions at sea, Hamilton led the Federalist cries for war. Jefferson and his Republicans, who had been supporting the French throughout Washington's administration, were in opposition. Recognizing that his country was not prepared for military action, John Adams sought a diplomatic solution to the crisis. He exercised his constitutional right to call Congress into special session to determine what action should be taken. They, too, backed sending diplomats to France, but also agreed to enlarge the army and the navy. Orders were placed for the construction of six new warships, including the USS *Constitution* and her sister ships. The president was taking no chances.

Once the diplomats arrived in France, the government refused to meet with them. Talleyrand, the French foreign minister, sent agents to demand a bribe of $250,000 before any further meetings could be arranged. Without hesitation, the Americans, including future chief justice John Marshall, indignantly refused and immediately sent their report to President Adams.

Upon receiving news of the diplomatic impasse, Adams moved forward with preparations for war. Jefferson and his fellow Republicans objected, unaware of the bribe, which the president had not publicly disclosed in the diplomatic report. Finally Adams felt compelled to reveal the information but, out of diplomatic courtesy, replaced the names of the three French agents with the letters X, Y, and Z. When the American people read of the French attempt at extortion, war fever flared hotter than ever. Now the Jeffersonians had to duck for cover as citizens cried, "Millions for defense, but not one cent for tribute!"

Although sympathetic to his countrymen's outrage, John Adams still desired to keep the peace. He never requested a declaration of war, but off and on for the next two years, the US and French vessels engaged in combat. The Quasi-War ended with another diplomatic mission and an agreement in 1800 providing the United States with neutral status at sea.

Fearful of enemies at home, Congress took action in 1798 with the passage of the Alien and Sedition Acts. The Alien Acts were aimed at making it more difficult for the growing number of immigrants (mostly pro-French and pro-Jefferson) to become citizens. The president also gained greater power to deport foreigners who he believed were endangering the nation. The Sedition Act was even more controversial as it became illegal for publications to print articles that were "false, scandalous, and malicious" about the government. Throughout the nation a handful of newspaper publishers were arrested; of course, they were Republicans, and by being jailed during the 1800 election, their viewpoints would be silenced. Or would they?

No one attacked the acts more vehemently than Vice President Jefferson. Understanding that these were directed against him and his party, he unleashed his anger in a whirlwind of letters to political allies. He and James Madison wrote the Kentucky and Virginia Resolutions, which argued

DID YOU KNOW?

Adams was the longest lived president at 90 years 253 days, until Ronald Reagan broke Adams's record on October 13, 2001. Reagan lived until June 5, 2004—93 years 119 days. (Gerald Ford broke Reagan's record on November 12, 2006, at 93 years, 120 days, and had outlived Reagan by 45 days when he died on December 26, 2006.)

XYZ AFFAIR (April 1798) ★ Faced with potential war against France, President John Adams sent three envoys to negotiate a peace treaty. French officials demanded outrageous bribes be paid before any negotiations could occur. Adams forwarded his diplomats' report of the bribery to Congress, but replaced the names of the three French officials with the letters X, Y, and Z; hence the name.

SEP 30: Convention of 1800 normalizes relations between the US and France, ends Quasi-War

NOV 1: John and Abigail Adams move into President's House in Washington, D.C.

NOV 11: Adams loses presidential election; Jefferson and Burr tie in Electoral College

NOV 17: Congress holds its first Washington, D.C. session

OCT 1: Spain cedes Louisiana Territory to France through secret treaty with Napoleon

DEC 3: Battle of Hohenlinden: French army defeats Austrian troops

DID YOU KNOW?

Adams dismissed his secretary of state, Timothy Pickering, for conspiring against him with Alexander Hamilton. Pickering is the only secretary of state to have been fired directly.

that states had the right to nullify any federal laws they found objectionable. This later provided the basis for the South's position on states' rights.

Not only did John Adams quarrel with Jefferson, he also found himself strongly disagreeing with Alexander Hamilton, who already despised the president for not sending the country to war against France. Both Adams and Jefferson feared Hamilton might stage a coup when he was appointed inspector general of the army. Republican Elbridge Gerry wrote of the president's concern that Hamilton would use the army as the means "to proclaim a regal government and place Hamilton as head of it, and prepare the way for a province of Great Britain."[8]

Fortunately, all fears of the "Second Bonaparte" proved groundless, but Hamilton was not yet finished with Adams. In the election of 1800, John Adams found himself deserted by the Federalists. Hamilton supported Charles Pinckney for president while the Republicans ran Thomas Jefferson and Aaron Burr. In the Electoral College, Adams came in third place. As he and many successors would learn, a reelection campaign is a referendum on their first term; if the people are unhappy, the result is victory by the opposing party.

> ***But a Constitution of Government once changed from Freedom, can never be restored. Liberty, once lost, is lost forever.***
>
> —*John Adams, in a letter to Abigail Adams, 1775*

Feeling betrayed and battered by the political experience, John Adams longed for the day when he and Abigail could retire to Braintree. For the last months of his presidency, they had been living in the unfinished hull of the President's House. Neither regretted leaving it or the small village of Washington. Their happiness, however, was greatly diminished with the news of their son Charles's death, who finally succumbed to his ongoing battle with alcoholism.

During his final weeks as president, Adams signed a number of appointments for judgeships. Obviously, they were for Federalist judges who he reasoned would maintain balance against the Republicans, who now controlled the other two branches of government. Not surprisingly, these "midnight judges" were not received kindly by his successor. The day of Jefferson's inauguration found John Adams on his way north rather than staying in town for the ceremony. The rift between the two former friends seemed final. Thankfully it was not.

RETIREMENT

John Adams would spend the next quarter century reading and writing in prodigious quantity. No correspondence, though, was more fulfilling than the one he and Thomas Jefferson began in 1812 at the instigation of mutual friend Dr. Benjamin Rush. Their ensuing letters, with Adams writing the majority, covered a variety of topics from the War of 1812 to slavery. Sometimes Abigail Adams also joined in the correspondence. But in 1818, John Adams's "Portia" died at the age of seventy-four. Her son John Quincy wrote in his diary, "My mother . . . had no feelings but of kindness and beneficence. Yet her mind was as firm as her temper was mild and gentle."[9]

Still John Adams persevered and continued his farm labors. He enjoyed hosting family members and chatting with visitors, including Jefferson's grandson. In 1824, he rejoiced at the news of John Quincy becoming president. The following year, John Adams celebrated a milestone—his ninetieth birthday. Both he and Jefferson knew their days were numbered and by spring 1826, both men refused invitations to attend the fiftieth anniversary celebrations of the Declaration of Independence. When asked to provide a suitable toast for the occasion, John Adams proclaimed, "Independence forever." John Adams breathed his last on July 4, 1826, at 6:20 p.m. He was buried beside Abigail at the Congregationalist church in Quincy, Massachusetts.

HIS LEGACY

As president, John Adams had the unenviable task of following George Washington; hence, Adams seems to become lost in the big general's shadow. The New Englander's presidency, however, was strong in its own right. He strove to maintain America's neutrality and sovereignty, while at the same time strengthening America's defenses in case he would be the first president to send troops into war. His greatest misstep was supporting the passage of the Alien and Sedition Acts to quell opposition. John Adams never cared for criticism, and his attempt to bypass civil liberties is still held as an example of what should never happen again.

Perhaps his most enduring legacy is the one he left in the White House. As its first occupant, he left a note with the following message that was then carved into the mantel of the State Dining Room: "I pray Heaven to bestow the best of Blessings on this House and all that shall hereafter inhabit it. May none but honest and wise Men ever rule under this roof."

ENDNOTES

1 David McCullough, *John Adams*, New York: Simon & Schuster, 2001, p. 61.

2 Ibid, p. 127.

3 Ibid, p. 142.

4 John Patrick Diggins, *John Adams*, New York: Times Books, 2003, p. 38.

5 James Grant, *John Adams: Party of One*, New York: Farrar, Straus and Giroux, 2005, p. 347.

6 William DeGregorio, *The Complete Book of US Presidents*, New York: Gramercy Books, 2005, p. 26.

7 McCullough, p. 272.

8 Ibid, p. 522.

9 Ibid, p. 623.

THOMAS JEFFERSON

★ ★ ★ THIRD PRESIDENT ★ ★ ★

LIFE SPAN

- Born: April 13, 1743, at Shadwell, in Virginia
- Died: July 4, 1826, at Monticello, in Virginia

NICKNAMES

- Father of the Declaration of Independence, Sage of Monticello, Man of the People

RELIGION

- Deist

HIGHER EDUCATION

- College of William and Mary, 1762

PROFESSION

- Lawyer, farmer

MILITARY SERVICE

- Colonel, Virginia militia 1770–1779 (not in active service)

FAMILY

- Father: **Colonel Peter Jefferson** (1708–1757)
- Mother: **Jane Randolph Jefferson** (1720–1776)
- Wife: **Martha Wayles Skelton Jefferson** (1748–1782); wed January 1, 1772, in Charles City County, Virginia
- Children: **Martha "Patsy"** (1772–1836); **Jane Randolph** (1774–1775); an infant son, died at birth (1777); **Mary "Maria"** (1778–1804); **Lucy Elizabeth** (1780–1781); **Lucy Elizabeth** (1782–1785)

POLITICAL LIFE

- Member, Virginia House of Burgesses (1769–1774)
- Delegate to the Continental Congress (1775–1776; 1783–1785)
- Delegate to the Virginia House of Delegates (1776–1779)
- Governor of Virginia (1779–1781)
- Commissioner and minister to France (1784–1789)
- Secretary of state (1790–1793)
- Vice president (1797–1801)

PRESIDENCY

- Two terms: March 4, 1801–March 4, 1809
- Democratic-Republican
- Reason for leaving office: completion of term
- Vice presidents: **Aaron Burr** (1801–1805); **George Clinton** (1805–1809)

ELECTION OF 1800

- Electoral vote: tied 73 with **Aaron Burr** (vice presidential candidate); won vote in House of Representatives. The deadlock led to passage of the Twelfth Amendment in 1804
- Popular vote: none

ELECTION OF 1804

- Electoral vote: **Jefferson** 162; **Charles C. Pinckney** 14
- Popular vote: none

CABINET

SECRETARY OF STATE
James Madison (1801–1809)

SECRETARY OF THE TREASURY
Samuel Dexter (1801)

Albert Gallatin (1801–1809)

SECRETARY OF WAR
Henry Dearborn (1801–1809)

ATTORNEY GENERAL
Levi Lincoln (1801–1804)

Robert Smith (1805)

John Breckinridge (1805–1806)

Caesar A. Rodney (1807–1809)

SECRETARY OF THE NAVY
Benjamin Stoddert (1801)

Robert Smith (1801–1809)

POSTMASTER GENERAL
Joseph Habersham (1801)

Gideon Granger (1801–1809)

Thomas Jefferson amazed and astounded his contemporaries, and continues to do the same today. This paradoxical man was truly a pragmatic idealist who left his imprint of liberty on the new nation. Jefferson saw America's future when it was still a patchwork of colonies; his eloquence inspired his countrymen to break from Britain; and he never lost hope in the darkest days of the Revolutionary War or when America took its first faltering steps as a truly independent nation. His was the dream of a nation founded on liberty; it is that ideal that guides America still.

EARLY LIFE

Peter Jefferson was descended from a long line of early Virginia settlers and was an established bachelor of thirty when he married nineteen-year-old Jane Randolph in 1739. Her family was considered one of the "FFVs" (First Families of Virginia), and she had lived most of her young life in England before returning to her father's native land. The Jeffersons had two daughters before Peter moved his family to the edge of the Virginia wilderness and the foothills of the Blue Ridge Mountains. He built a house he named Shadwell and there, on April 13, 1743, their first son was born. Thomas lived there his first two years, then Jane's cousin William Randolph died and his will requested the Jeffersons move to his home in the Tidewater, called Tuckahoe, to care for his orphaned children. Thomas and his siblings (who arrived at frequent intervals) played and attended school with their Randolph cousins. Seven years later, when the Jefferson family was ready to return to Shadwell, nine-year-old Thomas was sent away to school. There he became grounded in classical languages and mathematics.

Peter Jefferson was often away on surveying expeditions, including one with Joshua Fry to map Virginia's border with North Carolina. Peter Jefferson, from contemporary descriptions, was a huge bear of a man who was greatly admired by his oldest son. While fourteen-year-old Thomas was home on summer vacation in 1757, tragedy struck when Peter became gravely ill. He died in August, leaving behind eight children, including two-year-old twins. On his father's deathbed, Thomas had promised to continue his schooling, and he did. He attended another parson's school for the next three years, and then determined he was ready to attend the College of William and Mary in Williamsburg.

Thomas had never before been to such a large town. Williamsburg's population was normally about fifteen hundred people, but when the House of Burgesses or the General Court met, the number doubled. The town boasted several taverns and often hosted touring theatrical companies. Young Jefferson was eager to be accepted into the College of William and Mary. He easily passed the entrance examinations and quickly fell in with a number of fellow students who later would serve in a variety of public offices with him. His college instructors were impressed by the exceptionally bright and extremely talented student, and soon Jefferson was included in gatherings at the Governor's Palace. He would bring his violin and play in musical evenings with some of the colony's most influential men, including the governor. Here, among this company, Thomas also gained valuable insight into the world of political leadership; it was the most instructive classroom he would ever attend.

After two years, Thomas decided to pursue a legal career. One of his musical cohorts, George Wythe, agreed to be his teacher, and for the next five years Jefferson read law, attended courts, and regularly

	1801				
NATIONAL EVENTS	John Chapman arrives with apple seeds to plant in the Ohio valley, thus earning nickname "Johnny Appleseed"	**JAN 27:** US Senate confirms John Marshall to be chief justice of US Supreme Court	**FEB 13:** Judiciary Act passed **FEB 17:** House of Representatives finally—after 36 votes—chooses Thomas	Jefferson winner of the 1800 election; Aaron Burr will be vice president	**MAR 3:** President Adams makes last-minute appointments known as "midnight judges"
WORLD EVENTS	Guangzhou, China, world's largest city with 1.5 million people	**JAN 1:** Parliament creates United Kingdom of Great Britain and Ireland	**FEB 9:** Treaty of Lunéville between France and Austria	**FEB 27:** Spain declares war on Portugal	**MAR 1:** London Stock Exchange founded

met with Wythe. During this time, the colonies were beginning to exercise what they considered their rights as British subjects to oppose certain acts of Parliament, especially taxes. In May 1765, Wythe instructed his student to go to the capitol where the members of the House of Burgesses were debating their stance on the Stamp Act (p. 23). There in the doorway the tall redhead peered over the Burgesses to watch Patrick Henry (a member who had already won fame as a well-spoken attorney) incur the wrath of fellow members when he loudly voiced his opposition to Parliament and King George III in such strong terms that some Burgesses yelled "Treason! Treason!" To which Henry replied, "If this be treason, make the most of it!" Jefferson never forgot the spellbinding nature of Patrick Henry's speech, who he later said, "spoke as Homer wrote,"[1] nor would he ever be able to perform in such a manner himself, for public speaking was never his forte.

In 1767, Jefferson passed the bar and became one of the few lawyers privileged to try cases before the General Court. Two years later he was elected to the House of Burgesses. As a young man with a budding career, Thomas decided it was time to begin building a house. For years he had studied books by various architects but most admired the designs by the sixteenth-century Italian architect Andrea Palladio. Years before, he had decided to eschew the common practice of the day to build one's plantation home out of wood by a river. No, Jefferson wanted to be able to watch the weather and see the world sprawled out below him, so from the property he inherited from his father, he chose a mountaintop to construct his home out of brick. Building had scarcely begun when his birthplace, Shadwell, burned to the ground.

Work on his home, Monticello (Italian meaning "little mountain"), proceeded and picked up speed after he began courting Martha Wayles Skelton, a young Tidewater widow. From all accounts she was a vivacious, intelligent, and attractive woman who easily captured Jefferson's heart. They married on January 1, 1772, and settled in to their very unfinished home; in September, they welcomed their first child, a daughter also named Martha (nicknamed Patsy). Two years later, another daughter, Jane, was born, and the Jeffersons contentedly spent their time at Monticello and visiting relatives.

Their idyllic world, though, was abruptly halted by events far away in Boston as actions by the Sons of Liberty (p. 24) caused strained relations with Britain. Other colonies also watched with ever-growing concern as an entire shipment of tea was dumped into the harbor during the Boston Tea Party (p. 25), and the resulting Intolerable (Coercive) Acts closed the port in retaliation. In 1774, after the Coercive Acts took effect, Jefferson wrote a pamphlet, "The Summary View of the Rights of British America," which was published throughout the colonies, as well as in Great Britain. Thus, his name became associated with those liberals who were "fomenting rebellion," although he insisted he wanted nothing more than continued association with the mother country.

REVOLUTIONARY

In 1775, Jefferson became a delegate to the Second Continental Congress (p. 8) in Philadelphia, serving with Patrick Henry, John and Samuel Adams, John Hancock, Benjamin Franklin, and others. He spent eighteen months splitting his time between Monticello and Philadelphia. The delegates admired what John Adams called his "felicity of expression,"[2] and Adams went on to say that Jefferson was the best writer in Congress.

MAR 4: Thomas Jefferson inaugurated president

MAY 10: Tripoli declares war against US

NOV 16: The *New-York Evening Post* founded by Alexander Hamilton

DEC 8: Thomas Jefferson sends annual message to Congress in written form rather than in person; precedent continues until 1913

1802

Arlington House completed for George Washington Parke Custis, Martha Washington's grandson; his daughter and her husband, Robert E. Lee, will later inherit it; eventually, it becomes center of Arlington National Cemetery

MAR 11: Czar Paul I of Russia murdered; succeeded by his son Alexander I

JUN 7: Haitian Independence declared

JUN 14: Benedict Arnold dies in London

World population reaches 1 billion people

Madame Marie G. Tussaud opens wax museum in London

Consequently, in June 1776, when a committee met to determine who would write the document outlining the reasons for the colonies' separation from Great Britain, it was easily decided that Thomas Jefferson was best suited for the task. Seventeen days later, he had completed it, and was justifiably proud of his work. His colleagues, however, scrutinized the Declaration of Independence and made numerous changes to it, causing no small amount of discomfort to its writer. Still, he remained proud of his accomplishment and, fifty years later, would list it as one of only three achievements that he wished recorded on his tombstone.

The Declaration of Independence still resounds today and is considered by many a masterpiece of written political expression. Jefferson, however, always insisted that the thoughts were not anything new, just bits and pieces of philosophy he had absorbed over the years, since his purpose was "to place before mankind the common sense of the subject, in terms so plain and firm as to command their assent."[3] Once he was finished, he raced home to Virginia to rejoin his family, as well as help with the drafting of the state constitution and the overhaul of its penal code.

NOTES ON THE STATE OF VIRGINIA ★ Jefferson's answer to French diplomat François Marbois's questions about Virginia is remarkable in its depth of information. Originally written in 1781 and republished in Paris in 1784 after being expanded, it is mainly devoted to a thorough geographical description of Jefferson's native state, including its flora and fauna. Jefferson's descriptions of the native and African populations as being inferior races illustrate that he, too, was a product of his time.

One area of reform that Jefferson singled out for particular emphasis was that of religious freedom. Believing that the new state of Virginia would secure its liberty not only by breaking from its mother country, but from the Church of England as well, his Statutes on Religious Freedom aimed to create what is now known as "the separation of church and state." The times, however, were not ready for such a radical movement, and it would be several years before the newly created Virginia Assembly approved it—thanks to the efforts of Jefferson's protégé James Madison.

In 1779, Jefferson was elected to succeed Patrick Henry as governor of Virginia, so Thomas and his family moved to Williamsburg. Their stay was short-lived, for he and the Assembly believed that the state capital's location should reflect the westward movement of its citizenry, so the following summer, all packed and moved to Richmond. The first months there passed peacefully, but the clouds of war, distant at first, now moved ever closer. During the first six months of 1781, the British invaded Virginia, leaving destruction in their wake and causing the Jefferson family to repeatedly pack and flee or risk being taken prisoner. This was too much for their infant daughter, who died in April, the third of the Jeffersons' children to die in infancy.

The final flight occurred in June when the Assembly had adjourned to Charlottesville—the British decided to try to trap them, as well as the governor at his nearby mountaintop home. Jefferson barely escaped capture, but his reputation was not as lucky. By the end of the year, charges of cowardice and incompetence were flung at him and his seeming inability to handle the invasions adequately. Jefferson answered the charges but

NATIONAL EVENTS	**FEB 20:** James Callender publishes stories alleging President Jefferson has black slave mistress	**APR 6:** Whiskey tax abolished by Congress	**APR 14:** Congress nullifies Naturalization Act of 1798 and reinstates five-year citizenship requirement	**APR 30:** Enabling Act passed, allowing territories created under Northwest Ordinance of 1787 to become states	**JUL:** E.I. du Pont begins gunpowder plant along Brandywine River in Delaware, later the DuPont Corporation
WORLD EVENTS	**MAR 25/27:** Treaty of Amiens temporarily ends hostilities among France, Britain, Spain, and the Netherlands	**MAY 19:** Napoleon Bonaparte creates the Legion of Honor	**JUN:** General Nguyen Phuc Anh conquers Vietnam	**AUG 2:** Napoleon made consul for life	**SEP 11:** Italian region of Piedmont becomes part of the French First Republic

insisted to friends that his political career was done. Now he intended to retire to the comfort of his family, read his books and work on writing his own—*Notes on the State of Virginia*—and become a leisurely Virginia planter. In May 1782, Martha gave birth to their sixth child, Lucy Elizabeth, who joined her sisters Patsy and Mary (Polly). The deaths of her other three children, the flights from the British, and this last birth all took their toll, and Jefferson's "cherished companion" who had shared ten years with him in "unchecquered happiness"[4] died on September 6. His retirement plans instantly vanished. Hearing rumors of his friend's depression and fearing for his mental well being, James Madison was spurred to secure a position for Jefferson in France.

This position failed to materialize, but Jefferson did move—to Philadelphia—with ten-year-old Patsy and became a member of the Congress. There he threw himself into his labors and took particular interest in the development of the Northwest Territory (the land north and west of the Ohio River; current-day Ohio, Indiana, Illinois, Michigan, and Wisconsin). His efforts stood out in a congress populated by men of decidedly inferior abilities, but Jefferson remained, undoubtedly unwilling to return home where memories of his deceased wife were still fresh.

In 1784 the assignment in France finally came through; he was to depart for Paris, where he would be reunited with Benjamin Franklin and John Adams, developing commercial treaties between European powers and America. While serving in his capacity as minister to France, Jefferson also found time to travel to Italy and later, Great Britain, where he met King George III. During these travels, he enjoyed playing tourist, sightseeing at the usual stops and marveling at architecture that until then had only been sketches in his books; now his mind spun with possible ways he could implement these designs at Monticello.

Attending the court of Louis XVI allowed Jefferson to witness firsthand the extravagances of European high society. Here he met the powerful, but remained decidedly unimpressed, so he toured the backcountry to meet the French people. He also reestablished his friendship with the Marquis de Lafayette, whom he had met during his governorship. The two soon were meeting with others who wished to replicate the success of America's revolution in France. Before Jefferson's departure late in 1789, France was on its way to revolution, but already the signs of violence and fervor, unparalleled in America's revolution, were beginning to show.

From Philadelphia, James Madison wrote to his friend of the Constitutional Convention (p. 13) and, once their task was completed in September 1787, he forwarded a copy of the new Constitution. Jefferson devoured the document eagerly, but immediately became alarmed by the lack of a bill of rights. Protecting the people from their government was of paramount concern to him, and he found this omission unacceptable. Madison understood his distress and assured him that the problem could be rectified, but first the Constitution needed to be ratified.

SECRETARY OF STATE

Jefferson arrived home in December 1789, expecting to drop off his two daughters and then return to France, but to his surprise, a letter from President George Washington awaited him. In it he found his appointment to the position of secretary of state, which he accepted. Washington felt the best way to approach the presidency was to surround himself with knowledgeable men who could

SUPREME COURT APPOINTMENTS

William Johnson, 1804

Henry Brockholst Livingston, 1807

Thomas Todd, 1807

JUL 4: US Military Academy at West Point, New York, opens

OCT 18: Spanish officials in New Orleans prohibit Americans from right of deposit there

NOV: American representative Robert Livingston negotiates with French to use lower Mississippi River

OCT: French army enters Switzerland

1803

Cotton surpasses tobacco for first time as top American cash crop

FEB 24: Chief Justice John Marshall initiates judicial review (*Marbury v. Madison*) —Judiciary Act of 1789 declared unconstitutional

MAY 18: Hostilities resume between Great Britain and France

JUL: First public railway line opens outside London

STATE OF THE UNION

US POPULATION IN 1800
5,308,483

STATE ADMITTED TO UNION
Ohio, March 1, 1803

DID YOU KNOW?

Jefferson is on the nickel and the two dollar bill.

counsel him on the variety of topics that required his attention. In addition to Jefferson, he appointed old friend Henry Knox to secretary of war, fellow Virginian Edmund Randolph to attorney general, and of course, his former aide Alexander Hamilton as secretary of the treasury. Little did Washington know the powder keg he was about to ignite.

Hamilton and Jefferson disagreed philosophically about nearly every facet of the new government. Hamilton abhorred the idea of the people actually ruling themselves; instead, he thought they should be ruled by the elite and a strong central government. He wanted a moneyed class propped up by a growing industrial core, with cities developing as a result. On the other hand, Jefferson believed in the goodness of the common man and a society that allowed the people to be in control, with a weak central government allowing states more latitude. The two men made cabinet meetings a debating exercise—and often a great trial to the president's patience.

The pressing financial issues now facing the country were of deep concern for both Washington and Hamilton. Toward this end, the secretary of the treasury fashioned a series of proposals to gradually pay America's multi-million dollar debt and to secure a sound foundation for its future finances. Much of this involved bonds issued during the Revolution by the states, and Hamilton wanted the national government to assume these debts. Since most southern states had already retired their debts, the idea of repaying other states'—*northern* states'—bonds was an entirely unwelcome proposition. Enter Virginians Madison and Jefferson, who were also looking toward the debate regarding the site of the new nation's capital. Over dinner, the three men agreed to support each other: Hamilton's debt assumption would be passed, and the south would gain the new capital. Hamilton's next plan, however, could not be addressed so easily.

Believing that one of the primary building blocks of a new national economy would be the establishment of a national bank, Hamilton asked Congress to charter it. Immediately, Jefferson and Madison voiced strenuous opposition. Nowhere in the Constitution did it mention such a bank; therefore, it was unconstitutional, they argued. Hamilton pointed to Article 1 allowing Congress the authority to do whatever was "necessary and proper," thus beginning the debate between strict and loose interpretation of the Constitution, with Washington as referee. Ultimately he sided with Hamilton, as did Congress. The national bank was established and would continue until the administration of Andrew Jackson (p. 82).

The French Revolution (p. 15) created yet another rift in Washington's cabinet. Britain and its European allies fought France as they attempted to contain the ideas of revolution, and both sides attempted to ensnare the help of the United States by creating problems for the young nation. Hamilton still supported the British, in spite of the fact that they encouraged their Indian allies in the Northwest Territory to attack settlers. Jefferson, meanwhile, maintained his faith in the French people and their desire for liberty, even though news of the extreme violence waged daily in France frightened many Americans. Again in the uncomfortable middle, Washington chose not to side with either nation, as tilting either way could lead to war. Instead, he selected neutrality, which he fervently hoped would keep the United States at peace and away from the conflict that would soon enmesh Europe in decades of war.

Exhausted by the continual struggle to win the president's opinion (and usually failing in the

NATIONAL EVENTS

MAR: Fort Dearborn established on Lake Michigan; later becomes city of Chicago

MAR 1: Ohio becomes 17th state

APR 30: Louisiana Purchase negotiated—US buys entire Louisiana Territory including New Orleans for $15 million

OCT 31: American ship *Philadelphia* captured by Tripoli; crew taken prisoner

FEB 6: Lt. Stephen Decatur successfully burns the *Philadelphia* while in port in Tripoli

1804

WORLD EVENTS

AUG: Henry Shrapnel, British artillery officer, devises new exploding shell

AUG: British begin Second Anglo-Maratha War in India

NOV 29: Haiti declares independence from France

JAN 1: End of French rule in Haiti

FEB 12: German philosopher Immanuel Kant dies

attempt), Jefferson determined that it was time to retire. He wanted to oversee the renovations at Monticello and enjoy his new role as Grandpapa, so in 1793 he resigned and went home to Virginia.

NEW FOODS ★ Jefferson brought a taste of Europe to America when he returned after his five years in France. New foods to the American palate included vanilla ice cream, macaroni, figs, fried potatoes, anchovies, and broccoli. Jefferson also became a connoisseur of wines, and by the time he was president, over seven thousand dollars was spent on that item alone during his first term.

FIRST RETIREMENT

While completely removed from the political scene, Jefferson was far from forgotten. Differences between Hamilton and Jefferson had drawn battle lines for not only themselves, but their followers as well. In fact, these differences created the country's first two-party system. Washington decried its formation and worried that it could spell the demise of the nation by creating such division. The Federalist Party advocated Hamilton's ideas, and in 1796 when President Washington refused to run for a third time, they proposed John Adams for president. The Democratic-Republicans, anxious to gain the presidency, ran their founder Thomas Jefferson. According to the Constitution, whoever won the most electoral votes became president and the second highest became vice president. Thus John Adams became the second president and his mismatched vice president was Jefferson.

VICE PRESIDENT

Jefferson took the main duty of vice president seriously—to preside over the Senate. Believing that the senators needed guidelines for their daily business, the vice president undertook writing the *Manual of Parliamentary Practice*, which soon became the rule book for both houses of Congress and remains so today.

Starting with Washington's treatment of Adams, presidents historically did not allow their vice presidents into their confidence or even into their cabinet meetings. At a time when the two top officials of the government were from opposite parties, meetings between the men were usually rather cold. Although Jefferson and Adams had been friends during the Revolution and their time in Europe, more recent events had severed that friendship. Jefferson's pro-France stance came under attack with the disclosure of the XYZ Affair (p. 27). This involved demands by French officials (referred to by President Adams as Misters X, Y, and Z) for bribes from the American representatives. News of this shocked the nation, and Americans took to the streets yelling, "Millions for defense, but not one cent for tribute!" which put Jefferson and his pro-French party on the defensive.

Concerns regarding America's security grew, and Adams and the Federalist-controlled Congress passed two sets of bills collectively known as the Alien and Sedition Acts (p. 27). Under the Alien Act, citizenship requirements were tightened to prevent foreigners from gaining those rights too quickly. It also allowed the president to deport people he believed were a threat to national security. Causing greater consternation to Jefferson and his fellow Republicans was the Sedition Act, which curtailed first amendment rights of freedom of press and speech, making it illegal to publish or speak out against the Adams administration, although

MAY 14: Lewis and Clark begin three-year expedition with the Corps of Discovery

JUL 11: Vice President Aaron Burr kills Alexander Hamilton in a duel

SEP 25: Twelfth Amendment is ratified—voters choose both president and vice president to avoid replay of 1800 election

NOV: Thomas Jefferson reelected president; George Clinton is vice president

NOV: Supreme Court justice Samuel Chase served six articles of impeachment—first US Supreme Court justice to be impeached

MAR 21: Code Napoleon, a code of civil laws, enacted in France

MAY 18: Napoleon Bonaparte proclaimed emperor

JUN: Ludwig van Beethoven premieres Symphony No. 3

DEC 2: Napoleon Bonaparte crowns himself first emperor of the French in a thousand years at Notre Dame Cathedral

DEC 12: Spain declares war on Britain

DID YOU KNOW?

Jefferson was the first president to be inaugurated in Washington, D.C.

criticisms of the vice president were allowed. Jefferson and his good friend James Madison immediately collaborated to derail this outrageous legislation. Jefferson's Kentucky Resolutions, followed by Madison's Virginia Resolutions, argued that since the federal government was a collection of states, those states had the "final judgment" of any laws and could nullify any they deemed harmful or unconstitutional. The principles of these resolutions were virtually ignored by the other states; however, they would be resurrected years later by southerners to bolster their arguments favoring states rights and nullification. The Alien and Sedition Acts would be revoked for their unconstitutionality when Jefferson's administration took office.

ELECTION OF 1800

Jefferson and his party were now more determined than ever to win the presidency. Although presidents and vice presidents did not yet run as a single ticket, it was well understood that Jefferson was the Democratic-Republican's top candidate with New York's Aaron Burr as his running mate. When the votes were counted, to John Adams's embarrassment, he took third place, but Jefferson and Burr were tied at seventy-three votes apiece in the Electoral College. Now Aaron Burr saw an opportunity to win the highest position and availed himself the opportunity by refusing to step aside.

Americans viewed the unfolding drama with apprehension and concern. The next stop for the election was the House of Representatives. The House voted thirty-five times, and for thirty-five times it tied. The country feared the deadlock could go on indefinitely with no president chosen. Federalists composed the majority of House members, and none particularly liked their choices; but as nearly a week dragged on, more became convinced that Jefferson would be the better man. Finally on February 17, 1801, Thomas Jefferson was officially declared the winner of the 1800 election, and he took office three weeks later.

Keenly aware of the extremely close contest, Jefferson's inauguration speech spoke of reconciliation. "We are all Republicans, we are all Federalists. If there be any among us who would wish to dissolve this Union or to change its republican form, let them stand undisturbed as monuments of the safety with which error of opinion may be tolerated where reason is left free to combat it." For his audience, the speech was already printed, since his voice could scarcely be heard past the first few rows. Desiring to illustrate his Republican philosophy, Jefferson walked from his boardinghouse to the capitol for his inauguration, the first to be held in the capital city of Washington. John Adams, however, did not remain for his successor's ceremony, provoking many to speculate that the snub was a case of sour grapes.

PRESIDENT

Once he moved in to the President's House, which had just been completed the previous year, Jefferson's contradictory nature became even more pronounced. He received ambassadors in threadbare carpet slippers and dressing gown but entertained guests with French cuisine served by slaves. He and his secretary, Meriwether Lewis, found their new home rather cold and austere, so Jefferson soon began imploring his daughters and their families to come for visits. Both sons-in-law moved into the President's House when they came to Washington as Virginia congressmen.

With an eye to cutting the budget, the new president assigned Lewis, who was still a commissioned army officer, the task of reducing the military. He also made good his campaign promise

NATIONAL EVENTS

Mercy Otis Warren publishes first work on the American Revolution, *The Rise, Progress, and Termination of the American Revolution*

JAN 11: Michigan Territory created from part of Indiana Territory; Detroit chosen as new capital

MAR 1: Senate acquits Supreme Court justice Chase of impeachment

APR 27: US Marines land "on shores of Tripoli"

JUN 4: US wins war against Tripoli

AUG 21: Governor William Henry Harrison of Indiana Territory purchases large tracts of land from Delaware Indians

1805

WORLD EVENTS

Pasha Muhammad Ali (Mehemet Ali) begins to establish modern Egypt

MAY 26: Napoleon I of France crowns himself king of Italy

OCT 17: Battle of Ulm: Austria surrenders to Napoleon

OCT 21: Lord Nelson and the British navy defeat combined fleets of French and Spanish at Battle of Trafalgar

WINTER: First exportation of ice sent from New England to the West Indies; begins a lucrative trade

to cut taxes on items produced domestically, thus ending the hated whiskey tax originally levied during Washington's administration (p. 2). Many Federalists were kept on in the administration, but one group posed a particular dilemma for Jefferson and his new secretary of state James Madison.

On the last night of his presidency, John Adams worked late into the night signing judicial appointments, so while the Republicans might control two branches of government, the Federalists would still retain power over the judiciary. Some of these appointments were delivered before the exchange of power, but some were not. One who did not receive his appointment was William Marbury, who then filed suit with the Supreme Court to force the new government to grant his commission. Writing the Court's opinion was its chief justice and Adams appointee John Marshall. In *Marbury v. Madison*, Marshall argued that the Judiciary Act of 1789 allowing Congress to create the courts was unconstitutional. So while Jefferson won the battle of Marbury's appointment, he lost the war of judicial power, for in this one decision, Marshall extended the power of the Supreme Court dramatically by granting it the power of judicial review—determining whether laws are constitutional.

Another task for secretary Lewis to deal with was Richmond newspaper publisher James Callender, who had languished almost a year in jail after being charged with violating the Sedition Act when he referred to President Adams as a British spy. In an earlier and even more preposterous charge, Callender had insisted that Washington (whom he referred to as a "scandalous hypocrite") had "authorized the robbery and ruin of his own army."[5] As a loyal supporter of Jefferson, the publisher demanded the position of postmaster, which President Jefferson refused, but the president agreed to forward Callender a partial payment for his $200 fine. Upset by only receiving $50, Callender threatened to expose Jefferson's "secrets" to the world unless he received more money. Unwilling to be blackmailed, Jefferson ignored Callender.

By now the former Republican publisher worked for the opposition and he set his poisonous pen against the president. Soon Callender was printing stories of Tom and his "dusky Sally"—tales of the president's longtime slave mistress, Sally Hemings at Monticello. Jefferson never publicly addressed the charges, insisting that to answer one would merely cause his enemies to circulate new ones. His political foes believed that the widower kept a slave concubine, while his friends decried the tales as lies. According to the Hemings family, the story was true and Jefferson was the father of Sally's four children. The Jefferson family maintained that the story was false, and that cousins of theirs were the actual fathers of Hemings' children. In 1998, a DNA study proved that a Jefferson (others lived in the vicinity and frequently visited Monticello)—but not necessarily Thomas—was the father of at least one of the Hemings children. The study did, however, conclusively prove that Thomas Woodson, who tradition says was conceived in Paris, was not a Jefferson descendant. In 1803, a drunken Callender drowned in three feet of water, but his reporting would continue to stir controversy for centuries.

Jefferson worked to reduce the size of the military and, ironically, became the first president to send American troops to foreign soil to fight. For years the Barbary states of North Africa (Tripolitania (now Libya), Tunisia, Algeria, and Morocco) demanded tribute of any nation desiring to use the Mediterranean Sea. For safe passage of their vessels, all obliged. Then Tripoli announced it wanted more; Jefferson refused, and Tripoli declared war. In 1803,

DID YOU KNOW?

Jefferson and John Marshall, Chief Justice of the Supreme Court, 1801–1835, were second cousins once removed—Marshall's great-grandfather and Jefferson's grandfather were brothers.

AUG–OCT: Lt. Zebulon Pike searches for source of the Mississippi River, unsuccessfully

NOV 7: Lewis and Clark reach the Pacific Ocean

DEC 26: Peace of Pressburg between France and Austria

Noah Webster publishes *Compendious Dictionary of the English Language*

MAR 29: Congress authorizes construction of first federal highway (National Road or Cumberland Road) from Maryland to West Virginia; later, road is extended to Illinois

1806

Prussian pharmacist assistant introduces morphine as a pain reliever

English mills close due to lack of raw American cotton

JAN: British take over Cape Town and Cape Colony from Dutch

the American ship *Philadelphia* was seized by the pirates, its guns turned against other American vessels, and its crew held for ransom. The following year, Lieutenant Stephen Decatur boldly sailed into the port and set the ship on fire. Other American ships soon aided in what became the First Barbary War, and in 1805, Tripoli agreed to end the fighting and its tribute; in exchange a ransom of $60,000 was paid for the crew of the *Philadelphia*.

LOUISIANA

As more Americans moved to the fertile lands of Kentucky, Tennessee, and the Northwest Territory, transportation of their produce became an increasingly important issue. With roads across the Appalachians scarcely more than paths, farmers found river transportation much more efficient in terms of both time and money. Using the Ohio and Mississippi Rivers, then transferring to ships at New Orleans where their goods could then be sent either to the east coast or beyond was their preferred choice. During Washington's administration, Spain had closed New Orleans, but negotiations had reopened that port; however, alarm spread with the news that the entire Louisiana Territory had been transferred from Spain to France, one of the prizes of war gained by Napoleon when he conquered Spain. No one faced the threat of having Napoleon as its new neighbor with more trepidation than the American president. He determined that America must own that key piece of real estate—New Orleans. James Monroe was dispatched to France to aid American minister to France Robert Livingston in purchasing the port, as well as West Florida.

Just prior to Monroe's arrival, the French made the unbelievable offer to sell New Orleans *and* the vast Louisiana Territory beyond it. Unsure of what to do next, the two negotiators conferred with each other and hastily contacted bankers, since they had only been authorized to spend $10 million. Acting in the belief that the president and their countrymen would heartily approve, the two Americans successfully negotiated the purchase of the Louisiana Territory, including New Orleans (but not, as it turned out, West Florida) for the price of $15 million, which worked out to three cents an acre.

Once Jefferson heard of the acquisition, he was thrilled but also concerned about the constitutionality of purchasing territory. He prepared a constitutional amendment in case the Senate had qualms, but he did not need to fear—the Senate ratified the treaty 26–5. Doubling the United States would be considered the greatest achievement of Jefferson's presidency, but he would point with equal pride to the expedition that not only explored this new territory, but the land west to the Pacific Ocean as well. For at least twenty years, Thomas Jefferson had dreamed of sending an expedition to map this uncharted wilderness. He had contacted Revolutionary hero George Rogers Clark

NAPOLEON BONAPARTE (1769–1821) ★ By the time of the Louisiana Purchase in 1803, Napoleon was thirty-four years old, a famed military commander, conqueror, and recently proclaimed consul for life in France. At this time, his country enjoyed a respite from war, but bills—from previous conflicts in Europe and his defeat in Egypt—accumulated. Following slave uprisings in Santo Domingo, which prompted his troops to withdraw, Napoleon gave up his dream of creating an empire in North America, making the purchase of the Louisiana Territory negotiable.

NATIONAL EVENTS

MAY 30: Andrew Jackson kills Charles Dickinson of Tennessee in a duel

JUL 15: Lt. Zebulon Pike leaves on another expedition; explores the Southwest, including Colorado (where a mountain is named after him)

SEP 23: Lewis and Clark return to St. Louis and surprise many who assumed they were dead

SEP–OCT: General James Wilkinson informs President Jefferson that Aaron Burr is attempting to create his own nation in the West

WORLD EVENTS

JUN 5: Napoleon appoints his brother Louis Bonaparte as king of Holland

AUG 6: Emperor Francis I abdicates; end of Holy Roman Empire

OCT 27: French army enters Berlin

in the 1780s. His frontier and leadership skills were well known, and although Clark was interested in the mission, plans never materialized. Others were contemplated as well, but nothing happened until Jefferson was president.

Early in 1803—and *before* the Louisiana Purchase—Jefferson secured a budget of $2,500 to send a military expedition west. Meriwether Lewis was made its leader with the rank of captain, and Lewis appointed his former army superior William Clark as his co-captain. Ironically, Clark was the youngest brother of George Rogers.

Excited by the prospect of acquiring knowledge about all facets of the west, Jefferson instructed Lewis as to the types of information gathering he expected, including maps, and notes on the flora and fauna, soil, weather, and of course, the natives they encountered, who were to be treated "in the most friendly & conciliatory manner which their own conduct will admit."[6] Laying a foundation for peaceful trading among them was vital to the expedition's success, as well as the country's future as its people moved westward.

The Lewis and Clark expedition, officially known as the Corps of Discovery, pushed off from St. Louis at six a.m. on May 22, 1804, and began the journey up the Missouri River. Jefferson anxiously awaited hearing from Captain Lewis, who apparently neglected to write as frequently as his commander desired. But the following spring, ten members of the Corps returned and ensured that the president received journals from the captains and a wide variety of specimens both animal and botanical. Jefferson pored over the map of the Missouri River and the accounts of the expedition's relations with various native tribes. About a year later, Jefferson would be reunited with the co-captains and hear firsthand of their adventures and discoveries.

SECOND TERM

Jefferson won reelection in 1804, easily defeating Charles Pinckney, but this time his vice president would be George Clinton rather than Aaron Burr. Earlier in 1804, Burr had determined that his political fortune was being thwarted by his lowly status as vice president, so he announced he was running for governor of New York. This immediately set Alexander Hamilton into a fury, working feverishly to deny him the title. Burr suspected his old rival was badmouthing him, and wrote to Hamilton demanding the truth. Hamilton affirmed he had said something unflattering about Burr, so Burr countered with a challenge. Again Hamilton acquiesced, setting the stage for what became a historical duel. The two men met early on July 11 in Weehawken, New Jersey. There Burr fired a fatal bullet that not only killed Hamilton but Burr's political future as well.

Burr did little to help himself when he traveled westward to seek support for his scheme to seize land in the Louisiana Territory to either use as a base to attack Spanish territory if the United States went to war with that nation or create his own country. Which plan he truly intended is still unknown as he spread contradictory tidbits of information to a wide variety of people, including Andrew Jackson, during his intrigues. Burr conspired with General James Wilkinson, a double-dealer who earlier had worked for the Spanish by passing on information regarding the movements of the Corps of Discovery. Wilkinson now blew the whistle on Burr, who was soon arrested on charges of treason.

The grand jury convened in Richmond, Virginia, in May 1807. Chief Justice John Marshall presided and well-known orator Luther Martin headed Burr's defense team. The prosecution would fight an uphill battle to win conviction, for its judge was vehemently opposed to the president, and many had

DID YOU KNOW?

Jefferson was the first president to shake hands instead of bowing to others as a form of greeting.

MAR 2: Congress passes non-importation act against Great Britain to protest its impressments of American sailors

MAR 2: Congress passes legislation prohibiting importation of slaves after January 1, 1808

JUN 22: US relations with Great Britain worsen when USS *Chesapeake* is ordered to stop by HMS *Leopold*; when *Chesapeake* refuses, British open fire, killing 3, wounding 18

JUL: President Jefferson orders all British ships out of American waters

1807

JAN 7: Britain's Royal Council announces its prohibition of neutral nations' ships to trade with France or her allies; blockades French ports

JAN 28: London street lit with gaslights

FEB: Napoleon attacks Russia

FEB 23: British Parliament votes to ban slave trade

APR 27: French forces capture Danzig, Poland

DID YOU KNOW?

Jefferson wrote almost 20,000 letters in his lifetime.

been outraged when the president pronounced belief in Burr's guilt. Was not the accused innocent before being proven guilty? Martin in his defense of Burr compared Wilkinson to Satan, and the prosecution soon found themselves defending the administration more than actually prosecuting Burr. The defense asked and received Marshall's permission to subpoena the president and/or his papers regarding the case. Jefferson insisted the district attorney had the necessary papers, and as to attending the court in Richmond, he politely but firmly refused: "To comply with such calls would leave the nation without an executive branch . . . the sole branch which the constitution requires to be always in function."[7] Ultimately Aaron Burr was acquitted, much to the president's dismay and embarrassment, but to the pleasure and delight of both Burr and Marshall. Jefferson had little time to dwell on defeat, for international events threatened the peace at home.

PROBLEMS WITH BRITAIN

In June 1807, US ship *Chesapeake* was boarded by the British ship *Leopard* after being fired on, and four members of its crew were taken; three were Americans. Outrage spewed from American citizens demanding war against Britain. Jefferson, however, knew the country was in no condition to fight and pledged to retaliate with economic measures. Before the year was out, an embargo forbid American ships from sailing into foreign ports, and foreign ships were not allowed to trade in America. Expecting France and Great Britain to be especially stung by the economic sanctions, Jefferson believed the embargo would bring them to the negotiating table.

Unexpectedly, the ones most hurt by the embargo were Americans—shippers, sailors, farmers, planters—nearly all were victims of ships sitting and rotting in their berths. The national income dropped by over 50 percent, and increased trade with Russia fell far short of making up the difference. Americans decried the ruin they faced; consequently, before leaving office, Jefferson cancelled his embargo, and soon another took effect, which only prohibited trade between America and the two offending nations. Unfortunately, no embargo would prevent the march toward war, but Jefferson finished his term before actual fighting began. His secretary of state and good friend James Madison would inherit the impending crisis.

Anxious to be released from "the shackles of power,"[8] Jefferson relaxed at James Madison's inaugural ball, packed, and soon left Washington, never to return.

RETIREMENT AT LAST

Once he arrived at Monticello, he enveloped himself in the outdoors and spent most daylight hours tending his farm. He wrote the change brought him great happiness, as did the time he spent with his family. Unfortunately, his beautiful daughter Maria died in April 1804, leaving an infant daughter and a son. His older daughter Martha had married her cousin, Thomas Mann Randolph, and they had become parents to eleven children. Jefferson insisted the Randolphs live at Monticello, and so they did, much to his son-in-law's consternation.

Jefferson loved children and for years had worked on plans for educating the young, as he believed a democracy required an educated electorate. His crowning achievement of his retirement years would be the creation of a new state college—the University of Virginia. Jefferson oversaw every minute detail, from ensuring it was located in nearby Charlottesville, to determining its curriculum and selecting its faculty. As building progressed, he often traversed down the mountain to supervise construction; other times, he viewed it

NATIONAL EVENTS

AUG 17: Robert Fulton develops first commercially successful steamboat

SEP 1: Aaron Burr is acquitted for treason; he leaves for Europe

DEC 14: American Non-Importation Act of 1806 goes into effect, banning many British imports

DEC 18: Congress passes Embargo Act banning American trade with foreign nations

JAN 1: US stops importation of slaves

1808

WORLD EVENTS

JUN 14: Battle of Friedland: Napoleon defeats Russian army

JUL 7–9: Napoleon Bonaparte and Czar Alexander I of Russia sign the Tilsit Agreement, allying their nations

SEP 2-7: British navy bombs Copenhagen to prevent Denmark from surrendering its fleet to Napoleon

FEB 11: First use of anthracite coal as fuel

through his telescope from Monticello. Finally the long-awaited day arrived and the doors opened to greet the first students in 1825. Jefferson sometimes invited small groups of students to Monticello for dinner and conversation; perhaps one of his guests included seventeen-year-old Edgar Allen Poe, who matriculated there for most of 1826.

Being in debt had been a way of life for Jefferson since the Revolution, but over the years, it threatened to take his most prized possession—Monticello. With the burning of the Library of Congress during the War of 1812 (p. 54), he saw an opportunity to relieve some of his debt, as well as help his dear nation. He sold his extensive library of over 6,500 volumes to the government, which then formed the nucleus for today's Library of Congress collection. Since Jefferson could never be long without books, he soon began assembling a new library.

By this time, a reconciliation had occurred between Jefferson and John Adams. A mutual friend, Dr. Benjamin Rush, succeeded in encouraging the two men to begin a correspondence. (Several years before, Jefferson and Abigail Adams had a brief correspondence after his daughter Maria's death, but John Adams was not involved.) This they began tentatively at first, but as the letters went back and forth, the wall that had separated them for so many years came down. They chatted about family matters as well as national news; they reminisced and posed questions to each other. Would you live your life over again? When Abigail Adams died, Jefferson wrote a note of consolation, which Adams gladly accepted. Thus both were in each other's thoughts as the fiftieth anniversary of the Declaration of Independence approached.

Neither could leave home to celebrate; in fact, on July 4, 1826, both men breathed their last. The last words of John Adams were "Thomas Jefferson still survives."[9] Unbeknownst to him, his dear friend had died a few hours before. Unable to get out of bed for the previous days, Jefferson willed himself to live until the fourth and continually asked his grandson and namesake if it was the fourth yet. Finally it was affirmed, and Jefferson seemed relieved. He died at 9:50 a.m. that morning and was buried the following day in the graveyard at Monticello beside his wife and daughter Maria.

Jefferson's tombstone bore the epitaph he desired: a list of accomplishments he most wished to be remembered for and "not a word more":

Here was buried
Thomas Jefferson
Author of the Declaration of Independence
of the Statute of Virginia for
religious freedom & Father
of the University of Virginia.[10]

ENDNOTES

1 Adrienne Koch and William Peden, eds., *The Life and Selected Writings of Thomas Jefferson*, New York: The Modern Library, 1944, p. 6.

2 David McCullough, *John Adams*, New York: Simon & Schuster, 2001, p. 120.

3 Alf J. Mapp, Jr., *Thomas Jefferson, A Strange Case of Mistaken Identity*, New York: Madison Books, 1997, p. 111.

4 Koch and Peden, p. 53.

5 Virginius Dabney, *The Jefferson Scandals*, New York: Dodd, Mead & Co., 1981, p. 35.

6 Stephen Ambrose, *Undaunted Courage*, New York: Simon & Schuster, 1996, p. 95.

7 Dumas Malone, *Jefferson the President: Second Term, 1805-1809*, Boston: Little Brown & Company, 1974, p. 322.

8 Nathan Schachner, *Thomas Jefferson, A Biography*, New York: Thomas Yoseloff, 1969, p. 886.

9 Ibid, p. 1010.

10 Ibid, p. 1008.

APR 6: John Jacob Astor creates the American Fur Company

JUL 12: The *Missouri Gazette* begins publication in St. Louis, making it the first newspaper west of the Mississippi River

NOV 10: Osage Indians sign treaty granting their lands in Missouri and Arkansas; they move to area later known as Oklahoma

DEC 7: Democratic-Republican nominee James Madison wins presidential election; George Clinton is vice president

FEB 21: Russian troops invade Finland

APR: First typewriter built in Italy

DEC 22: Beethoven conducts his Fifth Symphony for first time at Vienna concert

JAMES MADISON

★ ★ ★ FOURTH PRESIDENT ★ ★ ★

LIFE SPAN
- Born: March 16, 1751, in Port Conway, Virginia
- Died: June 28, 1836, at Montpelier, in Virginia

NICKNAME
- Father of the Constitution

RELIGION
- Episcopalian

HIGHER EDUCATION
- College of New Jersey (now Princeton), 1772

PROFESSION
- Politician

MILITARY SERVICE
- Colonel, Virginia militia 1775–1776 (not in active service)

FAMILY
- Father: **James Madison** (1723–1801)
- Mother: **Eleanor "Nelly" Rose Conway** (1731–1829)
- Wife: **Dolley Payne Todd Madison** (1768–1849) a widow with a son; wed September 15, 1794, in Jefferson County, Virginia
- Stepchild: **John Payne Todd** (1792–1852)

POLITICAL LIFE
- Member of the Virginia Constitutional Convention (1776)
- Member of the Continental Congress (1780–1783)
- Member of the Virginia legislature (1784–1786)
- Member of the Constitutional Convention (1787)
- US representative (1789–1797)
- Secretary of state (1801–1809)

PRESIDENCY
- Two terms: March 4, 1809–March 4, 1817
- Democratic-Republican
- Reason for leaving office: completion of term
- Vice presidents: **George Clinton** (1809–1812), died while in office; **Elbridge Gerry** (1813–1814), died while in office

ELECTION OF 1808
- Electoral vote: **Madison** 122; **Charles C. Pinckney** 47
- Popular vote: none

ELECTION OF 1812
- Electoral vote: **Madison** 128; **DeWitt Clinton** 89
- Popular vote: none

CABINET

SECRETARY OF STATE
Robert Smith (1809–1811)

James Monroe (1811–1817)

SECRETARY OF THE TREASURY
Albert Gallatin (1809–1814)

George W. Campbell (Feb.–Oct. 1814)

Alexander Dallas (1814–1816)

William H. Crawford (1816–1819)

SECRETARY OF WAR
William Eustis (1809–1812)

John Armstrong (1813–1814)

James Monroe (1814–1815); briefly served dually as Secretary of State and War

William H. Crawford (1815–1816)

ATTORNEY GENERAL
Caesar A. Rodney (1809–1811)

William Pinckney (1811–1814)

Richard Rush (1814–1817)

"Little Jemmy," as his friends called him, stood less than five feet four inches and holds the title of America's shortest president. Always sickly, he would endure one of the worst events imaginable for any chief executive—foreign invasion. For the first time in our history, a war was given the president's name: Mr. Madison's War. Other presidents, including Lincoln, would also bear the burden of war, but only James Madison stood in the charred ruins of the capital city and encouraged the town's citizenry to rebuild. In the weary days of the War of 1812, James Madison stood taller than many successors, taking history's disastrous events and transforming them into opportunities for the new nation.

EARLY LIFE

James Madison was born March 16, 1751, the oldest of James and Nelly Conway Madison's seven children. Their plantation, Montpelier, was located in Orange County, Virginia, near the eastern edge of the Blue Ridge Mountains. James Madison Sr. was a leading member of Orange County's citizenry, as well as its principal landholder. For several years he supervised the construction of Montpelier. By age eleven, young James was sent to school in King and Queen County under the tutelage of Donald Robertson. Robertson taught Madison the normal curriculum of mathematics, philosophy, languages, history, and geography. Then for two years, he studied under a tutor as preparation for college. Madison pondered where to continue his education.

After considering various schools, including the College of William and Mary, Madison decided to attend the College of New Jersey (now Princeton University) and was admitted as a sophomore. There he came under the leadership of its new president, John Witherspoon. While at Princeton, Madison met other young men who demonstrated an interest in public affairs; they met and formed the American Whig Society. He participated in arguments and developed an interest in the law. Madison embraced his studies and worked feverishly to complete them in a short stretch of time. Leaving little time for sleep and recreation, his health suffered, but he still completed his coursework in two years and graduated in 1772. He remained in town and briefly studied Hebrew and ethics as the beginnings of a career in the clergy. That thought soon faded, and he returned to Montpelier.

Once home, Madison considered becoming a lawyer; after all, he had already read many of the works considered a necessity for its study. But soon that passion faded as well. His health remained poor, so the young man apparently grew melancholy as he pondered his fate. Uncertain of his future, he remained home and worked with his father managing the estate. Soon, events would determine the young man's destiny.

REVOLUTIONARY DELEGATE

By 1774, James Madison had made his choice—he would work to aid those wanting independence from Great Britain. He joined the Committee of Safety (local organizations that followed people and activities in the days leading up to the Revolution). Although Madison became a colonel in the Orange County militia, he never actually saw military duty because of his frequent bouts of poor health. Nevertheless, plenty of other tasks required the attention of someone with knowledge of the law and time to work on creating a new state government for

NATIONAL EVENTS — **1809**

FEB: Tecumseh and his brother Tenskwatawa (the Prophet) develop confederacy of Indian tribes to oppose encroaching American settlement

FEB 3: Congress creates Illinois Territory from western part of Indiana Territory

FEB 15: Congress passes Enforcement Act to halt smuggling

FEB 20: Supreme Court rules in *United States v. Peters* that federal government is supreme over states

MAR 1: President Jefferson repeals Embargo Act and replaces it with Non-Intercourse Act

WORLD EVENTS

JAN 5: Treaty of Dardanelles signed by Britain and Ottoman Empire

MAR 29: Swedish army officers force King Gustavus IV to abdicate; Duke of Sudermania becomes king, reigns until 1818

APR 25: Treaty of Amritsar (India) settles East India Company's northwest border

MAY: Napoleon captures Vienna, takes Pope Pius VIII prisoner, annexes Papal States

AUG: Ecuador declares independence from Spain

Virginia. Elected as a member to the Virginia House of Delegates in 1776, he soon caught the attention of Thomas Jefferson, newly returned from Philadelphia and drafting the Declaration of Independence. The two men met frequently and became best friends. No topic was beyond their discussion, and they often enjoyed a game of chess. Their friendship would continue uninterrupted the rest of their lives. Even then, Jefferson asked for Madison to "take care of me when dead."[1]

As a member of the Virginia Convention, Madison served on a committee drafting a declaration of rights, as well as the framework for their new state government. Once the new state constitution went into effect, the delegates stood for reelection. Madison decided not to continue the time-honored practice of serving whiskey to constituents on Election Day; his opponent won.

Nevertheless, Madison would not remain idle for long because within months, he was appointed to the Council of State for Governor Patrick Henry. Eight councilors served as advisors to the governor. Madison's first act was agreeing to respond to General Washington's desperate plea that food and provisions be sent posthaste to Valley Forge. Oftentimes the council met six days a week, and since the Assembly (the lower house of Virginia's legislative branch) was frequently not in session, more demands on the councilors' time were made. Madison grew increasingly unhappy with this type of leadership and called the council "the grave of all useful talents."[2] Although he relished working with Governor Thomas Jefferson, he dutifully relinquished the chains of councilor for those of a congressional delegate when he was appointed in 1780.

CONGRESSMAN

Even though he was the youngest member of Congress, Madison quickly impressed others with his diligence and hard work. Committee appointments, including the Admiralty Board, were soon his. Besides the ongoing demands of attempting to coordinate the war effort, the single major issue confronting the young Virginian was the matter of western land claims. The conflicting claims from various states threatened the already tenuous union. The matter required resolution before the Articles of Confederation would be ratified by the affected states. Madison understood the need to compromise for the greater good and worked diligently to win approval for Virginia to cede its claims to the country in return for its demands. It took the greater part of his four-year tenure to accomplish this, but ultimately his efforts gained the desired results and the states relinquished their disputed territories to the country to keep the peace.

Also while in Philadelphia, the thirty-year-old bachelor did the unexpected and fell in love with a young lady half his age. He pursued Kitty Floyd, daughter of a New York delegate, and seemingly, his affections were returned. He finally proposed; she accepted, and he hastened to make wedding plans. After a three-month engagement, the young lady's mind changed and she decided to wed another fellow closer in age. Madison accepted defeat, and probably assumed he would remain a bachelor for the rest of his life.

VIRGINIAN

Returning to Virginia in 1784 and elected to the Virginia House of Delegates, Madison quickly found himself immersed in state politics. Now debate raged over the question of the separation of church and state. Madison had worked previously

CABINET
★★★★★★★★★★

(continued)

SECRETARY OF THE NAVY

Paul Hamilton (1809–1812)

William Jones (1813–1814)

Benjamin Crowninshield (1815–1817)

MAR 4: Madison inaugurated as fourth president

JUN 8: Thomas Paine dies

SEP 7: Siam's king Phraphutthayotfa Chulalok dies after a 27-year reign

1810

US census shows more than 7 million people, including more than 1 million slaves

Prussia abolishes serfdom

New York City surpasses Philadelphia as largest American city

French chemist names active ingredient of tobacco nicotine

MAY: Congress repeals 1809 Non-Intercourse Act, resumes American trade with Britain and France

King Kamehameha I unifies Hawaii

JAN 10: Napoleon divorces his wife Josephine

FEDERALIST PAPERS (1787–1788) ★ The Federalist Papers were a series of eighty-five essays written by Alexander Hamilton, John Jay, and James Madison under the pseudonym Publius. Each paper argued in favor of the newly written Constitution and was published as a means to answer critics before state ratification conventions met. Hamilton and Madison drafted the majority of articles, which are still read today as fine examples of classic rhetoric.

with mentor Thomas Jefferson, but the proposal had stalled. Patrick Henry led the supporters of a religion tax to support a state church. After encountering opposition, Henry backtracked and suggested supporting teaching the "Christian religion."[3] Still considering this an offense to religious liberty, Madison continued to battle the famed speaker. Madison could not match Patrick Henry's impressive oratory, but he could defeat him with persuasive logic, and eventually he won passage of Jefferson's Statutes for Religious Freedom.

Following the Revolution, the nation faced new challenges that were as threatening as those during the war. Neither foreign nor interstate commerce were addressed in the Articles of Confederation (p. 26), thus creating problems whenever states disagreed on such matters. Britain closed its West Indian ports to the new nation, and Spain closed New Orleans and its right of deposit, which allowed American ships to use its port. Closer to home, Virginia and Maryland entertained divergent views about navigation rights on the Potomac River. Worried about such a conflict growing in scope, Madison agreed to attend an assembly in Annapolis to examine the trade issue. Although disappointed that only twelve delegates from five states attended, the men still agreed to have another meeting, with invitations sent to all thirteen states to assemble in May 1787 in Philadelphia to discuss problems with the current government and possible changes to the Articles of Confederation. Seizing upon the critical importance of the occasion, Madison stopped at Mount Vernon on his return to Virginia to urge Washington to attend the upcoming Philadelphia assembly. Although delegates would be elected, Madison knew if Washington agreed to have his name submitted, he would undoubtedly be selected. Then, he reasoned, news of Washington's attendance would create interest among the other states, and hopefully, a higher caliber of leaders would then be sent to Philadelphia. Madison's plan worked perfectly, and when the Constitutional Convention (p. 13) began, the delegates immediately elected George Washington as its chairman.

FATHER OF THE CONSTITUTION

The first to arrive in Philadelphia, Madison rented his normal lodging and began developing his thoughts of a new government. Other Virginia delegates soon joined him, and they assisted formulating what became known as the Virginia Plan. Immediately the stage was set: this convention would not simply revise the Articles of Confederation; instead, a new government would emerge. Nevertheless, some delegates remained unconvinced by Madison's ideas of a stronger central government, especially granting more representation proportional to population. Small states balked, and eventually, the "Great Compromise" was offered, creating the Senate and the House of Representatives. His ideas for a strong executive branch as well as a national judiciary found their way into the Constitution. Madison's role did not

NATIONAL EVENTS

OCT 27: After American settlers in Spanish West Florida rebel against Spain, President Madison annexes area to US with military occupation; later becomes part of Louisiana

JAN 10: New Orleans puts down a slave revolt involving 400 blacks

FEB 11: Congress reissues Non-Intercourse Act against Great Britain, but not France based on assurances by Napoleon

MAR: The Twelfth Congress meets, many demand Florida annexation; new member Henry Clay elected speaker of the house

1811

WORLD EVENTS

MAR 11: Napoleon weds Austrian archduchess Maria Luisa

JUL 20: Colombia proclaims its independence from Spain

Venezuela, Paraguay, and Bolivia declare their independence from Spain

Jane Austen publishes *Sense and Sensibility*

FEB 5: King George III is declared insane; his son George IV becomes his regent

end with proposals and debate; from the first day, he sat himself at the front and took copious notes of the debates in his private shorthand. Then he labored long into the night, writing his notes into longhand. These notes allow modern-day historians and readers a chance to peel back the curtain and watch the proceedings of that unbearably hot summer of 1787.

Although somewhat dismayed by the compromises necessary for the Constitution to be borne from the convention, Madison soon ascertained the critical need to plead its cause, as its ratification became a source of debate throughout the young nation. Since Madison's oratorical skills were limited, he turned to the quill to voice his thoughts. He joined with fellow New York delegates Alexander Hamilton and, to a lesser extent, John Jay to draft a series of essays under pseudonyms, defending the Constitution and the reasons why it was so sorely needed. *The Federalist Papers* played an invaluable part in appealing to the logical arguments for the new government. Still, Madison faced a worthy adversary during the ratification convention in his home state when Patrick Henry led the opposition, wielding his fiery oratory to win the emotions of his audience. Madison stood to oppose the legend and countered with reasoned rational arguments, much as he had during the convention's debates where Georgia delegate William Pierce said of Madison that though he "cannot be called an Orator . . . He is a most agreeable, eloquent, and convincing Speaker. From a spirit of industry and application which he possesses in a most eminent degree, he always comes forward the best informed Man of any point in debate."[4] Many a seasoned lawyer had lost a case to Patrick Henry because he outshone them in bombastic delivery, but James Madison held his ground and won the prize—Virginia's ratification of the Constitution. Due to his herculean efforts before, during, and after the Constitutional Convention, he gained the title "Father of the Constitution."

PUTTING THE CONSTITUTION INTO PRACTICE

Still smarting over his defeat, Patrick Henry pounced on a chance to avenge himself and worked to ensure Madison did not win a place in the new Senate. Undaunted, Madison simply returned to his Orange County home and won a seat in the US House of Representatives instead.

When Madison took office in 1789, he worked tirelessly in Congress to pilot through the one missing component of the Constitution—a bill of rights. The first ten amendments were ratified in 1791. Madison was also anxious about the nation's economy and worked to stabilize it. At first he and Secretary of the Treasury Alexander Hamilton were of similar minds, but over time, their ideas diverged. When Hamilton proposed the assumption of state debts by the federal government, meaning that some states such as Virginia would be required to pay the debt twice, Madison vehemently objected. While he fought Hamilton's plans in Congress, his old friend and now secretary of state Thomas Jefferson opposed them in the cabinet. The two Virginians fought vigorously but lost every fight. Their views, however, formed the basis of a new political party, the Democratic-Republicans.

Madison joined forces with Jefferson throughout the remainder of Washington's term, as well as during the presidency of John Adams. When the Alien and Sedition Acts (p. 27) were passed to quell opposition to government policies, the two friends launched a resonating salvo known as the Virginia and Kentucky Resolutions. Madison

SUPREME COURT APPOINTMENTS
★★★★★★★★★★

Joseph Story, 1811

Gabriel Duval, 1812

MAY 16: US and British ships fight off New York coast

NOV 7: Battle of Tippecanoe

NOV 16: Missouri is epicenter of one of the most powerful earthquakes in history; effects are felt in New York City and Boston; causes the Mississippi River to run backwards

FEB 11: Governor Elbridge Gerry of Massachusetts signs law allowing redrawing of district lines to ensure Democratic-Republican victory; redrawing district for political reasons, thus "gerrymandering"

1812

MAR 1: Mohammed Ali, ruler of Egypt, kills last mamluk (military) leaders

MAR 26: Earthquake destroys Carcas, Venezuela

MAY 28: Treaty of Bucharest signed, ending Russo-Turkish War (1806–1812)

BILL OF RIGHTS

One of the main arguments by those opposed to the Constitution was the lack of a bill of rights. Madison promised to rectify the situation, and in June 1789, he proposed twelve amendments. Congress made a few changes and ultimately accepted ten; these became the Bill of Rights. The first two proposed amendments, which concerned the number of constituents for each Representative and the compensation of Congressmen, were not ratified.

FIRST AMENDMENT ★ Congress shall make no law respecting an establishment of religion, or prohibiting the free exercise thereof; or abridging the freedom of speech, or of the press; or the right of the people peaceably to assemble, and to petition the Government for a redress of grievances.

SECOND AMENDMENT ★ A well regulated Militia, being necessary to the security of a free State, the right of the people to keep and bear Arms, shall not be infringed.

THIRD AMMENDMENT ★ No Soldier shall, in time of peace be quartered in any house, without the consent of the Owner, nor in time of war, but in a manner to be prescribed by law.

FOURTH AMENDMENT ★ The right of the people to be secure in their persons, houses, papers, and effects, against unreasonable searches and seizures, shall not be violated, and no Warrants shall issue, but upon probable cause, supported by Oath or affirmation, and particularly describing the place to be searched, and the persons or things to be seized.

FIFTH AMENDMENT ★ No person shall be held to answer for a capital, or otherwise infamous crime, unless on a presentment or indictment of a Grand Jury, except in cases arising in the land or naval forces, or in the Militia, when in actual service in time of War or public danger; nor shall any person be subject for the same offence to be twice put in jeopardy of life or limb; nor shall be compelled in any criminal case to be a witness against himself, nor be deprived of life, liberty, or property, without due process of law; nor shall private property be taken for public use, without just compensation.

NATIONAL EVENTS

MAR 14: Congress authorizes first set of war bonds

APR 4: Embargo with the UK goes into effect

APR 30: Louisiana becomes 18th state

MAY 14: Mississippi Territory established

JUN 14: Missouri Territory established

JUN 18: President Madison, after gaining congressional approval, declares war against Great Britain

NOV: Madison is reelected president; his vice president is Elbridge Gerry

WORLD EVENTS

JUN 16: Great Britain, unaware of America's declaration of war, votes to suspend its orders against neutral ships

JUN 24: Napoleon invades Russia; three months later he retreats from Moscow

SEP 21: Czar Alexander I of Russia offers to mediate the war between the US and Great Britain

DEC 26: British blockade Chesapeake and Delaware Bays

SIXTH AMENDMENT ★ In all criminal prosecutions, the accused shall enjoy the right to a speedy and public trial, by an impartial jury of the State and district wherein the crime shall have been committed, which district shall have been previously ascertained by law, and to be informed of the nature and cause of the accusation; to be confronted with the witnesses against him; to have compulsory process for obtaining witnesses in his favor, and to have the Assistance of Counsel for his defence.

SEVENTH AMENDMENT ★ In suits at common law, where the value in controversy shall exceed twenty dollars, the right of trial by jury shall be preserved, and no fact tried by a jury, shall be otherwise reexamined in any Court of the United States, than according to the rules of the common law.

EIGHTH AMENDMENT ★ Excessive bail shall not be required, nor excessive fines imposed, nor cruel and unusual punishments inflicted.

NINTH AMENDMENT ★ The enumeration in the Constitution, of certain rights, shall not be construed to deny or disparage others retained by the people.

TENTH AMENDMENT ★ The powers not delegated to the United States by the Constitution, nor prohibited by it to the States, are reserved to the States respectively, or to the people.

The two amendments that were not ratified:

ARTICLE THE FIRST... After the first enumeration required by the first article of the Constitution, there shall be one Representative for every thirty thousand, until the number shall amount to one hundred, after which the proportion shall be so regulated by Congress, that there shall be not less than one hundred Representatives, nor less than one Representative for every forty thousand persons, until the number of Representatives shall amount to two hundred; after which the proportion shall be so regulated by Congress, that there shall not be less than two hundred Representatives, nor more than one Representative for every fifty thousand persons.

ARTICLE THE SECOND... No law, varying the compensation for the services of the Senators and Representatives, shall take effect, until an election of Representatives shall have intervened.

JAN 22: Americans decisively defeated at Battle of Raisin River when British and Indians kill 400 and take 500 prisoner

MAR: Americans accept Russian offer for mediation, but British refuse

MAR 4: President Madison inaugurated for second term

APR 14: General James Wilkinson captures Spanish fort at Mobile, which British are using

MAY: British blockade extends to mid-Atlantic coast

1813

Simon Bolivar becomes dictator of Venezuela

Swiss writer Johann Rudolf Wyss publishes *Swiss Family Robinson*

Jane Austen publishes *Pride and Prejudice*

MAR 8: Royal Philharmonic gives its first concert in London

AUG 12: Austria declares war on France

DID YOU KNOW?

James Madison has the title of being the shortest president at five feet four inches tall.

wrote the first, arguing that the Alien and Sedition Acts were unconstitutional; therefore, they should be nullified by the states. Although their arguments were not widely adopted, southern states later proudly used these resolutions as the foundation for their states' rights position against northern tariffs.

MRS. MADISON

Most of James Madison's friends and acquaintances figured that the boyish looking scholar was destined to the life of a confirmed bachelor. He apparently had other plans, and during a congressional session in 1794, Madison asked a colleague to introduce him to the widow Dolley Payne Todd. Aaron Burr (p. 41) was happy to oblige. Dolley wrote a note to her sister that "the great little Madison" was coming to see her. The meeting went well, and Madison decided to pursue his suit vigorously. He asked for her hand after only a three-month courtship. She told him she would think about it while she journeyed to Virginia to see relatives. No doubt part of her hesitation was the seventeen-year difference in their ages, as well as the knowledge that she would be forced to leave her Quaker faith if they married, because Madison was Episcopalian. Moreover, she had a son from her first marriage, but she saw in Madison a worthy father for Payne. Dolley Todd sent her affirmative answer in August, and the couple wed a few weeks later. Their friends agreed that they made a wonderful couple, who complemented each other beautifully. Dolley Madison made the leap from somber Quaker threads to the vibrant fashions of the day; moreover, her winsome spirit and charm dazzled her husband's enemies. Over the years, she proved an invaluable asset for his political career. Disappointed that she and her husband never had children of their own, Dolley spared no expense or extravagance for her son Payne Todd, who grew up quite spoiled. As an adult, he liberally spent his stepfather's money, which ultimately led to the sale of Montpelier.

SECRETARY OF STATE

When Thomas Jefferson was elected president in 1800, James Madison was his first choice to head the State Department. Immediately, Madison became named in a lawsuit brought by William Marbury, who had been awarded a judgeship by President Adams in Adams's last days in office. Marbury's commission was never delivered, and with the transfer of power to a new party, Jefferson ordered Madison not to issue the remaining commissions for justices. The newly appointed chief justice Federalist John Marshall issued an order for Madison to act. Madison ignored the order, and because of a change in the Supreme Court's schedule, it would be nearly two years before a decision was announced. Marshall was furious at Madison for snubbing him; consequently, the chief justice handed down a decision in *Marbury v. Madison* that would forever alter America's government. Concerned that the executive branch felt it could disregard the judicial branch, Marshall scolded Jefferson and Madison for not commissioning Marbury. But Marshall stated that the law allowing Marbury's appointment was in fact unconstitutional, so Marbury would not become a justice. More importantly, though, by granting the Supreme Court the power of judicial review, Marshall strengthened the judicial branch to put it on a more equal footing with the other two branches of government. Jefferson and Madison won the battle but Marshall won the war.

In dealing with other nations, America attempted to maintain its neutrality, as well as keep

NATIONAL EVENTS

MAY 1–9: Tecumseh lays siege to Fort Meigs but is unable to penetrate General Harrison's defenses

JUN 1: USS *Chesapeake* captured by British

AUG 30: Creek Indians under command of Chief Red Eagle (William Weatherford) attack Fort Mims and massacre nearly half of the 550 people there

SEP 10: Americans regain control of Lake Erie after losing it three months earlier

OCT 5: General Harrison defeats British and Indians at Battle of the Thames; Tecumseh is killed

WORLD EVENTS

AUG 26–27: Battle of Dresden gives Napoleon his last major victory on German soil

OCT 16–19: Napoleon loses at Battle of Leipzig and must retreat after losing 30,000 men

OCT 24–NOV 5: Treaty of Gulistan ends first Russo–Persian War (1804–1813)

NOV 6: Mexico declares independence from Spain

NOV 11–DEC 30: Dresden, Stettin, Lübeck, Zamose, Modlin, Torgau, and Danzig surrender to Allied forces

its right to trade with warring nations Britain and France. Fortunately in 1802, the fighting ended, albeit briefly, allowing America to trade with less constraint. Problems still remained, though, with privateers from the North African Barbary Coast demanding tribute, or else they would attack American ships in the Mediterranean Sea. Jefferson and Madison agreed that bribery needed to stop, so they responded by sending warships to the region, and Tripoli declared war. The short-lived Barbary War resulted in a United States victory and freer trade in the Mediterranean.

Madison rejoiced with his friend at the amazing news of the Louisiana Purchase in 1803. The first term of Jefferson's presidency was relatively calm compared to the problems they faced in his second. By that time, Britain and France had resumed fighting and, in turn, attacking American ships. Both sides harassed ships using each other's West Indian ports. As secretary of state, Madison drafted numerous formal protests to their governments, which resulted in nothing but ridicule from Congress. With Britain's practice of kidnapping American sailors and forcing them into service in the Royal Navy, Madison agreed with Jefferson that they must take firm action; hence, the Embargo of 1807. This ended all trade for the United States and forbid foreign vessels from using American ports. Jefferson and Madison were convinced that such drastic action would so greatly hurt the French and British that they would forego their illegal measures. Instead, the embargo boomeranged and hit the American economy grievously. Businesses suffered tremendously, and in 1809, Jefferson repealed the embargo.

Throughout Jefferson's presidency, he turned to his old friend and protégé Madison for advice. They met frequently to discuss national affairs, so correspondence between the two is lacking for the period. Dolley Madison served as acting First Lady for the widower Jefferson. To no one's surprise, James Madison was the Democratic-Republican candidate in 1808 at the end of Jefferson's second term.

ELECTION OF 1808

The Embargo of 1807 was the key issue during the campaign, and Federalists used it to discredit Madison, but they failed to pull away his base of support. Madison won 122 electoral votes; his Federalist opponent, Charles Cotesworth Pinckney of South Carolina, won forty-seven electoral votes. James Madison took office on March 4, 1809, and that night the first inaugural presidential ball was held. Guests marveled at the beautifully elegant dress of Dolley Madison and the giddy demeanor of outgoing President Thomas Jefferson, which contrasted with the depressingly somber mood of his successor. No one doubted who had just inherited the mess known as the presidency.

PRESIDENT MADISON

During the last days of Jefferson's administration, Congress had passed the Nonintercourse Act, which resumed American exporting except to Britain and France, in an attempt to damage their economies. Since it actually had little effect on either nation, Madison repealed it in 1810 and replaced it with another act, saying that if either the French or British promised to honor neutrality of American ships, the United States would stop trading with the other nation. Napoleon agreed to this, so the US announced suspension of trade with Britain, resulting in further seizures and impressments by the British navy.

By 1812, Congress, led by a group of freshmen congressmen who came to be known as the War

STATE OF THE UNION
★★★★★★★★★★

US POPULATION IN 1809
7,239,881

NATIONAL DEBT IN 1809
$57,023.192

PRESIDENT'S SALARY
$25,000/year

STATES ADMITTED TO UNION
Louisiana, April 30, 1812

Indiana, December 11, 1816

NOV 4: British offer to begin peace negotiations with US

NOV 9: General Andrew Jackson destroys Creek village, killing more than 500

MAR 27: General Andrew Jackson, his Tennessee volunteers, and Cherokee warriors defeat Creek Indians at Battle of Horseshoe Bend

APR 14: Congress repeals both the Embargo and Non-Importation Acts

JUL 22: Indian Confederacy, including Delaware, Shawnee, Miami, Seneca, and Wyandot, agree to Treaty of Greenville

1814

The Times of India begins publication in Mumbai (Bombay)

JAN 14: Treaty of Kiel: Denmark cedes Norway to Sweden in exchange for west Pomerania

JAN 29: Battle of Brienne: French under Napoleon defeat Russian and Prussian forces

Hawks, including elected Speaker of the House Henry Clay of Kentucky and John C. Calhoun of South Carolina, demanded an end to the insulting treatment. American ships were constantly threatened by the far superior British navy, who boarded them and abducted sailors, as well as seized cargoes. Moreover, British-supported attacks by various Indian tribes on the northern and western frontiers demanded action. The year before, the Indiana governor William Henry Harrison had become famous for his winning the battle of Tippecanoe against the Shawnee tribe whose chief, Tecumseh, had gathered the support of a confederation of tribes. These Native Americans were thought to be aided by British agents. Madison increasingly believed war to be the answer, and one White House dinner guest at this time wrote, "He on every occasion, and to every body . . . says the time is ripe, and the nation, too for resistance."[5] After repeated petitions went unanswered, on June 12, 1812, Madison asked Congress to declare war. The War Hawks seized upon this as an opportunity to take Canada, so they eagerly voted for the declaration. Northeastern states disagreed and voted against the resolution, but it still passed.

First of American objectives was the capture of Canada. Obtaining this prize had been an elusive goal in the American Revolution, and it would prove no less unobtainable in this war. One campaign after another failed to reach Canada; in fact, America lost some of its own land when Detroit surrendered without firing a shot. This apparently made both William Henry Harrison and Jefferson's secretary of war Henry Dearborn, who Madison had appointed senior major-general of the army, too timid to push northward into Canada. Surprisingly, American superiority did appear in various naval engagements. The USS *Constitution*, in particular, demonstrated Yankee ingenuity in the form of a thickened hull. In its fight against the British ship *Guerriere*, cannonballs seemingly bounced off the American ship's sides and fell into the sea, prompting one sailor to yell that the sides must be made of iron; hence its nickname "Old Ironsides."

Then in 1813, a cocky young Commodore Oliver Perry obtained victory on Lake Erie even after his own ship was shot to pieces when he simply moved to a rowboat and headed to another ship with his banner flying, "Don't give up the ship." It took three hours before he could send the message to General William Henry Harrison, "We have met the enemy and they are ours." Soon after, Harrison won at the battle of the Thames, where the Shawnee chief Tecumseh met his demise.

Fortunately for the Americans, the war began while Britain still fought Napoleon in Europe, meaning they sent what they could spare since they

WAR HAWKS ★ In the congressional elections of 1810, a group of approximately twenty Democratic-Republican congressmen from western and southern states were elected. These young men, the War Hawks, were united in a common belief that war against Great Britain (including seizing Canada) was the only way America could avenge itself after years of being humiliated by the British practice of impressments (taking sailors by force) and crippling American trade. They successfully took leadership positions, including Kentuckian Henry Clay becoming Speaker of the House. The War Hawks also succeeded in convincing their fellow congressmen to vote for war, and so they did in June 1812.

NATIONAL EVENTS

JUL 25: Battle of Lundy's Lane stops American advance into Canada; bloodiest battle of the war

AUG 8: British and American peace commissioners begin meetings in Ghent, Belgium

AUG 24: British march on Washington, D.C., where they burn the President's House, capitol, and other buildings and homes; President Madison and his government flee to the countryside

SEP 11: Americans defeat British on Lake Champlain and end the British advance from the north

WORLD EVENTS

JAN 31: Gervasio Antonio de Posadas becomes supreme director of Argentina

FEB 11: Norway proclaims independence

APR 6: Napoleon is overthrown; now Britain can send 14,000 veterans to fight Americans

APR 11: Napoleon abdicates and is exiled to Mediterranean island of Elba; Louis XVIII becomes king of France

AUG 13: Anglo-Dutch Treaty signed

considered the Americans more a nuisance than a threat. British ships blockaded American ports, forcing the new country to develop its manufacturing capabilities. Meanwhile, Madison experienced continuing difficulties with his cabinet. Dissatisfied with his secretary of state, Robert Smith, who disliked Secretary of the Treasury Gallatin, Madison finally replaced Smith with his friend and sometime-rival James Monroe. Gallatin was soon dispatched to Europe to serve on a peace commission with Clay and John Quincy Adams. Secretary of War John Armstrong also lacked ability and would later resign at a most crucial moment.

In 1812, Madison faced reelection and was opposed by fellow Republican DeWitt Clinton, who enjoyed Federalist support. By now, many New Englanders disliked "Mr. Madison's War" and saw no reason why they should pay for it. Southerners and westerners disagreed and reelected Madison, but it was a closer contest than in 1808.

By 1814, the British were ready to continue the war in earnest since they had defeated Napoleon. They launched a three-pronged offensive: attack northern settlements from Canada; take the Chesapeake Bay; and seize New Orleans and the Mississippi River. Americans fought off attempts in the Great Lakes region, but the campaign in the Chesapeake was a different matter.

Secretary of War Armstrong insisted that the British were solely interested in Baltimore; the people of Washington, D.C., had nothing to fear. As the British neared the capital, Armstrong maintained his stance, so the area lacked defenders when British troops landed thirty-five miles southeast of the city on August 17. Inept commander General William Winder put up a pitiful defense at Bladensburg, Maryland, leaving Washington, D.C., open for the taking. At daybreak on August 24, President Madison left the city when he received a summons from General Winder. He left his wife packing, and she waited at the President's House for news. By mid-afternoon, she wrote her sister, "We have had a battle or skirmish near Bladensburg, and I am still here within sound of the cannon! . . . Two messengers covered with dust come to bid me fly."[6] Dolley would leave only after ensuring the safe removal of the full-length Gilbert Stuart portrait of George Washington. It would be many hours before she and her husband were reunited in the nearby countryside. British troops arrived soon after her departure and, after gathering souvenirs, they set the President's House ablaze. Then they proceeded to the Capitol, where they burned it, as well as other government buildings. That night and the following day, the president and First Lady attempted to reunite, but were unsuccessful until late in the day. By then a hurricane had ripped through the area, its rain dousing the fires, and its wind causing more destruction for both sides.

Outraged by the lack of defense for America's capital, many citizens demanded action against Secretary of War Armstrong. Madison sided with them and accepted Armstrong's resignation, and then appointed James Monroe acting secretary of war, as well as secretary of state. The president walked about the ruins of the President's House and met with the people of the town. One citizen wrote, "Our good President is out animating the troops and encouraging the citizens not to despair."[7]

Events soon turned in the Americans' favor as the British proceeded up the Chesapeake to attack Baltimore. In its harbor, blocking any offensive, was Fort McHenry (named after Washington's secretary of war). For twenty-five hours, the British

DID YOU KNOW?

Madison's wife Dolley was a popular hostess for both the widower Thomas Jefferson when he was president, as well as for her husband.

SEP 13: British attempt to take Baltimore by bombarding Fort McHenry; Francis Scott Key watches, pens "The Star-Spangled Banner"

DEC 24: Peace is declared on Christmas Eve with the Treaty of Ghent

1815

JAN 8: General Andrew Jackson becomes a national hero when he and his men trounce the British forces at New Orleans

JAN 30: Thomas Jefferson sells his private library of 6,500 volumes to replace Library of Congress, burned by British (he receives $23,950)

FEB 18: President Madison proclaims peace with Treaty of Ghent and its ratification by US Senate

Grimm's Fairy Tales is published

MAR 20: Napoleon arrives in Paris after escaping from Elba

APR: Largest volcanic eruption in recorded history occurs in East Indies, kills thousands; blamed for the "year without summer"

DID YOU KNOW?

The Madisons held the first inaugural ball in 1809.

bombarded the fort, but to no avail. Watching from the deck of a truce ship behind the British was an American lawyer, Francis Scott Key, who had come to Baltimore to negotiate the release of a civilian prisoner of war. Inspired by the huge flag seamstress Mary Pickersgill had made which flew over the fort and survived the bombardment, Key penned a poem, "The Star-Spangled Banner." Dismayed by their failure to secure the fort, the British departed, hoping that their offensive against New Orleans would be more successful.

New Englanders remained unimpressed by the events at Baltimore and demanded a swift end to the war. Delegates from New England states met secretly in Hartford, Connecticut, and debated possible action. Frustrated by years of embargoes, the British blockade, and the war in general, which had greatly harmed their trade and businesses, these men met to determine what action they could pursue to end the war, and just as importantly for them, the influence of southerners and the Democratic-Republican Party. They did not do anything, for they received good news, making any action unnecessary.

After months of negotiations, the British and Americans finally agreed to the Treaty of Ghent and signed it on December 24, 1814. This treaty gained no territory or promises for either side, but it simply ended hostilities and resumed prewar conditions. Since communication was slow, neither side was aware of the news when Andrew Jackson and his men provided the British with one of their worst defeats at the battle of New Orleans on January 8, 1815. On February 20, 1815, President Madison announced with no small amount of relief the end of the war.

The remaining year of Madison's presidency was one of extreme calm and, to some extent, jubilation. Although America had not won the war, they had not lost to Britain, and this knowledge provided the young nation with no small degree of self-confidence. The Madisons resumed entertaining, albeit on a smaller scale to fit in their reduced quarters at the Octagon house, another mansion in Washington, which stood in for the President's House. While few people disliked Dolley Madison, many were unimpressed by her husband. Often James Madison was described as "mean looking," but he was affable in conversation. Apparently after dinner and a few drinks, he could entertain all with his droll tales and anecdotes, often involving famous people. Looking to his retirement, the humor came more easily.

RETIREMENT

Madison renewed the charter for the Bank of the United States, ironic since he and his friend Thomas Jefferson had so vigorously opposed its creation twenty years before. He called for a constitutional amendment to grant Congress more power to authorize building canals and roads linking the country together. He also stated that tariffs might sometimes be needed. One Republican remarked that now Madison "out-Hamilton's Alexander Hamilton."[8] Unperturbed by anyone's criticism, he only looked to retire with his wife to his farm, Montpelier. He was happy to leave the worries of political life to the new president, James Monroe.

Once established at Montpelier, the Madisons soon received a steady stream of visitors. One remarked, "[Madison] has the reputation of being an excellent manager, and is a model of kindness to his slaves."[9] Madison sided with so many others on the need to extinguish slavery, but remained uncertain of the means to do so. He helped create

NATIONAL EVENTS

MAR 3: Congress declares war against Algeria (Second Barbary War)

JUL 19: Treaties of Portage des Sioux signed, ending hostilities with Indians in old Northwest Territory

Congress passes a bill authorizing the creation of a second Bank of the United States

APR 11: In Philadelphia, the first African Methodist Episcopal (AME) church is established by former slave Richard Allen, who becomes its first bishop

1816

WORLD EVENTS

JUN 18: Napoleon loses at Battle of Waterloo to extensive Allied army under Duke of Wellington

JUN 22: Napoleon abdicates—again—and is condemned to island of St. Helena

Tsultrim Gyatso becomes the 10th Dalai Lama

The British found Banjul, The Gambia as a trading post

East India Company begins importing opium to China

the American Colonization Society, which later sponsored moving freed blacks to Liberia.

At home, Madison fought ongoing poor harvests, as well as the accumulating debt of his stepson Payne Todd, which he kept hidden from Dolley.

One favorite project in his retirement was assisting Jefferson in the founding of the University of Virginia. Both men savored the opportunity to develop the college, selecting its faculty and curriculum. Finally seeing it open its doors in 1825 was a moment of great accomplishment. The two men had worked together for over a half-century, and it was with great sorrow that news reached the Madisons in 1826 that their dear friend had breathed his last on July fourth. Madison took Jefferson's place as rector of the university.

When Virginia decided to have a convention to draft a new state constitution, James Madison rode from Montpelier to attend. Later, he denounced South Carolina senator John C. Calhoun and other southerners who used the Virginia and Kentucky Resolutions to buttress their calls for nullification and secession.

With a growing concern about the time he had remaining, Madison worked feverishly to put his notes from the Constitutional Convention into order and ready for publication. Rheumatism made it nearly impossible for him to write legibly, so for hours he dictated to Dolley. He hoped that any money made from sales of the volumes would secure her for the rest of her life. (The government published the work four years after his death.)

James Madison's life ended on June 28, 1836, after a lengthy illness that left him bedridden for most of that year. He was buried in the Montpelier family burial plot. Dolley returned to Washington after his death and once again became the reigning hostess of the city. She was invited to various presidential receptions and became the favorite at gatherings. Still, her finances were drained by her son Payne, forcing her to sell her husband's papers to Congress, and later even Montpelier was sold.

Dolley Madison died in Washington on July 12, 1849. Her body was moved from there to Montpelier in 1858.

DID YOU KNOW?

Madison was a half-cousin twice removed of George Washington.

ENDNOTES

1 Robert A. Rutland, *James Madison*, New York: Macmillan Publishing Co., 1987, p. 244.

2 William DeGregorio, *The Complete Book of US Presidents*, New York: Gramercy Books, 2005, p. 59.

3 Ibid.

4 Rutland, p. 18.

5 Ralph Ketcham, *James Madison*, New York: Macmillan Publishing Co., 1971, p. 516.

6 Virginia Moore, *The Madisons*, New York: McGraw-Hill, 1979, pp. 315-316.

7 Ibid, p. 326.

8 Ketcham, p. 603.

9 Ibid, p. 608.

APR 16: Congress passes the Tariff Act of 1816 to protect American industry

SUMMER: Much of US experiences a "year without a summer" when frost and snow cover it in June and July

NOV: James Monroe is elected fifth president

DEC 11: Indiana becomes 19th state

DEC 13: In Boston, the first American savings bank is established

FEB 12: Fire nearly destroyed the Canadian city of St. John's, Newfoundland

FEB 20: In Rome, *The Barber of Seville* opera is performed for the first time

APR 14: Most significant slave revolt occurs at Bayleys Plantation on Barbados

JUL 9: Argentina declares its independence from Spain

JUL 17: The French passenger ship *Medusa* runs aground off the coast of Senegal; 140 perish

JAMES MONROE

★ ★ ★ FIFTH PRESIDENT ★ ★ ★

LIFE SPAN
- Born: April 28, 1758, in Westmoreland County, Virginia
- Died: July 4, 1831, in New York City

RELIGION
- Episcopalian

HIGHER EDUCATION
- College of William and Mary, 1776

PROFESSION
- Lawyer, senator

MILITARY SERVICE
- Continental Army 1776–1780; rose from lieutenant to major; wounded at Battle of Trenton
- Colonel, Virginia militia 1780–1781

FAMILY
- Father: **Spence Monroe** (d. 1774)
- Mother: **Elizabeth Jones Monroe** (d. ca. 1774)
- Wife: **Elizabeth Kortright Monroe** (1768–1830); wed February 16, 1786, in New York City
- Children: **Eliza Kortright** (1786–1835); **James Spence** (1799–1800); **Maria Hester** (1803–1850)

POLITICAL LIFE
- Member of the Continental Congress (1783–1786)
- US senator (1790–1794)
- Minister to France (1794–1796)
- Governor of Virginia (1799–1802)
- Minister to France and England (1803–1807)
- Secretary of state (1811–1817)
- Secretary of war (1814–1815)

PRESIDENCY
- Two terms: March 4, 1817–March 4, 1825
- Democratic-Republican
- Reason for leaving office: completion of term
- Vice president: **Daniel D. Tompkins** (1817–1825)

ELECTION OF 1816
- Electoral vote: **Monroe** 183; **Rufus King** 34
- Popular vote: none

ELECTION OF 1820
- Electoral vote: **Monroe** 231; **John Quincy Adams** 1
- Popular vote: none

CABINET

★★★★★★★★★★

SECRETARY OF STATE
John Quincy Adams (1817–1825)

SECRETARY OF THE TREASURY
William H. Crawford (1817–1825)

SECRETARY OF WAR
John C. Calhoun (1817–1825)

ATTORNEY GENERAL
Richard Rush (1814–1817)

William Wirt (1817–1825)

SECRETARY OF THE NAVY
Benjamin Crowninshield (1817–1818)

Smith Thompson (1819–1823)

Samuel L. Southard (1823–1825)

James Monroe has several distinctions as an American leader. He is the only person to serve as both secretary of state and secretary of war (defense) simultaneously; besides George Washington, he is the only president to win his election unopposed; and he was the main negotiator in America's greatest land deal—the Louisiana Purchase. Still, few Americans today can identify much about this man of whom Thomas Jefferson said, "Turn his soul wrong side outwards and there is not a speck on it."[1]

EARLY LIFE

James Monroe was born in Westmoreland County, Virginia, on April 28, 1758, and was the second of five children born to Spence and Elizabeth Jones Monroe. As the eldest son, James would inherit the lion's share of his father's modest accumulation of property. Little is known about Monroe's youth, and he shared few details in later years. Possibly his mother taught him the basics of reading, writing, and mathematics, but he did not begin his formal schooling until age eleven. At that time, he attended a nearby academy with twenty-four other boys, including John Marshall. The future chief justice and Monroe became close friends and remained so until political differences years later ended their association. In school, Monroe excelled in mathematics and Latin, yet he also found time for plenty of horseback riding and hunting.

In 1774, at the age of sixteen, Monroe went on to continue his education at the College of William and Mary. Prior to his entrance, James had endured the loss of his father, and it was his uncle's help that allowed Monroe to continue with his studies. No mention is made of his mother at this time, so apparently she preceded her husband in death. His uncle Joseph Jones made a powerful impression on the adolescent—Jones had been educated in England and served in various governmental positions, including deputy king's attorney for Virginia. By 1774, he was a member of the House of Burgesses and would later serve on the Committee of Safety, as well as in the Continental Congress.

The following year, the young student found many diversions from his studies during the turbulent time of 1775. As Virginia became swept up in events such as the governor removing gunpowder from the public magazine, the students grew more anxious to take an active role. Some formed a militia group, while others, including Monroe, marched on the Governor's Palace, taking possession of guns and swords stored there to be handed over to the militia. A year later, Monroe decided to take a break from his studies and enlist in the Third Virginia Infantry.

MILITARY LIFE

After weeks of intense training, Monroe's outfit marched northward to reinforce Washington's troops in New York. Five days after arriving, James Monroe had his first taste of combat during the fighting around Harlem Heights. Ashamed by the "disgraceful and dastardly" behavior of Connecticut recruits, he eagerly awaited his chance to show what Virginians could do. His company and two others reinforced troops and managed to force the British to withdraw. More fighting and marching was in store for the Americans as Washington attempted to keep his dwindling army together and not face a major engagement.

Although able to escape injury in combat, Monroe's luck ended on December 26, 1776, at the battle of Trenton. Junior officer Monroe volunteered to scout the roads into Trenton. He and

NATIONAL EVENTS

Executive Mansion rebuilt following its burning in War of 1812

Harvard opens law school

MAR 3: Alabama territory created from Mississippi territory

MAR 4: Monroe is inaugurated as fifth president

APR 15: Thomas Gallaudet founds first free school for deaf in Hartford, Connecticut (today's American School for the Deaf)

APR 30: US and Great Britain agree to limit number of warships on Great Lakes and Lake Champlain in Rush-Bagot Treaty

1817

WORLD EVENTS

Typhus epidemic sweeps Edinburgh and Glasgow, Scotland

Potato famine in Ireland leads to mass emigration from that country

Elgin Marbles displayed at British Museum

First Waterloo Bridge is completed across the Thames

FEB 12: Chile wins liberation from Spain at the Battle of Chacabuco

his men ensured that no one could warn of their arrival. In Trenton, he met a doctor who offered to feed the soldiers and provide surgical skills. Once the fighting started, Monroe was one of two officers ordered to prevent the Hessians from readying their cannons. Both officers were wounded; in fact, Monroe would have died from the severed artery in his shoulder if not for the quick action of their volunteer surgeon.

After a period of recuperation, Monroe rejoined the army and became aide-de-camp with a rank of major to Major General Lord Stirling. As he helped in planning major operations, Monroe came in contact with a wide circle of military officers, many of whom he would cross paths with politically in years to come. Among these were Alexander Hamilton, Aaron Burr, Lafayette, and, of course, his old friend John Marshall who was serving as judge advocate. Monroe was present at both defeats at Brandywine and Germantown, and suffered the long winter at Valley Forge. At the battle of Monmouth in June 1778, Monroe served as commander of a scouting party, but he felt unhappy without a field command and no prospects of acquiring one. He decided to return to Virginia and recruit a regiment in which he would serve as lieutenant colonel, and march them southward into the Carolinas, where British General Cornwallis had moved the fighting. George Washington wished him well and wrote him a recommendation.

Once Monroe arrived in Virginia, he found recruiting to be a nearly impossible task. Early in 1779, he met with Governor Thomas Jefferson, who sympathized with his plight. While unable to aid in the recruiting, Jefferson did help the young man with his future. Through discussions with the governor, Monroe began contemplating a different path for himself—reenrolling at the College of William and Mary and reading law with Jefferson. He wrote his uncle about the plan, and Joseph Jones responded positively, noting, "You do well to cultivate his friendship, and cannot fail to entertain a grateful sense of the favors he has conferred upon you, and while you continue to deserve his esteem he will not withdraw his countenance."[2] Monroe moved with Jefferson to Richmond when the Virginia capital was transferred from Williamsburg in 1780. This friendship would last fifty years and, over time, benefit both men.

In June 1780, Monroe rode into the South to establish an express route for dispatches to be forwarded north to Richmond in case of British movement in that direction. Monroe was successful, but still hoped for a combat command. He was later disappointed to learn that his expertise would not be needed at Yorktown. Knowing that his military career had truly ended, he determined his destiny lay in politics. He started by winning election in the spring of 1782 to the Virginia House of Delegates.

POLITICAL LIFE BEGINS

As Monroe's political star began its ascent, his mentor Jefferson's was on the decline. After serving two terms as governor, ending within months of the January 1781, British invasion of Virginia, Jefferson no longer cared for the demands of politics, preferring to tend his family and farms instead. Monroe understood this and was deeply concerned over the news of Mrs. Jefferson's precarious health following a difficult birth in May 1782. Monroe empathized with the misery Jefferson was enduring and wrote a sincere and touching letter saying, "I necessarily suppose you are entirely engaged in an attention and discharge to those tender duties which her situation unhappily requires from you . . . I shall forebear to trouble you with an answer

DID YOU KNOW?

★★★★★★★★★★★

Monroe's 1817 inauguration was the first to be held outside.

JUL 4: Construction begins on Erie Canal

NOV 20: First Seminole War breaks out in Florida

DEC 10: Mississippi admitted as 20th state

DEC 27: General Andrew Jackson takes control in Florida

Congress passes first pension plan for American Revolutionary War veterans

National (Cumberland) Road completed from Cumberland, Maryland, to Wheeling, Virginia

1818

APR: Earthquake rocks Palermo, Italy

OCT 31: Emperor Ninkō becomes the 120th emperor of Japan

NOV 22: Fredric Cailliaud discovers old Roman emerald mines at Sikait, Egypt

First successful blood transfusion performed in London

The third Anglo-Maratha War ends when the independent kingdom of Maharashtra comes under British control

Smith Thompson, 1823

. . . which respects your retreat from publick [sic] service."[3] He added the news as a postscript that he had been appointed to the Executive Council (the upper house of the Virginia Assembly which advised the governor); at the age of twenty-four, it was a great honor.

Elected the following year to the Confederation Congress, which served as the nation's sole governing body as set forth in the Articles of Confederation, Monroe traveled to New York City and began a three-year stint. There he developed an interest in the West and chaired committees toward that end. He pushed for western land grants for veterans and open navigation on the Mississippi River. Monroe also toured the Great Lakes region and began putting ideas together for developing effective territorial government. Parts of his plan were written into the Land Ordinance of 1787, which established the process for territories to become states.

While serving in Congress, James Monroe met and was captivated by a young lady, Elizabeth Kortright. The daughter of a former British officer, the eighteen-year-old was considered cold and reserved yet beautiful. Theirs was a short courtship before they married on February 16, 1786. After living in New York with her family for a few months, Monroe decided to return to Virginia and begin practicing law in Fredericksburg. Still, he kept his political life active by serving at the Ratification Convention (each state held one to decide whether to ratify the US Constitution). Monroe voted against the Constitution as a moderate anti-Federalist, but his fears of creating a national government whose power would crush the states and their people were soon allayed, and he accepted the ratification and the new government without misgivings. He then allowed friends to persuade him to run for the Senate. To the surprise of many, this meant he opposed James Madison, who easily beat his young friend. However, in the fall Monroe won election in his own right to fill a vacant seat after the death of Virginia's other senator.

Once established in the Senate, Monroe rapidly became its leader of the anti-Federalists after differences between Hamilton and Jefferson began to emerge. He opposed a national standing army, as well as Washington's Neutrality Proclamation, issued in 1793 in response to France's declaration of war against Britain. After originally accepting this stance, Monroe switched to Jefferson's side when they discussed the possible constitutional ramifications of a precedent being set if the executive branch simply acted arbitrarily. Both men were also in agreement regarding the French Revolution. Both believed that if the United States favored anyone, it should be the French, who were fighting to obtain their *liberté*.

DIPLOMAT

Monroe's preference for the French cause led to his appointment by President Washington to serve as minister plenipotentiary to that country. There his partiality toward that nation drew a rebuke from fellow Americans who believed he should act more objectively. Monroe also worked to gain the release of Thomas Paine from French prison (Paine had been imprisoned for not endorsing the execution of Louis XVI). Once freed, Paine immediately set his quill against Washington, whom he felt had abandoned him. This, too, diminished Washington's affection toward Monroe. He eventually was recalled for failing to enthusiastically support America's early attempt at negotiating with Britain in Jay's Treaty. With genuine regret, the Monroes said adieu to France in 1796.

NATIONAL EVENTS

- **JAN 5:** First transatlantic crossing on monthly basis begins between Liverpool, England, and New York City
- **APR 4:** Congress agrees to limit number of stripes on American flag to 13 and add stars with each new state
- **MAY 24:** General Jackson captures Pensacola and executes two British subjects
- **OCT 19:** Chickasaw tribe signs over its lands between Mississippi and Tennessee Rivers to US
- **OCT 20:** US and Great Britain agree to Convention of 1818—northern boundary settled as 49th parallel

WORLD EVENTS

- **FEB 12:** Chile officially declares its independence from Spain
- **MAR 11:** Mary Wollstonecraft Shelley publishes *Frankenstein*
- **MAY 11:** Charles XIV crowned king of Sweden
- **NOV 21:** Czar Alexander I of Russia petitions for a Jewish state in Palestine
- **DEC 24:** Franz Gruber sets "Stille Nacht, Heilige Nacht" (Silent Night) to music

GOVERNOR

Smarting over his recall and blaming Federalists, including Washington and Hamilton, for having engineered it, Monroe returned to Virginia to lick his wounds. He and his family returned to the small house on their land near Charlottesville near their neighbor Thomas Jefferson. Working on his farm and rebuilding his law practice occupied Monroe's time but not his thoughts. He yearned to return to the political arena and hoped to gain vindication. This he did by easily winning election to the governorship in 1799.

The governorship was not a powerful post according to Virginia's state constitution, yet Monroe worked to mold the office into something more. He introduced the first state of the state address and oversaw the construction of an armory in Richmond. During his tenure, James and Elizabeth Monroe experienced personal loss when their infant son died from complications of whooping cough. The Monroes still had two daughters, Eliza and Maria, who would provide comfort and solace to their parents.

The ominous threat that southerners feared more than any other—slave insurrection—grew nearer on August 30, 1800, when Monroe received word that slaves were planning a revolt (known as "Gabriel's Rebellion") for that night. As governor, he assumed authority to mobilize militia troops to patrol the state during the coming weeks. Later, the slave leader, Gabriel, was caught, tried, and hanged without naming any accomplices, but that did not prevent thirty-five other slaves from being executed in what Governor Monroe termed "this unpleasant event in our history." He anticipated similar incidents would occur—"While this class of people exists among us we can never count on with certainty on its tranquil submission."[4] Later he endorsed the idea of ending slavery through repatriation of freed slaves to Africa.

SLAVE INSURRECTIONS ★ During Monroe's tenure as governor of Virginia (1799–1802), his state witnessed two slave revolts. After the first occurred in Southampton County in 1799, Monroe worked to ensure that the accused leaders were represented by counsel and treated humanely in prison, and investigated claims that they had been freedmen from Maryland. At a time when many of his countrymen considered slaves inferior and not entitled to rights, Monroe's efforts stood out for his interest in justice and fairness to the defendants. (The slaves were prosecuted, found guilty, and executed.)

Upon completion of his third year as governor, Monroe planned to return to practicing law; however, his plans changed immediately upon receipt of a letter from old friend and now president Thomas Jefferson. He was being sent to France as special envoy to Robert Livingston to negotiate terms to gain the port of New Orleans. By March 1803, Monroe, his wife, and two daughters were on their way to France, and as it turned out, into history.

REAL ESTATE BROKER

Monroe left Washington, D.C., with instructions from Secretary of State Madison that he could offer up to $10 million[5] for New Orleans and West Florida. Once Monroe arrived in France, he learned from his colleague, Robert Livingston, that Napoleon had other ideas. Fighting multiple wars had created a tremendous deficit for France, so the First Consul now needed income. He and his finance minister, Talleyrand, dangled the

DID YOU KNOW?

Monroe was the first president to have previously served as a US senator.

DEC 3: Illinois admitted as 21st state and its northern portion transferred to Michigan territory

Financial panic hits US

Maine separated from Massachusetts

JAN 25: University of Virginia founded by Thomas Jefferson

FEB 22: US acquires Florida from Spain

FEB 28: Congress refuses to support Henry Clay's resolution condemning Jackson's actions in Florida

1819

French physician invents stethoscope

Poet John Keats publishes "Ode to a Nightingale"

Simón Bolívar elected president of Venezuela

First part of *Don Juan* published by Lord Byron

STATE OF THE UNION
★★★★★★★★★★

US POPULATION IN 1817
9,638,543

STATES ADMITTED TO UNION
Mississippi, December 10, 1817

Illinois, December 3, 1818

Alabama, December 14, 1819

Maine, March 15, 1820

Missouri, August 10, 1821

NUMBER OF STATES IN 1825
24

tempting offer of the entire Louisiana territory, although West Florida still remained Spanish, so Napoleon argued he was unable to sell it. Monroe and Livingston negotiated with the French, and as any good prospective buyer, they balked at the asking price. Eventually the French relented and, instead of 100 million francs, they agreed to eighty million, which was ten million more than the Americans wanted to spend. Still, the total of fifteen million dollars still resounds as a remarkable real estate deal, especially when calculated to three cents an acre. Talleyrand bemusedly told Livingston, "You have made a noble bargain for yourselves and I suppose you will make the most of it."[6]

DIPLOMAT EXTRAORDINAIRE

After concluding the treaty granting the Louisiana Purchase, Monroe left for England in July 1803. He was there to gain British cooperation regarding American shipping rights, particularly the curtailment of impressments, but he was unsuccessful in winning any concessions from the government. Monroe returned to France, attempting to encourage their aid in securing West Florida. The French now were cool to this idea, so America decided to push the notion that since the boundaries of the Louisiana Territory were vague (and always had been), then West Florida was included in the recent acquisition. Wanting to gain in writing the territory, and the monetary claims of Americans against the Spanish when the port of New Orleans had been closed, Monroe then traveled to Spain in early 1805.

The Spanish were under Napoleon's thumb and dared not go against the newly self-appointed emperor's wishes. Both Spain and France insisted that West Florida was never part of Louisiana and the Spanish balked at paying American claims. Negotiations soon broke down, and Monroe had to consider this mission, too, a failure.

The American diplomat now returned to Britain, hoping this time to be more successful gaining their support in observing American neutrality at sea. After receiving a cool reception in London, he wrote to Jefferson his belief that Britain would continue to bully the United States at sea because it knew it could, and Monroe warned, "All will insult us, encroach on our rights, and plunder us if they can do it with impunity."[7] The British refused to include any concessions regarding impressments, but a commercial treaty was signed and forwarded to President Jefferson, who refused to submit it to the Senate since it omitted any mention of impressments. This decision surprised and upset Monroe, who felt his efforts were not appreciated, and he returned to America late in 1807 a disgruntled diplomat.

VIRGINIAN

As 1808 began, so did the party politics to determine their candidates for the presidential election. Madison seemed the acknowledged heir apparent, but Monroe also gained a following. Still smarting from the recent treatment of his treaty with Britain, he decided to be open to any offers. Jefferson looked upon both Madison and Monroe as his close friends and protégés, so the possible rupture that such a contest might cause greatly distressed the president and he wrote to Monroe, "I have ever viewed Mr. Madison and yourself as two principal pillars of my happiness. Were either to be withdrawn, I should consider it as among the greatest calamities which could assail my future peace of mind."[8] Monroe reasserted his friendship with Jefferson, but for the next few years, his friendship with Madison was notably distant. This

DID YOU KNOW?
★★★★★★★★★★

Monroe was the first president to ride on a steamboat.

NATIONAL EVENTS

MAR 2: Congress passes its first law regulating immigration, including registration

MAR 2: Arkansas Territory established

DEC 14: Alabama admitted as 22nd state

Fourth census shows US population at 9.6 million

MAR 3: Missouri Compromise adopted; slavery now illegal north of 36°30′ in Louisiana Territory; proposes admitting Missouri as a slave state and Maine as a free state

1820

WORLD EVENTS

FEB 6: British trading post established in Singapore

Venus de Milo statue discovered on Greek isle of Milos

Spain's King Ferdinand VII announces end of Inquisition started by Queen Isabella in 1477

Census shows Great Britain has population of 20.8 million, France 30.4 million

did not improve with the election of 1808, where Madison won easily over both Monroe and his Federalist opponent.

Contented to return to his Virginia farm in Albemarle County and be among friends and family, Monroe still yearned to play a key role in the nation. Republicans, including Madison, thought his reputation and Republican status needed reaffirming. Toward this end, Monroe won election to the Virginia House of Delegates and then was appointed to fill the vacancy of governor. He stayed in that post only three months before receiving news that President Madison wanted him as secretary of state. James Monroe was ready.

THE WHITE HOUSE ★ Following the burning of the White House by the British in 1814, the Monroes moved back into the rebuilt home in 1817. They began furnishing the house in the Empire style, as they believed the president's home should be formal as well as stylish. Pieces included gilded furniture, carpets, silver, and chandeliers; many of these items continue to be used in the White House today. Monroe also supervised the planting of more trees on the grounds and hired the first gardener for the White House. The south portico was added in 1824.

SECRETARY OF STATE

Strained relations between the United States, Britain, and France continued to grow worse as the European nations refused to acknowledge American claims of neutrality. Both Madison and Monroe became increasingly "determined to make itself (America) respected."[9] Monroe worked as liaison between Congress and the executive branch, meeting with War Hawks (p. 54), including newly elected Speaker of the House Henry Clay and South Carolinian John C. Calhoun. The secretary of state assured them that the president would support a declaration of war should nothing improve in the coming months. Monroe also met frequently with British and French diplomats, but none were forthcoming in providing assurances.

President Madison decided the time for action had arrived and sent a message to Congress on June 1, 1812, asking for a declaration of war against Great Britain, citing the ongoing issues regarding blockade of American shipping, sailors being impressed, and the overall lack of respect of American neutrality rights at sea. Once Congress agreed to war, Monroe's desire to lead men into battle resurfaced again.

With so many military officers complaining to Monroe and the president about the lack of preparedness of troops and fortifications, the pressure was on Secretary of War William Eustis to resign, which he did in December 1812. Monroe then switched jobs temporarily and became acting secretary of war. While in that capacity for ten weeks, he amassed an impressive record of developing plans for coastal fortifications, suggesting recruiting guidelines, and planning for the invasion of Canada, which he hoped to lead personally. To his disappointment, he was passed over for that role and in February 1813, he returned to the State Department when John Armstrong became secretary of war.

Monroe continued to juggle his concerns for the ongoing negotiations occurring in Ghent, Belgium, with the warfront at home. His negotiating team complained of British unwillingness to allow any mention of impressing sailors; this

MAR 15: Maine admitted as 23rd state

APR 24: Congress passes Public Land Grant Act to allow more settlers opportunity to go west—minimum price cut from $2 to $1.25 an acre with minimum amount cut in half from 160 acres to 80

DEC 3: James Monroe and Daniel D. Tompkins reelected as president and vice president

JAN: Republic of Liberia is founded by American Colonization Society

1821

JAN 29: Britain's King George III dies at age 81 and is succeeded by his son George IV

MAY 11: HMS *Beagle* leaves England with Charles Darwin on board

Czar Alexander I of Russia proclaims his nation's claim to all American Pacific coastland north of 51st parallel, including Oregon Territory

LIBERIA ★ Beginning in 1816, the American Colonization Society (ACS) began to repatriate slaves to Africa, but their first attempts to relocate Africans to Sierra Leone failed. A few years later, the ACS bought land in Africa that ultimately became Liberia. In 1825, the capital of the new colony was named Monrovia on behalf of the current US president. Twenty years later, Liberia became Africa's first republic, but its citizens were divided between those native to the area and the former American slaves; the latter group controlled the former.

probably came as no surprise to the secretary of state, who had had the same difficulty in 1806. At home, Monroe argued repeatedly that the British planned to move against Washington, D.C. Armstrong disagreed, insisting that their objective was Baltimore. Madison sided with Armstrong, so defenses and troops were not expanded as Monroe had urged. By late August, Monroe's prediction was proven correct, and the capital city braced for an enemy attack. Not having any information regarding enemy troop movements or strength, Monroe volunteered to lead a cavalry troop to do just that. After reporting to the president, he then ordered clerks to begin packing important government papers, including the Declaration of Independence, to be moved for safekeeping.

The secretary of state attempted to assist at the Battle of Bladensburg, but Madison ordered him and other cabinet members to vacate the area. After the debacle (the Americans' defeat allowed the British to capture and burn the capital), Monroe remained to help evacuate troops and was the last cabinet member to leave that night. Three days later, when the two Virginians returned to Washington and its ashes, they were greeted by a frightened citizenry who insisted that the capital be surrendered. Incensed by such a statement, Monroe fumed, "Any deputation moved towards the enemy would be repelled by the bayonet."[10] The secretary of war did not return immediately; he lacked anyone's confidence, including the president's, who told Armstrong to take a vacation. Armstrong resigned soon after, and again, James Monroe resumed both critical positions.

Immediately, the new secretary of war worked tirelessly toward plans to defend Baltimore, and with great success. He introduced a plan for a conscription army, believing militias inadequate in numbers and training, but the Senate refused. Monroe also worked to create funding sources for the war. Once the Treaty of Ghent (the document that ended the War of 1812, but did little else since neither side was acknowledged as a true victor) was signed, some, including Monroe, may have been displeased not to see British concessions, but no one was surprised. In February 1815, the secretary of state/war wrote, "The demonstration (war) is satisfactory that our Union has gained strength, our troops honor, and the nation's character, by the contest."[11] He could have added that the war had secured him a place in the nation's gratitude, as well as a nomination to become the next president.

During the last months of his tenure under Madison, Monroe resumed only heading the state department and worked to restore his health, for the war had taken its toll. He was exhausted and had lost considerable weight, looking more like someone suffering from a terminal disease. He continued his duties while others worked to put his name forward as the Republican candidate for 1816. The main argument against his candidacy by some New Englanders was the dislike of yet

NATIONAL EVENTS	**JAN 17:** Moses Austin is granted land and permission by Spanish government in Mexico to bring 300 families to settle land in Texas	**MAR 5:** Monroe's second inauguration; "Hail to the Chief" first played using words from Walter Scott's poem "Lady of the Lake"	**AUG 10:** Missouri admitted as 24th state	**SEPT 21:** William Becknell leads first wagon train from Independence, Missouri, to Santa Fe	**NOV:** Andrew Jackson appointed governor of Florida, but resigns
WORLD EVENTS	Panama, Peru, Costa Rica, Guatemala, and Honduras declare independence from Spain	**FEB 24:** Mexico gains its independence from Spain	**MAR 25:** Greece declares independence from Ottoman Empire, starting Greek War for Independence	**MAY 5:** Napoleon Bonaparte dies	**AUG 30:** Simón Bolívar becomes president of Gran Colombia (present-day Panama, Ecuador, Venezuela, and Colombia)

another Virginian occupying the presidency, but he still won by an overwhelming majority. Monroe's Federalist opponent, Rufus King, only gained the electoral votes of three states, and his native New York was not one of them.

PRESIDENT MONROE

After taking the oath of office from his old friend Chief Justice John Marshall, James Monroe embarked on a presidency that would be called the "Era of Good Feelings," because, following their defeat in 1816, the Federalist party collapsed, eliminating the rancorous partisanship that had existed between the Federalists and the Republicans. The country, more self-confident now, concentrated on ways to expand itself. The new president's attention turned to Florida, where Seminole Indians frequently launched raids against neighbors in Georgia and runaway slaves sought refuge. Monroe sent the new hero from New Orleans, Andrew Jackson, to attend to the situation along the Georgia–Florida border. Jackson decided to go farther into Florida and went so far as to hang two British subjects who he said were inciting the Seminole raids. Jackson's action angered both British and Spanish governments and created a definite diplomatic challenge for the new secretary of state John Quincy Adams. Adams succeeded in convincing the Spanish that problems would only multiply in the future if they attempted to maintain their tenuous hold on Florida. They agreed to cede the territory in return for five million dollars that the United States would assume in American claims against the Spanish government. The two governments also managed to agree that the western boundary of the Louisiana Territory extended all the way to the Pacific Ocean.

Monroe faced another diplomatic challenge with the US–Canadian border. In 1818, the British and Americans agreed to the border as the forty-ninth parallel from the Lake of the Woods area (in today's Minnesota) west to the Rockies; shared fishing rights in Canadian waters; and the joint occupancy of the Oregon territory.

The president continued the practice begun when he was secretary of state of meeting with congressmen, and they were frequent visitors to the White House. The two groups tangled; however, when Congress wanted to pass an internal improvements package, which included the construction and maintenance of roads and canals, Monroe argued that the national government could not be responsible for manning toll booths and sustaining the transportation routes, so he vetoed the bill.

Now that the White House had been rebuilt and glistened from its new white paint, visitors flocked to see the changes, and they were suitably impressed. The Monroes had outfitted the house with furniture collected from their European sojourn. Their manners also reflected their stay in Europe's capitals as they insisted diplomats could only visit the president on official occasions. Receptions were more formal affairs than those in the past under Jefferson and Madison. Visitors found Mrs. Monroe much more reserved and aloof than Dolley Madison, but they still ventured to see the exquisitely dressed First Lady. When her frail health precluded her from attending functions, her daughter Eliza Hay stood in for her. Mrs. Hay soon became the talk of Washington society because of her refusal to call on people and her often mercurial temperament. Her sister Maria became the first White House bride when she married her cousin Samuel Gouverneur there in 1820. The two sisters were not close, and Maria

DID YOU KNOW?

Monroe's daughter Maria was the first to marry in the White House.

1822

- The Democratic-Republicans trounce Federalist Party in US House election
- **MAR 8:** President Monroe and Congress agree to recognize newly independent republics of Latin America
- Jean-François Champollion decodes Egyptian hieroglyphics using Rosetta Stone
- **FEB:** Haiti invades Dominican Republic
- **SEP 7:** Brazil becomes independent of Portugal

1823

- Philadelphia financier and editor Nicholas Biddle appointed to head Bank of the United States
- **DEC 2:** Monroe Doctrine issued, president tells the world western hemisphere is closed to European colonization
- **DEC 23:** First publication of "'Twas the Night Before Christmas," written by Clement C. Moore
- Scottish chemist Charles Macintosh develops a waterproof fabric that will be used to make raincoats
- **SEP 10:** Simón Bolívar named president of Peru
- **SEP 28:** Pope Leo XII succeeds Pope Pius VII

MISSOURI COMPROMISE ★ The new nation had maintained an equal number of slave and free states since its inception. This balance threatened to be disrupted when Missouri petitioned for statehood. The idea of allowing a state from the West to allow slavery was anathema to many Americans, and the issue was debated extensively in Congress. In 1820, Speaker of the House Henry Clay proposed a compromise—allow Missouri to enter as a slave state and Maine as a free state. All other lands north of the 36°30′N latitude would be free. (This law was later overturned by the 1854 Kansas–Nebraska Act and the Dred Scott Supreme Court decision.)

and her husband moved to New York. Whenever the Monroes could, they slipped to their property at Oak Hill in Loudoun County, which was an easy drive from Washington.

As Monroe's first term wound down, it became obvious that the nation was in the midst of a depression caused by postwar economic woes, including overextension of credit. The rising numbers of low-cost imports put American factories out of business, creating more unemployment. Fighting the nation's first peacetime depression was a new experience for the government. Monroe did propose allowing some relief for those paying mortgages on lands bought from the government.

During his presidency, Monroe decided to imitate Washington and make a Grand Tour of the nation. Shortly after he took office, he traveled through New England, stopping to see the ever-growing factories and cities. Two years later, he toured the South and then looped through Kentucky and Tennessee, making stops to see Clay and Jackson in their home states. These trips convinced Monroe of the distinctive differences between the nation's sections, much of it attributable to slavery. This concern was even more pronounced when Missouri asked to join the union as a slave state.

Immediately, Congress erupted into furor. Northerners demanded that slavery not extend into the new states, while southerners protested any restriction of slavery. Not desirous of war, some in Congress worked to create a compromise. The president, as well, accepted the need for the Missouri Compromise to keep the union intact. Slavery continued to be on Monroe's mind, and he worked with others to create a colony of freed American slaves in West Africa named Liberia. In honor of his work, the capital was named Monrovia.

In his reelection in 1820, James Monroe became the only person besides George Washington to run unopposed. Voter apathy hit and election turnout was low. One elector did cast his vote against Monroe because he simply did not like the president.

The crowning achievement of Monroe's presidency occurred in 1823, when he and his secretary of state were increasingly alarmed by the threats of European nations taking possession of territories in Latin America and the Russians claiming both Alaska and Oregon. The two men fashioned a document that became known as the Monroe Doctrine, which proclaimed to the world the United States' opinion that Europe should stop attempting to colonize the western hemisphere. The British had already agreed to support the words with their navy. This policy shaped American foreign policy from that point forward. With such a legacy, James Monroe left the presidency after refusing a third term, in March 1825.

NATIONAL EVENTS

- First reported strike by female workers occurs at Pawtucket, Rhode Island
- Mountain man Jedediah Smith discovers South Pass, which later will be used by thousands of wagon trains for easy access through the Rocky Mountains
- Fellow mountain man Jim Bridger discovers the Great Salt Lake
- **MAR 2:** Supreme Court rules that federal government controls interstate commerce in *Gibbons v. Ogden*

1824

WORLD EVENTS

- Singapore becomes a British colony
- **FEB 10:** Simón Bolívar named dictator of Peru
- **MAR 4:** John Cadbury opens a tea and chocolate shop in Birmingham, England
- **MAR 17:** Anglo-Dutch Treaty of 1824 signed
- **MAY 11:** British occupy Rangoon, Burma; beginning of Burmese War

RETIREMENT

The Monroes retired to their newly constructed home at Oak Hill, which had been designed by Thomas Jefferson. After nearly fifty years of public service, some of which he had never been compensated for, James Monroe embarked on his retirement years some $75,000 in debt. He spent some of those years wrangling with Congress to regain his rightful monies from expenditures he made for the United States. Ultimately, a fraction was paid to him.

He worked to improve Oak Hill, having already sold his Albemarle County property. Monroe also happily became a member of the Board of Visitors for his dear friend Jefferson's new project, the University of Virginia. In 1825, soon after retiring from the presidency, Monroe greeted Lafayette on his grand tour along with President John Quincy Adams. Monroe joined Madison for the state constitutional convention held in Richmond in 1829, and Monroe was promptly elected its president. Unfortunately, health concerns caused him to resign that post two months later.

Eliza Monroe may have been a victim of epileptic seizures, one of which may have caused her to fall into a fireplace and be severely burned in 1826. She died four years later, and the memories of happier days were too powerful for her husband, so he moved to New York to live with their younger daughter, Maria Gouverneur. There, he worked on writing two books, including his memoirs, but never finished either project.

On July 4, 1831, James Monroe became the third president to die on the nation's birthday. He was buried first in New York City, but in 1858, the body was reinterred at Hollywood Cemetery in Richmond, Virginia. In 1903, Eliza Monroe's body was moved next to her husband from their home in Oak Hill.

In his eulogy, John Quincy Adams praised Monroe's public service and said after "strengthening and consolidating the federative edifice of his country's Union, till he was entitled to say, like Augustus Caesar of his imperial city, that he had found her built of brick and left her constructed of marble."[12]

ENDNOTES

1 Julian P. Boyd, ed., *The Papers of Thomas Jefferson*, Princeton, NJ: Princeton University Press, 1950, vol. XI, p. 97.

2 Harry Ammon, *James Monroe*, New York: McGraw-Hill, 1971, p. 31.

3 Julian P. Boyd, ed., *The Papers of Thomas Jefferson*, Princeton, NJ: Princeton University Press, 1952, vol. VI, p. 192.

4 Ammon, p. 189.

5 Gaye Wilson, "Jefferson's Big Deal: The Louisiana Purchase," *Monticello Newsletter*, vol. 14, number 1, Spring 2003.

6 Ibid, p. 214.

7 Ibid, p. 250.

8 Dumas Malone, *Jefferson the President, Second Term 1805-1809*, Boston: Little, Brown & Company, 1974, p. 552.

9 Ammon, p. 297.

10 Ibid, p. 335.

11 Ibid, p. 344.

12 Ibid, p. 573.

APR: US and Russia sign a treaty granting America claim to Pacific coast south of 54th parallel

APR 30: Congress passes General Survey Bill to allow federal government to survey land for possible roads and canals

MAY 22: Congress raises tariffs to protect American industries

NOV: Presidential election ends with no candidate winning majority of electoral votes, but Andrew Jackson carries majority of popular vote

SEP 13: Arrival of 29 convicts in Queensland, Australia, to start a colony

SEP 16: Charles X succeeds Louis XVIII as king of France

OCT 4: Mexican constitution enacted for the new Mexican Republic

John Quincy Adams.

John Quincy Adams

★ ★ ★ SIXTH PRESIDENT ★ ★ ★

LIFE SPAN

- Born: July 11, 1767, in Braintree (now Quincy), Massachusetts
- Died: February 23, 1848, in Washington, D.C.

RELIGION

- Unitarian

HIGHER EDUCATION

- Harvard, 1787

PROFESSION

- Lawyer

MILITARY SERVICE

- None

FAMILY

- Father: **John Adams** (1735–1826)
- Mother: **Abigail Smith Adams** (1744–1818)
- Wife: **Louisa Catherine Johnson Adams** (1775–1852); wed July 26, 1797, in London, England
- Children: **George Washington Adams** (1801–1829); **John Adams II** (1803–1834); **Charles Francis Adams** (1807–1886); **Louisa Catherine** (1811–1812)

POLITICAL LIFE

- Minister to the Netherlands (1794–1797)
- Minister to Prussia (1797–1801)
- Massachusetts state senator (1802)
- US senator (1803–1808)
- Minister to Russia (1809–1814)
- Head negotiator of Treaty of Ghent (1814)
- Minister to Great Britain (1815–1817)
- Secretary of state (1817–1825)

PRESIDENCY

- One term: March 4, 1825–March 4, 1829
- Democratic-Republican
- Reason for leaving office: lost election to **Andrew Jackson** in 1828
- Vice president: **John C. Calhoun** (1825–1829)

ELECTION OF 1824

- Electoral vote:
  Jackson 99;
  Adams 84;
  William Crawford 4;
  Henry Clay 37
- Popular vote:
  Jackson 153,544;
  Adams 108,740;
  Crawford 46,618;
  Clay 47,136
- Due to lack of a majority, election decided by House of Representatives, who voted for **Adams**

CABINET
★★★★★★★★★★

SECRETARY OF STATE
Henry Clay (1825–1829)

SECRETARY OF THE TREASURY
Richard Rush (1825–1829)

SECRETARY OF WAR
James Barbour (1825–1828)

Peter B. Porter (1828–1829)

ATTORNEY GENERAL
William Wirt (1825–1829)

SECRETARY OF THE NAVY
Samuel Southard (1825–1829)

The first American political dynasty was that of John and John Quincy Adams. Both men became president, but to their chagrin, each only served one term. Father and son were close and shared a similar temperament, and in later years, John Quincy Adams described himself: "I never was and never shall be what is commonly termed a popular man. . . . I have no powers of fascination; none of the honey which the profligate proverb says is the true fly-catcher."[1] The same self-examination could easily have been stated by his father. While both served their country in a myriad of roles, they never felt the adoration of their nation's countrymen.

EARLY LIFE

John Quincy Adams was the oldest son and second child born to John and Abigail Smith Adams in Braintree (today Quincy), Massachusetts, on July 11, 1767. John Quincy saw little of his father in the very early years since John Adams practiced law in Boston and, as the times became increasingly hostile toward Britain, his father's absences grew longer. Then at age seven, he said goodbye to his father, who rode off to Philadelphia to attend the First Continental Congress and would continue as a delegate to the Second Congress, as well.

John Quincy remained at home, taught first by his mother and then by tutors. He played with his two younger brothers, and in June 1775, he witnessed a remarkable sight—the Battle of Bunker Hill, with his mother at his side. Two years later, his world changed drastically when his father was sent to France to negotiate French aid.

John and Abigail Adams agreed that John Quincy should accompany his father to gain an extraordinary educational opportunity. During his tenure in France, John Quincy became fluent in French and studied the arts and classics at the well-known Passy Academy near Paris. His fluency in French provided him with a rare opportunity—accompanying his father's private secretary, Francis Dana, to St. Petersburg, Russia, where he could be a translator for Dana, although John Quincy was merely fourteen years of age. His time in Russia was short-lived when the Russians refused to receive the American representative, so he traveled throughout Europe and eventually rejoined his father in the Netherlands. There, John Quincy attended Leyden University, where he excelled in mathematics and added Dutch to his language repertoire, which also included Greek, Latin, Spanish, and French.

By 1785, John and Abigail Adams determined that Harvard was the best place to send their son to complete his education, but owing to their strained financial resources, they expected him to enter as an upperclassman. He returned to Massachusetts, where he found, to his embarrassment, that he required extra tutoring with an uncle before he would pass the entrance examination as an upperclassman. Five months of hard work culminated in his entrance to Harvard, which would be his home for the next two years. There he developed new friendships and was elected to the Phi Beta Kappa Society. In 1787, John Quincy graduated the second in his class of fifty-one; his commencement speech was entitled "The Importance and Necessity of Public Faith to the Well-Being of a Nation." Now the twenty-year-old had to decide what path to pursue for his life's work.

It seemed almost certain that John Quincy would follow in his father's footsteps and become an attorney. He studied law for three years and passed the bar in 1790. He began practicing in Boston, but few appeared eager to hire the fledgling lawyer. Perhaps they could see that he lacked

NATIONAL EVENTS

First US representative, Joel R. Poinsett, sent to Mexico and is namesake for poinsettia plant

FEB: Removal of Native American tribes from east of Mississippi River to western lands begins

FEB 9: House of Representatives selects John Quincy Adams as president; John C. Calhoun vice president

MAR 4: John Quincy Adams inaugurated as sixth president

OCT 26: Erie Canal opens

1825

WORLD EVENTS

AUG 6: Bolivia breaks from Peru

AUG 25: Uruguay declares independence from Brazil

SEP 7: Portugal recognizes Brazil's independence

SEP 27: World's first modern railway opens in England

DEC 14: Decembrist Revolt begins in St. Petersburg against the new Czar Nicholas I

fervor for the law and much preferred other reading. By the early 1790s, newspapers abounded with the conflict between pro-British and pro-French factions in President Washington's government. The president decried their politics and insisted the only course was neutrality. Finding Washington's position sound and reasonable, John Quincy Adams put quill to paper to defend the president in a series of essays published throughout the nation under the pen name "Publicola." His rhetoric won him a fan and a new job—President Washington needed a representative to travel to the Netherlands and to be a correspondent reporting on the trouble brewing in Europe, specifically France. With John Quincy's fluency in the Dutch language and his previous experience in Europe, Washington believed him to be the best candidate. Young Adams was not so certain, but his proud father congratulated his son and wished him well.

DIPLOMAT

While serving in the Netherlands, John Quincy Adams frequently crossed the English Channel and traveled to London. There he often found himself in the home of the American consul Joshua Johnson, who had been living in Europe for twenty years and had three attractive and marriageable daughters. John Quincy soon found himself drawn to the middle daughter, Louisa Catherine. She had been born in London on the brink of the American Revolution in February 1775; the family moved to France during the war. There, Louisa was educated and became fluent in French. Her charm and intelligence impressed the young American, and he began writing home of his difficulties accomplishing his work. Once his parents surmised the identity of his beloved, they wrote for him to end the affair and wait to marry a true American lady when he returned. Earlier John Quincy had allowed his mother's insistence to end a romance; he was determined that history not repeat itself. He wrote that if this affair did not work out, he would be doomed to "perpetual celibacy." Abigail Adams relented and insisted that she would welcome another daughter.

Louisa Johnson's family lived in grand style, leading her prospective bridegroom to deduce that her father was a man of means. On the contrary, Joshua Johnson's fortune was in shambles; in fact, he had no dowry for Louisa. Perhaps because of this, the Johnson family seemed more inclined to see a wedding occur sooner rather than later, which was John Quincy's preference. Ultimately John Quincy and Louisa were wed in London on July 26, 1797. Their married life began with a stint in London before traveling on to Prussia for John Quincy's new assignment as minister to that nation.

Dismayed to be sent to Prussia rather than Portugal as he had been told earlier, the couple managed to enjoy their time in Berlin. While serving, Adams successfully negotiated the Prussian-American Treaty of 1799 promoting peace and commerce between the two nations. Still he yearned to do more, but after his father's unsuccessful reelection bid in 1800, he found that he and Louisa would

JOHN QUINCY ADAMS'S DIARIES ★ Starting in 1779 when the twelve-year-old boy and his famous father sailed from Boston to France, Adams began recording the events of his days. He continued this practice until a few weeks before his death in 1848. His entries are a treasure trove of anecdotes and observations of famous people during this era.

DID YOU KNOW?

John Quincy Adams owned a pet alligator that he kept in the White House.

James Fenimore Cooper publishes *Last of the Mohicans*

Sing Sing prison opens in New York

FEB 13: Founding of American Temperance Society

APR 1: Samuel Morey patents first internal combustion engine

JUL 4: 50th anniversary of Declaration of Independence; death of both John Adams and Thomas Jefferson

AUG 22: Jedediah Smith leads first expedition west to California

1826

Cholera epidemic in India

André Ampère publishes *Electrodynamics* about his studies of electromagnetism

FEB 11: University of London founded

JUN: First true photograph made

JUN 14–15: Sultan Mahmud II of Ottoman Empire crushes last mutiny in Constinople

ANTI-MASON PARTY ★ Founded in New York in 1827, the Anti-Masons were a response to a perceived threat that some believed was posed by the secretive Freemason organization. The Anti-Mason Party was formed by those who thought too many public officials filled the ranks of the Freemasons. It was the first "third party," but outside New York and Ohio, it failed to win any votes. The party collapsed in 1834.

return home, for John Adams did not want to presume that President-elect Jefferson wanted to keep his son in any government position. The new president likely would have asked John Quincy to remain, for he appreciated the negotiation skills he had developed and remembered kindly the entire family, who had treated him so well during their time together in France in the mid-1780s. Yet after seven years abroad, John Quincy Adams finally returned home.

POLITICAL OFFICE

To his relief, Abigail and Louisa Adams accepted each other, and both were happy to dote over the newest addition to the family—George Washington Adams. After numerous miscarriages, Louisa and John Quincy had two other sons, as well as a daughter who died in infancy. With the needs of a growing family weighing on his mind, John Quincy Adams needed to earn a living, and the only profession he knew was the law. Unfortunately, he did not like it and wrote, "The bar is not my element."[2] Apparently clients agreed, and they did not flock to him any more than they had before. By the following year, he was considering entering the political arena and ran for the state senate. He won, which encouraged him to try for the US House later that year, but he was defeated. The next year, however, he won a US Senate seat as the Federalist candidate. During this time, he was appointed first Boylston Professor of Rhetoric and Oratory at Harvard.

As senator, John Quincy Adams's actions would not be dictated by party or local politics, and he broke with the Federalists to cast his vote in favor of the Louisiana Purchase. He also disagreed with the ideas of the Twelfth Amendment but lined up with Republicans to approve the Embargo in 1807. This last move ended his Senate career, for New England interests knew any embargo would greatly harm their shipping concerns, so they expected their senators to vote accordingly. In June 1808, he resigned his seat after the Massachusetts legislature voted for another to take his place.

The following year brought a new administration, and President James Madison wanted a seasoned diplomat to become the first US minister to Russia. John Quincy Adams soon impressed the court of St. Petersburg, and more importantly, Czar Alexander I. Working to secure more European ports for trade, Adams successfully gained Russia's support, but French emperor Napoleon Bonaparte viewed this development, which ran specifically against his orders to the Czar, as an outrage. He resolved to take action against this and other affronts, and in 1812 marched his troops into Russia. Again, John Quincy Adams had a front row seat to the historic invasion, and he drafted numerous dispatches describing events and his elation at the defeat of the French.

John Quincy served as a paid diplomat, but his compensation was not nearly enough to cover the expenses of housing, staffing, and entertaining. Louisa Adams and her husband lamented the high costs to Abigail Adams, who in turn wrote to

DID YOU KNOW?

Adams was the first president to be photographed.

NATIONAL EVENTS

OCT 7: First horse-powered American railroad opens in Quincy, Massachusetts

NOV: Davy Crockett elected as congressman from Tennessee

1827

United States and Great Britain agree to renew treaty for joint occupation of Oregon Territory

Sam Houston elected governor of Tennessee

Fort Leavenworth, Kansas, built as military post for patrolling Santa Fe Trail

WORLD EVENTS

JUN 22: Panama Conference of Latin American States meets without US representatives; they unsuccessfully attempt to unify various countries

JUL 16: Beginning of Russo-Persian War

King of Laos declares war on Siam

Cairo University School of Medicine opens, first African school of medicine

Matches introduced in England

Madison asking him to recall her son. He agreed, but had another job offer in mind: associate justice of the Supreme Court. All were surprised when John Quincy declined the help and insisted on staying in St. Petersburg; he and his wife also longed to have their two older boys, George and John, sent from their grandparents in Massachusetts, to join them and their younger brother Charles Francis, but they would not be reunited for another five years.

By 1813, the United States was steeped in war with Britain; this bothered Czar Alexander I and harmed Russia's burgeoning trade with America. Desiring to help end the conflict, the czar inquired of Adams if Russia might mediate the war. Immediately, Adams sent word to President Madison, who eagerly accepted the kind offer and ordered John Quincy to become chief negotiator along with two others. Great Britain balked at Russia's offer, so the negotiators cooled their heels in St. Petersburg awaiting further instructions. Eight months later, the news arrived that the British were willing to discuss peace in Ghent, Belgium.

PEACE COMMISSIONER

Attempting to negotiate with the British would try John Quincy Adams's patience, but working with his own team of Americans, now including Speaker of the House Henry Clay, created even more consternation. Adams was offended by their socializing, including Clay's late-night poker parties, which ended nearly at sunrise, and Adams's temper often flared against his colleagues. Part of his anger arose from always being outnumbered in decision making, and he complained bitterly in his journal of how the other three commissioners always took the opposite position of whatever he proposed. Still, as the actual peace talks dragged on, he successfully convinced his countrymen that the best deal they could achieve was to agree to terms that returned to prewar status—in effect, a truce. With "peace on earth" in their hearts, both delegations signed the Treaty of Ghent on December 24, 1814. Understanding that many issues remain to be determined later, Adams still said, "I would cheerfully give my life for a Peace on this basis."[3]

President Madison had promised Adams that his next duty would be representing the United States in Great Britain, just as his father had done thirty years before. Arriving in May 1815, the couple was finally reunited with all three sons. Their time in London provided a restful reunion and allowed Adams more time with his boys. After two years of near bliss, the family learned that the new president Monroe had appointed John Quincy Adams as his secretary of state. The family would be returning home.

SECRETARY OF STATE

After arriving in Washington in September 1817, John Quincy Adams quickly plunged himself into work as President Monroe's secretary of state. The two men met daily, for the president continued his interest in the position that he had held for two terms. Surprising to Adams was the rather hostile response he engendered from various congressmen who viewed his title as prerequisite to the presidency. Conceding that Monroe would serve two terms, they already looked ahead to the 1824 election. Since the past three presidents had all served as secretaries of state, potential candidates eyed with hunger Adams's position. No one coveted it more than Henry Clay, who expected Monroe to grant him the honor; instead, Clay was offered the War Department, which he refused so he could remain in his more powerful seat as Speaker of the

SUPREME COURT APPOINTMENTS

★★★★★★★★★★

Robert Trimble, 1826

DID YOU KNOW?

★★★★★★★★★★

John Quincy Adams liked to skinny dip in the Potomac River.

John James Audubon publishes *Birds of America* in Europe (unable to find US publisher)

Edgar Allen Poe publishes his first book of poetry

New York City begins public transit with the operation of a 12-seat horse-drawn "bus"

Massachusetts requires high schools for every town with 500 families

Sarah Hale publishes *Northwood*, America's first anti-slavery novel

Englishman Frederick William Herschel develops first contact lenses

MAR 7: Brazilian marines attack naval base in Argentina, are defeated

MAR 26: Beethoven dies

APR: Ottoman dey in Algeria slaps French consul, eventually leading to war and French rule in Algeria

APR 7–8: Battle of Monte Santiago, major Brazilian victory over Argentina

STATE OF THE UNION
★★★★★★★★★★

US POPULATION IN 1825
12,866,020

NATIONAL DEBT IN 1825
$83,788,433

PRESIDENT'S SALARY
$25,000/year

NUMBER OF STATES IN 1829
24

House. From this vantage point, Clay vowed to monitor Adams and, hopefully, knock him out, so Clay could replace him. Secretary of the Treasury William Crawford also yearned for the same job and challenged Adams frequently at cabinet meetings. Adams wrote, "I ought to lay it down as a rule to myself never to oppose any opinion advanced by Crawford . . . when it is unnecessary to effect the result, and to leave absurdity to die a natural death."[4]

Matters of state early in Monroe's term primarily dealt with conflicts with America's neighbors in Canada and Florida. The Treaty of 1818 with Great Britain agreed to the forty-ninth parallel as the boundary with Canada to the Rocky Mountains; moreover, the Oregon territory would be one of shared occupation. Furthermore, fishing rights to Canadian waters around Labrador and Newfoundland were granted to Americans.

Prickly negotiations involved the Spanish in East Florida, where southerners complained of slaves running to the Spanish for freedom. More problematic, however, were the increasing raids by the Seminole tribe sponsored by the Spanish. General Andrew Jackson tackled the challenge of ending the problem and made headlines from Washington to Madrid when he executed two British subjects he called "unprincipled villains"[5] for inciting the Seminole. Secretary of State Adams condoned Jackson's action and prevented the president from reprimanding him. Furthermore, Adams convinced the Spanish that it would be prudent to vacate Florida, and in 1819, the Senate ratified the Adams-Onis Treaty, which paid the Spanish five million dollars in claims that Americans had against them. The treaty also spelled out the precise boundaries of the Louisiana territory with Spain, since the original Louisiana Purchase treaty was vague in outlining the western and southern boundaries that would be shared with Spain. The Spanish also agreed to renounce any claim to Oregon.

While Adams was winning victories diplomatically, he and his wife were undeniably losers in the social arena of Washington, where the mud roads were so treacherous their carriage upturned on one occasion, and Adams wrote, "It was a mercy that we all got home with whole bones."[6] They deigned not to venture among the town's social circles but preferred staying at home, instead. Louisa Adams refused initiating social calls and was soon summoned to the White House and chastised by Mrs. Monroe. The secretary of state and his lady rehabilitated their image by hosting social gatherings, including a three-hundred-person ball. Still, John Quincy admitted that small talk was not his forte. He blamed his mother for instilling at an early age the practice of not talking but listening; he also believed his failing to learn to dance as a child hurt him socially. John Quincy never felt especially close to his mother, but when he learned of her passing on November 2, 1818, he recorded in his diary: "She had no feelings but of kindness and beneficence. Yet her mind was as firm as her temper was mild and gentle." The ill feelings slipped away as he wrote that his mother, more than anyone he had ever known, lived "so unremittingly to do good."[7]

The year 1823 was pivotal for American foreign policy. Starting two years earlier in an Independence Day address, John Quincy Adams had broached the subject that the western hemisphere was now closed to European domination. By November 1823, the president and cabinet were debating what type of policy to pursue, with some believing that a joint declaration with

DID YOU KNOW?
★★★★★★★★★★★

John Quincy Adams was the only president to later be elected to the House of Representatives.

NATIONAL EVENTS

FEB 8: First American ballet performance in New York City (scanty costume of the French dancer Mme. Hutin causes uproar)

FEB 23: Incorporation of first US railroad, the Baltimore and Ohio

FEB 27: New Orleans celebrates Mardi Gras for first time

MAR 16: First African American newspaper, *Freeman's Journal*, begins publication

JUL 4: State of New York outlaws slavery

WORLD EVENTS

APR 24: Battle of Phaleron, Greek War of Independence

JUL 6: Treaty of London between France, Britain, Russia, demands Turks agree to armistice in Greece

OCT 1: Russians end a millennium of Muslim domination in Armenia with victory

OCT 20: Battle of Navarino, French, British, Russian navies destroy Turko-Egyptian fleet in Greece

Great Britain would best serve the interests of all. Adams insisted that the United States must issue a statement solely making it more "dignified to avow our principles explicitly . . . Than to come in as a cockboat in the wake of the British man-of-war."[8] In December 1823, President James Monroe announced in his message to Congress that the United States would remain out of the affairs of Europe; likewise, European powers should now consider the western hemisphere off limits to further colonization and/or intervention. The Monroe Doctrine (p. 68) had been born.

ELECTION OF 1824

As Monroe's presidency wound down, the presidential election of 1824 geared up, with candidates emerging from across the nation. Henry Clay of Kentucky vied against Andrew Jackson of Tennessee to gain western support; William Crawford of Georgia and, briefly, John C. Calhoun of South Carolina represented southern interests; and John Quincy Adams emerged as the voice of New England. Now that the Federalist Party was dead, no party label was employed, so the voters had little to differentiate the candidates besides regional appeal. Once the popular votes were counted, Andrew Jackson emerged the winner, but in the Electoral College, no candidate enjoyed the majority of votes. In accordance with the Twelfth Amendment, the House of Representatives voted from the top three vote-getters, with Henry Clay fourth and supposedly out of the picture. Jackson supporters worried over the considerable power that the Speaker of the House wielded, and on February 9, 1825, their fears were realized. John Quincy Adams was elected on the first ballot by the House of Representatives. Jackson and his followers were further incensed by the appointment of Clay to his long-coveted position of secretary of state in Adams's cabinet. Cries of a "corrupt bargain" between Adams and Clay started in February and were not silenced over the next four years, although both men denied any wrongdoing.

TWELFTH AMENDMENT ★ Following the fiasco of the 1800 presidential election, in which the electoral college tied, leaving the House of Representatives to decide the winner, Congress decided to change the electoral system. According to the Twelfth Amendment, separate ballots were cast for president and vice president beginning with the 1804 election. Any time a candidate did not receive a majority of electoral votes, however, the House of Representatives would decide the outcome, as they did in 1824.

PRESIDENT JOHN QUINCY ADAMS

While John Quincy Adams busied himself settling into the nation's role of chief executive, Andrew Jackson wasted little time in preparing for his next campaign—the presidential election of 1828. He was helped in this by the Tennessee legislature, which nominated him in October 1825. Jackson's supporters worked in Congress to defeat any legislation that smacked of Adams's approval. The president desired to send a delegation to attend a conference in Panama, but the matter was postponed long enough to ensure that it would be too late to attend. Critics took him to task when he delivered his first annual message, in which he declared that the nation's government should build more roads and canals linking the country and educate its citizens, including building a national university and an astronomical observatory.

DID YOU KNOW?

Louisa Adams is the only foreign-born First Lady.

1828

First recorded strike by American factory workers demanding 10-hour work-day, in Paterson, New Jersey	Construction begins on Baltimore and Ohio Railroad	**FEB 28:** Cherokee newspaper *Cherokee Phoenix* becomes first American Indian publication	**MAY 19:** Congress passes Tariff of 1828, better known as the Tariff of Abominations	**DEC 3:** Andrew Jackson defeats John Quincy Adams for the presidency
Greeks win War of Independence from Ottoman Empire	**JAN 22:** Duke of Wellington becomes Britain's prime minister	**FEB 2:** Treaty of Turkmanchai ends Russo-Persian War	**APR 26:** Russia declares war on Ottoman Empire	**DEC 28:** Earthquake in Japan kills 30,000

> *"Individual liberty is individual power, and as the power of a community is a mass compounded of individual powers, the nation which enjoys the most freedom must necessarily be in proportion to its numbers the most powerful nation. But our distribution of the powers of government is yet imprefect . . . We have not succeeded in providing as well for the protection of property as of personal liberty. Our laws between debtor and creditor are inefficacious and secure justice to neither. Our banks are for the most part fradulent bankrupts. Our judiciary is not independent in fact, though it is in theory; and according to the prevailing doctrine our national government is constituted without the power of discharging the first duty of a nation, that of bettering its own condition by internal improvement."*
>
> —*John Quincy Adams, in a letter to James Lloyd, 1822*

Immediately, Congress and newspapers derided his lofty ideas as grabs for power and compared him to Julius Caesar.

Wounded by the continual barbs, Adams slumped into a state of depression. His journal entries grew increasingly terse and his appetite declined. He continued his daily routine of walking at least four miles every morning, often with Chief Justice John Marshall. He also enjoyed swimming in the Potomac and puttering in the White House garden. In July 1826, he returned home to Quincy, Massachusetts, to visit his father, but arrived too late—John Adams had died on the fourth of July. The president stayed to take possession of his father's house and make upgrades on the property. He hoped that his oldest son George would oversee the property, but George was well on his way to mental instability. Worries about his son and helplessness over the continual stalemate with Congress worsened the president's own mental state, as well as his physical health. Adams lost weight and experienced difficulties sleeping. These problems were to linger until the 1828 election.

Another round of political rancor accompanied Adams's proposal to increase the tariff on imported goods, thereby helping protect the industry of New England. Anxious to quash such a plan, Jackson supporters amended the tariff to raise the duty of raw materials that the North needed to import. Instead of opposing the altered tariff bill, northern congressmen approved it, believing its benefits protecting their industries far outweighed paying more for raw materials. Southern opposition to what they dubbed the Tariff of Abominations would create havoc for the nation and the next administration.

By 1828, at least part of his plan for internal improvements was beginning to be implemented, and a pleased President Adams broke ground for the Chesapeake and Ohio Canal. When he took off his coat, "and resuming the spade, raised a shovelful of the earth . . . a general shout burst forth from the surrounding multitude"; he considered that this action had struck a chord with the common man more than "all the flowers of rhetoric in my speech."[9] A spontaneous demonstration in Philadelphia where hundreds cheered and extended their hands for him to shake greatly moved him. Yet Jackson's supporters were tireless in their drive to ensure Adams's defeat for reelection. The president himself believed the future meant a new occupant in the White House, so he told his cabinet they were free to flee his administration. Henry Clay was deeply touched by Adams's offer and predicament since he, too, was suffering from various mental and emotional problems and took a medical leave.

Vitriolic campaigns by both Adams and Jackson were waged in 1828. The Adams faction brought out the old charges against Rachel Jackson of adultery (she and Jackson married when they believed she had received a divorce from her first husband. They were later notified that was not the case; the divorce was granted and they married again). Jackson's supporters continued to remind everyone of the "corrupt bargain" between Adams and Clay, and Adams's ties to New England wealth and Europe, implying the common man needed someone more in touch.

The election results were resoundingly in favor of Old Hickory, who captured the western and southern votes, as well as New York. Perhaps relieved to soon be rid of his presidential burden, Adams and his wife now appeared more relaxed and comfortable with themselves and entertaining, yet, still hurt by the campaign, Adams refused to visit Jackson or to stay for his inauguration. He and his father would remain the only presidents not to observe that courtesy.

The Adamses would only be going a few miles away to a home he had recently purchased called Meridian Hill. They had asked for their son George to travel to Washington to help with the move, but to their great shock, they received word of George's death. Apparently en route, he had committed suicide by jumping off the steamboat, and his body washed ashore in the Long Island Sound. Undoubtedly the parallel between this death and that of his uncle just prior to John Adams leaving office must have come to mind.

The couple returned to Quincy the following year while John debated what to do with his life next and grew morose over a lack of direction. Friends from the Boston area asked if he would be willing to run for Congress, and he agreed he would serve if the people desired it. He ran as an Anti-Mason (p. 74) (then later joined the new Whig Party) and won handily over the Democratic candidate. He recorded, "No election or appointment conferred upon me ever gave me so much pleasure."[10] The former president lamented that his wife and children did not share in his joy.

DID YOU KNOW?

John Quincy Adams wrote *The Lives of James Madison and James Monroe* in 1850.

CONGRESSMAN

The congressional session began in November 1831; ultimately John Quincy Adams would serve seventeen years in the House of Representatives, and during his tenure, he would cast his vote on many vital issues of the times. He worked to create a lower, more universally acceptable tariff bill. He supported the Bank of the United States and vehemently opposed Jackson's use of the state banks in an effort to kill it. Adams opposed the annexation of Texas, fearing that it and the possibility of its division would create a multiplicity of slave states. Congress, weary of the slave debate and southerners, concerned of where it could lead, successfully passed the gag rule, which tabled any petition opposing slavery. Decrying the move as unconstitutional by preventing the right of petition, John

AMISTAD ★ In 1839, forty-nine enslaved Africans aboard the ship *Amistad* overwhelmed their Spanish slave captors off the Cuban coast. After killing the captain and his mate, they ordered the two slave traders to sail the ship back to Africa. Two months later, the *Amistad* arrived in New York harbor. The Africans were seized and Spanish officials demanded extradition to Cuba, but American abolitionists strenuously objected. A legal team was organized to argue for the slaves' freedom, and the case began its journey through the legal system. Championing the Africans' cause was John Quincy Adams, who argued their case before the US Supreme Court, which soon declared them free. They returned to their homeland in January 1842.

Quincy Adams spent the next eight years employing a variety of ruses to circumvent it. Ultimately the gag rule was repealed in 1844.

In 1841, Adams defended his clients, the slaves aboard the Spanish ship *Amistad*, before the United States Supreme Court. He was successful in his defense, and the slave mutineers were freed, with most returning home to Africa.

Five years later, Adams cast his vote with Congressman Abraham Lincoln and other opponents of going to war against Mexico. Adams believed President Polk had provoked the war by sending troops to the disputed border, thus taking away the power of Congress to declare war.

One vote that Adams delighted in casting created a national institution based on the bequest of an Englishman, James Smithson. Although thwarted by his idea for a national observatory, Adams was thrilled to be present at the birth of the Smithsonian Institution.

Serving in Congress took its toll, as did fretting over his family. Their second son, John Adams II, died in 1834, leaving behind a widow and two daughters. This death was a great blow for his father, who wrote, "A more honest soul, or more tender heart, never breathed on the face of the earth."[11] The third son, Charles Francis Adams, now became the financial advisor for his father, who often disagreed with his son's thrifty ideas.

Louisa Adams lamented her husband's tireless efforts working with congressmen, especially since "the energies of his fine mind (were lost) upon a people who do not either understand or appreciate his talents."[12] Still, Louisa enthusiastically rejoiced when she learned that Dolley Madison would be their new neighbor. The widow Madison returned to Washington to be among friends after her husband's death, and the two former first ladies presided over Washington society for years.

In November 1846, John Quincy Adams suffered a stroke, leaving his right side paralyzed and his speech greatly impaired. Within three months he had regained his wits and was back in Congress. During the coming year, Adams's health fluctuated, but all realized his time was limited. He collapsed on the House floor on February 21, 1848, and was carried to the Speaker's chamber, where he lingered two days before dying at 7:15 p.m. on February 23. Adams's last words were either "I am content" or "I am composed" before he lapsed into a coma. His body lay in state in the capitol and then was transported to Quincy, Massachusetts, where he was interred in his family's vault.

Louisa Adams returned to Washington and remained there until her death in May 1852, when she was also buried in the Adams family vault. Their descendants would continue the tradition of public service for the coming generations.

> ***"Within a few days one of the most distinguished statesmen of the age has passed away; a man who has long been before the public, familiarly known in the new world and the old. He was one of the prominent monuments of the age…there is one sentiment which runs through all his life: an intense love of freedom for all men; one idea, the idea that each man has unalienable rights.… The slave has lost a champion who gained new ardor and new strength the longer he fought; America has lost a man who loved her with his heart; Religion has lost a supporter; Freedom an unfailing friend, and Mankind a noble vindicator of our unalienable rights."***
>
> *—"A Discourse Occasioned by the Death of John Quincy Adams," delivered by Theodore Parker, clergyman, March 5, 1848*

ENDNOTES

1 Adrienne Koch and William Peden, eds., *Selected Writings of John and John Quincy Adams*, New York: Alfred A. Knopf, 1946, p. 320.

2 Paul C. Nagel, *John Quincy Adams*, New York: Alfred A. Knopf, 1997, p. 155.

3 Ibid, p. 220.

4 Ibid, pp. 245-246.

5 Andrew Burstein, *The Passions of Andrew Jackson*, New York: Alfred A. Knopf, 2003, p. 131.

6 Nagel, p. 251.

7 David McCullough, *John Adams*, New York: Simon & Schuster, 2001, p. 622.

8 William A. DeGregorio, *The Complete Book of US Presidents,* New York: Gramercy Books, 2005, p. 96.

9 Nagel, pp. 318-319.

10 Ibid, p. 336.

11 DeGregorio, p. 90.

12 Nagel, p. 356.

Andrew Jackson

★ ★ ★ SEVENTH PRESIDENT ★ ★ ★

LIFE SPAN

- Born: March 15, 1767, in Waxhaw region along North/South Carolina border
- Died: June 8, 1845, at the Hermitage, Tennessee

NICKNAME

- Old Hickory

RELIGION

- Presbyterian

HIGHER EDUCATION

- None

PROFESSION

- Lawyer, soldier

MILITARY SERVICE

- American Revolutionary War: enlisted and was a messenger at age 13; taken prisoner in April 1781 and held two weeks
- War of 1812: appointed major general of US volunteers and later promoted to major general in regular army; hero after winning battle of New Orleans
- First Seminole War (1817–1818)

FAMILY

- Father: **Andrew Jackson** (d. 1767)
- Mother: **Elizabeth "Betty" Hutchinson Jackson** (d. 1781)
- Wife: **Rachel Donelson Robards Jackson** (1767–1828); wed in August 1791 in Natchez, Mississippi; second ceremony on January 17, 1794, in Nashville
- Children: None, but adopted a nephew of Rachel's and named him **Andrew Jackson, Jr.** (1808–1865); and **Lyncoya Jackson**, (a Cherokee child, adopted c. 1812 and died 1828)

POLITICAL LIFE

- Public prosecutor western district of North Carolina
- US representative (1796–1797), served as first congressional representative from Tennessee
- US senator (1797–1798, resigned after five months)
- Justice of Tennessee Superior Court (1798–1804)
- US senator (1823–1825)

PRESIDENCY

- Two terms: March 4, 1829–March 4, 1837
- Democrat
- Reason for leaving office: completion of term
- Vice presidents: **John C. Calhoun** (1825–1832, resigned); **Martin Van Buren** (1833–1837)

ELECTION OF 1828

- Electoral vote: **Jackson** 178; **John Quincy Adams** 83
- Popular vote: **Jackson** 647,286; **Adams** 508,064

ELECTION OF 1832

- Electoral vote: **Jackson** 219; **Henry Clay** 49; others 18
- Popular vote: **Jackson** 687,502; **Clay** 530,189

CABINET

SECRETARY OF STATE
Martin Van Buren (1829–1831)
Edward Livingston (1831–1833)
Louis MacLane (1833–1834)
John Forsyth (1834–1837)

SECRETARY OF THE TREASURY
Samuel D. Ingham (1829–1831)
Louis MacLane (1831–1833)
William J. Duane (June–Sept. 1833)
Levi Woodbury (1834–1837)

SECRETARY OF WAR
John H. Eaton (1829–1831)
Lewis Cass (1831–1836)

ATTORNEY GENERAL
John M. Berrien (1829–1831)
Roger B. Taney (1831–1833)
Benjamin F. Butler (1833–1837)

Few presidents raised as much passion among their countrymen as Andrew Jackson: people either loved him or hated him. Jackson himself often ran the spectrum of emotions as he dealt with people. Today, sociologists would point to his fatherless childhood, war-torn home, and early violent encounter with a British enemy that left him facially scarred as roots for what his critics condemned as unpredictable and erratic behavior. But Andrew Jackson lived in a time before sociology; all he knew was he had to make his own way in life. And that he did.

EARLY LIFE

Andrew and Elizabeth Hutchinson Jackson left Ireland in 1765 to try for a better life for themselves and their two sons, Hugh and Robert. They settled on the Waxhaw lands along the North Carolina–South Carolina border. There, in 1767, Andrew died of fatigue and overwork on his farm, and a few days later on March 15, his widow gave birth to a son she named for her husband. Andrew's birthplace is not clear, as Elizabeth Jackson may have been visiting one of two sisters when she delivered—one lived in South Carolina and the other in North Carolina. Andrew Jackson later believed it was South Carolina, but the two states still contest it.

As a child, Andrew was combative but quick witted. If a fight occurred at school, chances were good that he was in the midst of it. One fellow wrestler said that even when he was thrown to the ground, "He would never stay throwed."[1]

Elizabeth Jackson wanted her son to become a Presbyterian minister, so she sent him to nearby schools, where his ease of reading often made him a favorite to read newspapers aloud to the adults. In 1776, the nine-year-old boy read the Declaration of Independence to his fellow citizens. He continued his schooling until 1780 when the war came to South Carolina, and he and Robert joined the militia.

Andrew rode as a scout and courier for a company of South Carolina mounted militia, but in 1781 he and Robert were taken prisoner when visiting their cousins' home. A British officer ordered the young teen to polish his boots, but the insolent lad refused and received a cut on the hand and a gash along his face for his impudence. He later said he was reminded of how much he hated the British every time he shaved. The British took the Jackson brothers prisoner and forced them to march forty miles to Camden, South Carolina. There, after two weeks, Elizabeth Jackson won their release. Unfortunately, relief was short lived, for Robert died soon after from smallpox. After burying Robert and nursing Andrew, Elizabeth traveled to Charleston to help the patriots' cause by nursing Americans held on a British prison barge. She soon contracted smallpox, died, and was buried in an unmarked grave. Elder brother Hugh had been killed earlier in the war, so at the age of fourteen, Andrew Jackson was on his own.

He drifted between two uncles and tried a saddlery apprenticeship, but gave up after six months. Then, at the age of fifteen, he inherited an impressive £250 from his Irish grandfather. Deciding to enjoy himself, he moved to Charleston and quickly gambled it away. Humbled by the experience, he returned to the Waxhaw area and taught school for one year, but again decided that it was not to be his life's work. Jackson finally decided he wanted to become a lawyer, so for the next three years he studied law with two attorneys, and in 1787, he was admitted to the North Carolina bar.

NATIONAL EVENTS

MAR 4: Andrew Jackson inaugurated as the seventh president; John C. Calhoun of South Carolina is vice president

MAR 4: Jackson's inauguration reception hosts common citizens who crowd into the President's House, nearly destroying it, and causing the president to escape

JUL 29: United States gains lands in Michigan Territory from Chippewa, Ottawa, and Pottawatomi tribes

AUG 25: Mexico rejects Jackson's offer to buy Texas, but exempts the territory from its anti-slavery decree three months later

1829

WORLD EVENTS

Juan Manuel de Rosas becomes dictator of Argentina

MAR 22: Greece gains its independence from the Ottoman Empire

MAR 31: Pope Pius VIII succeeds Pope Leo XII

SEP 29: First "Bobbies" appear on the streets of London to help ensure safety

During his time "studying the law," Andrew found plenty of opportunity to enjoy himself, as well. He was known for being "the most roaring, rollicking, game-cocking, horse-racing, card-playing, mischievous fellow that ever lived in Salisbury."[2] He courted the ladies, studied dancing, and played practical jokes, including moving outhouses and removing signposts. Not surprisingly, when news of his presidential candidacy reached the townspeople years later, they greeted the announcement with disbelief. One lady exclaimed, "When he was here, he was such a rake that my husband would not bring him into the house! . . . Well, if Andrew Jackson can be President, anybody can!"[3]

After a frustrating year of few clients, Andrew accepted a friend's offer to become the prosecutor for the Western District of North Carolina, which encompassed present-day Tennessee. Deciding that his future lay in the west, Jackson moved in the spring of 1788 to Tennessee.

TENNESSEE LAWYER

Jackson first stopped to take care of legal work in Jonesborough. While there, his short fuse ignited when opposing counsel used sarcasm. An outraged twenty-one-year-old Andrew scrawled a challenge (note spelling and grammar): "My charector you have injured; and further you have Insulted me in the presence of a court and larg audianc. I therefore call upon you as a gentleman to give me Satisfaction for the Same."[4] Thus, Jackson fought his first duel, but neither man was injured since both fired into the air, and Andrew felt vindicated. He soon moved deeper into the territory to a settlement started only a decade before—Nashville.

One of Nashville's founders was John Donelson, who had arrived in the region in 1779 with his family of eleven children; his youngest was a daughter named Rachel. The Donelsons and other families braved ongoing strife with the local Indians as they attempted to farm the fertile land along the Cumberland River. John Donelson had been killed a couple of years before Jackson arrived, and his widow lived in a blockhouse but rented rooms in a nearby cabin. Andrew rented one of those rooms and soon became friends with fellow boarder John Overton. But more importantly, Andrew became acquainted with Rachel Donelson Robards.

Rachel had married Lewis Robards and lived in Kentucky until her husband's overly protective and jealous nature created such tension that Rachel returned to her family. Lewis Robards soon became contrite and followed his wife to Nashville, where he apologized, and they decided to try again, but remained in widow Donelson's home. Andrew found Rachel Robards a captivating young lady brimming with fun and eager for adventure—in short, a kindred spirit. Her husband, however, watched Andrew's interest in his wife with mounting jealousy, and one day confided in a friend that he believed Jackson was "too intimate with his wife."[5] When told of Robards's comment, Jackson angrily threatened Robards with violence, specifically, cutting off his ears if any other statements were made about Andrew and Rachel. Frightened by Jackson, Robards swore out a complaint for Jackson's arrest. When the guard was leading him away, Andrew asked for a knife, which amazingly was granted, then with a wicked smile and staring straight at Robards, Jackson ran his finger along the knife. Unnerved, Robards ran away, with Jackson in hot pursuit. Only Jackson returned, and he was soon freed because Robards failed to appear in court. Later Jackson took lodging elsewhere, and Lewis Robards returned to Kentucky.

CABINET
★★★★★★★★★★

(continued)

SECRETARY OF THE NAVY
John Branch (1829–1831)

Levi Woodbury (1831–1834)

Mahlon Dickerson (1834–1837)

POSTMASTER GENERAL
William T. Barry (1829–1835)

Amos Kendall (1835–1837)

JAN: Senators Robert Hayne of South Carolina and Daniel Webster of Massachusetts debate states' rights versus federal sovereignty

JAN 28: Jackson signs Indian Removal Act to force Eastern Indians to relocate to Oklahoma

APR 13: President Jackson provides a toast at Jefferson Day banquet revealing his feelings on states' rights debate: "Our Federal Union—It must be preserved!"

JUL 15: Sioux, Sauk, and Fox cede lands, including parts of Iowa, Missouri, and Minnesota

1830

A Frenchman, Barthélemy Thimmonier, invents the first practical sewing machine

MAY 13: Ecuador is created from Gran Colombia

JUN 26: King George IV dies and is succeeded by his brother, William IV

JUL 5: France begins its occupation of Algiers

JUL 31: In Paris, revolutionaries depose Charles X; he is replaced by the duc d'Orleans

DID YOU KNOW?

US currency: Jackson is on the twenty dollar bill.

When news of Robards's plans to return and take his wife back to Kentucky reached Rachel's family, they decided to take action and included Jackson in the execution of their plan. Rachel was escorted to Natchez (on the lower Mississippi in Spanish-claimed territory) by family acquaintance Colonel Robert Stark and his family, as well as Andrew. There she remained with friends while Jackson returned to Nashville, where he learned that Robards had obtained a divorce. Without confirming it, Jackson quickly returned to Natchez, where he and Rachel married in the summer of 1791, or so they said. No record of such a marriage exists, and neither did a record of the divorce. It was not until September 27, 1793, that the official divorce decree reached Lewis Robards. It had been granted on the condition that his wife had committed adultery with an unmentioned man, who all understood was Jackson. The dates of certain events are suspect, as evidence points one way and the spin by Jackson's defenders points another. In piecing the story together, it seems likely that Andrew and Rachel wed prior to January 1791, when she is listed in county records as Rachel Jackson. Obviously, this put their wedding before her divorce, making their marriage illegal. They did officially marry again, on January 18, 1794, but the harm had been done. Andrew Jackson would spend the rest of his life as a medieval knight defending his lady, risking all to ensure her honor. The two began life on a small plantation named Poplar Grove. Then in 1795, he bought a more extensive plantation that would become the basis for the home they called the Hermitage, about twelve miles east of Nashville.

In Nashville, both Andrew's prosecuting duties and his law practice grew steadily. At times he was called away to defend the area against Native Americans, and his comrades said he was "bold, dashing, fearless."[6] Early in 1796, he traveled to Knoxville, where he worked with others to draft a constitution for the proposed state of Tennessee. Jackson favored granting suffrage to any freeman, but requiring office seekers to own property, and it was decided that two hundred acres was the minimum for any public office except governor—that required owning five hundred acres. President Washington signed the bill into law on June 1, 1796, making Tennessee the sixteenth state, and its first congressman elected to its one seat in the House of Representatives was Andrew Jackson.

POLITICAL CAREER BEGINS

Jackson's career in Congress can be termed brief and lackluster. He managed to secure passage of a bill granting Tennessee reimbursement for military expenses against the Cherokee. After hearing of their twenty thousand dollar windfall, the state legislature elected him to the Senate. Unfortunately, he was ill suited to this post and desperately wanted a position closer to home. He got his wish when he was appointed to the Superior Court. Now he could travel throughout Tennessee and hold court, meet people, and get paid six hundred dollars a year!

In 1802, Jackson cast his eyes on another prize—major general of the state militia. Revolutionary War hero John Sevier also wanted the job and certainly had the military qualifications, but Jackson decided to attack it with all his political might. Since officers elected the major general, Jackson campaigned and won a tie. Governor Archibald Roane, a friend of Jackson's who had originally traveled to Tennessee with him, broke the tie. Sevier felt cheated and worked to defame Jackson. One day in Knoxville the two saw each

NATIONAL EVENTS

SEP 15: Choctaw tribe agrees to cede lands east of Mississippi River in return for land in Oklahoma

US population is 13 million; outnumbers Great Britain

MAR 4: Former president John Quincy Adams begins his term in the House of Representatives; works to publicize abolitionist cause

MAR 18: Supreme Court rules it does not have jurisdiction to hear case from the Cherokee suing to stop Georgia from removing them from their lands

1831

WORLD EVENTS

AUG 25: Belgium independence declared from the Netherlands

Victor Hugo publishes *Notre-Dame de Paris*

MAR 9: French Foreign Legion is created

JUL 21: Belgian king Leopold I is first to reign in that country

JUL 21: Belgium gains independence from Netherlands

other and Sevier mocked his opponent and claimed the only service Jackson had provided was "taking a trip to Nashville with another man's wife." Flushed with fury, Jackson yelled, "Great God! Do you mention *her* sacred name?"[7] He fired his gun in exclamation and challenged Sevier to a duel, but Sevier refused to respond. Jackson pushed for action by publishing an advertisement claiming that Sevier was "a base coward and poltroon."[8] The two men finally met in a comedy of errors that included abundant cursing, a horse that ran off with Sevier's pistols, and Sevier's son threatening Jackson while Jackson's second drew his gun on the son. Amazingly, no one was hurt; moreover, the two men finally made amends of sorts and all returned to Knoxville without anyone trying to kill each other.

Another duel ended in much unhappier circumstances in May 1806. This one was prompted by a forfeited horse race between local leader and horseman Joseph Erwin and Jackson. Erwin paid the forfeit fee, but there had been some problem with the monetary notes he originally presented. A friend of Jackson's made some nasty comments about it, which reached the ears of Erwin's son-in-law, Charles Dickinson, who was known as a crack shot. He challenged Jackson to a duel and threw in malicious comments about Rachel for good measure. The two men met just across the state line in Kentucky. Jackson wore a huge overcoat, and Dickinson fired first, hitting Jackson but not killing him. Andrew gritted his teeth and leveled his pistol while his second had to remind Dickinson to resume his place. Jackson's shot hit Dickinson in the ribs and left him in a pool of blood that quickly drained away his life. Jackson himself had blood pouring from his chest wound; he would carry the bullet from that duel in him the rest of his life. When people pronounced amazement at Jackson's deadly shot, considering he did it after just being wounded, Jackson replied, "I should have hit him if he had shot me through the brain."[9] This duel would affect Jackson's reputation for years to come.

PLANTER JACKSON

By 1804, Rachel convinced Andrew to relinquish his court appointment and settle down to the life of a planter. By now his property holdings of land and slaves were considerable, and his financial status much improved. Jackson, however, was dissatisfied with his life and longed for excitement, so he wagered on game cocks and horses, and in 1805 nearly bet on the wrong man.

Former vice president Aaron Burr (p. 41), disgraced after killing Alexander Hamilton in a duel, now lived in exile in the west. He yearned to create his own empire in league with the Spanish, and stayed with Jackson while he tested the waters of Tennessee. Jackson liked Burr and pledged his support until Burr's accomplice General James Wilkinson blew the whistle on Burr's scheme. President Jefferson ordered Burr's arrest, and he was taken to Richmond for trial. Jackson was summoned as a witness and testified that Burr had discussed the possibility of war with Spain and the subsequent need to have a prepared militia (led by Jackson). Moreover, Jackson stressed that he told Burr he would only take action upon word from the secretary of war. Burr was found not guilty of treason, a verdict with which Jackson concurred.

The Jacksons never had any children of their own, but in 1808 they adopted a nephew of Rachel's and named him Andrew Jackson, Junior. Since both parents were forty-one and comfortable in their life together, the boy never lacked for attention, love, or anything he desired.

SUPREME COURT APPOINTMENTS

★★★★★★★★★★

John McLean, 1829

Henry Baldwin, 1830

James M. Wayne, 1835

Philip P. Barbour, 1836

Roger B. Taney, 1836

John Catron, 1837

APR: Secretary of war resigns; many other cabinet members follow within months, including secretary of state and attorney general

DEC 27: Charles Darwin, British naturalist, departs for the Galapagos Islands and South America

1832

MAR 3: Supreme Court takes case and rules in *Worcester v. Georgia* that Georgia laws "have no force" for the Cherokee tribe, so state cannot force them from their lands; Georgia and President Jackson disregard Chief Justice John Marshall and the ruling

MAR 24: Creek tribe cedes its lands east of the Mississippi River

APR 6: Black Hawk leads Sauk trying to regain land from settlers in Illinois; Abraham Lincoln serves during this four-month war

FEB 12: Cholera outbreak in London kills 3,000; later spreads to France and North America

MAR 23: British extensively reform their voting laws and enfranchise a million new voters

MAY 1: Greek monarchy begins with reign of Otto I, son of Bavarian king Ludwig I

MAY 7: Treaty of Constantinople

STATE OF THE UNION

US POPULATION IN 1829
12,866,020

NATIONAL DEBT IN 1837
$336,958

NUMBER OF STATES IN 1837
26

STATES ADMITTED TO UNION
Arkansas, June 15, 1836

Michigan, January 26, 1837

WAR

When the War of 1812 (p. 54) erupted, Tennessee militia major general Jackson eagerly offered his services. The War Department was hesitant to trust a possible co-conspirator of Burr, and so they acknowledged his offer but did nothing to reward it until it was determined to beef up military support in New Orleans. Jackson and fifteen hundred Tennesseans were ordered south. The night before they left Nashville was bone-chilling cold, and Jackson spent the night walking among his men, seeing to their comfort, and at about dawn, he went to a tavern for a warm drink. Once inside, a fellow made rude comments about how terrible the conditions were for the men while their officers enjoyed a comfortable tavern. In a flash, the unsuspecting civilian was hurled against the wall with a defiant Jackson staring down at him, yelling, "You d----d infernal scoundrel, sowing disaffection among the troops. My quartermaster and I have been up all night, making the men comfortable. Let me hear no more such talk, or I'm d----d if I don't ram that red hot hand iron down your throat."[10]

Jackson and his volunteers proceeded southward and were ordered to stop in Natchez by General Wilkinson. They waited a month for orders to continue to New Orleans; finally orders arrived. The new secretary of war John Armstrong ordered Jackson to dismiss his men and go home. The return home was no easier than the original journey, but his men were impressed by their commander's sheer will and determination. He and his officers gave their horses to the sick and walked alongside the men. All agreed that Jackson was as tough as hickory, and thus his nickname was born, "Old Hickory."

Once Jackson returned, conflict found him once again; this time he aided one of his officers by acting as a second in a duel against Jesse Benton, brother to attorney and fellow officer Thomas Hart Benton. Since Jesse was a master marksman and his opponent was an amateur, they shot at ten feet, and agreed to wheel around to face each other. Each was shot but not mortally. For Benton, the wound was as painful to his pride as to his anatomy, since he took a shot across the buttocks. Howls of laughter greeted the news, infuriating his brother, who held Jackson responsible for the mishap. Jackson threatened Thomas Benton with a horsewhipping and was ready to administer it when they came upon one another in Nashville. The Bentons drew their pistols, shooting Jackson in the shoulder and arm. Jackson's friends in town made life unpleasant for the Bentons, so after the war, Thomas Hart Benton moved west to Missouri. Later he would become reacquainted with Jackson as the two men served in the Senate. They agreed to let bygones be bygones, an amazing feat considering Jackson still bore the lead in his shoulder from Thomas's pistol. (The bullet was eventually removed and jokingly returned to Benton. Keeping in the spirit, he refused it, saying Jackson had possession of it longer and should retain it.)

While Jackson lay in bed recuperating from his wound, news of the massacre at Fort Mims by Creek Indians reached Nashville. The deaths of more than 250 settlers galvanized the surrounding areas, including the Tennessee militia, and a weak Andrew Jackson took command and once again led his men southward. They systematically destroyed Creek villages in retaliation. One of his volunteers, a young Davy Crockett, said, "We shot them like dogs."[11] Morale among the troops suffered from a lack of supplies and a group announced they were going home. Jackson stopped them with a gun and threatened that he would shoot anyone

NATIONAL EVENTS

MAY: Democratic Party unanimously nominates Andrew Jackson for a second term with Martin Van Buren as his vice president

MAY 9: Seminole chiefs agree to cede Florida lands

JUL 14: Tariff of 1832 is passed and angers the South

OCT 14: Chickasaw cede lands east of Mississippi River

NOV: Andrew Jackson wins reelection by a landslide

NOV 14: Last surviving signer of the Declaration of Independence—Charles Carroll of Maryland—dies at age 95

WORLD EVENTS

Cholera epidemic in India spreads to UK and then American cities, including NYC and New Orleans

MAY 27: War between Ottoman Empire and Egypt

JUN 5: Anti-monarchist riot breaks out in Paris

JUN 15: Egyptian forces seize Damascus

AUG 30: London Protocol marks end of Greek War of Independence

THE SEMINOLE WARS

Although sometimes referred to as the Seminole War, there were actually three wars over a forty-year span between the Seminole tribe in Florida and the US Army. The First Seminole War was from 1817 to 1818; the Second Seminole War from 1835 to 1842; and the Third Seminole War from 1855 to 1858. The Second Seminole War, often referred to as the Seminole War, was the most expensive, and lasted longer than any war involving the United States between the American Revolution and the Vietnam War.

THE FIRST SEMINOLE WAR (1817–1818) ★ Sparked by a belief that the Spanish in Florida were aiding the Seminoles to attack nearby American settlements in Georgia, General Andrew Jackson was dispatched to Florida. Once there, he soon created an international incident by executing two British men he claimed were aiding the Seminoles. Jackson and his militia razed native villages and forced the Spanish government to flee Pensacola.

THE SECOND SEMINOLE WAR (1835–1842) ★ Following the end of the first war, the United States had acquired Florida, and in 1835, now-President Jackson had ordered the relocation of various southeastern tribes to lands west of the Mississippi. The Seminoles began raiding farms, settlements, and attacked Army patrols; the Second Seminole War had begun. Colonel Zachary Taylor earned commendation for his victory over the Seminoles in the Battle of Lake Okeechobee on Christmas Day, 1837. Over the next five years, fighting continued, and in 1842, the US government authorized the creation of a reservation in southwestern Florida.

THE THIRD SEMINOLE WAR (1855–1858) ★ An uneasy peace began and ran for a dozen years. When an attack on a small Army patrol by a band of Seminole warriors became known, citizens of Florida demanded revenge. Secretary of the Army Jefferson Davis answered pleas from the governor for additional troops to squash the rebellion but many of these men were soon sent to help staunch the bloodshed in Kansas in 1856. Consequently, some militia troops were federalized as they pursued the Seminoles into the swamps, burning crops and destroying the Indian villages, capturing their leaders, and forcing their followers to move west. Some Seminole, however, managed to remain in their homeland. The Seminole tribe never surrendered.

NOV 24: South Carolina holds a special convention that nullifies the Tariff Acts of 1828 and 1832

DEC 10: President Jackson threatens to use force if South Carolina moves to secede

DEC 28: John C. Calhoun wins election to the Senate; resigns as vice president

Sketches and Eccentricities of Col. David Crockett is published, making him a national hero; at this time he is serving in Congress

MAR 2: Jackson signs Henry Clay's compromise tariff bill as well as a "force bill" to resolve South Carolina nullification crisis

1833

DEC 4: Battle of Antwerp: French attack Dutch citadel

DEC 21: Battle of Konya: Egyptians defeat Ottoman army in Anatolia

DEC 23: The Netherlands lose Antwerp; battle of Antwerp ends

Prussian general Karl von Clausewitz's *On War* is posthumously published

Slaves in British colonies are freed; Parliament compensates slaveholders

BLACK HAWK WAR (1832) ★ The Sauk and Fox Indians native to the Illinois area were forced to relocate west of the Mississippi River in 1831. When food became scarce that winter in their new Iowa home, their leader Black Hawk decided that they should return home. Hearing of the return of the Indians, the Illinois governor summoned the militia in April 1832. Many—including Abraham Lincoln—answered the call. Then in May, they were joined by 1,000 regular soldiers under General Winfield Scott. Negotiations failed, but so did Black Hawk's attempt to recruit warriors from other tribes. Fighting over the summer moved across northern Illinois into Michigan Territory (present-day Wisconsin). There in August, Black Hawk surrendered, and on September 21, a peace treaty was signed between the US government and the Sauk and Fox nations.

who kept moving. Later, when he heard a brigade threatened mutiny, he had his gunners light their matches, implying the cannons would be fired at the men. Most men left anyway with the end of their one-year enlistment, but to Jackson's surprise and joy, they were replaced with new volunteers. So in March, he moved his troops and friendly Cherokees to attack the Creek camp at Horseshoe Bend, which left nine hundred Creek dead. One of Jackson's officers, Sam Houston, led part of the forces against the Creeks even after taking an arrow in his thigh.

Later, the Creek leader, Chief Red Eagle, surrendered and helped Jackson to convince others to do likewise. Jackson worked with the remaining tribes of the Creek nation once he was made major-general in the US army and commander of the Seventh Military District, including Tennessee, Mississippi Territory, and Louisiana. He utilized his position to negotiate a treaty with the friendly Creeks to give up land, which later would compose most of Alabama and part of Georgia. Seeing no recourse except war, the Creeks reluctantly agreed, although the hostile members of their nation had already escaped to Florida and the protection of British and Spanish authorities.

Unable to tarry long, Jackson braced for a British invasion of the south through one of its ports. He raced to Mobile Bay and reinforced garrisons there, then veered to Pensacola, which was neutral Spanish territory, yet they permitted the British to use their ports. The British retreated, the Spanish capitulated, and Jackson left. He returned to Mobile and decided that the British objective had to be New Orleans, so there he led his troops.

Quickly Jackson assessed the situation and declared martial law. He began assembling an unusual assortment of "volunteers" to supplement his forces. These included the elite Creoles of New Orleans society, free blacks, and Jean LaFitte's band of pirates. All together, they comprised a fighting force of five thousand men. In December, nearly nine thousand British soldiers, fresh from their victorious campaigns against Napoleon, landed, and on the twenty-third, the two armies met in a two-hour engagement seven miles from New Orleans. Helping in Jackson's attack were two American ships. Once the British commander Lieutenant General Sir Edward Packenham arrived and was apprised of the situation, he immediately ordered one destroyed, and the Americans towed the other out of harm's way. The major British offensive was launched early on the morning of January 8, 1815, but their plans went awry as the river was too dangerous to allow them to cross it in great numbers, and others marched off to attack, only

NATIONAL EVENTS	**MAR 4:** Jackson and Van Buren are inaugurated	**APR:** Americans in Texas agree to separate from Mexico	**SEP:** Jackson presses for the end of the Second Bank and its funds to be distributed among smaller state "pet" banks	**SEP:** Clay introduces censures for Secretary of Treasury Taney for using the pet banks and Jackson for exceeding his authority	**DEC:** William Lloyd Garrison organizes first national anti-slavery conference
WORLD EVENTS	English mathematician Charles Babbage imagines the concept of a calculator	Chopin writes *Piano Concerto in E Minor*	**JAN 1:** Britain claims the Falkland Islands off Argentina's coast	**AUG 29:** British Parliament limits child labor with Factory Acts	**SEP 29:** Isabella II becomes queen of Spain at age 3; first Carlist War begins when her uncle challenges her claim to the throne

to find they were missing some of their equipment to scale the breastworks. Precious time was lost as they had to retrieve the items. Jackson was not a great tactician, and some of his men paid for it as they were attacked on the flanks, but the main British force marched up the center and straight into twenty cannons, which blasted them to eternity. About 40 percent of the British force was casualties, while only thirteen Americans lay dead and another thirty-nine wounded. Overall, Jackson's performance was exemplary, as explained by historian and future president Theodore Roosevelt (p. 300):

> *The promptness and skill with which he attacked, as soon as he knew of the near approach of the British, undoubtedly saved the city . . . Instead of being able to advance at once, they were forced to delay three days, during which Jackson entrenched himself in a position from which he was never driven. but after this attack the offensive would have been not only hazardous, but useless, and accordingly Jackson, adopting the mode of warfare which best suited the ground he was on and where he was strongest, and confined himself strictly to the pure defensive—a system condemned by most European authorities.*[12]

News of the victory in New Orleans reached Washington, D.C., in February and was soon followed by news from Europe of a peace treaty signed on Christmas Eve. Jackson was hailed as the conquering hero, and Congress jubilantly agreed to grant him a gold medal. The scar on his cheek from a British sword thirty years before had indeed been vindicated.

Jackson left New Orleans in April and was soon appointed as one of two divisional leaders. He ruled from the Hermitage, but occasionally ventured to Washington and Virginia. He was toasted by many, including Thomas Jefferson, and Jackson greeted the attention with modesty.

FLORIDA

After the war, the Seminoles continued to create havoc along the Georgia–Florida border; moreover, slaves frequently crossed the border to gain their freedom. The new president James Monroe offered to buy Florida, but the Spanish were not interested—yet. Two British traders arrived to help the Seminoles, and warfare continued between the settlers and the Seminoles. When a group of forty soldiers and their families were killed, the United States decided it was time to summon the man for action, and Andrew Jackson was ordered to take command.

Jackson's actions in Florida were later the subject of international condemnation and rebuke by his own government. Nonplussed, Jackson insisted that he had the president's blessing when he invaded Florida and hanged the two British traders. He retook Pensacola while dispatches flew among the diplomats of Britain, Spain, and America. Ultimately, the Spanish decided they could no longer adequately control Florida, so selling it would be more beneficial than having it seized. In 1819, the Spanish ceded Florida to the United States in the Adams–Onis Treaty (p. 76). Two years later, Jackson was made its military governor, but he served only a few months before resigning, so he could make preparations for a presidential campaign in 1824.

PRESIDENTIAL CANDIDATE

Tennessee leaders believed no one had a better chance to win the presidency than Jackson, so in 1822 they began laying the foundation to make

DID YOU KNOW?

Jackson was the only president to serve in both the Revolutionary War and the War of 1812.

JAN 3: Stephen Austin arrested in Mexico after traveling there to push for separation of Texas from Mexico; he is held for eight months

JAN 29: Jackson becomes first president to order troops to break up labor unrest. Workers building the Chesapeake and Ohio Canal riot to protest low pay and poor working conditions

MAR 28: Senate approves censures regarding the pet banks

APR 14: Whig party begins in the US with Henry Clay and Daniel Webster as its leaders; members oppose Andrew Jackson and his policies

1834

First settlements in South Australia and Victoria

London's Baring Brothers begins competing with East India Company for China trade

MAR 6: York, Canada, is incorporated as Toronto

MAY 6: Sikh forces take over the Muslim city of Peshawar

MAY 26: Portugal's civil war ends

DID YOU KNOW?

Jackson smoked a corncob pipe.

this a reality. State senator Sam Houston proclaimed to Jackson, "The next President will be the 'People's Choice.'"[13] First they elected Jackson to the Senate to provide him a national forum. There he backed western interests while trying to avoid confrontations with his enemies, who worked to provoke his temper. Their efforts failed; instead, people were astonished at the fine manners and gentle presence of this man of the frontier who did not appear to be a frontiersman.

When the election of 1824 finally occurred, Jackson won in popular votes as well as electoral votes, but he lacked a majority in the Electoral College. Jackson, John Quincy Adams, and William Crawford of Georgia (all members of the Jeffersonian Republican Party) had to wait for the House of Representatives to make its decision. There another presidential hopeful, Henry Clay, held power as its Speaker. Pennsylvania congressman James Buchanan went to Jackson to see if he would be willing to grant Clay the coveted position of secretary of state, but Jackson refused any deals. Later, Adams met with Clay and the two men came to an understanding; when the House votes were tallied, John Quincy Adams was named the new president. Soon he announced his choice of secretary of state—surprise!—Henry Clay. Andrew Jackson smelled a rat and decried the two men for making a "corrupt bargain"—a charge that both men spent the rest of their lives denying.

Bitterly disappointed by what he thought was a stolen election, Jackson quickly began plotting his next campaign, and this time, he expected to win a total victory. His first step was resigning his seat and coordinating efforts with his Tennessee cronies. Still, all their hard work could not prevent the storm of slander that befell Andrew and Rachel Jackson beginning in March 1827, when an Ohio newspaper publicized the rather questionable circumstances of their marriage. His dueling and his military career were questioned, but Jackson supporters fought back and encouraged demonstrations, as well as hickory tree plantings. All of the efforts paid off and the people voted Andrew Jackson as their overwhelming favorite to be the seventh president.

Andrew had worked to ensure that Rachel was prevented from seeing the worst of the libelous charges against her, but when she traveled to Nashville to shop for her impending position as First Lady, she encountered a pamphlet that revealed the full scope of the vitriolic attacks on her character. Stunned by its content, she wept uncontrollably and soon became physically ill, as well, first from a cold and then, a heart attack felled her. Rachel Jackson died December 22, leaving behind a very emotionally stricken husband who wrote, "My heart is nearly broke."[14]

PRESIDENT JACKSON

Accompanied by his nephew, Andrew Jackson Donelson, and his nephew's wife, Emily, who would serve as presidential hostess, Jackson arrived in Washington dressed in black from head to toe.

The people, nevertheless, intended to celebrate the arrival of their man into the President's House. After cheering their hero with thunderous huzzahs at his inauguration, the masses then trod down Pennsylvania Avenue to partake in the festivities. The mansion soon exceeded its limitations as all forms of humanity shoved their way in to shake the hand of Old Hickory. Jackson was nearly consumed by the people, and fled from the scene, leaving the house and its staff on their own. The mob of twenty thousand or so continued their

NATIONAL EVENTS

JUN 28: Second Coinage Act passed and leads to shortage of silver coins

JUN 30: Congress establishes the Bureau of Indian Affairs to manage the Indian Territory (Oklahoma)

OCT 28: US orders Seminoles to leave their homeland in Florida and relocate to Oklahoma

WORLD EVENTS

AUG 1: 35,000 former slaves of the British go free in South Africa

AUG 18: Mt. Vesuvius erupts

AUG 23: British Parliament outlaws slavery in its colonies

OCT 16: Massive London fire destroys part of the city, including Houses of Parliament

OCT 20: Persia's Fath Ali Shah dies; he is succeeded by Hajji Mirza Aghasi

chaotic party outside, and the staff raised the windows so the partygoers could exit more quickly. There was no doubt that the people's president now ruled the nation.

Jackson's choices for cabinet appointees included recently elected New York governor Martin Van Buren as secretary of state, Samuel D. Ingham of Massachusetts as secretary of the treasury, and John Eaton as secretary of war. This last choice provoked a maelstrom of protests from all quarters, including Jackson's own family, in a matter that became known as the "Petticoat Affair." Eaton had recently married a young widow who, gossips insisted, had been not only Eaton's mistress, but also on "friendly" terms with many other men. Washington society put up a wall that Eaton's wife could not penetrate, nor could the president on her behalf. Her situation appealed to his sensibilities as being similar to Rachel's, and Andrew adamantly insisted on defending her honor even if it tore apart his cabinet in the process. He increasingly leaned more on what became known as his "Kitchen Cabinet" of informal advisors, including his nephew Donelson, Van Buren, Eaton, and other associates to provide him with information and advice.

Demanding reform for officeholders, the president soon announced that he was replacing men who had been using their position for corrupt practices. This became the basis for the critics who termed this the spoils system for its rewarding political patronage; in fact, Jackson replaced less than 20 percent of officeholders. To his embarrassment, one of these appointees absconded with over one million dollars in public funds from his position as the collector for the Port of New York.

In 1830, Congress passed the Indian Removal Act, granting the president the authority to move southeast Native American tribes west to Indian Territory (Oklahoma). One of these tribes was the Cherokee, who faced relocation because gold had been found on their land in the Smoky Mountains, and Georgia demanded their removal. The tribe took the issue to court in *Worcester v. State of Georgia*, and Chief Justice John Marshall wrote that Georgia had no authority to dictate to the Cherokee. Georgia and the president determined otherwise, and as the majority of the tribe traversed the eight hundred miles to Oklahoma, they lost a quarter of their people. The route they took and the journey itself became known as the Trail of Tears.

Looking ahead to the next election, Clay and his supporters decided to launch the campaign on the rechartering of the second Bank of the United States. The president had already made noises about its demise, so Clay and the Bank's president, Nicholas Biddle, decided to act preemptively. Congress passed the recharter, and as promised, the president vetoed it. The battle lines were drawn. Jackson denounced the Bank as a hand puppet of the rich, and worked to "kill" it by distributing its funds to smaller state banks, or as his detractors called them, "pet" banks. Biddle exercised his power by restricting the credit of the state banks and calling in their loans,

INDIAN REMOVAL ACT (1830) ★ President Jackson wholeheartedly supported the Indian Removal Act, which pushed for the voluntary relocation of southeastern Native American tribes. Soon, however, the removal became mandatory, and a long, arduous process ensued of forcing thousands of native people from their homeland and relocating to the newly organized Indian Territory (Oklahoma).

JAN 30: Richard Lawrence assassination attempt on President Jackson; pistols misfire; Lawrence is arrested but sent to an insane asylum

MAR 3: Congress creates three new US mints

MAY: Democrats nominate Martin Van Buren for president

JUN 2: Phineas Taylor (P.T.) Barnum begins his career in show business

JUL 6: Chief Justice John Marshall dies at 80 after serving 35 years (legend says Liberty Bell cracked the final time when tolling for his death)

OCT 2: Texas begins its revolution for independence from Mexico

1835

Alexis de Tocqueville, French political scientist, publishes *Democracy in America*

SEP 7: HMS *Beagle* and Charles Darwin arrive on Galapagos Islands

DEC 1: Danish author Hans Christian Andersen publishes *Fairy Tales*

DEC 15: Mexican president Santa Anna issues a new constitution for Mexico, including Texas

creating a tightening around their fiscal necks. They appealed to the president, but he refused intervention, claiming they needed to go to the source—Biddle.

The elimination of the national bank was the main issue in the 1832 campaign between Jackson of the Democratic Party and Henry Clay of the National Republican Party. Clay and his supporters referred to their opponent as King Andrew and denounced Jackson's use of the veto—he had used it over a dozen times, significantly more than any predecessor. Still, the common folk flocked to Jackson and voted for him overwhelmingly, especially in the western and southern states. But he would soon face a showdown in the South.

During his first term, Jackson and his vice president, John C. Calhoun of South Carolina, grew increasingly distant. The main discontent stemmed from Calhoun's steadfast belief in nullification (state nullification of federal law), which he proposed should be done with the Tariff of Abominations, passed in 1828. Their differences finally emerged on the occasion of the Jefferson Day Banquet (the annual Democratic celebration on Thomas Jefferson's birthday) on April 13, 1830, when Jackson gave his toast: "Our Federal Union: It must be preserved!" Calhoun countered with, "The Union, next to our liberty, the most dear!"[15]

In 1832, another tariff, albeit lower, was passed; Calhoun and his southern colleagues issued threats of nullification and secession. No one threatened Andrew Jackson without receiving a threat in return. He pledged (and Congress supported) to send troops into South Carolina or anywhere else that refused to collect tariff duties. Earlier, he had pledged to another South Carolinian that he would "hang the first man I can lay my hand on engaged in such treasonable conduct, upon the first tree I reach."[16] Henry Clay stepped in and provided a compromise tariff that ended the crisis in 1833. By then Calhoun had resigned as vice president, so he could resume having more of a vocal position as South Carolina's senator.

With one crisis averted, another loomed ahead as the country's financial situation grew shaky with the demise of the national bank. Gaining more money and power, the pet banks now inaugurated a new wave of speculation as they issued more paper money (specie) than they had backing of gold or silver. The federal government became its

RICHARD LAWRENCE'S ASSASSINATION ATTEMPT (1835) ★ On January 30, 1835, a funeral procession for South Carolina congressman Warren R. Davis made its way from the House chamber toward the Capitol rotunda with President Jackson and Secretary of the Treasury Levi Woodbury directly behind the casket. Suddenly, thirty-five-year-old unemployed house painter Richard Lawrence jumped out and fired a pistol at the president, but when it misfired, Jackson immediately began whacking the would-be assassin with his cane. Lawrence managed to pull out another pistol, which also misfired, and Jackson resumed hitting Lawrence with his cane until aides pulled him away while congressmen subdued Lawrence. Richard Lawrence insisted he wanted to kill the president because Jackson had slain his father a few years before. This and other wild claims led to a verdict of "not guilty" due to insanity. Lawrence would be committed to an insane asylum for the remainder of his life.

NATIONAL EVENTS

DEC 28: Osceola leads his people against the US Army in Second Seminole War

DEC 30: Cherokees sign a treaty giving their eastern lands for $5 million and agreeing to move to Oklahoma

1836

JAN: Equal Rights Party (Loco-Focos) meet and choose their own platform, which they believe is more egalitarian than the Democrats'

FEB 22–23: Whigs nominate three regional presidential candidates: Daniel Webster (Northeast); William Henry Harrison (West); and Hugh Lawson White (South)

WORLD EVENTS

Boer farmers found Natal, Transvaal, and Orange Free State in South Africa

British Chartist movement begins demanding suffrage for males

City of Adelaide, Australia, founded

own victim as it accepted specie payment for sales of western lands. Jackson tried to avert the calamity by issuing his Specie Circular, demanding only gold or silver payment for western lands, thereby halting speculators from buying huge plots. Inflation, nevertheless, continued to climb and in 1837 would take the country into a downward spiral.

One western area demanding America's attention during Jackson's presidency was Texas. He had attempted to buy it from Mexico during his first term, but the Mexican government had been unreceptive. Then, when the Texans gained their independence from Mexico and asked to be annexed by the United States, Jackson had to disappoint his old friend Sam Houston, for the addition of another slave state was too much for many northerners to stomach. Moreover, the United States had a treaty with Mexico pledging neutrality, and in January 1837, General Santa Anna was sent to Washington, D.C., by Sam Houston to discuss a way for Texas to be recognized without further upsetting Mexico. Jackson and the Mexican general discussed options, but nothing materialized. A few weeks later, however, Congress approved recognition and funds to send a diplomat to Texas.

In 1835, Chief Justice John Marshall died after serving nearly thirty-five years as the supreme jurist of the land. Andrew Jackson appointed his successor, Roger Taney of Maryland; Jackson also appointed four associate justices during his tenure.

Although not running for a third term, Jackson still kept a close connection to the Democratic Party, ensuring that his successor was Martin Van Buren. As he left the White House one last time as the outgoing president, he was leaving a much different house than he had found. Magnolia trees now adorned the grounds, as well as a formal garden, the north portico was finished, and running water was pumped into the presidential residence. For the first time, the East Room was decorated in lavish style; furnishings throughout were refurbished, and staggering amounts of china and silver were purchased to keep up with the vast numbers who flocked to see their president. One of Jackson's New York supporters gave him a fourteen-hundred-pound block of cheese. After allowing it to age for two years, he had a cheese tasting for the public at the President's House, and the mob did its duty. Within two hours, the cheese was gone.

The people never forgot their hero, and on Van Buren's inauguration day, they again appeared in thousands, not to see the incoming president but rather to bid farewell to the outgoing one. His old foe Senator Thomas Hart Benton described the scene as one of the people giving "a collective thanks for lifting the nation to a new level of freedom and democracy."[17]

RETIREMENT

A grateful public greeted Jackson as he traveled homeward. His beloved Hermitage, now rebuilt from a fire over two years before, stood ready to welcome its owner. During his absence, his adopted son Andrew Jackson Jr. had been the caretaker and manager; he did neither well. Jackson's financial status deteriorated for two major reasons: Andrew Jr.'s imprudent investment in various schemes and frauds, and the Panic of 1837, which caused widespread bank failures, unemployment, and a drastic reduction of the money supply that wiped out many family fortunes.

Jackson's health also created concern, as it had during his presidency. Periodically, he experienced episodes of hemorrhaging and difficulties breathing, for which he was bled. Through the years, his

DID YOU KNOW?

Jackson was the first president to ride on a train.

FEB 24–MAR 6: Siege of the Alamo

MAR 2: Texas declares its independence, writes its own constitution, and elects its first government

APR–SEP: Narcissa Whitman and Eliza Spalding, accompanying their Methodist missionary husbands, become first women to travel west along the Oregon Trail

APR 14: Congress establishes Wisconsin Territory from western portion of Michigan

Dickens writes *Pickwick Papers*

JAN 12: Charles Darwin reaches Sydney, Australia

MAY 31: English farmer patents screw propeller

JUL 6: Battle of Sikkah: French colonial forces defeat Algerian emir Abdul-Qadar

JUL 21: The first Canadian railroad opens, between Laprairie and St. John

THE BATTLE OF THE ALAMO (1836) ★ On March 6, 1836, troops under Mexican president General Santa Anna ended a thirteen-day siege at the San Antonio mission known as the Alamo. There, 189 defenders died, including former Tennessee congressman Davy Crockett. Their deaths spurred fellow Texans to rally and seek revenge. The cries of "Remember the Alamo" pierced the air at San Jacinto on April 21, when the Mexican forces were overwhelmed, and Texas independence was achieved.

physical health weakened, but his political acumen remained strong, and he was called upon by the Democrats frequently to help with campaigns and issues. In 1844, during John Tyler's presidency, Jackson was outraged by Van Buren's refusal to support Texas annexation, so he cast about for someone who did support it, and summoned fellow Tennessean James K. Polk to the Hermitage. Dumbfounded by Jackson's decision that he should be the Democratic candidate, Polk traveled on to the Democratic convention, where the Jackson contingent made Old Hickory's wishes a reality once more.

> ***There are no necessary evils in government. Its evils exist only in its abuses."***
>
> *—Andrew Jackson, on vetoing the Second National Bank, July 10, 1832*

Pleased by Polk's nomination and then his election, Jackson remarked, "The Republic is safe."[18] Now he only had one more piece of unfinished business—annexing Texas and allowing it to join the United States. In mid-March 1845, Andrew received word that this, too, had been achieved.

Jackson's health continued to decline, and by spring of 1845, dropsy had bloated his body, leaving him unable to lie down. Propped up by pillows, his respiratory ailments continued to plague him. On Sunday, June 8, 1845, Andrew Jackson said goodbye to friends, family members, and slaves. His last words were, "Oh, do not cry—be good children & we will all meet in heaven."[19] Sam Houston, who brought his young son, did not arrive in time. They missed Jackson's passing by minutes, but after weeping at Jackson's prostrate body, the elder Houston told his son: "Try to remember that you have looked upon the face of Andrew Jackson."[20]

Two days later, Andrew Jackson's body was laid to rest beside his beloved Rachel in their vault in the garden. More than three thousand mourners attended his funeral, a mix of all the people who had welcomed back the Hero of New Orleans and Old Hickory from the White House. Andrew Jackson was ever appreciative of "the patriot's reward."[21]

NATIONAL EVENTS

APR 21: Battle of San Jacinto; Sam Houston defeats Santa Anna, who grants Texas its independence in return for his life but reneges soon after his return to Mexico

MAY 18: House of Representatives votes in favor of a "gag rule" blocking the discussion of slavery, much to dismay of John Quincy Adams

JUN 15: Arkansas is admitted as the 25th state

SEP 9: Ralph Waldo Emerson publishes his first book, *Nature*; he, Nathaniel

WORLD EVENTS

JUL 30: The first English-language newspaper is published in Hawaii

NOV 11: Chile declares war on Peru and Bolivia

DEC 28: Spain recognizes Mexican independence

DEC 30: Lehman theater in St. Petersburg catches fire; hundreds die

ENDNOTES

1 H. W. Brands, *Andrew Jackson, His Life and Times*, New York: Doubleday, 2005, p. 17.

2 James Parton, *Life of Andrew Jackson* (3 vols), Boston, 1866, vol. I, pages 104-105.

3 Ibid, p. 109.

4 Robert V. Remini, *The Life of Andrew Jackson*, New York: Harper and Row, Inc., 1988, pp. 14-15.

5 Ibid, p. 18.

6 A.W. Putnam, *History of Middle Tennessee*, Nashville, 1859, p. 318.

7 Ibid, p. 46.

8 Ibid, p. 47.

9 Amos Kendall, *The Life of General Andrew Jackson*, New York, 1844, p. 117.

10 Remini, p. 63.

11 Davy Crockett, *Life of Davy Crockett*, New York, 1854, p. 75.

12 Theodore Roosevelt, *The Naval War of 1812*, Annapolis, MD: Naval Institute Press, 1987, p. 433.

13 Brands, p. 374.

14 Remini, p. 171.

15 John C. Fitzpatrick, ed., *Autobiography of Martin Van Buren*, Washington, D.C., 1920, p. 415.

16 Remini, p. 197.

17 Thomas Hart Benton, *Thirty Years View*, New York, 1865, 2 vols, vol. I, p. 735.

18 Remini, p. 352.

19 Ibid, p. 358.

20 Ibid, p. 359.

21 Brands, p. 532.

Hawthorne, and Henry David Thoreau form the Transcendental Club

OCT 22: Sam Houston becomes the first president of the Republic of Texas

OCT 24: Alonzo Phillips of Massachusetts patents a prototype of phosphorous matches

NOV: Martin Van Buren is elected as the eighth president of the US

Martin Van Buren

★ ★ ★ EIGHTH PRESIDENT ★ ★ ★

LIFE SPAN
- Born: December 5, 1782, in Columbia, New York
- Died: July 24, 1862, in Kinderhook, New York

NICKNAMES
- The Little Magician, Old Kinderhook, Martin Van Ruin

RELIGION
- Dutch Reformed

HIGHER EDUCATION
- None; studied law with an attorney

PROFESSION
- Lawyer, senator

MILITARY SERVICE
- None

FAMILY
- Father: **Abraham Van Buren** (1737–1817)
- Mother: **Maria Hoes Van Alen Van Buren** (1747–1818)
- Wife: **Hannah Hoes Van Buren** (1783–1819); wed February 21, 1807, in Catskill, New York
- Children: **Abraham** (1807–1873); **John** (1810–1866); **Martin** (1812–1855); **Winfield Scott** (1813); **Smith Thompson** (1817–1876)

POLITICAL LIFE
- Columbia County attorney (1808–1813)
- New York state senator (1812–1813)
- US senator (1821–1828)
- Governor of New York (January–March 1829)
- Secretary of state (1829–1831)

PRESIDENCY
- One term: March 4, 1837–March 4, 1841
- Democrat
- Reason for leaving office: lost 1840 election to **William Henry Harrison**
- Vice president: **Richard M. Johnson** (1837–1841)

ELECTION OF 1836
- Electoral vote: **Van Buren** 170; **Harrison** 73; **White** 26; **Webster** 14
- Popular vote: **Van Buren** 765,483; **Harrison** 549,508; **White** 145,352; **Webster** 41,287

CABINET
★★★★★★★★★★

SECRETARY OF STATE
John Forsythe (1837–1841)

SECRETARY OF THE TREASURY
Levi Woodbury (1837–1841)

SECRETARY OF WAR
Joel R. Poinsett (1837–1841)

ATTORNEY GENERAL
Benjamin Butler (1837–1838)

Felix Grundy (1838–1839)

Henry D. Gilpin (1840–1841)

SECRETARY OF THE NAVY
Mahlon Dickerson (1837–1838)

James K. Pauling (1838–1841)

POSTMASTER GENERAL
Amos Kendall (1837–1840)

John M. Niles (1840–1841)

Among the ranks of America's lesser-known presidents is Martin Van Buren. Many consider his contribution to the political system prior to his presidency greater than any later accomplishment. Earlier in his career, Van Buren created America's first political machine, known as the Albany Regency. Subsequently, he molded the Democratic Party into that of the common man, who would elect Van Buren's predecessor, Andrew Jackson. These two men and their party shared the belief that, while national power was necessary to be respected on the international stage, its scope should be limited at home to allow states more autonomy. This belief would lead to his failure to secure a second term when a financial panic befell the nation, and the people felt their government offered precious little aid.

EARLY YEARS

The first seven presidents were all British subjects by birth. Martin Van Buren, born December 5, 1782, became the first American-born president. Ironically, he is also the only president whose first language was not English—it was Dutch. Born in what later became known as the "sleepy hollow" region of New York, Martin's Dutch father operated a tavern on the road between New York City and Albany. There, young Van Buren heard the tavern guests gossip, debate, and entertain one another with news and stories. Two of the frequent guests included Alexander Hamilton and Aaron Burr. Here the future president heard his first political discussions.

The small Dutch village of Kinderhook, in the Hudson Valley, boasted an academy young Martin attended until he reached fourteen years of age, when he left to begin his study of law. Van Buren's excellent speaking abilities allowed him the opportunity to give his first summation before a jury at the tender age of fifteen. After six years of study, he passed the bar and began practicing law in Kinderhook with his half-brother.

Over the next five years, Martin Van Buren's life changed tremendously. In 1807, he married his childhood sweetheart and distant cousin, Hannah Hoes. By the end of the year, they welcomed the first of four sons. Sadly, his Dutch bride contracted tuberculosis and died twelve years later. He never remarried.

By 1812, attorney Van Buren ran for state senator against well-known and respected Edward Livingston. Early election returns confirmed the expected—Livingston as the winner. Van Buren learned the news of his upset victory from his brother-in-law en route to New York City to resume his law career; thus began a political career that would span the next thirty years.

EARLY POLITICAL CAREER

Representing Jefferson's Democratic-Republican Party (a precursor to the modern Democratic Party) in the state senate meant championing its causes. Foremost among these in 1812 was the war against Britain (p. 54). The young senator also worked to end the age-old system of punishing debtors by putting them into prison. Such punishment seemed aimed against these people "for the misfortune of being poor."[1] In 1815, Van Buren served double duty when he became New York's attorney general while continuing in the state senate.

It was also during this time that Van Buren started building a network of supporters, which eventually coalesced into his own political machine. One factor brought these men together—their collective dislike of fellow New Yorker and rival DeWitt Clinton. Clinton and Van Buren had been allies at one time, but each perceived a threat

NATIONAL EVENTS

Native American tribes along the upper Missouri River fall victim to a smallpox epidemic that kills thousands

Cotton prices decline by nearly 50 percent

JAN 26: Michigan becomes the 26th state

MAR: Banks fail in New York and other major eastern cities, starting the Panic of 1837; this economic depression lasts for seven years

MAR 3: President Jackson recognizes Republic of Texas on his last full presidential day

1837

WORLD EVENTS

Treaty of Tafna signed between French and Algerian emir Abdul-Qadar

Japan's shogun Tokugawa Ienari resigns; he is succeeded by his son Tokugawa Ieyoshi

World's first kindergarten opens in Germany

Ancient Persian cuneiform is deciphered by German archaeologist Georg Friedrich Grotefend

Englishman Isaac Pittman develops first shorthand system

in the other. Clinton served in the double capacity of New York City mayor and lieutenant governor. Power accompanied these positions, and Clinton expected it to carry him to the presidency in 1816. Van Buren, however, skillfully maneuvered the Democratic-Republican Party to nominate another candidate for the lieutenant governor's position, thus unseating Clinton.

As the War of 1812 continued, Van Buren maintained his support and worked behind the scenes to make a Tennessean, Andrew Jackson, a major player. At one point, both Aaron Burr and Winfield Scott were guests at Van Buren's in Albany. The talk among the three men turned to Jackson, and Burr wanted Scott to encourage President Madison to commission Jackson in the US Army. Burr acknowledged that Madison might still resent the fact that Jackson had supported Burr during his trial for treason a few years before. Still, Burr pushed for Scott to submit Jackson's name. Andrew Jackson would soon become a major general and hero of the Battle of New Orleans.

After the war, Martin Van Buren worked tirelessly to build his political clout. He and his fellow Clinton opponents became known as the Bucktails for the bucks' tails they used to adorn their hats. Years later a local journalist, Thurlow Weed, began referring to them as the "Albany Regency." Weed described its members as "men of great ability, great industry, indomitable courage, and strict personal integrity."[2] The Federalists, though not in power, were far from impotent in New York politics. They maneuvered various political appointments between Clinton and Van Buren, keeping the balance of power ever swaying. When Clinton was elected governor in 1817, the centerpiece of his administration was the building of the Erie Canal. He and Van Buren both understood the need for this enterprise and agreed to abide by a truce in its support.

> *"For myself, therefore, I desire to declare that the principle that will govern me in the high duty to which my country calls me is a strict adherence to the letter and spirit of the Constitution as it was designed by those who framed it."*
>
> —*Martin Van Buren*

Still, each man continued his machinations to oust the other. Clinton toyed with making Van Buren a justice on the state supreme court, while Van Buren proposed that Clinton should accept an appointment to some foreign nation. Neither happened, but Martin Van Buren experienced a twin loss—his wife of twelve years died, and he was removed from his office as attorney general by Governor Clinton.

Although saddened by his losses, Van Buren remained immersed in New York politics. He worked with others to conduct a second state constitutional convention. One of the main products of this new constitution was the extension of suffrage to more potential male voters, including black voters who had $250. Also in 1820, Martin Van Buren earned his first trip to Washington, D.C., when he was elected to the United States Senate.

DID YOU KNOW?

For Van Buren's inauguration, the outgoing president rode in a carriage with the incoming president, establishing a tradition that continues today.

Van Buren's inauguration was the first to have floats in its parade.

MAR 3: Congress adds two Supreme Court justices, bringing the total to nine

MAR 4: Martin Van Buren is inaugurated as eighth president; Richard M. Johnson as vice president.

SEP 18: Lewis Tiffany opens a "Stationery and Fancy Goods Store" in New York City; later he begins to make jewelry and moves to Broadway

SEP 23: Samuel F.B. Morse receives patent for his telegraph

OCT: Republic of Texas applies for annexation but is refused because of the slavery issue

English brothers begin Tetley Tea

English banks stop issuing credit to Americans

French mathematician Simeon Denis Poisson establishes rules of probability

Daguerreotype, early form of photography, invented by Louis Daguerre

JUN 6: Chile's dictator is assassinated

DID YOU KNOW?

Instead of being paid annually as president, Van Buren took his salary in one lump payment at the end of his term.

WASHINGTON POLITICIAN

Once Van Buren's term commenced, he quickly grew dissatisfied with the "era of good feelings." President James Monroe's attempts to unite the country under one political party and appoint former Federalists to key positions only infuriated the junior senator from New York. Moreover, he believed that Monroe was not true to Jefferson's principles of limited government in size and scope. Van Buren envisioned a reenergized Democratic Party that espoused true Jeffersonian beliefs—not the watered-down moderate ideas made to be palpable to all. During his years in the Senate, he worked to develop what historians now call Jacksonian Democracy.

After the 1824 presidential election, Van Buren galvanized Senate opposition to the new president John Quincy Adams and spent much of Adams's term thinking of how to unseat him in the next election. Working with vice president John C. Calhoun, the men agreed that the best candidate from the new Democratic Party was Andrew Jackson. With thoughts of his own political future, Van Buren absented himself from the Senate on the day of a key vote on a tariff. He knew that a vote either way would antagonize North or South, so he decided the best vote was none.

With his eye on the 1828 presidential election, Van Buren toured the South to build a network of support for Jackson, and then did the same in the North. Jackson's men did well throughout the nation in the congressional election of 1827. This enabled Van Buren to be elected Senate majority leader, in which capacity he worked to ensure that the Speaker of the House was a fellow Democrat. Now with the party securely in control of both houses, committee leadership positions followed.

The Albany Regency worried they might lose the governorship of New York, so they begged Van Buren to run. Keeping his options open, he bargained that he would do so only with the understanding that if Jackson won the presidency, he would only serve as governor for a short time, then resign and join Jackson's cabinet.

With Jackson's overwhelming victory over John Quincy Adams in 1828, Martin Van Buren's tenure as governor ranked as one of the shortest on record. Soon he was jostling in a stagecoach en route to Washington. There he quickly assumed his new role as secretary of state and worked to reward party supporters with government jobs—the spoils system had begun. President Jackson appreciated his secretary's handling of delicate issues, including the Peggy Eaton affair (p. 93).

Secretary Van Buren managed the state department with no small degree of skill. The United States brokered its first peace treaty with the Ottoman Empire, which granted the country access to the Black Sea. Van Buren negotiated a trade treaty with Great Britain involving the West Indies. From the French, he won agreement to pay reparations for American shipping ruined during the Napoleonic Wars. Just as important, Van Buren had the president's ear. The two men frequently rode around Washington on horseback and discussed the issues. Martin Van Buren was, without a doubt, a key member of Jackson's "Kitchen Cabinet."

Counting himself as part of Jackson's inner circle was not without its hazards. Following on the heels of the Tariff of Abominations (p. 78) and repeated at the Jefferson Day dinner (p. 94) in 1830, the strain between Jackson and Calhoun grew to a breaking point. Fearing for

NATIONAL EVENTS

NOV 7: Elijah Lovejoy, abolitionist newspaper publisher in Alton, Illinois, is slain by a mob

DEC: Attempted rebellion in Canada spills into the US when Canadian authorities kill an American, setting off anti-British sentiment in the US

DEC 25: General Zachary Taylor defeats Seminoles in Florida fighting

President Van Buren sends troops to Canadian border under General Winfield Scott

House of Representatives refuses to allow Rep. John Quincy Adams to present 350 abolitionist petitions under its gag rule

WORLD EVENTS

JUN 20: Victoria becomes Queen of England following death of her uncle King William IV; she will reign until 1901

JUL 13: Queen Victoria is first monarch to make Buckingham Palace her official residence

AUG 16: Dutch win the Padri War in Indonesia

1838

Ongoing famine in Ireland kills thousands

Charles Dickens publishes *Oliver Twist*

his own political future if Jackson's troubles grew, Van Buren devised his own exit strategy. After much persuasion, Van Buren convinced the president to allow him to resign and ask for the resignations of his other cabinet members, allowing Jackson the opportunity to clean house. Then the president rewarded his former secretary with a foreign post, minister to the court of St. James.

Van Buren and his son, John, arrived in London and were touted by various luminaries. They were received at the court of Queen Victoria and enjoyed touring the sights with Washington Irving as their guide. Then, less than six months after their arrival, stunning news arrived. Something had occurred that no one could have possibly foreseen—a Senate rejection of Van Buren's appointment led by Clay, Webster, and Calhoun.

Instead of returning as a dejected loser, Van Buren left Britain and returned to the United States as a sympathetic soul who had been innocently caught in a web of political intrigue. The three forces who had worried about Van Buren's growing threat now had him much closer and the threat became more ominous—Van Buren would be Andrew Jackson's next vice president!

VICE PRESIDENT VAN BUREN

As vice president to Andrew Jackson, Martin Van Buren continued his role as advisor and confidante to the president. Jackson's second term involved serious issues—the National Bank and the removal of Native Americans among them—and his vice president remained steadfast. Most suspected that Van Buren was the heir apparent, and the political cartoons and editorials grew more numerous. One outspoken critic was Tennessee congressman Davy Crockett, who wrote a biography of the vice president. According to Crockett, "When he [Van Buren] enters the senate-chamber in the morning, he struts and swaggers like a crow in the gutter."[3]

The election of 1836 would see the dawn of a new political party—the Whigs. Opposition to Andrew Jackson and his policies were the main tenets of this new party, which had actually made its debut two years before. The Whig Party's first presidential election illustrated the lack of organization within the party. Instead of agreeing on one candidate, they decided to have several who were strong in their home regions. The Whig strategy was to prevent Van Buren from carrying the majority of electoral votes, thus throwing the election to the House. The Whig's disorganization was no match for the strong foundation the Democrats enjoyed, thanks to Van Buren himself.

SUPREME COURT APPOINTMENTS
★★★★★★★★★★

John McKinley, 1837

Peter V. Daniel, 1841

PANIC OF 1837 ★ Financial changes during the Jackson presidency, including "killing" the second Bank of the United States and issuing the Specie Circular (restricting the use of state bank notes) in 1836, caused many banks to reduce their credit and call in their loans. This created a "panic," which worsened when depositors withdrew funds, and companies began closing. Double-digit unemployment resulted, as did mob violence. New York City witnessed rioting as hungry people raided warehouses of food. The depression lasted about six years, and the Democratic Party lost the 1840 election when people voted for the Whigs, whom they hoped would be able to "fix" the economy.

MAY: Trail of Tears begins when 14,000 Cherokees are forcibly removed from their homes in Georgia, western North Carolina, and eastern Tennessee and relocated to Oklahoma; approximately 4,000 die along the way

MAY: Congress repeals the Specie Circular of 1836 to help restore banks and increase supplies of gold and silver

JUN 12: Wisconsin Territory is divided, and its western region becomes Iowa Territory

SEP 3: Frederick Douglass escapes from slavery

British troops invade Afghanistan and take the emir to India as their prisoner

Arc de Triomphe completed in Paris

Christian Schonbein discovers ozone

London's National Gallery opens

NOV 30: Mexico declares war on France

STATE OF THE UNION

US POPULATION IN 1837
17,069,453

NATIONAL DEBT IN 1841
$5,250,876

PRESIDENT'S SALARY
$25,000/year

PRESIDENT VAN BUREN

Martin Van Buren took the oath of office on March 4, 1837. His honeymoon with the country was extremely short-lived because by summer, the economy collapsed and plunged the nation into a depression that outlasted his term. As with many previous and future presidents, Van Buren inherited a vexing set of problems, but the voters blamed him for their banks closing and rising unemployment. The Panic of 1837 (the worst economic depression suffered in the United States in its early years) was the keystone of Van Buren's presidency, which he could never solve or escape. Ironically, many of the issues at work against him were ones he had supported when Jackson was president.

> *"As to the presidency, the two happiest days of my life were those of my entrance upon the office and my surrender of it."*
>
> —*Martin Van Buren*

With the ever-growing demand for western land, cash sales had escalated dramatically. But in 1836, under Jackson's direction, the Treasury issued a Specie Circular. This meant gold or silver, not cash, would be used for land sales. Such a drastic order created distrust toward the nation's currency, and in turn, undermined the banking system. President Van Buren angrily pointed to the nation's bankers, especially the director of the Bank of the United States, Nicholas Biddle, as the primary reason for the country's distress. Biddle paid a visit to the president and later told a reporter that the president was so disinterested in the nation's economic status that he never broached the subject during their conversation.

One victory for President Van Buren was the passage of his Independent Treasury bill to allow the country's money to be put in its own banks, rather than trusting those owned privately; in short, the president was reversing Jackson's policy of utilizing the state banks. The economy, however, continued to plummet.

Citizens across the country grew increasingly disgusted with the president and his party. The Whigs won handily in the congressional elections of 1838, including Van Buren's own Albany Regency domain of New York. There the Whig Party claimed all but twenty-seven seats of the 128 assemblymen.

Diplomatic matters also demanded the president's attention. Many of the people heading west were going to Texas. Months before Van Buren's election, Texas had won its independence. Now it was ready for the next step—statehood. This threw the nation into a quandary, since adding a slave state would upset the balance in Congress in the South's favor. Such a notion was anathema to the North, and in this matter, the president agreed, fearing such debate would sever the country. He would leave that thorny issue for another time, and another president. In the meantime Texas became its own nation, the Republic of Texas.

During Van Buren's presidency, the United States and Great Britain found themselves at loggerheads, for different reasons. In 1837, a group of Canadian rebels wanting independence

DID YOU KNOW?

Van Buren and his wife spoke Dutch in their home.

NATIONAL EVENTS

1839

Samuel F.B. Morse returns to America from France with photographic equipment so he can produce America's first daguerreotype portraits

President Van Buren sends John Lloyd Stephens to Central America to study Mayan ruins

FEB: Bloodshed is prevented along US-Canadian border by General Winfield Scott, who negotiates a truce so a boundary commission can develop a peaceful solution

MAR 23: First published appearance of the term "OK" appears in *Boston Morning Post*

WORLD EVENTS

Swiss chemist Christian F. Schönbein names his new discovery ozone

"Swedish nightingale" Jenny Lind makes her English singing debut

French Utopian socialist Louis Blanc writes "To each according to his needs, from each according to his abilities," in his essay "L'Organisation du Travail"

Charles Darwin publishes *Journal and Remarks* (*The Voyage of the Beagle*)

from Great Britain created a situation that required a bit of diplomatic finesse. They set up their headquarters on an island in the Niagara River and happily received supplies from helpful Americans. Canadian authorities, who did not share in this enthusiasm, confiscated an American steamship, the *Caroline*, loaded with cargo for the revolutionaries. They burned it and sent it over Niagara Falls. All of this occurred while the *Caroline* was in American waters. Van Buren protested but also issued a neutrality proclamation in regards to the Canadian uprising. Many Americans were disappointed that no other action occurred. But two years later, the two nations nearly came to blows again.

The United States and Canada had never officially determined the border between Maine and New Brunswick. Maine farmers wanted to plow its fertile lands and Canadian lumberjacks moved to cut down its trees. When Canadian authorities arrested an American agent sent to oust them, tempers flared. Militias on both sides were summoned, and war talk filled the air. Immediately, President Van Buren dispatched General Winfield Scott, commander of the US Army's Eastern Department, to solve the crisis diplomatically. This issue would be permanently settled by a treaty in 1842.

Van Buren continued the Indian removal of the Southeastern tribes begun in earnest by Jackson (p. 93). In Florida, the Seminole's resistance outlasted Van Buren's presidency, continuing into 1842.

Learning from their prior presidential election, the Whigs understood that they needed one strong candidate to oppose Van Buren in his bid for reelection in 1840. They proudly put forward William Henry Harrison, a hero from the War of 1812. Supporters quickly pointed to the vast differences between the two men. Van Buren had often been depicted as a dandy, a man who cared more about his clothes than the people he served. One Whig newspaper in Van Buren's home state warned readers, "If you wish to be poor and trodden down, and to see your wife starving and your children in ignorance, vote for Martin Van Buren."[4] Another favorite tune contained the refrain, "For Tippecanoe and Tyler, too, Tippecanoe and Tyler, too. And with them we'll beat little Van, Van, Van; Van is a used-up man."[5] ("Tippecanoe" referred to the famous military victory for General William Henry Harrison over Indians of the Northwest Territory in 1811, and John Tyler was his running mate.) When the votes were counted, William Henry Harrison was the overwhelming winner. Van Buren lacked even the support of his home state. He might be the first—but certainly not the last—president to lose an election because of the economy.

TRAIL OF TEARS ★ Following the directive of the US government, the Army marched into Cherokee lands of North Carolina and Georgia in the fall of 1838 to forcibly remove the natives from their homeland. This came after years of legal wrangling that ultimately involved the state of Georgia, the US Supreme Court, and President Andrew Jackson. The majority of Cherokee were forced at gunpoint to leave their homes in the Smoky Mountains and travel west to Indian Territory. Of the fifteen thousand people making the long, arduous journey that stretched over the winter, four thousand perished; thus, it was named the Trail of Tears.

DID YOU KNOW?

Van Buren was the first president born in the newly declared United States of America (after 1776).

JUL–AUG: *Amistad*, a Spanish slave ship where slaves killed the crew, sails into American waters and escorted to New London, Connecticut

NOV: Abolitionists form their own political party, the Liberty Party, so they can run their own candidate for president—James Birney

DEC: Whigs meet to decide their presidential candidate—although Henry Clay hoped for the honor, William Henry Harrison is chosen instead

Florida sees its first grapefruit trees thanks to Don Philippe, a Spanish nobleman

Independent Treasury Act is passed and signed into law

1840

Kirkpatrick Macmillan builds first bicycle in Scotland

British-Afghan War escalates

NOV: China and Great Britain launch an Opium War when Chinese order illegal Indian opium to be destroyed

Antoine-Joseph Sax, a Belgian instrument maker, develops the brass saxophone

First law of thermodynamics formulated by English physicist James Joule

AROOSTOOK WAR AND WEBSTER-ASHBURTON TREATY, 1842 ★ In 1839, ongoing disagreement between Americans and Canadians regarding the Maine-New Brunswick border threatened to become violent. The border had never been officially determined since the Treaty of Paris of 1783, and loggers on both sides desired the timberlands. President Van Buren dispatched General Winfield Scott to the region to prevent bloodshed. Then in 1842, representatives of both the British and American governments agreed to the Webster-Ashburton Treaty to split the disputed territory (some twelve thousand square miles), with New Brunswick receiving the majority of the land. The two nations also decided to survey and mark the border of the United States from the Lake of the Woods eastward.

RETIREMENT

Leaving Washington, former president Martin Van Buren stopped in Manhattan, where he was greeted by a crowd described with loathing by Whig supporter George Templeton Strong as "a disgusting assemblage of the unwashed democracy, they were, generally speaking, a . . . rowdy draggletailed, jailbird-resembling gang of truculent loafers."[6] While in the city, Van Buren enjoyed being wined and dined by his public. Finally, in early May, he trekked up the Hudson to his hometown of Kinderhook, where he began remodeling a house he had bought in 1839.

Try as he might, his interests kept escaping the confines of his new home and stretched far beyond the Hudson Valley. For a thirty-year veteran of politics, he yearned to reenter the rough-and-tumble world of a campaign. In 1842, the former president began a journey that he hoped would culminate in his victory to reclaim the presidency.

He toured the various cities of Philadelphia, New York, Baltimore, and then south to Charleston. He traveled through the Deep South to visit New Orleans and then north to Tennessee. There he stopped to see his aging friend and fellow former president Andrew Jackson. Going up the road to Kentucky, he visited Henry Clay and ventured as far north as Chicago.

Perhaps one of the most memorable visits of his tour was a stopover in Rockford, Illinois. There he passed an evening that no one present likely forgot. Feeling they ought to entertain their distinguished guest, the locals brought in a fellow well known for spinning entertaining yarns. He and the former president spent the evening swapping stories. Van Buren reminisced about his early days with Burr and Hamilton while the other guest related humorous stories that sent his listeners into side-splitting laughter. Van Buren claimed later that he had never spent a more enjoyable evening. Such was the night when former president Martin Van Buren met future president Abraham Lincoln.

Van Buren had laid the groundwork for political support, but it was insufficient to win the nomination for president. John C. Calhoun also desperately desired to win the Democratic nod. Issues and circumstances arose that would deny both men their wish.

The most looming issue involved Texas and the question of annexation. Many feared such a move would not only add another slave state, but antagonize Mexico to war. Expansionist fever was sweeping the country. It, however, did not "infect" Van Buren. He wrote a letter to a Mississippi congressman saying he did not believe that Texas annexation was the correct move at the

NATIONAL EVENTS	James Fenimore Cooper writes *The Pathfinder*	The Underground Railroad is in full force	**JAN 13:** The steamship *Lexington* sinks off the coast of Long Island; 139 die	**JAN 19:** Charles Wilkes, leading an American expedition, sights Antarctica, and claims part for US	**MAY:** Democrats renominate Martin Van Buren as their presidential candidate
WORLD EVENTS	New Zealand's Maori tribe cedes sovereignty to Great Britain	Duchess of Bedford establishes the afternoon tea ritual in Britain	Rafael Carrera becomes the dictator of Guatemala, where he will rule for the next quarter century	**FEB 10:** Queen Victoria marries her cousin Prince Albert of Saxe-Coburg-Gotha	**MAY 1:** World's first adhesive stamps are issued in Great Britain

moment. The southerners broke from his ranks, creating a wild Democratic convention in Baltimore. The two-thirds rule of the party prevented Van Buren from winning the nomination, but no second choice was immediately clear. After days of dead-lock votes, a victor emerged as the "dark horse." Andrew Jackson's protégé James K. Polk became the nominee.

Van Buren worked in New York to elect Polk. His efforts went unrecognized as the new president failed to reward Van Buren with the cabinet position he desired. Feeling hurt and disenfranchised, his son John now worked to ensure the Van Buren name still held sway in New York politics. The slavery issue divided the state's Democratic Party into two camps—those who were pro-slavery became known as the Hunkers, while the anti-slavery group was the Barnburners. Martin Van Buren moved to New York City and began writing "The Barnburner Manifesto." Here he argued forcibly against the expansion of slavery as contrary to the founding fathers' wishes.

In 1848, the Democratic Party divided, leaving the Northern Democrats and Whigs looking for a party and a candidate. They found it with the Free Soil Party (Barnburners) and Martin Van Buren. They lost the presidential election but began the precedent of third parties spotlighting issues that the major parties refused to consider.

Van Buren lived his remaining years at Kinderhook and watched with dismay and foreboding the ominous clouds of the Civil War gather on the horizon. His days of campaigning and elections were over, but he wanted to tell his tale. He wrote his autobiography and modernized his home. He voted for Lincoln in 1860 and called for his fellow New Yorkers to support the new president when war was declared. Sadly, Martin Van Buren did not live to see the war's outcome, for he died on July 24, 1862, and was buried in Kinderhook, New York.

DID YOU KNOW?

The expression "OK" began being heard about the time of Van Buren's presidency and some believe it refers to a nickname for him, "Old Kinderhook." More likely, though, it is from a popular expression used in New York and Boston to mean "oll korrect" (intentionally misspelled).

ENDNOTES

1 Denis Tilden Lynch, *An Epoch and a Man: Martin Van Buren and His Times*, Port Washington, NY: Kennikat Press, 1971 (originally published 1929), pp. 236-237.

2 Ted Widmer, *Martin Van Buren*, New York, NY: Times Books, 2005, p. 47.

3 William A. DeGregorio, *The Complete Book of US Presidents*, New York, NY: Gramercy Books, 2005, p. 133.

4 Edwin P. Hoyt, *Martin Van Buren*, Chicago: Reilly & Lee Co., 1964, p. 121.

5 Oliver Perry Chitwood, *John Tyler, Champion of the Old South*, New York, NY: Russell & Russell, Inc., 1964, p. 181.

6 Widmer, p. 142.

MAY 7: Deadliest tornado as of that date in US history strikes Natchez, Mississippi, killing 317 people

NOV: Whig candidate William Henry Harrison and his vice president John Tyler are elected

JUN: Britain declares war on China

JUN: Abolitionists attending a convention in London are shocked by English refusal to allow women to attend; Lucretia Mott and Elizabeth Cady Stanton will then begin working on women's rights issue after this snub

OCT 7: Willem II becomes king of the Netherlands

William Henry Harrison

★ ★ ★ NINTH PRESIDENT ★ ★ ★

LIFE SPAN
- Born: February 9, 1773, at Berkeley Plantation, Charles City County, Virginia
- Died: April 4, 1841, in Washington, D.C.

NICKNAME
- Old Tippecanoe

RELIGION
- Episcopalian

HIGHER EDUCATION
- Hampden-Sydney College, Virginia, 1787–1790, did not graduate
- University of Pennsylvania Medical School (briefly)

PROFESSION
- Soldier, military officer

MILITARY SERVICE
- Enlists in US Army as an ensign (1791)
- Promoted to lieutenant, then captain before resigning (1797)
- General in War of 1812; became national hero at the Battle of the Thames

FAMILY
- Father: **Benjamin Harrison V** (1726–1791)
- Mother: **Elizabeth Bassett Harrison** (1730–1792)
- Wife: **Anna Tuthill Symmes Harrison** (1775–1864); wed November 25, 1795, in North Bend, Ohio
- Children: **Elizabeth Bassett** (1796–1846); **John Cleves Symmes** (1798–1830); **Lucy Singleton** (1800–1826); **William Henry** (1802–1838); **John Scott** (1804–1878); **Benjamin** (1806–1840); **Mary Symmes** (1809–1842); **Carter Bassett** (1811–1839); **Anna Tuthill** (1813–1845); **James Findlay** (1814–1817)

POLITICAL LIFE
- Secretary of the Northwest Territory (1798–1799)
- Nonvoting delegate to US House (representing Northwest Territory, 1799–1800)
- Governor of Indiana Territory (1800–1812)
- US representative (1816–1819)
- Ohio state senator (1819–1821)
- US senator (1825–1828)
- US minister to Colombia (1828–1829)

PRESIDENCY
- One term: March 4, 1841–April 4, 1841
- Whig
- Reason for leaving office: died in office
- Vice president: **John Tyler** (March–April 1841)

ELECTION OF 1840
- Electoral vote: **Harrison** 234; **Van Buren** 60
- Popular vote: **Harrison** 1,274,624; **Van Buren** 1,127,781

CABINET

SECRETARY OF STATE
Daniel Webster (1841–1843)

SECRETARY OF THE TREASURY
Thomas Ewing (March–Sept. 1841)

SECRETARY OF WAR
John Bell (March–Sept. 1841)

ATTORNEY GENERAL
John J. Crittenden (March–Sept. 1841)

SECRETARY OF THE NAVY
George E. Badger (March–Sept. 1841)

POSTMASTER GENERAL
Francis Granger (March–Sept. 1841)

DID YOU KNOW?

Harrison was the first president to die in office and served the shortest term of any president—thirty-one days.

Harrison delivered the longest inaugural speech on record—it lasted one hour and 40 minutes in freezing cold rain.

In 1838, William Henry Harrison wrote in a letter a list of promises he would make if elected president. The first on the list was, "I will confine my service to a single term."[1] He did not need to worry about keeping that promise.

EARLY LIFE

The president who is first on the list for the shortest term in office began life in a historic Virginia home, Berkeley, on February 9, 1773. This comfortable two-story brick home had been the residence of the Harrison family for generations. William's father, Benjamin V, was a signer of the Declaration of Independence and later served as governor of Virginia. Ironically, Benjamin Harrison was defeated for assemblyman in the Virginia legislature by John Tyler, father of the future vice president to Harrison's son.

Enduring wartime hardships was a major factor in young Harrison's childhood. In early 1781, he and his siblings fled their home in the face of a British invasion that left their home standing, but their possessions, animals, and slaves carried away. His father's new position as governor required the family's move to Richmond, where William Henry Harrison continued the education he had begun with tutors at Berkeley.

By the age of fourteen, young Harrison had decided on a career in medicine. He began training at Hampden-Sydney College and then later apprenticed himself to a doctor in Richmond. Still desiring better instruction, Harrison moved to Philadelphia where he could study under America's preeminent physician, Dr. Benjamin Rush, at the Pennsylvania Medical School. Unfortunately, no sooner had Harrison arrived in the city than he heard of his father's death. He attempted to stay, but funds ran out before his schooling finished, so he decided to pursue a different calling—an army career.

ARMY CAREER

William Henry Harrison began his military career in 1791 when he enlisted as an ensign for the First Infantry Regiment. The following year he became a lieutenant.

Twenty-one-year-old Harrison tasted combat for the first time in 1794 when he served as an aide-de-camp to General "Mad" Anthony Wayne at the Battle of Fallen Timbers. There in the Ohio territory, American forces defeated an alliance of Native American tribes from the region including the Shawnee, Ottawa, and Chippewa. Wayne was impressed by the young officer's service as well as his "conduct and bravery in exciting the troops to press for victory."[2] The following year, Harrison attended the Treaty of Greeneville signing (the surrender of Indian lands in southern and eastern Ohio), which brought a temporary peace to the region.

Also in 1795, William Henry Harrison married young Anna Symmes of North Bend, Ohio. Her father objected to his daughter marrying a man of such modest means and forbid the couple from seeing each other. They ignored him and married when he was out of town. The Harrisons welcomed ten children over the next seventeen years. One son, John Scott, would later be the father to yet another president—Benjamin Harrison.

In 1797, Harrison became captain, but chose to leave the army the following year.

POLITICAL CAREER BEGINS

President John Adams awarded Harrison his first political appointment—secretary of the Northwest Territory. The twelve-hundred-dollar annual salary helped the young man with his growing family obligations, but he did not care for the work. He was relieved when he won an election (by one vote) for Northwest Territory delegate to the House of Representatives. As a nonvoting member, Harrison could only debate and introduce legislation. This he did with the Harrison Land Act of 1800, which made land purchase in the Northwest Territory more affordable for Americans hungering for land.

Harrison's military and political experiences in the Northwest Territory impressed President John Adams, who appointed him governor of the Indiana Territory in 1800. This spacious territory encompassed what later became three states (Indiana, Illinois, and Wisconsin), as well as parts of Michigan and Minnesota. An able civil servant, Harrison kept this post through the change of political parties as well as presidents and served for the next twelve years.

As governor, one of Harrison's main duties was keeping the peace between increasing numbers of settlers and the Native Americans who had called the same lands home for generations. He negotiated several treaties, including the Treaty of Fort Wayne, in which native tribes ceded 2.5 million acres to the United States. During his tenure, Harrison acquired fifty million additional acres for settlement. Still, violence erupted from time to time, and its threat increased with the growing popularity of the Shawnee chief Tecumseh and his brother Tenskwatawa, also known as the Prophet. These two men worked to convince other tribes of the absolute necessity to unite and drive away the encroaching white settlers.

In 1810, Harrison and his nemesis Tecumseh met face to face at Harrison's home in Vincennes, Indiana. There the two leaders squared off for days under the hot August sun. Tecumseh delivered a speech telling Harrison that he did not desire to fight Americans and understood that the British goading his people into war was not in their favor. He assured Harrison, "If you will prevail upon the president to give up the land in question and agree never again to make a treaty without the consent of all the tribes, I will be your faithful ally." When Harrison admitted that was not likely, Tecumseh responded: "It is true, he [president] is so far off he will not be injured by the war; he may sit in the town and drink his wine, while you and I will have to fight it out."[3] Later, violence seemed imminent when Tecumseh announced Harrison was a liar. Both sides drew weapons and waited for the other side to act. They withdrew, and the meeting ended. Tecumseh then decided to travel further to enlist the aide of southern tribes in their confederacy against the Americans.

Harrison, too, understood the need for quick action. He explained the situation to the Madison administration, which authorized the governor to attack the main encampment at Tippecanoe. On the morning of November 7, 1811, the Prophet and his followers were not idle. They decided to surprise Harrison's force of 950 men by encircling them and attacking just before dawn. Many of the soldiers and militia were cut down by this bold move. Still, Harrison reacted quickly and ordered his men to rally and hold the line. This they did, and the warriors broke off their attack and retreated into the woods. The fighting continued as Harrison and his men now went on the offensive. When the battle ended, Harrison ordered the burning and destruction of Prophetstown.

Later Harrison became known as the hero of Tippecanoe. At the time, not everyone was so certain of his "heroism" or good judgment. Word spread among the tribes, and raids on settlements increased, as did the recruiting efforts of Tecumseh.

The following year saw the beginning of the War of 1812 (p. 54). Harrison was ultimately commissioned a major general and commanded all forces in the Northwestern territories. Now he had two major enemies—the Native Americans under Tecumseh, and the British.

DID YOU KNOW?

Harrison was the grandfather of the twenty-third president, Benjamin Harrison.

BATTLE OF THE THAMES (October 5, 1813) ★ On October 5, 1813, General William Henry Harrison led a force of 3,500 Americans against 700 British and 1,000 Indians led by Tecumseh. Already defeated at the Battle of Lake Erie, the British were disheartened, but agreed to Tecumseh's demand that all should make a stand near Moraviantown. There in Ontario, Canada, the British quickly capitulated, and the Shawnee warrior met not only defeat, but death. With his demise ended his dream of an Indian confederation, and native resistance in the Ohio territory ended. The victor, William Henry Harrison, became an American hero.

WAR OF 1812

Harrison's orders demanded that he retake Fort Detroit, which had fallen without a fight in August 1812. After enduring the defeats of two divisions in early 1813, Harrison decided to be prudent and allow the navy a chance for victory. This occurred on September 10, 1813, when Captain Oliver H. Perry defeated the British at Put-in-Bay. Now with

None

Lake Erie open to the Americans, General Harrison moved forward. Successfully retaking Detroit, he pushed on into the Ontario province. Here in October 1813, he and Tecumseh met one last time on the Thames River. Kentucky riflemen comprised the majority of Harrison's force, and they blazed their way through the poorly placed British and Native American forces. Tecumseh died, and his warriors were either killed or captured. The Battle of the Thames catapulted Harrison to fame, and he probably would have been the hero of the war if not for the daring victory a little more than a year later in New Orleans by Andrew Jackson. Disagreements between Harrison and Secretary of War John Armstrong, however, led Harrison to resign his commission. He toured the East and then returned to resume farming in North Bend, Ohio.

POLITICAL CAREER RESUMES

During the coming years, William Henry Harrison worked to develop a résumé of political positions. He began by winning the House seat for the Cincinnati area in 1816. Being in Congress allowed Harrison the opportunity and means to clear his name. His quarrel with Secretary of War Armstrong involved the latter's charge that Harrison had profited from selling army supplies. At Harrison's request, a House committee investigated the allegations, and finding no evidence, cleared his name. Military matters interested Harrison most, and he worked to improve pensions for veterans and their widows. He also worked to develop better military training, but Harrison broke from the ranks when he voted to censure his rival, Andrew Jackson, for his part in the First Seminole War (p. 89). Jackson would not forget this.

INAUGURAL TRIVIA ★ In contrast to Harrison's very lengthy inaugural speech, George Washington holds the record for the shortest inaugural speech (135 words). Although weather at Harrison's inauguration was cold and rainy, it was coldest at Ronald Reagan's second inauguration in 1985, when the thermometer registered a very chilly seven degrees!

After completing his term, Harrison returned to his home in North Bend. He did not remain there long, for costs for building the sixteen-room house demanded funds that he concluded could best be attained by a salaried political position.

He served two years in the Ohio state senate, but was defeated in 1822 when he attempted to regain his US House seat. The Ohio senate elected Harrison US senator in 1825, and he again worked to improve the army and expand the navy. He supported internal improvements such as the construction of badly needed roads and canals that President John Quincy Adams and Henry Clay proposed. Subsequently, in 1828, President Adams rewarded Harrison by making him US minister to Colombia. Unfortunately, he had only one year at this post before the next president, Andrew Jackson, spitefully recalled him.

BACK TO OHIO

Retiring to his farm, William Henry Harrison kept a watchful eye on the political situation. He kept busy at home by becoming the clerk of the court of common pleas for Hamilton County in 1834. Two years later, he made his first attempt to win the presidency but was defeated by Democratic candidate Martin Van Buren.

Four years later, at the Whig convention in Harrisburg, Pennsylvania, Henry Clay was his party's leader. Nevertheless, Clay's political choices and stances on various issues created too many enemies, which worried the party. Consequently, the Whigs decided the nomination would best be served by a war hero. So William Henry Harrison became their nominee for a second time. In 1840, he again faced Martin Van Buren.

For the first time in American history, the two parties launched a major advertising and campaign blitz. Songs and newspaper advertisements popped up with catchy slogans. "Tippecanoe and Tyler too" (p. 105) sang the refrain of one campaign song. Harrison's supporters worked to convince voters of Harrison's humble origins, telling of his log cabin birthplace, and his homespun image drew a visible contrast to the dandy reputation of President Van Buren. Never mind that his birthplace was a mansion or that Harrison had his own mansion—with slave labor—in Ohio. Truth became a casualty of the campaign, as did the incumbent president. Harrison captured 53 percent of the popular vote to Van Buren's 47 percent, but the spread of electoral votes was even more impressive. Harrison won 234 to Van Buren's mere 60.

THE CURSE ★ Shawnee chief Tecumseh is said to have put a curse on Harrison that lived long past him: Harrison would be the first president to die in office, but not the last—those elected every twenty years after him would share the same fate: Lincoln (elected 1860), Garfield (elected 1880), McKinley (elected 1900), Harding (elected 1920), Roosevelt (elected 1940), and Kennedy (elected 1960). Reagan (elected 1980) is credited with breaking the curse, although he, too, nearly met death when John Hinckley, Jr., shot him, but he survived the assassination attempt.

PRESIDENT HARRISON

On March 4, 1841, William Henry Harrison delivered the longest inaugural address ever. This 8,445-word speech was delivered on a raw, blustery March day. The sixty-eight-year-old president had refused to wear either coat or hat, perhaps hoping to show he was in robust health. Harrison again reaffirmed his pledge that he would only serve one term, which seemed reasonable considering his age.

Harrison assembled a cabinet that featured Daniel Webster in the influential secretary of state position. Southerners John Bell and John Crittendon were appointed to the Departments of War and Justice, respectively. For the only time in history, the president and vice president were from the same county; however, John Tyler had continued to remain in Charles City County, Virginia, whereas the Harrison family had moved west.

A few weeks after his inauguration, President Harrison was caught in a downpour, which soon led to him getting a cold. This worsened and greatly weakened the president, who said, "I am ill, very ill, much more so than they think me."[4] Ultimately pneumonia developed, and his life ebbed away. He uttered his final words on April 4, 1841: "I wish you to understand the true principles of the government. I wish them carried out. Nothing more."[5]

After displaying his body in the East Room and then the Capitol, he was buried temporarily in Washington but removed a short time later and moved to North Bend, Ohio.

Sadly, Anna Harrison never saw her husband during his presidency because she was ill and too busy packing for the move to Washington. Due to his extraordinarily short term, and upon the request of President Tyler, Congress granted her the first-ever pension for a president's widow. She continued living in their home at North Bend until it burned in 1855, then she moved in with her son John Scott Harrison and his family. There she died at the age of eighty-eight on February 25, 1864, and was buried beside her husband.

DID YOU KNOW?

Harrison was the oldest man elected president at the age of 68 until Ronald Reagan won election at the age of 69.

ENDNOTES

1 Caroline Thomas Harnsburger, *Treasury of Presidential Quotations*, Chicago: Follett Publishing Co., 1964, p. 239.

2 Dorothy Burne Goebel, *William Henry Harrison: A Political Biography*, Indianapolis: Indiana Library and Historical Department, 1926, p. 34.

3 Allan W. Eckert, *A Sorrow in Our Heart, The Life of Tecumseh*, New York: Bantam, 1992, pp. 327-328.

4 William A. DeGregorio, *The Complete Book of US Presidents*, New York: Gramercy Books, 2005, p. 145.

5 Ibid.

John Tyler

★ ★ ★ TENTH PRESIDENT ★ ★ ★

LIFE SPAN

- Born: March 29, 1790, at Greenway Plantation, Charles City County, Virginia
- Died: January 18, 1862, in Richmond, Virginia

NICKNAMES

- His Accidency, Accidental-President

RELIGION

- Episcopalian

HIGHER EDUCATION

- College of William and Mary, 1807
- Studied law under an attorney

PROFESSION

- Lawyer

MILITARY SERVICE

- Captain of Charles City Rifles (militia) during War of 1812

FAMILY

- Father: **John Tyler Sr.** (1747–1813)
- Mother: **Mary Armistead Tyler** (1761–1797)
- First wife: **Letitia Christian Tyler** (1790–1842); wed March 29, 1813, at Cedar Grove plantation, New Kent County, Virginia
- Children: **Mary** (1815–1848); **Robert** (1816–1877); **John** (1819–1896); **Letitia** (1821–1907); **Elizabeth** (1823–1850); **Anne Contesse** (1825); **Alice** (1827–1854); **Tazewell** (1830–1874)
- Second wife: **Julia Gardiner Tyler** (1820–1889); wed June 26, 1844, in New York City
- Children: **David Gardiner** (1846–1927); **John Alexander** (1848–1883); **Julia Gardiner** (1849–1871); **Lachlan** (1851–1902); **Lyon Gardiner** (1853–1935); **Robert Fitzwalter** (1856–1927); **Pearl** (1860–1947)

POLITICAL LIFE

- Virginia House of Delegates (1811–1816)
- US representative (1816–1821)
- Virginia House of Delegates (1823–1825)
- Governor of Virginia (1825–1827)
- US senator (1827–1836)
- Virginia House of Delegates (1838–1840)
- Vice president (March–April 1841)

PRESIDENCY

- One term: April 4, 1841 (took office upon death of President William Henry Harrison)–March 4, 1845
- Whig
- Reason for leaving office: completion of Harrison's term
- Vice president: none

CABINET
★★★★★★★★★★

(Original members continued from President Harrison's cabinet)

SECRETARY OF STATE
Daniel Webster (1841–1843)

Abel P. Upshur (1843–1844); killed in explosion aboard the *Princeton*

John C. Calhoun (1844–1845)

SECRETARY OF THE TREASURY
Thomas Ewing (March–Sept. 1841)

Walter Forward (1841–1843)

John C. Spencer (1843–1844)

George M. Bibb (1844–1845)

SECRETARY OF WAR
John Bell (March–Sept. 1841)

John C. Spencer (1841–1843)

William Wilkins (1844–1845)

John Tyler was born in the same Virginia county as William Henry Harrison, his predecessor whose presidential term of thirty-one days left the nation and its government in shock as they attempted to determine what role Vice President Tyler should play.

EARLY LIFE

John Tyler was the first president to be born under the United States Constitution, on March 29, 1790, at his father's plantation in Charles City County, Virginia. His father, Judge John Tyler, had been a classmate of Thomas Jefferson's at the College of William and Mary. The two men remained lifelong friends, and Jefferson's philosophy shaped the politics of both Tylers for years to come.

At the age of seven, young Tyler became motherless. Still, in a household of seven children, it is unlikely that John lacked companionship. At school, he applied himself but revealed a bit of rebelliousness against his Scottish schoolteacher, William McMurdo, who frequently applied the whip to his charges. The pupils decided one day to turn the tables. Led by ten-year-old John Tyler, they pushed the man on the floor, tied him up, and locked him in the closet. After hearing the reasons for his son's extreme behavior, Judge Tyler refused to punish the boy, and soon after he sent his son to his alma mater to continue his studies.

In 1807, John Tyler graduated from the College of William and Mary. While there, he had become a disciple of Adam Smith's economic theories. Deciding to follow in his father's footsteps, the seventeen-year-old began studying law, first with his father and then with his cousin. When Judge Tyler was elected governor, the family moved to Richmond, where John Tyler began practicing law in the prestigious office of former US attorney general Edmund Randolph.

POLITICAL LIFE BEGINS

Wasting no time in beginning his political career, twenty-one-year-old John Tyler sought his first elected office to the Virginia House of Delegates. He had hardly taken his seat before the United States declared war on Great Britain. In 1813, Tyler volunteered for the militia. His unit defended Richmond, but since the British chose not to attack that city, they saw no action.

On his twenty-third birthday, March 29, 1813, he married Letitia Christian, daughter of a fellow planter and merchant. They had been courting for five years, and Tyler was quite the gentleman. Their first kiss—he kissed her hand—was only a few weeks before they wed. The Tylers had eight children, seven of whom survived, and enjoyed nearly thirty happy years together, marred only by Mrs. Tyler's strokes in 1839 and again in 1842, which resulted in her death.

In 1816, John Tyler won his first election to Congress and served in the House of Representatives for the next five years. As a vocal Jeffersonian, he worked to defeat the Bank of the United States, high tariffs, and internal improvements—all endemic, he believed, of mushrooming federal power. Tyler also opposed the Missouri Compromise (p. 68) and argued against any limitations of slavery. By early 1821, he felt defeated, frustrated, and exhausted, so he resigned his seat and returned to his family and home in Virginia.

Unable to stay out of the political scene, Tyler soon returned to the Virginia state capital, first as a member of the House of Delegates and then, in

NATIONAL EVENTS

FEB 18–MAR 11: First continuous filibuster in US Senate

MAR 4: William Henry Harrison is inaugurated as ninth president; John Tyler is his vice president

MAR 9: Supreme Court orders release of the slaves who revolted on the ship *Amistad*

APR 4: After a 31-day presidency, 68-year-old President Harrison dies of pneumonia

APR 4: John Tyler becomes the first vice president to take office upon a president's death

1841

WORLD EVENTS

Scottish surgeon James Braid discovers hypnosis

JAN 26: British begin occupying Hong Kong

FEB: Final installment of *The Old Curiosity Shop* by Charles Dickens

MAR 15: Englishman David Livingstone arrives at the Cape of Good Hope

MAY 3: Great Britain creates a new colony, New Zealand

1825, he was elected governor, but did not finish his term before being elected US senator by the state legislature.

RETURN TO WASHINGTON

Tyler had broken with his party to support John Quincy Adams for the presidency in 1824. This conversion lasted but a short time because of Adams and Henry Clay's push for internal improvements. Consequently, Tyler switched and now backed Andrew Jackson for president in 1828.

Jackson enjoyed Senator Tyler's support when he vetoed the rechartering of the Bank of the United States. Later, though, Tyler opposed Jackson's action of removing the Bank's money and placing it in state banks, arguing the president had overstepped his authority. Tyler also broke very publicly from the administration regarding the South Carolina nullification issue. When Jackson determined that South Carolina's threat to secede over the tariff of 1832 (the Tariff of Abominations, p. 78) demanded the use of force, Tyler disagreed quite vocally. In a speech on the Senate floor, Tyler asked, "The Federal Union must be preserved. But how? Will you seek to preserve it by force?"[1] He cast the only dissenting vote against the Force Bill.

By the following year, Tyler's break with Jackson and the Democrats was complete, and he voted to censure the president for his removal of public funds from the Bank of the United States, which were then placed in smaller state banks. Two years later, Democrats controlling the Virginia House of Delegates told their senators to expunge Jackson's censure as a means of rehabilitating Jackson's image; this put Tyler in a quandary. They felt he no longer supported them and hoped to force him into resigning his Senate seat. Their plan worked, and Tyler, disgusted by this betrayal of principles, resigned rather than do their bidding.

Now John Tyler considered himself to be a member of the Whig Party, whose principal leader was Henry Clay. They bound themselves together with a shared dislike of Andrew Jackson and his policies. In 1836, they attempted a daring maneuver: submit four slates of candidates throughout the country, which they figured would allow them to deprive the Democrats of a majority, thus throwing the election to the House of Representatives, where they could hope for a victory. John Tyler's name appeared on two of the vice presidential ballots. Their attempt, however, failed, and Democrat Martin Van Buren defeated William Henry Harrison for the presidency.

Returning to Virginia, John Tyler contented himself with his family and legal career for a brief interim before once again being sent back to the Virginia House of Delegates, where they chose him to be their speaker. In 1839, he lost in an election for a US Senate seat. The following year, though, his name was the Whig party vice presidential candidate under William Henry Harrison.

ELECTION OF 1840

Fighting a severely depressed economy, Martin Van Buren faced a formidable challenge in his reelection campaign. Moreover, this campaign featured cartoons and slogans touting the Whig challenger as a man of the people, with his humble log cabin (never mind the truth) beginnings, and a winning warrior of the War of 1812, versus the stuffy incumbent. "Tippecanoe and Tyler too!" sailed into the presidency with 234 electoral votes to Van Buren's sixty.

After being sworn in and enjoying the inaugural festivities, John Tyler returned home to

CABINET

(continued)

ATTORNEY GENERAL

John J. Crittenden (March–Sept. 1841)

Hugh S. Legaré (1841–1843)

John Nelson (1843–1845)

SECRETARY OF THE NAVY

George E. Badger (March–Sept. 1841)

Abel P. Upshur (1841–1843)

Thomas W. Gilmer (Feb. 19–28, 1844); killed in explosion aboard the *Princeton*

John Y. Mason (1844–1845)

POSTMASTER GENERAL

Francis Granger (March–Sept. 1841)

Charles A. Wickliffe (1841–1845)

AUG 16: President Tyler vetoes a bill to reestablish the Second Bank of the United States

SEP 11: Tyler's entire cabinet resigns except Secretary of State Daniel Webster

US opens trade with China

Congress sets the fiscal year as beginning July 1

MAR: Tariff of 1842 passed to protect American industry

MAR: Senator Henry Clay of Kentucky and Whig party leader resigns to prepare for 1844 election

1842

JUL 5: Thomas Cook of Great Britain begins a travel service

JUL 17: *Punch*, a humorous magazine, begins publication in London

Paris church, La Madeleine, is completed

British and Indian forces massacred by Afghan forces on road from Kabul to Jalalabad

Lord Nelson's statue is dedicated in London's Trafalgar Square

DID YOU KNOW?

Altogether, Tyler was the father of 15 children, more than any other president before or after him; his youngest child, Pearl, died 100 years, 1 week, and 6 days after the death of his eldest daughter, Mary.

Virginia. Unaware of the president's rapidly failing health, he was shocked by the arrival of Secretary of State Daniel Webster's son Fletcher, chief clerk of the State Department, to inform Tyler of President Harrison's death.

John Tyler immediately left Williamsburg and traveled by horse and steamboat to reach the capital city in twenty-one hours. There he was sworn in as president. This ceremony, though, did little to settle the dispute that had already begun among the powers of Washington.

HIS ACCIDENCY

According to Article 2, Section 6 of the Constitution:

> *In case of the removal of the President from office, or of his death, resignation, or inability to discharge the powers and duties of the said office, the same shall devolve on the Vice-President, and the Congress may by law provide for the case of removal, death, resignation or inability, both of the President and Vice-President, declaring what officer shall then act as President, and such officer shall act accordingly, until the disability be removed, or a President shall be elected.*

The wording left the succession in doubt. Should the vice president automatically become president? Should he serve only temporarily until a new president is elected or chosen? John Tyler believed the answer was simple. When the president died, the vice president assumed the office and its inherent duties, as well as its perks—salary, President's House, title, etc. Unfortunately, others disagreed. Many thought of him as merely an interim executive until another was selected. At most, they looked upon Tyler merely as a rubber stamp to whatever policies Harrison's cabinet desired. Tyler disagreed. At his first cabinet meeting, he told the men, "I shall be pleased to avail myself of your counsel and advice. But I can never consent to being dictated to as to what I shall or shall not do. . . . When you think otherwise, your resignations will be accepted."[2]

Some people continued to refer to Tyler as "acting president." Others were nastier and called him "His Accidency." Tyler stayed true to his belief and insisted that it was the others who needed to change their minds. Eventually most did, and the crucial precedent for presidential succession was established. The vice president would become president upon the death, removal, resignation, or inability of the chief executive.

PRESIDENT TYLER

Major challenges soon appeared for the new president—and most could be traced to Henry Clay. As the Whig party leader, Clay wielded enormous power and used this as Senate leader. Determined to reinstate the Bank of the United States, Clay and the Whigs passed two bank bills, which Tyler vetoed. Outraged by the president's refusal to follow the party line, Clay attempted to discuss his position with Tyler. After Clay's berating, Tyler had enough. He stood and pointed toward the capitol: "Then go to your end of the capital and perform your duty as you think proper. So help me God, I shall do mine at this end—as I think proper."[3] Clay exited and soon Tyler's cabinet followed suit, undoubtedly at Clay's insistence. His Whig cabinet (except Daniel Webster) resigned in protest. Outraged by Tyler's open break from Whig policy, the party disowned him. No longer a Whig, and definitely not a Democrat, President Tyler now found himself a president without a political party.

NATIONAL EVENTS

MAR 3: Massachusetts passes child labor laws setting workday at a maximum of 10 hours

MAR 31: First recorded use of general anesthesia in surgery in Georgia

APR: Rhode Island becomes divided as two governments are elected

AUG 9: Webster-Ashburton Treaty signed

AUG 14: Second Seminole War ends

NOV 22: Mount St. Helens erupts

WORLD EVENTS

JAN 4: Charles Dickens arrives in America for a five-month tour

MAY: Alfred Tennyson's *Poems* is published

AUG 29: Treaty of Nanjing ends Opium War; China cedes Hong Kong to Great Britain

Without party protection, Tyler was now prey to congressional action. This soon began in the form of a committee headed by former president and now representative John Quincy Adams to look at the possible abuse of presidential veto power. They also contemplated a constitutional amendment making the override of a veto an easier process—a simple majority vote by Congress. In January 1843, the House voted down beginning impeachment proceedings against Tyler by a vote of 127 to eighty-three.

Secretary of State Daniel Webster remained, believing that he needed to continue his negotiations with Great Britain to definitively determine America's northern border with Canada. In 1842, this matter was decided in the Webster-Ashburton Treaty. The border between Maine and New Brunswick province was resolved, as well as the border to the Rockies. Thanks to Webster's patient negotiations, the United States gained over half of the area in question, but the thorny Oregon issue remained to be decided at a later date.

In 1844, the United States moved forward in its relations with China. American envoy Caleb Cushing negotiated trading rights with China in the Treaty of Wanghia. Originally, Cushing planned to continue on to Japan and do the same there. Ill health, however, forced his premature return to the United States.

> ***"If the tide of defamation and abuse shall turn, and my administration come to be praised, future vice presidents who may succeed to the presidency may feel some slight encouragement to pursue an independent course."***
>
> —*John Tyler in a letter to his son, 1848*

Closer to home, Tyler pushed for annexation of Texas. A treaty to do this was voted down by the Senate. Concerns abounded regarding upsetting the delicate balance between slave and free states that would occur should Texas become a state. Americans' feelings ran counter to the worries of its congressmen and they clamored for annexation. Democratic candidate James K. Polk recognized this and campaigned to annex Texas when he ran for president in 1844. Polk won the election, but Tyler was determined to make annexation a legacy of *his* administration, so three days before leaving the presidency, John Tyler signed a joint resolution from Congress to allow the annexation of Texas and its inclusion under the Missouri Compromise. This measure circumvented the need for Senate treaty ratification.

THE PRESIDENT'S LADIES

While First Lady, Letitia Tyler remained sequestered upstairs due to a stroke she endured in 1839. She ventured downstairs once to see the wedding of their daughter Elizabeth. Then in September of 1842, she suffered a second stroke and died soon after. John Tyler mourned his quiet, somber wife of twenty-nine years and the mother of his seven children. She shrank from public life, content to remain in the background raising their children.

SUPREME COURT APPOINTMENTS
★★★★★★★★★★

Samuel Nelson, 1845

DID YOU KNOW?
★★★★★★★★★★★

Tyler was the first vice president to take office upon the president's death; he never ran for the highest office.

1843

Yellow fever epidemic kills 13,000 in the Mississippi Valley

Henry Cole of London designs and sends the first Christmas cards

JUN–NOV: Frémont leads expedition into Northwest along the Oregon Trail

MAR 15: Victoria, British Columbia, founded

JUL: Mexican president Santa Anna tells US that any annexation of Texas would be invitation to war

NOV 17: Shanghai opens for foreign trading

1844

FEB 28: Explosion aboard the USS *Princeton* kills the secretary of state and the secretary of the navy, but President Tyler is unharmed

Carlos Antonio Lopez becomes dictator of Paraguay

APR 12: US and Texas sign annexation treaty

French writer Alexandre Dumas publishes *The Three Musketeers*

STATE OF THE UNION

US POPULATION IN 1841
17,069,453

NATIONAL DEBT IN 1845
$15,925,303

PRESIDENT'S SALARY
$25,000/year

STATE ADMITTED TO UNION
Florida,
March 3, 1845

NUMBER OF US STATES
27

Probably no one, including the widower, would have imagined the next act in his personal drama.

Less than six months later, Tyler was busily wooing and courting the young Julia Gardiner, daughter of a New York state senator. Washington tongues wagged as they watched the fifty-five-year-old president in eager pursuit of a lady thirty years his junior. In less than a month after their first meeting, he proposed, but Julia refused. Undaunted, Tyler continued the pursuit. Ultimately, Julia consented, as did her parents. They urged the couple to wait as a way of ensuring that Julia was not acting impulsively. A year later, the president, Julia, and her father, as well as four hundred other dignitaries, including former First Lady Dolley Madison and Senator Thomas Hart Benton of Missouri, were aboard the USS *Princeton* to observe a display of this new state-of-the-art warship, featuring the very first screw propellers. Besides its twenty-four 42-pound carronades, the *Princeton* featured two long guns, named by the ship's captain as the "Oregon" and the "Peacemaker." The latter was just a bit bigger, making it the world's largest naval gun. During the festivities, refreshments were served below deck in the salon. Then the secretary of the navy urged everyone to go above for another demonstration of the gun. As he moved upstairs, Tyler was stopped in conversation and handed a drink. Meanwhile, the gun fired and exploded, sending hot metal around the deck. Both Secretary of the Navy Thomas Gilmer and Secretary of State Abel Upshur were killed, as was Julia's father, David Gardiner, and three other men.

> ***"So far as it depends on the course of this government, our relations of good will and friendship will be sedulously cultivated with all nations."***
>
> *—John Tyler*

The couple waited four months before marrying under a cloak of secrecy. President Tyler arrived quietly in New York City without fanfare or entourage. He was the first president to marry while in office. The only Tyler family member accompanying him was his son, John Tyler Jr. The others were not told, and the Tyler daughters were especially resentful of their father's marriage to a woman younger than his eldest daughter. After a short honeymoon trip to Philadelphia and the new Tyler estate of Sherwood Forest in Virginia, the president and new First Lady Julia Tyler made their home in Washington.

During his last months of the presidency, John Tyler found solace in his new wife. She entertained lavishly, and the couple upset the sensibilities of many by their open affection toward each other. She bought French furniture and wine. Julia and her sisters hosted receptions where they received their guests from a raised platform, making some wonder if the new First Lady considered herself a queen. Just weeks before the end of his term, the Tylers gave a farewell reception. The house and Julia sparkled, while the president gazed on with obvious affection. When he was congratulated on the party's success, John Tyler replied with a laugh, "Yes, they cannot say now that I am a president without a party!"[4]

DID YOU KNOW?

Tyler did not give an inaugural address.

Tyler's second wife began the practice of playing "Hail to the Chief" to signal the president's arrival at a state function.

NATIONAL EVENTS

MAY: Whigs nominate Henry Clay as their presidential candidate

MAY: Democrats nominate James K. Polk for president

MAY 24: Samuel F.B. Morse successfully sends the first telegraphic message, "What hath God wrought," testing telegraph lines between Washington, D.C., and Baltimore

JUN 26: President Tyler becomes first president to marry while in office; he weds Julia Gardiner

WORLD EVENTS

German socialist Karl Marx writes "Religion is the . . . opium of the people" while in exile in Paris; meets Friedrich Engels there

FEB 27: Dominican Republic gains independence from Haiti

MAR 8: King Oscar I ascends to throne of Sweden-Norway

APR: Fleet Prison for debtors is abolished in London

JUN 6: Young Men's Christian Association (YMCA) is founded in London

RETIREMENT

John Tyler left the presidency to return to his recently purchased plantation at Sherwood Forest. He and Julia greeted the arrival of seven children during the next fourteen years. He also worked with the College of William and Mary and later became its chancellor. He considered himself a Democrat now, but remained contentedly quiet in the background. This changed in 1861 when he traveled to Washington to chair a convention of twenty-one states in the hopes of avoiding a civil war. The mission failed and Tyler returned to his beloved Virginia, believing no other solution possible. He urged secession and served in the Provisional Congress of the Confederacy.

Elected to the Confederate House of Representatives, Tyler traveled to Richmond to attend. Julia Tyler had remained home, but after experiencing a terrifying nightmare of her husband taken deathly ill, she immediately made haste to Richmond. She found her seventy-one-year-old husband in good health, but that changed two days later when he developed debilitating nausea and dizziness. The doctor diagnosed him with bronchitis and gave Tyler morphine. This provided little relief, so again the doctor was summoned. Tyler informed him, "Doctor, I am going."[5]

John Tyler died at 12:15 a.m. on January 18, 1862. His body lay in state at the Confederate capitol, draped under its flag. He was buried at Hollywood Cemetery in Richmond next to James Monroe. Refusing to acknowledge the president whom many northerners considered a traitor, scarcely any mention was made of his passing. No official monument would accompany his grave until 1915.

Julia Tyler returned to New York for the remainder of the Civil War, and then later moved back to Virginia to live with her grown children since the family's wealth had been destroyed in the Panic of 1873, which left thousands destitute following bank failures and the tightening of credit. Julia died on July 10, 1889, and was buried beside her husband.

DID YOU KNOW?
★★★★★★★★★★★

Tyler joined the Confederacy during the Civil War and became the only president who later became a sworn enemy of the US.

ENDNOTES

1 William DeGregorio. *The Complete Book of US Presidents*, New York: Gramercy Books, p. 154.

2 Oliver Perry Chitwood, *John Tyler, Champion of the Old South*, New York, NY: Russell & Russell, Inc., 1964, p. 270.

3 Donald Barr Chidsey, *And Tyler Too*, Nashville: Thomas Nelson Inc. Publishers, 1978, p. 60.

4 Edward P. Crapol, *John Tyler, The Accidental President*, Chapel Hill: University of North Carolina Press, 2006, p. 221.

5 DeGregorio, p. 158.

JUL 3: Treaty of Wanghia is America's first treaty with China and opens five ports for American trading

NOV: James K. Polk is elected president

DEC: John Quincy Adams successfully wins repeal of the gag rule in the House of Representatives

JUL 3: Last pair of Great Auks killed on island off Iceland's coast; they were hunted to extinction

JUL 3: Unites States and China sign first diplomatic agreement between the countries, The Sino-American Treaty of Wanghia

NOV 3: Debut of Verdi's *I due Foscari* in Rome

NOV 6: Dominican Republic drafts its first Constitution

James K. Polk

★ ★ ★ ELEVENTH PRESIDENT ★ ★ ★

LIFE SPAN
- Born: November 2, 1795, Mecklenburg County, North Carolina
- Died: June 15, 1849, Nashville, Tennessee

NICKNAME
- Young Hickory

RELIGION
- Presbyterian (but on his deathbed baptized as a Methodist)

HIGHER EDUCATION
- University of North Carolina, 1818

PROFESSION
- Lawyer

MILITARY SERVICE
- Commissioned as captain of militia cavalry regiment (1821) and later promoted to colonel

FAMILY
- Father: **Samuel Polk** (1772–1827)
- Mother: **Jane Knox Polk** (1776–1852)
- Wife: **Sarah Childress Polk** (1803–1891); wed January 1, 1824, in Murfreesboro, Tennessee
- No children

POLITICAL LIFE
- Tennessee House of Representatives (1823–1825)
- US representative (1825–1839)
- Speaker of the US House (1835–1839)
- Governor of Tennessee (1839–1841)

PRESIDENCY
- One term: March 4, 1845–March 4, 1849
- Democrat
- Reason for leaving office: completion of term; refused to run for second term
- Vice president: **George M. Dallas** (1845–1849)

ELECTION OF 1844
- Electoral vote: **Polk** 170; **Henry Clay** 105
- Popular vote: **Polk** 1,338,464; **Clay** 1,300,097

CABINET

SECRETARY OF STATE
James Buchanan (1845–1849)

SECRETARY OF THE TREASURY
Robert J. Walker (1845–1849)

SECRETARY OF WAR
William L. March (1845–1849)

ATTORNEY GENERAL
John Y. Mason (1845–1846)

Nathan Clifford (1846–1848)

Isaac Toucey (1848–1849)

SECRETARY OF THE NAVY
George Bancroft (1845–1846)

John Y. Mason (1846–1849)

POSTMASTER GENERAL
Cave Johnson (1845–1849)

Following in the footsteps of his mentor, Andrew Jackson, James K. Polk projected an unwavering faith in America and managed to accomplish more in his one presidential term than many of his successors did in two. During his four years, he doubled the size of the country following a successful war and negotiated a treaty with Great Britain for the Oregon territory. Harry Truman later wrote admiringly of Polk: "Said what he intended to do and did it."[1] Only another president could appreciate how very difficult such a task could be.

EARLY LIFE

Although James Knox Polk began his life in Mecklenburg County, North Carolina, on November 2, 1795, he would call Tennessee his home. His parents, Samuel and Jane Knox Polk, moved to central Tennessee with their growing family in 1806. They began acquiring land around Columbia, and Samuel eventually accumulated a sizable estate, as well as more than fifty slaves.

Young James was sickly and remained at home rather than attend school. When he was seventeen, his father took him to a frontier doctor of some renown who decided that the malady plaguing Polk was gallstones and suggested surgery as the remedy. Without anesthesia, an extremely dangerous and painful operation ensued, but the offending gallstones were removed, and young Polk's health rebounded.

With improved health and stamina, James now sought an education. He enrolled at a nearby school to acquire the basic skills, then transferred to a better school in Murfreesboro. After mastering that program, he decided to enter the University of North Carolina and was admitted into the sophomore class, where he studied the classics and mastered mathematics. Forensics and debate were two skills he also developed while in college, and he planned to put them to ready use in a legal career. Polk graduated in 1818 with full honors and the following year began studying law with one of Nashville's most prominent attorneys and a friend of Andrew Jackson, Felix Grundy.

Polk gained his first taste of politics working at the lowly job of clerk for the state senate, which met in Murfreesboro. His salary from this position helped him pay bills until he was admitted to the Tennessee bar in 1820. He soon opened his own law practice in Columbia but continued to work for the state assembly. Keeping an eye toward gaining key connections, Polk joined the Masons, as well as the local militia, where he eventually became a colonel, although few but Andrew Jackson referred to him as "Colonel Polk."

While in Murfreesboro, Polk became reacquainted with a young lady he had met years before while attending school. Sarah Childress was the daughter of a wealthy local merchant, and her intelligent conversation captivated the serious young attorney. The two were wed on January 1, 1824; he was twenty-eight and she was twenty. Theirs was an extremely happy union marred only by their childlessness. Sarah became her husband's assistant and gracious hostess, and sometimes worried over her husband's propensity toward overwork.

Although his law practice steadily grew in volume, James found himself increasingly interested in the political arena. Toward that end, he wrote in 1823, "I am a candidate for the H. Rept. in the Tennessee Legislature."[2] He won his first election and embarked on a political career that would span the next quarter century.

NATIONAL EVENTS

Congress sets a uniform date for presidential elections to be the first Tuesday following the first Monday of November

FEB 1: The *Rainbow* begins the clipper ship era

MAR 1: Congress passes Texas annexation bill

MAR 3: Florida added as 27th state; it is a slave state

MAR 4: James K. Polk inaugurated as 11th president

JUN 8: Andrew Jackson dies at his Tennessee home, The Hermitage, at age 78

JUL: President Polk sends troops under General Taylor to southwestern border of Texas in case of possible Mexican attack

1845

WORLD EVENTS

Irish potato famine causes many to flee to America

Alexandre Dumas publishes *The Count of Monte Cristo*

Friedrich Engels publishes *The Condition of the Working Class in England*—about how capitalism exploits labor

Republic of Yucatan separates (for the second time) from Mexico

British annexation of Natal leads to renewed emigration of most Afrikaan and Dutch pioneers

POLITICAL CAREER

When Polk took office in the Tennessee Legislature, the nation was still struggling to regain its financial equilibrium following the Panic of 1819 (p. 68). Many of Polk's friends and neighbors found themselves in ruin because banks refused to exchange paper money for gold and silver (specie). To the young Tennessee lawyer, this battle between the bankers and the farmers was the same struggle waged years before between Hamilton and Jefferson, the moneyed class versus the average man. Even though his family counted themselves as part of the business class, James Polk championed the debtor class of farmers, which cast him politically against his mentor Felix Grundy. Although Grundy won a delay, forcing the banks to resume payments in gold and silver, Polk's determined opposition against the banking lobby gained the attention of many in Tennessee politics, including Andrew Jackson.

> ***No president who performs his duties faithfully and conscientiously can have any leisure.***
>
> —*James K. Polk*

In 1824, Andrew Jackson ran for president against John Quincy Adams; no better time to run for Congress, believed Polk, who planned to capitalize on the Tennessee wave of popularity. To the dismay of many, Jackson's popular victory did not translate into an electoral landslide; instead, the House of Representatives decided the presidency and cast their votes for Adams.

Still Polk won his seat and arrived in Washington after just having celebrated his thirtieth birthday and with the purpose of changing the current system of presidential election that allowed the election to move to the House when no candidate won a majority of electoral votes. For his maiden speech before the House of Representatives, Polk argued against the recent election by the House, "The majority should rule and the minority should submit."[3] He continued his argument saying that having Congress determine the presidency left itself vulnerable to corruption. Undoubtedly this caused some to shift uneasily in their seats because weeks before, they had cast their lot with Speaker Clay in what Jackson had termed a "corrupt bargain" making Adams president and Clay his secretary of state. When Representative Edward Everett rose in rebuttal, he fumed that the process prevented men from taking office who were not suited, including a "military chieftain."[4] Polk shot back an angry retort, "By some military chieftain whose only crime it was to have served his country faithfully at a period when that country needed . . . his services."[5] Polk failed to win the support of his fellow House members.

He continued his crusade against the administration as reflected in his voting record. He opposed internal improvements (believing it was best handled on a state level), high tariffs, and the bank. His views were popular with his constituents and they returned Polk to the House in 1826 and again in 1828.

The 1828 election also finally crowned Andrew Jackson president, and Polk worked tirelessly to gain support from House members for the president's programs and preferences. In the nullification debate, he agreed with the president that states

DID YOU KNOW?

Gaslights were installed in the White House while Polk was a resident.

JUL: Term "manifest destiny" is coined by John L. O'Sullivan

OCT 10: US Naval Academy opens at Annapolis, Maryland

OCT 13: Republic of Texas approves a constitution

NOV: US sends representative to Mexico to purchase Texas, New Mexico, and California, but the Mexican government refuses

DEC 29: Texas joins the US as 28th state; it is a slave state

FEB 7: An intoxicated visitor smashes the Portland Vase from the first century BC at the British Museum

MAR 17: Rubber band is invented in England

MAR 28: Mexico severs diplomatic relations with the US upon news of Texas annexation

AUG 9: Aberdeen Act passed in Britain to stop Brazilian slave trade

DEC 22–23: Battle of Ferozeshah: British forces defeat Sikhs in Punjab, India

DID YOU KNOW?

Sarah Polk held the first annual White House Thanksgiving dinner.

could not secede even though Polk understood the concerns South Carolina and other southern states felt toward the Tariff of Abominations. He also opposed a major internal improvements bill that Jackson later vetoed. And when the president decided to wage war against the Bank of the United States, he knew that he could count upon Representative Polk for leadership in the House.

In 1833, Polk became chairman of the powerful House Ways and Means Committee, where his well-written minority report attacked the abuses by the Bank of the United States and its chief, Nicholas Biddle. Polk pointed to instances where Biddle financed newspapers to write scathing editorials against Jackson and Polk. When that failed to stop the bank war, Biddle tightened the economy hoping that the president would flinch. He didn't. But the economy spiraled downward, and Polk denounced Biddle's ploy, warning that if left unchecked, the bank's power would only grow and become such a force that it would overshadow the national government with its influence. So the decision now before them was "whether we shall have the republic without the bank or the bank without the republic."[6]

Biddle's influence was felt again the following year when Polk ran for House Speaker. Biddle supported his opponent, Whig John Bell, while Vice President Van Buren backed Polk. Former vice president John C. Calhoun intensely disliked Van Buren, so he spitefully supported Bell, making him the winner. Yet Bell lasted only a year before he was turned out and Polk was elected to the coveted position. Bell did manage, however, to undermine the power wielded by Jackson back in Tennessee, which overwhelmingly voted for Whig party candidates in the 1836 election.

SPEAKER OF THE HOUSE

When James K. Polk took over as Speaker of the Twenty-fifth Congress, he had the unenviable task of working with a divided House: 108 Democrats, 107 Whigs, and twenty-four independents. Polk believed in rewarding loyal partisans, so he granted powerful chairmanships to fellow Democrats, and lesser chairs to Whigs, including former president John Quincy Adams. The latter never was an admirer of Polk and said he had "nothing that can constitute an orator, but confidence, fluency, and labor."[7]

The Speaker worked to push Van Buren's agenda through Congress while the shadow of a worsening economy and the ongoing gag rule dominated much of the House's business. After winning reelection to the Speaker's chair in 1837, the Whigs' frustration spilled out into House sessions and they directed their venom at Polk. Bell's friends attempted to engage Polk in a duel, but he refused to be manipulated onto the field of honor. They called him names and hurled insults, but Polk refused to allow his temper to guide his actions.

Meanwhile back home in Tennessee, fellow Democrats desperately desired to regain the governorship, but only one man appeared capable of winning the election. After considering his options—and foreseeing that the Whigs would likely win the next congressional election and depose him as Speaker—running for governor seemed logical, as well as helpful to the party. He toured the state giving speeches and bested his opponent in debates. By more than two thousand votes, Polk won a two-year term as governor of Tennessee.

GOVERNOR

As governor, Polk toiled less in matters of state than as steward of the Democratic Party. In the days when the state legislatures selected the US senators, Gover-

NATIONAL EVENTS

1846

JAN 13: After American attempt to purchase lands from Mexico has been rebuffed, Polk orders General Taylor to move his troops south of Rio Grande River

APR 4: General Taylor sends a message of hostile action against his troops

MAY 13: Congress declares war on Mexico

MAY 18: General Taylor crosses Rio Grande River and invades Mexico

WORLD EVENTS

The Corn Laws (import tariffs) are repealed in Britain ushering in free trade

Historian Jules Michelet writes *The People*, celebrating France's revolutionary ideals

FEB 21: Emperor Ninko of Japan dies

MAR 10: Prince Osahito becomes Emperor Kōmei in Japan

APR 27: Train travel begins in the city of Celje (Slovenia)

nor Polk oversaw the replacement of Tennessee's two Whig senators with two Democrats. The nation and his home state were still in the throes of the Panic of 1837; consequently, Polk's hopes of improving Tennessee education and roads were thwarted, as was his plan to regulate the state's banks. In 1841 and again in 1843, the voters refused to reelect him as governor. In 1840, Polk had pinned his hopes on becoming Martin Van Buren's vice presidential candidate, but again he was disappointed. The political future of James K. Polk appeared bleak.

ELECTION OF 1844

Should Texas be annexed? That was the question on every politician's mind in the spring of 1844. Soon sides were being chosen, beginning with Polk stating early in April that he favored annexation. Within weeks, both Henry Clay and Martin Van Buren, the likely candidates for the presidency, had both issued statements of opposition to the annexation. Polk found himself isolated from the frontrunners but in plenty of company with the average voter. Current president John Tyler also favored annexation and attempted to get the bill through Congress, but was unable to overcome the power exerted by Clay and Van Buren against it.

Baltimore became the focal point for political conventions in May where the Whigs nominated Clay, and the Democrats came to town assumingly to bless Van Buren. Andrew Jackson had other plans after hearing of Van Buren's stance on Texas. Determined to have a pro-annexation man as their standard bearer, Jackson and Polk, with other Tennessee party operatives, worked for the weeks preceding the convention to thwart the nomination of Van Buren, although Polk acknowledged that once the delegates bolted, "In the confusion that will prevail . . . there is no telling what will occur."[8]

Once the Democratic convention convened, they immediately approved a measure requiring that two-thirds of the delegates must approve the candidate, meaning Van Buren was already in trouble. After seven ballots, the former president failed to garner a majority, leaving the door open for the country's first dark horse candidacy. On the eighth ballot, Polk's name appeared, and when Van Buren's supporters pledged their support, he captured the majority on the ninth and final ballot. The governor of Pennsylvania, George Dallas, became his running mate, and the Democratic Party stood united on a platform of annexation of Texas and the acquisition of Oregon. This led to the party's slogan "54°40' or Fight!" referring to the northern line of latitude, which the United States believed should become the border of Oregon. Northern Democrats worried over Polk's anti-tariff stance and demanded reassurances. Polk allayed their fears, claiming that he favored duties, which provided "reasonable incidental protection to our home industries."[9]

SUPREME COURT APPOINTMENTS
★★★★★★★★★★

Levi Woodbury, 1845

Robert C. Grier, 1846

DARK HORSE CANDIDACY ★ "Dark horse" is an expression thought to have been first used by British politician and future prime minister Benjamin Disraeli in his 1831 novel *The Young Duke* to describe an unknown horse that won the race. This term then was transferred to the political spectrum in 1844 for the unexpected presidential candidacy of James Polk. From that point, a dark horse candidate would refer to one who is not the frontrunner, but is nominated unexpectedly. Other successful presidential "dark horse" candidates include Franklin Pierce, Rutherford B. Hayes, James A. Garfield, and Warren G. Harding.

JUN 15: US and Great Britain end boundary dispute of Oregon and settle on 49th parallel as northern border

JUN 19: First baseball game played

JUL 7: Naval force under Commodore John Sloat claims California for the US

AUG 8: David Wilmot introduces legislation known as Wilmot Proviso, which prohibits slavery in any territories gained in war with Mexico

AUG 10: Smithsonian Institution founded by Congress upon bequest by Englishman James Smithson

MAY 17: Antoine Joseph Sax patents the saxophone

JUN 16: Pope Pius IX succeeds Pope Gregory XVI

AUG: General Santa Anna takes command of Mexican army

SEP 23: Johann Galle discovers the planet Neptune

OCT 1: Christ College is founded in Tasmania, Australia

STATE OF THE UNION
★★★★★★★★★★

US POPULATION IN 1845
23,191,876

NATIONAL DEBT IN 1849
$63,061,859

PRESIDENT'S SALARY
$25,000/year

STATES ADMITTED TO UNION
Texas, December 29, 1845

Iowa, December 28, 1846

Wisconsin, May 29, 1848

NUMBER OF STATES IN 1849
30

Henry Clay asked rhetorically, "Who is James K. Polk?" The American voters knew that Polk's views represented their views of expansionism and manifest destiny. Polk's ties to Jackson earned him the nickname "Young Hickory," which was used both affectionately, as well as derisively. Both Clay and Polk were slave owners, so it was to Clay's disadvantage when an abolitionist party formed and took many Whig party votes in northeastern states, particularly New York, where Polk won. The dark horse took the election (although he became the only president not to win his home state) and the presidency.

PRESIDENT POLK

Polk had pledged during the campaign that he would serve only one term; therefore, he threw himself into his work unlike any president before or since. He once commented in his diary, "Though I occupy a very high position, I am the hardest working man in this country."[10] He expected staff members to keep up his pace, which meant being prepared to stay in town and meet with him daily. He laid out to his friend and new secretary of the navy, George Bancroft, his four goals: settlement of the Oregon boundary dispute; reduction of tariffs; the reestablishment of an independent treasury; and the acquisition of California from Mexico.

Since the annexation of Texas had been accomplished in the waning days of President Tylor's administration, Polk now focused on the Oregon territory. Great Britain disagreed with his demands of the fifty-fourth parallel as the northern boundary, and negotiations broke off with the threat of war a possibility. Tyler had previously offered the forty-ninth parallel as a compromise and Polk reiterated the offer, but the British wanted the line drawn at the Columbia River. Incensed at the refusal, Polk now argued with Secretary of State James Buchanan over the feasibility of waging war on the issue. Buchanan pointedly rejected the idea that Oregon was worthy of such action, but Polk would not back down. Against his better judgment, Buchanan delivered the ultimatum to the British, and the waiting game began. Within months, the administration learned they had won the game of chicken when Britain asked if the forty-ninth parallel would still be agreeable. Polk's cabinet voted to accept the offer (except Buchanan, who did a reversal), and the treaty was forwarded to the Senate for approval. By mid-June 1846, the Oregon Territory officially became the sole property of the United States north to the forty-ninth parallel, and the first of Polk's goals became reality.

Believing that tariffs should be levied principally as revenue producers, Polk balked at those wanting them for protectionist purposes. Alarmed by the threat of a lower tariff protecting their industries, northern businessmen swooped down on Washington, attempting to bribe congressmen into voting against the Walker Tariff. Polk's argument that high tariffs not only harmed southerners who imported more, but also westerners who needed to export their grain, swayed some. Nevertheless, Polk still had to twist a few arms of fellow Democrats to ensure their vote; a few even decided to leave town instead. The Senate tied, and Vice President Dallas cast his vote for the tariff in July 1846. Later in the year, many of the Democrats who had favored the tariff were then rejected in elections at home.

As president, Polk hoped to implement an improved fiscal policy with its basis in the reestablishment of the Independent Treasury System, which Van Buren had briefly started, only to have the

NATIONAL EVENTS

OCT: Mexican citizens revolt against the US and take Los Angeles and San Diego, but are soon taken over by Colonel Kearny

DEC 28: Iowa becomes 29th state; it is a free state

John Curtis of Maine develops the first American commercial chewing gum (made from spruce tree resin)

JAN 1: Michigan becomes first state to abolish capital punishment

JAN 13: John C. Frémont named governor of Republic of California

1847

WORLD EVENTS

Louis François Cartier opens a jewelry shop in Paris

Emily Bronte publishes *Wuthering Heights*; her sister Charlotte publishes *Jane Eyre*

Europe's oldest covered shopping center opens in Brussels, Belgium

Whigs dismantle it in 1841. He wanted to move away from the pet banks begun by Jackson and instead make the government the depository for its funds, breaking the cycle of corruption when private banks held the deposits. Congress agreed, and the third of his goals was met in August 1846. His treasury plan would be implemented until replaced by the Federal Reserve System in 1913.

HENRY DAVID THOREAU (1817–1862) ★

Massachusetts writer Henry David Thoreau opposed the Mexican War, arguing that it was merely a way for the United States to increase its slave territory. When required to pay a poll tax to help with the war's expenses, Thoreau refused and landed in jail. His later essay "Civil Disobedience" reflects on this experience and provided arguments that others would use in the future to oppose laws they believed to be morally wrong.

WAR

With the annexation of Texas came the dispute over what was truly the southern border of that state and, thus, the United States. Americans claimed it was the Rio Grande River, while Mexico insisted that its land ran north to the Nueces River. Polk wanted to settle the matter and acquire the provinces of New Mexico and California, so in late 1845, he dispatched a representative to negotiate. The Mexican government, furious over the Texas annexation, refused the diplomatic overture, and America began preparations for war.

In June 1845, Polk ordered General Zachary Taylor to the disputed region. Six months later they took up position on the northern side of the Rio Grande and waited. Meanwhile, Texas officially was granted statehood, and the Mexican government deliberated on what course of action to take. The answer came on April 24, 1846, when Mexican troops crossed the Rio Grande and killed eleven Americans in an ambush. Polk had already issued orders allowing "Old Rough and Ready" (the nickname Taylor had acquired in the Second Seminole War in the late 1830s) permission to retaliate if attacked, and ordered Taylor to prepare to cross the Rio Grande and take Matamoras. The president received news of the Mexican attack in early May and Congress declared war four days later. By then, General Taylor had already won additional victories and was pushing southward into Mexico.

Polk insisted that America needed to fight the Mexican invaders because they had "shed American blood upon American soil."[11] Not all in Congress bought his reasoning, and many Whigs, including Abraham Lincoln, claimed it was a veiled attempt to expand territory for slavery. Pennsylvania congressman David Wilmot twice introduced his Proviso, which banned slavery from any lands gained from the war, but Congress rejected it both times.

Throughout the war, Americans were outnumbered in battle, but their skill and better use of artillery provided victory after victory. While Taylor fought his way south from Texas, Stephen Kearny marched from Fort Leavenworth and captured Santa Fe, then moved west to San Diego. John C. Frémont, meanwhile, seized northern California and created the Bear Flag Republic. These victories, combined with naval help, ensured US possession of that region.

During this period, President Polk was duped by a Spaniard, A.J. Atocha, now a naturalized American citizen, who proposed that the American government help return the former Mexican president, General Antonio Lopez de Santa Anna,

DID YOU KNOW?

★★★★★★★★★★★

As a devout Presbyterian, Sarah Polk banned alcohol and dancing at official White House functions.

JAN 19: Charles Bent, fur trader and new governor of New Mexico territory, is slain by Pueblos and Mexicans

FEB 13: Relief group reaches members of Donner party; rescuers find that some have survived through cannibalism

FEB 22: General Taylor defeats forces under General Santa Anna at Battle of Buena Vista

JUN 10: *Chicago Tribune* begins publication as *Chicago Daily Tribune*

JUN 22: Maine baker's apprentice, Hanson C. Gregory, creates the first ringed doughnut

Nitroglycerin is discovered by Ascanio Soberro, an Italian chemist

Ottoman Empire cedes Abadan Island to Persia

Algerian Abd al-Kader imprisoned by French

First Chinese immigrants arrive in New York City and start to build Chinatown

MAR 1: Faustin Soulouque declares himself Emperor of Haiti

to power. Atocha reassured Polk that the former Mexican dictator would be amenable to ending the war and granting American requests. After several months Polk agreed, and Santa Anna returned to his native land from his Cuban exile. He then seized power and proceeded to confront American forces for the remainder of the war.

Taylor continued his drive into Mexico's interior, but Polk grew increasingly dismayed by him. The president confided his concerns in his diary, complaining that Taylor lacked initiative and seemingly waited for the government to send his orders. Polk decided to give Winfield Scott, the Army's highest-ranking general, command and wrote, "I am now satisfied that anybody would do better than Taylor. . . . [he] is not fit for a higher command."[12] Scott had been furious with the president only a few months earlier and had written the secretary of war a scathing letter: "I do not desire to place myself in the most perilous of all positions—a fire upon my rear from Washington, and the fire in front from the Mexicans."[13] Apparently, the general had changed his mind. General-in-chief Winfield Scott's troops landed on Mexico's east coast, where he soon became the victor at Vera Cruz and then led Americans to victory in Mexico City.

Now the debate in Congress raged over whether or not the United States should seize all of Mexico. Others who had opposed the war throughout its duration, including Whigs Abraham Lincoln and John Quincy Adams, approved a measure that said the war had been "unnecessarily and unconstitutionally begun by the President of the United States."[14] Still, Polk pressed forward to achieve his fourth goal, and in March 1848, California and New Mexico became territories of the United States as part of the Treaty of Guadalupe Hidalgo, which also paid Mexico fifteen million dollars and assumed claims by US citizens; the border was now fixed at the Rio Grande River.

PRESIDENCY

Throughout Polk's administration, he and Secretary of State James Buchanan endured an extremely contentious relationship that is baffling to explain. His diary provides numerous instances of disagreements between the men, especially when Buchanan desired a seat on the Supreme Court. Twice Polk had the opportunity to appoint him, but twice he refused. Buchanan was extremely upset, insisting that the appointment was the one position he wanted more than any other, including the presidency. Yet he remained at his post, and they continued to argue frequently at cabinet meetings and shout each other down. Most presidents would likely ask for a resignation after such sessions, but Polk kept him. Perhaps he found Buchanan the best advisor available; perhaps he believed he needed someone from such a key northeastern state as Pennsylvania to serve in a primary position; or perhaps he did as the ancient Chinese military tactician advised: "Keep your friends close and your enemies closer." No one knew Polk's reasoning, except very possibly his wife.

First Lady Sarah Polk enjoyed her position, for it granted her the opportunity to meet and discuss serious matters with the power players of the day. Sometimes during White House dinners she became so engrossed in the conversation that she forgot to eat, and on one occasion, she neglected to notice that no napkins graced the table. She also instituted the practice of no hard liquor served at the White House, and dancing was also banned because she did not believe it befit the decorum of the president's home.

NATIONAL EVENTS

JUL 1: US issues its first postage stamps

SEP 12–13: American forces under General Winfield Scott defeat Santa Anna at Mexico City

NOV 27: Cayuse Indians kill Methodist missionaries Marcus and Narcissa Whitman and 11 others in a massacre that shocks the nation

DEC 3: Frederick Douglass, fugitive slave from Maryland, begins publishing abolitionist newspaper, *The North Star*

DEC 24: Congressmen introduce idea of "popular sovereignty" to determine slavery in new territories

WORLD EVENTS

APR 15: Lawrence School, Sanawar is established in India

JUN 1: First congress of the Communist League in London

JUL 26: Liberia declares its independence from the US

SEP 20: Vegetarian Society formed in Britain

When entertaining, Sarah Polk was more interested in what various congressmen were thinking than conversing with their wives. Some men, including Henry Clay, admitted they preferred talking to her rather than her husband; undoubtedly they knew whatever they said would be related later to the president. Often Sarah acted as secretary for her husband and drafted correspondence; she reviewed upcoming speeches and voiced her opinion. Yet she still fulfilled her obligation as the hostess of the White House and worked to improve its furnishings, which were left over from the Monroe administration over twenty years before and terribly worn. As her husband looked forward to retirement, she did also. Sarah traveled to New York to purchase new furniture for the home they had acquired and were remodeling in Nashville. They called it Polk Place, and both anxiously anticipated spending the rest of their time together there.

TREATY OF GUADALUPE HIDALGO ★ Nicholas P. Trist (a grandson-in-law of Thomas Jefferson) negotiated the Treaty of Guadalupe Hidalgo with the Mexican government over several months (August 1847–February 1848). Eventually the treaty was signed to promise the cession of over 50 percent of Mexican land (states of New Mexico, Arizona, California, and parts of Utah, Nevada, and Utah) in return for fifteen million dollars. It also set the Rio Grande River as the border between Texas and Mexico. The United States promised to police its side of the river and to respect the rights of those Mexican people who would now become part of the United States.

RETIREMENT

Rebuffing attempts to make him run for reelection, Polk watched with dismay at Zachary Taylor's election to the presidency. Upon meeting the general, Polk's low estimate of his former commander was only reinforced. After the inauguration ceremonies concluded and farewells to friends were said, the Polks began their lengthy journey home.

By now James K. Polk was totally exhausted from his constant worries and the demands of the presidency. He had frequently suffered from stomach ailments and diarrhea, which only increased on the journey home. Along the way, well-wishers welcomed them with parties and dinners, which only prolonged his discomfort. He also fretted over reports of cholera in New Orleans and elsewhere as they traveled by steamboat up the Mississippi. After nearly a month, they arrived in Nashville. Neighbors were shocked by how much Polk had aged and commented he looked older than his mother. His hair was now white, and soon illness, possibly cholera, felled him. For days he lay bedridden, and when asked if he finally wanted to be baptized, he agreed, but with the stipulation that it be done by a Methodist clergyman rather than a Presbyterian minister preferred by both his mother and wife. His wish was granted, and on June 15, 1849, after only three months' retirement, James K. Polk died at the age of fifty-three.

Sarah Polk continued residing at Polk Place for the next forty-two years. She raised a grandniece and entertained other nieces and nephews, their children, and grandchildren. During the Civil War, Sarah claimed she was neutral and received both Confederate general Don Carlos Buell and Union general William Tecumseh Sherman. After the war, the first telephone in Nashville was installed in her home. Sarah enjoyed regaling visitors with tales of the past and taking them through the house on a

DID YOU KNOW?

Polk's nomination and his victory were the first to be reported by telegraph.

JAN 26: Henry David Thoreau delivers a lecture that will later be titled "Civil Disobedience"

JAN 31: Captain John C. Frémont is court-martialed and relieved of duty

FEB 2: Treaty of Guadalupe Hidalgo ends the war with Mexico and US gains over 500,000 square miles

FEB 2: First Chinese immigrants arrive in San Francisco

FEB 23: John Quincy Adams dies at the Capitol; he is 81 years old

1848

Revolutions of 1848 occur in Paris, Vienna, Prague, Rome, and Milan as well as parts of Latin America

John Stuart Mill, British economist, publishes *Principles of Political Economy*

British novelist William M. Thackeray publishes *Vanity Fair*

British troops in India begin wearing khaki-colored clothing as camouflage

JAN 3: First president of African Republic of Liberia sworn in

tour through history, including her husband's study, which she left untouched as a shrine. By 1891, Sarah had survived a bout of pneumonia but was left considerably weakened. She died on August 14, 1891, at the age of eighty-seven, and was buried beside her husband on their lawn. Later they were moved to the capitol grounds, and Polk Place was torn down.

HIS LEGACY

Among America's presidents, James K. Polk emerges as one of the most productive, but also one of the least remembered. This lack of acknowledgement began soon after his death. He died in the middle of 1849, when Americans cast their eyes west to California and many became "forty-niners" in search of gold. In December 1848, President Polk had received a gold nugget and promptly sent the news to Congress, which set the publicity into motion. A few months later, his death was overshadowed by people enjoying the fruits of his labor during a new surge of westward movement. He would have understood.

NATIONAL EVENTS

- **MAY:** Democrats select Lewis Cass to be their presidential candidate since Polk would only serve one term
- **MAY:** Group of New York newspapers combine with a telegraph, which will soon become known as the Associated Press
- **MAY 29:** Wisconsin enters as the 30th state, a free state
- **JUN:** Whigs meet and nominate General Zachary Taylor, hero of the Mexican War, for president
- **JUL:** First women's rights convention held at Seneca Falls, New York; leaders are Lucretia Mott and Elizabeth Cady Stanton

WORLD EVENTS

- **FEB 21:** Karl Marx publishes *The Communist Manifesto*
- **FEB 22:** French King Louis Philippe faces revolt in Paris and abdicates two days later
- **MAR 4:** First constitution signed in the Kingdom of Sardinia (Italy)
- **MAR 7:** King Kamehameha III signed the Great Mahele (land redistribution act) in Hawaii
- **MAR 12:** France creates its Second Republic

> *The passion for office and the number of unworthy persons who seek to live on the public is increasing beyond former example, and I now predict that no president of the United States of either party will ever again be reelected. The reason is that the patronage of the government will destroy the popularity of any president, however well he may administer the government.*
>
> —*James K. Polk, 1847*

ENDNOTES

1 Robert H. Ferrell, ed., *Off the Record: The Private Papers of Harry S. Truman*, New York: Harper & Row, 1980, p. 390.

2 John Seigenthaler, *James K. Polk*, New York: Times Books, 2003, p. 25.

3 Eugene Irving McCormac, *James K. Polk: A Political Biography*, Berkeley: University of California, 1922, p. 14.

4 Seigenthaler, p. 38.

5 Ibid.

6 Ibid, p. 53.

7 Charles Grier Sellers, Jr., *James K. Polk, Jacksonian*, Princeton, NJ: Princeton University Press, 1957, p. 217.

8 Seigenthaler, p. 80.

9 Charles A. McCoy, *Polk and the Presidency*, New York: Haskell House Publishers Ltd., 1973, p. 45.

10 Allan Nevins, ed., *Polk: The Diary of a President, 1845-1849*, New York: Longmans, Green and Co., 1929, p. 195.

11 Henry Steele Commager, ed., *Documents of American History*, New York: Crofts, 1945, Doc. No. 168, p. 311.

12 Nevins, p. 174.

13 Ibid, p. 101.

14 Seigenthaler, p. 146.

AUG 9: Anti-slavery groups combine and form the Free Soil Party and nominate Martin Van Buren

AUG 19: *New York Herald* announces a gold rush to California

NOV 7: Zachary Taylor wins the presidential election; Millard Fillmore is his vice president

DEC 5: President Polk announces the discovery of gold in California

MAY 18: First German National Assembly in Frankfurt, Germany

JUL 26: Matale Rebellion in Ceylon (Sri Lanka) against British

AUG 17: Yucatan officially united with Mexico

AUG 28: Mathieu Luis joins French Parliament as its first black member, representing Guadaloupe

DEC 2: Emperor Ferdinand I of Austria abdicates

Zachary Taylor

★ ★ ★ TWELFTH PRESIDENT ★ ★ ★

LIFE SPAN

- Born: November 24, 1784, in Orange County, Virginia
- Died: July 9, 1850, at the White House, Washington, D.C.

NICKNAME

- Old Rough and Ready

RELIGION

- Episcopalian

HIGHER EDUCATION

- None

PROFESSION

- Soldier

MILITARY SERVICE

- Career military officer (1808–1848)
- Entered as a first lieutenant and retired as major general
- Served in War of 1812, Black Hawk War, Second Seminole War, Mexican War

FAMILY

- Father: **Richard Taylor** (1744–1829)
- Mother: **Sarah "Sally" Dabney Strother Taylor** (1760–1822)
- Wife: **Margaret "Peggy" Mackall Smith** (1788–1852); wed June 21, 1810, near Louisville, Kentucky
- Children: **Ann Mackall** (1811–1875); **Sarah Knox** (1814–1835); **Octavia P.** (1816–1820); **Margaret Smith** (1819–1820); **Mary Elizabeth** (1824–1909); **Richard** (1826–1879)

PRESIDENCY

- Less than one term: March 5, 1849–July 9, 1850
- Whig
- Reason for leaving office: died in office
- Vice president: **Millard Fillmore** (1849–1850)

ELECTION OF 1848

- Electoral vote: **Taylor** 163; **Lewis Cass** 127
- Popular vote: **Taylor** 1,360,967; **Cass** 1,222,342

CABINET

★★★★★★★★★★

SECRETARY OF STATE
John M. Clayton (1849–1850)

SECRETARY OF THE TREASURY
William M. Meredith (1849–1850)

SECRETARY OF WAR
George M. Crawford (1849–1850)

ATTORNEY GENERAL
Reverdy Johnson (1849–1850)

SECRETARY OF THE NAVY
William B. Preston (1849–1850)

POSTMASTER GENERAL
Jacob Collamer (1849–1850)

SECRETARY OF THE INTERIOR
Thomas Ewing (1849–1850), first to serve in this new post

Among America's presidents, Zachary Taylor holds the distinction of being one of the extremely few men to hold the nation's highest elected office without any political experience whatsoever—years of working his way up the army's career ladder comprised the background of this unassuming man who served in a variety of posts, including his final one as commander in chief.

EARLY LIFE

Zachary Taylor was born on November 24, 1784, in Orange County, Virginia, son of Richard and Sarah Strother Taylor. James Madison, their famous kinsman (a second cousin), also resided in that county, but Richard Taylor had decided to use his land grant from the Revolution to move his family westward to Kentucky. The family soon settled on a plantation east of Louisville they called Springfield.

Over time the Taylor family grew at regular intervals to include four brothers and three sisters. Father and mother provided the early instruction for their children, and private tutors were employed sporadically; consequently, Zachary's schooling was limited, a fact reflected in his writing. Growing up on the Kentucky frontier provided its own classroom—learning how to live off the land, run a plantation, and hearing stories of Indian attacks were more to young Zachary's liking. At age seventeen, the young man demonstrated remarkable endurance when he swam across the Ohio River to Indiana and back to prove to himself that he could accomplish such a feat.

After serving briefly in the Kentucky militia in 1806, Taylor decided he wanted to enlist in the regular army as an officer. He appealed to his cousin James Madison, who secured a commission for him as lieutenant in the Seventh Infantry Regiment.

MILITARY LIFE

Taylor's first position was recruiting troops in his native Kentucky, followed by transfers to Fort Pickering in Memphis, Tennessee, and then to Natchez, Mississippi. He was promoted to captain in 1810 and transferred to Vincennes in the Indiana Territory to serve under William Henry Harrison.

Becoming a captain and gaining a pay raise was helpful for Taylor and his new bride, Margaret "Peggy" Smith, whom he wed on June 21, 1810, in Louisville. During their forty years together, their happiness was marred only by Peggy's concern for her husband's safety. They were parents to three daughters and one son who lived to adulthood.

During this time, Shawnee leader Tecumseh busily traveled from tribe to tribe, weaving together a confederacy to halt further white encroachment on native lands. In 1812, Captain Taylor and his fifty men successfully defended Fort Harrison against Tecumseh's force of four hundred warriors. Impressed by such a feat, the War Department took notice by awarding Taylor the rank of brevet major, the first in US history. He fought in numerous engagements in the Northwest Territory during the War of 1812, but in 1814, he and his men retreated when they found themselves facing a superior force of Native Americans and British troops.

With the dismantling of the army after the war, Taylor's rank reverted to captain, and deciding that it was time to pursue other interests, he resigned his commission and moved home to the Springfield plantation. Civilian life, however, quickly lost its appeal, and he rejoined the army in 1816 at the rank of major and was sent to Fort Howard, in Green Bay, Wisconsin.

Three years later, he relocated again to Louisiana, where he served at different forts. Newly

NATIONAL EVENTS

US and Hawaii sign a trade and friendship treaty

JAN 23: Elizabeth Blackwell becomes the first American woman to graduate from medical school

FEB 14: James K. Polk becomes the first president to be photographed

FEB 28: First wave of forty-niners arrive in California

MAR 3: Congress creates Home Department, later changed to Department of Interior

1849

WORLD EVENTS

Henry C. Harrod buys and begins to operate a London grocery store

JAN 1: France issues its first postage stamp

MAR 28: Four Christians burned alive in Madagascar by order of Queen Ranavalona I, fourteen others are executed

MAR 29: United Kingdom annexes the Punjab

APR 14: Hungary declares its independence from Austria

promoted Lieutenant Colonel Taylor admired the rich soil of Louisiana and purchased land near Baton Rouge to begin building a cotton plantation. Over the years, both his lands and his slaveholdings grew, making Zachary Taylor one of the major slave owners of the South. During the coming years, he maintained his home in Louisiana even as he was transferred to posts in Minnesota and Wisconsin.

In 1832, Taylor was promoted to colonel, and while in Wisconsin, he went to war again, this time against Black Hawk, the Sac chief. In northwestern Illinois, ever-growing numbers of settlers pushed the Sac and Fox people off their lands and westward. Tired of the encroachment, the natives decided to retake their homeland. Soon the Illinois frontier was ablaze with war, and Colonel Taylor was ordered to put an end to the outbreak. He and his men trekked through the wilderness looking for the elusive chief, and they finally met in Wisconsin at the Battle of Bad Axe on August 2, 1832. There Taylor's men defeated the natives, and hundreds of Indians surrendered, including Black Hawk. Peace was restored, the troops returned to their forts, and militiamen, including Abraham Lincoln, went home.

Five years later, Colonel Taylor moved again, this time to Florida where another uprising was underway. Osceola and his Seminole tribe chafed at giving up their land to settlers and began fighting the Second Seminole War (p. 89). Taylor was ordered to take one thousand men to subdue them. Marching east into the heart of Florida from Tampa Bay meant wading through dense swamps and marshes. The soldiers finally located their enemy on Christmas Day, 1837, at Lake Okeechobee. A three-hour battle culminated in the Seminoles retreating, although they had fewer casualties. While some surrendered during the coming months, resistance continued for years.

In recognition of his triumph, Taylor received a brevet promotion to brigadier general and was given command of all troops in Florida. During his three-year stint, he oversaw a massive construction campaign of bridges, roads, and posts. While in Florida, he gained the nickname "Old Rough and Ready" in recognition of his willingness to serve alongside his men, no matter the circumstance. His uniform was often unkempt and he surprised many a new officer who had no idea that he was the commander.

One young officer who did not meet Taylor's approval was Lieutenant Jefferson Davis. When Davis began spending time in the Taylor household courting daughter Sarah, Zachary Taylor announced he was not welcome, and he attempted to convince Sarah that she did not want to marry an army officer. Another one of his daughters had already married an officer, and the idea of losing a second daughter to a soldier caused him to rant, "I will be damned if another daughter of mine will marry into the Army. I know enough of the family life of officers. I scarcely know my own children or they me. I have no personal objection to Lieutenant Davis."[1] Rumors of settling the matter by dueling flew about briefly, but all was settled peacefully, although not to Taylor's liking. Jefferson Davis wed the twenty-one-year-old Sarah Taylor, but her parents did not attend. Tragically, the couple enjoyed only three months of wedded life before malaria attacked both. Davis eventually healed physically, but took years to emotionally recover from the loss of his beloved bride, who had succumbed to the disease.

Exhausted by the continual fighting with the Seminole and ill from disease, Taylor sought a transfer in 1839. The army's plans for his future differed, however, so he grudgingly remained in Florida until May 1840, when he finally received

DID YOU KNOW?

Taylor was a descendant of England's King Edward III.

MAR 5: Zachary Taylor is inaugurated as twelfth president

APR 10: Walter Hunt patents the safety pin

OCT 13: California drafts its constitution and applies to the US to be admitted as a free state

DEC 6: Harriet Tubman successfully escapes slavery

MAY 3: Beginning of May Uprising in Dresden, Germany

JUN 5: Denmark becomes a constitutional monarchy

JUL 3: French troops occupy Rome; Roman Republic surrenders

JUL 6: Prussian/Danish War ends (until 1864)

DID YOU KNOW?

Taylor voted for the first time when he was sixty-two years old; prior to that he had not voted because he was constantly being transferred to different locations and did not have a permanent voting address.

his transfer. General Taylor made his new headquarters for the Second Department, Western Division, at Fort Smith, Arkansas. This posting placed Taylor in charge of overseeing Louisiana, Arkansas, Indian Territory (land in America set aside for Native American use), and the US border with the republic of Texas. Much of his time was taken arbitrating disputes between settlers and Native Americans who had been moved in the 1830s; usually he sided with the Indians. Impressed by the fertile land along the Mississippi, Taylor decided to purchase another plantation; this one was double the size of his land near Baton Rouge. Cypress Grove was located north of Natchez, Mississippi, and its acreage and number of slaves greatly increased Taylor's holdings. Nevertheless, his family continued living in the modest cottage on the Louisiana farm.

Early in 1844, Taylor was transferred to Fort Jesup, Louisiana, to take command of the First Department. Of primary importance was the issuance of new orders from President John Tyler: take troops to the border of Texas and inform President Sam Houston that the US Army was ready and willing to take action should Mexico attack Texas while critical debates regarding Texas annexation raged in Congress. The issue dominated the 1844 presidential campaign, and the American people voted for the Democratic expansionist candidate James K. Polk. Using the election as a mandate, Congress passed the annexation resolution in March 1845 just prior to Polk taking office. Meanwhile, the War Department prepared itself for the very real possibility of a war with Mexico.

MEXICAN WAR

As part of the preparation, General Zachary Taylor was ordered to be on alert for action should Texas vote for annexation. While waiting for further orders, Taylor determined that he and his troops would travel to Corpus Christi on the Nueces River. But as more soldiers swelled the camp, marching orders did not arrive, and the men's inaction and boredom became rather troublesome for their commanding officer. For six months, the four-thousand-man army drilled and waited; finally word arrived in February 1846 for Taylor to take his men further into Texas, since diplomatic efforts had failed.

In March, Taylor led them to the Rio Grande River, where they were to await Mexican action. If the Americans were fired upon, they were to return fire. They did not need to linger long, for hostile action began almost immediately when Mexican troops ambushed small groups of Americans. In late April, a dragoon force of more than sixty men was either killed or captured by Mexican forces. In Taylor's mind, the Mexican War had begun, and he implemented his plans accordingly.

From his position at Matamoros, he learned that the Mexican Army was moving across the Rio Grande to cut the Americans off from their supply line. Taylor moved to block this and save the supply base at Port Isabel. His message to Washington was quickly transmitted across the country: "If the enemy oppose my march in whatever force, I shall fight him."[2] The opposition occurred as his troops marched back to Matamoros. They found the enemy at Palo Alto, and when the Americans drew closer, the Mexican artillery initiated its shelling. Immediately, Taylor ordered his artillery to respond, and for the next five hours the countryside reverberated with the continual pounding of cannons. The Mexicans suffered from outdated artillery that lacked the range of the Americans', whose firepower was deadly accurate. When the fighting ended, American casualties numbered less than sixty with only nine dead, while the Mexican Army of six thousand had lost 10 percent of its men, nearly all to artillery fire.

The next day, the two armies clashed again at Resaca de la Palma, where Americans defeated the Mexican soldiers in hand-to-hand combat after their dragoons silenced the enemy's guns. Many of the Mexican troops were shot as they fled toward the Rio Grande River for safety then tried vainly to swim across.

When word spread eastward of Taylor's consecutive victories, America decreed him a hero. Instantly he was promoted to major general and Congress bestowed two gold medals. Others began mentioning his name as a potential presidential candidate. Taylor ignored most of the talk and focused on the lack of supplies being sent. Troops continued to pour in, but he still lacked vital equipment and transportation. One factor that General Taylor could count on was the support and loyalty of his men, even though he never looked the part of a commander. One officer wrote, "He looks more like an old farmer going to market . . . jovial and good natured."[3] He was not West Point spit and polish, but an officer who was experienced, tough, and reliable. His men liked him and were fiercely loyal. They would go willingly wherever he led them.

Moving to Monterrey in northern Mexico was the next strategic objective, but the Americans had to cool their heels awaiting boats. Once they arrived in Monterrey, Taylor lacked wagons to haul supplies overland, causing him to split his forces. For five days, the two countries' armies tangled as Americans engaged in street fighting through the town. When the Mexican commander asked for surrender terms, Taylor was generous, granting a two-month armistice and allowing the soldiers to take their guns and artillery. While his magnanimous spirit was well received by the enemy, Taylor's commander in chief was not pleased.

Furious that Taylor was already gaining in stature and prestige and would likely become the Whig candidate in 1848, President Polk took action. He ordered Winfield Scott to take Veracruz and then follow in the footsteps of the explorer Hernando Cortés all the way to Mexico City and victory. Such aggressive movement required more men, which Polk triumphantly pulled from Taylor. Feeling greatly disheartened by such disgraceful treatment, Zachary Taylor still vowed to continue fighting rather than give up and retire as he assumed the president desired.

Although he had fewer than five thousand men, "Old Rough and Ready" refused to give in and hold a defensive position as his orders directed. General Santa Anna learned of the relatively small army and decided to strike with his force, which was triple the Americans'. On February 23, 1847, the two armies squared off at Buena Vista after Taylor refused Santa Anna's demand for surrender. Unable to defeat the Americans, Santa Anna ordered his troops to retreat from the field, leaving two thousand of his men behind as casualties. More than seven hundred American soldiers were killed and wounded, and Taylor received a slight grazing on the inside of his left arm. This additional victory all but assured him of the presidential nomination if he would accept it, as well as the continued wrath of an ungrateful president.

CANDIDATE TAYLOR

After his victory at Buena Vista, Taylor remained in Mexico, but inactive, as Winfield Scott marched victoriously with Taylor's troops from Veracruz to Mexico City. By November, Taylor had left Mexico to go home to Baton Rouge and contemplate his future. At first he refused talk of political ambition, but bitterness stemming from his treatment by Polk caused Taylor to reconsider. Important issues of the day such as the tariff, the National Bank, etc., were ones he had never pondered; in fact, he had never voted in a presidential election. Whig party leaders hesitated to allow such an uninformed candidate represent their party; in fact, Henry Clay at age seventy desperately wanted one more try at the race and tried to convince Taylor not to run. But the presidential bug bit Taylor early in 1848 and, while telling people he would not seek the nomination, he also employed the reliable refrain that he would serve if asked.

Meeting in Philadelphia, the Whig party chose Zachary Taylor as their presidential candidate and Millard Fillmore of New York as his vice president. Taylor remained at home in Louisiana and was

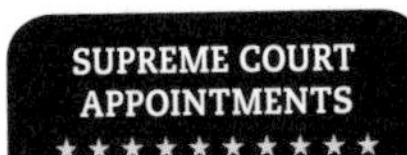

None

BATTLE OF BUENA VISTA (February 23, 1847) ★ Taylor impressed his men with his courage at the Battle of Buena Vista. One wrote: "I must mention one circumstance that happened there, which shows the extraordinary coolness of Gen. Z. Taylor in battle. He saw a small cannon ball coming directly towards his person. Instead of spurring [his horse] 'Old Whitey' out of its way, he coolly rose in his very short stirrups and permitted the ball to pass between his person and the saddle."[4]

STATE OF THE UNION

US POPULATION IN 1849
23,191,876

NATIONAL DEBT IN 1850
$63,452,774

PRESIDENT'S SALARY
$25,000/year

NUMBER OF STATES IN 1850
30

unaware of the news for some time. Since one had to pay postage upon receipt and his mail had increased dramatically, he allowed the letters to pile up, including the official notification of his nomination. When the Whigs did not receive a response, they sent a second letter via another post so it would *not* go to the Baton Rouge dead letter office.

The Democrats offered Michigan senator Lewis Cass, who had narrowly lost the nomination to Polk four years earlier. His platform included opposing the Wilmot Proviso to ban slavery from any territory acquired through the Mexican War; instead, he offered the idea of allowing the settlers to decide the issue. Taylor could not argue against slavery since he was a significant slave owner, nor could he talk knowledgeably about the issues, so he was promoted as purely and simply a war hero.

The Democrats were hindered by the entrance of former president Martin Van Buren running as the Free Soil candidate. His anti-slavery stance pulled votes from Cass, especially in New York, opening the door for Taylor's victory.

PRESIDENT TAYLOR

The issue of how to handle the expansion or prohibition of slavery in territory gained in the Mexican War occupied the attention of the Congress, its president, and the nation. California eagerly sought statehood, but only as a free state. Taylor saw no problem with the people there making that decision rather than Congress, but southerners indignantly pointed to the Missouri Compromise line and insisted that it must be followed, thus creating more slave territory. The president disagreed, and Congress was split, with John C. Calhoun announcing once again that South Carolina would secede if California was not divided. Taylor angrily replied that he would send troops to oppose any state that attempted secession.

Some congressmen, including Henry Clay and Stephen Douglas, sought a compromise to keep the Union intact. President Taylor disapproved of any compromise, believing it granted the South more power to dictate policy. He also believed that the executive branch was better suited than the legislative to settle such matters. Clay disagreed and denounced the president on the floor of the House, as did southern Whigs. Abandoned by his party, Taylor refused to abandon his principles and steadfastly maintained that he would do whatever necessary to preserve the Union.

One proud achievement of his administration was the Clayton-Bulwer Treaty with Great Britain. The two nations agreed to keep a neutral stance in Latin America, as well as begin building a canal across Nicaragua. This project was later superseded by the construction of the Panama Canal during Theodore Roosevelt's administration.

Other proposals of Taylor's included a transcontinental railroad, improvements to the army, and raising the tariff. His ideas received little acknowledgement or consideration, for the debate concerning slavery overshadowed all else, and finding jobs for Whig party members required much of the president's time. One of the party's rising stars was offered the governorship of the Oregon Territory, but Abraham Lincoln declined the honor eleven years before his own presidential election.

Another matter weighing heavily on Taylor was the serious threat of civil war erupting along the New Mexico–Texas border. Again, Taylor contemplated using force to prevent the threatened Texas invasion of its neighbor, as New Mexico worked to create a constitution and become eligible for statehood.

By the spring of 1850, "Old Rough and Ready" felt he was neither, as three members of his cabinet were implicated in a scandal that shook his presidency. The Galphin family of Georgia had previously been paid by the US government a claim they had dating to the 1770s. Now the family's heirs demanded an interest payment of $191,000. The treasury secretary paid it after it was approved by the attorney general. Soon word leaked that Secretary of War George Crawford had previously represented the Galphin family and stood to receive part of the award. Congressmen gleefully cried "Foul!" and demanded the removal of the offending cabinet members; some also mentioned impeaching the president. Distraught by such a betrayal, Taylor contemplated replacing the three men, but did not live long enough to do so.

DID YOU KNOW?

Taylor refused to be inaugurated on a Sunday (March 4), so David Rice Acheson, the Senate's President Pro Tempore, unknowingly served as the unofficial president for a day.

DEATH

All of the turmoil weighed on the sixty-four-year-old Taylor. His health had never been good after his Florida service, and now it grew worse, with intermittent spells of serious illness. Still, he attended the dedication ceremony for the Washington Monument on July 4, 1850, despite the heat and humidity, which he commented was even worse than Florida's. Afterward, he strolled along the Potomac and returned to the White House famished. Taylor ate considerable quantities of raw fruits and vegetables, washed down by either ice water or ice milk. His stomach rebelled soon after, and a doctor was summoned. The president was prescribed the normal calomel and opium, and seemed somewhat improved the next day. Soon afterward, though, his health deteriorated, despite the efforts of the retinue of physicians called in to prevent the feared fate. The doctors diagnosed him with cholera morbus and monitored him as best they could as he grew increasingly dehydrated.

Taylor was able to speak near the end, declaring, "I am about to die. I expect the summons very soon. I have tried to discharge my duties faithfully. I regret nothing, but I am sorry that I am about to leave my friends."[5] He died at 10:35 p.m. on July 9, 1850. His body lay in state in the East Room, but his widow refused its embalming. Ironically, those who had days before denounced her husband now carried his coffin. After a brief interment at the Congressional Burying Ground, he was moved to the family plot near Louisville, Kentucky.

Her husband's passing greatly distressed the First Lady, whose health had also been poor since he took office. In fact, during his presidency, she had stayed on the second floor of the White House as a semi-invalid while her daughter, Mary Elizabeth "Betty" Bliss, performed as hostess. Now Mrs. Taylor's health declined more rapidly, and she died two years later in August 1852, in Mississippi. She was laid to rest beside her husband in what is now called the Zachary Taylor Cemetery.

Rumors circulated that the president had been poisoned with arsenic. In 1991, a Taylor descendant granted permission to exhume his body. Arsenic did, in fact, appear in the analysis, but its level was no greater than that of the typical nineteenth-century figure, so the death again was determined to be by natural causes.

One indirect legacy of President Taylor's death was the Compromise of 1850. As long as he lived, Taylor vowed he would not acquiesce to the ideas that later became the basis for this famous bill. His successor, Millard Fillmore, disagreed and signed it into law two months after Taylor's death. The Civil War would be delayed.

CLAYTON-BULWER TREATY (April 19, 1850) ★ Concluded between American representative John Clayton and British plenipotentiary Sir Henry Bulwer on April 19, 1850, the Clayton-Bulwer Treaty was mainly concerned with eliminating any rivalry between these two nations in building a canal in central America. Some in the United States, however, were displeased with the wording, which denied either country "exclusive control over the said ship canal." Future negotiations resulted in attempts to remove this stipulation, but it would take a half-century before it was replaced by the Hay-Pauncefote Treaty, which stipulated the rule of neutralization for the Panama Canal.

DID YOU KNOW?

Sometimes White House visitors would take home an unusual souvenir—horsehairs from Whitey, the president's old Army horse that was kept on the White House lawn.

ENDNOTES

1 Holman Hamilton, *Zachary Taylor: Soldier in the White House*, Indianapolis: Bobb-Merrill, 1951, vol. I, p. 101.

2 Edwin P. Hoyt, *Zachary Taylor*, Chicago: Reilly & Lee Company, 1966, p. 79.

3 Hamilton, p. 320.

4 Samuel McNeil, *McNeil's Travels in 1849, To, Through and From the Gold Regions, in California*, Columbus: Scott & Bascom, 1850, vol. I, p. 15.

5 Silas Bent McKinley and Silas Bent, *Old Rough and Ready: The Life and Times of Zachary Taylor*, New York: Vanguard Press, 1946, p. 287.

MILLARD FILLMORE

★ ★ ★ THIRTEENTH PRESIDENT ★ ★ ★

LIFE SPAN
- Born: January 7, 1800, in Locke Township, Cayuga County, New York
- Died: March 8, 1874, in Buffalo, New York

NICKNAME
- The American Louis Philippe

RELIGION
- Unitarian

HIGHER EDUCATION
- None

PROFESSION
- Lawyer

MILITARY SERVICE
- During the Civil War, he served as major in the Union Continentals (home guard of Buffalo)

FAMILY
- Father: **Nathaniel Fillmore** (1771–1863)
- Mother: **Phoebe Millard Fillmore** (1780–1831)
- First wife: **Abigail Powers Fillmore** (1798–1853); wed February 5, 1826, in Moravia, New York
- Children: **Millard Powers** (1828–1889); **Mary Abigail** (1832–1854)
- Second wife: **Caroline Carmichael McIntosh Fillmore** (1813–1881); wed February 10, 1858, in Albany, New York; no children

POLITICAL LIFE
- New York assemblyman (1829–1831)
- US representative (1833–1835; 1837–1843)
- New York state comptroller (1848–1849)
- Vice president (1849–1850)

PRESIDENCY
- One term: July 9, 1850–March 4, 1853
- Whig
- Reason for leaving office: lost party's nomination
- No vice president

NO ELECTION
- Took office upon death of President **Zachary Taylor**

CABINET
★★★★★★★★★★

SECRETARY OF STATE
Daniel Webster (1850–1852)

Edward Everett (1852–1853)

SECRETARY OF THE TREASURY
Thomas Corwin (1850–1853)

SECRETARY OF WAR
Charles M. Conrad (1850–1853)

ATTORNEY GENERAL
John J. Crittenden (1850–1853)

SECRETARY OF THE NAVY
William A. Graham (1850–1852)

John P. Kennedy (1852–1853)

POSTMASTER GENERAL
Nathan K. Hall (1850–1852)

Samuel D. Hubbard (1852–1853)

SECRETARY OF THE INTERIOR
Thomas M. T. McKennan (Aug. 1850)

Alexander H.H. Stuart (1850–1853)

Millard Fillmore personified the Horatio Alger model of personal success. Fillmore was born into poverty, apprenticed to a tradesman, managed to educate himself and learn the law, became a successful attorney, then embarked on a moderately successful political career that eventually led him to the White House.

EARLY LIFE

Tired of battling the rocky soil of Vermont, Nathaniel Fillmore uprooted his family from their farm near Bennington and moved them to a log cabin in Cayuga County, New York. There on January 7, 1800, a second child was born and named Millard. Unfortunately, Nathaniel's luck did not improve, for his land title was fraudulent, so the Fillmores moved again a few years later to land near Lake Skaneateles in northern New York, where Nathaniel worked as a tenant farmer. Meanwhile, the Fillmore family continued to grow and eventually numbered nine children.

Millard was a farmer's son and that was his principal education during childhood. A precious few books were in the family's cabin, for his school was the outdoors. He learned the seasons of farming, from planting to harvesting. He was a strong boy, more comfortable helping his father in the fields than sitting still at a school desk. He managed to gain the fundamentals of reading and arithmetic, but very little beyond that. When he was fourteen years old, his father decided to apprentice him to a cloth maker in Sparta, New York. Millard hated the experience and left after only four months. His father believed his son needed to learn a trade to spare him a farmer's life, so he apprenticed him to another clothier, and soon Millard was off to work in New Hope, New York.

Mindful of his educational shortcomings, young Millard decided to work on improving his vocabulary. One of his first purchases was a dictionary, which he put to use at work. In between tending the machines, he would look up an unfamiliar word and then concentrate on committing it to memory as he continued his work. At the age of seventeen, he happily purchased a share in a lending library begun by people in the community. Books became his constant companions, yet he knew he still had so much more to learn. He had attended school sporadically in the past years, and had even taught school himself briefly in 1818, but desiring to further his education, he enrolled the next winter at New Hope's recently opened academy, where twenty-one-year-old Miss Abigail Powers became his teacher. Millard Fillmore soon became her star student and more, for the two fell in love. Yet Millard knew he was unable to provide for a wife.

During this time, Nathaniel Fillmore continued experiencing difficulties farming and moved his family to Montville, New York, where he met Judge Walter Wood, a wealthy Quaker who spent more time being a prosperous landlord than an attorney. Although Millard worked diligently in his apprenticeship, Nathaniel suspected that his son needed more in his future. One evening at dinner, his mother announced the news—Judge Wood had agreed to teach Millard law. Finding the study of law much more to his liking than carding wool, Fillmore negotiated ending his apprenticeship early, so he could devote more time to his legal studies. To finance this, he taught school during the winter terms. In 1821, he and Judge Wood came to an amicable parting, and Fillmore decided to move east, where his family had relocated, to pursue his future.

NATIONAL EVENTS

Brooklyn, NY, imports English sparrows to kill caterpillars in their trees, but when they overpopulate, starlings will be imported to kill the sparrows in Central Park

An immigrant can now come to the US for only $10 to ride in steerage

San Francisco experiences a series of devastating fires

A Massachusetts schoolteacher invents anagrams

Levi Strauss invents "bibless overalls" made from canvas material for the miners in the California goldfields

1850

WORLD EVENTS

German Hermann L.F. von Helmholtz invents the ophthalmoscope to examine the retina and the eye's interior

French colonists begin to settle in Algeria

German physicist Rudolf Clausius defines second law of thermodynamics

Modern acoustic guitar invented in Spain

French battleship *Le Napoleon* is launched

LAWYER

For two more years, Fillmore taught school and studied law in Buffalo. There he gained respect by his modesty and solidness of character. Still, after passing the bar in 1823, he admitted that he lacked "sufficient confidence in [himself] to enter into competition with the older members of the Bar."[1] Instead, he opened a law office in East Aurora, where he faced no legal competition. In this small community, his legal talents were utilized in collecting debts and working with land deeds. Toward the latter, he won appointment as commissioner of deeds for the area, which was his first public office.

Now earning enough money, he believed, to support himself and a wife, Millard Fillmore married Abigail Powers on February 5, 1826, in Moravia, New York. The couple soon moved to East Aurora, and within the year were able to move out of his parents' home to their own house, which Millard helped construct. Abigail continued teaching school to supplement their income. The Fillmores welcomed a son on April 25, 1828, whom they named Millard Powers Fillmore; to avoid confusion, they called him by his middle name.

> *"God knows that I detest slavery, but it is an existing evil, for which we are not responsible, and we must endure it, till we can get rid of it without destroying the last hope of free government in the world."*
>
> *—Millard Fillmore, 1850*

During these same years, events were transforming the political landscape of New York that would have a profound impact on Fillmore's career. In 1826, William Morgan became famous when he announced that he was planning to publish the secrets of the Masonic Order. He was arrested in September on charges of stealing a shirt and cravat from the master of a Masonic lodge. He went to jail, was rearrested on other petty charges, put in another jail, bailed out, and when released from jail, kidnapped by an unknown person and thrown into a carriage. He was last seen alive at Fort Niagara on September 18, 1826, but not seen again for months until his body was pulled from the Niagara River. Still his book was published and created a notable stir when it revealed a definite anti-societal bent against government institutions. Days after Morgan's appearance at Fort Niagara, an Anti-Mason convention convened in New York and soon emerged as a new political party and driving force in New York politics. Thurlow Weed, a newspaper publisher who had earlier aided John Quincy Adams with his backroom dealing, now joined the Anti-Mason group. In 1828, Weed and Fillmore met at an Anti-Mason convention, and Fillmore attended others throughout the year. By fall, Weed was sufficiently impressed to place Fillmore's name as the Anti-Mason candidate for state assembly. Millard Fillmore won his first political race.

POLITICIAN

In his first term as assemblyman, Fillmore utilized his time to learn parliamentary procedure and how state politics operated. He accomplished little

Emmanuel Leutze finishes painting *Washington Crosses the Delaware*	**JAN 29:** Senator Henry Clay introduces a series of resolutions hoping to preserve the Union	**MAR 16:** Nathaniel Hawthorne publishes *The Scarlet Letter*	**MAR 19:** American Express started in New York City as a business express delivery service	**APR 19:** Clayton-Bulwer Treaty signed between US and Great Britain
World's first exhibition hall opens in Birmingham, England	**APR 23:** Poet William Wordsworth dies	**MAY:** Alfred Tennyson writes "In Memoriam"	**JUL:** Taiping Rebellion against China's Qing Government	**AUG:** Charles Dickens publishes *The Personal History of David Copperfield*

DID YOU KNOW?

Fillmore refused an honorary doctorate of law degree from Oxford University because he felt he had "neither literary nor scientific attainment."

for his constituents and was assigned to the most inconsequential of committees. His next term, on the other hand, witnessed the transformation of Fillmore into an active politician. He devoted more of his energies to Anti-Mason causes, including its attempts to embrace the voters of the Working Men's Party (Workies). He gave more speeches during this time, and although he would never be considered a gifted orator, the people of western New York listened to his slow, deliberate delivery and believed his words came straight from the heart. No superfluous flattery or verbiage, he spoke in short sentences that drove home his points. During his final term in the assembly, Fillmore made his mark on New York when he co-wrote and sponsored a bill finally extinguishing the centuries-old practice of debtors prisons. He effectively worked to gain Democratic members' cooperation and shepherded the bill through the assembly.

In 1830, the Fillmores moved to the city they would call home the remainder of their lives, Buffalo. The growing city seemed ideal for a man whose ambition was on the move, as well. They enjoyed the varied cultural opportunities the city afforded, and he soon joined the Lyceum, where he could hear lectures and attend other educational offerings. On March 27, 1832, their daughter Abigail, nicknamed Abby, was born. The following year Fillmore joined with Nathan K. Hall to start a law practice in Buffalo. Hall would be the main lawyer, since Fillmore had been elected to the US House of Representatives.

By this time, the Anti-Masons had lost most of their following; many joined the Whig party. Millard Fillmore did so as well, putting him in direct opposition to the party and policies of the current president in 1833, Andrew Jackson. When he returned home to Buffalo, he worked to consolidate the Whig Party's base, including convincing the remaining Anti-Masons to join them. Fillmore worked at home and in Congress on measures to improve Buffalo, including bettering its harbor and enlarging the Erie Canal. In 1836, he added another name to his law firm when Solomon G. Haven joined, and their law firm became the most prominent one in Buffalo for more than twenty years. Fillmore added to his income by being an insurance agent for New York Life and Buffalo Mutual Fire.

CONGRESSMAN

Once Martin Van Buren became president, Fillmore opposed his Independent Treasury System and lambasted the fiscal policies of Jackson, which he said had caused the financial panic of 1837 (p. 95).

Fillmore won reelection the following year and found the anti-slavery faction growing in political clout. He worried this would work against the Whig candidate for president, Henry Clay, since Clay was a slave owner. Determined not to let an opportunity pass for his party to capture the White House, Fillmore began working with others to convince Henry Clay not to run but rather to allow William Henry Harrison the nomination instead. It worked, and "Tippecanoe" won the election of 1840. Elation over their victory proved short-lived for the Whigs, for Harrison died a month after his inauguration. John Tyler quickly proved he was not a Whig philosophically, and Henry Clay decided to use the next three years championing causes to ensure his successful election to the presidency in 1844. Fillmore was no fan of Clay's and disagreed with many of Tyler's proposals. Believing he could do the most good from the Speaker's chair, he ran for that post in 1840. He lost, but as runner-up, he became chairman of the House Ways and Means Committee.

NATIONAL EVENTS

JUN: *Harper's Magazine* begins publication

JUL 9: President Taylor dies and Vice President Millard Fillmore takes over

SEP: Congress passes the Compromise of 1850

SEP 9: California admitted as the 31st state; it is a free state

SEP 11: P.T. Barnum contracts with opera singer "Swedish Nightingale" Jenny Lind for an American tour

WORLD EVENTS

AUG: Elizabeth Barrett Browning writes *Sonnets from the Portuguese*

AUG 28: Wagner premiers his opera, *Lohengrin*

SEP 29: Pope Pius IX reestablishes Catholic hierarchy in England

OCT 1: First university of Australia, University of Sydney, founded

DEC 16: Canterbury Pilgrims land at Port of Lyttelton in New Zealand and found Christchurch

As one of the top congressmen, Fillmore now took the lead in introducing various bills backed by Whigs, but as it turned out, not supported by their new president, John Tyler. Fillmore voiced his frustration regarding the president's lack of support, and the Whigs agreed that Tyler could not be their nominee in the next presidential election.

In 1842, Fillmore was inspired by Samuel F.B. Morse, who had asked Congress for an appropriation of thirty thousand dollars to lay an underground wire from Washington, D.C., to Baltimore to test his new invention, the telegraph. At first Fillmore was not impressed, but he changed his mind, and then guided the bill through both houses. Morse's invention would proceed.

That same year, Fillmore sponsored a tariff bill, which Tyler vetoed; a second tariff was also vetoed, creating much animosity in Congress toward the chief executive. A third tariff was passed, raising the duties to 30 percent on many items. New Englanders rejoiced at the protectionist tariff of 1842, while southerners bitterly complained that the Whigs "carry their reason, patriotism, conscience, and religion in their purses."[2]

Deciding that he could do more good back home in New York, Fillmore chose not to run for reelection in 1842. Instead, he returned to Buffalo, his family, and his law practice. He also hoped to be named the vice presidential nominee in the 1844 Whig presidential campaign. The convention met and considered Fillmore as one of the three finalists, but chose instead Theodore Frelinghuysen of New Jersey. Fillmore was disappointed upon hearing the news, yet he also suspected what his friends reported was true: he had been denied the nomination because New York Whig party leaders thought he would make the strongest candidate for the governor's race. So as gubernatorial candidate, Fillmore wrote, "Though I had no desire for the office and still less for the nomination, yet being nominated I am not anxious to be defeated."[3] Defeated he would be, however, for he vehemently opposed Texas annexation, the main issue of the election. Throughout New York, Democrats, from Polk on down, won their elections. Clay wrote from his home, Ashland, "May God save the country, for it is evident that the people will not."[4]

Once the Mexican War started, Fillmore watched with disdain as the country's debt mounted to add "another slave territory." He wrote in the *Buffalo Express* his concern regarding the lopsided nature of American politics and stated, the "North has a majority of the votes, the South has managed to have the Speaker of the House about two-thirds of the time, and the Presidency about two-thirds of the time. Through the President they control the patronage and foreign missions and are able to veto [northern] legislation. Through the speaker they control the committees," and ended with, "Shall we submit to our servile condition?"[5] Clearly Fillmore yearned to correct the wrongs done by southern leadership in all branches of government.

Two years later, Whigs successfully began reclaiming certain positions, including the governorship. Still Fillmore remained busily traveling throughout the state, tending to legal matters as well as attending to Whig business. Then in 1847, friends approached him with the idea of running for comptroller. This was the key political position in New York, for it oversaw nearly every aspect of the state's affairs and supervised its banks, canals, and all financial departments. Fillmore easily won over his Democratic rival and began his $2,500 job (a significant pay cut, for he made more than $10,000 annually from his law practice).

SUPREME COURT APPOINTMENTS

★★★★★★★★★★

Benjamin R. Curtis, 1851

JAN 31: Gail Borden announces the invention of evaporated milk

FEB 15: Mob in Boston rescues a fugitive slave from jail in protest of the Fugitive Slave Act

APR: Publication of *The House of the Seven Gables*, by Nathaniel Hawthorne, about his hometown of Salem, Massachusetts, during the witch trials (one of his ancestors was a judge)

AUG 12: Isaac M. Singer patents a new sewing machine

1851

Cubans and Americans attempt to overthrow Spanish rule in Cuba, but are unsuccessful

James Young, Scottish chemist, patents paraffin

JAN 11: Taiping Rebellion begins

APR 2: Phra Chom Klao Mongkut becomes king of Siam (and inspiration for the Yul Brynner character in *The King and I*)

MAY 1: Crystal Palace opens at London's Great Exhibition

STATE OF THE UNION
★★★★★★★★★★

US POPULATION IN 1850
23,191,876

NATIONAL DEBT IN 1853
$59,803,118

PRESIDENT'S SALARY
$25,000/year

STATE ADMITTED TO UNION
California, September 9, 1850

NUMBER OF STATES IN 1853
31

Fillmore took office on January 1, 1848, and found himself inundated by men asking for clerkships in his office. He replaced the previous ones with clerks he found more competent. His varied duties included the Erie Canal as well as dealing with New York's Native American tribes. Then in June 1848, the Whig convention nominated Millard Fillmore as their vice presidential candidate to serve on the ticket with Zachary Taylor.

ELECTION OF 1848

By nominating Taylor, the Whig party fronted a candidate with no real political views; his appeal was hero status from the Mexican War. They nominated a northerner, Fillmore, to balance their slaveholder presidential candidate. Many Whig delegates identified Fillmore with their party's standard bearer, Henry Clay, although Fillmore had differed with him repeatedly. The Whigs also determined that slavery was too divisive of an issue; therefore, they ignored it and decided to forego a platform.

The Democratic Party followed suit, hoping that the voters would be content with their candidates, Lewis Cass of Michigan and William Butler of Kentucky. Cass believed in popular sovereignty for the territories, but little more was said. Frustrated by the two main political parties' reticence, a third party, the Free Soil Party, loudly demanded the abolition of slavery and ran former president Martin Van Buren and Massachusetts congressman Charles Francis Adams (son and grandson of two presidents). Numerous anti-slavery Democrats fled their party to join ranks with the Free Soilers, which translated to victory by the Whigs in New York as they won with 163 electoral votes to 127 for the Democrats.

THE FREE SOIL PARTY ★ A short-lived political party (1847–1848) formed by a variety of groups, including Democrats (Barnburners), anti-slavery Whigs, and members of the former Liberty party, the Free Soil Party opposed extending slavery into the Mexican Cession territories and wanted a homestead act passed. Free Soilers nominated Martin Van Buren as their presidential candidate in 1848. Though defeated in the election, they split enough votes from the Democrats to allow Zachary Taylor and the Whigs to win.

VICE PRESIDENT

Zachary Taylor first met his vice president one week before they were to be sworn in. Their meeting was brief; they saw each other again at a White House dinner given by outgoing president James K. Polk. Again, only pleasantries passed between them. Vice President Fillmore soon learned that his counsel was not welcomed by the Taylor administration.

During the opening months of his vice presidency, Fillmore was unaware that he was being undermined at every turn by the New York Whig party boss Thurlow Weed. They had once been friends, but when Fillmore refused Weed's wishes and advice, the Whig leader decided he would gain retribution with the help of newly elected William Seward and Governor Hamilton Fish. Seward soon ingratiated himself with Taylor and his brother and worked to exclude the vice president. They obtained the right to dole out the patronage appointments of New York, preventing Fillmore from exercising that power and with it, the ability to garner party loyalty.

Fillmore retaliated by creating a newspaper, the *New York State Register*, to counter Weed's paper,

NATIONAL EVENTS

AUG 31: Clipper ship *Flying Cloud* sets a new record sailing from New York to San Francisco in 89 days, eight hours

SEP 18: *New York Daily Times* begins publication; it will later drop "Daily" from its name

NOV 14: Publication of *Moby Dick*, by Herman Melville

DEC 9: First US Y.M.C.A. opens in Boston

DEC 24: Fire in Library of Congress destroys two-thirds of its volumes, including part of Thomas Jefferson's collection

WORLD EVENTS

AUG: Gold discovered in Australia

OCT: German Paul Julius Reuter begins Reuters News Service

OCT: Moons of Uranus discovered

the *Albany Evening Journal*. Then Fillmore met with President Taylor, explaining the situation and how Weed's patronage was undercutting Fillmore's power within the New York Whig party. He demanded to know whether in the future he would "be treated as friend or foe." Taylor assured him that he would be treated better, but he still did not receive invitations to consult the president or visit him. Instead, the president still looked to Weed's man, Senator Seward, for guidance.

Meanwhile, the Congress and the president were embroiled in determining whether to allow slavery in the Mexican Cession territories (today's southwestern United States, ceded to the United States by Mexico in 1848 following the Mexican-American War). Vice President Fillmore's role was simply to preside over the debates raging in the Senate. A variety of proposals and compromises were offered and discussed, while Fillmore maintained a deafening silence regarding his position. Then Henry Clay offered his omnibus of legislation, which became known as the Compromise of 1850. This series of congressional legislative actions allowed territories gained in the Mexican War to determine slavery by popular sovereignty; permitted California to enter as a free state; ended slave trade in Washington, D.C.; and, most controversial of all, contained the Fugitive Slave Act, which allowed southerners to pursue their runaway slaves into the north and outlawed anyone attempting to help with their escape. Taylor insisted that not only California must be free, but he desired the territories to enjoy the same status, and threatened to veto any measure that fell short of his goal. So divisive was the issue that it soon became apparent that the Senate could well be divided in half, leaving the key vote to be cast by its presiding officer. Aware of this very real possibility, Fillmore visited with Taylor and warned him that he might vote for the compromise but "I wished him to understand, that it was not out of any hostility to him or his Administration, but the vote would be given, because I deemed it for the interests of the country."[6] The country watched, but it would have to wait a bit longer, for the Congress recessed to enjoy Independence Day. No one could predict what would happen next.

UNDERGROUND RAILROAD ★ The Underground Railroad was a system of "stations" and "stationmasters" providing safe stops for fugitive slaves escaping the South. It is believed to have begun late in the eighteenth century with the aid of Quakers. The network expanded, and by 1860, more than 100,000 people had escaped to freedom.

On Tuesday, July 9, a messenger arrived in the Senate chamber and summoned the vice president to the President's House. Fillmore arrived and joined the other cabinet officials, who were told that President Taylor's condition was grave. The president had become ill July 4 after possibly suffering heat stroke and what doctors termed "cholera morbus." Although he rallied at first, his situation soon declined, and he grew ever weaker. On the evening of the ninth, Millard Fillmore was informed that President Taylor had expired. Hearing the news left the new president with the feeling others in the same circumstance described before and since: "The shock is so sudden and unexpected that I am so overwhelmed."[7] He stayed up that night and pondered his fate, as well as his country's. He later wrote that he "reviewed during those hours . . . his own opinions and life."[8] Believing that the nation now was held together very

"Go West, young man, go West" first appears in a newspaper

Some Sioux leaders agree to give US lands in Minnesota and Iowa

Wells, Fargo & Co. begins in New York

Clement Studebaker and his brother Henry begin manufacturing wagons

Hydraulic mining begins in California

1852

Argentina recognizes the independence of Paraguay

Devil's Island penal colony established by the French in French Guiana

David Livingstone explores the Zambezi, Africa's fourth-longest river

JAN 17: United Kingdom recognizes independence of the South African Republic (Transvaal Republic)

FEB 15: Great Ormond St. Hospital for Sick Children opens in London

FUGITIVE SLAVE LAW OF 1850 ★ The Fugitive Slave Law of 1850 angered northern residents by forcing them to help the authorities recover runaway slaves. Anyone who aided a fugitive slave could be sentenced to six months in jail and a $1,000 fine. With its passage, runaway slaves now had to escape to Canada to be truly free, and so thousands trekked farther north.

tenuously, he resolved to find the means to keep the fabric from tearing even more.

PRESIDENT FILLMORE

At noon on July 10, 1850, Millard Fillmore took the oath of office before a joint session of Congress. He accepted the resignations of Taylor's cabinet, but requested they remain for a month while he assembled a new one. Since they had sided with the president and Seward against Fillmore, they were in no mood to oblige; instead, they agreed to serve him one week. Fillmore's first appointment was Daniel Webster as secretary of state, and his opinion was valued by the new president in weighing the qualifications of other potential cabinet members. Fillmore's main concern was finding men who pledged themselves to serve their country first rather than their sectional interests, although he drew men from various parts of the nation.

Throughout the month of September 1850, the US Congress approved the five measures of the Compromise of 1850. These were sent on to the White House for the president's signature. Fillmore promptly signed the first four: 1) Allowing California to be a free state; 2) The creation of the territories of Utah and New Mexico (both could allow slavery); 3) Abolishing the slave trade in Washington, D.C.; 4) Payment of ten million dollars to Texas for its claims to adjoining territories. The last measure, the Fugitive Slave Act, greatly troubled the president. Fillmore referred the matter to his attorney general, Kentuckian John J. Crittenden, who determined it was in fact constitutional. So with heavy heart, President Fillmore affixed his signature to the last of the compromise bills. Now, he believed the country could truly be at peace with itself, for the determination of how to treat slavery in the Mexican Cession territories was complete after four years of wrangling.

Unfortunately, the Compromise had not solved the ills of the nation; in fact, it had inflicted a new open sore with the enactment of the Fugitive Slave Law. When northern law enforcement attempted to arrest fugitive slaves, they often met with violent resistance from mobs defending the slave. Fillmore received a request in late October for federal troops to help enforce the measure. Unsure how to proceed, the president convened his cabinet for advice, and they told him to go ahead and send in the military. Torn by such a dilemma, Fillmore wrote to Secretary of State Webster, "God knows I detest slavery, but it is an existing evil . . . and we must . . . give it such protection as it is guaranteed by the constitution. . . . I have therefore commenced . . . authorizing this force only in the last resort, but if necessary I shall not hesitate to give greater power, and finally to bring the whole force of the government to sustain the law."[9]

The president also deployed military troops to South Carolina to supplement various companies in Charleston, as well as New Mexico and other parts of the South. General Winfield Scott had advised the reinforcement in Charleston as the administration had been advised of plans to seize

NATIONAL EVENTS				
First Holstein cow arrives in the US	**MAR 14:** Uncle Sam first appears in cartoon form	**MAR 20:** Harriet Beecher Stowe publishes *Uncle Tom's Cabin*	**MAY 18:** Massachusetts passes first compulsory school attendance law in the US	**JUN:** Democrats nominate Franklin Pierce for president and William King for vice president

WORLD EVENTS				
MAR 1: Archibald William Montgomerie, 13th Earl of Eglinton appointed Lord Lieutenant of Ireland	**APR 1:** Start of Second Burmese War	**APR 29:** British physician and scholar Peter M. Roget publishes *Thesaurus of English Words and Phrases* at age 73	**SEP 24:** French engineer Henri Giffard pilots first dirigible from Paris to Trappes	**NOV 11:** New Palace of Westminster opens in Britain

one of the forts there. The president strongly believed in his duty "to preserve, protect, and defend the Constitution."

Millard Fillmore took a historic position in foreign trade when he endorsed the plan to send an envoy to the closed empire of Japan. For more than two hundred years, that nation had refused to trade with other nations, with the exception of the Dutch, who were allowed one ship per year. Commodore Matthew Perry was given the assignment, and he was briefed on his momentous undertaking by the president when they dined together numerous times. Fillmore also requested information from the Dutch, hoping to avoid any breach in protocol with the Japanese. He drafted letters for the emperor and promised him that the aim of the United States was not to "disturb the tranquility of your majesty's dominion,"[10] but rather to start a temporary trade relationship for the next ten years. Perry met with representatives of the emperor in July 1853, but was refused the opportunity to meet the ruler himself. Greeted by warriors and warships, Perry continued undaunted with his mission. He left Tokyo with the promise that the Japanese would have an answer for President Fillmore's invitation when Perry returned. He would do so under the administration of the succeeding president, Franklin Pierce.

ELECTION OF 1852

With the passage of the Fugitive Slave Law and its subsequent violence, northern Whigs parted company with Fillmore, although the rest of the Whig party still supported him. Fillmore, however, was determined to refuse the nomination. Concerned that such a stand would jeopardize the Compromise of 1850, he kept the thought to himself, but later revealed he made the decision when told of Taylor's death.

When Whigs met in Baltimore, Fillmore kept quiet until the party had composed its platform, which supported the Compromise. Reassured of his party's support, Fillmore then announced he was releasing his delegates to vote for Daniel Webster. Another candidate, though, vied for the nomination; Seward pushed General Winfield Scott for the presidential nominee. Ballot after ballot, day after day, the Whigs met, bargained, argued, and voted again. On the fifty-third ballot, they nominated Scott as their candidate with William Graham, Fillmore's secretary of the navy, his running mate. Party members throughout the nation lamented the ticket and believed they were simply handing the election to the Democrats and Franklin Pierce. A New York newspaper said what many thought, "The election will show that the [Whig] party will no longer have a show of existence."[11] The words were true, for this was the final presidential election for the Whigs; four years later a new party would replace it, the Republican Party.

While president, all four members of the Fillmore family resided at the White House. The First Lady helped her husband order books (including two copies of the newly published *Uncle Tom's Cabin*) and organized the first White House

DID YOU KNOW?

Abigail Fillmore established the first permanent White House library.

UNCLE TOM'S CABIN ★ After visiting Kentucky and living several years across the Ohio River in Cincinnati, Harriet Beecher Stowe wrote *Uncle Tom's Cabin*, which depicted the horrors of slavery in a story of a slave's attempt to escape from her wicked master. The book immediately became a bestseller. Though reviled by southerners, who denounced it as slanderous, this seminal novel is credited with inspiring countless Americans to join the abolitionist movement.

JUN: Whigs nominate General Winfield Scott for president and William Graham for vice president

AUG: Free Soil Party nominates John Hale for president and George Julian for vice president

AUG 3: First rowing match held between Harvard and Yale (Harvard wins)

NOV 2: Democrat Franklin Pierce wins the presidential election

DEC 29: Emma Snodgrass arrested in Boston for wearing pants

DEC 2: Louis Napoleon becomes Napoleon III when he proclaims a second French Empire

DEC 23–29: Taiping Rebellion takes Hanyang and Hankou and begins siege on Wuchang

library, which was established on the second floor in the oval room, above the Blue Room. The first family spent much of their time together listening to daughter Abby play the piano, harp, or guitar, and she often performed at White House functions. Son Millard Powers worked as his father's secretary. All enjoyed the various receptions and dinners held at the White House, and daughter Abby frequently substituted for her mother at these functions. An injury to Mrs. Fillmore's ankle in 1842 had left it weak, making it difficult for her to remain standing long. Still she managed to attend many White House entertainments and dinners.

On March 4, 1853, the Fillmores said goodbye to the White House and attended the inauguration of President Franklin Pierce. The gusty raw March wind bit through the skin, and for Abigail Fillmore, who had not been well, standing in the freezing damp wind only worsened her situation. As soon as possible, the former president and First Lady rode to the Willard Hotel, where she nursed her cold, but was unable to prevent it from developing into pneumonia. For three weeks, the close-knit family could only stand by helplessly while Abigail slipped away. She died on March 30; the following day her family escorted her body to Buffalo, and Millard Fillmore contemplated how to spend his retirement.

> *"It is a national disgrace that our presidents, after having occupied the highest position in the country, should be cast adrift, and, perhaps, be compelled to keep a corner grocery store for subsistence."*
>
> *—Millard Fillmore*

RETIREMENT

For months, Fillmore had fretted about how to fill his retirement years. Should he return to his law practice as his partner Nathan Hall suggested? Become a bank president? Travel? None of his options appealed to him following his wife's death, and though his situation was financially secure, he wanted to do something meaningful. Later he lamented: "It is a national disgrace that our Presidents . . . should be cast adrift, and perhaps be compelled to keep a corner grocery for subsistence. . . . We elect a man to the Presidency, expect him to be honest, to give up a lucrative profession, perhaps, and after we have done with him we let him go into seclusion and perhaps poverty."[12] He recommended Congress appropriate an annual presidential pension of twelve thousand dollars. That idea would not become reality until the retirement of Harry S. Truman a century later.

By the spring of 1854, Fillmore decided the time had arrived for him to make a contribution. He would travel the country and judge its pulse, working to ensure communication remained open as Congress now debated the Kansas–Nebraska Act, which allowed the people of those two territories to vote on whether to allow slavery. This law, in effect, nullified the earlier Missouri Compromise. Fillmore and his entourage toured the upper Midwest and most major cities of the South. He talked to political leaders and came to the conclusion that the idea of political parties representing national interests appeared to be increasingly cast aside in favor of parties supporting sectional priorities. This development alarmed the former president.

Tragedy struck the Fillmore family yet again when daughter Abby died from cholera. Perhaps hoping to escape the memories of home, he undertook a long-awaited trip to Europe. There he visited the pope and met with former president Martin Van Buren in London, where he also was presented to Queen Victoria and her family. Then he continued on to savor the sites of Paris.

While enjoying his European sojourn, he received notice that the pro-nativist/anti-Catholic political party, the Know-Nothings, had nominated him to be their presidential candidate in

1856. The Know-Nothings were strongly opposed to the ever-increasing immigrant population, who were also predominately Catholic. The nativists hid behind secrecy, and when anyone asked them about their activities, members were to reply, "I know nothing." He accepted and returned home in June. Democrat James Buchanan won the election over Republican John C. Frémont, and Fillmore took a very distant third place, winning only the state of Maryland.

On February 10, 1858, Millard Fillmore took Caroline McIntosh, a wealthy widow from Troy, as his second wife. They soon established themselves in a fine mansion on Niagara Square, and their home became the gathering point for society's prime gatherings and meetings. One guest was president-elect Abraham Lincoln en route to Washington, D.C., in February 1861.

Once the Civil War began, Fillmore rallied the people of Buffalo to enlist. He organized and commanded the Union Continentals to function as the city's home guard, which was mainly to act as an escort. Worried by the possibility of British invasion from Canada, the former president flooded Washington with letters reminding them to be vigilant about Buffalo and the northern border. While working on the war effort, he still believed that it could have been avoided. But in a speech early in 1864, he spoke as Lincoln did the following year in his second inaugural speech, of the need to forgive the South and "extending to them every act of clemency and kindness in our power, and by restoring them to all their rights under the Constitution" as the only way that "can ever restore this Union."[13] Later in the year, he believed a change in administration imperative for the nation's future and pledged himself to Democrat and former Union general George B. McClellan. People branded him as a Copperhead (a Confederate sympathizer) for this, and he faced more harassment following Lincoln's assassination. The people of Buffalo draped their doors in black, but not the Fillmore home because they were out of town. Once he returned, it was done, but someone had already covered it in black ink. Nevertheless, when the funeral cortege arrived, Fillmore was the leader of the city's delegation.

During his final years, Fillmore worked with a variety of charitable organizations in Buffalo. He became first chancellor of the University of Buffalo and founded Buffalo General Hospital. Always interested in improving his city, he helped start the Buffalo Fine Arts Academy, Buffalo Historical Society, and also co-founded Buffalo's chapter of the Society for the Prevention of Cruelty to Animals.

On February 13, 1874, Millard suffered a stroke on his left side. He recovered somewhat, but two weeks later another stroke befell him, this time paralyzing his throat, making it nearly impossible for him to swallow. He became unconscious the night of March 8 and died soon after. He was buried beside his first wife in Forest Lawn Cemetery in Buffalo. His son survived him, but never married, so there are no descendants. Caroline McIntosh Fillmore continued living in their mansion and survived her husband by seven years.

ENDNOTES

1 Robert J. Rayback, *Millard Fillmore, Biography of a President*, East Aurora, NY: Henry J. Stewart, Inc., 1972, pp. 13-14.

2 Ibid, p. 135.

3 Robert J. Scarry, *Millard Fillmore*, Jefferson, NC: McFarland & Co., Inc., Publishers, 2001, p. 83.

4 Ibid, p. 86.

5 Rayback, p. 162.

6 Ibid, p. 237.

7 Ibid, p. 239.

8 Ibid, p. 241.

9 Ibid, p. 271.

10 Scarry, p. 214.

11 Rayback, p. 362.

12 Ibid, p. 416.

13 Ibid, p. 428.

Franklin Pierce

★ ★ ★ FOURTEENTH PRESIDENT ★ ★ ★

LIFE SPAN

- Born: November 23, 1804, in Hillsborough (Hillsboro), New Hampshire
- Died: October 8, 1869, at Concord, New Hampshire

NICKNAME

- Young Hickory of the Granite Hills

RELIGION

- Episcopalian

HIGHER EDUCATION

- Bowdoin College, 1824

PROFESSION

- Lawyer

FAMILY

- Father: **Benjamin Pierce** (1757–1839)
- Mother: **Anna Kendrick Pierce** (1768–1838)
- Wife: **Jane Means Appleton Pierce** (1806–1863); wed on November 19, 1834, in Amherst, New Hampshire
- Children: **Franklin** (1836); **Frank Robert** (1839–1843); **Benjamin** (1841–1853)

MILITARY SERVICE

- Mexican War: enlisted as a private in New Hampshire volunteers, but commissioned as a colonel in regular army in February 1847, then promoted to major general. Resigned commission in 1848

POLITICAL LIFE

- New Hampshire legislature (1829–1833); Speaker (1831–1832)
- US representative (1833–1837)
- US senator (1837–1842)

PRESIDENCY

- One term: March 4, 1853–March 4, 1857
- Democrat
- Reason for leaving office: not nominated for second term
- Vice president: **William Rufus De Vane King** (1853); died before serving; position remained vacant

ELECTION OF 1852

- Electoral vote: **Pierce** 254; **Winfield Scott** 42
- Popular vote: **Pierce** 1,601,274; **Scott** 1,386,580

CABINET

SECRETARY OF STATE
William L. Marcy (1853–1857)

SECRETARY OF THE TREASURY
James Guthrie (1853–1857)

SECRETARY OF WAR
Jefferson Davis (1853–1857)

ATTORNEY GENERAL
Caleb Cushing (1853–1857)

SECRETARY OF THE NAVY
James C. Dobbin (1853–1857)

POSTMASTER GENERAL
James Campbell (1853–1857)

SECRETARY OF THE INTERIOR
Robert McClelland (1853–1857)

Franklin Pierce was the second "dark horse" candidate to win the presidency. In contrast to the first, James K. Polk, who entered office knowing his precise objectives, Pierce entered office less sure of himself, which allowed others the opportunity to sway his opinion regarding the controversial issues facing the nation in the days before the Civil War. Although he hoped to avoid war, by signing the Kansas-Nebraska Act, Franklin Pierce moved the country on an accelerated pace toward it.

EARLY LIFE

Benjamin Pierce, father to the president, was descended from early Massachusetts settlers. He later described how he was plowing a field when he heard of the fighting at Lexington and Concord, so he stopped the team, grabbed his gun, and started walking toward the Boston area. He served as a militia commander throughout the Revolution. Afterward, he moved his family to New Hampshire, where his son Franklin was born on November 23, 1804, to Benjamin's second wife, Ann Kendrick. (They had seven children who survived to maturity.)

Franklin attended school in his hometown of Hillsborough and was a fine student. He continued his education in nearby academies at Hancock and Francestown, New Hampshire, then in 1820 entered Bowdoin College in Maine. He did very little during his first two years—including attending class—and he dropped to the bottom of his class. He did, however, find time to make friends, including Nathaniel Hawthorne and Henry Wadsworth Longfellow. Finally his grades improved, and he completed his liberal arts curriculum while remaining active in other activities, including serving as captain of the military company that the young men formed on campus. Franklin graduated in July 1824, but without his father's company, since the elder Pierce was off to Portsmouth to meet Lafayette on his grand tour of the country.

That fall, Franklin began studying law while serving as the postmaster of Hillsborough, a job which his father had but was happy to hand over to his son. From this vantage point, he watched with extreme dismay the election of John Quincy Adams. By now, Pierce considered himself a solid Democrat in the mold of Jefferson and Jackson, and was horrified by the corruption of the 1824 presidential election.

POLITICAL CAREER

In 1825, Franklin moved to Portsmouth to continue studying law under the supervision of Levi Woodbury, who soon was elected senator. In his quest to further his legal education, Franklin relocated to Northampton, Massachusetts, and then returned to Hillsborough where, in September 1827, he was admitted to the bar. Earlier that year, Benjamin Pierce was elected governor. During this time, son Franklin gained his first political experience when he was elected as the moderator of the Hillsborough Convention, an annual gathering of eligible voters to vote for governor, the legislature, and to tend to local matters. For six years, Franklin Pierce served in this significant local role.

Pierce took his first steps as a lawyer, and his friend Nathaniel Hawthorne later recorded, "Pierce's distinction at the bar . . . did not immediately follow; nor did he acquire what we may designate as positive eminence until some years after this period."[1] He soon found success in the political arena when, at the age of twenty-four, he was elected to the New Hampshire legislature. By now Andrew Jackson had been elected president. The Democratic Party was likewise

NATIONAL EVENTS

Yellow fever kills nearly 8,000 in New Orleans

Elizabeth Jennings, an African American woman in New York, is ordered off a public streetcar; she hires an attorney, future president Chester A. Arthur, and sues; they win

JAN 6: Train wreck involving Pierce family near Andover, Massachusetts; son Ben is killed

FEB 21: Congress passes Coinage Act

1853

WORLD EVENTS

Taiping Rebellion continues in China (internal strife partly due to disagreement about western influences)

Brazilian slave woman discovers largest diamond (262 carats) ever found in that country

JAN 29: Napoleon III marries the Spanish Countess Eugènie at the Tuileries

MAR 6: In Venice, Giuseppe Verdi's opera *La Traviata* premieres

JUL 8: Arrival in Edo (Tokyo) Bay of fleet of ships under American Commodore Matthew Perry on orders from President Fillmore

strengthened in New Hampshire, and Pierce benefited as well. In 1831 and 1832, he was elected speaker. He was hailed by his townsmen, and the local newspaper reported:

> *Frank Pierce is the most popular man of his age that I know of in NH . . . he has a handsome person, bland and agreeable manners, a prompt and off-hand manner of saying and doing things, and talents competent to sustain himself in any station.*[2]

Franklin's political future outpaced his legal career when the following year he was elected to the US House of Representatives. He found himself working with fellow Jacksonians, toiling to ensure that the president's agenda passed, including "killing" the national bank.

Hoping now to find domestic happiness, as he found himself lonely and often turning to alcohol to fight off depression and boredom, he decided to wed. The lady was Jane Appleton of Amherst, New Hampshire, who was a shy, introverted young lady and also prone to depression. Their marriage was often strained and, in addition to the usual travails of marriage, they endured extraordinary tragedy. The Pierces began their married life on November 19, 1834, and although they had three sons, none lived to adulthood—two died early from disease and one perished during a train derailment. Jane Pierce never enjoyed the rough world of politics and would beg her husband to end his career. She later would blame his insistence to continue in politics as the reason for the greatest loss of her life.

Once James K. Polk became Speaker of the House, Pierce's future brightened as well. Polk placed Pierce on select committees including the Judiciary, but the main topic of debate was slavery. By now, Pierce's patience was exhausted by what he termed "abolitionist Fanatics," and he approved of the House's gag rule preventing abolitionist petitions from being read before the House. True to Jackson's policies, Pierce voted against internal improvements and was pleased to become friends with southerner and fellow congressman Jefferson Davis.

When not attending Congress, Pierce returned home to see his wife and continue his law practice. In Hillsborough, he became reacquainted with a promising young man named Albert Baker, who studied law under Franklin. Baker's younger sister Mary also met Franklin and was impressed by the learning of both men. Owing to her ill health, Mary had not attended school but had a keen mind. She later became known as Mary Baker Eddy, the founder of the Christian Scientist church.

In 1837, Franklin Pierce was elected to the US Senate and became its youngest member at the age of thirty-two. Here he caught the attention of many southern senators who were pleased by the northerner's understanding of the delicate slavery issue. In fact, he voted against any attempts to limit slavery anywhere in the United States. Pierce supported President Van Buren's legislative program and actively worked in New Hampshire toward his reelection. But when this was unsuccessful, and Whigs became the majority party in the Senate, Pierce decided to heed his wife's pleas and go home, which was now Concord, New Hampshire. Another magnet drawing him home was their two sons, Frank and Benjamin. So in early 1842, Pierce resigned his seat and resumed his law practice. Tragically, both boys grew gravely ill the following year from typhus,

DID YOU KNOW?

Pierce was the first president to be born in the nineteenth century.

The Pierces were the first family to enjoy hot and cold running water in the family bathroom on the second floor of the White House.

The Pierce family had the first Christmas tree in the White House.

MAR 2: Washington Territory is organized after separating from Oregon Territory

MAR 4: Franklin Pierce becomes the 14th president

APR 18: Vice President William R. King dies

JUL 14: Pierce opens World's Fair in New York

AUG 24: Chef George Crum creates the potato chip at a Saratoga Springs, New York, restaurant

AUG 8: Russian fleet arrives in Nagasaki, Japan, to attempt to open trade talks

to open relations with Japanese

OCT 5: Crimean War officially begins when Ottoman Empire declares war on Russia

NOV 15: Maria II of Portugal succeeded by her son Pedro

NOV 30: Battle of Sinop: Russian fleet destroys Turkish fleet

DID YOU KNOW?

Fort Pierce, Florida, is named after Pierce's older brother Benjamin Kendrick Pierce (1790–1850), a lieutenant colonel in the US Army.

and four-year-old Frank died. The Pierces had already experienced sorrow upon the death of their first son at the age of only three days. Pierce wrote himself an admonishment: "We were living for our children. . . . We should have lived for God and have left the dear ones to the care of Him who is alone able to take care of them and us."[3] The Pierces would now center their world on their sole son, two-year-old Benjamin, known affectionately as "Bennie."

At about this time, Franklin became involved in the temperance movement. He worked with others in the crusade to make Concord a dry town, like the villages surrounding it. In the process, some of his adversaries charged that Pierce was hypocritical, claiming that he often drank. His stand also created problems within his own party. Nevertheless, Pierce was still the Democratic state chairman in 1844 when he actively campaigned for former colleague James K. Polk in his presidential bid. Once Polk won, Pierce reaped the benefit by being appointed district attorney for New Hampshire.

Mid-May 1846 brought stories of Americans dying at the hands of Mexican soldiers on American soil. By the end of the month, the declaration of war was announced, and volunteers began enlisting to fight; among them was Franklin Pierce. He, however, did not march off immediately, but remained in New Hampshire to monitor Democratic Party business, which was not going well. Whigs and Free Soilers were making inroads on the state's political landscape, including the state house, where Democrats were no longer in control. In August, Polk offered him the post of attorney general, but sensitive to his wife's dislike of Washington, Pierce refused the post.

GENERAL PIERCE

On February 15, 1847, Franklin Pierce received a colonel's commission for one of ten infantry regiments. He accepted the post, but admitted in his acceptance letter that he had yet to tell his wife. When he finally took his leave, he wrote Jane that his heart would be with her and Bennie "wherever duty may lead my steps."[4] With the sword that the ladies of Concord had presented him and the black horse given by fellow Democrats, Franklin Pierce sailed toward Veracruz, and what he hoped would be glory.

By late June, now General Pierce and his 2,500 men landed in Mexico, where many immediately fell victim to the unaccustomed heat. It would be nearly six weeks before his troops began their march toward the interior of the enemy's country. Along the way, they occasionally encountered small skirmishes, in which Pierce was pleased to report of the fine conduct of his men. After a 150-mile march that took three weeks, they joined with others en route to Mexico City.

In August, Pierce was leading his men in battle at the Battle of Contreras when his horse reared. Pierce slammed hard against the pommel of the saddle, and then fell to the ground, wrenching his knee. The intense pain prompted Pierce to faint. A fellow officer yelled that he was a "damned coward," a characterization that would taint Pierce for the rest of his political career. He regained consciousness, received some first aid, and was helped back into his saddle. He then rode back to the field and continued there late into the night.

After scarcely any sleep and spending a day in agonizing pain, he reported to General Winfield Scott, who was shocked at the commander's woebegone appearance and decided to send him behind the lines for rest. Pierce protested, "For

NATIONAL EVENTS

DEC 30: US and Mexico sign Gadsden Purchase granting the Americans a tract of land (southern Arizona and New Mexico) to build a railroad; US pays $10 million

Samuel Maverick, a Texas cattleman, is told to brand his cattle; the word "maverick" is then used to label an animal that has not been branded or a politician who does not do what is expected

Godfrey Keebler begins making cookies at a Philadelphia bakery

1854

WORLD EVENTS

MAR 27: Crimean War: Great Britain declares war on Russia

MAR 28: France declares war on Russia

AUG 26: British explorer Elisha Kent Kane passes 80° North, the closest to the North Pole yet reached

God's sake, General, this is the last great battle, and I must lead my brigade."[5] Scott relented and Pierce soon rejoined his men, but on the uneven terrain, he had to dismount, and while leading them against enemy fire, he twisted his injured knee again, causing him to faint once more. When he regained consciousness, he warned his men against trying to move him to safety. Better to be shot than remembered as a coward, so he stayed in the midst of the battlefield, which his officers allowed to dissolve into chaos as they lost control. His men fled.

One army officer who was impressed by Pierce was Lieutenant Ulysses S. Grant, who years later wrote of General Pierce:

> *This circumstance [fainting] gave rise to exceedingly unfair and unjust criticisms of him when he became a candidate for the Presidency. Whatever General Pierce's qualifications may have been for the Presidency, he was a gentleman and a man of courage. I was not a supporter of him politically, but I knew him more intimately than I did any other of the volunteer generals.*[6]

General Scott allowed Pierce another opportunity to honor himself by serving with two others to draft surrender terms for Santa Anna rather than have the Americans march on Mexico City. The armistice failed, but not before dragging Pierce's reputation further into the mud as word of his ignominious battlefield behavior quickly traveled through camp. Trying to end the war seemed to many another act of cowardice, further defiling his name.

When Americans, including Pierce's Ninth Regiment, stormed the heights of Chapultepec, a castle-fort protecting Mexico City from the west, he would not accompany them. This time their commander had fallen victim to dysentery and lay sick in bed. Once Santa Anna's army surrendered, General Pierce longed to return home. The army, however, insisted he remain, for he became commander of the Third Division while General Gideon Pillow convalesced from a wound to his left ankle. Finally, on December 8, Winfield Scott treated him to a farewell dinner, and by January he returned safely home to the bosom of friends and family in Concord.

RETURN TO POLITICS

Now with his military career behind him, Pierce quickly resumed his civilian life. His earlier legal partnership had dissolved, but he soon had another partner, and their practice flourished. Pierce was a master at pleading a case to the jury while keeping the facts of the case simple for their consideration. Such a successful practice often led him to work long hours, which often prompted son Bennie to go fetch his father home.

Pierce also renewed his command of New Hampshire's Democratic Party; moreover, he and some other key state Democrats became known as the Concord Clique, or the Regency. They worked to regain the governorship, although Pierce turned down the chance to run for it himself. Democrats could not compete against war hero Zachary Taylor in the 1848 presidential election, but they regained hopes for victory when Taylor died in 1850. Maybe they could regain the White House in 1852 if they could only find the right candidate.

PRESIDENTIAL CANDIDATE

When the Democrats met in Baltimore in June 1852, they had four frontrunner potential nomi-

SUPREME COURT APPOINTMENTS
★★★★★★★★★★

John A. Campbell, 1853

MAR 31: Treaty of Kanagawa signed between US and Japan

MAY 26: Boston mob attempts to rescue fugitive slave Anthony Burns by attacking the federal courthouse, but they are unsuccessful

MAY 30: Kansas-Nebraska Act becomes law

JUN 10: First class of US Naval Academy graduates at Annapolis, Maryland

JUL 6: First convention of newly formed Republican Party is held in Wisconsin

JUL 13: Khedive Abbas I of Egypt assassinated

SEP 20: Battle of the Alma: British-French alliance wins first battle of Crimean War

OCT 18: Ostend Manifesto (created in Belgium) declares US needs to annex Cuba, and fight Spain for it if necessary

OCT 21: British nurse Florence Nightingale leaves with more than 30 nurses for Crimea

OCT 25: Battle of Balaclava

STATE OF THE UNION

★★★★★★★★★★

US POPULATION IN 1853
23,191,876

NATIONAL DEBT IN 1857
$28,699,832

PRESIDENT'S SALARY
$25,000/year

NUMBER OF STATES IN 1857
31

nees: Lewis Cass of Michigan, Stephen Douglas of Illinois, James Buchanan of Pennsylvania, and William Marcy of New York. Each man represented regional and business interests, and those sections vied against each other as delegates voted repeatedly, with no candidate receiving a decided majority. Pierce's avowed support of the Compromise of 1850, including the Fugitive Slave Law (p. 150), appealed to the southerners within the party; consequently, on the thirty-fifth ballot, the Virginia delegation placed Pierce's name before the convention. Having a northerner who had repeatedly declared himself as pro-slavery seemed a winning combination for the delegates, and they hoped, the nation. So on the forty-ninth ballot, Franklin Pierce was unanimously elected the Democratic presidential candidate, and William King of Alabama was chosen as his running mate. Pierce had attended the convention earlier but then left for Boston. He and his wife were taking a carriage ride when the news was shouted that he was the nominee; Jane Pierce promptly fainted.

Democrats now gleefully named Pierce as "Young Hickory of the Granite Hills," hoping the reference to Andrew Jackson would win votes. The candidate asked old friend Nathaniel Hawthorne to pen a biography of him, which was done, but not apparently to Hawthorne's total satisfaction. Hawthorne was rewarded with the post of consul in Liverpool—a job he hated although it allowed him ample time to write.

General Winfield Scott won the Whig nomination as an anti-slavery candidate, yet their platform endorsed the Compromise of 1850, as well as the Fugitive Slave Law, much to the horror of many of its members. Still, they remained loyal to their candidate, hoping that he would stay true to his principles once he became president. Whigs portrayed Pierce as a drunk and a coward in stark contrast to the courageous and extensive military service of Scott. The Democrats countered with calling Scott a drunk and pro-Catholic because his daughter had become a nun. Their slogan was, "We Polked you in 1844; we shall Pierce you in 1852!" Indeed they did, for Franklin Pierce captured 51 percent of the popular vote to Scott's 44 percent. There were probably no people sorrier for the victory than Jane and son Bennie Pierce.

Earlier when eleven-year-old Bennie heard of his father's candidacy, he had written his mother, "I hope he won't be elected for I should not like to be at Washington and I know you would not either."[7] Little would the eleven-year-old boy know that he need not worry, for he would not live to see his father become president. In January 1853, the three Pierces were traveling by train from Andover, Massachusetts, to Concord. Soon after departure, the train derailed, hurling the passenger car down an embankment. Only one fatality occurred—Bennie Pierce. Added to the loss for his parents were the horrific memories of seeing his death before their eyes. Jane Pierce, never a stable woman emotionally under the best of circumstances, now sunk under the weight of grief. She insisted that God had caused the death of their beloved son to prevent any distractions for Franklin as president. Her husband's political ambition had taken their son's life. Neither parent would ever be the same.

PRESIDENT PIERCE

After taking the oath of office, President Franklin Pierce delivered his inaugural address from memory. In it he proclaimed his belief about slavery:

I believe that involuntary servitude, as it exists in different States of this Confederacy, is

NATIONAL EVENTS

Poet Walt Whitman publishes his book of poems, *Leaves of Grass*

Actress Laura Keene opens her own theater in New York (she will be the star of the play that Lincoln sees on the night of his assassination)

Frederick Douglass publishes his autobiography, *My Bondage and My Freedom*

German immigrant Frederick Miller begins brewing his own beer in Milwaukee

1855

WORLD EVENTS

DEC 9: Alfred Tennyson publishes "Charge of the Light Brigade" about events in October at the Battle of Balaclava

JAN 1: The city of Ottawa, Ontario is incorporated

JAN 23: Earthquake with a magnitude of 8.1 strikes Wairarapa, New Zealand

JAN 27: First railway opens in Panama connecting Pacific and Atlantic Oceans

FEB 5: Lord Palmerston becomes Prime Minister of United Kingdom

recognized by the Constitution. I believe that it stands like any other admitted right, and that the States where it exists are entitled to efficient remedies to enforce the constitutional provisions. I hold that the laws of 1850, commonly called the "compromise measures," are strictly constitutional and to be unhesitatingly carried into effect.

He and his newly formed cabinet now began the business of governing the country. The cabinet was a mix of northerners and southerners, but the man Pierce desired most to serve, Jefferson Davis, required much persuasion but finally consented to become secretary of war and the president's chief advisor. During his term, Pierce relied on Davis to such an extent that he feared criticism, so sometimes he sneaked out at night to confer with Davis at his home.

One area of concern was restructuring and modernizing the army. Davis supervised these plans, and he was so successful in accomplishing these goals that his improvements would later be a factor in the Confederacy's defeat under his presidency. Davis also pushed for a transcontinental railroad and supervised surveying expeditions to map possible routes. Toward this aim, in 1853, the United States purchased a strip of land along southern New Mexico and Arizona from Mexico for ten million dollars for a southern rail line. The Gadsden Purchase completed the outline of the continental United States. Concerned about the arid conditions of the southwest, Davis also devised an unusual experiment—importing thirty-three camels to aid southwestern cavalry units. Deserts needed desert animals he reasoned, but US soldiers quickly learned that riding camels was no easy task, and the men soon returned to using horses and mules.

KNOW-NOTHING PARTY ★ The Know-Nothing Party (so called because its members were to keep their beliefs private—when asked to explain their party, they replied "I know nothing") in response to fear of waves of immigrants entering the nation, many of whom were Catholic. Many Americans feared these new arrivals would be more loyal to the pope than to the United States. Others worried that the immigrants would take away American jobs, so party membership consisted mainly of the working class of the North. In 1854, the Know-Nothings gained control of the Massachusetts legislature. They ran former president Millard Fillmore as their presidential candidate in 1856, and he captured about 9 percent of the votes. Still, when the party refused to take a stand on slavery, many abandoned the Know-Nothings and joined the new Republican Party instead. The Know-Nothings died out by the early 1860s.

The transcontinental railroad presented yet another challenge to the Pierce administration when Senator Stephen Douglas of Illinois proposed the Kansas-Nebraska Act. Arguing that a railroad's success depended upon business provided by settlers along its lines, Douglas proposed organizing the lands into the territory of Nebraska and allowing popular sovereignty to determine the slavery question. Southerners sensed change in the political winds and jumped at the chance to repeal the Missouri Compromise with its prohibition against slavery north of the 36°30' latitude. No better time, they reasoned, for such a measure than when a fellow Democrat sat in the White House. After initial misgivings about the act, Pierce changed his

Elmira Female College established as the first higher institution of learning for women

John Bartlett publishes the first edition of *Familiar Quotations*

JAN 10: US citizenship laws amended to include children born to US citizens abroad

JAN 23: First bridge opens across the Mississippi River in present-day Minneapolis

MAR 3: Congress appropriates $30,000 to create a camel corps on recommendation of Secretary of War Jefferson Davis

FEB 11: Kassa Hailu is crowned Tewodros II, Emperor of Ethiopia

MAR 2: Czar Nicholas I of Russia dies; he is succeeded by his son Aleksandr II

MAR 30: Treaty of Peshawar signed, creating an Anglo-Afghan alliance against Persia

MAY 15: Great Gold Robbery of 1855 pulled off by perpetrators who stole gold bars and coins during a train transfer from London to Paris; they were never apprehended

TREATY OF KANAGAWA ★ The Treaty of Kanagawa was signed on March 31, 1854, between Commodore Matthew Perry and the Japanese, allowing the United States to use the island nation as a coal refueling stop, as well as provide other supplies as necessary in two ports. The Japanese also promised favorable treatment toward any shipwrecked American crews or those needing help with repairs. Trading rights would be granted in a treaty a few years later.

mind and then worked steadily to ensure Democratic support in Congress. Ironically, he had stated in his inaugural speech, "I fervently hope that the question is at rest, and that no sectional or ambitious or fanatical excitement may again threaten." To the dismay of both sides, "fanatical excitement" was just beginning with the stroke of Pierce's pen signing the Kansas-Nebraska Act into law.

Irate over repeal of the Missouri Compromise, abolitionists now pledged to ignore the Fugitive Slave Act. The day after the Kansas-Nebraska Act became law, a Boston mob attempted to rescue fugitive slave Anthony Burns from a courthouse. He was returned to his master, but it took the US Army, Marines, and twenty-two companies of state militia to accomplish it. No other runaway slaves would be returned from Massachusetts.

Nowhere was violence more prevalent than in the newly formed Kansas territory. Both sides assumed Nebraska would be a free territory, but Kansas was not a foregone conclusion, not with slave-holding Missouri as its next-door neighbor. Pro- and anti-slavery forces now sprang into action, vying to fill the territory and the ballot box. Missourians traversed the line and committed voter fraud to ensure Kansas would not become a refuge for their runaway slaves. Once the votes were counted, it was official— Kansas was to be a slave territory, thanks in large part, to their neighbors' illegal votes. Two state governments were created, and Pierce supported the pro-slavery group, to the dismay of many. Political disagreement very quickly devolved into war, and "bleeding Kansas" became the battleground, a precursor to the Civil War. Violence worsened with the arrival from North Elba, New York, of abolitionist John Brown and his sons when they killed five pro-slavery men, then mutilated their bodies. This action only led to increased attacks on both sides of the state line, as Missouri "border ruffians" fought Kansas "jayhawkers." The president watched helplessly from Washington, and his inability to handle the situation in Kansas effectively would be a key factor in Pierce's political decline.

DID YOU KNOW?

Pierce is the only president to keep his cabinet intact for his entire term.

Pierce is the only elected president not nominated by his party for reelection.

FOREIGN POLICY

During the Fillmore administration, Commodore Matthew Perry had been tasked with journeying to Japan on a mission of opening trade with the "hermit kingdom." He arrived there with his four warships in July 1853, then returned seven months later with seven warships. The two countries exchanged gifts, including the Americans giving a model steam locomotive and the Japanese sending two hundred sacks of rice to Pierce. (The rice, however, was depleted of its germinal properties, so it could not be planted.) Reluctantly, the Japanese agreed to open the door of trade—but only a crack, with two of its smaller ports, Shimoda and Hakodate. Still, it was the beginning of what would become a vital commercial relationship.

While improving trade in Asia, Pierce kept his eye closer to home—Cuba. Many a president discussed the possibility of annexing Cuba, for

NATIONAL EVENTS

MAR 3: Ostend Manifesto is published in the US

MAR 30: First election in Kansas territory, with pro-slavery outcome, partly owing to neighboring Missourians crossing the border to vote

JUN 18: Opening of Sault Ste. Marie shipping canal to link Lakes Huron and Superior

SEP 3: American William Walter tries to set up his own state in Mexico

NOV–DEC: Wakarusa War begins in Kansas between pro- and anti-slavery forces

WORLD EVENTS

JUN 29: London's *Daily Telegraph* begins publication

SEP 11: Russian forces abandon Sevastopol

NOV 17: Traveling throughout Africa, Scottish missionary and explorer David Livingstone becomes first European to see Victoria Falls, which he names in honor of his queen

DEC 22: Battle of Santomé; 3,000 Dominicans defeat Haitian force 10 times larger

its location made it quite desirable, especially to southerners who viewed it as another slave territory. Spain, however, still had strong ties to the island and intended to keep it. After an American ship was seized off the Cuban coast, tension between Spain and the United States intensified, but Spain released the ship and its crew and paid damages. War talk in the United States was buoyed by Pierce, but northerners grew more outspoken against such a ploy to gain more slave territory by forcibly obtaining Cuba from Spain. Some in the government argued they wanted to help the slaves of Cuba, while others nervously worried over a possible slave revolt there that could easily spread to American shores. American ambassador to Great Britain, James Buchanan, met with American envoys to Spain and France in the summer of 1854 in Ostend, Belgium, to determine their recommendations regarding Cuba. They wrote that if Spain refused to sell the island, "We shall be justified in wresting it from Spain if we possess the power."[8] The document became known as the Ostend Manifesto and was leaked to the press, causing great consternation in Congress and for the president. Secretary of State William Marcy immediately began damage control, and reassured the world that the United States was not contemplating war with Spain, although it would definitely be interested in acquiring Cuba. Said March, "We cannot afford to get it by robbery or theft."[9]

SUMNER-BROOKS EPISODE ★ In May 1856, Senator Charles Sumner of Massachusetts, a staunch abolitionist, berated southerners in a lengthy speech and singled out his colleague, Senator Andrew Butler of South Carolina, for particular criticism. Butler was not in attendance that day, but his nephew, Congressman Preston Brooks, decided to take action. Brooks entered the Senate chamber on May 22, and began beating Sumner unmercifully with his cane, leaving him unconscious. Brooks resigned, but was soon reelected and considered a hero by many southerners, who enthusiastically sent him canes. Sumner, too, won acclaim for having suffered for the cause of abolitionism.

ELECTION OF 1856

By the time of the presidential election of 1856, there were multiple political parties. The Democrats remained the largest, but some of their membership in the North and West grew so dissatisfied after the Kansas-Nebraska Act that they joined with Free Soilers in creating the Republican Party. A much smaller party was the Know-Nothings, who exploited fears of increasing numbers of immigrants and Catholics in the nation. By 1856, the Whig party had virtually disappeared; its members joined one of the other parties. Each group represented a sliver of society, but whether any one group could manage to win a majority remained to be seen.

While Democrats debated each other on the issues, they agreed on one matter—nominate anyone but Pierce! In fact, one Democrat wrote of the president, "He has no real strength but there is much weakness in him *personally*. . . . There is undoubtedly an *active* opposition to Pierce in our ranks which we are bound to respect."[10] Delegates concurred, and the Democratic convention nominated James Buchanan as its presidential candidate for 1856. Pierce had hoped he could win the nomination, but gracefully accepted the decision.

Undoubtedly Jane Pierce heard the news with happiness, since she had not experienced that

I.M. Singer Company offers the first trade-in allowance for sewing machines	Gunsmiths Horace Smith and Daniel Wesson design a revolver	Margaret Schurz opens America's first kindergarten in Wisconsin	Western Union Telegraph begins	FEB 18: Know-Nothing (American) Party nominates their first presidential candidate, Millard Fillmore
1856				
Balmoral Castle completed in Scotland and will be used by Queen Victoria and her family	Gregor Mendel begins his research on genetics	Neanderthal skull discovered near Dusseldorf, Germany	National Portrait Gallery opens in London	JAN: Britain's Victoria Cross created as an award for valor

DID YOU KNOW?

Pierce had the lowest grade at Bowdoin College at the end of his sophomore year, but after changing his habits, he graduated third in his class, which also included Nathaniel Hawthorne and Henry Wadsworth Longfellow.

emotion during her time in Washington. For the first two years of his term, Jane had remained secluded upstairs in the White House, a victim of intense grief from Bennie's tragic death. Gradually she began attending a few social functions and performing her role as hostess. One guest noted, "Everything in that mansion seems cold and cheerless. I have seen hundreds of log cabins which seemed to contain more happiness."[11] Sadly, Jane Pierce's melancholy would remain with her the rest of her days.

RETIREMENT

On March 4, 1857, Franklin Pierce ceased being America's president, but he and his wife remained in Washington for a few weeks, allowing for winter to pass in New England. Returning home to Concord, however, held little attraction after hearing that plans for a welcome reception were halted by townspeople decrying his administration. They finally did travel to New England and, later that year, sailed to the island of Madeira and then on to Europe. Both hoped that such an extensive trip would improve Jane's spirits, but upon returning home in the summer of 1859, she remained depressed. Although they resumed living in Concord for a time, memories of their sweet son haunted her, so she spent more time with relatives in Andover.

Franklin Pierce deemed Lincoln's election in 1860 unfortunate for the nation, and argued that war was unnecessary. He denounced Lincoln as having "limited ability and narrow intelligence,"[12] and was aghast at the issuance of the Emancipation Proclamation, which he believed was unconstitutional. His last attempt to condemn the Lincoln administration occurred on July 4, 1863, in which he spoke out on this "fearful, fruitless, fatal civil war . . . How futile are all our efforts to maintain the Union by force of arms."[13] In the midst of his speech, however, the crowd's attention drifted from Pierce's words to news fresh from telegraph wires of the Union's grand victory at Gettysburg. The former president had lost his audience and any support the nation might have given him.

Jane Pierce died later that year, and longtime friend Nathaniel Hawthorne came to console Pierce. Then the following year Hawthorne died, but Franklin was not offered the honor of pallbearer because of his unpopularity. Illness plagued him for the next five years, sapping his energies with each new attack. He breathed his last on October 8, 1869, in his Concord, New Hampshire, home. He was buried beside his wife and sons at the Old North Cemetery in Concord.

NATIONAL EVENTS				
MAY 21: Missouri border ruffians attack Lawrence, Kansas, and sack the town	**MAY 22:** Congressman Preston Brooks attacks Senator Charles Sumner in senate chamber and beats him unconscious with a cane	**MAY 24:** Abolitionist John Brown leads a group to attack, kill, and mutilate five pro-slavery men near Pottawatomie Creek in Kansas	**JUN:** Democrats meet in Cincinnati and nominate James Buchanan as president; John C. Breckinridge is his running mate	**JUN:** Republicans nominate John C. Frémont at their convention in Philadelphia; William L. Dayton is the vice presidential nominee

WORLD EVENTS				
MAR 5: Fire destroys London's Covent Garden Theatre, later renamed the Royal Opera House	**MAR 31:** Crimean War ends with signing of Treaty of Paris	**APR 11:** Battle of Rivas: Costa Rica defeats invading Nicaraguans	**APR 21:** Masons march on Melbourne, Australia's Parliament House to push for an eight-hour day	**OCT 8:** Second Opium War begins

> *"We have to maintain inviolate the great doctrine of the inherent right of popular self-government; ... to render cheerful obedience to the laws of the land, to unite in enforcing their execution, and to frown indignantly on all combinations to resist them; ... to uphold the integrity and guard the limitations of our organic law; to preserve sacred from all touch of usurpation, as the very palladium of our political salvation, the reserved rights and powers of the several States and of the people; to cherish with loyal fealty and devoted affection this Union, as the only sure foundation on which the hopes of civil liberty rest..."*
>
> —*Franklin Pierce, December 4, 1854, in his second annual message to the Senate and the House*

ENDNOTES

1 Roy F. Nichols, *Franklin Pierce, Young Hickory of the Granite Hills*, Philadelphia: University of Pennsylvania Press, 1931, p. 36.

2 Ibid, p. 58.

3 Ibid, p. 124.

4 Ibid, p. 149.

5 Ibid, p. 162.

6 Ulysses S. Grant, *Personal Memoirs of Ulysses S. Grant*, vol. I, New York: Charles L. Webster & Co., 1894, p. 89.

7 Ibid, p. 205.

8 Larry Gara, *The Presidency of Franklin Pierce*, Lawrence: University Press of Kansas, 1991, p. 153.

9 Ibid, p. 154.

10 Nichols, p. 454

11 Ibid, p. 313.

12 Ibid, p. 521.

13 Ibid, p. 522.

JUL 17: "Great Train Wreck of 1856" occurs in Pennsylvania, killing about 60 and injuring 100

AUG 18: Congress authorizes US to annex any small island unclaimed by other governments

NOV 4: James Buchanan elected as 15th president

NOV 1: War declared between Great Britain and Persia

JAMES BUCHANAN

★ ★ ★ FIFTEENTH PRESIDENT ★ ★ ★

LIFE SPAN
- Born: April 23, 1791, at Cove Gap, (near Mercersburg) Pennsylvania
- Died: June 1, 1868, in Lancaster, Pennsylvania

NICKNAME
- Old Buck

RELIGION
- Presbyterian

HIGHER EDUCATION
- Dickinson College, 1808

PROFESSION
- Lawyer

MILITARY SERVICE
- War of 1812, volunteered with Pennsylvania dragoons

FAMILY
- Father: **James Buchanan, Sr.** (ca. 1761–1821)
- Mother: **Elizabeth Speer Buchanan** (1767–1833)
- Wife: None

POLITICAL LIFE
- Pennsylvania House of Representatives (1815–1816)
- US representative (1821–1831)
- Minister to Russia (1832–1833)
- US senator (1834–1845)
- Secretary of state (1845–1849)
- Minister to Great Britain (1853–1856)

PRESIDENCY
- One term: March 4, 1857–March 4, 1861
- Democrat
- Reason for leaving office: did not win party's nomination
- Vice president: **John C. Breckinridge** (1857–1861)

ELECTION OF 1856
- Electoral vote:
  Buchanan 174;
  John C. Frémont 114;
  Fillmore 8
- Popular vote:
  Buchanan 1,832,955;
  John C. Frémont 1,339,932;
  Fillmore 871,731

CABINET
★★★★★★★★★★

SECRETARY OF STATE
Lewis Cass (1857–1860)

Jeremiah S. Black (1860–1861)

SECRETARY OF THE TREASURY
Howell Cobb (1857–1860)

Philip F. Thomas (1860–1861)

John A. Dix (Jan.–March 1861)

SECRETARY OF WAR
John B. Floyd (1857–1860)

Joseph Holt (Jan.–March 1861)

ATTORNEY GENERAL
Jeremiah S. Black (1857–1860)

Edwin M. Stanton (1860–1861)

Becoming president in the bleak days leading up to the Civil War could not have been an easy task. James Buchanan's ambition had led him to this high office, and once there he found himself ill-equipped to face the crisis that enveloped the country by the end of his term; little wonder that his name usually ranks near or at the bottom of any list of presidents.

EARLY LIFE

James Buchanan was born in a log cabin on April 23, 1791, to Scotch-Irish immigrant parents James and Elizabeth Speer Buchanan, who were living in southern Pennsylvania. When young James was five years of age, they moved to nearby Mercersburg, where his father prospered as a merchant. The family grew to eight children over the years, with James the eldest. He attended local schools to study the classics, then entered Dickinson College as a junior at sixteen and finished college in two years. His collegiate career might easily have been cut short by the hijinks in which he and some classmates participated during his first year, and he later recalled, if not for his father's influence, "I would have been expelled from college."[1] Young James pledged to improve his conduct, but apparently committed more transgressions his last year, provoking the college to refuse to grant him any honors. He still received his degree, and by the end of 1809, he was in Lancaster studying law. Three years later he was admitted to the Pennsylvania bar.

EARLY CAREER

The War of 1812 erupted just as Buchanan began his legal career. Although he opposed the war in the beginning, his beliefs changed once news of the British burning of Washington, D.C., reached Lancaster. He volunteered to join a company marching to defend Baltimore. Once that was accomplished, he returned home with military service now on his record.

Using this service, albeit short-lived, to his advantage, Buchanan won election to the state legislature as a Federalist. After serving two terms there, he attempted to make the jump into national politics and ran unsuccessfully for a congressional seat. During this time, he also found the opportunity to court a wealthy young lady, Ann Coleman. Her family disapproved of the young attorney, believing him to be a fortune hunter, and they encouraged Ann to break the engagement. She did, and apparently died soon after, very possibly by her own hand, which prompted the family to ban Buchanan from attending her funeral. Saddened by her death, James wrote, "I have lost the only earthly object of my affections. . . . I feel that my happiness will be buried with her in the grave."[2] His name would never again be linked seriously with another woman.

After failing his first bid for Congress, Buchanan returned to Lancaster and his flourishing law practice. This success made him a fairly wealthy gentleman, but the desire to run for office still remained, so in 1820, he ran again and this time won. Although originally running as a Federalist, Buchanan had to change his allegiance, since his party died during this era. He switched to the hero of the day—Andrew Jackson—and became a lifelong Democrat.

CONGRESS

During his decade in Congress, Buchanan tended to be a fiscal moderate. He supported the tariff, but in moderation, and his views tended to side with southerners rather than his northern colleagues. He disavowed slavery, yet strongly believed that people

NATIONAL EVENTS

New Yorkers begin buying the first commercially produced toilet paper

FEB 21: Congress outlaws the use of foreign currency as legal tender in the US

MAR 4: James Buchanan becomes the 15th president

MAR 6: US Supreme Court delivers its decision in *Dred Scott v. Sanford*

MAR 23: First Otis elevator installed in a New York City building on Broadway

1857

WORLD EVENTS

Work begins in London to dig a tunnel under the city for a subway system

Giuseppi Garibaldi starts the Italian National Association as a first step toward the unification of Italy

MAR 21: Major earthquake hits Edo (Tokyo) Japan and kills more than 100,000 people

APR 12: Publication of *Madame Bovary*, by French author Gustave Flaubert

MAY 10: Sepoy Rebellion begins in India against control by the British East India Company

should have the right to continue that institution, and desperately hoped that any differences on the issue could be addressed peacefully.

In Congress, Buchanan increasingly enjoyed more power and influence, which also made him a target. Speaker of the House Henry Clay disliked him, probably owing to his inserting himself into the political turmoil surrounding the election of 1824. When the election went to the House of Representatives to determine the president between Jackson and John Quincy Adams, Buchanan had visited Jackson and implied that Clay could be a power broker. Jackson declined; Adams soon was declared the winner with Henry Clay his secretary of state, and the country cried "Foul!" Jacksonians would remain convinced that a deal had been struck between Adams and Clay, benefiting both.

On the floor of the House, Clay belittled Buchanan for being single and having crossed eyes. Still, the Pennsylvanian managed to win appointment as chairman of the important House Judiciary committee, where he worked as chief prosecutor on the impeachment trial of US District Court judge James H. Peck, who was being tried for abuse of judicial powers; the Senate acquitted him early in 1831. More importantly, going against his committee, Buchanan worked to defeat a bill that would have drastically limited the Supreme Court's power by taking away its authority to hear appeals and exercise judicial review. He rejoiced when the House voted down the bill.

DIPLOMAT

In 1831, Buchanan decided to forego another run for Congress, telling friends and family that he preferred returning to private life and his law practice. Very possibly he was hoping the rumors of Jackson selecting him as his running mate were true. They were not. But even though Martin Van Buren became the vice president, Buchanan was not forgotten. The United States needed a minister sent to Russia, so in the spring of 1832, he was bound for St. Petersburg.

During his eighteen months as America's representative, Buchanan was successful in negotiating a commercial treaty, but found a maritime treaty more troublesome, for the Russians were not welcome to the notion of "free ships make free goods." Still, he explored the countryside some, met Czar Nicholas I, and appreciated his own country all the more.

SENATOR

Buchanan returned home in 1833 and soon was voted by the Pennsylvania legislature to be US senator. He served three terms and was a Jackson booster, including aiding the president's efforts to kill the national bank, and opposing the Senate's censure of Jackson. Three years later, the Senate expunged the censure, largely because of Buchanan's efforts.

President Van Buren also enjoyed Senator Buchanan's support, and in 1837, he became chairman of the Senate's Foreign Relations committee. The following year Buchanan was offered the position of attorney general, but turned it down, insisting he had reached the height of his political ambition.

During the late 1830s and early 1840s, Buchanan advocated manifest destiny, and in one speech proclaimed: "Providence has given to the American people a great and glorious mission to perform, even that of extending the blessings of Christianity and of civil and religious liberty over the whole North American continent. . . . We must fulfill our destiny."[3] This desire for more land caused him to

CABINET
★★★★★★★★★★

(continued)

SECRETARY OF THE NAVY
Isaac Toucey (1857–1861)

POSTMASTER GENERAL
Aaron V. Brown (1857–1859); died in office

Joseph Holt (1859–1860)

Horatio King (Feb.–March 1861)

SECRETARY OF THE INTERIOR
Jacob Thompson (1857–1861)

OCT: Financial panic begins after an insurance company goes bankrupt; other banks and businesses fail, causing widespread unemployment and economic depression

OCT 24: World's first football (soccer) team is founded in Sheffield, England

DEC 31: Queen Victoria announces that Ottawa, Ontario, will become the capital of Canada

OCT–NOV: Kansans draft a state constitution that allows slavery; it's approved by pro-slavery forces but rejected by opponents, creating a quandary for Congress

Nathaniel Currier and James M. Ives begin selling lithographic prints

1858

Last black-maned Cape Lion seen in South Africa's Cape Town province

DID YOU KNOW?

Buchanan is the only bachelor president in American history.

When the Prince of Wales visited the White House in 1860, his entourage was so extensive that the president was forced out of his bedroom and slept in the hall.

be one of nine senators opposed to the Webster-Ashburton Treaty, which determined the border between Maine and Canada. In fact, he called it a "dishonorable" treaty for its ceding of over five thousand square miles to Canada, much of it in today's New Brunswick province.

Buchanan's lust for land made him one of the very few northern senators supporting Texas annexation. He argued that not allowing this annexation would create an unstable environment that very likely would lead to European intervention. Perhaps part of his posturing was the hope of gaining southern votes to capture the Democratic presidential nomination. He lost the gambit, and, to his surprise, James K. Polk won both the party's nomination and the election. The new president then asked Buchanan to serve in his cabinet as secretary of state. As an enthusiastic supporter of Polk's expansionist views, Buchanan agreed.

SECRETARY OF STATE

The relationship between Polk and Buchanan was one of the most strained of a president and his secretary of state. One marvels at why Polk kept Buchanan so long considering that he often found fault with his ideas and actions. Still his secretary supported Polk when it counted and successfully negotiated a treaty for the Oregon territory. Originally Buchanan balked at insisting that the United States maintain the "54°40' or fight!" posturing, worried that war might result. Polk reassured his nervous secretary that a compromise short of war would be reached. Eventually the British came around and accepted the previous offer of using the forty-ninth parallel as the border. Probably no one breathed a sigh of relief louder than Buchanan.

The Texas question proved thornier than anticipated. Buchanan wrote a message for US envoy John Slidell to deliver to the Mexican government that Mexico would recognize US annexation of Texas, including the border of the Rio Grande River, and would agree to pay its claims to US citizens. Additionally, Slidell was to covertly secure the purchase of California and New Mexico; however, when word of the mission became public knowledge, Mexican president José Joaquin de Herrera refused to see Slidell. Ultimately, American troops took position along the Rio Grande River in a show of force that was calculated to create a negative response from Mexico. And so the Mexican War began. Once the fighting started, some in Polk's government argued to seize territory southward into Mexico, but Buchanan disagreed. Yet once the war was won, the secretary of state insisted that the Mexican Cession was not enough, since American blood had been spilled; more territory should be taken. This time the rest of the administration disagreed.

During his presidency, Polk twice had vacancies to fill on the Supreme Court, and twice Buchanan clearly announced he was interested in becoming a justice. Both times he then withdrew his name from the nomination process. His reasons are unclear, although the second time, he wrote, "I cannot desert the President."[4] Polk probably was somewhat relieved, for having a Supreme Court justice who changed his mind as frequently as Buchanan did on weighty issues would not have been reassuring. The president once confided in his diary his thoughts regarding the secretary of state: "Buchanan is an able man, but in small matters without judgment and sometimes acts like an old maid."[5] An additional reason for Polk's concern was the very real possibility that Buchanan planned to run for president in 1848; after all, Polk had made it clear he would not seek a second term.

NATIONAL EVENTS

Yellow fever epidemic in New Orleans kills more than 7,000

Boston begins filling in its Back Bay to provide more land for the city

George Pullman begins building train sleeper cars in Chicago

William Tweed becomes the "boss" of Tammany Hall

Frederick Law Olmsted is hired to design New York's Central Park

WORLD EVENTS

JAN 14: Unsuccessful assassination attempt on France's Napoleon III and his wife leaves them unhurt, but 10 others are killed and 150 wounded in bombing

JAN 25: British Princess Royal Victoria weds Prussian Crown Prince Frederick Wilhelm

JAN 25: Mendelssohn's *Wedding March* played at the wedding of Queen Victoria's daughter; the piece is quickly embraced by other brides and grooms

Buchanan's decision not to serve on the Supreme Court might also be explained by the fact that such a position was not seen as a stepping-stone to the presidency. Another Polk diary entry warned, "No candidate for the presidency ought ever to remain in the cabinet. He is an unsafe advisor."[6]

The Democrats met in 1848, and while Buchanan attempted to curry votes, he lacked the numbers needed for a nomination. Instead, Michigan senator Lewis Cass gained the nod, and Buchanan swallowed his pride and campaigned for Cass, who lost to Mexican War hero Zachary Taylor.

SAGE OF WHEATLAND

Deciding it was an opportune moment for retirement, James Buchanan bought a three-story brick home on an estate of over twenty acres outside of Lancaster. He relied on his niece, Harriet Lane, to furnish the home he named Wheatland. She and a housekeeper ran the household, where its twenty-two rooms often had the sounds of children playing as many relatives soon came to stay with Uncle James. Here the "Sage of Wheatland" kept himself busy puttering about in his extensive gardens, reading from his considerable library, hosting a variety of guests, but most importantly, jockeying himself into position for the 1852 presidential race.

Frequent trips to Washington and continual correspondence with power brokers aided his efforts. He wrote letters to the public, including one in 1850 in which he discussed why he welcomed the defeat of the Wilmot Proviso, which would have prohibited slavery in any lands gained in the Mexican War, and explained how this was good for the nation. He worried that the slavery issue would continue dividing the nation, especially if left to the "fanatical abolitionists." Buchanan disapproved of slavery, but continued to hold to the belief that it was the constitutional right of American citizens. His views advocating states' rights and slavery angered many of his fellow Pennsylvanians; in fact, thirty-three delegates signed a petition against his nomination, preferring another Pennsylvanian, David Wilmot, author of the Wilmot Proviso, instead. The Baltimore Democratic convention of 1852 reflected the increasing division of the party and the nation. Neither Cass nor Buchanan garnered the necessary majority, so once again, a dark horse candidate, Franklin Pierce, was nominated. Once more, James Buchanan conceded defeat, but insisted, "I shall go into retirement without regret, and with a perfect consciousness that I have done my duty faithfully to my country. . . . I shall never hold another office."[7]

ENVOY TO GREAT BRITAIN

Newly elected President Pierce appointed Buchanan as minister to Great Britain. Buchanan accepted, then changed his mind, changed it again, rejected the position a second time, but finally agreed to go. Once overseas, he met frequently with British foreign minister Lord Clarendon, who was overseeing the Crimean War. The new American representative found himself in a quandary when

SUPREME COURT APPOINTMENTS
★★★★★★★★★★

Nathan Clifford, 1858

REPUBLICAN PARTY ★ The first official meeting of the Republican Party occurred in Jackson, Michigan, on July 6, 1854. Its membership consisted of former Whigs and those opposed to slavery, including Free Soilers and Know-Nothings. New York senator William Seward and publisher Thurlow Weed were among the early leaders. In 1856, they ran their first presidential candidate, John C. Frémont.

MAY 11: Minnesota enters as the 32nd state

JUN 16: Senate candidate Abraham Lincoln delivers his famous "House Divided" speech

JUL 29: US and Japan sign Harris Treaty to open additional Japanese ports to trade

AUG 16: First transatlantic cable is sent—President Buchanan and Queen Victoria exchange greetings

AUTUMN: Gold discovered in Cherry Creek in Colorado Territory and a new gold rush follows

FEB: Gold rush begins to British Columbia's Fraser River region

JUL 1: Darwin and Wallace's theories of Evolution read at London's Linnean Society

AUG 2: British Empire assumes control of India from British East India Company

OCT 21: Can-Can dance first performed in Paris

STATE OF THE UNION
★★★★★★★★★★

US POPULATION IN 1857
31,443,321

NATIONAL DEBT IN 1861
$90,580,874

STATES ADMITTED TO UNION
Minnesota, May 11, 1858

Oregon, February 14, 1859

Kansas, January 29, 1861

NUMBER OF STATES IN 1861
34

ordered by his own office to dress in the manner of a typical American, but since British protocol demanded formal dress for many occasions, this directive meant he could not attend the majority of functions normally required of a foreign diplomat. Newspapers in London complained when Buchanan did not attend the opening of Parliament, but he had no choice. The American press, nevertheless, praised his efforts, and one called him a "true man—a republican in fact and truth."[8]

While in Britain, Buchanan was ordered to meet fellow American diplomats regarding Cuba and its acquisition, which he had long advocated. He saw this rendezvous as a fruitless exercise since America already knew it wanted the island and was willing to purchase it, but Spain remained adamant against its sale. So what could three Americans do? The answer was to meet in Ostend, Belgium, and draft a report calling for the purchase of Cuba for one hundred million dollars; if Spain refused, then take it by force. As Buchanan had written earlier, "We must have Cuba."[9]

Once the report, called the Ostend Manifesto, was published, northerners decried another attempt to annex more slave territory. This added to their already flammable temperament from the Kansas-Nebraska Act, which permitted popular sovereignty to determine the slave question; it seemed everywhere they turned, southerners were gaining in power and slave territory. President Pierce and his administration quickly attempted to distance themselves from the report, while southerners applauded it. Buchanan requested permission to return home but was refused since the British had sent a fleet to the Caribbean. No doubt he desired to arrive in plenty of time to build support prior to the 1856 Democratic convention, and his ship docked in New York harbor one day after his sixty-fifth birthday. He soon heard the news that Pennsylvania Democrats had unanimously chosen him as their presidential candidate. The first step toward capturing the nomination was complete.

ELECTION

In May 1856, Democrats met in Cincinnati to determine their ticket, and quickly three contenders emerged: incumbent Franklin Pierce; Illinois senator and architect of the Kansas-Nebraska Act, Stephen Douglas; and James Buchanan. All three had established themselves as supporting southern rights, but Buchanan had the added advantage of not being in the country most of the past four years, so, besides the Ostend Manifesto, there was little to attack. His floor manager (the person designated to lead and organize consideration of the measure) skillfully kept Buchanan's name as the frontrunner of possible candidates, where he remained and finally captured the nomination on the seventeenth ballot. Kentuckian John C. Breckinridge was nominated to be his vice president. The Republican Party held its first presidential convention and submitted John C. Frémont of California and William Dayton of Ohio as their ticket. A third party, the Know-Nothings or American Party, nominated former president Millard Fillmore.

The two main parties differed on the expansion of slavery, with Democrats favoring the principle of popular sovereignty and the Republicans remaining vehemently opposed to any plan that could open new territories to slavery. But both parties opposed the Know-Nothings and their pro-bigotry stance, and both agreed that a transcontinental railroad was essential for the nation. Slavery was the key issue, and Democrats pandered to voters' fears by reminding them that a victory for the Republicans would likely mean civil war. Democrats

NATIONAL EVENTS

OCT 27: R.H. Macy opens his store on Sixth Avenue in New York City

Steinway family begins producing pianos

FEB 14: Oregon becomes the 33rd state

FEB 27: Rep. Daniel Sickles murders the son of Francis Scott Key because he believes Key was having an affair with his wife. Sickles pleads a new defense—insanity—and wins acquittal (later serves as general in Union Army during Civil War)

JUN 11: Comstock Lode, the country's richest silver deposit, discovered in Nevada

1859

WORLD EVENTS

JAN 24: Moldavia and Wallachia combined to create Romania

FEB: Ongoing fighting in Vietnam between French and Vietnamese; French seize Saigon

APR 25: French begin construction of Suez Canal

APR: Charles Dickens publishes *A Tale of Two Cities*

insisted that voting for their party would benefit the country and provide continued financial stability. Although he only captured 45 percent of the popular vote, Buchanan succeeded in winning the majority of electoral votes (including all of the South except Maryland, which was the sole state that Fillmore won).

COMSTOCK LODE ★ The Comstock Lode was the richest silver deposit found on US soil. First, gold was discovered in 1859 by two miners, and a third miner, Henry Comstock, managed to convince them they were on his land. The gold was difficult to mine because it was laced with a silver blue clay that was determined to be high-grade silver. The mining towns of California were abandoned as men headed east to Nevada, where Virginia City became a boomtown. Eventually $300 million in silver would be mined from the area.

PRESIDENT BUCHANAN

In his inaugural speech, the incoming president mentioned the pending Supreme Court decision regarding the slave Dred Scott suing for his freedom, promising to "cheerfully submit" to the Court's decision. Very shortly, that decision would rock the nation with its insistence that the Missouri Compromise was unconstitutional, as were any limitations on the spread of slavery. This coincided perfectly with Buchanan's beliefs that slavery was permitted by the Constitution; therefore, it should be allowed.

Kansas continued to be the battleground for this volatile issue. Buchanan sent a southerner, Robert J. Walker of Mississippi, to become the new territorial governor of Kansas. Refusing to recognize Governor Walker, the anti-slavery forces boycotted the constitutional convention in Lecompton. Not surprisingly, the convention adopted a pro-slavery constitution, which was submitted to Congress. The seemingly pleased president announced, "Kansas is therefore at this moment a slave state as Georgia and South Carolina."[10] He then urged its adoption, but many congressmen, led by Stephen Douglas, rejected it, saying that it did not truly represent the views of Kansans, so in 1858 a referendum was held that vindicated Congress. Buchanan remained unconvinced, but another referendum provided the same result. Ultimately, Kansas would enter the Union in 1861 as a free state.

The Kansas question revealed the increasing tension between the Democratic Party's top two men—Buchanan and Douglas. Already many had fled the party over the Dred Scott decision, but both men understood the crucial need for their cooperation with each other. A truce was called so Douglas could run for reelection to the Senate. This campaign became national news as it magnified the slavery issue in a series of debates between him and his opponent, Abraham Lincoln. Although Douglas won reelection, Lincoln gained fame and respect, which would soon catapult him into the White House.

In 1857, the country plunged into a depression worsened by runs on banks, many of which lacked proper state supervision. Falling gold prices compounded the shaky financial foundation of the nation, particularly for the North and West. The federal government and its president refused to aid the people, saying it was "without the power to extend relief."[11] The South, however, escaped relatively unscathed, which bolstered their confidence for what they considered their superior economy.

DID YOU KNOW?

Buchanan was the first president to send a transatlantic telegram.

JUL 1: First intercollegiate baseball game played; Amherst defeats Williams 73–32

AUG: Edwin Drake strikes oil in Pennsylvania and America's first oil well begins pumping

OCT 16: Abolitionist John Brown leads a raid on federal arsenal at Harpers Ferry, Virginia; troops under Colonel Robert E. Lee suppresses the attempted insurrection two days later

DEC 2: John Brown is hanged; he becomes a martyr to abolitionists

MAY 31: The Great Clock of Westminister, "Big Ben," begins announcing the time in London

JUL: Alfred Tennyson begins a series on the King Arthur legends with *The Idylls of the King*

NOV 12: World's first flying trapeze circus act performed in Paris

NOV 24: Charles Darwin publishes *On the Origin of Species*, creating debate about natural selection and evolution

DRED SCOTT DECISION ★ Dred Scott, a slave, was owned by an Army doctor who took him to the various posts he was assigned, some of which were in northern territories. When his owner died in 1846, Scott attempted to buy his freedom from the widow, but she refused. So a few months later, with help from slavery opponents, Scott brought his suit against his owner in St. Louis. A succession of trials ensued, followed by appeals that ended with the US Supreme Court ruling in March 1857. Chief Justice Roger Taney declared that Scott had no right to bring his case to court since slaves were not citizens and so held no rights. Furthermore, Taney argued that the Missouri Compromise was unconstitutional since it barred citizens from taking their "property" anywhere they wished to settle. Abolitionists could scarcely believe the ruling and understood it had set back their cause immeasurably.

That same year, Buchanan had to send American troops against Mormons in the Utah territory. Non-Mormons who held government positions complained of the church's refusal to respect their authority. President Buchanan removed the Mormon leader Brigham Young from his position as territorial governor and ordered army troops to enforce federal authority. The Mormons launched a series of harassing attacks against the army marching from Fort Leavenworth, which effectively slowed the soldiers' advance. By the spring of 1858, negotiations successfully ended the conflict, and a federal appointee became the new territorial governor while Young remained the head of the Mormon Church.

The following year, 1859, would see the president utilizing federal troops yet again to put down another attempted insurrection. This time, however, the target was much closer—Harpers Ferry, Virginia. There the arsenal was seized by abolitionist John Brown and eighteen of his followers who hoped to take the weapons to instigate a widespread slave uprising. Local militia surrounded them, but the governor requested reinforcements, so Buchanan sent word to Colonel Robert E. Lee, who was home on leave at Arlington. He led a contingent of marines and quickly ended the standoff. Brown was apprehended, tried, and hanged. (Ironically, one of the Virginia volunteers on duty as a guard at Brown's hanging was John Wilkes Booth, future assassin of Abraham Lincoln. Booth said he "looked at the traitor and terrorizer with unlimited, undeniable contempt."[12])

The election year of 1860 proved to be the most divisive ever for the nation. Democrats split on slavery: Douglas represented the Northern Democrats and their view of popular sovereignty; Breckinridge represented the Southern Democrats who wanted to preserve the status quo for the South. The Constitutional Union Party made its singular appearance with its nominee, John Bell; and Republicans nominated Abraham Lincoln, who won the election.

South Carolina led seven states in seceding from the Union upon news of Lincoln's election. Buchanan took no action, believing he had no authority to keep states in the Union. In his last message to Congress, he explained, ". . . all for which the slave states have ever contended, is to be let alone and permitted to manage their domestic institutions in their own way. . . . As sovereign States, they, and they alone, are responsible before God and the world for the slavery existing among them. For this the people of the North . . . have no more right to interfere than with similar institutions in Russia or in Brazil."

NATIONAL EVENTS

FEB 27: Abraham Lincoln delivers speech against slavery at New York's Cooper Union

MAY: Constitutional Union Party (former Whigs and Know-Nothings) nominate John Bell for president and Edward Everett for VP

MAY: Republicans meet in Chicago and nominate Abraham Lincoln and Hannibal Hamlin

JUN: Democrats meet in Baltimore and nominate Illinois senator Stephen A. Douglas as their presidential candidate; Herschel Johnson of Georgia is his running mate

1860

WORLD EVENTS

Englishman Frederick Walton begins producing linoleum

Louis Pasteur develops "pasteurized" milk

OCT 17: First playing of the British Open

OCT 25: British win the Opium War and rights to opium trade

DEC 1: First installment appears of *Great Expectations* by Charles Dickens

When Buchanan was informed of the need to resupply US troops stationed in Charleston harbor at Fort Sumter, he sent a supply ship. However, once it was fired upon and returned, the president took no further action. Instead, he was content to allow his successor to determine his own course of action regarding Fort Sumter and other aggressive southern acts.

In March 1861, Buchanan watched as Abraham Lincoln took the oath of office and reminded his countrymen that he had just pledged to "preserve, protect, and defend (the constitution)." Afterward the outgoing president told Lincoln, "If you are as happy on entering the White House as I on leaving, you are a very happy man indeed."[13]

RETIREMENT

Buchanan retired to his palatial home near Lancaster, passing his days quietly. Niece Harriet, now married, continued in her role as hostess for her uncle as she had for the past twenty years, including his presidency. He supported the nation and President Lincoln but felt he needed to defend his own presidential actions. Consequently, he authored *Mr. Buchanan's Administration on the Eve of the Rebellion*, which was published just after the Civil War. He also decided that he needed a biography, which was commissioned but would not be published until 1883.

Buchanan suffered from gout and other ailments before pneumonia ended his life at the age of seventy-seven on June 1, 1868. He died peacefully at home and left behind an estate estimated at around three hundred thousand dollars, which was divided principally among his relatives. Buchanan was buried at Woodward Hill Cemetery in Lancaster.

Toward the end of his life, Buchanan remarked, "History will vindicate my memory." Perhaps this may happen in time, but meanwhile historians consistently rank Buchanan's presidency as a failure.

DID YOU KNOW?

Buchanan had one nearsighted eye and one farsighted, so he would tilt his head to one side when talking to people and often closed one eye.

ENDNOTES

1 George Ticknor Curtis, *Life of James Buchanan: Fifteenth President of the United States*, 2 vols., New York: Harper & Bros., 1883, vol. I, p. 4.

2 Ibid, p. 18.

3 Jean H. Baker, *James Buchanan*, New York: Henry Holt and Co., 2004, p. 35.

4 Ibid, p. 39.

5 Allan Nevins, ed., *Polk: The Diary of a President, 1845-1849*, New York: Longman's Green, 1929, p. 79.

6 Ibid, p. 306.

7 John Bassett Moore, ed., *The Works of James Buchanan*, 12 vols., New York: Antiquarian Press, 1960, vol. 2, p. 451.

8 Baker, p. 62.

9 Ibid, p. 43.

10 Moore, vol. 10, p. 190.

11 Baker, p. 90.

12 David S. Reynolds, *John Brown, Abolitionist*, New York: Alfred A. Knopf, 2005, p. 397.

13 John G. Nicolay and John Hay, *Abraham Lincoln: A History*, New York: Century, 1890, vol. II, p. 394.

JUN: Southern Democrats also meet and decide to split from the party to form one that demands federal protection of slavery; they nominate Vice President John C. Breckinridge of Kentucky for president and Oregon senator Joseph Lane as vice president

NOV 6: Abraham Lincoln elected president

DEC 20: South Carolina secedes from the US

DEC 17: Kingdom of the Two Sicilies annexed to the Kingdom of Italy

Abraham Lincoln

Abraham Lincoln

★ ★ ★ SIXTEENTH PRESIDENT ★ ★ ★

LIFE SPAN

- Born: February 12, 1809, near Hodgenville, Kentucky
- Died: April 15, 1865, Peterson House, Washington, D.C.

NICKNAME

- Honest Abe

RELIGION

- No formal affiliation; attended Presbyterian services in Springfield and Washington, D.C.

HIGHER EDUCATION

- None

PROFESSION

- Lawyer

MILITARY SERVICE

- Enlisted in April 1832 to serve in Black Hawk War; elected to be captain of a company of Illinois volunteers; reenlisted twice more as a private

FAMILY

- Father: **Thomas Lincoln** (1778–1851)
- Mother: **Nancy Hanks Lincoln** (1784–1818)
- Stepmother: **Sarah Bush Johnston Lincoln** (1788–1869); wed **Thomas Lincoln** in 1819
- Wife: **Mary Todd Lincoln** (1818–1882); wed November 4, 1842, in Springfield, Illinois
- Children: **Robert Todd** (1843–1926); **Edward Baker** (1846–1850); **William Wallace** (1850–1862); **Thomas "Tad"** (1853–1871)

POLITICAL LIFE

- Postmaster of New Salem, Illinois (1833–1836)
- Illinois legislature (1834–1842)
- US representative (1847–1849)

PRESIDENCY

- Two terms: March 4, 1861–April 15, 1865
- Republican
- Reason for leaving office: assassinated
- Vice presidents: **Hannibal Hamlin** (1861–1865); **Andrew Johnson** (1865)

ELECTION OF 1860

- Electoral vote: **Lincoln** 180; **John C. Breckinridge** 72; **John Bell** 39; **Stephen Douglas** 12
- Popular vote: **Lincoln,** 1,865,908; **Breckinridge** 848,019; **Bell** 590,901; **Douglas** 1,380,202

ELECTION OF 1864

- Electoral vote: **Lincoln** 212; **George McClellan** 21
- Popular vote: **Lincoln** 2,218,388; **McClellan** 1,812,807

CABINET

SECRETARY OF STATE
William H. Seward (1861–1865)

SECRETARY OF THE TREASURY
Salmon P. Chase (1861–1864)

William P. Fessenden (1864–1865)

Hugh McCullough (1865)

SECRETARY OF WAR
Simon Cameron (1861–1862)

Edwin M. Stanton (1862–1865)

ATTORNEY GENERAL
Edward Bates (1861–1864)

James Speed (1864–1865)

SECRETARY OF THE NAVY
Gideon Welles (1861–1865)

POSTMASTER GENERAL
Montgomery Blair (1861–1864)

William Dennison (1864–1865)

SECRETARY OF THE INTERIOR
Caleb B. Smith (1861–1862)

John P. Usher (1863–1865)

"I happen temporarily to occupy this big White House. I am living witness that any one of your children may look to come here as my father's child has."[1] When Abraham Lincoln spoke these words in 1864, he was mindful of the extraordinary journey that had begun on the Kentucky frontier, taken him through the fields and hamlets of Indiana to the capital of Illinois, and finally to the seat of national power in Washington, D.C. There, today, he is honored at his memorial, and at Mount Rushmore his likeness is carved in granite. These monuments attempt to express the thanks of a grateful nation, but, as Lincoln himself said, it is beyond our "poor power to add or detract." Abraham Lincoln's words and actions live on to ensure that "a government of the people, by the people, for the people, shall not perish from the earth."

EARLY LIFE

Abraham Lincoln was born in a small log cabin of rough-hewn logs cut by his father, Thomas Lincoln, in western Kentucky. His mother, Nancy Hanks Lincoln, gave birth to their son, and second child, on February 12, 1809; a daughter, Sarah, was born in 1807. Within two years, the family was on the move to another farm ten miles away. Problems with land titles kept Thomas Lincoln moving, again when Abe was seven, to Spencer County, Indiana, where Thomas built a permanent cabin for his family.

Young Abe learned his ABCs and basic "ciphering" at whatever school was briefly available, and although his parents were nearly illiterate, he later insisted, "All I am or hope to be I owe to my sainted mother."[2] Tragedy touched the family when Nancy Lincoln died; Abe was nine years old. Mourning was a luxury his father could not afford with two young children, so Thomas married widow and old friend Sarah Bush, who came with three children of her own. Sarah encouraged young Abe's inquiring intellect and explained to her husband that the boy's learning to read was as essential as his being able to clear and plow fields. Thomas may not have fully understood, but he grudgingly accepted that his son was exceptional. The neighbors, however, were more interested in Abe's physical strength and would sometimes employ him to help on their farms, where he spent many hours wielding an ax splitting rails. By the age of seventeen, Abe yearned to see more of the world, and he hired on to build a flatboat and carry produce down to New Orleans.

Four years later, Thomas Lincoln and his family were once again on the move, this time to Illinois and the Sangamon River. They moved yet again the following year to Coles County, but by this time, Abe had struck out on his own. He had been hired once again to take a flatboat to New Orleans, this time in the employ of Denton Offut, who had settled in a small Illinois village named New Salem. Offut offered Abe a job in his New Salem store, which Abe accepted.

Abe had never before lived in a community, and he found New Salem very much to his liking. The townspeople enjoyed his company as well, especially his ability to tell a good joke or an amusing story. When Offut decided to close his store, Lincoln enlisted as a volunteer to fight in the Black Hawk War (p. 90). He had become such a popular figure that he easily won the captaincy of his company. The soldiers wandered through northern Illinois and southern Wisconsin looking for the elusive Sac chief, but Lincoln saw no actual fighting, admitting that his only combat had been against swarms of mosquitoes. Still, he and his men did witness the tragic results of the conflict when they had to bury

NATIONAL EVENTS

Gatling gun developed (but not used until 1864)

Massachusetts Institute of Technology (MIT) founded in Cambridge, Massachusetts

"Dixie" becomes unofficial song of the Confederacy after being played at Jefferson Davis's inauguration

Gilbert C. Van Camp, a grocer, wins an Army contract to provide canned pork and beans to Union soldiers

Henry Wadsworth Longfellow publishes the poem "Paul Revere's Ride"

1861

WORLD EVENTS

Louis Pasteur publishes a paper that explains his theory of germs causing disease

French troops arrive in Lebanon

Abortion ruled a crime in Ireland

JAN 1: Benito Juarez captures Mexico City

JAN 2: Friedrick Wilhelm IV of Prussia dies; he is succeeded by Wilhelm I

five men who had been slain and scalped by Indians the day before. Lincoln mustered out in July to return to New Salem in time to campaign for his first public office, the Illinois state legislature.

Lincoln's campaign audiences were struck by the odd sight of a man so tall he nearly touched the treetops, with pants that missed the top of his shoes by a good half-foot. He traveled the countryside doing whatever he could to earn their trust—pitching hay, wrestling, and plain talking. He told a crowd, "My politics are short and sweet, like the old woman's dance. I am in favor of a national bank. I am in favor of the internal improvements system and a high protective tariff. . . . If elected, I shall be thankful; if not, it will be all the same."[3] He lost the election but gained friends and respect.

Abe returned to New Salem and became a partner in another store where his customers were the townspeople, many of whom bought items on credit with balances that were never paid. To help cover his own expenses, Abe worked other jobs and even learned surveying, but he still spent time in the store, sometimes just reading. One day a wagon stopped and, although he was not in the market for anything, Abe bought a barrel. Later, to his delight, he found books at the bottom of the barrel, and better still, law books—Blackstone's *Commentaries on the Laws of England,* the foundation for all legal education. At one point Lincoln had toyed with the idea of becoming a lawyer, and these books seemed a sign that it was his destiny.

In 1833, Lincoln became postmaster of New Salem. Although the pay helped with expenses, the main benefit of the job for this young student of the law was ready access to newspapers. Lincoln eagerly devoured each issue as soon as it arrived, paying particular attention to political news.

While postmaster, Lincoln ran again for the state legislature, and this time he won, going on to serve three additional terms; his allegiance was to the Whig Party and its spokesman, Henry Clay. Meanwhile, he continued to read the law. In 1836, he passed the bar, and the following year, moved to the growing town of Springfield, which soon replaced Vandalia as the state capital.

SPRINGFIELD ATTORNEY

While serving in the state legislature, Lincoln continued to support the Whig platform, but rarely spoke on the floor. He was, however, a compelling public speaker, as courtroom audiences throughout the Illinois countryside could testify. Lincoln advised lawyers that, "extemporaneous speaking should be practiced and cultivated. It is the lawyer's avenue to the public. However able and faithful he may be in other respects, people are slow to bring him business if he cannot make a speech."[4] Lincoln honed this skill through conversing with constituents and fellow assemblymen and discoursing on the reasons for his clients' innocence. His cases included all types of civil and criminal law, and he won the majority, resulting in a growing caseload.

By the time Lincoln moved to Springfield, he had already experienced at least two unhappy romances in New Salem. Ann Rutledge was the daughter of the town's innkeeper, and her death from typhoid fever in 1835 left him distraught. Another acquaintance from his New Salem days, Mary Owens, originally interested him, but when she left and returned three years later, she was considerably heftier and minus some teeth—not an enticing sight for Lincoln, and they parted, never to meet again.

Once the young, aspiring lawyer had established himself in Springfield, busily practicing

JAN 29: Kansas enters the Union as the 34th state

FEB 4: Provisional government formed by six states seceding from the US

FEB 18: Jefferson Davis named president of the Confederate States of America

MAR 4: Abraham Lincoln is inaugurated as the 16th president

APR 12: Confederate forces in Charleston's harbor fire at Fort Sumter; Union forces surrender the fort the next day

FEB 1: Dike breaks in Gelderland, Netherlands

FEB 18: Victor Emmanuel II assumes title of king of Italy, the first king of a united Italy

FEB 19: Russia abolishes serfdom

FEB 23: Dutch Premier Floris A van Hall resigns

FEB 27: Russians fire on crowd demonstrating against Russian rule of Poland, the Warsaw Massacre

DID YOU KNOW?

Lincoln well understood failure: he failed as a shopkeeper in New Salem; he failed in his first attempt to win a seat in the Illinois legislature; later, when he was in the legislature, he lost a bid to become Speaker; he lost his first nomination to Congress; he lost in an attempt to gain a nomination for the US Senate; he lost when he ran for the Senate four years later; and he failed to win the nomination for vice president in 1856. Lincoln truly personified the adage: "If at first you don't succeed, try, try again!"

law, he was invited to a variety of social functions. One of these was a dance in 1839, where he met a young Kentucky belle who later laughingly told of a lanky man walking up to her saying he wanted to dance with her "in the *worst* way." Mary Todd was refined and well educated, the daughter of a Lexington, Kentucky, banker, and raised in a household run by slave labor. She knew the art of sparkling conversation, but also practiced the unladylike skill of talking politics. The couple's courtship worried Mary's sister and brother-in-law, Ninian Edwards, with whom she lived in Springfield. According to Elizabeth Edwards, she "warned Mary that she and Mr. Lincoln were not suitable. . . . They had no feelings alike. They were so different that they could not live happily as man and wife."[5] From the reports of countless friends, acquaintances, co-workers, and relatives, the Edwards' hesitation was rather well-founded and would prove itself repeatedly during the Lincolns' marriage. Nevertheless, even through the rocky episodes of their lives together, each seemed to seek solace from the other. On November 4, 1842, the couple stood before an Episcopal minister and repeated their vows, and Lincoln slipped a gold band engraved with the words "love is eternal" on Mary's finger.

After living in a boardinghouse for a year, the Lincolns moved into a small rental cottage with their infant son, Robert. Soon after, they were visited by Mary's father and the baby's namesake, whose financial help enabled the couple to move into their own home in Springfield. They were soon joined by another son, in March 1846. The child was named Edward Baker, after Abe's good friend, who had in fact just defeated Lincoln for the Whig nomination to Congress.

Lincoln's affable manner and homespun humor made him a favorite among his colleagues and juries. One of his cases involved a woman who had stumbled and fallen in Alton, Illinois, and badly injured her ankle. She wanted to sue the town for five thousand dollars for having a faulty sidewalk, and she hired Lincoln as her attorney. He and the town's mayor discussed a possible settlement. Abe proposed three thousand dollars, to which the mayor balked, pleading that Alton did not have that kind of money. Lincoln decreased the amount to fifteen hundred dollars, which prompted the exasperated mayor to ask if Abe would throw in the injured limb for such a sum. Smiling, Abe countered that he could probably have the entire woman for fifteen hundred dollars!

Another case concerned the son of Lincoln's former New Salem wrestling opponent, Jack Armstrong. Duff Armstrong was accused of murder, and an eyewitness claimed to have seen him commit the crime by the light of the moon. With the witness on the stand, Lincoln read from the *Farmer's Almanac* entry for that night. The moon was setting at the time of the murder, so the witness was clearly lying, and Duff Armstrong was freed.

Lincoln had enormous respect for the law and he firmly believed in protection for every citizen under its tenets, but the role of lawyer as protector of one's civil rights was not without its challenges. Lincoln did sometimes refuse a case that he did not believe in. He once confided to a fellow attorney, "I couldn't do it. All the while I'd be talking to that jury I'd be thinking, 'Lincoln, you're a liar,' and I believe I should forget myself and say it out loud."[6]

Lincoln spent some evenings debating with his fellow lawyers on various national issues, on which he took the standard Whig position. One

NATIONAL EVENTS

APR 20: Robert E. Lee resigns from the US Army

APR 23: Robert E. Lee named commander of Virginia's forces

APR 27: Lincoln suspends the writ of habeas corpus

MAY 8: Richmond, Virginia, selected as the capital of the Confederacy

JUL 21: First major battle of the Civil War occurs at Bull Run, Virginia; Confederates win

WORLD EVENTS

MAR 10: El Hadj Umar Tall takes Segou, crushing the Bambara Empire of Mali

MAR 20: Mendoza, Argentina is completely destroyed by an earthquake

MAR 23: Tramcars begin operation in London

MAY 13: Queen Victoria declares a proclamation of neutrality regarding the American Civil War

JUN 15: Benito Juarez formally elected president of Mexico

such time, he and a Chicago attorney discussed politics late into the night until they tired. Later, the lawyer from Chicago awoke to see Lincoln still sitting there, ready to resume the discourse, and irritably told him, "Oh, Lincoln, go to sleep."[7] Lincoln yearned to debate the issues on the national stage.

CONGRESSMAN

Although unsuccessful in his effort to gain the congressional nomination in 1844, Lincoln won not only the nomination but the election as well in 1846. The following December, Abe, Mary, and the boys traveled to Washington, where they took up residence in a cramped room of a boardinghouse. Robert struck the other boarders as being spoiled, and his mother fared no better. Edward was a sickly baby, and by spring it was agreed that Mary and the boys would visit her family in Lexington. Abe, on the other hand, relished his time in Washington and worked diligently on his committees. He opposed President Polk and the Mexican War and gave speeches denouncing it, although by the time he arrived in Washington, the war was winding down. Still Lincoln was keenly aware that the Whigs needed to have visible speakers and a platform to build on. The next election was never far away, and Lincoln wanted to lay the foundation for reelection.

The accomplished public speaker from Illinois was a bit nervous facing the House for the first time, so he decided to speak on a familiar subject, his committee work with the post offices. As he told his law partner, "I find speaking here and elsewhere about the same thing. I was about as badly scared, and no worse, as I am when I speak in the court."[8] He would soon address much weightier matters that would receive national attention.

Before Lincoln's first month was through, he had introduced a series of Whig resolutions against the Democratic Party and its leader, James K. Polk. He attacked the president for beginning the war under doubtful circumstances—questioning whether the US Army deliberately provoked the Mexican army to attack on the Rio Grande River. These became known as the "spot resolutions," for he demanded that the president tell if the "particular spot of soil on which the blood of our citizens was so shed was, or was not, our own soil."[9] He continued to criticize the president, hoping to win some points back home. Lincoln did not realize that not only were the Democratic papers hostile to his remarks, but neither were the Whigs nor their papers impressed by his oratory. Lincoln wrote to his law partner, William Herndon, that he would not be running again—adding, however, "if it should so happen that nobody else wishes to be elected, I could not refuse the people the right of sending me again."[10]

In 1848, Lincoln's primary focus was ensuring the election of Zachary Taylor, the Whig presidential candidate. He not only traveled throughout the north extolling the glories of his party, he also allowed his humor to shine through on the floor of the House, much to the pleasure of his fellow representatives. His anti-war stance had prevented his party from nominating him for reelection, but Lincoln still remained pleased by Taylor's victory. Now Lincoln could resume his congressional term and the issues before it—namely, expansion and slavery.

Although Lincoln was silent on the Congressional Record regarding his position on slavery, he told others that he believed in the eventual demise of slavery due to economic concerns of southerners because it was becoming unprofitable. Lincoln

SUPREME COURT APPOINTMENTS
★★★★★★★★★★

Noah H. Swayne, 1862

Samuel F. Miller, 1862

David Davis, 1862

Stephen J. Field, 1863

Salmon P. Chase, 1864

JUL 26: General George B. McClellan takes command of the Army of the Potomac (main Union Army)

AUG 5: First income tax levied in US to pay for the Civil War

OCT 1: John Ericsson begins building the Union's first ironclad ship (*Monitor*)

OCT 22: Telegraph fully connects the east and west coasts

OCT 24: West Virginia secedes from Virginia

OCT 26: Pony Express ceases service

JUN 25: Sultan Abdul Mejid of the Ottoman Empire dies; he is succeeded by his brother Abdul Aziz

JUN 28: Leipzig Observatory discovers Comet D'Arrest

AUG 1: Brazil recognizes the Confederacy

OCT 6: Russian students riot and shut down University of Petersburg

OCT 24: The world's first ocean-going iron-hulled armored ship, the Royal Navy's H.M.S. *Warrior,* is completed outside London

STATE OF THE UNION
★★★★★★★★★★

US POPULATION IN 1861
31,443,321

NATIONAL DEBT IN 1865
$2,680,647,870 (first time over $1 billion, due to Civil War costs)

STATES ADMITTED TO UNION
West Virginia, June 20, 1863

Nevada, October 31, 1864

NUMBER OF STATES IN 1865
36

opposed the extension of slavery into new territories and voted in favor of the Wilmot Proviso, which prohibited such expansion in any lands gained from Mexico. This measure, however, failed to pass.

Slavery had existed in the District of Columbia since the city was founded, and many, including Lincoln, found it the height of hypocrisy that people were being bought and sold and kept in bondage in the capital city of "the land of the free." He attempted to rectify this enormous wrong by drafting a compromise bill that would work toward gradual emancipation in the capital, but congressional backing dissolved before it could be presented.

Lincoln faced further frustration from the newly inaugurated Whig president, who did not understand that part of his job was rewarding supporters with political appointments. He was besieged by Illinois party members who wanted their hard work and patronage rewarded, but with Lincoln's defeat for a second term, Taylor had little interest in the lame-duck congressman. The most desirable position was one that Abe was encouraged by his friends to seek—commissioner of the General Land Office, with an annual salary of three thousand dollars and the possibility of future political advancement. Though not interested initially, when another Whig was discussed as a strong candidate, Lincoln pushed his own bid. The other candidate (who ironically had not even supported Taylor) won the position.

Lincoln's loss might be partly attributed to letters written by his Whig Party supporters in Springfield denouncing him for his vocal opposition to the Mexican War, which had rendered him "very unpopular."[11] Another position was tendered him, that of governor for the Oregon Territory, but Lincoln declined the offer. Instead, he returned to Springfield and resumed his law practice.

ATTORNEY AND FAMILY MAN

For the next five years, the law firm of Lincoln and Herndon prospered; in fact, Lincoln was offered a position with a Chicago firm but turned it down. Not only was he riding the circuit, he was also appearing before the state supreme court; his reputation was growing among the legal circles in the state. Lincoln's professional success was tempered by personal tragedy, however, as he and Mary watched their sickly Eddie slowly worsen from tuberculosis and finally die on February 1, 1850, a month shy of his fourth birthday. By the end of the year their grief was assuaged somewhat by the joy of welcoming a third son, William Wallace, named for a relative and physician who tended Eddie and Mary. Willie, as he was known, was then joined in 1853 by another brother, Thomas, whose nickname was "Tad," owing to his seemingly abnormally large head that reminded his father of a tadpole. Willie and Tad became their father's favorites and could do no wrong in his eyes. Neither parent was a firm disciplinarian, much to the consternation of others. Owing to Lincoln's frequent absences earlier in his career, his elder son Robert never enjoyed his father's playful nature and as a result, the two were never close.

Lincoln's legal career flourished, reflecting the high regard in which he was held by others. The top client for any lawyer in the mid-1800s was the burgeoning railroad industry that soon engaged Lincoln's legal services. When he submitted a bill of five thousand dollars to the Illinois Central, they balked, claiming that they could hire an eastern attorney—even Daniel Webster—for a sum as high as that. So Lincoln sued in court, stating that he had been paid only two hundred dollars. Eventually he won his case and was awarded forty-eight hundred dollars. Yet, on another occasion, when

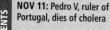

NATIONAL EVENTS

NOV 8: US Navy stops a British mail ship, the *Trent*, and arrests two Confederate envoys, creating diplomatic crisis between the United States and Great Britain

NOV 19: Julia Ward Howe writes "Battle Hymn of the Republic"

1862

FEB 6: General Ulysses S. Grant wins first Union victory when he captures Fort Henry, Tennessee

FEB 20: Willie Lincoln, 11-year-old son of the president, dies

WORLD EVENTS

NOV 11: Pedro V, ruler of Portugal, dies of cholera

DEC 14: Britain's Prince Albert dies of typhoid fever

Anna Leonowens, widow of a British officer living in India, agrees to serve as governess to the children of King Mongkut of Siam (Thailand)

he was paid twenty-five dollars for drafting legal papers, he returned ten dollars to the client with a note: "You must think I am a high-priced man. You are too liberal with your money. Fifteen dollars is enough for the job."[12]

Still Lincoln yearned for a starring role on the political stage. In 1854, he began as a supporting player helping Richard Yates in his reelection bid to the House of Representatives. The Whigs vehemently opposed Democrat Stephen Douglas's Kansas-Nebraska Act, which allowed those territories to determine slavery through popular sovereignty, thus reversing the Missouri Compromise with its insistence of no slavery north of Missouri. Although Lincoln could have run for Congress himself, he knew that would take him out of running for the Senate two years later. Competing against Douglas was an opportunity not to be missed, so instead he stumped for Yates, and in one speech declared: "No man is good enough to govern another man without that other's consent. I say this is the leading principle—the sheet anchor of American republicanism."[13] Although Yates lost the election, Lincoln gained exposure and revealed, as one newspaperman reported, "that he was an honest man, and second, that he was a powerful speaker."[14]

MARY LINCOLN'S CONFEDERATE BRETHREN ★ Mary Todd Lincoln supported the Union, but her Kentucky kinsmen served the Confederacy. One brother labored through the war as a Confederate surgeon. Two half-brothers served and one was killed at Shiloh, another at Baton Rouge. Another half-brother was wounded at Vicksburg, and a fourth served for a time as the commandant of Richmond's Libby Prison. Emilie Helm, Mary's half-sister, was married to a Confederate general who died at Chickamauga. When Emilie visited the White House, the Lincolns experienced a great deal of criticism for providing refuge to a rebel. These circumstances only fueled speculation that the unpopular First Lady was a Confederate spy; in fact, Lincoln testified before a congressional committee regarding his wife's allegiance to the United States.

SENATE CANDIDATE

Since US senators were still elected by their state legislature, Lincoln began lobbying for his own bid to run, telling Illinois legislators, "It has come around that a Whig may, by possibility, be elected to the US Senate, and I want the chance of being the man."[15] He turned down election to the Illinois legislature, knowing that the closely divided legislature would be electing the next senator. If he were a member, it would not be considered proper for him to vote for himself, and that could be enough to lose him the election. Those opposed to Douglas were angered by Lincoln's desire to place his success above that of his party. He angered them again when he refused to join the newly formed Republican Party state committee. Calculating his chances, Lincoln believed forty-three of one hundred were Douglas Democrats, so he needed to convince at least fifty-one of the remaining that he was a better candidate. He managed to gain forty-seven votes, but five Democrats refused to leave Congressman Lyman Trumbull. Lincoln realized that this deadlock would probably result in Douglas's man being picked to run, so Lincoln regretfully released his votes to Trumbull, who would never forget Abe's generosity. Mary Lincoln, on the other hand, refused to speak to her once good friend and bridesmaid Julia Trumbull.

FEB 22: Jefferson Davis inaugurated as president of the Confederacy

MAR 10: US issues its first paper money (greenbacks)

APR 4: Union forces land on Virginia peninsula under command of General McClellan

APR 6–7: Battle of Shiloh (Pittsburg Landing), Tennessee; General Grant wins after two days of intense fighting

APR 25: US Navy under Commodore David Farragut takes New Orleans

King Mongkut writes to President Lincoln offering to send elephants to help in the Civil War

Les Misérables published by French writer Victor Hugo

First Monte Carlo casino opens in Monaco

Alfred Nobel begins experimenting with nitroglycerin

JAN 1: Britain annexes Lagos in modern-day Nigeria

JAN 6: French, Spanish, and British forces arrive in Mexico

DID YOU KNOW?

Lincoln remains the tallest American president at 6'4".

Legal work—and more disappointment—occupied Lincoln for the rest of 1855. He was hired as a local attorney in a major case to break the patent of Cyrus McCormick's mechanical reaper. However, once Lincoln arrived in Cincinnati for the trial, he was completely shut out of the proceedings by the other eastern attorneys, including Edwin M. Stanton of Pittsburgh. After being paid for services, Lincoln returned the check with a curt note stating he had not earned it. The lead patent attorney insisted otherwise, and Lincoln kept the money when it was offered the second time. He and Stanton would meet again.

Lincoln pondered the ongoing debate over the slavery issue. He felt the Whig Party was not adequately addressing the question and began meeting with disgruntled members with various political affiliations. In 1856, the Republican Party met nationally for the first time to select its ticket for the upcoming election. John C. Frémont was chosen as president, and though some attempted to push Lincoln for the vice presidency, he lost to William Dayton of New Jersey. Faced with disappointment yet again, Abe put his feelings aside and campaigned for the ticket, but Democratic candidate James Buchanan won the election.

Back in Springfield, Lincoln worked on his practice, and Mary remodeled and enlarged their house. As usual, she overspent and was reprimanded by her husband. But she did now have a more spacious and fashionably decorated house that allowed the First Lady to feel more comfortable entertaining. The couple extended their hospitality, including hosting a birthday party for Lincoln—and inviting five hundred guests.

In March 1857, two major events occurred on the national level: the inauguration of President Buchanan, and the Supreme Court decision regarding a slave named Dred Scott. When the Court's decree invalidated the Missouri Compromise and argued that no slave was a citizen and able to sue in court, many throughout the North, including Illinois, were outraged. Lincoln sensed the time was growing ripe for a Republican victory.

Stephen Douglas understood he was in trouble both because of the Kansas-Nebraska Act, as well as his support for the Dred Scott decision. He redeemed himself in the eyes of many, though, when he opposed Buchanan regarding the Lecompton Kansas Constitution. "Bleeding Kansas" was a battleground that only became more contentious on election day when abolitionists were surprised that the state voted in favor of slavery. The winning delegates then met in Lecompton and drafted a constitution. Other Kansans said the election was a fraud and set up their own government in Topeka. Buchanan allowed the Lecompton results to stand, but Douglas led the charge against it, pleasing many within his state and also gaining favorable press coverage, much to the dismay of Lincoln and his fellow Republicans.

In June 1858, Lincoln accepted the nomination of Illinois Republicans and campaigned vigorously for the Republicans to win the statehouse, an event that would send him to Washington as senator from Illinois. For his acceptance speech, Lincoln initiated a theme he would use throughout his campaign: "'A house divided against itself cannot stand.' I believe this government cannot endure, permanently half slave and half free. I do not expect the Union to be dissolved—I do not expect the house to fall—but I do expect it will cease to be divided. It will become all one thing, or all the other." He went on to warn that slavery's supporters might "put [slavery] forward, till it shall become alike lawful in all the States, old

NATIONAL EVENTS

MAY 15: President Lincoln signs legislation creating the Department of Agriculture

MAY 20: Homestead Act passed

JUN 25–JUL 1: Seven Days' Battle in Virginia; Union troops lose seven times in seven days and end their push toward Richmond

JUL 1: Lincoln signs legislation to begin building a transcontinental railroad

AUG 14: McClellan is ordered to retreat from the peninsula

WORLD EVENTS

JAN 24: Romania formed under rule of King Alexander Cuza

MAR 10: United Kingdom and France recognize Zanzibar's independence

MAY 5: Battle of Puebla: Mexico defeats French army (commemorated annually as Cinco de Mayo)

MAY 7: Massive fire destroys large portion of Enschede, Netherlands

JUL 1: Princess Alice, second daughter of Queen Victoria, marries Prince Ludwig

as well as new—North as well as South." Little doubt that chief among those to watch was his rival, Stephen Douglas.

For six weeks Douglas toured the state with Lincoln close behind. Dubbed "the little giant" for his small stature but large chest and booming voice, Douglas would make his speech, and Lincoln would respond either then or the next day. This tactic proved ineffective, so the Republican challenged his opponent to a series of debates. Douglas reluctantly agreed to participate in seven debates with Lincoln, with both men continuing to crisscross the state campaigning for their parties. When the votes were counted, Republicans had failed to win the majority of the legislature; Lincoln had lost his hope of winning a Senate seat.

PRESIDENTIAL CANDIDATE

Lincoln worked to ensure that his loss would not weaken the Republican Party in Illinois. Newspapers from across the nation had spotlighted the Illinois race since it appeared a good barometer of the rhetoric that would occur in the next presidential campaign. Because of this press coverage, Lincoln had gained national notoriety, and invitations to speak came in from various northern cities. Many supporters were already looking forward to even greater prospects for Lincoln two years down the line. When asked about his ambition for higher office, Lincoln replied, "I must, in candor, say I do not think myself fit for the Presidency."[16] Others, undoubtedly, would share his trepidation, considering that his only national office was a single congressional term and he had never served in any type of executive capacity—on any level.

Lincoln's audiences, nevertheless, had no doubts about his ability. At Cooper Union in New York City, the fifteen hundred people gathered were initially surprised by the odd-looking man before them who was clothed in an ill-fitting new suit and capped by a shock of disheveled hair. But once he began speaking, they no longer cared about his appearance, for his oratory resonated with them, and their thunderous applause shook the hall as he ended his speech: "Let us have faith that right makes might, and in that faith, let us, to the end, dare to do our duty as we understand it."

By May 1860, the Illinois Republican convention agreed to support Lincoln's candidacy for president at the upcoming national convention in Chicago (Lincoln had shrewdly proposed the site). Many believed that William Seward of New York would capture the nomination, but their expectation ran against the opposition posed by states including Indiana, Illinois, Pennsylvania, and Iowa, who voiced concern that Seward was too strong of an abolitionist. Lincoln's team in Chicago met with state delegations and convinced them that he was a better choice, much to the chagrin of another hopeful—Ohioan Salmon P. Chase. On the third ballot, Lincoln the "Rail Splitter" won the nomination, and Springfield erupted in celebration.

The Democratic Party hosted two conventions. The first had dissolved when southern states bolted, upset by the unwillingness of others to preserve the federal protection of territorial slavery in their platform. Ultimately, the party itself split in two: the regular (Northern) Democrats nominated Stephen Douglas, and the newly formed National (Southern) Democrats picked John C. Breckenridge of Kentucky. Yet another party melded together parts of disgruntled Whigs and Know-Nothings (anti-Catholic/pro-nativists) to form the Constitutional Union Party, who fronted John Bell of Tennessee as its candidate.

DID YOU KNOW?

Lincoln was the first president born outside of the original thirteen colonies.

AUG 28–30: Second Battle of Bull Run ends in defeat for Union forces under General John Pope

SEP 17: Battle of Antietam, Maryland, the single bloodiest day of the war ends with General Robert E. Lee and his Confederate forces retreating back to Virginia

SEP 22: Preliminary Emancipation Proclamation issued by Lincoln; will take effect on January 1, 1863, to free all slaves in rebelling states

NOV 7: General Ambrose Burnside replaces General McClellan as Union commander

JUL 1: Russian State Library founded

AUG 9: Berlioz' opera *Beatrice et Benedict* premieres in Baden-Baden, Germany

SEP 22: Otto von Bismarck becomes prime minister of Prussia; he plans to unite Germany

SEP 29: Prime Minister Bismarck delivers famed speech in which he insists that future world issues would not be settled diplomatically, but rather by "blood and iron"

DID YOU KNOW?

Lincoln and Charles Darwin were born on the same day.

Only Douglas actively campaigned; the other three employed the time-honored tradition of allowing others to "stump" for them. Although the candidates and their proxies discussed various subjects, the focus remained on slavery and the possible secession of southern states if Lincoln won. When the votes were counted, Southern fears were realized as Lincoln captured the majority of the electoral vote.

In the months leading to his inauguration, Lincoln could only stand by as an observer to events that would be at the core of his presidency. President Buchanan did little, believing he had no authority to prevent the calamity that threatened the nation. Some members of Congress discussed possible compromises, including amending the Constitution to placate southerners, but Lincoln was solely interested in preserving the Union.

On February 11, 1861, Lincoln bid farewell to his friends and neighbors in Springfield and began his journey east. En route Lincoln received the feared news—seven states had seceded and chosen Jefferson Davis as president of the Confederate States of America. In Baltimore, Pinkerton detectives moved Lincoln from the inaugural train and stealthily whisked him into Washington for fear of a possible assassination. Threats had been arriving since before his election, and the growing hostility within the nation made the possibility of assassination seem very real.

PRESIDENT LINCOLN

In his inaugural speech on March 4, 1861, Lincoln reminded his fellow Americans that the nation's fate rested with the South: "In *your* hands, my dissatisfied-fellow countrymen, and not in *mine*, is the momentous issue of civil war. The Government will not assail you. You can have no conflict without being yourselves the aggressors. *You* have no oath registered in heaven to destroy the Government, while I shall have the most solemn one to 'preserve, protect, and defend it.'"

Scarcely a month later, the South replied by firing on the US Army's garrison based at Fort Sumter in Charleston harbor. After a thirty-four-hour bombardment by Confederate guns, the fort's commander surrendered. The country not only lost a fort, but four more states also seceded, bringing the total to eleven. Border states, including Delaware, Maryland, Kentucky, and Missouri, did not withdraw, and Lincoln was determined to avoid provoking any such action. West Virginia was also created when western counties of Virginia decided not to secede.

Less than twenty miles from the nation's capital, the two armies met in the first (and many hoped only) major battle of the war. Here at Bull Run, the northern army proved itself untrained and unprepared to face its southern counterpart in war. Lincoln refused to keep General Irvin McDowell in charge and sent for another commander, Major General George B. McClellan.

More impressive was the Union naval blockade to prevent the Confederates from exporting their cotton and importing war materiel. The blockade would take years to complete, as the southern coastline stretched over three thousand miles, but its effectiveness was a key component in the Confederacy's eventual capitulation.

After McClellan's appointment, Lincoln allowed his general the rest of 1861 to train the new recruits and mold them into a fighting army. Come spring, the president expected these troops to bring the war to the South. When McClellan hesitated, his commander in chief prodded him a bit harder, and then ultimately relieved him of

NATIONAL EVENTS	**DEC 13:** Battle of Fredericksburg, Virginia, ends in Union defeat and General Burnside is replaced by General "Fighting" Joe Hooker	Dome installed on the top of the national capitol	New song published, "When Johnny Comes Marching Home"	**JAN 1:** Emancipation Proclamation goes into effect (at least on paper)	**JAN 8:** Central Pacific Railroad breaks ground in California and begins laying track east
		1863			
WORLD EVENTS	**DEC 16:** Kingdom of Nepal ratifies its Constitution	Scarlet fever wipes out 30,000 in England	Twelve-year worldwide Cholera epidemic begins	French army occupies Mexico City and offers Mexican throne to Austrian Archduke Maximilian	Cattle disease in Britain sends the cost of beef soaring

supreme command. McClellan was left in charge of the Army of the Potomac, and he was ordered to take Richmond. To add to the Union's troubles, the rebels unleashed their newly outfitted ironclad, the *Virginia* (formerly the *Merrimack*), which proceeded to sink two wooden Union ships. Fear of the damage such an invention could inflict permeated Washington, and the city breathed a sigh of relief when the Union's own ironclad, the *Monitor*, met the *Virginia* in a battle that forced the Southern vessel to withdraw.

Meanwhile, McClellan, who Lincoln said had "the slows," finally arrived in Virginia by sea with one hundred thousand troops to begin his Peninsula campaign. Although the Confederates had built some defensive works, their position was weak. Confederate commander General Joseph Johnston wrote to Robert E. Lee, "No one but McClellan could have hesitated to attack,"[17] but McClellan's timidity allowed the Confederates to effectively counterstrike and protect their capital in Richmond. Ironically, when Lee took command of the Confederate army, McClellan remarked that Lee would be "cautious and weak."[18] Repeatedly, the Union commander begged for more troops. Lincoln promised them but then had to send the men to the Shenandoah Valley in the vain hope of blocking or even capturing General Thomas "Stonewall" Jackson. Lincoln and his secretary of war Edwin Stanton micromanaged the Union military in the east and their cause suffered for it. Troops in the west, however, under the command of Ulysses S. Grant, won a hard-fought victory at Shiloh, Tennessee, and, farther south, Admiral David Farragut's fleet took control of New Orleans.

By July, a new commander, John Pope, promised the president decisive action. Unfortunately that soon happened at the Second Battle of Bull Run, where the Union met a decisive loss, thus allowing Lee to push northward into Maryland. During this time, Lincoln grew more determined to free the slaves but was concerned about the impact of such a move on the border states who, thus far, were still part of the Union. Both he and his cabinet believed that such a decree must be delivered following a victory to prevent talk that the action was only done out of desperation. Now he needed to wait for that victory.

Against the advice of his cabinet, Lincoln put his trust in McClellan once more; this time the general was to pursue Lee northward. By chance, Lee's plans were found and given to McClellan, but again he failed to fully utilize the information. The two armies finally met along Antietam Creek in Maryland, where they fought a day-long battle ending in a marginal northern victory. Unsure of when another victory might occur,

LINCOLN'S BEARD ★ During the election season of 1860, Abraham Lincoln received a letter from eleven-year-old Grace Bedell, who offered advice for him to "let your whiskers grow . . . you would look a great deal better for your face is so thin. All the ladies like whiskers and they would tease their husbands to vote for you and then you would be President." A few days later the candidate replied, "Having never worn any [whiskers], do you not think people would call it a piece of silly affection if I were to begin it now?" Apparently he liked the advice, grew the beard, and showed it off to Grace when his train stopped in her hometown of Westfield, New York, en route to Washington.

FEB 4: First publication appears by Mark Twain, pen name for Samuel L. Clemens

FEB 26: President Lincoln signs National Currency Act to allow US government to print "greenbacks"

APR: Bread riots in Richmond, Virginia

MAY 1: Confederate government passes a resolution to execute any black soldiers who are taken prisoner

MAY 1–5: Battle of Chancellorsville, Virginia, where Union forces are defeated by General Lee

Cunard Line offers low rate transatlantic passage aboard its ships; Irish fleeing another potato famine take advantage and travel to America

Perrier water is introduced commercially

"Football" association formed in England to standardize the rules for soccer

JAN 10: London Underground opens (Paddington to Farringdon Street)

JAN 19: General Mieroslawski installed as Polish dictator

LINCOLN'S SUBSTITUTE ★ Beginning in March 1864, the provost marshal general announced that those men not required to serve in the army could pay a $500 bounty and hire substitutes as a way to be "personally represented." In September 1864, John Summerfield Staples, a twenty-year-old, was walking down Pennsylvania Avenue and was asked if he would be the president's substitute. Staples accepted and served the next eleven months as part of the defenses of Washington. He was discharged in September 1865. Sadly, he never received a pension and dropped dead from a heart attack in 1888 at the age of forty-three. He is buried in Stroudsburg, Pennsylvania.

Lincoln decided the time had come to issue his Emancipation Proclamation.

In September 1862, President Lincoln announced that slaves in the rebelling territories would be freed as of January 1, 1863. Border states were excluded, as well as areas under Union occupation, and Tennessee. Some abolitionists complained that the order did not go far enough. Within days, its news was overshadowed by the president's next announcement—the suspension of the writ of habeas corpus and the right of the government to arrest anyone who it believed was disloyal. Democrats used both developments to their advantage in state and congressional elections. Lincoln blamed the significant Republican setbacks on the poor showing in the war, and many Republicans blamed their losses on Lincoln.

After McClellan failed to move out of Maryland, Lincoln visited him, and while viewing the Army of the Potomac in camp, remarked that the unit should be renamed "McClellan's bodyguard." Their meeting yielded no change in the general's attitude. "Little Mac" despised Lincoln and what he believed were the president's misguided attempts to conduct a war with no military expertise. Lincoln's patience exhausted, he fired McClellan and appointed Ambrose Burnside.

Burnside led the army to Fredericksburg, Virginia, where they were soundly defeated. Lincoln then turned to "Fighting Joe" Hooker, who took the field in May 1863. Once more the Union army met defeat, this time at the Battle of Chancellorsville, Virginia. Unfortunately for the South, the rebels lost one of their top generals, "Stonewall" Jackson, as a result of friendly fire. Hooker was soon replaced by George Meade as Lincoln continued to seek a winning commander.

The president faced more criticism on the home front with the passage of the conscription act, which made men ages twenty to forty-five eligible for military service. Outrage over this and the provision that allowed wealthy men to pay a substitute rather than serve themselves generated considerable political dissension. Rioting ensued in New York City over the draft, but quickly turned into an excuse for violence against its black population, who were viewed by immigrant laborers as competitors for the same jobs. During a three-day period in mid-July 1863, hundreds were killed and scores of buildings burned before troops from the Gettysburg battlefront were able to restore order. During this time, Congress also passed the National Banking Act, creating for the first time a national currency; passed the Homestead Act (the opening of public domain lands to settlement—160 acres of free land granted to the adult head of household); authorized a transcontinental railroad; established land-grant colleges; inaugurated an income tax; and established the Department of Agriculture—proof that the

NATIONAL EVENTS

MAY 2: Confederate General Stonewall Jackson is accidentally shot by his own men

MAY 10: Stonewall Jackson dies of pneumonia

MAY 22: General Grant begins siege of Vicksburg, Mississippi

JUN 17: Incorporation of Travelers Insurance of Connecticut makes it America's first accident insurer

JUN 20: West Virginia enters the Union as the 35th state

WORLD EVENTS

JAN 22: January Uprising, a national movement to regain commonwealth of Poland, Lithuania, and Belarus from Russian occupation

FEB 10: World-famous General Tom Thumb and Lavinia Warren marry; P.T. Barnum charges admission

MAR 10: Albert Edward, Prince of Wales, marries Princess Alexandra of Denmark

MAR 30: Prince Wilhelm George of Denmark elected King George I of Greece

APR 30: Battle of Camarón, Mexico

business of government continues even as soldiers march to war.

Lincoln's sons, Willie and Tad, did succeed in occasionally helping to take their father's mind off the war. The boys had never experienced much parental supervision, and their life in the White House was no different as they enjoyed the run of the mansion, including their father's office. Mary allowed them to keep a variety of animals outside. Two of their favorites were goats, one of which Tad yoked to his sled and rode through the East Room in the middle of a reception. Tragedy struck the family suddenly on February 20, 1862, when Willie died from typhoid fever. Mary was inconsolable and spent months in mourning; Lincoln kept to himself in his office where he could weep in private, while Tad lay grieving in his room. Eldest son Robert continued his studies at Harvard (and was also criticized for not serving in the war), so both parents lavished their attention on nine-year-old Tad.

Criticism was nothing new to Mary. Soon after becoming First Lady, she was taken to task for her overspending of the appropriation for White House furnishings. At times she ventured to New York, where she often spent lavish sums on clothing and household items. She attempted to keep the expenditures a secret from her husband and tried to gain as much as possible through gifts. Whenever Abe learned of Mary's extravagances, he would chastise her, but as he told a guest once, "My wife is as handsome as when she was a girl and I, a poor nobody then, fell in love with her and once more, have never fallen out."[19] Few could understand his devotion to a woman whose mercurial temperament often frightened everyone else. Lincoln's attention to his wife remained steadfast, however. Once, when Mary fell from a carriage during an accident, Lincoln stayed by her side as long as he possibly could, considering his other, weighty responsibilities. To her credit, Mary did work at the hospitals in Washington, serving as a listener, scribe, and waitress, and one acquaintance remarked that if journalists had accompanied her on those trips, her reputation might have been greatly enhanced. The First Lady endured more gossip and negative remarks when her half-sister, Emilie Helm, visited the White House after being widowed. The lady's late husband had been a Confederate officer, and many criticized the Lincolns sharply for allowing her to visit.

The president's unflinching devotion to his wife was returned in kind. Mary's main concern was always her husband. She fretted over his health, his lack of eating, his long hours, sleepless nights, and rapid aging. Lincoln tried to reassure her—and the country—claiming things would be better once the North was winning the war.

Secretary of State William Seward also did what he could to minimize the strain on the president by dealing with international issues that might otherwise occupy him. Seward skillfully steered the State Department away from foreign entanglements that could be especially problematic for the administration. Keeping Britain out of the war was essential, and Lincoln dispatched Charles Francis Adams (son of one president and grandson of another) to convince the British to remain on the sidelines of the Civil War, even if it meant losing their precious imported southern cotton.

TURNING POINT

Fresh from his victories in Virginia, Robert E. Lee moved north once more into Pennsylvania, and newly appointed General George Meade followed. The two armies met for three brutally hot days

JUN 28: General Hooker is replaced with General George Meade to lead the Union Army

JUN 29: George A. Custer promoted to brevet rank of brigadier general at age 23

JUL 1–3: Battle of Gettysburg, Pennsylvania, where Union forces under General Meade stop Lee's invasion of the north and deal his army a devastating loss

JUL 4: After weeks of fighting, Vicksburg, Mississippi, surrenders to General Grant

MAY 15: *Le dejeuner sur l'herbe* by Edouard Manet is exhibited at Paris's *Salon des Refuses*

MAY 23: First socialist workers party formed in Germany

MAY 25: Playwright Colin H. Haslewood's *Lady Audley's Secret* premiers at London's Royal Victoria Theatre

JUN 7: French troops capture Mexico City

JUL 1: Slavery abolished in Suriname and Netherlands Antilles

around the quiet town of Gettysburg. When the battle was over, the Union had struck a major victory, causing Lee to retreat back to Virginia. The next day, July fourth, news arrived that Ulysses S. Grant had finally taken Vicksburg on the Mississippi River. Soon Grant moved to eastern Tennessee and broke the siege at Chattanooga, opening the way for General William Sherman to cut a wide swath of destruction through the South during his "march to the sea."

In November 1863, the people of Gettysburg wished to dedicate their new cemetery and invited Edward Everett, a well-known orator, to speak. They tendered an invitation to Lincoln out of courtesy, and were surprised by his acceptance. On November 19, Everett spoke for two hours, and then Lincoln rose. His speech, which he expected that "people would little note nor long remember," did not receive much attention at the time because of its brevity. Fortunately, however, it was published, and in time, was acclaimed as perhaps the most stirring oration in American history.

Throughout the war, Lincoln had steadfastly stood by Grant even though rumors swirled about the general's drinking and criticism of his abnormally high casualty rate was widespread. The president refused to replace the general because, stated simply, "He fights." Once Chattanooga fell, Lincoln felt secure in his next move and invited Grant to Washington, where he bestowed the rank of lieutenant general (not used since George Washington) to head the Union armies. In private, Lincoln told the new commander that he had always wanted someone in charge who would be willing to "take the responsibility and act"[20] knowing that the president would provide support.

Feeling that the war was in capable hands, Lincoln now turned his attention to his reelection. Some Republicans worried that Lincoln's renomination would spell disaster, for they doubted he could be reelected. Still, when the party met in Baltimore, it was agreed by overwhelming majority that Lincoln should remain their man. The nomination for vice president presented more of a problem. Hannibal Hamlin wanted to remain vice president, but Lincoln had other ideas. He pushed for an unlikely man—Andrew Johnson of Tennessee, a Democrat who had stayed in Congress because he believed his loyalty should lie with the Union. Johnson became the vice presidential nominee, but within the year, many would question the wisdom of this decision.

The Democrats met in Chicago, denounced the president and the war as failures, and then nominated the man who had both denounced the president and failed in the war—George B. McClellan. He pledged to win a negotiated peace rather than continue the tragic loss of lives; George Pendleton of Ohio was selected as his running mate.

With the prospect of an extended war looming ahead, the political climate seemed to favor McClellan; in fact, Lincoln himself believed his former general would soon be president and wrote a memorandum to that effect: "General, the election has demonstrated that you are stronger, have more influence with the American people than I. Now let us together, you with your influence and I with all the executive power of the Government, try to save the country."[21] McClellan's hopes, however, evaporated with Sherman's capture of Atlanta in September. Americans now wondered why the Democrats wanted to negotiate a peace, so McClellan started backtracking from his own party's platform, arguing that he would do no such thing. Democrats still clung to the hope that "Mac

NATIONAL EVENTS

JUL 11: Union Army begins drafting men

JUL 12: Worst draft riot in US history in New York City

JUL 18: Union forces fail to take Battery Wagner; the 54th Massachusetts, an African American regiment, bears brunt of the casualties, losing nearly half its men including its commander, Colonel Robert Gould Shaw

AUG 21: Raid on Lawrence, Kansas, by Quantrill's Raiders

SEP 2: General William T. Sherman captures Atlanta, Georgia

WORLD EVENTS

JUL 11: Japanese battleship shoots at warship *Medusa* under the Dutch flag, kills four

AUG 11: Cambodia becomes French protectorate

AUG 12: Lumber shipments begin out of the Burrard Inlet near Vancouver, B.C., Canada

OCT 1: Dutch railway opens

OCT 26–29: Resolutions of the Geneva International Conference signed

Will Win the Union Back," while Republicans countered, "Don't swap horses in the middle of the stream." With the introduction of absentee voting, Union soldiers, wanting to ensure that they were not risking their lives unnecessarily, helped turn the prevailing tide. (Interestingly, although McClellan had been a popular general among his men, they still overwhelmingly favored the president, who won 120,000 of the soldiers' 154,000 votes.) With no splintering of political parties, but lacking the eleven Confederate states (parts of Union-occupied Tennessee and Louisiana voted, but their results were not counted), Lincoln won 55 percent of the popular vote and 212 electoral votes to McClellan's twelve.

Gratified and bolstered by the country's mandate, Lincoln resumed his duties, anxiously planning the South's postwar reconstruction. Others, however, were not as pleased with the election results and the number of threats against the president increased. Would-be conspirators discussed kidnapping and holding him for the ransom of a negotiated peace, while others contemplated assassination. Security was enhanced, as more Army guards were assigned to the president (the Secret Service was not commissioned until July 5, 1865, and only became responsible for the safety of the president after the assassination of President McKinley in 1901), but his safety was still a critical issue. A shot was fired at the president while he was riding his horse one evening, but except for a hole in his hat, Lincoln remained unscathed. When asked about the incident, Lincoln admitted to a reporter, "I know I am in danger, but I am not going to worry over threats like these."[22] Rather than succumb to fear, the president was determined to move forward with the country's future.

1865

Among the letters Lincoln wrote in early 1865 was one addressed to Grant, the purpose of which was more fatherly than presidential. Robert Lincoln had graduated from Harvard and desired a place in the Army. Worried that having an officer's rank might incur jealousy among those who had served longer, the president, and concerned father, asked, "Could he, without embarrassment to you, or detriment to the service, go into your Military family with some nominal rank?"[23] Grant honored the president's request, and Robert Lincoln entered the Army as a captain, soon winning respect as a hard worker and dedicated soldier.

Also in January 1865, the floor of the Congress was hot with debate regarding the Thirteenth Amendment, which abolished slavery throughout the United States. Lincoln was determined, and worked tirelessly, to gain support from border state congressmen; eventually his efforts were rewarded. Journalist and social reformer William Lloyd Garrison hailed the president as the "chain breaker for millions of the oppressed."[23]

At the same time, Lincoln was involved, at first indirectly, with peace negotiations on the international front. Francis Blair, a seventy-three-year-old former editor and member of Andrew Jackson's "Kitchen Cabinet," offered to unofficially discuss the possibility of halting the war in the United States long enough to unite the two armies and attack French forces in Mexico. (The French, capitalizing on the United States' attention to its own civil war, had seized power—and the profitable mines—in Mexico and placed Emperor Maximilian in charge.) Some American leaders hoped that such unified action (the Union and Confederate armies, fighting together in Mexico against the French) would lead to a unified nation.

DID YOU KNOW?

Lincoln was the first president to be assassinated.

SEP 19–20: Battle of Chickamauga, Tennessee, is won by Grant and his Union forces

OCT 3: Lincoln proclaims the last Thursday in November as a day of Thanksgiving

NOV 19: Lincoln delivers his famed "Gettysburg Address" at the dedication of its new national cemetery

NOV 23–25: Battle of Chattanooga, Tennessee, is won by Grant and General William T. Sherman

DEC 2: Union Pacific Railroad begins breaking ground in Nebraska Territory to build a railroad west

OCT 29: International Red Cross formed in Geneva by sixteen countries

NOV 15: King Frederick VII of Denmark dies

DEC 8: Jesuit church in Chile catches fire during service, nearly 2,500 perish

DID YOU KNOW?

Lincoln is the only president to receive a patent; his was a device to move boats over shoals.

Jefferson Davis agreed to consider it to win peace between the two countries. This last point was not amenable to Lincoln and Secretary of War Stanton, who argued the country had never been two nations but always one. Davis maintained his stance but agreed to move forward with sending peace commissioners to Fort Monroe, including Confederate Vice President Alexander Stephens. They met in Petersburg with General Grant and were impressed by his desire to end the war. Although Secretary of State Seward was to meet them, Grant implored Lincoln to attend as well. So the president quietly slipped down to the fort and met with the Confederate delegation for four hours. Although the talks were civil and informal, neither side was willing to concede its position, and the men adjourned acknowledging that they had reached an impasse.

Radical Republicans were incensed when they heard what had occurred, berating the executive branch for attempting to sell out for a dishonorable peace. The House Republicans demanded full disclosure from the president, which he provided via his correspondence. As the documents were read, the House listened intently and approvingly to the exchange; their fears were put to rest.

Lincoln still desperately desired a peaceful solution and end to the nearly four-year-long nightmare that the country had experienced. He proposed paying slave owners reparations for the loss of their slaves, and calculated it would cost the country four million dollars, payable by means of a tax; he insisted the same amount would be spent if the war were continued. Lincoln's cabinet adamantly vetoed the idea, so the president sadly pushed aside his hope to end the casualties, which numbered more than 490,000 by 1865.

SECOND TERM

On March 4, 1865, braving a steady rain, crowds attended the second inauguration of the sixteenth president. First outgoing vice president Hamlin spoke, then the new vice president, Andrew Johnson, stood, albeit unsteadily, and proceeded to launch into a twenty-minute incoherent, rambling speech. The uncomfortable situation prompted Secretary of the Navy Gideon Welles to whisper, "Johnson is either drunk or crazy"[24] to Secretary of War Stanton. After Johnson's swearing-in, the president took the oath administered by newly appointed Chief Justice Salmon P. Chase (a former cabinet member). Then Lincoln read his second inaugural speech, ending with the promising words: "With malice toward none, with charity for all, with firmness in the right as God gives us to see the right, let us strive to finish the work we are in, to bind up the nation's wounds, to care for him who shall have borne the battle and for his widow and his orphan, to do all which may achieve and cherish a just and lasting peace among ourselves and with all nations."

A few weeks later, Lincoln eagerly accepted an invitation from Grant to visit City Point, Virginia, close to Petersburg. The president met with Grant, and later, Sherman arrived from North Carolina. The group, along with Admiral David Porter, chatted, the military leaders asking the president what would happen to the rebels after the war. Lincoln answered that he desired only to defeat the troops and return the men to their homes. "I want no one punished; treat them liberally all around. We want those people to return their allegiance to the Union and submit to the laws."[25]

Lincoln's ideas about the South's reconstruction did, however, differ from those of his cabinet and

NATIONAL EVENTS

FEB: First Navajos arrive at their New Mexico reservation after being forced on the "Long Walk" of over 300 miles by Colonel Kit Carson

FEB 17: Confederate submarine *H.L. Hunley* sinks in Charleston harbor after ramming the USS *Housatonic* with explosives

FEB 27: Andersonville POW camp in Georgia accepts its first group of Union prisoners

MAR 10: Ulysses S. Grant takes command of all Union armies

APR 22: Treasury Secretary Salmon P. Chase orders the phrase "In God We Trust" to be printed on all money

1864

WORLD EVENTS

New Zealand Settlements Act enacted—large areas of land confiscated from Maori tribes by the government

Imperial forces attack capital of Nanking in last great civil war battle of Taiping Rebellion

Dostoyevsky writes the novel *Notes from Underground*

Tolstoy writes *War and Peace*

Pope Pius IX condemns socialism and cautions followers against liberal agendas

Congress. He believed in keeping southern legislatures, as well as their court system, arguing that in the latter's absence, "the disbanded armies would turn into robber bands and guerrillas."[26] Stanton voiced his objections repeatedly, and when Lincoln heard of the proposed meeting of the Virginia legislature, he acknowledged that they might possibly plot against the victors, so ordered that the body should not be allowed to assemble.

LINCOLN'S DREAMS ★ According to one of Lincoln's friends, Ward Hill Lamon, a few days before Lincoln's assassination, Lincoln experienced a disturbing dream that he related to his friends and family. Lincoln said in his dream he was asleep, but awakened to the sound of sobbing. He rose from his bed and wandered the rooms of the White House looking for its source and finally went downstairs to the East Room. "There I met with a sickening surprise. Before me was a catafalque, on which rested a corpse wrapped in funeral vestments." Crowds of mourners filled the room, and Lincoln said he asked one of the guards on duty who had died. He was told it was the president—"He was killed by an assassin." Lincoln awoke from the dream, but admitted it preyed on his mind afterward.

FINAL DAYS

During the first two weeks of April 1865, Grant and the Union Army pursued Lee as he abandoned Petersburg and Richmond; Lee surrendered the Army of Northern Virginia on April 9, 1865. The war was nearly at an end.

The next day, guns bellowed a salute and jubilant crowds besieged the White House, where they heard a few remarks from the president, who requested the band to play "Dixie." That night crowds returned to hear prepared remarks by the president, who addressed how the former enemy should be treated. Standing among the listeners was actor John Wilkes Booth and a few of his friends. These southern sympathizers had long hated the president and discussed possibly kidnapping him. Now with the war all but over, something more final seemed appropriate.

General Grant received a hero's welcome in the city of Washington, and he was invited to the cabinet meeting on the following day, Good Friday. Lincoln felt it was better to consider the terms of Reconstruction when Congress was not in session, because "there were men . . . who possessed feelings of hate and vindictiveness in which he did not sympathize and could not participate. He hoped there would be no persecution, no bloody work, after the war was over."[27] The president also informed those in attendance that he was opposed to the hanging of Confederate leaders since it would only serve to propagate the bloodshed.

The Lincolns wanted to celebrate, and agreed that seeing the final performance of the hit comedy *Our American Cousin* would be a fine way to do it. They invited various people to accompany them, including the Grants and officers of the War Department, but none could attend. Finally Clara Harris, daughter of a senator, and her fiancé, Major Henry Rathbone, accepted. A messenger carried word to Ford's Theater that the president would attend; the management quickly began publicizing their featured guest. One who was keenly interested in the news was well-known actor John Wilkes Booth, who immediately began making his plans.

MAY: Fighting near Fredericksburg, Virginia, between Grant's and Lee's forces in the battles of the Wilderness and Spotsylvania Courthouse

JUN: Congress adopts measure to protect California's Yosemite Valley as a "scenic reserve"

JUN 12: Grant moves southward after losing Battle of Cold Harbor, Virginia

JUN 15: Siege of Petersburg, Virginia, begins (south of Richmond)

JUN 15: Creation of Arlington National Cemetery (on grounds of former home of Robert E. Lee and Mary Custis Lee)

Napoleon ends French ban on workers' associations

Norwegian Sven Foyn devises harpoon gun with explosive heads

JAN 11: Charing Cross Station opens in London

FEB 1: Danish-Prussian War begins with invasion of Denmark by Prussian and Austrian troops

MAR 1: Alejandro Mon Menendez sworn in as Spain's Prime Minister

JOHN WILKES BOOTH (1838–1865) ★ John Wilkes Booth was the second generation of an acting family. His father, Junius Brutus Booth Sr., came to America in 1821; his three sons carried on the tradition. John was his middle son, born in 1838. He began acting in stock companies in Baltimore and Philadelphia at the age of seventeen, but was considered an inferior actor, especially when compared to his father and older brother Edwin. Booth went to Richmond to hone his skills and while there he enjoyed the southern lifestyle. He briefly served in the Richmond Grays, a military unit that witnessed John Brown's hanging in 1859. Booth left Richmond, but his sympathies remained with the Confederacy, and he possibly smuggled items into the South. For months prior to the assassination, Booth schemed to kidnap Lincoln and then trade him for Confederate prisoners. After Lee's surrender, his plans changed—he would now assassinate the president.

ASSASSINATION

Booth was familiar with the play and knew precisely when he planned to kill the president. His access to the president's box was fairly easy since the Washington policeman functioning as the president's bodyguard was absent from his post. The only person outside the box was a White House footman, to whom Booth presented his card before being allowed to enter. Booth stepped inside quietly and stood in the shadows, waiting for the biggest laugh of the evening, at which point he moved directly behind Lincoln and fired a derringer aimed at the president's head. After warding off Rathbone's lunge with a large knife, Booth leapt to the stage, but his spur caught in the flag bunting and he took an awkward fall, breaking his left leg. He fled the theater, yelling "*Sic semper tyrannis*" (Thus ever to tyrants!).

Two doctors on the scene pronounced Lincoln's wounds to be fatal but wanted him moved to where he could be examined more fully. He was carried across the street to the Petersen boardinghouse and stretched across a bed. While physicians labored over the president's near lifeless body, others had been summoned to the home of Secretary of State Seward. He, too, had been attacked in the evening by one of Booth's partners, Lewis Paine. Seward had been in bed recuperating from a carriage accident when Paine posed as a deliveryman with medicine to gain access to his victim, then slashed both Seward and his son. Fortunately, a surgical collar on Seward's neck protected him from a fatal stabbing.

Lincoln never regained consciousness and, at 7:22 a.m., the president died. Stanton's words were, "Now he belongs to the ages."[28] On the following Wednesday a funeral service was held, but Mary was too distraught to attend. The president's body was taken home to Springfield, Illinois, and buried at the new Oak Ridge Cemetery outside of town.

On April 26, John Wilkes Booth was found in a Virginia tobacco barn by men of the 16th New York Cavalry Regiment. Sergeant Boston Corbett disobeyed orders and mortally wounded Booth. Three other conspirators and Paine were found guilty in the plot and hanged; others were imprisoned.

AFTERWARD

Mary remained at the White House for more than a month, and then with trunks and boxes packed, she and her sons moved to Chicago. There in a hotel, she replayed the assassination continually in her mind, and to the precious few visitors she was willing to receive. Eventually she and Tad

NATIONAL EVENTS	**JUN 27:** General Sherman loses the Battle of Kennesaw Mountain outside of Atlanta	**JUL 14:** Gold discovered in Helena, Montana	**JUL 30:** Union soldiers try to break siege of Petersburg by blowing up part of Confederate line (Battle of the Crater)	**AUG 5:** Union Admiral David Farragut takes Mobile Bay	**AUG 31:** Democratic Party meeting in Chicago nominates George B. McClellan as presidential candidate
WORLD EVENTS	**MAR 29:** Britain returns Corfu and Ionian islands to Greece	**APR 10:** Archduke Maximilian of Austria made emperor of Mexico	**JUN 12:** Maximilian arrives in Mexico City to become emperor	**AUG 22:** Geneva Convention signed; rules for treating prisoners of war is accepted by twelve nations	**SEP 28:** British and French trade unions, the International Working Men's Association, meet in London for the first time

traveled to Europe, but upon their return, she had to endure the loss of yet another beloved family member. Tad succumbed to a heart ailment at the tender age of eighteen.

Mary quarreled constantly with her surviving son, Robert, about expenses and her behavior. He ultimately committed her to an insane asylum, where she stayed for four months before being released to her sister. After suffering a stroke, Mary Todd Lincoln died on July 16, 1882, at the age of sixty-three. She was entombed along with her husband and three of their sons at Oak Ridge Cemetery. Robert died in 1926 and was buried at Arlington Cemetery. Today there are no direct descendants of Abraham Lincoln, but he left an enduring legacy in his words and his actions.

Historians consistently rank Lincoln as the greatest president in American history, and he continues to be revered to this day for his determined perseverance in pursuing the Civil War to its ultimate victorious conclusion and insisting that the former enemy be treated as brothers once more. When Lincoln first ran for public office in 1832, he wrote: "I can say for one that I have no other [ambition] so great as that of being truly esteemed of my fellow men, by rendering myself worthy of their esteem."[29] Abraham Lincoln assuredly achieved his ambition.

ENDNOTES

1 Roy P. Basler, ed., *The Collected Works of Abraham Lincoln*, vol. VII, New Brunswick, NJ: Rutgers University Press, 1953, p. 512.

2 William H. Herndon and Jesse W. Weik, *Herndon's Lincoln: The True Story of a Great Life*, Chicago: Belford-Clarke, 1890, vol. I, p. 3.

3 Carl Sandburg, *Abraham Lincoln, The Prairie Years*, vol. I, New York: Hartcourt, Brace & World, Inc., 1926, p. 161.

4 Abraham Lincoln, *Selected Speeches and Writings*, New York: Vintage Books, 1992, p. 81.

5 Jean H. Baker, *Mary Todd Lincoln*, New York: W.W. Norton & Co., 1987, p. 89.

6 Sandburg, p. 335.

7 Sandburg, vol. II, p. 24.

8 Sandburg, vol., I, p. 367.

9 David Herbert Donald, *Lincoln*, New York: Simon & Schuster, 1995, p. 123.

10 Basler, vol. I, p. 431.

11 Donald, p. 140.

12 Ibid, p. 148.

13 Ibid, p. 176.

14 Ibid, p. 178.

15 Ibid, p. 179.

16 Ibid, p. 235.

17 Bruce Catton, *Mr. Lincoln's Army*, New York: Doubleday & Co., 1962, p. 109.

18 Stephen W. Sears, ed., *The Civil War Papers of George B. McClellan*, New York: Ticknor & Fields, 1989, p. 244.

19 Baker, p. 198.

20 Doris Kearns Goodwin, *Team of Rivals, The Political Genius of Abraham Lincoln*, New York: Simon & Schuster, 2005, p. 616.

21 Tyler Dennett, ed., *Lincoln and the Civil War in the Diaries and Letters of John Hay*, New York: Dodd, Mead, & Co., 1939, p. 428.

22 Donald, p. 550.

23 Goodwin, p. 690.

24 Ibid, p. 698.

25 David D. Porter, *Incidents and Anecdotes of the Civil War*, New York: D. Appleton and Company, 1886, p. 314.

26 Goodwin, p. 729.

27 Ibid, p. 732.

28 Donald, p. 599.

29 *Sangamon Journal*, March 9, 1832.

SEP 2: General Sherman takes Atlanta

OCT 31: Nevada admitted as 36th state

NOV 8: Lincoln reelected

NOV 16: Sherman's troops begin their infamous "march to the sea"

NOV 29: Cheyenne encampment is attacked by Colonel John Chivington; more than 150 Cheyenne are massacred, mainly women and children

DEC 15–16: Union forces win the Battle of Nashville

DEC 22: Sherman takes Savannah

OCT 5: Cyclone kills more than 60,000 in Calcutta

OCT 30: Prussia wins war against Denmark and gains several territories

DEC: Beginning of Latin America's bloodiest conflict when dictator of Paraguay, Francisco Solano López, declares war on Brazil

Andrew Johnson

★ ★ ★ SEVENTEENTH PRESIDENT ★ ★ ★

LIFE SPAN
- Born: December 29, 1808, in Raleigh, North Carolina
- Died: July 31, 1875, in Carter's Station, Tennessee

RELIGION
- No formal affiliation

HIGHER EDUCATION
- None

PROFESSION
- Tailor

MILITARY SERVICE
- Civil War: served as military governor of Tennessee, 1862–1864, with rank of brigadier general

FAMILY
- Father: **Jacob Johnson** (1778–1812)
- Mother: **Mary "Polly" McDonough Johnson** (1783–1856)
- Wife: **Eliza McCardle Johnson** (1810–1876); wed May 17, 1827, in Warrensburg, Tennessee
- Children: **Martha** (1828–1901); **Charles** (1830–1863); **Mary** (1832–1883); **Robert** (1834–1869); **Andrew** (1852–1879)

POLITICAL LIFE
- Greeneville, Tennessee alderman (1828–1830)
- Greeneville mayor (1830–1833)
- Tennessee House of Representatives (1835–1837, 1839–1841)
- Tennessee state senator (1841–1843)
- US representative (1843–1853)
- Governor of Tennessee (1853–1857)
- US senator (1857–1862)
- Military governor of Tennessee (1862–1864)
- Vice president (March–April 1865)

PRESIDENCY
- One term: April 15, 1865–March 4, 1869 (assumed presidency upon death of President Abraham Lincoln)
- Democrat
- Reason for leaving office: did not win party's nomination
- Vice president: none

CABINET

SECRETARY OF STATE
William H. Seward (1865–1869)*

SECRETARY OF THE TREASURY
Hugh McCullough (1865–1869)*

SECRETARY OF WAR
Edwin M. Stanton (1865–1868)*

John M. Sheffield (1868–1869)

ATTORNEY GENERAL
James Speed (1865–1866)*

Henry Stanberry (1866–1868)

William M. Evarts (1868–1869)

SECRETARY OF THE NAVY
Gideon Welles (1865–1869)*

POSTMASTER GENERAL
William Dennison (1865–1866)*

Alexander W. Randall (1866–1869)

SECRETARY OF THE INTERIOR
John P. Usher (1865)*

James Harlan (1865–1866)

Orville H. Browning (1866–1869)

***Holdover from Lincoln's cabinet**

While some presidents grew up in humble circumstances, none had a more modest beginning than Andrew Johnson. His family in North Carolina was dirt poor and ridiculed as "white trash" by the townspeople. But he would raise himself above his past to reach the highest pinnacle in America, only to be cast down from it in the first-ever impeachment of the presidency.

EARLY LIFE

Jacob Johnson barely kept his family clothed and fed through his menial jobs, including working as a bank janitor and porter at an inn in Raleigh, North Carolina. Jacob and Polly McDonough Johnson already had one four-year-old son, William, when another arrived on December 29, 1808, in a room at the back of the inn where both parents worked. Three years later, Jacob died after rescuing three men from drowning, and Polly struggled to keep her sons, but was unable to send them to school since the only schools available required tuition. Later Johnson would say, "I have grappled with the gaunt and haggard monster called hunger."[1] Once they were teenagers, she was able to indenture them as apprentices to a tailor, James Selby. There they gained the rudiments of an education, some training in the tailor trade, and for Andrew, an appreciation for oratory. Sometimes the town's gentlemen visited the shop and debated, or one of them would read from various oratorical books. The Johnson boys' apprenticeships were unfortunately cut short when both boys ran away after a neighbor threatened to sue them for vandalizing her house. Selby ran an advertisement offering a ten-dollar reward for both, or Andrew alone. The boys did not return.

They eventually decided to move out of state for safety and landed in South Carolina, where Andrew found work as a tailor. There he also fell in love and proposed marriage; again misfortune struck as the mother adamantly opposed her daughter marrying a pauper. So Andrew left and decided the time was ripe to return home to clear his name. He visited his former master, hoping to be released from his indenture, but was refused. Again, Johnson felt it unwise to remain, so he cast his lot west—over the mountains to Tennessee.

TAILOR

Now eighteen, young Johnson was able to "hitch a ride" with others headed westward. He moved about and finally landed in Columbia, Tennessee, where he worked a few months, but ultimately decided to take his mother and stepfather to eastern Tennessee where older brother William had already settled. They loaded all of their worldly belongings into a two-wheeled cart and came upon Greeneville, a village named for Revolutionary War hero Nathaniel Greene, and spent the night. The next morning, Andrew walked around, liked what he saw, and began plying his tailor trade.

He soon moved on, but love brought him back to Greeneville. Eliza McCardle was the sixteen-year-old daughter of a cobbler who had no prejudice against a craftsman, and Andrew proposed. Andrew and Eliza were married in May 1827 by Reverend Mordecai Lincoln, cousin to the future president.

The young couple developed a partnership in which she tutored him in reading and writing while he worked in his tailor shop. His work, however, did not suffer as he proudly recalled, "My work never ripped or gave way."[2] Their first child, a daughter Martha, was born in 1828, and the Johnsons had three more children in two-year intervals—two boys and another girl. Then twenty-

NATIONAL EVENTS

John D. Rockefeller opens the first oil refinery	Oregon's Mount Hood erupts and then falls silent	John B. Stetson, Philadelphia hatmaker, creates the ten-gallon hat	**JAN 7:** Union Pacific advertises in a Sacramento newspaper for 5,000 laborers to build the railroad eastward	**JAN 13:** Second Battle of Fort Fisher: Union forces launch major amphibious assault against Confederate stronghold in North Carolina

1865

WORLD EVENTS

First pay toilets open outside the London Exchange, cost one cent	Au Printemps department store opens in Paris	Francis Galton introduces eugenics	Gregor Mendel explains heredity	Peruvian general Mariano Ignacio Prado ousts President Juan Antonio Pezet

four years after Martha's birth, their fifth child, Andrew Jr. (known as Frank), was born.

EARLY POLITICAL CAREER

Johnson thoroughly enjoyed his political discussions with men who would come to his tailor shop and discuss politics. He soon joined a debating society at Greeneville College and took part in forensic activities at Tusculum College four miles away, activities that provided Andrew with a means of networking with the more intellectual and powerful men in the area. The germination of a political career was beginning to take root.

Johnson took his first political step in 1828 by winning the seat of alderman for Greeneville. He served in that position for six years before capturing the mayoral seat and remaining there for three years. Always keeping the benefit of the working class uppermost in his activities became the hallmark for the young tailor. Still, he was eager to emerge from that label, and gradually earned a reasonable income from real estate investing in addition to his tailoring. Accordingly, he then moved his family into a bigger home and began buying domestic slaves.

Johnson's political career prospered as well, and in 1835, he was elected to the Tennessee state assembly, where he voted mostly as an independent. He argued against measures that increased government spending, but contrary to the views of many of his constituents, he opposed the extension of railroads, believing they would spell the demise of roadside inns. Tennesseans were not pleased and refused to reelect him in 1837.

Although unseated, Johnson still kept informed and in contact with men throughout the state. In 1839, he made the decision to become a Jackson Democrat, announced himself as such and returned to Nashville. There he was part of the welcoming committee for the newly elected governor and fellow Democrat James K. Polk. While serving in the legislature, Andrew opposed any bills supporting the national bank or independent treasury, and he often extolled the virtues of Thomas Jefferson and the Democratic Party, whose "constant aim has been to preserve our Government in its original purity."[3] He also backed Martin Van Buren's unsuccessful reelection bid in 1840. Johnson shocked party members with his stance against the prayers said at every session and was labeled an "atheist." But what sent many into a tailspin was when he suggested removing the three-fifths provision of counting slaves when figuring representation in the redistricting of the state. Another "A" word was used—abolitionist. His own slaveholding argued against the charge, but many remained unsure about where exactly his loyalties lay.

Back home in Greene County, he enjoyed the power of party leadership. On occasion, he would call for a meeting, and men would come in from miles to hear Johnson speak. He would address the topic of the day, and one eyewitness described Johnson's public speaking: "He was forcible and powerful without being eloquent. He held his crowd spellbound. There was always in his speeches more or less wit, humor, and anecdote which relieved them from tedium and heaviness."[4] No doubt this was useful in speeches that usually ran from two to three hours. Helping guide the audience was the Greene County sheriff standing to the side, prodding them when to laugh, shout, or applaud. The Democrats of eastern Tennessee were always an appreciative audience and would be content to follow his lead in the years to come.

DID YOU KNOW?

Johnson lacked a formal education, but his wife Eliza taught him the basics of reading, writing, and arithmetic.

JAN 15: Union forces capture Fort Fisher

JAN 31: Robert E. Lee becomes general-in-chief of Confederate forces

MAR 3: Congress authorizes the creation of the Freedmen's Bureau

MAR 4: Lincoln inaugurated for a second term; Andrew Johnson of Tennessee as vice president

MAR 18: Confederate Congress meets for the final time

Bhutan signs a treaty ceding control of southern passes to Britain

India is linked to Britain by telegraph

Economic depression hits South Africa

American mapmaker A. J. Johnson makes map of northwestern South America

Waikato and Taranaki Wars end in New Zealand

DID YOU KNOW?

The first state visit by a monarch occurred during Johnson's term when Queen Emma of the Sandwich Islands (Hawaii) visited.

CONGRESSMAN

Andrew Johnson made his national debut in 1842 when he won election to the US House of Representatives, and remained for a decade as the voice for the working class. Johnson pressed hard for a measure he had long wanted—a homestead act. Allowing people 160 acres of free land to start a new life appealed to his desire to help those in need, so long as they were willing to farm and improve it. After a great deal of work, he finally saw it pass the House; the Senate, on the other hand, was not so willing. Southerners feared such a law would open the floodgates of more abolitionists moving westward; consequently, they voted it down.

Continuing his record of voting against increased government expenditures, Johnson did so as often as possible, including public improvements and protective tariffs. As a southerner, he upheld the right to own slaves and voiced his beliefs that blacks were inferior to whites. He also spoke out in favor of the "gag rule" in the House preventing abolitionist petitions from being read because of their possible incendiary effect.

As the election of 1844 loomed, Johnson supported his fellow Tennessean although the relationship between him and Polk had grown strained. He stumped for Polk across the state, but apparently it was not enough, for Clay won Tennessee.

Still Johnson won reelection and was happy to vote in favor of Texas annexation and, as a true expansionist, totally approved of going to war against Mexico. He also enthusiastically opposed the Wilmot Proviso with its mandate to keep slavery from any new territories gained from the war. Yet, adding the Oregon territory was just as critical, he believed, which put him at odds with fellow southerners.

Congressman Johnson continued his crusade against government spending and voted against appropriations for the Smithsonian Institution and raising soldiers' pay. He ridiculed West Point officers and decried taxes on tea and coffee as being offensive to the poor. In a speech answering the assault on West Point graduates, newly elected congressman (and West Point graduate) Jefferson Davis responded with a spirited defense of those men and ended with his doubt that "a blacksmith or tailor" could have constructed the necessary defense works as required by the nation. Wounded by the implied insult, Johnson answered by insisting that Davis had insulted a portion of the American population that included Johnson, who "was not ashamed to avow that he was a mechanic."[5] Davis apologized, but the harm had been done, and Johnson would not forget it.

Another person who apparently had crossed Johnson's path and never understood how was President Polk, who wrote in his dairy in 1849: "He is very vindictive and perverse in his temper and conduct. . . . I am not aware that I have ever given him cause for offense."[6] Others had a low opinion of Johnson, including a fellow congressman from North Carolina who described him as a "filthy, slimy being."[7] Refusing to yield to critics,

HOMESTEAD ACT ★ A popular law enacted in 1862, the Homestead Act settled 10 percent of the United States. This law enabled poorer Americans and new immigrants to own land. The only requirements: individuals must be at least 21 years of age, live on the claimed land for five years, and improve it (i.e., build a house, dig a well, plow at least 10 acres). At the end of five years, they owned their 160-acre parcel.

NATIONAL EVENTS

- **APR 2:** Siege of Petersburg, Virginia, ends with Confederates retreating
- **APR 3:** Richmond falls to Union troops
- **APR 9:** Lee surrenders to Grant at Appomattox Courthouse, Virginia
- **APR 14:** Lincoln signs a law creating the US Secret Service (to fight counterfeiting) as part of the Treasury Department (his final act as president)
- **APR 14:** Lincoln shot at Ford's Theater by John Wilkes Booth

WORLD EVENTS

- **APR 24:** Grand Duke Nicholas Alexandrovich of Russia dies
- **MAY 19:** Triple Alliance formed of Argentina, Brazil, and Uruguay to fight Paraguay
- **JUN 11:** Brazilian navy defeats Paraaguay
- **JUL 2:** Salvation Army started in London
- **JUL 4:** Lewis Carroll publishes *Alice in Wonderland*

Andrew continued to be unbending, although he had changed his views regarding railroads. After losing his election years before on the issue, he now voted in favor of railroad appropriations.

The 1850 congressional session required give and take by everyone because of a variety of contentious pending bills and the increasingly apparent battle lines between North and South. Johnson voted in favor of the Compromise of 1850 (p. 150), saying, "The preservation of this Union ought to be the object which is paramount to all other considerations."[8]

Johnson would not run again in 1852, for the Tennessee legislature, now Whig-controlled, had redrawn his district to benefit their party. He bemoaned the change and wondered what he could do next. The answer was quick in coming.

GOVERNOR

Tennessee Democrats determined that a race for the governorship would be just the ticket for their man from Greeneville. His opponent was the man responsible for the redistricting forcing him from his House seat. The two held a series of debates throughout the state, and on election day it was "the masses . . . the mechanic, the day laborer . . . [who came] to the rescue"[9] by electing Johnson.

Wanting to follow Jefferson's example at his inauguration, Andrew Johnson decided to forego using a carriage and walked instead. While the crowd appreciated the gesture, many found the new governor's speech lacking. One quipped that while he did not expect much from it, "[Johnson's] inauguration is below my expectations."[10]

Soon the governor was at work appointing men to various state positions, but he also had an agenda of legislation. First and foremost was a need to improve schools, and Johnson proposed levying a tax to pay for the necessary changes. He also wanted an office of weights and measures. The legislature was slow to act on his proposals, but both were eventually passed.

Then Johnson ran for reelection against a candidate of the Know-Nothing party, which was opposed to foreigners and Catholics. Johnson railed against their platform, reminding audiences of the contributions of immigrants and the protection of all religions by the First Amendment. Again Johnson could claim victory, and during this term he

SUPREME COURT APPOINTMENTS

None

JEFFERSON DAVIS (1808–1889) ★ Confederate president Jefferson Davis had established both a military and political record for himself prior to leading the South. He graduated from West Point in 1828 and served on the frontier before leaving the Army in 1835, and marrying the daughter of his commander. General Zachary Taylor disapproved of the match, and tragically, Sallie Taylor Davis died unexpectedly within three months of the wedding. Jeff Davis became a cotton planter and began taking part in Democratic politics, and was elected to Congress in 1845. There he took offense at derogatory remarks about soldiers made by Congressman Andrew Johnson. Davis enlisted to fight in the Mexican War and served with distinction. Once home, he was elected to the US Senate. Then in 1852, President Franklin Pierce appointed him secretary of war. During this time, Davis introduced camels to Army troops stationed in the Southwest, but the experiment was short-lived. Then, in 1857, Davis returned to the Senate, where he served until Mississippi voted for secession in January 1861. A month later, Jefferson Davis became the president of the Confederacy.

APR 15: Lincoln dies; Andrew Johnson is sworn in as new president

APR 27: Steamship *Sultana* blows up in Mississippi River killing 1,700 of her 2,300 passengers (many of whom are released prisoners from Andersonville)

MAY 10: Jefferson Davis captured near Irwinville, Georgia

MAY 12: Trial begins for Booth conspirators; all are found guilty; four are sentenced to death by hanging, including Mrs. Mary Surratt

JUL 5: Britain introduces first speed limit

JUL 6: Sophie of Sweden, Grand Duchess of Baden, dies

JUL 14: British mountain-climbing expedition becomes first to successfully scale the Matterhorn

JUL 27: Welsh settlers arrive in Argentina

AUG 25: Meteorite from Mars falls on India

STATE OF THE UNION
★★★★★★★★★★

US POPULATION IN 1865
39,818,449

NATIONAL DEBT IN 1869
$2,588,452,214

STATE ADMITTED TO UNION
Nebraska, March 1, 1867

NUMBER OF STATES IN 1869
37

proposed a few unusual ideas: shut down all banks in the state; no currency for any amount less than five dollars; and pay for road upkeep with taxation rather than the utilization of poor labor.

Still he yearned to move higher on the political continuum and started pondering running for the US Senate. Since senators were then elected by state legislatures, he worked to ensure the majority of those were Democrats and again stumped for candidates across the state. His efforts were successful, and in October 1857, Andrew Johnson was elected senator.

SENATOR

Returning to Washington after a five-year absence, Johnson resumed his campaign to pass a homestead bill. Finally one cleared both houses, only to be vetoed by fellow Democrat, President James Buchanan. To Johnson's dismay, southerners again blocked its passage by preventing an override of the veto. Johnson also continued his longstanding campaign against what he considered wasteful government spending, including the construction of a transcontinental railroad, which he insisted would make the United States incur a tremendous debt.

During this critical era, Johnson spoke out repeatedly of the need to preserve the Union while still preserving slavery. All eyes turned to the Democratic National Convention in Charleston to see who would be their nominee, but Johnson could not attend as he was working on securing passage of his homestead bill. Others who attended kept him informed of the convention proceedings. For years Johnson had hungered for the presidency and thought that he, as a moderate southerner who was also working to pass the Homestead Bill, would be a more viable candidate than the esteemed Stephen Douglas. Tennessee nominated Johnson, but they were unable to garner more support. Ultimately the convention was deadlocked and agreed to meet again a few weeks later in Baltimore, where it divided into two factions—Northern Democrats for Douglas and Southern Democrats for Breckenridge. After a great deal of consideration, Johnson cast his lot for Breckenridge and half-heartedly campaigned for him in Tennessee. Nevertheless, Constitutional Union Party nominee and Tennessee native John Bell claimed the state, but Abraham Lincoln took the election. The country held its breath for what would happen next.

Andrew Johnson made his decision and spoke to the Senate on the topic of secession. Although he believed southern states had the right to continue slavery, he felt they did not have the right to leave the Union. "It is treason, nothing but treason, and if one State, upon its own volition, can go out of this Confederacy without regard to the effect it is to have upon the remaining parties to the compact, what is your Government worth?"[11] He reminded his audience of the constitutional and legal election of president-elect Lincoln and ended his speech with Andrew Jackson's quote: "The Federal Union, it must be preserved!" While northern newspapers applauded Johnson's efforts, southern ones called him a traitor. Within his own state, supporters commended the speech while opponents burned him in effigy.

During the first weeks of 1861, various southern senators lined up to attack Johnson and his speech. He finally replied to them in early February, and news of his address caused the galleries to fill, mainly with Republicans to hear what the Tennessee senator might say. This time, Johnson reiterated his longstanding belief that secession was treason and that southerners would be as much at fault if the nation disintegrated as the abolitionists

NATIONAL EVENTS

JUL 6: First US train robbery occurs on railway between New York and Boston

JUL 7: Four Booth co-conspirators are hanged

NOV 10: Henry Wirz, commandant of Andersonville POW camp, is hanged for war crimes

NOV 18: Mark Twain publishes *The Celebrated Jumping Frog of Calaveras County*

DEC 6: Thirteenth Amendment goes into effect, abolishing slavery

WORLD EVENTS

OCT 11: Morant Bay rebellion in Jamaica

OCT 20: Ottawa proclaimed seat of Canadian government

NOV 26: Spanish ship *Covadonga* captured by Chile and Peru at Battle of Papudo

DEC 10: Léopold II becomes king of the Belgians

they blamed. He added that when his time came, he wanted "no more honorable winding sheet than that brave old flag, and no more glorious grave than to be interred in the tomb of the Union."[12] Cheers broke out in the galleries and his speech created news back home, where it also swayed voters to reject the idea of a convention to vote on secession. The good feelings were to be short-lived.

WAR

President Lincoln had been pleased by Johnson's stand and rewarded him with patronage appointments for Tennessee. Once Fort Sumter was attacked, however, Tennesseans began having second thoughts about secession. Johnson decided to return home to try to talk sense into his fellow citizens, but twice along the way his train was attacked by mobs threatening to lynch the senator; at one point, he had to defend himself with his pistol. He arrived home safely, and once reassured that his family was well, traveled about making speeches on the need to remain in the Union. This time a convention was held, and Tennessee voted for secession; the eastern portion, however, remained true to Johnson and the Union.

Returning to Washington required careful planning as well as an armed escort part of the way, but Johnson reached the capital safely. Soon, though, reports of Confederate harassment of Unionists in eastern Tennessee reached him, and he feared for the safety of his family and friends. Meanwhile, he urged Union commanders to send troops into that beleaguered region, but all pleas fell on deaf ears.

By early 1862, federal troops had regained control of Nashville and beyond, so President Lincoln decided to establish a military governor there; his choice was Andrew Johnson. For this position, Johnson was commissioned a brigadier general and arrived in the disheveled city in March. He quickly began rounding up the most prominent and wealthy of secessionists and putting them in prison while fending off attacks from Confederate raiding parties. Continually petitioning to the president and secretary of war for more men and supplies, he warned of the very real threat that the area might once more fall to enemy troops. At one point, Johnson made it clear the rebels would find his remains under a burned-out capitol for he would set fire to it rather than surrender. Fortunately nothing so drastic was required.

Of course his family's welfare also concerned the military governor, and he was greatly relieved when Eliza and their young son, Frank, joined him. For years, Eliza had been suffering from tuberculosis and now attempting to stay ahead of the enemy only weakened her infirm state.

Lincoln pressed Johnson to push reconstruction ahead in Tennessee, including emancipation of slaves. At first Johnson opposed this and convinced Lincoln to exclude Tennessee as one of the states

DID YOU KNOW?
★★★★★★★★★★★

Johnson is one of two presidents to be impeached.

RED CLOUD'S WAR ★ During much of Johnson's presidency, Oglala Sioux Chief Red Cloud led warriors against the Army, which attempted to patrol the Bozeman Trail running from Fort Laramie, Wyoming, to the Montana gold fields. After a two-year war, the US Army signed the Treaty of Fort Laramie in 1868, making Red Cloud one of the few Native American leaders to defeat the US Army. The Army agreed to abandon its forts along the Bozeman Trail; the Sioux were granted their hunting grounds forever. The discovery of gold in the Black Hills in 1874 would end the "forever."

DEC 24: Ku Klux Klan formed by several ex-Confederates

Cattle trail drives beef west to Denver for Army to give to Indians on reservations

FEB 13: First US daylight bank robbery in Missouri by Jesse James and his gang

APR 9: Congress passes Civil Rights Act; President Johnson vetoes it; Congress overrides the veto

MAY 16: Charles E. Hires invents root beer

1866

Alfred Nobel invents dynamite

JAN 6: Ottoman troops defeated in Lebanon

JAN 12: Royal Aeronautical Society founded in London

APR 4: Czar Alexander II of Russia barely escapes an attempted assassination

MAY: Failed assassination attempt on Otto von Bismarck in Berlin

DID YOU KNOW?

Johnson never had a vice president.

Johnson is the only former president to be elected to the US Senate.

where the Emancipation Proclamation was to take effect. Soon after, however, Johnson worked on behalf of slave emancipation and promoted the creation of black regiments. Another part of reconstruction required the oath of allegiance; it was a simple pledge, but Johnson instituted his own, which was more forceful and angered many who were required to take it. The governor remained unyielding, and resentment of the people prevented him from moving Tennessee forward to take its place again as a free state. In short, Johnson had failed in his job, but northerners still swarmed to hear him speak whenever he stopped on his trips to and from Washington. Attention now turned to the election of 1864.

VICE PRESIDENT

The Republicans hoped to win the support of War Democrats such as Johnson, and when their convention met, they called themselves the Union Party. Lincoln won the nomination as the presidential candidate and Johnson quickly followed as his running mate. Meanwhile, the Democrats nominated General George B. McClellan for president. Lincoln and Johnson won the election easily. Johnson hastened preparations for transferring the government of Tennessee from military to civil authority, resigned his military commission, and headed for Washington.

The vice president-elect had been in poor health for some time and now had to leave his family behind. Feeling unwell and perhaps a bit insecure, he accepted a friend's offer of whiskey to celebrate his inauguration the following day. Before being escorted to the dais for the ceremony the next day he downed three more glasses. Johnson's inebriated state quickly became apparent to the audience, and he was led away from the podium as his speech rambled. His swearing in was nearly comical as he roared, "I kiss this Book (Bible) in the face of my nation of the United States."[13]

Attempting to rehabilitate his image, Johnson soon took his place as president of the Senate and in early April visited City Point and later, Richmond, the conquered Confederate capital. On April 14, Johnson met with Lincoln urging the president not to be too easy on the former rebels, but that was their last meeting. Later that evening, Lincoln attended a play at Ford's Theater, where he fell mortally wounded at the hands of the assassin John Wilkes Booth.

Johnson was awakened by a knocking at his hotel door to learn that the president had been shot. He dressed quickly and went to the Petersen House, where Lincoln lay dying. The next morning, Andrew Johnson, unlike at his inaugural appearance six weeks earlier, comported himself in a most dignified and calm manner when taking the oath of the presidency. His first business was to plan Lincoln's funeral and request cabinet members to remain in their positions to ease the transition.

PRESIDENT JOHNSON

While the country mourned the fallen president, Johnson enjoyed a honeymoon with Congress. Radical congressional leaders visited him and reported they were pleased with his attitude acknowledging the need to punish those who had committed the crime of treason. He won more praise by allowing Mary Lincoln time to grieve before having to vacate the White House. The new president's family joined him there in June.

Multiple issues required the president's attention during the early days of his term in office: Lincoln's funeral; the surrender of General Joseph Johnston's troops in North Carolina; the reward

NATIONAL EVENTS

MAY 16: US Treasury authorizes creation of the nickel

JUL 24: Tennessee becomes first former Confederate state to be readmitted to the Union

JUL 25: Ulysses S. Grant becomes a five-star general (General of the Army)

DEC 21: Sioux warrior Crazy Horse leads US Army troops into an ambush; all 79 soldiers killed

WORLD EVENTS

MAY 11: London bank collapses

JUN 14: Start of Austro-Prussian War

JUN 20: Kingdom of Italy declares war on Austria

AUG 23: Treaty of Prague ends Austro-Prussian War

OCT 12: Treaty of Vienna ends war between Italy and Austria

OCT 14: In first military contact between Korea and a Western force, French troops land on Korean island

> *There are some who lack confidence in the integrity and capacity of the people to govern themselves. To all who entertain such fears I will most respectfully say that I entertain none… If man is not capable, and is not to be trusted with the government of himself, is he to be trusted with the government of others… Who, then, will govern? The answer must be, Man—for we have no angels in the shape of men, as yet, who are willing to take charge of our political affairs.*
>
> —*Andrew Johnson, 1853*

and capture of Booth and his co-conspirators; and the reward and capture of Confederate president Jefferson Davis and his cabinet. Each task was eventually accomplished, although Johnston's surrender had to be renegotiated as General Sherman's original terms of surrender had included provisions that President Johnson and his cabinet deemed inappropriate. For two days in late May, the new president could stand back and enjoy the Grand Parade of federal troops marching past on their way to being dismissed from service. Undoubtedly the country and its leader were relieved at the war's end and now could look ahead to the future.

A few days later, the president's reconstruction program was unveiled (without the approval of Congress, as it was not in session). Johnson hoped to smooth the states' reentry to the Union by putting few restrictions on them: he would appoint a governor, and a state constitutional convention would be called once 10 percent of the 1860 voting population had sworn the oath of allegiance. The state conventions would then draft new constitutions ending slavery, repudiate their Confederate debt, and denounce secession. Citizenship rights would be granted to southerners taking the required oath, which the president hoped would mean the states could resume self government without delay. Johnson fervently believed that suffrage should be left up to each state to decide. Southern leaders and the Democratic Party praised Johnson's plan. But for radicals, his proposal was preposterous as it said nothing about black voting rights, and they feared business would all too quickly resume as usual.

Johnson garnered yet more disfavor by granting pardons to former wealthy Confederates who requested his assistance. Once the states began holding their conventions, public opinion dropped even further as many refused to abide by the president's wishes, and soon they were electing former rebel leaders and passing "Black Codes" as law. Restrictions such as denying African Americans the right to serve on juries or vote were passed by southerners hoping to block citizenship rights to their former slaves. Since the states' first bold steps met with no noticeable negative response from

James A. Church of Brooklyn, New York, begins producing a baking soda under the name Arm & Hammer

First elevated railroad begins operation in New York City

FEB: Congress passes Tenure of Office Act to prevent president from removing any cabinet officer unless the Senate concurs

MAR: Congress passes two Reconstruction acts over President Johnson's vetoes

MAR 1: Nebraska enters as the 37th state

1867

Diamonds discovered in South Africa

JAN 30: Emperor Kōmei of Japan dies

FEB 17: First ship sails through Suez Canal

MAR 16: British surgeon Joseph Lister describes antiseptic surgery in his article "The Lancet"

APR 1: Singapore becomes a Crown Colony of the British

the president, a change in their attitude began to emerge. Initially submissive, assuming that any type of punishment, including black suffrage, might be levied for their refusal to conform to the president's directives, observers now noted a distinct arrogance on the part of the states, and "the old feeling of hatred returned."[14]

Radical Republicans in Congress, in response to the southern attempt to prevent blacks from gaining their civil rights, wasted no time and swiftly moved on the Civil Rights Act. The President vetoed the act, claiming it was dictating policy to the states when they were not yet represented in Washington. Congress responded by overriding the veto, just as they did to Johnson's veto of the Freedman's Bureau bill, which offered educational opportunities and relief for freedmen and refugees. War raged between the executive and legislative branches as bills were passed, vetoed, and sometimes overridden. Concerned that basic rights needed to be safeguarded to all regardless of race, the Fourteenth Amendment passed both houses and was sent to the states with the president's advice that it should be voted down. All the southern states did just that, except one—Johnson's home state of Tennessee voted for ratification.

The congressional elections of 1866 were critical to the president. He attempted to campaign in the Midwest, but was often greeted with heckling and sometimes snubbed by local politicians. Mary Lincoln was forced to receive him, which did not please her at all. Johnson's attempts to sway public opinion against the radicals failed miserably. They actually won more seats in Congress, which translated into an adequate number of votes to implement their plans and override any presidential vetoes.

One of the new bills was a Tenure of Office Act, which required the Senate's permission before the president could remove any cabinet officer. Johnson vetoed the act, and his veto was overridden. Displeased with this outcome, the president's rancor was more evident with the passage of the comprehensive Reconstruction Act, which divided the South into five military districts ruled by military governors. The president objected to the passing of a law that had not been voted on in the affected states. Once the act became law, cabinet members urged him to act with haste in appointing the five commanders. According to one witness, "He got very angry and swore vehemently, and said that they might impeach and be damned—[he] was tired of being threatened—that he would not be influenced by any such considerations."[15] At the same time, Johnson's power as commander in chief was stripped when another law requiring that orders go through the Army's commanding general took effect. The man who had molded his own destiny now refused to submit and accepted the inevitable showdown.

IMPEACHMENT

For most of Johnson's presidency, Secretary of War Edwin Stanton had grown increasingly distant and opposed to the president's policies. In fact, Stanton refused to repudiate the radicals' reconstruction program, which heightened Johnson's suspicions. Once it became clear that the secretary and General Grant were working together behind the president's back to make their own policy, Johnson knew the time had come to act. He was reluctant to oppose the extremely popular Grant and instead waited until Congress was in recess to write a brief note to Stanton asking for his resignation. Stanton refused. Before pressing the issue, Johnson asked Grant if he would be willing to replace Stanton, but Grant was hesitant. A week after the original

NATIONAL EVENTS

AUG: First running of New York's Belmont Stakes

AUG: President Johnson dismisses Secretary of War Edwin Stanton

SEP 25: Congress creates all-black college, Howard University, in Washington, D.C.

SEP 30: Midway Islands in the Pacific become a US possession

OCT: Chef at New York's Delmonico's restaurant creates Baked Alaska in honor of "Seward's Folly"

WORLD EVENTS

MAY 15: Due to world pressure, emperor Maximilian surrenders to Mexican troops after French forces had been withdrawn, ending Napoleon III's dream of empire

JUN 19: Maximilian killed by a firing squad

JUL 1: Canada united with Ottawa as its capital

OCT 1: *Das Kapital* by Karl Marx is published

request for resignation, Johnson sent another note to Stanton informing him that he was suspended and needed to transfer his power to General Grant, to which Stanton acquiesced. Johnson, however, soon developed misgivings about Grant as the general attempted to stay clear of the cabinet and disagreed on some matters pertaining to the removal or transfer of the five military commanders in the South. Many suspected Grant of attempting to bide his time until the presidential election in 1868. Ultimately Grant resigned, denouncing Johnson for attempts to "involve me in the resistance of the law,"[16] and he turned their correspondence over to the press for publication.

By November 1867, the House Judiciary Committee began hearings to determine whether to move closer toward impeachment. In February, the president himself took a step by advising Stanton of his permanent removal. Stanton in turn informed Grant and Republican leaders in Congress of the president's action; Stanton was advised to stand his ground and refuse to leave. On February 24, the House voted to impeach the president for "high crimes and misdemeanors." Eleven charges were filed, mostly concerned with violations of the Tenure of Office Act. Johnson's defense team asked for a one-month delay and received ten days. Johnson, meanwhile, fired off his own retorts, citing the fact that he was being put on trial for attempting to uphold the Constitution while the traitor Jefferson Davis had never even seen the inside of a courtroom.

The trial began in the Senate on March 30, 1868, with Chief Justice Salmon P. Chase presiding. The defense decided to keep Johnson out of the proceedings. The focal point of the charges was the Tenure of Office Act, which Johnson's attorneys argued was not constitutional, nor was it applicable to Stanton's firing as the Secretary of War had been appointed by Lincoln rather than Johnson. For six weeks the trial dragged on as each side interrogated witnesses and espoused at length. Finally the votes on impeachment were taken. Republicans had believed that as long as they kept ranks, the two-thirds majority was theirs for conviction. Johnson's defense team and the Senate Democrats had calculated that they had to win at least seven Republicans to avoid removal. Three articles were voted on, and each time, seven Republicans sided with the Democrats against removal of the president. On May 26, Secretary of War Stanton "relinquished" his post.

Congress recessed during the impeachment trial so the Republicans could meet for their convention—Ulysses S. Grant was chosen as their presidential candidate. Johnson had hoped to win the Democratic nomination, but New York governor Horatio Seymour, a less noteworthy—and controversial—public figure, was their choice. Johnson thus headed into the final months of his administration.

MYERS V. UNITED STATES ★ *Myers v. United States* was the 1926 Supreme Court decision that struck down the premise of the Tenure of Office Act. The Court ruled that the Senate could not require approval before non-Cabinet officials were removed by the president. (The ruling was supported by Supreme Court Chief Justice—and former president—William H. Taft.)

FINISHING THE JOB

Johnson, pleased by his victory over his congressional rivals, could also cite other successes. In 1867,

OCT 18: Alaska officially becomes a US territory (purchased from Russia for $7.2 million)

Autobiography of Benjamin Franklin is published

FEB 24: House of Representatives votes to impeach President Johnson for his dismissal of Secretary of War Stanton, which violated Tenure of Office Act of 1867

APR: George Westinghouse patents the air brake

1868

OCT 14: Last of the Tokugawa Shogun resigns

Sir Joseph Lockyer names a newly discovered element, helium

French workers discover 30,000-year-old bones

JAN 3: Meiji emperor of Japan declares "Meiji Restoration" to regain power against the supporters of the Tokugawa Shogunate

JAN 5: War of the Triple Alliance: Brazil takes Paraguay's capital

Secretary of State William Seward negotiated the purchase of Alaska for $7.2 million from Russia; at the time, however, many, believed it a waste of money and nicknamed the acquisition "Seward's folly" or "Seward's Icebox." Seward also managed to invoke the Monroe Doctrine to pressure France to remove its emperor Maximilian from Mexico. In 1868, the United States also acquired Midway Islands in the Pacific.

As Johnson's term wound down, he surprised visitors by his calm appearance and pleasing demeanor. He still hosted parties at the White House with his daughter usually presiding, since Eliza was by now nearly an invalid and remained upstairs. The couple worried over their eldest son's alcoholism, but their grandchildren were a constant source of joy. In fact, one of Johnson's favorite activities was taking the children to wade in Rock Creek, and on one occasion, a children's party was held (bipartisan) and a good time was had by all (except Grant would not allow his children to attend).

The hostility between the outgoing president Johnson and the president-elect Grant reached a climax on inauguration day, when Grant refused to share a carriage with Johnson, who determined that it would be best if he left before the inaugural festivities began. By mid-March the former president and his family were on their way home to Tennessee.

RETIREMENT

Johnson was returning home for the first time since the war, when he had been called a traitor. He was pleased to find himself welcomed with open arms and called a patriot, but his triumphant return soon turned to sorrow when word arrived that his troubled son Robert had committed suicide. Robert's younger brother Charles had died in the war, so Andrew and Eliza's sole surviving son was Frank, who was about to graduate from college and pledged he would stay away from spirits.

Johnson found it impossible to stay away from the political fray and traveled throughout Tennessee denouncing Grant and the Republicans. He made a bid for a US Senate seat in 1869 but was defeated by a narrow margin. Johnson finally determined it was time to go home to Greeneville, but his life there was terribly dull. Again he tried a run for Congress, in 1872, but was defeated. A cholera epidemic the following year seriously sickened him, but he slowly recovered. His financial health was not so fortunate, as many of his investments were lost in the Panic of 1873.

Still desiring to win political office, Johnson worked to make sure he was considered when the newly elected Democratic state legislature met in 1875 to elect a new US senator. Johnson won the election and felt truly vindicated by the victory. He soon departed for Washington, for Congress had been called into special session by President Grant to take action on a variety of matters, including a trade treaty with Hawaii. Once Johnson arrived in Washington, he wasted no time in attacking Grant and his policies.

Johnson then returned to Greeneville to check on his various business ventures, after which he took a train to see one of his daughters. During his visit, he suffered two strokes within two days, and died, on July 31, 1875. On August 3, Andrew Johnson's body led a procession of more than five thousand mourners to his final resting place in Greeneville. Eliza died six months later.

As Johnson had requested, in his casket, his head reposed on his personal copy of the Constitution while his body lay draped in the flag of the country that he had served for forty years.

NATIONAL EVENTS

MAY 16: By one vote, President Johnson is acquitted and remains in office

MAY 30: First observance of Memorial Day (Decoration Day) to remember Civil War dead

JUL 28: Enactment of Fourteenth Amendment granting blacks rights as US citizens

JUL 28: Burlingame Treaty signed between United States and China regarding immigration/emigration

OCT: Louisa May Alcott publishes *Little Women* (first part)

WORLD EVENTS

JAN 10: Shogun Tokugawa Yoshinobu declares emperor's action "illegal" and attacks Kyoto; pro-emperor forces drive his troops away and he surrenders in May

APR 9: Emperor Theodore of Abyssinia massacres at least 197 of his own people

APR 10: British-Indian task force kills 700 and defeats Abyssinian army of Emperor Theodore

APR 13: Abyssinian-British War ends with the suicide of Theodore

> *"I have performed my duty to my God, my country, and my family. I have nothing to fear in approaching death. To me it is the mere shadow of God's protecting wing... Here I will rest in quiet and peace beyond the reach of calumny's poisoned shaft, the influence of envy and jealous enemies, where treason and traitors or State backsliders and hypocrites in church can have no peace."*
>
> —*Andrew Johnson, July 1875*

ENDNOTES

1 Albert Castel, *The Presidency of Andrew Johnson*, Lawrence, KS: Regents Press of Kansas, 1980, p. 2.

2 Ibid, p. 3.

3 Hans L. Trefousse, *Andrew Johnson, A Biography*, New York: W.W. Norton & Co., 1991, p. 47.

4 Ibid, p. 42.

5 Ibid, p. 64.

6 Milo M. Quaife, ed., *The Diary of James K. Polk During His Presidency, 1845-1849*, 4 vols., Chicago, 1910, 4:264.

7 Trefousse, p. 74.

8 Ibid, p. 76.

9 Ibid, p. 88.

10 Ibid, p. 90.

11 Ibid, p. 131.

12 Ibid, p. 136.

13 Ibid, p. 190.

14 Ibid, p. 233.

15 Castel, p. 114.

16 Trefousse, p. 309.

OCT 28: Thomas Edison applies for his first patent (electric vote recorder for Congress)

NOV 3: Republican Ulysses S. Grant wins presidential election over Horatio Seymour

NOV 27: Lieutenant Colonel George A. Custer leads soldiers to attack Cheyenne at the Washita River

DEC 25: President Johnson grants unconditional pardon to all former Confederates

AUG: Earthquake kills 25,000 in Peru and Ecuador

AUG 22: Riot in China almost leads to war with Britian

SEP: Queen Isabella II of Spain is sent into exile

OCT 10: Cuba begins a ten-year war against Spain

Ulysses S. Grant

★ ★ ★ EIGHTEENTH PRESIDENT ★ ★ ★

LIFE SPAN

- Born: April 27, 1822 at Point Pleasant, Ohio
- Died: July 23, 1885 at Mount McGregor, New York

NICKNAMES

- "Unconditional Surrender" Grant, Hero of Appomattox

RELIGION

- Methodist

HIGHER EDUCATION

- US Military Academy at West Point, 1843

PROFESSION

- Soldier

MILITARY SERVICE

- Second lieutenant, 1843
- First lieutenant, Mexican War (1846–1848); after the war, served in variety of posts and rose to Captain; resigned in 1854
- Civil War: appointed colonel of Twenty-first Illinois Infantry; promoted to brigadier general
- After his victory at Shiloh, Tennessee, he was promoted to major general
- In March 1864, **President Lincoln** appointed him lieutenant general and commander of all Union armies
- He was promoted to general of the army in July 1866 (**Grant** was only the second man to hold this title; **George Washington** was the first)

FAMILY

- Father: **Jesse Root Grant** (1794–1873)
- Mother: **Hannah Simpson Grant** (1798–1883)
- Wife: **Julia Boggs Dent Grant** (1826–1902); wed on August 22, 1848, in St. Louis
- Children: **Frederick Dent** (1850–1912); **Ulysses Simpson** (1852–1929); **Ellen Wrenshall** (1855–1922); **Jesse Root** (1858–1934)

POLITICAL LIFE

- Interim secretary of state under President **Andrew Johnson** (1867–1868)

PRESIDENCY

- Two terms: March 4, 1869–March 4, 1877
- Republican
- Reason for leaving office: completion of term
- Vice presidents: **Schuyler Colfax** (1869–1873); **Henry Wilson** (1873–1875); died in office

ELECTION OF 1868

- Electoral vote: **Grant** 214; **Horatio Seymour** 80
- Popular vote: **Grant** 3,013,650; **Seymour** 2,708,744

ELECTION OF 1872

- Electoral vote: **Grant** 286; **Horace Greeley** 0 (**Greeley** had died after the popular election, but before the electoral college vote)
- Popular vote: **Grant** 3,598,235; **Greeley** 2,834,761

CABINET

★★★★★★★★★★

SECRETARY OF STATE
Elihu B. Washburn (Mar. 5–16, 1869)

Hamilton Fish (1869–1877)

SECRETARY OF THE TREASURY
George S. Boutwell (1869–1873)

William A. Richardson (1873–1874)

Benjamin H. Bristow (1874–1876)

Lot M. Morrill (1876–1877)

SECRETARY OF WAR
John A. Rawlins (Mar.–Sept. 1869) (died in office)

William T. Sherman (Sept.–Oct. 1869)

William W. Belknap (1869–1876)

Alphonso Taft (Mar.–May 1876)

James D. Cameron (1876–1877)

The life of the nation's eighteenth president was a rollercoaster of successes and failures. His childhood nickname was "Useless," and that was precisely how he felt as a child and later as an adult, when a reputation for heavy drinking nearly destroyed his military career. A better nickname, however, would have been "Phoenix," for just as the mythical bird rose from the ashes, Ulysses S. Grant would remake himself and rise to heights greater than anyone could have imagined.

EARLY LIFE

On April 27, 1822, a baby boy was born to Jesse and Hannah Simpson Grant in their two-room cabin in Point Pleasant, Ohio. Unsure of what to name their son, they hesitated for several weeks before finally deciding on Hiram Ulysses Grant; the boy would be haunted through childhood by his initials—H.U.G.—but within the family he was known as "Lyss."

The Grants soon moved to nearby Georgetown, and over the years the family grew to include six children: three boys and three girls. The boys were expected to help their father in his tannery business, but eldest son Ulysses balked at doing so, for the blood-soaked environment sickened him, as did the idea of killing any living thing. His favorite pastime was riding horses, and he became well known for having a unique ability to quiet seemingly unmanageable animals. At age eight, he bought his first horse.

Young Grant preferred the outdoors to sitting still in a small schoolhouse, reciting his lessons, although he did do well in mathematics and took part in a debating society when he was fourteen. He later criticized his mediocre education, saying, "They were all supported by subscription and a single teacher—who was often a man or a woman incapable of teaching much, even if they imparted all they knew."[1]

AN OFFICER AND A GENTLEMAN

Unbeknownst to him, Ulysses' father requested their local congressman to recommend his son to West Point. Thanks to Representative Thomas L. Hamer, Grant gained not only the appointment, but a new name, too. Hamer accidentally confused Grant's given name, believing Ulysses was the first name and the mother's maiden name was the middle: Ulysses S. Grant was born. The initials U.S. pleased the young cadet, so he neglected to correct the mistake. Grant's new buddies at West Point decided the U.S. stood for "Uncle Sam," and soon his nickname became Sam, and so he would be known to his friends. Many of these classmates included young men who later would serve with him in the Mexican War, and some against him in the Civil War—James Longstreet, John Pope, William Rosecrans, and Richard Ewell.

Come graduation, Grant was twenty-first in his class of thirty-nine. A fellow cadet said he was "lazy and careless" in his studies; on the other hand, he surpassed everyone in horsemanship. "He used to take great delight in mounting and breaking the most intractable of the new horses . . . He succeeded in this . . . by patience and tact."[2] Grant's great-great-grandson and namesake also insisted that he "developed considerable skill in drawing and painting" and "was always much pleased to have anyone compliment his drawings, but . . . seemed to take no special interest in any compliments on his military achievements."[3]

Lieutenant Grant graduated from West Point in 1843 and naturally asked for appointment to the cavalry, but was refused and instead was sent to the infantry as brevet second lieutenant. His first assignment was Jefferson Barracks in St. Louis, where he was commanded by Stephen Kearny. A previous roommate from West Point, Frederick

NATIONAL EVENTS

Thomas B. Welch develops a method of pasteurizing grape juice

Barbed wire invented

Joseph A. Campbell Preserve Company started by a vegetable merchant in Camden, New Jersey, and later becomes Campbell Soup Company

Henry John Heinz begins bottling horseradish with a partner in Sharpsburg, Pennsylvania

MAR 4: Ulysses S. Grant inaugurated as 18th president

1869

WORLD EVENTS

New York Herald newspaper sponsors expedition of Henry Stanley into Africa to look for Dr. David Livingstone

Great Britain abolishes debtors' prisons

Jonathan Scobie, an American Baptist minister in Yokohama, invents the rickshaw

French chemist creates margarine to be used by the French navy

MAY 4–10: Naval Battle of Hakodate in Japan between the Ezo Republic and the newly formed Imperial Japanese Navy

Dent, invited Grant to his family home near St. Louis. There Sam was welcomed by Mrs. Dent and Frederick's siblings, including seventeen-year-old sister Julia. The young lady had received a proper education for young females but probably lacked suitors as she was plain in appearance and had crossed eyes. Still, she excelled where others failed to bring out the quiet young man; Sam felt comfortable in her presence and often traveled to the Dent plantation west of St. Louis. Her father, a southerner and slaveholder, was not so welcoming, and worried that his daughter was being courted by a Yankee.

The Mexican War interrupted the courtship, but not before Grant was able to ask Julia for her hand in marriage as he was "too shy," Julia later said, to ask her father. Still Colonel Dent suspected the seriousness of the relationship and tried to dissuade it, telling his daughter that Grant was too poor to afford a wife. Nor did Dent desire his daughter to face the long separations he knew were inevitable, but Julia would not be deterred. Although Grant was now in Louisiana preparing for likely hostilities after the forthcoming annexation of Texas, he did return on leave to request Colonel Dent's permission to marry Julia. Fortunately, Grant managed to arrive at an opportune moment and received a positive response; nevertheless, the couple would have to settle for what turned out to be a four-year engagement.

MEXICAN WAR

Grant later wrote that he disagreed with the Mexican War: "I was bitterly opposed to the measure, and to this day regard the war, which resulted, as one of the most unjust ever waged by a stronger against a weaker nation."[4] Undoubtedly, his disagreement with the impending military action caused him to request transfer to West Point as a mathematics instructor, but the war intervened, and off he went to report for duty in Louisiana, where the men awaited further orders.

Eventually Grant, newly promoted to second lieutenant of the Fourth Infantry, was ordered to the Rio Grande River. There General Taylor had amassed a force of nearly three thousand men as he waited for the Mexican Army to make its first move. Fighting finally erupted, prompting Grant to have second thoughts about his enlistment. He would come under fire multiple times in the coming weeks at the battles of Palo Alto and Resaca de la Palma.

During this time, Lieutenant Grant was made quartermaster for his regiment, which meant he had the onerous duty of attempting to corral and manage the mules bearing supplies that the army needed. Not an easy task for anyone, he admitted that while he never used profanity, he could certainly understand why someone might under those circumstances.

In September 1846, Americans attacked Monterrey. As the fighting dragged on, his outfit needed more ammunition, and horseman Grant volunteered to retrieve it. Since he had to slip by the enemy and through gunfire, Grant rode over to one side of his horse, with one arm hanging onto the horse's neck and one foot in the stirrup—a ride that only a very few could duplicate. The young second lieutenant may have been against the war, but once in it, could barely be held back.

Grant resumed his duties as quartermaster under his new superior, General Winfield Scott. President James K. Polk had sent Scott to replace Zachary Taylor, who Polk feared could be a powerful political rival in the 1848 election. At Veracruz, Grant watched the lopsided battle that ended in

CABINET
★★★★★★★★★★

(continued)

ATTORNEY GENERAL
Ebenezer R. Hoar (1869–1870)

Amos T. Akerman (1870–1871)

George H. Williams (1872–1875)

Edwards Pierre Pont (1875–1876)

Alphonso Taft (1876–1877)

SECRETARY OF THE NAVY
Adolph E. Borie (Mar.–June 1869)

George M. Robeson (1869–1877)

POSTMASTER GENERAL
John A.J. Creswell (1869–1874)

James W. Marshall (July–Aug 1874)

Marshall Jewell (1874–1876)

James N. Tyner (1876–1877)

SECRETARY OF THE INTERIOR
Jacob D. Cox (1869–1870)

Columbus Delano (1870–1875)

Zachariah Chandler (1875–1877)

MAY 10: Transcontinental railroad completed and ceremony held at Promontory Point, Utah

MAY 15: National Women's Suffrage Association founded by Susan B. Anthony and Elizabeth Cady Stanton

JUN 1: Cincinnati Red Stockings become first professional (paid) baseball team

SEP 24: Financial panic hits Wall Street

DEC 10: Wyoming Territory adopts a constitution permitting women's suffrage

MAY 29: British parliament abolishes public hangings

AUG 9: Social Democratic Workers' Party of Germany founded by August Bebel and Wilhelm Liebknecht

SEP 5: Foundation stone laid for Neuschwanstein Castle in Bavaria; it's now the most photographed building in Germany

NOV 17: Suez Canal officially opens, linking Red Sea to the Mediterranean

NOV 23: One of the last clipper ships to be built, the *Cutty Sark* is launched in Dumbarton, Scotland

DID YOU KNOW?

Grant's real name was Hiram Ulysses (initials HUG), which he detested; a clerical error later gave him the name he used for the rest of his life.

the garrison's capitulation. Awed by the fighting and carnage, he wearily wrote an inquisitive friend, "You say you would like to hear more about the war. If you had seen as much of it as I have you would be tired of the subject."[5]

Fearful that his role as quartermaster might relegate him to being little more than a spectator in the battles to come, Grant attempted to be reassigned. Unsuccessful, he nevertheless found reasons to be close to the action, and fellow officer James Longstreet later admitted, "You could not keep Grant out of battle."[6] When the fighting moved closer to Mexico City in the area near Chapultepec, Grant reconnoitered and pondered how to take the hill. He and a column of men commandeered a church, much to the dismay of the local priest. Grant was determined, however, and in broken Spanish convinced the priest that he might as well agree to the soldiers' requests as they would do as they liked regardless. Grant's men lugged the pieces of a cannon up the bell tower, assembled it, and soon began pouring shot into the Mexican ranks. Grant was later escorted to his division commander, General William Worth, who congratulated the young lieutenant on his actions. Grant was one of many officers who received an intense combat education at the series of engagements—among them Chapultepec—known as the Battle for Mexico City. Others who would achieve fame later in the Civil War included James Longstreet, George Meade, Thomas J. Jackson, George McClellan, John Pemberton, and of course, Robert E. Lee, who wrote, "Lieutenant Grant behaved with distinguished gallantry on the 13th and 14th [of September 1847 at the Battle of Mexico City].[7]

BATTLE OF CHAPULTEPEC ★ Perched on a mountaintop to the west of Mexico City sat Chapultepec Castle. This citadel was the scene of vicious fighting between Americans and Mexicans. Since the castle was also the Mexican military academy, many of Chapultepec's defenders were its cadets, including boys as young as 13. After an artillery barrage on September 12, 1847, Americans advanced on the citadel at dawn the next day, and once the troops moved up the hill and gained a foothold, Mexican troops retreated to the city. Five of the cadets refused to retreat and fought to the death; another cadet, seeing he was the sole survivor of his group, wrapped the Mexican flag around himself and jumped off the cliff. They are remembered in Mexican history as Los Niños Héroes (child heroes).

ARMY LIFE

Now with peace talks progressing, the young lieutenant longed to return to St. Louis and marry Julia; he wrote to be granted a short leave from the army, but was denied. Permission was granted several months later, and on August 22, 1848, Julia became Julia Dent Grant. The couple traveled to Ohio to meet Grant's parents, but in November it was time to report to new quarters in Detroit. Julia returned to St. Louis in the spring of 1850 to give birth to their first child, a son they named Frederick; mother and son joined Grant when he was transferred to Sackett's Harbor, New York. He would journey alone for his next transfer to San Francisco and then Fort Vancouver, Oregon. According to one of the officers' wives, he was a fine cook and would attend social evenings, but never took part in the dancing. He smoked cigars and talked about how he missed his wife and children (a second son, Ulysses Jr., nicknamed "Buck," was born in 1852); sometimes he would take long walks

NATIONAL EVENTS

Frederick A.O. Schwarz opens a toy store in New York City

Margaret "Mattie" Knight begins production of square-bottom paper bags (predecessor to grocery bags)

Benjamin F. Goodrich starts producing rubber products; the first is a rubber hose

JAN 3: Construction begins on the Brooklyn Bridge

JAN 15: First appearance of Democratic donkey drawn by political cartoonist Thomas Nast for *Harper's Weekly*

1870

WORLD EVENTS

Diamonds discovered in South Africa

British transatlantic steamship company, White Star Line, begins passenger service from Liverpool to New York City

British Education Act makes elementary education compulsory for boys and girls

MAR 2: Fighting ends in Paraguay and War of the Triple Alliance is over

JUN 25: Queen Isabella II abdicates Spanish throne

or ride his horse for hours. A sergeant's wife, Mrs. Sheffield, noted that Grant handled his men firmly, but never with anger. "In manner," she added, "he was unassuming and approachable, and his language was always plain and straightforward."[8] He dressed simply, as he was known to do a decade later serving the Union in the Civil War.

Grant spent a year near the Columbia River and received a promotion to captain. He was then transferred to Humboldt Bay, California. Within six months, Grant resigned his commission. Rumors circulated in military circles that Captain Grant left the service because of an increasingly debilitating drinking problem. No official written documentation exists to support this, and many eyewitnesses who knew him during this period did not mention that any such condition existed. Indisputable, however, is the fact that Grant was miserable in California serving under a superior he despised, and with plenty of time to ponder his future, he finally decided to go home and pick up the plow. Letters to Julia reveal his impatience to rejoin his family. As he explained in his memoirs, "I saw no chance of supporting them on the Pacific coast out of my pay as an army officer. I concluded, therefore, to resign."[9] By late summer, 1854, he was back with his beloved family, ready to begin life as a farmer.

CIVILIAN LIFE

Julia's father offered his son-in-law a farm of a hundred acres west of St. Louis, and Grant accepted. He cleared the land and built a modest home, which he called "Hardscrabble." The happy family was soon joined by a third child, Ellen, known as "Nellie," who was born in 1855. For nearly four years, Grant plowed his fields and harvested crops alongside slaves he hired from neighbors. He probably would have been content to continue such a tranquil existence except for an illness that struck most of the family. Grant was ill for over a year with fever and chills, making him unable to attend the farm. Consequently he determined to rent out the land and went to work with a cousin of Julia's in a real estate firm. The family moved to a modest home in the city, but real estate failed to provide much of a living, and Julia later wrote of her husband's difficulty collecting money. He left the business and applied for other jobs, including teaching mathematics at Washington University. Nothing came of these attempts.

Ultimately, a reluctant Grant swallowed his pride and accepted an offer of employment at his father's leather store in Galena, Illinois. Grant worked with his two brothers and hoped to become a partner; meanwhile, though, he had to be content with the miserly sixty dollars his father paid him each month. This did not stretch far enough to care for the family of six (another son, Jesse, was born in 1858), but contributions from the Dent family helped ease their situation somewhat.

Grant kept close watch on the events that were unfolding in the fall of 1860, but as a new resident of Illinois, he was not allowed to vote in the presidential election; he later stated that he would have voted for Lincoln. When Fort Sumter fell, and the new president's call for volunteers went out in April 1861, the men of Galena decided to hold a meeting. Looking about the room, they quickly agreed that Grant should preside, as he was the sole man with military experience; he reluctantly took the podium, and by the end of the evening a company of volunteers had been raised, with Ulysses S. Grant as their unofficial leader. He, as well, understood that his destiny lay

SUPREME COURT APPOINTMENTS
★★★★★★★★★★★

William Strong, 1870

Joseph P. Bradley, 1870

Ward Hunt, 1873

Morrison R. Waite, 1874

FEB 25: Hiram Revels, senator from Mississippi, becomes first African American in Congress

MAR 30: Fifteenth Amendment ratified

JUN 22: Department of Justice is created

JUN 26: Christmas is declared a federal holiday

JUN 26: First section of Atlantic City famed boardwalk opens

NOV 1: First forecast by Weather Bureau

JUL 15: Province of Manitoba created in Canada

JUL 19: Franco-Prussian War begins when France declares war on Prussia

STATE OF THE UNION

US POPULATION IN 1869
39,818,449

NATIONAL DEBT IN 1877
$2,205,301,392

PRESIDENT'S SALARY
$25,000/year; increased to $50,000/year in 1873

STATE ADMITTED TO UNION
Colorado, August 1, 1876

NUMBER OF STATES IN 1877
38

in the war, and later wrote, "I never went into our leather store after that meeting, to put up a package or do other business."[10]

CIVIL WAR

In the days that followed, Grant helped the good ladies of Galena in procuring material for sewing uniforms and began the laborious process of training the recruits while awaiting his own commission. He escorted the trainees to Springfield and assumed his duty was done, but Governor Richard Yates requested Captain Grant to stay and work in the adjutant-general's office. His duties there were tedious, but sometimes he was able to get out and aid with the new regiments reporting to Camp Yates. Grant then traveled to the St. Louis area, where his volunteers were to report. Grant visited his in-laws, whom he found to be staunch rebels, and learned that the army, for now, had no place for him. He yearned for a colonelcy in a regiment, but none was forthcoming. He sought out former colleague George B. McClellan, but gave up after cooling his heels for two days waiting to speak with him. Grant's father again attempted to gain a position for his son, but none resulted.

On June 15, Grant was appointed colonel of the Seventh District Regiment in Illinois, replacing an officer who spent a great deal of his time drinking instead of supervising his men properly. A month later the unit left Illinois to rescue another regiment from being taken by rebel forces in Missouri. This would be the Seventh Regiment's first taste of battle, and their commanding officer was anxious about what lay ahead. His feelings were soon assuaged, however, when he found that the rebels had already abandoned the field. "From that event to the close of the war," Grant stated, "I never experienced trepidation upon confronting an enemy,"[11] having realized that the opposing forces were as afraid of battle as were he and his own troops. Grant continued his march into Missouri, and while there, he received the surprising news of his promotion to brigadier general. By fall, he was back in Illinois, and in November, his troops saw action in battle in Belmont, Missouri. They continued down the Mississippi.

The rebels were not Grant's only problem. A steamboat captain and traders who had been accused of dealing with the rebels began to spread rumors about the general's drinking. Grant's chief of staff, John Rawlins, took issue with these reports and assured the leaders of Galena that liquor had never made his commander "unfit for business" and that he would leave his post if Grant ever became "an intemperate man or an habitual drunkard."[12]

In February 1862, Grant captured Forts Henry and Donelson on the Cumberland River, initiating the offensive that would launch him onto the national stage. The defeated rebel commander was greatly distressed by what he termed Grant's "ungenerous" and "unchivalrous" terms of unconditional surrender—Grant's new nickname became "Unconditional Surrender" Grant. Spurred on by his victories, Grant headed to Nashville, but received orders from his superior, General Henry W. Halleck, to retreat to Fort Henry. Halleck, jealous of Grant's victories, attempted to take credit for them as a way to sway the growing popular support for the Illinois commander. Hoping to undermine Grant, Halleck wrote to his superiors in Washington that Grant was uncooperative and uncommunicative. Instead of receiving a reprimand, though, Grant received a promotion to major general of volunteers, making him second in command to Halleck. Grant then resumed moving southward toward Pittsburg Landing.

NATIONAL EVENTS

Post of Surgeon General created

Barnum's Circus opens in New York City

C.A. Pillsbury Company started by Charles Pillsbury, a Minneapolis miller

MAY 18: Chinese victims of race riots in Los Angeles

JUL 8: Exposé of Boss Tweed's corruption of Tammany Hall published in *New York Times*

OCT 2: Mormon leader Brigham Young is arrested in Utah Territory for polygamy; he has 27 wives

1871

WORLD EVENTS

Japan passes a law allowing intermarriage between members of different social classes

JAN 18: German Empire (Second Reich) established, with Prince Wilhelm I as its emperor and Otto von Bismarck its first chancellor

JAN 28: Paris falls to German troops

MAR 1: Napoleon III officially deposed by French Assembly

MAY 10: Treaty signed between France and Germany; France cedes territories of Alsace and a portion of Lorraine

The sixth and seventh of April 1862 were two of the bloodiest days of the bloodiest war in American history. At Shiloh, Tennessee, Grant faced a tenacious enemy led by General Albert Sydney Johnston, and he later described the battlefield "so covered with dead that it would have been possible to walk across the clearing, in any direction, stepping on dead bodies, without a foot touching the ground."[13] The Confederates endured two fatal blows—the loss of Johnston on the first day and the arrival of Union reinforcements that night. They were unable to recover from either, providing the North and Grant with a much-needed victory. This was also the first opportunity for Grant to work with Brigadier General William Tecumseh Sherman; their alliance would ensure future success for the country.

In July 1862, Grant took over as commander of the District of West Tennessee and continued to defend Memphis against guerrilla fighters throughout the area. He also wrestled with the ongoing problem of what to do with the former slaves who flooded across Union lines. Grant proposed paying them wages to pick cotton and work in other capacities as needed; their families would live in camps that were created under his direction. The general's solution showed great compassion and forethought, extending beyond any proposed by the Lincoln administration at the time. Unfortunately, General Grant was not as enlightened when it came to the Jewish population, whom he blamed for speculating in the cotton market. He therefore issued a directive on December 17, 1862, ordering Jews to move out of Tennessee; fortunately, the order was countermanded by the Department of State, but it remained a dark blot on Grant's record.

By the end of the year, Grant was planning an attack on the key Confederate stronghold of Vicksburg, which dominated the Mississippi River and the railroad links to the city. He worked with

DID YOU KNOW?

While president, Grant was ticketed for driving his horse too fast and fined $20.

CHRONOLOGY OF GRANT'S CIVIL WAR BATTLES

- ★ February 1862: Captures Forts Henry and Donelson in Tennessee
- ★ April 1862: Wins Battle of Shiloh (Pittsburg Landing), Tennessee
- ★ May 1863: Captures Jackson, Mississippi, and moves toward Vicksburg
- ★ July 1863: Vicksburg surrenders after six-week siege
- ★ November 1863: Chattanooga, Tennessee, falls after two-month siege
- ★ May 1864: Campaign in Virginia: Wilderness and Spotsylvania
- ★ June 1864: Costly Union victory at Cold Harbor, Virginia
- ★ June 1864: Siege of Petersburg, Virginia, ("backdoor" to Richmond) begins
- ★ March 1865: Petersburg falls to Grant and Union Army
- ★ March 1865: Fall of Richmond
- ★ April 1865: Lee surrenders to Grant at Appomattox Court House, Virginia

OCT 8: Great Chicago Fire destroys over 17,000 buildings and leaves 100,000 people homeless

OCT 27: Boss Tweed arrested for graft

NOV 24: National Rifle Association founded in New York City

Income tax abolished by Congress

Apache chief Cochise surrenders to US Army

Cornelius Vanderbilt buys controlling stock of the Union Pacific railroad

JUL 20: British Columbia joins Confederation of Canada

NOV 10: Henry Stanley locates Dr. David Livingstone near Lake Tanganyika and greets him with, "Dr. Livingstone, I presume?"

1872

Louis Ducos du Hauron creates first color photograph

JAN 12: Yohannes IV crowned Emperor of Ethiopia

APPOMATTOX "SOUVENIRS" ★ On April 9, 1865, the Wilmer McLean house in Appomattox Court House, Virginia, was the site of the historic surrender of General Lee and his Confederate Army to General Grant. Following the signing of surrender terms by Lee, he and his staff departed, as did General Grant. Afterward, some of the Union commanders who witnessed the historic occasion decided to acquire some "souvenirs." General Ord paid $40 for the marble-topped table next to where Lee had sat. General Sheridan bought the wooden table used by Grant to draft surrender terms. Other officers "appropriated" smaller items in the drawing room, including chairs used by the two leaders and even the "silent witness"—a doll left by one of the McLean daughters.

the navy's gunboats to secure the area, but had to wait until spring to advance, as the winter weather had caused abnormally high water levels on the Mississippi. The Union troops advanced in March and April, moving closer and then laying siege to Vicksburg for six weeks before the city finally surrendered on July 4, 1863. The Confederacy was now severed, and the Mississippi River was once more securely under Union control.

For his efforts, Grant received news that he was now commander of the Military Division of the Mississippi, including lands from the Mississippi east to the Allegheny Mountains. By late October he was on his way to Chattanooga, a major southern railroad hub where the Union Army was under siege, but Grant successfully broke the logjam at the end of November, adding another victory for the general.

Grant passed an uneventful winter in Nashville before being ordered to Washington in early March 1864. There Grant and Lincoln met for the first time, the president having decided to promote Grant to the rank of lieutenant general and general in chief of all armies. After receiving assurances from advisors that Grant was not interested in running for the presidency, Lincoln felt satisfied that he had the man who could finally bring the South to its knees—though he preferred not to know the specific details of Grant's plans to achieve that goal.

DID YOU KNOW?

Grant is a cousin to later presidents Franklin D. Roosevelt and Grover Cleveland.

COMMANDER OF ALL UNION ARMIES

In early May the Union Army crossed the Rapidan River on its way to Richmond. A few miles beyond Chancellorsville, Virginia, Generals Grant and Lee opposed each other for the first time at the Battle of the Wilderness. Unlike his fellow commanders, Grant was not awestruck by Robert E. Lee. When another officer attempted to tell Grant that he should be more cautious in dealing with General Robert E. Lee (who now commanded the Confederacy's Army of Northern Virginia) and the Confederates, Grant took his cigar out of his mouth and replied, "Oh, I am heartily tired of hearing about what Lee is going to do. Some of you always seem to think he is suddenly going to turn a double somersault, and land in our rear and on both our flanks at the same time. Go back to your command, and try to think what we are going to do ourselves instead of what Lee is going to do."[14]

The Battle of the Wilderness was fought in dense underbrush and rugged terrain. No clear winner emerged from the two days of intense fighting, which left 18,000 Union Army soldiers dead. But Grant did the unexpected—he refused to retreat. Instead, he simply shifted his army to the east. Within a couple of days, the armies were fighting, this time at Spotsylvania. Grant's refusal to quit came as no surprise to Lee's second in

NATIONAL EVENTS

MAR 1: America's first national park established at Yellowstone

OCT 9: Aaron Montgomery Ward starts a mail-order business in Chicago

NOV 5: Grant reelected president defeating Horace Greeley

NOV 5: Susan B. Anthony fined for attempting to vote

MAR 1: Production of first modern typewriters by Remington

1873

WORLD EVENTS

APR 24: Mount Vesuvius erupts

OCT 19: World's largest gold nugget discovered in New South Wales, Australia

United Kingdom declares war against Ghana, and after it is defeated, Ghana becomes the Gold Coast colony

command, "Pete" Longstreet, a friend of Grant's from West Point, who admonished other Confederate officers not to "underrate him . . . for that man will fight us every day and every hour till the end of this war."[15] Lee, whose losses were also severe, moved to keep his army between Grant and Richmond.

Apparently Grant's patience expired by early June when he faced Lee yet again, this time at Cold Harbor, Virginia. In an ill-planned and poorly executed advance, more than 7,000 Union soldiers died in less than thirty minutes. The experience haunted Grant, and he wrote in his memoirs that he "regretted that the last assault at Cold Harbor was ever made . . . no advantage whatever was gained to compensate for the heavy loss we sustained."[16]

Grant's strategic shifting of his army to his left, or eastern flank, had steadily brought it closer to the Confederate capital. The best way to make the final approach into Richmond was, he determined, from the south through the town of Petersburg, which, with its five railroads, was also a vital link in the southern supply system. To Grant's dismay, his Union commanders failed to press the attack, which gave Lee the opportunity to reinforce his troops there. As a result, the two armies dug in for a siege that would last the next ten months. Systematically, the Union cut the rail lines and taunted Lee with skirmishes near the city, forcing him to divide his already depleted troops. Once spring arrived, Grant's troops punched through Confederate trenches, prompting Lee to send word to President Jefferson Davis to evacuate Richmond.

On April 3, 1865, the capital of the confederacy was under Grant's control, and President Lincoln arrived to walk amid the rubble. Lee's all-but-defeated army fled west, their desperately needed food supplies intercepted by Union cavalry under Brigadier General George A. Custer. Finally, on April 9, Grant and Lee met in the front parlor of a home in the hamlet of Appomattox Court House, Virginia, to negotiate Lee's surrender. The two men discussed old times in the army and the Mexican War before settling down to the business at hand. In Grant's estimation, Lee seemed satisfied by the terms of surrender and asked for food for his starving troops, which Grant gladly provided. When the two leaders met again, Grant urged Lee to seek the surrender of the remaining southern troops, but Lee deferred, insisting such action was a matter for Confederate president Davis.

Grant reported to President Lincoln later that week and also received an invitation to attend Ford's Theater the night of April 14 with the Lincolns. Grant declined as he and his wife wished to visit their children in school in New Jersey. While en route, Grant learned of Lincoln's assassination and hurried back to Washington.

JOHNSON ADMINISTRATION

Though Andrew Johnson was a disappointment compared to Lincoln, Grant stayed in Washington to serve the new president and his administration whose members had served in Lincoln's cabinet. Johnson determined to institute his own Reconstruction Plan, which allowed former Confederates to participate in their new governments provided they took a loyalty oath. Southern states were also required to abolish slavery before regaining admittance to the United States. The plan's terms were less punishing to the South than many northern congressmen believed appropriate, and the president became the prime target for attack. Once elections were held in 1866, a majority of Republicans could override his vetoes, which they did on a regular basis. By this time, Grant

DID YOU KNOW?

Grant established the first national park when he created Yellowstone in 1872.

MAR 3: Comstock Law enacted, forbidding the mailing of anything considered "obscene, lewd, or lascivious"

MAR 4: President Grant inaugurated for his second term

AUG 1: World's first cable car begins operation in San Francisco

SEP 18: Financial panic triggered by collapse of Jay Cooke and Company

APR: Madison Square Garden opens in New York City

1874

Puerto Rico abolishes slavery

MAY 23: Canadian law creates North-West Mounted Police (later renamed Royal Canadian Mounted Police "Mounties")

JUL 1: Prince Edward Island joins the Canadian Confederation

SEP 16: German troops evacuate France after French complete paying their indemnity following Franco-Prussian War

Thomas Hardy publishes *Far from the Madding Crowd*

DID YOU KNOW?

Grant's habit of smoking seven to ten cigars daily led to his developing throat cancer.

Grant's memoirs were completed a few weeks before his death and ultimately gave his family $450,000.

had received yet another promotion to a new post created by Congress: General of the Armies of the United States.

Early in Johnson's presidency, the chief executive and his secretary of war Edwin Stanton became enemies because of their differing views on Reconstruction. Stanton sided with the Radical Republican element in Congress, who demanded a punitive, long-term military occupation. Grant was dragged into the fray when Johnson suspended Secretary Stanton and asked Grant to take his place. Grant reluctantly agreed to serve in the interim, which lasted from August 1867 to January 1868. The removal of Stanton led to the impeachment of President Johnson by Congress for violating the recently passed Tenure of Office Act; the president only narrowly escaped being convicted. Not wishing to remain in the middle of the power play between the executive and legislative branches, Grant refused to remain in the cabinet once Congress ordered the president to reinstate Stanton. Johnson felt betrayed by Grant and suspected that his general had political ulterior motives; indeed, Grant was looking to the 1868 presidential election and the Republican nomination.

ELECTION OF 1868

In May, the Republicans met in Chicago and nominated General Ulysses S. Grant as their presidential candidate and Schuyler Colfax of Indiana as vice president. Democrats fronted former New York governor Horatio Seymour and former Union commander Francis Blair Jr. as their ticket, but fully expected to be defeated. Grant had ended his letter accepting the nomination with the phrase "Let us have peace," which became his campaign slogan. The Republican candidate did not actively campaign, but, rather, allowed his military experience and status to carry him. The Republicans promised to continue the Reconstruction programs begun during Johnson's presidency; the Democrats pledged to end Reconstruction quickly, eliminate the Freedman's Bureau, which provided relief and educational assistance for refugees and freed slaves, and allow the South to determine its voting rights.

The popular vote was a modest victory for Grant—53 percent to Seymour's 47 percent—but the electoral vote was a landslide, with 214 for Grant to 80 for Seymour. Grant would now join Washington, Jackson, Harrison, and Taylor as former generals and war heroes elected to the presidency.

PRESIDENT GRANT

In the eight years since Abraham Lincoln's inauguration, the United States had endured the deadliest war in its history, an assassination of its leader, an impeachment of his successor, and the divisiveness of Reconstruction. In short, the country was ready and willing for peace and tranquility to reign. Grant had no particular strategy for his administration; he appointed friends and relatives to various political positions and planned to sit back while the wheels of government rolled along. Having never served in elected office before, Grant was ill equipped to handle the various problems of a country still healing, with much of its population still recovering from its wounds of war. Grant's hands-off policies would create disastrous circumstances for the nation's economy, and his poor choice of cabinet and political appointments would make his presidency one of the most scandal-ridden in history.

The economy was of primary concern as Republicans had promised to pay off the war debt with "hard" money, while the Democrats, who favored the debtors—the farmers and laborers—

NATIONAL EVENTS	**MAY 20:** Levi Strauss receives patent for jeans with copper rivets	**JUL 1:** First zoo opens in US in Philadelphia	**NOV 7:** First appearance of the elephant as the Republican symbol drawn by Thomas Nast	**NOV 18:** Women's Christian Temperance Union founded in Cleveland	**NOV 19:** Boss Tweed convicted of corruption and sentenced to 12 years in prison
WORLD EVENTS	First Impressionist exhibition in Paris	Agra Canal opens in India	**JAN 23:** Duke of Edinburgh marries Grand Duchess Marie Alexandrovna (only daughter of Emperor Alexander II of Russia)	**APR 5:** In Vienna, world premiere of Johann Strauss's opera *Die Fledermaus*	**OCT 10:** Fiji Islands annexed by the British

pledged "soft" money or the issuance of more greenbacks. The value of greenbacks to gold varied considerably and led to a fluctuating market. Two New York financiers, Jay Gould and Jim Fisk, devised a scheme to corner the gold market of the New York City Stock Exchange. In September 1869, they implemented their plan and caused the price of gold to rise 20 percent, sending businessmen who had to use greenbacks (which did not increase in value) to purchase the gold, to go into bankruptcy. A crisis developed on September 24, which came to be known as Black Friday: commodities and foreign trade suffered and the stock market plummeted. Grant and his secretary of the treasury attempted to rectify the situation by dumping four million dollars of the US gold reserve onto the market to drive down the price. Later it was learned that Fisk and Gould had paid the president's brother-in-law in the hope of influencing the timing of Grant's response to the crisis, but their efforts were to no avail.

Hoping to improve the nation's health and jump the hurdle of Reconstruction, Grant supported the Fifteenth Amendment, which granted citizens the right to vote regardless of "race, color, or previous condition of servitude," while also backing amnesty for former Confederate leaders. The president was concerned about resistance occurring in various areas of the South, especially the violence attributed to a new organization called the Ku Klux Klan. In 1870 and 1871, new laws were passed that allowed the use of armed force, if necessary, to curb the terror. Martial law was declared in part of South Carolina, but enforcement was nearly impossible with the army so greatly reduced in numbers. The fates of the recently freed slave population of the South were more or less at the hands of former owners, and those whose freedoms had just been won saw them slip away, as intimidation and terror gripped the region and lasted for nearly a century.

TRANSCONTINENTAL RAILROAD (May 10, 1869) ★ At Promontory Point, Utah, the Union Pacific and Central Pacific railroads met, joining the nation by rail.

Most of President Grant's cabinet were incompetent in their positions, but one member—Hamilton Fish of New York—rose above the rest and proved an extremely effective diplomat. He managed to convince the British to use an arbitration panel to determine what damages, if any, the British owed the United States for destruction caused by British-built Confederate ships. The panel awarded the United States $15.5 million.

Attempting to improve the nation's government, Grant tried to push civil service legislation through Congress, but its members were less than enthusiastic about losing patronage; consequently, reform would have to wait until the aftermath of President Garfield's assassination. Grant also wanted to set aside land for the country's future recreation, so he supported the bill creating Yellowstone as the nation's first national park.

President Grant eagerly pledged himself to a second term; however, this announcement was not greeted with enthusiasm by all Republicans. Dissatisfied with the corruption that seemed to pervade Grant's administration, some liberal Republicans held their own convention in Cincinnati and chose newspaper publisher Horace Greeley as their candidate and B. Gratz Brown as his running mate. The Democrats, in disarray and unable to determine their own candidate, also endorsed Greeley-Brown. Grant won reelection—with a

NOV 24: Joseph Glidden patents a double-stranded barbed wire

Ice cream soda invented in Philadelphia

R.J. Reynolds begins producing tobacco products in Winston, North Carolina

MAR 1: Civil Rights law passed making it illegal to discriminate against African Americans in public places

APR 22: Arbor Day begins in Nebraska, but soon recognized nationally as people plant trees in its honor

1875

JAN 12: Kwang-su becomes emperor of China

MAR 3: Bizet's opera *Carmen* premieres in Paris

MAY 7: Treaty of Saint Petersburg signed between Russia and Japan; gives Russia Sakhalin Island and

Japan receives control of Kuril Islands as far as Kamchatka Peninsula

AUG 2: Opening of world's first roller skating rink in London

DID YOU KNOW?

Fred Grant, Grant's eldest son, served as minister to Austria under President Benjamin Harrison, and as the New York City Commissioner of Police.

wider margin than he had four years earlier. Horace Greeley died between the popular and electoral elections, so all the electoral votes went to Grant.

SECOND TERM

During Grant's second presidential campaign, yet another scandal rocked the country, this one involving the construction of the transcontinental railroad and the Union Pacific, one of the nation's two major railroad companies. Concerned that the railroad might not be a financially sound investment, the Union Pacific created its own company, Crédit Mobilier, which won the construction contracts. The firm then turned around to charge the Union Pacific grossly inflated prices, making its top investors millionaires. When a hint of scandal reached Congress, discounted shares of stock were sold or given to congressional leaders as bribes to halt an investigation into the matter. As with the earlier gold market scandal, Grant was not involved, but the fact that it occurred while he was in office further tainted his administration.

Financial difficulties resurfaced in the country as Grant settled into his second term. The banking firm of Jay Cooke and Company, primary investors of the overextended Northern Pacific Railroad, collapsed in September 1873, precipitating a depression that lasted five years. European economic woes, as well as the drain on insurance payouts from the great Chicago fire of 1871 and a major fire that scorched Boston in 1872, worsened an already bleak economic outlook. One quarter of the nation's burgeoning railroad business failed during the five-year depression. Countless businesses and factories declared bankruptcy, leading to double-digit unemployment. Naturally, the man who received the blame was President Grant.

To help pay for the staggering cost of the Civil War, taxes had been raised, particularly the tax on distilled liquor. The industry found a way to circumvent the tax, however—bribe Treasury officials. When the secretary of the treasury, Benjamin Bristow, suspected the problem, he hired outside investigators, and in May 1875, more than two hundred arrests were made, including the president's personal secretary, who was only saved from indictment by Grant's intervention. Still, more than a hundred were convicted.

Secretary of War W.W. Belknap soon found himself mired in his own scandal when it was discovered that he had taken kickbacks from the post trader at Fort Sill, Oklahoma. In 1870, his wife had worked out this arrangement; after her death, her sister, who was to become Mrs. Belknap, continued the practice, apparently with Belknap's knowledge. In all, they received an additional twenty thousand dollars before the scheme was uncovered in 1876. Grant accepted the secretary's resignation, but still the House impeached Belknap; the Senate failed to reach the required two-thirds vote for conviction.

During the trial, Lieutenant Colonel George Custer testified against Belknap, repeating the rumors he had heard about the secretary's illegal financial dealings. Scandal came uncomfortably close to the presidential family when Custer also testified against Orvil Grant, the president's brother. Grant became incensed and ordered Sherman, who was in charge of the armies, to keep Custer from taking command of the Seventh Cavalry as they were to join with General Terry in the valley of the Little Bighorn to stop Crazy Horse and the Sioux. Custer, however, successfully lobbied General Sheridan to win his command, and off he galloped to the Little Bighorn and infamy.

NATIONAL EVENTS

MAY 17: First running of Kentucky Derby at Churchill Downs

DEC: Boss Tweed escapes from jail and flees to Cuba; later is arrested and returned to US

JAN 31: All American Indians ordered to reservations by US government

FEB 2: National league of baseball founded with teams in Boston, Chicago, Cincinnati, Hartford, Louisville, New York, Philadelphia, and St. Louis

MAR 7: Alexander Graham Bell receives patent for telephone

1876

WORLD EVENTS

AUG 25: Captain Matthew Webb is the first person to swim the English Channel

SEP 7: Ethiopian Emperor Yohannes IV defeats Egyptian invasion in Battle of Agurdat

German inventor Nicholas Otto develops the four-stroke internal combustion engine

Samurai are banned from carrying swords in Japan

Nikolaus Otto invents internal-combustion engine in Germany

As the 1876 election approached, the question arose whether Grant, still immensely popular, would seek a third term. He insisted that he was not interested: "I would not accept a nomination if it were tendered, unless it should come under such circumstances as to make it an imperative duty—circumstances not likely to arise."[17] Julia, on the other hand, was perfectly content to remain in the White House and continue serving as First Lady. Surgeon General William Barnes described an occasion close to the end of Grant's second term when the president was returning from Capitol Hill and stated, "I wish this was over . . . I wish I was out of it altogether. After I leave this place, I never want to see it again." Julia replied, "Why, Ulyss, how you talk! I never want to leave it!"[18]

Though Julia was not granted her wish to remain in the White House for a third term, the White House was the breathtaking setting for the wedding of daughter Nellie to Englishman Algernon Sartoris in May 1874. The bride and the groom each thought they were marrying into money, but each was mistaken. Nellie, to her parents' sorrow, moved to England, where she bore four children. Unfortunately, years later the marriage ended in divorce.

Grant did not seek a third term in 1876. Voting fraud tainted results from four states in the national election, and eventually a committee determined the winner. Grant, to his great relief, could finally leave the presidency. He later admitted, "I felt like a boy getting out of school."[19] The president was eager to move on to the next stage of his career and travel the world.

WORLD TRAVELER

The former president and First Lady looked forward to an extensive world tour. A timely purchase of twenty-five shares in the Consolidated Virginia Mining Company, and the discovery of the Comstock Lode in 1859, yielded the Grants twenty-five thousand dollars in 1876, which they used to finance their trip.

BATTLE OF THE LITTLE BIGHORN (June 25, 1876) ★ Troops under command of Colonel George A. Custer attacked the camp of Sioux and Cheyenne along Little Bighorn River in Montana. The Indians under the command of Crazy Horse retaliated, killing Custer and 265 men in his command.

The couple visited the old world of Europe. They were entertained by its leaders, and Grant resigned himself to enduring the obligatory military displays held in his honor (he wore a specially made uniform for such occasions). He abhorred small talk among the "smart set"; he acted the typical American tourist and visited the key sites and art museums, but often simply sat and watched the people or wandered the streets of the cities. The pyramids of Egypt were next on the itinerary, followed by visits to Palestine and Turkey, where Grant was thrilled to receive two horses from Sultan Abdul Hamid II. They eventually traveled through the Suez Canal to India, then China, Siam, and Japan. Although Grant planned to continue to Australia, Julia decided that two years of traveling was plenty; now it was time to go home.

CIVILIAN IN RETIREMENT

The Grants docked in San Francisco, visited the Comstock mine, and then traveled by train to Galena, Illinois. There they were greeted by old war buddies Sherman and Sheridan, and another fellow who had become a famous writer—Samuel Clemens, a.k.a. Mark Twain. While there, friends

MAR 10: Alexander Graham Bell makes first successful telephone call, saying "Mr. Watson, come here, I want you."

MAY 10: Centennial Exposition opens in Philadelphia and includes new products such as Heinz Catsup, bread and rolls made with Fleischmann yeast, Hires root beer, and Budweiser beer

JUN 17: At Battle of the Rosebud, General George Crook's forces defeated by Sioux and Cheyenne warriors under Crazy Horse

JUN 25: Lt. Col. George Custer's force of nearly 300 men is wiped out by Crazy Horse at the Battle of the Little Bighorn

FEB 18: Telegraph link completed between Britain and New Zealand

FEB 24: Henrik Ibsen's play *Peer Gynt* premieres in Oslo, Norway

FEB 26: Japan recognizes independence of Korea from China in Treaty of Kanghwa

MAR 7: Egyptians beaten out of Ethiopia during the Battle at Gura

APR 16: The April Uprising in Buglaria begins; leads to the nation's independence in 1878

DID YOU KNOW?

Grant's funeral procession in 1885 was seven miles long as it wound through New York City. President Grover Cleveland led the procession, accompanied by Congress, the Supreme Court, his cabinet, and former presidents Hayes and Arthur. The procession took over five hours to pass by the 1.5 million people watching.

Grant was buried in a temporary tomb in Riverside Park while his permanent resting place was designed and constructed. On April 27, 1897, President William McKinley presided over the dedication of Grant's Tomb, with Mrs. Julia Grant, her family, and thousands of others in attendance.

and party members attempted to draft the former president for the 1880 election. Grant was not at all interested and was relieved when James A. Garfield was chosen instead.

The Grants, who had literally seen the world, had outgrown Galena's small-town charm, and wealthy friends purchased a property in New York City on East 66th Street for them. Grant became president of the Mexico Southern Railroad and walked to his Wall Street office every day. Monetary problems continued to plague him; nevertheless, he unwisely agreed to help fund his son Buck's partnership with young Wall Street tycoon Ferdinand Ward in an investment firm. Neither Grant knew that Ward was simply running a scheme, which ended in significant financial loss for both father and son. Worried that his son's brokerage firm was nearly bankrupt, the former president prevailed upon William Vanderbilt for a loan of $150,000. Eventually, all involved lost their investments and Ward was sent to jail. Vanderbilt accepted some of Grant's military memorabilia as repayment on the loan and then turned the artifacts over to the government.

In February 1885, Ulysses S. Grant received numbing news: he had cancer of the esophagus and throat, which had gone too long unchecked. His concern now turned to his wife's financial security after his death. The previous summer, Grant had been contracted to write descriptions of key Civil War battles for *Century* magazine. Pleased by the readership's response to the accounts, the publisher now asked Grant to write his memoirs. While considering the offer, he was visited by Twain, who proposed an attractive counteroffer from his publishing firm. Grant finally agreed to write the book in return for 70 percent of the profits. With pencil in hand and son Fred as his assistant, he worked feverishly to complete the two volumes before death claimed him. Losing his voice and wracked by pain, he refused to admit defeat and sometimes rejected morphine, which would help the pain but cloud his thinking.

On July 19, 1885, Grant considered his task completed. He then wrote to his doctor, "My life is precious of course to my family and would be to me if I could entirely recover. There never was one more willing to go than I am."[20] The tranquil environment of the Adirondacks was calming, but over the next few days Grant's condition steadily declined. With his family gathered around, Ulysses S. Grant died at 8:08 a.m. on July 24. His body was taken to Albany, past West Point where cadets lined up and saluted, and then on to New York City, where he was buried. In 1897, President Garfield dedicated Grant's Tomb on Riverside Drive, and seven years later, Julia was buried beside her beloved husband.

Grant's *Memoirs* proved to be a huge publishing success and provided the family with nearly $450,000.

NATIONAL EVENTS

JUL 4: Centennial of US

AUG 1: Colorado admitted as 38th state

AUG 2: "Wild Bill" Hickok killed in a Deadwood, South Dakota, saloon while playing poker by Jack McCall; Hickok was holding aces and eights, which will become known as the "Dead Man's Hand"

SEP 7: Jesse James and gang attempt bank robbery in Minnesota; two are killed and three of the Younger brothers are captured

NOV 7: Presidential election, but disputed results between candidates Rutherford B. Hayes and Samuel

WORLD EVENTS

MAY 8: The last Tasmanian aboriginal, Truganini, dies

JUL 1–2: Serbia and Montenegro declare war on Turkey

AUG 13: Richard Wagner's *Ring* cycle opens in Germany

AUG 31: Murat V, sultan of the Ottoman Empire is deposed and succeeded by his brother, Abdul Hamid II

OCT 31: Cyclone hits Bengal (Bangladesh); 200,000 perish

> *"The right of revolution is an inherent one. When people are oppressed by their government, it is a natural right they enjoy to relieve themselves of oppression, if they are strong enough, whether by withdrawal from it, or by overthrowing it and substituting a government more acceptable."*
>
> —*U.S. Grant in his personal memoirs published in 1885*

ENDNOTES

1 Ulysses S. Grant, *Personal Memoirs of U.S. Grant,* New York: Charles L. Webster & Company, 1894, p. 19.

2 Ulysses S. Grant, 3rd, *Ulysses S. Grant, Warrior and Statesman*, New York: William Morrow & Company, 1969, p. 28.

3 Ibid, p. 29.

4 Grant, *Memoirs*, p. 37.

5 Brooks D. Simpson, *Ulysses S. Grant,* New York: Houghton Mifflin & Co., 2000, p. 40.

6 Ibid, p. 41.

7 Grant, *Warrior and Statesman*, p. 78.

8 Ibid, p. 90.

9 Grant, *Memoirs,* p. 125.

10 Ibid, p. 138.

11 Ibid, p. 149.

12 Simpson, p. 107.

13 Grant, *Memoirs*, p. 211.

14 Grant, *Warrior and Statesman*, p. 218.

15 Simpson, pp. 287-288.

16 Grant, *Memoirs*, p. 503.

17 Grant, *Warrior and Statesman*, p. 340.

18 Geoffrey Perret, *Ulysses S. Grant, Soldier & Statesman*, New York: Random House, 1997, p. 444.

19 Ibid, p. 446.

20 Mark Perry, *Grant and Twain*, New York: Random House, 2004, p. 225.

J. Tilden will necessitate a committee to decide the election, and ultimately Hayes is declared the winner

NOV 29: Mexican general Porfirio Diaz overthrows President Lerdo de Tejada

Rutherford B. Hayes

★ ★ ★ NINETEENTH PRESIDENT ★ ★ ★

LIFE SPAN
- Born: October 4, 1822, in Delaware, Ohio
- Died: January 17, 1893, in Fremont, Ohio

NICKNAME
- Dark-Horse President

RELIGION
- No formal affiliation, but attended Methodist services after his marriage

HIGHER EDUCATION
- Kenyon College, 1842
- Harvard Law School, 1845

PROFESSION
- Lawyer

MILITARY SERVICE
- Civil War: served with Twenty-Third Ohio Volunteer Infantry Regiment June 1861 to June 1865; began as a major and rose to rank of major general

FAMILY
- Father: **Rutherford Hayes** (1782–1822)
- Mother: **Sophia Birchard Hayes** (1792–1866)
- Wife: **Lucy Ware Webb Hayes** (1831–1889); wed on December 30, 1852, in Cincinnati, Ohio
- Children: **Birchard "Birch" Austin** (1853–1926); **James Webb Cook** (1856–1934); **Rutherford "Ruddy" Platt** (1858–1927); **Joseph Thompson** (1861–1863); **George Crook** (1864–1866); **Frances "Fanny"** (1867–1950); **Scott Russell** (1871–1923); **Manning Force** (1873–1874)

POLITICAL LIFE
- Cincinnati city solicitor (1858–1861)
- US representative (1865–1867)
- Ohio governor (1868–1872; 1876–1877)

PRESIDENCY
- One term: March 4, 1877–March 4, 1881 (inauguration held on March 5 since the 4th was a Sunday)
- Republican
- Reason for leaving office: announced at start of presidency he would not seek second term
- Vice president: **William A. Wheeler** (1877–1881)

ELECTION OF 1876
- Electoral vote (disputed and went to committee which determined results): **Hayes** 185; **Samuel Tilden** 184
- Popular vote: **Hayes** 4,036,572; **Tilden** 4,284,020

CABINET

SECRETARY OF STATE
William M. Evarts (1877–1881)

SECRETARY OF THE TREASURY
John Sherman (1877–1881)

SECRETARY OF WAR
George W. McCrary (1877–1879)

Alexander Ramsey (1879–1881)

ATTORNEY GENERAL
Charles Devens (1877–1881)

SECRETARY OF THE NAVY
Richard W. Thompson (1877–1880)

Nathan Goff (Jan.–Mar. 1881)

POSTMASTER GENERAL
David M. Key (1877–1880)

Horace Maynard (1880–1881)

SECRETARY OF THE INTERIOR
Carl Schurz (1877–1881)

The year was 1876 and the presidential election was mired in controversy. Both parties contested the results, each accusing the other of fraud. The final result was not yielded through the democratic process, but, rather, by deals made behind the scenes. The winner, and new president, was Republican candidate Rutherford B. Hayes.

EARLY LIFE

Rutherford Hayes Jr. and his wife, Sophia Birchard, moved to Ohio in 1817 and settled in the town of Delaware. He became part owner in a distillery (ironic, since his son and daughter-in-law would later become famous for prohibiting alcohol in the White House). Hayes died five years later, before the birth of his son on October 4, 1822. Rutherford Birchard Hayes, whom family and friends would call "Rud," had three older siblings: a sister, who died the year before his birth; a brother, who died while ice skating; and his sister Fanny, who became her little brother's nursemaid, protector, best friend, and confidante.

Sophia Hayes managed to keep her small family comfortable. She rented out a farm and received considerable assistance from her wealthy brother, Sardis Birchard, who became a father figure to young Rutherford. The family lived modestly, but both Hayes children seldom felt the economic pinch, and especially enjoyed visiting their farm outside of town where they could eat their fill and play to their hearts' content. Fanny was a bit of a tomboy and could ride and shoot a gun as well as any boy. She taught Rud how to play chess, and they passed the hours in pleasant recreation.

Attending school for the first time was rather traumatic for the Hayes children. Their schoolmaster, Daniel Granger—Hayes described him as "a demon of ferocity" with "piercing black eyes"[1]—would whip his students, big or small, and at least once threw a knife near Rutherford to get the attention of a boy who was talking. Fanny and her brother feared for their lives and begged to be excused from attending, but to no avail.

In 1834, Sophia Hayes took her children on an extensive journey through New England to visit relatives; young Rutherford was impressed by the superior intellect and abilities of the Hayes girl cousins over their male counterparts. Once they returned home, Rutherford attended high school, and Fanny attended a female academy.

In 1836, Rutherford was sent to a Methodist academy in Norwalk, Ohio, and the following year, he moved on to Middletown, Connecticut, where he attended a college preparatory academy that enabled him to enter Kenyon College in Gambier, Ohio, at the age of sixteen. The schoolmaster at Middletown wrote to Mrs. Hayes that her son would do well in his future: "He is well informed, has good sense, and is respected and esteemed by his companions."[2]

At Kenyon College, the affable young man excelled in his studies, improved his public speaking abilities, made friendships, and in general had a very successful experience. He believed that a legal career was his best choice, and after graduation, moved to Columbus (now also the home of his beloved sister Fanny, who had married), where he read law for a year in one of the city's law firms. Uncle Birchard, however, believed he should engage in a more systematic study, so off Rutherford went to Harvard Law School.

For three semesters he studied in Cambridge and thoroughly enjoyed the experience: reading and attending lectures, participating in moot court sessions, and learning German. Upon his return to Ohio, he moved to his uncle's town of Lower

NATIONAL EVENTS

JAN 29: Fifteen-man presidential commission appointed to determine winner of the presidential election

MAR 2: Rutherford B. Hayes announced as the presidential winner

MAR 4: Hayes inaugurated as 19th president

MAR 4: Emile Berliner invents the microphone

APR 27: Federal troops withdrawn from the South, ending Reconstruction

MAY 5: Lakota Sioux follow Sitting Bull to Canada

1877

WORLD EVENTS

Leo Tolstoy publishes *Anna Karenina*

Anna Sewell publishes *Black Beauty*

German physicist, Wilhelm Pfeffer, discovers the process of osmosis

JAN 1: Queen Victoria proclaimed empress of India

JAN 29: Satsuma Rebellion begins in Japan as samurai warriors rebel against the emperor's advisors

Sandusky (Frémont), as the Harvard men had been cautioned not to move to cities. He passed the bar examination and became a practicing attorney.

All of this intensive hard work took its toll, though, and Rutherford's health deteriorated. He considered joining the army and going to fight in Mexico (a warmer climate), but was advised not to and went to Texas with his uncle instead. The fresh air and wide-open spaces of the range were invigorating for the young man, and his health improved.

ATTORNEY

Hayes returned again to Ohio, his strength regained, but this time decided he wanted to be part of a growing city, so in 1849 moved to Cincinnati. His legal practice grew steadily, and he handled both civil and criminal cases. While enjoying the various benefits of a bigger community, including membership in a literary society, Rutherford desired to find a wife. Earlier he had courted a young lady from Connecticut, but that relationship ended when she was unable to convince him to move there.

Another young lady, Lucy Webb, captivated him with her grace and charm; moreover, her natural intelligence, and the fact that she had a college education, made her prominent among the young ladies of Cincinnati. They courted for more than three years before they wed on December 30, 1852. The marriage lasted over forty years, and both described themselves as perfectly happy while experiencing life's ups and downs.

During the 1850s, Hayes took an increasingly more active role in the various issues of the day. He gave speeches for a temperance society and denounced the activities of the anti-Catholic, anti-immigrant Know-Nothing Party. He opposed slavery and his marriage into Lucy's family provided him with a more personal perspective on the issue. Her family was originally from Kentucky; in fact, she was only two years old when her father, Dr. James Webb, died after returning to his home state to help slaves that he had inherited to be repatriated to Liberia (an African colony founded by Americans for former slaves). With her husband's death, Lucy's mother was advised to sell the slaves for much-needed cash. Maria Cook Webb answered, "Before I will sell a slave, I will take in washing to support my family."[3] The slaves were freed, and were hired by the family from time to time.

Lucy inherited her family's views on slavery, and her husband was in complete agreement, both personally and professionally. On one occasion, he successfully argued a case with Senator Salmon P. Chase in favor of a fugitive slave girl. The courtroom broke into applause after Hayes concluded his argument. He made his legal expertise available to all runaway slaves and wrote, "My services were always freely given to the slave and his friends in all cases arising under the Fugitive Slave Law."[4] He did, however, keep his involvement with the Underground Railroad low-key so as to keep his law firm from suffering any ill effects.

Politically, Hayes was not an active member of the newly formed Republican Party, although he made speeches for their candidate, John C. Frémont, in 1856 and bemoaned Frémont's loss to James Buchanan. The next year Hayes refused a nomination for Congress, and in 1858 he was appointed Cincinnati city solicitor (prosecutor). Reelected two more times to the position, he was very appreciative of the guaranteed annual income of $3,500.

By 1860 threat of war loomed, and the divisiveness within the Democratic Party only worsened

DID YOU KNOW?

Although Hayes was not the first war veteran to be president, he was the first veteran to have been wounded in combat (he received four wounds while fighting in the Civil War).

MAY 6: Sioux leader Crazy Horse surrenders he and his people to the US Army at Ft. Robinson, Nebraska

JUL 24: Federal troops fire on striking railroad workers; more strikes begin across the US

SEP 5: Crazy Horse bayoneted by soldier at Fort Robinson

OCT 5: Promising "I will fight no more forever," Chief Joseph of the Nez Perce surrenders his tribe to the US Army; the Nez Perce were less than 40 miles from the Canadian border when their escape was halted

APR 24: Russia declares war on the Ottoman Empire

MAY 16: French political crisis of the Third Republic

MAY 21: Romania declares its independence from the Ottoman Empire

JUN 3: Dutch queen dies

JUL 9: First Wimbledon tennis championship

DID YOU KNOW?

Hayes was the only president whose election was decided by a congressional commission.

the already sharp divisions throughout the country. After meeting Lincoln on a few occasions, Hayes professed support, but in general admitted, "I cannot get up much interest in the contest,"[5] a strange reaction considering the enormous importance of the outcome. A few weeks later, on the day of the election, he seemed more fatalistic on the question of whether the South would secede. His diary entry reads, "I feel as if the time had come to test this question. If the threats are meant, then it is time the Union was dissolved or the traitors crushed out. I hope Lincoln goes in."[6] Lincoln was elected and the country was poised for war.

WAR

In February, Lincoln arrived in Cincinnati, where Hayes and his wife met occasionally with the president-elect. Hayes described Lincoln as "in good health; not a hair gray or gone; in his prime and fit for service, mentally and physically," and the president's public speeches more general and "wary" than in the "discreet but frank"[7] discussions the two shared in private. Hayes was more confident about his country's future knowing that Lincoln would be at the helm.

Once Fort Sumter fell and the new president called for 75,000 volunteers, Hayes pondered his fate. His family was divided on the issue: his mother thought the war was punishment from God; his mother-in-law fretted over it; and his wife enthusiastically proclaimed she wished she could take part in it. A month after the attack on Fort Sumter, Hayes wrote that he was accepting a commission to become a major of the Twenty-third Regiment of Ohio Volunteers, the reason being, "I would prefer to go into it if I knew I was to die or be killed in the course of it, than to live through and after it without taking any part."[8]

For the next four years, Hayes experienced army life with all of its dirt, grime, and glory. For a few weeks in the fall of 1861, he was transferred from combat to the judge advocate's office to try cases. After receiving a promotion to lieutenant colonel, he returned to the Twenty-Third. At the Battle of Antietam, his regiment came under heavy fire. Undaunted, Lieutenant Colonel Hayes ordered a charge, and the rebel line fell apart, but only briefly. Twice more his men charged, and then Hayes felt "a stunning blow." He had been shot in the left arm above the elbow. The loss of blood made him weak and, feeling faint, he laid down. He continued giving commands when conscious and attempted to move a short distance. His men retreated, leaving their commander pinned down under fire from both sides. During a lull, he called, "Hallo Twenty-third men, are you going to leave your colonel here for the enemy?"[9] Eventually he was moved off the field, and the regimental surgeon, who happened to be his brother-in-law, dressed the wound. Unfortunately, Lucy received word that he was dead; later she was told he was indeed alive, but was misinformed of his location. Eventually they were reunited, and Lucy enjoyed the first of many visits to her husband's camp. His men appreciated the kind-hearted woman's words of encouragement and her tender ministration to the wounded, and she became a popular figure among his men.

After recovering from his wounds, Hayes became a full colonel and better acquainted with newly promoted second lieutenant William McKinley. Hayes was impressed by the young man and wrote that he was "exceedingly bright, intelligent . . . and promised to be one of our best."[10] The Twenty-third continued to fight in Virginia and what soon became West Virginia. Now commanding the

NATIONAL EVENTS

DEC 6: *Washington Post* begins publishing

DEC 7: Thomas Edison demonstrates his new invention, the phonograph

Maximilian Berlitz opens a school for languages in Providence, Rhode Island

Louis Tiffany, son of the jeweler, begins creating his own type of glass

FEB 16: Congress makes silver legal tender in the US

1878

WORLD EVENTS

JUL 19: First battle in the Siege of Pleven, Russo-Turkish War

JUL 30: Second battle in the Siege of Pleven

Henry Stanley publishes a two-volume work, *Through the Dark Continent*, detailing his travels in Africa

Gilbert and Sullivan's opera *H.M.S. Pinafore* premieres in London

Catastrophic famine strikes Asia, killing more than 10 million people in China

First Brigade of the 2d Kanawha Division, Hayes served under General George Crook, whom he so admired that he named a son after him.

Colonel Hayes and his men took an active role in the Shenandoah Valley campaign, where Hayes was wounded again, but suffered even more when his horse was shot out from under him and fell on Hayes's ankle. With Lincoln's first term coming to a close, Hayes campaigned—vigorously this time—for the president's reelection, encouraging his troops to make use of the newly available absentee ballots. He understood, and wanted his troops to understand, that their commander in chief needed their vote as much as they needed his leadership.

In late summer 1864 Hayes learned that he had been nominated for election to Congress. He won the congressional seat in October, but his term would not start until December 1865. He was determined to stay in the army until Grant took Richmond. In November, Hayes became brigadier general and was promoted once more as brevet major general in recognition of "his distinguished and gallant services in the Campaign of 1864."[11]

Hayes was shocked to receive the news of Lincoln's assassination in April 1865, and pondered what the fate of the South would now be under President Johnson. In June, Hayes resigned his command and returned to Cincinnati.

CONGRESSMAN

For the first months after his return to civilian life, Hayes could immerse himself in the joys of family life, but then it was time to travel to Washington and become part of the Reconstruction Congress. His admiration for President Johnson soon waned, and he threw in his lot with fellow Republicans who consistently overrode the president's veto on such measures as the Civil Rights Bill, which declared that all born in the United States were citizens regardless of race or color and had rights of citizens, and the Freedman's Bill (p. 206). In 1866, Hayes campaigned for his congressional reelection. In one of his speeches, Hayes argued that there were two plans for Reconstruction: the one that Lincoln had wanted, and the one Jefferson Davis would like. President Johnson, argued Hayes, proposed a Reconstruction plan more in line with what Davis and the South wanted, and Hayes's Ohio constituency agreed. Hayes was reelected and continued his support of the Radical Republican agenda, including the Tenure of Office Act, forbidding the president from removing any federal official whose appointment required Senate confirmation, and Radical Reconstruction Acts, which divided the South into military districts ruled by martial law and granted blacks the right to vote three years prior to adoption of the Fifteenth Amendment.

FREEDMEN'S BUREAU ★ Created in March 1865 to help refugees and former slaves with procuring clothing, medicine, and other needed items, the Freedmen's Bureau also provided schools for African Americans during the Reconstruction era. Reuniting slave families after the Civil War was another of its functions.

Hayes's personal congressional record was lackluster, as he rarely gave a speech, and his highest committee assignment was chairing the Library Committee, where he managed to garner support to add two wings to the Library of Congress, as well as to increase appropriations for more acquisitions.

SUPREME COURT APPOINTMENTS
★ ★ ★ ★ ★ ★ ★ ★ ★ ★

John Marshall Harlan, 1877

William B. Woods, 1881

FEB 18: Lincoln County War begins in New Mexico Territory

APR: First Easter egg roll held on White House lawn

AUG 21: American Bar Association formed in Saratoga Springs, New York

OCT 15: Edison Electric Company opens for business

DEC 1: White House receives its first telephone

FEB 2: Greece declares war on Turkey

FEB 10: Cuba's ten-year rebellion ends against Spain

JUN 4: Turkey cedes Cyprus to Great Britain

JUL 13: Treaty of Berlin recognizes independence of Serbia, Montenegro, and Romania

SEP 12: Cleopatra's Needle installed in London

NOV 21: Second Afghan War begins between Afghanistan and Great Britain when British invade Khyber Pass

STATE OF THE UNION
★★★★★★★★★★

US POPULATION IN 1877
50,155,783

NATIONAL DEBT IN 1881
$2,069,013,570

PRESIDENT'S SALARY
$50,000/year

NUMBER OF STATES IN 1881
38

Still he was popular with the Republican Party in Ohio and he was nominated for governor.

As the Republican nominee, Hayes traversed the state making frequent speeches, but the audience he most enjoyed were those men of the Twenty-third whom he encountered along the way. The campaign schedule was temporarily—and happily—interrupted by the birth of Rutherford and Lucy's only daughter, named Fanny for his beloved sister who had died many years before. Contrary to initial reports of a Democratic Party win, Hayes did clinch the win and he girded himself to confront the legislature's Democratic majority. Before the inauguration, he also had to travel to Columbus and find a suitable house to rent, as there was no governor's mansion.

GOVERNOR

Inauguration day—January 13, 1868—was a bitterly cold and snowy day in Columbus, and, perhaps out of consideration for the audience, who were standing outside, the new governor delivered the shortest inaugural speech in Ohio's history. He pledged himself to voting rights that were granted regardless of color. He also understood his power was considerably limited as the governor was unable to exercise the power of a veto.

Governor Hayes found his new position as the state's chief executive "the pleasantest (office) I have ever had. Not too much hard work, plenty of time to read, good society, etc."[12] Hayes spent much of his time trying to convince the men of the Ohio legislature to support an amendment to the Ohio state constitution to allow suffrage for African American males. The Democratic majority, however, voted down the measure. Governor Hayes found the Republican Party giving him more consideration for his new stature. He was consulted on national matters, including the president's impeachment trial, which he attended. At the Republican national convention, Hayes headed the Ohio delegation and was pleased by its choice of Ulysses S. Grant as their candidate for the 1868 election.

Hayes faced stiff competition when he ran for his own reelection against George Hunt Pendleton. Earlier, Ohio had ratified the Fifteenth Amendment, granting blacks the right to vote, but the Democratic legislature subsequently attempted to rescind it; Hayes pointed to such an action as an example of the ruling party's desire to deprive citizens of their right to vote. To help turn the tide, he argued that a Republican legislature was needed as well. Democrats stood fast on their position of Negro suffrage and also countered with the demand for paying debts in greenbacks rather than gold. In October, Hayes and the Republicans won elections for the governorship as well as a slim majority in the Ohio legislature.

The reelected governor rejoiced at the ratification of the Fifteenth Amendment, and was instrumental in helping other groups of citizens

CIVIL WAR AMENDMENTS ★ Amendment 13 (1865) ended slavery everywhere in the United States (the Emancipation Proclamation only ended slavery in actual Confederate states, but allowed it to continue elsewhere). Amendment 14 (1868) granted citizenship to Americans born here (Native Americans were excluded until 1924). Amendment 15 (1870) allowed African American males the right to vote. (Many southern states ignored this and created barriers to disenfranchise blacks. This was not corrected for nearly 100 years with the passage of the Voting Rights Act of 1965.)

NATIONAL EVENTS	**EXODUS OF 1879:** More than 20,000 African Americans flee the oppressive conditions in the South and move to Kansas	Mary Baker Eddy founds the Church of Christ, Scientist Henry James publishes *Daisy Miller*	Joel Chandler Harris, whose pen name was Uncle Remus, writes "The Tar Baby"	James Ritty invents the first cash register for his Dayton, Ohio, bar	**JAN 1:** Specie Resumption Act—greenbacks equal gold in value for first time since Civil War
1879					
WORLD EVENTS	William Murrell, British physician, discovers that nitroglycerin is effective for cardiac problems	*A Doll's House* by Henrik Ibsen premieres in Copenhagen	**JAN 11:** Zulu War begins against the British in South Africa	**JAN 22:** Battle of Rorke's Drift; 140 British soldiers fight off over 4,000 Zulu warriors for hours	**FEB 14:** War of the Pacific begins between Chile and joint forces of Peru and Bolivia

better themselves as well. He supported the establishment of the Agricultural and Mechanical College, which later became Ohio State University. Lucy had helped to create the Soldiers' and Sailors' Orphans' Home at Xenia, and with her husband's endorsement, the state legislature took over its operation. He commuted the death sentences of a few prisoners, as well as transferred juveniles from adult facilities to reform schools. Hayes attempted to treat his constituents as well as he could and traveled among them whenever possible.

Hayes retired from the governorship in January 1872, and bragged to his uncle Sardis, who had built a home for the Hayes family in Frémont, "True or not, the common remark is that I am the most esteemed of the governors within the memory of people living."[13] Now the question was what to do next. Many begged the former governor to run for the US Senate against John Sherman, but he felt uncomfortable in doing so. Instead he worked for the campaign to reelect Grant and, against his wishes, was himself nominated for Congress. While Grant won in 1872, Hayes lost his first election.

RETIREMENT

Thanks to the fortune and generosity of Uncle Sardis, Hayes was able to enjoy the luxury of a political life without being overly concerned about the modest pay that came with it. But the Hayes family was still growing and the oldest boys would soon attend college, so the now retired governor contemplated a legal career in the growth industry of the late nineteenth century—railroads. President Grant offered him the position of assistant secretary of the treasury for the Cincinnati district, but Hayes refused the appointment, believing it was a step down after being governor. Instead he decided the best course of action was to return to his hometown of Frémont.

Once in northern Ohio, Hayes convinced his uncle to donate money for a town library. He also began dabbling in the real estate business in the greater Toledo area, as he believed growth there would make such investments profitable. In the fall of 1873, he attended military reunions and remarked that he had been invited by Generals Sheridan and Custer to tour the Great Plains the following year. The Hayes family also welcomed their eighth and final child, who sadly died a year later (the third of their children to die in infancy), and retired to their home at Spiegel Grove, which they inherited upon the death of Uncle Sardis.

In the off-year election of 1874 Hayes once again campaigned for Republican congressional candidates, but the results were disappointing. For the first time since the Civil War, the Democrats took the majority in Congress. After returning home to continue historical and genealogical research, Hayes was once again called upon by the Ohio Republican Party, who drafted him to run a third time for governor. The prospect of winning a post that no one had ever successfully claimed three times was too tempting for the savvy politician, as was the talk that very likely the winner of this contest could possibly be the next presidential candidate. Hayes allowed his name to be submitted, and on a platform of sound money, he won an unprecedented third term.

GOVERNOR AGAIN

On January 10, 1876, Rutherford B. Hayes was inaugurated governor. He worked with a Republican legislature to decrease the state budget while continuing his efforts to reform the penal system and suggested creating workhouses as halfway houses

DID YOU KNOW?

Hayes was the first president to be inaugurated in the White House.

New technologies introduced at the White House: typewriters and telephones.

The official title of "First Lady" was first used for Lucy Hayes.

JAN 28: New Haven, Connecticut, hosts the world's first commercial telephone exchange and the first telephone directory (it has 21 listings)

FEB 12: First artificial ice rink in North America opens at New York's Madison Square Garden

FEB 27: Chemists at Johns Hopkins University discover artificial sweetener saccharin

MAR 3: Belva Lockwood becomes first female lawyer to present a case before US Supreme Court

FEB 18: In Toronto, Canada, Sandford Fleming, an engineer, proposes creating standard time zones

MAR 13: Duke of Connaught and Strathearn, third son of Queen Victoria, marries Princess Louise Marguerite of Prussia

MAY 26: Treaty of Gandamak establishes an Afghan state

JUL 4: Zulu War ends in British victory

OCT 7: Germany and Austria-Hungary form Dual Alliance against Russia

DID YOU KNOW?

Hayes was the first president to travel to the West Coast during his term as president.

for prisoners. Again, some prisoners received commuted sentences or pardons from the benevolent governor. He had other ideas for his state, but those were shelved when the Republican Party decided it had more plans for him.

ELECTION OF 1876

James G. Blaine of Maine was initially the Republican frontrunner for the presidential nomination in 1876, but when his opponents threw in their lot with Hayes's supporters, the newly elected governor of Ohio was dubbed the Republican candidate when the party met in Cincinnati. New York representative William Wheeler was the vice presidential nominee. The Democrats chose Samuel J. Tilden of New York to head their ticket. Tilden had recently served as the leader of the New York Democratic Party and had effectively ended the power and corruption of the Tweed Ring; his vice presidential candidate was Thomas Hendricks of Indiana.

Hayes and his supporters effectively waved the "bloody shirt," contrasting their candidate's meritorious war record with Tilden's failure to serve in the war. But former New York governor Tilden had his impressive victory busting the corrupt Tweed Ring to bolster his record as a reformer. The country seemed ready to elect the first Democrat since Buchanan, and most indications pointed to a Tilden victory; in fact, Hayes went to bed on Election Day believing he had lost the election. But as dawn broke, the outcome was still in doubt.

Popular vote totals showed a majority of 51 percent going to Tilden and 48 percent to Hayes; electoral votes were, however, more problematic. Tilden was one vote shy of winning the Electoral College, and results were disputed in three southern states—South Carolina, Louisiana, and Florida. Owing to the fact that the Constitution did not provide instruction for any such occurrence, a national crisis loomed as Congress debated its course of action. Ultimately it was decided to create a bipartisan commission of fifteen to settle the matter—five representatives, five senators, and five supreme court justices and broken down to seven Republicans (including future president James Garfield), seven Democrats, and one independent. The attempt at equal representation immediately failed when the independent justice chose not to serve and was replaced by another justice who was also a Republican. Keeping March 5 as their deadline (inauguration day), the commission began its work.

States' electoral results were opened and certified in alphabetical order. The first problem was Florida with two sets of returns—one showing Tilden the winner; the other Hayes. After holding testimony and hearing arguments, the commission decided 8–7 that Hayes was the winner. The roll call resumed. Next were Louisiana's electoral votes, and the commission again voted 8–7 in favor of Hayes. The issue surrounding Oregon's returns regarded just one of its electors, but he was kept in the Hayes column. Finally the commission turned to South Carolina and again ended in the same vote. The final determination of the group was held for a few days while men on both sides met, deciding on certain actions that would later become known as the Compromise of 1877. On March 2, the country heard that the next president would be Republican Rutherford B. Hayes, with an electoral vote of 185 to Tilden's 184.

The result brought relief to some, joy to Hayes and his supporters—and proclamations of "Fraud!" from the Tilden camp. In fact, the *New York Sun* ran the headline, "Mr. Hayes is not President."[14] (The newspaper continued its campaign during the

NATIONAL EVENTS

APR 8: Echo Farms Dairy in Brooklyn, New York, introduces milk bottles

JUN 21: Frank W. Woolworth opens his first successful five-and-ten-cent store in Lancaster, Pennsylvania

JUL: James Gamble begins selling Ivory soap

OCT 21: Thomas Edison demonstrates his new invention, the light bulb

Former Civil War general and current New Mexico territorial governor Lew Wallace writes *Ben-Hur, A Tale of the Christ*

1880

WORLD EVENTS

OCT 19: Afghan's emir Mohammed Yakub forced to resign

NOV 28: Battle at Lydenburg South Africa

DEC 30: *Pirates of Penzance* premieres in London

Efforts to dig an English Channel tunnel end after 1.5 miles

next four years by frequently repeating the word "Fraud" when Hayes's picture was run.) Tilden responded to his supporters by saying, "I can retire to private life with the consciousness that I shall receive from posterity the credit of having been elected to the highest position in the gift of the people, without any of the cares and responsibilities of the office."[15]

Over a century later, consensus has not been reached regarding who was the true winner. Evidence of violence and intimidation against black voters in the South, as well as accusations of the possible bribery of electors, continue to raise questions of Hayes's legitimacy as the president.

WHITE HOUSE EASTER EGG ROLL ★ In the early 1870s, the Easter egg roll was held on the grounds of the Capitol, but too many children led to vast destruction of the lawn, so in 1878, they were banned. Two versions exist of how the White House revived the tradition. One states that the children next ran down Pennsylvania Avenue to the White House and demanded that the gates open and allow them their Easter egg roll. Another (more likely) version states that President Hayes heard of the youngsters' plight and announced the White House would serve as the setting. Starting that year and continuing for all succeeding years (except during World War II and while the White House was undergoing renovation during the Truman years), the tradition has grown and evolved to become the largest outside public gathering of the year at the White House.

PRESIDENT HAYES

Hayes began the duties of his new office satisfied that his election was a valid mandate of the people. The first order of business was to end Reconstruction, as had been promised to the southern Democrats. This involved the withdrawal of federal troops and the reestablishment of home rule. Republicans immediately objected to what they perceived as their defeat, and many within the party abandoned the president for his betrayal of their principles. Hayes countered with the promises he exacted from southern Democrats promising to help blacks gain voting and civil rights.

Fulfilling a pledge that Hayes was committed to, his second month in office saw a push for civil service reform. First on the agenda was Tilden's backyard—New York City and the New York Custom House, where party boss and U.S. senator Roscoe Conkling ruled with the power of patronage. Unlike Conkling, Hayes wanted positions to be based on merit rather than political favors. The senator waged a political war of power against the president. Although Conkling won the early skirmishes, Hayes claimed victory in the war by successfully replacing the top two men of the customs house (including future president Chester A. Arthur) with his own appointments based on merit.

In October 1877, the president called a special congressional session to deal with a critical problem—the U.S. Army had not been paid since June. Congress had used the military as a political football, with Democrats determining that the military should not be used to patrol the South and enforce Reconstruction. The military's presence was now needed in the West. In 1876, a force under Custer had been nearly wiped out, and earlier in 1877, US troops had forced the return of the Nez Perce under Chief Joseph, who, in an attempt to avoid being moved to a reservation had come within forty miles of the Canadian border. Problems along the

MAR 4: First photo in a newspaper appears in *New York Daily Graphic*

MAR 31: Wabash, Indiana, becomes first town to be lit by electricity

MAY 13: Thomas Edison demonstrates his electric railway at Menlo Park

JUNE 18: Johann Sutter dies penniless in Washington, D.C. (California gold rush began on his land, but 49ers quickly overran his property)

AUG 30: First complete railroad trip made from Houston to New Orleans on the Texas and New Orleans Railroad

Fedor Dostoyevsky publishes *The Brothers Karamazov*

Marthe Distel opens Le Cordon Bleu cooking school in Paris

MAR 8: Conservatives in Britain suffer major defeat at the polls and Liberals take control of the government

JUN 24: First performance of "O Canada," song that will become Canadian national anthem

JUN 29: France annexes Tahiti

DID YOU KNOW?

President and Mrs. Hayes began the "Easter Egg Roll" for children on the White House Lawn (1878). Mrs. Hayes was the first wife of a president to graduate from college.

Mexican border were also intensifying, with the Army receiving authority to pursue marauders into Mexico if necessary. (This disagreement was soon resolved diplomatically.) The Army was also called into service to aid in restoring order where railroad strikes had created unsafe conditions. Curiously, the key question put before Congress was not whether to pay the soldiers but whether the size of the Army—which obviously were needed on many fronts—should be reduced. Congress debated this question for days when finally Ohio congressman James A. Garfield rose and asked, "Is it not enough that our poor, unpaid, starving Army shall, by the delay of the House, be doomed to many days of starvation while their numbers are reduced by sickness and Indian warfare, only to learn that a merciful Congress proposes still further to reduce them?"[16] Finally, it was determined to keep the staffing at 25,000, and to pay them.

President Hayes had long been a proponent of "hard money," keeping the currency backed with gold. Congress, on the other hand, wanted to buy silver from recent silver strikes in the West to inflate the currency, thereby helping debtors. Hayes vetoed the measure, but Congress overrode the veto, and the Bland-Allison Act was passed in 1878 as a compromise. It did not allow unlimited coinage of silver, as desired by many in Congress, but the Bland-Allison Act did permit the Treasury to buy between $2 and $4 million in silver bullion every month. That silver was then coined and could be used as legal tender to pay any debts. The president supported the Resumption of Specie Act (actually passed four years earlier), which allowed people to redeem their currency "greenbacks" to gold as of January 1, 1879. These differences over finance and civil service issues revealed the deep division between the president and his party, and he remarked, "I am not liked as a President by the politicians in office, in the press, or in Congress."[17]

Plagued by divisiveness at work, at home Hayes never questioned the love and devotion of his family. In fact, he and Lucy repeated their vows on their silver anniversary in 1877 and the next day held a magnificent reception to celebrate. Lucy enjoyed updating the White House and even had the first telephone installed. They entertained, but she soon received the nickname "Lemonade Lucy" for her efforts to make the president's home an example of temperance. Children descended on the White House in 1878 for the first official Easter egg roll there (previously they had been held on the grounds of the Capitol). And thus began another White House tradition.

On the international front, the United States received word that the same French company that had successfully built the Suez Canal was preparing to build a similar waterway in Central America. President Hayes voiced the country's concern and issued a statement saying, "The policy of this country is a canal under American control." It would be more than thirty years before his idea became reality when the Panama Canal opened in 1914.

Closer to home, Hayes was concerned by the growing anti-Chinese sentiment, which in 1879 manifested itself in congressional passage of a bill that nearly excluded Chinese immigration. Hayes vetoed the measure and, concerned about America's relations with China, sent a new team of diplomats there to negotiate the Treaty of 1880, which limited, but did not exclude, further Chinese immigration. This issue of Chinese immigration would continue and the entry of Chinese into the United States would be further curtailed two years later, with the Chinese Exclusion Act.

As the election of 1880 approached, some were

NATIONAL EVENTS

OCT: Blizzard of 1880

OCT 1: John Philip Sousa becomes conductor of US Marine Corps Band

NOV 2: James A. Garfield elected president

NOV 4: First cash register patented in Ohio

NOV 17: Chinese Exclusion Treaty is signed, severely limiting Chinese emigration to the US

WORLD EVENTS

JUL 3: Madrid Convention signed by leading European powers and US; Moroccan independence recognized

JUL 16: First woman licensed to practice medicine in Canada

JUL 22: The British recognize Abdur Rahman Khan as emir of Afghanistan

AUG 2: Greenwich Mean Time officially becomes the standard time of Great Britain

AUG 14: Cologne Cathedral is finally completed; construction had begun 600 years earlier, in 1248

surprised by Hayes's steadfast opposition to running for a second term. When the Republicans met in Chicago, Conkling pushed for Grant to run for a third term; others pointed to an array of potential candidates. The anti-Grant faction finally agreed on a dark horse, James A. Garfield, and the former New York port collector, Chester A. Arthur, as his vice president. Hayes supported the ticket and was thrilled with Garfield's victory in both the popular and electoral elections. After attending Garfield's inauguration, the president and Lucy returned to Ohio and Spiegel Grove.

RETIREMENT

For the next dozen years, the former president continued to travel widely, as he had done during his presidential term. Among his favorite causes were education (he served as trustee for several Ohio colleges), prison reform, and improving Negro education, but he opposed women's suffrage. While attending one of his meetings at Ohio State University, Lucy suffered a debilitating stroke. The couple remained together until her death on June 25, 1889, and her burial at Spiegel Grove.

Hayes was disconsolate over the loss of his wife of forty years, but finally agreed to travel with his daughter to Bermuda. He enjoyed himself and soon resumed visiting friends and family throughout the country. In January 1893, while visiting in Cleveland, he suffered a heart attack. He insisted on returning home, and successfully reached Spiegel Grove as family members began pouring in. His last words were of his wife, "I know that I am going where Lucy is."[18] Rutherford B. Hayes died on January 17, 1893, and was buried four days later beside his beloved Lucy.

ENDNOTES

1 Charles Richard Williams, ed., *Diary and Letters of Rutherford Birchard Hayes*, vol. I, Columbus, OH: Ohio State Archaeological and Historical Society, 1922, p. 9.

2 Hans L. Trefousse, *Rutherford B. Hayes*, New York: Times Books, 2002, p. 5.

3 Ari Hoogenboom, *Rutherford B. Hayes, Warrior and President*, Lawrence, KS: University Press of Kansas, 1995, p. 95.

4 Ibid.

5 Williams, ed., p. 564.

6 Ibid, p. 566.

7 Hoogenboom, p. 113.

8 Williams, vol. II, p. 17.

9 Hoogenboom, pp. 146-147.

10 Trefousse, p. 30.

11 Ibid, pp. 36-37.

12 Hoogenboom, p. 215.

13 Ibid, p. 238.

14 Trefousse, p. 82.

15 Irving Stone, *They Also Ran*, Garden City, NY: Doubleday, 1966, p. 210.

16 S.E. Whitman, *The Troopers, An Informal History of the Plains Cavalry, 1865-1890*, New York: Hasting House, 1962, p. 116.

17 Arthur B. Tourtellot, *The Presidents on the Presidency*, New York: Russell and Russell, 1964, p. 44.

18 Trefousse, p. 146.

DEC 20: Lights shine on Broadway for the first time, making it the "Great White Way"

SEP 5: First successful test of an electric tram in St. Petersburg, Russia

SEP 13: Britain's Parliament passes Employers' Liability Act (workmen's compensation)

NOV 11: Australian outlaw Ned Kelly is hung in Melbourne

DEC 30: The Transvaal becomes a republic

James A. Garfield

★ ★ ★ TWENTIETH PRESIDENT ★ ★ ★

LIFE SPAN

- Born: November 19, 1831, in Orange Township, Cuyahoga County, Ohio
- Died: September 19, 1881, in Elberon, New Jersey

RELIGION

- Disciples of Christ

HIGHER EDUCATION

- Eclectic Institute at Hiram, Ohio
- Williams College,1856

PROFESSION

- Teacher, lawyer

MILITARY SERVICE

- Civil War (1861–1863); commissioned as a lieutenant colonel in Ohio Forty-second Regiment and rose to major general
- Resigned his commission in 1863 to take a seat in Congress

FAMILY

- Father: **Abram Garfield** (1799–1833)
- Mother: **Eliza Ballou Garfield** (1801–1888)
- Wife: **Lucretia "Crete" Rudolph Garfield** (1832–1918); wed on November 11, 1858 in Hiram, Ohio
- Children: **Eliza Arabella** (1860–1863); **Harry Augustus** (1863–1942); **James Rudolph** (1865–1950); **Mary** (1867–1947); **Irvin McDowell** (1870–1951); **Abram** (1872–1958); **Edward** (1874–1876)

POLITICAL LIFE

- Ohio state senator (1859–1861)
- US representative (1863–1880)

PRESIDENCY

- One term: March 4, 1881–September 19, 1881 (shot on July 2, 1881, and died September 19)
- Republican
- Reason for leaving office: assassinated
- Vice president: **Chester A. Arthur** (1881)

ELECTION OF 1880

- Electoral vote: **Garfield** 214; **Winfield Scott Hancock** 155
- Popular vote: **Garfield** 4,453,295; **Hancock** 4,414,082

CABINET

SECRETARY OF STATE
James G. Blaine (1881)

SECRETARY OF THE TREASURY
William Windom (1881)

SECRETARY OF WAR
Robert Lincoln (1881)

ATTORNEY GENERAL
I. Wayne McVeigh (1881)

SECRETARY OF THE NAVY
William H. Hunt (1881)

POSTMASTER GENERAL
Thomas L. James (1881)

SECRETARY OF THE INTERIOR
Samuel J. Kirkwood (1881)

Journalists and political spectators often point to the first hundred days as the critical period in a presidential term. It is the time when the new president pushes forward the agenda that has brought him to that high office. In the case of James A. Garfield, however, his hundred days were even more critical, since he fell victim to an assassination less than four months after he took the oath of office.

EARLY LIFE

James A. Garfield was born November 19, 1831, in rural Orange Township near present-day Cleveland, Ohio. He never knew his father because when he was only eighteen months old, Abram Garfield became ill after fighting a nearby forest fire and died. Eliza Ballou Garfield determined not to parcel out her four children to others or lose the farm. Methodically she sold most of their acreage, keeping thirty acres for the family's use. Ten-year-old Thomas Garfield became the male head of the household and main farmhand.

As the baby in the family, James was coddled by all. His ability to read at age three encouraged his mother to enroll him in school. In fact, Eliza Garfield donated land for the small school cabin. Although he was an exceptional student, James frequently encountered difficulties with the other boys and began complaining of headaches and stomachaches. Reading became his favorite escape, especially the world of *Robinson Crusoe.*

James started working on neighboring farms when he was twelve to help earn extra money for the family. As he grew from small boy to strong lad standing six feet tall, his strength and wages grew, as well. But Cuyahoga County held little attraction for the sixteen-year-old, so he bid his mother farewell and headed to Cleveland to begin a sailor's life. When this prospect failed, Garfield decided the next best job was working on a canal boat, and for three months he worked aboard the *Evening Star*, carrying copper ore to Pittsburgh. His canal days ended, however, when a serious fever developed, keeping young Garfield bedridden for the next several months.

While her son convalesced, Eliza Garfield endeavored to encourage him to reinvigorate his studies. Aided by a mathematics tutor, the two convinced Garfield to resume his education at a nearby academy. The next several years found him attending, as well as teaching, school. In 1854, the twenty-three-year-old enrolled as the oldest junior at Williams College in Massachusetts. He excelled in debate and seriously considered the ministry. Instead, after graduation, he returned to the Eclectic Institute in Hiram, Ohio, as instructor of Latin, Greek, and English grammar. Soon the conflict that threatened the nation confronted this small academic institution.

In 1857, the president of the Eclectic Institute retired. Many assumed that the second highest faculty member, Professor Norman Dunshee, would succeed him. Yet the board decided his credentials were inferior to his colleague's; consequently, James A. Garfield became president. Angered by losing the presidency, Dunshee worked to undermine his superior.

Nearby Oberlin College was well known for its strong abolitionist stance. Dunshee demanded the same at Hiram, but Garfield, although a stalwart Republican, refused to press the issue. Understanding the town's strong division, he wanted no conflict between the two. Ultimately, Dunshee lost his job because of his radical beliefs. Yet Garfield did not emerge unscathed either. He lost the support of many for not agreeing with the abolitionists.

	1881				
NATIONAL EVENTS	**MAR:** P.T. Barnum merges his circus with that of James Bailey to create Barnum & Bailey's Circus	**MAR 8:** Second transcontinental railroad completed	**MAY 21:** Clara Barton establishes the American Red Cross	**SUMMER:** Drought hits many parts of the US, leaving thousands of cattle dead in the West	New York City runs out of water, causing many of its residents to die from heat exhaustion
WORLD EVENTS	Italian writer, C. Collodi, writes *Pinocchio (Little Wooden Boy)*	Vatican archives opened to scholars for the first time	Romania and Serbia snatch independence from Constantinople	Japan forms its first political parties	Scotland Act grants women the right to vote in local elections

While a student at Hiram, Garfield had discovered that he had a talent for preaching. He had continued at Williams, and when he returned to Hiram. He believed that he was an effective evangelist preacher. His spell-binding sermons often focused on the nation's continuing woes over slavery. Garfield started pondering whether to change vocations. His mother had always encouraged him to become a minister, but he also began considering the law and politics as possible careers.

MARRIED LIFE

Although Garfield was a serious scholar, he had found time to court several young ladies. His first romance involved one of the students he taught while at a small school, after which they attended Eclectic Institute together. She and her family believed they were engaged, but in fact, Garfield had never proposed.

Instead Garfield married another Eclectic classmate, Lucretia "Crete" Rudolph. Her father was co-founder of the Institute. She, too, had taught school and agreed to postpone their wedding until her fiancé's financial circumstances improved. They finally wed on November 11, 1858, and began married life at Hiram. The Garfields became parents to five children who survived to maturity—four sons and a daughter.

The newlywed husband continued as president of the Eclectic Institute, but he also took up the study of the law. After two years, Garfield passed the bar.

EARLY POLITICAL LIFE

In 1859, James A. Garfield won his first political office and became a state senator. Talk still lingered about John Brown and his raid on Harpers Ferry at the time Garfield took his seat in 1860. Ohio Governor William Dennison, Jr., needed an exceptional speaker to address a gathering of legislators from Ohio, Kentucky, and Tennessee regarding the need for unity, and he chose the young state senator. Garfield skillfully argued the need for solidarity of the three western states and their common reliance on the Mississippi River.

Garfield also campaigned for Republican Party presidential candidate Abraham Lincoln. Lincoln's victory was cause for celebration, but within the following weeks, the hopeful words of his party's win evaporated into clouds of concern as the nation witnessed one state after another declaring its secession. Garfield now expressed doubt that the new president was up to the task at hand, writing to an old friend, "Just at this time we have no man who has the power to ride upon the storm and direct it. The hour has come, but not the man."[1] His opinion soon changed. After meeting with Lincoln in Columbus a few weeks later, Garfield wrote, "He has a peculiar power of impressing you that is frank, direct, and thoroughly honest. His remarkable good sense, simple and condensed style of expression, and evident marks of indomitable will, gives me great hopes for the country."[2]

In April 1861, Garfield and his cohorts were heartened by the news of the attack on Fort Sumter. Now the problem for Ohioans was arming its military force—and paying for it. Garfield sponsored a bill authorizing $500,000 to do just that. The governor then sent him to Illinois to request a loan of five thousand rifles. Garfield was also directed to ask the men of Illinois and Indiana to serve under an officer from Ohio—General George B. McClellan. After securing the needed funds, firearms, and military support requested by the governor, Garfield returned to find he had lost an election at home—not a political position as such, but, rather, the elected

DID YOU KNOW?

Garfield was the last president to be born in a log cabin.

JUL 2: President James A. Garfield is shot by Charles Guiteau

JUL 4: Booker T. Washington founds Tuskegee Institute in Alabama

JUL 20: Sitting Bull leads his band of Sioux to surrender to the US Army in Montana

SEP 19: President Garfield dies from infection and complications from his wound; Chester A. Arthur is sworn in as the next president

OCT 26: Gunfight at the O.K. Corral in Tombstone, Arizona

Cunard launches the S.S. *Servia*, the world's first ocean liner constructed of steel; it's also equipped with electric lights

The vaporetto (water bus) introduced in Venice; number of gondolas drop dramatically

MAR 13: Czar Alexander II of Russia assassinated; his son Alexander III succeeds him

MAY 12: Tunisia becomes a French protectorate

AUG 3: Pretoria Convention signed ending the war between the Boers and the British

DID YOU KNOW?

Garfield could write with either hand and sometimes amazed people by writing in Latin with one hand and writing in Greek with the other.

title of colonel. Another opportunity for military service, however, soon presented itself.

CIVIL WAR OFFICER

Although Garfield possessed no military experience, he nevertheless desired—and expected—a high rank. Others with comparable credentials had gained generalships; the thirty-year-old senator, therefore, expected the same and was insulted when the highest rank he was offered was that of lieutenant colonel by Governor Dennison. At first, he refused, but in the summer of 1861, he accepted the lower rank with the proviso that he would only serve under a West Point officer.

Within two months, Colonel Garfield headed a regiment; the only problem was that there were no men in the regiment. Garfield himself was required recruit the men to fill the ranks. (This was common practice for the military during the Civil War since the men were being recruited from areas near the hometowns of the regimental commanders.) His first stop was Hiram, where a company of men enlisted. As autumn progressed, more companies were added to the 42d Ohio Volunteer Infantry Regiment, and in January 1862, their actions to halt the Confederate advance won Garfield a promotion to brigadier general.

In April 1862, Garfield was among the reinforcements who arrived to bolster Grant's troops for the second day of fighting at Shiloh.

Now in charge of the Twentieth Brigade and serving under General Halleck, Garfield's attitude became increasingly disgusted with the pitifully slow pace of war. He despaired of the time spent on building entrenchments and patching roads and bridges. Instead he pushed for Lincoln to emancipate the slaves and transform the fighting to total war. He grew disheartened with the regular army officers and feared the war's outcome in such incapable hands.

Believing he could better serve elsewhere, by the summer of 1862, Garfield began pondering the possibility of running for Congress. He went to Washington and passed several weeks attempting to lobby for an independent command. Meanwhile, he also worked to improve his political connections. In October, General Garfield acquired a new title—Congressman Garfield. Now with his political future tied to his military service, Garfield reported again for active duty with the Army of the Cumberland under General William Rosecrans. Soon Garfield was chief of staff and winning his commander's praise: "Brigadier General Garfield, ever active, prudent, and sagacious. I feel indebted to him for both counsel and assistance in the administration of this army. He possesses the instincts and energy of a great commander."[3] Rosecrans's support helped Garfield to secure a promotion to major general; his new position did not, however, keep Garfield from blaming Rosecrans for the Union's loss at Chickamauga and arguing that his commander should be replaced.

Garfield reappeared in Washington and made the rounds to discuss his future. One stop was the White House, where Lincoln urged him to take his seat in Congress; looking ahead to Reconstruction, the president wanted every available vote. Garfield agreed and resigned his commission in December 1863.

BATTLE OF CHICKAMAUGA (September 18–20, 1863) ★ Union troops under General William Rosecrans attempted to push Confederates from their strongly held position at Chattanooga, Tennessee. Rosecrans's plans, however, were derailed by Confederate commander James Longstreet, who exploited a gap in the enemy's line, causing a third of the Union soldiers there to abandon the field, as did Rosecrans and Garfield. The Confederates won the battle.

CONGRESSMAN GARFIELD

Given Garfield's wartime experience, he immediately was assigned to the Military Affairs Committee. There he worked to pass a draft bill to add more troops to the Union Army. While not an impassioned supporter of Lincoln's reelection campaign, Garfield understood it would be politically ruinous for him not to back the president.

After Lincoln's assassination, Garfield used

his congressional pulpit to preach the need for reprisals: "It was not one man who killed Abraham Lincoln, it was the embodied spirit of treason and slavery, inspired with fearful and despairing hate, that struck him down."[4] Holding former Confederate leaders responsible only made sense to Garfield and his fellow northern congressmen.

The dilemma of Reconstruction now posed a major problem for the country as the legislative and executive branches fought over its purpose and execution. The Radical Republicans demanded punishment for the offending South. Garfield was no exception. He agreed with his colleagues that Johnson's treatment was much too soft and did nothing toward teaching their countrymen a lesson. When others argued against the military districting of the South, Garfield wrote, "It was written with the steel pen made out of a bayonet; and bayonets have done us good service hitherto."[5] When President Johnson continued to fight the Radical Republicans and their harsh Reconstruction policies, Garfield sided with those demanding the president's impeachment.

The Ohio congressman won plaudits when he and his House Committee on Banking and Currency investigated the allegations of railroad mogul Jay Gould and others conspiring to fix the gold market, resulting in the Black Friday scandal of September 24, 1869. Garfield's action snagged him a new appointment—the chairman of the House Appropriations Committee. As head of one of the two most important congressional committees, Garfield's influence and power was acknowledged.

While shedding light on one scandal, another broke a few years later that threatened to drag Garfield down and possibly end his political career. As Reconstruction woes plagued the South, the rest of the country watched the West, where the two major railroads, the Union Pacific and Central Pacific, laid track as fast as humanly possible. Congress had appropriated millions of dollars for this worthy goal, but for some of the principal stockholders of the Union Pacific, that was not enough. They formed their own company, named the Credit Mobilier, to function as the construction company. It was awarded the Union Pacific's building contract, and charged fifty million dollars more than it had cost.

Massachusetts congressman Oakes Ames was at the heart of the scheme, and when the whiff of scandal permeated the halls of Congress, he quickly set to work offering shares of Credit Mobilier stock to influential political figures including the vice president, Speaker of the House James G. Blaine, and the House Appropriations Committee chairman, James A. Garfield. Not desiring to be accused of bribery, Ames did not give away the stock, but rather sold it at par value of one hundred dollars a share. The recipient could then sell the stock for as much as a 500 percent profit. When the matter was investigated in 1873, Garfield denied any wrongdoing, but Ames insisted Garfield had $329 of stock. Apparently the House of Representatives believed the Ohio congressman and Garfield emerged from the scandal relatively unscathed, while Ames received a censure.

In the 1874 congressional election, Garfield faced closer competition than he had previously. Fed up with the scandals from Grant's government, the people voted in a Democratic majority, leaving Garfield out of his chairmanship. Still he managed to do well by becoming the minority party leader in the House.

SUPREME COURT APPOINTMENTS

★★★★★★★★★★

Stanley Matthews, 1881

ANDERSONVILLE ★ The Confederate government established this site in western Georgia as a prisoner of war camp, and began bringing Union prisoners there in February 1864. The camp soon became overcrowded with more than 30,000 men in an area designed to hold only 10,000. Starvation and disease caused the deaths of nearly 13,000 soldiers during the fourteen months that Andersonville operated. Once the inhumane conditions became public knowledge, northerners wanted revenge and demanded that someone pay for Andersonville. In August 1865, Henry Wirz, the commandant of the prison camp, was tried by a military tribunal, found guilty, and hanged on November 10.

US POPULATION IN 1881
50,155,783

NATIONAL DEBT IN 1881
$2,069,013,570

NUMBER OF STATES IN 1881
38

In 1876, Garfield became a leader of the "waving the bloody shirt" campaign. Here Republicans reminded the country that Democrats represented the slaveholders of the South. When a bill to grant amnesty to former Confederate soldiers was debated, Garfield argued strenuously against it, reminding all of the horrible treatment Union prisoners had received at the prisoner of war camp at Andersonville, Georgia. There the inhumane treatment of the Union prisoners led to a war crimes trial for the camp's commander, Captain Henry Wirz, and his execution in November 1865.

The presidential election of 1876 was a deplorable contest with both of the two parties attempting to paint the other as the brute. Republicans had nothing but scandals to show for their leadership, argued the Democrats. But don't vote for the same party that wanted slavery, argued the Republicans. It was little surprise that the final count for the election was very much in dispute and required a fifteen-man committee to decide whether Republican Rutherford B. Hayes or Democrat Samuel Tilden was the winner. Sitting on that committee at the request of President Grant was Congressman James A. Garfield. His maneuvering helped ensure the Compromise of 1876, including the election of Hayes.

ELECTION OF 1880

The next presidential election found the Republican Party split. Hayes was not seeking a second term, but Grant made it known he would be interested in a third term. John Sherman and James G. Blaine were the major frontrunners when the Republicans held their convention in Chicago. When Garfield gave Sherman's nominating speech, many began considering him as a possible compromise candidate. After thirty ballots, when no one had a majority, more delegates began moving toward supporting Garfield. On the thirty-sixth ballot, James A. Garfield was nominated as the presidential candidate and New Yorker Chester A. Arthur the vice presidential candidate.

Opposing Garfield was former Union general Winfield Scott Hancock. His Civil War service indisputably outshone Garfield's. Since the war, Hancock had served in the South as one of its military governors. There Garfield had criticized him for his soft handling of the former enemy. Hancock then continued his military career in the Dakota Territory. Now as a presidential candidate, Hancock campaigned for civil service reform, tariffs, and an end to monopolies.

Garfield, caught between the two factions of his party—one demanding patronage reform, and the other just as vocally insisting on keeping party politics the same as usual—promised to consult local party leaders before making any political appointments.

Not seeing much difference between the candidates, the popular vote reflected the small difference between the two, with Garfield winning 48.3 percent and Hancock 48.2 percent, but Garfield successfully won the majority of northern states, whose greater population translated to higher electoral votes.

PRESIDENT GARFIELD

Before becoming President, Garfield had to resign his seat as US senator. He had been elected to the post earlier in 1880, but never served. Instead John Sherman (brother to General William T. Sherman) served in that capacity.

In the weeks leading up to his taking office, Garfield attempted to keep all factions of his party satisfied as he chose men for his cabinet. He chose James G. Blaine as secretary of state. Angered at Blaine's appointment, Senator Roscoe Conkling of New York launched into a tug-of-war with the president-elect regarding the secretary of the treasury position. The two men argued over this key party position. Conkling desperately wanted it for a fellow New Yorker, but Garfield hesitated handing it to a Wall Street baron. Ultimately, Garfield appointed William Windom of Minnesota, thus incurring Conkling's wrath. This only worsened when Garfield sent the Senate a list of appointments, none of whom were approved by Conkling. The New York senator cried foul and President Garfield replied, "This brings on the contest at once and will settle the question whether the President is registering clerk of the Senate or the executive of the United States."[6] Eventually the showdown in the Senate ended with both New York senators resigning, and Conkling's political career ended. The constant

DID YOU KNOW?

Garfield was the second president to be assassinated.

demands on the president to satisfy office seekers continued in the following weeks.

While her husband struggled with the demands of his office, Lucretia Garfield studied plans to refurbish the White House. The presidential home had not been well tended, and she desired to restore the mansion to its earlier beauty. Her plans abruptly ended, though, when she developed malaria. By early July, Garfield believed his wife well enough that he could leave her for a short trip. He planned to take two of their sons to a class reunion at Williams College.

ASSASSINATION

Thirty-nine-year-old Charles Guiteau arrived in Washington soon after Garfield's inauguration. He was a Republican without a job and a rather shaky mental history who decided he would best be suited for the Paris consulate. He attempted to take his plea to various officials, including Secretary of State Blaine. He visited the White House numerous times, but only saw Garfield briefly once. As time progressed, Guiteau grew convinced that the president was dividing the Republican Party, and his death would reunite it. Guiteau decided he would be the instrument to bring about this outcome.

He bought a .44-caliber British Bulldog revolver whose appearance he thought fine for a museum and began following Garfield around Washington. Guiteau had opportunities to shoot, but he shrank from firing each time. He finally decided the time had come when he read of Garfield's planned trip, and awaited him in the Baltimore and Potomac rail station in Washington. About 9:30 a.m., Garfield and Blaine walked across the waiting room, with Guiteau in pursuit. Two shots felled the president. One glanced off Garfield's right arm, but the second bullet entered his back at the bottom of the rib cage, traveled through his abdomen, and lodged by his pancreas.

Policemen immediately grabbed Guiteau and found a note. In it Guiteau wrote that he was not acting out of ill will toward the president, but rather by desire to unite the Republican Party, calling the death "a political necessity."[7] He did not apologize to Mrs. Garfield, saying, "He is liable to go at any time anyway."[8]

But contrary to Guiteau's expectations, Garfield was not dead. He fainted and was carried to the White House. There he was probed by a physician's unclean hands and unsterilized instruments. Infection began and grew slowly over the summer months. Hoping the coastal breezes would be healthier for him, he was moved in September to the New Jersey coast. This was not enough, and on September 19, 1881, James A. Garfield breathed his last at 10:35 p.m. His body laid in state at the capitol, then was carried to Cleveland, where he was interred at Lake View Cemetery in Cleveland, Ohio.

Charles Guiteau's trial began in mid-November and lasted two months. At one point, a man tried to kill him, but only grazed Guiteau's arm with a bullet. He rejected any talk of insanity and claimed God told him to kill Garfield. The jury deliberated only an hour before determining he was guilty. Sentenced to death by hanging, Guiteau's execution was carried out June 30, 1882.

Chester A. Arthur received instructions from Guiteau regarding selecting his cabinet, as well as being told, with Garfield's death, that Arthur now had been raised "from political cypher to President of the United States."[9] As president, one of his first duties would be to oversee the transformation of the patronage spoils system to the civil service system based on merit. Thus Garfield's death was not in vain.

DID YOU KNOW?
★★★★★★★★★★★

Garfield is the only president to be a congressman, senator-elect, and president-elect at the same time.

ENDNOTES

1 John Clark Ridpath, *The Life and Work of James A. Garfield*, Cincinnati: Jones Brothers and Co., 1881, p. 85.

2 Edwin P. Hoyt. *James A. Garfield*. Chicago: Reilly and Lee, Co., 1964, p. 37.

3 Robert Granville Caldwell, *James A. Garfield*, Hamden, Conn.: Archon Books, 1965, p. 114.

4 Russell H. Conwell, *The Life Speeches and Public Services of General James A. Garfield of Ohio*, Boston: B.B. Russell & Co., 1880, p. 218.

5 Ibid, p. 89.

6 Ibid, p. 137.

7 Ibid, p. 153.

8 Ibid.

9 William DeGregorio, *The Complete Book of US Presidents*, New York: Gramercy Books, 2005, p. 303.

Chester A. Arthur

★ ★ ★ TWENTY-FIRST PRESIDENT ★ ★ ★

LIFE SPAN

- Born: October 5, 1829, in Fairfield, Vermont
- Died: November 18, 1886, in New York City

NICKNAMES

- Gentleman Boss, Elegant Arthur, Chet, The General

RELIGION

- Episcopalian

HIGHER EDUCATION

- Union College, 1848

PROFESSION

- Lawyer

MILITARY SERVICE

- Civil War: enlisted in New York state militia in February 1858 as brigade judge advocate; rose to quartermaster general by the time he retired in December 1862

FAMILY

- Father: **Reverend William Arthur** (1796–1875)
- Mother: **Malvina Stone Arthur** (1802–1869)
- Wife: **Ellen "Nell" Lewis Herndon Arthur** (1837–1880); wed October 25, 1859, in New York City
- Children: **William Lewis Herndon** (1860–1863); **Chester Alan** (1864–1937); **Ellen Herndon** (1871–1915)

POLITICAL LIFE

- Collector of the port of New York (1871–1878)
- Vice president (March–September 1881)

PRESIDENCY

- One term: September 19, 1881–March 4, 1885
- Not elected as president; was President **Garfield**'s vice president and assumed the presidency upon **Garfield**'s death
- Republican
- Reason for leaving office: lost party's nomination
- Vice president: none

CABINET
★★★★★★★★★★

SECRETARY OF STATE
James G. Blaine (Mar.–Dec. 1881)

Frederick T. Frelinghuysen (1881–1885)

SECRETARY OF THE TREASURY
William Windom (Mar.–Nov. 1881)

Charles J. Folger (1881–1884)

Walter Q. Gresham (1884–1885)

SECRETARY OF WAR
Robert T. Lincoln (1881–1885)

ATTORNEY GENERAL
Wayne MacVeigh (Mar.–Oct. 1881)

Benjamin H. Brewster (1882–1885)

SECRETARY OF THE NAVY
William H. Hunt (1881–1882)

William E. Chandler (1882–1885)

POSTMASTER GENERAL
Thomas L. James (Mar.–Dec. 1881)

Timothy O. Howe (1882–1883)

Walter Q. Gresham (1883–1884)

Frank Hatton (1884–1885)

SECRETARY OF THE INTERIOR
Samuel J. Kirkwood (1881–1882)

Henry M. Teller (1882–1885)

Chester A. Arthur entered office under a pallor of suspicion. President Garfield's assassin proclaimed that he had killed James Garfield so that Chester Arthur could become president and reunite the Republican Party. Arthur had nothing to do with his predecessor's death, but some hinted otherwise. It was no secret that Arthur had worked for New York senator Roscoe Conkling for many years. Once in office, President Garfield openly broke with Conkling, and kept his vice president at arm's length. Soon after, Garfield was shot by Charles Guiteau, clearing the way for Arthur to take office and possibly appoint Conkling to a key cabinet position. While in New York City awaiting further developments in Garfield's deteriorating condition, Arthur began receiving threatening notes. Very likely he ruminated during those dangerous days on the path that had led him to this unique place in history.

EARLY LIFE

William and Malvina Arthur welcomed their first son on October 5, 1829, in a small log cabin in North Fairfield, Vermont. They named him Chester Alan, for the physician who delivered him and his grandfather, respectively. William, a native Irishman, had migrated as a young man, first to Canada, where he met his wife, and then later the couple moved to Vermont. Prior to Chester's birth, his father had become a Baptist preacher, and he would move his family seven times in the coming years to parishes in New York and Vermont. The family grew over the years to include eight children who survived to maturity.

Fortunately Chester became adept at meeting people and getting along with various groups, although later he admitted to becoming involved in fisticuffs as a teen when someone badmouthed his favorite candidate in 1844—Henry Clay. His earlier education had been provided by his father, and when he was fifteen years old, he attended the Lyceum in Schenectady, New York. Chester was able to enter Union College as a sophomore. To help defray his schooling costs, he taught school during his college term breaks.

An average student, Arthur was involved in other activities, among them debating, writing, and acting mischievously. In one famous prank, Arthur dumped one of the school's bells in the Erie Canal. Other times he incurred punishments for skipping the required chapel services. Still he managed to join Phi Beta Kappa his senior year and graduated in 1848.

With years of studying the classics under his belt, Arthur knew he could teach but decided he wanted to become a lawyer instead. He attended law school briefly, returned home, and eventually taught and worked as a principal in two small communities in Vermont and New York until 1853. In New York he worked and studied under abolitionist attorney E.D. Culver. The following year, Arthur passed the New York bar.

LEGAL CAREER

New York State sat comfortably north of the Mason-Dixon Line in the 1850s and, as such, was a free state, but that did not preclude incidents involving acts of exclusion against blacks. One of Arthur's early legal cases was brought by Lizzie Jennings, an African-American schoolteacher who was physically ejected from a "whites only" streetcar. Determined not to allow this senseless action against a law-abiding lady to go unpunished, the black community urged Jennings to prosecute. She did, and her attorney was Chester A. Arthur. The young attorney successfully argued that his client

NATIONAL EVENTS

JAN 2: John D. Rockefeller incorporates the Standard Oil trust

FEB 6: Western Electric Company awarded contract to produce telephones for Bell Co.

MAR 29: Knights of Columbus founded

APR 3: Robert Ford shoots his friend Jesse James in the back to collect the reward money

APR 10: Jumbo the elephant performs for the first time in Barnum & Bailey's Circus

1882

WORLD EVENTS

Gottlieb Daimler, German engineer, develops the world's first internal combustion engine powered by gasoline

Robert A. Hadfield, British metallurgist, invents manganese steel (used for railway tracks)

JAN: New Zealand government begins compensating Taranaki tribes in exchange for their lands

MAR 24: Dr. Robert Koch, German bacteriologist, announces discovery of the germ causing tuberculosis

MAY: Explorer Adolphus W. Greely reaches the Arctic's 83° 24′ north

had done nothing to deserve being treated in such a shabby manner. The jury agreed, and although only half of the requested five hundred dollar settlement was awarded, one of the first civil rights cases ever tried had been won. The case pushed New York to draft legislation to desegregate its public transportation, no common feat in 1854.

In 1856, Arthur voted for John C. Frémont, the Republican candidate for president. The horrifying reports of "Bleeding Kansas" disturbed both him and his new law partner, Henry D. Gardiner, so they decided to continue their careers there. The legal team bid farewell to New York and journeyed to the land, not of Oz, but rather of Jayhawkers and border ruffians.

ARTHUR'S BIRTHPLACE ★ During the 1880 presidential election, a rumor circulated that Arthur had actually been born in Canada. No one cared since he was merely the vice presidential candidate, but once he succeeded to the presidency, the rumor surfaced again. Arthur's parents, Irish immigrants, had initially migrated to a farm 80 miles north of Vermont in Canada, before moving to Vermont. Arthur airily dismissed the charge, but some insisted that the president of the United States, while he was a son of American citizens, had been born in Canada.

BLEEDING KANSAS

Although motivated to help the abolitionists in Kansas, Arthur also dabbled in land speculation. After his arrival, he soon began procuring a few parcels of land, hoping to sell them later to settlers. As he traveled throughout the territory, he witnessed first-hand why Kansas was "bleeding." After arriving in Leavenworth, Arthur and Gardiner, as any good prospective citizens of the territory, attended a political meeting. But unlike similar gatherings in New York, this one was adjourned in a blaze of gunfire when discussions about the slavery issue became heated.

Arthur purchased some land in Leavenworth but decided to investigate other towns as well. He found the violent and volatile political climate widespread. Quickly understanding the dangers surrounding him, Arthur asked a sheriff to accompany him to Lecompton. En route they were approached by gunmen, who probably would have killed Arthur had he been alone. He did arrive safely in Lecompton but was soon presented again with the reality of life in the West. While eating dinner at his hotel, he witnessed a nearby patron being dragged from his table and taken to jail on a murder charge. The man begged Arthur to represent him. Arthur agreed and was appalled to find the jail overrun with countless others accused in a similar manner. Undoubtedly, the young attorney could have remained in Kansas and been kept busy defending these potential clients, but he was compelled to return to New York.

MARRIAGE

Before leaving for Kansas, Arthur had met the cousin of one of his fellow boarders, an attractive nineteen-year-old young lady visiting New York with her mother. Ellen Herndon (nicknamed Nell), of Fredericksburg, Virginia, hoped to embark on a singing career. She and Arthur fell in love and wrote frequently to each other after he journeyed to Kansas, but tragedy soon struck her family when her father, a ship's captain, went down in a storm off North Carolina. Upon receipt

MAY 6: Chinese Exclusion Act approved, severely limiting Chinese immigration to the United States

JUN 30: President Garfield's assassin, Charles Guiteau, is hanged

SEP 30: World's first hydroelectric power plant opens in Appleton, Wisconsin

OCT 6: First game of the first World Series is played (Cincinnati vs. Chicago)

NOV: Charles Dow and Edward Jones create the Dow Jones & Company

MAY 20: Triple Alliance formed between Germany, Austria-Hungary, and Italy

JUN 6: Catastrophic cyclone hits India, leaving 100,000 dead

JUL 11: British take over Suez Canal and Alexandria, Egypt

AUG: British Parliament pass Married Women's Property Act, allowing married British women the right to own property

AUG 20: Premiere performance in Moscow of Tchaikovsky's *1812 Overture*

DID YOU KNOW?

Arthur prided himself on his appearance and changed his clothes several times in one day; he had over 80 pairs of pants when president.

of his beloved's distress call, Arthur decided Nell, not Kansas, held his future, and he returned to New York without delay.

Arthur accompanied Nell to Virginia to meet her family, whom he assisted with a move to New York. He managed Nell and her mother's legal and business affairs, as well as rebuilt his legal career, while he continued the courtship. On October 25, 1859, Chester and Nell wed and began their married life living with her mother. They later moved to their own home in New York City.

CIVIL WAR POLITICS

Arthur's political life began about this time as he grew more active in the Republican Party. With an eye to the gathering storm, he also joined the local militia. Between both activities, Arthur gained the attention of New York's Republican Boss, Thurlow Weed. Ambitious and wanting to further his political future, Arthur associated himself with Weed, and in turn, with his puppet, Governor Edwin Morgan. Due to this association, the title of engineer in chief with the rank of brigadier general of the militia was conferred upon Arthur on January 1, 1861.

Within five months, the country was in the midst of war; Arthur's title was no longer purely ceremonial. He reported to the state quartermaster general and soon was promoted to assistant quartermaster general. Arthur's job was outfitting and supplying the soldiers in New York City—no small task considering it expanded to include ensuring that those passing through the city were also equipped. Within the year, Arthur was promoted to inspector general and in this position he toured fortifications and recommended changes. In the spring of 1862, he visited his in-laws' former home in Fredericksburg, Virginia, during the peninsula campaign.

Five months later, Arthur became quartermaster general but with Governor Morgan's defeat for reelection, Arthur's service in this capacity lasted less than six months. Morgan had nothing but praise for Arthur, saying, "He displayed not only great executive ability and unbending integrity, but great knowledge of Army regulations."[1] Arthur's successor reported that the state was "indebted to . . . Gen. C.A. Arthur, who, by his practical sense and unremitting exertion, at a period when everything was in confusion, reduced the operation of the department to a matured plan, by which large amounts of money were saved."[2]

As a man in his thirties, Arthur was certainly eligible to continue military service, but he refrained from doing so. Many believed his decision was explained by the ideological divisiveness at home. Nell Arthur was a rebel at heart and had relatives fighting for the Confederacy. Nell's mother-in-law fled to Europe, while his "little Rebel wife," as he called her, stayed home in New York and fumed about her husband fighting for the Yankees— who had destroyed part of her family home, killed family members, and imprisoned others. Friends detected a noticeable tension developing between the couple during those agonizing years. Tragedy brought them together as they mourned the loss their two-and-a-half-year-old son William in 1863, apparently resulting from a brain hemorrhage. The following year they welcomed another son, Chester Arthur Jr., and in 1871, Ellen, who, like her mother, was nicknamed "Nell."

NEW YORK CITY POLITICS

During the remainder of the 1860s, Arthur's law practice flourished, as did his association with Republican leaders. Arthur's personal appearance took on the aura of a dandy, always in the latest

NATIONAL EVENTS

DEC: Edward Johnson of New York hosts the world's first electrically lit Christmas tree

New Jersey becomes the first state to legalize labor unions

Sarah Winnemucca publishes *Life Among the Paiutes: Their Ways and Claims*, one of the first published works by a Native American woman

Emma Lazarus writes a poem, "The New Colossus," for a subscription drive to provide a pedestal for the Statue of Liberty: "*Give me your tired, your poor,/ Your huddled masses yearning to breathe free,/ The wretched refuse of your teeming shore./*

1883

WORLD EVENTS

SEP 13: Egypt becomes British protectorate in Anglo-Egyptian War

Ferdinand de Lesseps begins work on the Panama Canal (previously had built the Suez Canal)

Robert Koch discovers the bacterium causing cholera

Robert Louis Stevenson publishes *Treasure Island*

Russian revolutionary Vera Nikolaevna Figner is arrested and condemned to death,

fashion and with a cigar. He was not averse to alcohol, and perhaps that explained the flush in his face. Many enjoyed being in the "General's" easy-going company. Among his party acquaintances was Roscoe Conkling, a New York senator who aspired to the presidency.

Arthur campaigned for Lincoln's reelection, as well as Grant's election in 1868. By then he was state chairman of the Republican's executive committee. While steadily working on behalf of his party, Arthur's law practice suffered. His partnership with Gardiner ended, and Arthur's lifestyle necessitated a steady income of no modest means. Not least of his troubles was the new home he and his family of four now occupied on Lexington Avenue. In short, Chester Arthur needed a job that paid well.

He managed to procure the position of counsel to the New York tax commission, but for reasons unknown he left after a few months' time. Once more he was in need of a job. This time the president helped him by appointing him to the extremely lucrative position of collector of the Port of New York. With this, Arthur could be assured of a fifty thousand dollar income, but more importantly he collected fees from any shipper not paying the proper tariff (the collector was entitled to pocket a percentage of the fees charged). Considering that he supervised the busiest port in the United States, where as much as three-quarters of the country's duties were collected, Chester Arthur prospered. Moreover, he enjoyed increased political power, overseeing more than one thousand employees who were appointed as part of the "spoils system."

One requirement all of these patronage workers was paying their political party upon request. Arthur ensured that his people paid into the party coffers for both the 1872 reelection of Grant and Rutherford B. Hayes's campaign in 1876. By then, complaints of possible corruption in the customhouse were widespread, and Hayes promised to act. A commission investigated and determined that the charges were legitimate. So after seven years, Chester Arthur was once more unemployed.

For the next two years, Arthur resumed his law practice while continuing his work in the Republican Party. By 1880, he counted himself one of the top supporters of his old friend Roscoe Conkling. They called themselves Stalwarts and supported Grant to run for a third term. The Stalwarts and Half Breeds, led by Ohio senator John Sherman and Maine senator James Blaine, vied for the nomination, and ultimately James A. Garfield, a Half Breed backer, became the compromise candidate. Then Garfield required a compromise candidate of his own—someone from the Stalwart camp. To Conkling's dismay, Chester Arthur unabashedly agreed to Garfield's offer and become the vice presidential nominee.

News of Arthur's nomination drew harsh criticism from John Sherman, who called it "ridiculous burlesque"; *Harper's Weekly* said it was done "to placate the minority," and E.L. Godkin, editor for the *Nation,* wrote, "General Garfield, if elected, may die during his term in office, but that is too unlikely a contingency to be worth making provisions for."[3]

VICE PRESIDENT ARTHUR

Undoubtedly it was a sadder Arthur who was sworn in March 4, 1881. Just over a year earlier, his wife had died from pneumonia. At the time of their mother's death, Chester Jr. was fifteen and his sister Nell was only eight years old.

As president of the Senate, Arthur supported Garfield by casting tie-breaking votes to allow

SUPREME COURT APPOINTMENTS
★★★★★★★★★★

Horace Gray, 1882

Samuel Blackford, 1882

DID YOU KNOW?
★★★★★★★★★★

Arthur was the first president to take the oath of office in his home.

Send these, the homeless, tempest-tost to me," will later be inscribed on the pedestal

JAN: *Life* magazine begins publication

JAN 16: Pendleton Civil Service Reform Act passed requiring many government jobs to be filled based on merit

FEB 16: *Ladies Home Journal* begins publication

FEB 23: Alabama becomes the first state to enact an antitrust law

her sentence is commuted and she spends 20 years in solitary confinement

Zygmunt Florenty von Wroblewski, a Polish physicist, is the first to liquefy hydrogen

British engineer Hiram Maxim invents the automatic machine gun

Kristiania-Bergen railway across Norway's Hardanger mountain range is completed, connects Bergen and Oslo

MAR 13: Philosopher and socialist Karl Marx dies in London

STATE OF THE UNION

US POPULATION IN 1881
50,155,783

NATIONAL DEBT IN 1885
$1,863,964,873

NUMBER OF STATES IN 1885
38

Republicans to better control the chamber. Before long, however, Arthur was in the midst of a political brawl between Garfield and Conkling regarding patronage appointments—especially that of collector of the Port of New York. Arthur sided openly with his mentor, Roscoe Conkling. Garfield won the fight, a victory that ultimately proved to be the beginning of the end of Conkling's influence in national politics. Ironically, Arthur was in Conkling's company when word arrived of the attempted assassination of Garfield by Charles Guiteau. Unsure what to do and shaken by rumors of his possible involvement, Arthur decided to stay in New York until invited to Washington. Boys hawking newspapers crowded the street corners of the city. Many throughout the country were reading Guiteau's comment, "I am a Stalwart and Arthur will be President,"[4] with disgust. Cries of retribution against Arthur and Conkling abounded. Others speculated on their possible role in the assassination attempt.

Vice President Arthur struggled to maintain composure and addressed various newspaper reporters. He expressed his concern for the president and his family, and then went home. Death threats pursued him as he returned to Conkling's side. He awaited an invitation from Washington, which arrived from the cabinet later that evening. Arthur arrived the next day, desperately desiring to see Garfield, but doctors would not allow the president to receive visitors. Cabinet members welcomed Arthur, and later he met with Lucretia Garfield. Afterwards he expressed his sincere desire for the president's recovery, adding, "God knows I do not want the place I was never elected to."[5]

He remained in the capital until Garfield's health improved. Hoping that the crisis was over, Arthur returned to New York. By now he understood that many expected Conkling to pull the strings should Arthur ascend to the presidency. Determined for the first time in his political career to stand on his own, Arthur attempted to distance himself from Conkling.

Word of Garfield's death on the evening of September 19, 1881, reached Arthur about 11:30 that night. Newspaper reporters were turned away by the butler, who explained, "He is sitting alone in his room, sobbing like a child . . . I dare not disturb him."[6] Later a telegram arrived from the cabinet and detectives were posted at his door. At about 2:15 a.m., Chester A. Arthur was sworn in as the twenty-first president at his home. He and his secretary worked through the night. Fully aware that his own life might be cut short by another assassin's bullet, Arthur drafted a proclamation for the Senate to meet in special session to appoint a president pro tempore to succeed him if the unthinkable should occur.

DID YOU KNOW?

Arthur dedicated the Washington Monument in 1885.

ARTHUR'S PRESIDENCY

Arthur journeyed to Elberon, New Jersey, and accompanied Garfield's family and body back to Washington. The manner in which the new chief executive presided over the grief-stricken nation was greatly admired, prompting the *Chicago Tribune* to describe him "as a gentleman of the finest sensibility."[7] Refusing to move into the White House may have appeared as a genuinely sympathetic gesture toward the grieving First Lady, yet Arthur's primary reason was his disgust with the structure's shabby appearance. Instead he continued living elsewhere for the next four months while the antiquated plumbing was replaced. None other than Louis Tiffany was hired to redecorate the presidential home.

NATIONAL EVENTS

FEB 27: Rubber stamp is patented by William Purvis of Philadelphia

FEB 28: Boston is home to first vaudeville theater

MAY 19: *Buffalo Bill's Wild West* show premieres in Omaha

MAY 24: Brooklyn Bridge opens to traffic

OCT 15: US Supreme Court decides that parts of the Civil Rights Act of 1875 are unconstitutional and violate the Fourteenth Amendment

WORLD EVENTS

JUN 5: The Orient Express makes its first trip from Paris to the Black Sea

AUG 1: Electric lights installed at Amsterdam's Grand Hotel Krasnapolsky

AUG 26–28: Krakatoa (a volcanic island in the Indian Ocean) erupts, causing huge tidal waves leaving nearly 40,000 dead

AUG 28: Britain bans slavery

OCT 20: Treaty of Ancon ends fighting among Chile, Bolivia, and Peru over Atacama Desert, an area rich with nitrates and copper

By December, the White House was officially Arthur's residence. He and his ten-year-old daughter Nell moved in, with Arthur's sister acting as hostess four months of the year. The president soon became known for elegant dinner parties and his extensive wardrobe; he would change clothes several times in a day and was known to try on twenty pairs of pants before selecting one. Arthur's work day usually began about 10 a.m. and lasted until 4 p.m. The *Chicago Tribune* complained of the president's laziness: "Great questions of public policy bore him. No President was ever so much given to procrastination as he is."[8]

Arthur presided over a country at peace. No major crises threatened; no economic disasters befell him. One of his first tasks was asking Garfield's cabinet to remain intact. Most eventually left, but many stayed for a time to help the new president launch his administration. Consequently, reforms begun by Garfield continued with Arthur. One was a revamping of the US Navy and an order for sixty-eight new steel ships. Another involved the new secretary of state Frederick Frelinghuysen's negotiations with Nicaragua, which succeeded in gaining a treaty allowing the construction of a canal. To the president's dismay, however, the Senate rejected the agreement because of its proposed cost.

Closer to home, concern was rising over the growing number of Chinese immigrants to the United States and the government was called upon to take action. Congress passed a law banning Chinese from entering the country for twenty years. Arthur exercised his veto power, believing the time period too long. Congress tried again with the Chinese Exclusion Act, which only banned immigration for ten years. Arthur signed this, as well as another measure to formally exclude paupers, criminals, and lunatics from emigrating to the United States.

ROBERT LINCOLN (1843–1926) ★ Robert, the eldest son of Abraham Lincoln, was the only member of Garfield's cabinet to stay throughout the remainder of the term. Robert had been in the crowd at the train station when Charles Guiteau shot President Garfield. Ironically, Robert would be present at McKinley's assassination in 1901. After that incident, he refused to be in the company of presidents, saying that he only brought them bad luck. (Robert had been invited by his parents to attend Ford's Theater, but he declined and so was not present at his father's assassination. He never forgave himself.)

The president won praise for vetoing yet another bill, this one calling for nineteen million dollars in pork barrel improvement, even though ultimately Congress overrode the presidential veto and passed the legislation.

In 1883, Chester Arthur signed the Pendleton Act into law, which established the Civil Service Commission, creating examinations for applicants to take before they can be placed in certain government jobs. The president must have appreciated the irony in this statute, as this reform dealt a major blow to the old spoils system that Arthur had enjoyed and profited from handsomely. Still, with President Garfield's assassination fresh in the public's mind, Arthur broke with his Stalwart cronies and enthusiastically supported the measure.

The issue of tariffs, not unfamiliar to Arthur, emerged again, and in 1882, Arthur appointed a tariff commission to investigate the matter. Many wanting free trade pushed for lower tariffs, while protectionists wanted higher import taxes. Lobbyists from both sides kept Congress in check, thus ensuring that the overall bill, known as the

OCT 22: New York's Metropolitan Opera House opens

NOV 18: US railroads adopt standard time zones

Congress creates the Bureau of Labor in the Department of the Interior

Mark Twain publishes *The Adventures of Huckleberry Finn*

The "Louisville Slugger" baseball bat is introduced

Railroad connects the East to Seattle

1884

DEC 3: Harrods is gutted by fire in London; the store reopens in time for Christmas

Czar Alexander III commissions Peter Carl Fabergé to create an Easter egg for his wife

France takes over Madagascar and the French Congo

Russia ends poll tax

Ottmar Mergenthaler patents the linotype typesetting machine, which transforms newspaper publishing

FEB 1: First edition printed of the *Oxford English Dictionary*

DID YOU KNOW?

When Arthur became president, he refused to move into the White House until it was redecorated and refurbished. To help in this, he ordered for much of the old furniture to be loaded on wagons and sold at auction; twenty-four wagons hauled away the furniture, including some priceless pieces.

"Mongrel" Tariff for its assortment of duties, had very little impact, since it lowered overall duties less than 2 percent. Still, the political damage was done, and Americans believed the political parties represented both sides of the tariff debate: Republicans were protectionists, while Democrats supported free trade. The tariff issue promised to be one of the key campaign issues of the 1884 election.

Anxious to seek revenge for Arthur's betrayal of the patronage system, the Stalwarts under Roscoe Conkling ensured Arthur was not the Republican Party's presidential nominee for the 1884 election. Instead, they nominated James Blaine. For Arthur, the news was not entirely disappointing, for he knew he would not have survived a second term.

RETIREMENT

Chester Arthur left the White House in 1885 knowing that his days were numbered. Doctors had diagnosed him as suffering from Bright's disease, a fatal kidney ailment. He spent much of 1886 in bed or fighting the effects of his disease, as it raised his blood pressure and weakened his heart, as well as his kidneys. In July, Arthur managed to attend Grant's funeral, but he soon no longer felt strong enough to leave his house. During his final months, he directed the burning of many public and private papers. Then, after growing weaker and suffering a major stroke, Chester A. Arthur breathed his last at 5 a.m. on November 18, 1886. His funeral was four days later and he was buried beside his wife, Ellen, in the Rural Cemetery in Albany, New York.

ENDNOTES

1 William DeGregorio, *The Complete Book of US Presidents*, New York: Gramercy Books, 2005, p. 310

2 George Frederick Howe, *Chester A. Arthur, A Quarter Century of Machine Politics*, New York: Frederick Ungar Publishing Co., 1957, p. 28.

3 Zachary Karabell, *Chester Alan Arthur*, New York, NY: Times Books, 2004, p. 43.

4 Kenneth D. Ackerman, *Dark Horse, The Surprise Election and Political Murder of President James A. Garfield*, New York: Carroll & Graf Publishers, 2003, p. 381.

5 *Washington Evening Star*, July 4, 1881.

6 *New York Times*, September 20, 1881.

7 *Chicago Tribune*, September 21, 1881.

8 Thomas C. Reeves, *Gentleman Boss: The Life and Times of Chester Arthur*, New York: Alfred A. Knopf, 1975, p. 235.

NATIONAL EVENTS

Temple University founded in Philadelphia by Baptist clergyman Russell H. Conwell

Montgomery Ward publishes a catalog offering almost 10,000 household items

FEB 19: Devastating tornadoes rip through southern states and north to Indiana, killing more than 800

JUN 16: World's first roller coaster opens at Coney Island, New York

JUL 3: Dow Jones Average first appears in the *Afternoon News Letter*

WORLD EVENTS

MAR 12: Siege of Khartoum begins; British and Egyptian forces in the city are surrounded by a Mahdist Sudanese army; siege lasts until January 1885

JUL 4: France presents United States with Statue of Liberty in Paris

JUL 5: Germany takes over Cameroon

JUL 27: France legalizes divorce

> *"The wisdom of our fathers, foreseeing even the most dire possibilities, made sure that the Government should never be imperiled because of the uncertainty of human life. Men may die, but the fabrics of our free institutions remain unshaken. No higher or more assuring proof could exist of the strength and permanence of popular government than the fact that though the chosen of the people be struck down, his constitutional successor is peacefully installed without shock or strain except the sorrow which mourns bereavement."*
>
> —*Chester Arthur, on becoming president after President Garfield's death, 1881*

JUL 5: Congress passes a second Chinese Exclusion Act

AUG 5: Cornerstone laid on Bedloe's Island for Statue of Liberty

OCT 6: US Naval War College founded in Newport, Rhode Island

NOV 4: Democrat Grover Cleveland defeats Republican James Blaine for the presidency

DEC 6: Washington Monument is completed

AUG 9: Inaugural flight of world's first dirigible, *La France*

OCT 13: Meridian Conference establishes time zones around the world, beginning with Greenwich Mean Time

OCT 26: China declares war on France

NOV 25: First surgery to remove a brain tumor is performed in London

Grover Cleveland

★ ★ ★ TWENTY-SECOND & TWENTY-FOURTH PRESIDENT ★ ★ ★

LIFE SPAN
- Born: March 18, 1837, in Caldwell, New Jersey
- Died: June 24, 1908, in Princeton, New Jersey

NICKNAMES
- Uncle Jumbo, Big Steve

RELIGION
- Presbyterian

HIGHER EDUCATION
- None

PROFESSION
- Lawyer

MILITARY SERVICE
- None; although he was drafted in the Civil War, he paid a substitute to serve for him instead

FAMILY
- Father: **Reverend Richard Falley Cleveland** (1804–1853)
- Mother: **Ann Neal Cleveland** (1806–1882)
- Wife: **Frances Folsom Cleveland** (1864–1947); wed June 2, 1886, at the White House
- Children: **Ruth** (1891–1904); **Esther** (1893–1980); **Marion** (1895–1977); **Richard Folsom** (1897–1974); **Francis Grover** (1903–1995)

POLITICAL LIFE
- Sheriff of Erie County, New York (1871–1873)
- Mayor of Buffalo, New York (1882)
- Governor of New York (1883–1885)

PRESIDENCY
- Two separate terms
- Democrat
- First term: March 4, 1885–March 4, 1889
- Second term: March 4, 1893–March 4, 1897
- Vice presidents: **Thomas A. Hendricks** (1885–1889); **Adlai Ewing Stevenson** (1893–1897)

ELECTION OF 1884
- Electoral vote: **Cleveland** 219; **James G. Blaine** 182
- Popular vote: **Cleveland** 4,874,621; **Blaine** 4,848,936

ELECTION OF 1892
- Electoral vote: **Cleveland** 277; **Benjamin Harrison** 142; **James B. Weaver** 22
- Popular vote: **Cleveland** 5,553,898; **Harrison** 5,190,819; **Weaver** 1,026,595

CABINET (1ST TERM)

SECRETARY OF STATE
Thomas F. Bayard (1885–1889)

SECRETARY OF THE TREASURY
Daniel Manning (1885–1887)

Charles S. Fairchild (1887–1889)

SECRETARY OF WAR
William C. Endicott (1885–1889)

ATTORNEY GENERAL
Augustus H. Garland (1885–1889)

SECRETARY OF THE NAVY
William C. Whitney (1885–1889)

POSTMASTER GENERAL
William F. Vilas (1885–1888)

Donald M. Dickinson (1888–1889)

SECRETARY OF THE INTERIOR
Lucius Q.C. Lamar (1885–1888)

William F. Vilas (1888–1889)

SECRETARY OF AGRICULTURE
Norman J. Colman (Feb.–Mar. 1889), first to serve in this new post

Only once in American history has a president won the office, and then been voted out, only to be reelected four years later. Grover Cleveland was also the only president to be married in a fancy White House wedding and have a child born there. Unfortunately, Cleveland is better known for these facts than his accomplishments while president—for either term.

EARLY LIFE

Stephen Grover Cleveland was born March 18, 1837, in Caldwell, New Jersey, the fifth of nine children. His father, Reverend Richard Falley Cleveland, was a Presbyterian minister, and he named his newborn son in honor of his predecessor in Caldwell. By the time young Cleveland became an adult, he no longer used the first name.

During his earliest years, Cleveland was schooled at home. The family moved when he was four years old to Fayetteville, New York, and it was there, at the age of eleven, that he attended school for the first time. Two years later, the family moved again, this time to Clinton, New York. Their son attended the Clinton Liberal Institute for a year, but then returned to the Fayetteville Institute, where he enjoyed debate and organized a debating society. His collegiate plans ended, however, when his father died unexpectedly in 1853. Later Cleveland reflected on his father's religious impact and said, "I have always felt that my training as a minister's son has been more valuable to me as a strengthening influence than any other incident in my life."[1]

Young Cleveland's earliest employment was on the Erie Canal, where he performed various tasks. At age fifteen, he clerked in a store. But the following year he was teaching reading, writing, geography, and arithmetic at the New York Institute for the Blind. He quickly decided that teaching was not his calling and returned home. Still hoping to attend college, but unable to afford the costs involved, Cleveland decided to join friends who wanted to try their luck in the growing city of Cleveland, Ohio. Along the way he stopped in Buffalo and paid what turned out to be a fortuitous visit to a wealthy uncle, Lewis F. Allen. As a child, Cleveland had spent long summer visits with his uncle, who had been impressed by the young boy's quick mind and interest in the family cattle herds. The two struck a bargain—Allen hired his nephew to edit *The American Shorthorn Handbook* and Cleveland would remain in Buffalo. Soon he was studying law in the law office of Allen's attorney, and in 1859, Grover Cleveland was admitted to the bar.

EARLY LEGAL/POLITICAL CAREER

Cleveland joined Rogers, Bowen and Rogers, the same law firm where he had studied. While establishing himself as an attorney, he also began associating himself with the Democratic Party. In 1860, he supported the Northern Democratic candidate, Stephen A. Douglas, but once the Civil War started, he switched allegiance to the president while remaining a loyal party member in Buffalo. In 1862, he became ward supervisor, and the following year, assistant district attorney for Erie County. After two years in that position, Cleveland ran for district attorney, but lost the election.

Grover Cleveland did not serve in the military during the Civil War. He was drafted, but with the Conscription Act of 1863, he was able to pay a substitute to serve instead. Later he defended his actions by claiming he needed to continue working to help support his mother and siblings.

NATIONAL EVENTS

Three Johnson brothers—Robert Wood, James Wood, and Edward Mead—form Johnson & Johnson to produce special medicinal plasters in Brunswick, New Jersey

FEB 21: President Chester A. Arthur dedicates the Washington Monument

MAR 4: Grover Cleveland inaugurated as president

AUG: *Personal Memoirs of U.S. Grant* is published (Grant died on July 23)

1885

WORLD EVENTS

Banff National Park is created as the first of Canada's national parks

FEB 5: King Leopold II establishes Congo Free State

FEB 24: Berlin West Africa Conference ends with agreement to declare Congo River basin neutral

JUL 6: Louis Pasteur administers world's first rabies vaccine, saving the life of a six-year-old boy

NOV 14: Serbia and Bulgaria go to war

After 1865, Cleveland returned to private law practice. He ran for his next political office in 1871 and was elected Erie County sheriff. There he discovered that the position was rife with graft, and Cleveland worked tirelessly to clean up the office and the image. One task he despised but refused to shirk was that of public executioner. Grover Cleveland has the dubious distinction of being the only US president to personally have hanged two men. After serving for two years, Cleveland again returned to private practice where he continued to garner respect for his incorruptible spirit; ten years later, he used his success to win the mayoral election for Buffalo.

THE VETO MAYOR

After winning the election in 1882, Cleveland wasted no time in demonstrating that his platform to reform the mayor's position was no sham. He vetoed multiple contracts for city services, believing them to be overpriced, thereby earning the title of the "veto mayor." Instead, he recommended a more equitable bidding system and won praise when he vetoed a proposal to pay city councilmen to study Buffalo's poor sewage system—a problem that had resulted in the typhoid deaths of many citizens. The mayor insisted that experts be hired instead. Many residents applauded his efforts and urged him to consider continuing his good work in the state's highest office. Later in 1882, Grover Cleveland was elected governor of New York.

THE VETO GOVERNOR

Surprisingly Tammany Hall backed the election of the incorruptible Cleveland. Believing that he, too, had a price, the bosses waited to sway him until after the election, but to their great dismay, the 250-pound bulk of a governor would not be moved. Cleveland refused their requests—rather, their demands—for patronage appointments repeatedly. Interested in only appointing men who were qualified for the state's jobs, Cleveland found himself allied with a young Republican assemblyman, Theodore Roosevelt, who sponsored a bill to implement a state civil service program.

Cleveland's veto did not always boost his popularity. His most unpopular decision was rejecting a measure to reduce the New York City transit fare to five cents. He understood how the city's residents were in favor of such a bill, but his legal mind would not allow a measure that clearly was counter to the city's contract with Jay Gould, which set fees at ten cents for certain times of the day. Though he vetoed this bill, the governor happily signed another, which created a protected area of 1.5 million acres around Niagara Falls.

A governor who refused to cater to the whims of the party bosses quickly attracted the attention of the Democratic Party leaders when they met in Chicago in 1884. A candidate was needed who could break their long line of presidential losses; no Democrat had won since James Buchanan in 1856. Cleveland captured the nomination in only two ballots; the ticket included Thomas Hendricks of Indiana for vice president. The Democratic platform reflected the concern of workers—recognizing labor's rights, limiting Chinese immigration, and tariff revision.

The campaign focused closely on the two presidential candidates, with the Democrats quickly trumpeting James Blaine's questionable association with railroads and possible graft. Meanwhile, people scrambled to buy newspapers to read about Governor Cleveland's illegitimate son. He acknowledged an affair (although paternity was not certain) during the time he was sheriff. He also

CABINET (2ND TERM)

SECRETARY OF STATE
Walter Q. Gresham (1893–1895); died in office

Richard Olney (1895–1897)

SECRETARY OF THE TREASURY
John G. Carlisle (1893–1897)

SECRETARY OF WAR
Daniel S. Lamont (1893–1897)

ATTORNEY GENERAL
Richard Olney (1893–1895)

Judson Harmon (1895–1897)

SECRETARY OF THE NAVY
Hilary A. Herbert (1893–1897)

POSTMASTER GENERAL
Wilson S. Bissell (1893–1895)

William L. Wilson (1895–1897)

SECRETARY OF THE INTERIOR
Hoke Smith (1893–1896)

David R. Francis (1896–1897)

SECRETARY OF AGRICULTURE
J. Sterling Morton (1893–1897)

SEP 2: Anti-Chinese riot in mining town of Rock Springs, Wyoming, where white miners kill 28 and wound 15 more

MAY 4: Haymarket bombing in Chicago kills six policemen

MAY 8: John Stith Pemberton, Georgia pharmacist, invents a drink that will become known as Coca-Cola

JUN 2: White House wedding for President Grover Cleveland and Frances Folsom, 27 years his junior

SEP 4: Geronimo, Apache leader, surrenders to US Army

OCT 28: President Cleveland dedicates the Statue of Liberty

1886

DEC 28: Indian National Congress meets for the first time in Bombay

JAN 1: Great Britain annexes northern Burma

JAN 29: German Karl Benz patents the first successful gasoline-driven automobile

MAR 3: Four-month war between Serbia and Bulgaria ends with settlement by Council of Berlin

JUN 13: Bavaria's King Ludwig II found drowned in a lake three days after being declared insane

CIVIL WAR SUBSTITUTES ★ During the Civil War, the US government allowed for men to hire substitutes for $300 if called into service. This policy was permitted under the Conscription Act passed in March 1863. The one paying, though, was still liable for service when the next draft was held, so he would continue having to pay money if he wanted to remain a civilian. Therefore, those hiring substitutes were usually the wealthy. Cleveland hired a substitute, and so was the only president between Abraham Lincoln and William McKinley who did not serve in the Civil War.

agreed to take financial responsibility for the child. Later, the boy, Oscar Folsom Cleveland, was adopted, and the mother was paid five hundred dollars to relocate. Many worried that such an admission would cost Cleveland the presidency, but Blaine's behavior did little to encourage voters to elect him.

Republicans found themselves disenchanted by Blaine's nomination. As a result, a sizeable group broke and named themselves the Mugwumps. They instead rallied behind Cleveland, who they hoped would continue his reforms on the national level. Blaine himself managed to alienate two groups of voters—the Irish and the workers. He failed to object when a Protestant minister said, "We are Republicans, and don't propose to leave our party and identify ourselves with the party whose antecedents have been Rum, Romanism, and Rebellion."[2] Labor became outraged when they learned he was hobnobbing with John Jacob Astor, Jay Gould, and other robber barons.

DID YOU KNOW?

Cleveland is the only president to serve nonconsecutive terms.

By losing those two key groups, the Republicans lost their hope to win New York City, which meant New York went with its governor, Grover Cleveland. He won 49 percent of the popular vote with James Blaine claiming 48 percent. Cleveland carried the South, as well as some northeastern states—New Jersey, Delaware, Connecticut, and of course, New York. In two years, Grover Cleveland had gone from mayor to governor to president. A meteoric rise to be sure. But what happens when the meteor crashes into the halls of Congress?

PRESIDENT CLEVELAND: FIRST TERM

On March 4, 1885, Grover Cleveland took the oath of office. He delivered his inaugural address without the aid of any notes, and at least one of his points apparently fell on deaf ears when he proclaimed, "The people demand reform in the administration of the Government and the application of business principles to public affairs. As a means to this end, civil-service reform should be in good faith enforced. Our citizens have the right to protection from the incompetency of public employees who hold their places solely as the reward of partisan service." Since no Democratic president had held office for nearly thirty years, the capital city became deluged with office seekers who firmly believed "To the victors belong the spoils." At ten o'clock each morning, they laid siege to the White House, demanding to see the president. Cleveland, disgusted by the continual drain on his time, often compromised by allowing some political appointments but refusing to replace others strictly for rewarding party service and loyalty. He succeeded in doubling the number of federal workers covered by the Civil Service Commission.

Not satisfied with the enormous job of reforming political patronage, Cleveland worked to upgrade and modernize the US Navy. Meanwhile, his secretary of the interior, Lucius Lamar, tackled the extensive plundering by various western

NATIONAL EVENTS

DEC 8: American Federation of Labor (AFL) created, with 26 craft unions

1887

FEB 1: Interstate Commerce Act passed to end railroads giving preferential treatment to some customers and unfairly setting rates

FEB 8: Congress passes the Dawes Act providing reservation land to American Indians (160 acres) if they live on it for 25 years and renounce membership in their tribe

MAR 2: Annie Sullivan travels to Alabama to begin working with six-year-old Helen Keller

WORLD EVENTS

JUL 1: Canadian Railway opens

OCT 7: Slavery abolished in Cuba

In Berlin, Julius R. Petri introduces the "petri dish" as a means to grow bacteria cultures

JAN: Italian-Ethiopian War begins

MAR 4: Daimler motorcar introduced

JUN 18: Russo-German treaty signed

SEP 24: Emile Berliner patents gramophone

DEC 1: Sherlock Holmes appears in his first story, *A Study in Scarlet*, by Arthur Conan Doyle

interests, including the railroads, cattle barons, and lumber companies who vied to divide the western territories into their own fiefdoms. Cleveland had said in his inaugural speech that "Indians within our boundaries shall be fairly and honestly treated as wards of the Government," and by 1887, Congress and the president passed the Dawes Act. This well-intentioned law meant to help Native Americans assimilate. Reservation lands were divided and American Indians who renounced their tribal allegiance were allotted parcels that might be used as small farms or ranches. These plots could also be sold, which ultimately led to the extreme reduction of many reservations throughout the West.

> ***"A government for the people must depend for its success on the intelligence, the morality, the justice, and the interest of the people themselves."***
>
> *—Grover Cleveland*

One group who grew disenchanted with the president was the veterans. Hundreds of private pension bills crossed his desk. Some received his signature, but many were vetoed for the thinly veiled attempts at fraud by veterans wanting the government to pay for accidents they had suffered since the Civil War. Cleveland said no, and more than three hundred vetoes showed he meant what he said.

Taking center stage, as it had so often in the past, was tariffs. Should the United States raise its tariffs to protect industry, as the Republicans preached? Or should they be lowered to keep prices reasonable for average American workers, as the Democrats demanded? Cleveland sided with his party, but was not avid about reforming the tariff. He decided not to push the issue until after the 1886 congressional elections for fear of dividing his party, but the following year, his entire State of the Union message focused solely on the tariff. The president proposed that Congress should lower the tariff, especially since the US Treasury was enjoying a surplus. Afraid to hurt northern industry, Congress delayed action; thus, the debate extended into the 1888 presidential election.

Economic questions consumed a great deal of Cleveland's first term. Increasingly, farmers demanded expanding the country's money supply by issuing currency not backed in gold, so they could have the cash they needed to pay bills. They wanted "cheap money." After much deliberation, President Cleveland decided he must back supporters of the gold standard and "sound money," because those creditors had the right to be repaid in money of the same value that they loaned. He also worked to repeal the Bland-Allison Act of 1878, which required the US Treasury to purchase millions of dollars in silver each month and coin it. By repealing this, Cleveland hoped to slow the pace that gold was leaving the Treasury as payment for US bills and creating a serious drain on its reserves. Congress, however, disagreed and the Bland-Allison Act remained.

Not all of the president's time was consumed by matters of national importance. Grover Cleveland managed to fit courtship into his busy schedule. Frances Folsom was the daughter of his former law partner who had died in 1875. Cleveland had been the administrator the estate. Now she was twenty-one years old, and she and her mother visited the

SUPREME COURT APPOINTMENTS

★★★★★★★★★★

1st term:

Lucius Q.C. Lamar, 1888

Melville W. Fuller, 1888

2nd term:

Edward D. White, 1894

Rufus W. Peckham, 1896

Congress creates US Department of Labor, but will be 15 years before it is a cabinet post

JAN 27: National Geographic Society founded in Washington, D.C.; begins publishing in October

MAR 11: "Great Blizzard of '88" shuts down the northeast, killing an estimated 400

OCT 1: Congress passes the Scott Act to ensure any Chinese who have left the US would not return

NOV 6: Benjamin Harrison, Republican, declared winner of presidential election although Grover Cleveland won the popular vote

1888

Auguste Rodin sculpts *The Thinker*

AUG: Women's bodies found in London after having been brutally killed by "Jack the Ripper" (identity unknown)

DEC 23: Vincent van Gogh, French painter, cuts off part of his left ear

STATE OF THE UNION

US POPULATION IN 1885
62,947,714

NATIONAL DEBT IN 1897
$1,817,672,666

STATE ADMITTED TO UNION
Utah,
January 4, 1896

NUMBER OF STATES IN 1897
45

president at the White House. The Folsom ladies traveled on to Europe and when they returned, the president welcomed them home in their hotel. Soon an announcement told the world that the president and Miss Frances Folsom were engaged. Many people were astounded to hear that it was the young Miss Folsom, rather than her mother, who was the object of Cleveland's affection. A small group of family and friends assembled in the Blue Room of the White House on June 2, 1886, to witness the two exchanging their vows. John Philip Sousa and the Marine Band provided the music. The newlyweds enjoyed a five-day honeymoon in Maryland before the president and First Lady returned to their duties at the White House.

Frances Cleveland impressed Washington society and her husband's critics with her grace and charm. The White House hosted dinners and receptions that had been sorely missing during the year of Cleveland's bachelor presidency. Still the couple yearned for a more private home; therefore, he purchased twenty-seven acres in the countryside near Georgetown. Only three miles from the White House, the president and First Lady savored their breathtaking view of the city and the quiet of the country.

DID YOU KNOW?

Cleveland was the first president to enjoy his own White House wedding when he married Frances Folsom during his first term. He was also the first president to have a child born in the White House.

ELECTION OF 1888

The Democratic convention in St. Louis elected Cleveland as their presidential nominee. Republicans in Chicago voted to run Benjamin Harrison as theirs. The tariff issue divided the candidates, with Cleveland promising to lower it, and Harrison saying America needed a strong protective tariff to keep its industry vital. Cleveland's sound money policy cost him votes throughout the farming states of the Midwest and far west. This, combined with losing New York because of Tammany Hall's hatred of his reforms cost Cleveland the electoral election. Although he claimed the popular vote, losing his home state meant losing the presidency. Undaunted by this setback, Frances Cleveland told a White House worker, "I want you to take good care of all the furniture and ornaments in the house, for I want to find everything just as it is now when we come back again."[3]

INTERIM

The next four years were ones of bliss for the Clevelands and their growing family. Baby Ruth was born October 3, 1891, in New York City. There the former president worked at a prestigious law firm, and they acquired a vacation house on the Massachusetts coast where they could boat and fish in nearby streams.

Although far from Washington, Cleveland still kept a watchful eye on events. Increasingly dismayed by Harrison's spending policies, which had eaten away the Treasury surplus, as well as by the recently enacted McKinley Tariff raising taxes, Cleveland and the Democratic Party eagerly awaited the 1892 election.

The election of 1892 was a rematch of Democratic candidate Grover Cleveland against incumbent president Benjamin Harrison. For the first time, both candidates had held the nation's highest office. Another party developed from the frustrations of America's farmers, who felt betrayed by both Democrats and Republicans. The Populists ran as a third party with James B. Weaver as their candidate.

The campaign, however, became practically nonexistent with the death of Mrs. Caroline Harrison in October. Cleveland agreed to remain home out of respect for Benjamin Harrison and his family, yet when the votes were counted, Cleveland

NATIONAL EVENTS

JAN 17: US Marines overthrow Hawaiian queen Liliuokalani

FEB 1: Thomas Edison builds the first motion picture studio

MAR 4: Grover Cleveland returns to the presidency

JUN 27: Crash of New York Stock Exchange sets off the Panic of 1893

JUL 1: President Cleveland undergoes secret surgery to remove a mouth tumor

1893 (second term)

WORLD EVENTS

Laos conquered by France

MAR 10: France starts Ivory Coast as a colony

JUN 6: Prince George, Duke of York, marries Mary of Teck

JUN 17: Gold found in western Australia

SEP 19: New Zealand becomes the first country to grant women's suffrage

won both popular and electoral votes, including his home state of New York. Weaver and the Populists won three states and their electoral votes. Mrs. Cleveland's prediction had come true.

BABY RUTH ★ Popular myth says that the candy bar Baby Ruth was named for little Ruth Cleveland. This seems rather unlikely, since it premiered 17 years after she had died from diphtheria. More likely, the namesake was Babe Ruth, but the company did not want to be liable for any royalties that he might demand, nor risk any potential lawsuits and/or negative publicity; hence, they used the story of Ruth Cleveland.

PRESIDENT CLEVELAND: SECOND TERM

A month before Cleveland was sworn in for his second term, the Philadelphia and Reading Railroad failed. This was the first domino, and others fell in short order, plunging the country into a depression that would last through Cleveland's second term. Overexpansion of railroads and other industries were partly to blame, as was the ever-shrinking gold reserves. Failing banks and falling farm prices combined with European economic problems meant unemployment and poverty for millions of Americans.

The president believed that silver purchasing was the primary culprit and decided to try for the repeal of the Sherman Silver Purchase Act. He called Congress into special session in August to do just that.

Meanwhile, Cleveland faced his own crisis. Bothered by a sore spot in the roof of his mouth, he finally had doctors look at it, and they agreed it needed to be removed immediately. Worried that having the president undergo surgery when the country was experiencing such dire problems, Cleveland decided to have the work done clandestinely.

He boarded a yacht in New York, where he spent the night. The next day the operation was performed in the main cabin with Cleveland strapped to the main mast and under general anesthesia. Five doctors and a dentist operated. They found the cancerous growth to be greater than anticipated, so teeth were removed, as well as the left side of his jaw. Later in the summer, he experienced a smaller operation to remove more tissue and then was fitted with an artificial jaw. No one knew the extent of the president's operation or even that he had had one. As far as the public knew, Cleveland had cruised on a friend's yacht, and then continued to his vacation home at Gray Gables, in Massachusetts, to relax and escape the heat of the Washington summer.

Congress repealed the Sherman Silver Act, which angered many of Cleveland's fellow Democrats. Calling for a tariff reduction, Cleveland was pleased by Democratic representative William Wilson's bill to reduce the McKinley Tariff. But unwilling to allow a total reduction, Senator Arthur Gorman of Maryland tacked on a list of duties for various items to please the industries of eastern states. Desperately wanting the tariff reduction but dismayed by Gorman's addition, Cleveland took the unusual step of allowing the bill to become law without his signature.

Economic distress led to strikes throughout the nation. Steelworkers, miners, and textile workers walked off their jobs to protest low wages and poor working conditions. In Ohio, a group of twenty-five thousand disgruntled men left Massillon, Ohio, to march on Washington and convince the president to take action. By the time they reached their destination, their numbers

MAY 1: Coxey's Army (a protest march by unemployed workers) arrives in Washington, D.C.—the first significant popular protest march on Washington

MAY 11: Pullman Strike begins in Illinois

JUN 28: Congress votes to make Labor Day a national holiday

JUL 4: Republic of Hawaii proclaimed

AUG 27: Wilson Gorman Tariff lowers tariffs

1894

JUN 23: International Olympic Committee (IOC) founded in France

JUN 24: Sadi Carnot, French president, assassinated

AUG 1: Sino-Japanese War begins

NOV 1: Russian czar Alexander III dies; Nicholas II succeeds him

DID YOU KNOW?

Cleveland holds the presidential record of vetoes. During his first term, he vetoed over 400 bills, at least 200 more than the second highest.

had dwindled to less than four hundred. Those were chased away by the police, and the leader of "Coxey's Army," Jacob Coxey, was arrested for trespassing on the capitol lawn.

The country's attention soon shifted to Chicago, where workers struck the Pullman Palace Car Company. Angry and frustrated by having their wages cut, while at the same time paying higher prices at the employee store and for their company housing, the workers decided to strike. Led by American Railway Union leader Eugene V. Debs, strikes soon spread to other railroad companies and brought rail traffic between the west coast and Chicago to a standstill. Violence erupted, and the rail companies looked to Cleveland for assistance. Counter to the will of Illinois governor John P. Altgeld, the attorney general filed an injunction against the strikers and, claiming that the strike was hindering mail service, Cleveland said, "If it takes the army and navy of the United States to deliver a postcard in Chicago, that card will be delivered."[4] Consequently, army troops soon arrived to break up the strike. Debs was also arrested, and workers throughout the country noted the actions of the president, while the rail companies and businesses breathed a sigh of relief.

> *"I would rather the man who presents something for my consideration subject me to a zephyr of truth and a gentle breeze of responsibility rather than blow me down with a curtain of hot wind."*
>
> —*Grover Cleveland*

Another crisis threatened the nation's economy. When gold supplies continued to dwindle at an alarming rate, Cleveland knew action must be taken or the gold standard would be lost. Cleveland and J.P. Morgan agreed to a deal that allowed the United States to sell gold bonds to Morgan and his Wall Street cronies at a discount. They, in turn, would work to halt the flood of gold from the Treasury. Cleveland despised dealing with Morgan, but he had no choice after being told that the US sub-Treasury in New York had a gold supply of less than nine million dollars. Morgan reminded him that he "knew of an outstanding note for twelve million dollars. 'Mr. President . . . If that [note] is presented today; it is all over.'"[5] Cleveland's agreement with Morgan cost him support within his party and the Populists gained sway.

FOREIGN POLICY

Before Cleveland took office for his second term, a treaty to annex Hawaii awaited Senate approval. Angry that American business interests had forced out the native queen Liliuokalani, he withdrew the treaty and refused recognition of the Dole government in Hawaii.

In 1895, President Cleveland invoked the Monroe Doctrine to prevent a land grab by Great Britain in South America when the British territory of Guiana disputed its boundary with Venezuela. Cleveland and Secretary of State Richard Olney succeeded in convincing the British to submit the dispute for arbitration.

In nearby Cuba, Spain faced rebellion. Cleveland refused to commit the United States to

NATIONAL EVENTS

Ignaz Schwinn begins manufacturing bicycles in Chicago

Completion of Biltmore estate, George W. Vanderbilt's home in North Carolina

New York City opens its first pizzeria

JUL 4: "America the Beautiful" introduced

SEP 3: First professional football game played

NOV 5: George Selden receives first US patent for a car

1895

WORLD EVENTS

MAR 22: Moving pictures first play in a Paris theater

APR 17: Sino-Japanese War ends in victory for Japan

JUN 28: Central American Union formed of Honduras, Nicaragua, and El Salvador

NOV 8: German W.C. Roentgen discovers x-rays

becoming involved, but he did offer to be a mediator between the two. Spain refused, setting the stage for the next president, who would send troops to help Cubans fight the Spanish.

RETIREMENT

The *Indianapolis Sentinel* insisted that Cleveland was the most maligned president to have ever served. He probably empathized, for the country tended to blame him for its economic faults. The debate over the gold standard split the Democratic Party and led them to nominate William Jennings Bryan of Nebraska as their candidate in 1896. Bryan's passionate speech made headlines throughout the country when he proclaimed, "You shall not press down upon the brow of labor this crown of thorns. You shall not crucify mankind upon a cross of gold."[6] Bryan faced National Democrat John Palmer, as well as Republican William McKinley, who easily defeated the divided Democrats.

Meanwhile, the Clevelands made plans to move their family to Princeton, New Jersey. Their family had grown during the second term, as little Ruth now had additional siblings to play with—sister Esther was the only child of a president to be born in the White House, brother Marion was born in Massachusetts. Richard arrived in 1897 after Cleveland left office, and Francis in 1903 when Cleveland was sixty-five years old. The following year, Ruth died of diphtheria.

Cleveland joined one of the top law firms in New York City and made money from the stock market. He wrote magazine articles and books, fished, played with his children, survived cancer, and joined the board of trustees for Princeton University and later became its president. He served with Woodrow Wilson as the university's president.

In his last years, Cleveland faced a variety of health problems, including kidney ailments, digestive problems, and rheumatism. He died June 24, 1908, of heart failure. His last words were "I have tried so hard to do right."[7] In recognition of his help during their border dispute with Britain, Venezuela lowered their flags to half staff.

Cleveland's widow, Frances, remarried in 1913, to a Princeton professor. She died on October 29, 1947, and is buried beside Grover Cleveland in Princeton.

DID YOU KNOW?

Cleveland frequently answered the White House telephone personally.

ENDNOTES

1 John Sutherland Bonnell, *Presidential Profiles: Religion in the Life of American Presidents*, Philadelphia: Westminister, 1971, p. 147.

2 Eugene H. Rosebloom, *A History of Presidential Elections*, New York: MacMillan, 1957, p. 272.

3 Michael Beschloss, ed., *American Heritage Illustrated History of the Presidents*, New York: Crown, p. 287.

4 Ibid, p. 290.

5 Ibid, p. 289.

6 Rexford Guy Tugwell, *Grover Cleveland*, New York: MacMillan, 1968, p. 273.

7 William DeGregorio, *The Complete Book of US Presidents*, New York: Gramercy Books, 2005, p. 350.

1896

Kodak produces the Brownie camera and sells them for $1 each

JAN 4: Utah admitted as 45th state

MAR 20: US Marines go to Nicaragua

MAY 18: *Plessy v. Ferguson* Supreme Court decision declares "separate but equal" facilities are constitutional

JUN 4: Henry Ford drives his first car (the Quadricycle) in Detroit

NOV: William McKinley wins presidential election over William Jennings Bryan

APR: Summer Olympic Games open in Athens, Greece; first modern Olympic games

JUN 2: Italian Guglielmo Marconi patents the radio

JUN 15: Tsunami in Japan kills 27,000

Benjamin Harrison

★ ★ ★ TWENTY-THIRD PRESIDENT ★ ★ ★

LIFE SPAN
- Born: August 20, 1833, in North Bend, Ohio
- Died: March 13, 1901, in Indianapolis, Indiana

NICKNAMES
- Little Ben, Kid Gloves Harrison

RELIGION
- Presbyterian

HIGHER EDUCATION
- Miami (Ohio) University, 1852

PROFESSION
- Lawyer

MILITARY SERVICE
- Civil War: served with 70th Indiana Infantry Regiment, rising from second lieutenant to brigadier general (served July 1862 to June 1865)

FAMILY
- Father: **John Scott Harrison** (1804–1878)
- Mother: **Elizabeth Irwin Harrison** (1810–1880)
- Wife: **Caroline Lavinia Scott Harrison** (1832–1892); wed October 20, 1853, in Oxford, Ohio
- Children: **Russell Benjamin** (1854–1936); **Mary Scott** (1858–1930)
- Second wife: **Mary Scott Lord Dominick Harrison** (1858–1948); wed on April 6, 1896, in New York City
- Child: **Elizabeth** (1897–1955)

POLITICAL LIFE
- Indianapolis city attorney (1857–1860)
- Indiana supreme court reporter (1861–1862)
- US senator (1881–1887)

PRESIDENCY
- One term: March 4, 1889–March 4, 1893
- Republican
- Reason for leaving office: lost 1892 election to former president **Cleveland**
- Vice president: **Levi P. Morton** (1889–1893)

ELECTION OF 1888
- Electoral vote: **Harrison** 233; **Grover Cleveland** 168
- Popular vote: **Harrison** 5,443,892; **Cleveland** 5,534,488

CABINET
★★★★★★★★★★

SECRETARY OF STATE
James G. Blaine (1889–1892)

John W. Foster (1892–1893)

SECRETARY OF THE TREASURY
William Windom (1889–1891); died in office

Charles Foster (1891–1893)

SECRETARY OF WAR
Redfield Proctor (1889–1891)

Stephen B. Elkins (1891–1893)

ATTORNEY GENERAL
William H. Miller (1889–1893)

SECRETARY OF THE NAVY
Benjamin F. Tracy (1889–1893)

POSTMASTER GENERAL
John Wanamaker (1889–1893)

SECRETARY OF THE INTERIOR
John W. Noble (1889–1893)

SECRETARY OF AGRICULTURE
Jeremiah M. Rusk (1889–1893)

The two presidents Adams shared both a common familial bond and the misfortune not to win reelection to the nation's highest office—such also was the fate of the Harrison men.

EARLY YEARS

Benjamin Harrison never enjoyed the chance to visit his presidential grandfather owing to the extremely short nature of William Henry Harrison's term. Still, in his early years, young Benjamin had ample opportunity to learn from his grandfather.

Benjamin's father, John Harrison, and wife, Elizabeth Irwin Harrison, settled on land given to them soon after Benjamin's birth on August 20, 1833. The Point, a six-hundred-acre farm near North Bend, Ohio, was a fine place for the boy to enjoy childhood. His education was a blend of tutors and attendance at the nearby one-room schoolhouse. At the age of fourteen, he left his home and moved to Cincinnati to attend Farmer's College, a preparatory school. Here, and following, when he entered Miami University as a junior, Harrison honed his oratorical and debate skills. In 1852, he graduated and was ready to begin the study of law.

Harrison pursued his legal studies at a Cincinnati law firm for two years before being admitted to the bar in 1854. The year before, he wed Caroline Lavinia Scott. The couple had become acquainted when Harrison studied at Farmer's College, where her father, John Scott, was a professor. Caroline's father was also an ordained Presbyterian minister and so officiated at his daughter's nuptials on October 20, 1853.

After exploring various possibilities, the young couple decided that Indianapolis offered them the most opportunities, and they decided to settle there. A son, Russell Benjamin Harrison, was born in 1854, and a daughter, Mary Scott, known affectionately as Mamie, arrived four years later.

Harrison, not content with being a successful attorney, yearned for a political career. In 1856, the newly organized Republican Party ran its first presidential candidate, John C. Frémont. Harrison campaigned actively for his party's nominee. On one occasion, when party men demanded that Harrison leave his office to go outside and give a speech, he was given an enthusiastic introduction that reminded the crowd of his famous grandfather. Harrison bristled and announced, "'I want it understood that I am the grandson of nobody. I believe that every man should stand on his own merits.'"[1] He became secretary of Indiana's Republican committee in 1858, and in 1860, worked to elect the candidate from nearby Illinois—Abraham Lincoln.

While developing his political party affiliation, Harrison worked to build the foundation for his own political career. In 1857, he won his first election and became the city attorney for Indianapolis. During the first year of the Civil War, he served as supreme court reporter of Indiana, a rather tedious post in which he transcribed judicial opinions and trial records. Harrison's hard work paid off as he was able to make a tidy income from sales and afford a nice house for his family of four.

MILITARY CAREER

In July 1862, Benjamin Harrison was commissioned as a second lieutenant for the 70th Indiana Regiment and was ordered by Governor Oliver P. Morton to recruit the necessary men. The young lieutenant understood the need for advertising, so hired a fife player and hung a flag at his office. He also printed an appeal in the Indianapolis *Daily Journal* on July 18, 1862: "Boys, think quick and decide as patriots should in such an emergency."[2]

NATIONAL EVENTS

Bicycles go on sale in the US

Social worker Jane Addams opens Hull House in Chicago

Singer Company introduces first electric sewing machine

MAR 4: Benjamin Harrison inaugurated president

APR 22: Race to open Oklahoma Territory to settlers; those arriving early are nicknamed "sooners"

MAY 31: Johnstown Flood kills more than 2,000 people

JUN 6: Great Seattle Fire destroys 25 city blocks

1889

WORLD EVENTS

Fusajiro Yamauchi begins producing playing cards; later his company will become Nintendo

Pandemic flu begins to strike throughout the world and continues for two years

Mary Cassatt paints *Mother and Child*

Torakusu Yamaha starts the Japanese Musical Instrument Manufacturing Company

JAN 10: Ivory Coast becomes French protectorate

APR 6: Trinidad annexes Tobago

After deploying to Kentucky to help repel a Confederate attack, Harrison and his men settled in to the dull monotony of army life. They patrolled and safeguarded railroad tracks and trains, drilled and marched, and wondered when their turn would come to fight.

In February 1864, the regiment finally received their marching orders to reinforce General Sherman's troops in Georgia. There, the 70th Indiana faced the enemy in a number of engagements as the Union troops fought their way toward Atlanta. At Peach Tree Creek, brigade commander Harrison won praise for his determined defense against a determined enemy assault. Following intense fighting around Kennesaw Mountain, Harrison assumed a new role—surgeon. When his men moved, the surgeons had become separated from the troops, leaving the wounded without medical assistance. Harrison rolled up his sleeves and did the best he could to assist his men. As he wrote to his wife, "I was but an awkward surgeon, of course, but I hope I gave them some relief."[3] The 70th marched into Atlanta on September 1, 1864. Harrison's commander, General Joseph Hooker, recommended Harrison for promotion.

Harrison worried about the antiwar talk coming from a new political faction, the Copperheads. He took a leave of absence and returned to Indiana to campaign for both Lincoln's reelection and his return as supreme court reporter. In November, both outcomes were realized. Soon after, Harrison attempted to return to his men, now in South Carolina. He finally rejoined them in April after being detoured to help in the defense of Nashville. He then contracted scarlet fever. His recuperation took several weeks before he arrived on the Carolina coast and found himself ordered to train new recruits. General Harrison finally returned to his brigade on April 19, 1865, just as his men learned of President Lincoln's assassination. Two months later, Harrison and his soldiers marched in the Grand Review in Washington, D.C., and then on June 8, General Benjamin Harrison, who had seen more actual combat than his grandfather, was discharged.

GRAND REVIEW (May 23–24, 1865) ★ For two days, thousands of people crowded into Washington, D.C., to witness the Grand Review, a military parade of the Union Army. The first day saw George Meade and the Army of the Potomac marching in precision past the reviewing stand that included the new president, Andrew Johnson, and General-in-Chief Ulysses S. Grant. The next day, General William T. Sherman led his men, who had marched to the sea in Georgia and now were cheered by the people of Washington. This parade ended the official mourning period for the death of President Abraham Lincoln.

RETURN TO POLITICS

Harrison returned to Indianapolis and his dual positions as private attorney and supreme court reporter. He also continued his work with the Republican Party, including campaigning for Ulysses S. Grant's presidential campaign in 1868. Grant, in turn, appointed Harrison to be defense counsel for the army when it was sued by Lambdin Milligan. Milligan had been arrested in 1864 for working with pro-Confederate sympathizers. He was tried by a military tribunal and found guilty of inciting rebellion and sentenced to death, but the war ended before his execution. Then in 1866, the US Supreme Court ruled that no military

DID YOU KNOW?

Harrison was the grandson of the ninth president, William Henry Harrison.

NOV 2: North and South Dakota admitted as 39th and 40th states

NOV 8: Montana admitted as 41st state

NOV 11: Washington admitted as 42nd state

NOV 23: First jukebox plays tunes in a San Francisco saloon

John Hay and John Nicolay, former secretaries to President Lincoln, write a ten-volume biography about him

First book of Emily Dickinson's poems is published posthumously

1890

MAY 6: Eiffel Tower is completed in Paris

AUG 20: Beginning of Great London dock strike, which keeps Port of London closed for a month

Benzocaine developed in Germany

Emil von Behring develops vaccines for both tetanus and diphtheria

STATE OF THE UNION

US POPULATION IN 1889
62,947,714

NATIONAL DEBT IN 1893
$1,545,985,686

STATES ADMITTED TO UNION
North Dakota, November 2, 1889

South Dakota, November 2, 1889

Montana, November 8, 1889

Washington, November 11, 1889

Idaho, July 3, 1890

Wyoming, July 10, 1890

NUMBER OF STATES IN 1893
44

DID YOU KNOW?

Harrison became the first president to attend a baseball game when he watched the Cincinnati Reds beat the Washington Senators 7 to 4 on June 6, 1892.

tribunal had jurisdiction for a civilian so long as civil courts operated. Five years later, Milligan sued the military for one hundred thousand dollars in compensatory damages. The job fell to Harrison to convince jurors not to award Milligan the sum he demanded. Summoning his best oratorical skills, Harrison persuaded them to only award a token sum of five dollars to Mr. Milligan.

Harrison followed his legal success with political losses. He campaigned for Grant's reelection, but was unsuccessful in his own gubernatorial bid. Four years later, he lost his election for governor, but again worked to elect the Republican presidential candidate, Rutherford B. Hayes.

At the 1880 Republican convention, Harrison led the Indiana delegation and rallied support for James A. Garfield. His efforts did not go unnoticed. The following year, the Indiana legislature elected Benjamin Harrison to the US Senate.

The junior senator from Indiana quickly distinguished himself as the "soldier's legislator," pursuing more than a hundred pension plans for his fellow Civil War veterans. Harrison also campaigned for protectionist tariffs and favored the Pendleton Act (p. 253) to establish the civil service system. He unsuccessfully proposed creating a protected area along the Colorado River and attempted to gain statehood for Dakota.

Senator Harrison stood apart from many of his fellow senators. His landlord's son wrote, later, "I like President Harrison and I'll tell you why. At dinner frequently a group of Senators (whom I shall not name) passed Harrison by without speaking as though they didn't care a d--n for him. But what I liked about Harrison was, that he didn't seem to care a G-d d--n for them!"[4]

In 1884, some Hoosier delegates attempted to win the presidential nomination for Harrison, but instead it went to James Blaine. The election went badly for the Republicans, as they lost the presidency as well as the Indiana legislature. With that, Harrison lost his senate seat.

Refusing to yield to failure, Harrison decided to pursue the presidency in 1888. Thanks to skillful political maneuvering by Indiana's attorney general at the Republican convention, his backers were able to build support with each ballot. On the eighth ballot, Benjamin Harrison became his party's nominee with Levi P. Morton of New York as his vice president.

CAMPAIGN OF 1888

Incumbent Grover Cleveland believed he had little to fear and decided to sit out the campaign. Harrison also kept appearances to a minimum, usually only addressing delegations that visited his home in Indianapolis. The Republican platform embraced many of Harrison's beliefs—the use of tariffs, civil service reform, statehood for western territories, and, of course, pensions for veterans. Cleveland's reform practices ultimately cost him his reelection when the political machine of Tammany Hall worked to unseat him and deprive him of his home state's thirty-six electoral votes.

PRESIDENT HARRISON

The four years of Harrison's administration were ones of reform. The president was pleased to sign into law the Dependent and Disability Pensions Act in 1890, providing aid to veterans even if their disabilities were not the result of wartime service. This also compensated the widows and dependents of veterans.

One of Harrison's appointments may have later caused him some sleepless nights. Theodore Roosevelt became his civil service commissioner,

NATIONAL EVENTS

JAN 25: United Mine Workers formed

FEB 10: Part of Sioux lands in South Dakota (11 million acres) are opened to homesteaders

JUL 2: Sherman Antitrust Act is enacted

JUL 3: Idaho admitted as 43rd state

JUL 10: Wyoming admitted as 44th state

AUG 1: Yosemite and Sequoia National Parks created

AUG 6: First person executed by the electric chair in New York state

WORLD EVENTS

First tetanus inoculation developed in Berlin

Paul Cézanne paints *The Cardplayers*

JAN 1: Eritrea established by Italy as its colony in northeast Africa

JAN 15: *Sleeping Beauty* ballet by Pyotr Ilyich Tchaikovsky premieres in St. Petersburg

FEB 17: British steamship *Duburg* sinks in China Sea, 400 die

a position that Roosevelt said, "gave me my first opportunity to do big things."[5] While Roosevelt complained that he was being told that, "the law should be rigidly enforced where the people will stand it, and handled gingerly elsewhere,"[6] he was not willing to bend to any political agenda and insisted on following the civil service law to the letter. Reflecting on his achievements in correspondence to Harry Cabot Lodge in June 1889, Roosevelt noted that Harrison's administration was "in striking contrast to the facts under Cleveland, that there was no humbug in the law now."[7]

Reforms in business and industry came the following year when President Harrison signed the Sherman Antitrust Act. This marked the initial attempt by Congress to curtail some of the growing power by monopolies. Senator John Sherman also introduced and successfully passed the Sherman Silver Purchase Act in order to placate the western interests and win their support for the McKinley Tariff bill. The McKinley Tariff raised the rate to an all-time high of 48 percent. The American people soon felt the result in their pocketbooks as prices climbed. Sensing problems ahead, Harrison traveled throughout the Midwest hoping to gain support for his party and its congressional candidates in this off-year election. He addressed farmers and city dwellers. In Ohio, he pled for improved employer-labor relations. While his efforts proved futile, he refused to be discouraged, even after the voting resulted in Democratic gains throughout the nation, including the defeat of the tariff's sponsor, William McKinley.

Midway through Harrison's term, disturbing news reached Washington of activities on the Sioux reservation at Pine Ridge, South Dakota. There some of the Indians had been taking part in the "Ghost dance" in the belief that time could be turned back and erase any trace of the white man. Indian agents on the Sioux reservation became increasingly nervous, and tensions heightened, especially after the killing of Sitting Bull. The Army was summoned to restore order. In December 1890, the Seventh Cavalry, under Major General Nelson Miles, had orders to move a band of 350 Sioux, mostly women and children, back to the Pine Ridge reservation. The Sioux were camped along Wounded Knee creek; the group had been disarmed by Miles's men when suddenly shots rang out on the morning of December 29. When the shooting stopped, 150 Lakota Sioux lay dead in the snow. Upon hearing of this tragedy, Harrison sent a

SUPREME COURT APPOINTMENTS
★★★★★★★★★★

David J. Brewer, 1889

Henry B. Brown, 1891

George Shiras, 1892

Howell E. Jackson, 1893

SHERMAN SILVER PURCHASE ACT (1890) ★ Passed in 1890, the Sherman Silver Purchase Act required the US Treasury to buy 4.5 million ounces of silver per month, which meant most of the output of the western silver mines. The silver could be bought with notes that then could be redeemed in either silver or gold. When most people wanted to trade the notes for gold, the US gold reserve ran dangerously low. This law was repealed three years later.

SHERMAN ANTITRUST ACT (1890) ★ Ohio senator John Sherman sponsored this bill to attack monopolies by making any arrangements designed to increase the cost of goods to the consumer illegal and subject to a $5,000 fine and a one-year prison term. Little prosecution was done under this law until the administrations of Theodore Roosevelt and William H. Taft.

OCT 11: Daughters of the American Revolution (DAR) founded in Washington, D.C.

NOV 16: World's richest iron-ore deposit found in Minnesota

DEC: Construction begins on Ellis Island immigration station

DEC 15: Sioux chief Sitting Bull shot to death when Indian police attempt to arrest him

DEC 29: Massacre at Wounded Knee, South Dakota, where US Army gun down and kill more than 150 Lakota Sioux

MAR 18: Kaiser Wilhelm II forces Prime Minister Otto von Bismarck to resign

MAY 12: The first official County Championship cricket match is played in Bristol

JUL 11: Japan holds its first elections

JUL 27: Artist Vincent van Gogh shoots himself and dies two days later

NOV 23: Luxembourg declares its independence from the Netherlands

JOHNSTOWN FLOOD (May 31, 1889) ★ One of America's worst natural disasters occurred after days of heavy rains led to the collapse of a dam near Johnstown, Pennsylvania. This created a 40-foot wall of water (and debris) sweeping down on the town; more than 2,200 people were killed. The American Red Cross under the leadership of Clara Barton undertook its first massive aid effort.

message to Miles that he "heard with regret of the failure of your efforts to secure the settlement of the Sioux difficulties without bloodshed. . . . If there was any unsoldierly conduct, you will relieve responsible officers . . ."[8]

Harrison forged ahead in matters of defense. He supported enlarging the navy and developing armor-clad ships to protect the seas. Harrison also favored the annexation of Hawaii following the American-led revolt there against its ruling monarch, Queen Liliuokalani.

In 1892, a revolution occurred in Chile, and a new anti-American regime took charge. When American sailors were attacked in a Chilean bar, leaving two dead and seventeen others injured, Harrison demanded redress. At one cabinet meeting, Harrison addressed Secretary of State Blaine with a reprimand for his pacifistic attitude. "Mr. Secretary, that insult was to the uniform of the United States sailors."[9] He issued a message to Congress saying, "If the dignity as well as the prestige and influence of the United States are not to be wholly sacrificed, we must protect those who in foreign ports display the flag or wear the colors." America received its apology and seventy-five thousand dollars for the sailors and their families.

DID YOU KNOW?

During Harrison's presidency, electricity was installed in the White House, but his family was frightened by it after he received an electric shock. They sometimes refused to touch the switches.

As the election of 1892 loomed closer, Harrison made a difficult decision. He did not want to serve a second term, but believed he should remain the candidate rather than allow his secretary of state James Blaine to gain the nomination. Consequently, Harrison ran for reelection in 1892. It was a rematch of four years before, with Grover Cleveland once again as the Democratic nominee.

As before, both candidates waged low-key campaigns, but this time for a far different reason. Carrie Harrison lay dying of tuberculosis at the White House. Her husband had no desire to leave her side to campaign. Cleveland understood and pledged that he, too, would stay home.

While First Lady, Carrie Harrison oversaw major renovation in the White House, as well as a thorough cleaning, which it sorely needed. Electricity was added, but fear of shocks from the switches prevented the Harrisons from personally using them. Mrs. Harrison also taught china-painting classes and initiated the presidential china collection. The first White House Christmas tree appeared during the Harrison presidency. Caroline Harrison had made her imprint on the role of First Lady, but the demands of the job had exhausted her and now she fought for her life.

During that election-year summer, tempers flared as the temperatures rose. In Homestead, Pennsylvania, steelworkers struck the Carnegie Steel Company. Fights erupted when workers were locked out as the owners refused to recognize the union, and twenty men died in the violent conflicts between workers and guards. The same scenario repeated itself across the country in railroad and miners' strikes. All of the unrest demonstrated the belief of many workers: Benjamin Harrison and the Republi-

NATIONAL EVENTS

1891

MAR 15: First advertising firm opens in New York City

MAY 5: Music Hall in New York opens (later renamed Carnegie Hall)

AUG 24: Thomas Edison patents the motion picture camera

DEC 29: Thomas Edison patents electric transmission of signals (radio)

1892

JAN 1: Ellis Island opens as receiving station for immigrants

WORLD EVENTS

1891

Tess of the d'Urbervilles written by Thomas Hardy

Oscar Wilde publishes *The Picture of Dorian Gray*

Artist Henri de Toulouse-Lautrec produces his first music hall poster

FEB 26: Henrik Ibsen's play *Hedda Gabler* premiers in Oslo

MAY 31: Trans-Siberian railway begins construction

OCT 28: Earthquake hits Japan, killing over 7,000

1892

FEB 20: Lillie Langtry stars in play by Oscar Wilde, *Lady Windemere's Fan*, at London's St. James's Theatre

can Party were no friends to labor. The tariffs added profits to the owners' pocketbooks, but none of the additional wealth trickled down to the laborers who had made it possible. In November, labor had its say and voted to return Grover Cleveland to the presidency.

Caroline Harrison died shortly before the election. After losing the presidency, Harrison wrote, with some relief, to a friend, "Indeed after the heavy blow the death of my wife dealt me, I do not think I could have stood the strain a re-election would have brought."[10]

QUEEN LILIUOKALANI (1838–1917) ★ The last reigning monarch of Hawaii, Queen Liliuokalani, became queen in 1891 and, buckling to American business interests, agreed to the "bayonet constitution," which limited her power. When the McKinley Tariff began hurting sugar exports, American businessmen decided the time had come for the annexation of Hawaii. Queen Liliuokalani attempted to retain her power with a new constitution, but was deposed in January 1894 by American troops. Six months later, the Republic of Hawaii was created with American businessman Sanford Dole as its president. The queen remained in Hawaii and died there of a stroke in 1917.

RETIREMENT

The former president returned to Indianapolis and his law practice. He also found himself in demand as a speaker and writer, which required that he travel widely. In 1896, Harrison shocked his children by remarrying. His bride was a niece of Carrie Harrison and twenty-five years his junior. They had a daughter, who was younger than any of his grandchildren.

The Republican Party attempted to coax Harrison to run again for the presidency in 1896, but he refused and campaigned for William McKinley instead. He also worked as counsel on a boundary dispute between Venezuela and British Guiana. After the arbitration in Paris, he enjoyed a tour of the continent before returning home.

In March 1901, Benjamin Harrison became ill with influenza, which did not respond to treatment and worsened into pneumonia. He died on March 13 at the age of sixty-seven. He was buried next to Carrie Harrison at Crown Hill Cemetery in Indianapolis. His second wife survived him by nearly fifty years.

DID YOU KNOW?

During one thirty-day period, Harrison gave one hundred and forty different speeches.

ENDNOTES

1 Sievers, Harry J. *Benjamin Harrison*, Chicago: Henry Regency Company, 1952, p. 11.

2 Ibid, p. 183.

3 Ibid, p. 255.

4 Ibid., p. 9.

5 Sievers, Harry J. *Benjamin Harrison: Hoosier President*, Indianapolis, Indiana: The Bobbs-Merrill Company, Inc., 1968, p. 75.

6 Ibid, p. 80.

7 Ibid.

8 Socolofsky, Homer E. and Allan B. Spetter, *The Presidency of Benjamin Harrison*, Lawrence: University Press of Kansas, 1987, p. 107.

9 Ibid, p. 194.

10 Ibid, p. 250.

APR 15: Creation of General Electric Company

MAY 5: Congress passes a ten-year extension for Chinese Exclusion laws

JUN: Homestead Steel strike begins in Pennsylvania

AUG 4: Lizzie Borden's father and stepmother are found dead; each had been struck multiple times with a hatchet

NOV 8: Former president Grover Cleveland elected to return to the presidency, defeating incumbent Benjamin Harrison

MAR 31: World's first fingerprinting bureau founded in Buenos Aires

JUN 11: World's first film studio, Limelight Department, opens in Melbourne, Australia

OCT 31: Arthur Conan Doyle publishes *The Adventures of Sherlock Holmes*

DEC 17: In St. Petersburg, Russia, *The Nutcracker Ballet* premieres

William McKinley

★ ★ ★ TWENTY-FIFTH PRESIDENT ★ ★ ★

LIFE SPAN
- Born: January 29, 1843, in Niles, Ohio
- Died: September 14, 1901, in Buffalo, New York

NICKNAME
- Idol of Ohio

RELIGION
- Methodist

HIGHER EDUCATION
- Allegheny College, 1860 (did not graduate)
- Albany Law School, 1866–1867 (did not graduate)

PROFESSION
- Lawyer

MILITARY SERVICE
- Civil War: enlisted as a private in the Twenty-third Ohio Volunteer Infantry in June 1861 and rose to brevet major when he was discharged in July 1865

FAMILY
- Father: **William McKinley Sr.** (1807–1892)
- Mother: **Nancy Allison McKinley** (1809–1897)
- Wife: **Ida Saxton McKinley** (1847–1907); wed on January 25, 1871, in Canton, Ohio
- Children: **Katherine** (1871–1875); **Ida** (1873)

POLITICAL LIFE
- Stark County, Ohio, prosecutor (1869–1871)
- US representative (1877–1883, 1885–1891)
- Governor of Ohio (1892–1896)

PRESIDENCY
- Two terms: March 4, 1897–September 14, 1901
- Republican
- Reason for leaving office: assassinated
- Vice presidents: **Garret Augustus Hobart** (1897–1899), died in office; **Theodore Roosevelt** (March–September 1901)

ELECTION OF 1896
- Electoral vote: **McKinley** 271; **William Jennings Bryan** 176
- Popular vote: **McKinley** 7,112,138; **Bryan** 6,508,172

ELECTION OF 1900
- Electoral vote: **McKinley** 292; **Bryan** 155
- Popular vote: **McKinley** 7,228,864; **Bryan** 6,371,932

CABINET
★★★★★★★★★★

SECRETARY OF STATE
John Sherman (1897–1898)

John M. Hay (1898–1901)

SECRETARY OF THE TREASURY
Lyman J. Gage (1897–1901)

SECRETARY OF WAR
Russell A. Alger (1897–1899)

Elihu Root (1899–1901)

ATTORNEY GENERAL
Joseph McKenna (1897–1898)

John W. Griggs (1898–1901)

Philander C. Knox (1901)

SECRETARY OF THE NAVY
John D. Long (1897–1901)

POSTMASTER GENERAL
James A. Gary (1897–1898)

Charles Emory Smith (1898–1901)

SECRETARY OF THE INTERIOR
Cornelius N. Bliss (1897–1898)

Ethan A. Hitchcock (1898–1901)

SECRETARY OF AGRICULTURE
James Wilson (1897–1901)

Although overshadowed in history by his ebullient successor, William McKinley's legacy to Theodore Roosevelt was thrusting the United States into the world-power arena by sending the country to fight in "this splendid little war."

EARLY YEARS

William McKinley Jr. was born to William and Nancy Allison McKinley of Niles, Ohio, on January 29, 1843. There his father and grandfather operated a small pig-iron foundry. William's mother wanted her children to use their minds rather than their hands, so the family moved to the nearby town of Poland, Ohio, where William enrolled in a private seminary. There he did well and was even required to sit at the back, allowing those who were slower to absorb the lessons to sit close to the front.

The McKinley family prized reading and spent an hour each night taking turns reading aloud from periodicals such as *Harper's Weekly* or the *New York Weekly Tribune*. Nancy McKinley wanted her son to become a Methodist minister. He already excelled in public speaking and had developed a serious interest in religion. Events transpired, however, to lead young McKinley toward a different path.

In 1860, young McKinley left Ohio to attend college in nearby Meadville, Pennsylvania. He spent only one term at Allegheny College before being forced to leave because of exhaustion and possible depression. When he later desired to return, the family was unable to help, as their finances had suffered as a result of the financial Panic of 1857. After returning home, he taught school and worked at the local post office. Then in June 1861, President Lincoln's plea for federal troops prompted the eighteen-year-old to enlist in the 23rd Ohio Volunteer Infantry.

CIVIL WAR

Private McKinley spent his early enlistment in West Virginia and within a year rose in rank to quartermaster sergeant. At Antietam, McKinley drove a wagon through Confederate fire to bring supplies to isolated units. This act of heroism was noticed by his regimental commander and future president Rutherford B. Hayes, who promoted him to lieutenant. McKinley was soon made brigade quartermaster. McKinley's bravery at Kernstown won him further promotion to captain, and he began serving with Philip Sheridan's Army of the Shenandoah. Twenty-two-year-old McKinley ended the war as a brevet major. He was offered a peacetime lieutenancy but declined it, deciding to study law instead.

PUBLIC CAREER BEGINS

William McKinley Jr. passed the bar in 1867 and became a successful attorney. One who observed his legal skills noted, "He had the faculty of putting things so that the jury could easily comprehend and follow his arguments. He . . . appealed to their judgment and understanding, rather than to passion and prejudice."[1] These skills would soon help him climb the political ladder. The young lawyer wasted no time in rejoining his former regimental commander in Republican Party politics. In 1867, he campaigned for Hayes's gubernatorial campaign. Two years later, McKinley won his first political office—prosecutor of Stark County, Ohio.

He failed to win his reelection bid in 1871, but did succeed in winning the hand of Ida Saxton. While his law practice prospered, his family life turned tragic. William and Ida welcomed a daughter, Katie, in December 1871, and another daughter, Ida, early in 1873. Sadly, the infant

NATIONAL EVENTS

- Library of Congress building completed
- **FEB 17:** Parent Teachers Association (PTA) founded
- **MAR 4:** William McKinley inaugurated president
- **APR 19:** First Boston Marathon; won by John McDermott in 2:55:10
- **APR 27:** Grant's tomb is dedicated in New York City
- **JUN 1:** Beginning of miners' strike
- **JUL 17:** Klondike Gold Rush begins

1897

WORLD EVENTS

- English physicist J.J. Thompson discovers electrons
- France allows women to study at the Ecole des Beaux-Arts
- **FEB 10:** Freedom of religion proclaimed in Madagascar
- **MAR:** Emilio Aguinaldo becomes president of the Philippines
- **MAY 18:** Bram Stoker's book *Dracula* is published

only lived five months, and her mother suffered from convulsions and seizures, possibly epileptic, following the baby's traumatic delivery. The condition would afflict Ida McKinley for the rest of her life. She worried and fretted that their daughter Katie would die. In 1875, her fears were realized when Katie succumbed to typhoid fever. The McKinleys never had any other children, but William McKinley spent the rest of his life doting on his fragile wife.

Grabbing on to his former commander's coattails, McKinley won his first national office in 1876 when he became a congressman from Ohio. He served three terms, and then lost by eight votes in 1882. Still, two years later he returned to Congress, determined to push forward an agenda of protectionism. Although giving vocal support to sound currency, he sided with silver interests and voted for both the Bland-Allison Act and the Sherman Silver Purchase Act. Both of these required the purchase of silver, which then inflated the currency, helping debtors—mainly farmers—pay off their debts more easily. Congressman McKinley supported the Sherman Silver Purchase Act of 1890 in exchange for backing his upcoming tariff bill.

McKinley's personal goal had long been to curb the affordability of cheap foreign imports by adding tariffs to those products. As the new chairman of the House Ways and Means Committee, he worked tirelessly to pass the highest protectionist tariff up to that time. The average tariff now became a whopping 48 percent and drove prices to new highs. Undoubtedly his father's small furnace works in Niles, Ohio, colored his desire to protect American business from what many perceived as unfair foreign competition. Unfortunately, the tariff's "boomerang" effect resulted in excessively high prices and defeats at the polls for Republicans in the 1890 elections. McKinley was no exception and lost his seat to Ohio's lieutenant governor. Undaunted by this setback, he merely moved forward in a different direction and handily won the governorship of Ohio.

MCKINLEY TARIFF OF 1890 ★ As an Ohio congressman, McKinley sponsored this protectionist bill, which raised tariffs to 48 percent, setting a new record. The tariff went into effect one month before mid-term congressional elections, and unhappy American consumers voted out the Republicans, including McKinley. The tariff was lowered to 41 percent three years later with the Wilson-Gorman Tariff.

Citizens of Columbus marveled at two touching scenes McKinley performed daily. Every morning, when he left his hotel suite to walk across the street to his office, he stopped and bowed to the window where Ida sat. Then at 3 p.m. every afternoon, he stopped to wave out his office window to his beloved wife. Many remarked upon his devotion, which continued unfailingly until his death. This affection was reciprocated by the nearly bedridden woman who cast her eyes upon her husband's portrait as her last sight before she went to sleep at night and her first upon waking.

GOVERNOR MCKINLEY

During McKinley's two terms as governor, his primary focus was keeping the lid on labor disputes and unrest. At times he was moved to call out the National Guard to help in this endeavor. He tried to balance this stance by supporting legislation that limited employers' power over unions.

DID YOU KNOW?

McKinley usually wore a red carnation in his buttonhole for good luck.

JUL 24: Dingley Tariff Act passes, raising tariff rates over 50 percent

SEP 21: Francis P. Church's *New York Evening Sun* editorial "Yes, Virginia, there is a Santa Claus" is published

Four biscuit companies combine to form National Biscuit Company (Nabisco)

FEB 15: US battleship *Maine* explodes in Havana harbor

FEB 25: Asst. Sect. of the Navy Roosevelt cables

Admiral Dewey to take the Pacific fleet to Hong Kong in preparation to attack the Philippines

1898

JUN 12: Swiss army knife patented by Swiss inventor Karl Elsener

JUN 22: Queen Victoria celebrates her diamond jubilee

Henry James writes *The Turn of the Screw*

H.G. Wells publishes *The War of the Worlds*

First official game reserve, Sabi, designated in South Africa

DID YOU KNOW?

McKinley was the first president to ride in an automobile.

While monitoring his state, McKinley also kept a watchful eye on the national scene. Though he was an early Republican presidential nominee in 1892, Ohio's governor stood aside for Benjamin Harrison and worked in his campaign. This support was reciprocated four years later when William McKinley became the 1896 Republican presidential candidate against William Jennings Bryan, the thirty-six-year-old lawyer from Nebraska.

CAMPAIGN OF 1896

The centerpiece of the presidential campaign was the currency issue. After dazzling the audience at the Democratic national convention with his "Cross of Gold" speech, Bryan immediately became the spokesman for the free-silver movement. While Bryan launched a blitzkrieg campaign covering nearly twenty thousand miles in three months, McKinley retired to his home in Canton and spoke only a few times to groups gathered at his front porch. Instead, he allowed vocal supporters to do the bulk of his campaigning while he stayed home and looked after Ida.

YELLOW JOURNALISM ★ The sensational journalism practiced by newspapers of the late nineteenth and early twentieth centuries was nicknamed "yellow journalism" after a cartoon, "The Yellow Kid," that was printed in yellow ink. The leading publishers, Joseph Pulitzer (*New York World*) and William Randolph Hearst (*New York Journal*), were in a race to sell papers and encouraged their reporters to write stories that were extremely biased, rather than objective news. The papers were largely responsible for insisting on the involvement of the United States in the war against Spain.

Helping in this effort were newspaper editors and Republican stalwarts. They melded into one, touting Bryan as a socialist who would destroy the country with his reckless fiscal policy of coining more silver. McKinley himself insisted workers' wages would be eaten away in higher inflation and foreign investors would refuse to continue investing in American businesses.

McKinley's message was received by the voters, and he won 51 percent of the popular vote to Bryan's 47 percent.

PRESIDENT MCKINLEY

On March 2, 1897, President Grover Cleveland hosted President-elect William McKinley to a quiet dinner at the White House. There the two men discussed the country's concerns, which would direct the new president's attention when he took office two days later. Cleveland warned of the expansionist-minded Congress. Many there seemed eager to pull Cuba away from Spain and were being aided in this quest by American consul-general Fitzhugh Lee.

Two days later, William McKinley stood on the steps of the capitol and took the oath of office while his mother and wife looked on. He proclaimed, "We want no wars of conquest; we must avoid the temptation of territorial aggression. War should never be entered upon until every agency of peace has failed; peace is preferable to war in almost every contingency." Ironically, war would become the cornerstone of his presidency—a fight to gain a territory that had no interest in becoming an American possession.

WARTIME PRESIDENT

For years, Spain had waged war against Cuban rebels. Growing weary of the fight, Spain exerted

NATIONAL EVENTS

APR 19: Congress recognizes Cuban independence

APR 25: US declares war on Spain

MAY 1: Battle of Manila Bay between American and Spanish navies

JUL 1: Battle of San Juan (Kettle) Hill makes Theodore Roosevelt a national hero as he leads his group of volunteers, the "Rough Riders"

JUL 7: US annexes Hawaiian islands

JUL 25: US invades Puerto Rico

WORLD EVENTS

FEB 12: First fatality due to an automobile accident, Henry Lindfield dies in England

FEB 23: Emile Zola imprisoned in France for publishing "J'Accuse," a letter accusing the French government of anti-Semitism

MAY 5: Bava Beccaris Massacre in Milan—workers strike and demonstrate against the government

MAY 28: First photographs taken of the Shroud of Turin

JUL 2: Treaty signed between Britain and China for Hong Kong to be leased to the British for 99 years

more pressure and corralled many civilians into concentration camps. Although Spanish authorities appeared to bow under international pressure and removed the harsh commander, General Valeriano Weyler, other brutal realities remained. The countryside exhibited signs of scorched earth with no food or crops remaining. McKinley protested Spain's treatment of the Cuban people, but hesitated to volunteer American support. Opposing the president's efforts to keep peace were the pro-war newspapers (known as the "yellow press") and the war-mongering Congress. Both groups continually pounded the drumbeat of war.

The president decided to take the precaution of stationing the USS *Maine* off the shore of Havana, ready in case needed to evacuate American citizens. Already Congress had appropriated aid for those Americans in Cuba. The president personally donated five thousand dollars to a relief effort in late December 1897.

Events soon forced McKinley to take the action he had hoped to avoid. Early in February 1898, the *New York Journal*, flagship of William Randolph Hearst's publishing empire, printed a letter from Enrique Dupuy de Lôme, Spain's minister to the United States. In this stolen letter, de Lôme criticized the president and referred to him as "weak and a bidder for the admiration of the crowd, besides being a would-be politician who tries to leave a door open behind himself while keeping on good terms with the jingoes [pro-war faction] of his party." Such harsh criticism by an already unpopular country bolstered anti-Spanish feelings.

Then the powder keg burst open when the USS *Maine* exploded on the night of February 15, killing three-fourths of its 350-man crew. Americans immediately blamed the Spanish and their mines in Havana harbor. However, one American remained unconvinced—President McKinley. He attempted to tune out the ever-growing cry "Remember the *Maine*! To Hell with Spain!" (A congressional investigation eighty years later concluded that the explosion was most likely internal.)

McKinley pondered this situation for weeks. He wrote to Leonard Wood, "I shall never get into a war unless I am sure that God and man approve. I have been through one war; I have seen the dead piled up; and I do not want to see another."[2] The country, newspapers, and more importantly, Congress, clamored for war against Spain. The president still publicly vacillated while privately working the diplomatic channels. Not desiring to worsen the situation by angering other European nations, McKinley strove to ensure they understood America's position. Meanwhile, military preparations for a possible war with Spain proceeded.

Secretary of War Russell Alger took the unusual step of discussing the situation with a powerful senator and asked him to tell McKinley to go to war. Alger's main concern was the future of the Republican Party: "He is in danger of ruining himself and the Republican Party by standing in the way of the people's wishes. Congress will declare war in spite of him." The senator replied that the secretary should have more faith in the president for "he knows exactly what he is doing. There is no more sagacious man in the country."[3]

When negotiations floundered and the country demanded war, William McKinley wearily acquiesced and on April 11, he asked Congress to declare war on Spain. In his message, he repeatedly used the close proximity of Cuba to American shores as the primary reason for the action. "It is especially our duty, for it is right at our door."

SUPREME COURT APPOINTMENTS

★ ★ ★ ★ ★ ★ ★ ★ ★ ★

Joseph McKenna, 1898

DID YOU KNOW?

★ ★ ★ ★ ★ ★ ★ ★ ★ ★ ★

McKinley's picture was on the $500 bill from 1928 to 1946.

AUG 12: End of fighting between US and Spain

DEC 10: Treaty of Paris ends Spanish-American War; US gains Philippines, Guam, Wake Island, and Puerto Rico; Cuba granted independence

Ragtime music increases in popularity, with songs such as "Hello My Baby" and Scott Joplin's "Maple Leaf Rag"

FEB 12–14: Blizzard of 1899 leaves much of US blanketed in snow; record-breaking temperatures recorded

FEB 14: Congress approves use of voting machines

1899

SEP 10: Empress Elizabeth of Austria-Hungary is assassinated by Luigi Lucheni

DEC 26: Chemist couple Pierre and Marie Curie isolate radium

Rudyard Kipling publishes poem "The White Man's Burden" about recent US involvement in the Philippines

FEB 4: Rebellion breaks out in Philippines against US rule

FEB 7: Spanish troops leave Cuba

MAR 6: Bayer patents aspirin

STATE OF THE UNION

US POPULATION IN 1897
75,994,575

NATIONAL DEBT IN 1901
$2,143,326,934

NUMBER OF STATES IN 1901
45

He continued to justify the war by explaining America needed to protect its citizens and business interests in Cuba, as well as for humanitarian considerations for the Cuban people. He concluded with the US Naval Court of Inquiry's findings that the *Maine* had been sunk by a mine, showing "that the Spanish government cannot assure safety and security to a vessel of the American Navy in the harbor of Havana on a mission of peace, and rightfully there." Within two weeks, Congress declared war with an overwhelming vote of 310–6 in the House, but a closer 42–35 vote in the Senate. Some worried about the seemingly imperialistic tone of the war declaration, so the Teller Amendment was passed to silence those critics. This promised that the United States was only going to Cuba to pacify it, but promised to leave as soon as that was accomplished.

One government official who was practically giddy at the thought of war was Assistant Secretary of the Navy Theodore Roosevelt. When his superior was out of the office, Roosevelt had systematically sent messages to various naval commanders ordering them to prepare for war. President McKinley learned of this and canceled all the orders save one. Admiral George Dewey could steam ahead toward the Philippines. In Manila Bay on May 1, Dewey destroyed the Spanish fleet without any American losses. This event marked America's first fight in the Asian theater.

McKinley turned to the Pacific once again the following month when he told Congress that the United States needed to annex Hawaii. Comparing it to the need fifty years earlier for California, he echoed the same justification—manifest destiny.

Meanwhile, the war in Cuba lasted three months. Assistant Secretary of the Navy Roosevelt resigned his post to form his own regiment, which consisted of the elite of New York's society, as well as western cowboys. Roosevelt and his Rough Riders made the battle of San Juan Hill famous, and Theodore Roosevelt became a national hero. Other battles occurred, including the easy destruction of the Spanish fleet in Havana. During this time, President McKinley moved the commander in chief closer to the twentieth century when he had the first war room constructed in the White House. Improved communications allowed the president to easily access his commanders and the press by either telephone or telegraph.

By July, Spain had had enough of "this splendid little war," as it was dubbed by Secretary of State John Hay, and asked for peace terms. The prospect of acquiring new territories/possessions such as Cuba and Puerto Rico in the Caribbean interested the president. But he also wanted the United States to gain a foothold in the Pacific. Acquiring Guam and Hawaii were the first steps, but a territory closer to China was imperative. That territory was the Philippines.

Being closer to China was necessary for US interests. For the last half-century, European interests grew ever closer to carving up Asia much as they had already done to Africa, while American presidents insisted that China be allowed to remain whole. Fearing that increasing Japanese aggression might provoke conflict there, McKinley believed the United States needed to acquire nearby bases. The Philippines would serve such a purpose.

Taking the Philippines proved no easy task, neither there nor here at home. Immediately, Andrew Carnegie and others began an anti-imperialist movement. A showdown loomed ahead in the Senate, where the treaty would be ratified. Filipino Emilio Aguinaldo had fought the Spanish government for years and did not

DID YOU KNOW?

McKinley's pet parrot was named "Washington Post."

NATIONAL EVENTS

JUL 17: First juvenile court in US opens in Chicago

JAN 2: Secretary of State John Hay announces America's Open Door policy

MAR: First incident of bubonic plague in the US (begins in San Francisco)

MAR 3: Carnegie Steel founded by Andrew Carnegie

MAR 24: Construction of New York City subway begins

1900

WORLD EVENTS

OCT 11: Second Boer War starts in South Africa between British and Dutch

Dr. Sigmund Freud publishes *The Interpretation of Dreams*

FEB 14: World's Fair opens in Paris

FEB 27: British Labour Party formed

MAR 16: English archaeologist Sir Arthur Evans unearths ancient palace of Knossos on Crete

JUN 20: Boxer Rebellion against foreigners begins in China, will be put down by foreign troops on July 13

wish their domination to be replaced by America. Although McKinley had once considered only taking Manila, he later believed that American interests required all of the Philippines being taken. Early in February 1899, US soldiers were fired on by Aguinaldo's men. Even with this report, the treaty only passed by one vote in the Senate.

The treaty was the easy part—making it work proved much more difficult and costly in both lives and expense. For the first time, American troops attempted to wage war against a nearly unseen enemy in the jungles. The guerrilla fighters effectively frustrated American attempts to end the uprising. Knowing that the continued fighting could cost his reelection, McKinley appointed a new commander, General Arthur MacArthur (father to Douglas MacArthur of World War II and Korea fame). The following year, Aguinaldo was captured and a tense peaceful interim ensued.

Meanwhile, China faced its own problems when the Boxers (a Chinese religious society opposed to outsiders) waged war against foreigners and Christian missionaries, in particular. Concerned that such actions could prompt European powers to invade China, McKinley and his secretary of state John Hay worked quickly and issued their Open Door Policy. This policy requested the six foreign nations of Britain, France, Germany, Russia, Italy, and Japan who were already in China to allow equal trade and access to China. Surprisingly, they agreed. Then, when the same countries readied themselves to send troops and squelch the Boxer Rebellion, a second Open Door policy was initiated. This reminded Europe to preserve Chinese "territorial and administrative" integrity. Again, the response was positive. President McKinley added Americans to the foreign contingent moving into China. The rebellion was put down, and William McKinley was reelected, even though he had written in September 1899, that he was not anxious for a second term, since "I have had all the honor there is in this place and have had responsibility enough to kill any man."[4]

The campaign of 1900 was nearly a replay of the previous campaign. The same two men opposed each other. Again, William Jennings

WILLIAM JENNINGS BRYAN (1860–1925) ★ One of the most popular speakers in American history, William Jennings Bryan ran twice against McKinley for the presidency and lost. Theodore Roosevelt remarked, "By George, he would make the greatest Baptist preacher on earth." Instead of becoming a minister, Bryan became a lawyer, and in 1891, he became Nebraska's first Democratic congressman. Picking up the cause of farmers, he championed free silver. His speech proclaiming, "You shall not press down upon the brow of labor this crown of thorns; you shall not crucify them upon a cross of gold," won him the presidential nomination in 1896, making him the youngest candidate ever at the age of thirty-six. He ran then and again in 1900 unsuccessfully against McKinley; he tried once more in 1908 against Theodore Roosevelt and again lost. He later became secretary of state under President Woodrow Wilson. Bryan, though, is perhaps best known in his last role—assisting the prosecution in the case of John Scopes in 1925. Scopes was on trial for teaching evolution in his classroom. By this time, Bryan was old and ill and a poor foil to the quick-witted legal mind of Clarence Darrow. The Scopes trial emerged as one of the most famous events of the 1920s.

APR: Foraker Act passed making Puerto Rico a territory of the US

NOV 6: Willliam McKinley wins reelection over William Jennings Bryan; McKinley's vice president is Theodore Roosevelt

Booker T. Washington publishes his autobiography *Up from Slavery*

JAN 20: Spindletop oil well begins pumping in Beaumont, Texas, and soon

Texas is top oil-producing state in the US; owners start Gulf Oil Corp.

1901

JUL 19: Paris subway (Métro) begins service

JUL 29: Italy's King Umberto I is assassinated by an anarchist

Winston Churchill becomes a member of the House of Commons

JAN 1: Commonwealth of Australia created

JAN 1: Nigeria becomes British protectorate

JAN 22: Queen Victoria dies at the age of 81 and a reign of 64 years; her son Edward VII succeeds her

DINGLEY TARIFF ACT OF 1897 ★ One of McKinley's campaign pledges was to raise the tariff, so in July 1897, he called Congress into special session to enact new legislation. Maine congressman Nelson Dingley sponsored a bill that raised rates an average of 46 percent, but some were over 50 percent—the highest up to that time. During this high protectionist tariff era, US exports far outpaced imports, and the president began looking to develop reciprocal trade agreements with other nations.

Bryan attempted to make currency the main issue, but what worked in 1896 was not popular four years later. Earlier in the year, Congress had passed the Gold Standard Act, and the country was experiencing prosperity. When Bryan tried to argue otherwise, his words fell on deaf ears. The country overwhelmingly reelected William McKinley and his new vice president and war hero Theodore Roosevelt.

The opening months of 1901 found Congress passing the Platt Amendment, which authorized the use of American forces if necessary in Cuba. The country itself was now governed by a regime friendly to US interests. Farther south, McKinley and Secretary Hay began plans for building a canal that would cross either Nicaragua or Panama.

America's interests seemed to span the globe, as its products found markets across the continents. Fittingly, a Pan-American Exposition opened in September. President McKinley traveled to Buffalo, New York, to visit. McKinley arrived and was enthusiastically received. He reiterated his position that America needed more markets and trade reciprocity. Building an isthmian canal would help further this, as would a new merchant marine. The twentieth century was just beginning, and all signs pointed toward it being America's century, with McKinley at the helm.

Sadly, none of these ideas would be realized by William McKinley. The following day, September 6, 1901, while greeting guests to the exposition, he extended his hand to a man who held a gun in his hand concealed with a handkerchief. Self-proclaimed anarchist Leon Czolgosz fired twice directly into the president. McKinley lingered for eight days before finally succumbing to his wounds in the chest and stomach. Again, his concern was for Ida as he begged, "My wife—be careful how you tell her. Be careful!"[5] Although two operations seemed successful, gangrene set in, and the doctors agreed that the president's prognosis was fatal.

On September 14, 1901, President William McKinley died. His final words were "Goodbye. Goodbye to all. It is God's will. His will, not ours, be done."[6] Six weeks later, his assassin died in New York's electric chair after insisting he had killed the president because "he was the enemy of the people—the good working people. I am not sorry for the crime."[7]

President William McKinley is buried in Canton, Ohio, at the McKinley National Memorial. Mrs. McKinley was too distraught to attend her husband's funeral. She passed the rest of her days at their Canton home and died there on May 26, 1907. She was buried next to her beloved husband.

After winning his first presidential election, McKinley was asked by a fellow veteran of his unit what to call him now. Certainly the man had served a variety of offices—governor, congressman, and then president. McKinley replied, "Call me Major. I earned that. I am not so sure of the rest."[8]

NATIONAL EVENTS	**MAR 2:** Financier J.P. Morgan creates US Steel, the world's first billion-dollar corporation	**MAR 2:** Platt Amendment passed by Congress granting US right to take military action in Cuba if needed	**MAR 4:** President McKinley sworn in for his second term	**MAY 23:** American forces in the Philippines capture rebel leader Emilio Aguinaldo	**JUN 12:** Cuba becomes US protectorate
WORLD EVENTS	**MAR 6:** An assassin attempts to kill Wilhelm II of Germany in Bremen	**MAR 17:** A sensation is caused in Paris when 71 of Vincent van Gogh's paintings go on display in Paris, 11 years after his death	**MAR 31:** British Census accounts for 32 million people and 6 million households	**MAY 5:** Official end of the Castle War of Yucatan	**MAY 9:** Australia opens its first parliament in Melbourne

> *That's all a man can hope for during his lifetime—to set an example—and when he is dead, to be an inspiration for history.*
>
> —*William McKinley*

DID YOU KNOW?

McKinley was the first president to campaign by telephone.

ENDNOTES

1 Charles S. Olcott, *The Life of William McKinley*, vol. I, Boston, Houghton Mifflin & Co., 1916, p. 62.

2 Lewis L. Gould, *The Presidency of William McKinley*, Lawrence, KS: Regents Press of Kansas, 1980, p. 78.

3 Olcott, vol. II, p. 28.

4 Ibid, pp. 213–214.

5 William A. DeGregorio, *The Complete Book of US Presidents*, New York: Gramercy, 2005, p. 367.

6 Olcott, p. 324.

7 John Mason Potter, *Plots against the Presidents*, New York: Astor-Honor, 1968, p. 172.

8 William H. Armstrong, *Major McKinley: William McKinley and the Civil War*, Kent, Ohio: Kent University Press, 2000, p. 103.

JUL: Orville and Wilbur Wright test their first glider at Kitty Hawk, North Carolina

SEP 2: Vice President Roosevelt uses the phrase "Speak softly and carry a big stick"

SEP 6: President McKinley is shot by Polish-born anarchist Leon Czolgosz at Pan-American Exposition in Buffalo, New York

SEP 14: President McKinley dies from complications from his wound (after three presidential assassinations in 36 years, the Secret Service is now tasked with guarding the president)

MAY 25: Club Atlético River Plate discovered in Argentina

JUN 2: Katsura Taro becomes Prime Minister of Japan

SEP 7: Peace accord signed, formally ending Boxer Rebellion

SEP 26: Britain annexes Africa's Gold Coast (Ghana)

DEC 10: First Nobel Prizes awarded in Stockholm

Theodore Roosevelt

★ ★ ★ TWENTY-SIXTH PRESIDENT ★ ★ ★

LIFE SPAN
- Born: October 27, 1858, in New York City
- Died: January 6, 1919, in Oyster Bay, New York

NICKNAMES
- Teddy, TR, Trust Buster

RELIGION
- Dutch Reformed

HIGHER EDUCATION
- Harvard College, 1880

PROFESSION
- Lawyer, author, public official

MILITARY SERVICE
- Spanish-American War, commanded First US Volunteer Cavalry Regiment
- "Rough Riders" from May to September 1898; started as a lieutenant colonel and rose to colonel

FAMILY
- Father: **Theodore Roosevelt Sr.** (1831–1878)
- Mother: **Martha "Mittie" Bulloch Roosevelt** (1834–1884)
- Wife: **Alice Hathaway Lee Roosevelt** (1861–1884); wed October 27, 1880, in Brookline, Massachusetts
- Child: **Alice** (1884–1980)
- Second wife: **Edith Carow Roosevelt** (1861–1948); wed December 2, 1886, in London, England
- Children: **Theodore** (1887–1944); **Kermit** (1889–1943); **Ethel Carow** (1891–1977); **Archibald Bulloch** (1894–1979); **Quentin** (1897–1918)

POLITICAL LIFE
- New York state assemblyman (1882–1884)
- US Civil Service Commission (1889–1895)
- New York City Police Board commissioner (1895–1897)
- Assistant secretary of the Navy (1897–1898)
- Governor of New York (1898–1900)
- Vice president (March–September 1901)

PRESIDENCY
- Two terms: September 14, 1901–March 4, 1909 (succeeded to presidency upon **McKinley's** death and completed that term)
- Republican
- Reason for leaving office: declined third term
- Vice president: **Charles W. Fairbanks** (1905–1909)

ELECTION OF 1904
- Electoral vote: **Roosevelt** 336; **Alton B. Parker** 140
- Popular vote: **Roosevelt** 7,630,457; **Parker** 5,083,880

CABINET

SECRETARY OF STATE
John M. Hay (1901–1905); died in office
Elihu Root (1905–1909)

SECRETARY OF THE TREASURY
Lyman J. Gage (1901–1902)
Leslie M Shaw (1902–1907)
George B. Cortelyou (1907–1909)

SECRETARY OF WAR
Elihu Root (1901–1904)
William H. Taft (1904–1908)
Luke E. Wright (1908–1909)

ATTORNEY GENERAL
Philander C. Knox (1901–1904)
William H. Moody (1904–1906)
Charles J. Bonaparte (1906–1909)

SECRETARY OF THE NAVY
John D. Long (1901–1902)
William H. Moody (1902–1904)
Paul Morton (1904–1905)
Charles J. Bonaparte (1905–1906)
Victor H. Metcalf (1906–1908)
Truman H. Newberry (1908–1909)

A "bully" time (popular vernacular then that meant wonderful, first-rate) is precisely what Theodore Roosevelt had while in the White House. No other president possessed as much zest and pure fondness for the job. For Roosevelt, *carpe diem* was a dictum for life in and out of the presidency.

EARLY LIFE

The first Roosevelts arrived in the Dutch town of New Amsterdam in the 1600s, and their prosperity grew as the town evolved into New York City. The future president's grandfather invested heavily in real estate in Manhattan, which paid dividends for himself and his descendants. His son Theodore, Senior, had heard of a fine Georgia family, the Bullochs, who were known for both their hospitality at their plantation of Roswell as well as their attractive daughters. So Theodore journeyed to Georgia in 1850, met the Bullochs, and was especially enchanted by attractive fifteen-year-old Mittie. They fell in love, but were forced to spend the next three years apart and continued their courtship by mail. Then on December 22, 1853, they married and moved to a fashionable house on Twentieth Street given to them by his father, Cornelius Roosevelt.

There on October 27, 1858, Mittie gave birth to her second child and first son, whom they named Theodore but nicknamed Teedie. He and his older sister Anna, known as Bamie, grew close, and were joined by two more siblings—Elliott and Corinne. At the tender age of ten months, Teedie's maternal grandmother proudly pronounced him "one of the brightest little fellows I ever knew."[1] Although he was a healthy baby, by the time he was a toddler of three, he had developed a serious asthmatic condition, causing his parents to walk the floor with him at night and sometimes take him for buggy rides at high speeds through the city to encourage air into Teedie's lungs. As he grew older, the lad cautioned his father not to punish him for transgressions lest it bring on an attack. Small wonder that his mother wrote of Teedie, he is "brimming full of mischief and has to be watched all the time."[2]

The Roosevelt household viewed the Civil War with more immediate concern than many of their high-class neighbors since Mittie's relatives lived in Georgia, and many of them, including her brothers, were fighting for the Confederacy; in fact, one brother became a famed blockade runner. Theodore Sr. wanted to enlist in the Union Army, but Mittie begged him not to, fearful that one day he could be meeting a brother-in-law in battle. Instead, he engaged a substitute (the conscription laws permitted men with means to hire another man to fight in their place), but the stigma never left him (or his eldest son). In April 1865, Teedie and Elliott stood at their window to watch the funeral procession bearing the coffin of the assassinated president Lincoln. The Roosevelt home always hosted a steady stream of visitors, and this solemn occasion was no exception. Edith Carow, daughter of a family friend and frequent visitor to the Roosevelts, was with them that day. Although she was Corinne's age, she became best friends with Teedie, and when the family traveled to Europe four years later, the sight of Edith's picture stirred Teedie's homesickness like no other.

On first seeing Europe, at the age of ten, Teedie was unimpressed. His family toured the usual sights, from Great Britain to Germany and then south to Italy. There the boy described in his diary a situation in which his father made a game of feeding starving Italian women and children pieces of cake and made them open their mouths like little birds practically begging for the morsels.

NATIONAL EVENTS

Macy's begins construction of its new store in Herald Square

First Studebaker car appears

Animal crackers introduced

Crayola crayons produced by Edward Binney and C. Herald Smith

Muckraker Ida Tarbell writes exposé *History of Standard Oil Company*

West Wing added to the White House

Owen Wister publishes *The Virginian*

Helen Keller publishes *The Story of My Life*

1902

WORLD EVENTS

Joseph Conrad publishes *Heart of Darkness*

Arthur Conan Doyle publishes *Hound of the Baskervilles*

Beatrix Potter publishes the *Tale of Peter Rabbit*

Fish and chips shops open

German Robert Bosch invents the spark plug

Anglo-Japanese Alliance signed

To receive more they had to "give three cheers for the U.S.A."[3] The Roosevelt family apparently saw nothing wrong in the degrading activity, and son Teedie thought it great fun. But the problem of his asthma remained, and his father's solution was to force the boy to smoke cigars, which made him sick but somehow relieved some of the debilitating symptoms of the disorder. After visiting France, the family returned to America, where Teedie continued to fight his ongoing battle with poor health.

Determined that his son would not grow up a weakling, Theodore Sr. added a gym to the back of the house, and instructed Teedie, "You have the mind but not the body, and without the help of the body the mind cannot go as far as it should. You must make your body. It is hard drudgery to make one's body but I know you will do it."[4] Young Theodore would follow his father's advice to the letter and in time, his asthmatic condition improved.

Teedie lived for the summers on Long Island Sound at Oyster Bay, where he indulged his growing fascination with all things natural. He gathered specimens and fed newborn squirrels, but Mittie drew the line when his collection of dead mice was found in the icebox, and she ordered them to be disposed of, causing her son to mourn "the loss to science."[5] But he continued to hike the mountains, scouting for any creature to add to his collection. He donated part of his collection, including a bat, turtle, and red squirrel skull, to the new American Museum of Natural History, where his father was on the board.

Young Roosevelt learned the art of taxidermy from the taxidermist for John James Audubon, but his world truly transformed when he was fourteen years old. At that age, he was given a 12-gauge shotgun by his father and a pair of spectacles, which allowed him to see more clearly the beauty of the world around him. Another overseas trip soon followed, this time to cruise the Nile, then northward through the Continent. When the family returned, they moved into a more luxurious home uptown on Fifty-Seventh Street, two blocks from Central Park. Their summers were still spent on Oyster Bay, Long Island, where they rented a house but talked of building their own. The Roosevelt family was an active one, with horseback riding, sailing, rowing, and hours spent meandering through the nearby woods. In addition, Theodore Sr. would direct the children in theatrical productions. During the staid Victorian era, the Roosevelts were, according to a friend of the family, "without inhibitions to an unusual degree," and stood out for their "extraordinary vitality."[6]

While the oldest Roosevelt son excelled in the outdoors, knew French and German, and read voraciously, he still lacked the prerequisite subjects to pass Harvard's entrance exam, so a tutor was engaged to coach Teedie for the next two years. Mathematics was the focus of his lessons, but there was still time for his workouts and his naturalist activities. Brother Elliott, however, had developed his own physical problems of unknown origin and was sent to Texas, where its clean air and vigorous lifestyle was meant to cure him of any and all ills.

HARVARD

In September 1876, Theodore Sr. escorted his eldest son to catch the train to Cambridge, telling the young man, "Take care of your morals first, your health next, and finally your studies."[7] Teedie lived off campus, and in his first two years was not particularly popular. He was considered a bit of an oddity at Harvard. Of average height and slight in build, his most noticeable features were his blue eyes, piercing from behind his spectacles.

CABINET
★★★★★★★★★★

(continued)

POSTMASTER GENERAL

Charles E. Smith (1901–1902)

Henry C. Payne (1902–1904); died in office

Robert J. Wynne (1904–1905)

George B. Cortelyou (1905–1907)

George von L. Meyer (1907–1909)

SECRETARY OF THE INTERIOR

Ethan A. Hitchcock (1901–1907)

James R. Garfield (1907–1909)

SECRETARY OF AGRICULTURE

James Wilson (1901–1913)

SECRETARY OF COMMERCE AND LABOR

George B. Cortelyou (1903–1904), first to serve in this new post

Victor H. Metcalf (1904–1906)

Oscar S. Straus (1906–1909)

JAN 1: First Rose Bowl game played between Michigan and Stanford; Michigan wins 49–0

MAR 4: American Automobile Association (AAA) founded

APR 2: First American movie theater opens in Los Angeles, California

APR 14: James Cash Penney opens his first store in Kemmerer, Wyoming

MAY 12: United Mine Workers initiate a five-month strike

JAN 24: Virgin Islands sold to US by Denmark

MAY 10: Portugal declares bankruptcy, mainly due to fighting rebellion in Angola

MAY 20: Cuba becomes independent

AUG 9: Coronation of King Edward VII

DEC 9: British and German ships blockade Venezuelan ports as punishment for that country's refusal to pay its debts

DID YOU KNOW?

Roosevelt was the first president to ride in an airplane and a submarine.

Roosevelt was also known for his insistence on running rather than walking, and his insatiable appetite for debate, including in the classroom, where one professor admonished him, "Now look here, Roosevelt, let me talk! I'm running this course!"[8]

In December 1877, the family experienced the devastating loss of Theodore Sr. from stomach cancer. When Teedie returned to Harvard, he was sometimes overwhelmed with grief, remembering "the most wise and loving father that ever lived: I owe everything to him."[9]

His last years at Harvard saw Theodore grow in esteem and popularity among his fellow classmates. He joined the Hasty Pudding, the Porcellian (an ultra-exclusive social club that recruits a small number each year for membership), the Art Club and Rifle Club; he was an editor for the *Advocate*, and qualified for Phi Beta Kappa. When he went out on the town, he dressed fashionably and kept a horse stabled nearby with a cart to drive about. Theodore continued his physical fitness regimen and boxed for Harvard, but avoided any team sports because of his poor eyesight.

During his junior year, Theodore fell in love with a young lady he met at Oyster Bay. Alice Lee lived in Boston, so she and her suitor spent many hours enjoying long walks and attending Harvard functions. He boasted to one of his friends, "See that girl? I am going to marry her. She won't have me, but I am going to have *her*!"[10] The lovely young lady was not without other suitors, but she agreed to Theodore's marriage proposal.

The year 1880 was a whirlwind for Theodore, who graduated in June, traveled west for a hunting trip with his brother, and then, on his twenty-second birthday, married Alice. Once settled as a married man, he enrolled at the Columbia School of Law, but the more he learned, the less he liked it. He completed his first book, *Naval War of 1812*, but his future remained uncertain, until he decided to embark on a career in politics.

POLITICAL BEGINNING

At the age of twenty-three, Theodore Roosevelt won his first political office when he was elected to represent the Twenty-first District as an assemblyman in Albany. There Roosevelt quickly earned a name for himself by standing against railroad mogul Jay Gould, who owned the Manhattan Elevated Railroad as well as Missouri Pacific Railroad, Western Union, and the *New York World*. Gould's wealth and connections could easily derail a young politician's promising career. Undaunted, Roosevelt attempted to block a bill that would rebate one-third of taxes paid by the elevated trains back to Gould. Although unsuccessful in stopping its passage in the assembly, Theodore caused such an uproar that the governor vetoed it. Then Roosevelt launched an investigation of a judge who was reportedly in Gould's pocket, and gleefully wrote to his wife, "I have drawn blood."[11] Gould retaliated by hiring detectives to sniff out Roosevelt's dirty laundry, but they could find none. Thrilled by the reformer's refreshing sense of honesty and fair play, Roosevelt's constituents reelected him for two more terms.

In the summer of 1883, Theodore decided to go west again for hunting; this time he trekked to a town called Little Missouri in the Dakota Territory. Here his health improved, and he decided to buy cattle and build a ranch in the Badlands. He returned to New York, thrilled by his new acquisition and overjoyed by news that his beloved wife Alice was expecting a baby. A baby girl was born on February 12, 1884. Roosevelt was in Albany, and after receiving the news by telegram, made plans to return home. Earlier, he had been

NATIONAL EVENTS

JUN 28: US acquires rights from France to buy the Panama Canal

JUL 4: President Roosevelt declares Philippines rebellion to be officially over

AUG 12: Cyrus McCormick Jr. founds International Harvester

AUG 22: President Roosevelt becomes first president to ride in a car

Mary Mallon of New York earns nickname "Typhoid Mary" for passing on the disease as a food handler

1903

WORLD EVENTS

DEC 31: Antarctic explorers Robert Scott, Ernest Shackelton, and Edward Wilson reach the furthest southern point so far by man (82°17'S)

German coffee merchant develops a decaffeinated version of the drink and calls it Sanka

informed that his mother was seriously ill with typhoid; then a second telegram arrived, telling of his wife's unexpectedly poor condition. He arrived home the next day to find the two women dearest to him dying. They both died on Valentine's Day, and he marked a large black X on the date and added, "The light has gone out of my life."[12] After seeing to the funerals of both women, and giving his newborn daughter, whom he named Alice, to his sister Bamie, Theodore packed his bags and left for his new ranch in the West.

INTERIM

For two years, Roosevelt lived the life of a rancher in the Dakota Territory. He hunted and learned how to be a cowboy, but he was never particularly skilled at it. He found time to continue his writing and completed a volume on *Thomas Hart Benton* as well as one titled *Hunting Trips of a Ranchman.* Although an avid hunter, Theodore grew concerned over the dwindling numbers of large game. He lost a great deal of his herd to the drought and blizzards of the mid-1880s, which translated into a considerable financial loss for him, as well. Still, he treasured the time he spent on his Elkhorn ranch, as well as the many friends he gained there. He later declared that his time as a rancher enabled him to be elected president, for it stripped him of much of his eastern snobbishness. As president, he said, "No guests were ever more welcome at the White House than these old friends of the cattle ranches and the cow camps."[13]

By the summer of 1886, Theodore had returned to New York City and resumed his acquaintance with childhood friend Edith Carow. She journeyed to Europe, where Theodore pursued her. They wed in England in December and toured Europe for their three-month honeymoon. For the next two years, he continued writing various books, including the first volume of his proposed four-volume series *The Winning of the West.* Although he never finished all four volumes, he did complete other books, including *Gouverneur Morris* and *New York.* Theodore still yearned to resume his political career and quickly accepted the post of civil service commissioner, which was conferred upon him by President Benjamin Harrison. The annual salary of thirty-five hundred dollars was also welcome for a man with a growing family. Within ten years, five children arrived: Theodore Jr. arrived first, followed by Kermit, Ethel, Archibald, and Quentin.

POLITICAL CAREER RESUMES

Anxious to throw himself headlong into his task at the civil service, Roosevelt gladly extolled the virtues of the merit system to all, calling it "essentially democratic and essentially American . . ."[14] The young commissioner embarked on a trip to the Midwest, where he visited post offices and found examples of corruption that resulted in recommendations for firing several postmasters who were not obeying the provisions of the Pendleton Act (the law creating the civil service system). Theodore bragged, "We stirred up things well."[15] President Harrison, though, was not always eager to obey his appointee's suggestions. Roosevelt proudly admitted that even though he was not always supported, he refused to cater to any political whims, "when my duty is to enforce a law, that law is surely going to be enforced, without fear or favor."[16] Commissioner Roosevelt was proud of his civil service tenure; he transferred political offices from patronage to civil service positions, which improved the lives of more than twenty-five thousand citizens. He also improved testing and succeeded in putting women on equal terms

SUPREME COURT APPOINTMENTS
★★★★★★★★★★

Oliver Wendell Holmes, 1902

William R. Day, 1903

William H. Moody, 1906

Jack London publishes *The Call of the Wild*

First World Series played between American and National League winners (Boston defeats Pittsburgh)

Parker Brothers obtain rights to English game of table tennis and develop game of ping pong

King Gillette begins producing safety razors

Song "Sweet Adeline" introduced and sung by barbershop quartets

Henry James writes *The Ambassadors*

JAN 1: King Edward VII named Emperor of India

JAN 19: First transatlantic broadcast between England and US

FEB 13: Britain, France, and Italy sign a treaty agreeing to lift the blockade of Venezuelan ports

FEB 23: Cuba leases Guantanamo Bay to the United States "in perpetuity"

STATE OF THE UNION
★★★★★★★★★★

US POPULATION IN 1901
75,994,575

NATIONAL DEBT IN 1909
$2,639,546,241

STATE ADMITTED TO UNION
Oklahoma, November 16, 1907

NUMBER OF STATES IN 1909
46

with men by making qualifications for a job more important than connections.

The Theodore Roosevelts were often guests at the White House, and they entertained at their Washington home, as well. When he walked by the White House, Roosevelt later remembered, "My heart would beat a little faster as the thought came to me that possibly—possibly—I would some day occupy it as President."[17]

When Benjamin Harrison lost his reelection bid, President Grover Cleveland asked Roosevelt to remain as commissioner. By now, though, the young politician had grown bored with his job and cast about for a new challenge. New York reformers asked if he would consider running for mayor; while he was eager to do so, Edith vehemently objected, so he refused. Saddened by this, he escaped to the West once more, and Edith wrote to her sister-in-law Bamie of her guilt: "I never realized for a minute how much he felt over this, or that the mayoralty stood for so much to him. . . . This is a lesson that will last my life, never to give it [her opinion] for it is utterly worthless when given—worse than that in this case for it has helped to spoil some years of a life which I would have given my own for."[18] Such a division would never again occur in their thirty-three-year marriage.

In the spring of 1895, Theodore Roosevelt moved to a new post as New York City Police Commissioner with an annual salary of five thousand dollars. He now had two jobs—president of the Police Board and member of the Health Board—which he saw as serving two purposes: to oversee the Police Department and to help improve the city for its people—all of its people. Roosevelt became acquainted with the reporters whose offices were located across the street from the Police Department. He valued the friendship of one in particular—Jacob Riis, who wrote *How the Other Half Lives*, a descriptive and photographic account of New York City's slums. Theodore admired the work, calling it "an enlightenment and an inspiration."[19] Together they wandered the streets, viewing the unseemly areas of the city that Roosevelt had never before observed.

The commissioner also made surprise inspections to see if policemen were truly doing their duty, and those found lacking incurred his wrath. One reporter wrote: "When he asks a question, Mr. Roosevelt shoots at the poor trembling policeman, as he would shoot a bullet at a coyote."[20] Roosevelt spoke to various groups and congregations encouraging young men to become police officers. He allowed more women to be hired and organized a police academy. He standardized their weapons and developed squads trained in certain specialties. The reforms Roosevelt initiated in the two years he spent on the job continued long after his service was completed.

Elated by news of William McKinley's election over William Jennings Bryan, Theodore hoped for a position in the new president's government, specifically assistant secretary of the navy. He gained the nomination despite opposition by one of McKinley's key supporters, and was appointed to the position in April 1897.

RETURN TO WASHINGTON

Roosevelt had always been fascinated with naval operations and a few years prior to his appointment had struck up a friendship with leading naval authority Captain Alfred Mahan. Both men agreed that the United States must build up its navy and bases for protection as well as for power if it wanted to emerge as one of the world's

NATIONAL EVENTS

JAN: Sour Lake, Texas, produces major strike for new oil company Texaco

FEB: "Teddy" bear stuffed animals introduced

FEB 14: US Department of Commerce created as a cabinet post

FEB 19: Elkins Act passed to strengthen Interstate Commerce Act

MAR 30: US begins two-year military occupation of Dominican Republic

WORLD EVENTS

MAR 5: Turkey and Germany sign agreement to build the Constantinople-Baghdad Railway

MAY 18: Port of Burgas, Bulgaria opens

JUL: First Tour de France race

AUG 10: Paris Metro train fire, 84 perish

OCT 1: Introduction of Thermos bottle by German glassmaker

dominant countries. Roosevelt argued, "It is not economy—it is niggardly and foolish short-sightedness—to cramp our naval expenditures, while squandering money right and left."[21]

Not long after taking office, Roosevelt grew cautious, believing that war with Spain was imminent because of growing unrest in Cuba. He continued his crusade for naval expansion and was thrilled to visit the fleet in September 1897, where he witnessed the ship's weaponry in target practice. Then in February 1898, the USS *Maine* was blown up in Havana harbor by unknown causes; however, the American press insisted it was Spanish sabotage. Roosevelt hoped war would soon follow and admitted to a German friend, "I have been hoping and working ardently to bring about our interference in Cuba." The opportunity presented itself when Secretary of the Navy John Long left work one Friday afternoon, February 25. Roosevelt immediately sent a message to good friend Senator Henry Cabot Lodge requesting assistance. Ships of both the Atlantic and Pacific fleets received orders to move, and docks were placed on alert for war. Roosevelt then sent the most critical telegram, to Commodore George Dewey, commander of the Asiatic squadron in Japan:

> *Secret and confidential. Order the squadron except Monocacy to Hongkong. Keep full of coal. In the event of declaration of war Spain, your duty will be to see that the Spanish squadron does not leave the Asiatic coast, and then offensive operations in Philippine Islands. Keep Olympia until further orders.*

Once Secretary Long heard of his subordinate's actions, he wrote, "Roosevelt, in his precipitate way, has come very near causing more of an explosion than happened to the *Maine*."[22] Long, however, allowed Dewey's orders to stand. Soon after, McKinley asked Roosevelt's buddy, Army Surgeon Leonard Wood, "Have you and Theodore declared war yet?" Wood replied, "No, Mr. President, but we think you should."[23] War was declared in April 1898, and Theodore announced he would be going to join the action. Friends pleaded with him and begged him to stay home, but he adamantly refused. "For the last year I have preached war with Spain. I should feel distinctly ashamed . . . if I now failed to practice what I have preached."[24]

OFF TO WAR

Leonard Wood gained a colonel's commission of the First Volunteer Cavalry, with Roosevelt as his second in command as lieutenant colonel. They reported to San Antonio, where Camp Wood soon became home to cowboys and Indians, ranchers and New York society gentlemen. All were part of Roosevelt's world and wanted to be part of his new adventure. They were dubbed the Rough Riders, a regiment he said that looked "exactly as a body of cowboy cavalry should look."[25] They trained and slowly learned to trust each other, even coming from vastly different backgrounds. Although anxious to be on their way to Cuba, supplies and red tape were not as hurried. The men transferred to Florida, only to sit and wait again.

When they landed at Daiquiri on June 22 and disembarked, several of the horses and mules drowned in the water, so the Rough Riders became dismounted cavalry. They fought in a skirmish as they moved toward Santiago, and Roosevelt found himself promoted to commander of the Rough Riders when Wood was made brigadier general to take over the brigade from their ill commander.

On the night of June 30, a correspondent wrote: "Above us the tropical moon hung white and clear in the dark purple sky, pierced with millions

DID YOU KNOW?

Roosevelt hated the nickname "Teddy."

JUN 16: Incorporation of Ford Motor Company

NOV 18: Hay-Bunau-Varilla Treaty signed granting US rights to Panama Canal Zone

DEC 1: Motion picture *The Great Train Robbery* opens

DEC 17: Wright Brothers successfully fly a gasoline-powered airplane

DEC 30: Fire at Chicago's Iroquois Theater kills more than 600, mainly women and children attending a matinee

OCT 6: High Court of Australia sits for the first time

NOV 3: Panama declares independence from Colombia

DEC 10: Husband-and-wife team, Marie and Pierre Curie, receives the Nobel Prize

DID YOU KNOW?

Prior to Roosevelt's presidency, the presidential home was known as the Executive Mansion. After putting "White House" on his stationery, others then used it as the official name.

of white stars. . . . Before the moon rose again, every sixth man who had slept in the mist that night was either killed or wounded."[26] Roosevelt later remembered it as a "very lovely morning," with a setting that included "lofty and beautiful mountains hemmed in the Santiago plain, making it an amphitheatre for the battle."[27]

Once guns of both sides began pounding each other, Roosevelt received orders to move out and connect with a unit somewhere to his right. They crossed a stream where they found Spanish troops manning German guns on two hills—San Juan Hill on the left and Kettle Hill on the right. Pinned down by the deadly fire were other Americans, including regular troops. Theodore led his men forward, and when he could not convince the regular commander to storm Kettle Hill, he asked, "If you don't wish to go forward, let my men pass, please."[28] The Rough Riders ran and cheered their way up the hill as Spanish soldiers absconded. Although jubilant in their victory, they were still facing a shower of bullets from the enemy on San Juan Hill, so Colonel Roosevelt ordered his men to charge. He started running when he realized that no one was following. He returned and found his Rough Riders had not heard his original order. Now they tried it again and reached their destination, but by this time, the Spanish had fled. He wrote home, "I think I earned my Colonelcy and medal of honor, and I hope to get them."[29]

Attaining the medal of honor seemed assured at the time, but politics derailed his chances. Within weeks, the fighting ended, but troops were not immediately evacuated from Cuba, allowing more men to fall victim to the deadly yellow fever. Disgruntled officers, including Roosevelt, decided to voice their dissatisfaction. The young colonel penned a strong message that insisted if they remained, it "will simply involve the destruction of thousands. There is no possible reason for not shipping the entire command North at once."[30] A round-robin letter was signed by the officers and sent to Washington. There someone leaked it to the press, which infuriated President McKinley, who worried such knowledge could be used by Spain during peace negotiations. While the letter did little to affect peace talks, it did slam the door on Roosevelt's chance to be awarded the medal of honor—or at least for one hundred years. In January 2001, President William Clinton bestowed the medal on Theodore Roosevelt posthumously, making him the only president to receive such an honor.

While awaiting orders to return home, Roosevelt heard news that many in New York were mentioning his name as a gubernatorial candidate. He was greatly pleased by such a notion, as more reports of his popularity poured in. The boss of New York's Republican machine, Senator Tom Platt, faced the prospect with some trepidation. He admitted Roosevelt stood the best chance of being elected against a Democrat, but he still worried. "If he becomes Governor of New York, sooner or later, with his personality, he will have to be President of the United States. . . . I am afraid to start that thing going."[31] But Platt concurred with Republican wisdom that the former Rough Rider was the only one with the hope of beating a Democratic candidate, so he agreed.

Using his fighting experience, and with Rough Rider colleagues at his side, Roosevelt crisscrossed New York state, campaigning on an imperialist platform advocating annexation of the Philippines (something which no governor controlled) and denouncing the Democratic Tammany Hall machine. Sometimes a friend took the podium on his behalf.

NATIONAL EVENTS

- Lincoln Steffens publishes *The Shame of the Cities*
- Capitalizing on St. Louis fair, new song "Meet Me in St. Louis"
- **FEB 7:** Great Baltimore Fire destroys more than 1,500 buildings
- **APR 8:** Longacre Square in New York City is renamed Times Square
- **MAY 5:** Cy Young, pitcher of Boston Americans, pitches the first perfect game

1904

WORLD EVENTS

- Construction begins on Panama Canal
- **JAN 17:** St. Petersburg premiere of Anton Chekhov's play *The Cherry Orchard*
- **FEB 8:** Russo-Japanese War ignited with Japanese surprise attack on Port Arthur (Lushun)
- **FEB 17:** Puccini's *Madame Butterfly* makes a lackluster premier in Milan
- **MAR 4:** Russo-Japanese War begins

Former sergeant Buck Taylor told a crowd, "Vote for my Colonel! Vote for my Colonel! And he will lead you, as he led us, like sheep to the slaughter!" Recounting the speech in his autobiography, Roosevelt admitted, "This hardly seemed a tribute to my military skill; but it delighted the crowd, and as far as I could tell did me nothing but good."[32] On November 8, 1898, Theodore Roosevelt was elected governor of New York.

NEW YORK GOVERNOR

Once inaugurated as governor, Roosevelt soon demonstrated his desire to be independent of any political influence, including Republican boss Tom Platt. The first showdown involved a campaign promise to investigate possible illegal activities in the state's canal system. Platt decided who would be the next superintendent of public works, and when he handed the telegram of acceptance from the appointee to the governor, Roosevelt declined to accept Platt's candidate for the position and explained he was not going to have his administration run by someone else. When he tried to fill the job, however, few were willing to cross Platt and incur the party boss's wrath. Ultimately, a list of four candidates was given to Platt, who then picked one—such was the working relationship between the two for the remainder of Roosevelt's governorship.

The governor sought new solutions to old problems and instituted weekly cabinet meetings for the heads of departments. He also invited college professors to Sagamore Hill to elicit their opinions on various topics; it was here, at the family home at Oyster Bay, that Princeton professor Woodrow Wilson first met Roosevelt. Understanding the power of newspapers in molding public opinion, the new governor took the unusual step of courting the press. Twice a day, reporters trooped into the governor's office, where they chatted about issues and he sounded them out on ideas—Roosevelt, however, usually did all or most of the talking during their fifteen-minute sessions.

Three months into his term, Roosevelt launched a campaign to levy taxes on public utilities, something that Boss Platt had promised those corporations would never happen. Republican assemblymen now were being cajoled by the governor and threatened by their boss to gain their votes. Ultimately Roosevelt won, although he told an assemblyman he thought his actions probably had ended his political career. "You're mistaken, Governor," Assemblyman Nathaniel Ellsberg said, "This is only the beginning."[33]

During this legislative session, Roosevelt successfully championed a wide variety of bills: salary increases for teachers, prohibition of racial segregation in schools, stronger regulations of working conditions in clothing and cigar factories, civil service reform, and setting aside lands for preservation. The summer of 1899 found him touring the nation giving speeches, prompting some to think he planned to oppose McKinley's renomination. Roosevelt insisted he had no such plans, but famed Emporia, Kansas, newspaper editor William Allen White wrote that Roosevelt's presidential candidacy was "more than a presidential possibility in 1904, he is a presidential probability. He is the coming American of the twentieth century."[34]

As Republicans focused on the upcoming 1900 presidential campaign, Platt saw his opportunity to rid himself of Roosevelt. He pushed for the governor to be nominated as the vice president under McKinley, and his hopes were heightened by the death of incumbent vice president Garret Hobart. Roosevelt desired another gubernatorial

JUL 23: Ice cream cone invented by Charles E. Menches at the Louisiana Purchase Exposition in St. Louis; other new foods introduced—hamburger, hot dog, iced tea, and Dr. Pepper

AUG: Olympic games held in St. Louis

SEP 9: First use of mounted police in New York City

NOV 8: Theodore Roosevelt elected president

NOV 17: George M. Cohan opens on Broadway in show *Little Johnny Jones*

APR 18: Great Toronto Fire destroys much of the city's downtown

JUN 28: Danish ocean liner SS *Norge* runs aground and sinks off the coast of Ireland, 635 die

JUL 21: Trans-Siberian railway completed

DEC 27: Premiere of *Peter Pan* in London

DID YOU KNOW?

Roosevelt had extremely poor eyesight. When he went to Cuba in the Spanish-American War, he had several pairs of spectacles sewn into his uniform.

term instead, to continue his reform agenda, and saw the vice presidency as a dead end. McKinley still smarted from Roosevelt's criticism after the Spanish-American War and withheld support. When others were yelling for "Teddy!" the president asked, "Don't you realize there's only one life between that madman and the White House?" His political advisor and power broker Mark Hanna told the president he had a duty to survive the next four years. Platt's political maneuvering succeeded and the convention nominated the forty-one-year-old governor of New York to be vice president.

Although initially cool to the idea of trading the governorship for the vice presidency, once he was nominated to run with McKinley, Roosevelt enthusiastically threw himself into the campaign, traveling the country and giving hundreds of speeches in cities and small communities, while McKinley retired quietly to his Ohio home. Roosevelt spoke out in favor of McKinley's policies and attacked Democrat William Jennings Bryan for his tariff reduction proposal and tax reforms. In November, the McKinley-Roosevelt ticket claimed an impressive victory, winning 292 electoral votes to Bryan's 155. No small part of the win was due to the New Yorker's tireless campaigning.

VICE PRESIDENT

The one duty listed for the vice president in the Constitution is presiding over the Senate, which Roosevelt did for exactly four days before the congressional session adjourned. He was grateful for its brevity as he found the task inordinately boring. He wondered how he would fill the next four years and considered possibly studying law under Supreme Court Justice Edward White. The summer of 1901 found the Roosevelt clan enjoying themselves at Sagamore Hill. On September 6, he received word that President McKinley had been shot while visiting the Pan American Exhibition in Buffalo. Roosevelt immediately rushed to the president's bedside and was relieved to see the president's condition improving, so he joined his family vacationing in the Adirondacks. On the thirteenth, he went mountain climbing with friends and was sitting down to eat when he spied a guide hastening toward him, bearing a telegram from Buffalo asking him to return since the president's condition had worsened considerably. Roosevelt hiked twelve miles to the nearest telephone to confirm the news. The vice president raced on horseback to a waiting train, where he learned the president had died. He visited Mrs. McKinley and family, and then went to take the oath of office from Judge John R. Hazel. At the age of forty-two, Theodore Roosevelt had become the youngest president in American history.

PRESIDENT ROOSEVELT

The city of Washington was draped in black when Roosevelt arrived, but his youthful enthusiasm for his new job prevented him from staying in mourning for very long. One observer noted, "He strode triumphant around among us, talking and shaking hands, dictating and signing letters, and laughing . . . No doubt the President felt he should hold himself down; he didn't; he tried to, but his joy showed in every word and movement. . . . And he laughed with glee at the power and place that had come to him."[35] But not all would go smoothly.

Within a month of taking office, the new president found himself in the midst of a firestorm of protest from southerners who had heard of a supper guest at the White House. Booker T. Washington, renowned scientist, had been invited to share dinner with the president and First Lady. Roosevelt

NATIONAL EVENTS

DEC 6: Roosevelt Corollary to Monroe Doctrine introduced

DEC 31: First New Year's Eve celebration in Times Square

Diary from Dixie, Civil War memoirs kept by southerner Mary Chestnut, is published

Charles Schwab founds Bethlehem Steel

"Those who cannot remember the past are condemned to repeat it," writes George Santayana in his book *The Life of Reason*

1905

WORLD EVENTS

V.I. Lenin returns to Russia from exile

Maji-Maji warriors in Tanganyika attack German forces

World's largest diamond, Cullinan diamond (3,106-carat), discovered in South Africa

In France, Alfred Binet and Théodore Simon develop the Binet-Simon I.Q. (intelligence quotient) test

admitted later that he had first experienced misgivings about inviting a Negro, but chastised himself for giving the invitation a second thought. They discussed the president's desire for blacks to understand that the federal government supported them and their rights. But by daybreak, southern newspapers, having learned of the dinner, fired vicious salvos of outrage. The *Memphis Scimitar* called it a "damnable outrage" that Roosevelt allowed "a nigger to dine with him at the White House." It further argued that Roosevelt had dishonored both his mother (a southern woman) and his wife by having her sit at the table. The *Richmond News* disavowed his actions, claiming, "It will be impossible to feel, as we were beginning to feel, that he is one of us."[36] While the president insisted that he did not care what criticism he incurred and wanted to continue his association with Booker T. Washington, they would never again share a meal at the White House.

In November 1901, the country learned of a vast new conglomerate fashioned by three of the richest men in America to control the lucrative northern rail route. The men included James J. Hill (Great Northern Railroad), E.H. Harriman (Union Pacific Railroad), and J.P. Morgan (financier extraordinaire and owner of Northern Pacific Railroad). They put their businesses together and called it the Northern Securities Trust, which would function as a holding company for their earnings. Through the three rail routes, they would oversee thirty-two thousand miles of track; in addition, Hill managed trade routes overseas to China. The three tycoons considered that such an organization might violate the Sherman Antitrust Act of 1890, but their attorneys assured them that they need not fear the government. Their legal team forgot one key fact—they were dealing with Theodore Roosevelt.

TEDDY BEARS ★ During his first term, Roosevelt was hunting in Mississippi, but had no luck after three days. A guide found an old bear and, after exhausting it, tied it to a tree for Roosevelt to shoot. Roosevelt refused, since it lacked a sporting chance, but ordered its suffering ended. *Washington Post* cartoonist Clifford Berryman sketched the president's refusal to slay the bear. The cartoon immediately became popular, and in time, the bear appeared in a rounder, cuter form, which coincided with a new stuffed animal—the "Teddy bear."

In mid-February 1902, Attorney General Philander Knox announced that the Justice Department would be instituting an investigation of the Northern Securities Trust. Immediately, J.P. Morgan arrived at the White House to plead his case to Roosevelt and Knox. Morgan told the president, "If we have done something wrong, send your man to my man and they can fix it up." Roosevelt replied it wasn't possible, and Knox added, "We don't want to fix it up; we want to stop it."[37] Morgan asked if they would attack his other trusts, including US Steel, but Roosevelt said they would not, unless they believed the trusts to have committed wrongdoing. The government filed suit, and in March 1904, the US Supreme Court handed down its opinion that the trust had, in fact, violated the Sherman Antitrust Act, and so the Northern Securities Trust was dissolved. Theodore Roosevelt had begun his trust-busting career.

The president faced another crisis when the United Mine Workers went on strike in eastern Pennsylvania coal fields. At first, Roosevelt merely played the part of observer, but as winter approached, people grew more apprehensive at the

Mark Twain's *Huckleberry Finn* and *Tom Sawyer* are banned from the Brooklyn Public Library for "setting a bad example"

JAN 8: Five-and-a-half-month textile workers strike in Fall River, MA ends, workers win their demands

FEB 1: President Roosevelt creates Bureau of Forestry under Department of Agriculture

FEB 23: Founding of Rotary International in Chicago

MAR 4: Inauguration of President Theodore Roosevelt

1.3 million die in Bubonic plague in India

JAN 2: Russians at Port Arthur surrender to Japanese forces

JAN 14: Earthquake in Jamaica kills more than 1,000

JAN 22: "Bloody Sunday"—massacre of more than 100 demonstrators in St. Petersburg, Russia, outside the Winter Palace

MAR: Romanian peasants revolt in Moldavia to protest poor living conditions

WHITE HOUSE REMODELING ★ In 1902, Roosevelt decided that the president needed more office space than what he had on the second floor. He then ordered the demolition of greenhouses and the construction of a west wing to be used for presidential business. A large east entrance to the White House was also added. A major renovation of the first floor was done to rid the house of the Victorian touches added over the preceding thirty years and restore it more closely to its original appearance.

prospect of high coal costs or shortages. A meeting was called for early October for the two sides to meet at the White House. Roosevelt regretted that he had to appear in a wheelchair because of a recent leg operation resulting from a carriage collision, which had killed his Secret Service agent. While the UMW representatives said they would be happy for arbitration, the mine owners remained intractable and angrily insisted the government should serve an injunction forcing the miners to return to work. After threatening to send in federal troops to manage the mines, Roosevelt won support by the mine operators to agree to arbitration. Eventually, the miners won a 10 percent wage hike and reduction of hours to a nine-hour day, and the operators were allowed a 10 percent price increase of coal. When Roosevelt explained how the matter was settled, he used a phrase that would be heard frequently in future speeches. Both parties had wanted and arbitrated a "square deal" for themselves, and he insisted the president had the power to take "immediate and vigorous executive action" in his capacity as "steward of the people."[38] Roosevelt took his stewardship role very seriously, but only took action in future strikes when he deemed such action necessary.

With regard to both domestic and foreign matters, the president enjoyed quoting a favorite *West Afri*can proverb: "Speak softly and carry a big stick; you will go far." First used when describing New York politics, his "big stick" was felt as well by nations around the world. With an eye toward extending America's power and influence, Roosevelt ordered Secretary of State John Hay (who had also served as Lincoln's private secretary) to negotiate terms for a canal to be constructed in Panama. Colombia ruled Panama, however, and did not approve of America's terms. A revolt staged within Colombia resulted in a new Panamanian government that was pro-American and quite happy to agree to a canal treaty, which was signed in 1903. The United States gained the right to a ten-mile canal zone, and use of the canal; in return, they would pay ten millions dollars and an annual fee to the Panamanian government. Building began in 1904 and would continue for a decade. The Panama Canal opened in 1914 and remained under US control until 1979, when it was transferred to Panama.

Mindful of America's role in the western hemisphere as stated in the Monroe Doctrine, the president decided to add some meat to it by creating the Roosevelt Corollary. On the heels of repeated German blockades of Venezuela as punishment for that South American nation not repaying its debt in 1903, Roosevelt believed the United States needed to be more forceful regarding its role as protector of its hemisphere. In his annual messages to Congress in both 1905 and 1906, he announced that the United States had the right to intervene if a nation was victim of unwanted foreign aggression or it was violating the rights of the United States.

NATIONAL EVENTS

MAR 17: President Roosevelt attends wedding of cousin Franklin and gives away the bride Eleanor

MAR 28: US ends occupation of Dominican Republic but it continues as an American protectorate

MAY 15: Las Vegas founded

OCT 5: Wright Brothers third airplane, the Wright Flyer III, stays airborne for 39 minutes

DEC 16: *Variety* magazine begins weekly publication

WORLD EVENTS

MAR 3: Czar Nicholas II agrees to create an elected assembly (Duma)

JUN 7: Norway declares its independence from Sweden

JUN 30: Albert Einstein publishes paper discussing his theory of special relativity

SEP 5: Treaty of Portsmouth signed ending Russo-Japanese War; peace talks mediated by President Roosevelt

OCT 4: First arrest and prison sentence of English suffragettes

OCT 30: Czar Nicholas II agrees to Russian constitution

DEC 9: Russian revolt begins and Duma suspended until January

As the election season approached, Roosevelt announced both his candidacy and his declaration that he would not run again in 1908, saying he would have served two terms by then. He lived to regret this statement, and Edith later said had she known he was going to make such an announcement, she would have tried to convince him otherwise.

But in 1904, Roosevelt was the Republican candidate for president at the party's convention in Chicago, where they also nominated Indiana senator Charles Fairbanks as vice president. The Democratic presidential candidate, Alton B. Parker, was the chief justice for the New York Court of Appeals. The campaign lacked acrimony since the two platforms were almost identical in supporting the gold standard and independence for the Philippines, and both parties opposed monopolies. Neither candidate promoted his agenda actively, choosing instead to remain at home. When Americans voted on November 8, 1904, Theodore Roosevelt received their hearty endorsement as he clinched 56 percent of the popular vote to Parker's 38 percent; the electoral college advantage was even more pronounced, with Roosevelt winning 336 votes to Parker's 140. Roosevelt told his wife, Edith, "My dear, I am no longer a political accident."[39]

SECOND TERM

Roosevelt was surrounded by his family as he took the oath of office for the second time. Edith had grown more comfortable in her role as First Lady and worked to improve the living conditions of the White House; in fact, the family moved out for a time, so extensive remodeling could occur. The children's antics in the White House kept the nation, but probably not the White House staff, amused; they kept a menagerie of animals, including snakes, and at one point a pony rode the elevator to the second floor to cheer up a sick Archie. The beautiful inlaid parquet floor of the East Room doubled as a roller skating rink for the children. Daughter Alice was outspoken and seemingly incorrigible; she was often seen playing poker and smoking in public. Her father's quip that he could either run the country or control her but not both was not far from the truth. In February 1906, the White House served as a beautiful backdrop for her gala wedding to Senator Nick Longworth of Ohio, a man fifteen years her senior who had accompanied her on a tour of the Pacific on a four-month cruise with Secretary of War William H. Taft acting as chaperone. A year earlier, the president had given away another bride, his niece Eleanor, who was marrying distant cousin Franklin Roosevelt.

During the end of Roosevelt's first term, Russia and Japan had been fighting a war over control of Manchuria and Korea. Concerned over an imbalance of power and possible partitioning of neutral China, Roosevelt volunteered to act as mediator. At first his offer was refused by both combatants, but following their loss of Port Arthur to the Japanese, the Russians began to reconsider, though they were slow to act. Roosevelt wrote in disgust, "He [the czar] has been unable to make war, and he is now unable to make peace."[40] Finally, the two sides agreed to send representatives to the naval yard at Portsmouth, New Hampshire, in August 1905. Taft headed the US mediation team (Secretary of State Hay had recently died and his successor, Elihu Root, had not yet taken office). Roosevelt met with the representatives at a luncheon aboard the presidential yacht; then, as the talks progressed, the president monitored their progress. By late August, the parties had agreed to

DID YOU KNOW?

Roosevelt was the first president to travel overseas while in office. He visited Panama to inspect progress of the Panama Canal in 1906.

University of Chicago publishes its first *Manual of Style*

Song "Anchors Aweigh" written by US Naval Academy music director Charles Zimmerman and midshipman Alfred Miles

Jack London publishes *White Fang*

JAN 1: Alfred Fuller begins the Fuller Brush Company

FEB 17: White House wedding for presidential daughter Alice Roosevelt marrying Nicholas Longworth

FEB 28: Upton Sinclair publishes *The Jungle*, an exposé on Chicago's meat-packing industry

1906

MAR 7: Finland becomes first European nation to grant women's suffrage

MAR 15: Registration of Rolls-Royce Ltd.

APR 7: Mount Vesuvius erupts and buries nearby Naples under ash

JUL 4: Ethiopia becomes independent but is also divided among Britain, France, and Italy for spheres of influence

SEP 11: Mohandas Gandhi initiates nonviolent resistance in South Africa to protest treatment of Indians

BOOKS BY THEODORE ROOSEVELT ★ Roosevelt wrote 35 books on various topics ranging from history to outdoor life, including *The Naval War of 1812* (1882);*Hunting Trip of a Ranchman* (1885); *Life of Thomas Hart Benton* (1887); *Gouverneur Morris* (1888); *Ranch Life and the Hunting Trail* (1888); *The Winning of the West 1769–1807* (4 vols., 1889–1896); *New York* (1891); *Hero Tales from American History* (1895); *Rough Riders* (1899); *African Game Trails* (1910); *The New Nationalism* (1910); *History as Literature, and Other Essays* (1913); *Theodore Roosevelt, An Autobiography* (1913); *Through the Brazilian Wilderness* (1914); *Life Histories of African Game Animals* (1914); *America and the World War* (1915); *Fear God and Take Your Own Part* (1916); *The Foes of Our Own Household* (1917); *National Strength and International Duty* (1917).

the terms of the Treaty of Portsmouth, including the end of fighting; Japan returned the northern half of Sakhalin Island to Russia, but dropped its demand for an indemnity. In return, Russia returned southern Manchuria to the Chinese, and all agreed to recognize Japanese control of Korea. Korea protested the treaty and Japan's act of domination, but Roosevelt did not wish to anger Japan, fearing retribution against the Philippines or Hawaii. That would occur thirty-five years later. For his part, Roosevelt received word that he was a recipient of the Nobel Peace Prize of 1906.

In the following months, however, tensions between Japan and the United States grew, with the increasing hostility of Californians toward the Japanese. The president reached a "gentleman's agreement" with the Japanese government that would restrict emigration from their nation but avoid an exclusion act as had been earlier passed against Chinese immigration.

The president was concerned about the situation in the Pacific and decided this was an opportune time for the US Navy to go on a tour. He called it "a practice cruise around the world," which would have the navy in the Pacific by October 1907. Tensions relaxed, however, so the Great White Fleet did not depart until December from Hampton Roads, Virginia. As it sailed, Roosevelt appealed to Congress for an increase in the number of battleships and a reorganization of the navy's bureaucracy. Congress agreed to build two battleships instead of the four requested by the president, who admitted that two was all he actually had expected. In February 1909, the president proudly received the twenty-one gun salutes by the fleet's twenty-six ships returning to Hampton Roads. During his presidency, Roosevelt had overseen the dramatic increase of the US Navy from 19,000 to 45,000 men and a buildup of ten ships, elevating it to third place, behind the British and German navies. Still, he was concerned about its future and warned his successor, William H. Taft, "Under no circumstances divide the battleship fleet between the Atlantic and Pacific Oceans prior to the finishing of the Panama Canal."[41]

In October 1907, the economy took a nosedive with the failure of New York's Knickerbocker Trust, one of the nation's major banks, which collapsed following a run on the bank; public confidence in the banking industry sunk as well. Six years later the government would step in and create the Federal Reserve system, but during the interim, more banks failed and stock prices plummeted. Many business owners insisted the problems stemmed from government policies; the

NATIONAL EVENTS

APR 18: Catastrophic San Francisco earthquake (8.25 on Richter scale) leaves more than 3,000 dead and 200,000 homeless

JUN 30: Congress passes Meat Inspection Act and Pure Food and Drug Act (in reaction to *The Jungle*)

AUG 22: Victor Victrola phonograph introduced

SEP 24: President Roosevelt makes Devils Tower the first national monument

DEC 10: Roosevelt becomes first president to win Nobel Prize; it is awarded for his work mediating Russo-Japanese War

WORLD EVENTS

SEP 22: Tsunami kills more than 20,000 in Hong Kong

DEC 2: Commissioning of British warship HMS *Dreadnought*; first of its kind to have large guns mounted on turrets that can rotate 360°

DEC 30: Iran creates a constitutional monarchy

president disagreed. Recovery would not begin until the spring of 1908.

During the early twentieth century, journalists such as Ida Tarbell and Lincoln Steffens were awakening Americans to the unsanitary and unsafe practices in factories and tenements exercised by those interested only in profitable gains. Roosevelt named these journalists "muckrakers" when he compared them to characters in *Pilgrim's Progress* who raked the filth with muckrakes. Tarbell attacked John D. Rockefeller's Standard Oil Trust, which soon followed the way of the Northern Securities Trust, and Steffens attacked corruption found in city governments. But it was Upton Sinclair's book *The Jungle* which horrified readers with its account of appalling conditions in Chicago's meat-packing plants. Americans demanded government action, and Congress responded with two new laws to regulate the meat-packing industry and oversee the manufacture of other foods and drugs—the Meat Inspection Act and the Pure Food and Drug Act of 1906.

Not satisfied with just improving present conditions, Roosevelt looked toward the future and continued his lifelong passion for conservation. During his presidency he had toured Yosemite and Yellowstone National Parks. He wanted more lands set aside for future generations, and throughout his presidency he worked toward that goal. His conservation legacy was impressive: five national parks (including Crater Lake in Oregon and Mesa Verde ruins in Colorado); sixteen national monuments, beginning with Devil's Tower, Wyoming, and eventually adding the Grand Canyon, which was later made a national park; four game refuges; and fifty-one national bird reservations. He helped to oversee the vast timberlands by creating the National Forest Service, with Gifford Pinchot as its first administrator. Both men understood the need to be watchful conservators of America's vast but finite natural resources. The president also endeavored to help the southwest, where water was a premium, and worked to ensure new dams were constructed and a new government agency established, the Reclamation Service.

As his second term neared its completion, Roosevelt remained bound to his vow not to seek another term. The presidency had served as his "bully pulpit," enabling him to seek reform for the nation. "I do not believe that any President has ever had as thoroly [sic] good a time as I have had, or has ever enjoyed himself as much."[42] But it was time to move on, and he was happy to see his friend and cabinet appointee William H. Taft win the Republican nomination and then the presidency. Life was an adventure and the outgoing president was eager to continue on the journey.

RETIREMENT

Almost immediately after Taft took office, Roosevelt and his son Kermit departed for an African safari, which was also to benefit the Smithsonian Institution's collection. Scribner's agreed to pay him to write a series of articles about their adventures. Trip costs increased rapidly—more than anticipated—so Roosevelt wrote to former steel magnate Andrew Carnegie for additional funding—thirty thousand dollars, which Carnegie sent.

Edith and Ethel arrived to tour Egypt, then Italy. Next the family visited Germany, where they met Kaiser Wilhelm, who proved a gracious host. Over the next six weeks the party were guests of several heads of state in the various European capitals. Then word arrived of the death of King Edward VII followed by a request by President Taft

DID YOU KNOW?

Roosevelt was the first American and first president to win the Nobel Prize.

Chicago movie projectionist Donald Bell and camera repairman Robert Howell start a new company, Bell and Howell

Louis Maytag of Newton, Iowa, begins producing washing machines

Construction of Washington Cathedral begins (finished in 1976)

Hershey Chocolate Company introduces Hershey Kisses

JAN 23: Kansan Charles Curtis becomes the first Native American elected to US Senate

1907

German neurologist Alois Alzheimer researches dementia

French engineer Edouard Belin develops world's first facsimile (fax) machine

First major exhibition of Cubist paintings in Paris; major artist is Pablo Picasso

Winston Churchill calls for the abolition of Parliament's upper chamber

Royal Dutch Oil and Shell Transport and Trading Co. merge to create Royal Dutch-Shell

DID YOU KNOW?

Roosevelt liked coffee (he drank nearly a gallon a day) and coined the phrase "good to the last drop" when he drained a cup of Maxwell House coffee.

that Roosevelt represent the United States at the British king's state funeral. After serving in this official capacity, Roosevelt and his family finally returned home to their beloved estate at Sagamore Hill. Politics, however, soon recaptured the attention of the former president.

In the summer of 1910, Taft invited Roosevelt to the White House, but, thinking it would not be wise, he declined. Later they met at Taft's summer residence in Massachusetts, but the tone was entirely formal. Roosevelt confided to friends that he was disappointed in Taft's leadership and his removal of Gifford Pinchot from the Forestry Service. He was dismayed by the fractioning of the Republican Party into two camps, each of which wanted his support for their candidates in the 1910 congressional elections.

Attempting to remain neutral was no easy task for Roosevelt, but he did so as he contemplated his own future and wondered if he would hold office again. He traveled the country and made speeches, wrote articles in favor of progressive reforms, and, to his great enjoyment, reveled in his new role as grandfather. When troubles erupted across the border in Mexico, the former president immediately volunteered his services to lead troops once more, but the United States did not require the former Rough Rider's military assistance.

By early 1912, Roosevelt could fight the urge no more, and in February, he announced, "My hat is in the ring." Addressing a constitutional convention in Ohio, he openly declared himself a Progressive and advocated its reforms, which brought government to the people, including initiative, referendum, and the direct election of senators. Later he reiterated his position, saying, "I will accept the nomination for President if it is tendered to me."[43] Now the nation eagerly awaited a battle royal between the current occupant of the White House and the man who put him there.

ELECTION OF 1912

Lamenting the loss of Roosevelt's support, Taft wept, murmuring, "Roosevelt was my closest friend."[44] He never understood, nor did many others, what created such a chasm between the two men. They began attacking each other in speeches, Taft calling Progressives "neurotics." Later Roosevelt would respond with name-calling, including "puzzle wit" and "fathead." None of their oratory was fitting of the office they held (or had held). At the Republican convention in Chicago, it quickly became clear that Taft would prevail. Angered by what he perceived as an outrage, Roosevelt launched into a speech for his supporters, invoking Lincoln and God and ending with the phrase, "We stand at Armageddon, and we battle for the Lord!"

He determined that a new party would be born with him as its candidate and his agenda for its platform. The Progressive Party met in early August and did just that, although Democratic candidate Woodrow Wilson favored many of the same reforms. Roosevelt actively campaigned through the nation and was in Milwaukee on October 14. There a disgruntled tavern keeper from New York approached him and attempted to shoot him, but a bystander moved his arm. Believing he had been saved from harm, Roosevelt did not realize he had been shot until someone mentioned he had a hole in his overcoat. He reached in and felt blood but decided he would go ahead and speak. He told his audience about the assassination attempt and showed his bloodstained shirt, but in a hoarse voice reminded them, "It takes more than that to kill a Bull Moose."[45] That name stuck and

NATIONAL EVENTS

FEB 18: Roosevelt appoints Lt. Col. George W. Goethals of the Army Corps of Engineers to finish building the Panama Canal (two others had quit)

MAR 13: Stock prices drop sharply on NYSE and fears of further economic problems ahead

JUN 1: United Press created as competition to Associated Press

AUG 22: Ringling Brothers buys Barnum & Bailey Circus

WORLD EVENTS

French chemist Eugène Schueller launches L'Oreal

Ongoing genocide in Namibia (then known as German South-West Africa)

JAN 6: In Rome, Maria Montessori opens a school for children

MAR 22: Introduction of taxi meters in London cabs

JUN 10: The French and Japanese sign an "open door" treaty recognizing their respective interests in China

became the nickname for his party. Meanwhile, he was whisked away to a hospital to stay for a week-long observation, since doctors decided against removing the bullet. Thankfully, the manuscript of his speech and his spectacles case were in his coat pocket and deflected the bullet from hitting a vital organ and slowed its velocity. Although the assassination attempt definitely gained Roosevelt sympathy from all sides, it was not enough on election day. Due to the split of the Republican Party, Wilson captured the presidency with over six million votes, but Roosevelt won second place with four million, beating out Taft with three-and-a-half million votes.

JOHN HAY (1838–1905) ★ Only one man in Washington, D.C., could brag he began his government career serving President Abraham Lincoln and ended it by working for President Theodore Roosevelt. John Hay served as a personal secretary to Lincoln, and after the president's assassination in 1865, Hay traveled to Europe, where he worked for various American legations. When he returned to the United States, he briefly worked as a journalist before accepting a post in Grant's administration as assistant secretary of state. Then in the 1880s he returned to writing, and co-authored with fellow Lincoln secretary John Nicolay a major biography on their former boss, *Abraham Lincoln: A History*. Hay returned to government service in 1898 and became secretary of state for friend William McKinley and continued at that post for Roosevelt. In a letter to President Roosevelt, he coined the phrase "that splendid little war" when describing the Spanish-American War. Hay's distinguished career ended with his death in July 1905.

RETIREMENT AGAIN

Following his defeat at the polls, Roosevelt launched himself into new endeavors. He began drafting his autobiography. He found a worthwhile adventure: journeying once more into the Amazon rain forest and documenting the trip for Scribner's. He would also gather specimens for his benefactor, the American Museum of Natural History, and map the region for the Brazilian government. He and Kermit left with their party in October 1913 for this perilous undertaking. Although far from being in peak physical shape and fifty-five years old, Roosevelt proclaimed, "I had to go. It was my last chance to be a boy."[46]

The expedition was beset by a chain of difficulties, including one of its men drowning, another going insane and killing a companion, and, in April, Roosevelt developed jungle fever and hallucinated. When he injured his leg and it became too painful for him to walk, he told the others to save themselves and leave him; of course, they brought him out of the jungle alive, albeit thirty-five pounds lighter than he had started seven months before. The Brazilian government recognized Roosevelt's efforts and the River of Doubt was renamed Rio Roosevelt.

Scarcely had the adventurers returned than the world found itself embroiled in war. He continued writing books about his expeditions to Africa and Brazil, as well as commentaries for the *Kansas City Star*. He supported Charles Evans Hughes's bid for the presidency in 1916, and when the United States entered the war, he again offered his services to create and lead volunteers, but President Wilson denied his request. The four Roosevelt sons, however, did enlist.

In March 1918, the family received news of the Croix de Guerre bestowed upon Archie for heroism

AUG 28: James Casey of Seattle creates UPS (United Parcel Service)

SEP 17: Harley-Davidson, organized four years before, is incorporated

NOV 3-4: During the night, J.P. Morgan works with other bankers to avert economic crisis

NOV 16: Oklahoma becomes 46th state

DEC 31: Ball drops for the first time on Times Square for New Year's Eve

JUN 10: First long-distance motorcar rally leaves Beijing (Peking) for Paris; the winner arrives in Paris on AUG 10

JUL 19: Korea's emperor Kojong (I T'ae-wang) abdicates

JUL 25: Korea becomes protectorate of Japan

SEP 5: Eight-year-old Vinh San proclaimed emperor in Vietnam

SEP 7: Maiden voyage of Cunard's ocean liner SS *Lusitania* from Liverpool, England to New York City

NOV 13: First helicopter takes flight; designed by French engineer Paul Cornu

in battle. Although wounded, he was alive in a French hospital. Ted received the same commendation, as well as a silver star for his efforts to lead a battalion following being gassed. The British Military Cross was awarded to Kermit for his bravery in Mesopotamia. Then in July word came that Quentin's plane had been shot down; they soon learned that he had been killed. German pilots had buried him with full military honors in a village near Rheims, France.

Their other sons returned from the war, but Quentin's death, as well as numerous ailments, plagued Roosevelt. Inflammatory rheumatism crippled the former president, causing him to be hospitalized. While there, he continued writing and seeing various guests. He refused sympathy from anyone. "Have you ever known any man who has gotten as much out of life as I have? I have seen more than any other man. I have made the very most out of my life." And to his sister Corinne he said: "No matter what comes, I have kept the promise that I made to myself when I was twenty-one . . . That I would work up to the hilt until I was sixty, and I have done it."[47]

> ***"To announce that there must be no criticism of the president, or that we are to stand by the president, right or wrong, is not only unpatriotic and servile, but is morally treasonable to the American public."***
>
> —*T. Roosevelt, editorial in the* Kansas City Star, *May 7, 1918*

He was allowed to go home for Christmas and enjoyed spending time at his beloved Sagamore Hill. He spent January 5 reading and completing an editorial for the *Kansas City Star*. He went to bed and was peacefully sleeping when Edith later checked on him. About four o'clock the next morning, she was awakened by the nurse and told he had ceased breathing; a coronary embolism had killed him. Archie sent a simple telegram to his brothers still in Europe: "The old lion is dead."[48]

A modest funeral service was held at Christ Church in Oyster Bay following a funeral cortege bearing his coffin covered with Rough Rider flags. A short ceremony ensued for the guests before the casket was then taken to Young's Memorial Cemetery in Oyster Bay. There, former president William H. Taft remained at the graveside and wept.

Edith Roosevelt stayed at Sagamore Hill for the remainder of her life, save for a few trips to Europe, and visits to see her children and grandchildren. She lived to be eighty-seven years old and died September 30, 1948, and was buried beside her husband.

Forty years before, as her husband prepared to leave the presidency, he showed her a sample business card which only listed his name. Edith said the "Mr." was more appropriate for his status, but he and his friend Archie Butt disagreed. While she laughingly replied that she was not surprised that the men were sticking together, she asked, "Why should he not have 'Mr. Theodore Roosevelt,' as any other gentleman would have on his card?"

Archie Butt replied, "Because he is not like any other gentleman."[49]

	1908				
NATIONAL EVENTS	New Yorker Thomas Sullivan develops tea bags	Tuberculin test developed to determine if tuberculosis is present	**FEB 18:** US and Japan sign a "Gentleman's Agreement" to end Japanese immigration to US	**MAR 29:** "Mutt and Jeff" comic strip debuts in *San Francisco Examiner*	**MAY 10:** First observance of Mother's Day
WORLD EVENTS	German physicist Hans Geiger develops the Geiger Counter at Manchester University	Kenneth Grahame writes *The Wind in the Willows*	L.M. Montgomery publishes *Anne of Green Gables*	**FEB 1:** Portugal's King Carlos I and Crown Prince Luiz are assassinated	**MAY 26:** Drilling for oil begins in the Middle East

ENDNOTES

1 Nathan Miller, *Theodore Roosevelt, A Life*, New York: William Morrow & Company, 1992, p. 29.

2 David McCullough, *Mornings on Horseback*, New York: Simon and Schuster, 1981, p. 59.

3 Ibid, p. 88.

4 Miller, p. 46.

5 McCullough, p. 117.

6 Ibid, p. 143.

7 Miller, p. 64.

8 Donald Wilhelm, *Theodore Roosevelt as an Undergraduate*, Boston: John W. Luce, 1910, p. 35.

9 Miller, p. 186.

10 McCullough, p. 222.

11 H.W. Brands, *T.R., The Last Romantic*, New York: BasicBooks, 1997, p. 137.

12 Ibid, p. 162.

13 Theodore Roosevelt, *An Autobiography*, New York: Library of America, 2004, p. 374.

14 Brands, p. 224.

15 Miller, p. 213.

16 Brands, p. 224.

17 Ibid, p. 215.

18 Sylvia Jukes Morris, *Edith Kermit Roosevelt, Portrait of a Lady*, New York: Coward, McCann & Geoghegan, Inc., 1980, p. 153.

19 Roosevelt, p. 423.

20 Miller, p. 231.

21 Brands, p. 238.

22 Ibid, pp. 326-327.

23 Ibid, p. 327.

24 Miller, p. 274.

25 Ibid, p. 278.

26 Richard Harding Davis, *The Cuban and Puerto Rican Campaigns*, New York: Scribners, 1899, pp. 193-194.

27 Theodore Roosevelt, *The Rough Riders*, New York: Library of America, 2004, p. 97.

28 Davis, p. 214.

29 Brands, p. 356.

30 David Traxel, *1898, The Birth of the American Century*, New York: Alfred A. Knopf, 1998, p. 222.

31 Ibid, p. 229.

32 Roosevelt, *Autobiography*, pp. 379-380.

33 Miller, p. 329.

34 Ibid, p. 331.

35 Brands, p. 359.

36 Edmund Morris, *Theodore Rex*, New York: Random House, 2001, pp. 54-55.

37 Lewis L. Gould, *The Presidency of Theodore Roosevelt*, Lawrence, KS: University Press of Kansas, 1991, p. 51.

38 Miller, p. 377.

39 Miller, p. 436.

40 Elting E. Morison, ed., *The Letters of Theodore Roosevelt: The Square Deal 1901-1905*, vol. 4, Cambridge, MA: Harvard University Press, 1951, p. 1158.

41 Gould, p. 269.

42 Miller, pp. 492–493.

43 Brands, p. 705.

44 Ibid, p. 707.

45 Ibid, p. 721.

46 Stefan Lorant, *The Life and Times of Theodore Roosevelt*, Garden City, NY: Doubleday & Company, Inc., 1959, p. 590.

47 Sylvia J. Morris, p. 430.

48 Ibid, p. 434.

49 Edmund Morris, p. 541.

MAY 18: President Roosevelt signs a bill into law ordering "In God We Trust" to be inscribed on all US coins

MAY 30: First workmen's comp bill passed by Congress

JUL 6: Robert Peary embarks for the North Pole

JUL 22: Arthur Fisher founds Fisher Body Company

SEP 22: First Ford Model T rolls off assembly line

NOV 3: Republican William H. Taft wins presidential election over perennial Democratic opponent William Jennings Bryan

NOV 15: Roosevelt becomes first president to travel outside US when he visits Panama

JUL 13: First time women compete in Olympic games

OCT 5: Bulgaria declares independence

OCT 6: Austria annexes Bosnia and Herzegovina, much to dismay of neighboring nations including Russia and Turkey

OCT 18: Belgium annexes Congo

DEC 28: Earthquake in Sicily kills more than 70,000

William H. Taft

★ ★ ★ TWENTY-SEVENTH PRESIDENT ★ ★ ★

LIFE SPAN

- Born: September 15, 1857, in Cincinnati, Ohio
- Died: March 8, 1930, in Washington, D.C.

NICKNAME

- Big Bill

RELIGION

- Unitarian

HIGHER EDUCATION

- Yale, 1878
- University of Cincinnati Law School, 1880

PROFESSION

- Lawyer

MILITARY SERVICE

- None

FAMILY

- Father: **Alphonso Taft** (1810–1891)
- Mother: **Louisa "Louise" Maria Torrey Taft** (1827–1907)
- Wife: **Helen "Nellie" Herron Taft** (1861–1943); wed on June 19, 1886, in Cincinnati, Ohio
- Children: **Robert Alphonso** (1889–1953); **Helen Herron** (1891–1987); **Charles Phelps** (1897–1983)

POLITICAL LIFE

- Assistant prosecutor of Hamilton County, Ohio (1881–1882)
- Internal revenue collector of Ohio's First District (1882–1883)
- Assistant solicitor of Hamilton County (1885–1887)
- Cincinnati Superior Court judge (1887–1890)
- US solicitor general (1890–1892)
- Sixth US Circuit Court judge and ex officio member of Sixth US Circuit Court of Appeals (1892–1900)
- Commissioner (1900–1901) and Governor-General (1901–1904) of the Philippines
- Secretary of war (1904–1908)
- Chief Justice of the United States (1921–1930)

PRESIDENCY

- One term: March 4, 1909–March 4, 1913
- Republican
- Reason for leaving office: lost election to **Woodrow Wilson** (with the fewest popular votes of any incumbent president seeking reelection)
- Vice president: **James S. Sherman** (1909–1912)

ELECTION OF 1908

- Electoral vote: **Taft** 321; **William Jennings Bryan** 162
- Popular vote: **Taft** 7,676,320; **Bryan** 6,412,294

CABINET

SECRETARY OF STATE
Philander C. Knox (1909–1913)

SECRETARY OF THE TREASURY
Franklin MacVeagh (1909–1913)

SECRETARY OF WAR
Jacob M. Dickinson (1909–1911)

Henry L. Stimson (1911–1913)

ATTORNEY GENERAL
George W. Wickersham (1909–1913)

SECRETARY OF THE NAVY
George von Lengerke Meyer (1909–1913)

POSTMASTER GENERAL
Frank H. Hitchcock (1909–1913)

SECRETARY OF THE INTERIOR
Richard A. Ballinger (1909–1911)

Walter L. Fisher (1911–1913)

SECRETARY OF AGRICULTURE
James Wilson (1909–1913)

SECRETARY OF COMMERCE AND LABOR
Charles Nagel (1909–1913)

Few men entered the presidency less interested in obtaining the office than did William H. Taft. His goal for years before—and after—was to be appointed to the US Supreme Court. He finally achieved this and served on the bench for nine years, making him the only US president to have gained both honors.

EARLY LIFE

Alphonso Taft was a mainstay of the Republican Party in Ohio and a well-respected attorney when he married his second wife, Louisa "Louise" Torrey, in 1853. He had two sons by his first wife, who died of tuberculosis, and with whom he shared a comfortable home on Mount Auburn, the most fashionable neighborhood of Cincinnati. Alphonso married Louise, seventeen years his junior, less than two years later, and she gave him four children—three sons and a daughter. Their first child was born on September 15, 1857, and named William Howard. When Will was nearly two months, his mother wrote, "He is very large of his age and grows fat every day."[1] Little did the family realize that his "baby fat" would continue into adulthood, causing him health problems and embarrassment for most of his life. As a child Will was active, playing with his two younger brothers, who arrived in quick succession (to the family's great joy a sister finally joined them in 1865). Baseball was his favorite sport; he was a good hitter but slow base runner. Swimming occupied a good deal of his time in the summer.

Will was a smart boy and excelled in school, although he was cautioned about his tendency toward procrastination. He attended public school, including Woodward High School, where he graduated second in his class and also proved himself an apt pupil in the art of dancing. While at Woodward, he wrote an essay discussing the reasons why women should be granted more educational opportunities, and, just as importantly, the right to vote—certainly unusual thoughts for a young man of the 1870s.

Following in his father's footsteps, Will attended Yale University. Alphonso Taft, now in Washington serving in the Grant administration as secretary of war, expected high marks from his son, and Will wrote explaining how hard he was working, "You expect great things of me, but you mustn't be disappointed if I don't come up to your expectations."[2] Young Taft attempted to spend both his money and his time wisely; his only sport was a wrestling match against a sophomore, which he won. He was awarded various prizes for academics in literature and mathematics, and was voted the class orator. His greatest thrill, however, was being selected for Skull and Bones, the secretive society of Yale (co-founded by his father in 1832). Taft graduated in 1878, second in his class of 132 students.

For the next three years, Taft studied at the University of Cincinnati Law School. Since the school's program was structured to allow students plenty of time to work, he procured a job as a reporter for the court beat on the *Cincinnati Commercial* newspaper. Despite such a busy schedule, he still found plenty of time for leisure activities and socializing—too much time, as far as his father was concerned. But young Taft's efforts to prepare for the bar exam were rewarded, and he was admitted in May 1880.

Taft had a choice of careers: his newspaper offered him a full-time reporter's position, or he could practice law. Once he chose the latter, he picked a job in the prosecutor's office over private practice, and on January 3, 1881, Taft began a public career that would continue for more than thirty years.

NATIONAL EVENTS

J.L. Kraft begins producing pasteurized cheese

JAN 1: Drilling begins on Lakeview Gusher in Kern County, CA, largest US oil well gusher on record

JAN 16: Shackleton's expedition finds the magnetic South Pole

JAN 28: US troops withdraw from Cuba (they had been there since the Spanish-American War in 1898)

FEB 12: National Association for the Advancement of Colored People (NAACP) is founded

1909

WORLD EVENTS

Danish biologist Wilhelm Ludwig Johannsen introduces new terms—gene, genotype, and phenotype

World's first plastic, Bakelite, patented by Belgian chemist Leo Baekeland

JAN 5: Colombia recognizes Panama's independence

JAN 9: Irishman Ernest (Henry) Shackleton reaches Antarctica and within 100 miles of South Pole

MAR 31: Serbia accepts Austrian annexation of Bosnia-Herzegovina

PUBLIC OFFICE

After serving as assistant prosecutor and gaining a fair number of convictions, Taft acquired his second public office when President Chester A. Arthur appointed him as the collector for internal revenue for his district. Asked later how such a position came to him at such a young age and so early in his career, he replied, "I got my political pull, first, through father's prominence; then through the fact that I was hail-fellow-well-met with all the political people of the city convention-going type. I also worked in my ward."[3] He served in the office for over a year and later admitted to detesting it. The position was a patronage appointment and so were the office's employees whom he was ordered to replace. Taft was sickened by the political bickering and asked the president to be released so he could begin private practice at long last.

In 1883, he went into partnership with a man twenty years his senior, Harlan Page Lloyd. Theirs was a traditional practice of both civil and a few criminal cases. Taft, however, yearned to rejoin his parents, who had gone to Europe where his father was serving as American minister in Vienna, but returned in time for the political maneuverings for the Republican presidential nomination in the summer of 1884. To Taft's dismay, incumbent President Chester A. Arthur's reform policies had angered too many within the GOP, so the party chose Radical Republican James G. Blaine instead to run against Grover Cleveland. Although disappointed, Taft still stumped for his party's candidate.

Taft was appointed supervisor of the election for Cincinnati; his job was to ensure that no voting fraud occurred—never an easy task. Democrats controlled the city's politics and its police force, so Taft appointed his own force of more than sixty men to function as "special deputy US marshals" to police the polling places throughout the city. Although Democratic candidate Grover Cleveland took the presidency, Republicans won in Cincinnati's elections. Suspicious of possible fraud, the House of Representatives ordered an investigation and sent a committee (mainly Democrats) to look into any possible wrongdoing. Taft testified at their hearing, but admitted he learned late on election day that some of his deputies had intimidated voters. The committee found that a certain US marshal was guilty of misconduct. Taft was grateful to see the matter concluded; he had other concerns on his mind.

THE TAFT FAMILY IN POLITICS ★ The Taft family served in government for generations. President Taft's father, Alphonso Taft, was Grant's secretary of war. Taft's oldest son, Robert, represented Ohio for years in the US Senate while another son, Charles, served as Cincinnati's mayor in the 1950s. The president's grandson Robert Jr. was an Ohio senator in the 1970s. A great-grandson served as governor of Ohio (1999–2007). Other relatives have served in diplomatic positions and as advisors to the White House.

NELLIE

Women of the 1880s were considered to be frail things of beauty who should not indulge in vices or in stimulating intellectual activities. Helen Louise Herron, known as "Nellie," broke all the rules. Her family mixed in the same circles as the Tafts; in fact, her sister and Will's were good friends. But as she matured, she found herself increasingly

DID YOU KNOW?

Taft was the first president to preside over the 48 contiguous states.

MAR 4: Inauguration of William H. Taft; he is first president to earn $75,000 (presidential salary raised for the first time since Washington)

MAR 23: Former president Theodore Roosevelt departs for an African safari

APR 6: American Robert Peary claimed to reach the North Pole

MAY 1: Walter Reed Army Medical Center opens

JUL 1: US copyright law takes effect

JUN 9: First concert by London Symphony

JUN 26: Victoria and Albert Museum opens in London

JUL: Crete annexed by Greece

JUL 13: Gold discovered in Canadian province of Ontario

JUL 25: Louis Bleriot becomes first man to fly across the English Channel in a heavier-than-air craft

OLMSTEAD V. UNITED STATES (1928) ★ *Olmstead v. United States* was the US Supreme Court decision in which the majority opinion written by Taft found that the defendant's Fourth and Fifth Amendment rights were not violated by use of wiretaps of telephone conversations conducted by federal agents without a warrant. This decision stood until a later Supreme Court decision reversed it in 1967.

unhappy with the role society had defined for her. Nellie Herron wanted to study music, but her mother thought it wasteful. Determined to earn her own money, Nellie found a teaching position. She also gravitated to the many German beer halls of Cincinnati and thoroughly enjoyed the music and companionship found there. She drank beer and learned to smoke cigarettes with a couple of her Bohemian friends. Nellie feared marriage and the improbability of finding a mate who would be her intellectual equal. Her father had been a classmate of Benjamin Harrison's and a friend of Rutherford B. Hayes. In fact, John Herron had taken his family to the White House during Hayes's presidency. Perhaps it was then that she first set her mind to one day occupy the White House as First Lady.

In her twenties, Nellie hosted a salon on Saturday evenings, where serious discussion was encouraged and served with refreshments. Taft became a regular attendee and soon fell in love with this very unique young woman. At first she was hesitant, although she enjoyed their conversations and friendship. When he proposed, she refused, so he proposed again and received another refusal. And so it went until Nellie finally consented.

DID YOU KNOW?

Taft was the heaviest president and weighed over 330 pounds. After getting stuck in the White House bathtub, one was custom-made for him.

MOVING UP THE JUDICIAL LADDER

Will and Nellie married on June 19, 1886, at her parents' home in Cincinnati. After a honeymoon in Europe, they settled down to a quiet (and rather frugal) life as Taft worked as assistant solicitor for Hamilton County while continuing his private practice. At an early age, Taft had mentioned that his goal was to be appointed to the US Supreme Court bench, and he took the first step in this direction in 1887 when he was appointed to fill a vacancy on the lower superior court. Governor Joseph B. Foraker chose thirty-year-old Taft because he had been impressed by the young man's "keen, logical, analytical mind."[4] Within a year, Taft won the election to keep his judgeship.

While many of Taft's decisions were routine in nature, one case would be used against him in later years. In *Moores & Co. v. Bricklayers' Union*, he and his fellow judges found that the union had been guilty of conspiring against another company because the company had refused to hire certain bricklayers. When the union refused to work, the supply companies were affected, including the business, Moores & Co., a lime manufacturer. The original trial had found in favor of the plaintiff and awarded them $2,250 in damages. Taft and his colleagues upheld the verdict, later leading to cries of anti-union, anti-labor from Democrats.

Taft was pleased to be a judge, but still yearned to be a justice on the US Supreme Court and attempted to push his name with President Benjamin Harrison when a vacancy occurred. Again, Governor Foraker backed him, but this time, Taft's youth and judicial inexperience hindered him and he was refused. As a consolation prize, however, Harrison offered him the post of solicitor general, which Taft accepted.

NATIONAL EVENTS

JUL 29: General Motors acquires Cadillac for $5.5 million

AUG 2: Philadelphia mint begins coining Lincoln-head penny

AUG 5: President Taft signs Payne-Aldrich Tariff into law

NOV 11: US Navy starts a naval base at Pearl Harbor, Hawaii

Charles Walgreen's Chicago pharmacy introduces the soda fountain/lunch counter that will become popular in drugstores

1910

WORLD EVENTS

SEP 26: Auroras seen in Singapore

OCT 1: Britain creates intelligence agency (MI5)

Francis Hodgson Burnett publishes *The Secret Garden*

On Valentine's Day, 1890, Taft was sworn in to his new position. Nellie remained in Cincinnati with their six-month-old son Robert while Taft secured appropriate lodging. In Washington, the Tafts met another young couple, Theodore and Edith Roosevelt. The men hit it off, but the women never became friends. Theodore was serving on the Civil Service Commission, and Will was attracted to the human dynamo. Meanwhile, Taft was hard at work, aiding the attorney general, but he still found serving in a judicial capacity more rewarding. Nellie, however, urged him to become more involved in politics; thus, Taft came to a crossroads in 1892, and took the path more to his liking, securing an appointment to the US Sixth Circuit Court and its Court of Appeals. He was just as pleased that he and his family, which now included baby daughter Helen, could return home to Cincinnati.

In addition to holding court in Cincinnati, Taft traveled to various cities in the sixth circuit, including Nashville, Cleveland, Toledo, and Detroit. Nellie tended to their children, but also looked for some outside project. She found one that allowed her to indulge her love of music. She worked tirelessly to organize and oversee the Cincinnati Orchestra Association by not only raising money for it, but also by seeking talent to conduct and perform in the orchestra. Somehow, she managed to find time to teach kindergarten, as well, but her favorite pastime was monitoring the political scene and her husband's caseload.

Taft's most famous case involved the Pullman Strike of 1894, when Eugene V. Debs, leader of the American Railway Union, organized his workers to strike the Pullman Car Company of Chicago. After President Cleveland sent troops in to break up the strike, and Debs was sent to jail, another union man, Frank Phelan, traveled to Cincinnati to encourage other railroad workers to strike on behalf of their brothers. Phelan was arrested and tried before Taft. As news of bloodshed in Chicago made headlines, eyes now fixed on Taft, to see what position he would take. Republicans heartily approved when he ruled against the union, and the American Bar Association tapped him to make a speech before their assembly in 1895. He continued to acquit himself with distinction on the bench and dote on his family, which now included another son, Charles, who was born in 1897 and quickly became his mother's favorite.

In 1900, Taft received a summons from President McKinley to come to Washington; he hoped it was to discuss a position on the Supreme Court. Instead, the president offered him a different job—commissioner to the Philippines. When Taft hesitated to take on the task, reminding the president of Taft's own reluctance in taking the islands, McKinley replied, "You don't want them any less than I do, but we have got them and in dealing with them I think I can trust the man who didn't want them any better than I can the man who did."[5] McKinley made the offer more palatable by promising Taft that by taking this position, he would be in line for a future Supreme Court nomination—if one should arise. When Taft returned home with the news, his wife greeted it enthusiastically, and soon the family was busy packing for their move.

PHILIPPINES

En route to their destination, the family stopped first in Japan, where Taft met with the emperor and empress. His weight of over two hundred and fifty pounds created a stir wherever he went, and he required a double-seat rickshaw for traveling. He

SUPREME COURT APPOINTMENTS

Horace H. Lurton, 1910

Charles Evans Hughes, 1910

Edward D. White, 1910

Willis Van Devanter, 1911

Joseph R. Lamar, 1911

Mahlon Pitney, 1912

Duncan Black and Alonzo Decker start a company (Black & Decker) making tools

Chicago physician makes first diagnosis of sickle cell anemia

Joyce C. Hall moves to Kansas City and begins selling postcards, leading to a greeting card business—Hallmark Cards

Edward Stratemeyer introduces Tom Swift series of books about a boy inventor; character is modeled on Henry Ford

FEB 8: Boy Scouts of America chartered

JAN: Greece revises its Constitution, under force by the Military League

JAN 16: Heavy rains in Paris cause the Seine to flood the city

MAR: Albania rises up against its Ottoman rulers

MAR 10: China abolishes slavery

MAY 6: Britain's King Edward VII dies; he is succeeded by son George V

STATE OF THE UNION
★★★★★★★★★★

US POPULATION IN 1909
95,972,266

NATIONAL DEBT IN 1913
$2,916,204,914

PRESIDENT'S SALARY
$75,000/year

STATES ADMITTED TO UNION
New Mexico, January 6, 1912

Arizona, February 14, 1912

NUMBER OF STATES IN 1913
48

journeyed on to Hong Kong and finally to Manila to prepare for his family, who remained in Japan. Nellie was captivated by the Japanese and seemed in no hurry to rejoin her husband, but finally she and the children arrived. Together the Tafts worked to establish friendly relations with their hosts, as well as set up a civil government. Thwarting some of these efforts was the American military governor, General Arthur MacArthur (father of the World War II commander), who scarcely hid his dislike for the Filipinos, but was successful in squelching the insurrection led by guerilla leader Emilio Aguinaldo. Once that was accomplished, Taft moved forward to create a government which protected its citizens' rights.

Serving now as governor-general of the islands, Taft's diligent efforts improved the lives of the people. Furthering public education and teaching English was crucial for the success of the Filipinos, and again, both Tafts worked toward this goal. Since the Catholic Church owned much of the property, they traveled to Rome, where Taft negotiated with Vatican officials to sell nearly four hundred thousand acres, which were then sold at low rates to the Filipino people. Other improvements were made to help upgrade health standards and limit corruption. Overseeing such a grand scale project required a great deal of Taft's energies, and he refused to allow its discontinuance; consequently, Taft twice rejected offers to be appointed to the Supreme Court. Both of these offers were from his friend who had recently become president owing to McKinley's assassination—Theodore Roosevelt. Finally, Roosevelt convinced Taft that he could return home and serve in the new administration as secretary of war, the president adding, with his customary good humor, "If only there were three of you! Then I would have put one of you on the Supreme Court . . . one of you in Root's place as secretary of war . . . and one of you permanently governor of the Philippines."[6]

SECRETARY OF WAR

Taft returned to Washington, eagerly awaiting the opportunity to reacquaint himself with Roosevelt, whom he remarked was "just the same as ever."[7] He was somewhat concerned about being able to live and entertain in Washington on a cabinet member's modest pay. The president answered the new secretary's concerns with the advice to economize. Nellie did not appreciate Theodore's words, nor did she trust him or his wife, Edith. During the 1904 election, Taft was often away from home campaigning for his boss, and making speeches that his wife criticized as being excessively long and boring.

Among Taft's new War Department duties was supervision of the Panama Canal construction. Then in 1907, Taft returned to the Far East. He met with Japanese officials regarding the ongoing Russo-Japanese War, which centered on interests in Manchuria and Korea. On his own initiative, Taft informed the Japanese that they could keep Korea, with the blessing of the United States. Afterwards he continued on to the Philippines and wrote to the president his opinion that the islands should receive help as needed but be granted as much independence as possible. Though Roosevelt knew that the American people had very little interest in the Philippines, both he and his secretary of war understood the strategic importance of maintaining a presence in that part of the Pacific to keep an eye on Japan and Russia.

A year after Taft's return from the Pacific, he was sent on a mission to Cuba, the island now in turmoil because its president Palma had shut out

NATIONAL EVENTS

APR 15: President Taft starts a presidential tradition of throwing out the first baseball

MAY 16: Congress creates US Bureau of Mines

JUN 18: Congress passes Mann-Elkins Act

JUN 19: First observance of Father's Day

JUL 24: *Detroit News* publishes first Paul Bunyan story by James MacGillivray

OCT 1: Union leaders James B. McNamara and Joseph J. McNamara plant bomb at the *Los Angeles Times* building, 21 die and more are injured

WORLD EVENTS

MAY 11: Glacier National Park is established in Montana per a Congressional vote

MAY 18: The Earth passes through the tail of Halley's Comet

MAY 31: Republic of South Africa created

JUL 2: French citizens demonstrate against public executions

AUG 22: Japan establishes Korea as a protectorate

AUG 28: Montenegro declares its independence

the Liberal members of his government in favor of the Moderates. Fearing revolution, Palma asked for American help, so Roosevelt sent Taft and the acting secretary of state Robert Bacon. Taft arrived in mid-September 1906, worried that he was unequal to the task before him. He found the coastal areas relatively stable, but anarchy rampant in the interior. Discussions with leaders of both groups proved futile and Palma resigned, against Taft's advice, forcing the American secretary to reluctantly impose the Platt Amendment (which allowed for US military/political involvement in Cuba whenever the United States believed necessary) and became the country's provisional governor. Under strict instructions from Roosevelt, Taft was to go and appraise the situation in Cuba and, above all, avoid using the term "intervention" publicly; the last thing the president wanted was to send American troops to quell a revolution. Taft's diplomatic skills prevented such an occurrence, and within a few weeks, the crisis passed and Taft returned home. Preparations ensued for his run at the presidency.

PAYNE-ALDRICH TARIFF ACT (1909) ★ The Payne-Aldrich Tariff Act was originally meant to lower tariff rates, but as it passed through both houses, so many amendments were added that it actually raised duties on 220 imported items and lowered taxes on more than 600 others. Taft received a great deal of criticism from Progressives for signing the bill. This became one of the issues for the division in the Republican Party in 1912.

PRESIDENTIAL CANDIDATE

As Theodore Roosevelt neared the end of his second term, speculation increased about who would be the Republican nominee in 1908. In a statement that he would long regret, Roosevelt announced that he would not serve three terms, thereby taking him out of the running. So now the question remained, who would run? Taft insisted his ambition was to serve on the Supreme Court, but he had repeatedly turned down opportunities to join the bench. He did so again when Roosevelt offered him a justiceship on the Court on January 1, 1906. Initially Taft admitted that he wanted the position, but Nellie immediately opposed it, saying such an appointment would prevent his presidential nomination in two years. The story goes that Roosevelt, exercising no small amount of mischief, gathered the Tafts in the second-floor library after a small White House dinner. Then pretending to fall under a trance, the president intoned, ". . . I see a man of three hundred and fifty pounds. There is something hanging over his head. I cannot make out what it is; it is hanging by a single thread. At one time it looks like the presidency—then again, it looks like the chief justiceship." "Make it the presidency!" insisted Nellie, while her husband argued, "Make it the chief justiceship."[8] Nellie would not be dissuaded.

Roosevelt conspired with Nellie, extending an invitation to Taft to come to the White House for a talk. The president convinced his war secretary, citing their similar views on policy matters, that he made the best candidate for the job—and to Taft's amazement, others agreed. The only person who seemed to understand his judicial aspirations was his eighty-year-old mother, who explained that Roosevelt was "a fighter and enjoys it, but the malice of politics would make you miserable."[9] Louise Taft knew her son well.

DID YOU KNOW?

Taft kept a cow on the lawn of the White House to provide fresh milk.

OCT 11: Theodore Roosevelt becomes first (former) president to ride in an airplane

NOV 7: First commercial airplane flight for cargo travels between Dayton and Columbus, Ohio by the Wright Brothers

DEC 19: Edward Douglas White sworn in as 9th chief justice of the US Supreme Court

JAN 18: Plane flown by Eugene B. Ely takes off and lands on USS *Pennsylvania* to demonstrate use of ships carrying planes

FEB 1: Thomas Jennings becomes first person to be convicted of a crime on basis of fingerprints

1911

SEP 1: Vatican issues to priests a compulsory oath against modernism

OCT 5: Portugal becomes a republic; its king flees the country

DEC 11: First neon lamp goes on in Paris

DEC 26: London Palladium opens

JAN 21: First auto races at Monte Carlo

MAR 1: Jose Batlle y Ordonez is elected president of Uruguay

ROBERT LAFOLLETTE (1855–1925) ★ Wisconsin governor from 1901–1905, LaFollette was instrumental in introducing progressive ideas there, including a civil service commission, regulation of railroads, corporation tax, and primaries for state offices. When he became US senator in 1906, he pushed progressivism in Washington and unsuccessfully sought the Republican presidential nomination in 1908 and 1912. He opposed American involvement in World War I.

Roosevelt worked with Republican leaders to ensure that Taft won the Republican nomination when the convention met in Chicago in June 1908. On the first ballot, the man with little desire to become president was nominated. He allowed the convention to pick his running mate, and they chose James Sherman of New York. The Republican platform was a continuation of Roosevelt's themes, including breaking up the trusts, passing laws to improve workers' safety, and allowing the territories of Arizona and New Mexico to become states. Taft campaigned throughout the nation, and asked his wife to accompany him. Nellie, however, found being a candidate's wife rather tedious since she was often relegated to meeting local politicians' dull spouses. That did not mean she did not find the campaign interesting, for she kept close watch on the newspapers and tracked events. William Jennings Bryan, the Democratic challenger, was waging his third bid for the presidency. He, too, was a reformer, and insisted he would be more effective than Taft. But Bryan's ideas went too far, particularly when he stated that railroads should be nationalized. The business community was shocked by such a socialistic proposition and replied with a resounding "NO!"

Taft captured 52 percent of the popular vote and double Bryan's electoral vote (321–162). Nellie Taft could now realize her decades-long dream of becoming First Lady, and she was ecstatic. Her husband, on the other hand, worried that he was not fit for the job and would be a poor successor to his friend and predecessor Theodore Roosevelt.

PRESIDENT TAFT

On the eve of his inauguration, the Tafts spent the night as guests of the Roosevelts at the White House, where both couples passed a rather uncomfortable evening. A winter storm hit Washington that night, leaving ice, six inches of snow, and frigid temperatures, so the ceremony was moved inside to the Senate chamber for the first time since Andrew Jackson's inauguration. Taft faced the weather with some humor, telling friends, "I always said it would be a cold day when I got to be President of the United States."[10] Bucking tradition, Nellie insisted on riding with her husband back to their new home. Once there, the ebullient new First Lady toured the White House while her husband, in a dour mood, sank into an easy chair and bellowed, "I am president now and tired of being kicked around."[11]

Theodore Roosevelt made a swift departure, leaving just after the inauguration, and soon was headed overseas to Europe and Africa. When asked why he left town so quickly, the outgoing president admitted it was to prevent any talk that he might be pulling the strings of Taft's administration. After all, one of the jokes from the campaign was, "What does Taft stand for? Take Advice from Theodore."[12] Though physically removed from the scene, Roosevelt left with full confidence that Taft would continue his policies; in fact, he told one friend, "Taft will be me!"[13]

NATIONAL EVENTS

MAR: Serialization of Frederick Taylor's *The Principles of Scientific Management* makes his writings widespread

MAR 25: Fire at Triangle Shirtwaist Factory in New York City leaves more than 140 dead

APR 17: Record number of immigrants—11,745—land at Ellis Island

APR 30: Great Fire of 1911 destroys much of downtown Bangor, Maine

MAY 15: US Supreme Court orders dissolution of Standard Oil Co. for violating Sherman Antitrust Act

WORLD EVENTS

MAR 24: Denmark abolishes death penalty and flogging

MAY 25: Rebellion begins in Mexico

JUN 22: Coronation of King George V and his wife Queen Mary at Westminster Abbey

JUN 28: Nakhla meteorite, from Mars, lands in Alexandria, Egypt

JUL 24: Inca ruins of Machu Picchu discovered in Peruvian Andes by Yale archaeologist Hiram Bingham

When Taft took office, the Republican Party found itself divided between conservatives and progressives. In Congress, conservatives held sway. There, Speaker of the House Joe Cannon ruled his dominion with all of the power of a despot, and Republican Senate leader Payne Aldrich worked to keep business in power and labor under its thumb. Insurgents who were progressives from the West and Midwest desired to pierce through the power bubble and pass legislation more to their liking, including lowering tariffs, and this idea also appealed to the president. While his predecessor had kept himself far removed from such an inflammatory issue, Taft had campaigned on the promise to lower tariffs to help American workers. He called Congress into special session to take action; however, he neglected to tell anyone what action he wanted. Many concluded that while tariffs can go down, they can also go up, and so the wrangling began.

> ***"Next to the right of liberty, the right of property is the most important individual right guaranteed by the Constitution and the one which, united with that of personal liberty, has contributed more to the growth of civilization than any other institution established by the human race."***
>
> —*William H. Taft*

Senator Aldrich proposed a bill raising tariff rates, while another bill offered the opposite. With Congress debating the virtues of each and appearing increasingly deadlocked on the issue, Taft invited to dinner leaders of both sides, who agreed to keep the president's views in mind when they formed their conference committee. To Taft's dismay, the committee was merely a group of conservatives pledged to keep the tariff from lowering in any significant way. When a bill emerged that raised duties on more than six hundred items, Wisconsin senator Robert LaFollette went to Taft, begging him to take action, and was amazed at the president's response: "Well, I don't much believe in a president's interfering with the legislative department while doing its work. They have their responsibility and I have mine. And if they send that bill to me, and it isn't a better bill than it is now, I will veto it."[14] When LaFollette and his colleagues attempted to lower certain duties, the conservatives catcalled them and sneered when they spoke. The president then began excusing the bill and talked about the various parts he did like, including the corporate income tax and the creation of a tariff commission, while not remarking about the higher rates on products including sugar, iron, lumber, and cotton.

One unlikely participant in the conferences between the executive and legislative branches was Nellie Taft. She paid close attention to the maneuverings and attended the sessions when the actual voting occurred. A few weeks later, she and her husband were sailing with a small group on the presidential yacht when Nellie collapsed. She had fallen victim to a stroke rendering her speechless. After years of leaning on her

DID YOU KNOW?

Taft was the first president to inaugurate a new baseball season by throwing the first pitch.

MAY 23: Dedication ceremony for the New York Public Library

MAY 29: US Supreme Court orders dissolution of James B. Duke's tobacco trust

MAY 30: First running of Indianapolis 500

JUN 15: In New York, IBM incorporates as Computing Tabulating Recording Corporation (CTR)

AUG 8: Congress determines US House of Representatives' number will be set at 435 beginning in 1913

AUG 10: US House of Commons approves paying itself a salary for first time

AUG 22: Theft of *Mona Lisa* discovered at the Louvre

SEP 25: While anchored in Toulon, French navy ship *Liberté* explodes

SEP 29: Italy declares war on Turkey

OCT 10: Rebellion begins in China

OCT 18: Manchu dynasty overthrown in China

DID YOU KNOW?

Taft is the only president to later serve on the US Supreme Court and become chief justice.

guidance and advice, Taft now had to stand on his own and make decisions.

Hoping to bolster his popularity, Taft decided to travel the country, see the sites, and make a few speeches. Although it was planned before his wife's stroke, he went ahead anyway and toured the West. In Minnesota, Taft made headlines when announcing his pleasure with the tariff, stating it was "the best tariff bill that the Republican Party ever passed."[15] Many people (especially Republicans), however, remained confused about the president's change of heart and his unwillingness to veto a bill that did not fulfill his expectations.

Another problem threatened to disrupt the accord within his administration when the head of the Forest Service, Gifford Pinchot, informed Taft that the secretary of the interior, Richard Ballinger, should be fired because of how he handled the allotment of certain Alaskan coal field properties. Taft assigned his attorney general to investigate, but the president already tended to believe Ballinger had done nothing wrong. He and his interior secretary agreed that Roosevelt had acted unconstitutionally in appropriating lands for public domain, so they determined to go slower and more cautiously. When the Justice Department reported all was well, Taft refused to fire Ballinger, which enraged Pinchot (a holdover from the previous administration), and soon it was he who was asked to resign. Again, progressives felt betrayed by the president. Theodore Roosevelt proclaimed, "One of the heaviest counts against Taft is that by his actions he has produced a state of affairs in which the split is so deep that it seems impossible to heal it, and the most likely result is that the people will . . . turn to the Democrats."[16] How prophetic his words became.

Taft still wished to serve as a justice on the Supreme Court; ironically he, as president, had to appoint another for the position. Still, his choice may have been made with an eye toward his own future justiceship. Taft had told Charles Evans Hughes that if the chief justiceship opened, he would be nominated. But when the opportunity presented itself, Taft appointed an older judge instead, possibly with the hope that the elder justice would not live as long and therefore leave an opening for the president when he became available.

For the four years of his presidency, Taft found little joy in his work, and his increasing weight only made him more unhappy. To add to his problems, the Republicans had lost their majority in the House and Democrats had been added to the Senate after the midterm elections in 1910. On the plus side, he experienced some successes, albeit short-lived, when he rallied to encourage passage of a reciprocity agreement with Canada to ease tariff barriers. Many farmers opposed the possible increase of Canadian foodstuffs coming south, and fishermen also had similar concerns. Congress at first voted it down, but Taft called them back into session, and eventually they approved it, but Canada then refused to agree, fearing talk by Americans of annexing Canada.

Taft supported the antitrust measures of his predecessor; in fact, ninety lawsuits were filed under his administration, including against Standard Oil Company and the tobacco interests. He was happy to sign the Mann-Elkins Act, which placed the burgeoning communications industry under the Interstate Commerce Commission. Trying to make the federal government more efficient and helpful to its people, Taft divided the Department of Commerce and Labor into two; created the Bureau of Mines; started the Commission on Economy and Efficiency, which later became the Budgeting and Accounting office; and wrote a

NATIONAL EVENTS

AUG 15: Proctor & Gamble markets first solid hydrogenated shortening—Crisco

NOV 3: Chevrolet enters auto industry to compete with Ford

Leon Lenwood Bean begins L.L. Bean clothing store in Freeport, Maine

Salt Lake City is first to have traffic lights

Nabisco introduces Oreo biscuits to compete with a similar cookie, Hydrox

1912

WORLD EVENTS

NOV 6: Francisco Madero declares himself president of Mexico

DEC 14: Norwegian explorer Roald Amundsen reaches South Pole

German geologist Alfred Wegener proposes idea of continental drift and early continent of Pangaea

Lake Guatavita in Colombia is drained by British treasure hunters hoping to find gold; they come up empty

JAN 1: China becomes a republic; Sun Yat-sen becomes provisional president

paper telling why the country needed a national budget. He oversaw the entrance of Arizona and New Mexico into the Union as the forty-seventh and forty-eighth states, and the Sixteenth Amendment was passed allowing personal income tax.

After his background serving in the Philippines and Cuba, Taft had a particular interest in foreign affairs. He hoped to improve America's relations with other nations by using dollars rather than bullets, thus giving the program the name "Dollar Diplomacy." He pursued this policy of helping developing nations, particularly in Central and South America, because "this financial rehabilitation and the protection of their customhouses from being the prey of would-be dictators would remove at one stroke the menace of foreign creditors and the menace of revolutionary disorder."[17] Investments were encouraged for Haiti and Honduras, but Marines were sent into Nicaragua to ensure a government friendly to American interests remained in power, which would help ensure the safety of the nearby building project—the Panama Canal.

JUDGES' BILL (1925) ★ The Judges' Bill was recommended by Chief Justice Taft to lessen the onerous workload of the Supreme Court by limiting its caseload. After its passage, the Court could pick and choose which cases to hear, depending upon the constitutional questions raised or points of law requiring clarification.

ELECTION OF 1912

Speculation abounded in the spring of 1912 as to whom the two parties might nominate. Normally, the incumbent president was a certainty unless he expressly declined; however, Theodore Roosevelt now encouraged talk of his candidacy. The Republican convention in Chicago erupted with fistfights and police being summoned to break apart members of the two factions—Taft supporters and Roosevelt supporters. Their behavior was so wild that Democrat William Jennings Bryan humorously said it sounded more like a *Democratic* convention. Taft's men controlled the convention, causing Roosevelt and his people to bolt the party. The Progressives held their own convention a few weeks later, with Roosevelt as their candidate announcing he was "fit as a bull moose"; they became the Bull Moose Party. In stark contrast, the Democrats selected mild-mannered Woodrow Wilson, governor of New Jersey and former college professor.

During the campaign, Roosevelt and Wilson traveled around the nation while Taft did very little; most believed him to have nearly no chance of victory. He admitted, "If I cannot win, I hope Wilson will, and Roosevelt feels, that if he cannot win, he hopes Wilson will."[18] The other two candidates often differed little in substance and the Democrats argued they had more history and understanding of change than did any part of the Republican Party. A few weeks before election day, Roosevelt was shot during a speech, but in true "Teddy" fashion, he refused to quit. Instead, he completed his remarks before telling the audience that he in fact had been hit and required medical attention.

As Roosevelt had predicted a few years earlier, the Democrats won thanks to the split of the Grand Old Party. Wilson won 42 percent of the popular vote and 435 electoral votes; Roosevelt won 27 percent and eighty-eight electoral votes; Taft won 23 percent and only eight electoral votes (Utah and Vermont). The tide had turned against him and the Republicans.

DID YOU KNOW?

Taft is one of two presidents buried at Arlington National Cemetery (John F. Kennedy is the other).

Morton Salt begins production

The Blues is born when "The Memphis Blues" is published

JAN 6: New Mexico admitted as 47th state

JAN 9: US forces sent to Honduras

FEB 14: Arizona admitted as 48th state

FEB 19: Cracker Jack candy offers prizes in boxes for the first time

MAR 1: Albert Berry made his first parachute jump from a moving airplane in Missouri

JAN 8: South African Native National Congress convenes for first time

JAN 12: First international drug control treaty, the International Opium Convention, signed at The Hague

JAN 17: British explorer Robert Scott reaches South Pole, only to find Amundsen's flag (who had reached the point one month earlier)

FEB 12: China's boy emperor Pu Yi abdicates

MAR 5: Italy use airships for reconnaissance west of Tripoli, first military use of these crafts

DID YOU KNOW?

Taft was a cousin of Richard Nixon.

RETIREMENT

The person most disappointed by the election results (besides Theodore Roosevelt) was Nellie Taft. Her recovery was nearly complete from her stroke earlier and she hated to leave their home of the past four years. During her husband's presidency, Nellie had enjoyed entertaining groups large and small, inside as well as outside. She introduced the practice of having musical or theatrical entertainment for guests. And it was Nellie's idea that brought Japanese cherry trees to Washington, which still dazzle visitors in April.

> *We are all imperfect. We cannot expect perfect government.*
>
> —*William H. Taft*

Leaving the capital city meant deciding where to go next. They had considered Cincinnati, but she vetoed returning there; fortunately, Taft was asked to teach at Yale Law School, so they moved to New Haven. There they lived in peace and happiness for the next eight years, content to travel the world and enjoy life. Taft supported Wilson and his position to stay out of the war, but also later backed his decision to go to war. He also reconciled with Roosevelt, although their friendship was never as warm as it once had been (nor did the wives ever become friends).

Then in 1921, at the age of sixty-four, Taft's lifelong dream was realized. President Warren G. Harding asked if Taft would like to serve as the new chief justice of the Supreme Court. He and Nellie returned to Washington, where he served on the bench for the next nine years. Taft proved an efficient judicial administrator and drafted one-sixth of the court's opinions (about 250). While he mostly ruled as a conservative, he sometimes agreed to broaden the federal government's power, particularly involving interstate trade. Ironically, one of the main cases of his court involved the same Tenure of Office Act which provoked the impeachment of President Andrew Johnson. The Taft court found the act unconstitutional, just as Johnson had argued. Besides his work on the court, Taft also improved training for circuit court judges and urged construction of a building for the Supreme Court.

Although his health began deteriorating, Taft refused to resign because he feared the type of appointment Hoover would make to replace him, and told a friend, he wanted to "prevent the Bolsheviki from getting control of it."[19] But by early 1930, Taft could no longer delay his resignation; he was simply too sick and weak to work. He felt somewhat better when informed that Charles Evans Hughes was set to replace him. Suffering from high blood pressure, heart disease, and other ailments, there was little anyone could do for him, and on March 8, 1930, the former president and chief justice of the United States, William Howard Taft, peacefully passed away. His body lay in state at the capitol, then he was buried, as he had requested, at Arlington National Cemetery.

Nellie Taft continued to travel and live an independent lifestyle (including gleefully violating Prohibition). She died on May 22, 1943, and was buried next to her husband.

NATIONAL EVENTS

MAR 12: Girl Scouts of America founded

MAR 27: Gift from Japan of 3,000 cherry blossom trees to be planted in Washington, D.C.

APR 20: Fenway Park completed in Boston, home of the Red Sox; Detroit opens its Tiger Stadium

JUN 5: US Marines arrive in Cuba

JUL 19: A meteorite explodes over Holbrook, AZ, thousands of pieces of debris pelt the town

WORLD EVENTS

MAR 30: France establishes a protectorate over Morocco

APR 15: Sinking of British ocean liner *Titanic* after it strikes an iceberg in North Atlantic; 1,500 perish

APR 16: Harriet Quimby makes history as first woman to fly across the English Channel

APR 17: Russian army shoots striking goldfield workers near the Lena River

MAY 5: Stockholm, Sweden welcomes the Summer Olympics

ENDNOTES

1 Henry F. Pringle, *The Life and Times of William Howard Taft*, New York: Farrar & Rinehart, Inc., 1939, p. 3.

2 Ibid, p. 35.

3 Ibid, p. 58.

4 Ibid, p. 94.

5 Judith Icke Anderson, *William Howard Taft, An Intimate History*, New York: W.W. Norton & Co., 1981, p. 66.

6 Pringle, p. 252.

7 Anderson, p. 79.

8 Nathan Miller, *Theodore Roosevelt, A Life*, New York: William Morrow & Co., Inc., 1992, p. 483.

9 Pringle, pp. 319–320.

10 Anderson, p. 120.

11 Ibid, p. 121.

12 Ibid, p. 109.

13 Carl Sferrazza Anthony, *Nellie Taft: The Unconventional First Lady of the Ragtime Era*, New York: William Morrow & Co., 2005, p. 221.

14 Anderson, p. 173.

15 Ibid, p. 175.

16 Ibid, p. 190.

17 William A. DeGregorio, *The Complete Book of US Presidents*, New York: Gramercy Books, 2005, p. 402.

18 Anderson, p. 247.

19 Anthony, p. 381.

AUG 5: Progressive (Bull Moose) Party formed and nominates Theodore Roosevelt as its presidential candidate

AUG 14: Americans land in Nicaragua to protect American interests (remain until 1933)

OCT 14: Attempted assassination of Theodore Roosevelt, but he continues to deliver his prepared speech before seeking medical attention

NOV 5: Democrat Woodrow Wilson wins presidential election easily against incumbent Taft and Roosevelt

JUN 4: Constantinople burns, 1,120 buildings razed

JUL 12: Greek island of Icana declares independence

OCT 8: First Balkan War begins when Montenegro declares war on Turkey (Ottoman Empire)

OCT 17: Serbia, Bulgaria, and Greece (Balkan League) join to fight Turkey

NOV 28: Albania declares its independence from Ottoman Empire

DEC 3: Temporary end of First Balkan War (just as Austria and Russia begin mobilizing to help Turkey)

Woodrow Wilson

★ ★ ★ TWENTY-EIGHTH PRESIDENT ★ ★ ★

LIFE SPAN
- Born: December 28, 1856, in Staunton, Virginia
- Died: February 3, 1924, in Washington, D.C.

NICKNAME
- Schoolmaster in Politics

RELIGION
- Presbyterian

HIGHER EDUCATION
- College of New Jersey (Princeton), 1879

PROFESSION
- Professor, college administrator

MILITARY SERVICE
- None

FAMILY
- Father: **Joseph Ruggles Wilson** (1822–1903)
- Mother: **Janet "Jessie" Woodrow Wilson** (1830–1888)
- First wife: **Ellen Louise Axson Wilson** (1860–1914); wed on June 24, 1885, in Savannah, Georgia
- Children: **Margaret Woodrow** (1886–1944); **Jessie Woodrow** (1887–1933); **Eleanor Randolph** (1889–1967)
- Second wife: **Edith Bolling Galt Wilson** (1872–1961); wed on December 15, 1915, in Washington, D.C.
- No children

POLITICAL LIFE
- Governor of New Jersey (1911–1913)

PRESIDENCY
- Two terms: March 4, 1913–March 4, 1921
- Democrat
- Reason for leaving office: completion of term
- Vice president: **Thomas R. Marshall** (1913–1921)

ELECTION OF 1912
- Electoral vote: **Wilson** 435; **Taft** 8; **Roosevelt** 88
- Popular vote: **Wilson** 6,296,184; **Taft** 3,486,242; **Roosevelt** 4,122,721

ELECTION OF 1916
- Electoral vote: **Wilson** 277; **Charles Hughes** 254
- Popular vote: **Wilson** 9,126,868; **Hughes** 8,548,728

CABINET
★★★★★★★★★★

SECRETARY OF STATE
William Jennings Bryan (1913–1915)

Robert Lansing (1915–1920)

Bainbridge Colby (1920–1921)

SECRETARY OF THE TREASURY
William G. McAdoo (1913–1918)

Carter Glass (1918–1920)

David F. Houston (1920–1921)

SECRETARY OF WAR
Lindley M. Garrison (1913–1916)

Newton D. Baker (1916–1921)

ATTORNEY GENERAL
James C. McReynolds (1913–1914)

Thomas W. Gregory (1914–1919)

A. Mitchell Palmer (1919–1921)

Woodrow Wilson rose to the presidency more as a result of his academic rather than his political background. Before serving for two terms at the nation's top post, he spent eight years as president of Princeton University and became well known for lectures he gave across the country. His governorship of New Jersey was a mere way station on his trip to the grandest lecture podium of all, or what Theodore Roosevelt called, "the bully pulpit."

EARLY LIFE

Thomas Woodrow Wilson was the third of four children born to Dr. Joseph Ruggles Wilson and his wife Janet "Jessie" Woodrow. Joseph had become an ordained Presbyterian minister seven years before his son's birth, so his assignments took the family to various towns. Woodrow was born in Staunton, Virginia, on December 28, 1856, but the following year the family moved to Augusta, Georgia, where they remained until he was fourteen. They then moved to Columbia, South Carolina, and, later, Wilmington, North Carolina. While in Augusta, the Civil War raged and did affect their town, but, thankfully, it was not among those burned by Sherman's army. Woodrow was educated by his parents at home, where they could provide the extra help he needed learning to read and grasping fundamental arithmetic concepts. Today, most experts would say that Wilson suffered from a form of dyslexia, which hampered his early efforts. Once he jumped the hurdle of reading, however, he advanced steadily, and by age twelve, he was sent to school in Columbia. Four years later, he attempted higher education at Davidson College in North Carolina, where he developed debating skills, but ill health forced him to return home after his freshman year.

Both parents played important roles in Woodrow's young life. His father's strong Presbyterian beliefs remained with his son, who in later years said, "My life would not be worth living if it were not for the driving power of religion, for faith, pure and simple. . . . Never for a moment have I had one doubt about my religious beliefs."[1] His faith was a constant source of strength throughout his life, as was his connection to his parents. Although Jessie Wilson had four children, Woodrow was her particular favorite, and he clung to her, later admitting he had been a bit of a "mama's boy." She wrote to him frequently when he was at college. At Princeton, she sometimes worried, "I did not like to hear of your sleeping without first having fire—even in warm weather. Have you cover enough for very cold weather." She often complimented him on his fine oratorical success and reminded him that it was a gift: "It would be your own fault if you were not an orator—for you have not only a fine memory, but the *acting talent* . . . in such a degree that you can make yourself what you please in that line."[2] While their son chose not to pursue acting, he employed his oratorical skills to great effect over the course of his academic and political careers.

Once the Wilson family settled in Wilmington, North Carolina, it was also decided that Woodrow would follow in his father's footsteps and attend the College of New Jersey (Princeton). For the next four years, he applied himself to his studies, with pleasing results, although he continued to struggle in mathematics and science. Extracurricular activities were important to him, as well. Wilson played baseball and football, debated and performed in some theatrical ventures, but more significantly, he wrote and

NATIONAL EVENTS

FEB 3: Sixteenth Amendment ratified, creating income tax

MAR 4: Woodrow Wilson inaugurated president

MAR 4: US Department of Commerce and Labor split into two departments

APR 8: Seventeenth Amendment ratified, granting direct election of senators

DEC 23: President Wilson signs bill creating Federal Reserve banking system

1913

WORLD EVENTS

FEB 18: Mexican militant Victoriano Huerta seizes control of Mexico City and declares himself president

MAR 18: Assassination of King George I of Greece

JUN 16: Second Balkan War begins when Bulgaria attacks Serbian and Greek troops

AUG 10: Second Balkan War ends with Treaty of Bucharest (Bulgaria defeated)

DEC 1: Crete annexed by Greece

was published in a variety of journals, including *International Review*. He also edited the college's newspaper, the *Princetonian*. When graduation day arrived in 1879, Woodrow Wilson stood thirty-eighth in his class of 167.

Wilson assumed that one day he would become a politician, and since most politicians started as lawyers, he began the appropriate course of study at the University of Virginia law school. Before a year was out, he knew he had made a mistake. He found the law extremely tedious and amused himself by participating in the university's debating society and singing in the glee club. A few months before graduation, Woodrow fell ill again and returned to his family in Wilmington. He completed his legal studies on his own and passed the bar in 1882. Then he and a friend, Edward Ireland Renick, opened a practice in Atlanta, but this too was short lived. Even more boring than studying law was practicing it, a disillusioned Woodrow writing of "the depth and slime of the gulf that often separated the philosophy of law from its practice."[3] After eighteen months, the partnership dissolved, and Wilson moved north to Baltimore, where he enrolled at Johns Hopkins University to pursue a PhD in political science.

The atmosphere and curriculum at Johns Hopkins were much more to his liking, and Wilson flourished, academically and physically. Prior to receiving his degree in 1886, Wilson published an acclaimed book, *Congressional Government*, in which he argued against America's present system, which allowed for Congress to exercise dominative powers over the executive and judicial branches; instead, he reasoned the United States should adopt the British parliamentarian model. The book brought attention to the young scholar and would open crucial doors in academia.

PROFESSOR

Wilson began his career teaching political economy and public law at Bryn Mawr women's college, but he was dissatisfied during his three years there. Although he did not directly blame his unhappiness on the women in his classroom, because society did not welcome any true intellectual debate, he did feel that a "painful absenteeism of mind" created a need for him to find a new position elsewhere in 1888. By this point, however, he had to take into consideration the needs of the rest of his new family.

Five years earlier, while visiting Rome, Georgia, and attending to legal business, Wilson attended the Presbyterian church, and his eyes soon settled on the attractive young lady in front—the minister's daughter. He called on her father at the parsonage and happily became better acquainted with twenty-three-year-old Ellen Axson. Since losing her mother three years earlier, she had taken on the care of her siblings and acted as mistress of the household and her father's hostess; consequently, she never considered becoming a southern belle, or even marrying, believing that her duty was to her family. That is until a smooth-talking attorney appeared.

The two began a long-distance courtship and wrote many lengthy letters to each other. While Woodrow studied in graduate school, Ellen remained in Georgia, helping her father, who suffered from mental illness, including depression. With a heavy heart, Ellen committed him to the Georgia State Mental Hospital, where he soon committed suicide. She withdrew and decided to resume her passion—art. When Ellen went to New York to study at the Arts Students League, her fiancé wondered if she was having second thoughts about marriage. But she returned to Savannah,

CABINET
★★★★★★★★★★

(continued)

SECRETARY OF THE NAVY
Josephus Daniels (1913–1921)

POSTMASTER GENERAL
Albert S. Burleson (1913–1921)

SECRETARY OF THE INTERIOR
Franklin K. Lane (1913–1920)

John B. Payne (1920–1921)

SECRETARY OF AGRICULTURE
David F. Houston (1913–1920)

Edwin T. Meredith (1920–1921)

SECREARY OF COMMERCE
William C. Redfield (1913–1919)

Joshua W. Alexander (1919–1921)

SECRETARY OF LABOR
William B. Wilson (1913–1921)

JAN 5: Ford Motor Company declares it will have an eight-hour workday and $5 minimum wage per day

APR 9: American ship's crew held in Tampico, Mexico

APR 21: 3,000 Marines land in Vera Cruz, Mexico

AUG 6: First Lady Ellen Wilson dies from Bright's disease

AUG 18: President Wilson issues "Proclamation of Neutrality"

SEP 26: Federal Trade Commission (FTC) created

OCT 15: Clayton Antitrust Act passed

1914

JUN 28: Austro-Hungarian Archduke Franz Ferdinand and his wife are assassinated in Sarajevo by Serbian terrorist

JUL 28: World War I begins when Austria-Hungary declares war on Serbia

AUG 1: Germany declares war on Russia

AUG 3: Germany declares war on France

AUG 4: German troops march into neutral Belgium, prompting Britain to declare war on Germany

AUG 15: Panama Canal officially opens

AUG 23: Japan declares war on Germany

DID YOU KNOW?

Wilson was the first president to have earned a Ph.D.

Georgia, and on June 24, 1885, Ellen and Woodrow married. After spending the remaining summer near Asheville, North Carolina, they traveled north to Bryn Mawr. There Ellen gave birth to the first two of their daughters.

By 1888, the family was packing up for a move to Middletown, Connecticut, where Woodrow had taken the position of professor of political science and history at Wesleyan University. There they welcomed their third and final child, another daughter. Wilson was happier among his students, and his colleagues, at Wesleyan than at Bryn Mawr. He became involved in more than just academics, even drawing on his football experience to devise a play for the Wesleyan team to use against Pennsylvania. And, on one occasion, before facing Wesleyan's longtime adversary, Yale, he was heard to exhort, "You can lick Yale as well as any other team. Go after their scalps. Don't admit for a moment that they can beat you."[4] His tall form could often be found pacing the sidelines and leading the crowd in cheers for the Wesleyan players.

While at Wesleyan, Wilson published a second book, *The State: Elements of Historical and Practical Politics*, which was meant to be a comparative government textbook. In this, he advocated some of the principles of socialism and argued that government action was essential to righting society's wrongs—child labor, consumer's rights, breaking up monopolies and trusts, and operating the major transportation systems. Many of these views would form the basis for the progressive reforms of his presidency.

In 1890, a longtime desire of Wilson's became reality when he was offered a position at Princeton. He eagerly accepted the prized Chair of Jurisprudence and Political Economy. The Wilson household, which often included extended family members, moved once more to a large house, which they named Library Place. At Princeton, Wilson quickly gained notoriety as a professor in demand; in fact, half of the juniors and seniors enrolled in his classes. His lectures became legendary, as remarkable for their depth of content as much as for his captivating delivery. Every year, he took a six-week sabbatical to return to Johns Hopkins, where he taught administration. Wilson managed to find time to write, too, and in 1893 another volume appeared, this time a historical work on the Civil War, *Division and Reunion*. Here he argued that originally the United States was a federation, so southerners had been correct in their belief that they could legally secede. However, over time the country truly forged into a nation, resulting in Lincoln's assertion that secession was unconstitutional. Again, Wilson received critical acclaim for this and other essays that were published over the coming years.

PRINCETON PRESIDENT

Although pleased by his success in teaching and publishing, he scarcely had to think before accepting the presidency of Princeton when offered it in 1902. His installation was a national event with persons including J.P. Morgan and Booker T. Washington in the audience. President Theodore Roosevelt was also planning to attend but was delayed. Another member of the audience was Colonel George Harvey, a man of multiple talents, including publisher of *Harper's Weekly* and a major player in the Democratic national party. He was so impressed by Wilson's oratory that he read all of his books and began contemplating if Wilson could be molded into a political figure. Time would tell.

Meanwhile, the new president of Princeton threw himself into his work with a spirited

NATIONAL EVENTS

NOV 16: Federal Reserve banks open

NOV 20: Photographs now required for US passports

JAN 12: US House of Representatives votes down proposal allowing women's suffrage

JAN 25: Long distance telephone service now connects New York to San Francisco

FEB 8: Premiere of D.W. Griffith's controversial film *The Birth of a Nation*

JUL 28: US begins occupation of Haiti

1915

WORLD EVENTS

NOV 4: Britain and France declare war on Turkey

DEC 18: British declare protectorate over Egypt

JAN 19: First use of Zeppelins to bomb British cities by air

FEB 18: German U-boats begin blockading British coast

FEB 19: British attack Dardanelles

FEB 21: Battle of Verdun begins

APR 22: Second Battle of Ypres, Belgium—Germans introduce poisonous gas as a weapon

fervor. Fighting the growing tendency that allowed students to build their program from electives which varied greatly in rigor, Wilson proposed implementing required courses and developing more organization in their education, with the goal of students actually learning in a worthwhile manner. To facilitate this, he also planned to institute the British system of assigning students to young teachers, called preceptors, who would take the underclassmen under their wing and help them through all four years. Although this required funding, it became a positive experience for students and faculty. His next reform, however, met with decided resistance from all sides.

People of Princeton must have been rocked on their heels when they heard the college's president announce, "I have told the authorities I will not be the President of a Country Club. Princeton must either be an educational institution or I will not remain."[5] His target was the eating clubs on campus who invited students to join them. Those who were excluded were also shut out from other activities; thus, the campus was often divided along economic lines.

Wilson saw no reason to continue the division between the "haves" and "have nots" on campus, but current students and alumni strongly disagreed. They believed that his proposal of having a quad system where students of all classes lived in a dormitory with one of the professors as the head of the house was far too democratic and barred students from determining which young men they chose to eat and live with. Adding to the controversy was the gift of William Proctor of Proctor & Gamble of Cincinnati. He dangled five hundred thousand dollars in front of the trustees' noses with the requirement it be spent on a graduate school some distance from the undergraduate campus. Proctor offered this in collusion with the graduate dean and his former teacher, Andrew F. West, who disliked Wilson and desired to be far away from his control; to ensure this happened, Proctor stipulated that the grant would be awarded *if* the college provided matching funds and they chose a site to Proctor's liking. Not wishing to lose such a beneficent amount, the trustees allowed Proctor and West to place the graduate school a distance from campus and they refused Wilson's quad plan.

> *"For beauty I am not a star*
> *There are others more handsome by far*
> *But my face I don't mind it*
> *For I am behind it*
> *It's the people in front that I jar."*
>
> —*Limerick written by Woodrow Wilson to describe himself*

Upset and disappointed by the dual loss, the president now started wondering about blazing a new path for himself. It was a time for reflection. Wilson had recently turned fifty and suffered bouts of illness, including a frightening episode of temporary blindness in his left eye. Very likely this occurred because of severe hypertension, which later resulted in more serious strokes. Fortunately, Wilson accepted the diagnosis of rest and allowed himself time to recover, although his left eye never

SUPREME COURT APPOINTMENTS
★★★★★★★★★★

James C. McReynolds, 1914

Louis D. Brandeis, 1916

John H. Clarke, 1916

OCT 12: One-millionth Model T Ford rolls off assembly line

DEC 18: President Wilson marries Edith Bolling Galt

MAR 8–9: Mexican rebel leader Pancho Villa attacks Columbus, New Mexico, killing 17

MAR 15: 12,000 American soldiers sent into Mexico in pursuit of Pancho Villa

MAY 5: US Marines land in Dominican Republic to restore order

1916

MAY 7: British ocean liner *Lusitania* sunk by German U-boat, nearly 1,200 die

MAY 23: Italy joins the Allies

DEC 16: Albert Einstein publishes "General Theory of Relativity"

German potato blight leads to death by starvation for hundreds of thousands of Germans

JAN 8: Allied troops leave Gallipoli

JAN 29: Paris bombed from air by German Zeppelins

JUN 5: Arabs revolt (partly owing to British officer T.E. Lawrence's efforts) against Turks

STATE OF THE UNION

US POPULATION IN 1913
91,972,266

NATIONAL DEBT IN 1921
$23,977,450,553

NUMBER OF STATES IN 1921
48

regained full sight. While recuperating, he contemplated the direction he wished his future to take and opened himself to new opportunities.

POLITICS

The 1908 election found the Democratic Party the loser—again. They had not won an election since Grover Cleveland's victory in 1892. For three elections, they fronted William Jennings Bryan as their presidential candidate, and three times they watched Republicans, first William McKinley then Theodore Roosevelt, defeat them. It was definitely time for a change before the election of 1912. The question remained, who should be run this time? Colonel Harvey believed he might have found the man, but he needed to be tested in both a campaign and political office. When asked if he would be willing to run for governor, Wilson resigned his post at Princeton and gratefully accepted the nomination from the New Jersey Democratic convention, saying, "I did not seek the nomination. It has come to me absolutely unsolicited."[6] Unbeholden to anyone, his nonpolitical persona won many converts that day, including assemblyman Joseph Tumulty, who soon would be on Wilson's staff.

Another part of Wilson's appeal was his emphatic drive against the political machines and the boss system that had held the balance of power for years. Some voters were put off by his professorial appearance and somber demeanor, but approved of his strong progressive stance on issues, including direct election of senators and setting rates for public utilities. He barnstormed New Jersey using his honed oratorical skills to advantage. On November 5, he achieved what many believed impossible—a Democratic sweep of the state assembly and overwhelming victory for himself to the governorship.

DID YOU KNOW?

Wilson kept a flock of sheep on the White House grounds to provide wool during the shortages of World War I.

GOVERNOR WILSON

One of his first tasks as governor-elect was asserting power over the state's party machine. When Boss James Smith discussed with Wilson his desire to run for US senator, Wilson was not encouraging. This somewhat shocked Smith, who had received a public letter from Wilson during the campaign promising, "I would be perfectly willing to assure Mr. Smith that I would not, if elected Governor, set about 'fighting and breaking down the existing Democratic organization and replacing it with one of my own.' The last thing I should think of would be building up a machine of my own."[7] Smith later denounced him as "an ingrate and a liar."[8] The Democratic Party chairman also was removed as part of Wilson's progressive house cleaning.

The new governor pledged his wholehearted support to the Geran bill, which provided the means for granting the voters, rather than the party machines, political power in elections. Undaunted by the uphill fight to win support in the state legislature, Wilson pushed forward, going so far as meeting with the Democratic caucus and warning them, "You can turn aside the measure if you choose. You can decline to follow me; you can deprive me of office and turn away from me, but you cannot deprive me of power so long as I steadfastly stand for what I believe to be the interests and legitimate demands of the people themselves."[9] His efforts paid off when the bill passed the state assembly. Progressive reforms continued in the same legislative session with the passage of a workmen's compensation bill, public utilities law, and one against corrupt practices. He acknowledged the hard work of himself and others in their achievements but also insisted that timing was crucial, and his success was attributable to the fact that his term occurred "when opinion was ripe on all these matters, when both parties were com-

NATIONAL EVENTS

AUG 25: President Wilson signs a bill creating the National Park Service

AUG 29: Philippines Autonomy Act signed into law by President Wilson

SEP 7: Congress passes Workmen's Compensation Act

NOV 7: Wilson wins reelection over Republican challenger Charles E. Hughes

NOV 7: Jeannette Rankin of Montana becomes first woman elected to Congress

WORLD EVENTS

JUL 1–NOV 18: More than one million men die in the Battle of the Somme (including 60,000 British soldiers in the first day)

SEP: Manfred von Richthofen (the "Red Baron") begins flying and shooting down Allied aircraft

SEP 15: First British tanks roll into war at the Battle of the Somme

DEC 13: Avalanche in eastern Alps kills more than 10,000 Austrian and Italian soldiers

DEC 29: Gregori Rasputin (confidante and friend to Czarina Alexandra of Russia) is murdered

mitted to these reforms, and by merely standing fast, and by never losing sight of the business for an hour, but keeping up all sorts of (legitimate) pressure all the time, kept the mighty forces from being diverted or blocked at any point."[10] Now his message would be delivered on the national stage.

ESPIONAGE ACT (1917) ★ Passed soon after America's entry into World War I, this law prevented anyone from interfering in troop recruitment or conveying information to the enemy. Penalties included a twenty-year prison term and $10,000 fine. Those refusing to serve were also arrested under this act and imprisoned. Then the Sedition Act was passed in 1918 to curb any political dissent of the government and/or the war. This included verbal and written speech, and the postmaster general was granted power to ban any materials deemed subversive. Eugene V. Debs (1855–1926), socialist activist and outspoken critic of the war, was arrested for a speech encouraging people to ignore the call "to duty" and resist becoming cannon fodder. He was sentenced to a ten-year prison term under the Espionage Act, but was pardoned in 1921 by President Warren G. Harding.

PRESIDENTIAL CANDIDATE

For years, Colonel Harvey had run "Woodrow Wilson for President" under the *Harper's Weekly* masthead. As 1912 edged closer, he and other Democratic leaders planned to make the phrase popular across the country. Republican president William H. Taft decided to run for reelection, but his former mentor and predecessor, now angered and disappointed by Taft's lackluster performance, chose to run against him. The nation watched as Theodore Roosevelt bolted his beloved Republican Party to form the Progressive Party, which soon became better known as the "Bull Moose" Party. Democrats now only need find a reasonable alternative and the election would be theirs. Who better than a scholar and academic to market credibility and stability to voters?

When Democrats met at their convention in Baltimore, two names topped the list of potential presidential nominees—Representative James Beauchamp (Champ) Clark of Missouri, who was also the Speaker of the House, and Governor Woodrow Wilson of New Jersey. After much maneuvering and switching of delegates' votes, Wilson captured the nomination on the forty-sixth ballot, thanks in part to perennial candidate William Jennings Bryan, who released his delegates to Wilson. The vice presidential candidate was Indiana governor Thomas R. Marshall.

While Taft remained at the White House, Wilson and Roosevelt actively stumped around the country. Earlier, Wilson had coined the phrase "New Freedom" to describe his program against trusts and monopolies, as well as more power to labor. His party endorsed proposed constitutional amendments for income tax and direct election of senators and stricter regulations on food, drugs, and public utilities.

As predicted, the Republican Party split created the opening for Wilson to win with 42 percent of the popular vote and 435 electoral votes compared to second-place Theodore Roosevelt with 27 percent of the popular vote and 88 electoral votes. When one of the main political operatives from the Democratic convention met with the new president-elect, Wilson cautioned him that politicians would receive nothing from him: "I wish it clearly understood that I owe you nothing.

1917

JAN 25: US buys Danish West Indies for $25 million

JAN 30: General Pershing's troops begin leaving Mexico, not having found Pancho Villa

FEB 3: US ends diplomatic relations with Germany

FEB 24: British intercept Zimmerman telegram detailing Germany's plan to give southwest back to Mexico if they ally themselves with the Germans

JAN 31: Germany announces it will engage in unrestricted submarine warfare

MAR 5: Mexico adopts its constitution

MAR 8: Russian Revolution begins

MAR 15: Czar Nicholas II of Russia abdicates

MAR 17: Provisional government takes over Russia

APR: "Red Baron" Manfred von Richthofen shoots down 21 Allied aircraft in April

JUN 13: Germany bombs London

JUL: Germany begins using mustard gas

FEDERAL RESERVE SYSTEM (1913) ★ The Federal Reserve Act of 1913 established the Federal Reserve System. The "Fed" functions as the nation's money manager, mainly through raising/lowering interest rates. It also works as the banker of the Federal Treasury and is the "banker's bank."

Remember that God ordained that I should be the next president of the United States. Neither you nor any other mortal or mortals could have prevented that."[11]

PRESIDENT WILSON

Once he took office in March 1913, President Woodrow Wilson put his plans for progressive reforms into action. He announced these when he discarded the practice of sending the State of the Union message to Congress, as done by every president since Jefferson. Instead Wilson addressed the joint session himself and made the case for lower tariffs. This was accomplished with the passage of the Underwood Tariff, which reduced the rates substantially (from 41 to 27 percent on the average). An income tax also took effect since the Sixteenth Amendment was ratified the same year.

With his sights set next on the banking system, Wilson worked with both houses to pass a massive reform to help prevent economic crises by creating a Federal Reserve System of twelve regional banks governed by its own board of governors and chairman, all of whom were appointed by the president and confirmed by the Senate. They met regularly to determine if and when interest rates should be raised or lowered depending on the status of the money supply. With a few changes since 1913, the Federal Reserve System remains today a living, functioning part of Wilson's New Freedom reform.

Trusts were another target for the Democratic administration in conjunction with its members in Congress. Two new laws were passed to thwart big business and monopolies' power. First the Federal Trade Commission was created to promote fair business practices, overseen by its five-member bipartisan board appointed by the president with the Senate's approval. The other reform was the Clayton Antitrust Act, passed to add more meat to the Sherman Antitrust Act passed during President Benjamin Harrison's administration. By excluding labor from being designated a trust, this law guaranteed unions more powers, including collective bargaining, strikes, picketing, and boycotts. Agriculture organizations were also exempted from being classified as trusts.

Domestic reform warmed Wilson's heart, but news from Europe sent chills down his spine, for word of relentless fighting between Allied (principally Great Britain and France) and Central (mainly Germany and Austria-Hungary) Powers frightened Americans, who demanded assurances from their government that America would not be drawn into the European squabble. Wilson wholeheartedly agreed with the pacifists; for one reason, whose side should the United States take? Since the mid-nineteenth century, migration from central and Eastern Europe had dramatically risen and, of course, British immigration had continued to be significant. Keep the fighting contained to the continent, many reasoned, so American boys could stay safe at home. Hoping to keep America out of the sights of European guns, Wilson continued pursuing his progressive domestic initiatives.

Within his family, Wilson faced personal tragedy with the death of his beloved wife Ellen in

NATIONAL EVENTS

MAR 2: Puerto Ricans granted US citizenship

MAR 4: Wilson inaugurated for a second term

MAR 31: US takes possession of Virgin Islands

APR 6: US declares war on Germany

MAY 18: President Wilson signs conscription bill into law

JUN 4: First Pulitzer prizes awarded

JUN 15: Espionage Act goes into effect

German dishes renamed: German toast becomes "French toast" and sauerkraut becomes "liberty cabbage"

1918

WORLD EVENTS

JUL 17: King George V declares that the British royal family will become Windsor (replacing German name Saxe-Coburg-Gotha)

JUL 31–NOV 6: Third Battle of Ypres

OCT 17: First British bombing of Germany

NOV 2: Balfour Declaration proclaims British support of Jewish settlement in Palestine

NOV 7: Lenin leads October Revolution

NOV 7: British capture Gaza from Ottoman Turks

JAN–MAR: Ukrainian Republic, Lithuania, Estonia, Belarus, Armenia, Azerbaijan, and Georgia declare their independence from Russia

August 1914 of nephritis. Grieving intensely, he found himself scarcely able to function; this would pose special significance because at the same time as Ellen Wilson's passing, the countries of Europe were declaring war on each other. Meanwhile, the American president was wandering the White House grounds asking, "Oh my God, what am I to do?"[12]

> *There is a price which is too great to pay for peace, and that price can be put in one word: one cannot pay the price of self-respect.*
>
> —*Woodrow Wilson, 1916*

The president's depression lifted sooner than he expected with the introduction of a wealthy Virginia widow, Edith Galt, who became Wilson's friend, and within two months' of their meeting, his fiancée. Their courtship less than a year after Ellen's death provided great fodder for the gossipmongers. Woodrow and Edith were wed on December 18, 1915, at her Washington, D.C., home. Wilson's demeanor greatly improved, and his new wife would ultimately secure her own place in history.

Early in his presidency, Wilson found himself facing the very real threat of war against Mexico. Relations between the United States and its southern neighbor grew increasingly strained with the murder of the Mexican leader and the questionable election of his successor, Victoriano Huerta, in 1913. Although American business interests pressured Wilson to recognize the new leader, he refused, and Huerta grew belligerent. Tempers flared hotter when Mexican authorities arrested a group of American sailors in Tampico, but even though they were soon released, the American public was incensed. Officially the US government demanded an apology and a twenty-one-gun salute, which was refused, so President Wilson dispatched troops to Veracruz. Before shots were exchanged, Argentina, Brazil, and Chile offered to act as mediators. Violence was avoided, and Huerta resigned. The United States recognized the new leader, Venustiano Carranza, but not everyone in Mexico did. Revolutionary leader Pancho Villa led attacks in northern Mexico, and American forces were sent in under General John J. Pershing when the town of Columbus, New Mexico, was raided and seventeen Americans were killed. For nearly a year troops attempted to locate Villa but never succeeded; instead, they were called home by the president, who would have other orders for them.

In May 1915, America received shocking news of the German U-boat's attack on the British passenger liner *Lusitania* (covertly carrying munitions), which lost 1,200 lives, including 128 Americans. Wilson's advisors were divided as to the response—some believed the United States should enter the war, but Secretary of State William Jennings Bryan adamantly opposed such a move and ultimately resigned. Bryan disapproved of the president sending a letter to the German government chastising them for their conduct that resulted in the deaths of so many innocent people, and then, displeased with Germany's reply, Wilson warned any more such attacks would be considered attacks on America. Bryan could not tolerate a step away from neutrality and promptly resigned. He was replaced by pro-war advocate Robert Lansing.

DID YOU KNOW?

Wilson played golf regardless of the weather and used black golf balls in the snow.

United States commissions its first aircraft carrier

United Way of America is founded to coordinate philanthropic efforts among a variety of groups

JAN 8: President Wilson outlines his Fourteen Points for peace

MAR 11: First American cases of Spanish flu at Fort Riley, Kansas; soon spreads; will kill 675,000 Americans before it ends in 1919

MAR 19: US sets standardized time zones and will begin daylight saving time as of March 31

FEB 6: Britain grants suffrage to women over 30

MAR 3: Treaty of Brest-Litovsk signed by Bolshevist Russia to end its involvement in the war; Germany and Austria also sign

MAR 21: Second Battle of the Somme begins

APR 21: "Red Baron" flying ace shot down and killed

JUL 15–AUG 7: Second Battle of the Marne

JUL 17: Russian royal family Nicholas and Alexandra and their children are assassinated under orders of the Bolshevik Party

DID YOU KNOW?

Wilson was the first president to travel to Europe while serving as president.

ELECTION OF 1916

"He kept us out of the war" read the president's reelection campaign slogan. Wilson's Republican challenger was former New York governor and Supreme Court justice Charles Evans Hughes, who believed the United States should step up war preparations. The president's popularity received a boost when he personally intervened to prevent a railroad strike by proposing to both sides the idea of an eight-hour workday. Although US troops were in Mexico, American fears had been reduced, but many Americans still had doubts about the former university professor. Consequently, when Woodrow Wilson went to sleep on election night, he heard that Hughes had won, but he was also reminded that western states could change that status. And they did. Still, the election was close—Wilson won with 49 percent of the popular vote and 277 electoral votes to Hughes winning 46 percent and 254 electoral votes. Now how much longer could the president keep his campaign pledge?

SECOND TERM

Although Europe had been engulfed in war for the past thirty-one months, the Wilson administration had steadfastly maintained its neutrality, which translated to doing very little toward readiness because it was feared that such moves would provoke the belligerents. The navy was supposed to be increased with roughly two battleships and their complement annually, but one battleship and a few smaller craft were all the United States produced during the early war years. Wilson had not wanted to venture far from his message to the world in August 1914: "We are a true friend to all the nations of the world, because we threaten none. . . . We are the champions of peace and of concord."[13] Intermittent crises and news of ongoing warfare in the trenches and at sea crowded the headlines, but Americans still believed an ocean would keep them isolated. But then they learned that war could arrive at their own backdoor.

Mexico resurfaced in the news in February 1917, when British intelligence reported an intercepted message between German foreign minister Arthur Zimmerman and the German minister in Mexico discussing a possible alliance between Germany and Mexico should the United States enter the war on the side of Britain and France. When Americans read Zimmerman's words assuring "financial support" for Mexico "to reconquer the lost territory in New Mexico, Texas, and Arizona,"[14] their isolationist stance melted away and was replaced with firm resolve to fight.

Just weeks before, the United States received word that Germany intended to resume unrestricted submarine warfare, prompting Wilson to send the German ambassador home, saying "Let us be done with diplomatic notes. The hour to act has come."[15] On April 2, 1917, President Wilson walked into the joint session of Congress asking for a declaration of war and proclaimed: "The world must be made safe for democracy. . . . We desire no conquest, no dominion." Congress overwhelmingly granted his request, and the United States transformed itself from a land of peace to a war-making machine.

Allied leaders were gratified and greatly relieved by America's decision and planned to use its troops as replacements for their own, but Wilson promptly nixed the idea, insisting Americans would fight together and serve under their own leader, General John J. Pershing, who was named commander of the American Expeditionary Force (AEF). To fulfill required manpower quotas, a draft was

NATIONAL EVENTS

MAY 15: The Post Office Department begins regular airmail service between New York City, Philadelphia, and Washington, D.C.

MAY 18: Sedition Act of 1918 approved

JUL 1: US rations sugar to 8 oz. per person per week due to shortages

JUL 14: Roosevelt's youngest son Quentin is shot down over France; his father never recovers from the loss and dies in Jan. 1919

AUG 1: After the death of her husband, Emma Susan Daugherty Banister becomes the first woman sheriff in the United States

WORLD EVENTS

OCT 3: Bulgaria's King Ferdinand abdicates in favor of his son Boris III

OCT 28: Czechoslovakia declares its independence from Austria-Hungary

NOV 3: Armistice signed by Allies and Austria-Hungary

NOV 3: Poland declares its independence from Russia

NOV 7: Revolution erupts in Germany

NOV 9: German Kaiser Wilhelm II abdicates and moves to the Netherlands

NOV 11: Allies sign armistice with Germany in France

NOV 11: Fighting ends at 11 a.m. (11th hour of the 11th day of the 11th month)

introduced, and the War Industries Board was established to oversee war production. Americans at home were encouraged to do their part by planting victory gardens and having meatless Mondays and wheatless Tuesdays—examples of all were set by First Lady Edith Wilson.

Wilson oversaw the war and the massive export of men and materiel throughout early to mid-1918, then focused his attention on the peace. Here the philosopher took heart that out of such destruction and killing, a greater good could result. He had earlier termed it a "peace without victory" but did not understand such a notion is rarely amenable to parties who have lost millions of young men. In January 1918, the president announced his Fourteen Points, which he insisted would provide the foundation for the world to have peace. Terms of this included open treaties (ending secret alliances and pacts), open trade (no economic barriers) and open seas (navigation open to all in peacetime and war), arms reductions, the realignment of various territories and nations in Europe, and his favorite, the establishment of an international organization that would arbitrate disputes and ensure that the world would fight at most with words rather than weapons.

Historians agree that Wilson committed a huge mistake by foregoing American precedent and rather than sending delegates to wrangle with fellow diplomats, the president announced he would sail to France and participate in the peace conference. Now his personal credibility and prestige were more vulnerable as he negotiated at Versailles in 1919 with the other members of the Big Four—British prime minister Lloyd George, French premier Georges Clemenceau, and Italian premier Vittorio Orlando. Quickly their motives revealed themselves as quite different from America's idealistic president. Land grabbing for themselves and punishment for Germany held sway over any talk of "peace without victory." The leaders did agree to the League of Nations as part of the Treaty of Versailles signed in June 1919. Now Wilson need only gain the Senate's approval.

RED SCARE (1918–1921) ★ Shortly after the end of World War I and the Bolshevik Revolution in Russia, a "red scare" gripped the United States. Following anarchist bombs being sent to a variety of prominent Americans, including Chief Justice Oliver Wendell Holmes and Attorney General Mitchell Palmer, a nationwide fear developed. Later, when one of the men setting a bomb was killed and it was learned he was an Italian alien, concerns about immigrants heightened. From 1918 to 1921, the "Palmer Raids" were launched to round up and deport aliens and arrest those with Communist or radical connections. Helping in identifying targets was 24-year-old J. Edgar Hoover. More than 5,000 were arrested during the raids' two-year period.

TREATY FIGHT

Once he returned to the United States, Wilson began working to gain approval for the treaty, but he quickly learned that such action would not be easy. The Republican majority in the Senate felt uncomfortable about the League of Nations provision, worrying that such an organization might cause more problems than it solved. When the president was informed that it was unlikely to receive the required two-thirds vote, he railed, "Anyone who opposes me in that, I'll crush!"[16] Determined to win, Wilson toured the country taking

DID YOU KNOW?

Wilson suffered a debilitating stroke while in office.

SEP 11: Boston Red Sox win the World Series against the Chicago Cubs; the Red Sox wouldn't win the Series again until 2004

DEC 4: President Wilson becomes first US president to travel to Europe while in office; he will attend Paris peace conference

NOV 12: Austria becomes a republic

NOV 14: Czechoslovakia becomes a republic

NOV 16: Hungary declares itself independent of Austria

1919

JAN 16: Prohibition (Eighteenth Amendment) ratified

FEB 26: Congress creates Grand Canyon National Park

MAY–SEP: Race riots occur in 26 American cities

JAN 5–12: Spartacist (January) Uprising in Germany: General strike by workers leads to violent suppression

JAN–NOV: Civil war continues in Russia between White and Red Armies

JAN 18: Peace conference opens at Versailles

JAN 25: Wilson proposal for a League of Nations adopted at peace conference

the treaty to the people. In three weeks' time, he visited twenty-nine cities across the nation giving speeches, but it came to a stop in Pueblo, Colorado, where he collapsed. His train ran an express route straight to Washington, where he suffered a severe stroke leaving him paralyzed on the left side and his sight again impaired.

For weeks he lay nearly immobile and removed from the eyes of the nation or those in government. Edith Wilson functioned as gatekeeper and decided what matters required his attention; the country retreated to an "auto pilot" status through the crisis. Because the First Lady received correspondence addressed to the president and sent out missives seemingly from him, she has sometimes been referred to as America's first female president. She rejected the notion and insisted she was merely acting on behalf of her husband: "The only decision that was mine was what was important and what was not."[17]

Being unable to fulfill his constitutional duties, Wilson should have resigned, or at least allowed Vice President Thomas Marshall to take his place. Marshall had already substituted during Wilson's trip to France and intensely disliked it, so he contentedly stayed far away from 1600 Pennsylvania Avenue during Wilson's convalescence. In fact, he and the president did not meet again until the inauguration of President Harding.

Gradually, the president's health improved and passed muster when queried by two senators who represented others in the government wondering about Wilson's capabilities since it had been over a year since the stroke. Meanwhile, debate moved forward on the peace treaty and Article X—the League of Nations. Wilson's steadfast refusal to compromise on this provision and other points did not bode well for the Treaty's passage in the Senate. In March 1920, the Senate cast forty-nine votes approving it to thirty-four against, but still seven votes shy of the required two-thirds majority.

Both during and after the war, America witnessed a variety of attacks upon its own civil liberties. The passage of the Espionage Act of 1917 and the Sedition Act of 1918 worked to quash any opposition to the government or the armed forces. Anyone or anything German was distrusted, and the target moved to communists or "reds" when word of the bloody Russian revolution reached the United States. As a preemptive strike, Attorney General Mitchell Palmer launched a series of raids to find and deport thousands of immigrants and others with suspected communist tendencies. The president's ill health precluded him from knowing, let alone approving, of the Red Scare at the time. Across the country, violence erupted against labor leaders and African Americans. Race riots spilled out in urban centers, but again no response from the executive branch. His presidency was sputtering to a stop.

Some, including Wilson, briefly entertained thoughts of a third term, but they soon evaporated. With the inauguration of Republican Warren G. Harding as the new president, Woodrow Wilson could leave the White House and return to private life.

RETIREMENT

The former president and Edith Wilson moved to a house they purchased in Washington. There he thought he could resume his legal practice, but health concerns prohibited him. Writing projects never progressed; he simply lacked the strength and, sometimes, the interest he once had. He and Edith led a quiet existence, and he appeared in public only rarely. On one occasion, the couple rode in the procession to bury the Unknown Soldier at Arlington,

NATIONAL EVENTS

AUG 31: American Communist Party founded

OCT 2: President Wilson suffers massive stroke, but its effects are kept secret by his wife

OCT 28: Congress passes Volstead Act to enforce Prohibition

1920

JAN 3: Babe Ruth is traded by the Boston Red Sox to the New York Yankees for $125,000

JAN 9: George Polley, "The Human Fly," is arrested for climbing the New York Woolworth Building; he makes it to the 30th floor

WORLD EVENTS

MAR 23: Benito Mussolini founds Fascist Party in Italy

JUN 28: Treaty of Versailles signed

AUG: Allied forces invade Russia

AUG 11: Weimar Constitution creating a German republic adopted

AUG 19: Afghanistan gains its independence from Great Britain

APR: Britain granted mandates over Mesopotamia (Iraq) and Palestine

JUL 27–AUG 15: Red Army unsuccessfully invades Poland

and to their surprise, the crowds along the route broke into spontaneous applause, and thousands greeted them when they returned to their home. Wilson finally appeared and softly said, "I can only say, 'God bless you.'" Moved by the frail former president leaning on his wife's arm with tears in his eyes, the crowd hailed him with cheers.

Two years later, Wilson was in another funeral procession; he had amazingly outlived his successor and planned to attend Harding's funeral, but then felt too weak to do anything but stay outside in the car. Later that year he spoke on the radio to deliver a message on the fifth anniversary of the armistice.

Never fully recovered from his strokes or longtime stomach problems, his condition deteriorated with age. On February 1, 1924, his good friend and physician was summoned to the Wilson house, where he was greeted by a weak patient who explained, "The machinery is worn out," but then added, "I am ready."[18] He died on February 3 and was buried at Washington Cathedral in Washington, D.C. Edith Wilson lived nearly thirty-eight more years. She attended the inauguration of President John F. Kennedy in January 1961, and died later that year, on December 28. She was buried beside her husband.

DID YOU KNOW?

Wilson is the only US president to be buried in Washington, D.C. (he is buried at the National Cathedral).

ENDNOTES

1 Arthur Walworth, *Woodrow Wilson: American Prophet*, New York: Longmans, Green, 1958, p. 417.

2 Arthur S. Link, ed., *The Papers of Woodrow Wilson*, vol. I, Princeton, NJ: Princeton University Press, 1966, p. 250.

3 Josephus Daniels, *The Life of Woodrow Wilson*, Philadelphia: John C. Winston & Co., 1924, p. 60.

4 Ibid, p. 69.

5 Ibid, p. 76.

6 Louis Auchincloss, *Woodrow Wilson*, New York: Penguin Putnam, 2000, p. 31.

7 H.W. Brands, *Woodrow Wilson*, New York: Times Books, 2003, pp. 16-17.

8 Ibid, p. 19.

9 August Heckscher, *Woodrow Wilson*, New York: Charles Scribner, 1991, p. 227.

10 Ray Stannard Baker, *Woodrow Wilson, Life and Letters*, 8 vols., Garden City, NY: Doubleday, Page, & Company, Inc., vol. 3, p. 170.

11 Brands, pp. 24-25.

12 Heckscher, p. 335.

13 Daniels, p. 243.

14 William A. DeGregorio, *The Complete Book of US Presidents*, New York: Gramercy Books, 2005, p. 423.

15 Daniels, p. 262.

16 Auchincloss, p. 112.

17 Heckscher, p. 616.

18 Brands, p. 135.

JAN 16: Prohibition takes effect

JAN 19: US refuses to join the League of Nations

MAR 19: Congress refuses to ratify Treaty of Versailles

MAY 2: Negro National League plays first game in Indianapolis

AUG 26: Nineteenth Amendment ratified

NOV 2: Republican Warren G. Harding defeats James E. Cox in presidential election

AUG 11: Bolshevist Russia recognizes independence of Estonia and Latvia; earlier had recognized Lithuania

SEP 1: France creates Lebanon

NOV 15: First meeting of League of Nations in Geneva, Switzerland; among those not in attendance: US, Russia, and defeated nations of World War I

Warren G. Harding

★ ★ ★ TWENTY-NINTH PRESIDENT ★ ★ ★

LIFE SPAN

- Born: November 2, 1865, in Corsica (Blooming Grove), Ohio
- Died: August 2, 1923 in San Francisco, California

RELIGION

- Baptist

HIGHER EDUCATION

- Ohio Central College, 1882

PROFESSION

- Newspaper publisher, editor

MILITARY SERVICE

- None

FAMILY

- Father: **George Tyron Harding** (1843–1928)
- Mother: **Phoebe Elizabeth Dickerson Harding** (1843–1910)
- Wife: **Florence "Flossie" Mabel Kling DeWolfe Harding** (1860–1924); wed on July 8, 1891, in Marion, Ohio
- No children by his wife; one alleged illegitimate child, **Elizabeth Ann Christian** (1919–2005) with mistress Nan Britton

POLITICAL LIFE

- Ohio state senator (1899–1903)
- Lieutenant governor of Ohio (1903–1905)
- US senator (1915–1921)

PRESIDENCY

- One term; March 4, 1921–August 2, 1923
- Republican
- Reason for leaving office: died in office
- Vice president: **Calvin Coolidge** (1921–1923)

ELECTION OF 1920

- Electoral vote: **Harding** 404; **James M. Cox** 127
- Popular vote: **Harding** 16,147,885; **Cox** 9,141,535

CABINET

★★★★★★★★★★

SECRETARY OF STATE
Charles Evans Hughes (1921–1923)

SECRETARY OF THE TREASURY
Andrew Mellon (1921–1923)

SECRETARY OF WAR
John W. Weeks (1921–1923)

ATTORNEY GENERAL
Harry M. Daugherty (1921–1923)

SECRETARY OF THE NAVY
Edwin Denby (1921–1923)

POSTMASTER GENERAL
Will Hays (1921–1922)

Hubert Work (1922–1923)

SECRETARY OF THE INTERIOR
Albert B. Fall (1921–1923)

SECRETARY OF AGRICULTURE
Henry C. Wallace (1921–1923)

SECRETARY OF COMMERCE
Herbert Hoover (1921–1923)

SECRETARY OF LABOR
James J. Davis (1921–1923)

Warren G. Harding spent most of his life attempting to win people's favor rather than taking sides. In fact, his father once said, "Warren, it's a good thing you weren't born a gal because you'd be in the family way all the time. You can't say no."[1] Sadly, for all his goodwill, he would not be able to prevent his public approval from plummeting during his presidency owing to scandal connected to his friends. When Harding died in office, the country cared little about the cause, but rather felt relief knowing that a new man was president.

EARLY LIFE

The Harding family was descended from Puritans who had immigrated to Massachusetts in the 1620s. Some moved to New York, and by the early nineteenth century, the family was moving west again, this time to north central Ohio, where they settled in a small village known later as Blooming Grove. There George T. Harding and Phoebe Dickerson married and reared a family of six children; the oldest, Warren Gamaliel Harding, was born on November 2, 1865. When Warren was five, his father moved to Cleveland to attend the Western College of Homeopathy and completed three years of training before returning to Blooming Grove and beginning a medical practice. Phoebe assisted her husband and worked as a midwife in the area. At home, she taught her oldest son recitations before he began his schooling.

Warren and his siblings attended the town's one-room schoolhouse, where he learned the three Rs. His favorite activity was public speaking and reciting poetry, and he learned to play the cornet. Warren played with other children, swam, performed his farm chores, and worked outside of the home to earn extra money by helping farmers at harvest time and learning the printing business as a helper for the *Caledonia Argus*. As a teenager, he was hired on to a construction gang of the Toledo and Ohio Central Railroad.

Harding entered Ohio Central College in Iberia in 1880. There the fifteen-year-old continued studying the usual topics in history, composition, mathematics, and science, plus Latin, and found debating to be particularly satisfying. He also decided to work with other students to start a campus newspaper they named the *Iberia Spectator,* which ran only for six issues but whetted his appetite for the business. At seventeen, he was a college graduate and unemployed.

Harding decided his education had prepared him best to be a teacher; he soon began working at the White Schoolhouse near Marion. Long before the first term was over, he realized that molding young minds was clearly not to his liking, and, as the term came to a close, he wrote ecstatically to an aunt that he only had one week before "my career as pedagogue will close, and oh—the joy!"[2]

Selling insurance was next on Harding's list of employments, but that endeavor turned into a disaster when his boss made him return a policy he had underwritten for a new hotel. He read law briefly, but that too held little if any interest for the young man. However frustrating his search for a fulfilling profession may have been, Harding did, however, enjoy living in the town of Marion, where his family had moved. There he organized and played in the town band and took up the new roller skating craze at the town's rink. Harding learned to play poker with the guys and was not averse to having a few drinks, as well.

Harding's pursuits began heading in a new direction when, in May 1884, he started working for one of Marion's three small newspapers, the *Star*. As the printer of the railroad timetables,

NATIONAL EVENTS

Drano drain cleaner first produced

Band-Aids introduced

Goodyear launches its first blimp

Earl Wise begins packaging potato chips

JAN: San Francisco's DeYoung Museum opens in Golden Gate Park

JAN 2: First radio broadcast of a religious service

MAR 4: Warren G. Harding inaugurated as president

MAY 19: Congress passes Emergency Quota Act restricting immigration and instituting quotas

1921

WORLD EVENTS

First Bolshevik concentration camp opens at Archangel

English writer Agatha Christie publishes her first mystery

More than 3 million Russians die from ongoing famine; League of Nations refuses to send aid

Swiss psychiatrist Hermann Rorschach develops his famed inkblot test as a means to discern personalities

JAN 21: Italian Communist Party founded in Livorno

FEB 25: Invasion of Republic of Georgia by Russian Red Army

the *Star* granted its employees free passes, one of which Harding used to ride to Chicago to attend the Republican National Convention. He was now hooked on two vocations—newspaper publishing and politics. For a brief interval he worked for a rival paper, but was soon back at the *Star*, this time as a partner and editor.

NORMALCY ★ Although coinage of the term "normalcy" is frequently attributed to Harding, it apparently was used in the nineteenth century. Harding used it during the 1920 presidential campaign to mean a return to the relative calm that predated Wilson and the World War I era.

NEWSPAPERMAN

Harding worked hard to make his paper a profitable enterprise and was often seen around Marion visiting and, at the same time, selling advertising. This hands-on approach worked—circulation rose and so did his earnings. He built a home for himself, and seemed happy to remain single. Harding was considered a handsome man and had no trouble finding female companionship.

Then he met his sister's piano teacher, Florence Kling DeWolfe. Florence, or "Flossie" as she was called by friends, was the daughter of one of Marion's most prominent citizens, Amos Kling. She had disobeyed Kling years before to run off and marry Pete DeWolfe, and they had a son before divorcing six years later. Now Flossie was attempting to support herself by giving piano lessons. She fell for the newspaper editor, but apparently he, at first, did not share her infatuation. Soon, though, he succumbed to her charms, and again, Amos Kling stood defiantly against the match. His main objection was actually a rumor, but one that had existed for generations and, in the 1890s, was enough to kill a man's reputation. People whispered that Warren shared the supposed fate of his family—Negro blood ran in their veins. At one point, Kling yelled at Harding and called him a "nigger" on a city street and threatened to kill him should he continue to see Flossie. The couple disregarded Kling and married at Harding's Marion home on July 8, 1891. He was twenty-five years old; she was five years older. Her son, though, was kept and reared by the Klings.

Soon after they were married, Flossie Harding dropped by her husband's office and decided to lend a hand; she later wrote, "I went down there intending to help out for a few days, and I stayed fourteen years."[3] Her efficiency helped to streamline their delivery system and increase profits. Warren was probably grateful for her help because soon after their marriage, he had to escape—for the second time in two years—to the Battle Creek Sanitarium in Michigan, where he was under the care of Dr. Joseph Kellogg. In 1890, he had suffered a nervous breakdown, and over the next decade he visited the sanitarium four additional times, besides continuing to fight a nervous stomach.

By this stage in his life, Harding had worked to ingratiate himself into Marion society. He joined the Rotary and Elks clubs, continued playing in the town band, and was a member of the Baptist church. He served on a variety of boards of directors for local companies and organizations. And of course, he found time to help the county's Republican Party and used his newspaper to trumpet their agenda. He became the mouthpiece both in print and in oratory for the GOP and was rewarded in 1899 by being run for the Ohio Senate. He easily won his first elected office.

JUN 1: 85 people killed in Tulsa Race Riot, Oklahoma

AUG 3: Nine members of Chicago White Sox go on trial for taking bribes; although acquitted, they are banned from baseball

AUG 5: First radio broadcast of a baseball game, Pirates v. Phillies at Forbes Field, on KDKA Pittsburgh

AUG 10: Franklin D. Roosevelt develops polio and becomes paralyzed

SEP 7: First Miss America Pageant held in Atlantic City, New Jersey

MAR 8: Assassination of Spanish premier Eduardo Dato Iradier

MAR 13: Mongolia declares its independence from China

MAR 18: End of Polish-Soviet War

MAY 5: Coco Chanel introduces her new perfume, "Chanel No. 5"

JUL 1: Official date of beginning of China's Communist Party

DID YOU KNOW?

Harding was the first president to own a radio and speak on it.

POLITICIAN

Arriving in Columbus, Harding quickly became a popular politician, for he played the game exceedingly well. He liked the middle ground and attempted to stay in that locale as much as possible to keep both conservatives and progressives somewhat pleased by his performance. One observer wrote, "Harding proved a great harmonizer. He had the unusual gift of getting people together and inducing them to patch up differences."[4] This talent earned him a second term and, in 1903, a nomination for lieutenant governor.

Harding found the state's second highest position rather pleasant since it required very little of him, simply running the state senate, which left him plenty of time for other pursuits. He hoped to run for the top job the next election, but Governor Myron Herrick wanted to run for reelection, so with a sick wife recuperating from having a kidney removed, Harding decided it was time for a political sabbatical; after all, the newspaper needed its editor back at the helm. So he packed up and returned to Marion in 1905.

MARION

Back behind his desk at the *Star*, Harding monitored state politics and wrote his pro-Republican editorials. During this time, he also began a fifteen-year affair with a friend's wife, Carrie Phillips. The two couples often traveled together and were great friends; apparently the two other spouses were totally unaware of how "friendly" their partners were. The affair ended with Harding's election to the presidency.

With the presidential election of 1908, Harding had to do something that he always found particularly difficult—make a decision that would invariably generate significant dissatisfaction and criticism. His longtime supporter and mentor Senator Joseph Foraker wanted to run for the presidency, but Secretary of War William H. Taft (and fellow Ohioan) also planned to make a bid for the top job. Who should Harding support? He cast his lot with Taft, to his mentor's great distress. Taft won the state and would become a Harding booster. But two years later, Harding faced his first political defeat when he lost the gubernatorial race to his Democratic challenger, incumbent governor Judson Harmon.

In 1912, Harding gained the honor of placing Taft's name in nomination for the Republican ticket. This was the convention, however, that split at its seams between old guard Republicans under Taft and the progressive wing under Theodore Roosevelt. The latter booed and catcalled during Harding's speech, especially at moments when he attacked their man, calling Roosevelt "the greatest faker of all times."[5] Harding had backed the winner, though, and would be rewarded for his efforts.

By 1914, the Seventeenth Amendment had passed, so in that year, the first direct election of senators occurred across the country. Included in that election was Warren G. Harding, who had defeated the former senator and his mentor Joseph Foraker in the state primary. Now the fifty-one-year-old newspaper editor was ready for his move to the power center of the nation.

SENATOR

Harding decided to make himself comfortable in his new city, so bought a duplex on Wyoming Avenue and rented out the other half to pay the interest on his mortgage. Once the congressional session started in December 1915, he found himself popular once more and making new friends and allies. Determining his position on issues, however,

NATIONAL EVENTS

NOV 11: Tomb of the Unknown Soldier dedicated at Arlington National Cemetery

NOV 12: Opening of Washington Conference on Limitation of Naval Armaments

NOV 20: Film star Rudolph Valentino wins women's hearts in *The Sheik*

Kansas City opens world's first shopping center, the Country Club Plaza

F. Scott Fitzgerald publishes *The Beautiful and Damned* and *Tales of the Jazz Age*

1922

WORLD EVENTS

JUL 29: Adolf Hitler becomes leader of Germany's Nazi Party

AUG 23: King Faisal is crowned in Baghdad

SEP 10: Opening of Berlin's Autobahn

OCT 19: Many Portuguese politicians, including Prime Minister Antonio Granjo, are killed in massacre in Lisbon

DEC 6: Former grand vizier of Egypt Halim Pasha Said is assassinated by an American in Rome

JAN 11: First use of insulin for diabetes

was much more problematic as he again faced the dilemma of how to do so without offending people.

Harding developed different tactics for tackling this problem—he flip-flopped on issues, for instance voting for and against labor almost equally, and was an astute player of the ever-popular game of "avoid the roll call vote," which would place him "on the record" more than he considered wise. Harding's record showed him to miss votes about 40 percent of the time. Some matters, though, he could not evade, including the ongoing question of Prohibition. Harding liked to drink; cities approved of alcohol, but rural areas disliked it. So how was he to handle the issue? Let someone else decide it. Harding pushed to have the states determine whether the country should go dry. Then he also signed off on the Volstead Act to allow enforcement of Prohibition, which made the Anti-Saloon League happy. But Harding reminded people that he was "not a Prohibitionist"[6] nor did he view the debate as one based on moral grounds. This issue did not help Harding, noted one observer who said that it illustrated, "that vertebral weakness which is the one material infirmity in his character."[7]

This character flaw would be displayed in another key matter—women's suffrage. Again, he disliked taking a stand and living by it, but he admitted to a group of suffragettes that he was opposed to their cause because Ohio had disapproved amending it to its state constitution. Once more he decided to pass the buck, this time to the political parties. Harding explained, "Personally I am a believer in government through political parties . . . and my own conviction is that suffrage will never become a fixed thing until some political party . . . assumes sponsorship for the suffrage cause."[8] Soon others made Harding's mind up for him, and Republicans, himself included, could vote for women gaining the right to vote with a clear conscience. Ironically, the first time all women in the country could cast ballots would be when he ran for the presidency in 1920.

Harding's senate record was not particularly distinguished; he made few speeches and, of the 134 bills he introduced, all but twelve were vanity bills (of local interest only); none were national in scope. His committee assignments were undertaken with only moderate interest. He did, however, serve on the Foreign Relations committee and a subcommittee on the Philippines. That territory was the topic of his maiden speech as a US senator in which he argued that the United States should continue its rule over the islands for, in his opinion, they were not ready for independence.

With the advent of World War I, Harding broached the subject of internationalism at the 1916 Republican National Convention and told the audience that no longer could the United States feel isolated and it needed "a navy that fears none in the world." He went on to insist that Americans "must assume the responsibilities of influence and example, and accept the burdens of enlarged participation. . . . Americanism begins at home and radiates abroad."[9]

Life became more unpleasant for the nonconfrontational Senator Harding when he was criticized for speaking out in Ohio against the Liberty Bond campaign, calling it an unsound way to finance the war. Not wishing to offend the German voters of his state, he told them that he wished Americans were as patriotic for their country as Germans were for the Kaiser. Back in Congress he had to explain his remarks by insisting that he was by no means pro-German. Later he found himself in trouble again when he hinted of knowledge of some sinister secret regarding the

SUPREME COURT APPOINTMENTS
★★★★★★★★★★

William H. Taft, 1921

George Sutherland, 1922

Pierce Butler, 1922

Edward T. Sanford, 1923

English-born author Margery Williams publishes *The Velveteen Rabbit* in New York

Mah-jongg craze hits the US

Sinclair Lewis publishes *Babbitt*

T.S. Eliot publishes his poem "The Waste Land"

JAN 24: Ice cream treat Eskimo Pie patented

FEB 5: First issue of *Reader's Digest* published

FEB 6: Washington Naval Conference ends with Five Power Naval Disarmament Treaty signed by US, Britain, France, Italy, and Japan

FEB 8: First radio installed in the White House

JAN 13: In Britain, 804 die during a flu epidemic

JAN 21: First slalom ski race run in Switzerland

JAN 22: Pope Benedict XV dies

FEB 2: James Joyce's *Ulysses* published in France

MAR 11: Mohandas Gandhi arrested for sedition (will be found guilty and serve two years in prison)

STATE OF THE UNION
★★★★★★★★★★

US POPULATION IN 1921
105,710,620

NATIONAL DEBT IN 1923
$22,349,707,365

NUMBER OF STATES IN 1923
48

government's handling of the war, and although he was from the opposite political party, Harding vowed he would not betray the administration's confidence. When pressed to answer, he ultimately admitted that he had spoken in jest, but the joke was far from amusing.

As part of the Foreign Relations committee, Harding participated in the debate over the Treaty of Versailles ending World War I, as well as the key Article X, which created the League of Nations. Harding accompanied a group of senators to the White House to discuss the League with ailing President Woodrow Wilson, who was still recuperating from a massive stroke, and asked the president: Was it a legal or moral commitment to abide by the League? When the president demurred from answering, Harding pressed by asking what was the point of such an organization if the only obligation was moral. Obviously Harding was joining with the Republican majority to vote down the League.

ELECTION OF 1920

Now with the League of Nations, and Wilson, defeated, the question became, who would be the candidates running for the presidency in 1920? Many had predicted one more run by former president Theodore Roosevelt, but he died unexpectedly the year before. Now the Republican field was wide open, and former rival and lobbyist Harry Daugherty seized the opportunity to try to put Harding in the White House, and made himself campaign manager. Daugherty later insisted that after visiting with the newspaperman for a few minutes in 1899, he thought "what a great President he'd make!"[10] He also insisted that Harding looked like a president. Now their job became convincing others that Harding was the man.

The fact that the senator was not a front runner when he arrived in Chicago for the Republican National Convention did not distress either Harding or Daugherty. The main rivals ended in a deadlock with none able to break out of the pack, so Daugherty went to work convincing delegates that his dark horse, Harding, would be a prime choice. After all, he had worked hard his entire political career to avoid making enemies, so he was a popular man in his party. With only a few hours before the gavel came down opening the next session, a group of Republican leaders summoned Harding to ask if he had any reason he could not accept the nomination. Never mind that Carrie Phillips was attempting to blackmail him for her silence regarding their affair. Forget Nan Britton, the daughter of a friend whom he had helped and with whom he had very possibly had an affair (and a child). There were stories of other extramarital activities, his earlier nervous breakdowns, and of course, the old rumor that surfaced occasionally about his mixed blood. But after quick consideration, Harding replied there was no reason he could not accept.

The next day, the convention's front runner, General Leonard Wood, began losing support, while Harding gained in the balloting. On the tenth ballot, Harding was nominated as the Republican presidential candidate. When asked why this unknown was selected, Frank Brandegee, a top party leader, simply explained, "There ain't any first-raters this year."[11] Then another surprise occurred when Governor Calvin Coolidge of Massachusetts was selected as his running mate. The Democrats nominated another son of Ohio for their presidential candidate, James Cox, who was also a newspaperman and former governor. His running mate was Franklin D. Roosevelt of New York.

NATIONAL EVENTS

MAR 5: Sharpshooter Annie Oakley sets a record by hitting 98 clay pigeons out of 100

APR 29: Beginning of Teapot Dome scandal (government oil reserves leased)

MAY 5: Construction begins on Yankee Stadium in New York's Bronx neighborhood

MAY 23: Walt Disney incorporates his first film company, Laugh-O-Gram Films

MAY 30: Lincoln Memorial dedicated

WORLD EVENTS

APR 10: Genoa Conference of 34 nations to discuss monetary concerns in post World War I

JUN 28: Irish Civil War begins

JUL 28: France granted mandate over Syria by League of Nations

OCT 18: Formation of British Broadcasting Corporation (BBC)

OCT 28: Benito Mussolini becomes Italy's youngest premier

The candidates sparred over the League of Nations, which Cox enthusiastically supported, arguing that the United States needed to stay active in world affairs. After World War I, however, the majority of Americans seemed content to return to their prewar isolationist stance. In truth, the country lacked interest in both candidates, seeing them as basically mirror images of each other. Newspaper headlines decried the choices of the two parties; one said each man was "of mediocre ability and of unimpeachable party regularity."[12] One of the top Republicans advocated that Harding remain at home rather than actively campaign. He worried and cautioned others: "Don't let him make any speeches. If he goes on a tour, somebody's sure to ask him questions, and Warren's just the sort of damn fool that'll try to answer them!"[13] So Harding patterned his campaign—and his porch—to resemble that waged by McKinley, who had stayed at home.

Harding used his affable charm on reporters and won them over by sharing a smoke or playing some horseshoes with them. He gave them frequent interviews, but also would stipulate that certain items remain off the record. Because of his kind treatment and virtual open door policy, he would entertain an excellent relationship with the press that few presidents have equaled since.

When election day came, the expected happened—the Democrats were turned out of office, and Warren G. Harding was the next president. He captured the majority of states, losing only the southern votes, which were expected to remain solidly Democratic. Capturing 60 percent of the popular vote and a Republican majority in Congress seemed to portend success for all concerned.

EUGENE V. DEBS (1855–1926) ★ The presidential candidate for the Socialist Party in 1920, Eugene Debs ran his campaign from the penitentiary in Atlanta, where he was serving a ten-year sentence for breaking the Sedition Act of 1918. Debs had long been involved in the American Railway Union, which he helped create, and he had organized the famous strike against Great Northern Railroad in 1894. Later he helped with the Pullman Strike, and while in jail for interfering with the mail, read and embraced the writings of Karl Marx. Once released, he served five times as the presidential candidate for the Socialist Party. President Harding released Debs from prison in 1921. Debs died five years later.

PRESIDENT HARDING

When setting up his cabinet, Harding surrounded himself with able minds and others with only themselves in mind. Men such as Secretary of State Charles Evans Hughes, Secretary of the Treasury Andrew Mellon, and Secretary of Commerce Herbert Hoover were extremely talented in their fields and stayed into the next administration. Others, including Attorney General Harry Daugherty and Interior Secretary Albert Fall, would prove to be disastrous liabilities for the president.

Harding continued his opposition to the League of Nations, sealing that organization's death sentence. He did, though, attempt to win support for the United States to join the World Court, but was not backed in Congress. Without agreeing to the Treaty of Versailles, the United States needed to officially end its part in World War I. So on July 2, 1921, the president was summoned from a round of golf to come inside and sign a joint resolution ending the war between

JUL 11: The Hollywood Bowl opens

AUG: First radio commercials broadcast from a New York station

NOV 21: Georgia's Rebecca Felton becomes the first woman Senator

Robert Frost publishes poem "Stopping by Woods on a Snowy Evening"

NOV 1: Ottoman Empire abolished

NOV 4: King Tut's tomb found by British archaeologist Howard Carter

DEC 6: Irish Free State (Republic of Ireland) founded

DEC 30: Russia, Ukraine, Belarus, and Transcaucasia combine to form Union of Soviet Socialist Republics (USSR)

1923

JAN 11: Occupation of Germany's Ruhr Valley by French and Belgian troops demanding their reparations

DID YOU KNOW?

Harding was the first president to visit Alaska and Canada.

Germany and the United States. He quickly looked it over, affixed his signature, and headed back to his game.

One part of the original treaty dealt with arms limitation, and the United States under Secretary Hughes pursued this goal at the Washington Conference for the Limitation of Armament, which spanned late 1921 to early 1922. The nations of the United States, Great Britain, France, Italy, and Japan agreed to limit their fleet size, prompting one British naval officer to state, "Secretary Hughes sank in 35 minutes more ships than all the admirals of the world have sunk in a cycle of centuries."[14] The Five Power Pact (United States, Great Britain, France, Italy, and Japan) agreed to peaceful arbitration of any disputes and to respect each other's territories in the Pacific.

Another aftermath of the war was the continued imprisonment of people convicted of antiwar activities, the most prominent being the Socialist leader Eugene V. Debs. Opposed to wholesale pardoning, Harding announced that the cases would be examined individually by the Justice Department. Debs received his release and pardon just before Christmas 1921. The number of "Wobblies" (International Workers of the World) imprisoned started at seventy-six and decreased over the next two years to twenty-two who remained at the time of Harding's death.

Farmers were feeling crushed by falling prices and put their weight on Congress, who then insisted that the government needed to help. Harding disagreed, arguing that farmers sometimes had tough times but certainly it was no excuse for a government subsidy. The president and legislative branch did agree, however, to raise tariffs to an all-time high of 38 percent, but this protectionism only launched a tariff war with America's trading partners.

Labor did not care for Harding either, for he showed repeatedly that he sided with business. In 1922, strikes erupted across the country—textile workers in New England; 650,000 miners walking out of the coal mines; and railroad workers joining soon after. Commerce Secretary Herbert Hoover wanted to end the normal twelve-hour, seven-day workweek in the steel industry, but Harding balked at the government interfering in such matters. A committee met but accomplished nothing for a year, and it was only after Harding announced his displeasure in the inability to rectify the situation in 1923 that the steel industry finally abolished the twelve-hour workday.

Another group who received the president's attention were the people of the Deep South. For the first time in American history, a president traveled to the region to address racial inequality. In October 1921, Harding faced a segregated audience of twenty thousand whites and ten thousand blacks in Birmingham, Alabama, to discuss the progress made by the South, and the goals it still needed to reach. He advocated improved education for its black population and increased job opportunities, but he cautioned that integration was not the objective. His intention was to try and win votes to break the strong grip the Democratic Party had over the "Solid South." Harding told his audience: "Neither political sectionalism nor any system of rigid groupings of the people will in the long run prosper our country. I want to see the time come when black men will regard themselves as full participants in the benefits and duties of American citizenship."[15] Throughout his speech he pushed for blacks actively participating in the voting process, much to the disgust of southern congressmen.

Although his stand on this and other issues lost him support, he admitted to a friend that he was

NATIONAL EVENTS

Dance marathons gain in popularity

Harry Reese creates peanut butter cups

Pam American World Airways established in New York City by Juan "Terry" Trippe and John Hambleton

23 million acre National Petroleum Reserve established in Alaska by Congress with provisions that it will be tapped only under the most dire circumstances

MAR 3: First issue of *Time* magazine published

APR 5: Firestone begins producing inflatable tires

WORLD EVENTS

APR: End of Irish Civil War

APR 26: Price Albert marries Lady Elizabeth Bowes-Lyon at Westminster Abbey

JUN 18: Etna volcano erupts in Sicily, making 60,000 homeless

JUN 20: Mexican rebel leader Pancho Villo slain

JUL 6: Official beginning of the USSR (Soviet Union)

a changed man since becoming the nation's chief executive: "Responsibility has a strange effect. I am not boosting myself, but I do not believe anyone could come to the Presidency without being imbued with the desire to serve above and beyond most selfish aims. I find even myself growing less a partisan than I once was."[16] It would prove unfortunate that other members of his administration did not share this sentiment.

PROHIBITION (1920–1933) ★ On January 16, 1920, the Eighteenth Amendment went into effect, prohibiting the sale of alcohol. This action was years in the making, starting with the work of temperance societies earlier in the nineteenth century, combined with pleas by churches, some business owners, and progressives of the early twentieth century. Many states had already outlawed alcohol, and during World War I, some Prohibitionists argued that it was a patriotic measure since German Americans owned many of the nation's breweries. The actual amendment did not outlaw consumption but did prohibit the manufacturing, transporting, and selling of alcohol. Enforcement proved to be a time-consuming and expensive process, and eventually was one of the primary reasons for its repeal. President Harding did not observe prohibition, and alcohol continued to be served at the White House (albeit in private rooms). Prohibition was repealed in 1933 by the ratification of the Twenty-first Amendment.

SCANDAL

Attorney General Harry Daugherty strongly believed in "open shop" rather than labor demands for union-only closed shops, and when strikes broke out, Daugherty advocated using injunctions to stop pickets and break the strikes in any way possible. He did so successfully against the railroad strike in Chicago, much to the distress of the other cabinet members and the president. Still, Harding stood by him, which would soon prove unfortunate.

One of the first scandals of the Harding presidency involved the recently created Veterans Bureau and its head, Colonel Charles Forbes. When word got out of Forbes possibly skimming large amounts of funds, he fled to Europe, and his assistant committed suicide. Forbes was ultimately returned to the United States, where he went on trial for bribery and corruption and was found guilty of taking over two hundred million dollars. He was fined ten thousand dollars and sentenced to two years at Leavenworth Penitentiary.

During World War I, the office for Alien Property Custodian had been created to safeguard property belonging to the citizens that the United States was fighting. During Harding's presidency, Thomas Miller held the position and accepted a bribe from a friend of Attorney General Daugherty's involving disposition of certain property. Miller was later sent to prison.

Daugherty was also at the center of a group known as the Ohio Gang, a group of Ohio Republicans who lived and worked together in Washington. One of his associates was Jess Smith, and together they lived in a house lent by the owner of the *Washington Post*, Ned McLean, another former Ohio resident. But they usually met in a house on K Street and were sometimes guests of the president. None minded breaking Prohibition—liquor ran freely, as did the gambling. The Ohio Gang members made money by telling others they could gain the president's influence by

APR 18: New York's Yankee Stadium opens

JUN 4: US Supreme Court decides *Meyer v. Nebraska*, striking down the Nebraska law that stopped schools from teaching languages other than English

AUG 2: President Harding dies and is succeeded by Calvin Coolidge

OCT 15: New York Yankees win first World Series

OCT 16: Walt Disney starts the Walt Disney Company

SEP 13: Military coup and dictatorship created under Miguel Primo de Rivera in Spain

OCT 13: Ankara becomes capital of Turkey, replacing Constantinople

NOV 8: Beer Hall Putsch: Hitler unsuccessfully attempts a coup in Munich

NOV 23: Germany's coalition government collapses

DID YOU KNOW?

Harding enjoyed playing poker and reportedly lost a set of White House china in one game.

paying the gang, then going to the K Street house to see Harding. The president, though, was apparently only interested in relaxation. To ensure they were not pursued by anyone, a Daugherty crony was in charge of the FBI. William Burns was not averse to blackmailing anyone who threatened to expose the "gang."

Once Harding realized some of the Ohio Gang's activities, including selling influence and bribery in the Justice Department, he took action. He ordered Jess Smith to resign. Smith immediately destroyed incriminating paperwork, and then committed suicide. Still Harding was unable to take action against his longtime friend Harry Daugherty. But Daugherty was not the only cabinet member to cause the president grief.

The US government possesses various oil reserves throughout the nation for emergency purposes. In 1921, Interior Secretary Albert Fall and Navy Secretary Edwin Denby agreed that the Navy's oil reserves in California and at Teapot Dome, Wyoming, would be put under Fall's department. Harding signed the executive order after discussing the matter with his two secretaries. The following year, Fall leased the Teapot Dome reserve to Harry Sinclair without any competitive bidding; the interior secretary received over three hundred thousand dollars for the deal. Fall also made a similar deal with Pan-American Petroleum and Transport Company for the California reserve. By the spring of 1922, rumors were flying of Fall's corrupt dealings which he emphatically denied. Congress pressed for an investigation and hearings were slated to begin in October 1923. Looking to the likely headaches of the upcoming congressional investigation, Harding decided to take a summer vacation trip. Little did he know that its outcome would be the most surprising of all events from his administration.

WESTERN JOURNEY

In the summer of 1923, President Harding decided to embark on an extensive cross-country rail trip that would ultimately take him to Alaska. His wife's health was fragile, but she insisted on accompanying him. Undoubtedly he wished to remove himself from Washington and the political scene, which was threatening to destroy his presidency, although none of the scandals connected directly to him. Harding was clearly upset by events and remarked, "My God, this is a hell of a job! I have no trouble with my enemies. . . . But my damn friends, they're the ones that keep me walking the floor nights."[17]

The trip was taxing on the president, who had only recently had a bout of the flu. Still, he stayed up late and rose early; in six weeks, he gave eighty-five speeches. And though he was thousands of miles from the nation's capital, his situation kept haunting him. One night he confronted Commerce Secretary Herbert Hoover and asked, "If you knew of a great scandal in our administration, would you for the good of the country and the party expose it publicly or would you bury it?" Hoover instantly replied he would make it public and asked what Harding was referring to. The president mentioned the problems in the Justice Department but immediately dropped the subject when Hoover asked if Daugherty was involved. Nothing was mentioned again.

Harding suffered some type of collapse in Seattle. His close friend and surgeon general Dr. Charles Sawyer announced that the president had food poisoning from bad seafood. The presidential train continued its way south to San Francisco, where it arrived on July 29, and Harding and his entourage moved into the Palace Hotel. There he received around-the-clock medical care and was seen by other physicians, who believed he was suffering heart problems and probably had for years, as illustrated by his history of high blood pressure.

Mrs. Harding remained at his side, and on the evening of August 2, her husband appeared better, so she read aloud an article about him entitled "A Calm View of a Calm Man" by Samuel Blythe in the *Saturday Evening Post*. He liked its favorable treatment of the subject and told her, "That's good. Go on; read some more."[18] Those were to be his final words. The nurse saw his face jerk and his head roll to the side; Flossie Harding ran into the hall screaming for a doctor. But it was too late. President Warren G. Harding had died.

AFTERMATH

In the days and months that followed, whispers of a conspiracy and cover-up regarding the president's death would shroud the events. Was his death of natural causes? What were they? Was someone responsible? Did someone murder the president? Did he commit suicide? The questions were asked, but could not be definitively answered because no autopsy was performed; instead, his body was embalmed soon after his death. Gaston B. Means wrote a book in 1930 offering the notion that Mrs. Harding killed her husband, but nothing could be proven, nor does evidence make it likely. What is more probable is that because of increased weight, the pressures of the job, and high blood pressure, Harding suffered multiple heart attacks and possibly strokes. Moreover, Dr. Sawyer's negligence could have led to the fatal attack and very likely is the reason why no autopsy was done.

The country watched their fallen leader's funeral train traverse the last leg of his journey from Washington home to Marion. Within the year, Dr. Sawyer died from a blood clot; coincidentally, Mrs. Harding was at his home at the time. Six months later, she, too, was dead. Senate hearings and criminal trials of the men involved in the various scandals of the Harding administration continued for years.

When the Harding tomb was complete and ready for dedication, President Calvin Coolidge, disgusted by his predecessor's scandal-ridden administration, absolutely refused to attend its dedication. According to his successor and former Harding cabinet secretary Herbert Hoover, the mere mention of Harding's tomb brought an express of "furious distaste"[19] from Coolidge. So in 1931, it was Hoover who journeyed to Marion, Ohio, to dedicate the tomb of its most famous citizen.

Warren G. Harding was the fifth president to come from Ohio, following in the footsteps of Grant, Hayes, Garfield, and Taft. No wonder it was said, "Some men have greatness thrust upon them, some are born great, and some are born in Ohio."[20]

DID YOU KNOW?

★★★★★★★★★★★

Harding was the first president who did not outlive his father.

ENDNOTES

1 William A. DeGregorio, *The Complete Book of US Presidents*, New York: Gramercy Books, 2005, pp. 431–432.

2 Robert K. Murray, *The Harding Era: Warren G. Harding and His Administration*, Minneapolis: University of Minnesota Press, 1969, p. 7.

3 Francis Russell, *The Shadow of Blooming Grove: Warren G. Harding and His Times*, New York: McGraw Hill Book Company, 1968, p. 90.

4 Murray, p. 11.

5 Ibid, p. 12.

6 Andrew Sinclair, *The Available Man: The Life Behind the Masks of Warren Gamaliel Harding*, New York: MacMillan Company, 1965, p. 64.

7 Ibid, p. 65.

8 Ibid, p. 63.

9 Ibid, p. 68.

10 Russell, p. 109.

11 Charles L. Mee, *The Ohio Gang*, New York: M. Evans and Company, Inc., 1981, p. 89.

12 Sinclair, p. 159.

13 Ibid, p. 160.

14 DeGregorio, p. 438.

15 Sinclair, p. 233.

16 Ibid, p. 240.

17 *The Autobiography of William Allen White*, New York: Macmillan, 1946, p. 419.

18 Sinclair, p. 286.

19 Russell, p. 633.

20 Sinclair, p. 33.

Calvin Coolidge

★ ★ ★ THIRTIETH PRESIDENT ★ ★ ★

LIFE SPAN
- Born: July 4, 1872, at Plymouth Notch, Vermont
- Died: January 5, 1933, in Northampton, Massachusetts

NICKNAME
- Silent Cal

RELIGION
- Congregationalist

HIGHER EDUCATION
- Amherst College, 1895

PROFESSION
- Lawyer

MILITARY SERVICE
- None

FAMILY
- Father: **John Calvin Coolidge** (1845–1926)
- Mother: **Victoria Josephine Moor Coolidge** (1846–1885)
- Wife: **Grace Anna Goodhue Coolidge** (1879–1957); wed on October 4, 1905, in Burlington, Vermont
- Children: **John** (1906–2000); **Calvin** (1908–1924)

POLITICAL LIFE
- Northampton (Massachusetts) city council (1899–1900)
- Northampton city solicitor (1900–1902)
- Hampshire County clerk of courts (1903)
- Massachusetts General Court member (1907–1908)
- Northampton mayor (1910–1911)
- Massachusetts state senator (1912–1915); Senate president (1914–1915)
- Lieutenant governor of Massachusetts (1916–1918)
- Governor of Massachusetts (1919–1920)
- Vice President (1921–1923)

PRESIDENCY
- One term: August 3, 1923–March 4, 1929; became president upon death of **Warren G. Harding**
- Republican
- Reason for leaving office: declined to run for another term
- Vice president: **Charles G. Dawson** (1925–1929)

ELECTION OF 1924
- Electoral vote: **Coolidge** 382; **John W. Davis** 136; **Robert M. LaFollette** 13
- Popular vote: **Coolidge** 15,723,789; **Davis** 8,386,242; **LaFollette** 4,831,706

CABINET

SECRETARY OF STATE
Charles Evans Hughes (1921–1925)
Frank B. Kellogg (1925–1929)

SECRETARY OF THE TREASURY
Andrew W. Mellon (1923–1929)

SECRETARY OF WAR
John W. Weeks (1921–1925)
Dwight F. Davis (1925–1929)

ATTORNEY GENERAL
Harry M. Daugherty (1921–1924)
Harlan Fiske Stone (1924–1925)
John G. Sargent (1925–1929)

SECRETARY OF THE NAVY
Edwin Denby (1921–1924)
Curtis D. Wilbur (1924–1929)

POSTMASTER GENERAL
Harry S. New (1923–1929)

Politicians and presidents are not known for being quiet. Calvin Coolidge was an exception, his reserved, serious nature earned him the nickname "Silent Cal." But he was possessed of a quick, however subtle, wit and on one occasion turned it on himself when a dinner guest at the White House told President Coolidge that she had made a bet that she could make him say more than two words. In his nasal Yankee twang, the president replied, "You lose."

EARLY LIFE

The Coolidge family had called New England home since landing in Massachusetts in the 1630s. An ancestor fought at the Battle of Lexington and then later moved to Vermont. It was there that John Calvin Coolidge married Victoria Josephine Moor in 1868. They had two children, a son who was given his father's name, but, to prevent confusion, was called "Cal," and a daughter, Abigail, who was born four years later.

The Coolidge family lived in the small town of Plymouth Notch, where the elder Coolidge ran a store, farmed, and dabbled in state and local politics, serving in a variety of offices. Cal attended the local school for the equivalent of an eighth grade education, and the rest of the time helped with chores at home and on the farm; he especially enjoyed tapping maple sugar on wintry days. Naturally shy, Cal preferred to spend time alone. He refrained from participating in sports and often worked in a carriage shop where he made toys. He never outgrew his shyness, later telling a friend that he felt fearful whenever he heard visitors' unfamiliar voices in the kitchen: "The hardest thing was to have to go through that kitchen door and give them a greeting. . . . I'm all right with old friends, but every time I meet a stranger, I've got to go through the old kitchen door, back home, and it's not easy."[1]

At the age of fourteen, young Cal followed in his father's footsteps and trekked to Black River Academy in Ludlow, Vermont. He matriculated there for the next four years with nothing outstanding to distinguish his record, then failed the entrance examination to his college of choice—Amherst. Refusing to give up, Coolidge attended a college preparatory program at St. Johnsbury Academy, also in Ludlow, and upon completion, he was accepted to Amherst.

Again, Cal made no exceptional progress; in fact, his marks were mediocre for the first two years. His grades improved during his last years with rhetoric, history, and languages being among his top courses. He gained some recognition in his junior year. An Amherst tradition was the running of a footrace by its junior class, each fellow wearing a silk hat and carrying a walking stick. The seven who completed last had to serve a dinner to their classmates. Coolidge found himself in this bottom group and then was selected to write a speech he titled, "Why I Got Stuck." In it he explained how life on a farm and in a store had little prepared him for running a race, but ended with a quotation that would prove prophetic over the course of his life: "Remember, boys, the Good Book says that the first shall be last and the last shall be first."[2]

In his senior year, Cal joined the new campus fraternity Phi Delta Gamma, but still kept mainly to himself. When he won the Amherst medal for the Sons of the American Revolution essay "The Principles Fought for in the American Revolution," he bragged to no one, nor did he do so when he won the national prize.

Coolidge also won the honor of being Grove Orator to speak at the Class Day activities that

NATIONAL EVENTS

Columbia Pictures founded

Zenith produces first portable radio for household use

Herman Melville's book *Billy Budd* is published

JAN 5: First appearance of a Chrysler automobile

FEB 12: First radio broadcast by a president

FEB 12: First performance of George Gershwin's *Rhapsody in Blue*

FEB 14: IBM incorporated

APR 17: Founding of Metro-Goldwyn-Mayer (MGM) studios

1924

WORLD EVENTS

JAN 10: British sub *L34* sinks in the English Channel, 43 lose their lives

JAN 21: V.I. Lenin dies and will be buried in a mausoleum at Red Square in Moscow

JAN 25: First Winter Olympic Games opens at Chamonix, France

JAN 26: Petrograd renamed Leningrad

MAR 3: End of Ottoman dynasty

preceded his class's graduation the following day. He entertained his classmates with humorous anecdotes of their times at Amherst, his stories colored with his characteristic biting sarcasm. The next day, Calvin Coolidge became the first member of his family to graduate from college. Now he had to decide his destiny.

Coolidge wrote to his father that he was not sure of what direction to take—should he work in the family store or go to law school? He ultimately decided to do neither. Because of the expense of attending law school, reading law with a practicing attorney seemed a more practical alternative. So in the fall of 1895, Calvin moved to Northampton, Massachusetts, to learn the law from two fellow Amherst alumni, John Hammond and Henry Field. After two years of studying, Coolidge successfully passed his Massachusetts bar examination.

ATTORNEY AND NORTHAMPTON POLITICIAN

Northampton seemed a good place to open a law practice, so by the spring of 1898, he had hung up a shingle and rented two rooms for his office. Clients were not exactly waiting in line to retain his services, but he made a little money here and there handling the tedious paperwork that forms the backbone of the legal profession.

Though Coolidge had had some exposure to politics through his father's activities, he took his first real steps into the political arena while he was studying with Field and Hammond. Soon after he began his law studies, Coolidge assisted Field in a run for mayor. For the 1896 election, Coolidge gave a speech at home and wrote articles arguing against the Democrats and William Jennings Bryan. The following year, he was tapped by the Northampton Republicans to join their five-man committee, and in 1898, he attended the state's convention. Later that year he was elected to an unpaid position on the city council. Looking for a more financially feasible alternative, he ran successfully for city solicitor, a job that gained him an additional six hundred dollars annually. He served two terms in this capacity, but was defeated for his third term.

Coolidge was soon back on the political scene. In 1903, he won appointment as court clerk for an annual salary of $2,300, but since it precluded him from practicing law, he only finished the term and refused to run for election. In 1904, he was the Republican local chairman, in which capacity he helped ensure a victory in the presidential race, although the party did lose the governorship. He lost in a three-way race the following year for the local school committee but at that point was less concerned with losing an election than gaining a wife.

Meeting women was no easy task for the naturally shy Cal. Fortunately, lady luck smiled on him when a young woman across the street looked into an open window and saw him, clad in long underwear and a hat, shaving his face. Grace Goodhue burst out laughing and later asked to be introduced to the unusual figure. They took an instant liking to each other. Grace was a college graduate from the University of Vermont and was currently teaching at the Clarke Institute for the Deaf in Northampton. Perhaps it was her work with the deaf, who often were withdrawn and alone in society, that made Grace better suited to draw out the innately shy Cal, but her natural charm and vitality totally captivated him, and the two made plans for a future, much to her mother's dismay. The couple married on October

CABINET

★★★★★★★★★★

(continued)

SECRETARY OF THE INTERIOR
Hubert Work (1923–1928)
Roy O. West (1928–1929)

SECRETARY OF AGRICULTURE
Henry C. Wallace (1921–1924)
Howard M. Gore (1924–1925)
William M. Jardine (1925–1929)

SECRETARY OF COMMERCE
Herbert Hoover (1921–1928)
William Whiting (1928–1929)

SECRETARY OF LABOR
James J. Davis (1923–1929)

MAY 10: J. Edgar Hoover appointed to head Federal Bureau of Investigation

JUN 2: Indian Citizenship Act grants citizenship rights to Native Americans

OCT 5: Little Orphan Annie comic strip introduced

NOV 4: Calvin Coolidge wins presidential election, defeating John W. Davis

Development of Scotch tape

Introduction of the Charleston dance

1925

MAR 25: Greece declares itself a republic

JUN 3: Writer Franz Kafka dies in Vienna, Austria

DEC 24: Albania becomes a republic

Britain declares Cyprus a crown colony

DID YOU KNOW?

The Coolidge family used sign language to communicate so others would not know what they were "saying."

4, 1905, at her parents' home in Burlington, Vermont, enjoyed a one-week honeymoon to Montreal, and then returned to begin their life together in Northampton.

In 1906, the Coolidges settled into a duplex, where they would remain until moving to Washington years later. In September, they welcomed the arrival of a son, John. Then in November, Coolidge won his first state election to the Massachusetts House of Representatives.

STATE LEGISLATOR

In the early 1900s, President Theodore Roosevelt wielded executive power and, on the national level, progressive reforms were initiated; states followed the lead. In the Massachusetts General Court, Coolidge joined others who believed that change was necessary to improve life for its citizens. He supported a six-day workweek for labor, constitutional amendments favoring the direct election of senators, and the right to vote for women. During his second term, he was appointed to more significant committees, including banking and judiciary, where he continued his pro-labor stance. He stayed in a boardinghouse and lived frugally, then returned home on weekends to see his family, which meant Grace was the main parent rearing their children (a second son, Calvin, was born in 1908). He took a break from the legislature to return to his law practice and hopefully bolster the family's income.

RETURN TO NORTHAMPTON

Retirement from public office was short lived as Coolidge was asked to run for mayor of Northampton. The main issue of the campaign was whether the candidates were for or against the prohibition of liquor. The Democratic challenger offended the "wets" when he took the side of the temperance advocates in a debate, but Coolidge remained silent on the issue, offending no one, and he won the election. It would not be the last time that he would use silence to his advantage.

The town of Northampton found itself much improved following Coolidge's two mayoral terms. He managed to make capital improvements, including upgrading the city's sidewalks and expanding police and fire departments, as well as increasing teachers' salaries, while at the same time, his budgeting allowed the town to reduce its debt and enjoy a tax reduction. Coolidge also sold some of the city's property, investing the proceeds to provide future income. His administration was free of scandal and corruption, and his party believed he had higher offices in his future.

STATE SENATOR

Coolidge's next step on the political ladder was running for the state senate, which he handily won. He returned to his earlier frugal lifestyle in Boston, taking up residence in the same boardinghouse he occupied during his second term as state representative. One of the freshman senator's first assignments was heading a committee to settle a textile strike in Lawrence. Both sides worked with his group for weeks to hammer out a settlement, which allowed for an increase in workers' wages and the institution of paid overtime. Coolidge's cool head in a volatile situation gained him recognition.

The 1913 state senate session was, as Coolidge stated, "the most enjoyable session I ever spent with any legislative body,"[3] because he breathed the sweet air of victory. The year before a bill that would provide trolley service to Northampton and much of Coolidge's district had been vetoed

NATIONAL EVENTS	New songs: "Yes Sir, That's My Baby," "Sweet Georgia Brown," and "St. Louis Blues"	First appearance of Burma-Shave signs on roadsides Al Capone becomes Chicago's boss	**FEB 21:** First issue of *New Yorker* magazine **MAR 4:** Inauguration of Calvin Coolidge	**MAR 18:** Nearly 700 killed in nation's deadliest tornado ripping across Missouri, Illinois, and Indiana	**APR 10:** F. Scott Fitzgerald publishes *The Great Gatsby*
WORLD EVENTS	Turkmenistan and Uzbekistan become Soviet Socialist republics	**JAN 3:** Benito Mussolini declares himself dictator of Italy	**MAY 1:** Cyprus named a British Crown Colony	**JUL 18:** Publication of *Mein Kampf (My Struggle)* by Adolf Hitler	**JUL 25:** Telegraph Agency of the Soviet Union (TASS) is established

by Democratic governor Eugene Foss. Upset by the loss but not defeated, Coolidge persevered; he was appointed to head the senate committee on railroads and worked through their summer recess to develop his case and gain allies. His actions triumphed in the overriding of the governor's second veto of the trolley bill. Coolidge's hard work paid off in other ways as well, earning him further acclaim and important political contacts.

Coolidge's record in the state senate reveals strong support of progressive issues, including women's suffrage. He also backed widows' pensions, minimum wage for women, and assistance for indigent mothers; moreover, he voted for workmen's compensation and legalized picketing. Other reforms calling for direct election of senators and the income tax also had his support.

Coolidge took another step up when, in 1914, he was nominated by the Republican caucus and then voted in by the Massachusetts senate to become their president, which he accepted in a characteristically short address. He would be the one to determine committee assignments and decide where bills would be sent. His position was one of influence, and he often used his negotiation skills to gain compromises.

He returned the following year for his fourth senate term and was again elected as its president. This time his address to the group was even shorter—forty-two words. He ended it with "Be loyal to the Commonwealth and to yourselves. And be brief; above all things, be brief."[4] The General Court was not as productive during its 1915 term, but Coolidge continued pushing committees to complete their assigned duties. A diligent and dedicated politician, he always retained his characteristic wit. When, during his term of office, one senator complained that another had told him to go to hell, Coolidge replied, deadpan, "I've examined the Constitution and the Senate rules, and there's nothing in them that compels you to go."[5] His tenure in the senate made him a bit of a political anomaly—he was a worker who made very few enemies along the way. Still, by the end of the 1915 term, he was ready to resume his private practice and live with Grace and their sons in Northampton.

While Coolidge was returning to his family, fellow alumni from Amherst were discussing how they could gain some of the political clout that their rivals from Harvard enjoyed in the statehouse, so they convinced the senate president to make a bid for the lieutenant governorship. Samuel McCall, an experienced politician and fine orator, was Coolidge's running mate. The two traveled across Massachusetts making stump speeches, all of which amply displayed Coolidge's poor speaking ability. A saying became popular: "McCall could fill any hall in Massachusetts, and Coolidge could empty it."[6] But still the voters liked both and overwhelmingly said so on election day.

LIEUTENANT GOVERNOR

In Massachusetts, the lieutenant governor heads the governor's council, which is mainly concerned with judicial appointments and pardons. Coolidge discharged these duties, but was called upon to perform others, as well. In 1916, he chaired a committee to revamp the financial structure of the Boston Elevated Street Railway. His group proposed creating a board of trustees to oversee the El's operations and fares to ensure they were affordable. Also, with American involvement in World War I, Coolidge now stumped for war bonds and rallied the citizens of Massachusetts to support their nation and state, in addition to campaigning twice

SUPREME COURT APPOINTMENTS
★★★★★★★★★★

Harlan Fiske Stone, 1925

JUL 10–21: Scopes trial, regarding the teaching of evolution

AUG 4: End of American occupation of Nicaragua

AUG 18: Forty thousand Ku Klux Klan members march in Washington

NOV 28: First radio broadcast of *Grand Ole Opry* show

First college exam, SAT, administered

AUG 14: Norway annexes Spitsbergen per a treaty in 1920

DEC 1: Locarno Treaty signed determining boundaries for Germany-France and Germany-Belgium

DEC 26: The excavation of the Great Sphinx of Giza is finally completed

1926

John L. Baird of Scotland invents an early television

STATE OF THE UNION

US POPULATION IN 1923
105,775,046

NATIONAL DEBT IN 1929
$16,931,088,484

NUMBER OF STATES IN 1929
48

for reelection. But by 1918, Coolidge was ready for a higher position, and when Governor McCall announced he would run for the US Senate, the way was open for the lieutenant governor to move up. He narrowly defeated his Democratic opponent, winning the governorship, while most of the rest of the ticket went Democratic. A few days after his victory, Coolidge had more cause for celebration—the end of the fighting in Europe.

GOVERNOR

With the end of war came the return of the fighting men—and the appearance of related issues requiring the attention of state governors. With housing at a premium, many landlords seized the opportunity to increase their profits, resulting in former soldiers with little or no income having nowhere to live. Coolidge worked with the General Court to pass legislation cracking down on such loathsome practices. A state commission was created to investigate profiteering charges dealing with basic necessities, and profiteering was deemed a criminal enterprise. Coolidge was also known to serve as mediator when labor and management were at loggerheads, always with an eye to improving the average wage for laborers, state employees, and teachers. He oversaw a broad spectrum of improvements, among them the reduction of the workweek to forty-eight hours for women and children, the reforestation of one hundred thousand acres, and the granting of more home rule to local municipalities. As a result of measures adopted during the recent constitutional convention, Coolidge now also had to enact the reduction of the state government, which caused significant distress to politicians across the political spectrum who stood to lose jobs and political clout.

The pivotal event of Coolidge's governorship came seven months into his term, when tempers flared and strikes plagued the nation. Just as he and his family were leaving for a summer vacation in Maine, conditions in Boston rapidly deteriorated for one of its largest municipal groups—the policemen, whose working conditions were deplorable and their pay less than that of trolley car operators. Concluding their situation was untenable, the angry members of the department met and decided to join the American Federation of Labor. This news antagonized the police commissioner, Edwin Curtis, who then expressly forbade the policemen from joining any type of union. Now passions were thoroughly inflamed, and the police pressed forward to organize. Nineteen were arrested for their efforts, and Boston remained a city unsure of what might happen next.

Coolidge believed he had no jurisdiction over the city of Boston's police force, so he refused to involve himself despite others' pleas for him to step in. On Tuesday, September 9, the police went on strike, and that night, under cover of darkness, the city fell into lawlessness, with vandals looting stores and turning Boston Common into a gambling park. The State Guard was called out to patrol the city, and the next day, the governor was again pressured to intervene, but again he refused. After consulting with advisors, however, he issued executive orders that gave him command of the situation, called out the rest of the State Guard, and instructed Commissioner Curtis to assist him with maintaining law and order. When the head of the AFL, Samuel Gompers, asked Coolidge to reconsider and submit the matter for arbitration, including rehiring the nineteen dismissed, his reply was that the officers had been fired because they "abandoned their sworn duty" and as governor, "I

DID YOU KNOW?

While president, Coolidge had a pet raccoon (Rebecca) that was often found riding around on the president's shoulder.

NATIONAL EVENTS	Ernest Hemingway writes *The Sun Also Rises*	Vaudevillians George Burns and Gracie Allen form a comedy team	Miniature golf invented	Gene Tunney wins heavyweight championship	First two volumes of Carl Sandburg's six-volume series on Abraham Lincoln is published
WORLD EVENTS	Mercedes-Benz created	A.A. Milne publishes *Winnie-the-Pooh*	**JAN 6:** Lufthansa begins operations with a fleet of 162 aircraft	**JAN 16:** BBC radio play about worker's revolution causes a panic in London	**MAR 6:** The Shakespeare Memorial Theatre in Stratford-upon-Avon is destroyed by fire

have no authority to interfere."[7] But it was the next exchange that captured the nation's attention. After days of following the news story, and worried that other cities could also fall victim, the American people rallied around the Massachusetts governor's quote: "There is no right to strike against the public safety by anybody, anywhere, any time."[8] This was reprinted throughout the nation and soon Calvin Coolidge became a household word. He easily won reelection in 1919, and Republicans in Massachusetts and elsewhere began touting his name for the presidential nomination of 1920.

Unlike other members of his party, Coolidge supported the League of Nations, which had been proposed by the outgoing Democratic president, Woodrow Wilson. Under advisement from other Republicans who supported him, Coolidge attempted to be more impartial toward the question. Many names were offered for the presidential slot when Republicans met in Chicago in June 1920. House Speaker Frederick Gillett placed Coolidge's name in nomination, comparing him to other favorite Republican presidents—Lincoln, Grant, McKinley, and Roosevelt. The delegates were unmoved by Gillett's speech, but they also became deadlocked among the three leading contenders, who included fellow Massachusetts Republican, General Leonard Wood. Party leaders worked late into the night in the back rooms of their hotel, attempting to find a compromise candidate. They finally selected Ohio senator Warren G. Harding; now the rush was on to pick his running mate. Several favored Wisconsin senator Irvine Lenroot, but his was not the only name being discussed. Coolidge supporters demanded to be heard; Oregon delegate Wallace McCamant announced that there was "a son of Massachusetts who has been much in the public eye in the last year, a man who is sterling in his Americanism and stands for all that the Republican Party holds dear . . . I name Governor Calvin Coolidge of Massachusetts."[9] When Coolidge received the call in his Boston boardinghouse room, he told his wife the news. Grace replied, "You aren't going to take it, are you?" He answered, "I suppose I'll have to."[10]

THE ROARING TWENTIES ★ The 1920s was a time of outrageous fads and fashions, including flagpole sitting, dance marathons, and mah jong. Some young women became "flappers," whose behavior defied the conventions of the day. They bobbed their hair, wore bright red lipstick, and painted their knees that showed below their short skirts, listened to jazz, smoked cigarettes, and drank alcohol. Listening to the radio began growing in popularity. More automobiles than ever before crammed the narrow roadways of the nation. America was on the move!

ELECTION OF 1920

In late June, the Republican ticket met in person for the first time. Harding addressed the reporters saying, "I think the vice president should be more than a mere substitute in waiting. . . . and I have been telling Governor Coolidge how much I wish him to be not only a participant in the campaign but a helpful part of a Republican administration."[11] Coolidge put in campaign appearances throughout New England, but his stumping was kept to a minimum. The Democratic challengers, Ohio governor James Cox and his running mate, assistant navy secretary Franklin D.

MAR 16: Robert Goddard launches his first rocket propelled by liquid fuel

MAY 20: Air Commerce Act regulating air carriers

SEP 25: Ford Motor Company announces they will operate on a five-day workweek

NOV 11: National Broadcasting Company (NBC) founded

NOV 27: John D. Rockefeller begins providing money for restoring Colonial Williamsburg, Virginia

APR: German-Soviet Treaty of Berlin is signed

MAY 13: Coal miner's strike begins in Britain sparking general strike throughout the United Kingdom in support of the miners

MAY 23: Lebanon declared a republic

JUL 1: Kuomingtang begins a campaign in northern China for unification

OCT 7: Benito Mussolini and his Fascist Party take full control of Italy

DID YOU KNOW?

Coolidge is the only president to be sworn into office by his father, a justice of the peace.

Roosevelt, made a better speaking team, but their views supporting the League of Nations and opposing Prohibition were unpopular among the voters who turned out on November 2 and gave Harding and Coolidge a landslide victory.

VICE PRESIDENT COOLIDGE

President Harding made good on his campaign pledge to grant his vice president more authority; Coolidge was included in the cabinet meetings, although he declined to take an active role, preferring to merely sit and listen; his role as the Senate's presiding officer was equally unimpressive. Coolidge furthered Harding's policies, but hurt his own reputation among Progressives by mishandling a proposed bill by Nebraska Senator George Norris that would aid farmers who were facing problems as they converted from wartime to peacetime production. The Harding administration, however, opposed this measure and backed a different one pushing domestic markets, sponsored by Senator Frank Kellogg of Minnesota, who intended to derail the Norris bill with his own. Hearing of Kellogg's plan, Norris asked Coolidge to allow Senator Joseph Ransdell to speak first on the Nebraskan's bill before Kellogg. The vice president agreed. But just before the debate began, Coolidge absented himself from the Senate chamber and left Senator Charles G. Curtis to preside. Following the wishes of the president, Curtis called on Kellogg, who was *not* asking to speak, and flagrantly ignored Norris, who was demanding the floor. After Kellogg was recognized, Coolidge returned to his chair, but the damage was done. Progressives and Democrats who backed Norris were outraged, and the incident seriously eroded Coolidge's credibility as a man who would keep his word.

The vice president traveled about giving speeches, attending dinners, and generally becoming better known to the voting public. Supporting these efforts was his wife Grace, whose easy charm was welcome wherever they went. Throughout their marriage, his frugality knew only one luxury—dressing his wife in style, and Grace Coolidge became a popular guest and hostess. Meanwhile, the teenage Coolidge boys attended Mercersburg Academy in Pennsylvania.

By 1923, some Republicans were discussing dumping Coolidge for another candidate when Harding made his reelection bid. The vice president was not particularly happy in his job anyway and was glad to return home to Massachusetts in the spring. The Coolidge family then spent part of the summer at his father's farm in Plymouth Notch, Vermont. There he helped with the chores, and on the night of August 2, easily drifted off to sleep, not knowing that the president had suffered a fatal heart attack in San Francisco and died. In the absence of telephone lines to Colonel Coolidge's house, a group of three—the vice president's stenographer, his chauffeur, and a reporter, who received the news off the wire—drove to Plymouth Notch. There they awakened the senior Coolidge, who in turn awoke his son to deliver the shocking news. The vice president and his wife dressed, prayed, and then went downstairs. The attorney general insisted Coolidge should take the oath of office as soon as possible, Secretary of State Charles Evans Hughes adding that it needed to be administered by a notary. So Colonel John Calvin Coolidge, local justice of the peace and notary public, became the only father in history to give his son the presidential oath of office. Having been duly sworn in as the president of the United States, Coolidge and his family went back to bed.

NATIONAL EVENTS — 1927

- First 7-Eleven store opens
- Nan Britton publishes *The President's Daughter* claiming she had a child by Warren G. Harding
- **JAN 7:** First transatlantic phone call between New York and London
- **MAY 20–21:** Charles Lindbergh makes first solo transatlantic flight (NYC–Paris)
- **AUG 23:** Sacco and Vanzetti executed for payroll robbery and killing two guards in Massachusetts; some believe they were innocent

WORLD EVENTS — 1927

- **JAN 19:** British troops sent to China
- **FEB:** Uprisings in China led by Chiang Kai-shek, who successfully takes Shanghai and Canton
- **MAR 4:** Diamond rush in South Africa
- **MAY 13:** "Black Friday" in Germany when its economy plummets
- **MAY 20:** Saudi Arabia gains independence from United Kingdom

PRESIDENT COOLIDGE

Coolidge returned to Washington and attended the funeral services for Harding. He reassured Mrs. Harding that she need not be in a hurry to vacate the White House. Once she did leave, the Coolidges waited four days before moving their belongings from their hotel suite at the New Willard Hotel.

> *I have found it advisable not to give too much heed to what people say when I am trying to accomplish something of consequence. Invariably they proclaim it can't be done. I deem that the very best time to make the effort.*
>
> —*Calvin Coolidge*

As president, Coolidge thought he would be best served by keeping Harding's cabinet in place; he would soon, however, make changes of his own owing to scandals erupting from his predecessor's administration. Although Harding had been a newspaperman, it was Coolidge who began holding weekly press conferences. Within the White House, orders were given to return the first floor rooms to the public and reserve the upstairs for the family, following a precedent broken only by the Hardings, who utilized the entire house for their pleasure. The White House staff soon learned a new type of president was in residence, one who looked everywhere for signs of waste and even specified that food was to be purchased from large suppliers; he also inspected gifts that arrived and carefully peered over guest lists for various functions. Coolidge was also known to amuse himself at the staff's expense. Customarily, the president would press a buzzer to notify the residence staff that he was leaving his office and on the way upstairs. According to the presidential bodyguard, Coolidge would occasionally send the message, necessitating a bustle of activity in preparation for his arrival, after which he would, instead, "stroll out West Executive Avenue and leave them."[12]

Soon after taking office, the president received news that Japan had suffered a catastrophic earthquake and typhoon. Coolidge called the Department of the Navy and ordered the Asiatic fleet to sail to Japan and render any assistance. He also cabled the emperor with his condolences on the nation's tragedy. Closer to home, he decided to help the embattled Mexican government, which was attempting to ward off attacks by militants, by granting its request to lift the American arms embargo. Relations with America's southern neighbor seemed much improved since Wilson's presidency, and the trend promised to continue.

Each president develops his own style working with Congress; for President Coolidge it included going through the membership alphabetically and inviting them to the White House for breakfast. The congressmen soon dreaded receiving the invitation—the meal (always with pancakes and Vermont maple syrup) seemed pointless since their host rarely chatted with them, and promptly dismissed them once they finished eating. Coolidge, however, considered the breakfasts valuable since they afforded him an opportunity to meet with the legislative branch on a more personal level.

Congress made headlines when it launched investigations into various deals made during the

DID YOU KNOW?

As president, Coolidge refused to use the telephone.

OCT 6: Premiere of talking motion picture, *The Jazz Singer*, making silent pictures obsolete

DEC 2: End of Model T production, Model As replace it

DEC 27: Jerome Kern and Oscar Hammerstein's musical *Show Boat*, based on Edna Ferber's novel, premieres

Al Capone declared wealthiest American with annual income of $105 million

First highway cloverleaf built in New Jersey

1928

MAY 22: Catastrophic earthquake in China kills 200,000

MAY 24: Britain ends relations with Soviet Union

Chiang Kai-shek victorious in Chinese Civil War and takes Beijing (Peking)

World population reaches 2 billion

DID YOU KNOW?

Coolidge lighted the first national Christmas tree in 1923 on the White House lawn.

Harding administration, the most infamous being that involving Teapot Dome. The matter in question involved the former secretary of the interior Albert Fall, who leased from navy secretary Edwin Denby oil reserves in California and Wyoming (Teapot Dome). Fall then turned around and leased the land to oil companies and apparently was paid hundreds of thousands of dollars. Democrats loosely talked of the possibility of the oil scandal involving more of Harding's government, including Coolidge, hoping to derail any plans he might have of running in the 1924 election. The president maintained his distance as well as his innocence and applauded Congress for its investigation; he appointed bipartisan special prosecutors to delve more deeply into the matter.

> *"Nothing in the world can take the place of persistence. Talent will not; nothing is more common than unsuccessful men with talent. Genius will not; unrewarded genius is almost a proverb. Education will not; the world is full of educated derelicts. Persistence and determination alone are omnipotent. The slogan 'press on' has solved and always will solve the problems of the human race."*
>
> —*Calvin Coolidge*

When word became more widespread of unethical dealings by the attorney general's office, pressure mounted for the president to remove Harry Daugherty from that position. Coolidge refused at first, but ultimately he summoned Daugherty, whose insolence toward the president only aggravated the situation. Soon after Daugherty stepped out of the meeting, he received a note from the president's secretary, saying, "The president directs me to notify you that he expects your resignation at once."[13] The resignation arrived the following day. Coolidge named as his new attorney general a classmate from Amherst, Harlan Fiske Stone, who restored respect to the Justice Department, as well as revamped the Federal Bureau of Investigation, including appointing a young lawyer, J. Edgar Hoover, as its new director.

The president kept an eye on the economy and believed that, with war appropriation ended and a much lower budget requested than in recent years, he should grant the American people a tax cut. He explained, "I have in mind that the taxpayers are the stockholders of this business corporation of the United States, and that if this business is showing a surplus of receipts the taxpayer should share therein in some material way that will be of immediate benefit."[14] He trusted that these funds would, in turn, lead to an economic boom. He and treasury secretary Andrew Mellon were vindicated when they were successful at this first attempt at supply-side economics. People put their money to use purchasing, saving, and speculating. By the end of the decade, the latter would lead to trouble and disaster, but for the remainder of Coolidge's tenure, the economy moved along smoothly.

NATIONAL EVENTS	Rudy Vallee becomes first "crooner"	Welcome Wagon begins in Memphis	Daniel Gerber develops baby foods	Margaret Mead publishes *Coming of Age in Samoa*	**APR 9:** Mae West opens in her play *Diamond Lil*
WORLD EVENTS	D.H. Lawrence publishes *Lady Chatterly's Lover* in Italy; it is too risqué for British publication	British bacteriologist discovers penicillin in mold	**AUG 27:** Kellogg-Briand Pact signed by 15 nations, agreeing to outlaw war	**OCT 1:** Josef Stalin orders collectivization of farms in the Soviet Union	**NOV 10:** Hirohito becomes emperor of Japan

Coolidge was the president who signed into law the Immigration Act of 1924, which greatly reduced the numbers of certain immigrant groups, specifically those from eastern and southern Europe, especially Jews and Italians. Japanese immigration was banned entirely, to the dismay of the Coolidge administration and the Japanese government, who protested and threatened "grave consequences" should no quota be included. This only inflamed anti-Asian sentiment among congressmen who refused to acquiesce. Reluctantly, the president signed the bill into law.

In the spring of 1924, Coolidge took an unpopular stand, fully aware that it could end in defeat at the polls. The American Legion and veterans' groups were pushing Congress for two bills: one would pay additional pension to veterans of earlier wars; the second was a bonus for those serving in World War I in the form of insurance that would be available in twenty years. Coolidge disliked both proposals and vetoed them. The first veto was sustained, but the second made Congress nervous. The president maintained that the veterans should not complain, arguing, "Service to our country in time of war means sacrifice."[15] The Republican members of Congress, however, were not about to "sacrifice" votes to curry the president's favor, so members of his own party voted to override his veto.

Soon after the Veterans Bonus became law, both parties geared up for their presidential conventions. The Republicans met in Cleveland, where they became the first to broadcast their convention on the radio. As expected, Coolidge won the nomination, but deciding on his running mate was not so easy. Coolidge's first two choices for the position, Senator William Borah of Idaho and Governor Frank Lowden of Illinois, rejected his offer. Lowden's rejection was particularly embarrassing for the president since he had assumed Lowden would accept the nomination, having just been approved by the delegates. Commerce secretary Herbert Hoover then lost on the third ballot to Charles Dawes, who had been director of the Bureau of Budget and admitted his selection as vice presidential candidate was "about the most unexpected thing in my life." Dawes had served as brigadier general in World War I and was the army's purchasing agent. He was questioned by a postwar congressional committee regarding possible overpayment for supplies and became well known for his response: "Sure we paid. We didn't dicker. . . . Hell and Maria, we weren't trying to keep a set of books, we were trying to win the war!"[16] Such a man was slated to be the running mate for the taciturn president.

The Coolidge family had more than politics on their minds in the summer of 1924. Younger son Calvin Jr. played tennis one day without wearing socks and developed a blister. He ignored it until blood poisoning and infection set in. The boy was hospitalized, but there was little anyone, including the president, could do. Later the heartsick Coolidge wrote, "In his suffering he was asking me to make him well. I could not."[17] The sixteen-year-old died on July 7. No longer did the campaign or even the presidency seem all-important. Later, when a boy arrived at the White House grounds asking to accompany the president on his walk, Coolidge's bodyguard ushered him to the president's side. Hearing that the boy wished to express his condolences on his son's death, tears welled in Coolidge's eyes, and once the lad was on his way, the president instructed his guard, "Whenever a boy wants to see me always bring him in. Never turn one away or make him wait."[18]

JUN 29: Democrats nominate New York Governor Alfred E. Smith as first Catholic candidate for president

NOV 7: Republican Herbert Hoover defeats Al Smith in presidential election

NOV 18: First appearance of Mickey Mouse in animated sound film *Steamboat Willie*

DEC 6: Bolivia and Paraguay begin fighting a war

THE KKK ★ For the first half of the 1920s, the Ku Klux Klan experienced a burst of popularity throughout the United States, and in 1925, 40,000 marched on Washington, D.C. Following World War I, the Klan enlarged its scope of enemies to include various types of foreigners, especially Jews, Catholics, and anyone considered a Communist or socialist. Several Klansmen became elected public officials in the South as well as in Oregon, Maine, and Indiana. With the Great Depression, people's interest waned, and the Klan's membership went from an all-time high of more than 4 million in 1925 to so few that the organization disbanded in 1944, only to resume during the civil rights movement in the 1950s.

Political campaigns wait for no one, including grieving fathers. Coolidge seldom made a speech and told reporters it was a good tactic because "I don't recall any candidate for President that ever injured himself by not talking."[19] His Democratic opponent was John Davis of West Virginia, a former member of the Wilson administration, whose running mate was Charles W. Bryan, brother of William Jennings Bryan of Nebraska. The Democratic ticket supported the League of Nations, Prohibition, tariff reduction, and a public works program. Davis never enjoyed much support beyond the South, and his popularity there waned even further when he denounced the Ku Klux Klan, whose numbers had skyrocketed in recent years.

Progressive senator Robert LaFollette of Wisconsin and Senator Burton Wheeler of Montana headed their party's ticket. Their platform supported additional help for farmers and labor, government ownership of utilities, and multinational disarmament.

With the economy healthy and thriving, the American people seemed satisfied to "Keep Cool with Coolidge" and he captured 54 percent of the popular vote; the Democrats were second with 29 percent. The president handily won the electoral college with 35 states for a total of 382 electoral votes.

SECOND TERM

Coolidge's inauguration began badly when his new vice president stood at the podium and denounced Congress. The president and the legislative body never saw eye to eye, but Coolidge had attempted to smooth relations by not vetoing their salary hike approved shortly before his inauguration; he had, however, utilized his veto power numerous times—twelve to be exact—during the 1927–1929 congressional sessions. He was opposed by Progressives and Democrats alike, including his own nominee for attorney general, Charles Beecher Warren, who was denounced because of his legal work for the Michigan Sugar Company. Vice President Dawes apparently believed there was not enough opposition to be concerned and returned to his suite at the Willard Hotel for a nap. The Senate voted and was tied at 40-40, ready for Dawes to cast the determining vote. Dawes arrived too late, and one of the senators chose to change his vote, both incidents resulting in Warren's defeat. The president was understandably embarrassed and angry at his vice president and the defection of Senate Republicans.

The president waged another battle in Congress when he insisted that more should be done to help and regulate the burgeoning aviation industry. With more airplanes flying, railroad interests were scrambling to block competition, as were buses and trucking companies. But Coolidge strongly believed the future was in the air (although he refused to fly) and recommended creating a Bureau of Civil Aeronautics under the Commerce Department. He faced criticism by some citizens, who believed taxpayer money would be wasted on research and development of airplanes. Coolidge hoped the players in the aviation industry would put aside their competitiveness and work together instead. More attention was turned to the skies after Colonel William "Billy" Mitchell charged that the United States was lagging behind in its national defense and aviation. The president appointed a board headed by former Amherst buddy Dwight Morrow (future father-in-law of Charles Lindbergh) to look into the allegations. The board drafted recommendations that

Coolidge passed on to Congress, including a budget increase. In 1926, the commerce department took over civil aviation and the first commercial air traffic routes were created.

> ***If you don't say anything, you won't be called on to repeat it.***
>
> —*Calvin Coolidge*

In an effort to help the farmers who were not enjoying the nation's growing prosperity, Congress passed the McNary-Haugen Bill, which propped up prices that had dropped considerably because of extensive surpluses. Price fixing was "economic folly,"[20] according to the president, so he vetoed the farm bill twice. The midterm elections of 1926 saw a decrease in the Republican majority in both houses, meaning the president would encounter even greater difficulties in future legislation.

In foreign affairs, the president and his state department skirted possible conflict with China, which was undergoing its own internal strife. The Philippines were also posing problems, partly owing to friction between its people and Governor General Leonard Wood, who left in 1927 and was replaced by Henry Stimson, a more capable diplomat who had earlier monitored elections in Nicaragua. His presence eased tensions considerably. Associations with Mexico had also become strained due to legislation recently passed involving foreign oil and land rights. Once more Coolidge turned to friend Dwight Morrow who readily agreed to become America's ambassador to Mexico. He was a great success because he fulfilled his promise, "I know what I can do for the Mexicans. I can *like* them."[21] And that he did, as he and his family became immersed and enthralled with the culture and its people.

Coolidge believed the United States should do as Harding desired and join the World Court, but certain senators strenuously opposed such a move and ultimately it died. The president similarly failed at his attempts to set up a disarmament conference in Geneva, Switzerland, involving the nations of Great Britain, France, Italy, Japan, and the United States. Italy and France declined to attend; additionally, the Americans and British could not agree on cruiser tonnages. In short, there was no agreement among nations. More successful was the Kellogg-Briand Pact of 1928 in which Secretary of State Frank Kellogg and the French foreign minister Aristide Briand drew up an agreement that its nations would "condemn recourse to war for the solution of international controversies, and renounce it as an instrument of national policy in their relations with one another."[22] Fifteen nations signed the pact, including the United States, France, Great Britain, Italy, Japan, India, Poland, and South Africa. Other countries from around the globe also ratified the agreement, although, within the decade, its significance had evaporated.

In the summer of 1927, the first family vacationed in the South Dakota Black Hills, where, within a few months, work would commence carving out the heads of four presidents from the granite mountainside. Speculation was rampant regarding the upcoming campaign in 1928 and whether Coolidge would run again. He answered that question definitively on August 2 when the press was summoned to the Rapid City High School, and as they filed by the president, Coolidge handed each a thin slip of paper that read "I do not choose to run for President in nineteen twenty-eight."[23] This was news to the nation, as well as his wife. He told Kansas senator Arthur Capper later that day, "It's four years ago today since I became President. If I seek another term, I will be in the White House till 1933. . . . Ten years in Washington is . . . too long!"[24] Admittedly his enthusiasm had waned after his son's death; both his and Grace's health had also suffered during his presidency. No one received much of an explanation, but it was plain that Calvin Coolidge was ready to go home.

RETIREMENT

After attending the inaugural festivities of his successor, Herbert Hoover, the former president

THE SCOPES "MONKEY" TRIAL ★ In the summer of 1925, the country's attention focused on the small community of Dayton, Tennessee, where a high school biology teacher, John Scopes, was on trial for teaching the theory of evolution to his students. Scopes agreed to be prosecuted as a means to promote the trial, since the "hot" topic would certainly bring in a crowd. And it did. William Jennings Bryan, frequent presidential hopeful, volunteered to help prosecute, and famous defense lawyer Clarence Darrow leaped at the chance to help the ACLU defend Scopes. People swarmed into Dayton for the trial and some made money selling lemonade and providing entertainment for the crowd. Soon the proceedings were moved outside to accommodate more than 5,000 people. They watched a war of wits between the two legendary attorneys, especially when Darrow cross-examined Bryan and had him admit that the Bible should not be taken literally. Ultimately Scopes was convicted, but on appeal, the ruling was overturned. No further action was recommended by the court because, "Nothing is to be gained by prolonging the life of this bizarre case."

and Mrs. Coolidge returned to their home in Northampton, but after the grandeur of the White House, the duplex seemed much too modest. For the first time, they purchased a home, or rather an estate on nine acres, named the Beeches. The Coolidges continued their simple lifestyle, although they were well off financially, thanks to savings over the years and careful investing. He wrote some, including publishing his autobiography and a daily syndicated column called "Thinking Things Over with Calvin Coolidge," where topics ranged from the stock market crash and Depression to the alarming arms buildup in Europe. After a year, he tired of the column and quit but still longed for something worthwhile to fill his time. Coolidge consented to head the Harding Memorial Association, but refused to travel to Marion, Ohio, for the initial dedication of his predecessor's monument. But four years later, sufficient time had elapsed for Coolidge to agree to accompany President Herbert Hoover for the formal dedication ceremony of Harding's monument. Coolidge also agreed to serve on the National Transportation Committee, which examined the need for increased regulation and policy for the growing needs of transportation.

In 1932, Coolidge refused to play an active role in the Republican campaign, arguing if he helped one candidate, everyone else would want his help. Some party members wanted him to run as vice president, a rumor he quickly squashed. After denying requests to talk at the convention, he reluctantly agreed to speak before an audience at Madison Square Garden in New York City, but a raspy throat and his overall weakened condition meant the end of any public speaking. Spending time at the Vermont family farm failed to heal him—various respiratory ailments continued to plague him into the first days of 1933. Those who visited him in his final days said he told them, "I feel worn out."[25] On January 5, Grace went to tell him lunch was ready, but he was lying on the floor of his dressing room, dead from a heart attack.

Calvin Coolidge was buried at the family plot at Plymouth Notch, Vermont, and his funeral attendees included President and Mrs. Hoover, Mrs. Eleanor Roosevelt, and Chief Justice Charles Evans Hughes, among other dignitaries.

Grace Coolidge resumed her earlier work helping the deaf of the Clarke School, and during World War II, she assisted the Red Cross and other domestic efforts. Mrs. Coolidge also became well known as a baseball fan and attended Red Sox games as long as she was able and would listen to them on the radio. She died at the age of seventy-eight in the midst of baseball season on July 8, 1957, and was buried beside her husband.

ENDNOTES

1 Calvin Coolidge, *The Autobiography of Calvin Coolidge*, New York: Cosmopolitan Book Corporation, 1929, p. 12.

2 Claude M. Fuess, *Calvin Coolidge, The Man from Vermont*, Boston: Little, Brown and Co., 1940, p. 52.

3 Coolidge, p. 49.

4 Donald R. McCoy, *Calvin Coolidge, the Quiet President*, Lawrence, KS: University Press of Kansas, 1988, p. 58.

5 Fuess, p. 122.

6 McCoy, p. 66.

7 Robert M. Washburn, *Calvin Coolidge, His First Biography*, Boston: Small, Maynard and Company, 1923, p. 141.

8 McCoy, p. 94.

9 Ibid, p. 120.

10 Ibid, p. 121.

11 Louis C. Hatch and Earl L. Shoup, *A History of the Vice-Presidency of the United States*, New York: American Historical Society, 1934, p. 378.

12 McCoy, p. 158.

13 Robert H. Farrell, *The Presidency of Calvin Coolidge*, Lawrence, KS: University Press of Kansas, 1998, p. 50.

14 McCoy, p. 202.

15 Ibid, p. 233.

16 Donald Young, *American Roulette, The History and Dilemma of the Vice Presidency*, New York: Holt, Rinehart and Winston, 1965, p. 155.

17 Coolidge, p. 190.

18 McCoy, p. 252.

19 Ibid, p. 255.

20 William A. DeGregorio, *The Complete Book of US Presidents*, New York: Gramercy Books, 2005, p. 458.

21 Farrell, p. 129.

22 McCoy, p. 374.

23 DeGregorio, p. 459.

24 McCoy, p. 388.

25 Ibid, p. 412.

Herbert Hoover

★ ★ ★ THIRTY-FIRST PRESIDENT ★ ★ ★

LIFE SPAN

- Born: August 10, 1874, in West Branch, Iowa
- Died: October 20, 1964, in New York City

NICKNAME

- Bert, The Chief

RELIGION

- Quaker (Society of Friends)

HIGHER EDUCATION

- Stanford University, 1895

PROFESSION

- Engineer

MILITARY SERVICE

- None

FAMILY

- Father: **Jesse Clark Hoover** (1846–1880)
- Mother: **Huldah Randall Minthorn Hoover** (1848–1883)
- Wife: **Lou Henry Hoover** (1874–1944); wed on February 10, 1899, in Monterey, California
- Children: **Herbert Charles** (1903–1969); **Allan Henry** (1907–1993)

POLITICAL LIFE

- Relief efforts during World War I: Belgium Relief (1914–1919); US Food administrator (1917–1918); War Trade Council (1917–1920); Sugar Equalization Board (1918–1920); European Coal Council (1919); American Relief Administration (1919–1920); economic director of Supreme Economic Council (1918–1920); economic advisor to President **Woodrow Wilson** at Versailles Peace Conference
- Secretary of commerce (1921–1928)

PRESIDENCY

- One term: March 4, 1929–March 4, 1933
- Republican
- Reason for leaving office: defeated by **Franklin D. Roosevelt** in 1932 election
- Vice president: **Charles Curtis** (1929–1933)

ELECTION OF 1928

- Electoral vote: **Hoover** 444; **Alfred E. Smith** 87
- Popular vote: **Hoover** 21,427,123; **Smith** 15,015,464

CABINET

SECRETARY OF STATE
Henry L. Stimson (1929–1933)

SECRETARY OF THE TREASURY
Andrew W. Mellon (1929–1932)

Ogden L. Mills (1932–1933)

SECRETARY OF WAR
James W. Good (Mar.–Nov. 1929)

Patrick J. Hurley (1929–1933)

ATTORNEY GENERAL
William D. Mitchell (1929–1933)

SECRETARY OF THE NAVY
Charles Francis Adams (1929–1933)

POSTMASTER GENERAL
Walter F. Brown (1929–1933)

SECRETARY OF THE INTERIOR
Ray L. Wilbur (1929–1933)

SECRETARY OF AGRICULTURE
Arthur M. Hyde (1929–1933)

SECRETARY OF COMMERCE
Robert P. Lamont (1929–1932)

Roy D. Chapin (1932–1933)

SECRETARY OF LABOR
James J. Davis (1929–1930)

William N. Doak (1930–1933)

Ironically, the president whose name became synonymous with the stock market crash of 1929 and the Great Depression is the same one who worked tirelessly both before and after his presidency around the world to improve conditions for those less fortunate. His life was an American dream come true—the boy of modest means who works his way through school and then, with a driving determination to succeed, becomes a self-made millionaire.

EARLY LIFE

Herbert Clark Hoover arrived around midnight of August 10, 1874, in his parent's home in West Branch, Iowa. There his father Jesse worked as a blacksmith and sold farm equipment while his mother Huldah reared the children. Herbert was the second of three children, and he nearly died from croup at the age of two. His parents believed him dead; however, a physician uncle managed to revive the toddler.

Herbert was an active youngster with an inquisitive mind that occasionally got him into trouble. One time he wondered what would happen if a hot iron was added to a cauldron of boiling tar. His answer came quickly, along with the town's fire brigade in response to the billowing clouds of smoke. When Hoover later wrote his autobiography, he did not describe many of his childhood experiences as pleasant ones, with the exception of sledding and making popcorn balls in the wintertime. He attended services at the Quaker meetinghouse, which he found rather tedious and admitted, "I was a Quaker but I didn't work very hard at it."[1]

When Herbert was six years old, his father died from an apparent heart attack, leaving his widow to rear their three children. Huldah took in sewing for a meager income and retreated to her Quaker faith to heal her aching soul. Over the years, Herbert was sent to other relatives to live while his mother traveled and preached. But then, three years after losing their father, the Hoover children became orphaned when Huldah died of pneumonia. The three children were parceled out to family members; Herbert was first sent to an uncle near West Branch. But the following year, Herbert moved west to live with the man who had saved his life years before. Now Dr. John Minthorn lived in Oregon and wanted Herbert to live with his family, so a ticket was purchased, and the nine-year-old embarked on a weeklong railroad journey across the country with only two dimes in his pocket and a basket of food.

Starting at five, Herbert had begun his formal schooling at the West Branch Free School, where he liked recess the best. He was an average student there, as well as in Newberg, Oregon, where he attended the Friends Pacific Academy, finding math his favorite part of the day. His next stop was a business school, but he could only go at night because during the day he was working for his uncle. Minthorn owned a land office in Salem, and Herbert worked as an office boy. He kept the books, ran errands, and learned to type. One day a visiting engineer took him around the Cascades looking for mining possibilities. This adventure sparked an interest in Hoover, and after mulling it over for a year, he made his decision. He would apply for admission to the new Stanford University in Palo Alto, California, which had an engineering program. His lack of a formal education, however, stood in his way, and he failed the entrance exam; his examiner wrote he was "none too well prepared . . . but showing remarkable keenness."[2] Promising to study with a tutor, Hoover was granted acceptance on the condition

NATIONAL EVENTS

Lynchings continue in the South: a black man in Mississippi is burned alive by a mob of 2,000, but coroner's jury says cause of death unclear

FEB 14: Valentine's Day Massacre—seven rival gangsters of Al Capone gunned down

MAR: Buck Rogers becomes first science fiction comic strip

MAR 4: Herbert Hoover's presidential inauguration

OCT 24: "Black Thursday," beginning of the stock market crash

NOV 29: Admiral Richard Byrd is first person to fly over the South Pole

1929

WORLD EVENTS

Japan holds last parliamentary election for 16 years

JAN 18: Leon Trotsky expelled from the Soviet Union

JAN 26: Indian National Congress proclaims goal of independence

FEB 11: Lateran Pacts: Vatican City created as a sovereign state

MAR 4: Beginning of a new Mexican political party: the Institutional Revolutionary Party led by Plutarco Elías Calles

he pass the entrance examination the next time, and in 1891, the seventeen-year-old became a member of Stanford's first freshmen class.

EARLY OPPORTUNITIES

His mediocre grades continued into his collegiate career, but he passed everything except German. Since he was a geology major, he worked during the summers to earn money and experience. The US Geological Survey became his summer employer. The first summer found him mapping the Arkansas Ozarks, then the next two summers he worked in California and Nevada. During his time at Stanford, he managed to squeeze in some extracurricular activities, including managing the freshman baseball and football teams and being treasurer for the junior class. He earned extra money clerking in the registration office and started a student laundry service and a newspaper route.

In 1892, Dr. John Branner came to Stanford to head the geology department, and he needed a part-time secretary. Since he could type, Hoover got the job and thirty dollars a month. The close relationship between Branner and Hoover created jealousy among other students, but Branner told them Hoover's advantage was his character: "I can tell Hoover to do a thing and never think of it again."[3]

As a young man of modest means, Herbert did not join a fraternity, which made him a "barbarian." The two groups vied for power on the campus, and under Hoover's leadership, the barbarians won most of the elected class offices; moreover, he wrote a student constitution. As treasurer, Hoover collected fees at the gate for athletic events. He made sure no one was allowed in without paying; in fact, he pursued former president Benjamin Harrison, "my first public contact with a great man,"[4] for his fee and later did the same to multimillionaire Andrew Carnegie.

His last summer found him unemployed, so he and some friends decided to create a business making billboards for San Francisco businesses in the Yosemite Valley. As soon as they arrived, Hoover received a telegram telling him to report to the survey team. Not having money for a stage, he walked eighty miles to catch the train, but he made his connection and worked in the Sierra Nevada Mountains. Once the maps were published, Hoover's name was beside that of geologist Dr. Waldemar Lindgren. The experiences and friendships he gained from these surveying expeditions were treasured by Hoover.

In May 1895, Herbert C. Hoover received his Bachelor of Arts in Geology, and he later wrote that he sat listening to the commencement speech while pondering that he had "only forty dollars in cash and the need for finding an immediate job."[5] Additionally, he needed work because he had recently met a coed freshman, Lou Henry, who was also majoring in geology. After attending one of Dr. Branner's lectures, she decided on geology and Herbert was her assistant. They soon fell in love, but agreed that he would work while she finished her college education.

Meanwhile another freshman, Will Irwin, later recorded his initial impression of senior Herbert Hoover:

> *"Hoover, while he walked humanly among us, was a kind of legend too . . . The crown of that personality was shyness. Even men who opposed him in that 'great frat-barb war,' coming afterward into association with him, began to lean on his sane and unruffled judgment. The whimsies of life have permitted*

DID YOU KNOW?

Hoover's Secretary of the Navy Charles Francis Adams was the great-grandson of John Quincy Adams and great-great-grandson of John Adams.

Hoover was an eighth cousin once removed of Richard Nixon.

DEC 3: President Hoover tells Congress that the worst of the Depression is over

DEC 31: Guy Lombardo and his band play *Auld Lang Syne* for the first time

Grant Wood paints *American Gothic*

Air conditioning installed in the White House

Dick and Jane readers are first published and used in schools

Teenage detective Nancy Drew debuts in her first mystery novel

1930

OCT 3: Official creation of Yugoslavia from kingdoms of the Serbs, Croats, and Slovenes

MAR 12–APR 5: Salt March: Mohandas Gandhi leads a 200-mile march to the sea protesting the British monopoly on salt

MAR 28: Constantinople renamed Istanbul

APR 14: Spain's King Alfonso XIII leaves Spain, and the nation becomes a republic

SUPREME COURT APPOINTMENTS
★★★★★★★★★★

Charles Evans Hughes, 1930

Owen J. Roberts, 1930

Benjamin N. Cardozo, 1932

some of us to follow him since in affairs and struggles whose actors were kings, principalities and powers, dynasties and armies, violences of which the nineteenth century never dreamed."[6]

With diploma in hand, Hoover headed to the same area he had recently passed two summers—the Sierras. There he attempted to find work in the mining camps, but they considered a college graduate overqualified. Finally he was hired at the Mayflower Mine, where he was told "Get in there and dig. You need a nose for gold. It can't be learned by sticking your nose in a book. You'll develop it by working where the gold is."[7] After doing this for a time, Hoover wanted more and decided to look for opportunity in San Francisco, where the reputed richest mining expert was to be found. He met Louis Janin and discussed employment over lunch. Since the only job in Janin's engineering office was that of copyist, Janin figured Hoover would not be interested. Hoover responded by explaining that he knew how to type and could begin immediately. And so he did.

Although typing skills got him the job, it was Hoover's mining expertise that soon pulled him outdoors. He worked in California, Colorado, and New Mexico. The last assignment was as a mine manager, which meant working with a tough group of men who he described as having "practiced a good deal of original sin, especially after paydays,"[8] wearing his pair of six-guns on his belt, and carrying a rifle in his saddle. This territory had been under Indian control until only recently, when Geronimo was forced off the land.

After about a year tramping about the mines of the Great American West, Hoover was summoned to work in Janin's main office and assisted legal counsel in preparing for a major mining case, which was won primarily thanks to Hoover's expertise. Then in 1897, Janin received a cable from London's premier mining consulting firm of Berwick, Moreing and Co., asking for his recommendation of someone with knowledge of American mining methods who could be sent to the mining fields of Australia. Janin asked Hoover if he wanted the job, and although he would miss Lou Henry, he desperately yearned for the adventure and experience (not to mention the six hundred dollars a month), so he eagerly agreed. His journey took him first to West Branch, then New York, London, and finally Australia.

MINING OVERSEAS

In the Australian Outback—a land of deserts and camels—Hoover endured harsh conditions, including temperatures over 100 degrees. He inspected mining operations and upgraded them, brought in equipment and experts, and discovered a gold mine that netted his company over sixty million dollars. But after two years, he was ready to return home; however, his home office had other ideas—they wanted him to move to China. He agreed, but first stopped in California to marry Lou Henry on February 10, 1899. Their honeymoon was a month-long voyage to China.

Once in Peking, Lou immersed herself in the language, culture, and art of the land, while her husband journeyed into the countryside overseeing coal mines. The Minister of Mines, Chang Yenmao, desperately wanted to find gold to impress his empress, so he sent Hoover to various sites looking for the elusive ore. The American engineer preferred going with only a couple of assistants, but Minister Chang adamantly refused, insisting they must have an entourage to symbolize the impor-

NATIONAL EVENTS

JAN 20: First broadcast of radio program *The Lone Ranger*

FEB 18: Pluto discovered by Clyde Tombaugh from photographs

JUN 17: President Hoover signs Hawley-Smoot Tariff into law

DEC 2: President Hoover asks Congress for $150 million in aid to employ Americans

Pearl Buck publishes *The Good Earth*

Hawaiian "aloha" shirts become popular

1931

WORLD EVENTS

APR 22: London Naval Treaty signed by US, Britain, and Japan limits shipbuilding

JUL 30: First World Cup soccer championship game played—Uruguay defeats Argentina 4–2

AUG–OCT: Coups overthrow governments of Peru, Argentina, and Brazil

FEB 10: New Delhi becomes new capital of India

tance of their station, as well as their mission. They traveled to Manchuria, the Gobi Desert, Shantung, the Grand Canal, and the Great Wall. Often Lou accompanied the expeditions. Hoover met with the Dalai Lama, but still he had no great discoveries of gold. He did, however, succeed in convincing the Chinese to test the lands west of Peking for coal, where it was discovered in greater quantity than all other deposits in the world combined.

In May 1900, the Hoovers were living in Tientsin when they heard the horrifying tales of foreigners being murdered by Chinese known as the "boxers." Hoover ordered his men to come in from the field, and the foreigners living within the city hoped they would be safe with their contingent of over one thousand sailors and marines on board warships. An Imperial Army force of twenty-five thousand with foreign officers was stationed nearby, but on June 13, the soldiers slayed some of their officers while others fled to the foreign compound of Tientsin. There the civilians looked to who they considered the leading man—twenty-six-year-old Herbert Hoover. Fortunately, a Russian colonel was there to take charge militarily while Hoover worked out the logistics of keeping the people in the compound supplied with food. They managed to maintain their position for more than a month while being bombarded night and day. Hoover wrote, "I do not remember a more satisfying musical performance than the bugles of the American Marines entering the settlement playing 'There'll Be a Hot Time in the Old Town Tonight.'"[9]

Although the Boxer Rebellion collapsed in July, it was the ensuing grab for wealth by the foreign nations that created Hoover's next task in China. After being promoted to general manager with a higher salary, including stocks, he redoubled his efforts to demand the return of property or reparations by the foreign governments who had seized it. He succeeded in this endeavor, which earned him yet another promotion—junior partner. The Hoovers traveled first to America and then continued to London, where they welcomed their first child, a son whom they named Herbert Hoover Jr., and four years later, another son, Allan, was born.

As a consultant, Hoover constantly moved from place to place across five continents. He excelled in finding other superb engineers and talented individuals to work for him; he was also helped by what some called his "card index memory," which kept details of a variety of mining operations straight in his mind. He continued

THE BOXER REBELLION (1899–1901) ★ Discontented Chinese peasants in Shandong province who were starving because of a drought started this uprising. Some joined a group known as Fists of Righteous Harmony, but were often called Boxers because of their use of martial arts. Boxers blamed their problems on the empress and foreigners. The empress convinced them to turn their anger on the "foreign devils," and they began attacking and slaughtering Christian missionaries in the countryside, moving ever closer to Beijing. The empress assured the foreigners in their compound near the Forbidden City that she would allow no harm to come to them, but as the Boxers approached, she did nothing to stop them. For almost two months, the group of foreigners had to defend themselves against thousands of Boxers. Then a contingent of American marines and sailors arrived, followed by military forces of other countries who drove away the Boxers and freed the foreigners from the barricades.

MAR 3: "The Star-Spangled Banner" becomes US national anthem

MAR 17: Gambling legalized in Nevada

MAY 1: Official opening of the Empire State Building

AUG 21: 600th home run hit by Babe Ruth

OCT 4: "Dick Tracy" comic strip first appears

OCT 17: Al Capone receives eleven-year prison sentence for tax evasion

First use of pacemaker

1932

JUL: Huang He (Yellow River) Flood becomes world's deadliest disaster—over 850,000 estimated dead, maybe 4 million

JUL 16: Emperor Haile Selassie of Ethiopia signs its first constitution into law

AUG: Yangtze River floods, causing homelessness and famine for hundreds of thousands

NOV 7: Mao Tse Tung proclaims the Chinese Soviet Republic

Swiss balloonist Auguste Piccard is the first person to enter the stratosphere

STATE OF THE UNION

US POPULATION IN 1929
122,775,046

NATIONAL DEBT IN 1933
$22,538,672,560

PRESIDENT'S SALARY
$75,000/year

NUMBER OF STATES IN 1933
48

to read on his travels; additionally, he and his wife translated a Latin text on metallurgy as a hobby. Hoover's income increased not only after making partner but also by locating more profitable mines in Australia and Burma. But not all of his mining adventures panned out. Moreover, he lost a sizeable amount of money paying back the monies embezzled by another partner in the firm. Nevertheless, by 1908, Hoover decided it was time to develop his own engineering firm.

Hoover's consulting firm had offices in the United States and Europe. Although he still traveled extensively, he managed to have more time at home in Palo Alto, where he could stay active as a Stanford alum and as a member of their board of trustees. He also wrote a textbook and frequently lectured in his field. With all the success that "the doctor of sick mines" found, including becoming a millionaire, Hoover started tiring of "playing the game for the game's sake."[10] He was forty years old and ready for a change of direction. He simply did not know what that might be, but his answer came in June 1914, when shots were fired in Sarajevo that would soon result in the first world war.

WAR RELIEF

Earlier in 1914, Hoover had traveled to London to hopefully build interest in the upcoming Panama-Pacific International Exposition to be held in San Francisco. The American consulate knew he was in town and frantically called him on August 3. Thousands of Americans were attempting to flee the continent and impending war. They flooded embassies and consulates everywhere. Could Hoover help? He agreed and later recorded, "I did not realize at that moment, but on this Monday my engineering career was over. I was on the slippery road of public life."[11]

Deciding that the main problem was lack of cash, Hoover and some friends pooled their monies and gave out loans to grateful Americans. When the embassy heard of his actions, the ambassador decided to relinquish his refugee responsibilities to Hoover. Accustomed to moving staffs and commandeering supplies, the former engineer soon had a smooth operation that oversaw the needs of thousands of distraught Americans. He supplied food, clothing, medicine, money, shelter, and passage to the United States. On his honor, banks in London agreed to cash checks; although over $1.5 million was spent, he lost only three hundred dollars, for all the rest was paid back. Hoover had to perform a multitude of tasks, including writing a note guaranteeing that the ship an elderly lady was to travel on would not be sunk by a U-boat. Once the Hoover committee had completed this momentous task, his family began packing for their own return home.

In September, a group of Belgians and Americans asked Hoover for help. Here he was at a crossroads; he could easily continue his mining career and become one of the richest men in the United States or dedicate his services to others. He announced his decision to friend and *Saturday Evening Post* reporter Will Irwin, "Let the fortune go to Hell."[12] For the remainder of the war, Hoover supervised the Commission for the Relief of Belgium, which fed fifteen million people in the most massive humanitarian relief program the world had ever witnessed. He insisted that food was not a bargaining chip to be used against anyone; nor could anyone be deprived of it based on race or religion. He described the constant struggle to complete the Herculean task in a letter to a priest:

> *"To beg, borrow, and buy nearly $1,800,000 worth of food every week; to ship it overseas*

DID YOU KNOW?

Hoover donated his presidential salary to charity.

NATIONAL EVENTS

World's first drive-in movie theater opens in Camden, New Jersey

MAR 1: Charles Lindbergh Jr. is kidnapped from New Jersey home; body found two months later

MAY: Veterans calling themselves the Bonus Army begin amassing in Washington, D.C.

JUN 28: President Hoover orders the Army to disband the Bonus Army in Washington

NOV 7: Supreme Court strikes down convictions of "Scottsboro Nine" due to lack of legal representation

WORLD EVENTS

JAN 22: First Communist revolt in Western Hemisphere—El Salvador's president puts down rebellion

JAN 28: Shanghai occupied by Japan

FEB 2: Disarmament conference begins in Geneva

FEB 11: Pope Pius XI and Benito Mussolini meet in Vatican City

FEB 27: Austrian Adolf Hitler gains German citizenship

MAR 9: Manchuria declares its independence, but its government is actually run by Japan

MAR 19: Sydney Harbour Bridge opens

from America, Australia, the Argentine, and India; to traverse three belligerent lines; to transport it through a country with a wholly demoralized transportation service; to distribute it equitably to over 7,000,000 people; to see that it is adapted to every condition from babyhood to old age."[13]

The task changed somewhat with the entrance of the United States into the war in 1917. At that time, President Woodrow Wilson summoned Hoover home and asked him to head the American Food Administration allocating food to the troops and nations overseas, as well as the civilian population at home. Hoover agreed, but did not want to lead a bureaucracy of employees; instead, he preferred enlisting the help of volunteers. He also opposed rationing items, hoping people would do it on their own. They did economize, only they called it "Hooverize."

Once the war ended, Hoover became director of the American Relief Administration, whose duty was to distribute food, clothing, and other items to war-torn Europe, including the unpopular defeated Germany. The allies placed multiple diplomatic roadblocks to prevent Germans from receiving aid, but Hoover ultimately prevailed. Finally in 1919, he returned once more to the United States. He reopened his office in San Francisco, and the following year was elected president of the American Institute of Mining and Metallurgy, as well as head of the American Engineering Council. Men started discussing his name as a possible candidate for the presidency. Franklin D. Roosevelt wrote, "Herbert Hoover is certainly a wonder, and I wish we could make him President of the United States. There could not be a better one."[14]

POLITICAL CAREER BEGINS

In the wake of the country's animosity toward Democratic president Wilson and the League of Nations, Republican candidate Warren G. Harding won the election. He offered Hoover his choice to head either the interior or commerce departments in his cabinet. While being tempted by this offer, another was given him: the Guggenheim brothers owned the top mining enterprise in the world and they needed someone to take over their business. Since no one else in their family was interested, they thought of Hoover. He would receive a half million dollars annually as a minimum salary, as well as become full partner in the business. Now he had to determine whether to plunge back into his business and enrich himself further or follow the path of public service at fifteen thousand dollars a year for a cabinet position. After a week of consideration and discussion with Lou, he decided to accept the post of secretary of commerce.

Starting with President Harding, and then continuing under Calvin Coolidge, Hoover spent eight years making wide-ranging reforms affecting all Americans. His office standardized parts of American automobiles to make them interchangeable and easier to access as spare parts; he did the same for electric light bulbs, lumber, doors, windows, and many other items. He focused attention on the health of American children and presided over the American Child Health Association, while his wife headed the American Girl Scouts. He worked to improve labor conditions and housing. With the increased interest in radio, he advocated government regulation and issuance of broadcasting licenses. He called for a system of inland waterways for several areas, including the Columbia River basin, the Great Lakes and St. Lawrence Seaways, and the Colorado River basin, as a cheaper means

DID YOU KNOW?

Hoover was the first president to have been born west of the Mississippi River.

NOV 8: Democratic candidate Franklin D. Roosevelt defeats incumbent Herbert Hoover for president

NOV 24: FBI Crime Lab opens

DEC 27: Radio City Music Hall opens in New York City

APR 10: Paul von Hindenburg is elected president of Germany

APR 17: Emperor Haile Selassie of Ethiopia abolishes slavery

MAY 16: Thousands killed or injured in Bombay during riots between Hindus and Muslims

JUN 24: Siam becomes a constitutional monarchy

SEP 23: Kingdom of Saudi Arabia formed

NOV 30: German Enigma cipher code broken

DID YOU KNOW?

President and Mrs. Hoover spoke in Chinese if they wanted no one to know what they were saying.

of transporting goods. Later in Coolidge's administration, Hoover called for a dam to be built on the Colorado River in Nevada, but it would not be started until his own presidency.

In 1923, the Hoovers accompanied President and Mrs. Harding on their western trip to Alaska and California. One day the two men had the following conversation with the weary-looking Harding asking, "Hoover, if you knew of a great scandal in our Administration, would you for the good of the country and the party expose it publicly or would you bury it?"

Hoover immediately responded, "Blow it out at once. The blowing will prove the integrity of the Administration."[15] Although Harding provided a few details to his query, he did not spell out exactly what he meant. In the months following Harding's death, news of scandals would rock the nation, since they included various high-ranking officials such as Attorney General Harry Daugherty and Secretary of the Interior Albert Fall.

Hoover served Coolidge, but apparently he was not particularly appreciated by his boss. While Harding had referred to the commerce secretary as "the smartest 'geek' I know," Coolidge said, "That man has offered me unsolicited advice for six years. All of it bad."[16] Republicans, however, were ready for him to advise the nation on a grander scale, and with the announcement that President Coolidge would not seek reelection in 1928, the push was on to make Herbert Hoover the candidate.

At the Republican convention in Kansas City, Missouri, Hoover won the nomination on the first ballot. His acceptance speech was one of optimism, promising that America was headed in the right direction. "Given a chance to go forward with the policies of the last eight years, we shall soon with the help of God be in sight of the day when poverty will be banished from this nation."[17] No doubt he would recall those words in the years to come with no small amount of irony. Charles Curtis of Kansas, his main rival for the nomination, became his running mate. The Democrats picked Alfred Smith, past governor and Tammany Hall operative of many years; his vice presidential candidate was Arkansas senator Joseph Robinson.

While Hoover did not personally attack Smith for his Catholic faith or his opposition to Prohibition, which Hoover called "a great social and economic experiment,"[18] others took the initiative in doing so, especially in the strongly Protestant South. Smith was also hurt by his connections to Tammany Hall, while Hoover was bolstered by the country's prosperity on the heels of eight years of Republican leadership with promises he would continue the same policies with an emphasis on what he termed "rugged individualism." Americans chose not to mess with success and came out solidly in support of Hoover, giving him 58 percent of the popular vote to Smith's 41 percent; moreover, Hoover won forty out of forty-eight states in the electoral college. All indications pointed to another Republican term of economic prosperity.

RECONSTRUCTION FINANCE CORPORATION (RFC) ★ Hoover's primary response to the Depression was the creation of the RFC to loan money to business, industries, and agricultural interests. Most of the $2 billion loaned was repaid. President Franklin D. Roosevelt kept the RFC and expanded its scope and its funding. It then primarily helped banks and railroads to stay solvent. It also provided loans to states as needed to run their own relief projects. The RFC continued to operate throughout World War II.

PRESIDENT HOOVER

Hoover's public speaking abilities were poor, for he seldom looked at his audience, staring at his text instead and scarcely modulating his voice out of its monotone. So it was on March 4, 1929, his inauguration day, when he pronounced "I have no fears for the future of our country. It is bright with hope." Within eight months, hopes would be crushed, replaced by a nation fearful of its future.

During his first months in office, Hoover busily began instituting changes and reforms, including directing the FBI to focus on cleaning up Chicago and ending Al Capone's control of the city; as a precaution against history repeating itself, he canceled private leases on government oil lands; and he signed the Agricultural Marketing Act, which included a provision to create the Federal Farm Board, which was to help prevent farm surpluses and encourage cooperatives. Hoover also voiced support for a new cabinet position of Education and the reduction of income taxes; he worked to reform and improve prison facilities; he wanted to see Native Americans given better educational opportunities; and began working toward creating pensions for older Americans. His main concern was the raising of the tariff. After Congress made its changes, the Hawley-Smoot tariff (a protectionist tariff raising rates an average of 40 percent) doubled the rates the president wanted. Consequently, Americans were hit hard by higher prices on raw materials, and this came nearly a year after the stock market crash. Its protectionist objective was sidetracked by igniting a tariff war among America's trading partners.

In the autumn of 1929, the president advised Wall Street to stop allowing widespread stock purchasing on the margin (paying only a fraction of the purchase price). They refused, and the bull market continued until Black Thursday, October 24, 1929, when the stock prices drastically fell, but were soon propped up by investment bankers. Conditions improved Friday, but on Monday and Tuesday, stocks crashed. Ramifications from this event would not be immediately understood.

Within a month, Hoover hosted a meeting of labor, business owners, and agricultural leaders to discuss current conditions and plot future strategy. The president defined the economic crisis as a depression and stated his belief that it would last for a while and boost unemployment. Both he and the business leaders agreed to work against this with increased building contracts. The economy improved, albeit modestly, so Hoover felt confident when he announced in March 1930, that the depression would be over by summer. Sadly his prediction fell far short of reality—unemployment rose steadily, banks closed, and people found themselves broke and homeless. Farmers experienced worse when summer droughts repeatedly hit the Great Plains in the early 1930s, leading to the dust storms that then created the Dust Bowl of the mid-1930s. By that time, over four million Americans found themselves unemployed. By 1933, numbers increased until one out of every four Americans was out of work.

World War I veterans were among the unemployed, and fifteen thousand decided to visit Washington to demand immediate payment of their bonuses rather than wait for their 1945 due date. The men and their families settled in Anacostia across the Potomac River from the capitol. Conditions were deplorable for the inhabitants, who lived in cardboard boxes and tents, but overall, few problems developed. Although they voted against the bonus bill, the Senate did appropriate one hundred thousand dollars to help defray expenses for the marchers returning home. Many then packed and left the city. Some remained, and violence became more widespread. Hoover grew tired of the demonstrations near the White House and ordered the Washington, D.C., police to move them. Shots were fired and two marchers were killed. President Hoover then verbally ordered Secretary of War Patrick Hurley to take care of the situation, but "to use all humanity consistent with the execution of the law." Hurley then turned to Chief of Staff General Douglas MacArthur and his two aides—Colonel Dwight D. Eisenhower and Major George S. Patton. Tanks and troops rolled in; tear gas was fired into the crowd, some marchers were bayoneted, then the camp was burned. These militaristic actions were taken by MacArthur on his own initiative, but the president paid the price. Since the incident occurred just three months prior to the 1932 election, the Democratic candidate, Franklin D. Roosevelt, took great glee in watching Hoover become the scapegoat and exclaimed, "This elects me."[19]

Blamed for the Depression, Hoover was no stranger to being a scapegoat. While he steadfastly maintained that the federal government should not become too involved in bailing out the economy, he did create the Reconstruction Finance Corporation to provide a source of money for loans to financial institutions and governments.

DID YOU KNOW?

Hoover had never run for elected office until he ran for the presidency in 1928 and 1932.

DID YOU KNOW?

Humorist Will Rogers joked that if someone bit into a wormy apple, president Hoover would get the blame. Hoover's name was used to describe new sights of the Depression: "Hoover flags" were empty pants pockets turned inside out, "Hoover blankets" were newspapers used by the homeless; and "Hoover Pullmans" were boxcars used by hobos catching rides across the country.

Since this did little to help the man on the street, his efforts were ridiculed, and the shantytowns that sprang up in ever-increasing numbers became known as "Hoovervilles."

The Depression and the government's response were on everyone's mind when they cast their votes in 1932. Hoover ran for reelection against charismatic Franklin D. Roosevelt, who promised to help the beleaguered citizenry with government aid and simultaneously balance the budget. While the logic of it eluded some, it was music to the ears of many. Hoover gave few political speeches during the campaign and was not surprised by its outcome. He won 40 percent of the popular vote and six states in the electoral college to Roosevelt's 57 percent and forty-two states.

For the remaining four months of his presidency, Hoover attempted to keep the economy from worsening; earlier in 1932 it actually had improved, only to decline with the election. Now the incumbent tried to convince the president-elect to announce some of his planned policies to help allay fears; this FDR refused to do. In the days and weeks preceding the end of his term, Hoover presided over a country whose banks grew increasingly more insolvent and were failing at alarming rates. Again he begged his successor to calm the people, but his pleas were answered by silence. On March 4, 1933, the economic calamities besetting the nation were no longer Hoover's headache; he could now return home to California and relax—but not for long.

RETIREMENT

Although he and Lou first retired to their Palo Alto home, they moved to the Waldorf-Astoria Hotel in New York City to be closer to friends and events. By the mid-1930s, Hoover was regularly criticizing his successor's New Deal policies. Roosevelt's staff, on the other hand, was just as busy working to create the myth that the depression was all Herbert Hoover's fault; moreover, he had done nothing to help. Adding insult to injury, the name of the newly constructed Hoover Dam was changed to Boulder Dam, and the former president was not allowed to attend its dedication. (It was renamed Hoover Dam by Congress and President Truman in 1947.)

Desiring to help in a positive way, Hoover gladly accepted the chairmanship of Boys Clubs of America in 1936; he served in that capacity for the next twenty-eight years. The organization flourished under his leadership, expanding its numbers and membership by over 300 percent.

In 1938, the Hoovers traveled to Europe, visiting fourteen nations including France, Poland, and Germany. There he met with Adolf Hitler for an hour. Hoover recorded that Hitler was not the "dummy" he expected, but also noted how he could immediately be set off "in furious anger."[20] The former president voiced optimism that the continent could avert war with appeasement. In less than two years, many of the same nations that Hoover had just visited would beg for his help once more in gathering humanitarian aid as they fell victims to another world war. While opposed to direct American involvement, he did advocate assisting those in need, but the Roosevelt administration was not interested, even after Hoover launched a campaign to win public support. After the Japanese attack on Pearl Harbor, he became a staunch ally of the war effort. He also continued his humanitarian efforts to help those in need overseas.

On January 7, 1944, Lou Hoover died of heart failure. While grieving over his tremendous loss, Hoover continued his work, as well as his writings for magazines and authoring books including *The Problems of Lasting Peace* and *The Basis of Lasting Peace* (both with Hugh Gibson).

The following year the nation experienced the death of Roosevelt, and with Truman came the end of Hoover's exile. Over the years, the former president's expertise had been sought by members of Congress and military staff who in turn kept Hoover briefed on classified information. Secretary of War Henry Stimson wanted to see his former boss (Stimson had been secretary of state for Hoover) meet with his current one, but Hoover insisted he could not stop by the White House unless he had an invitation. After meeting with Stimson in May, Hoover composed a memorandum discussing the end of the war against Japan. In it, he gave "500,000 to 1,000,000 lives" as his casualty estimate, which doubled the Army's projection. The paper was circulated as being written by "an economist."[20] After discussion with Stimson, President Harry Truman decided it was time for Hoover to visit. Not trusting the Roosevelt staff holdovers, Truman wrote out the invitation, slapped a stamp on it, and personally carried it to the mailbox. They met on May 28, 1945, and at Truman's request, Hoover prepared memoranda addressing the topics they discussed: two discussed food organizations, one proposed a War Economic Council, and the fourth was titled "The Japanese Situation," which addressed ending the war in the Pacific and was the basis for Truman's discussion with senior advisors.

After the war, President Truman appointed Hoover to head the Famine Emergency Commission to try to prevent that crisis from occurring in regions ravaged by years of war. Following this task, Truman next put the former president in charge of a task group to revamp the executive branch of the federal government and improve its efficiency following the growth of New Deal agencies. The Hoover Commission met again at the request of President Dwight D. Eisenhower to make recommendations about the powers and scope of the federal government in general.

TWENTIETH AMENDMENT (ratified in 1933) ★ Also known as the Lame Duck amendment, the Twentieth Amendment moved up presidential inaugurations from March 4 to January 20 and also moved the opening session of Congress to meet January 3.

For his remaining years, Hoover continued to give speeches and write; in fact, his volume *The Ordeal of Woodrow Wilson* was acclaimed by many who were impressed by a former president writing about another president—from the opposite political party. He also authored three volumes of his memoirs. Then on his eighty-eighth birthday he proudly opened the Herbert Hoover Presidential Library in West Branch, Iowa.

Slowly his health deteriorated requiring removal of his gallbladder, and then intestinal cancer was discovered. Severe intestinal bleeding put Hoover into a coma for two days, and then he died on October 17, 1964. His funeral was a simple Quaker service. After his body lay in state at the capitol, he was buried at West Branch next to his wife.

DID YOU KNOW?

"Star-Spangled Banner" became America's national anthem during Hoover's presidency.

ENDNOTES

1 Richard Norton Smith, *An Uncommon Man: The Triumph of Herbert Hoover*, New York: Simon & Schuster, 1984, p. 65.

2 Ibid, p. 68.

3 Eugene Lyons, *Herbert Hoover: A Biography*, Garden City, NY: Doubleday & Company, Inc., 1964, p. 26.

4 *Memoirs of Herbert Hoover*, New York: Macmillan, 1951-1952, vol. I, p. 21.

5 Eugene Lyons, *Herbert Hoover: A Biography*, Garden City, NY: Doubleday & Company, Inc., 1964, p. 34.

6 Ibid, pp. 31-32.

7 Ibid, p. 37.

8 Smith, p. 73.

9 Ibid, p. 75.

10 Ibid, p. 77.

11 Lyons, p. 75.

12 Smith, p. 81.

13 George H. Nash, *The Life of Herbert Hoover, The Humanitarian, 1914-1917*, New York: W.W. Norton & Company, 1988, p. 93.

14 Lyons, p. 143.

15 Ibid, p. 169.

16 Smith, p. 44.

17 Ibid, p. 105.

18 David Burner, *Herbert Hoover: A Public Life*, New York: Knopf, 1979, p. 218.

19 Smith, p. 140.

20 Lyons, p. 357.

21 D.M. Giangreco, "A Score of Bloody Okinawas and Iwo Jimas: President Truman and Casualty Estimates for the Invasion of Japan," in *Hiroshima in History*, Robert J. Maddox, ed., Columbia: University of Missouri Press, 2007, pp. 92-95.

Franklin D. Roosevelt

★ ★ ★ THIRTY-SECOND PRESIDENT ★ ★ ★

LIFE SPAN

- Born: January 30, 1882, in Hyde Park, New York
- Died: April 12, 1945, at Warm Springs, Georgia

RELIGION

- Episcopalian

HIGHER EDUCATION

- Harvard, 1903
- Columbia Law School, 1905–1907, did not graduate (dropped out in 1907 after passing NY bar exam)

PROFESSION

- Lawyer, senator, governor

MILITARY SERVICE

- None

FAMILY

- Father: **James Roosevelt** (1828–1900)
- Mother: **Sara Delano Roosevelt** (1854–1941)
- Wife: **(Anna) Eleanor Roosevelt** (1884–1962)
- Children: **Anna Eleanor** (1906–1975); **James "Jimmy"** (1907–1991); **Franklin Delano Jr.** (1909; died at eight months); **Elliott** (1910–1990); **Franklin D. Jr.** (1914–1988); **John Aspinwall** (1916–1981)

POLITICAL LIFE

- New York state senator (1911–1913)
- Assistant secretary of the Navy (1913–1920)
- Governor of New York (1923–1933)

PRESIDENCY

- Four terms: March 4, 1933–April 12, 1945
- Democrat
- Reason for leaving office: died in office
- Vice president: **John Nance Garner** (1933–1941); **Henry A. Wallace** (1941–1945); **Harry Truman** (1945)

ELECTION OF 1932

- Electoral vote: **Roosevelt** 472; **Hoover** 59
- Popular vote: **Roosevelt** 22,821,277; **Hoover** 15,758,901

ELECTION OF 1936

- Electoral vote: **Roosevelt** 523; **Alfred Landon** 8
- Popular vote: **Roosevelt** 27,752,648; **Landon** 16,681,862

ELECTION OF 1940

- Electoral vote: **Roosevelt** 449; **Wendell Willkie** 82
- Popular vote: **Roosevelt** 27,307,819; **Willkie** 22,347,744

ELECTION OF 1944

- Electoral vote: **Roosevelt** 432; **Thomas Dewey** 99
- Popular vote: **Roosevelt** 25,612,474; **Dewey** 22,017,929

CABINET

SECRETARY OF STATE
Cordell Hull (1933–1944)
Edward R. Stettinius Jr. (1944–1945)

SECRETARY OF THE TREASURY
William H. Woodin (1933)
Henry Morgenthau Jr. (1934–1945)

SECRETARY OF WAR
George H. Dern (1933–1936)
Henry H. Woodring (1936–1940)
Henry L. Stimson (1940–1945)

ATTORNEY GENERAL
Homer S. Cummings (1933–1939)
Frank Murphy (1939–1940)
Robert H. Jackson (1940–1941)
Francis B. Biddle (1941–1945)

POSTMASTER GENERAL
James A. Farley (1933–1940)
Frank C. Walker (1940–1945)

Mourners poured out in record numbers as the train bearing Franklin D. Roosevelt's body wound its way across the nation. For many, they could recall no time when he had not sat at the helm of the nation; they feared the future without the man who gave reassurances over the radio through the Depression and World War II. To the multitudes, Franklin D. Roosevelt was America.

EARLY LIFE

Franklin Delano Roosevelt was born on January 30, 1882, in his family's comfortable home in Hyde Park, New York. His father, James, was a Harvard-trained lawyer who decided he much preferred the life of a country squire and financier to that of a busy attorney. His first wife had died in 1876. He then married his sixth cousin, Sara Delano (who was twenty-six years his junior), in 1880. Franklin was their only child, and he received his parents' *complete* devotion.

When he was five years old, Franklin was taken to the White House, where he met an acquaintance of his father's, President Grover Cleveland, who looked down at the lad and said, "My little man, I am making a strange wish for you. It is that you may never be president of the United States."[1] Cleveland was only one of a number of his parents' circle who were people of power and influence. Not all though, were welcome; in fact, Sara had to turn down an invitation to visit the "nouveau riche" Vanderbilts because her husband feared it meant they would have to invite them to their home in return.

The three Roosevelts were often traversing the Atlantic Ocean to visit Europe, and so by an early age, Franklin was well acquainted with the various cosmopolitan centers, as well as certain mineral baths, especially in Germany, that his father visited. He attended a German school, where he was punished by the teacher for making a caricature of Kaiser Wilhelm II, and militaristic lessons occupied much of the curriculum—including how close the French border was and the need for German expansion. Since they were often moving, Franklin also had a succession of governesses and tutors. His mother, though, doted on him for the rest of her life; she introduced her son to the lifelong hobby of stamp collecting. Franklin also developed an enduring interest in the sea and sailing, and his father gave him his first sailboat at the age of fourteen. That same year his life changed drastically when he was sent off to study at Groton.

EDUCATION

From 1896 to 1900, Franklin made the relatively new preparatory school in Groton, Massachusetts, his home. He was an average student, and although not a star athlete, he became a manager for the baseball team; while Franklin repeatedly failed to make the top teams in a variety of sports, he instead sang in the choir and debated. In his spare time, he helped the poor by volunteering at the Groton Missionary Society. Cousin Theodore Roosevelt, now the governor of New York, gave the commencement speech at Franklin's graduation. His future was determined; his next stop would be Harvard.

At Harvard, Roosevelt kept his average grades, but dabbled in other activities, as well: Glee Club, third crew captain of the Newell Boating Club, member of the Hasty Pudding Club, class chairman, and editor-in-chief of *The Harvard Crimson*. This last position was his favorite; in fact, he stayed at Harvard an extra year doing graduate work so he could continue working on the *Crimson*. Although he was a Democrat, he proudly campaigned for the Republican ticket in 1900, since cousin Theodore

NATIONAL EVENTS

Ruth Wakefield invents chocolate chip cookies at her Toll House Inn

JAN 23: Twentieth Amendment ratified, changing opening dates of Congress (and later inaugurations) from March to January

FEB 15: In Miami, Giuseppe Zangara attempts to assassinate president-elect Roosevelt but misses, hitting five others, including Chicago mayor Anton Cermak, who is mortally wounded

MAR 2: Premiere of movie *King Kong*

MAR 3: Dedication of Mount Rushmore

1933

WORLD EVENTS

JAN 30: Adolf Hitler appointed chancellor of Germany by President von Hindenburg

FEB 27: Germany's Reichstag building (home of German parliament) set ablaze

FEB 28: Hitler uses the fire to issue a decree ending civil rights protections of the Weimar Constitution

MAR 4: Austria's Parliament is suspended

MAR 22: First Nazi concentration camp opened at Dachau

was running as McKinley's vice presidential candidate. He graduated in 1904 with majors in political history and government.

The next step of his education was attending Columbia Law School, although his interest seemed to wane, and he failed two courses. During this time, he courted his sixth cousin, Eleanor Roosevelt, niece to Theodore. His mother, however, was far from pleased with his choice and did what she could to break up the couple, but Franklin refused to change his mind. He and Eleanor married on March 17, 1905, in New York City with President Theodore Roosevelt giving away the bride, and the couple enjoyed a three-month honeymoon trip to Europe before returning to New York for Franklin to continue his legal studies. They welcomed their first child, a daughter Anna, in 1906 and a son James the following year. In time, three more boys joined the family—Elliott, Franklin Jr., and John.

In 1907, Franklin took the New York bar exam and passed. Finding no reason to continue at Columbia, he then dropped out of law school and joined the Wall Street law firm of Carter, Ledyard, and Milburn, whose specialty was corporate law. At this time they were busily engaged in representing various major trusts against his trust-busting cousin, President Theodore Roosevelt. For the first year, Franklin received no salary but lived on Roosevelt trust funds and his mother's assistance. Another law clerk in the firm recalled Roosevelt "saying with engaging frankness that he wasn't going to practice law forever, that he intended to run for office at the first opportunity, and that he wanted to be and thought he had a real chance to be President. I remember that he described very accurately the steps which he thought could lead to this goal."[2]

STATE POLITICS

Roosevelt took his first step by running for state senator from the Hyde Park district in 1910. Since no Democrat had won the seat in a quarter of a century, he was definitely considered an underdog. He traveled back and forth across his district. For the first time, "FDR" met people who his mother would have insisted were his social inferiors, but who held his political future in their work-worn hands. Roosevelt won his election, as did another Democrat, Woodrow Wilson, who became governor of New Jersey. Wilson said, of young Roosevelt, "He'll bear watching. I think he has a political future."[3]

Franklin's future may have appeared somewhat dimmed when, immediately upon his arrival in Albany, he refused to side with the Tammany machine to back its nominee for the US Senate. The fledgling politician soon became known as a leader of the insurgent movement in New York politics. He often hosted meetings of the group in his rented home and was quoted in *The New York Times* as bragging, "There is nothing I love as much as a good fight. I never had as much fun in my life as I am having right now."[4] Eventually a compromise candidate was found, and Roosevelt became a supporter of the Seventeenth Amendment, the direct election of senators.

As a state senator, he did not pursue any specific cause or purpose, and many people found him to be irritatingly snobbish. Frances Perkins, a young woman of a proper New England family, needed Roosevelt's support on a bill limiting the workweek for women and children to fifty-four hours. When she attempted to talk to him, he waved her aside, insisting, "More important things. Can't do it now. More important things."[5] Over time, FDR would improve his rapport with people and later admitted

CABINET

★★★★★★★★★★

(continued)

SECRETARY OF THE NAVY
Claude A. Swanson (1933–1939)
Charles Edison (1940)
Frank Knox (1940–1944)
James V. Forrestal (1944–1945)

SECRETARY OF THE INTERIOR
Harold L. Ickes (1933–1945)

SECRETARY OF AGRICULTURE
Henry A. Wallace (1933–1940)
Claude R. Wickard (1940–1945)

SECRETARY OF COMMERCE
Daniel C. Roper (1933–1938)
Harry L. Hopkins (1938–1940)
Jesse H. Jones (1940–1945)
Henry A. Wallace (1945)

SECRETARY OF LABOR
Frances Perkins (1933–1945)

MAR 4: Franklin D. Roosevelt inaugurated as president

MAR 4: Frances Perkins becomes first female cabinet member when she takes office as Secretary of Labor

MAR 12: First of FDR's "Fireside Chats"

MAR 31: Civilian Conservation Corps (CCC) created

APR 7: Beer legalized prior to ending Prohibition

JUN 16: National Industrial Recovery Act (NIRA) passed

DEC 5: Twenty-first Amendment takes effect, repealing Prohibition

MAR 23: German Reichstag proclaims Hitler as dictator of Germany

MAR 27: Japan leaves League of Nations

APR 26: Nazi Gestapo created

JUN 17: Non-Nazi political parties banned in Germany

OCT 16: Germany announces it will leave League of Nations

OCT 17: Albert Einstein flees Germany to the US

DEC 26: Nissan is started in Japan

ELEANOR ROOSEVELT (1884–1962) ★ With FDR's continued political involvement despite his paralysis, his wife Eleanor took a greater role in helping him by traveling the country to visit people, learn of conditions, and report back to him. She started in the 1920s as the governor's wife and expanded her role as the nation's First Lady. Eleanor went deep into coalmines and often was found on assembly lines. During World War II, she visited troops at home and abroad. She worked to gain a greater voice for women in the political process and helped African Americans as well. Mrs. Roosevelt made her anti-segregationist feelings clear when she sat between whites and blacks at the Southern Conference for Human Welfare in Birmingham and later invited Marian Anderson to sing at the Lincoln Memorial. During World War II, the First Lady convinced the Army nursing corps to allow black nurses to serve. Following her husband's death, Mrs. Roosevelt continued her work to help the oppressed of the world, and often served on panels for the newly formed United Nations.

to Perkins, when she served as secretary of labor during his presidency, "I was an awfully mean cuss when I first went into politics."[6] In the New York senate, he grew more outspoken toward helping the poor and sponsored a series of bills to aid farmers, including providing low-interest improvement loans. Sometimes he backed Tammany Hall; other times he opposed them, but he did make a name for himself. In 1911, he trekked to New Jersey to discuss Democratic politics with Governor Wilson. By this time, FDR had also attracted the attention of a newspaperman, Louis Howe, who became his chief advisor from 1912 until Howe's death in 1936. Howe wrote a note to Roosevelt calling him the "Beloved and Revered Future President."[7]

Although sick in bed with typhoid fever, FDR won reelection in 1912, but he was hopeful that he would not remain in Albany; instead, he cast his eyes toward Washington and soon visited with Wilson, who had just won the presidential election. Following in his famous cousin's footsteps, Franklin secured an appointment as assistant secretary of the navy.

ASSISTANT SECRETARY OF THE NAVY

Roosevelt's main duties in his new office were ensuring the "Great White Fleet" created by cousin Theodore was well supplied and overseeing civilian personnel. The new assistant secretary enjoyed reminding people of his cousin's tenure in the same job and how Theodore had exercised initiative in ordering Admiral Dewey to the Philippines; unlike Theodore, however, Franklin saw his chance to win glory in Mexico fade away when President Wilson refused to go to war because of internal strife there. Still, he and Eleanor attended various parties and functions, and he made contacts with politicians and military personnel, many of whom would continue to intersect his life. He reveled in having seventeen-gun salutes when he boarded naval vessels and ordered the battleship *North Dakota* to Maine when his family was vacationing nearby.

Eager to scramble up the next step of his political career, FDR ran in the Democratic primary for US senator in 1914. He lost to another Wilson appointee, American ambassador to Germany James Gerard, who was unable to cross the ocean in time to campaign; later he was defeated by the Republican candidate in the general election.

After returning to his Washington post, Roosevelt grew more irritated by President Wilson's

NATIONAL EVENTS

MAY: Dust Bowl conditions worsen across the Great Plains

MAY 23: Outlaw couple Bonnie and Clyde gunned down by police

JUN 6: Securities and Exchange Commission (SEC) created

JUN 10: Federal Communications Commission (FCC) created

AUG: American forces withdrawn from Haiti after a 19-year occupation

1934

WORLD EVENTS

JAN 26: German-Polish Non-Aggression Pact signed

FEB 12–16: Austrian Civil War

MAY 28: Canada's Dionne quintuplets are world's first quints to survive

AUG 2: Hitler becomes Germany's Fuehrer

DEC 27: Persia renamed Iran

refusal to become involved in the war in Europe. Here he disagreed with his boss, Secretary of the Navy Josephus Daniels, who opposed American intervention, and would sometimes enter his boss's office saying, "We've got to get into this war." Daniels always responded, "I hope not."[8] While away on an inspection tour of the Marine facilities in Haiti, Roosevelt learned that the United States had taken its first step toward war by ending diplomatic relations with Germany. Once America did declare war, FDR immediately offered his resignation (on cousin Theodore's advice) so he could obtain a military command and win glory, but Wilson rejected this move, so Roosevelt remained in office, helping to ensure that men were trained and appropriate wartime materiel gathered. Moreover, he oversaw the mining of the North Sea to prevent German submarine attacks and was excited to be invited overseas in the summer of 1918, where he visited Belleau Wood battlefield. Evidence of destruction lay everywhere. FDR recorded in his diary what he found:

> ". . . rusty bayonets, broken guns, emergency ration tins, hand grenades, discarded overcoats, rain-stained love letters . . . many little mounds, some wholly unmarked, some with a rifle stuck bayonet down in the earth, some with a helmet, and some too, with a whittled cross with a tag of wood or wrapping paper hung over it and in a pencil scrawl an American name."[9]

Franklin returned to Europe the following year, accompanied by Eleanor. They toured the sights and met a variety of dignitaries, including King George V, Prime Minister Lloyd George, and Minister of Munitions Winston Churchill. Franklin also took care to perform his official duty of inspecting bases and disposing of certain naval property.

By the end of 1919, FDR was casting about for new ways to further his political career. His cousin had become vice president, so perhaps that was his destiny as well.

PAINFUL INTERLUDE

With Wilson's refusal to run for a third term and Theodore Roosevelt's unexpected death, both parties now were open for candidates. FDR happily resigned from the Navy Department to accept the Democratic nomination for vice president to run with Governor James Cox of Ohio. Both campaigned in support of the League of Nations, which was unpopular among the people; consequently, the Democrats lost to Ohio senator Warren G. Harding. Roosevelt then returned to New York City, resuming his law practice and dabbling in other business ventures while he contemplated his next political move.

In July 1921, his future took a drastic turn when he arrived at the family's vacation home feeling ill. Within a few days, he could no longer walk, and a physician pronounced what the family feared—FDR had fallen victim to the dreaded disease poliomyelitis. At first he indulged in self-defeatist feelings of helplessness, but soon pushed those aside and began rehabilitation in earnest. For the next three years he underwent intensive physical therapy to develop whatever movement was still possible in his legs. He also experienced a change in mental attitude, and others remarked on the difference. One said, "It mellowed him, and it certainly added to his spiritual nature and his willingness to listen to other people's views." Eleanor agreed, and told one audience, "Anyone who has gone through great suffering is bound to have a greater sympathy

SUPREME COURT APPOINTMENTS
★★★★★★★★★★

Harlan Fiske Stone, Chief Justice, 1941

Hugo Lafayette Black, 1937

Stanley Forman Reed, 1938

Felix Frankfurter, 1939

William Orville Douglas, 1939

Frank Murphy, 1940

James Francis Byrnes, 1941

Robert Houghwout Jackson, 1941

Wiley Blount Rutledge, 1943

SEP 4: Largest US strike when half-million textile workers leave their jobs

DEC 29: Japan renounces its participation in earlier disarmament treaties

1935

MAR 1: US Army Air Corps begins

MAY 6: Works Progress Administration (WPA) created

World's first lobotomy performed in London

MAY 11: Rural Electrification Administration created

MAY 25: Jesse Owens breaks three track world records

MAR 16: Hitler proclaims right of Germany to arm itself (in direct violation of Treaty of Versailles)

MAY 27: Supreme Court rules NIRA unconstitutional

MAY 30: Babe Ruth plays his final professional game

SEP 15: First German laws limiting rights of Jewish citizens passed

AUG 14: Roosevelt creates Social Security Administration

SEP 30: Roosevelt dedicates Boulder (Hoover) Dam

OCT 3: Italy invades Ethiopia

NOV 9: Japan attacks Shanghai

STATE OF THE UNION
★★★★★★★★★★

US POPULATION IN 1933
125,578,763

US POPULATION IN 1945
139,928,165

NATIONAL DEBT IN 1945
$258,682,187,410

PRESIDENT'S SALARY
$75,000/year

and understanding of the problems of mankind."[10] She explained such was true of her husband, and that he had gained a greater sense of patience, rather than always demanding instant results. Now he had to wait to see if his body would allow him to pursue his political career.

Roosevelt meanwhile had become vice president of a surety bond business on Wall Street, where he could use his contacts gained in politics to further business interests. There he suggested and took part in investments—some succeeded; others went bust in the 1920s speculative fever.

At the Democratic national convention in New York City, Franklin Roosevelt made his political comeback by giving a rousing nomination speech for Al Smith's candidacy for the 1924 presidential election. Kansas City political boss Tom Pendergast was impressed and said that if FDR had been "physically able to [withstand] the campaign, he would have been named in acclamation in the first few days of the Convention. He has the most magnetic personality of any individual I have ever met."[11] But Roosevelt believed his own political career had to remain on hold while he worked to regain full use of his legs, citing the difficulty of being in a wheelchair or moving on crutches when one had to campaign. To help with his recovery, he journeyed to Georgia and Florida.

FDR AND POLIO ★ During the first half of the twentieth century, scores of American families were struck by the polio virus; usually children were its victims, and often their legs were left useless. Occasionally adults were affected, and Franklin Roosevelt was nearly forty years old when he developed polio in the summer of 1921. FDR wanted something done for all the others who could not afford the fine care available to him at Warm Springs, Georgia. So in 1938, President Roosevelt helped start an organization, the National Foundation for Infantile Paralysis, whose purpose was to find a cure for the disease and help those who were afflicted. Appeals for money were broadcast on the radio, and people were asked to send in dimes, so comedian Eddie Cantor called it the March of Dimes (a popular radio show was the "March of Times"), and that became the new name of the organization. Later FDR's picture was put on the dime since he was so closely associated with the crusade.

He found Georgia more to his liking and decided to make himself a long-term resident. To help himself and others afflicted with polio, FDR purchased a facility in Warm Springs, and created the Georgia Warm Springs Foundation with charitable donations from his well-connected friends and associates. Owing to the location and the times, it was a white-only establishment, although he attempted to rectify the situation when he was president by suggesting building a separate cottage for black residents. He withdrew the idea when it was pointed out how unfavorably it would be viewed by southern congressmen whose support he needed to pass his New Deal programs.

Although FDR himself did not feel ready, New York Democrats pushed him to run for the governorship in 1928, replacing Al Smith, who was again campaigning for the presidency. Roosevelt won the race, by a narrow margin.

GOVERNOR

Al Smith expected to continue running New York State through FDR, but the new governor had other plans. Immediately, Smith was put on alert

NATIONAL EVENTS

Supreme Court moves to new building

JUN 30: Margaret Mitchell publishes *Gone with the Wind*

NOV 3: President Roosevelt enjoys landslide victory over Republican Alf Landon of Kansas

NOV 23: *Life* magazine publishes first issue

DEC 30: UAW organizes first sit-down strike

JAN 19: Howard Hughes sets flying speed record from Los Angeles to New York in 7 hours, 28 minutes

1936

1937

WORLD EVENTS

JAN 20: Britain's King George V dies and his eldest son Edward VIII succeeds him

MAR 7: Hitler reoccupies Rhineland

JUL 18: Spanish Civil War begins

AUG 9: Jesse Owens wins his fourth medal at the Berlin Olympics; Hitler refuses to congratulate him

DEC 11: King Edward VIII abdicates throne in favor of younger brother Albert (George VI) to marry American divorcée Wallis Simpson

MAY 12: Coronation of King George VI and Queen Elizabeth

that Roosevelt would exercise his own judgment by writing his own inauguration speech rather than the one written by a Smith staffer. FDR also refused to keep many other Smith appointees in office, preferring to have his own group of advisors.

Progressive reforms were on Roosevelt's agenda, but they also had to pass muster from the Republican-controlled legislature. Farmers were one of FDR's targets to receive greater assistance through tax relief and cheaper electric power that would be available if his plans regarding hydroelectricity were implemented. He also threatened that the state would run the utility if private companies gouged the public. The first step was getting agreement from the legislature to create a commission that would investigate harnessing the power of the St. Lawrence River. FDR won the right to appoint all five members of the commission. Other ideas of his met with less enthusiasm, including judicial and prison reform. In the latter effort, he enlisted help from his wife, Eleanor, who toured various facilities and reported on their conditions. He also created a commission to study another of his pet projects—old-age pensions.

In 1930, Roosevelt ran for reelection in a country whose immediate concerns were different from when he had run previously. Now the country was slipping into a depression following the stock market crash in October 1929. The voters gave FDR a much larger margin of victory this time—more than eight hundred thousand separated him from his rival, Charles Tuttle. Roosevelt had grown familiar to New Yorkers owing to the increased popularity of radios; at least once a month, the governor went on the air and spoke to the public as if he were sitting across from them in their own living rooms. The day after FDR's victory, humorist Will Rogers quipped, "The Democrats nominated their president yesterday, Franklin D. Roosevelt."[12]

THE GOLDEN AGE OF RADIO ★ Although begun in the 1920s, the 1930s and '40s saw radio make its presence felt throughout the nation's living rooms. Music programs were most popular, but during the Depression, daytime serials began. Afternoon shows often featured comic strip characters such as Little Orphan Annie and Dick Tracy. In the evenings, families gathered to hear dramatic presentations performed by well-known actors of both stage and Hollywood. One program was almost "too dramatic" when, on Halloween night, 1938, Orson Welles and the Mercury Theater performed "War of the Worlds." Although a disclaimer ran throughout the program, many disregarded it and believed that New Jersey was truly under an attack by aliens from outer space. Any question of the power of radio disappeared after that night.

Roosevelt's second term was mainly concerned with helping those who were suffering the most from the Great Depression's disastrous effects. FDR saw government work programs as the best way to handle unemployment, as he was not a proponent of direct government payouts. During his travels he outwardly criticized the Hoover administration's reluctance to involve the government in economic relief for the American people. In New York, he supervised the development of the Temporary Emergency Relief Administration (TERA), which in time aided about 40 percent of New York's population. FDR increasingly assumed the posture of a presidential candidate, and throughout his two terms, he attended governor's conferences, where he worked to ingratiate himself with his

JAN 20: President Roosevelt begins second term

MAR 15: Chicago opens world's first blood bank

MAY 6: Zeppelin airship *Hindenburg* lands at Lakehurst, New Jersey, and bursts into flames

MAY 27: Golden Gate Bridge opens

JUL 2: Amelia Earhart disappears over the Pacific Ocean, attempting to become first female to fly around the world

JUL 22: US Senate refuses "court packing" scheme of FDR to prevent future rulings outlawing New Deal legislation

JUL 7: Second Sino-Japanese War begins when Japan invades China

SEP 21: First edition published of J.R.R. Tolkien's *The Hobbitt*

NOV 6: Italy joins Japan and Germany in Anti-Comintern Pact

NOV 9: Japan takes Shanghai

DEC 11: Italy withdraws from League of Nations

DEC–FEB: Nanjing (Nanking) Massacre by Japanese troops ends in the deaths of more than 250,000 Chinese

AMERICAN POW CAMPS ★ During World War II, prisoners from the European theater were frequently shipped to the United States, where they were held in POW camps that existed in nearly every state. Although the camps had originally begun in the southern states, they expanded to accommodate the Italian and German prisoners, numbering over 400,000. Some of these prisoners remained in the United States after World War II rather than return to their war-torn homes.

colleagues and build support nationally. His goal was to achieve the nomination in 1932 when the Democrats met in Chicago.

Although FDR was the favorite at the Democratic convention, he was not a clear-cut winner for the nomination. Among others who controlled delegates was his former friend, predecessor, and now rival, Al Smith. Another was House Speaker John Nance Garner of Texas, who agreed to become the vice presidential candidate to FDR and release his delegates to the New Yorker. Roosevelt flew to Chicago to give his acceptance speech, and in it he mentioned for the first time a promise to America of a "new deal." What that might involve remained to be seen.

1932 CAMPAIGN

Opposing FDR in the campaign was incumbent president Herbert Hoover, and of course, the issue was the Great Depression and how the government should try to handle it. Roosevelt supporters rallied around the song "Happy Days are Here Again," underscoring their faith in the man who promised to help them—though he remained vague on what form that help would take. Hoover, on the other hand, found his popularity plummeting, with crowds booing him at campaign appearances. Many Republicans abandoned their leader to join the Democrats. To no one's surprise, Roosevelt easily won the election, with 57 percent of the popular vote and 472 of 531 electoral votes.

Between the election and FDR's inauguration in March, a group of advisors—known as the Brain Trust—worked to flesh out the details of the New Deal that had been promised to the American people.

A few weeks before the inauguration, an Italian immigrant, Giuseppe Zangara, fired five shots at the president-elect as the presidential motorcade drove through Miami. Roosevelt was not hurt, but the mayor of Chicago was killed and four others were wounded. The assassin was found guilty of murder and was executed a little over a month later.

The nation listened to the broadcast of FDR's inaugural speech on March 4, 1933, in which he made a statement that was to resonate throughout his terms in office: "First of all, let me assert my firm belief that the only thing we have to fear is fear itself—nameless, unreasoning, unjustified terror which paralyzes needed efforts to convert retreat into advance." He assured an economically troubled people that he planned to put them to work with government-subsidized projects. Now the country watched to see what the first hundred days would bring.

PRESIDENT—FIRST TERM

First on the agenda was the banking crisis, which had worsened in the weeks preceding the president's inauguration. FDR turned to the medium that had proven so effective in explaining new policies when he was governor. Two days after taking office, he delivered his first radiobroadcast "fireside chat," starting with the simple words, "My

NATIONAL EVENTS

1938

JUN 14: National Labor Standards Act signed into law by President Roosevelt

JUL 3: 75th anniversary of the Battle of Gettysburg and final reunion of survivors

OCT 30: Mass hysteria results from Orson Welles's radio presentation of *War of the Worlds* causing listeners to fear there is an invasion of space aliens

1939

Pocket Books, Inc., begins publishing first American paperbacks

WORLD EVENTS

1938

MAR 3: Oil discovered in Saudi Arabia

MAR 14: Germany annexes Austria

SEP 29: Munich Agreement by Italian, French, and British officials appeasing Germany in granting it the Sudetenland

NOV 9: Kristallnacht ("Night of Broken Glass") occurs when German Jews experience looting of their businesses by German troops

1939

JAN 26: During Spanish Civil War, Francisco Franco takes Barcelona

friends," and ending with the national anthem. The president explained he was calling a special session of Congress to deal with the banking crisis. Congress convened three days later, and within eight hours, the Emergency Banking Act that FDR's staff had drafted had passed both houses and was on his desk for signature. The banks were closed temporarily so that each could be evaluated on its soundness—those in good fiscal shape would be allowed to reopen. The following month, the president took further action by removing the United States from the gold standard and forbidding its export. In May, the Federal Securities Act was enacted to regulate the stocks and bonds market.

Roosevelt had promised to put people to work, and later in March he launched the Civilian Conservation Corps (CCC), a work project geared toward young men, ages eighteen to twenty-five, of poor urban families, who were taken to rural areas and employed on conservation projects. They earned one dollar a day and were expected to send most of their wages back home. Over the years, more than three million young men worked for the CCC.

Farmers were helped by the Agricultural Adjustment Act (AAA), which paid them to lower production, thereby causing prices to rise, giving them a greater income and more ability to pay off their debts. Three years later the Supreme Court ruled the law unconstitutional, stating it violated the Tenth Amendment, and should have been levied by states. The AAA was not popular among many of America's citizens who did not see the wisdom of destroying food when so many were going hungry.

Following on his support of hydroelectricity in New York as governor, Roosevelt now advocated doing the same in the Tennessee Valley as a means of using the river and its tributaries to provide power to the depressed people living in that region. The Tennessee Valley Authority (TVA) became a mammoth operation and covered seven states; its success continues today as it remains the largest utility in the United States.

With various programs now in place, the centerpiece of the New Deal was introduced on the one hundredth day of FDR's presidency: the National Industrial Recovery Act (NRA) was passed to revitalize business and outlaw price fixing. Companies who participated had to agree to limit working hours and provide safe conditions in return for their federal grant money. The larger corporations refused to play along, and consumers were unhappy about higher prices. Two years later, part of the measure was ruled unconstitutional by the Supreme Court, which stated that Section 3 of the NIRA overstepped its constitutional bounds by granting the president legislative authority to set hours, wages, and minimum ages of employees.

Part of the NRA (not in dispute) included creating the Public Works Administration (PWA), which concentrated on "priming the pump" by putting people to work on major building projects such as dams, hospitals, schools, city pools, and even aircraft carriers. The PWA was later discontinued during World War II when the nation's resources were required for providing military materiel.

Another public employment program enacted was the Civilian Works Administration (CWA), which employed people on public works projects; however, this resulted in tremendous cost overruns. One observer reporting to the administration wrote, "When CWA came in, the men were 'tickled to death.' Their morale jumped about a hundred points. . . . Now they are beginning to be bitten by the urge to get even more. . . . I guess it's true that, the more you do for people, the more

FEB 27: US outlaws sit-down strikes

APR 14: *The Grapes of Wrath* by John Steinbeck is published

JUN 12: National Baseball Hall of Fame opens in Cooperstown, New York

JUL 13: Frank Sinatra begins a recording career at age 23

AUG 2: Albert Einstein writes to President Roosevelt about possibility of developing atomic bomb

FEB 27: France and Britain recognize Franco's government in Spain

MAR 14: Slovakia declares its independence

MAR 15: End of Czechoslovakia; German troops take over Moravia and Bohemia

APR 1: End of Spanish Civil War

APR 7: Italy invades Albania

MAY 7: Spain leaves League of Nations

JUN 24: Siam changes name to Thailand

they demand."[13] The CWA was dissolved within months of its implementation.

Other legislation allowed easier refinancing of home loans to help those paying mortgages. Congress agreed to create the Federal Deposit Insurance Corporation (FDIC) to protect bank deposits, and the National Labor Relations Board (NLRB) was initiated to ensure that labor was not denied its right to collective bargaining. To cap it all, Prohibition officially ended with the ratification of the Twenty-first Amendment.

During Roosevelt's second year as president he expanded on the foundation he had established in his first year in office. Farmers received additional relief through production limits; assistance increased for labor; and homeowners were aided by the creation of the Federal Housing Administration (FHA). The Securities and Exchange Commission (SEC), whose purpose was to regulate the stock market, was also established.

To FDR's delight, the New Deal proved popular with the voters in the 1934 congressional election, and Democrats gained seats in both houses. When Congress met in 1935, they found more legislation waiting for them from the executive branch, among them the Works Projects Administration (WPA), which put "artists" to work using their talents in a variety of projects.

The Rural Electrification Administration (REA) brought electricity to those without in America's poorer rural regions. And, finally, after years of pushing for a pension to help older citizens, Roosevelt won the passage of the Social Security Act, which was funded by contributions paid by both employers and employees.

FDR did suffer a setback at this point, however, with the Supreme Court decision finding the NRA unconstitutional; it would not be the last time he and the Court would disagree on the New Deal.

Nevertheless, the American people supported their president and reelected Roosevelt in a landslide over his Republican challenger Kansas governor Alf Landon, who secured only two states in the electoral college—Maine and Vermont—for a total of eight votes to 523 electoral votes won by FDR.

PRESIDENT—SECOND TERM

With the Supreme Court overturning the AAA, citing that government was overstepping its authority by controlling farm production, President Roosevelt decided to take action by reorganizing the federal judiciary and adding more justices to the Supreme Court. News of this attempt to "pack the court" with his own appointees more inclined to approve the New Deal shocked Americans as well as the justices. The court, in turn, soon found in favor of certain programs, including Social Security. Although no additional justices were appointed to the Supreme Court, a smaller-scale reorganization of the lower federal courts occurred.

Across the nation, labor unrest increased throughout 1937. Sit-down strikes became a favorite weapon, and violence often erupted between strikers and police. In the Hershey plant, fighting occurred between the striking plant workers and the dairy farmers who were unable to sell their product as long as production was halted.

By the winter of 1937–1938, the country's economy was sliding downward with unemployment numbers rising, and the stock market falling. The resulting recession put aside FDR's plans to have a balanced budget by 1939. Republicans gained seats in the 1938 election, but Democrats still held sway in Congress, and the Fair Labor Standards Act was

NATIONAL EVENTS

- **AUG 17:** *The Wizard of Oz* movie starring Judy Garland opens
- **SEP 5:** President Roosevelt reassures the American people that the US will remain neutral in World War II
- **NOV 4:** Neutrality Act adopted by Congress, but allows warring nations to buy American materials for cash
- **DEC 15:** Premiere of blockbuster film *Gone with the Wind* in Atlanta
- Ernest Hemingway publishes *For Whom the Bell Tolls*

1940

WORLD EVENTS

- **AUG 23:** Nonaggression Pact signed between Germany and Soviet Union agreeing to divide Eastern Europe
- **SEP 1:** Germany invades Poland, igniting World War II; Soviets attack from east on September 17
- **NOV 30:** Soviet Union invades Finland, prompting League of Nations to expel USSR
- **DEC 1:** Nazis demand that Polish Jews must wear Star of David
- **MAR 12:** Winter War between USSR and Finland ends with signing of a peace treaty

passed in 1939. The act helped workers by enacting a minimum wage of twenty-five cents an hour and a forty-four-hour workweek, which was to ultimately decrease to forty hours, and the minimum wage raised to forty cents by 1945.

Late in Roosevelt's second term, many New Deal programs were fading away while world events became more prominent. In his first term, FDR had granted official recognition of the Soviet Union, hoping to ensure good diplomatic relations with that communist nation. Then he initiated the Good Neighbor policy to build on Hoover's efforts to develop improved ties with Latin America. The United States demonstrated its willingness to put words into actions by removing American forces from Haiti, passing a new treaty which nullified the former Platt Amendment granting US intervention to Cuba, and refusing to practice "Dollar Diplomacy" when Mexico took over American-owned oilfields. Roosevelt personally attended the 1936 Pan American Conference in Buenos Aires, Argentina, and promised improved cooperation with its neighbors, which would be needed when the second world war began.

Meanwhile, Roosevelt warily viewed events in Europe, and his British counterparts did likewise. Neville Chamberlain, chancellor of the exchequer, told Prime Minister Stanley Baldwin and his cabinet, "I look upon him [FDR] as a dangerous and unreliable horse in any team."[14] Lord Runciman, president of the Board of Trade, met with FDR in 1937 and returned with the impression (as told by Chamberlain) that Roosevelt was "very friendly, very afraid of war, very anxious to avoid if it came, but likely, if we should be involved, to be in it with us in a few weeks."[15] The two powers collided over possession of certain Pacific islands, looking ahead to which ones might be useful as bases and refueling stops.

After Japan moved into China, FDR addressed an audience in Chicago about the Asian war and the threat of it spreading elsewhere: "If those things come to pass in other parts of the world, let no one imagine that America will escape . . . that this Western Hemisphere will not be attacked." He went on to reassure the people that he would pursue a policy of peace and use "quarantine" against the "epidemic of world lawlessness"[16] that threatened all. The problem was that neither he nor anyone else quite knew what the quarantine might entail.

The last days of the 1930s found European powers practicing appeasement toward Adolf Hitler and Nazi Germany. Wanting to save Jews from hostile Nazis was foremost on Roosevelt's mind as he pushed for the refugees to be welcomed by nations around the globe. It was during this time that Albert Einstein emigrated to the United States.

Worried that eventually he might have to lead the American people into war, FDR wrote to his friend William Phillips, now America's ambassador to Italy, that the United States might have to "pick up the pieces of European civilization." He made clear, though, that the Italian fascists of Benito Mussolini must not be misled by American neutrality because "if we get the idea that the future of our form of government is threatened by a coalition of European dictators, we might wade in with everything we have to give."[17]

To be prepared for any eventuality, FDR ordered increased arms production and especially advocated greatly increasing the number of warplanes manufactured to be ready for American use, or use by any other country needing them to fight Germany. Many others held to their belief that the United States could remain true to the Neutrality Act of 1935 but, in 1939, it was amended to allow

DID YOU KNOW?

FDR was an avid stamp collector—he helped design some US postage stamps while president, approved all new stamps during his presidency, and his stamp collection was purchased for more than $200,000 after his death.

A 24-year-old John F. Kennedy writes *Why England Slept*

Ronald Reagan stars in *Knute Rockne, All American* movie

FEB 29: Hattie McDaniel becomes first African American to win Academy Award

APR 1: First demonstration of an electron microscope

APR 7: Booker T. Washington becomes first African American to be depicted on a US postage stamp

MAR 18: Benito Mussolini and Adolf Hitler meet and agree to jointly fight France and Great Britain

APR 9: Germany attacks Norway and Denmark

MAY 10: Winston Churchill succeeds Neville Chamberlain as Britain's prime minister

MAY 14: Queen Wilhelmina and her Dutch government flee Netherlands as German Luftwaffe bombs the country; Dutch army surrenders

MAY 17: Brussels falls to Nazi troops

MAY 20: Auschwitz death camp opens in Poland

the British and French to purchase needed items from America on a "cash and carry" basis.

Looking for opportunities to build relations among allies, British King George VI and his wife, Queen Elizabeth, accepted an invitation from FDR to visit Hyde Park in June 1939. The press, however, was more interested in the menu (and many expressed disdain toward a host who would dare serve hot dogs to their majesties!). One evening the men talked late into the night; afterward, the king asked Canadian prime minister Willliam Lyon MacKenzie King, "Why don't my ministers talk to me as the president did tonight? I felt exactly as though a father were giving me his most careful and wise advice."[18]

By 1940, European nations erupted into war, as Hitler seized Czechoslovakia, Austria, Poland, and then attacked northern and western Europe. Britain became the target of air raids, and FDR concluded that he could not abandon his post; moreover, he had concerns that the New Deal might disappear if he were not in office. Therefore, he made the unprecedented decision to run for a third term, but without Vice President John Nance Garner, who had become increasingly hostile toward Roosevelt. The Democrats nominated Roosevelt on the first ballot, and Henry Wallace, secretary of agriculture, became his running mate. They promised to continue New Deal reforms and keep America out of the war.

Republicans nominated Wendell Willkie of Indiana, who had made a name for himself when his utility company opposed the creation of the TVA. Senator Charles McNary of Oregon became the vice presidential nominee. A few voices from both parties even proposed a joint ticket of Roosevelt–Willkie, but this was not seriously considered, so campaigning went on as usual. Republicans argued that now there were too many regulations because of the New Deal and also denounced the country's military unpreparedness. Of course, another criticism was leveled at Roosevelt for seeking a third term, but to no avail, as Americans again voted to return him to the White House. This time he captured 55 percent of the popular vote and 449 electoral votes to Willkie's eighty-two. After successfully leading the country through the Great Depression, they now looked to their president to guide them against the ever-growing threat of war.

In December, FDR created the lend-lease program to aid Great Britain, and he told his Fireside Chat radio listeners, "The people of Europe who are defending themselves do not ask us to do their fighting." But, he went on to explain, Americans could provide them with the tools to do so because, "We must be the great arsenal of democracy." Later British prime minister Winston Churchill echoed the president when he broadcast a personal message to the United States that Britain did not require the sacrifice of American soldiers, rather, "Give us the tools and we will finish the job."[19]

PRESIDENT—THIRD TERM

With the ratification of the Twentieth Amendment, presidential inaugurations were now held in January to shorten the lame-duck session after elections. So on January 20, 1941, Roosevelt once more delivered an inaugural address, but this time its focus was on world politics rather than the country's economy. Now the cabinet discussed the very real possibility of war and determined that chances were one in five that the United States would be attacked by either Germany or Japan; consequently, military planning moved forward, as did contingency plans for aiding Great Britain.

NATIONAL EVENTS

- **MAY 15:** First McDonald's restaurant opened in San Bernadino, California, by two brothers, Dick and Mac McDonald
- **JUN:** Rubber Reserve Co. created by the president in case US loses its supply from Far East
- **JUN 22:** First Dairy Queen opens selling soft serve ice cream in Joliet, Illinois
- **JUN 27:** Debut of Bugs Bunny in *The Wild Hare*
- **SEP 16:** President Roosevelt signs into law first peacetime draft in American history

WORLD EVENTS

- **MAY 26:** Dunkirk evacuation begins of British forces and continues until June 4, rescuing more than 300,000 soldiers
- **MAY 28:** Belgium army surrenders
- **JUN 10:** Italy declares war on Britain and France
- **JUN 10:** Norway surrenders to Germany
- **JUN 14:** German troops march into Paris
- **JUN 21:** France and Germany sign armistice in same railcar used to end World War I
- **JUN 28:** General Charles DeGaulle recognized by British as leader of Free French movement

Through the spring of 1941, FDR grew increasingly worried about the war, specifically the Germans in the Atlantic, and decided against sending naval escorts with convoys carrying supplies to Great Britain, fearful that attacks would mean war. Concerns weighing on him began taking their toll on his health, and his assistant, Missy LeHand, suffered a stroke. In June, he received the news that Hitler's new target was US treaty partner, the Soviet Union. The United States then expanded the lend-lease program to include that nation, and FDR added to the bill's provisions calling for heightened appropriations for defense, knowing Congress would dare not decline. Also Roosevelt was keeping an eye on the Japanese, since their expansion across much of China and now French Indochina was on par with Germany's. An American embargo against Japan for war materiel and oil heightened tension between the two nations.

Strikes increased at war production plants, and the president soon began to lose his patience. In June 1941, the North American Aviation Company in California, which manufactured bombers, experienced a wildcat strike that ended in a presidential order to send in 2,500 soldiers, armed with bayonets, to subdue the action (one striker was indeed bayoneted). As FDR hoped, not only was this strike quelled, but potential walkouts elsewhere did not materialize. Still, war production was behind schedule.

In August 1941, an anticipated meeting finally occurred between FDR and Winston Churchill at Placentia Bay, Newfoundland. The Atlantic Conference allowed the two leaders to meet and discuss each of their positions. They also jointly issued the Atlantic Charter calling for a better world, where no nation sought world domination; where an arms race did not exist; and where international cooperation was supreme. The British delegation left the meeting somewhat disappointed in not receiving all they desired. One wrote, "I think the general opinion in our party would be that the Americans have a long way to go before they can play any decisive part in the war. . . . Both their Army and their Navy are standing like reluctant brothers on the brink." When FDR bragged about how well he had done in his meetings with Churchill, a staffer reminded him, "You may want to look out, Mr. President, Churchill may be pulling your leg by letting you win the first round."[20]

Roosevelt did agree that the United States would take over part of the patrol duties for convoys headed to Britain, and Marines moved into Iceland to free their British counterparts for other duties. Congress also passed an extension to the Selective Service Act, which greatly upset isolationists who were extremely vocal in their opposition to supporting the British.

In September, while FDR was grieving over the loss of his beloved mother, Sara Delano Roosevelt, he heard of an American destroyer being targeted (but not hit) by a German U-boat. A few weeks later, another destroyer was not so lucky; the *Kearney* was torpedoed and eleven men died. The president responded by telling the nation, "We Americans have cleared our decks and taken our battle stations."[21] Another destroyer, the *Reuben James*, went down on convoy duty with a hundred men at the same time Congress was debating modifying the Neutrality Act.

Meanwhile Secretary of State Cordell Hull continued to meet with Japanese representatives, and while their talks were not expected to be fruitful, FDR supported any effort that would give the United States more time to build up its forces. By late November, many cabinet members agreed with

OCT 15: *The Great Dictator*, film by Charlie Chaplin lampooning the German dictator, premieres

NOV 5: FDR becomes only president to win a third term, defeating Wendell Wilkie

DEC 29: President Roosevelt tells American people they are "the arsenal of democracy"

DEC 26: *The Philadelphia Story* starring Katharine Hepburn, Cary Grant, and James Stewart premiers at Radio City Music Hall in New York City

DEC 30: First modern freeway, California State Route 110, opens to traffic in Pasadena

JUL 9: British begin retaliatory air strikes on German targets

AUG 20: Leon Trotsky, former associate of Stalin, assassinated in Mexico

SEP 7: London Blitz begins (nightly German aerial bombing of London); lasts for 57 consecutive nights

SEP 12: Lascaux cave paintings discovered

SEP 27: Tripartite Pact signed by Germany, Italy, and Japan, making them the Axis powers

Roosevelt that a surprise Japanese attack was a real possibility, and most believed the target would be the Philippines. Chief of Staff General George C. Marshall issued a warning to the Pacific command, telling commanders, "The United States desires that Japan commit the first overt act."[22] Thanks to the American cryptologists, US intelligence could decipher the top-secret code used by Japan to communicate with their diplomats and military officers. Still they could not learn the location of the planned attack, and the Japanese ships moving stealthily across the northern Pacific were under strict orders to maintain radio silence.

The president was soon to learn the exact target of Japan's military might—America's naval base at Pearl Harbor, Hawaii. As the first bombs fell on the morning of December 7, 1941, Japanese representatives met with Secretary Hull at about 2:20 p.m., Washington, D.C. time. Hull had just read the initial bombing reports, and when presented by Japan's declaration of war (which was supposed to have preceded the attack), the Secretary of State exploded: "In all my fifty years of public service I have never seen a document that was more crowded with infamous falsehoods and distortions—on a scale so huge that I never imagined until today that any government on this planet was capable of uttering them."[23]

Eleanor Roosevelt later wrote, "In spite of his anxiety, Franklin was in a way more serene than he had appeared in a long time. I think it was steadying to know finally that the die was cast."[24] His serenity was soon shattered with an evening cabinet meeting where tempers flared as details emerged of the navy's unpreparedness at Pearl Harbor. FDR demanded to know why the ships were berthed in long, exposed rows; others complained that the planes were easily bombed because they were parked wingtip to wingtip; and the first casualty numbers were coming in. The country was at war.

The next afternoon, in a special session of Congress, Roosevelt referred to the Sunday morning attack as a "day of infamy" and asked "that the Congress declare that since the unprovoked and dastardly attack by Japan on Sunday, December 7, 1941, a state of war has existed between the United States and the Japanese Empire."[25] All except Senator Jeannette Rankin of Montana voted to go to war.

As Japan began its conquest of Pacific islands, the administration decided it prudent to take into custody Japanese Americans and move them to relocation centers scattered in remote regions of the West. The Canadian government did likewise.

Germany and Italy honored their pact with Japan and declared war on the United States on December 11, so Roosevelt sent a note to Congress asking for recognition that war now existed between the United States and those two nations. Eleven days later, Churchill arrived in Washington to meet with FDR and formulate strategy. The two leaders decided that their most dangerous enemy, Nazi Germany, had to be defeated before the push against Japan. The first target for the Allies would be the German and Italian armies in North Africa during 1942. The men also spent considerable time discussing the world after the war and agreed on a charter for a United Nations, which they hoped would be more successful than the League of Nations in preventing future wars.

WARTIME LEADER

Along with ordering the internment of Japanese Americans, Roosevelt made other decisions that would later be questioned, or in many cases, denounced. With war came new bureaucratic agencies—for war production, price controls, and

NATIONAL EVENTS

JAN 6: In his State of the Union speech, President Roosevelt discusses the "Four Freedoms"

FEB 4: United Service Organization (USO) created

MAR 11: Lend-Lease Act passed providing loans of American-made war materiel to Allies

MAY 1: Orson Welles's film *Citizen Kane* premieres

MAY 6: Bob Hope performs in his first USO show

AUG 9: President Roosevelt and Winston Churchill meet to sign Atlantic Charter

1941

WORLD EVENTS

JAN 22: British and Australian forces take Tobruk, Libya, from Italians

APR 6: Invasion of Yugoslavia and Greece by Germany

APR 21: Greece surrenders to Nazi troops

JUN: Allies invade Iraq, Syria, and Lebanon

JUN 22: Germany attacks Soviet Union

SEP 8: Siege of Leningrad begins

NOV 26: Six Japanese aircraft carriers begin steaming toward Pearl Harbor

censorship. At this time, work on the Manhattan Project, which had been given the green light in the 1930s to develop an atomic bomb, was also stepped up and given almost unlimited funding. In April 1942, FDR ordered the production of poisons for biological warfare.

The president needed the support of the nation, so the White House announced that on February 23, he would give a Fireside Chat to discuss the progress of the war and advised all to have a map close at hand to refer to during the address. Americans flocked to buy world maps in record numbers, and more than sixty-one million sat down to listen to FDR's account of America's war aims. He explained to his audience that the world was embroiled in "a new kind of war . . . Not only in its methods and weapons but also in its geography" because it extended to "every continent, every island, every sea, every air lane in the world."[26] Then he outlined strategic places in the Pacific, referring listeners to their maps. He ended his lecture with the famous quotation from Revolutionary War pamphleteer Thomas Paine, reminding all, "These are the times that try men's souls."

At the same time, Roosevelt was negotiating the often-delicate web of coalition politics. As part of a team, America had to put the needs of all of the coalition above its own desires, which FDR understood could create hazardous political fallout for himself. Because the British already had a Combined Chiefs of Staff, the Americans had to create something similar, and so the Joint Chiefs of Staff was born. Military advisors were invaluable to both Roosevelt and Churchill, according to Secretary of War Henry Stimson, because they "were men whose great talents required the balancing restraint of carefully organized staff advice."[27] Sometimes the British disagreed with their Yankee allies, but pretended to go along, fearful that any overt opposition would result in America's emphasis switching to the Pacific.

The Russians, meanwhile, agitated for a second front to take the heat off of their war with Germany. Stalin sent Foreign Minister Molotov to meet with Roosevelt and put pressure on the United States for more aid, which the president promised. Moreover, FDR confided his hope that after the war, the Allied powers—Great Britain, the United States, and the Soviet Union—would function as the sentinels of peace for the world. He explained that he wanted to see the demise of the colonial empires and those territories becoming independent.

Both Secretary Stimson and General Marshall believed that the United States should build up its forces in England in preparation for a cross-channel invasion. Roosevelt wavered between supporting their plan and Churchill's proposed invasion of Northwest Africa, Operation TORCH. Much to Marshall's disgust, Churchill eventually

JAPANESE INTERNMENT CAMPS ★ Following the hysteria of the attack on Pearl Harbor on December 7, 1941, the US government quickly ordered a round-up of more than 100,000 Americans of Japanese descent; they were put in "relocation" centers based in several western states. People were crowded into barracks that often were devoid of plumbing or heating. Then in 1944, President Roosevelt signed an executive order to begin closing the camps. In 1988, Congress passed a reparations bill granting all survivors of the detainment a one-time payment of $20,000 and an apology from the US government.

SEP 11: President Roosevelt signs executive order allowing naval vessels to shoot on sight any Axis vessels in US waters

OCT 17: USS *Kearney* sunk near Iceland and 11 sailors die, first American casualties of World War II

OCT 31: Mount Rushmore completed

DEC 6: President Roosevelt appeals to Japanese emperor Hirohito for peace

DEC 7: Massive attack on Pearl Harbor by Japanese killing 2,300, sinking 5 battleships, and destroying 200 planes

DEC 8: China declares war on Japan

DEC 8: Japan attacks Hong Kong, Malaya, Singapore, and Manila

DEC 11: Germany declares war on US

DEC 23: Wake Island falls to Japanese; more than 1,600 Americans taken prisoner

DEC 25: Hong Kong falls to German troops

HOME FRONT ★ During World War II, Americans were exhorted to do their part to win the war by rationing, buying war bonds, and planting "victory gardens." Children at school and adults at work were constantly reminded of the boys overseas who needed everyone at home to help. Women served in a variety of military organizations: WACS (Women's Auxiliary Army Corps); WASPs (Women's Airforce Service Pilots); and WAVES (Women Accepted for Volunteer Emergency Service). They provided priceless assistance in the factories, making "Rosie the Riveter" an American icon.

won, and the general considered resigning. Also frustrated by the seeming inaction on the Allied front, many Americans decided to vote against the administration, so Republicans gained a total of fifty-three seats in both houses of Congress. A few weeks later, German commander Erwin Rommel lost at El Alamein in Egypt, and Churchill proudly proclaimed, "Before Alamein we never had a victory. After Alamein we never had a defeat."[28]

Other good news was coming in. American forces experienced victory against the Japanese at Midway in the summer and Guadalcanal in the fall. Now Germany was experiencing its own frustration with the siege of Stalingrad, and Operation TORCH succeeded with the Allies racing across North Africa from both east and west toward Tunisia.

In January 1943, Churchill and Roosevelt met again, this time near Casablanca, where they discussed where to take the war. Again Churchill feared a premature landing in France, insisting that Sicily was a preferable alternative. At a press conference, Roosevelt perhaps startled his ally by announcing the desire of the Allies to have the "unconditional surrender" of Germany and Japan by "the destruction of the philosophies in those countries which are based on conquest and the subjugation of other people."[29]

Around this time, FDR was also beginning to change his mind about the world order to follow the war; he believed France was too weak and should be replaced by China as the fourth world power.

Another conference was called with Churchill regarding how to follow up an invasion of Sicily; the British wanted to take Italy, but Americans argued that such action could jeopardize the major invasion they planned for the following year. Both leaders rejoiced upon hearing of Mussolini's overthrow, but disagreed on which successor to support. US and British forces had invaded Italy in September after an armistice was signed with the Italians, and the German army moved in force to secure as much of the country as possible. Roosevelt and Churchill met again in Canada, and Roosevelt pressed for Operation Overlord, the invasion of France, although Churchill still remained hesitant. The president maneuvered the situation so an American would be its commander.

In November 1943, Roosevelt finally met face to face with Soviet premier Joseph Stalin in Tehran, Iran. The meeting yielded mixed results, with Stalin discussing his desire to add the Baltic States to the USSR, but he also promised to join the Allies in the war against Japan once Germany was defeated. Tired of Churchill's continual plea for an Eastern Mediterranean offensive, FDR worked on convincing Stalin to side with him, so the two could better encourage the prime minister to support Overlord; the operation was to be launched in May 1944, and its commander was to be Marshall (both would later change as the invasion was

NATIONAL EVENTS

DEC 8: US declares war on Japan

FEB 9: Daylight savings time adopted

FEB 19: Executive Order issued by FDR to begin taking Japanese-Americans into custody and putting them into internment camps

FEB 22: President Roosevelt orders General Douglas MacArthur to leave the Philippines to avoid capture by the Japanese

FEB 24: Voice of America initiates broadcasting

1942

WORLD EVENTS

JAN: Japan attacks Netherlands East Indies, Kuala Lampur, and Burma

JAN 7: Japan begins its siege of Bataan peninsula in the Philippines

JAN 22: Wannsee Conference in Berlin determines to utilize "final solution"—extermination of Jews

FEB 15: Japan takes Singapore

rescheduled for June, and Roosevelt decided to put General Dwight D. Eisenhower in charge and keep Marshall in Washington). The three leaders also discussed the postwar world, including dividing Germany into occupation zones administered by the British, Americans, and Soviets.

The invasion of Italy begun late in 1943 continued into the new year with Allied forces becoming increasingly bogged down in the rugged mountainous terrain by growing numbers of German troops. Roosevelt and Churchill saw the operations in Italy as useful in pulling some of the Nazi war machine southward and away from where the main invasion was planned for the following spring.

By early 1944, those near the president could perceive the toll the war was taking on his health. He had permanent dark circles under his eyes, his hands trembled, and he was often ill. Doctors ordered him to reduce his smoking and all wondered if FDR would run a fourth time—and if he did, would he survive? For himself, he was not particularly pleased by the prospect of running once more and told a friend, "God knows I don't want to, but I may find it necessary."[30]

At his State of the Union message in January, Roosevelt unveiled his campaign, The Economic Bill of Rights, which called for equality of opportunity to "all—regardless of station, race, and creed." These included the right to work and housing, to be educated, to have medical care, to be secure in retirement and old age, and for farmers to receive reasonable payment for their produce and businessmen to be free from monopolistic competition. He admitted that pressing for legislation would have to wait, but maintained: "After the war is won, we must be prepared to move forward, in the implementation of these rights, to new goals of human happiness and well being."[31]

First, though, the war had to end. Toward that objective, Allied forces were gathering in England for the long-anticipated Operation Overlord to retake Europe from Hitler, which would involve a cross-channel assault by paratroopers and an armada of ships landing thousands upon thousands of men to gain a foothold on the beaches of Normandy, France. The Allied leaders, however, still disagreed about where else to conduct a supporting attack to better utilize troops in the Mediterranean, with Churchill pushing for launching east and north from Italy to block Stalin from taking the Balkans. Roosevelt disagreed, arguing that they had already promised to attack southern France, which would also shorten the supply line to the United States. Although the prime minister acquiesced to the American position, he later gloomily noted, "Except in Greece, our military power to influence the liberation of southeastern Europe was gone."[32]

HOLLYWOOD ★ Throughout FDR's administration, Hollywood played a key role in boosting American morale. During the Great Depression, movies were turned out in astonishing frequency; especially popular were musicals with Fred Astaire and Ginger Rogers, the escapades of German shepherd Rin Tin Tin, and the ever-cute little pixie, Shirley Temple. The star system created by the studios reached its zenith during the 1940s and fans flocked to see their favorite stars. Then during World War II, Hollywood became a propaganda machine to help America's war effort. Stars went on tours and attended rallies to boost sales of war bonds, while many of its leading men, including Clark Gable and Jimmy Stewart, enlisted.

MAR 9: United States Army reorganized into Army Ground Forces, Army Air Forces, and Services of Supply (Army Service Forces)

MAY: Congress creates Women's Army Auxiliary Corps (WAAC)

MAY: Sugar rationing begins

JUN 7: Japanese invade Aleutian Islands

JUN 13: US opens Office of War Information to disseminate propaganda

SEP: Gasoline rationing begins

OCT 28: The Alaska Highway is completed

APR 9: Bataan falls to Japanese; American and Filipino prisoners begin Bataan Death March

APR 18: Doolittle bombing raid on Tokyo

MAY 4–8: Battle of Coral Sea—Americans defeat Japanese

JUN 4–7: Battle of Midway—victory for US when it sinks three of Japan's five aircraft carriers

JUN 12: Jewish teenager Anne Frank receives a diary for her 13th birthday; her family goes into hiding a few weeks later

AUG 7: Battle of Guadalcanal begins

SEP: German troops move into Stalingrad

In July, FDR traveled to Honolulu to meet with military leaders regarding future actions in the Pacific. Admiral Chester Nimitz and General Douglas MacArthur met with the president for two and a half hours. Nimitz and the US Navy advocated invading Formosa (Taiwan); MacArthur and the Army, on the other hand, backed island hopping toward Japan by way of the Philippines and Okinawa. The general particularly favored this plan since he strongly desired returning to the Philippines, as he had promised when he was forced out by the Japanese earlier in the war. Roosevelt was concerned that the Nimitz plan could lengthen the war without a firm deadline, whereas MacArthur's seemed better suited to a timeline that would support the planned invasion of Japan. So the decision was made to strike the Philippines. Meanwhile the island hopping continued, and the Navy dealt the Japanese devastating twin defeats at the Battles of the Philippine Sea in June and Leyte Gulf in October.

The summer also meant convention time for the political parties, and FDR officially agreed to one more term. The question remained who should serve as his vice president, and with the president's declining health, this choice became even more critical. Roosevelt voiced support for different candidates, including the current vice president Henry Wallace, but Democratic leaders emphatically refused, claiming Wallace only divided the party. Another possibility was war mobilization director James Byrnes, who had long been loyal to the president. A third possibility was Senator Harry S. Truman of Missouri, who had earned respect and attention through his chairmanship of the Special Committee to Investigate the National Defense Program, which exposed fraudulent waste by defense contractors totaling around fifteen billion dollars.

For weeks the president waffled among his choices, telling Byrnes he supported him, while Wallace was told the same. Ultimately FDR instructed the political bosses to throw their support to Truman, but the Missouri senator was skeptical of supporters' claims that Roosevelt actually wanted him on the ticket. Democratic chairman Robert Hannegan met with the senator, and when FDR phoned to see if Truman had accepted, Hannegan replied, "He's the contrariest goddamn mule from Missouri I ever saw." Roosevelt replied, "Well you tell him if he wants to break up the Democratic Party in the middle of the war and maybe lose that war that's up to him."[33] Truman accepted and was nominated for vice president by the convention on the second ballot.

Republicans nominated "racket buster" New York governor Thomas Dewey as their presidential candidate and Ohio governor John Bricker as his running mate. Fearful of being portrayed as unpatriotic, Dewey declined to run against the war, but he did run against the "tired old man" and argued it was time for new ideas and leadership. His worst mistake was attacking the president's dog, Fala, by saying naval resources had been abused in sending a destroyer to pick up the dog when accidentally left behind on an inspection tour. FDR replied in an address to the Teamsters Union: "These Republican leaders have not been content with attacks on me, or my wife, or on my sons. No, not content with that, they now include my little dog, Fala."[34] For the fourth time, Franklin D. Roosevelt won a presidential election, but this time it was by the smallest margin: 53 percent of the popular vote to Dewey's 46 percent, but in the electoral college, Roosevelt easily won with 432 votes to Dewey's ninety-nine.

During the second half of 1944, Allied leaders met at Dumbarton Oaks in Washington and

			1943		
NATIONAL EVENTS	**NOV 28:** Fire at Cocoanut Grove nightclub kills 491 people in Boston	**DEC 2:** Nuclear chain reaction completed for first time in development of Manhattan Project	**JAN 14:** FDR becomes first president to fly in an airplane out of the country when he attends Casablanca Conference	**JAN 15:** Pentagon is dedicated; it is world's largest office building	**FEB 11:** Dwight D. Eisenhower named allied leader in Europe
WORLD EVENTS	**NOV:** Russians launch counteroffensive, trapping Germans and forcing them to winter in Stalingrad	**NOV 3:** Second Battle of El Alamein ends and German general Erwin Rommel retreats from British	**FEB 2:** German Sixth Army surrenders at Stalingrad	**FEB 8:** American forces successfully take Guadalcanal after months of tough fighting	**FEB 14:** Americans lose Battle of the Kasserine Pass in Tunisia

again in Quebec to discuss the formation of the United Nations and how representation would be determined for war planning. Roosevelt seemed to take a less active interest in many of the issues and became somewhat forgetful of details. Meanwhile the fighting dragged on, with news of Americans being caught by surprise during the last German offensive of the war in the Battle of the Bulge.

PRESIDENT—FOURTH TERM

Deciding to cut expenses and time, FDR decided to take his oath of office at the White House rather than the capitol. His speech was only five minutes long, and many left the ceremony shocked by his frail appearance. He had recently lost twenty pounds and admitted to close friends he no longer had an appetite. Edith Wilson, widow of President Woodrow Wilson, told labor secretary Frances Perkins, "He looks exactly as my husband looked when he went into his decline." Others later remembered the total solemnity of the occasion; Colorado senator Ed Johnson said, "There wasn't any smiling."[35]

In February, against doctor's advice, Roosevelt flew six thousand miles to the Crimean Sea resort of Yalta to meet with Churchill and Stalin once more. He believed that the other two Allied leaders were working against America's hope for a stronger China, and he wanted to discuss Europe and Palestine as well as the Russian entry into the Pacific war. This last matter was his main objective, for he considered Eastern Europe already under Stalin's rule.

Dealing with Europe after the war divided the leaders. Churchill pushed for France to share in an occupation zone of Germany, whereas Stalin had been adamant that the French should be excluded for they had done comparatively little fighting against the Germans, but he agreed to the British proposal. When asked how long the Americans would remain after the war, FDR answered two years; undoubtedly, Stalin thought he could endure anything for such a short time. When the matter of reparations came up, disagreements over how much to force Germany to pay postponed a decision.

Poland presented another formidable problem, with FDR and Churchill reluctant to, in effect, give it to Stalin. They negotiated and ultimately, the Soviet leader agreed to free elections in the nation within a month. (An election did occur in January 1947, but it was far from "free".)

For Roosevelt, the toughest negotiations took place during his successful attempt to gain the Soviet Union's direct participation in the war against Japan. Stalin's demands included obtaining use of certain railroads in Manchuria, which would give the Soviets a stronger post-war presence there. Stalin also demanded access to Port Arthur and Darien, and ultimately Stalin won.

Consensus was also secured on the role of the new United Nations, but the lack of provisions for international observers to monitor elections in Eastern Europe was taken advantage of by the Soviets, who moved quickly to establish communist regimes in the areas under their military control. Even before the war ended, criticism increased regarding the State Department and Roosevelt's handling of the negotiations, especially his decision to make the trip to Yalta knowing he was extremely ill. Still the administration believed itself successful, as illustrated by a War Department memo dated April 3, 1945: "The State Department feels that Stalin made very big concessions at Yalta."[36]

The president continued to Egypt to meet with King Ibn Saud to petition for more Jewish settlements in Palestine, but the king insisted that peace

APR 13: President Roosevelt dedicates Thomas Jefferson Memorial

JUN 2: Tuskegee Airmen (all African Americans) go into battle for first time

JUN 14: Supreme Court rules that reciting Pledge of Allegiance cannot be compulsory

JUN 25: Smith-Connally Anti-Strike Act passed over Roosevelt's veto allows US to take over any defense industry threatened by a strike or lockout

MAR 22: Entire population (149) of Khatyn, Belarus, burned to death by German troops

APR 16: Albert Hofmann, Swiss chemist, discovers hallucinogenic properties of LSD

APR 19: Warsaw Ghetto Uprising begins and lasts for 6 weeks (but all inhabitants will ultimately be killed or put in death camps)

MAY 13: German Afrika Corps and Italian troops surrender to Allies in North Africa

JUL 5–13: Largest tank battle in history at Kursk between Soviets and Germans, involves more than 6,000 tanks and ends in Nazi defeat

could not occur between Jews and Arabs, nor would Arabs willingly give up their land for the Jews.

Back home, FDR was forced to confront Stalin through cables as the United States and Britain watched the Soviet leader break his Yalta promise of free elections in Poland. Stalin also refused to release American troops who had been liberated by the Red Army. Stalin fired back angry missives, insisting that the British and Americans could not be trusted and that he had information regarding a treaty between Germany and the Allies against the Russians. FDR admitted to *New York Times* columnist Anne O'Hare McCormick that either Stalin could not be trusted or did not have the faith of his government. Either way, Roosevelt now understood that any agreement based on discussions at Yalta was unreliable.

Exhausted by his travels and weakened by the country's concerns, FDR decided he needed to go to Warm Springs, Georgia, to rest. For nearly two weeks, the president relaxed but also kept himself apprised of the world's events. He welcomed President Sergio Osmeña of the Philippines, and at a press conference, he promised to grant Filipinos their independence once Japanese forces in the islands were defeated. Looking to the end of April and the conference in San Francisco, which would draft the United Nations charter, Roosevelt chatted with visitors about his hopes.

With him at Warm Springs were a few staff members and old friends, including Lucy Mercer Rutherford, with whom he had conducted an adulterous relationship a quarter century earlier. Eleanor Roosevelt had learned of it and threatened divorce, but Sara Roosevelt had reminded her son that a divorce would end his political career, so he had agreed to break off the affair and never see Lucy again. Franklin and Eleanor had drifted apart, and during his presidency he resumed playing host to Lucy when Eleanor was out of town (which was frequently). Sometimes she also accompanied him to Warm Springs, and so she was there on April 12. This time she brought a friend, Elizabeth "Mopsy" Shoumatoff, a portrait artist who was painting FDR's picture that afternoon when he said, "I have a terrific headache," then slumped in his chair. The president was carried to bed; Lucy and Mopsy left.

Dr. Howard Bruenn, the president's cardiologist, examined Roosevelt and immediately concluded the president had experienced a massive stroke. FDR worsened during the next two hours, and at 3:35 p.m., Dr. Bruenn pronounced him dead. About ninety minutes later, Vice President Harry Truman was summoned to the White House, where Eleanor Roosevelt told him the news. Truman was sworn in two hours later.

In Germany, Hitler was told of the news by his propaganda minister Joseph Goebbels: "My Fuhrer, I congratulate you! Roosevelt is dead. . . . It is the turning point!"[37] Convinced that the alliance between the Western Allies and the Soviets would now collapse, a jubilant Hitler gushed to his armaments minister, Albert Speer: "Here it is. Here we have the miracle I always predicted. . . . The war isn't lost."[38] But the course of the war did not change with the death of the American president; instead, both Hitler and Goebbels would die at their own hands less than three weeks later, and Speer, convicted of war crimes, would spend twenty years in prison.

On April 13, Roosevelt's body was placed onto a railroad parlor car, which was illuminated at night for its journey to Washington. An honor guard accompanied the casket, and an estimated two million people along the way stopped and paid their respects to the man they had called President for twelve years. Once in Washington, representatives from

NATIONAL EVENTS

SUMMER: Race riots in Detroit and Harlem

AUG 2: *PT-109* commanded by John F. Kennedy rammed in South Pacific

AUG 3: Gen. George Patton makes headlines when he slaps a soldier in a hospital for being a coward

DEC 24: Eisenhower named Supreme Allied Commander

WORLD EVENTS

JUL 10: Allied invasion of Sicily begins

JUL 25: RAF planes bomb Hamburg, Germany, with incendiaries creating massive firestorms

SEP 3: Allied invasion of Italy begins

SEP 8: Italy surrenders to Allies

NOV 28: Tehran Conference: meeting of Churchill, FDR, and Stalin to discuss strategy and agree to Allied invasion of Europe

JUN 6: D-Day: more than 155,000 Allied troops land on beaches of Normandy as part of world's largest amphibious invasion

all three branches, including President Truman and the cabinet, met the train and followed the funeral cortege to the White House. There the coffin was placed in the East Room, and at 4 p.m., a funeral service was conducted. In London, the British had a memorial service as well, attended by the royal family and Churchill. After the White House service, the coffin was loaded onto a train once more, for the last leg of the journey, to Hyde Park. There Franklin Roosevelt was buried with a simple tombstone as he had requested, inscribed only with his name and years of birth and death.

Eleanor Roosevelt spent her remaining seventeen years traveling, writing, and serving at President Truman's request as a delegate to the United Nations. She died in 1962 and is buried beside her husband.

ENDNOTES

1 Arthur M. Schlesinger Jr., *The Age of Roosevelt: The Crisis of the Old Order 1919-1933*, Boston: Houghton-Mifflin, 1957, pp. 319-320.

2 Ted Morgan, *FDR, A Biography*, New York: Simon & Schuster, 1985, p. 108.

3 Ibid, p. 116.

4 Ibid, p. 119.

5 Ibid, p. 127.

6 Frances Perkins, *The Roosevelt I Knew*, New York: Viking Press, 1946, p. 12.

7 Frank Freidel, *Franklin D. Roosevelt, A Rendezvous with Destiny*, New York: Little, Brown & Company, 1990, p. 22.

8 Morgan, p. 175.

9 Freidel, pp. 30-31.

10 Morgan, pp. 259-260.

11 Ibid, p. 271.

12 Frank Freidel, *F.D.R., Vol. III, The Triumph*, Boston: Little, Brown, & Co., 1956, p. 167.

13 Kenneth S. Davis, *FDR, The New Deal Years 1933-1937*, New York: Random House, 1986, p. 313.

14 Freidel, *Rendezvous*, p. 260.

15 Ibid, p. 261.

16 Ibid, pp. 263-264.

17 Ibid, p. 299.

18 John W. Wheeler-Bennett, *King George VI*, New York: St. Martin's Press, 1958, p. 389.

19 Freidel, *Rendezvous*, pp. 360-361.

20 Morgan, p. 598.

21 Samuel I. Rosenman, ed., *Public Papers and Addresses of Franklin D. Roosevelt*, (13 vols.), *The Call to Battle Stations: 1941*, New York: MacMillan, 1950, p. 444.

22 Gordon W. Prange, *At Dawn We Slept*, New York: Penguin Books, 1981, p. 402.

23 Prange, p. 554..

24 Eleanor Roosevelt, *This I Remember*, New York: Harper & Brothers, p. 233.

25 Freidel, *Rendezvous*, p. 406.

26 Kenneth S. Davis, *FDR, The War President, 1940-1945*, New York: Random House, 2000, p. 434.

27 Morgan, p. 636.

28 Ibid, p. 649.

29 George J. McJimsey, *The Presidency of Franklin D. Roosevelt*, Lawrence, KS: University Press of Kansas, 2000, p. 224.

30 Robert Dallek, *Franklin D. Roosevelt and American Foreign Policy, 1932-1945*, New York: Oxford University Press, 1979, p. 442.

31 Nathan Miller, *FDR, An Intimate History*, Garden City, NY: Doubleday & Co., Inc., 1983, p. 498.

32 Dallek, p. 457.

33 Harry S. Truman, *Memoirs, Vol. 1: Year of Decision*, Garden City, NJ: Doubleday, 1955, p. 193.

34 William A. DeGregorio, *The Complete Book of US Presidents*, New York: Gramercy Books, 2005, p. 493.

35 Morgan, p. 742.

36 Ibid, p. 755.

37 William L. Shirer, *The Rise and Fall of the Third Reich*, New York: Simon and Schuster, 1960, p. 1110.

38 Albert Speer, *Inside the Third Reich*, New York: Avon Books, 1971, p. 586.

Eastman Kodak develops Kodacolor film

JUL 6: Jackie Robinson arrested when he refuses to sit at the back of a segregated Army bus; he is court-martialed but later acquitted

NOV 7: FDR wins unprecedented fourth term over Republican Thomas Dewey; vice president is Missouri senator Harry S. Truman

DEC 16: George C. Marshall becomes America's first five-star general

1944

AUG 24: Allies liberate Paris

SEP 3: Brussels liberated by Allies

OCT 20: Americans begin to retake Philippines led by General Douglas MacArthur

OCT 21: Aachen becomes first German city to fall

DEC 16: Germany launches winter offensive in the Ardennes—the Battle of the Bulge

Harry S. Truman

★ ★ ★ THIRTY-THIRD PRESIDENT ★ ★ ★

LIFE SPAN
- Born: May 8, 1884, in Lamar, Missouri
- Died: December 26, 1972, in Kansas City, Missouri

NICKNAME
- Give 'Em Hell Harry

RELIGION
- Baptist

HIGHER EDUCATION
- University of Missouri at Kansas City Law School, 1923–1925, did not graduate

PROFESSION
- Farmer, businessman

MILITARY SERVICE
- Served with Missouri National Guard (1905–1911)
- World War I: rejoined National Guard in May 1917, which was absorbed into US Army
- Served with 129th Field Artillery (Aug. 1917–May 1919); entered as a lieutenant, promoted to captain; commanded Battery D
- He stayed in the US Army Officers' Reserve Corps and commanded an artillery regiment as a full colonel in the 1930s

FAMILY
- Father: **John Anderson Truman** (1851–1914)
- Mother: **Martha Ellen Young Truman** (1852–1947)
- Wife: **Elizabeth "Bess" Wallace Truman** (1885–1982); wed on June 28, 1919, in Independence, Missouri
- Child: **Margaret** (1924–2008)

POLITICAL LIFE
- Jackson County, Missouri, judge (administrative position) 1922–1924
- Jackson County Presiding judge (chief county executive) 1926–1934
- US senator (1935–1945)
- Vice president (January–April 1945)

PRESIDENCY
- Two terms: April 12, 1945–January 20, 1953 (took office upon death of President **Franklin D. Roosevelt**)
- Democrat
- Vice president: **Alben Barkley** (1949–1953)

ELECTION OF 1948
- Electoral vote: **Truman** 303; **Thomas E. Dewey** 189; **Strom Thurmond** 39
- Popular vote: **Truman** 24,179,347; **Dewey** 21,991,292; **Thurmond** 1,175,930

CABINET
★★★★★★★★★★

SECRETARY OF STATE
James F. Byrnes (1945–1947)
George C. Marshall (1947–1949)
Dean Acheson (1949–1953)

SECRETARY OF THE TREASURY
Frederick M. Vinson (1945–1946)
John W. Snyder (1946–1953)

SECRETARY OF WAR
Robert P. Patterson (1945–1947)
Kenneth C. Royall (July–Sept. 1947), then integrated into new Department of Defense

SECRETARY OF DEFENSE
James V. Forrestal (1947–1949)
Louis A. Johnson (1949–1950)
George C. Marshall (1950–1951)
Robert A. Lovett (1951–1953)

ATTORNEY GENERAL
Thomas C. Clark (1945–1949)
J. Howard McGrath (1949–1952)
James P. McGranery (1952–1953)

Harry Truman never graduated from an Ivy League university, or any university for that matter. He was not from a wealthy family nor was he from the East Coast or Ohio, which were the main breeding grounds for the nation's chief executives. Instead, Harry Truman grew up on a farm in rural Missouri, served in World War I, became a failed businessman, then a small-time politician who rapidly rose within little more than a decade to become US senator, vice president, and president. His presidency became one of the most pivotal administrations in our nation's history, and all the world came to know "the man from Independence."

EARLY LIFE

On May 8, 1884, in the small rural community of Lamar, Missouri, Martha (Mattie) Young Truman gave birth to the first of three children with John Anderson Truman. They named their son Harrison for his uncle and gave him the middle initial of "S," which stood for his maternal grandfather Shipp and paternal grandfather Solomon (Young). John Truman was a mule trader in Lamar, and before Harry had his first birthday, he and his parents moved to a farm in rural Cass County, and the following year they moved in with Mattie's family. By now, two siblings had joined Harry—John Vivian and Mary Jane.

The family moved again in 1890, this time to the town of Independence some twenty miles away, where John could resume his livestock trading, and the children would have better educational opportunities. Harry liked school and later insisted all of his teachers were wonderful; he read all of the books in the library and managed to skip the third grade. He now wore spectacles for his bad eyesight, which an optometrist attributed to his having "flat eyeballs."

Harry tended to avoid the rough and tumble of male sports and stuck with mostly feminine company instead. He especially liked spending time with his female cousins, the Nolands, and later another young lady joined them—Elizabeth "Bess" Wallace, whom he had originally met at Sunday school. Bess excelled in tomboy activities and was extremely popular, yet also enjoyed spending time with the bookworm. As he grew older, he also struck up a lifelong friendship with classmate Charlie Ross.

At fourteen, Harry was hired to work at Clinton's Drug Store, where he cleaned from 6:30 to 7:00 every morning, and he called his first payday, "the biggest thing that had ever happened to me"[1] when three silver dollars were placed in his hand. He stayed only three months, for his father feared his studies might suffer. So Harry's life continued to center around school, the library, home, and his piano lessons with a teacher who pushed her student to practice seriously two hours daily. Young Harry displayed great potential and both of them believed that he might become a concert pianist.

In 1900, Harry accompanied his father to Kansas City for the Democratic National Convention where William Jennings Bryan received the party's nod for the second time to face William McKinley for the presidency. Both Trumans enjoyed their convention experience, and the son contentedly followed in his father's footsteps to become a loyal Democrat.

After his high school graduation in May 1901, Harry had to determine his future course. No longer planning on playing the piano for a living, he considered an appointment to West Point, but his poor eyesight prevented his acceptance. Meanwhile, John Truman had been engaged in some futures speculat-

NATIONAL EVENTS

US women lose their jobs as men return from the war and resume their former occupations

Streptomycin first used to treat tuberculosis at Mayo Clinic

Percy Spencer invents the microwave oven

George Orwell publishes *Animal Farm*

Philadelphia department store introduces the Slinky

1945

WORLD EVENTS

JAN 17: Soviets liberate Warsaw, then Auschwitz concentration camp ten days later

FEB 4–11: Yalta Conference held with FDR, Churchill, and Stalin; Stalin agrees to help fight in Pacific after war is won in Europe

FEB 23: Battle of Iwo Jima—classic photograph taken of Marines raising American flag on Mount Suribachi

MAR 9–10: American B-29s drop incendiary bombs on Tokyo, killing more than 70,000

MAR 19: Hitler orders destruction of all German military installations, factories, transportation, and communication facilities

ing, and the summer of 1901 saw his fortune depleted. The family now sold its property and moved to Kansas City, where John found work as a night watchman for a grain elevator; Harry worked in the *Kansas City Star*'s mailroom. The following summer he switched jobs to work for the Santa Fe Railroad as a construction timekeeper. For the first time, Harry was exposed to the working class with men who toiled for ten-hour days, six days a week, liberally exercised their knowledge of profanity, then drank their wages. Although the men's behaviors were alien to his world, Harry soon accepted them and they him. One foreman proclaimed that Harry was "all right from his asshole out in every direction."[2]

Harry's next work experience was as a clerk at the National Bank of Commerce in Kansas City. Again he received sterling performance reviews, albeit in less colorful language. "I do not know of a better young man in the bank than Trueman [sic]," wrote his superior A.D. Flintom, who also said, "He is an exceptionally bright young man."[3] At this time, the twenty-one-year-old joined the National Guard. When he went home proudly wearing his new blue uniform, the appearance of such a "Yankee" garment greatly offended his grandmother, whose farm had been repeatedly pillaged by men in Union blue during the Civil War. He never wore it in her presence again. His parents resettled farther south, so Harry now moved into a boardinghouse, where he became friends with fellow lodger Arthur Eisenhower, older brother to future president Dwight. Truman's world abruptly changed in early 1906 when his father called to ask his oldest son to come and help on their farm near Grandview.

FARMER

Although the change in his fortune was unexpected, the young man accepted it with grace and never complained. He plowed and harvested, then went inside to help the women in the kitchen. Invited to join the Masons, he did so with pride and was respected by his fellow lodge members. In the summer of 1910, he began officially courting Bess Wallace. He wrote extensive letters to his beloved back in Independence, detailing his farming activities, as well as anything unusual in his life—including an account of digging a grave. He proposed to her in another letter and waited three weeks for her response, which eventually came as a refusal. Still they continued their correspondence, and he chatted extensively about a great variety of topics. Explaining his deep affinity for music, he wrote, "Did you ever sit and listen to an orchestra play a fine overture, and imagine that things were as they ought to be and not as they are?"[4]

Anxious to attempt a new venture, Truman and his namesake uncle invested in a zinc mine in Oklahoma. Unfortunately, the mine lost everyone's money, including his mother's, who had advanced his original investment. Soon he tried another scheme, this time as treasurer of the Morgan Oil and Refining Company, a venture that also flopped but produced lifelong friendships. Fortunately none of these financial disasters included losing title to the farm, and although farming was not his first choice of career, Truman later admitted that his decade of tilling the soil paid dividends in helping him to develop as a person.

SOLDIER

Once the call to war was issued to American men in the spring of 1917, Harry Truman knew he must heed it. Although he had left the National Guard six years earlier and was thirty-three years old, he believed he must do his duty and serve. He enlisted, and was elected a first lieutenant of the

CABINET
★★★★★★★★★★

(continued)

SECRETARY OF THE NAVY
James V. Forrestal (1945–1947), then integrated into new Department of Defense

POSTMASTER GENERAL
Robert E. Hannegan (1945–1947)

Jesse M. Donaldson (1947–1953)

SECRETARY OF THE INTERIOR
Harold L. Ickes (1945–1946)

Julius A. Krug (1946–1949)

Oscar L. Chapman (1949–1953)

SECRETARY OF AGRICULTURE
Clinton P. Anderson (1945–1948)

Charles F. Brannan (1948–1953)

SECRETARY OF COMMERCE
Henry A. Wallace (1945–1946)

W. Averell Harriman (1946–1948)

Charles Sawyer (1948–1953)

SECRETARY OF LABOR
Lewis B. Schwellenbach (1945–1948)

Maurice J. Tobin (1948–1953)

Grand Rapids, Michigan, is first community to fluoridate its water

Frozen juices developed

Coke becomes new trademark for Coca-Cola

Penicillin becomes available on a large scale; other antibiotics soon follow

JAN 20: Unprecedented fourth inauguration for President Franklin Roosevelt

APR 10: Buchenwald concentration camp liberated by Allies; two days later Bergen-Belsen liberated

APR 28: Benito Mussolini executed in Italy

APR 30: Hitler and Eva Braun commit suicide in their bunker

MAY 2: Soviet troops take Berlin

MAY 5: Canadian troops liberate Amsterdam

MAY 7: German General Alfred Jodl signs surrender terms

MAY 8: V-E Day (Victory in Europe) celebrated

MAY 8: Beginning of Sétif Massacre in Algeria by French troops who killed at least 20,000 Algerian citizens

newly formed Battery F of the 129th Field Artillery Regiment of the 60th Brigade attached to the 35th Division. They were sent to Camp Doniphan near Fort Sill, Oklahoma, for training, where he worked with his men on the handling of horses as well as acquiring vital knowledge of trench warfare and artillery. Additionally, Truman was put in charge of the regiment's canteen and decided to ask Sergeant Edward Jacobson to be his partner. The two men excelled in the enterprise and became great friends as well as business partners. Truman proudly wrote to Bess about his new Jewish friend.

After some fast talking with an Army optometrist who failed Truman on the eye exam, he managed to stay in the Guard. He also endured the grueling examination by US Army general Lucien D. Berry, won promotion to captain, and was selected for advanced artillery training in France. After a whirlwind trip to New York City, he bid farewell to his homeland on the night of March 29, 1918, as he sailed on a troopship to Europe and the war.

After undergoing additional training in France, Truman took command of Battery D, known as the "Dizzy Ds"—a group of wild Irishmen from Kansas City who boasted of having run off a succession of other commanders before their new bespectacled captain's arrival. He later recalled his first meeting with the corporals and sergeants and explained his intentions: "I told them I knew they had been making trouble for the previous commanders. I said, 'I didn't come over here to get along with you. You've got to get along with me. And if there are any of you who can't, speak up right now, and I'll bust you right back now.'" Later, he reported, "We got along."[5]

Six weeks after he took command of Battery D, he and his men faced combat in the Vosges Mountains in what later became jokingly known as "the Battle of Who Run" because one of his sergeants yelled for the men to flee when they came under German artillery fire. Truman's vocabulary impressed his men that night as he illustrated his considerable repertoire of cursing and questioned the courage of his Irish battery. Although involved in heavy fighting at various times, no one in Battery D was killed while under his command during the war.

After the armistice of November 11, 1918, Truman had the unenviable task of keeping tabs on his men for the next five months as they awaited orders to go stateside. During his military service, Truman met several men whose paths he would cross many times in the coming years, including James Pendergast, who was nephew to Kansas City political boss Tom Pendergast. Meanwhile he and his officer buddies struggled to keep their men occupied, often passing the evenings in an ongoing poker game, until they finally shipped home.

BUSINESSMAN

Shortly before his thirty-fourth birthday, Truman returned home and six weeks later wed Bess Wallace at Trinity Episcopal Church on June 28, 1919. After a short honeymoon, they moved in with her mother at 219 North Delaware Street. The Wallaces had been one of the wealthiest families in Independence and their home reflected their gentility, although years before their world had been shattered by the suicide of her father, a subject that would remain taboo within the family.

In the fall, Truman entered the haberdashery business with former sergeant and canteen partner Eddie Jacobson. The two men enjoyed economic success in the first two years, only to see it lost by the deflation of the early 1920s. While contemplating the closing of their business and its

NATIONAL EVENTS

JAN 31: Private Eddie Slovik executed for desertion in France

MAR 1: Roosevelt addresses Congress for the last time, briefing them on the Yalta Conference

APR 12: President Roosevelt dies at Warm Springs, Georgia, and Harry Truman becomes president

MAY 5: Five people killed in Oregon when Japanese balloon bomb explodes

JUL 16: Trinity Test conducted of atomic bomb near Alamogordo, New Mexico

WORLD EVENTS

JUN 21: After nearly three months of fighting, American and Allied troops take Okinawa

JUL 1: Division of Germany for occupation

JUL 5: Liberation of Philippines is complete

JUL 17–AUG 2: Potsdam Conference

JUL 26: Allied leaders issue Potsdam Declaration

JUL 28: Japan rejects the Potsdam Declaration

AUG 6: Atomic bomb lands on Hiroshima, Japan

disastrous personal economic effect, Michael Pendergast, brother of Democratic Party boss Tom, came by the store. He asked Truman if he wanted to be county judge, which in Jackson County, Missouri, meant a county administrator. Truman accepted, and Mike introduced him to his own Tenth Ward Democratic Club: "Now I'm going to tell you who you are going to be for, for county judge. It's Harry Truman. He's got a fine war record. He comes from a fine family. He'll make a fine judge."[6] Once a Pendergast had spoken, the deed was done. They wanted someone they trusted in office since the county judge awarded public works contracts for the county, especially its roads, and was comptroller of its finances. Truman would always be grateful to Mike Pendergast, whom he considered his political mentor. He won election to a two-year term and took office on January 1, 1923.

JACKSON COUNTY POLITICIAN

During this time, the Ku Klux Klan was enjoying a resurgence of popularity, including in western Missouri. They, like the veterans, wielded no small amount of political clout, so Truman decided to join and gave them his ten-dollar fee. When he learned they would not allow him to hire Catholics, he told them flatly that he would not turn down the Catholic fighting men of Battery D and stomped out. His walkout was the end of the story—until 1944, when Truman was the vice presidential candidate and Hearst newspapers published the story of Truman being a Klansman. The Klan would not forget his pointed rebuff and aggressively campaigned against him during his 1924 reelection bid (which he lost) and his 1926 race for presiding judge (which he won).

Truman had another new responsibility as of February 17, 1924, when he and Bess welcomed their one and only child, a daughter they named Margaret. Thinking he needed a true professional career, Truman had attempted law school only to face so many interruptions from friends and constituents that he gave it up after two years of class work. This was also the year that he was defeated for reelection to county judge by a Republican whom the Klan supported.

During the next two years, Truman worked for the Kansas City Automobile Club, where he sold memberships and earned commissions. He did well but was less successful picking business schemes for investments and was burned twice investing with a former Guard comrade, Spencer Salisbury. Later when Truman referred federal investigators to check into Salisbury's dealings, which lead to a conviction and a term at Leavenworth, Salisbury did his best to sully Truman's reputation.

In early 1926, Tom Pendergast met with Truman to discuss the young politician's future. It was determined that Truman would run for presiding judge of Jackson County, which was the overall county administrator for an office that paid a six thousand dollar annual salary. With Pendergast's support, Truman had no problem winning in the primary or the general election and enjoyed job security for the next four years. Then he won a second term in 1930.

Once in office, Truman oversaw various Jackson County offices, including the sheriff's department, roads, the health department, the county treasury, tax collection, schools, elections, and the county hospital, as well as the two jails and homes for problem youth. He was the face of the administration and his knowledge and willingness to work with all factions impressed many. Wanting to boost

SUPREME COURT APPOINTMENTS
★★★★★★★★★★

Harold H. Burton, 1945

Frederick M. Vinson, 1946

Thomas C. Clark, 1949

Sherman Minton, 1949

JUL 21: Truman approves use of atomic bomb

JUL 28: B-25 bomber crashes into Empire State Building, 14 people are killed

JUL 30: USS *Indianapolis* sunk by Japanese sub; 600 of 900 men die before being rescued (ship was returning from delivering first atomic bomb)

AUG 8: US ratifies UN Charter, becomes the third nation to join the new international organization

AUG 9: Second atomic bomb hits Nagasaki after Japanese government fails to respond to Truman's call for surrender

AUG 9: Soviet troops move into Japanese-controlled Manchuria

AUG 15: Japanese emperor Hirohito announces his country's capitulation

AUG 15: V-J Day (Victory in Japan)

AUG 19: Ho Chi Minh and Viet Minh take over in Hanoi, Vietnam

SEP 2: Japanese surrender signed aboard USS *Missouri* in Tokyo Bay

STATE OF THE UNION
★★★★★★★★★★

US POPULATION IN 1945
151,325,798

NATIONAL DEBT IN 1953
$275,168,120,129

PRESIDENT'S SALARY IN 1948
$100,000/year

NUMBER OF STATES IN 1953
48

Kansas City's economy, he managed to woo the Republicans to hold their 1928 convention there. (Democratic boss Tom Pendergast was not pleased.) Truman went to the voters to approve road-building bonds. He campaigned extensively for the measure, promising to use the lowest bids and ensure they were built properly. He won, and rural Jackson County soon boasted hundreds of square miles of fine roads paved with Pendergast concrete.

Overseeing a variety of construction projects for the county, plus continuing his association with the National Guard and the Masons, kept Truman extremely busy, yet he found time to join the Veterans of Foreign Wars and the Elks. Daughter Margaret later explained his preference to living in town rather than the city because "he genuinely liked people and he liked to talk to them."[7] He began looking ahead to the next political office and believed he would enjoy being governor. Tom Pendergast, however, saw a different future for him.

SENATOR

After conferring with Tom's older bother Jim Pendergast, who offered Truman the chance to run for US senator, Harry pondered his abilities. He decided he could handle the job. "If the Almighty God decides that I get there, I am going to pray, as King Solomon did, for wisdom to do the job."[8] The summer of 1934 was the hottest on record with temperatures over 100 degrees for three weeks in July. Still Truman crisscrossed the state and gave speeches in cities and small towns. In the August primary, the St. Louis candidate John Cochran won his city; Truman won Jackson County; and the rural voters cast their ballot for the man who had braved the heat and the dusty roads to see them. Truman won their votes and was now a US senator. Fellow senator Hamilton Lewis of Illinois told him, "Harry, don't you go to the Senate with an inferiority complex. You'll sit there about six months, and wonder how you got there. But after that you'll wonder how the rest of them got there."[9]

Truman's main concern when he reached Washington was fighting the nickname bestowed on him: "the senator from Pendergast." He was slow to make friends in the Senate, but one colleague, Burton Wheeler, senior senator from Montana, was a rarity and befriended Truman. That gesture was remembered, and later when Truman was president, he explained that although he and Wheeler were often opposite in their views, "You must understand that sixteen years ago Burt Wheeler was one of the few Senators in the Senate who was in any way decent to the junior Senator from Missouri and I can't forget that. . . . I shall continue to like him as long as I live."[10]

Truman usually voted for whatever bills the administration deigned appropriate and twice came flying back to Washington to cast his vote for those in a close race. He believed, however, that the president did not appreciate him and told press secretary Stephen Early, "I think the President ought to have the decency to treat me like the Senator for Missouri and not like a God-damned office boy, and you can tell him what I said. If he wants me to, I'll come down and tell him myself."[11] The next day Truman sat down with Roosevelt and enjoyed a seven-minute conversation, after which both men had a better appreciation of the other. However, two members of the cabinet, Agriculture Secretary Henry Wallace and Interior Secretary Harold Ickes, completely ignored the presence of the senator from Missouri. They would later regret their inattention.

NATIONAL EVENTS

NOV 15: Truman supports the UN Atomic Energy Commission (AEC) to foster peacetime development of atomic technology

NOV 16: US invites 88 German scientists to assist in the production of rocket technology, inciting controversy

DEC 4: US Senate approves the entry of the United States into the United Nations

DEC 21: President Truman appoints Eleanor Roosevelt as a US representative to the UN

JAN 19: 750,000 steelworkers leave their jobs and strike

1946

WORLD EVENTS

SEP 8: Soviet troops move into northern Korea while American forces move into southern Korea

SEP 20: Gandhi orders British to withdraw from India

OCT 11: Beginning of Chinese Civil War (Chiang Kai-shek vs. Mao Tse-Tung)

OCT 18: Nuremberg war trials begin

OCT 24: United Nations chartered

JAN 7: Division of Austria into four occupation zones

Within the Senate, Truman continued his interest in transportation and served on that committee, helping to create the Civil Aeronautics Act of 1938, which governed aviation for the next forty years. The Wheeler-Truman Transportation Act of 1940 reorganized railroads and governed them.

Throughout Truman's term, the Pendergast machine was under fire in Missouri, partly for voter fraud, and partly because of the ongoing campaign against it by Governor Lloyd Stark. The governor turned his sights on Truman's senate seat, confident that he could win the 1940 election now that Pendergast had been locked away at the federal penitentiary at Leavenworth for income tax evasion.

During his campaigning, Truman made clear his intention to grant rights to the nation's black citizens. In the heart of the Bible belt, Truman addressed his all-white crowd at the Missouri State Fair in Sedalia: "In giving Negroes the rights which are theirs we are only acting in accord with our own ideals of true democracy."[12] Twenty years earlier his views had been more in line with his audience, but experiences in war, business, and politics had altered his perception of the world. As president, he would work diligently to put his views into practice.

As an incumbent senator scrambling to keep his seat, Truman perceived that he would have to win on his own—no party machine, no president to lend support. Roosevelt sent word to Truman that if he dropped his candidacy, he would be appointed to the Interstate Commerce Commission for a higher salary than he currently made. The senator responded, "Tell them to go to Hell because I've made up my mind that I'm going to run for the Senate."[13] He busily cobbled together his own campaign organization composed of men from around the state. Truman called upon a National Guard buddy, Harry H. Vaughan, to come to Missouri and head his finance committee, where contributions trickled in, while his opponent, Governor Lloyd Stark, enjoyed plentiful funds and endorsements.

Truman stumped the state in between his working in Washington and serving in the National Guard as a colonel. His speeches discussed the war in Europe, the ongoing plight of farmers, and the need for young men to enlist in the military. Helping in the campaign was senior senator Bennett Clark, who had also tangled with Roosevelt and did not mind aiding the man bucking the administration. Ultimately Truman defeated Stark for the Democratic nomination by seven thousand votes. Truman had believed he would lose and confided his fear to friends. It was late in the day after the election before it was confirmed that he had won the Democratic primary, and he duplicated the victory in November with a margin of forty-four thousand votes over Republican opponent Manvel Davis.

SECOND-TERM SENATOR

Missourians had written to Truman telling of what they thought were misappropriations of funds at Camp Leonard Wood in central Missouri. He decided to take a look and went on his own fact-finding mission, driving from Washington to Florida then northward again to Michigan. He toured facilities and took notes; at every stop he found more evidence of slipshod management and extravagant price markups and cost overruns. Contractors were taking advantage of their defense contracts on the backs of the American taxpayer, and Senator Truman was ready to avenge the wrong.

First he told Roosevelt, who warmly greeted him, but did not take any particular interest

DID YOU KNOW?

Truman met his future wife in Sunday school when they were children.

MAR 5: At a speech in Fulton, Missouri, Winston Churchill proclaims the world is divided by an "iron curtain"

MAY 17: US government seizes railroads, fearful that impending strike will shut them down

JUN 3: US Supreme Court rules that Jim Crow laws allowing segregation on interstate buses are unconstitutional

JULY 25: First underwater test of atomic bomb near Bikini Atoll in Pacific Ocean

NOV 6: Off-year elections result in Republican majorities in both Senate and House

JAN 10: United Nations General Assembly meets for the first time in England

JAN 11: Albania becomes a "People's Republic"

JAN 17: First meeting of UN Security Council

JAN 31: Yugoslavia uses Soviet Union as a model for its government

FEB 1: Trygve Lie of Norway becomes UN's first secretary-general

FEB 2: Hungary becomes a republic

FEB 24: Juan Peron elected president of Argentina

in the senator's news. Truman consulted his colleagues and worked tirelessly on his speech, which he delivered to the Senate on February 10, 1941. In March, the Senate Special Committee to Investigate the National Defense Program was created with Truman as its chairman and a membership of seven, including five Democrats. They heard testimony from the US Army and its contractors; they traveled to factories and posts acquiring information but not hunting for something wrong. Truman wanted it understood that he did not conduct fishing expeditions. Through its investigations, his committee was said to have saved the nation considerable money—hundreds of millions of dollars. It also gave its chairman free publicity, although the president was not always pleased by its results, especially when the senator admitted that a great deal of fault for the waste lay with the administration and its Office of Production Management, which would have been more aptly named "Mismanagement." Roosevelt agreed to its disbandment and replaced it with the War Production Board, which kicked into service just after Pearl Harbor was bombed on December 7, 1941.

Although some wanted Truman's committee ended now that the country was at war, Roosevelt insisted that its work should continue. Their information frequently came from employees who knew of wrongful practices, including inferior metal being used to build ships and causing one to fall apart off the Oregon coast. Defective aircraft engines were investigated, as were the wings of B-26 bombers. Truman was proud of his committee work and told Bess they were aiding in the war effort and increasing efficiency: "That means fewer of our young men killed and a chance for a more honorable settlement."[14]

By early 1944, Truman's outstanding effort had placed him on the short list for possible vice presidential candidates. Current vice president Henry Wallace had become a political liability, forcing Democrat power brokers to tell Roosevelt he needed to find another man. Each potential candidate had problems with their background, religious affiliation, etc., except the man from Independence. Political boss Ed Flynn saw Truman as the answer to their dilemma because of his fine record in the Senate, good relations with labor, plus, "He came from a border state, and he had never made any 'racial' remarks. He just dropped into the slot."[15] Roosevelt remained somewhat unconvinced and still preferred his old friend and experienced politician Jimmy Byrnes. Truman himself figured Byrnes would be nominated; in fact, Byrnes asked him to make the nominating speech in Chicago, to which Truman happily agreed. The Missourian felt his future lay in the Senate and planned to run for reelection in 1946.

The Democratic convention promised suspense, as no one was certain who would be the next vice president. Roosevelt kept dropping different names, and politicians worked busily to further certain ones. Truman continued a top contender, but he insisted, "I'm satisfied with where I am."[16] He told those around him that he feared becoming president and had absolutely no interest in that job. Widely understood but not openly discussed was a keen concern many party leaders felt in 1944 about the president's rapidly declining health, and they believed that the man who was nominated must be one who could lead the country when the time came. More backroom politics ensued before the night of July 18, when Truman was finally informed that President Roosevelt had indeed chosen him as his running mate.

NATIONAL EVENTS

DEC 5: President Truman forms Civil Rights Commission to investigate possible intimidation/violence against southern blacks preventing them from voting

DEC 14: President Truman lifts price controls causing inflation to rise

DEC 31: President Truman officially announces end of World War II

END OF YEAR: Movies resume full production: Jimmy Stewart stars in *It's a Wonderful Life*; first pairing

WORLD EVENTS

MAR 2: Ho Chi Minh elected leader of North Vietnam

APR 1: Singapore becomes British Crown Colony

APR 7: Syria officially is independent of France

APR 18: Final meeting of League of Nations then it disbands; UN will now fulfill its mission

APR 29: War crimes trial in Japan

MAY 10: Nehru becomes leader of India

MAY 22: Transjordan founded (later renamed Jordan)

Truman accepted the nomination, and newspapers broke the news of "the Missouri Compromise" to the nation. Many remarked about the power of the political bosses who made him the candidate, a foreshadowing of the Republican campaign to remind all of his Pendergast connection. Others expressed concern about his lack of experience, but usually also admitted that he was an effective senator and a decent, honest man.

Within a month, Truman was dining with Roosevelt on the White House lawn, providing photographers with an opportunity to catch the two candidates in pleasant but meaningful discussion. A worried Truman returned to his office and confided to his military aide his concern about Roosevelt's health. The same sentiment was expressed by another friend the following month, who told Truman he would soon be living in the White House. "I'm afraid you're right, Eddie," he replied, "and it scares the hell out of me."[17]

Although Roosevelt did make a few appearances and speeches against Republican Tom Dewey, Truman shouldered the bulk of the campaigning throughout the country. Sometimes he addressed crowds of thousands; on other occasions, only a handful of people, but he still gave a speech. People liked his down-to-earth attitude and demeanor. Republicans tried to stir up the Pendergast association and denounce him as a failed businessman and hinted he might be part Jewish. He shrugged off most of the lies, but when they attacked Bess for being on his payroll, Truman was unforgiving to her critics. The stories, however, did little to stop Americans from voting for their beloved president a record fourth time.

On January 20, 1945, the inauguration of Franklin D. Roosevelt occurred at the White House and was over in a matter of minutes. Vice President Harry S. Truman of Missouri was now only a heartbeat away from the nation's highest office.

POSTWAR UNITED STATES ★ The GI Bill passed in 1944 and greatly helped returning veterans go to college and buy homes. The postwar baby boom created a great need for housing, and places like Levittown, New York, sprang up with look-alike houses. Pent-up demand for consumer goods now could be unleashed, and so people bought cars, appliances, televisions, clothing, and food—and inflation rose. Another major problem for the postwar economy was finding jobs for the more than 20 million who were returning from serving in the war or working in defense plants. Conflicts arose between ethnic/racial groups for jobs, and some women resented having to give up working outside of the home. Soon the sales-at-home industry blossomed, so housewives could remain homebound but earn extra spending cash at the same time.

VICE PRESIDENT

Following the inauguration, Truman did not see the president for several weeks, nor was he informed about the secret meeting of Roosevelt, Churchill, and Stalin taking place at Yalta to discuss the postwar world. For the first time, a Secret Service agent was assigned to the vice president. Truman seemed to simply mark time in his new job and wrote to his family in Missouri about his duties:

"I go over to the Capitol gold-plated office and see Senators and curiosity seekers for an hour and then the Senate meets and it's my job to get 'em prayed for—and goodness knows they need it, and then get the business going by staying in the chair

of Humphrey Bogart and Lauren Bacall, in *The Big Sleep*; and a postwar drama, *The Best Years of Our Lives*

JUN 10: Italy becomes a republic; king goes into exile

JUL 4: Philippines granted full independence

AUG 19: Violence in Calcutta between Hindus and Muslims ends in deaths of more than 3,000

OCT 2: Communists take power in Bulgaria

NOV 15: Netherlands grants Indonesia its independence

DEC 5: UN decides New York City will be its permanent home

DEC 11: UNICEF founded

Margaret Wise Brown writes children's classic *Goodnight Moon*

1947

The Dead Sea Scrolls are discovered in a cave in the West Bank

DID YOU KNOW?

Truman once boarded in Kansas City with Arthur Eisenhower, Dwight's older brother.

for an hour and then see more Senators and curiosity people who want to see what a V.P. looks like and if he walks and talks and has teeth."[18]

He also made news early in his vice presidency. In late January, Truman learned of Tom Pendergast's death, so he decided to fly home and attend the funeral. Reporters snapped his photograph, so newspapers could show the vice president "disgracing his office" by being there. Then photographers had a field day two weeks later capturing Truman playing the piano with the lovely actress Lauren Bacall splayed across it. Both were entertaining servicemen at the Washington Press Club's canteen; however, Bess was not amused.

The occasion was definitely more solemn on March 1 when President Roosevelt reported on his mission to Yalta to a joint session of Congress. Again, Truman and others watched their frail leader quiver when he reached to drink from his glass or lost his place in the speech. No one then was surprised by the announcement that Roosevelt would soon be headed to recuperate at Warm Springs, Georgia. The two top executives met twice before Roosevelt's trip, but the president did not take Truman into his confidence regarding the war or any of its developments.

On April 12, Truman observed his normal schedule. He dictated letters in the morning, and then presided over the Senate for the remainder of the day except for an hour to meet with a constituent. At five o'clock he left to visit Speaker Sam Rayburn and cronies, where he was told to call Steve Early at the White House. When Truman returned the call, Early told him to "quickly and quietly" come over. Hanging up the phone, Truman muttered, "Jesus Christ and General Jackson," and then ran through the capitol and jumped into his car. He arrived at the White House at 5:25 p.m. where Mrs. Roosevelt greeted him with the news he had dreaded since his nomination—Franklin Roosevelt was dead. Concerned about the widow, Truman asked if he could do anything for her. Eleanor Roosevelt looked at him and replied, "Is there anything we can do for you. For you are the one in trouble now."[19] Harry Truman had been vice president for exactly eighty-two days.

Within twenty minutes of his hearing the news, it was released to the rest of the world. Meanwhile, preparations were made for his swearing in, which took place a little after seven o'clock in the cabinet room, with its members watching and Bess and Margaret next to him. Afterward he met with the cabinet and decided to go forward with the San Francisco Conference scheduled to meet in twelve days, whose purpose would be to charter the United Nations. Secretary of War Henry Stimson mentioned they would need to meet about an urgent matter involving a new weapon. Afterward, Truman returned to their five-room apartment on Connecticut Avenue while Bess and Margaret stayed with neighbors.

PRESIDENT TRUMAN

Wrapping up the war in Europe and winning the war in Japan were the most pressing issues before the new president. Immediately Truman worked to catch up in his learning curve so he could discuss matters intelligently at Potsdam, Germany, with British prime minister Winston Churchill (who was replaced by Clement Atlee during the conference when he lost his reelection bid) and Soviet premier Josef Stalin via cables. The three leaders met in person in July and August of 1945 in Potsdam, and there they reached agreement on how to administer defeated Germany, on operations against Japan, and the postwar world order. Here

NATIONAL EVENTS	Tupperware introduced First microwave oven goes on sale	**JAN 3:** First televised session of Congress **FEB 21:** Introduction of Polaroid camera	**APR 15:** Jackie Robinson becomes first African American to play professional baseball when he joins Brooklyn Dodgers	**MAY 22:** President Truman signs the Truman Doctrine into force sending aid to Turkey and Greece	**JUN 5:** Secretary of State George Marshall introduces the Marshall Plan to rebuild Europe
WORLD EVENTS	**JAN 31:** Communist Party takes power in Poland	**FEB 17:** Voice of America begins broadcasting into Soviet Union	**MAR 1:** International Monetary Fund begins operations	**JUL 18:** British troops capture the *Exodus* carrying 4,500 Jewish Holocaust survivor refugees, barring them from Palestine	**AUG 14:** Pakistan becomes independent from British Empire and India

Truman was informed of the successful test in the New Mexico desert of the newly developed atomic bomb. He told Stalin of it, and as he later wrote, "I casually mentioned to Stalin that we had a new weapon of unusual destructive force. The Russian Premier showed no special interest. All he said was that he was glad to hear it and hoped that we would make 'good use of it against the Japanese.'"[20]

Contrary to popular belief, Truman did know about the atomic bomb's development long before he became president. As chairman of the Senate Special Committee to Investigate the National Defense Program, he had been privy to secret intelligence. At one point in 1943, he had become too inquisitive about the Manhattan Project owing to its high price tag and had called Secretary of War Henry Stimson, who refused to give a comprehensive explanation. Truman received enough information from other sources, however, to know what only a handful of men knew. In a July 1943 exchange of letters with his future labor secretary, Lewis Schwellenbach, who was growing suspicious of mysterious government land acquisitions, Truman told him not to worry and said as much as he could without using the word "atomic" or divulging the name of the top secret Manhattan Project. The "tremendous land deal," said Truman, was "for the construction of a plant to make a tremendous explosi[ve] for a secret weapon that will be a wonder."[21]

Before the successful atomic bomb test, there were serious questions as to whether the bomb would work and what the cost might be if Japan were invaded. Plans had been honed and were being implemented for Operation Downfall, the massive series of invasions stretching into 1946. Truman had earlier requested former president Herbert Hoover to draft a report about the possible consequences for US casualties for an invasion. Hoover believed between 500,000 and one million Americans would die as a result of invading the islands of Japan. Truman's subsequent meeting with his senior advisors at a June 18 White House meeting confirmed that casualties would be huge, but that an invasion was essential for the defeat of Imperial Japan. At the meeting, Stimson said he "agreed with the plan proposed by the Joint Chiefs of Staff as being the best thing to do, but he still hoped for some fruitful accomplishment through other means." Those other means ranged from increased political pressure brought to bear through a display of Allied unanimity at the imminent Potsdam Conference to the as-yet-untested atomic weapons that might

FOUNDING OF THE UNITED NATIONS

(1945) ★ One of Truman's first actions as president was to insist that the United Nations Conference on International Organization in San Francisco proceed as scheduled. Its purpose was to charter a new international organization that would prevent any world wars in the future. The United States proposed to take a leading role, rather than isolate itself as it had done by refusing to join the League of Nations. President Truman attended the final session of the conference in June 1945, and then urged the Senate to approve the charter without delay; they overwhelmingly voted in favor of joining the United Nations in July 1945. As the Cold War unfolded, the UN often found itself cast between the two superpowers in various parts of the globe. Many of its early issues were shared with Truman while he was president, including the creation of Israel and the Korean War.

JUN 23: Congress passes Taft-Hartley Act over Truman's veto; new law restricts labor's right to strike

JUL: Containment policy explained by George Kennan in *Foreign Affairs*

JUL 18: President Truman signs Presidential Succession Act into law

JUL 26: National Security Act creates CIA and Department of Defense

SEP 18: Creation of US Air Force

DEC 27: *Howdy Doody* begins its television run

AUG 15: India gains its independence from Great Britain

AUG 31: Communists take control of Hungary

OCT 30: The General Agreement on Tariffs and Trade (GATT), a precursor to the World Trade Organization (WTO), is founded

NOV 20: Wedding of Princess Elizabeth and Prince Philip, the Duke of Edinburgh

NOV 29: UN decides to partition Palestine into areas for Jews and Arabs

"shock" the Japanese into surrender. As for Truman, he responded that he "was clear on the situation now and was quite sure that the Joint Chiefs of Staff should proceed" but expressed hope "that there was a possibility of preventing an Okinawa from one end of Japan to the other."[22]

On July 26, 1945, the Potsdam Declaration was issued; this was an ultimatum to Japan to surrender or face "prompt and utter destruction."[23] When no response was forthcoming, Truman authorized the use of the atomic bomb, and it was dropped on Hiroshima on August 6, 1945. When Japan continued its silence to pleas for surrender, the second bomb was dropped on Nagasaki three days later. The following day, Japan announced it would surrender, and that ceremony took place on the USS *Missouri* in Tokyo Bay on September 2 with General Douglas MacArthur presiding.

> ***You members of this Congress are to be the architects of the better world. In your hands rests our future. By your labors at this conference, we shall know if suffering humanity is to achieve a just and lasting peace.***
>
> *—Harry Truman, April 25, 1945*

Although the war was over, its fallout would continue to form the primary backdrop for the remainder of Truman's first term. Hoping to prevent any future world wars, Truman gladly supported the chartering of the United Nations and worked to ensure that, unlike the fate of the League of Nations, this charter was ratified by Congress. With the UN's establishment in 1946, Truman would utilize it through his administration. Through it, the president pushed for the creation of the State of Israel and an Arab state from the British mandate of Palestine. Once Israel came into existence on May 14, 1948, the United States became the first country to recognize the Jewish state, but not all championed its formation, and Israel's territory was immediately invaded by its Arab neighbors, which incorporated into their own territory all portions of the mandate not held by the Israelis at the time of the cease-fire.

Change was also occurring in Eastern Europe as the Soviet Union's influence encompassed many previously independent nations. In 1947, Winston Churchill made a speech at William Woods College in Fulton, Missouri, where he proclaimed "an iron curtain had descended across the Continent" because the Soviet Union wanted "the indefinite expansion of their power and doctrine."[24] Concerned that more might fall victim to the USSR, Truman decided to take action and introduced to Congress a $400 million aid package to help Greece fight a Communist insurgency and for Turkey to resist the direct threat of the Soviets; this plan became known as the Truman Doctrine. Later, Clark Clifford, special counsel to the president, would say that the 1947–1948 era was "one of the proudest moments in American history. What happened during that period was that Harry Truman and the United States saved the free world."[25]

In 1948, American aid poured into Europe and continued for the next four years in what was called the Marshall Plan, named for Secretary of State

NATIONAL EVENTS

- Abstract expressionism created by Jackson Pollock
- Cadillac cars introduce tail fins
- **JAN:** "Kinsey Report" by Alfred Kinsey is first major study on sexuality
- **JAN 19:** Presidential salary increased from $75,000 to $100,000
- **APR 3:** President Truman authorizes the Marshall Plan
- **JUN 2:** *Ed Sullivan Show* premieres
- **JUL 26:** President Truman issues Executive Order ending segregation in the armed forces

1948

WORLD EVENTS

- **JAN 30:** Gandhi assassinated
- **FEB 25:** Communists take over Czechoslovakia
- **APR 7:** World Health Organization started by the UN
- **MAY 14:** State of Israel officially established with a proclamation of independence from its British mandate
- **MAY 15:** Beginning of Arab-Israeli War when Egypt, Saudi Arabia, Transjordan, Lebanon, Syria, and Iraq attack Israel

George Marshall. Since the end of the war, how to rebuild Europe had been a topic of considerable deliberation, and the time to act could not be delayed any longer. Truman concurred and told an audience at Baylor University, "We are the giant of the economic world. Whether we like it or not, the future pattern of economic relations depends upon us." Churchill was saying the same in London, calling Europe "a rubble-heap, a charnel house, a breeding ground of pestilence and hate."[26] Billions of American dollars would eventually be pumped into the reconstruction of the devastated continent, to the dismay of Stalin, who waited to pick up the pieces of a European collapse, and also insisted that America was simply attempting to buy its way into the hearts of Europeans; consequently, he refused to allow any of his Soviet satellites to accept money from the Marshall Plan.

The summer of 1948 was one of political conventions; the Republicans met in June and picked Governor Thomas Dewey as their presidential candidate. On the same day they selected him, the Soviet Union blockaded the former German capital of Berlin, which was located deep within the Soviets' occupation zone in the defeated country and jointly administered by American, French, British, and Soviet forces. Within days, a full-scale airlift had been implemented to ensure that not all of Berlin would be swallowed up by the Soviets.

Meanwhile at home, Truman faced opposition as he prepared for the Democratic convention. Many southern Democrats vehemently opposed his candidacy because of his recent proposal that strongly pushed for Congress to implement civil rights legislation, particularly outlawing lynching and the poll tax, and ending segregation in the armed forces. At the convention, all of the Mississippi and half of the Alabama delegations walked out, and their defection became the basis for the States' Rights Party or Dixiecrats, who nominated Strom Thurmond as their presidential candidate; meanwhile, Progressives nominated Henry Wallace, and he was endorsed by the Communist Party. Other Democrats were hopeful that recent Allied commander General Dwight D. Eisenhower could be enlisted to run; many were unenthusiastic about campaigning for Harry Truman. But Eisenhower declined, and Truman won the nomination, giving a fighting acceptance speech at 2 a.m. In his speech, the president announced he was calling Congress into special session to handle parts of his agenda that he had dubbed the "fair deal."

Congress met but made little progress on his plans for improved housing, increasing the minimum wage from forty to seventy-five cents an hour, extending Social Security coverage, and imple-

VISIT TO MEXICO (March 1947) ★ Truman became the first American president to make a state visit to Mexico, and received a warm reception, but his gesture the day after his arrival made him a hero among the Mexican people. Although not on his itinerary, Truman decided to visit Chapultepec Castle, the site of fighting during the Mexican War, where Americans led by George Pickett stormed the heights, and where legend says six Mexican military cadets committed suicide rather than surrender to the Americans. Truman laid a wreath at the memorial for Los Niños Héroes and bowed his head in respect to their sacrifice. Word rapidly spread through the city and newspaper headlines proclaimed the beginning of a new era of friendship between the two neighbors, started by the simple act of an American president.

JUN 24: Berlin Blockade begins

AUG 15: Republic of Korea proclaimed with Seoul as its capital and Syngman Rhee its president

NOV 2: Truman defeats Dewey in the presidential election that pollsters had predicted Dewey would easily win

DEC 1: Scrabble introduced

DEC 10: UN issues Universal Declaration of Rights

1949

JAN 4–FEB 22: Major winter snowstorms blanket the Great Plains

JAN: Chiang Kai-shek and his Nationalist followers begin evacuating to Taiwan

JAN 5: President Truman announces his Fair Deal program

JAN 23: Communist troops move into Peking

APR 4: Formation of North Atlantic Treaty Organization (NATO)

BERLIN AIRLIFT (June 26, 1948–May 12, 1949) ★ At the end of World War II, the Allies split Germany into four occupation zones—Soviet, American, British, and French. Berlin was deep in the Soviet zone but split between East (Soviet) and West (the other three Allies). Dismayed by the presence of the Allies in the Russian sector, the Soviets decided to take action to push out their unwelcome visitors. So on June 22, 1948, Soviets stopped all ground traffic to Berlin and figured that without necessities, West Berlin would soon succumb and join the rest of Communist East Germany. The Allies, however, were not willing to passively accept this act of aggression. On June 26, 1948, the first plane flew into West Berlin, starting an Allied airlift, which lasted the next 11 months and included more than 270,000 missions. Truman approved this action as essential to proving not only to Germany and the Soviet Union, but the rest of the world, that the Communist threat would not be ignored.

menting national health insurance. Not surprised by the lack of support by the Republican Congress for his program, he now felt emboldened to use their inaction as the main issue for his campaign. The president crisscrossed the country, covering thirty thousand miles by train in what was dubbed the "whistle-stop campaign," castigating the "Do Nothing Eightieth Congress." Often the crowd would yell, "Give 'em hell, Harry!" and Truman flashed back a smile.

Labor favored the president since he had vetoed the Taft-Hartley Act (although Congress overrode the veto) and its anti-labor stance. Blacks and farmers also supported Truman and his vice presidential candidate Alben Barkley, but pollsters and pundits agreed—Thomas Dewey would certainly become the next president. Presidential aide George Elsey recounted that on board the presidential train, the *Ferdinand Magellan*, Truman had Elsey write the electoral votes for the candidates as the president recited the numbers of each state by memory. Once that was done, Elsey calculated Truman and Dewey's numbers and found Truman the winner.

On election night, the *Chicago Tribune* printed the banner headline, "Dewey Defeats Truman," believing that to be the inevitable result of the day's voting. The next morning Truman's smile was nearly as wide as the headline as he held it up to reporters, joyous in the news that he was, in fact, the winner. He carried 49 percent of the popular vote to Dewey's 45 percent, but in the electoral college Truman's lead was 303 votes to 189 for Dewey.

SECOND TERM

For his inaugural speech, the president addressed the evils of communism and referred to it as a "false philosophy which purports to offer freedom, security, and greater opportunity to mankind. Misled by this philosophy, many peoples have sacrificed their liberties only to learn to their sorrow that deceit and mockery, poverty and tyranny, are their reward." The expansion of communism would be the key issue of Truman's second term, and fear of its spread within the United States created near hysteria within the nation, culminating in the rise and fall of Senator Joseph McCarthy.

The long civil war in China ended in a Communist victory shortly after Truman began his second term, and "Who lost China?" immediately became a rallying cry for McCarthy and other administration critics (as if the mammoth nation

NATIONAL EVENTS

JAN 11: First snowfall on record in Los Angeles

JAN 20: Inauguration of President Truman

JAN 31: President Truman orders the development of a hydrogen bomb

1950

WORLD EVENTS

MAY 25: Shanghai falls to Communist forces

JUN 2: Transjordan changes its name to Jordan

JUN 29: Apartheid laws begun in South Africa

AUG 29: First atomic bomb detonated by Soviet Union

SEP 7: Federal Republic of Germany founded

OCT 1: People's Republic of China proclaimed by Mao Tse-tung

OCT 16: Greek Civil War ends

C.S. Lewis publishes the first of the *Chronicles of Narnia—The Lion, the Witch, and the Wardrobe*

had been America's to lose). However, the establishment of the North Atlantic Treaty Organization (NATO) in April 1949, was generally greeted with great relief since it created a military alliance that both enhanced America's security and acted as an effective bulwark against further Soviet expansion in western Europe, which was only just beginning to feel the effects of the Marshall Plan. This was followed only a few months later by the detonation of a Soviet atomic bomb, an event that only fueled increased tensions and enraged those who claimed—with some justification, as was later proven—that US atomic secrets must have been spirited away to the Soviets for them to have developed the weapon long before it was thought possible to do so.

The McCarran Internal Security Act of 1950 was vetoed by Truman, but the veto was overridden by the Republican Congress because they wanted tougher restrictions against Communists. The following year saw the trial and conviction of Julius and Ethel Rosenberg for espionage involving passing on secrets involving the atomic bomb. Senator McCarthy seized the opportunity to feed the frenzy of fear and announced he had a list of 205 suspected Communists within the State Department. More hearings resulted, which led to the ruination of careers and lives for numerous Americans.

In June 1950, Communist forces from North Korea struck south across the 38th parallel and invaded South Korea, and Truman immediately sought help from the United Nations to push back the North Koreans. Although the force was to be international, Americans and South Koreans composed most of it with American general Douglas MacArthur leading. An offensive operation was successfully launched at the port of Inchon which pushed North Korean troops back north of the parallel. President Truman flew to Wake Island in the Pacific to meet MacArthur and discuss the next phase of the war. Both men wrote of being impressed by the other. Truman recorded, "I found him a most stimulating and interesting person. Our conversation was very friendly—I might say much more so than I had expected."[27] The general recorded that Truman "radiated nothing but courtesy and good humor during our meeting. He has an engaging personality, a quick and witty tongue, and I liked him from the start."[28]

Their good relations would deteriorate with the flood of thousands of Chinese soldiers crossing the Yalu River in January 1951. Their numbers overwhelmed the coalition. MacArthur announced that the war should be carried to China, and advocated the use of the atomic bomb against them—an idea that was anathema to the president. Galled by his general's willingness to sidestep his chain of command through press statements and contacts in Congress, Truman decided to fire America's favorite general. Although he understood the firestorm of protest that such action would incur, Truman felt compelled to take it, and the criticisms poured into the White House. He received far more negative letters from this than he had on his dropping the atomic bomb. General Matthew Ridgway replaced the popular commander, but the war showed no signs of ending; in fact, it dragged on into the beginning of President Eisenhower's term.

On the home front, Truman faced myriad problems stemming from the country trying to regain its pre–World War II normalcy. With the GIs return and a record number of weddings soon following, housing shortages grew across the country; additionally, inflation skyrocketed as the wartime rationing of goods ended and the country

DID YOU KNOW?

Truman's eyesight was so poor, he memorized the eye chart for the Army entrance exam.

FEB 9: Senator Joseph McCarthy announces Communists are employed by the State Department

FEB 12: Einstein warns that nuclear war could lead to destruction of both sides

MAR 14: FBI issues first "Ten Most Wanted" list

MAY 9: L. Ron Hubbard, founder of the Church of Scientology, publishes *Dianetics: The Modern Science of Mental Health*

MAY 11: Beginning of the Kefauver Committee hearings about the current state of, and ways to fight, organized crime in the US

FEB 14: USSR and People's Republic of China sign a mutual defense pact

FEB 27: Chiang Kai-shek, now in Taiwan, elected as president of Nationalist China

MAR 8: Soviet Union claims to have atomic bomb

MAR 22: British ordered to leave Suez Canal by Egypt

APR 24: West Bank annexed by Jordan

DID YOU KNOW?

Senator Truman was named one of the ten best-dressed senators.

attempted to shift back to a peacetime economy. Men needed jobs, but there were not enough to go around. Then, no longer bound by wartime pledges against strikes, the labor unions struck, and the presidential temper exploded.

The first union to feel Truman's wrath was the United Mine Workers under the leadership of John L. Lewis. Coal was the prime energy source, so when coal workers went on strike in 1946, factory production declined significantly, as did railroad service; office buildings were dimmed, including the White House, prompting the president to state he might have to conduct business outside. With the miners on strike, the railroad workers threatened similar action, which threw the country into a panic. Truman countered with the warning that the government would take over the railroads if such action occurred. He told the two railroad labor leaders, Alvanley Johnston and Alexander Whitney, "If you think I'm going to sit here and let you tie up this country, you're crazy as hell."[29]

Ignoring the president's ultimatum, railroad workers left their jobs, and the following day, the president announced to his cabinet his plan to deal with the crisis—draft the rail workers, so then the government could order them to work. Truman delivered his message to a joint session of Congress the next day, and just as he uttered the words, "I request the Congress immediately to authorize the President to draft into the Armed Forces of the United States all workers who are on strike against the government," he was handed a message. "Word has just been received that the railroad strike has been settled, on terms proposed by the President!"[30] The railroad union leaders pledged to use their treasury to defeat Truman in '48 but by then tempers had cooled considerably. Lewis and his United Mine Workers also won a settlement that gave them most of their demands.

Steel workers in 1952 struck for wage increases, which they had not had in two years; they demanded a raise of thirty-five cents an hour. When the Wage Stabilization Board recommended a twenty-six-cent raise, the steel companies objected, arguing it would result in $12-a-ton increase in price, something which the US defense industry, struggling to meet the needs of the war in Korea and the NATO buildup in Europe, would acutely feel. With negotiations at loggerheads, and not seeing any other way to prevent the strike from beginning on April 8 (the deadline given by the United Steel Workers), Truman decided the only course of action was for the government to seize the steel mills. Once the US government acted on April 9, denunciations of Truman became the dominant theme of newspaper headlines, and talk of impeachment filled the halls of Congress. The steel companies sued, and on June 2, the US Supreme Court backed them in a 6–3 ruling, stating that the president did not have the power to seize private property to avoid strikes. "This is a job for the Nation's lawmakers, not for its military authorities,"[31] wrote Justice Hugo Black.

By now, Truman felt exhausted by the burdens of the job. Some attempted to entice him to run for the Senate, but he declined, saying Bess was against it. The Truman family was an especially close-knit one with both parents doting on daughter Margaret, and they wholeheartedly supported her launching a singing career. Two years earlier, on December 5, 1950, the president learned of the passing of his childhood friend and press secretary Charlie Ross. Although devastated by the loss, he knew he had to hide his sorrow, for Margaret was performing that night at Constitution Hall. When

NATIONAL EVENTS

SEP 30: National Security Council Report 68 enacted by Truman, sets US foreign policy during the Cold War for the next 20 years

OCT 2: First appearance of comic strip *Peanuts* by Charles Schulz

OCT 11: CBS granted first license by FCC to broadcast in color

NOV 1: Assassination attempt on President Truman's life

NOV 11: Harry Hay founds the earliest pro-homosexual organization, the Mattachine Society, in Los Angeles

WORLD EVENTS

APR 27: Formal segregation takes effect in South Africa

JUN 25: Korean War breaks out

JUN 27: North Korean troops capture Seoul

JUL 8: Douglas MacArthur named commander in chief of UN forces in Korea

SEP 15: Allied troops land at Inchon

the president opened the *Washington Post* the next morning and read the review by its music critic Paul Hume, his blood pressure skyrocketed. "Miss Truman cannot sing very well," Hume wrote. "She is flat a good deal of the time. . . . She cannot sing with anything approaching professional finish." With the crushing loss of Ross and now this scathing review, Margaret's father put pen to paper and wrote to Hume. He referred to Hume's column as a "lousy review," and after criticizing his writing, ended with this threat: "Some day I hope to meet you. When that happens you'll need a new nose, a lot of beefsteak for black eyes, and perhaps a supporter below!"[32] Once he finished, he kept it from his staff, affixed a three-cent stamp, and mailed it himself. Hume gleefully published its contents, and again the criticism poured in, although some voiced their support of a proud parent.

A week after his reelection, the president was informed that his home had been declared unsafe. Fortunately, Congress quickly agreed to appropriate the necessary funds, and plans were implemented to rebuild the White House. The presidential family moved to the nearby Blair House as the executive mansion was disassembled piece by piece. Concrete was added, as well as 660 tons of steel reinforcement to ensure a strong future. The remodeling took three-and-a-half years, and was completed in March 1952.

While the family lived in Blair House, tragedy nearly struck Truman on November 1, 1950, when two Puerto Rican men decided to slay the American president, believing he was preventing their island from gaining its independence. Oscar Collazo and Girsel Torresola arrived at Blair House armed and ready to shoot; they opened fire on two policemen on duty, seriously wounding one and killing the other, although both officers had mortally wounded the would-be assassins. The Trumans were in Blair House, and the president immediately went to the window when Bess yelled, "Harry, someone's shooting our policemen,"[33] but he pulled back when Secret Service agents ordered him away from the window.

Other incidents occurred during Truman's administration, including a serious threat of his being shot when he attended the Army-Navy game and made the customary crossover from the Army side to the Navy's at halftime. The Secret Service, D.C. police, FBI, and even the US Air Force (in the form of two F-51 fighters) took extra precautions, and all went well on game day.

With 1952 came talk of the November election, and Truman restated his desire to retire, but he wanted to select the Democratic candidate. Since Eisenhower announced his intention to run as a Republican, the president knew he had to find a viable opponent. Illinois governor Adlai Stevenson was advanced by some in his circle, and although initially cool to the idea, Stevenson did accept the party's nomination and ran unsuccessfully against Eisenhower.

On January 20, 1953, the Truman family said goodbye to the recently refurbished White House. The president was irritated by his successor's refusal to come inside and escort him out; Eisenhower insisted it was to keep the attention focused on Truman. The family said its goodbyes and left once more on the presidential train, heading west toward Independence and home.

RETIREMENT

Once they were back at 219 North Delaware, Truman busied himself with his presidential papers in preparation for writing his memoirs and looked forward to developing a presidential library. Thanks to

DID YOU KNOW?

George Washington, James Monroe, Andrew Jackson, James K. Polk, James Buchanan, Andrew Johnson, James A. Garfield, William McKinley, Theodore Roosevelt, William H. Taft, Warren G. Harding, Franklin D. Roosevelt, Harry S. Truman, Lyndon B. Johnson, and Gerald R. Ford were all Masons.

DEC 6: President Truman writes scathing response to music critic Paul Hume about his critical review of Margaret Truman's concert

DEC 19: Dwight D. Eisenhower named head of NATO

FEB 27: Twenty-second Amendment ratified limiting presidential term to two terms

APR 5: Julius and Ethel Rosenberg convicted of conspiracy to commit espionage, sentenced to death

APR 11: Gen. MacArthur relieved of his command in Korea by President Truman

1951

NOV 21: US troops reach Yalu River

NOV 26: Invasion of Chinese Communist forces moving into North Korea

JAN 4: Seoul taken by Communists

JAN 9: UN headquarters opens in New York City

MAR 7: UN forces attack Chinese troops

DID YOU KNOW?

Truman was the first president to have a television in the White House.

the donations of many, the Truman Library opened in 1957, and he enjoyed planning its many details, including asking Missouri artist Thomas Hart Benton to paint a mural. Over the years, Truman wrote his memoirs: *Year of Decisions* (1955); *Years of Trial and Hope* (1956); and *Mr. Citizen* (1960).

The former president also delighted in continuing his famous brisk walks around his neighborhood and visiting old friends. He and Bess traveled to England and saw the Churchills; he went to the newly opened Disneyland; and they enjoyed a road trip to Washington, D.C.

Lecturing at colleges and universities was another favorite pastime, and often the question would be asked: do you regret dropping the atomic bomb? During one of these sessions, Truman responded, "It was a question of saving hundreds of thousands of American lives. . . . I could not worry about what history would say about my personal morality. I made the only decision I ever knew how to make. I did what I thought was right."[34]

Truman continued to support the Democratic Party and its candidates. Although he opposed John F. Kennedy's nomination, he campaigned for him because he utterly abhorred his opponent, Richard Nixon. Struck by the tragedy of Kennedy's assassination, he and Bess attended the funeral with the Eisenhowers. A result of the assassination was legislation that granted Secret Service protection to former presidents, so to the Truman's dismay, a contingent arrived to protect them.

In 1964, Truman celebrated his eightieth birthday, and although he had gallbladder surgery and a near-fatal reaction to the antibiotics, his health remained in good form. A fall on icy streets resulted in some broken ribs; the injury was then repeated a few years later. He welcomed President Lyndon B. Johnson to the Truman Library in 1965. Johnson was there to pay homage to the man who had first attempted to win national health insurance, and the president had traveled to Independence so he could sign the Medicare Act with Truman at his side. Although not a fan of the next president, Truman welcomed Nixon to his home, but the visit did not last long as tension was felt by all.

The Trumans celebrated their fiftieth wedding anniversary in 1969, but seeing his feeble steps, all knew there would not be many more. He ceased his daily visits to the Truman Library. Twice in the summer of 1972 he was hospitalized—for gastrointestinal problems and injuries from another fall. Then on December 5, he was taken by ambulance to the hospital for congested lungs, which was complicated by bronchitis and hardening of the arteries. After three weeks of decline, Harry S. Truman died on December 26, 1972.

His body laid in state at the Truman Library where over seventy thousand people lined up in the freezing cold to pay their last respects. Then on December 28, he was buried in the courtyard of the library, as he had wanted. Bess continued to live in their home until her death on October 18, 1982, at the age of ninety-seven. She was buried beside her husband.

When Margaret Truman Daniels asked her father for a quote to end her biography of him, he replied with the comparison of three southern (Tennessee) presidents—Jackson, Polk, and Andrew Johnson, all of whom he said had been misunderstood, as he believed his actions often had been. But he added the lesson to be learned was, "Do your duty and history will do you justice."[35]

NATIONAL EVENTS

JUN–JUL: Worst flooding to date in central part of the nation

JUL 16: J.D. Salinger publishes *The Catcher in the Rye*

OCT 15: *I Love Lucy* premieres

1952

Mylar developed

Amy Vanderbilt's *Complete Book of Etiquette* is published

Dr. Norman Vincent Peale writes *The Power of Positive Thinking*

Milk/juice cartons begin replacing bottles

WORLD EVENTS

MAR 15: UN forces retake Seoul

SEP 1: ANZUS pact signed by US, Australia, and New Zealand

English cryptologist Michael Ventris becomes first to decipher Mycenaean language

FEB 6: British King George VI dies and is succeeded by his daughter Queen Elizabeth II

FEB 26: Prime Minister Winston Churchill announces that UK has an atomic bomb

ENDNOTES

1 Harry S. Truman, *Memoirs. Vol. I: Year of Decisions*, Garden City, New York: Doubleday, 1955, p. 121.

2 David McCullough, *Truman*, New York: Simon & Schuster, 1992, p. 68.

3 Ibid, p. 69.

4 Ibid, p. 86.

5 Jonathan Daniels, *The Man from Independence*, Columbia, Mo.: University of Missouri Press, 1998 (original copyright 1950 by J.B. Lippincott), p. 95.

6 Ibid, p. 114..

7 Ibid, p. 191.

8 Margaret Truman Daniels, *Harry S. Truman*, New York: William Morrow & Co., 1973, p. 86.

9 Robert H. Ferrell, *Truman and Pendergast*, Columbia, Mo.: University of Missouri Press, 1999, p. 34.

10 Ibid.

11 Conrad Black, *Franklin Delano Roosevelt, Champion of Freedom*, New York: Public Affairs, 2003, p. 508.

12 Jonathan Daniels, p. 339.

13 Ferrell, p. 83.

14 McCullough, p. 282.

15 Ibid, p. 297.

16 Ibid, p. 308.

17 Jonathan Daniels, p. 255.

18 Ibid, p. 335.

19 Robert H. Ferrell, *Harry S. Truman and the Modern American Presidency*, Boston: Little, Brown & Co., 1983, p. 42.

20 Harry S. Truman, p. 416.

21 D.M. Giangreco and Kathryn Moore, *Dear Harry: Letters from Truman's Mailroom, 1945-1953*, Mechanicsburg, PA: Stackpole Books, 1999, p. 280.

22 D.M. Giangreco, "Harry Truman and the Price of Victory: New Light on the President's Biggest Decision," *American Heritage*, April-May 2003, pp. 13-14.

23 Truman, p. 392.

24 McCullough, p. 489.

25 Ibid, p. 554.

26 Ibid, p. 562.

27 Truman, p. 365.

28 Douglas MacArthur, *Reminiscences*, New York: McGraw-Hill, 1964, p. 361.

29 Robert J. Donovan, *Conflict and Crisis: The Presidency of Harry S. Truman, 1945-1948*, Columbia, Mo.: University of Missouri Press, 1996, p. 211.

30 Ibid, p. 215.

31 McCullough, p. 901.

32 Ibid, p. 829.

33 Ibid, p. 488.

34 Ibid, p. 567.

35 Ibid, p. 581.

SEP 2: World's first open heart surgery performed

OCT 24: President Truman establishes National Security Agency (NSA)

NOV 1: US tests world's first hydrogen bomb

NOV 4: Dwight D. Eisenhower wins presidential election and defeats Democratic challenger Adlai Stevenson

NOV 29: President-elect Eisenhower flies to Korea to see what can be done to end the conflict

JUN 15: First publication of *The Diary of Anne Frank*

JUN 30: End of Marshall aid to Europe

JUL 25: Puerto Rico becomes self-governing commonwealth

NOV 25: Agatha Christie's play *The Mousetrap* begins its run in London; it will be the longest-running play (55+ years) in history

Dwight D. Eisenhower

★ ★ ★ THIRTY-FOURTH PRESIDENT ★ ★ ★

LIFE SPAN

- Born: October 14, 1890, in Dennison, Texas
- Died: March 28, 1969, in Washington, D.C.

NICKNAME

- Ike

RELIGION

- Presbyterian

HIGHER EDUCATION

- US Military Academy at West Point, 1915

PROFESSION

- Soldier

FAMILY

- Father: **David Jacob Eisenhower** (1863–1942)
- Mother: **Ida Elizabeth Stover Eisenhower** (1862–1946)
- Wife: **Marie "Mamie" Geneva Doud Eisenhower** (1896–1979); wed on July 1, 1916, in Denver, Colorado
- Children: **Doud Dwight** (1917–1921); **John Sheldon Doud** (1922–)

MILITARY SERVICE

- Commissioned second lieutenant in 1915; promoted to first lieutenant in 1916, then captain in 1917; remained in US during World War I. After WWI, promoted to major in 1920; became lieutenant colonel in 1936 and then colonel in 1941
- World War II: promoted to major general and then made commander of all US forces in Europe with promotion to lieutenant general. In February 1943, promoted to general and in December 1943, President **Franklin D. Roosevelt** selected Eisenhower as the Supreme Allied Commander to plan the invasion of Europe (Operation Overlord). After success of D-Day, he won promotion to five-star general in December 1944. He accepted Germany's surrender in May 1945 and then resigned from the army in February 1948

POLITICAL LIFE

- Supreme Commander of the North Atlantic Treaty Organization (NATO) (1951–1952)

PRESIDENCY

- Two terms: January 20, 1953–January 20, 1961
- Republican
- Reason for leaving office: completion of term
- Vice president: **Richard M. Nixon** (1953–1961)

ELECTION OF 1952

- Electoral vote: **Eisenhower** 442; **Adlai Stevenson** 89
- Popular vote: **Eisenhower** 33,778,963; **Stevenson** 27,314,992

ELECTION OF 1956

- Electoral vote: **Eisenhower** 457; **Stevenson** 73
- Popular vote: **Eisenhower** 35,581,003; **Stevenson** 25,738,765

CABINET

SECRETARY OF STATE
John Foster Dulles (1953–1959)
Christian A. Herter (1959–1961)

SECRETARY OF THE TREASURY
George M. Humphrey (1953–1957)
Robert B. Anderson (1957–1961)

SECRETARY OF DEFENSE
Charles E. Wilson (1953–1957)
Neil H. McElroy (1957–1959)
Thomas S. Gates Jr. (1959–1961)

ATTORNEY GENERAL
Herbert Brownell Jr. (1953–1957)
William P. Rogers (1957–1961)

POSTMASTER GENERAL
Arthur E. Summerfield (1953–1961)

SECRETARY OF THE INTERIOR
Douglas McKay (1953–1956)
Frederick A. Seaton (1956–1961)

SECRETARY OF AGRICULTURE
Ezra Taft Benson (1953–1961)

Though Dwight D. Eisenhower lacked a political background prior to being elected president, his service as the Supreme Allied Commander in Europe, where he worked with a broad coalition of forces and personalities, allowed him the opportunity to hone his negotiation and diplomatic skills—all vital for the nation's chief executive.

EARLY LIFE

Dwight David Eisenhower was born on October 14, 1890, to David and Ida Stover Eisenhower in Dennison, Texas. Dwight was the third of six sons, all of whom matured into extremely successful men, including a future president of Johns Hopkins University. The family moved with baby Dwight to Abilene, Kansas, where David Eisenhower worked for a local creamery and later as a manager for a gas company. His son later described his father as the "breadwinner, Supreme Court, and Lord High Executioner,"[1] and admitted the last was necessary in riding herd over his brood of six boys. Ida Eisenhower organized the boys into an efficient unit, with each assigned specific chores that were rotated weekly, allowing all six to gain proficiency in the running of the household and farm.

Dwight, or "Ike" as he was nicknamed, attended Abilene schools and liked spelling and arithmetic, but earned mediocre marks in other subjects. Recess was his favorite part of the school day for it allowed the boy to let off some steam and play hard. He and his brothers were known for being tough scrappers in fights and they were also referred to as being "from the wrong side of the tracks." In high school, Ike played football and baseball, and he even organized an athletic association. One of his schoolmates later remembered him as "a natural leader. But Ike was no miracle child; he was just a strong, healthy boy with a serious mind."[2] On his own, he read history and biographies voraciously; his two favorites were Hannibal and George Washington—he especially devoured tales of their battles and campaigns and details about their military strategies. His mother was a pacifist and rather displeased by her son's militaristic interests. She was known to lock his books in a cabinet when she felt he was spending too much time buried in them.

Not sure of his future after graduation in 1909, but knowing he wanted to pursue a college education, as did brother Edgar, the boys agreed to alternate attending college with working and earning tuition money. Ike found various menial jobs around Abilene and apparently also played some semi-pro baseball under an assumed name in another town. A friend suggested that he apply for appointment to either the US Military Academy at West Point or the Naval Academy at Annapolis. He passed the initial West Point examination and then traveled to St. Louis to take the entrance test. Some back in Abilene were dismayed by his decision, as one friend told him: "There's just no future in the Army. You're just throwing your life away."[3] Although his parents likely felt the same, they withheld their thoughts, and received the anticipated news: Dwight D. Eisenhower had been accepted to West Point to enter as a member of the class of 1915 (along with another who took the test with him in St. Louis, Omar Bradley).

At West Point, Ike continued his average scholastic performance, but earned higher marks for engineering, drilling, and gunnery. He incurred a variety of demerits and later admitted, "I enjoyed life at the Academy, had a good time with my pals, and was far from disturbed by an additional demerit or two."[4] His favorite activities

NATIONAL EVENTS

JAN 7: President Truman announces US has developed a hydrogen bomb

JAN 20: President Eisenhower inaugurated

JAN 22: Arthur Miller's *The Crucible* opens on Broadway

FEB 11: President Eisenhower denies Ethel and Julius Rosenberg's appeal for clemency

FEB 19: First literature censorship board in US approved in Georgia

1953

WORLD EVENTS

JAN 14: Josip Broz Tito becomes second president of the Socialist Federal Republic of Yugoslavia

JAN 15: Foreign minister of East Germany arrested for spying

JAN 31–FEB 1: North Sea flood kills more than 2,200 people

FEB 11: Soviet Union breaks off diplomatic relations with Israel

FEB 28: Structure of DNA molecule discovered

MAR 5: Josef Stalin dies

were athletics—playing baseball and football—but after a near-disastrous injury to his right knee in a football game against Tufts, his dreams of winning glory on the field ended. As graduation neared in the spring of 1915, he received his commission as second lieutenant in the infantry, signed by President Woodrow Wilson.

ARMY CAREER

Eisenhower had a few months to relax before he received his first assignment—the 19th Infantry Regiment based at Fort Sam Houston in San Antonio, Texas. When he arrived, the regiment had just returned from patrolling the border, searching for Mexican bandit Pancho Villa and his men who had been raiding the area. Eisenhower had not yet met his commanding officer when he made a five-dollar bet with another young soldier that he could scale the flagpole. Partway up in his climb, Colonel Millard Fillmore Waltz arrived and ordered the junior officer to come down, then he browbeat him for being "foolhardy," "undignified," and "ignorant."[5] Eisenhower soon became sought after to coach football teams. In fact, Major General Frederick Funston "asked" the young infantryman to coach the nearby Peacock Military Academy's team, and the following year Eisenhower was recruited by the local Saint Louis College team. They went from a five-year losing streak to playing in the finals of the city championship.

Although busy with his duties, Eisenhower still found time for a social life, and on his first afternoon as officer of the day (a typical chore for junior officers requiring inspection of guard posts), he was introduced to Miss Mamie Doud. He asked the nineteen-year-old if she wanted to walk the post with him. Not comprehending the distance involved, she agreed, and off the couple went on a three-mile hike. They had plenty of opportunity to chat, and Eisenhower learned that Mamie's family lived in Denver during the warmer months and kept their home in San Antonio from fall to spring. They were soon found together constantly, and anytime he was off duty, he headed to the Doud home. Within four months of meeting, they were engaged, but it was nearly ended when he announced his intention to join the aviation section of the Signal Corps. To Mamie and her father John Doud, this was unthinkable, so she told her fiancé he had to make the choice—either flying or her. The wedding took place on July 1, 1916, moved up from their original date in November because of the growing threat of war for the United States either in Europe or with Mexico.

Soon after their marriage, Eisenhower received orders that the 19th Infantry was moving to a new post near Austin named Camp Wilson. Mamie was upset that her new husband was leaving her, and Eisenhower explained: "There's one thing you must understand. My country comes first and always will. You come second."[6] Once at Camp Wilson, the men formed a new regiment, the 57th Infantry, and Eisenhower was soon promoted to captain. He also served as the regimental supply officer, but with the United States declaring war on Germany, men desperately needed training, and Eisenhower was chosen. Off he went to Georgia to instruct "ninety-day wonders," a.k.a. officer candidates.

While at Camp Oglethorpe, Ike received news that he was a father. Doud Dwight was born in September 1917. Mamie tried to call him Little Ike, then tried Ikey, and finally decided his nickname was Icky. Father and son met when Eisenhower was en route to his new assignment at Fort Leavenworth, Kansas, to train more officers.

CABINET
★★★★★★★★★★

(continued)

SECRETARY OF COMMERCE
Sinclair Weeks (1953–1958)

Frederick H. Mueller (1959–1961)

SECRETARY OF LABOR
Martin P. Durkin (Jan.–Sept. 1953)

James P. Mitchell (1953–1961)

SECRETARY OF HEALTH, EDUCATION, AND WELFARE
Oveta Culp Hobby (1953–1955), first to serve in this new post

Marion B. Folsm (1955–1958)

Arthur S. Flemming (1958–1961)

MAR 17: Nuclear test in Nevada

MAR 26: Jonas Salk announces his discovery of a polio vaccine

MAY 18: Jacqueline Cochran is first woman to break sound barrier, in California

MAY 25: US conducts first and only nuclear artillery test at the Nevada Test Site

JUN 19: Julius and Ethel Rosenberg executed by electric chair at Sing Sing prison, New York

MAR 14: Nikita Khrushchev becomes general secretary of Soviet Communist Party

APR 7: Dag Hammarskjöld elected UN secretary general

APR 8: Jomo Kenyatta is sentenced to seven years in jail for organizing Mau Mau Rebellion

APR 13: Ian Fleming publishes first James Bond novel, *Casino Royale*

MAY 2: Hussein crowned king of Jordan

SALK VACCINE (1955) ★ For eight years, Dr. Jonas Salk toiled to create a vaccine against polio, and he finally succeeded in 1955. American children were inoculated and within a generation, the disease had been eradicated from the United States.

Upset by being denied the opportunity to fight in Europe, he was then reprimanded by his superior at Leavenworth for his numerous requests to leave. Ultimately he did receive transfer orders—to Camp Meade, Maryland, where he had been requested to help train men for the 301st Tank Battalion. While at first dismayed by the transfer, Eisenhower was thrilled to hear he would lead the men into combat once these soldiers were trained, but he did such a fine job that his superior refused to let him go.

Soon he received a promotion to major and another transfer; this time to Camp Colt, Pennsylvania, adjacent to the Gettysburg battlefield. There he trained future tankers, even though he was given no tanks. Refusing to allow this minor point to distract him, he improvised by using trucks over hazardous terrain and asked the Navy to loan small three-pound cannons when the Army failed to assign similar weapons to him. Eisenhower's tankers used the Gettysburg battlefield for target practice, with men and machine guns on Little Round Top firing on trucks below. Again he won plaudits and commendations from his superiors, as well as another promotion, so in October 1918, he became Lieutenant Colonel Eisenhower, and he finally received his long-awaited orders: "You will proceed to Camp Dix, New Jersey, for embarkation on November 18, 1918."[7] No shipping out, however, would occur, for they received word that hostilities would end on November 11. Knowing he would never be able to list "The Great War" on his resumé, Eisenhower angrily wrote his friend Norman Randolph, "I suppose we'll spend the rest of our lives explaining why we didn't get into this war. By God, from now on I am cutting myself a swath and will make up for this."[8]

Now Eisenhower faced the monumental challenge of disbanding Camp Colt and assisting with the Army's demobilization. Lieutenant Colonel Ira Welborn recommended him for the Distinguished Service Medal and wrote, "I regard this officer as one of the most efficient young officers I have ever known."[9] His rank was reduced as part of the switch to peacetime, and he was a captain again.

BETWEEN THE WARS

Besides the millions of soldiers leaving the armed forces, many of the officers decided to join the business world of a peacetime economy. Eisenhower briefly contemplated such a change, but Mamie counseled him to stay with his Army career, so off they went to the new home of the US Army Tank Corps at Camp Meade. There Eisenhower was disappointed to learn that he was required yet again to resume coaching football. In 1919, he volunteered to accompany an Army convoy of various vehicles on a transcontinental cavalcade to promote the armed forces, as well as highlight the very real need for an improved road system. At that time, no highways linked the nation, and most roads that existed were dirt. The country definitely needed to modernize its roads, but that would not occur for another thirty years, when the Interstate

NATIONAL EVENTS

AUG 18: Second Kinsey Report released

OCT 30: President Eisenhower formally approves top-secret document to maintain and expand US nuclear weapons arsenal to counter Communist threat

DEC 8: President Eisenhower gives his Atoms for Peace speech to the UN

DEC 17: FCC approves color television

WORLD EVENTS

MAY 29: Sir Edmund Hillary and Tenzing Norgay make first successful ascent to the summit of Mount Everest

JUN 2: Coronation of Elizabeth II at Westminster Abbey

JUN 18: Egypt declared a republic

JUL 27: Korean War ends

AUG 19: CIA helps overthrow Mohammed Mossadegh, Shah Mohammed Reza Pahlavi remains on throne in Iran

AUG 20: French government ousts sultan of Morocco, exiles him to Corsica

Highway Act of 1956 was signed into law by President Eisenhower.

Once Eisenhower returned to Camp Meade, he and Colonel George S. Patton, newly returned tank officer from France, met for the first time. Eisenhower later recalled, "From the beginning, he and I got along famously. Both of us were students of current military doctrine. Part of our passion was our belief in tanks—a belief derided at the time by others."[10] This belief in the future of tank warfare bonded the men together at a time when scarcely anyone else among the Army leadership shared their vision. The two experimented with a stripped-down tank and narrowly missed being injured on a few occasions. Still they continued to construct what Eisenhower later called "a comprehensive tank doctrine that in George Patton's case would make him a legend. Naturally, as enthusiasts, we tried to win converts. This wasn't easy, but George and I had the enthusiasm of zealots."[11]

This infectious spirit nearly ended their careers. Both men published articles advocating tank warfare in *Infantry Journal* in 1920, which explored the importance that tanks would play in future wars and the tactics demanded by then. Major General Charles Farnsworth, the chief of infantry, directed that Eisenhower meet him in Washington. There he ordered the captain never to write such an article again and told Ike that his ideas were "dangerous" and "incompatible with solid infantry doctrine. If I did, I would be hauled before a court-martial."[12] Patton and Eisenhower refused to give up their ideas and agreed not only that they were correct, but that another war would rise from the ashes of the Treaty of Versailles. For that war, Patton told Eisenhower, "This [next] war may happen just about 20 years from now. This is what we'll do. I'll be [Stonewall] Jackson, you'll be Lee. I don't want to do the heavy thinking; you do that and I'll get loose among our #%&%$# enemies."[13]

Sadly, the Eisenhowers' world shattered when Icky died on January 2, 1921. What at first seemed only a minor complaint was soon diagnosed as the very serious and contagious scarlet fever. The three-year-old was quarantined away from his parents, who could only blow him kisses from the other side of a glass window. Then meningitis set in, and Eisenhower sat on his son's death watch. Icky's death devastated both parents, and they rarely spoke of the tragedy. Eisenhower admitted that it nearly led him to a breakdown, and Mamie was not far behind. He later said that his son's death was "the greatest disappointment and disaster of my life, the one I have never been able to forget completely."[14]

After a year of grieving, the Eisenhowers bid farewell to Camp Meade and prepared themselves for a journey to Panama and a transfer to the Canal Zone's garrison. There the tropical conditions made life extremely unpleasant for pregnant Mamie, who was frightened by the bats that flew everywhere. She shrieked and Eisenhower would assail them with his sword, refusing to obey a law forbidding their demise. Meanwhile his commanding officer Brigadier General Fox Connor tutored Eisenhower in military history and how its lessons could be applied to other situations. Since Connor had served as Pershing's second-in-command in Europe, he had his own ideas about working with allies and counseled his protégé about not allowing American troops to become subservient to another country's.

SUPREME COURT APPOINTMENTS
★★★★★★★★★★

Earl Warren, Chief Justice 1954

John Marshall Harlan, 1955

William J. Brennan, 1956

Charles E. Whittaker, 1957

Potter Stewart, 1959

DEC 30: First color televisions go on sale for $1,175

NOV 5: David Ben Gurion resigns as prime minister of Israel

NOV 9: Cambodia gains independence from France

NOV 9: King Abdul Aziz of Saudi Arabia dies

NOV 29: French paratroopers capture Dien Bein Phu

1954

JAN 14: Marilyn Monroe and Joe DiMaggio marry

JAN 25: Berlin Conference of US, UK, France, and Soviet Union

MAR 1: American hydrogen bomb tested in the Pacific Ocean

FEB 25: Lt. Col. Gamal Abdel Nasser become premier of Egypt

STATE OF THE UNION
★ ★ ★ ★ ★ ★ ★ ★ ★ ★

US POPULATION IN 1953
151,325,798

NATIONAL DEBT IN 1961
$296,168,761,215

PRESIDENT'S SALARY
$100,000/year + $50,000 non-taxable expense account

STATES ADMITTED TO UNION
Alaska, January 3, 1959

Hawaii, August 21, 1960

NUMBER OF STATES IN 1961
50

By the time Eisenhower received orders transferring him stateside, the family now included infant son John. Eisenhower, however, was annoyed about being sent back to Camp Meade and extremely dismayed that it was for the sole purpose of coaching the football team in the 1924 season. His stay was shortened by a transfer to Colorado, where he worked briefly as a recruiting officer before reporting to where he wanted and knew he needed to attend—the Command and General Staff School at Fort Leavenworth. Although assignment there was renowned as being a grueling year, it was imperative that an officer successfully complete it if he wanted to continue as a career army officer. Thanks to Patton's notes from the previous session, Eisenhower found he excelled at the Staff School, and graduated first in his class in 1926. Besides the knowledge gained there, the men also met others and networked. These relationships would be revisited in the years—and the war—ahead.

After a brief tenure at Camp Benning, Georgia (where again he was recruited to coach football), he was appointed to the American Battle Monuments Commission (ABMC), which was overseen by Army Chief of Staff General John J. Pershing. It meant moving to Washington, D.C., where he also received advanced training at the Army War College. After graduation in 1928, he returned to the ABMC, but soon he, Mamie, and six-year-old John were en route to Europe for a yearlong tour to write a guidebook of the various battlefields in France.

Upon his return in the fall of 1929, Eisenhower accepted a transfer to the General Staff of the War Department, where he worked with General Pershing and first met Lieutenant Colonel George C. Marshall, another former protégé of Fox Connor. The following year, Eisenhower had a new superior when General Douglas MacArthur became chief of staff and ordered Major Eisenhower and Brigadier General George Van Horn Moseley to draft the Army's mobilization plan in case the nation went to war. Once completed, however, the plan never was read by President Herbert Hoover because he could not fathom why such an occurrence would ever need to happen. After all, hadn't the country fought "the war to end all wars."

ON MACARTHUR'S STAFF

In 1932, Eisenhower officially became a member of General MacArthur's staff and would remain with him for the next seven years. In the spring of that year, veterans from World War I marched to Washington from across the nation, demanding the bonus promised them for 1945. The Great Depression was hurting them now, they argued, so they needed their money. When violence broke out on July 28, Eisenhower was with MacArthur, who ordered the troops, clad in riot gear, including the 3d Cavalry led by Patton, into the city. Photographs of tear gas and the burning of squatters' shacks by police ended Herbert Hoover's hopes of reelection, and although MacArthur also received blame, he continued as chief of staff, with Eisenhower remaining at his post, as well.

In late 1935, Eisenhower followed his commanding officer to the Philippines. Now a lieutenant colonel, he increasingly found himself on opposite sides from MacArthur, whose task was planning for not only Filipino independence, but the future nation's ability to defend itself if attacked. After going home for a few months in 1938 (and surprising all with his bald head, which he had begun shaving to keep cool), Eisenhower returned to find someone else in his place—he was

NATIONAL EVENTS

APR 1: President Eisenhower authorizes creation of the US Air Force Academy in Colorado

APR 7: President Eisenhower gives "domino theory" speech

APR 22: Senator Joseph McCarthy begins hearings

MAY 17: US Supreme Court declares segregation is unconstitutional in *Brown v. Board of Education of Topeka, Kansas*

JUN 14: "Under God" added to the Pledge of Allegiance

WORLD EVENTS

MAR 30: Canada's first subway opens in Toronto

MAY 7: Battle of Dien Bien Phu ends in French defeat

MAY 20: Chiang Kai-shek reelected president of Republic of China

JUN 17: CIA-sponsored military coup in Guatemala; triggers civil war for next 35 years

JUL 21: Geneva Conference divides Vietnam into North and South

SEP 8: Southeast Asia Treaty Organization (SEATO) established

no longer MacArthur's chief of staff. Although distrustful and unhappy with his commander, Eisenhower truly respected and liked the Philippine president Don Manuel Quezon, who begged him to remain at his post. In 1939, Eisenhower finally received transfer orders to report for duty at Fort Lewis, Washington, and heard that Hitler had invaded Poland. A new world war had begun, just as he and Patton had predicted years before.

WARTIME

Eisenhower served only briefly at Fort Lewis before moving to Fort Ord, California, where he commanded a battalion of the 3d Division. Eisenhower found commanding men "a lot of fun."[15] Meanwhile old friend George Patton was practically giddy at the prospect of going to war. He wrote to Eisenhower, "No matter how we get together we will go PLACES." Then he ended his letter: "hoping we are together in a long and BLOODY War."[16] Soon thereafter, Eisenhower also won his first star—promotion to brigadier general.

On December 7, 1941, after spending the morning plowing through paperwork, the brigadier general ate a quick lunch and laid down for a nap. He awakened to the news of the Japanese attack on Pearl Harbor. A few days later, he received a call from Colonel Walter Bedell Smith, in the War Department's General Staff office, who ordered Eisenhower to Washington immediately. Disappointed that this probably meant another stint as a war planner, he reluctantly bid farewell to Mamie and headed for Washington, D.C.

Eisenhower reported to General Marshall, who was now the chief of staff for the War Plans Division, and accompanied Marshall to the Arcadia (Canada) conference later in December, between President Franklin Roosevelt and British prime minister Winston Churchill. Continuing into 1942, Eisenhower toiled at formulating strategic plans that would be carried out in the coming months. Marshall was a demanding taskmaster, and in March, he and Eisenhower faced off in a discussion regarding promotions. Only field commanders would gain promotions, Marshall told him, so he might as well face the facts: "You are going to stay right here on this job, and you'll probably never move." Eisenhower turned crimson and faced down his commanding officer, telling him, "I don't give a damn about your promotion plans,"[17] and then proceeded to insist that if his duty was to remain at his desk, he would do it. To his astonishment, Eisenhower soon learned that Marshall had recommended him for promotion to major general.

Eisenhower traveled to England to improve communications between the United States and its prime ally. He met with Churchill and the chief of the Imperial General Staff, Sir Alan Brooke, as well as General Bernard Law Montgomery, top trainer for the British, and Lord Louis Mountbatten, commander of Combined

NATO (1949) ★ The North Atlantic Treaty Organization was created in 1949 with its headquarters in Brussels, Belgium, and its mission to protect the security of its member nations (primarily western Europe, Iceland, the United States, and Canada). An attack upon any one of its members would be considered an attack upon all. In 1952, Greece and Turkey joined, and in 1954, NATO rejected the Soviet Union's overture to also join. The following year, West Germany became a NATO member.

DID YOU KNOW?

Eisenhower is the only president to win an Emmy award, given in recognition of his use of television.

AUG 16: First *Sports Illustrated* published

NOV: Ellis Island closes

DEC 2: US Senate votes to condemn Joseph McCarthy

DEC 2: Mutual Defense Treaty signed between Taiwan and US

SEP 9: Earthquake in Algeria

SEP 14: USSR tests nuclear weapon

OCT 11: Viet Minh takes control of North Vietnam

OCT 23: West Germany joins NATO

OCT 26: Attempted assassination of Gamal Abdel Nasser

OCT 31: Algerian War of Independence begins

NOV 14: Gamal Abdel Nasser replaces Mohammed Naguib as Egyptian president

DEC 24: Laos gains independence

1950s FADS ★ Young people of the 1950s enjoyed a variety of new games and activities, including the Hula Hoop, Frisbee, spud guns, and going to drive-ins, where car hops rollerskated about with their orders. Girls wore poodle skirts and saddle shoes while guys wore letter sweaters (or the ones imitating James Dean cruised around in their rolled-up jeans, leather jackets, and hair greased back in a D.A.). Coonskin hats from the hit television show *Davy Crockett* were all the rage, and televisions became common in America's households.

Operations. He deeply understood the need for developing equipment and tactics to coordinate a large-scale Allied invasion into German-occupied France. In June 1942, Eisenhower presented Marshall with his report, including a recommendation that the United States establish a European Theater of Operations in London. Marshall concurred, and gave its command to a delighted Eisenhower, who a few days later told a friend, "They're sending me over to command the whole shebang!"[18]

OFF TO EUROPE

The allies determined to open a second front to aid the Russians and thus take some of the heat from their brutal fight with Nazi Germany. Operation Torch would occur as a landing in North Africa; Eisenhower was its commander and in charge of its planning. To help with this, he decided to form the Allied Force Headquarters, and Brigadier General Bedell Smith joined him as chief of staff. Soon Eisenhower told Marshall that he wanted General George Patton to head the invasion at Casablanca. During the coming months, Eisenhower coordinated allied efforts and cajoled military and political leaders in this first effort to mount a united front and invasion. By November 1942, Operation Torch was launched into northern Africa. Although the operation failed to go as quickly as planned—and many blamed Eisenhower for that—President Roosevelt disagreed and sent word that he wanted Eisenhower to be awarded the Medal of Honor for his efforts. Eisenhower, however, saw this as a slap to the fighting men and replied: "I don't want it and if it is awarded I won't wear it. I won't even keep it."[19] In February 1943, though, a different honor was bestowed upon him—his fourth star, which he wore proudly.

Managing the coalition war effort proved a monumental task throughout the war, but it was most difficult for its commander during its infancy. British chief of the Imperial General Staff, Field Marshal Sir Alan Brooke, gleefully said that his countrymen "were pushing Eisenhower up into the stratosphere and rarified atmosphere of a Supreme Commander, where he would be free to devote his time to the political and inter-allied problems . . . whilst we inserted our own commanders to deal with the military situations."[20] But Eisenhower was determined to keep himself involved on all levels and closely monitored their actions.

The next objective was the invasion of Sicily, known as Operation Husky, launched in July 1943. Mediating between two prima donnas—British general Montgomery and General George Patton—about who would take the key city of Messina elevated Eisenhower's blood pressure to alarmingly high levels and he was ordered to bed, where he received the welcome news that Marshall had promoted him to permanent

NATIONAL EVENTS

JAN 28: Congress authorizes President Eisenhower to use force to protect Formosa from China

FEB 12: President Eisenhower sends first US advisors to Vietnam

APR 18: Albert Einstein dies

JUL 17: Disneyland opens in California

AUG 19: Hurricane Diane hits the Northeast

1955

WORLD EVENTS

JAN 2: President José Antonio Remón Cantera of Panama is murdered

APR 5: Winston Churchill resigns

MAY 14: Warsaw Pact formed by Communist states of Eastern Europe and USSR

JUL 13: Last woman to be executed in UK hanged for murder

JUL 18–23: Geneva Summit between US, UK, USSR, and France

brigadier general (earlier "wartime" promotion had been temporary). Patton took Messina, but soon after grabbed unwanted headlines by slapping a GI in a hospital for cowardice. Although a firestorm of criticism erupted, Eisenhower stood by his old friend, put a reprimand in Patton's file, and ordered him to apologize. Patton would stay in Europe, provided such an incident never happened again. Afterwards Patton wrote an apology to Eisenhower: "I am at a loss to find words with which to express my chagrin and grief at having given you, a man to whom I owe everything and for whom I would gladly lay down my life, cause to be displeased with me."[21]

OPERATION OVERLORD

After agreeing to a cross-channel invasion into the Normandy peninsula of France, the British and Americans had to decide who would be its commander. General George Marshall coveted the honor, as did Churchill's chief of staff, General Brooke. Roosevelt told Churchill that Americans demanded an American commander but could have a Brit as second in command. All signs indicated that Roosevelt was selecting Marshall, and Eisenhower would return to Washington to serve as chief of staff. This dismayed Eisenhower, who believed he would fail miserably at the post and told friends he would be buried at Arlington within six months of the appointment. Finally FDR decided on the commander and asked if Eisenhower wanted the job because, as Roosevelt explained, Marshall was badly needed at home. Later when the president's son James asked why Eisenhower was selected, FDR replied, "Eisenhower is the best politician among the military men. He is a natural leader who can convince other men to follow him, and this is what we need in his position more than any other quality."[22] Montgomery conceded that while he did not respect Eisenhower's soldierly qualities, "He has the power of drawing the hearts of men towards him as a magnet attracts the bit of metal. He merely has to smile at you, and you trust him at once."[23]

After a trip back to Washington to see Roosevelt, Marshall, and Mamie, Eisenhower returned in January 1944 to London to assemble the men and supplies required for the invasion, Operation Overlord. He now worked out of what was officially called Supreme Headquarters, Allied Expeditionary Force. Its staff worked in three shifts around the clock and eventually its size grew to sixteen thousand strong. As the time edged nearer to the planned May invasion, Eisenhower's health spiraled downward, as he suffered from a variety of ailments including insomnia and coughing. He did not appear healthy and his aide said, "The strain is telling on him. He looks older now that at any time since I have been with him."[24]

From time to time, Eisenhower ventured out of London and visited the thousands of troops training for this historic event. It was a welcome break from the tedium of planning this logistical nightmare, which had been delayed because of supplies not being ready. The end of May or the first few days of June now were targeted, and Eisenhower was the one person who would decide when D-Day occurred in Normandy, France. This heavy burden weighed on him continually, adding to his health problems, including a ringing in the ear and a sore left eye. He chain-smoked several packs of Camel cigarettes daily and downed fifteen cups of coffee.

On May 15, the Allies met for a banquet with King George VI, the guest of honor. Before leaving, the king talked briefly to Eisenhower,

SEP 24: President Eisenhower suffers a heart attack on vacation in Denver

SEP 30: Actor James Dean dies in a car accident

DEC 1: Rosa Parks refuses to give up her bus seat and is arrested in Montgomery, Alabama

DEC 5: AFL-CIO is formed

AUG 20: Anti-French rioting in Algeria and Morocco

SEP 6: Istanbul's Greek minority is the target of a government-sponsored pogrom

SEP 19: President Juan Peron of Argentina is ousted in a military coup

OCT 26: Austria declares permanent neutrality

OCT 26: Ngo Dinh Diem proclaims himself president of Republic of Vietnam

DID YOU KNOW?

Eisenhower was the first president of the *fifty* United States.

who reassured His Majesty, "There will be eleven thousand planes overhead on D-Day and Overlord is backed by the greatest armada in history. It will not fail."[25]

Weather predictions, phases of the moon, and timing of the tides were the key determinants in launching the invasion. Eisenhower received daily reports and increasingly it appeared that early June would be the best time. Following a crucial one-day delay because of a storm blowing through the English Channel, Eisenhower ordered that the airborne troops could commence the night of June 5, to be followed by the rest of the invasion force the next morning. Otherwise, weather reports indicated a minimum delay of two weeks, which Eisenhower and others feared would be deadly in terms of losing the element of surprise, as well as severely damaging the morale of their own men.

FINISHING THE WAR

The assault succeeded, and Allied troops soon found themselves bogged down in the Normandy hedgerow country, but as the summer wore on, Patton's Third Army broke through the German barrier and led the way eastward across France. Montgomery, who commanded the British and Canadian field armies, clamored for more support that would enable him to move toward the German capital. An exasperated Eisenhower replied, "If I give you all the supplies you want, you could go straight to Berlin. Right straight to Berlin? Monty, you're nuts. You can't do it!"[26] Apparently, the Supreme Allied Commander no longer felt bound to couch his words in soft terms for his Allied leaders.

By December, most Allied generals were satisfied that there would be no major enemy offensive, partly due to snow that had fallen earlier in the month. On December 16, Eisenhower received notification of his promotion to the five-star rank making him General of the Army. He soon heard ominous reports of German movement in Belgium; the last German offensive, the Battle of the Bulge, had begun. The German attack was beaten back in heavy fighting that lasted nearly two months. The approach of spring brought improved weather, and the push to cross the Rhine River finally occurred late in March 1945. With this, the last great obstacle to an assault into Germany itself was removed.

British military and political leaders wanted the Americans to push as far eastward into Germany as possible, fearing possible ramifications if the Russians made great inroads. Eisenhower and Army Chief of Staff Marshall, on the other hand, were concerned only about destroying Germany's industrial complex and forcing its surrender and redeploying many of Eisenhower's soldiers to the Pacific to fight Imperial Japan. This strategy would haunt Eisenhower in the future, for critics would maintain that he could have prevented the Soviets from being the first to enter Berlin. But for now, Eisenhower—and Washington—merely saw the German capital as a city that had very little strategic value.

Events began happening rapidly in May 1945. First Adolf Hitler committed suicide on the third, but his commanders refused to surrender, hoping that a delay would permit many of their troops to surrender to the Americans rather than the Soviets. Eisenhower repeatedly told them that all had agreed to immediate and unconditional surrender. On May 7, the Germans acquiesced to his demands, and General Alfred Jodl met with Eisenhower, who told the German

NATIONAL EVENTS

FEB 22: Elvis Presley's "Heartbreak Hotel" puts him on the music charts for the first time

MAR 12: Ninety-six Congressmen protest the *Brown v. Board of Education* ruling

JUN 29: Marilyn Monroe marries Arthur Miller

JUN 29: President Eisenhower signs Federal-Aid Highway Act, creating Interstate Highway System

JUL 30: "In God We Trust" becomes US national motto

1956

WORLD EVENTS

JAN 16: President Nasser of Egypt vows to reconquer Palestine

MAR 2: Morocco declares independence from France

MAR 20: Tunisia gains independence from France

MAR 23: Pakistan becomes first Islamic republic

APR 19: Prince Rainier III of Monaco marries American actress Grace Kelly

JUL 26: Egyptian President Nasser nationalizes Suez Canal

general that he would be held responsible should any violations of the surrender occur. Afterward Eisenhower sat down and wrote, "The mission of this Allied force was fulfilled at 0300, local time, May 7th, 1945."[27]

DEMOBILIZATION

With victory came the parades and plaudits; speeches lauding Eisenhower as a great commander were spoken on both sides of the Atlantic. When he met with President Harry Truman, he was told, "General, there is nothing that you may want that I won't try to help you get. That definitely and specifically includes the presidency in 1948."[28] Ike was taken aback by the suggestion and quickly reassured Truman that they would not face each other in the next presidential election. Others, however, had similar thoughts of running the successful general, but Eisenhower harbored no such ideas.

In November 1945, George C. Marshall retired as chief of staff, and Truman appointed Eisenhower as his replacement. He soon learned that this duty was in many respects more difficult than being the Supreme Allied Commander, and he complained to his son John that the Pentagon "was a sorry place to light after having commanded a theater of war."[29] Eisenhower's life changed dramatically in his new role—he lived better and dined with millionaires. Although he felt unqualified, he gave numerous public speeches. He and President Truman would never be close, and Eisenhower disagreed with many advisors who insisted that the Soviet Union was a viable threat to the security of the United States. Eisenhower had met Stalin after the war and believed the Soviets had their hands full rebuilding. He also disliked the introduction of the atomic bomb and hoped the newly created United Nations would control it. Optimistic of the UN's powers, Eisenhower also favored the development of a large peacekeeping force, with the United States contributing a sizeable contingent of troops.

> *"I feel impelled to speak today in a language that in a sense is new—one which I, who have spent so much of my life in the military profession, would have preferred never to use. That new language is the language of atomic warfare."*
>
> —*Dwight D. Eisenhower*

As the election of 1948 approached, speculation rose regarding an Eisenhower presidential bid. But in July 1947, Eisenhower again stated, "I say flatly, completely, and with all the force I have—I haven't a political ambition in the world. I want nothing to do with politics."[30] This pronouncement did little to squelch the hopeful talk by members of both parties, since Eisenhower had never formally declared which one he preferred. But he remained steadfast, leaving the Republicans to run New York governor Thomas Dewey unsuccessfully against incumbent president Harry Truman.

On February 7, 1948, General Dwight D. Eisenhower left his Pentagon post and entered civilian life. He had agonized over what to do next, knowing he needed something that would provide

OCT 17: Thirteen-year-old Bobby Fischer wins "The Game of the Century" (chess tournament)

OCT 29: IBM creates first hard disk drive (5MB)

NOV 6: Incumbent President Eisenhower defeats Adlai Stevenson in rematch of 1952 presidential election

OCT 23: Hungarian revolution; Hungary attempts to leave Warsaw Pact

OCT 26: Red Army troops invade Hungary

OCT 29: Israeli troops invade Sinai Peninsula; start of Suez Crisis

OCT 31: UK and France start bombing Egypt to force the reopening of the Suez Canal

NOV 7: UN calls for UK, France, and Israel to withdraw from Arab lands

DID YOU KNOW?

A putting green was installed on the White House lawn for President Eisenhower.

a reasonable income for his family. Nearly two years earlier, Tom Watson, a trustee for Columbia University, had discussed with him the possibility of becoming its president, but Eisenhower had declined. Now he decided to accept the offer, especially after the assurance that he could begin several months later, allowing time for him to begin writing his memoirs. This he wanted to do as a way of creating a future retirement nest egg. *Crusade in Europe* was published in 1948 and was well received. Eisenhower had modeled his book after Ulysses S. Grant's memoirs, and the two books were often compared.

At Columbia, professors had little use for this general in charge. He lacked the proper collegiate philosophy and resented all the piles of paperwork and bluster generated by the academicians. Eisenhower briefly returned to the Pentagon at Truman's request to help with the organization of the newly formed Defense Department. Unhappy at Columbia, Eisenhower accepted the invitation by Truman in December 1950 to head NATO, the North Atlantic Treaty Organization of western European nations, the United States, and Canada, to preserve peace in Europe and be ready should the Soviet Union take military action.

Immediately, Eisenhower began touring the NATO nations to drum up support and confidence in their future and willingness to defend it. He also encouraged the various leaders to work with others even if they had centuries of hatred and distrust behind them. In time he advocated for a United States of Europe as a means of pulling the continent together to work toward the common goal of "human betterment."

Meanwhile people in the United States were looking toward the next presidential election. Organizations like Ike Clubs and Citizens for Eisenhower dotted the country, and party leaders vied with each other to win his promise to be their candidate. When Truman asked if he wanted the nomination, Eisenhower replied, "What reason have you to think I have ever been a Democrat? You know I have been a Republican all my life and that my family have always been Republicans."[31]

In May 1952, he resigned from his NATO post and in July, resigned his Army commission to become a full-time politician and Republican presidential candidate. Ohio senator Robert Taft (son of former president William H. Taft) and spokesman for the "Old Guard" of the Republican Party, fought for the nomination, but owing to Eisenhower's strong showing in the primaries (including winning New Hampshire without campaigning), and Thomas Dewey's behind-the-scenes political manipulations, Eisenhower won the nomination on the first ballot. Dewey also proposed that Senator Richard Nixon of California be his running mate, and so the Eisenhower-Nixon ballot was born. Their platform proposed a balanced budget, a vigorous defense program to oppose the growth of communism, and lower taxes.

1952 ELECTION

Democrats chose Illinois governor Adlai Stevenson as their presidential candidate with Senator John Sparkman of Arkansas as his running mate. The Democrats echoed Republican calls for strong defense against communism but also argued for disarmament and increased public assistance for women, children, minorities, and those with disabilities.

Both Eisenhower and Stevenson campaigned throughout the nation, as did their running

NATIONAL EVENTS

JAN 3: First electric watch introduced

JAN 14: Humphrey Bogart dies

JAN 20: President Eisenhower inaugurated for second term

MAR 7: Congress approves Eisenhower Doctrine

JUN 27: Hurricane Audrey hits Louisiana

1957

WORLD EVENTS

DEC 12: Japan becomes UN member

DEC 23: British and French troops withdraw from Suez Canal region

JAN 11: African Convention political party founded in Dakar

JAN 22: Israel withdraws from Sinai Peninsula

FEB 4: France prohibits UN involvement in Algeria

MAR 6: UK colonies Gold Coast and Togoland become Ghana

mates, with Nixon frequently used as an "attack dog" against the Democrats and their twenty-year reign of power in Washington. Eisenhower, however, lost the respect of many former colleagues when he failed to come to the defense of General George C. Marshall, who had just been maligned and called a "traitor" by Joseph McCarthy, the Republican senator who had won fame and fear by calling people communists and permanently ruining their reputations.

Two weeks before the election, Eisenhower made a public speech about the ongoing war in Korea, pledging that only with a personal visit there could the war be stopped. His pledge, "I shall go to Korea,"[32] though ambiguous, helped his campaign tremendously. Voters wore their "I like Ike" buttons and arrived at the polls to vote for him; in fact, he won 55 percent of the popular vote and 442 electoral votes to Stevenson's 44 percent and 89 electoral votes. This election marked the beginning of the end of the Democratic Party's lock on the Solid South; five southern states voted Republican, and in the future, more would follow.

PRESIDENT EISENHOWER—FIRST TERM

The presidential inauguration was as icy between the incoming and outgoing presidents as the weather outside. Eisenhower declined to come inside and chat with Truman before making the trip together to the capitol, so Truman angrily walked out to the waiting car. En route, Eisenhower asked who had ordered his son John back from Korea to attend, and Truman admitted he had done it, saying, "The President thought it was right and proper for your son to witness the swearing-in of his father to the Presidency."[33] The two men said little else; they may have grown up in the same part of the country but their personalities and beliefs were worlds apart.

Prior to his inauguration, Eisenhower had pieced together his cabinet with a variety of faithful Republican civil servants, but one refused his offer of becoming interior secretary: Earl Warren of California wanted a post in the judiciary instead, and the new president promised him that he would receive the first vacancy on the US Supreme Court.

Two months after his inauguration speech, the world heard the news from the Soviet Union—Josef Stalin was dead. Secretary of State John Foster Dulles distrusted Soviets and suspected Stalin's immediate successor Georgi Malenkov to be insincere when he promoted a possible summit meeting with the West, and Dulles refused the offer. Malenkov would be replaced within two years with a man of bluster—Nikita Khrushchev.

Eisenhower wanted the world to be one of peace; he had seen enough of war and spoke out for the need to disarm. This became a popular stance and was welcome news to allies around the world.

Utilizing his military experience, Eisenhower built on an idea from Truman's administration—the National Security Council. He added the treasury secretary to those who were included in its meetings and insisted that the group meet weekly. Various scenarios and possible trouble spots in the world were studied and discussed and strategies developed to handle emergencies. These were filed away and ready should the occasion arise; Eisenhower wanted no chaotic flustering.

As promised in his campaign, Eisenhower traveled to South Korea in December 1952, a few weeks before taking office as president. There he visited American and UN troops and decided

JUL 16: New transcontinental speed record set: California to New York in 3 hours, 23 minutes by plane

AUG 21: President Eisenhower suspends nuclear testing for two years

AUG 28: Senator Strom Thurmond sets record for longest filibuster (24 hours, 18 minutes; against civil rights bill)

SEP 24: Federal troops go to Arkansas to protect Little Rock Nine

NOV 25: President Eisenhower suffers a stroke

MAR 8: Egypt reopens Suez Canal

MAR 25: Treaty of Rome establishes European Economic Community (EEC)

JUL 25: Tunisia becomes a republic

JUL 29: International Atomic Energy Agency established

OCT 4: Soviet Union launches Sputnik I

that he could not support troops remaining there indefinitely or worse, launching an all-out invasion as proposed by the UN's commander in chief General Mark Clark. United States negotiators took advantage of the new Soviet leadership's desire for a thaw in relations, and the Chinese Communists' economic weakness after years of war and revolution. By the end of his first six months in office, Eisenhower could proudly point to a major achievement—the armistice ending the Korean conflict, which left the nation divided North and South almost at the thirty-eighth parallel.

However, hardly did one war stop than another was heating up. French Indochina had been mired in fighting for years, with America supporting the French, who were losing against the Viet Minh. In May 1954, Americans learned of the shocking French loss in northern Vietnam at Dien Bien Phu. This placed the United States in the uncomfortable position of either stepping up to combat communism in Indochina or allowing it to begin taking over the region. For the moment, the president insisted on no further action.

While Eisenhower disapproved of fighting a ground war in Asia, fearing it could never be won, he also opposed giving up another nation to communism. He explained this in a 1954 press conference as the domino principle—if one country falls to communism, the others in the region will follow. The president favored the creation of the Southeast Asia Treaty Organization (SEATO) composed of various powers including the United States, France, Great Britain, Australia, New Zealand, the Philippines, Thailand, and Pakistan to protect Laos, Cambodia, and South Vietnam. Soon after the treaty signing, South Vietnam's prime minister, Ngo Dinh Diem, received Eisenhower's promise of support.

> ***"I hate war as only a soldier who has lived it can, only as one who has seen its brutality, its futility, its stupidity."***
>
> —*Dwight D. Eisenhower*

The year before, Eisenhower had fought communism by non-traditional means; he determined that the Central Intelligence Agency (CIA) could be used effectively and actively to topple regimes considered friendly to communism. In 1953, Iranian prime minister Mohammed Mossadegh had taken the lucrative oil fields owned by the British and terminated relations with that nation. Immediately the British and American governments conferred about what action should be taken toward this regime that Eisenhower was told supported the communists. Codenamed Ajax, the CIA launched a coup that saw Iran's prime minister arrested and Iran returned to the control of the shah, who then agreed to an oil deal with America. Eisenhower also promised foreign aid for Iran and praised the CIA for its handling of the situation. A new chapter in US covert operations had begun.

In the fall of 1954, Eisenhower discussed the recent successful test of a Russian hydrogen bomb. He wanted the American public to know that the Soviets had such capabilities, but he also feared the hysteria it could generate in this increasingly hostile Cold War world. The president opposed an arms race, believing it was madness, but Secretary of State Dulles emphati-

NATIONAL EVENTS

NOV 27: Gaither Report calls for more US missiles and fallout shelters

Jim Henson, creator of the Muppets, founds the Jim Henson Company

1958

JAN 31: Explorer I launched (first successful US satellite)

MAR 17: US launches Vanguard I satellite

MAR 26: US Army launches Explorer III

WORLD EVENTS

NOV 3: Soviet Union launches Sputnik II with dog onboard—first animal to enter space

JAN 1: Singapore gains self-rule

JAN 4: Sputnik I falls to Earth

JAN 13: More than 9,000 scientists publish a plea to stop nuclear bomb tests

JAN 23: Dictator of Venezuela overthrown

FEB 1: Egypt and Syria unite to form the United Arab Republic

cally disagreed. Any sign of weakness would be seized upon, Dulles argued, so it was imperative that the United States maintain a strong defense program. Eisenhower hoped that the superpowers would scale down their weaponry to halt "racing toward catastrophe."[34] He proposed the creation of an International Atomic Energy Agency that would use isotopes contributed by both the United States and USSR, and a team of scientists would study ways to utilize atomic energy for peaceful, beneficial purposes. His proposal to the UN General Assembly was well received, but a cool reception from the Soviet Union halted the plan immediately. The arms race would continue.

At home, another type of explosion was occurring. California governor Earl Warren had received a pledge from Eisenhower prior to his inauguration that he would have the first vacancy on the Supreme Court. In 1954, a vacancy occurred when Chief Justice Fred Vinson died, and Earl Warren received his appointment, although he had no prior judicial experience. Soon a decision by the Warren court would rock the nation. In *Brown v. Board of Education of Topeka*, the Supreme Court handed down its unanimous decision that "separate but equal" was unconstitutional for schools and other public facilities. Desegregation had begun.

During the 1950s, Americans experienced economic prosperity; consumer goods were bought at record rates, but inflation was not a problem. George Meany, AFL-CIO chief, proclaimed, "American labor has never had it so good."[35] New car sales were selling at record rates, which pushed the antiquated road system to its limits. When passed in 1956, the Federal Aid Highway Act authorized construction of forty-two thousand miles of interstate highways. Eisenhower had admired the German autobahn system during World War II and witnessed its help in providing quicker and safer mobility. He later reflected on this accomplishment as the most important of his administration and wrote: "More than any single action by the government since the end of the war, this one would change the face of America. . . . Its impact on the American economy—the jobs it would produce in manufacturing and construction, the rural areas it would open up—was beyond calculation."[36]

In the summer of 1955, Eisenhower flew to Geneva, Switzerland, to meet with Soviet leaders to discuss trade, open air space above their countries, German reunification, and of course, the arms race. The Soviets were not open to the American president's suggestions, but the fact that both sides met and talked was significant and reassuring to the world.

A few weeks later, Ike and Mamie traveled to a Colorado ranch for some relaxation. While there, he was also contemplating whether he should run for reelection; he was leaning against it, fearing that another term might take too much of a toll

WARSAW PACT (1955) ★ This organization of the USSR and its satellite states was created in response to the addition of West Germany to NATO. A primary difference between the two organizations was that all NATO members were members because each chose to be; the Warsaw Pact nations enjoyed no such autonomy. The presence of both of these organizations emphasized the line drawn by the Cold War, the line between democracy and communism.

MAY 30: Remains of unidentified soldiers killed in action in WWII and the Korean War are buried in Arlington National Cemetery at the Tomb of the Unknowns

JUL 7: First International House of Pancakes (IHOP) opens in Toluca Lake, CA

JUL 15: Five thousand US Marines land in Beirut, Lebanon, to protect the pro-Western government

JUL 26: Explorer IV launched

FEB 5: Gamal Abdel Nasser nominated first president of the United Arab Republic

FEB 14: Hashemite kingdoms of Iraq and Jordan unite

MAR 27: Nikita Khrushchev becomes premier of Soviet Union

JUL 14: Iraqi monarchy overthrown by Arab nationalists (King Faisal II murdered)

JUL 26: Charles given title Prince of Wales by his mother, Queen Elizabeth II

BOMB SHELTERS ★ Promoted by the Federal Civil Defense Administration as a means to supplement fallout shelters for the population in case of nuclear attack, some Americans built bomb shelters in their homes (or nearby). The government suggested guidelines for the bomb shelter's construction (including one wall of 18-inch concrete with a second wall to act as protection against radiation) and also recommended keeping at least two weeks' of food staples on hand at all times. At school, children would practice "duck and cover" drills. Signs for fallout shelters were visible so people knew where to go if notified of an impending attack, and these, too, were to be kept stocked at all times.

on his mental and physical health. Then on the night of September 23, Eisenhower suffered a heart attack and was transported to a Denver hospital, where he remained for a month before being flown to Washington. He continued his convalescence at their Gettysburg farm.

By the end of the year, Eisenhower was back at work but still uncertain about his political future. Advisors were telling him that if he ran again, he should do so with a different vice president. Eisenhower did not agree that he should dump Nixon, yet he rather hoped that his vice president would choose to leave the ticket for another post. Nixon, however, believed his political future was tied to keeping his vice presidency and argued that he should be kept on the ticket, but Eisenhower was still uncertain. By early 1956, Eisenhower decided his own political future after receiving a clean bill of health from his doctors and announced he would run for reelection.

During this time, the South was experiencing unrest stemming from the *Brown* decision; in fact, in Montgomery, Alabama, a bus boycott was underway. Reverend Martin Luther King Jr. had initiated the action following the arrest and forcible removal of one his congregation members, Rosa Parks, from a city bus. Eisenhower had worried earlier that the Supreme Court decision could create a furor in the South. The president believed that people who had never lived in the South could not understand the depth of prejudice found there. Those feelings would not be easily erased by legislation, Eisenhower argued. Years later, he wrote, "I did not agree with those who believed that legislation alone could institute instant morality, [or] who believed that coercion could cure all civil rights problems."[37] He was unsure how to proceed or how much action he as president could or should take. He supported a civil rights bill, although he was disappointed by the watered-down version ultimately handed him by Congress, and he reluctantly signed it into law in September 1957. This created a nonpartisan Civil Rights commission and emphasized eliminating voting restrictions for black voters, especially in the South.

1956 CAMPAIGN

Republicans meeting in San Francisco replayed the 1952 convention by nominating both Eisenhower and Nixon for reelection. Democrats also chose their 1952 presidential candidate, Adlai Stevenson, to try again. The vice presidential running mate was a hard-fought race between Estes Kefauver, Tennessee senator, and Massachusetts senator John F. Kennedy, but Kefauver won the nomination. They campaigned against the Republicans as a party "dominated by representatives of special privilege."[38] They believed

NATIONAL EVENTS

JUL 29: Congress officially creates National Aeronautics and Space Administration (NASA)

OCT 11: Pioneer I first spacecraft launched by NASA

DEC 9: Conservative John Birch Society founded by Robert Welch

JAN 3: Alaska admitted as 49th state

1959

WORLD EVENTS

OCT 1: Morocco and Tunisia join the Arab League

OCT 2: Guinea declares its independence from France

NOV 25–28: French Sudan, Chad, the Republic of Congo, and Gabon become autonomous republics

DEC 1: Central African Republic gains independence from France

DEC 21: Charles de Gaulle elected president of France

JAN 2: Fidel Castro's troops advance on Havana

more could be done to promote mutual disarmament and that spending should be increased for domestic programs.

Throughout the campaign season of 1956, Eisenhower attempted to keep up with the quick pace of unfolding world events. After Egyptian president Gamal Abdel Nasser seized the Suez Canal from the French and British companies who owned it, he blocked Israel's only outlet to the Red Sea. Consequently, the British, French, and Israeli governments were determined to take action. Days before the election, Israeli troops invaded Egypt's Sinai Peninsula. The British and French soon followed by seizing the Suez Canal. Eisenhower was not consulted before any of these actions, and he was surprised by what he considered the audacity of the three powers. Fearful of possible Soviet intervention, Eisenhower attempted to encourage the Europeans to back down. The Soviets, however, had their hands full with uprisings against the communist regimes in Poland and Hungary, and the United States decided to push for a UN cease-fire resolution to end hostilities in the Middle East. Monitoring the world situation kept Eisenhower too busy to continue campaigning in the final week before the election. Secretary of State Dulles went into the hospital for emergency surgery at this crucial juncture, and gloomy news poured into the White House. British prime minister Anthony Eden refused Eisenhower's pleas to withdraw troops, insisting they had to remain until a UN force arrived to take charge of the Canal; meanwhile, the Red Army marched into Budapest to regain control of their satellite nation. The Soviets also warned of their taking action against the British and French if they did not withdraw from the Suez. Talk of World War III now hung in the air, and the next day was the presidential election. Eisenhower stated, "If those fellows start something, we may have to hit 'em—and, if necessary, with everything in the bucket."[39] Such action, fortunately, was not necessary, as the Europeans accepted the cease-fire, and the United States remained aloof from the Hungary situation.

The Soviets, however, were not totally placated because they resented the ongoing flights by American U-2 reconnaissance aircraft flying over Eastern Europe and the Soviet Union, snapping pictures. Eisenhower decided that the information gained from these flights was not worth the risk and ordered them to cease, although they would be periodically resumed.

On November 6, 1956, the American people rewarded Eisenhower with another four years as their president. He received an overwhelming mandate with 57 percent of the popular vote and 457 electoral votes to Stevenson's 73 from six southern states and Missouri. Democrats, however, would control Congress.

SECOND TERM

Keeping peace at home in September 1957 was no easier than trying to preserve it elsewhere in the world. News arrived from Little Rock, Arkansas, that its governor, Orville Faubus, was refusing to allow Central High School to be integrated; in fact, Faubus had empowered the state's National Guard to keep any black students from entering the school. Eisenhower talked to Attorney General Herbert Brownell about what actions he could take. Simply ignoring the governor's defiance of a federal court order was not possible; Brownell argued that sending Army troops into Little Rock might be the solution, but the president dreaded

DID YOU KNOW?

Eisenhower is the only president to have served in the military during both World Wars.

JAN 7: US recognizes Fidel Castro's new Cuban government

FEB 3: Buddy Holly, Richie Valens, the Big Bopper, and their pilot die in plane crash

MAR 9: Barbie doll debuts

APR 9: NASA selects seven military pilots to become first US astronauts

APR 9: Architect Frank Lloyd Wright dies

FEB 1: Female suffrage defeated in referendum in Switzerland

FEB 16: Fidel Castro becomes premier of Cuba

FEB 18: Women vote for the first time in Nepal

FEB 19: UK grants Cyprus independence

MAR 17: The 14th Dalai Lama flees Tibet for India

APR 10: Japanese prince Akihito marries

JUN 3: Singapore becomes self-governing

such a scenario. Mob rule then took over and the lives of the black students were in jeopardy. Little Rock mayor Woodrow Wilson Mann begged the president for help. Eisenhower first federalized the Arkansas National Guard and ordered the 101st Airborne Division to Little Rock. Within hours, the city was occupied and the mobs dispersed. Southerners screamed in protest; one senator proclaimed, "The President's move was an attempt to destroy the social order of the South."[40] Within a few weeks, nine black students were attending Central High School, paratroopers had withdrawn, and Attorney General Brownell resigned, hoping such action would help diffuse the situation.

> ***A people that values its privileges above its principles soon loses both.***
>
> —*Dwight D. Eisenhower*

Hardly had one near-disaster been handled when another even greater one loomed overhead. On the night of October 3, 1957, a satellite flew over the towns and cities of the United States for the first time in history. Although American technology had the ability to launch a satellite, Eisenhower had refused, saying it would merely be a publicity stunt. Nikita Khrushchev, however, had no such hesitation and lauded the coup his country had gained over the United States. Eisenhower did not consider Sputnik to be of any importance, but the American people were of a different mind. They feared this new space age technology and demanded to know what their president and government planned to do in retaliation. Sputnik II went into space, and the United States soon followed with its first satellite, which ingloriously rose from its launch pad only to fall back down and collapse into flames. Now what? More rockets, more failures, but finally *Explorer* sailed into the sky in January 1958; the United States had joined the space race. In April, Eisenhower sent a proposal to Congress that created the National Aeronautics and Space Administration (NASA), whose purpose would be to oversee US projects in space. (Those of a military nature would be under the auspices of the Defense Department.)

More problems erupted in the Middle East as Nassar sponsored coups in the region, one of which saw the bloody massacre of Iraq's royal family. Lebanese president Camille Chamoun requested American help against a possible attack by Syria. Meanwhile the British parachuted troops in to bolster support for Jordan's King Hussein. Kuwait was under the watchful eyes of the US Navy, who were also ensuring no one seized control of that small country's bountiful oil fields.

With such unrest in the world and the advent of Sputnik, the American people sent even more Democrats to Congress in the off-year election of 1958, and they now outnumbered Republicans by nearly two to one.

A few days after the election, another crisis loomed with the Soviet Union when Khrushchev announced that his nation would sign a treaty with East Germany and end the Allied presence in Berlin. Eisenhower believed that Khrushchev was merely doing some saber rattling and ignored the congressmen in Washington, including Senator Jack Kennedy, who demanded increased defense spending. Such a

NATIONAL EVENTS

JUL 8: First Americans killed in action in Vietnam

JUL 15: Jazz singer Billie Holiday dies

AUG 14: First picture of Earth from space taken by Explorer 6

AUG 21: Hawaii admitted as 50th state

OCT 21: Solomon R. Guggenheim Museum opens in NYC

WORLD EVENTS

JUL 2: Prince Albert of Belgium marries Italian princess Paola Ruffo di Calabria

AUG 4: Martial law declared in Laos

AUG 8: Two thousand die in flooding in Taiwan

AUG 15: Cyprus gains independence

SEP 13: Luna 2 crashes onto the moon

OCT 7: First photos of far side of the moon sent back by USSR probe Luna 3

DEC 1: Antarctic Treaty signed by 12 countries; first arms control agreement of the Cold War

move, the president argued, was nonproductive and only benefited the defense industry. Instead, Eisenhower believed the path to peace was continued talks and negotiations with the Soviets. Toward that end, he invited Khrushchev to the United States, and the Soviet leader arrived in September 1959. Khrushchev toured the country, but insisted he was unimpressed by anything in America—especially his visit to a Hollywood set, where he witnessed a musical number done by scantily clad dancers. No agreement was reached by the two leaders, but the world felt a little safer knowing that at least the men were talking.

Closer to home, a revolt in Cuba to overthrow its dictator, Fulgencio Batista, had succeeded and the rebel leader Fidel Castro had seized control of the island nation. The man that the United States had originally thought would be friendly now spouted hatred toward America. Fearing he would create a communist regime, Eisenhower decided to take action. Plots to remove him were undertaken by the CIA, but none succeeded. Other plans moved ahead for a coup and the transfer of power to a government friendly to the United States.

As Eisenhower neared the end of his presidency, he wanted to leave a legacy of peace, and proposed a test-ban treaty that would ultimately result in disarmament. A summit was arranged for the United States, France, Great Britain, and the Soviet Union to attend and discuss such a treaty. Many within the United States, however, disagreed with the proposal and argued that testing should be increased. The intelligence community needed more pictures from reconnaissance flights, and on May 1, 1960, Major Francis Gary Powers flew over the Soviet Union in his U-2 aircraft. The next day, the president was informed that the plane was missing, and over the next several days the truth emerged. The Soviets had downed his plane and taken him prisoner. Khrushchev angrily denounced the American "spy mission," which Eisenhower at first denied had occurred and tried to cover up the flight. But Khrushchev produced pictures to support his statements, and Ike had to admit what had happened. Although the four countries' leaders met at the Paris summit, Khrushchev seized the occasion to denounce America and its president, and then walked out. With him went any hope of an early end to the Cold War.

In the summer of 1960, Republicans chose Richard Nixon as their presidential candidate, though many preferred New York governor Nelson Rockefeller. Eisenhower constantly fielded reporters' questions regarding his vice president and if he was qualified for the nation's highest job. When asked for "an example of a major idea of his that you had adopted in that role, as the decider," Eisenhower broke in testily, "If you give me a week, I might think of one. I don't remember."[41] Although he apologized to Nixon, the harm of his comment was done. Still the president campaigned for Nixon, admitting he was doing it as much against Kennedy as to help his own candidate, but his efforts were in vain as Kennedy won the presidential election.

Before leaving office, Eisenhower delivered a farewell address in which he warned of the dangers resulting from the Cold War and the creation of a vast "military-industrial complex." He also apologized for his failure to secure an arms agreement, but hoped that it would still be accomplished in the future.

DID YOU KNOW?

President Eisenhower supported adding the phrase "under God" to the Pledge of Allegiance.

JAN 3: US Senator John F. Kennedy declares his candidacy for the Democratic nomination for president

JAN 19: US signs Treaty of Mutual Cooperation and Security with Japan

JAN 25: Radio payola scandal hits Washington, D.C., and the National Association of Broadcasters threatens to fine any DJ accepting money in exchange for playing certain records on the air

FEB 1: Sit-in at Woolworth's lunch counter protesting segregation

1960

JAN: Mau Mau Rebellion officially ends in Kenya

JAN 1: Cameroon gains independence

JAN 9: Construction of Aswan High Dam begins in Egypt

FEB 13: France tests its first atomic bomb in the Sahara

MAY 11: Fugitive Nazi Adolf Eichmann abducted by Mossad agents in Buenos Aires

MAY 15: Sputnik IV launched

DID YOU KNOW?

Eisenhower's picture was on the dollar coin from 1971 to 1978.

RETIREMENT

Following the inauguration of John F. Kennedy, Ike and Mamie slipped away to their Gettysburg farm and their new life. They enjoyed hosting their son John, his wife Barbara, and their three children (the oldest, David, had been the namesake for the presidential retreat in Maryland, Camp David). Eisenhower spent a good deal of his time working on his memoirs of his presidency, which were published in two volumes: *Mandate for Change* (1953–1956) and *Waging Peace* (1956–1961). He also spent many enjoyable hours on the putting green or playing golf at the nearby country club. Friends would drop in, and the Eisenhowers traveled a good deal, as well. Both Presidents Kennedy and Johnson consulted Eisenhower about foreign affairs, and he opposed increasing American involvement in Vietnam.

In 1965, he suffered his second major heart attack (he also had had a major stroke eight years earlier), but he slowly recovered and resumed his activities. With his health worsening, Eisenhower decided to begin putting his affairs in order. Already his papers and archives had been moved to the recently constructed Eisenhower Library and Museum in Abilene. A meditation chapel was also built across from his childhood home, and he decided that would be the final resting place for Icky, Mamie, and him.

Eisenhower suffered a third heart attack in April 1968 and again in August. Still he monitored the 1968 presidential campaign with Nixon again as the Republican candidate, and he was happy about Nixon's victory. From his Walter Reed Hospital room he watched the wedding of his grandson David to Nixon's daughter Julie on closed-circuit television.

His health continued to deteriorate in the coming months, and on March 28, 1969, Dwight D. Eisenhower was surrounded by his family when he looked at his son John and murmured, "I want to go; God take me." Wearing his full military uniform and in an Army coffin, Eisenhower made his last trek to Abilene.

Mamie continued to live on the Gettysburg farm for the next ten years. She suffered a stroke in September 1979, but lingered nearly six weeks before dying on November 1, 1979. She is buried beside her husband at Abilene.

NATIONAL EVENTS

FEB 9: Actress Joanne Woodward receives the first Hollywood Walk of Fame star

FEB 11: The ZPG-3W airship is destroyed during a storm in Massachusetts

FEB 18: The Winter Olympics open in Squaw Valley, California

APR 1: The first weather satellite, TIROS-1, is launched

MAY 1: US spy plane shot down by Soviet missile

WORLD EVENTS

MAY 22: Great Chilean Earthquake is largest earthquake ever recorded

JUN 30: Belgian Congo gains independence from Belgium, then civil war breaks out

JUL 20: First elected female head of government in Ceylon (Sri Lanka)

AUG: Burkina Faso, Cote d'Ivoire, Chad, Central African Republic, Congo-Brazzaville, Gabon, and Senegal all gain their independence

SEP 14: Iran, Iraq, Kuwait, Saudi Arabia, and Venezuela form OPEC

ENDNOTES

1 Dwight D. Eisenhower, *At Ease: Stories I Tell Friends*, Garden City, NY: Doubleday, 1967, p. 31.

2 Carlo D'Este, *Eisenhower: A Soldier's Life*, New York, NY: Henry Holt and Co., 2002, p. 43.

3 Ibid, p. 56.

4 Eisenhower, p. 10.

5 D'Este, p. 95.

6 Geoffrey Perret, *Eisenhower*, New York: Random House, 1999, p. 65.

7 Alden Hatch, *General Ike*, New York: Henry Holt and Co., 1944, p. 64.

8 D'Este, p. 136.

9 Ibid, p. 137.

10 Eisenhower, p. 169.

11 Ibid, p. 170.

12 Ibid, p. 173.

13 Ibid.

14 Ibid, p. 181.

15 Perret, p. 138.

16 Ibid, p. 139.

17 Eisenhower, p. 249.

18 Perret, p. 160.

19 Ibid, p. 187.

20 Ibid, p. 197.

21 Dwight D. Eisenhower, *Crusade in Europe*, New York: Da Capo Press, 1979, p. 183.

22 D'Este, p. 467.

23 Bernard Law Montgomery, *The Memoirs of Field-Marshal the Viscount Montgomery of Alamein*, Cleveland, OH: World Book Publishing Co., 1958, p. 484.

24 Perret, p. 270.

25 Ibid, p. 324.

26 Ibid, p. 320.

27 Dwight D. Eisenhower, *The Papers of Dwight D. Eisenhower* (17 vols.), Alfred Chandler, ed., Baltimore: Johns Hopkins University Press, 1996, vol. IV, p. 2696.

28 Eisenhower, *Crusade*, p. 444.

29 Stephen E. Ambrose, *Eisenhower, Soldier and President*, New York: Simon & Schuster, 1990, p.219.

30 Ibid, p. 227.

31 Ambrose, p. 260.

32 William Bragg Ewald, Jr., *Eisenhower, the President*, Englewood, NJ: Prentice-Hall, 1981, p. 224.

33 Ambrose, p. 296.

34 Ibid, p. 340.

35 Dwight D. Eisenhower, *Mandate for Change*, Garden City, NY: Doubleday & Co., Inc., 1963, p. 491.

36 Ibid, pp. 548-549.

37 Ibid, p. 235.

38 William A. DeGregorio, *The Complete Book of US Presidents*, New York: Gramercy Books, 2001, p. 535.

39 Ambrose, p. 431.

40 Ibid, p. 447.

41 Perret, p. 597.

MAY 6: President Eisenhower signs Civil Rights Act of 1960 into law

MAY 9: Sale of birth control pill approved by FDA

SEP 26: Nixon and Kennedy participate in the first televised presidential debate

OCT 29: Cassius Clay wins his first professional fight

NOV 8: JFK elected president

DEC 12: Supreme Court rules segregation unconstitutional

SEP 22: Mali gains independence

OCT 1: Nigeria gains independence

OCT 30: First successful kidney transplant, in the UK

NOV 28: Mauritania gains independence

DEC 13: Revolt in Ethiopia to overthrow Emperor Haile Selassie while he is in Brazil

DEC 17: Ethiopian revolt suppressed; Selassie returned to power

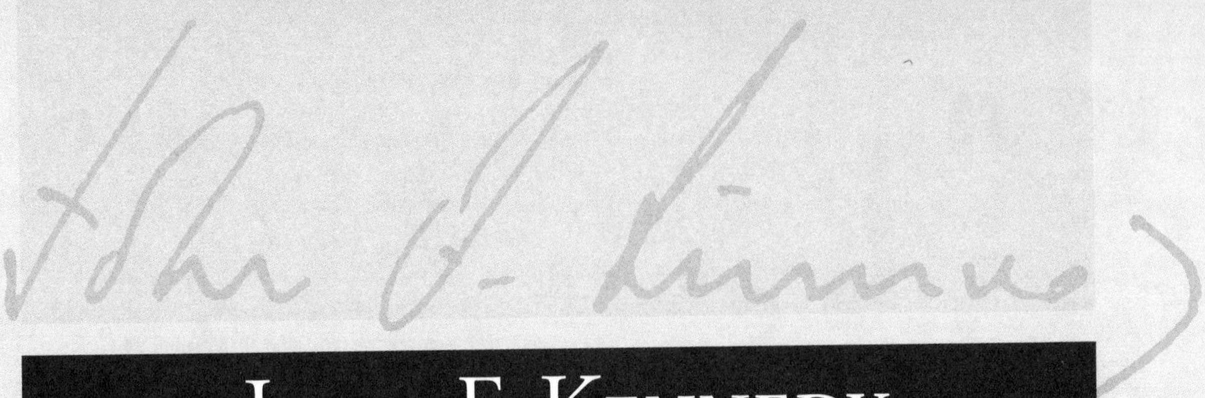

John F. Kennedy

★ ★ ★ THIRTY-FIFTH PRESIDENT ★ ★ ★

LIFE SPAN

- Born: May 29, 1917, in Brookline, Massachusetts
- Died: November 22, 1963, in Dallas, Texas

NICKNAMES

- Jack or JFK

FAMILY

- Father: **Joseph P. Kennedy** (1888–1969)
- Mother: **Rose Fitzgerald Kennedy** (1890–1995)
- Wife: **Jacqueline Lee Bouvier Kennedy** (1929–1994); wed on September 12, 1953, in Newport, Rhode Island
- Children: **Caroline Bouvier** (1957–); **John Fitzgerald Jr.** (1960–1999); **Patrick Bouvier** (1963)

RELIGION

- Roman Catholic

HIGHER EDUCATION

- Harvard College, 1940

PROFESSION

- Politician, author

MILITARY SERVICE

- World War II: enlisted in the navy in September 1941 as an ensign; later promoted to lieutenant; earned Purple Heart in August 1943 off Solomon Islands as skipper of ***PT-109***
- Discharged April 1945

POLITICAL LIFE

- US representative (1947–1953)
- US senator (1953–1961)

PRESIDENCY

- One term: January 20, 1961–November 22, 1963
- Democrat
- Reason for leaving office: assassinated
- Vice president: **Lyndon B. Johnson** (1961–1963)

ELECTION OF 1960

- Electoral vote: **Kennedy** 303; **Richard M. Nixon** 219
- Popular vote: **Kennedy** 34,226,731; **Nixon** 34,108,157

CABINET

SECRETARY OF STATE
Dean Rusk (1961–1963)

SECRETARY OF THE TREASURY
C. Douglas Dillon (1961–1963)

SECRETARY OF DEFENSE
Robert S. McNamara (1961–1963)

ATTORNEY GENERAL
Robert F. Kennedy (1961–1963)

POSTMASTER GENERAL
J. Edward Day (1961–1963)

John A. Gronouski (1963)

SECRETARY OF THE INTERIOR
Stewart L. Udall (1961–1963)

SECRETARY OF AGRICULTURE
Orville L. Freeman (1961–1963)

SECRETARY OF COMMERCE
Luther H. Hodges (1961–1963)

SECRETARY OF LABOR
Arthur J. Goldberg (1961–1962)

W. Willard Wirtz (1962–1963)

SECRETARY OF HEALTH, EDUCATION AND WELFARE
Abraham A. Ribicoff (1961–1962)

Anthony J. Celebrezze (1962–1963)

On November 22, 1963, the American people were shocked to learn of the assassination of their youthful president in Dallas, Texas. The tragic death of John F. Kennedy buoyed his waning popularity, and immediately the circumstances and speculation surrounding his demise overshadowed the life he had led prior to that fateful day.

EARLY LIFE

John Fitzgerald Kennedy was born on May 29, 1917, at the home of Joseph and Rose Fitzgerald Kennedy in Brookline, Massachusetts. John or "Jack," as he was called, was their second son, and he eventually had seven younger siblings, many of whom were very close to him. Kennedy's father was quite wealthy, the president of a local bank, the Columbia Trust Company, and he later branched into other businesses, including real estate, bootlegging alcohol during Prohibition, and stock market investing. As a Broadway and movie producer, Joe Kennedy had public affairs with actresses, including silent screen star Gloria Swanson.

Rose was a devout Catholic and reared her children in the faith, but she was not a doting mother; in fact, she ascribed to the child-rearing authority of the time and refused to coddle or even hug her children. Between her lack of affection and the obvious preference by his parents for his older brother Joseph Jr., Jack felt neglected and soon exhibited physical ailments. At an early age he developed intense gastrointestinal problems that required multiple hospitalizations.

When Jack was five, he began attending a nearby public elementary school but after two years, he and Joe Jr. transferred to the private Dexter School. There the boys encountered anti-Catholic prejudice and were often targets for abuse and frequently fought with other children in the schoolyard.

The Kennedy siblings loved their summers when the family traveled to their rambling home on Cape Cod, providing plenty of room for the growing brood and any others who might drop by. There Jack spent much of his time reading, a passion he shared with his mother. Unfortunately, this did not ensure high scores on school entrance exams. His father wanted his oldest sons to attend Choate preparatory school, but Jack was not ready in 1930, so he was sent instead to Canterbury in New Milford, Connecticut. Although he was unhappy there, he did learn how to play football, even though he was slight in build. His health also took a beating as he suffered from hives and had to undergo an emergency appendectomy. After months of tutoring, Jack passed his entrance tests and entered Choate in 1931 at the age of fourteen.

For the next four years, Jack tried to find his niche among his classmates and decided his schoolwork could be neglected in favor of fun. His headmaster wrote, "Jack has a clever, individual mind. When he learns the right place for humor and learns to use his individual way of looking at things as an asset instead of handicap, his natural gift of an individual outlook and witty expression are going to help him. . . . Jack is not as able academically as his high IQ might lead us to think."[1] Jack's teasing nature stood him in stark contrast to his older brother Joe, who was willing to "play the game" and win the support of the faculty and administration, as well as their father. Although Joe Jr. went to England while Jack finished his Choate career, the shadow of his older brother still loomed large over him. When his studies faltered, Joe Sr. wrote to Jack: "Don't let me lose confidence in you again because it will be nearly impossible to restore it."[2]

NATIONAL EVENTS

Ray Kroc buys the McDonald's hamburger stands

The Misfits, screenplay by Arthur Miller, is final movie for its stars Clark Gable and Marilyn Monroe

JAN 3: Atomic reactor explodes in Idaho Falls, ID at the National Reactor Testing Station, killing three

JAN 17: President Eisenhower delivers his final State of the Union message and warns the American people to be wary of the "military industrial complex"

1961

WORLD EVENTS

JAN 1: The UK bids farwell to the farthing, its legal tender since the 13th century

JAN 3: President Eisenhower announces that US will cease diplomatic ties with Cuba

JAN 7: Five African heads of state create the Charter of Casablanca, a NATO-like organization

FEB 4: Portuguese Colonial War begins

FEB 15: Entire US figure skating team and several coaches are killed near

He did finish (sixty-fourth in his class of 112) and was preparing to attend Princeton, but his father insisted that once more he follow in his elder brother's footsteps and journey to England to spend a year studying at the London School of Economics. He had hardly arrived before his old bowel ailment hit, and he became seriously ill. Joe Kennedy decided to let his son return home and enroll at Princeton. Health ailments continued to plague him, and at one point, he was diagnosed with leukemia but Jack refused to believe it. He left for Palm Beach and later worked on a ranch in Arizona and spent the rest of his summer in one of his favorite pursuits—sailing off Cape Cod. Then in the fall of 1936, he entered Harvard University.

HARVARD AND ENGLAND

Jack threw himself into athletics at Harvard and joined the freshman football, swimming, and golf teams. Swimming was his best sport of the three. The following year he ran for his first elected office and was trounced.

The summer before his sophomore year, Jack took his father's advice and took a road trip across Europe with a friend. Joe Kennedy believed, as many did by 1937, that war was on its way, and the continent would likely never be the same in its wake. The tour took Jack and friend LeMoyne Billings across France, Spain, Italy, Austria, and Germany, but on the Riviera, their car got stuck in the sand, and it took two hours to push it out. This was also the first recording of Kennedy's persistent back problems, and it remained sore for several days. The young men returned to England, where Jack's father was now the American ambassador to the Court of St. James. This appointment seemed rather shocking to some, including President Roosevelt who, when he first contemplated sending a full-blooded Irishman to the English court, laughed and called it "the greatest joke in the world."[3]

Back at Harvard, Kennedy resumed his studies, where he majored in political science with international relations as his emphasis. He joined the secret club the Spee, and his sports activities also continued, but this was his last year of football, for his slight stature was not strong enough to withstand the blows of his opponents, and a ruptured disc decisively ended his playing. He and brother Joe took Harvard to the top with their sailing skills and won the Intercollegiate Sailing Championship in the waters off Cape Cod in June 1938.

His junior year found Jack on the Dean's list, and he was also dating an heiress, Frances Ann Cannon of the Cannon textiles of North Carolina. The courtship ended, though, when Frances turned down Kennedy's marriage proposal. The news of their breakup was welcome to both families, who were concerned about religious differences. The Cannons were Presbyterian and wanted their daughter to avoid marrying a Catholic; the Kennedys felt equally strong that their future daughter-in-law must be Catholic.

Jack returned to England to work for his father at the American embassy, and he took another road trip across the continent at his father's behest to learn firsthand what the situation was following Germany's seizure of Czechoslovakia. "Everyone thinks war is inevitable before the year is out. I personally don't though Dad does,"[4] wrote Kennedy in the spring of 1939. During the trip, he seriously injured his back again when his car overturned. Then, traveling to Germany, the reception turned violent as Germans pelted his car with stones when they spied its English license plate.

JAN 20: John F. Kennedy inaugurated president

JAN 24: A US B-52 Stratofortress carrying two nuclear bombs crashes near Goldsboro, NC

JAN 25: President Kennedy conducts the first live televised presidential news conference

JAN 26: President Kennedy appoints Dr. Janet G. Travell to be his physician, the first woman to hold this distinction

JAN 31: NASA sends a chimpanzee into space to test the Mercury space capsule

Brussels, Belgium, when the Sabena Boeing 707 plane they're traveling in crashes

MAR 1: Uganda holds its first general election

MAR 3: Hassan II is crowned King of Morocco

APR 11: Adolf Eichmann's war crimes trial begins in Jerusalem

APR 12: Yuri Gagarin, a Soviet cosmonaut, becomes the first human to go into space

Kennedy returned to London at the end of August, and a few days later Germany invaded Poland. Forty-eight hours later, a German U-boat sank the British liner *Athenia* traveling between Liverpool and New York. More than one hundred people died, including twenty-eight Americans. Joe sent his son to see the injured Americans scattered in the Glasgow hospitals. The twenty-two-year-old attempted to offer solace and comfort to those he found, but some refused it, shouting down his words of neutrality and peaceful open seas. They remembered the days of World War I and now the world seemed plunged into war once more.

> ***"A revolution is coming—a revolution which will be peaceful if we are wise enough; compassionate if we care enough; successful if we are fortunate enough—but a revolution which is coming whether we will it or not. We can affect its character, we cannot alter its inevitability."***
>
> *—John F. Kennedy*

When Jack returned to Harvard, he resumed his work at the school of government and joined the editorial board of Harvard's newspaper, *The Crimson*. He also plunged into researching and writing his honors thesis. In "Appeasement at Munich," he echoed his father's belief in the need for England to appease Hitler and avoid fighting his Nazi war machine. He received high honors for his thesis, but his father's appraisal was less complimentary: "It seems to represent a lot of work, but it does not prove anything."[5] Still Joseph Kennedy had it reworked and published in book form. *Why England Slept* became a modest seller and gained Jack recognition as a writer. After graduating magna cum laude with a bachelor of science in economics in 1940, Jack looked to his future with uncertainty.

In the fall of 1940, Jack drove his new car to Stanford University and briefly enrolled there, as well as registered for the draft. He still lacked direction. He tried traveling, but then decided to attend law school, only to learn that his brother Joe Jr. had enlisted in the Naval Reserve. Jack wanted to enlist, too, but kept failing his physicals. Finally, his father pulled strings; in October 1941, the Navy accepted Jack and commissioned him as an ensign into the Naval Reserve. The twenty-four-year-old was ecstatic—he now was an officer, but his older brother was a seaman second class; in short, Joe would be required to salute Jack.

WAR AT SEA

While Joe, by now a naval airman, went to Europe to fly reconnaissance planes against Germany, Jack reported for duty in October 1941 at Naval Intelligence in Washington, where he summarized information and prepared reports. Within a month his group was tasked with determining the most likely target of the Japanese, since intercepted dispatches indicated such an attack was imminent. Soon after that

NATIONAL EVENTS				
MAR: President Kennedy starts the Alliance for Progress to help Latin America	**MAR 1:** President Kennedy creates the Peace Corps	**MAR 29:** Ratification of Twenty-third Amendment permitting residents of Washington, D.C., to vote in presidential elections	**APR 23:** Singer Judy Garland makes her comeback at New York's Carnegie Hall	**MAY 4:** Freedom Riders begin their journey to protest segregation of transportation in the South

WORLD EVENTS				
APR 17–19: Bay of Pigs invasion in Cuba fails	**APR 27:** Sierra Leone becomes independent	**JUN 19:** Kuwait becomes an emirate	**JUN 21:** Russian ballet dancer Rudolf Nureyev visits Paris with the Kirov Ballet and asks France for asylum	**JUL 5:** Shavit 2, the first Israeli rocket, is launched

day of infamy at Pearl Harbor—December 7, 1941—Jack Kennedy was transferred to Charleston, South Carolina. Some believed it was to separate him from his current lady, Inga Arvad, who the FBI was monitoring because she had won a Berlin beauty contest and had been given her award by Herman Goering, a member of the Nazi party. Bored with his work of coding and decoding messages, Kennedy itched to go into active duty and applied for midshipman's training. He was accepted and went to Northwestern University in July 1942.

Once in training, he soon decided he wanted to command PT-boats and his request was granted. In Rhode Island, the PT-trainees had to learn how to operate their boats, guns, and torpedoes mainly on the basis of theory rather than hands-on experience. In short, their training did little to prepare them for what lay ahead. Jack's popularity among the men grew with his organization of football games for their downtime. He too would play, although the activity wrecked havoc on his back. One of his friends there later remembered that he was impressed because Kennedy "pulled strings" to leave his cushy desk job to go into combat while others were doing the opposite.

When the men received their assignments, Kennedy was most disappointed to learn he was to remain there and train future recruits. Whether he was kept because of extraordinary skill or rather fear that his back would not endure combat has been debated. Pulling strings once again, he was transferred to the Solomon Islands as an officer replacement in March 1943.

Rose Kennedy worried about her son and wrote, "He is quite ready to die for the U.S.A. . . . He also thinks it would be good for Joe [Jr.]'s political career if he [Jack] died for the grand old flag."[6] Although Jack would not die in war, he would certainly win glory for himself and his family.

On the night of August 1, 1943, Kennedy commanded PT-109 near New Georgia Island, along with fourteen other boats. Reports vary about what happened and who was at fault during the confused night action. Their mission was to intercept a Japanese convoy, but few torpedoes were fired by the Americans and no damage inflicted. Then an incident occurred that only happened once in the war—a PT-boat was rammed and cut in half by a Japanese destroyer. (While some praised Kennedy for keeping his cool under such duress, others blamed his inexperience for causing the incident in the first place, and Lieutenant Commander Thomas G. Warfield later said, "He wasn't a particularly good boat commander."[7] A few weeks earlier Jack had found himself in trouble when racing his engines. The engines cut out when thrown into reverse, causing PT-109 to slam into the dock—taking off a piece of it—and other boat commanders good-naturedly nicknamed him "Crash" Kennedy.)

In a split second, the Japanese destroyer *Amagiri* split PT-109, killing two men. Kennedy yelled for his crew to jump into the water while he destroyed the codebook. The men clung to the hull in the water, ringed by flaming fuel. He swam out to help two of his crew to the hull, where they bobbed in the ocean until the next afternoon when they decided to paddle toward an island some miles away. It took four hours, and Jack swam with the straps of his engineer Patrick Henry McMahon's life jacket in his teeth, towing him, for the man's hands were too burned to use. Kennedy (again towing McMahon) and his crew swam to another island where they found coconuts, which the men subsisted on. On August 5, they found a barrel of

SUPREME COURT APPOINTMENTS

Byron R. White, 1962

Arthur J. Goldberg, 1962

DID YOU KNOW?

Kennedy was the first president born in the twentieth century.

MAY 5: Alan Shepard is first American in space

MAY 24: Freedom Riders arrested in Jackson, Mississippi

JUN 3–4: Meeting between President Kennedy and Soviet leader Nikita Khrushchev in Vienna

JUL 2: Ernest Hemingway commits suicide

AUG 5: Six Flags over Texas theme park opens

AUG 10: Britain applies for membership in the European Economic Community

AUG 13: Russia builds Berlin Wall in East Germany

SEP 17: Turkish military leaders hang former president Adnan Menderes

SEP 18: UN secretary general Dag Hammarskjöld is killed in a plane crash

OCT 12: New Zealand abolishes the death penalty

STATE OF THE UNION

US POPULATION IN 1961
179,323,031

NATIONAL DEBT IN 1963
$309,346,845,059

NUMBER OF STATES
50

fresh water and Japanese crackers on another island. Jack continued watching the sea for other PT-boats that he could flag down, but none appeared. Two native islanders, however, took a message he carved on a coconut shell to an Australian "coast watcher" tracking the movement of Japanese ships and planes. The men were soon rescued.

Following a brief convalescence, Kennedy was reassigned to PT-boat 59 on September 1. His task was to convert it to a gunboat, and five of his former crewmembers volunteered to serve under him again. Nine guns of varying sizes were mounted, so he required a bigger crew than before; others joined him from another PT-boat. A few weeks later, his Gunboat One was tasked with intercepting Japanese traffic in the northern Solomons. They often functioned as a rescue crew for those pinned down under enemy fire, and on one occasion, Kennedy and another boat raced to the assistance of a trapped Marine patrol, even though PT-59 was dangerously low on fuel and ultimately had to be towed the final miles back to base. By now, Jack's stomach was in terrible shape, as was his back, so his commander decided to send him stateside in January 1944.

His family was disappointed by the honors he received, thinking he deserved more and higher ones than the Purple Heart and the Navy and Marine Corps Medals for saving the lives of his men and many Marines. He was on duty in Miami, and then returned to New England, where his aching back landed him once more in the hospital. He was interviewed extensively by reporter and writer John Hersey about his naval experiences. Hersey's article ran in *Life* magazine and publicized the youthful naval officer's exploits. Although duty in Miami was hoped to heal his back, it failed to work, and finally the long-delayed operation was performed in Boston, but it, too, failed to relieve his chronic pain.

LOOKING FOR A FUTURE

Meanwhile the family learned from daughter Kathleen with the Red Cross in England that Joe Jr. had decided to enlist for a second tour. Although his continual naval flights against submarines were extremely dangerous and taxing, he wanted even more daring duty—bombing the V-1 rocket sites in Germany. The United States and Britain had created aircraft carrying tons of explosives that were to be detonated by remote control. On their first mission, Joe's plane exploded in midair; no one ever was certain how it happened.

The Kennedy family was devastated by the news; fortunately, John was home from the hospital recuperating, but all were aware that their parents felt their oldest son's death most keenly. Joseph admitted, "All my plans for my own future were all tied up with young Joe and that has gone to smash."[8] Now Jack felt he could never win favor over his brother in his father's eyes: "I'm shadowboxing in a match the shadow is always going to win."[9] More health problems prompted him to resign from the Navy in late December 1944. Following Joe Jr.'s death, Joseph Kennedy told Jack, "It is your responsibility to go into politics,"[10] and his son agreed.

First, Jack wrote a tribute to his brother, *As We Remember Joe*. He also penned an article, "Let's Try an Experiment in Peace," which was run by *Atlantic Monthly*. Then Joe Sr. arranged for his son to report from San Francisco on the UN conference establishing that organization in April 1945, and the *Atlantic Monthly* asked him to travel to London and write about the election there, which resulted in the unseating of Winston Churchill.

NATIONAL EVENTS	**SEP 26:** Bob Dylan debuts in New York	**NOV 18:** President Kennedy orders 18,000 military advisors to South Vietnam	General Motors installs first industrial robots on its assembly lines	K-Mart opens its first store Trident introduces sugarless gum	Ken Kesey publishes *One Flew Over the Cuckoo's Nest* Biologist Rachel Carson writes *Silent Spring*
			1962		
WORLD EVENTS	**OCT 31:** Hurricane Hattie destroys Belize City, killing almost 300	**DEC 2:** Cuban leader Fidel Castro proclaims that he is a Communist	**JAN 3:** Pope John XXIII excommunicates Fidel Castro	**JAN 9:** Soviet Union and Cuba sign a trade pact	**JAN 10:** A massive avalanche kills 4,000 on Nevado Huascaran in Peru

Afterward, Kennedy traveled to his ancestral homeland of Ireland, made a quick tour of Europe, and returned to see what political future Joseph Kennedy had mapped for his son.

POLITICS

Using the experience gained by his grandfather Fitzgerald, Jack set off to conquer the Eleventh District—a working-class area of Boston (although it also included Harvard and MIT across the Charles River in Cambridge). He stumped the area and shook hands with one person after another; he gave speeches in schools and touted his war experience. His youthful charm was warmly received by many; however, the Democratic machine had tried to prevent his run, fearing once a Kennedy was elected, the family would control the area rather than the party. Kennedy was one of the first to specifically target women voters, and he found himself a popular figure among them. Campaigning was difficult and wearing on his health, but Kennedy plunged ahead, and at night plunged into a hot bath at his Ritz-Carlton suite. His family enthusiastically campaigned on his behalf, the first of innumerable elections for their clan. All efforts paid off, and he won the Democratic primary in June 1946 and easily won the general election in November.

CONGRESSMAN KENNEDY

Kennedy took office in January 1947 and soon was busy meeting constituents, playing football, and dating a bevy of beauties. One of his committee assignments placed him on the House Committee on Education and Labor, giving him the opportunity to speak against the Taft-Hartley Act, which opposed the growing power of labor by curbing collective bargaining. On the opposite side of the bill was another freshman congressman, Richard Nixon. The two men debated the bill in the heart of steel mill country in Pennsylvania. In a precursor of future debates, thanks to his youthful charm, Kennedy claimed victory.

Jack supported the Truman Doctrine, stating, "If Greece and Turkey go down, the road to the Near East is open. We have no alternative but to support the President's policy."[11] He backed Truman again a few months later on the creation of the Jewish state of Israel.

In September 1947, Kennedy journeyed once more to Ireland and then to London. While there he fell seriously ill, and doctors diagnosed him with Addison's. This disease attacks the adrenal glands and at that time was often fatal. He was shipped back to the United States, and in New York, received experimental treatment with cortisone. Thoughts of his death weighed on him, and he told a friend, "The doctors say I've got a sort of slow-motion leukemia. They tell me I'll probably last till I'm about forty-five." But he also admitted to friends that he believed his end would come in an automobile accident.[12]

Upon returning to Congress, he worked on veterans' issues, including providing more housing for low-income families. His support, however, had limits and he took on the American Legion when they backed a proposal by House Democrats to raise veterans' pensions even higher than Truman requested. "The American Legion hasn't had a constructive thought since 1918!"[13] argued Kennedy on the House floor.

The spring of 1948 brought sad news of sister Kathleen's death in a plane crash over the Rhône Valley with her boyfriend. She had been his favorite sister, and her loss now made him dwell again on his own mortality.

DID YOU KNOW?

Kennedy was the first president to have served on active duty in the US Navy.

Kennedy was the first Roman Catholic president.

FEB 3: US issues a trade embargo against Cuba

FEB 10: American pilot Gary Powers is exchanged for a Soviet spy

FEB 14: First Lady Jackie Kennedy takes American television viewers on a tour of the White House

FEB 20: John Glenn becomes the first American to orbit Earth

APR 16: Walter Cronkite becomes anchor of *CBS Evening News*

JAN 16: A military coup is staged in the Dominican Republic

JAN 26: Mafia boss Lucky Luciano dies at Naples Airport in Italy

FEB 3: US puts a trade embargo to Cuba in place

FEB 9: The Taiwan Stock Exchange opens for business

MAY 14: Spain's Juan Carlos marries Greek princess Sophia in Athens

DID YOU KNOW?

Kennedy was the first president to hold a televised news conference.

Kennedy had won a Pulitzer Prize prior to becoming president for his book *Profiles in Courage.*

Kennedy only gave lukewarm support to the Marshall Plan and traveled to Berlin to witness the Soviet blockade of the city. In 1950, he bemoaned the conversion of China to communism, stating, "The basic question that must be answered is not whether the Chinese did their best to save themselves, which they most certainly did not. The question is whether we did our best to save China."[14]

He made more trips to Europe to inspect NATO facilities and meet with General Dwight D. Eisenhower. In October 1951, he, his brother Bobby, and sister Patricia traveled to Yugoslavia and met with Tito, who expounded his belief that the Soviet Union hoped for a showdown between the United States and China. Kennedy also understood the key part to be played in the future by Middle Eastern states, so he visited that region, as well. He visited Asia, including India, Thailand, and French Indochina. There he heard guns being fired by the Viet Minh. A bout of Addison's put him in the hospital with a temperature of 106 degrees, and he fell into a coma. Once he recovered, though, Kennedy insisted that he resume the trip and see Korea and Japan. Upon completing his globe-trotting trek, he was convinced that Stalin would attempt to take western Europe, and he was shocked by the lack of professional knowledge on the parts of the ambassadorial staffs of the various countries he had visited. Kennedy had a new appreciation for the role of foreign affairs and noted, "Foreign policy—in its impact on our daily lives—overshadows everything else."[15]

Joe Kennedy and his son now looked to the 1952 election as the time when Jack would make a run for the Senate by challenging long-term Republican Henry Cabot Lodge. Joe believed this was the logical steppingstone in the path to the White House that he was preparing his son to follow. The campaign occurred in the midst of McCarthyism and McCarthy's crusade to rid America of all Communists—real and imagined. The Kennedys and Joe McCarthy had been long-time friends and their families frequently socialized together. Jack needed to attack him to win voters, but he felt uncomfortable going after him. Rather than attack McCarthy, Kennedy backers trumpeted their candidate's own anti-Communist stance. The Kennedy charisma worked its charm, and when the votes were counted, many Republican voters had crossed over to elect the thirty-five-year-old to his first term in the US Senate.

SENATOR

Kennedy gained national coverage for his defeat of Henry Cabot Lodge, but when he was sworn in on January 3, 1953, he found himself in the minority, for the senatorial elections of 1952 had been overwhelmingly won by Republicans. *The Saturday Evening Post* featured him in an article, "The Senate's Gay Young Bachelor," which called him "just about the most eligible bachelor in the United States."[16] Kennedy disliked the article and its emphasis on his playboy image rather than the serious work he was doing in the Senate; however, a few days after it appeared, his engagement to Jacqueline Lee Bouvier was announced.

The attractive lady had grown up in wealth and attended the best private schools, including Vassar. After her graduation from George Washington University, she had worked for the Washington *Times-Herald* as a photographer taking pictures of everyday people, whom she asked the day's question, such as, "Do you think a wife should let her husband think he's smarter than she is?" She had been introduced to Congressman

NATIONAL EVENTS

APR 21: World's Fair and the Space Needle open in Seattle

JUL 2: Sam Walton opens the first Wal-Mart store in Rogers, Arkansas

SEP 12: President Kennedy announces goal of the US to send a man to the moon by the end of the decade

OCT 1: Johnny Carson takes over duties as host of NBC's *Tonight Show* with sidekick Ed McMahon

OCT 1: US marshals accompany African American student James Meredith to the University of Mississippi

WORLD EVENTS

JUN 1: Adolf Eichmann is hanged in Israel

JUL 1: Rwanda and Burundi gain their independence

JUL 5: Algeria gains its independence from France

JUL 12: Debut of the Rolling Stones

AUG 5: Nelson Mandela arrested by the South African government

Kennedy at a dinner party, and their courtship had been off and on. But when he proposed to her during a call to London where she was covering Queen Elizabeth II's coronation, she readily accepted. After their wedding in Newport, Rhode Island, and honeymoon in Acapulco, Jack resumed his work in the Senate.

Meanwhile Kennedy's staff prepared a 159-page book entitled *The Economic Problems of New England: A Program for Congressional Action*. Here they set down issues confronting not just Massachusetts but the entire northeastern region, part of a strategy that Kennedy's advisors believed would help build support for his later presidential bid. But he soon angered some of his constituents when he pledged support to President Eisenhower's plan to develop the St. Lawrence Seaway, which opponents argued would divert shipping from Boston. After Kennedy spoke in favor of the seaway in a Senate speech, criticism from Massachusetts poured in, but he maintained his stand.

During these Senate years, Kennedy worked to improve his knowledge of foreign affairs, especially in the evolving Third World, where dangerous situations seemed most likely to threaten the world's peace. He advocated increasing defense spending in 1954 by an additional $350 million to ensure military superiority. Kennedy also opposed Secretary of State Dulles's avowed policy of massive retaliation, believing that such a threat would not prove feasible in Southeast Asia, where the French were losing the war against communism and its leader, Ho Chi Minh. In a Senate speech, Kennedy argued, "that no amount of American military assistance in Indochina can conquer an enemy which is everywhere and at the same time nowhere, 'an enemy of the people' which has the sympathy and covert support of the people."[17] He continued in the same vein in other speeches around the country, and the traveling took its toll on his back and often required the use of crutches.

> ***"And so, my fellow Americans, ask not what your country can do for you; ask what you can do for your country."***
>
> *—John F. Kennedy*

In October 1954, Kennedy underwent major back surgery although its risks were magnified even further because of Addison's disease. On the third day of his recovery, infection set in and his situation rapidly deteriorated. Last rites were administered at the hospital with the Kennedy family gathered, but the danger slowly ebbed. Meanwhile the Senate was passing a condemnation of Senator Joe McCarthy, and since Kennedy was sufficiently recovered to phone his desire to his aide Ted Sorenson, many expected him to do so. However, no such action occurred, and he would later be known as the one Democrat who did not vote against McCarthy. Critics would assail him for years for failing to take action and seemingly ducking the issue.

Once he returned home, Kennedy and Sorenson worked on a collection of biographies of famous politicians who exhibited bravery and courage by their unpopular stands on a variety of issues. Published in early 1956, *Profiles in Courage* was well received by the critics and the public; moreover, he was awarded the Pulitzer Prize. Speculation questioning Kennedy's authorship of the book soon followed, but he and Sorenson insisted that the work was Kennedy's. Undoubtedly,

OCT 14–28: Cuban Missile Crisis

NOV 7: Richard Nixon loses election for governor of California

NOV 17: President Kennedy dedicates Dulles International Airport in Washington, D.C.

Smiley face first appears

New Hampshire becomes first state to conduct a lottery

Kodak introduces Instamatic cameras

First multiplex movie theater built in Kansas City

1963

AUG 6: Jamaica gains its independence

OCT 5: Beatles release their first single "Love Me Do"

NOV 6: UN condemns apartheid policy of South Africa

Roald Dahl publishes *Charlie and the Chocolate Factory*

The Bell Jar published by Sylvia Plath

the idea for it was, but significant research and writing was done by Sorenson and professor Jules Davids. Kennedy remained sensitive for the rest of his life, arguing that he was the one true author of the book. His family threatened ABC and columnist Drew Pearson with a lawsuit when Pearson announced on a television program hosted by a young newsman, Mike Wallace, his belief that the book had been "ghostwritten." Both Pearson and the network soon issued retractions, but the whispers lingered.

Kennedy wanted the talk quieted before the Democratic convention in Chicago met in July 1956. With his additional popularity, Jack's name was being bandied around as the running mate for Adlai Stevenson, former Illinois governor. Kennedy's chances had two obstacles: his vote against price supports for farmers and his Catholic religion. He attempted to gain the support of former First Lady Eleanor Roosevelt and former president Harry Truman, but failed. Kennedy had narrated the film *The Pursuit of Happiness*, shown on the opening night of the convention, and he immediately won the crowd's appreciation. Stevenson, however, remained lukewarm and believed his ticket required a southerner, so he asked Senator Estes Kefauver of Tennessee instead. Although he had lost the nomination, he gained the nation's attention and many newspapers reported that the real star of the convention had been Jack Kennedy.

He returned to the Senate determined to try and change his anti-farmer image. He also became more vocal in supporting immigration causes, labor, and civil rights reform. After Sputnik's launch, he crusaded for the improvement of American education to counter the Soviets.

In November 1957, he and Jackie celebrated the birth of daughter Caroline. (Earlier Jackie had suffered a miscarriage after the 1956 convention.) With Caroline's birth, the forty-year-old senator seemed happier and more relaxed than he had in years. The couple and Caroline soon moved into a home in Georgetown, Virginia, and improved their image by dressing in well-tailored clothing of the latest styles. He consulted photographers to learn his best angles and most effective looks for the camera. Traveling throughout the country, Kennedy gave speeches and made his name better known, for he was looking ahead to the 1960 presidential election. First, however, he had to win reelection to his Senate seat, but he easily managed this, winning with a margin of nearly 875,000 votes, the largest winning margin in Massachusetts history.

1960 CAMPAIGN

Kennedy entered seven Democratic primaries including Wisconsin, which was considered a lock for its neighboring senator Hubert Humphrey. Kennedy toured the state and shook hands with thousands of its citizens; he visited their workplaces and discussed their concerns. He joked about the telegram he received from his father: "Dear Jack: Don't buy a single vote more than is necessary. I'll help you win this election, but I'll be damned if I'm going to pay for a landslide."[18] He managed to win six of Wisconsin's ten districts, leaving Humphrey the remaining four and little reason to stay in the fight. Later Kennedy told Humphrey in Washington that he should consider dropping out because he would never win the nomination.

Jack traveled through the mountains and coal mining regions of West Virginia. A young West Virginian asked Kennedy his thoughts about going into space. The candidate replied, "Well some of my opponents think I should go into space. But I'll

NATIONAL EVENTS

FEB 8: President Kennedy forbids Americans from traveling to Cuba or conducting business transactions with that nation

MAR 18: *Gideon v. Wainwright* Supreme Court decision rules that all are entitled to legal representation in court, including the poor

MAR 21: Federal prison of Alcatraz closes

APR 16: Dr. Martin Luther King Jr. writes "Letter from Birmingham Jail"

MAY 2: Protests by African Americans in Birmingham end with police dogs and fire hoses being used

WORLD EVENTS

JAN 29: French President Charles De Gaulle vetoes Britain's entry into the EEC

MAR 16: Mount Agung in Bali erupts and kills 11,000

APR 7: Josip Broz Tito named "President for Life" when Yugoslavia is proclaimed a Socialist republic

APR 15: Seventy thousand demonstrators against nuclear weapons march from London to Aldermarston

APR 22: Canada votes in Lester B. Pearson as their 14th prime minister

ask you, young man—what do you think we ought to do in space?" The boy enthusiastically replied, "We should go to the moon!" Kennedy replied, "I think maybe we will go to the moon."[19] (The young man was Homer Hickam Jr., who would later work for NASA and write his own book, *Rocket Boys*.) By winning this primary and his other primaries, Kennedy forced his detractors to admit that his Catholic faith would not impede his chances of being a presidential candidate.

Robert "Bobby" Kennedy arrived early in Los Angeles to set up the campaign operation for his brother, including installing sixty telephone lines linking the floor to various people within the Kennedy organization. Senator Lyndon B. Johnson of Texas was another serious contender for the nomination, but the Senate minority leader's hopes were dashed with the clinching of the Democratic nomination on the first ballot by the young Massachusetts senator. Then Kennedy asked Johnson to be his vice president, and LBJ accepted. Kennedy looked out to the eighty thousand people assembled in the Coliseum and announced, "We stand today at the edge of a New Frontier, the frontier of the 1960s—a frontier of unknown opportunities and perils—a frontier of unfulfilled hopes and threats." The crowd cheered their candidate with his eloquent rhetoric, and the "Kennedy for President" campaign was officially underway.

Republicans nominated Eisenhower's vice president, Richard Nixon, as their candidate, with Henry Cabot Lodge as his running mate. Both men campaigned actively, but for most Americans their decision was based on four televised debates. The first was broadcast from Chicago, where Nixon believed the backdrop would be dark so he dressed in a light-colored suit. Instead, the backdrop was light, so he tended to blend into the set, whereas Kennedy appeared suave in his dark suit, which contrasted nicely. Appearances can be deceiving, and for those who listened to the debate, Nixon was the clear winner; viewers watching it on television, however, insisted that Kennedy won. The lights were hot, and Nixon perspired; every time he wiped his brow, he lost more viewers. Kennedy felt pity for his former friend and confided to Ben Bradlee, "Anyone who can't beat Nixon doesn't deserve to be President."[20]

Steadily Kennedy insisted that the Eisenhower administration had not spent enough on weaponry, causing the United States to lag behind the Soviet Union in the development of medium- and long-range missiles. Although Eisenhower ordered the Joint Chiefs to brief the nominee, Kennedy refused to believe their insistence that the United States was well prepared to defend itself, and that the Soviets had not yet developed anything that

PEACE CORPS (Established March 1, 1961) ★ On October 13, 1960, candidate John F. Kennedy asked an audience of 10,000 at the University of Michigan if they would be willing to devote part of their time and energies to serving overseas for humanitarian causes. Once Kennedy became president, he quickly moved forward to create this organization of youthful volunteers, which some derisively called "Kennedy's Kiddie Korps." Sargent Shriver, Kennedy's brother-in-law, headed the new organization and ensured that the Peace Corps fulfilled its mission of promoting a better understanding of the world by sending young Americans to help people in underdeveloped nations.

against them by police under commissioner "Bull" Connor

JUN 8: American Heart Association votes to begin working on an educational campaign to discourage smoking

JUN 9: President Kennedy makes Winston Churchill an honorary American citizen

JUN 11: Governor George Wallace refuses to admit African American students from entering the University of Alabama by standing in the doorway blocking their entrance

MAY 23: Fidel Castro visits the Soviet Union

JUN 3: Pope John XXIII dies

JUN 16: Valentina Tereshkova, Soviet cosmonaut, becomes first woman in space

JUN 21: Pope Paul VI succeeds Pope John XXIII

AUG 5: Nuclear Test Ban Treaty signed by Soviet Union, UK, and US takes effect

DID YOU KNOW?

Kennedy was the first former Boy Scout to be elected president.

could actually hit the United States. Instead, he maintained that the country had to increase its defense spending.

Throughout the campaign, Nixon had rebuffed Eisenhower's offers to stump for him, but the close election made him change his mind. With the ever-popular Ike now entering the fray, the numbers grew even closer.

Kennedy won support when upon hearing of the arrest of civil rights leader Dr. Martin Luther King Jr., in Atlanta, he called Mrs. Coretta King to offer his support. His brother Bobby worked to gain King's release from jail. Reverend Martin Luther King Sr. issued his own statement: "Jack Kennedy has the moral courage to stand up for what he knows is right."[21]

The election promised to be extremely close, and on election night, no one had a clear victory. Mayor Richard Daley of Chicago told Jack, "With a little bit of luck and the help of a few close friends, you are going to carry Illinois."[22] Kennedy went to bed uncertain of his outcome, but the next morning daughter Caroline came tumbling into his room, saying, "Good morning, Mr. President."[23] Thanks to Johnson and his southern support, Kennedy had won the election with 49.7 percent of the popular vote to Nixon's 49.5 percent, but in the electoral college, the margin widened with Kennedy collecting 303 electoral votes to Nixon's 219. The narrow nature of the victory bothered Kennedy, who believed that more of the American electorate should have realized he was a far better choice than Nixon.

In December the two former candidates met in Washington. Then Eisenhower and Kennedy had a one-hour meeting where they discussed various issues, and Ike told JFK, "No easy matters will ever come to you as President. If they are easy, they will be settled at a lower level."[24] They met again a couple of days prior to the inauguration, when Kennedy was briefed on the world's trouble spots, and he asked Eisenhower's opinion about Cuba. "Should we support guerrilla operations in Cuba?" Ike replied, "To the utmost. We cannot allow the present situation to go on." JFK also received the instructions for using the "football"—the briefcase containing codes to launch a nuclear strike. The president tried once more to lecture Kennedy that there was no need to fear a "missile gap" with the Soviets. It simply did not exist.

PRESIDENT KENNEDY: FIRST YEAR

On Friday afternoon, January 20, 1961, John F. Kennedy was sworn in as the youngest-elected president in history. In the raw twenty-degree cold, minus his overcoat, Kennedy delivered his inaugural speech emphasizing the change: "The torch has been passed to a new generation of Americans. . . . Let every nation know, whether it wishes us well or ill, that we shall pay any price, bear any burden, meet any hardship, support any friend, oppose any foe in order to assure the survival and success of liberty." He ended his speech with a phrase that would ring immortal: "And so, my fellow Americans: ask not what your country can do for you—ask what you can do for your country."

That night the Kennedys lit up the evening's festivities at each of the record five inaugural balls that they attended. Then the next day, the life of the new president began in earnest as he began tackling the challenges of what he called the New Frontier.

The first major event of his presidency was the invasion of Cuba, which had already been planned during the Eisenhower administration, and Kennedy felt duty-bound to allow it to continue. For a year, more than a thousand Cuban exiles had

NATIONAL EVENTS

JUN 12: NAACP organizer Medgar Evers is shot to death in his driveway in Jackson, Mississippi

JUN 26: President Kennedy travels to Berlin and tells its people: "Ich bin ein Berliner"

JUL 1: Zip codes introduced

AUG 28: Civil rights "March on Washington" culminates in Dr. King's "I Have a Dream" speech in front of Lincoln Memorial before a crowd of 250,000

SEP 15: Bombing of 16th Street Baptist Church in Birmingham kills four girls

WORLD EVENTS

AUG 8: The Great Train Robbery of 1963 is executed in Buckinghamshire, England

AUG 30: "Hot line" between Washington and Moscow goes into effect for instant communication in times of emergency

SEP 16: Formation of Malaysia by combining Federation of Malaya, Singapore, North Borneo, and Sarawak

NOV 1: Military coup against South Vietnam's leadership under President Diem

NOV 2: South Vietnamese president Ngo Dinh Diem is assassinated

trained with the Central Intelligence Agency (CIA) in the Sierra Madre Mountains of Guatemala. Many of these men had originally fought the cruel Cuban dictator Fulgencio Batista in favor of Fidel Castro, but when Castro took control and revealed his true belief in communism, these former supporters fled the island. The CIA had originally planned to put the Cubans back into their country and become guerrilla fighters who could link with other underground members of the Cuban resistance. But increasingly the CIA grew concerned that the anti-Communist guerrillas could have Castro's people infiltrate their ranks and lead them to defeat. So the strategy shifted from being an undercover operation to one that included an amphibious landing across a beach with combat aircraft for protection.

Kennedy ordered a report by the Joint Chiefs regarding the planned invasion. This report admitted that it had a "fair chance" of succeeding, but it was dependent upon support by the Cuban people staging an overthrow of Castro. The CIA informed the president that his window for action was closing because intelligence indicated that the Soviets were about to give Castro MIG fighter jets and pilots to fly them. After that point, American fighting men would be required to launch a Castro overthrow. Moreover, calling off the operation would cause great discontent among the Cubans who had been trained by the CIA. What then would happen to them? Go to the United States where they could tell what they had been doing? Dissolve into other parts of Latin America where they might stir others to take action against the Americans who had betrayed them?

Kennedy decided to move forward with the invasion, and then announced, "There will not be, under any conditions, an intervention in Cuba by the United States Armed Forces. . . . The basic issue in Cuba is not one between the United States and Cuba. It is between the Cubans themselves."[25] The attack would be on Cochinos Bay (Bay of Pigs) on April 17, 1961. A preemptive air strike occurred three days earlier against three airfields but found few planes to hit. The cover story by the CIA quickly fell apart, and the president felt that another air strike during the invasion would be too obviously an American tactic that would drastically hurt its international relations, so he canceled it.

The invasion took place, but without air support, the men were pinned down in a hopeless situ-

FIRST FAMILY ★ The newly elected president was forty-three years old. With two small children in tow, the new first family exemplified youth in a White House that had not heard the laughter of young children since Teddy Roosevelt's term. Jackie modeled haute couture, and her sense of style was applauded in the United States as well as on the world stage. Women copied her bouffant hair topped with a pillbox hat. She traveled more than any previous First Lady, and when accompanying her husband to France, he quipped that he was only "the man who accompanied Jacqueline Kennedy to Paris." News cameras rolled and captured the delight on the president's face whenever he saw Caroline or John Jr. running toward him. The proud parents determinedly attempted to keep their children living as normal a life as possible, and the lawn boasted a swing set and trampoline. A preschool was established in the executive mansion, so the two could meet and play with other children.

NOV 22: Assassination of President John F. Kennedy as his motorcade rides through Dallas; Texas governor John Connally is also shot but will recover; Lyndon B. Johnson is sworn in as president aboard Air Force One; Lee Harvey Oswald is arrested

NOV 24: Lee Harvey Oswald is shot to death by Jack Ruby (broadcast live on national television)

NOV 25: President Kennedy is laid to rest at Arlington National Cemetery

NOV 29: President Johnson creates the Warren Commission to investigate Kennedy's assassination

DEC: First miniskirts appear in London

DEC 12: Kenya gains its independence

DEC 19: Zanzibar gains its independence

DEC 21: Fighting breaks out in Cyprus between Turkish and Greek Cypriots

WHITE HOUSE RESTORATION ★ Once she began residing in the White House, Jackie Kennedy immediately made plans to improve its appearance, which she believed had been allowed to deteriorate, and update its worn and outdated furnishings. Working with interior designers and private donations to supplement the $50,000 allocated by Congress, she managed to transform the mansion into a stately residence. Mrs. Kennedy also created the White House Historical Association, which developed a guidebook of the mansion that was sold to provide ongoing funding of this restoration, as well as future projects. On Valentine's Day, 1962, the First Lady took television viewers on a tour of the newly redecorated home and displayed some of the treasures she had found in storage rooms, including the desk in the Oval Office presented to President Hayes by Queen Victoria.

ation while Castro's tanks and thousands of troops bore down on them. Within three days, the bulk of the exiles had been taken prisoner, and Kennedy received a great deal of criticism and acknowledged that he was the one responsible for the debacle. He and the CIA, as well as the other parts of his administration, had underestimated Castro; they would not do so again.

Military intervention was not the only method to conquer communism. Two programs were created by the Kennedy administration in 1961 that would combat the threat in two very different ways. The Peace Corps began in March as an agency within the State Department whose mission was to utilize the talents and energies of Americans by sending them to Third World nations and poor areas within the United States. There they could serve in a variety of capacities—teaching, medical aid, farming, etc. Sargent Shriver, Kennedy's brother-in-law, became its first director. The other program, Alliance for Progress, provided financial aid specifically for Latin American nations and began in August. This effort would later be abandoned owing to insufficient funds when monies were increasingly diverted to the Vietnam War, and the reluctance of the receiving nations to institute required reforms. It ended in 1973.

Five days before the Bay of Pigs invasion, the United States awoke to the news that the Soviets had successfully launched a man into space—Yuri Gagarin had orbited the earth three times before returning home. Vice President Johnson, who had been appointed the chairman of the National Space Council, was the man on the hot-seat when Kennedy met him that morning demanding answers to why the American space program lagged behind. The United States must catch up immediately, the president insisted.

With those two black eyes on the United States, Kennedy was informed that the Southeast Asian nation of Laos was about to fall to Communist forces. The possibility of an American invasion loomed over him during the spring of 1961, but after the Bay of Pigs, Kennedy hesitated to launch another attack. Other countries in the vicinity were in danger of falling to communism, and the president announced, "If we have to fight in Southeast Asia, let's fight in Vietnam. The Vietnamese, at least, are committed and will fight. Vietnam is the place." He admitted to his counsel, Ted Sorenson, "We would have troops in Laos right now if it weren't for the Bay of Pigs."[26]

Kennedy approved of the cease-fire agreement signed to end hostilities in Laos and turn its control over to a UN force. *Time* magazine took the president to task for his apparent caving on such a vital issue. "Laos—with a Communist sympathizer at the head of the government, with Communists in posts of government power, and with Communists troops already holding half the nation—will quickly go behind the Iron Curtain."[27] Using Kennedy's words against him, it reminded its readers that he had promised to "pay any price to assure the survival and success of liberty." The words rang hollow when compared to his recent actions. Upset by the criticism, Kennedy determinedly ordered more troops to aid and train the South Vietnamese military, as well as more money for the US Army's Special Forces known as the "Green Berets," and training of guerrilla units.

Hearing mostly bad news, the president was buoyed by the success of Alan Shepard's first American manned flight on May 5. A few weeks later he addressed the nation and a joint session of Congress. His speech discussed the need for increased civil defense spending and more funding for the space program and its new goal: going to the moon by the end of the decade "not because it is easy but because it is hard."[28] Kennedy's New Frontier had just reached to the heavens.

> ***History is a relentless master. It has no present, only the past rushing into the future. To try to hold fast is to be swept aside.***
>
> *—John F. Kennedy*

Also in May, Kennedy spoke with Vice President Johnson about visiting South Vietnam; the VP, however, was extremely cool to the idea of traveling to a country where he might well be shot. Kennedy smiled and said, "Don't worry, Lyndon. If anything happens to you, Sam Rayburn and I will give you the biggest funeral Austin, Texas, ever saw."[29] Johnson was to be a special envoy to President Diem of South Vietnam and carried a letter from Kennedy promising increased assistance, including "military, political, economic, and other fields."[30]

At home, Kennedy was caught unawares when a group of thirteen members of the Congress of Racial Equality (CORE) decided to test segregation in buses and bus stations throughout the South. They left Washington, D.C., on May 4 and intended to end in New Orleans thirteen days later to coincide with the seventh anniversary of the *Brown v. Topeka Board of Education* Supreme Court decision ending school desegregation. They encountered no problems until Rock Hill, South Carolina, where one of the white Freedom Riders was beaten at the Greyhound terminal. More hostilities continued as they traveled into Georgia, where tires were slashed, a firebomb exploded, and the riders beaten.

News of this reached President Kennedy the same way it reached everyone else—on the front page of the newspaper. Upset that he had not been forewarned that such an action was going to take place, Kennedy was irate. He and his brother Bobby, the attorney general, decided to send someone from the Justice Department to Birmingham, Alabama, to ensure their safety leaving town since its police commissioner, "Bull" Connor, ruled the city and was known to be antagonistic toward African Americans and anyone associated with the civil rights movement.

The situation deteriorated after Bobby sent his administrative assistant John Siegenthaler, a southerner, to Alabama. There after meeting the governor in Montgomery, the Justice Department official was beaten unconscious; something had to be done. Ultimately the president authorized federal marshals to go to Alabama, and by the time they arrived, the situation had inflamed further with the arrival of Reverend Martin Luther King. Also working against the Kennedy administration was the FBI, whose leader J. Edgar Hoover saw nothing wrong in segregation and refused to allow his men to act in a timely manner.

On the night of May 21, Reverend King addressed a black crowd at the First Baptist Church, and as the evening wore on, more whites gathered outside the building. The marshals used tear gas on the crowd, then the Alabama National Guard moved out to take control, and the marshals retreated with Reverend King yelling over the phone to Bobby Kennedy, "You betrayed us."[31] Kennedy assured him he had not, but the president was still irritated by the chain of events and believed that the civil rights leaders were undermining his position as he prepared to travel to Vienna to hold a summit meeting with Soviet premier Nikita Khrushchev. The president complained, "I've done more for civil rights than any President in American history. How could any man have done more than I've done?"[32]

Khrushchev was an older and more experienced politician than his American counterpart,

BERLIN WALL CONSTRUCTION ★ The East German government decided to take action rather than continue to watch the constant flood of the country's professionals and skilled workers leave for West Germany. Early in the predawn hours of August 13, 1961, barbed wire began being strung and roadblocks established, cordoning off East Berlin from the rest of the city. Movement was severely restricted between the sectors. A few days later, the first concrete blocks were erected of the permanent barrier that would become known as the Berlin Wall. Berliners were no longer permitted to pass between the two sectors of the city from August 1961 until November 1989, when the Berlin Wall came down.

and when the two men met in Vienna in June 1961, Kennedy felt sorely outmatched. Repeatedly, Khrushchev kept the topic to his advantage and did his best to prod and poke the young American onto the defensive. They discussed Cuba and Laos, as well as the ongoing push by NATO and the United States to prevent communism from expanding. Kennedy admitted to his staff that the meetings were going poorly and that the Soviet leader treated him "like a little boy." Khrushchev told his companions that the American was "not strong enough. Too intelligent and too weak."[33]

They discussed a nuclear test ban treaty but Khrushchev was not receptive, fearing it would open doors for espionage into his country. Then they tackled Berlin, a tender subject for the Soviet Union since the city's legal status and location in the middle of Communist East Germany allowed many citizens from the East to flee to the West. He issued an ultimatum: either sign a treaty with East Germany or the Soviet Union would close the city to the West and a state of war would begin. Kennedy said the idea of abandoning Berlin was unacceptable. As the men prepared to leave the summit, they reiterated their stances on Berlin, and Kennedy replied to the Soviet's position that the United States would decide on war or peace. "Then, Mr. Chairman, there will be war. It will be a cold winter."[34]

Within two months, the Soviet's reaction to Berlin became world news as a wall began to be constructed separating the eastern, Communist-controlled sector from the western sector under the jurisdiction of the British, French, and American military authorities. Although unhappy by the appearance of the wall, Kennedy felt some measure of relief because a wall precluded the need for a war. West Germany, however, was far from pleased and demanded assurances from the American government, which reacted by sending more American troops as a symbolic gesture that the United States still stood behind its allies. Lyndon B. Johnson flew to Berlin to meet with Chancellor Willy Brandt and to pledge his government's support.

The Soviets alarmed the world that summer in another way—the resumption of nuclear testing, which they insisted was their right to keep safe from the American nuclear threat. Kennedy attempted to cool the rhetoric and reminded the United Nations General Assembly: "Mankind must put an end to war—or war will put an end to mankind."[35]

War and the various sites where it was being fought continued to demand the president's attention, particularly in Vietnam. Some advisors warned the president against becoming involved—troops could be thrown into a guerrilla conflict that likely would not be won. Others argued that American troops should be sent to "reverse the deteriorating situation."[36] The president listened to more viewpoints, but while the majority insisted that such a war could not be won, the idea of the first domino in Southeast Asia falling to communism was an image that continued to haunt the White House. At a National Security Council meeting, the president "asked how he could justify the proposed courses of action in Vietnam while at the same time ignoring Cuba."[37] On November 15, 1961, the president decided his course of action and wrote to President Diem that he would send more military equipment, as well as double the number of American military personnel (to nearly 3,500) already committed to training the South Vietnamese, but who themselves were not to be used in combat. The White House remained less than candid about the role of Americans in Vietnam, especially after they learned that many were being sent on missions when they lacked South Vietnamese personnel. The situation would only worsen in the months and years ahead.

PRESIDENCY: SECOND YEAR

Beginning in the fall of 1961, the president had begun discussing with the steel industry the need to keep down prices as it had historically led all others in hiking prices, and, being the linchpin for other industries, its actions would be continued down the line. Labor agreed not to demand a wage increase, and the steel industry agreed to keep prices down. Days after the AFL-CIO agreed to no wage increase, the steel companies announced a 3.5 percent price hike. Again Kennedy felt he appeared weak, and this time, double-crossed, so he went on the attack. Using his own resources, he called a press conference the next day to garner public opinion by denouncing the steel corporations' greed. He won the fight and the American public. The Defense Department pressured their contractors, and the FBI began investigating the industries' top executives with threats of IRS audits hanging over them. Soon the companies decided to roll back their prices, although the president of one steel corporation complained about the strong-armed tactics by the Justice Department, to which the president replied that the attorney general would not resort to such measures. The two brothers enjoyed a good-hearted laugh, and Bobby explained, "They were mean to my brother. They can't do that to my brother."[38]

On May 19, John F. Kennedy celebrated his forty-fifth birthday at a Democratic gala and fundraiser held at Madison Square Garden. Celebrities including Jack Benny, Henry Fonda, Ella Fitzgerald, and Harry Belafonte led the guest list, but the one everyone would remember that night was Marilyn Monroe (rumors had been circulating of a possible affair between her and Kennedy). Shoehorned into her five thousand dollar sequined gown, the "blonde bombshell" breathily sang "Happy Birthday" to the president. Kennedy was reputed to have had numerous and frequent sexual liaisons with women, including at the White House. The marriage between him and Jackie, which already showed signs of strain, was damaged considerably by his infidelities. She and the children (son John F. Kennedy Jr. was born just three weeks after his father's presidential election) were often elsewhere, for Jackie found life at the White House too tedious and onerous; instead, she preferred to take Caroline and John to their Virginia farm for fresh air and plenty of horseback riding. In fact, that was where they were when Marilyn was singing to her husband.

PHYSICAL FITNESS ★ Although President Eisenhower initially established a council on physical fitness, it was President Kennedy who made its goals a priority. Before taking office, JFK wrote an article for *Sports Illustrated* telling of his plans to reorganize the council and become more involved. The President's Council for Physical Fitness developed standards and curriculums for the nation's youth, which were not mandated, but implemented by many school districts across the nation. Presidents since Kennedy have continued to sponsor the council and its efforts to improve the health and fitness of Americans of all ages.

On Wall Street, following the steel fight, Kennedy became known as anti-business, a belief only reinforced at the end of May when stock prices tumbled sharply. Some called it the "Kennedy crash." The president worried about deficit spending while at the same time needing money for programs he had promised, and ultimately decided to send to Congress a tax-cut package to reinvigorate the economy.

In September, civil rights again took center stage when African American college student James Meredith arrived at the University of Mississippi to enroll—and for extra insurance, he carried a court order demanding the institution grant him this right. He arrived at Ole Miss with a two-man escort, but was refused entrance by the

DID YOU KNOW?

Kennedy is one of two presidents buried in Arlington Cemetery; the other is William H. Taft.

administration. Kennedy had border patrol and federal prison guards sworn in as US marshals and sent to the Oxford campus, where Governor Ross Barnett ordered his two hundred highway patrolmen to abandon their job holding back the mob. Violence erupted, but the president refused requests for the marshals to respond with their guns. They could only do so if Meredith were threatened. The siege ended the next day with two dead and others injured; Meredith was allowed to register.

Hardly had this crisis been handled before another loomed on the president's horizon. It began with a group of photographs given to him on the morning of October 16, 1962, showing missile bases under construction in Cuba. The Joint Chiefs explained that the threat was a grave one as it meant that at least 85 percent of US cities could be destroyed on a first strike; moreover, Cuban missile bases allowed the Soviets power to eliminate the Strategic Air Command (SAC) bases. Rather than confront this threat with military might, which very possibly would push Khrushchev into a corner and likely escalate into a nuclear crisis, Kennedy decided to use a naval blockade around Cuba to prevent the missiles from entering the nation from the Soviet Union. The American people were told of the crisis on October 22 when Kennedy addressed the nation and, using the term Secretary of State Dean Rusk advised, said the United States was "imposing a strict quarantine on all offensive military equipment under shipment to Cuba."[39]

The quarantine was to begin at 9 a.m. eastern time on October 24. As the time approached, the two Kennedy brothers discussed the situation, and Jack wanted reassurance that he was doing the right thing. Bobby answered, "There wasn't any choice. You would have been impeached."[40] All within the Oval Office held their breath that morning when eight Soviet ships with their escort of four submarines approached the US naval blockade and then stopped in the water. Secretary of State Rusk said, "We are eyeball to eyeball, and I think the other fellow just blinked."[41] Khrushchev ordered the ships to turn back the next day. Meanwhile United States ambassador to the UN Adlai Stevenson was demanding that the Soviet ambassador Valerian Zorin answer questions about the missiles. Zorin replied that Stevenson would have to wait for his answer on whether Soviet missiles were actually in Cuba. Stevenson answered, "I am prepared to wait for my answer until hell freezes over."[42] His boss in Washington wholeheartedly approved.

The danger, however, was far from over as building continued in Cuba; moreover, a U-2 reconnaissance plane was shot down over Cuba. Khrushchev proposed swapping missiles—giving up Cuba for NATO bases in Turkey, as well as American assurance that no invasion of Cuba would occur. By Sunday, prospects for peace appeared bleak with more Soviet posturing and Kennedy trying to decide whether to order an air strike and invasion. He believed that the obsolete missiles in Turkey were a fine swap for Soviet ones in Cuba, and it became clearer that the Soviets did not want war, which could very possibly go nuclear. The missile swap remained secret for years, possibly to protect Bobby Kennedy from any embarrassment when he ran for public office. But on October 30, the Cuban missile crisis had passed, and the president finally had a victory worthy of the leader of the free world.

Another Kennedy came to Washington as a result of the election of 1962. Younger brother Ted was elected to Jack's former Senate seat. Although happy about his victory, the president was a bit dismayed by the overall results, since it did little to change the conservative configuration, which continued to block his legislative agenda, including civil rights reform and the creation of Medicare. Still he was hopeful as he looked to 1963.

PRESIDENCY: THIRD YEAR

One result of the Cuban Missile Crisis was the belief that the Soviets acted in a belligerent manner because they were afraid; the answer, Kennedy and defense secretary Robert McNamara believed, was the establishment of a nuclear test ban treaty. This would ease the fears of the Soviets, they reasoned, if the Americans were not jumping ahead of them in the arms race.

Although the country's economy was strong as it entered his third year, Kennedy still pushed Congress for tax cuts, which its Democratic leaders vehemently opposed, arguing that they would only aid the rich. (They would finally be approved after Kennedy's death.)

The civil rights movement attempted to move forward when Dr. King announced they would travel to Birmingham, Alabama, in early May 1963, to bring attention to the city's segregated facilities. "Bull" Connor still ruled the police, and all knew a showdown would occur. Police dogs and fire hoses were unleashed on the demonstrators, but the president was reluctant to involve himself or use his power. Angered by the federal government's inaction, King wrote disgustedly from his Birmingham cell (imprisoned for having taken part in the nonviolent protest) of the "white moderate, who is more devoted to 'order' than to justice."[43]

Bobby Kennedy sent a Justice Department official to Birmingham to help negotiate a compromise, but this only infuriated its population more. The Ku Klux Klan rallied, bombs exploded, and violence in general gripped the city, and the country waited for the president's response. Aware that Alabama governor George Wallace would do nothing to help, Kennedy weighed his options. An uneasy truce began with the threat of federalized National Guard troops moving in and the assurance of Dr. King to keep his supporters under control so nothing further would occur while the president asked the nation and Congress for civil rights legislation. He had determined that southerners had to be pushed to integrate because "when an outsider intervenes, they'll tell him to get out; they'll take care of it themselves, which they won't."[44]

As promised, Governor Wallace stood at the schoolhouse door, blocking the entrance of two black students from the University of Alabama, and arguing with Justice Department official Nicholas Katzenbach about his action, all of which was captured on film and shown on the evening news. Ultimately the Alabama Guard ordered the governor to move, and he did.

SPACE PROGRAM ★ On May 25, 1961, President Kennedy addressed a joint session of Congress and said, "I believe that this nation should commit itself to achieving the goal, before this decade is out, of landing a man on the moon and returning him safely to the earth. No single space project in this period will be more impressive to mankind." Kennedy's goal was attained on July 20, 1969, when Neil Armstrong and Edwin "Buzz" Aldrin landed on the moon, and from the Sea of Tranquility, Neil Armstrong proclaimed, "That's one small step for man, one giant leap for mankind."

The president also took action, although many believed it political suicide, by insisting that his comprehensive civil rights reform be passed by Congress. Hoping that the American people could sway their elected officials, Kennedy delivered a televised address that night explaining why he believed civil rights legislation was needed. Fears that southern congressmen would block it were realized when a package to help improve the poverty-stricken people of Appalachia went down in defeat the day after the broadcast because southern congressmen refused to support anything backed by Kennedy. Vice President Johnson advised him to travel through the South to deliver his message in person; after a meeting with Texas governor John Connally, the three agreed that the president would travel to Texas for Democratic fundraising in October or November.

Later in June, the president traveled to Europe, including Berlin, where he received cheers and applause form his audience when he proclaimed in his thick Boston accent, "Freedom has many difficulties and democracy is not perfect, but we have never had to put up a wall to keep our people in. . . . All freemen, wherever they may live, are citizens of Berlin, and therefore as a free man, I take pride in the words 'Ich bin ein Berliner [I am a Berliner].'"[45] His next stop was Ireland where he visited cousins. After stops in England and Italy, he returned home in early July.

Kennedy was the only president to appoint his brother to a cabinet position.

At this time, American diplomat Averell Harriman was dispatched to Moscow on the president's behalf to negotiate with Khrushchev on a nuclear test ban treaty. After several days of discussions and wordsmithing, the document was produced to the satisfaction of both parties. Each feared Communist China and hoped this treaty would isolate it in the world. The Limited Test Ban Treaty prohibited nuclear testing in space and underwater. Both the US and Soviet governments were pleased by the accomplishment. (Secretary of State Dean Rusk had to wait to discuss the politics of sending the treaty to the Senate while the president met a group of Boys Nation participants that included future president William Jefferson Clinton of Hot Springs, Arkansas.)

Meanwhile, news from Vietnam poured in, with each report more alarming than the last. Earlier in the summer, Buddhist monks had set themselves on fire to protest South Vietnamese president Diem. Pictures of this event flashed around the world, as reporters had been told earlier to be on the scene, and the Buddhists' protests prompted some American citizens to begin their own protests against involvement in Vietnam. Some on the president's staff reminded him of Eisenhower and MacArthur's advice to avoid ground wars in Asia, and Senator Mike Mansfield wrote to Kennedy a report that warned, "We are in for a very long haul to develop even a modicum of stability in Vietnam."[46]

During this trying summer, the president and First Lady endured a heartbreaking loss. In early August, Jackie went into labor and delivered Patrick Bouvier Kennedy by caesarian section. He was born five weeks premature and suffered hyaline membrane (respiratory distress), which did not improve in his two days of life. A funeral mass was said in Boston while Jackie recuperated at Cape Cod, where she had borne Patrick. His tiny body was laid to rest at Holyhood Cemetery in Brookline, Massachusetts.

Later in August, the president and city braced for an event they feared could tear apart the capital: Dr. Martin Luther King's March on Washington. At the same time, the Kennedy administration was also dealing with a crisis in South Vietnam of whether to continue supporting the Diem government. Secretary of State Dean Rusk put it simply: "We must actually decide whether to move our resource out or to move our troops in."[47] Plans to launch a coup against the South Vietnamese government disintegrated when word of it leaked out, and the president and his staff feared that too much of the plot was known.

Meanwhile Attorney General Robert Kennedy was monitoring the arrival of Dr. King and a quarter of a million participants in King's demonstration and parade. Fearful that there could be violence and bloodshed, President Kennedy refused to meet with any of the civil rights leaders prior to the march, nor would he accept their invitation to speak at the gathering before the Lincoln Memorial. Perhaps this was just as well, for the nation watched and heard the Reverend King proclaim his immortal words: "I have a dream." One of the millions of television viewers that August day was the president, who said, "He's damned good. Damned good."[48] A short time later, King arrived at the White House, where Kennedy greeted him, and they discussed the proposed civil rights legislation. The president admitted it would require a crusade to convince Congress to pass the law. The civil rights leaders gathered there in the cabinet room told the president that he would be the one leading the crusade.

At a press conference in early September, the president was asked about American aid for South Vietnam. He replied, "Some 25,000 Americans have traveled 10,000 miles to support in that struggle. . . . We want the war to be won, the Communists to be contained, and the Americans to go home." At the same conference he was asked about desegregation in schools and a recent Gallup poll, which said half the country believed he was "pushing too fast." The president responded by pointing to the other side, which thought, "it was more or less right. I thought that was rather impressive, because it is change; change always disturbs, and therefore I was surprised that there wasn't greater opposition."[49] Sadly the opposition was heard a few days later when a bomb blasted the 16th Street Baptist Church, killing four girls on a Sunday morning.

As autumn progressed, the president appeared in various television interviews discussing the need to stay in Vietnam. Defense secretary Robert McNamara and Chairman of the Joint Chiefs of Staff General Maxwell Taylor went on a fact-finding mission there and returned with their assessment—if training of South Vietnamese troops were increased, then American involvement could be ended within two years; moreover, the situation was stable enough to allow one thousand troops withdrawn. Kennedy liked the idea, for he feared the possibility of Vietnam becoming a major focus of the 1964 election. He hesitated to announce it lest events change, but on October 31, the president did admit they would take action if possible. It did not take long for such change to occur. On November 2, word arrived of a military coup in South Vietnam and the deaths of both President Diem and the military chief General Nhu. Special Assistant to the President Arthur Schlesinger Jr. later wrote that this news left Kennedy "somber and shaken. I have not seen him so depressed since the Bay of Pigs. No doubt he realized that Vietnam was his great failure in foreign policy, and that he had never really given it his full attention."[50]

> ***"Let every nation know, whether it wishes us well or ill, that we shall pay any price, bear any burden, meet any hardship, support any friend, oppose any foe to assure the survival and the success of liberty."***
>
> *—John F. Kennedy*

Within a week the US government granted formal recognition to the new South Vietnamese government—General Duong Van Min, president, and Nguyen Ngoc Tho, premier. Kennedy and his administration pledged to increase economic and military aid to that embattled nation, as well as withdrawing some American troops by year's end. A new twist emerged, however—operations could extend within thirty miles inside Laos, and Cambodia's significance was also placed higher.

ASSASSINATION

On November 21, the president and Mrs. Kennedy flew to San Antonio, Texas, then Houston, and on to Fort Worth, where they spent the night. The next morning was rainy but the weather failed to dampen the spirits of the growing crowd outside the Texas Hotel. Kennedy marveled at his warm reception "in nut country." When he spied his speaking platform, he commented, "With all these buildings around it, the Secret Service couldn't stop someone who really wanted to get you."[51] He spoke briefly outside to the crowd, and then Jackie joined him in her pink suit and matching pillbox hat for the flight to Love Field in Dallas. There a motorcade began which would snake ten miles through downtown Dallas and end at the Trade Mart for a scheduled luncheon.

The top of the presidential limousine was put down so the crowd could more easily see Kennedy. Governor and Mrs. Connally rode in the front seat, with the presidential couple in back; the vice president and Mrs. Johnson rode in a car farther back in the procession. Thousands lined both sides of the route, waving and cheering. Just before 12:30 p.m., Mrs. Connally turned to the president and said, "Mr. President, you can't say Dallas doesn't love you." He replied, "That is very obvious."[52] Passing by the Texas School Book Depository, the air was punctured by shots fired. One bullet pierced the president's neck and he immediately grabbed it, and then a second tore out the back of his head.

Governor Connally also was bleeding from wounds to his chest, thigh, and wrist. Immediately the limousine raced to Parkland Hospital, where doctors gave the president blood transfusions and oxygen, then a cardiac massage once his heart stopped. All failed to revive Kennedy;

he was administered last rites and pronounced dead at 1 p.m. A few hours later aboard Air Force One, Lyndon B. Johnson took the oath of office with Jackie Kennedy looking on, still wearing her bloodied suit. Her husband's casket had been loaded onboard for the trip back to Washington. There his body lay in state at the rotunda of the Capitol, where a quarter of a million people filed by, paying their last respects. After a funeral mass at St. Matthew's Roman Catholic Cathedral in Washington, his body was carried on a cortege and taken to Arlington Cemetery led by his widow and brother Bobby, with scores of foreign dignitaries and well-known Americans in the procession. At Arlington, Jackie lit the eternal flame, which still burns today over his grave.

Jacqueline Kennedy retreated to a quiet life to rear their two children, Caroline and John Jr. She remarried in 1968 to Greek tycoon Aristotle Onassis and upon his death in 1975 began working for Doubleday publishers as an editor. In January 1994 she was diagnosed with non-Hodgkin's lymphoma, a form of cancer, and died in May. She is buried at Arlington Cemetery beside President Kennedy and their two children who died in infancy—Patrick Bouvier and a stillborn daughter.

> ***"A man may die, nations may rise and fall, but an idea lives on."***
>
> *—John F. Kennedy*

Controversy still pervades the assassination, with scores of theories and tales of conspiracy continually emerging. Lee Harvey Oswald, a former Marine sharpshooter who had recently returned after a lengthy visit to the Soviet Union, was arrested within the hour after the assassination, hiding in a Dallas movie theater after he had shot Dallas police officer J.D. Tippit. Oswald had purchased a rifle and left it behind at the Texas School Book Depository, but he insisted he was innocent. Two days later when he was being transferred from the Dallas Police Department to a county jail, a Dallas nightclub owner, Jack Ruby, stepped forward and fired point-blank at Oswald's stomach. Oswald died, and Ruby was taken into custody, where he died four years later.

A commission was formed to study evidence and determine the "facts" of the Kennedy assassination. Its name derived from the head of the group, Chief Justice Earl Warren. After months of testimony and discussions, it published its findings, insisting that Oswald acted alone and killed the president with two out of three shots (the other one hit Connally). Many remained unconvinced, and suspects range from Castro to the CIA, the Mafia to the FBI, the Soviet Union to LBJ. None can be definitively proven and it's unlikely any ever will be.

ENDNOTES

1 Joan Blair and Clay Blair Jr., *In Search of JFK*, New York: Berkley/Putnam, 1976, p. 30.

2 Geoffrey Perret, *Jack, A Life Like No Other*, New York: Random House, 2001, p. 39.

3 Michael R. Beschloss, *Kennedy and Roosevelt*, New York: Norton, 1980, p. 157.

4 Perret, p. 73.

5 Ibid, p. 81.

6 Robert Dallek, *An Unfinished Life: John F. Kennedy*, New York: Little Brown & Co., 2003, p. 88.

7 Blair, p. 235.

8 Dallek, p. 107.

9 Doris Kearns Goodwin, *The Fitzgeralds and the Kennedys*, New York: Simon and Schuster, 1987, p. 698.

10 Perret, p. 125.

11 Ibid, p. 144.

12 Ibid, p. 148.

13 Dallek, p. 144.

14 Perret, p. 157.

15 Ibid, p. 171.

16 Herbert S. Parmet, *Jack: The Struggles of John F. Kennedy*, New York: Dial Press, 1980, p. 258.

17 Congressional Record, 83rd Congress, 2nd Session, p. 4674.

18 Perret, p. 246.

19 Homer Hickam Jr., *Rocket Boys*, New York: Delta, 1998, pp. 335-336.

20 Benjamin C. Bradlee, *Conversations with Kennedy*, New York: Norton, 1975, p. 32n.

21 William A. DeGregorio, *The Complete Book of US Presidents*, New York: Gramercy Books, 2001, p. 553.

22 Perret, p. 270.

23 Ibid, p. 271.

24 Ibid, p. 273.

25 Arthur M. Schlesinger Jr., *A Thousand Days*, Boston: Houghton Mifflin Company, 1965, p. 262.

26 Richard Reeves, *Profile of Power*, New York: Simon & Schuster, 1993, p. 112.

27 Ibid, p. 116.

28 Dallek, p. 333.

29 Reeves, p. 119.

30 Ibid.

31 Ibid, p. 131.

32 Thomas Wofford, *Of Kennedy and Kings*, Pittsburgh: University of Pittsburgh Press, 1980, p. 126.

33 Dallek, pp. 407-408.

34 Ibid, p. 413.

35 Schlesinger, p. 485.

36 Dallek, p. 447.

37 Ibid, p. 453.

38 Ibid, p. 487.

39 *Public Papers of the Presidents: John F. Kennedy, 1962*: Washington, D.C., 1963, p. 808.

40 Robert F. Kennedy, *Thirteen Days: A Memoir of the Cuban Missile Crisis*, New York: W.W. Norton, 1969, p. 67.

41 Reeves, p. 401.

42 *New York Times*, October 26, 1962.

43 Dallek, p. 596.

44 Ibid, p. 600.

45 Reeves, p. 536.

46 Ibid, pp. 556-557.

47 Ibid, p. 568.

48 Ibid, p. 584.

49 Reeves, pp. 597-598.

50 Schlesinger Jr., p. 997.

51 Reeves, p. 661.

52 DeGregorio, p. 559.

LYNDON B. JOHSON

★ ★ ★ THIRTY-SIXTH PRESIDENT ★ ★ ★

LIFE SPAN
- Born: August 27, 1908, near Stonewall, Texas
- Died: January 22, 1973, near Johnson City, Texas

NICKNAME
- LBJ

FAMILY
- Father: **Sam Ealy Johnson Jr.** (1877–1937)
- Mother: **Rebekah Baines Johnson** (1881–1958)
- Wife: **Claudia Alta "Lady Bird" Taylor Johnson** (1912–2007); wed November 17, 1934, in San Antonio, Texas
- Children: **Lynda Bird** (1944–); **Luci Baines** (1947–)

RELIGION
- Disciples of Christ

HIGHER EDUCATION
- Southwest Texas State Teachers College, 1930
- Georgetown Law School, 1934

PROFESSION
- Teacher, lawyer

MILITARY SERVICE
- World War II: joined naval reserve in January 1940
- Lieutenant commander in US Navy (December 1941–July 1942)

POLITICAL LIFE
- National Youth Administration in Texas administrator (1935–1937)
- US representative (1937–1939)
- US senator (1949–1961)
- Vice president (1961–1963)

PRESIDENCY
- One term: November 22, 1963–January 20, 1969 (took office upon **President Kennedy**'s assassination)
- Democrat
- Reason for leaving office: declined to run for second term
- Vice President: **Hubert Humphrey** (1965–1969)

ELECTION OF 1964
- Electoral vote: **Johnson** 486; **Barry Goldwater** 52
- Popular vote: **Johnson** 43,129,566; **Goldwater** 27,178,188

CABINET
★★★★★★★★★★

SECRETARY OF STATE
Dean Rusk (1963–1969)

SECRETARY OF THE TREASURY
C. Douglas Dillon (1963–1965)

Henry M. Fowler (1965–1968)

Joseph W. Barr (Dec. 1968–Jan. 1969)

SECRETARY OF DEFENSE
Robert S. McNamara (1963–1968)

Clark Clifford (1968–1969)

ATTORNEY GENERAL
Robert F. Kennedy (1963–1964)

Nicholas B. Achenbach (1965–1968)

Ramsey Clark (1967–1969)

POSTMASTER GENERAL
John A. Gronouski (1963–1965)

Lawrence F. O'Brien (1965–1968)

W. Marvin Watson (1968–1969)

SECRETARY OF THE INTERIOR
Stewart L. Udall (1963–1969)

SECRETARY OF AGRICULTURE
Orville L. Freeman (1963–1969)

Prior to being selected by John F. Kennedy as his vice presidential candidate in 1960, Lyndon B. Johnson (LBJ) had been known as a consummate politician, the master leader of the US Senate. As president, he would use his legislative skill to pass his Great Society programs, but it did little to endear him to the American people as the Vietnam War escalated under his leadership.

EARLY LIFE

From both sides of his family, Lyndon inherited a passion for politics. His ancestors moved to Texas in 1846, and his paternal grandfather, Sam E. Johnson, founded Johnson City; his maternal grandfather, Joseph Baines, served as Texas secretary of state in the 1880s and later as a state representative. Sam Johnson, LBJ's father, was serving in the Texas House of Representatives when he married Rebekah Baines in 1907, and they lived in a small farmhouse on the Pedernales River. The following year, they welcomed Lyndon Baines Johnson to their family, and over the coming years, four additional children were born.

Besides being a state legislator, Sam Johnson worked as a farmer and cotton broker and invested in real estate. Money was often tight in the household, causing a great deal of tension between the couple. Additionally, Sam sometimes drank and squandered the family's money. In later years, Lyndon recalled how his father's erratic behavior upset his mother, and she would cry for hours. Usually the one who comforted her was her eldest son. She made him promise that he would not repeat the mistakes of his father. He agreed and vowed, "I would be there to protect her always."[1]

Rebekah Johnson educated her son at home, teaching him his alphabet at age two, and he was reading two years later. He entered school at the age of four but was rather frightened, so his mother told the teacher to have him sit in the teacher's lap for reading and doing his lessons. This worked, but only briefly as a case of whooping cough abruptly ended his schooling that year.

When he was five years old, the family moved from their small farmhouse to a bigger home in Johnson City, where he reentered school. His mother taught debate at the high school, wrote a newspaper column, and earned extra income by giving elocution lessons. Lyndon hated spending his days in a classroom and his behavior deteriorated, resulting in frequent punishment. He refused to do his lessons, but Rebekah would walk with him to school, drilling him along the way.

One of the boy's favorite pastimes was chatting with the adults, particularly the men who came to discuss politics with his father. Later LBJ said his mother wanted Sam to run for national office, but his father had no interest; in fact, he skipped serving the legislature for a decade before returning after World War I. There he made a name for himself by speaking out against a loyalty bill that was aimed at the German population, and he forever won the appreciation of the German community in Texas.

Lyndon graduated from high school at the age of fifteen in 1924. Rebekah expected her son to enter college, but he was sick of school and wanted to do something different. So he and a group of his buddies drove to California and worked there at various odd jobs for the next two years. He then returned home to Texas and after enduring the harsh conditions of working on a road crew, Lyndon decided to abide by his mother's wishes and enrolled at the Southwest Texas State Teachers College at San Marcos.

NATIONAL EVENTS

G.I. Joe action figure produced

JAN 8: Johnson announces "War on Poverty"

JAN 11: First warning by US surgeon general saying that, "Smoking may be hazardous to your health"

JAN 23: Twenty-fourth Amendment ratified outlawing poll taxes

FEB 9: *Ed Sullivan Show* hosts the Beatles

APR 8: Unmanned Gemini I is launched

APR 22: World's Fair opens in New York City

1964

WORLD EVENTS

Palestine Liberation Organization (PLO) formed

JAN 7: British automaker Leyland Motor Corp. challenges US blockade of Cuba with the sale of 450 buses to that government

JAN 27: China and France establish diplomatic relations

JAN 28: A jet training mission strays into East Germany; Soviet fighters shoot down the plane and all three US crewmen are killed

FEB 1: Beatles land at #1 on American music charts for the first time with their hit "I Want to Hold Your Hand"

COLLEGE

He was always short on money, so LBJ worked as a janitor and secretary to help defray expenses. During the 1928–1929 term, he left school to work as principal and teacher at the predominately Mexican American Welhausen School in Cotulla. There he flourished while introducing the children to new experiences—baseball, volleyball, spelling contests, and public speaking events. He believed the children had to learn English to succeed, so he forbade the use of Spanish at school or in the schoolyard.

After his year there, he returned to college, where he finished his degree in a little over a year. During this time, he also ventured into a new world of fighting the power base of the elite. A group known as the Black Stars controlled all of the campus activities, so if one was not selected to join, he would not likely be able to serve on the newspaper staff or student government. Once rejected, Johnson decided to create a rival organization—the White Stars. The group was kept secret until they had done their research and were ready for action. Most of the Black Stars were athletes, and the White Stars soon learned that others disliked the power wielded by this small select group. Once they learned that the majority of student activity funds went to support athletics (i.e., Black Stars), LBJ could see the way to undermine their position. He increased the membership of his White Stars, which openly opposed their rival for membership to the various campus organizations and began winning slots in those groups. They in turn recruited even more fellow White Stars, and the Black Stars saw their power erode thanks to a certain young man from Johnson City. LBJ asked a friend to run for senior class president and Johnson continually took polls, chatted with students, and refused to give up even when they figured they would lose by a narrow margin. Thanks to his perseverance, the White Stars won. Additionally LBJ became editor of the college newspaper and continued to emerge as a talented debater. Although originally intending to become a teacher, the college president deterred him from that path, saying it was not competitive enough for Johnson and counseled him to become a politician instead. But teaching was his first job upon graduation in May 1930.

TEACHING AND POLITICS

Lyndon taught briefly at Pearsall High School before moving to Sam Houston High School in Houston, Texas. There he taught public speaking, and his students won the district title in 1931. But he would soon leave his teaching career, never to return.

In 1928, he and some of his college friends had traveled to Houston for the Democratic National Convention. They used their college newspaper credentials to get in the door, and Johnson was captivated by what he experienced in the convention hall as Franklin D. Roosevelt nominated Al Smith as the Democratic presidential candidate. Johnson was hooked.

Then in 1930, at one of LBJ's favorite events, the all-day political picnic in Henley, Texas, the young man gave his first speech. A politician named Pat Neff was supposed to speak to the crowd on his candidacy for state railroad commissioner, but when they called his name, he was nowhere to be found. Suddenly Johnson yelled, "By God, I'll make the speech for Neff,"[2] and so he did. The crowd enthusiastically applauded his speech, and one member of the audience was keenly impressed by LBJ's performance. Willy Hopkins

CABINET
★★★★★★★★★★

(continued)

SECRETARY OF COMMERCE
Luther H. Hodges (1963–1965)

John T. Connor (1965–1967)

Alexander B. Trowbridge (1967–1968)

C.R. Smith (1968–1969)

SECRETARY OF LABOR
W. Willard Wirtz (1963–1969)

SECRETARY OF HEALTH, EDUCATION, AND WELFARE
Anthony J. Celebrezze (1963–1965)

John W. Gardner (1965–1968)

Wilbur J. Cohen (1968–1969)

SECRETARY OF HOUSING AND URBAN DEVELOPMENT
Robert C. Weaver (1966–1969), first to serve in this new post

SECRETARY OF TRANSPORTATION
Alan S. Boyd (1967–1969), first to serve in this new post

MAY 2: First major student protests in American cities against the Vietnam War

JUN 21: Three civil rights workers are slain in Mississippi by local KKK members

JUL 2: President Johnson signs the Civil Rights Act of 1964 into law

JUL 30: Medicare Act signed into law by President Johnson

AUG 4: Two American ships attacked in the Gulf of Tonkin

AUG 7: Tonkin Gulf Resolution passed granting president powers to take care of threats against US forces in Vietnam

APR 26: Tanzania formed from Tanganyika and Zanzibar

MAY 19: US announces it has found more than 40 hidden microphones in its new embassy in Moscow

JUN 12: Nelson Mandela sentenced to life imprisonment in South Africa

JUL 6: Malawi becomes independent

SEP 21: Malta granted its independence

was running for the state legislature, and he asked Johnson to manage the campaign, an opportunity that LBJ quickly accepted. Hopkins won his election, and the following year, he suggested Johnson's name to congressman Richard Kleberg of the 14th Congressional District to serve as his legislative secretary. Johnson eagerly accepted the opportunity to work for the heir of the biggest ranch in Texas, the King ranch, and he was soon on a train bound for Washington and his destiny.

LEGISLATIVE AIDE

For the next three years, Johnson learned the operations of America's legislative process. He quickly made friends and learned his way around the capital. He absorbed facts and read voraciously from three newspapers; he asked questions and listened. He became a doorkeeper of the Democrats in the House so he could observe its members more closely. In Kleberg's office, Johnson was also the one to contact if anything needed to be accomplished, and he used his skills in the Little Congress, a group of legislative secretaries. They had become a rather tired organization that accomplished little and relied on seniority for leadership, but Johnson challenged this and decided to run for speaker, but knew he would need more votes. So in a repeat of his performance at college, he recruited more aides to join, and it worked. At the tender age of twenty-three, Johnson became the youngest speaker of the Little Congress.

The following year Lyndon briefly studied law at Georgetown University, but he quickly tired of the night class which, in his opinion, taught him nothing he had not already seen working with Congress, so he gave up and considered other possibilities.

In early September 1934, Johnson was visiting Austin, Texas, when a friend introduced him to Claudia Taylor, and he was immediately smitten with the attractive young woman. The next day he proposed to her, but she "thought it was some kind of joke."[3] He was serious and the couple wed by year's end.

Congressman Kleberg worried that his ambitious secretary might well try to take away his own congressional seat, so he was amenable to Johnson's interest in becoming the Texas director of the National Youth Administration, one of Roosevelt's New Deal programs. Johnson expressed definite interest and began conveying this to various Texas congressmen including Sam Rayburn, who was happy to push for Johnson's appointment in July 1935, making him the youngest state director.

NATIONAL YOUTH ADMINISTRATION (NYA) (1935–1943) ★ Started in June 1935 with Lyndon B. Johnson as its first state director, the purpose of the National Youth Administration was to employ the youth of the state, as well as provide education and counseling to them during the Great Depression. Many worked on building projects, including construction of highways, playgrounds, and other recreational areas and parks. The program was disbanded during World War II.

NATIONAL YOUTH ADMINISTRATION (NYA)

For the next two years, LBJ worked to improve the lives of young people during the Depression. He worked long hours seven days a week attempting to find work programs for numerous youth and help others to stay in high school and college by providing vocational training opportunities; moreover, he ensured that young people were not denied help

NATIONAL EVENTS

AUG 20: Johnson signs Equal Opportunity Act into law

AUG 28–30: Race riots in Philadelphia

SEP 24: Publication of Warren Commission, which insists only one gunman, Lee Harvey Oswald, was involved in the Kennedy assassination

NOV 3: Lyndon B. Johnson elected president defeating Republican Barry Goldwater of Arizona

DEC 10: Dr. Martin Luther King Jr. awarded Nobel Peace Prize

JAN 1: US discontinues using any silver in its coins

1965

WORLD EVENTS

OCT 5: More than 50 East Germans escape through a tunnel under Berlin Wall

OCT 13: Soviet Union coup d'état ousts Nikita Khrushchev from power and installs Leonid Brezhnev as party leader and Aleksei Kosygin is the new premier

OCT 24: Northern Rhodesia becomes Zambia

JAN 14: For the first time in 43 years, the prime ministers of Northern Ireland and the Republic of Ireland meet

based on race. His work impressed all, including Eleanor Roosevelt, who visited him in one of his training centers in Austin. Later when he left the position in 1937, his successor was told, "You haven't got but one way to go and that's down. This man Johnson was operating the best NYA program in all of the states."[4]

Although he found his work for the NYA meaningful, the desire to run for political office appealed to him. He had his chance when the Tenth District congressman James "Buck" Buchanan died in February 1937, and a special election was called for April. Johnson ran in the special election and campaigned tirelessly, driving across the district of eight thousand square miles, meeting people and shaking hands all along the way. When he started having abdominal pains, he refused to quit, but two days before his election, the doctors insisted he have his appendix removed. So he was in the hospital recuperating when he learned he was now Congressman Johnson.

Impressed by Johnson's victory, President Roosevelt decided to meet him when the presidential yacht docked in Galveston following a cruise in the Gulf of Mexico. The two men chatted and bantered, creating a friendship that would last for years. The only dark cloud for LBJ was the death of his father in October 1937. Earlier his father had told him, "Measure each vote you cast by this standard: Is this vote in the benefit of the people? What does this do for human beings?" He then added, "Now you get up there, support FDR all the way, never shimmy and give 'em hell."[5]

US REPRESENTATIVE

Johnson had barely landed in Washington before his dogged determination to help his constituents became well known. He worked tirelessly to gain federal funds to help the folks back home in Travis County, including paved roads, streetlights, schools, and public buildings. The first contract from the newly formed US Housing Authority was awarded to Austin. Johnson continued to work to improve life for the rural communities by securing monies for building dams and winning a contract from the Rural Electrification Administration (REA) to bring electricity to the poor. LBJ also vocally supported the Fair Labor Standards Act, which created a minimum wage of forty cents an hour. He bucked considerable opposition against established congressmen to help the Roosevelt administration ultimately win victory with its passage in the House in June 1938; moreover, he could be depended on to back FDR on any of the New Deal legislation he wanted enacted.

By 1940, Johnson felt stymied by the seniority system in the House kept in place by House Speaker Sam Rayburn (and fellow Texan) and Carl Vinson, chairman of the powerful Committee on Naval Affairs. He yearned for more and decided to seize the opportunity when a special election was called after Senator Morris Sheppard unexpectedly died from a brain hemorrhage. LBJ's opponent for the Senate seat was Texas governor Wilbert "Pappy" O'Daniel, who narrowly squeaked by with a victory.

Johnson, smarting from his first electoral defeat, later remarked that it was "the most miserable time in my life. I felt terribly rejected, and I began to think about leaving politics and going home to make money." He ultimately decided to remain in Washington and keep his House seat because "with all those war clouds hanging over Europe, I felt that someone with all my training and preparedness was bound to be an important figure."[6]

SUPREME COURT APPOINTMENTS
★★★★★★★★★★

Abe Fortas, 1965

Thurgood Marshall, 1967

JAN 4: President Johnson discusses plans for the "Great Society" in his State of the Union address

JAN 20: Inauguration of Lyndon B. Johnson for his first (and only) full presidential term

FEB 21: Malcolm X assassinated

MAR 7: March on Selma (Alabama) ends in violence by state troopers against the protesters

MAR 23: Launch of Gemini 3, first space capsule, carrying two Americans

JAN 24: Death of Winston Churchill

FEB 7: US initiates bombing of North Vietnam

FEB 15: New maple leaf flag of Canada flown for the first time

MAR 18: Russian cosmonaut becomes first person to walk in space

APR 9: Parliament of West Germany extends the statute of limitations on Nazi war crimes

STATE OF THE UNION
★★★★★★★★★★

US POPULATION IN 1963
179,323,031

NATIONAL DEBT IN 1969
$368,225,581,254

NUMBER OF STATES IN 1969
50

Those war clouds determined his next position. After the Japanese attacked Pearl Harbor on December 7, 1941, Lyndon B. Johnson enlisted the next day in the US Navy. The newly commissioned lieutenant commander was sent to a desk job in San Francisco, where he yearned to leave the safety of his office for the dangers of combat. He complained to the president, who decided to send LBJ on a fact-finding mission to the South Pacific and gain information about whatever deficiencies American troops suffered in that theater of war. He was to report to FDR any information regarding problems, including shortages of equipment that troops faced there.

The Southwest Pacific commander, General Douglas MacArthur, accommodated the requests of Johnson and provided information confirming suspicions that more supplies were desperately needed. Later, when the opportunity to ride along on a combat mission arose, LBJ eagerly demanded to go and scrambled on board the *Wabash Cannonball*. Answering a call of nature, he jumped off briefly and his place was taken by someone else, so LBJ went to the *Heckling Hare* instead. On June 9, 1942, both planes encountered numerous Japanese Zeros, and the *Wabash Cannonball* was shot down over the Pacific, with no survivors. Although minus its right engine and various other hits, Captain Walter Greer managed to pilot the *Heckling Hare* to base. After hearing of its near-disaster, MacArthur decided to award Johnson the Silver Star; understandably, this political move did not please the plane's crew, who received no commendations whatsoever. For the rest of his life, LBJ would proudly trot out his wartime experience and speak in campaigns of having "seen the horrors of war."[7] He soon returned to Capitol Hill, as the president had decreed that American congressmen were needed there more than with the Armed Forces.

At this time, Johnson decided he and his family needed another source of income, so they invested their money in the purchase of a radio station, KTBC in Austin. Part of his reasoning for the acquisition was his belief that the Roosevelt administration would be amenable to any requests by the Johnsons; moreover, they could expect favorable rulings by the FCC, and within the coming years, the station would make millions of dollars in profit for the family. LBJ's investment proved sound, and over the years, they acquired both radio and television stations. By the time Johnson was president, he was earning over $1 million in profits annually. (In 2003, the Johnson family sold six Austin radio stations for $103 million.)

The Johnsons were pleased by another addition—in March 1944, a baby daughter, Lynda, was born to the couple, who had experienced numerous miscarriages during their ten-year marriage. Three years later another daughter, Luci Baines, joined the family. Tragedy, however, struck the family and the country the following year with the death of President Roosevelt. Whereas Johnson had supported FDR throughout his presidency, now LBJ backed some of Truman's policies, while opposing others. Johnson backed the Taft-Hartley Act, which prohibited the closed shop (not hiring non-union workers), and joined other congressmen who overrode Truman's veto of the bill. He did, however, support the Marshall Plan and Truman Doctrine as the ways to rebuild war-ravaged nations and develop allies to freedom rather than converts to communism.

Now forty years old, Johnson longed for new challenges and decided to run again for the US Senate in 1948 against another incumbent governor,

NATIONAL EVENTS

APR 28: American troops sent to Dominican Republic when a coup occurs, to ensure Communists do not take over the government

MAY 5: First burning of draft cards occurs at University of California at Berkeley

JUN 3: Ed White is first American astronaut to walk in space

JUL 28: Escalation of American involvement in Vietnam when President Johnson doubles number being drafted and announces increasing troop strength from 75,000 to 125,000

WORLD EVENTS

APR 15: Indian forces move across border and attack Pakistan-controlled Kashmir launching a war

APR 29: Australia sends military support to the South Vietnam government in the form of an infantry battalion

MAY 12: Israel and West Germany establish diplomatic relations

MAY 30: Viet Cong offensive against American base at Da Nang begins

SEP 2: Pakistani troops enter Indian sector of Kashmir

Coke Stevenson. Less than a month prior to the election, LBJ was hospitalized for kidney stones. The election itself was uncomfortably close—Johnson won by 87 votes, and his opponent cried foul, demanding a recount; a demand that was heard by the Supreme Court, who ruled against his opponent. So LBJ won the election as well as a derogatory new nickname, "Landslide Lyndon."

CIVIL RIGHTS WORKERS SLAIN IN MISSISSIPPI (August 4, 1964) ★ The bodies of three civil rights workers were found in a partially constructed dam about six miles from the town they were last seen visiting six weeks earlier. Michael Schwerner and Andrew Goodman were from New York, and James Chaney, an African American from Meridian, Mississippi, had been accompanying them as they traveled through Mississippi trying to encourage blacks to register to vote. Their actions prompted local KKK members to lure them to a church site on June 21, 1964, and slay them. Forty years later, a jury convicted a now-elderly Edgar Ray Killen for manslaughter of the three men and sentenced him to 60 years imprisonment.

SENATOR

Cultivating friendships with the Senate leaders became a top priority for the freshman senator from Texas. Helping with his contacts was his encyclopedia-like mind, which catalogued countless details about others that he could later retrieve and use, and he courted the leader of the southern caucus, Georgia senator Richard Russell, who also chaired the powerful Armed Services Committee. Johnson understood that any hope for advancement in the Senate rested on the opinion of Russell, and LBJ's efforts paid off in 1951 when he was rewarded with the position of Democratic whip. Then in 1953, he was elected as the Democratic minority leader.

In his new position, Johnson worked to create a cohesive Democratic Party within the Senate and strove to reconcile the positions of liberals, conservatives, and moderates to work together. Although Dwight D. Eisenhower was a Republican president, that was no excuse for the Democrats to quit working, and in foreign policy matters, Johnson believed in bipartisanship. He also crafted new policy that took aim at the seniority system, which he saw as ill-serving for energetic new senators, and he ensured that many of them received some of the plum committee assignments.

Johnson's main opponent was Wisconsin senator Joseph McCarthy and his continuous diatribe against Americans he insisted were acting in the interests of Communists. To a friend, LBJ remarked that McCarthy was "the sorriest senator up here. Can't tie his goddamned shoes. But he's riding high now, he's got people scared to death some Communist will strangle 'em in their sleep."[8] The minority leader seized his opportunity to bring down McCarthy when the Wisconsin senator attacked the US Army, and Johnson ensured that the hearings were televised, allowing the American people to witness for themselves "what the bastard was up to."[9] Then Johnson worked with the president's staff, Chief Justice Earl Warren, and fellow senators to create a bipartisan commission to pull the plug on McCarthyism. It worked, and a few months later in November 1954, the American people responded by rewarding the Democrats with control of the House and one additional seat in the Senate. Then two years later, the Democrats won the Senate and Johnson was elected Senate majority leader.

JUL 30: President Johnson signs Social Security Act of 1965 establishing Medicaid

AUG 6: President Johnson signs into law Voting Rights Act of 1965

AUG 11: Race riots begin in Watts section of Los Angeles and last nearly a week

OCT 3: New law abolishes immigration quotas based on national origin

OCT 16: Major antiwar protests in more than 80 cities involving more than 100,000

SEP 7: China announces its plan to reinforce its troops on the Indian border

SEP 9: China is recommended for United Nations membership by the organization's secretary general, U Thant

SEP 22: UN ceasefire stops fighting between India and Pakistan

OCT 8: Indonesian army performs a sweep of arrests and executes communists

NOV 6: Cuba and US agree to start an airlift program for Cubans wanting to emigrate to US

DID YOU KNOW?

Johnson liked to give presents to friends, especially electric toothbrushes, since that would ensure that they would think of him both in the morning and at night.

Johnson logged innumerable hours on the telephone, wheeling and dealing; when he met others in person, they were subjected to "the treatment": while standing next to the tall Texan and shaking his hand, their other arm was being held by LBJ while his southern drawl worked its magic in gaining their cooperation. He insisted that the only power he had was the "power of persuasion. There is no patronage; no power to discipline; no authority to fire senators like a President can fire [Cabinet] members."[10] He was intimately acquainted with the intricacies of proposed bills and the needs that senators had in their home states.

In the summer of 1955, a massive heart attack struck Johnson, but he refused to allow it to sidetrack his political career. A journalist wrote that Einstein's formula might be $E=mc^2$, but in Washington, D.C., "E=LBJ."[11] Three months later President Eisenhower also had a heart attack, and both men pondered how their health might impact the upcoming presidential election. Joseph Kennedy asked Johnson if he wanted to run for president, and stated that he would provide necessary funds, with the only provision being that LBJ choose his son John to be the vice presidential candidate. When LBJ turned down Joe Kennedy's offer, he made an instant enemy of younger son Bobby Kennedy—a relationship that did not improve with time.

Looking ahead to the next presidential election, Johnson decided to find issues with national importance that he could support and thus win widespread recognition. The first was civil rights, which he supported. He believed blacks, especially in the South, needed to be treated more equitably, and as Dr. Martin Luther King Jr. was becoming increasingly well known for the Montgomery bus boycott and other efforts, he believed the time had come for action. A civil rights act needed to pass the Senate as it had the House. Johnson saw this as crucial for the South to develop economically, but he lied to his Texas constituents and insisted he was not doing any such thing. Meanwhile in Washington he worked tirelessly to ensure the bill's passage. However, the watering down of the bill to make it more appealing included removing the section addressing the integration of schools by the federal government. Eventually the bill passed and was signed into law in September 1957, but its effect was minimal.

That same year, Johnson took the initiative to begin a congressional investigation through the Preparedness Committee to determine why the United States had suddenly taken second place in the space race following the successful launch of the Soviet satellite Sputnik. As the leader on the committee, he became the outspoken critic of the Eisenhower administration's lack of response. Then in February 1958, he pushed a resolution through the Senate creating a Special Committee on Space and Astronautics, which he then chaired. Two months later, he co-sponsored the bill creating the National Aeronautics and Space Administration (NASA).

During this time, Massachusetts senator John Kennedy enjoyed relating an anecdote in which God told him in a dream that he was going to be the next Democratic presidential candidate and win. When he told fellow senator Stu Symington about it, the Missourian laughed and said he had had the same dream. Then they told LBJ about the dream and he replied, "That's funny. For the life of me I can't remember tapping either of you two boys for the job."[12]

Johnson refused to publicly admit his candidacy for the presidency, afraid that he could

NATIONAL EVENTS

US Department of the Interior issues its first "List of Rare and Endangered Species"

NIH (National Institute of Health) introduces rubella vaccine

JAN 13: Robert Weaver is first African American to serve in the cabinet when appointed as Secretary of Housing and Urban Development

MAR 26: Massive anti-war demonstrations held across the US

JUN 13: *Miranda v. Arizona*—Supreme Court rules that all suspects must be informed of their rights before being interrogated by police

1966

WORLD EVENTS

JAN 17: Nigerian government overthrown by a military coup

JAN 19: Indira Gandhi elected Prime Minister of India

FEB 23: Ba'athists replace Syria's government after a military coup

MAR 11: Indonesian President Sukarno transfers all executive powers to General Suharto

MAR 11: President Charles de Gaulle announces France will withdraw from NATO

not face running and losing. Not entering any primaries certainly hurt his chances and allowed for the younger Jack Kennedy to take the lead among the Democratic hopefuls. Later Johnson admitted that he was unable to understand the attraction for Kennedy and referred to him as "a young whippersnapper . . . He never said a word of importance in the Senate and he never did a thing." Johnson went on to admit that Kennedy had "a good sense of humor and that he looked awfully good on the goddamn television screen."[13] A problem for Johnson was his southern roots, while Kennedy's foreseen handicap was his Catholic faith. Ultimately, the Democratic Party chose the pleasing presence of the young senator and his glamorous wife Jackie rather than the tall and rather unmannerly behavior of LBJ. Once Kennedy was selected, he needed to pick his vice president, and he believed that Johnson would not be inclined to accept the position and lose all of his power in the Senate, but LBJ was agreeable to Kennedy's offer, which was hoped would gain them the South.

ELECTION OF 1960

By acclamation, the Democratic convention approved the choice of Lyndon B. Johnson for their vice presidential candidate. He imitated Truman's whistle-stop campaign tour of 1948 by taking a train across eight southern states and delivering sixty speeches, but he worried about the very real possibility that Texas would not vote Democratic, and told his friend and aide John Connally, "We must not win the nation and lose Texas."[14] An incident in a Dallas hotel four days before the election helped ensure his state's support. Hecklers yelled, spit, and one hit Lady Bird with a picket sign as they walked through the lobby of the Adolphus Hotel. Camera crews caught the incident on film, and Americans were shocked by the behavior of Republican supporters.

When Kennedy won the election, he carried seven southern states, including Texas. But with the victory, Johnson felt no satisfaction that he would now be the man in the office of the vice president.

VICE PRESIDENT

Vice presidents lack direction, and Johnson hoped that Kennedy would provide him with the opportunity to be useful. However, whenever he visited the president, "I felt like a goddamn raven hovering over his shoulder." He went on to describe his office as being "filled with trips around the world, chauffeurs, men saluting, people clapping, chairmanships of councils, but in the end, it is nothing. I detested every minute of it."[15]

The new Senate majority leader, Senator Mike Mansfield of Montana, attempted to help LBJ by changing the Senate rules and allowing the former leader to become the head of the Democratic Senate meetings, but its members soundly rejected the idea, which also stung Johnson personally. Kennedy included him in Cabinet meetings and National Security Council briefings. The president was sympathetic to Johnson's dissatisfaction and told his staff, "You are dealing with a very insecure, sensitive man with a huge ego. I want you literally to kiss his fanny from one end of Washington to the other."[16] Johnson, however, still felt unnecessary, and friends remarked about how sullen and depressed he appeared. The LBJ exuberance no longer exhibited itself; instead, he rarely talked unless a question was specifically addressed to him. The cosmopolitan flavor of the Kennedy White House left him feeling uncomfortable and ill suited for their gala dinners.

Johnson was appointed as the chairman of the

SUMMER: Race riots in Cleveland, Chicago, and Atlanta

JUN 30: National Organization for Women (NOW) founded

OCT: Black Panther Party started

OCT 15: Department of Transportation created

NOV 8: Ronald Reagan elected governor of California

Historian William Manchester writes *Death of a President* at Jackie Kennedy's request, who provides him access to papers not before seen

1967

JAN 27: US and Soviet Union agree not to place weapons in space or on the moon

MAR 23: Pope and Archbishop of Canterbury meet; it is first official meeting between those churches in over 400 years

APR 14: South Vietnam promises free elections within the next 3–5 months

APR 21: Haile Selassie travels to Jamaica for the first time to meet with Rastafarian leaders

AUG 13: Mao Tse-Tung begins China's Cultural Revolution

DID YOU KNOW?

LBJ was the first president to appoint an African American to the cabinet and to the Supreme Court.

Johnson's swearing in was the first by a woman and the only one on an airplane.

Committee on Equal Employment Opportunity and was also tasked to head the National Aeronautics and Space Council. When these opportunities did little to please the vice president, Kennedy and his staff decided to send him abroad, where he could make headlines. So during his tenure, LBJ was sent on eleven foreign trips and visited thirty-three nations; his previous enthusiastic persona returned, only to be shelved once he returned to Washington, D.C. On one of these trips, he visited Vietnam and its president Ngo Dinh Diem. In Saigon, LBJ insisted on having his motorcade halt numerous times so he could greet the onlookers and hand out cigarette lighters and passes to the US Senate, so the next time they were in Washington, the Vietnamese could watch democracy in action. He also shocked foreign correspondents when he disrobed in front of them, toweled himself off, and then dressed in fresh clothes while giving a press conference. As one diplomat traveling with the vice president remarked, the Asian cities he visited "would never be the same."[17] In August 1961, LBJ visited the recently constructed Berlin Wall to deliver the president's message that the German people had America's support.

Although he flourished whenever traveling abroad, he did not do as well when on his home turf. Moving closer to the 1964 election, rumors bounced through Washington that Kennedy planned to dump Johnson from the ticket and replace him with North Carolina governor Terry Sanford. Those close to the president have differed on the issue, but apparently Johnson believed the rumor might very well be true.

But with declining poll numbers among Texans for the president, the decision was made to travel there to bolster his standing and raise money for the party coffers. The president, vice president, and their wives flew to Texas in November 1963, where they found the reception much warmer than anticipated. On the twenty-second, the car carrying Governor and Nellie Connally in the front seat and President and Mrs. Kennedy in the back was hit by multiple gunshots. Upon hearing the first shot, a Secret Service agent in the next car threw the six-foot-three vice president on the floor of his car and held him down while the cars zipped through the streets of Dallas to Parkland Memorial Hospital. Once they arrived, Johnson could finally stretch out of his uncomfortable contortionist position, and he rubbed his chest, causing some to speculate that he, too, had been shot or suffered a heart attack, but he and Senator Ralph Yarborough had escaped unscathed.

Once Kennedy was declared dead, LBJ moved quickly to legitimize his authority by taking the oath of office aboard Air Force One with his wife and Jackie Kennedy (still wearing the suit splattered with her husband's blood) watching. The plane soon departed, carrying the deceased president, and Johnson worked in the coming days to begin running the country while leading the mourning process. Jackie Kennedy was grateful for his compassion, especially for the kind letters he wrote both Kennedy children the night of their father's death. Caroline and her friends continued using the White House for their kindergarten class through the end of the year, although the Johnsons moved into the presidential residence on December 7. Years later LBJ admitted that, "I felt from the very first day in office that I had to carry on for President Kennedy. I considered myself the caretaker of both his people and his policies."[18]

NATIONAL EVENTS

JAN 27: Apollo 1 capsule burns while testing on the launch pad at Cape Kennedy; all three astronauts die on board

FEB 10: Twenty-fifth Amendment ratified outlining presidential succession and what to do in case of incapacity of the president

APR 28: Boxer Muhammad Ali refuses to report for duty when drafted and is arrested and stripped of his boxing title

SUMMER: Race riots in many American cities

AUG 30: Thurgood Marshall becomes first African American appointed to the US Supreme Court

WORLD EVENTS

FEB 24: USSR forbids its satellite nations from conducting diplomatic relations with West Germany

MAR 4: Oil begins being pumped from North Sea

MAR 9: Defection by Stalin's daughter to the US

APR 24: Soviet capsule Soyuz I crash-lands killing cosmonaut on board

JUN 5–10: Six Day War fought between Israel and its Arab neighbors of Jordan, Iraq, Syria, and Egypt; Israel

PRESIDENT JOHNSON

Johnson decided to keep his predecessor's staff, and years later, Lady Bird admitted that was a poor decision. Some of the members left of their own accord while others remained and were faithful to their new president. One who stayed for another year but was not happy was Attorney General Robert Kennedy. Still looking to the 1964 presidential election, he hoped to be the vice presidential candidate, but LBJ abhorred the idea. When he told Kennedy personally of his decision, Bobby refused to withdraw publicly, so Johnson issued a statement saying no one on the current cabinet would be considered. Bobby later apologized to the others, tongue in cheek, saying he was "sorry [he] took so many nice fellows over the side with me."[19] The two men would collide on future issues, as well.

Meanwhile, Johnson was determined to push John Kennedy's agenda through Congress, where it had stalled. Here the former majority leader worked his magic once more by chatting on the phone with its members, their wives, and on occasion their children, to win support of the proposed legislation. It worked and the logjam broke. Chief among these was the Civil Rights Act of 1964, aimed to stop discrimination in employment and in the use of public facilities. While it originally meant to prohibit discrimination based on race, a Virginia congressman tacked on an amendment against sexual discrimination, thinking that would sink it. Instead it, too, became law. Race riots spread across northern cities that summer, the first of several long hot summers to come.

The following year the Voting Rights Act was passed to end the unconstitutional use of literacy tests, poll taxes, and any other means to prohibit black Americans from exercising their right to vote. This law came on the heels of the shocking deaths of three young men—two New Yorkers and one black man from Mississippi, all working there in Mississippi to convince more African Americans to register to vote in the 1964 election. Johnson ordered J. Edgar Hoover and the FBI to investigate; they ultimately determined that a conspiracy existed between the local sheriff's department and the Ku Klux Klan, but the civil rights movement continued forward in spite of the intimidation tactics.

Shortly after Johnson took office, he told his staff that he wanted to "fight the war on poverty," and instructed them to develop a program. He confided to the head of the Council of Economic Advisors, Walter Heller, that he was "a Roosevelt New Dealer." He went on to say that "John F. Kennedy was a little too conservative for my taste."[20] Johnson returned to his Depression-era roots and his strong belief that those New Deal plans provided essential help to those in need. With that in mind, in May 1964, the president announced his social program, entitled the Great Society, which would end poverty and erase racial discrimination. It would uplift the lives of the poor and improve education for all. The Office of Economic Opportunity was one of the first, and its original administrator was Kennedy brother-in-law Sargent Shriver. Great Society programs included the Job Corps, which provided job training to young people ages sixteen to twenty-one; Volunteers in Service to America (VISTA), a domestic version of the Peace Corps that utilized volunteers to aid the poor in the United States; and Community Action Program, which created Head Start for preschool children of low-income families and legal aid services.

Another of Kennedy's plans languishing in Congress was his proposed tax cuts, which ran

OCT 21: Antiwar demonstration in Washington, D.C., draws thousands

NOV 30: Senator Eugene McCarthy announces he will seek Democratic nomination for president against LBJ

DEC 9: White House wedding of Lynda B. Johnson to Charles Robb

Air Force doctor writes book *Aerobics* describing ways to exercise

New York first to use 911 emergency calling system

takes Sinai Peninsula, West Bank, Golan Heights, and Gaza Strip

JUN 17: China announces it has completed a successful test of a hydrogen bomb

JUN 27: British Barclays Bank installs first automated teller machine (ATM)

1968

Japan becomes world's second strongest economic power behind the United States with a gross national product of $140 billion

Yasir Arafat of the Al Fatah movement becomes leader of the Palestine Liberation Organization

THE GREAT SOCIETY ★ The "Great Society" was a term coined by President Johnson in 1964 to describe new social programs to fight his "war on poverty" and improve the lives of Americans. The Social Security Act of 1965 established Medicare, which helps pay health care expenses for Americans over 65 years of age. Medicaid also was created by this law and provides health care to citizens unable to afford it themselves. Other significant Great Society programs included the 1965 Elementary and Secondary Act, earmarking federal funds to help defray costs for local school districts; Head Start to provide preschool education for lower income children; Job Corps, giving disadvantaged youth job training; Vista Volunteers, a domestic version of the Peace Corps; Corporation for Public Broadcasting; 1968 Fair Housing Act prohibiting discrimination in housing; and many others.

counter to Johnson's Great Society programs. Senator Harry Byrd of Virginia worried about the possible deficit that would be incurred and pushed Johnson to find cuts in his budget. LBJ decided that cutbacks could be done everywhere, and while his staff streamlined some of the program budgets, the president began turning off the lights in the White House to reduce wasteful energy consumption. The tax cuts were finally approved in early 1964.

In foreign affairs, Johnson continued implementing policies approved by his predecessor, as well as those of administration officials in Vietnam. Everyone said that to allow Vietnam to fall to communism would set the "domino theory" in motion and soon all of Southeast Asia would be behind the "bamboo curtain." Johnson did not want to see the war escalate, for he saw that as creating a barrier toward implementing the Great Society. Repeatedly presidents lost their domestic agenda to pressing foreign problems, but soon events would push him in that direction.

In 1964 few Americans perceived Vietnam as a major threat or even a campaign issue. This changed, however, when the USS *Maddox* was fired on by North Vietnamese gunboats on August 2 in the Gulf of Tonkin. The destroyer returned fire and radioed for help from the carrier USS *Ticonderoga*, whose jets badly damaged the enemy gunboats. Two days later the *Maddox* and another destroyer, the *Turner Joy*, radioed torpedoes were being fired at them. Although the first attack went unanswered, Johnson decided the second demanded a swift response. He ordered American jets to bomb North Vietnamese bases and told the American people in a television address that the United States was now facing "open aggression on the high seas," which was being met with "firm but limited response."[21] Ironically, many, including defense secretary Robert McNamara, later stated that a second attack never occurred, but rather that jittery crews only thought an attack had been launched.

Five days after the original attack, Congress passed the Gulf of Tonkin Resolution allowing the "President as Commander in Chief, to take all necessary measures to repel any armed attack against forces of the United States and to prevent further aggression."[22]

Besides Vietnam, the main topic on Johnson's mind was the Democratic National Convention in late August. Speculation grew as to who would be his choice for vice president; he ultimately selected Minnesota senator Hubert Humphrey. They were opposed by Barry Goldwater of Arizona, whose running mate was New Yorker Thomas Miller. Goldwater's unabashedly conservative stance drove

NATIONAL EVENTS	Arthur C. Clarke writes *2001: A Space Odyssey*	**FEB 8:** First flight by a Boeing 747	**FEB 21:** Delta flight hijacked to Cuba, first of many resulting in increased airport security	**MAR 12:** LBJ defeats Eugene McCarthy in first presidential primary	**MAR 16:** Robert Kennedy announces his candidacy for Democratic nomination
WORLD EVENTS	Cunard launches the SS *QE2* to replace the *Queen Elizabeth*	**JAN 2:** Most successful complete heart transplant to date performed by Christian Barnard in South Africa	**JAN 5:** Alexander Dubcek elected leader of Czechoslovakia's Communist Party	**JAN 23:** North Korea seizes ship USS *Pueblo* and its crew	**JAN 25:** Israel's INS *Dakar* submarine sinks in the Mediterranean Sea

many into Johnson's camp, especially when the Arizona senator mentioned making Social Security voluntary, and his opposition to civil rights legislation angered many. Democrats proclaimed "All the Way with LBJ," and the voters agreed. Johnson received 61 percent of the popular vote to Goldwater's 39 percent. Of the electoral votes, LBJ won 486 to Goldwater's fifty-two, which consisted of Arizona and five southeastern states.

Since Democrats controlled both Houses, Johnson had high hopes for the 89th Congress when it met in January 1965.

PRESIDENT IN HIS OWN RIGHT

With the new year, Johnson focused Congress on his domestic agenda, asking for increased federal funding of public education, and in April he proudly signed the Elementary and Secondary Education Act into law. A few months later the Higher Education Act was signed granting scholarships and student loans for college students.

Worried about the health care of the country's aging population, Johnson proposed a program to help those receiving Social Security benefits. Some, including Ronald Reagan, loudly opposed the idea, believing it was moving the country toward socialism. Some changes were made to the Medicare bill, but the program that Harry Truman had earlier proposed was signed into law at the Truman Library on July 3, 1965, with the former president looking on. It would be one of the few triumphs that Johnson could enjoy before Vietnam consumed his presidency.

Two days before the election, five American B-57 bombers were destroyed and more than a dozen other aircraft damaged by a mortar attack by Communist guerrillas while the planes sat on an airfield in South Vietnam. Fearful that a retaliatory strike could be interpreted as escalation, thus jeopardizing the election, Johnson decided against taking action. After the election, members of his staff wrote position papers on possible actions/scenarios that could be taken should the conflict develop further, and on December 7, he approved the memo that moved the United States closer to war; yet he still maintained the status quo when queried by reporters. To Tom Wicker of the *New York Times*, Johnson insisted that he did not want to see the war expanded, but to another *Times* reporter, Turner Catledge, he said, "Whether we spread military operations across North Vietnam is yet to be decided. We certainly haven't decided against it."[23]

On Christmas Day, Communist Viet Cong guerrillas set off a bomb in Saigon at the Brinks Bachelor Officer's Quarters, killing two Americans and injuring fifty more. Again, Johnson's advisors and cabinet split on what response was needed. Once more the president hesitated, arguing that retaliatory bombing was not necessarily the best action; instead, "I have never felt that this war will be won from the air, and it seems to me that what is much more needed and would be more effective is a larger and stronger use of Rangers and Special Forces and Marines, or other appropriate military strength on the ground and on the scene."[24]

Reports of more violence by the Viet Cong against the South Vietnamese came in, and led to more vacillating by the administration. The South Vietnamese government was in a quandary and offered little aide of their own, and then in late January 1965, it was overthrown in a coup. The time had come for action by the president, and he authorized a prolonged bombing campaign dubbed Operation Rolling Thunder. It began on February 13, but no announcement was made to

DID YOU KNOW?

Johnson patrolled the White House at night turning off the lights to save the taxpayers money.

MAR 31: President Johnson announces he will not seek reelection

APR 4: Dr. Martin Luther King Jr. is assassinated on motel balcony in Memphis

APR 11: President Johnson signs Civil Rights Act of 1968

JUN 5: Robert Kennedy shot after an appearance in a Los Angeles hotel; he dies the next day

JUN 7: Sirhan Sirhan indicted for murder of Robert Kennedy

JAN 30: US forces launch Tet Offensive in Vietnam

JAN 31: Viet Cong forces attack American embassy in Saigon

FEB 11: Israel and Jordan clash over their border

FEB 24: Tet Offensive ends

MAR 16: My Lai Massacre occurs when American troops gun down civilians in South Vietnamese village

CIVIL RIGHTS ACT OF 1964 ★ Originally proposed by President Kennedy, the House Rules committee chairman had stalled the Civil Rights Act, but after the president's assassination, Johnson pushed for its passage and gained public support for it as well. Its purpose was to eliminate discrimination against any group for voting, employment, or use of public services such as city buses. President Johnson signed it into law on July 2, 1964.

the American people. James Reston told the *New York Times* readers that America had begun "an undeclared and unexplained war in Vietnam."[25] Soon afterward, LBJ ordered Marines to guard the air base at Da Nang, but refused to commit them to combat duty.

Closer to home, Marine paratroopers were dispatched to the Dominican Republic for the safety of Americans living there when the pro-American government fell victim to a coup. This situation soon quieted and the Marines left, unlike the increasingly violent situation in Vietnam.

In March the president finally made a public statement regarding his administration's policy in Southeast Asia when he addressed an audience at Johns Hopkins University. He explained that America was in Vietnam because of previous pledges to help the South Vietnamese, and espoused the domino theory. Then Johnson called for Hanoi to sit down and negotiate a peace, something which North Vietnamese leader Ho Chi Minh absolutely ignored. Americans had little regard for Johnson's speech either and remained unconvinced.

At this time, Marines were landing in Vietnam, and more troops arrived the following month, and by summer, a commitment was made by the administration to send young American men into combat after the South Vietnamese experienced several defeats. In July, defense secretary McNamara presented the president with three options: "1) Cut our losses and withdraw; 2) Continue at about the present level; or 3) Expand promptly and substantially the US military pressure against the Viet Cong."[26] Others, including General William Westmoreland, who was commanding US forces in Vietnam, and Secretary of State Dean Rusk, advised Johnson to support the third option, and he fell in line. Westmoreland wanted a total of 175,000 soldiers, an increase of over ninety thousand men. He maintained these were necessary to "take the war to the enemy."[27] Fearful of losing the momentum of the Great Society, LBJ also decided to tell the American people as little as possible and wait to consult Congress or the National Security Council. Buried in an afternoon press conference was the announcement of increased troops being deployed. Enlistment tours were extended and more young men were to be drafted.

By mid-1965, a few college campuses sprouted antiwar protests with vocal demonstrators, and LBJ worried that their actions could erode his support. Now people spoke of the "credibility gap" as the difference between what the president said and what actually was occurring. The president worked to keep the media on his side, as well as Congress; the support of both would be imperative to win the war. By the end of the year, various opinion polls showed widespread public support of Vietnam, but some administration staffers discounted it, arguing that many of those "people probably do not even understand what they are supporting."[28]

Ebullient by the passage and signing of the Voting Rights Act in August 1965, Johnson's happiness soon evaporated with news of bloody riots in the

NATIONAL EVENTS

SUMMER: Race riots occur in major American cities including Kansas City, Chicago, Boston, and Miami

AUG 8: Republican National convention nominates Richard Nixon as presidential candidate

AUG 22–30: Demonstrators clash repeatedly with police in Chicago while Democratic convention is held; Hubert Humphrey becomes the party's nominee for president

OCT 11: First manned Apollo mission launches (Apollo 7) with three astronauts

WORLD EVENTS

MAR 17: Brits demonstrate in Grosvenor Square, London against US military action in Vietnam

APR 20: Pierre Elliott Trudeau elected Canada's 15th prime minister

MAY 19: Italy holds general elections

JUN 29: Pope Paul VI publicly condemns birth control

JUL 1: Non-Nuclear Proliferation Treaty signed by Britain, US, and Soviet Union

Watts section of Los Angeles. The president could not believe what was happening, and his aide Joseph Califano later said, "He refused to look at the cable from Los Angeles describing the situation. He refused to take the calls from the generals who were requesting government planes to fly in the National Guard."[29] More riots and more violence spread throughout the country, and the president was powerless to stop it.

The Great Society initiatives began winding down in 1966, and although a few small reforms were achieved, the one major change was the creation of the Department of Transportation, which combined a score of government agencies under one umbrella. Along with this, Johnson pushed for laws to research and improve highway safety, and two were passed.

Determined to attain Kennedy's goal of landing a man on the moon by the end of the decade, NASA moved the space program forward, and in 1965, the United States watched five Gemini flights safely orbit the world with their two-man crews. The Soviets, however, had three-men missions and beat the Americans by three months with the first spacewalk. Five more Gemini flights successfully flew in 1966, leading the way to the testing of the Saturn rocket, which would ultimately launch crews to the moon. Then tragedy shook the nation when fire broke out on board the Apollo I capsule where astronauts Gus Grissom, Ed White, and Roger Chaffee were running through a test as it sat on top of the Saturn rocket on Pad-34 at Cape Kennedy. Engulfed in a flash fire, the astronauts died immediately. The future of the space program hung in the balance while Congress and NASA investigated and worked to correct the myriad problems that were exposed under the scrutiny. By November 1967, the redesigned Saturn V rocket flew successfully in an unmanned mission; two more in the coming year led to the first manned Apollo mission—Apollo 7, launched on October 11, 1968.

The space program, the war, and the Great Society all led to spiraling costs and inflation was on the rise. Economic advisors told the president he needed a tax increase; he attempted to ignore the problem, and when he finally did ask Congress to pass the increase in 1967, LBJ found himself mired in a dispute pitting the liberals, who wanted monies only spent on social programs, against conservatives, who wanted funding increased for Vietnam.

By early 1967, the American people's support of Vietnam was steadily declining, and with it, the president's popularity. Johnson desperately desired to end involvement there, hoping to stage peace talks prior to the 1968 election. The North Vietnamese were not receptive to negotiations, so LBJ decided to escalate the war instead, with more attacks launched and scheduled. News of this only further damaged the president's standing, but he remained adamant that the United States would not leave without achieving victory. Casualties mounted to nearly seventy thousand by the summer of 1967, and Johnson asked defense secretary McNamara, "Are we going to be able to win this goddamned war?" upon his return from the battlefront. McNamara reported General Westmoreland's insistence that "We are winning slowly but steadily."[30]

Johnson felt overwhelmed by the growing criticism from seemingly all quarters—Congress, the press, and students on college campuses. McNamara began harboring doubts, and Johnson decided it was time for his secretary of defense to find employment elsewhere—he became the new director of the World Bank. Other former Kennedy

DID YOU KNOW?

Johnson would sometimes pull up his shirt to show off his scar from gall bladder surgery.

OCT 20: Jackie Kennedy weds Greek tycoon Aristotle Onassis

NOV 1: President Johnson orders cessation of bombardment of North Vietnam

NOV 5: Nixon wins presidential election

DEC 22: Wedding of former president Dwight Eisenhower's grandson David to president-elect Richard Nixon's daughter Julie

DEC 24: Crew of Apollo 8 become first humans to see the far side of the moon

JUL 17: Saddam Hussein becomes vice chairman of Iraq's Revolutionary Council

JUL 29: In Costa Rica, the Arenal Volcano erupts for the first time in hundreds of years

NOV 11: Extensive bombing of Laos begins to interrupt transportation of supplies along Ho Chi Minh trail

DEC 23: Crew of USS *Pueblo* released by North Korea

DID YOU KNOW?

LBJ received criticism for picking up one of the family beagles by its ears.

staffers exited as well, sensing that this presidency was on its way down. One very vocal critic of the president and the war was Bobby Kennedy, who was jockeying into position for the 1968 Democratic nomination. Kennedy decried Johnson's lack of willingness to discuss peace and called for immediate negotiations with the North Vietnamese. LBJ later replied that the American people would not tolerate "a dishonorable peace . . . bought at the price of a temporary lust for popularity."[31]

Elsewhere in the world, peace also seemed illusory. In the Middle East, Egyptian president Gamal Abdel Nasser convinced UN secretary general U Thant to remove UN troops who were guarding the Egyptian-Israeli border. Foreseeing war, Johnson pled for both sides to remain calm, but Nasser had already moved against Israel and talked of war. Fearing that Egypt would receive help from its ally, the Soviet Union, Israel moved first on the fifth of June and launched blistering attacks against Egypt. Soon Egypt's Arab neighbors were on the offensive against Israel. Johnson refused to intervene, which angered many American Jews, but by the fourth day of fighting, Israel had pushed into Syria and the Golan Heights, with the UN attempting to broker a cease-fire. Two days later, negotiations succeeded, ending the Six Day War.

Amid war and protests, Johnson managed a few occasions of more pleasant events. In June, he proudly announced the appointment of the first African American to the Supreme Court, Thurgood Marshall. In December he gave away daughter Lynda in a grand-scale White House wedding to Marine captain Charles Robb. The president always enjoyed spending time with his one grandchild, Patrick Nugent, son of his other daughter Luci and her husband Patrick.

With the new year dawning and its upcoming election, the family worried about LBJ's health and were concerned that another term would very possibly kill him. Johnson apparently also began thinking of not running for reelection, but was still vacillating. Events soon transpired that would help make up his mind.

In January 1968, the USS *Pueblo*, a US intelligence-gathering vessel, was operating in waters off North Korea when it was captured by a group of that nation's gunboats, and its eighty-three-man crew imprisoned. Johnson protested the North Koreans' belligerent actions, and insisted that the UN demand sanctions. He called up reservists but fortunately the crisis passed, and the crew was freed.

Scarcely had the country recovered from one emergency when the next broke. Throughout the war, both North and South Vietnam had celebrated the Tet holiday (lunar New Year) with a week-long celebration and cease-fire. Tet 1968 began at midnight January 30, and within the hour, South Vietnam was under siege by more than seventy thousand North Vietnamese troops and Viet Cong guerrillas. One target was the American embassy in Saigon, where US Marines kept the Viet Cong from entering the building in a six-hour gun battle that left seven Americans dead. Although expected groundswell of public support among the South Vietnamese never materialized, and the Communists suffered brutal losses, the North Vietnamese still claimed victory.

One who believed that the United States needed to withdraw was CBS news anchor Walter Cronkite, who visited the troops in February and told his audience that it was time for the American troops to leave. Bill Moyers, aide to LBJ, said later that after hearing Cronkite's report, Johnson stated: "If I've lost Cronkite, I've lost middle America."[32] Still the commander in chief ordered reinforcements, as the military warned that an additional 206,000 troops were required to continue the war and cautioned of reversals if this was not done. The new defense secretary, Clark Clifford, grew increasingly dovish in his new job. And the chorus of "Hey, hey LBJ, how many kids did you kill today?" grew ever louder with the rising number of protests coast to coast.

Sensing weakness, Democratic challengers began encircling the president like vultures eyeing a carcass. Minnesota senator and antiwar candidate Eugene McCarthy ran a close second to Johnson in the New Hampshire primary; Robert Kennedy joined the hail of criticisms against

LBJ and proclaimed that he was running for the highest office "to propose new policies . . . to end the bloodshed in Vietnam and in our cities."[33] In a televised address on Sunday evening, March 28, the president finally announced his plans: "I have concluded that I should not permit the Presidency to become involved in the partisan divisions that are developing. . . . Accordingly, I shall not seek, and I will not accept, the nomination of my Party for another term as your President."[34]

Hardly a week later, the country and its president heard the sobering news of the assassination in Memphis of Dr. Martin Luther King Jr., and the president reminded the people that King's "dream" should not die but continue to live. Not all agreed, and race riots erupted throughout the nation's cities. A few days later, LBJ signed the Fair Housing Act into law, which was designed to end racial discrimination in the housing market. Later in the summer the Housing and Urban Development Act was also passed, opening the way for lower-income families to own or rent homes through government subsidies.

By late April, a third prominent Democrat threw his hat into the ring—Vice President Hubert Humphrey. The campaigning was in full swing by early June when more tragic news arrived: Robert Kennedy had been shot in a Beverly Hills hotel kitchen that he was using for his exit following a speech. The president and Mrs. Johnson attended the funeral mass, as well as his burial at Arlington.

The gloom that pervaded the summer lifted a little for LBJ's address to the UN General Assembly to announce his pleasure upon their approval of the Nuclear Nonproliferation Treaty to prohibit non-nuclear nations from obtaining the technology and means to produce their own nuclear weapons. This was followed by the United States–USSR Consular Treaty, which allowed both to begin the process of establishing consulates in each other's countries; moreover, the two were discussing possible future negotiations regarding arms limitations.

No longer a candidate, Johnson planned to take a back seat to the Democratic convention proceedings in Chicago. Others, however, seized the opportunity to bask in the glow of the media spotlight, creating headlines with daily coverage of protestors versus police in riot gear. Behind the scenes Johnson still wielded power and insisted on removing the doves' plank to immediately cease the bombing of North Vietnam and withdraw American troops. LBJ adamantly refused any wording that would undercut the current administration's position; instead, a plank was adopted allowing for peace talks and bombing reduction only when troops were not in harm's way.

CHAOS OF 1968 ★ While voices grew in number and volume protesting the Vietnam War, the country's fabric of civility seemed to tear itself apart during the spring and summer of 1968. Following the assassination of Dr. Martin Luther King Jr. in April, riots broke out in more than 100 cities, including Chicago and Washington, D.C. Chicago experienced more violence when it hosted the Democratic convention in August. Antiwar protests attracted thousands and police responded in riot gear with mace and clubs. Americans, including the president, watched the brawling in horror on television. It seemed the country was spiraling out of control.

The two top contenders for the nomination, Hubert Humphrey and Eugene McCarthy, did not please Johnson, and although many figured Humphrey would be nominated, they feared he would lose to Nixon in the general election because of his association with Johnson. The president stayed at his ranch in Texas and watched the convention on television, including Humphrey's nomination. Later when asked if he would be willing to campaign on his vice president's behalf, LBJ replied, "Why? Nixon is supporting my Vietnam policy stronger than Hubert."[35]

Still Johnson remained loyal to his party and worked to develop peace talks with North Vietnam, as well as to halt the bombing. Worried that such negotiations might smack of manipulating the election, the president called the three candidates (Alabama governor George Wallace ran as an independent) to explain his plan. The

South Vietnamese believed they would do better under the Nixon regime, so they refused to attend peace talks organized by the Johnson administration. Still LBJ moved forward and on October 31 announced there would be an end to the bombing campaign beginning the next day. (Peace talks would begin—after Nixon took office, but the talks would be intermittent and the bombing would resume.) Although the news brought many into Humphrey's camp, it fell short of victory, and LBJ consoled the loser: "You fought well and hard. . . . In twenty years of national service, you have had no finer hours than those of the past few weeks—in which you awakened the support and interest of millions of our people."[36]

For Johnson's remaining weeks, he worked with Nixon on the transition, although the president found it a difficult task since his successor began to insert himself in the decision-making process for Vietnam before his term began. The Johnsons greeted a new granddaughter and rejoiced in the inspiring journey of Apollo 8, whose crew read from the Book of Genesis on Christmas Eve while they showed the world for the first time a view of earth from space. When he handed over the reins of power to Nixon on January 20, 1969, he did so with regret that he was also transferring the Vietnam War, and later wrote in his memoirs, "I regretted more than anyone could possibly know that I was leaving the White House without having achieved a just, an honorable, and a lasting peace in Vietnam."[37]

RETIREMENT

LBJ and Lady Bird Johnson flew from Washington to their ranch near Johnson City. Through sound investments, the couple had acquired an impressive portfolio of over fifteen million dollars in assets, so their future was financially sound. The former president was eager to begin on the LBJ Library in Austin, the state capital, near the University of Texas. He shunned the press and its constant pressing of him on Vietnam. He attended the July launch at Cape Kennedy of the Apollo 11 crew to the moon, but disliked sharing the attention with Vice President Spiro Agnew.

Johnson also began working on his memoirs with the aid of Harvard professor Doris Kearns, and in 1971, *The Vantage Point: Perspectives of the Presidency, 1963–1969*, was published. In May the Johnson Library opened to a long line of celebrities and more than two hundred antiwar protestors and hecklers. But they did not spoil the festivities, and Johnson proudly led tours of the new School of Public Affairs.

The next spring, while visiting daughter Lynda and her family in Virginia, LBJ suffered a massive heart attack. After staying in a local hospital, he was flown to one in San Antonio, and then soon released to go home although he would continue suffering irregular heartbeats and chest pains. He refused surgery and experts agreed that his heart was irreparably damaged.

Although feeling unwell, the politician in Johnson could not resist the upcoming presidential campaign. He rooted for Edmund Muskie to win the nomination and was disappointed when liberal South Dakota senator George McGovern won it instead. When the two men sat down for lunch, LBJ opined that he believed the Democratic candidate was "crazy as hell"[38] regarding the war and his willingness to accept "peace at any price."

In December, Johnson granted the National Park Service his ranch for historical tours. A two-day civil rights symposium in early December tired him greatly. In January, he attended three funerals, including former president Harry Truman's in Independence, Missouri. He greatly admired Truman and remarked that the Missourian had been helpful and supportive throughout LBJ's presidency.

On January 22, 1973, after eating his lunch, Johnson retired to his bedroom for a nap. At 3:50 p.m., he called asking for a Secret Service agent to come "immediately." By the time two agents arrived, he was unconscious on the floor. Mouth to mouth resuscitation was applied, but to no avail. He was airlifted to San Antonio, but was pronounced dead before they exited the plane.

Johnson's body was returned to Austin, where it laid in state at the capitol. Then two days later, a horse-drawn caisson bore his body to Washington, where it remained for the next day for national leaders to pay their respects. Then one last time, LBJ was flown to Texas, where he was buried beside his family members in the family plot near Johnson City, Texas.

Sadly, Johnson did not live to witness the end of the Vietnam War, but he came close. Five days after he found his peace, the cease-fire was announced.

Lady Bird Johnson continued being active in a variety of organizations and valued spending time with her family. A stroke in 2002 left her somewhat debilitated but she continued to divide her time between her Texas ranch and Austin home. In late June 2007, she became ill and died on July 11. She is buried beside her husband.

ENDNOTES

1 Doris Kearns, *Lyndon Johnson and the American Dream*, New York: Harper and Row, 1976, p. 24.

2 Ibid, p. 69.

3 Robert Dallek, *Lyndon B. Johnson: Portrait of a President*, New York: Oxford University Press, 2004, p. 24.

4 Ibid, p. 31.

5 Irwin and Debi Unger, *LBJ, A Life*, New York: John Wiley & Sons, 1999, p. 66.

6 Kearns, pp. 93-94.

7 Ronnie Dugger, *The Politician, The Life and Times of Lyndon Johnson*, New York: W.W. Norton & Co., 1982, p. 252.

8 Robert A. Caro, *The Years of Lyndon Johnson, Master of the Senate*, New York: Alfred A. Knopf, 2002, p. 546.

9 Dallek, p. 81.

10 Ibid, p. 86.

11 Ibid, p. 92.

12 Ibid, p. 111.

13 Doris Kearns Goodwin, *The Fitzgeralds and the Kennedys*, New York: Simon & Schuster, 1987, p. 780.

14 Dallek, p. 119.

15 Kearns, p. 164.

16 Dallek, p. 124.

17 Ibid, p. 128.

18 Lyndon Johnson, *The Vantage Point: Perspectives of the Presidency, 1963-1969*, New York: Holt, Rinehart and Winston, 1971, p. 19.

19 Unger, p. 324.

20 Paul R. Henggeler, *In His Steps: Lyndon Johnson and the Kennedy Mystique*, Chicago: Ivan R. Dee, 1991, p. 109.

21 James S. Olson and Randy Roberts, *Where the Domino Fell: America and Vietnam, 1945 to 1995*, New York: St. Martin's Press, 1996, p. 117.

22 Unger, p. 322.

23 David Kaiser, *American Tragedy, Kennedy, Johnson and the Origins of the Vietnam War*, Cambridge, MA: Belknap Press of Harvard University Press, 2000, p. 381.

24 Ibid, p. 385.

25 Dallek, p. 210.

26 Kearns, p. 280.

27 Dallek, p. 218.

28 Ibid, p. 225.

29 Kearns, p. 305.

30 Dallek, p. 307.

31 Henggeler, p. 217.

32 Walter Cronkite, *A Reporter's Life*, New York: Alfred A. Knopf, 1996, p. 258.

33 Unger, p. 455.

34 Ibid, p. 458.

35 Ibid, p. 484.

36 Ibid, p. 493.

37 Lyndon B. Johnson, *The Vantage Point: Perspectives of the Presidency, 1963-1969*, New York: Holt, Rinehart and Winston, 1971, p. 529.

38 Unger, p. 529.

to believe otherwise. Hiss was later found guilty of two counts of perjury and sentenced to a federal penitentiary. The Senate, meanwhile, created its own committee and soon Senator Joe McCarthy's insidious influence stretched across the country and through every level of society, recklessly hurling accusations and causing numerous people to lose their jobs, homes, and reputations.

After winning reelection in 1948, and gaining widespread notoriety thanks to the HUAC, Nixon decided to run in 1950 for one of California's senate seats. Using his links to the committee, he papered California with a half million "pink sheets" hoping to connect his opponent's voting record to the Communist Party. Helen Gahagan Douglas was a longtime Democrat and friend of the Roosevelts. She and her husband, actor Melvyn Douglas, were guests at the White House before she began her career in Congress in 1944, and her public criticism of HUAC invited talk of her entertaining Communist sympathies. During the hard-fought campaign, a nickname for Nixon would surface for the first—but definitely not the last time—"Tricky Dick." Promoting propaganda against Douglas and insinuating Communist leanings at the height of the Red Scare paid off for Nixon, who won the election by more than 680,000 votes.

SENATOR

Nixon was the nation's youngest senator in 1951, and the thirty-eight-year-old was soon appointed to Joe McCarthy's committee investigating communism. The war in Korea focused his attention, and in one speech, he spoke with unintended irony: "Asia may not be the place to defeat communism in a war, but Asia is a place where we can lose to communism without a war, and it is a place where we can lose to communism with a war—either way."[7] Soon he was denouncing President Harry Truman for the abrupt dismissal of General Douglas MacArthur. Nixon warned that a White House smear campaign would soon emerge from a president producing "secret papers" to support his action, and the senator again spoke words that would return to haunt him years later: "The new test for classifying documents now seems to be not whether the publication . . . would affect the security of the nation, but whether it would affect the political security of the administration."[8] He also led a crusade against perceived corruption in the Democratic Party and unsuccessfully introduced legislation to help investigate such crimes. By the spring of 1951, his political career and speaking engagements had worn down Nixon, and friends feared a possible collapse. He traveled to Florida for a vacation, and there he met Miami entrepreneur Charles "Bebe" Rebozo, who would become one of Nixon's trusted associates. The senator returned to Washington, rested and ready to resume his career, which was about to take yet another step forward.

Over the years, Nixon and Dwight D. Eisenhower's paths had crossed a handful of times. They had chatted a bit, but in 1951 both men were in Geneva, Switzerland, attending the World Health Conference, and engaged in a lengthy discourse. Both men emerged with a favorable opinion of the other. Eisenhower later said he was impressed by Nixon's fairness in dealing with Alger Hiss. "He did not persecute or defame. This I greatly admired."[9] The respect was mutual, and Nixon later wrote that he believed that Eisenhower was the "most qualified of the potential Presidential candidates." He went on to say, "I came away convinced that he should be the next President. I also decided that if he ran

SUPREME COURT APPOINTMENTS

Warren E. Burger, Chief Justice, 1969

Harry A. Blackmun, 1970

Lewis F. Powell Jr., 1972

William H. Rehnquist, 1972 Chief Justice, 1986

OCT 15: Nationwide protests against the Vietnam War

OCT 16: New York Mets defeat heavily favored Baltimore Orioles in the World Series

NOV 10: PBS series *Sesame Street* debuts

NOV 15: First Wendy's opens in Columbus, Ohio

DEC 1: First draft lottery held since end of World War II

First computer floppy disk developed

1970

SEP 1: Col. Muammar al-Qaddafi seizes power following a military coup in Libya

SEP 3: North Vietnamese leader Ho Chi Minh dies

APR 10: Paul McCartney announces the Beatles have disbanded

STATE OF THE UNION

US POPULATION IN 1969
203,302,031

NATIONAL DEBT IN 1974
$492,665,000,000

for the nomination I would do everything I could do to help him get it."[10]

Although officially pledged to vote for fellow Californian and Governor Earl Warren for the presidency (a possibility if the delegates deadlocked between Eisenhower and Robert Taft at the convention), Nixon also planned to secure Eisenhower's nomination after the release of delegates by California's "favorite son." Once in Chicago, Warren complained to Eisenhower that Nixon was acting undercover for Ike, and Warren demanded they stop allowing the deceptive activities. Ike agreed but was also talking to his associates about having Nixon as his running mate.

Pat Nixon attempted to talk her husband out of accepting any such nomination, fearful of the long campaign season and separation from their very young daughters, ages four and six. She believed he was no longer a likely candidate when she was eating lunch with a friend the next day, only to see "Ike chooses Nixon" appear on the TV in the restaurant. Her food fell from her mouth as she sat in disbelief and later said, "I guess I was one of the last to learn that he had accepted."[11] The convention approved the choice, and Richard Nixon was officially the Republican Party's candidate for vice president—a thankless job, many have believed. Theodore Roosevelt's daughter Alice Longworth told Nixon before the convention: "Father used to tell me that being Vice President was the most boring job in the world." But, she warned, if Ike were the nominee, "someone will have to go on that ticket who can reassure the party regulars and particularly the conservatives that he won't take everyone to hell in a handcart, and you are the best man to do it."[12]

1952 CAMPAIGN

During the convention and soon afterwards, rumors of a Nixon slush fund floated around, and finally a journalist asked him about it. He admitted that some contributors sent money to help with his expenses, but he did not know amounts or names; consequently, he referred the columnist Peter Edson to his attorney Dana Smith. Again the questions were asked and innocently answered. More reporters delved into the story and found some of the contributors had paid Nixon hundreds to thousands of dollars because they saw him as their best defense against the growing threat of communism within the United States. Once the story broke, while Nixon was traveling by train across the West, it threatened to derail the campaign. He told the crowds that the allegations of misuse of funds were spearheaded by Communists upset by his congressional activities against them. Newspapers began suggesting that Eisenhower dump his running mate, and some of Ike's advisors agreed, but he refused to consider changing candidates. Nixon also thought of resigning, but Pat talked him out of it, insisting that such an action would bring disgrace to him and his family.

At Eugene, Oregon, hecklers held signs that on one side read, "SH-H-H, Anyone who mentions $16,000 is a Communist" and on the other side said, "No mink coats for Nixon—just cold cash." Pointing to the protestors, Nixon told them, "That's right, there are no mink coats for Nixon, nothing for which the taxpayer has paid, no mink coats for Nixon and no mink coats for Pat Nixon, his wife. I'm proud of the fact that Pat Nixon wears a good Republican cloth coat, and she's going to continue to."[13] Within days he would use this phrase again in front of television cameras to a nationwide audience to explain his finances. He

NATIONAL EVENTS

Maya Angelou publishes *I Know Why the Caged Bird Sings*

MAR 18: Beginning of two-week strike by postal workers across the nation

APR 1: President Nixon signs a bill that will end cigarette advertising on television as of JAN 1

APR 21: Earth Day celebrated for first time

MAY 4: Four students at Kent State are gunned down by National Guard troops

WORLD EVENTS

MAY 17: Thor Hyerdahl attempts another Atlantic crossing; this one is successful

JUN 28: US troops leave Cambodia

SEP: "Black September"—numerous terrorist activities by Popular Front for the Liberation of Palestine (PFLP), including attempted assassination of King Hussein of Jordan, airline hijackings

SEP 16: King Hussein announces Jordan under martial law as he moves against Palestinian forces (backed by

laid out the finances of his family, emphasizing that he was not a wealthy man, and his family lived quite modestly. He added that they had recently acquired a cocker spaniel dog that six-year-old Tricia had named Checkers for his black and white coloring. "I just want to say to this right now that regardless of what they say about it, we're going to keep him."[14] Hence the speech would forever be known as the "Checkers" speech. The American people rewarded Nixon's humbling discourse with overwhelming support, and the campaign regained its momentum, propelling the Republican ticket to victory in November.

VICE PRESIDENT

Richard Nixon was sworn in as vice president on January 20, 1953, with Pat holding two family Bibles. In the spring, President Eisenhower sent the couple on a two-month visit to Asia, where they were received by heads of state and toured sites from Australia to French Indochina (Vietnam), Indonesia to India and Pakistan.

World and national events made 1954 a busy year for the Eisenhower administration. In May 1954, they learned of the shocking French loss in northern Vietnam at Dien Bien Phu. This placed the United States in the uncomfortable position of either stepping up to combat communism in Indochina or allowing it to begin taking over the region. For the moment, the president insisted on no further action.

Nixon crisscrossed the nation campaigning for Republican candidates in the off-year election. Eisenhower wrote a letter of appreciation to his vice president: "You will have to consider these burdens I impose upon you the penalty for being such an excellent and persuasive speaker. One thing that is coming out of this is that you are constantly becoming better and more favorably known to the American public. This is all to the good."[15] Nixon's efforts, however, could not thwart the wave of Democratic victories, and both houses of Congress now belonged to them. The campaigning took its toll on the vice president, who increasingly resented being the "bad guy" of the administration, speaking out against the Democrats so Eisenhower could maintain his affable image. Nixon began thinking of stepping off the political stage after his term was finished.

Then in September 1955, he received a phone call from presidential staffer James Haggerty with the news that Eisenhower had suffered a heart attack while vacationing in Denver. The next day Nixon learned more of the president's condition and now had the uneasy task of negotiating his way through his constitutional duties and the expectations of the cabinet, the press, and the American people. The country needed leadership, but not an usurping of Eisenhower's authority. Nixon attended cabinet and National Security Council meetings but was careful not to sit in the president's chair, and worked from his capitol office rather than the Oval Office of the White House. Two months later the president returned to Washington.

With an eye to the coming election, Eisenhower discussed the prospect of Nixon taking a cabinet post rather than run again as vice president. Ike told him that this would provide more valuable experience that would benefit him later should he want to run for president. Nixon was surprised by the president's suggestion and later wrote, "Eisenhower's staff or his friends had evidently been sowing doubts in his mind, suggesting that I might . . . be a drag on the ticket if I were his running mate again. It was hard not to feel that I was being set up."[16] In public, the president

DID YOU KNOW?

Nixon was a distant cousin to both William H. Taft and Herbert Hoover.

JUN 10: President Nixon signs a law allowing voting age to drop to 18 from 21

JUN 24: Senate repeals Gulf of Tonkin Resolution

OCT 5: Public Broadcasting Service (PBS) goes on the air

OCT 30: Amtrak created

NOV 3: Democrats victorious in midterm elections

NOV 17: Lt. William Calley's trial begins for My Lai massacre

DEC 2: Clean Air Act signed into law by President Nixon

Syria) and requests American backup support; ultimately Palestinians move their operation to Lebanon

SEP 28: Egyptian President Gamal Nasser dies; Anwar Sadat becomes new president

OCT 9: Khmer Republic declared in Cambodia

OCT 30: Fighting halts temporarily in Vietnam when a monsoon hits

NOV 13: Bhola cyclone hits East Pakistan (later named Bangladesh) killing an estimated half million people

equivocated about whether he would have the same running mate, and at a news conference he stated that he wanted Nixon to "chart out his own course."[17] Upset by Ike's words, Nixon told staffers he would not fight to stay part of the team, but then decided he could not withdraw without hurting Eisenhower's chances for reelection. So in late April, the two men met and Nixon told the president he would willingly run again, and Eisenhower voiced his approval.

A "Dump Nixon" attempt by Harold Stassen to place Governor Christian Herter of Massachusetts on the ticket instead was thwarted by the administration prior to the Republican convention, where Nixon was nominated by a vote of 1,323 to one.[18] Again he took on the bulk of campaigning duties for the ticket and toured the country speaking against his Democratic opponent, Adlai Stevenson. Once more, he and Eisenhower won, but were disappointed by the Democrats retaining control of Congress.

> ***"The people's right to change what does not work is one of the greatest principles of our system of government."***
>
> *—Richard M. Nixon*

While Americans were casting their votes in November 1956, Hungarian revolutionaries were attempting to overthrow the tyranny of the Communists, but their efforts were brutally quashed. A hundred thousand had fled to Austria, and Eisenhower offered asylum to a fifth of the refugees. Now he sent Nixon to Austria to assess the situation and determine what further action should be taken. The vice president urged the relaxation of immigration limits to allow more refugees to enter the United States; although the president concurred, Congress and the American people did not.

The vice president had more responsibilities and duties placed on him during the second term. Part of this shift was due to Eisenhower's deteriorating health; in fact, in November 1957, he suffered a stroke. Although he did recover from this setback, Ike decided to create a plan that he and Nixon could use should any further health concerns arise. If feeling he could not perform his duties, Eisenhower would ask Nixon to "become acting president with full authority until he decided he was able to resume his duties."[19] But if he were unable to make such a decision, Nixon was authorized to do so. (Such plans would no longer be necessary after the ratification of the Twenty-fifth Amendment in 1967.)

In the spring of 1958, Nixon was tasked to attend the inauguration of Argentina's new president, Arturo Frondizi, and to stop in other Latin American nations, as well. The vice presidential party traveled to Uruguay, Argentina, and Bolivia without problems and encountered minimal protests. The reception was usually quite warm and friendly, but all changed when they reached Lima, Peru. There Communist students greeted Nixon with chants of "Muera Nixon! Muera Nixon" (Death to Nixon!) and rocks were thrown at the entourage. When Nixon returned to his hotel, one student spat in his face. The riotous reception continued in Caracas, Venezuela, where more students catcalled and assailed the vice presidential couple in a literal shower of spittle. He rode through the city with the foreign minister (Pat's car was behind) and a mob caught up to them, broke windows, and rocked the

NATIONAL EVENTS

FEB 8: Nasdaq, a new stock market index, begins

FEB 9: Satchel Paige is first African American player to be inducted into Baseball Hall of Fame

FEB 9: Apollo 14 successfully returns to earth after landing on the moon

MAR 1: Weather Underground terrorist organization takes credit for bombing in men's room of the White House

MAR 29: Lt. William Calley found guilty for My Lai massacre and sentenced to life imprisonment

1971

WORLD EVENTS

JAN 15: Egypt's Aswan High Dam opens

JAN 18: Polish workers strike to oust Interior Minister Kazimierz Switala; he resigns on JAN 23 and is replaced by Franciszek Szlachcic

JAN 25: Idi Amin deposes Milton Obote in a coup in Uganda and becomes president

FEB 13: South Vietnamese troops invade Laos

MAR 12: Hafez a-Assad installed as president of Syria

car in an attempt to turn it over. Fortunately the traffic jam keeping the cars stopped opened, and they sped away to the American embassy. When the Nixons returned home to the United States, the American people frequently greeted them with applause and standing ovations.

Now at his highpoint of popularity, Republican leader Tom Dewey and others advised Nixon not to campaign in 1958, since it could possibly hurt his chances for a presidential run in two years. He stumped for candidates anyway, but his efforts were futile as Republicans lost even more seats to the Democrats in Congress and most of the gubernatorial races.

In April 1959, the president asked Nixon to receive a new leader whom the administration was uneasy about recognizing—the former guerrilla commander in Cuba, Fidel Castro, who led the overthrow of a regime friendly to the United States. The two men met for three hours, during which the vice president urged the Cuban leader to hold elections and prove to the people they had not traded one dictator for another. The talk would do nothing to encourage Castro to create a democracy for his people; instead, it soon became obvious that his brand of communism would be just as despotic as his predecessor Batista's regime had been.

A few months later, Nixon would be sent on the most critical foreign trip of his vice presidency—he was to represent the United States at the opening of the American National Exhibition in Moscow and meet Nikita Khrushchev, premier of the Soviet Union and principal leader of world communism. Added to the already tense atmosphere of the Cold War, Eisenhower issued the Captive Nations resolution (as had been done each year since 1950), reminding the world of those countries under Communist rule and of the need "to recommit themselves to the support of the just aspirations of those captive nations." Nixon worried that such words, proclaimed a week before his visit, would do little to calm the waters.

No reception or fanfare greeted the vice president and his wife when his plane landed in Moscow. The next morning, determined to meet the common Russian people, Nixon journeyed to the city's farmer's market, where he interacted with the customers. The following day he met with Khrushchev, who launched into a tirade, berating Nixon for the Captive Nations resolution. Afterward they drove to preview the American Exhibition before its opening that evening. There Khrushchev mugged before the television cameras and bragged that the Soviets would catch up to the Americans within the next seven years in terms of productivity and technology. The group then moved to a model of a typical American home priced at fourteen thousand dollars. Khrushchev derided it as an inaccurate representation of what an average American worker could afford, while Nixon insisted it was typical. The exchange that followed was widely reported as the "kitchen debate," wherein the two men argued over the merits of communism versus capitalism. Attempting to keep the tone civil, Nixon told Khrushchev that it was better to argue about washing machines than missiles, but that only further infuriated the chairman. The two men did agree on one point—neither liked jazz music. Later they ended their discussion with another agreement—both nations desired peace.

After leaving the Soviet Union, the Nixons flew to Poland. There they were greeted warmly by throngs of well-wishers who yelled in Polish, "Long live America!" This was remarkable considering the strong military presence of the Soviets, but the

DID YOU KNOW?

Nixon was the first president to visit China.

APR 20: US Supreme Court decrees that busing can be used to promote racial balance in schools

JUN 30: *New York Times Co. v. United States*—Supreme Court rules that the Pentagon Papers may be published

JUL 1: Twenty-sixth Amendment ratified granting 18-year-olds the right to vote

JUL 19: South Tower of the World Trade Center completed, making it and the North Tower the tallest buildings in the world

AUG 15: President Nixon imposes wage and price freeze

MAR 25: Pakistani Army attacks East Pakistan, resulting in widespread killings

MAR 26: East Pakistan declares its independence, but fighting with Pakistan continues

APR 19: Sierra Leone declares itself a republic

APR 19: Soviet Union launches world's first space station, Salyut I, but its crew dies two months later

JUN 10: End of trade embargo between China and US

DID YOU KNOW?

Nixon was the first president to travel to all 50 states.

heartfelt greetings of the Polish people touched the vice president and his wife.

1960 CAMPAIGN

In July 1960, Republicans chose Richard Nixon as their presidential candidate, and from a list of possible running mates including, ironically, Gerald Ford, Nixon chose United Nations ambassador Henry Cabot Lodge. They faced stiff competition from the Democratic ticket: John F. Kennedy and Lyndon B. Johnson. Nixon made a campaign pledge to visit all fifty states, but the pace required to fulfill this pledge soon made the candidate extremely ill. First he suffered from a knee infection, which forced him to spend two weeks in the hospital. To catch up, he zipped across the country visiting twenty-five states in two weeks. Then he had his first debate with Senator Kennedy. Nixon's clothes hung loosely on him since he had lost weight, and he refused make-up for his television appearance; consequently, his appearance was a stark contrast to the tanned, relaxed, youthful Massachusetts senator who captured the television audience. People listening to the radio believed Nixon to be the victor in the debate, however.

The experience taught Nixon the valuable lesson of appearance; for debates that followed, he wore make-up, and his self-confidence and experience stood him in good stead. The final confrontation, however, did not go well for Nixon. Both candidates had been briefed on the US government's plans to covertly train Cuban exiles and then send them back to their nation to retake their government from Castro. Disregarding the secrecy of the plans, Kennedy openly called for US intervention in Cuba and help for the exiles. Nixon, on the other hand, could not publicly admit to the administration's actions, so he countered by saying the United States should take no action, even though he knew what Eisenhower was planning. Nixon's words now made him look soft on communism—unthinkable for any viable presidential candidate in 1960.

Earlier, Nixon and the president had agreed that Eisenhower would campaign close to the election in the hope of winning undecided voters in key swing states. At a press conference, Ike answered a reporter's question about what major policy idea of Nixon's had been adopted by the administration by saying that if he had a week, he could probably think of something. This prompted great hilarity among the Democrats and the press corps. Eisenhower apologized profusely, but the harm was done. Prior to Nixon's departure on the campaign trail, Mamie Eisenhower asked Pat Nixon to convince her husband not to use the president because his health was not strong enough for traveling and campaigning. A call from Eisenhower's physician confirmed this, so Nixon politely but firmly told the president his presence was not needed on the campaign.

The election results showed Kennedy the winner, but by a thin margin of 113,000 votes, and rumors of widespread voter fraud in Texas and Illinois began to circulate. Many urged Nixon to withhold any concession speech and instead demand a recount. He considered their advice, but decided the country would not be well served by a president who was under such a cloud of illegitimacy. A recount might not be completed until possibly a year later. He, therefore, sent a telegram of congratulations to President-elect John F. Kennedy. How much fraud existed in this election would never be known, and as *New York Times* columnist Tom Wicker wrote years later: "Nobody knows to this day, or ever will, whom the American people really elected President in 1960."[20]

NATIONAL EVENTS

AUG 26: Second Women's Rights March in New York City attracts more than 6,000

OCT 1: Opening of Walt Disney World in Florida

NOV 12: President Nixon announces 45,000 more troops will return from Vietnam in February

NOV 13: Mariner 9 becomes first spacecraft to successfully enter orbit around Mars

NOV 15: Intel develops world's first microprocessor

DEC 11: Libertarian Party founded

WORLD EVENTS

AUG 12: Syria cuts diplomatic ties with Jordan

AUG 18: Ongoing violence in Northern Ireland between IRA and British troops

OCT 25: UN General Assembly admits People's Republic of China; expels Republic of China (Taiwan)

DEC 2: Creation of United Arab Emirates (UAE)

DEC 3: Beginning of Indo-Pakistani War

DEC 16: Pakistan Army surrenders

INTERIM

For the next year, Nixon returned to the legal profession and practiced law with a Los Angeles firm. Yet within months of his return to private practice, he was being sought out as a Republican Party leader to make speeches and by President Kennedy for advice following the Bay of Pigs debacle. Nixon was back in Washington when he found a phone message left by fifteen-year-old daughter Tricia: "JFK called. I knew it! It wouldn't be long before he would get into trouble and have to call on you for help."[21] The two men met in the Oval Office, where Kennedy vented his frustration about the failure of the Cuban invasion. He argued that he could not propose going into Laos if Cuba were allowed to remain Communist within ninety short miles of the American coastline. Although disagreeing with this, Nixon still offered the beleaguered president words of encouragement. A couple of weeks later, Nixon traveled to Chicago and addressed the Executives Club, where he urged that in the future, the United States "must be willing to commit enough power to obtain our objective even if all of our intelligence estimates prove wrong. Putting it bluntly, we should not start things in the world unless we are prepared to finish them."[22]

In 1962, Republicans worked to convince Nixon to run for governor of California, a job for which he had no desire, but they insisted was necessary to keep his name famous and poise him for the 1964 presidential election. Although Pat was not in favor of his running, she ultimately supported his decision. Campaigning across the state, he was badgered this time by John Birch Society members, the ultra-right wing of the Republican Party. Incumbent governor Pat Brown also raised the issue of possible financial dealings with defense contractor Hughes Tool Company. Nixon explained that the matter involved his bankrupt brother and their mother putting up her property for collateral for the loan, which was defaulted to Hughes.

> ***A man is not finished when he is defeated; he's finished when he quits.***
>
> *—Richard M. Nixon, November 11, 1960*

Then shortly before the election, Cuba again took the headlines, only this time it was owing to the Soviets and their attempts to build missile bases on the island. Nixon supported Kennedy, and the election went to Brown. With his fate sealed, reporters wanted him to appear one last time. Although he declined at first, Nixon grew increasingly bitter and finally decided to address them. He thanked his many supporters and then turned to the reporters and berated them for never giving his opponents the tough treatment they gave him: "For sixteen years, ever since the Hiss case, you've had a lot of—a lot of fun—that you've had an opportunity to attack me, and I think I've given as good as I've taken. . . . You won't have Nixon to kick around anymore, because gentlemen, this is my last press conference."[23]

A few months later, the IRS visited Nixon with a tax audit, and the agent assigned to the case later told Nixon's secretary that on three separate occasions, he was told to audit again based on various news articles, but he had refused. Meanwhile Attorney General Robert Kennedy attempted to use his resources at the Justice Department to criminally indict Nixon's brother and mother for

Greenpeace founded

Magnetic resonance imaging (MRI) patented

JAN 5: President Nixon authorizes development of space shuttle

FEB 1: First hand-held calculator goes on sale ($395)

FEB 5: Passengers and luggage begin to be inspected at US airports

FEB 18: California Supreme Court commutes all death penalties to life imprisonment sentences

1972

JAN: Bangladesh declares itself a sovereign nation

JAN 13: Thirteen unarmed Catholics killed by British troops in Northern Ireland

JAN 24: Japanese soldier Shoichi Yokoi is found in Guam after wandering in the jungle for 28 years

FEB 2: Movement 2 June, a German militant group, throws their support to the Irish Republican Army

FEB 20: President and Mrs. Nixon arrive in China for historic visit

DID YOU KNOW?

Nixon was the first president to resign from office.

the Hughes loan, but again this led to nothing.

After his California defeat, advisors urged Nixon to relocate to New York, where he could work for the law firm now named Nixon, Mudge, Rose, Guthrie and Alexander and have more visibility as a leader of the GOP. This move also virtually ruled out any races in New York politics—an idea that Pat Nixon greatly favored. Later, on November 22, 1963, Nixon was leaving Dallas after meeting with his law firm's client, Pepsi-Cola, and upon returning to New York, he learned of John Kennedy's assassination. The former rival then penned a letter of condolence to the widow, who responded gratefully to his kind words.

Nixon traveled extensively throughout the world on behalf of the firm's international clients and often mixed these visits with stops to meet national leaders, including President Chiang Kai-shek of Taiwan, Prime Minister Hayato Ikeda of Japan, and other Asian heads of state, who kept him apprised of their situations and relations with the United States.

At the 1964 Republican convention, Nixon won the honor of giving the speech presenting their nominee, Barry Goldwater, as a true conservative and the candidate to unite the party. Within moments, however, Nixon felt betrayed by Goldwater, who plunged into a speech that alienated many of his party, as well as the nation, with terms such as "Extremism in the defense of liberty is no vice! . . . Moderation in the pursuit of justice is no virtue!"[24] Such inflammatory rhetoric failed to heal the party's divisions. In the coming months, Nixon grew increasingly disenchanted with Goldwater's speeches and considered him a poor presidential choice. The country agreed, and voted for Johnson and the Democrats in overwhelming numbers. Instead of being disheartened by his party's poor showing, Nixon took heart that it provided opportunity for the Republicans to rebuild and come back stronger in 1966 and be ready to retake the White House in 1968. Once LBJ announced his plans to establish the "Great Society," Nixon knew that the liberal spending to fund these programs would present the perfect foil for the conservatism of the Republicans. He spoke out against the president's policy in Vietnam, and Nixon argued that the administration was losing the war. Johnson launched a nasty personal attack against the former vice president that even the press found particularly distasteful. This may have helped elect numerous Republicans to Congress and state legislatures, just as Nixon had hoped for and worked to accomplish.

1968 ELECTION

In January 1967, Richard Nixon told his friends that he wanted to be considered a candidate for the Republican presidential nomination. At this time, his law firm joined another, and one of its senior partners was John Mitchell. Nixon was immediately impressed by Mitchell's contacts as well as his legal knowledge and used him increasingly as a consultant.

In February 1968, he officially opened his presidential campaign with a press conference in New Hampshire. His main challengers were New York governor Nelson Rockefeller and California governor Ronald Reagan, who vied with Nixon for southern support. The blood of two prominent men colored the atmosphere that spring with the assassinations of Dr. Martin Luther King Jr. and Robert Kennedy. Johnson decided not to run for reelection, and George Wallace attempted to court southern voters. When Republicans met in

NATIONAL EVENTS

MAR 2: Pioneer 10 launched and will become first satellite to leave the solar system

MAR 3: Stone Mountain, Georgia, completed with faces of Robert E. Lee, Stonewall Jackson, and Jefferson Davis

APR 3: First cellular phone (Motorola) callMAY: First video game console (Magnavox Odyssey) goes on sale

MAY 15: Assassination attempt on Governor George Wallace by Arthur Bremer leaves Wallace paralyzed

JUN 17: Five arrested for breaking into office in Watergate building in Washington, D.C.

WORLD EVENTS

FEB 21: Luna 20, the Soviet unmanned spacecraft, lands on the Moon

FEB 22: IRA bombing in Aldershot, England kills seven

MAR 2: Jean-Bedel Bokassa becomes president of Central African Republic

MAR 4: Soviet Union and Libya sign a treaty of cooperation

MAR 26: An avalanche on Japan's Mount Fuji kills 19

Miami, Nixon was nominated on the first ballot. He chose Maryland governor Spiro "Ted" Agnew for his running mate, saying later his choice was based on "a good record as a moderate, progressive, effective governor."[25]

In his acceptance speech, Nixon told the delegates that it was time for a change: *"When the strongest nation in the world can be tied down for four years in a war in Vietnam with no end in sight, when the richest nation in the world can't manage its own economy, when the nation with the greatest tradition of the rule of law is plagued by unprecedented racial violence, when the President of the United States cannot travel abroad or to any major city at home, then it's time for new leadership for the United States of America."*

The party's platform avoided specific proposals for the problems in Vietnam and those at home to avoid any open division between the party's moderate and conservative elements. Nixon pledged to bring an honorable end to the Vietnam War but declined to explain how. Johnson's vice president, Hubert Humphrey, was the Democratic candidate, and he attempted to support the president's stand in Vietnam, but at the same time, distance himself from the increasingly unpopular president. Alabama governor George Wallace headed the American Independent Party and vowed to fight court-imposed busing as a way to achieve racial integration in schools. President Johnson boosted Humphrey's chances when he announced a few days before the election that the bombing of North Vietnam would be stopped immediately. Still this announcement was not enough to push Humphrey over the top in a very tight race. Less than one percentage point separated the two top candidates: Nixon won 43.4 percent of the popular vote and Humphrey captured 42.7 percent, while Wallace took 13.5 percent. The margin of victory in the electoral college was more pronounced: Nixon won 301 votes; Humphrey won 191; and Wallace won forty-six.

WOODSTOCK (August 15–18, 1969) ★ Thousands drove or hitched their way to upstate New York near the small town of Bethel in mid-August 1969 to listen to music performances by popular rock bands such as Santana, Blood, Sweat & Tears, Joe Cocker, Fleetwood Mac, and Jimi Hendrix. Many in the audience also imbibed in the drugs and free love that abounded.

Before taking on the duties of his new office, Nixon had a more personal one to perform—father of the bride. Daughter Julie wed David Eisenhower, grandson of the former president, on December 22 in New York City with Reverend Norman Vincent Peale officiating. Sadly Ike's health did not permit him to attend, but he and Mamie watched the ceremony on closed-circuit television in his Walter Reed Hospital room.

PRESIDENT NIXON

The theme for Nixon's inauguration was peace as the two Milhous family Bibles were both turned to Isaiah 2:4: "They shall beat their swords into plowshares, and their spears into pruning hooks: nation shall not lift up sword against nation, neither shall they learn war any more." His speech reflected his thoughts: "The greatest honor history can bestow is the title of peacemaker." He talked not only of

JUN 29: US Supreme Court rules death penalty is unconstitutional

JUL 10–14: Democratic National Convention selects George McGovern as presidential candidate and Thomas Eagleton as vice presidential candidate

AUG: Bob Woodward and Carl Bernstein of *Washington Post* begin reporting on Watergate and possible connection to Committee for the Reelection of the President

MAR 30: Easter Offensive—North Vietnamese troops cross into South Vietnam

APR 10: A massive 7.0 earthquake kills 5,000 in Iran

APR 16: US renews bombing of Hanoi and Haiphong

MAY: More than 500,000 Hutus die in Burundian genocide

MAY 22: Ceylon becomes Sri Lanka

APOLLO PROGRAM ★ Plans for the Apollo spacecraft to reach the moon seemed out of reach when on January 27, 1967, Apollo I crew members were killed in a fire as their Saturn V sat on the launch pad. Months of reviewing plans, making changes, and altering designs resulted in a reworked and safer spacecraft that debuted in October 1968. Two months later, Apollo 8 showed everyone a picture never before seen—earth from space. Once Apollo 11 and Apollo 12 flew successful round-trip missions to the moon, Americans became blasé about the operation, only to be reminded of space travel's dangers when Apollo 13 nearly became lost in space in April 1970 when an oxygen tank exploded on the service module. The world put aside its differences and prayed for the safe return of the crew. Four more missions were successfully completed, and the final footprints were left on the moon in December 1972. The United States would now turn its attention to other space endeavors.

the country's opportunity "to help lead the world at last out of the valley of turmoil and onto that high ground of peace" but also the need for Americans to stop spewing hate-filled speech at each other: "To lower our voices would be a simple thing."

Apparently demonstrators along the inaugural route were far from interested in lowering their volume; as the presidential limousine drove its way from the capitol to the White House, protestors yelled, "Four more years of death!" and burned American flags that the Boy Scouts had provided along the parade route. Some threw beer cans, bottles, and rocks at the car while others in the crowd yelled "Communist swine!" at the disruptive demonstrators.

The rest of the day went on as planned, and the Nixons attended all four inaugural balls, braving the bone-chilling cold rain that capped the raw day. When they returned to the White House at about 1:30 a.m., David Eisenhower gleefully showed his in-laws the note he had tucked away on the third floor: "I will return." Then the president played the piano, and Pat said, "Dick, let's turn on all the lights in the White House and make it cheery."[26] He agreed, and soon the first floor was awash in light, a stark change from the drab darkness dictated by Johnson's cost-cutting measures.

In the coming days, the new president illustrated other ways in which his administration would differ from those in the past. Before the inauguration, Nixon had determined his staff members. For personal secretary he chose the woman who had been with him since his Senate days—Rose Mary Woods. His chief of staff was Bob Haldeman, whose job was "gatekeeper of the Oval Office."[27] The two staffers did not like each other, and this pattern would be repeated throughout the Nixon White House, for he apparently saw it as a way of keeping control by encouraging competition within the staff and allowing them to use their energies fighting each other rather than ganging up on the president.

Approaching foreign affairs, Nixon was determined to keep his own counsel and was quite leery of the State Department, insisting that they had kept him blocked out during his vice presidency. He also distrusted the CIA, believing their Ivy League personnel were liberal, and instead, he decided to build up the National Security Council (NSC), and chose a Harvard professor, Henry Kissinger, to be national security advisor. Longtime friend William Rogers became secretary of state, setting the stage for a major

NATIONAL EVENTS

AUG 1: Eagleton withdraws from race after it is disclosed he had earlier been treated for mental illness

OCT 8: Sargent Shriver becomes new Democratic vice presidential candidate

NOV 7: Richard Nixon wins reelection in a landslide victory

DEC 19: Return of Apollo 17 ends manned space missions to the moon

DEC 25: "Christmas bombing" of North Vietnam by US

DEC 26: Former president Harry S. Truman dies

WORLD EVENTS

MAY 26: Leonid Brezhnev and President Nixon sign SALT I treaty in Moscow

MAY 28: Death of Duke of Windsor (former King Edward VIII)

JUN 17: US returns Okinawa to Japan

JUL 8: Soviet Union buys grain from US

SEP 5–6: Munich Massacre at Summer Games—Israeli Olympic team kidnapped from Olympic village by Black September Arab terrorist group; 11 athletes slain

antagonistic rivalry between him and Kissinger. Another friend, John Mitchell, took the post of attorney general although he had at first declined the offer, citing his wife's health as his reason (Martha Mitchell would later play a role in the saga that would bring down the president). For the key post of defense secretary, Nixon chose Wisconsin congressman Melvin Laird, who had experience and was a "shrewd politician."[28] Other cabinet members included Maurice Stans heading Commerce; George Schultz in Labor; and Robert Finch, Health, Education, and Welfare. But regular cabinet meetings were anathema to the president, who explained, "I had attended hundreds of cabinet meetings as Vice President, and I felt that most of them were unnecessary and boring."[29] Instead he would meet with members as needed and usually conducted business via memos. Nixon believed in delegating authority to those under him in a position to better make decisions. This choice would ultimately lead to his own downfall.

The ongoing Vietnam War required the most immediate attention of the new chief executive. He had promised voters to get Americans out of the mire, but had never told how. His staff now needed to formulate a plan, but circumstances would intervene. The first step was "Vietnamization" of the war—train more South Vietnamese troops to fight, thereby releasing Americans from duty. The president spoke to "the silent majority" for support of his program, and asked for their support: "North Vietnam cannot humiliate the United States. Only Americans can do that."[30] His words rang prophetic when Lieutenant William Calley was charged with multiple counts of premeditated murder in the village of My Lai on March 16, 1968, and weeks later, journalist Seymour Hersh broke the story, prompting public opinion of the war to take a definitive nosedive.

Still, troop strength was reduced by two hundred thousand from 1969 to 1970, but bombing campaigns were increased and the scope of the war broadened owing to Communist incursions being launched from Cambodia. Secretary of State Rogers argued against attacking North Vietnamese staging areas in Cambodia: "It will cost us great casualties with very little gain."[31] Taking such action was nearly pointless since it would not directly affect North Vietnam, but others urged the president to go ahead, so on April 30, 1970, a joint American and South Vietnamese force invaded Cambodia to disrupt Communist supplies feeding into South Vietnam. That night he addressed the nation, giving rationale for the action and reassuring Americans that we were not invading Cambodia or planning to occupy it. Instead the purpose was to rid the enemy of its sanctuaries that "gravely threaten" US troop withdrawals. The immediate response to his speech was positive, but soon the opposition was heard, especially when it was learned that America had resumed bombing North Vietnam.

Four days later a group of thirty-seven college presidents from New York University, Princeton, Notre Dame, Johns Hopkins, and others petitioned Nixon to end the war. Later that day, National Guardsmen at Kent State opened fire on a noontime rally of students, killing four and wounding nine others. Now the country's campuses erupted into massive demonstrations requiring some to be totally shut down to avoid further violence. National Guardsmen in sixteen states were called out to restore order on twenty-one campuses.

In June 1970, the Senate voted to repeal the 1964 Gulf of Tonkin Resolution, and Nixon

Nike started in Oregon

US stops routine vaccinations against smallpox; disease is considered eradicated

JAN 22: Former President Lyndon B. Johnson dies

JAN 22: *Roe v. Wade*—US Supreme Court overturns state bans on abortion

FEB 27: American Indian Movement (AIM) begins occupation at Wounded

1973

JAN 17: Philippine President Ferdinand Marcos becomes president for life

JAN 21: The Communist League founded in Denmark

JAN 27: Paris Peace Accords signed ending Vietnam War

JAN 28: End of direct US involvement of ground troops in Vietnam

FEB 11: American POWs begin to be released from North Vietnam

replied with an announcement that troops would be withdrawn by June 30, claiming victory for the actions taken in Cambodia.

In between protests and nightly body counts on the television news, the country looked heavenward and rallied behind the space program. On July 20, 1969, attention throughout the world focused on the fuzzy images transmitted from the surface of the moon, where Neil Armstrong made the first human footprint and announced, "That's one small step for man, one giant leap for mankind." The president decided to make a phone call to congratulate Armstrong and his partner Edwin "Buzz" Aldrin, and critics decried Nixon's attempt to steal the limelight from the astronauts. Once they splashed down in the South Pacific, the president greeted them (from the other side of their quarantined quarters): "This is the greatest week in the history of the world since Creation."[32] Ironically, the administration would soon propose budgetary cutbacks for the space program, and that, combined with a quickly dwindling interest by the public, meant the beginning of the end for the Apollo program.

In answer to a new awareness of the fragility of the environment, the administration responded with new policies. The keystone was the creation of the Environmental Protection Agency in 1970, whose duty was to monitor pollution, with its aim to not only control but to reduce it over time. The National Air Quality Standards Act of 1970 was key to this and began restricting auto emissions and initiating standards for clean air. A Water Pollution Act was added in 1972, which focused on building waste treatment plants and stopping the industrial waste discharges polluting the waterways.

On the world stage, Nixon embarked on a period of remarkable negotiations between two of America's enemies—the Soviet Union and China. Building on work done by the Johnson administration, the new president desired to work on an arms treaty with the Cold War rival. By now, the MAD (mutual assured destruction) doctrine was accepted in both camps. Should there be a nuclear war, neither nation would triumph; instead, the two would simply destroy each other. Therefore, an arms treaty seemed most sensible in lowering the level of hostility. Soviet leader Leonid Brezhnev was receptive to a proposal that would help dampen the spiraling spending of his nation's defense program. He was also keenly interested in opening trade with the United States allowing imports of grain to his country as well as other consumer goods that were in short supply. Greatly aiding in this effort was Soviet ambassador Anatoly Dobrynin, who met regularly with NSC adviser Henry Kissinger. Following a series of high-level meetings over two years, the first SALT (Strategic Arms Limitation Talks) Treaty was finally signed in May 1972, and later ratified by the Senate. The two superpowers agreed to limit ABMs (antiballistic missile) sites to two each and freeze their strategic offensive ballistic missiles at present levels. The treaty would be the foundation for future talks upon which succeeding presidents would build.

In February 1970, Nixon sent the first Foreign Policy Report to Congress and stated: "The Chinese are a great and vital people who should not remain isolated from the international community. . . . It is certainly in our interest, and in the interest of peace and stability in Asia and the world, that we take what steps we can toward improved practical relations with Peking."[33] So now Congress was aware of the president's desire to open the door to

NATIONAL EVENTS				
Knee, South Dakota, to bring attention to plight of American Indians	**APR 4:** Official opening of World Trade Center	**MAY 3:** Sears Tower in Chicago completed, making it world's tallest building	**MAY 8:** Standoff between Indian activists and law enforcement ends at Wounded Knee	**MAY 14:** Launch of Skylab I, America's first space station

WORLD EVENTS				
MAR 8: Bombings in London by IRA	**MAR 11:** Governor of Bermuda, Sir Richard Sharples, assassinated in Government House	**MAR 17:** London Bridge opens in England	**MAR 29:** The last US solider leaves Vietnam	**APR 10:** Israeli operatives assassinate three Palestinian Resistance Movement leaders in Beirut

China, and in private, Nixon and Kissinger began creating back-channel communications, using various mutual friendly nations to start negotiations with Pakistan and Romania being key players. In April 1971, China replied by extending an invitation to the American table tennis team to visit them. A few days later, Nixon announced the end of America's trade embargo with the People's Republic of China. Relations improved radically over the coming months, allowing for the historic visit by President and Mrs. Nixon to China in February 1972. For a week, diplomatic talks were held between Chinese leaders, including, briefly, the ailing Chairman Mao Zedong, and Nixon and Kissinger. At other times, the Nixons played tourists, to the delight of the press and the Chinese people. The visit was touted as a great success.

At home, Nixon was experiencing difficulties that can spell disaster for a president—the economy was struggling. Following the return of some of the troops, unemployment began climbing along with inflation. Ultimately wage and price controls were initiated in August 1971, and the dollar was taken off the gold standard. In the short run the measures worked and inflation dropped to under 2 percent and unemployment declined a percentage point; however, once the controls were removed, rates soared again. Nixon wrote in his memoirs that imposing economic controls "in the long run was wrong."[34] His successor would pay dearly.

On June 12, 1971, the president traded in his normal duties to play father of the bride once more when elder daughter Tricia wed Edward Cox in a White House wedding conducted between rain showers in the rose garden. Afterward festivities moved inside, where the proud parents danced, and people remarked that Nixon had not appeared so happy and relaxed in quite a while.

VIETNAM PROTESTS ★ The early 1970s was a period of protests, sometimes violent, occurring across the United States. Dissenters against the Vietnam War marched and college students staged sit-in strikes and even set fire to campus buildings to show their displeasure with America's continued involvement in the war. The most famous incident on a campus was May 4, 1970, at Kent State University in Ohio, when four students died after being shot by National Guardsmen.

As it turned out, he would soon have reason for the smile to fade.

In the next day's *New York Times*, a series of articles called the *Pentagon Papers* began running to the right of a picture from Tricia Nixon's wedding. These classified documents had been commissioned by Johnson defense secretary Robert McNamara about American involvement in Southeast Asia. Much of this was critical of past administrations and their unwillingness to be honest with the American people about what was being done in that region. Upset by their appearance, Attorney General John Mitchell attempted to thwart their publication by injunction, but the court refused, citing the First Amendment guarantee of freedom of the press. Determined to punish the ones responsible, the government then indicted former government employee Daniel Ellsberg, who had released the information to *The New York Times*. This case, too, would go nowhere, and charges against him were dismissed in May 1973, but by then, much more was at stake than the publication of secret documents.

Distressed by Ellsberg's actions, Nixon ordered White House aide (officially head of the Domestic Affairs Council) John Ehrlichman to plug the

MAY 17: Senate hearings on Watergate begin and are televised

JUL 1: Drug Enforcement Administration (DEA) created

JUL 16: Watergate committee hears that meetings in Oval Office are taped

OCT 10: Vice President Spiro Agnew resigns because of charges of income tax evasion

NOV 7: Congress passes War Powers Act, over President Nixon's veto

APR 17: GSG 9 counter-terrorism unit formed in Germany

JUN 16: Talks begin between Soviet leader Brezhnev and President Nixon

JUL 17: Afghanistan becomes a republic following a coup

AUG 15: End of bombing over Cambodia by US

OCT 6: Yom Kippur War starts when Egyptian and Syrian forces attack Israel on the holy day of Yom Kippur

IMPROVED U.S.-CHINA RELATIONS ★ In April 1971, an unexpected invitation by the Chinese for the American ping pong team to come and play in China led to a warming between the two nations, and later the visit was reciprocated. Then in February 1972, President and Mrs. Nixon visited the Communist nation. They visited the typical tourist sites, including the Forbidden City and the Great Wall of China. While her husband was participating in diplomatic talks, Pat Nixon visited schools, hospitals, and factories. At the end of the trip, the two nations issued a joint announcement (Shanghai Communique) asserting that Taiwan was part of China. Nixon then returned to the United States from what he called "the week that changed the world."

leaks. Forming a group known as the "plumbers" with their own office in the Executive Office Building, Ehrlichman recruited others, including former FBI agent G. Gordon Liddy and former CIA operative E. Howard Hunt. Once they discovered that Daniel Ellsberg had been under psychiatric care, they decided to break into the doctor's office to pull his file. The break-in occurred on September 3, 1971, but they came up empty. Although Nixon denied knowing of this illegal activity, others near him insist that he was fully apprised of the plumbers' intentions and actions. He wanted Ellsberg stopped, and Hunt hired thugs to beat up Ellsberg when he came to speak on the capitol steps; they never reached him, but did rough up some demonstrators.

Most important to the administration was the upcoming reelection campaign, and in March 1971, the Committee to Reelect the President was created. William Safire had named it and figured it would use the acronym CRP; the media preferred "CREEP" instead.

Orders were issued to dig up any dirt on possible Democratic candidate Edward Kennedy, and a disguised E. Howard Hunt began spying on him. Dirty tricks to alienate voters against Edmund Muskie and George McGovern were employed by CRP, which was led by former attorney general John Mitchell. Their ultimate caper would prove their downfall when they decided to break into the Democratic Headquarters located in the posh Watergate building in the early hours of June 17, 1972. A night watchman phoned police, who apprehended five men there and two other men (Hunt and Liddy) across the street in the Howard Johnson hotel. Four of the five from the Watergate building were Cubans and the fifth was a former CIA operative, James McCord, who was in charge of security for CRP.

The purpose of the break-in was apparently to either remove or improve surveillance devices planted there on an earlier occasion. Press Secretary Ron Ziegler told reporters that this was a "third rate burglary attempt. . . . nothing the President would be involved with, obviously."[35] But the president was keeping tabs on the various people involved, and Watergate became the major focus of the Nixon White House. On July 20, 1972, when he and his aide H.R. Haldeman conferenced, his aide insisted that those who knew what was going on included only a small group. "There's no need for anybody to know. There's nothing they can do about it." Nixon replied, "That's right. It's enough for just a few of us that know to worry about it." Then he added, "I can't believe that they can tie this thing to me."[36]

Working to do just that were two junior reporters for *The Washington Post*—Carl Bernstein and

NATIONAL EVENTS

NOV 16: President Nixon authorizes construction of Alaskan pipeline

NOV 21: Gap of 18 ½-minutes discovered in key White House tape recording of discussions on Watergate

DEC 6: Gerald R. Ford confirmed as vice president

Cincinnati surgeon Jay Heimlich develops technique to help choking victims

Post-it notes invented

1974

WORLD EVENTS

OCT 17: In retaliation for western aid to Israel, Arab nations initiate an oil embargo

OCT 20: Sydney Opera House opens in Australia

OCT 26: End of Yom Kippur War

World population reaches 4 billion

Somalia and Soviet Union sign a friendship treaty

Bob Woodward. When the report of the initial burglary had come in, they were assigned to the seemingly innocuous story, but both decided to pursue it wherever it went, and ultimately it led them to the White House.

Meanwhile, the administration greeted the Democratic nomination of South Dakota liberal senator George McGovern and his running mate Missouri junior senator Thomas Eagleton with glee. The press chimed in since all believed McGovern had no chance whatsoever in winning, especially after announcing he wanted all American troops withdrawn from South Vietnam regardless of the status of any prisoners of war. McGovern's prospects declined even more when Eagleton admitted to seeking psychiatric care, including electric shock therapy for depression. He was soon replaced by Kennedy in-law Sargent Shriver. Eagleton later called the White House in appreciation for a note the president had sent the senator's teenage son: "What matters is not that your father fought a terribly difficult battle and lost. What matters is that in fighting the battle he won the admiration of foes and friends alike because of the courage, poise, and just plain guts he showed against overwhelming odds."[37]

In August, Republicans meeting in Miami renominated Nixon on the first ballot, and Agnew, too, was nominated for vice president. Promises of "Peace with Honor" resonated far more with the American public than the image of McGovern begging for peace. Although the Democrats had high hopes for support from a marginally younger electorate (since this was the first election in which eighteen- to twenty-year-olds could vote), the change scarcely made a difference. In a markedly lopsided race, Nixon won 61 percent of the popular vote and captured 520 electoral votes to McGovern's 38 percent of popular vote and seventeen electoral votes (only Massachusetts and the District of Columbia). It seemed smooth sailing for Nixon to enter his second term with a strong mandate, but his world was about to be upended.

SECOND TERM

By the end of August 1972, the last American combat troops had been withdrawn from Vietnam. Attempting to secure a peace accord that included the release of prisoners was another matter. When faced with foot dragging by North Vietnam, the United States responded with the "Christmas bombing" of areas previously off-limits to US aircraft in December 1972, and the North Vietnamese returned to negotiations. By February, the first prisoners were being released.

Congress was taking its own action early in February 1973 when the Senate created a committee to investigate Watergate. The televised hearings began in May, with committee chairman Democratic senator Sam Ervin in charge, and would last until August 7. Under the light of television cameras, witnesses were sworn in and testified, and Tennessee senator Howard Baker repeatedly asked, "What did the president know and when did he know it?" It was a question that all the nation wanted answered, and Nixon insisted he had been ignorant of the break-in and innocent of any wrongdoing, including a cover-up.

The American people heard of an enemies list of celebrities including Jane Fonda, Daniel Schorr, Bill Cosby, Paul Newman, and others who were monitored for any possible advantage the administration might glean from their activities. News of the "dirty tricks" and the White House "plumbers" emerged, as did details of payoffs to those involved to keep their silence. The prime witness was

Scientists warn that ozone layer of atmosphere being harmed by CFC pollutants

New books: *Jaws* by Peter Benchley, *Carrie* by Stephen King, *The Killer Angels* by Michael Shaara, and *All the President's Men* by Bob Woodward and Carl Bernstein

JAN 2: President Nixon signs law to lower highway speed limits to 55 mph

JAN 4: Nixon refuses to surrender subpoenaed Watergate tapes and documents

FEB 7: Grenada gains independence after 200 years under British rule

MAR 8: Charles de Gaulle Airport opens in Paris

MAR 10: Japanese WWII soldier Hiroo Onoda surrenders in the Philippines, nearly 30 years after the end of the war

MAR 18: Oil embargo ends

APR 10: Golda Meir resigns as Israel's prime minister

APR 25: A coup—the Carnation Revolution—in Portugal restores democracy to the country

EQUAL RIGHTS AMENDMENT (ERA) (March 22, 1972) ★ The Equal Rights Amendment passed Congress and was sent to the states for ratification. The amendment stated, "Equality of rights under the law shall not be denied or abridged by the United States or by any State on account of sex." It did not win ratification by the deadline of 1979, so an extension was granted for 1982, but it, too, was not met. Opponents argued that such an amendment would eliminate single-sex schools, restrooms, sports, organizations, etc. Proponents insisted these were merely scare tactics to keep a needed amendment, ensuring equal rights for all regardless of gender, from being ratified.

White House counsel John Dean, who insisted the president was unaware of the initial Watergate break-in but worked to conceal it once he was told. Figuring out who was telling the truth—witnesses or the president—was nearly impossible until the committee subpoenaed the tapes secretly recorded in the Oval Office. Their existence was made known by White House aide Alexander Butterfield. They were made by the president for historic purposes, but Nixon refused to turn them over, citing executive privilege.

The Justice Department appointed Archibald Cox as special prosecutor to investigate Watergate, and throughout the committee's hearings, Cox frequently sided with them and their demands for the tapes. By October 1973, Nixon tired of this lack of support, and in what became known as the "Saturday Night Massacre," ordered the current attorney general Elliott Richardson to fire Cox. Richardson refused and resigned instead. Nixon then ordered Deputy Attorney General William Ruckelshaus to fire Cox; he, too, refused and was fired. Then the president ordered Solicitor General Robert Bork to do the deed, and he followed orders. (This would later ruin Bork's chances to be appointed to the US Supreme Court under President Reagan.)

By now, the White House had also endured the disgrace of Vice President Spiro Agnew's resignation following charges of accepting bribes and falsifying income tax returns years earlier. He pled no contest to the latter charge and resigned October 10. Two days later, Nixon nominated House Republican minority leader Gerald Ford of Michigan to be his new vice president. Citing in his memoirs the reasons for the choice, Nixon stated: "I felt that Jerry Ford was qualified to be President if for any reason I did not complete my term; I knew that his views on both domestic and foreign policy were very close to mine and that he would be a dedicated team player; and there was no question that he would be the easiest to get confirmed."[38] The following month at a news conference, Nixon told the reporters, "I am not a crook. I have earned everything I've got." He also attempted a feeble joke and said he would not allow a back-up plane for Air Force One saying, "If this one goes down, they don't have to impeach."[39]

October 1973 was a difficult period on the world stage, for the Middle East dissolved into violence once more in the sixteen-day Yom Kippur War when Egypt and Syria launched a joint assault against Israel on this holy Jewish holiday. Helped by other Arab states in the region and a Soviet airlift, the attackers quickly gained the upper hand. The Israelis fought back but were losing ground until the United States stepped in with its own airlift following an Egyptian refusal to back a cease-fire. Outraged by the American "interven-

NATIONAL EVENTS

FEB 4: Symbionese Liberation Army (SLA) kidnaps heiress Patty Hearst

FEB 27: First issue of *People* magazine published

MAR 1: Indictments handed down for seven Watergate conspirators

APR 3: Nearly 150 tornadoes rip through 13 states, killing more than 300 and injuring 5,000

APR 8: Hank Aaron breaks Babe Ruth's homerun record when he hits #715

WORLD EVENTS

MAY 7: German chancellor Willy Brandt resigns, several days later Foreign Minister Walter Scheel is elected president

MAY 18: India successfully tests its first nuclear weapon

JUN 17: Provisional IRA claims responsibility for bombing Houses of Parliament in London

JUL 1: Juan Peron, president of Argentina, dies; his wife Isabel Peron becomes president and the first female head of state in South America

tion," Saudi Arabia and other Arab nations then announced an oil embargo against the United States and other western nations. Henry Kissinger ushered in the era of "shuttle diplomacy" as he flew back and forth between various capitals in the region, attempting to negotiate a lasting settlement. Ultimately this was achieved and the oil embargo ended by May 1974. It was a success that would come at a time when the administration had little good news to celebrate.

In February, the House of Representatives voted to authorize its Judiciary Committee to begin its determination if grounds existed to impeach the president. In the last week of July, the committee approved three articles of impeachment: obstruction of justice, abuse of power, and contempt of Congress.

Within days, the long-awaited Oval Office tapes appeared, and the "smoking gun" was quickly found, revealing that the president definitely knew more than he had admitted, much earlier than he had said. Impeachment proceedings were now definite, and congressional support to save him evaporated. To prevent himself from being the first president to be forcibly removed from office, Nixon had to become the first to resign. For a few days, he waffled between fighting the impeachment and resigning. Part of his decision hinged on financial concerns, for a resignation would mean he kept the presidential pension and other perks. Earlier in 1973, he had told White House counsel Chuck Colson, "You know that if I am impeached, I'll be wiped out financially—no pension—and now with all I owe in taxes."[40]

On August 8, 1974, an exhausted Richard Nixon announced, "I shall resign the presidency effective at noon tomorrow. By taking this action, I hope that I will have hastened the start of that process of healing which is so desperately needed in America. I regret deeply any injuries that may have been done in the course of the events that led to this decision."[41] The next morning, the Nixons bid farewell to the White House staff and wished the new president and First Lady well, then boarded the Marine helicopter that would take them to Andrews Air Force Base and the final journey on Air Force One, which would take them to California. As they flew over Jefferson City, Missouri, Gerald Ford officially became president.

EXILE

The next stage for the president was in Gerald Ford's hands. Earlier Ford had been urged by Nixon chief of staff Alexander Haig to grant Nixon a pardon, but Ford refused. The Nixon family also campaigned for a pardon, and David Eisenhower warned without it, his father-in-law was in danger of a breakdown. If any of the possible cases were brought to court, could Nixon receive a fair trial? Could a jury pool be untainted? What if he were found guilty, could he be sent to jail? Worried about the troublesome answers to these questions and believing that most Americans believed in allowing the disgraced president to live in peace, Ford pardoned Nixon on September 8.

The next tangle between the former president and the government involved his papers and tapes; he demanded them, and many feared they would be destroyed. Ultimately the National Archives won possession of them, but the tapes themselves were not fully disclosed until 1996, and they were far from favorable to the president.

Needing money to pay legal expenses and back taxes, Nixon looked for ways to earn some cash.

APR 15: Patty Hearst helps her kidnappers rob a San Francisco bank

MAY 9: Beginning of formal impeachment hearings against President Nixon

JUN 26: First use of Universal Product Code (UPC)

JUL 24: US Supreme Court rules that Nixon must surrender subpoenaed tapes

JUL 27–30: US House of Representatives decides on three articles of impeachment against the president

JUL 17: IRA bombs explode at the Tower of London and outside a government building in South London

JUL 20: Turkey invades Cyprus

JUL 22: Mikael Imru replaces Ethiopian Prime Minister Endelkachew Makonnen

AUG 30: 150 passengers killed in a train derailment in Zagreb, Yugoslavia on route from Belgrade to Germany

SEP 5: Caribbean island Martinique receives région status from France

SEP 8: TWA flight 841 crashes into Ionian Sea after take off in Athens, a bomb explodes killing 88 people

In 1977, he made a series of interviews with David Frost and was paid six hundred thousand dollars, as well as 20 percent of the profits. More lucrative were Nixon's book deals for eight books, nearly all of which were bestsellers. He made speeches around the world (including China), which created criticism, as well as praise, for his efforts to rehabilitate his image.

In 1980, he and Pat moved to New York City to be nearer their daughters and grandchildren. Pat had suffered a stroke four years earlier when reading the Woodward and Bernstein book *The Final Days*, which presented her marriage as a loveless travail. Through therapy she regained her speech and use of her left side.

> ***I let down my friends. I let down the country. I let down our system of government and the dreams of all those young people that ought to get into government, but think that it's all too corrupt.***
>
> —*Richard M. Nixon in the* New York Times, *May 5, 1977*

Nixon desperately desired to have his own presidential library, but various possible sites backed out after initially expressing interest. Finally his hometown of Yorba Linda agreed. In July 1990, the privately funded Nixon Presidential Library and Birthplace opened with presidents Bush, Ford, and Reagan and their wives in attendance.

Desirous of maintaining an advisory capacity with the presidents, Nixon attempted to influence their foreign policy either directly (through meetings or letters) or indirectly (through articles in newspapers). Although a visitor to the Ford White House, he was never invited there again by a resident, although he did lead a delegation of former presidents to attend the funeral of slain Egyptian president Anwar Sadat in 1981.

In 1993, Pat Nixon died, and her husband followed ten months later. At his funeral in April 1994, current president William Jefferson Clinton and his wife Hillary attended, as well as the four other living presidents with their wives. The Nixons are both interred at the Nixon Presidential Library and Museum.

In 1978, when Nixon visited Oxford Union, he told the crowd, "Some people say I didn't handle [Watergate] properly, and they're right. I screwed it up. And I paid the price. Mea culpa. But let's get on to my achievements. You'll be here in the year 2000 and we'll see how I'm regarded then."[42]

Ironically, in 2004, Nixon's name was in the forefront again at the Republican National Convention. He may not have been welcome to attend one in person after 1972, but his spirit was there as California Governor Arnold Schwarzenegger told the delegates his personal story about his arrival in the United States from Austria and why he decided to become a Republican:

> *I finally arrived here in 1968. What a special day it was. I remember I arrived here with empty pockets, but full of dreams, full of determination, full of desire. The presidential campaign was in full swing. I remember watching the Nixon and Humphrey presidential race on*

NATIONAL EVENTS

AUG 5: Watergate tape reveals cover-up by Nixon, ending any hope to defeat impeachment

AUG 8: President Nixon announces to American people that he will resign effective the next day

AUG 9: Nixon becomes first president to resign; Gerald R. Ford sworn in as 38th president

SEP 8: President Ford pardons Nixon

NOV 5: Democrats enjoy victory in congressional midterm elections

WORLD EVENTS

SEP 13: The French Embassy in The Hague is seized by members of the Japanese Red Army

OCT 9: Oskar Schindler, who worked to rescue many from the Holocaust, dies in Germany

OCT 30: Heavyweight boxing fight "Rumble in the Jungle" in Kinshasa, Zaire, between Muhammad Ali and George Foreman; Ali reclaimed his title

NOV 22: Palestine Liberation Organization granted observer status at the United Nations General Assembly

NOV 27: The United Kingdom passes the Prevention of Terrorism Act

TV. A friend of mine who spoke German and English translated for me. I heard Humphrey saying things that sounded like socialism, which I had just left. But then I heard Nixon speak. He was talking about free enterprise, getting the government off your back, lowering the taxes, and strengthening the military. Listening to Nixon speak sounded more like a breath of fresh air. I said to my friend, I said, 'What party is he?' My friend said, 'He's a Republican.' I said, 'Then I am a Republican.'[43]

ENDNOTES

1 Richard Nixon, *The Memoirs of Richard Nixon*, New York: Grosset & Dunlap, 1978, p. 23.

2 Earl Mazo, *Richard Nixon: A Political and Personal Portrait*, New York: Harper & Bros., 1959, p. 31.

3 Nixon, p. 26.

4 Kornitzer, Bela. *The Real Nixon*, New York: Rand McNally, 1960, p. 144.

5 William A. DeGregorio, *The Encyclopedia of US Presidents*, New York: Gramercy Books, 2005, p. 585.

6 Nixon, p. 42.

7 Roger Morris, *Richard Milhous Nixon*, New York: Henry Holt and Co., 1990, p. 631.

8 Ibid.

9 Ibid, p. 666.

10 Nixon, p. 82.

11 Julie Nixon Eisenhower, *Pat Nixon: The Untold Story*, New York: Simon & Schuster, 1986, p. 115.

12 Nixon, p. 84.

13 Morris, p. 785.

14 DeGregorio, pp. 586-587.

15 Nixon, p. 161.

16 Ibid, p. 167.

17 Ibid, p. 170.

18 Ibid, p. 176.

19 Ibid, p. 185.

20 Ibid, p. 224.

21 Ibid, p. 234.

22 Ibid, p. 236.

23 Ibid, p. 245.

24 Ibid, p. 260.

25 Ibid, p. 312.

26 Eisenhower, pp. 253-254.

27 Nixon, p. 337.

28 Ibid, p. 339.

29 Stephen E. Ambrose, *Nixon, The Triumph of a Politician 1969-1972*, New York: Simon & Schuster, 1989, p. 239.

30 Melvin Small, *The Presidency of Richard Nixon*, Lawrence, KS: University Press of Kansas, 1999, p. 75.

31 Ambrose, p. 343.

32 Small, p. 231.

33 Nixon, p. 545.

34 Ibid, p. 521.

35 Richard Reeves, *President Nixon, Alone in the White House*, New York: Simon & Schuster, 2001, p. 502.

36 Ibid, p. 516.

37 Nixon, p. 644.

38 Ibid, p. 926.

39 *Washington Post*, November 18, 1973.

40 Small, p. 294.

41 Nixon, p. 1083.

42 Small, p. 305.

43 Arnold Schwarzenegger, 2004 Republican Convention speech, August 31, 2004.

NOV 20: US files antitrust suit against AT&T, which results in its breakup into smaller Bell systems

DEC 19: Nelson Rockefeller sworn in as vice president

NOV 30: Lucy, a skeleton from the hominid species Australopithecus afarensis, is discovered in Ethiopia; she is estimated to have lived nearly 3.2 million years ago

DEC 23: Former British minister John Stonehouse arrested in Melbourne, Australia; he had faked his own drowning in Florida earlier in the year

DEC 24–25: Darwin, Australia nearly destroyed by Cyclone Tracy

Gerald R. Ford

★ ★ ★ THIRTY-EIGHTH PRESIDENT ★ ★ ★

LIFE SPAN

- Born: July 14, 1913, in Omaha, Nebraska
- Died: December 26, 2006, in Rancho Mirage, California

NICKNAME

- Jerry

RELIGION

- Episcopalian

HIGHER EDUCATION

- University of Michigan, 1935
- Yale University Law School, 1941

PROFESSION

- Lawyer

MILITARY SERVICE

- World War II: enlisted in US Navy in April 1942 as ensign and rose to lieutenant commander by the time he was discharged in February 1946

FAMILY

- Father (Biological): **Leslie L. King** (1882–1941)
- Father (Adoptive): **Gerald R. Ford Sr.** (1890–1962)
- Mother: **Dorothy A. Gardner King Ford** (1892–1967)
- Wife: **Elizabeth "Betty" Anne Bloomer Warren Ford** (1918–); wed on October 15, 1948, in Grand Rapids, Michigan
- Children: **Michael Gerald** (1950–); **John Gardner** (1952–); **Steven Meigs** (1956–); **Susan Elizabeth** (1957–)

POLITICAL LIFE

- US representative (1949–1973)
- House minority leader (1965–1973)
- Vice president (1973–1974)

PRESIDENCY

- One term: August 9, 1974–January 20, 1977
- Republican
- Reason for leaving office: defeated by **Jimmy Carter** in 1976 election
- Vice president: **Nelson A. Rockefeller** (1974–1977)
- No inauguration; took oath of office following **Richard Nixon's** resignation
- No electoral vote: not elected to either presidency or vice presidency

CABINET

SECRETARY OF STATE
Henry Kissinger (1974–1977)

SECRETARY OF THE TREASURY
William E. Simon (1974–1977)

SECRETARY OF DEFENSE
James R. Schlesinger (1974–1975)

Donald H. Rumsfeld (1975–1977)

ATTORNEY GENERAL
William B. Saxbe (1974–1975)

Edward H. Levi (1975–1977)

SECRETARY OF THE INTERIOR
Rogers C. B. Morton (1974–1975)

Stanley K. Hathaway (June–July 1975)

Thomas S. Kleppe (1975–1977)

SECRETARY OF AGRICULTURE
Earl L. Butz (1971–1976)

John A. Knebel (1976–1977)

SECRETARY OF COMMERCE
Frederick B. Dent (1973–1975)

Rogers C. B. Morton (April–Dec. 1975)

Elliot L. Richardson (1975–1977)

Entering office on the heels of the first presidential resignation in history, Gerald R. Ford faced a particular challenge—restoring confidence to the nation, while at the same time attempting to steer the country back on its normal course. In the process, one of his actions would have damaging consequences to his future political career.

EARLY LIFE

The man who later would be known to the world as Gerald R. Ford actually was given the name Leslie L. King Jr. when he was born in Omaha to Leslie King Sr. and his wife Dorothy on July 14, 1913. King had begun to abuse Dorothy on their honeymoon and the abuse continued after her son's birth. Ultimately she was forced to flee the mansion where they were living in the dead of night with only her two-week-old baby in her arms, and in December 1913, she managed to secure a divorce based on grounds that her husband had been "guilty of extreme cruelty."[1] Soon Dorothy, her parents, and her infant son moved to Grand Rapids, Michigan, for a new start.

The family settled into a comfortable life in Grand Rapids, and at a church social, Dorothy met Gerald Ford and dated him for a year before they married on February 1, 1916. He welcomed her son, whom the family affectionately called "Junie," and soon called him Junie Ford. Gerald Ford Sr. would be the only father the boy would know: "He was the father I grew up to believe was my father, the father I loved and learned from and respected. He was my Dad."[2] Over time, the boy not only learned to fish and throw a football from his father, but he also acquired his most prized possession—his name—and became Gerald Ford Jr.

In first grade, Ford learned he wrote better with his left hand, but the teacher and his parents disapproved and forced him to write with his right hand. Junie soon began stuttering, so adults backed off from forcing his writing, and the stuttering soon ended. He emerged from this with an unusual quirk—he wrote right-handed standing up and left-handed sitting down. He joined the Boy Scouts and within three years attained the status of Eagle, and in the summers worked as a camp counselor.

Gerald Ford Sr. worked as a paint salesman and later established his own business, the Ford Paint and Varnish Company, and managed to keep the business through the lean Depression years. The family grew with the addition of three half-brothers, so money was often tight. When he was about thirteen years old, Junie learned from his mother that Ford was not his biological father, but the news barely made an impression on the teen since Ford was the only father the boy had known or loved.

Although the Fords could have sent their son to a nearby high school that catered to the wealthier set, they chose instead to send him to the working-class South High School, where he attended classes with a mix of immigrants, blacks, and the poorer whites. There Ford received high grades in history and government, but struggled through Latin. He worked odd jobs, including flipping burgers at a local restaurant, but his favorite pastime was playing football. He was the star center and a defensive linebacker for South High's football team and was selected for the all-city squad.

One day on the job in the midst of serving the lunchtime crowd, Gerald found himself face to face with his biological father. Leslie King introduced himself and asked if the two could go and talk. Outside, he met King's second wife, and they drove to a Grand Rapids restaurant, where Leslie steered the conversation into small talk. At the end of their

NATIONAL EVENTS

JAN 1: US attorney general, White House chief of staff, and assistant to the president for domestic affairs found guilty of Watergate cover-up

JAN 2: US Congress approves Federal Rules of Evidence

JAN 8: Ford appoints Vice President Rockefeller to head a special commission to look into alleged domestic abuses by the CIA

JAN 8: Ella Grasso of Connecticut becomes first woman governor in the US who did not succeed her husband

JAN 12: Pittsburgh Steelers take their first pro football championship when they win Super Bowl IX 16–6 against the Minnesota Vikings

1975

WORLD EVENTS

UN declares 1975 International Women's Year

JAN 1: Channel Tunnel work abandoned on British end

JAN 15: Portugal grants Angola's independence

JAN 20: Final North Vietnamese military offensive against South Vietnam

FEB 28: Lomé Convention financial and economic treaty signed by EEC and 46 African, Caribbean, and Pacific countries in Togo

time together, he gave his son—whom he had not seen or supported in fifteen years—twenty-five dollars and disappeared again out of Gerald's life. The experience left the young man shaken and upset.

During his senior year, Ford was selected as the most popular high school senior in Grand Rapids and was allowed to travel with thirty midwestern students to Washington, D.C. He thoroughly enjoyed the experience, particularly attending sessions of Congress and watching the debates from the gallery.

He was also elected captain of the South High football team and later named to the all-state team and chosen as their captain; coach Cliff Gettings said of him, "Jerry was one of the hardest-working kids who ever played football for me, and totally dependable in every game." Ford learned from Gettings some basic rules for life: "You play to win. You give it everything you've got, but you always play within the rules."[3]

Ford graduated in 1931 and earned a partial scholarship to the University of Michigan, where he earned money working odd jobs, including waiting tables in the interns' dining room and donating blood a few times a year. He was grateful for the help he received, but added, "Football was my ticket to college. That's the only way I got to Michigan, and that was the luckiest break I ever had."[4]

Michigan was undefeated in football when Gerald played his freshman year and was awarded the Meyer Morton Trophy for outstanding freshman player in spring practice. Although he was not a star player, he did manage to badly injure his knee his sophomore year, and had to endure an operation. By his senior year, the team was no longer undefeated, but Ford still was successful, and was selected by his teammates as the most valuable player. A guard from Northwestern's team told his coach that Ford was "the best damn center"[5] he had ever played against, so the coach tapped Gerald to participate in the annual Shriners East-West Collegiate game. Two minutes into the game, the star center was injured, leaving Ford to play center the rest of the game, but despite his efforts the East team lost 19–13.

In his later years, Ford wrote that if he had it to do again, he would concentrate his studies on speaking and writing: "Nothing in life is more important than the ability to communicate effectively."[6] Weekends were spent composing one-thousand-word themes for his Monday English class, and he was pleased to receive a C for the course. He pledged Delta Kappa Epsilon, a fraternity known for its athletic rather than academic abilities. In the 1935 yearbook, senior Gerald Ford was listed in the Hall of Fame for his football record, good grades, and because "he never smokes, drinks, swears, or tells dirty stories . . . and because he's not a bit fraudulent and we can't find anything really nasty to say about him."

As graduation approached, he now had to decide which road to take for his future—both the Green Bay Packers and Detroit Lions offered him a contract of $2,800 to begin playing in the fall of 1935. Ford, however, declined their offers and decided he would take his bachelor of science in economics with an emphasis in political science to study law. When he was twenty-one, Gerald decided to take the formal step and legally change his name to Gerald Rudolph Ford Jr. Perhaps part of his decision lay with the knowledge that when he desperately needed financial assistance for college, he wrote to his father, now living in Wyoming, but never received a response.

CABINET

★★★★★★★★★★

(continued)

SECRETARY OF LABOR

Peter J. Brennan (1973–1975)

John T. Dunlop (1975–1976)

W. J. Usery, Jr. (1976–1977)

SECRETARY OF HEALTH, EDUCATION, AND WELFARE

Caspar W. Weinberger (1973–1975)

F. David Matthews (1975–1977)

SECRETARY OF HOUSING AND URBAN DEVELOPMENT

James T. Lynn (1973–1975)

Carla A. Hills (1975–1977)

SECRETARY OF TRANSPORTATION

Claude S. Brinegar (1973–1975)

William T. Coleman Jr. (1975–1977)

FEB 13: The World Trade Center's North Tower catches fire on the 11th floor and spreads to other floors but is contained, no one is injured

FEB 23: Daylight saving time starts two months early owing to energy crisis

MAR 9: Work begins on the Trans-Alaska Pipeline

MAR 10: *The Rocky Horror Picture Show* opens in New York City

JUN 10: Rockefeller Commission issues its report on CIA abuses

MAR 6: Algiers Accord: Iran and Iraq settle their border dispute

MAR 8: UN proclaims International Women's Day

MAR 13: Mass exodus of troops and civilians ("Convoy of Tears") from Central Highlands in South Vietnam

MAR 25: Saudi Arabian king Faisal is shot and killed by his mentally ill nephew, who is beheaded on June 18; King Khalid succeeds Faisal

APR 13: President of Chad is overthrown and killed in military coup d'état

DID YOU KNOW?

Ford survived two assassination attempts within one month—both made by women.

Since money was in short supply, Gerald approached his football coach asking for a job to help defray the costs of attending law school. Soon the coach offered another possibility. Yale was looking for an assistant line coach, so Gerald went to the campus to meet the coaches. He was offered the job for $2,400. It also meant being assistant boxing coach, even though he had no experience; he promised to gain some at the YMCA. Still wanting to enter law school, he broached the subject with the coaches, who were doubtful he could work full time and be a law student—a conclusion with which the law school dean concurred.

Ford began working at Yale in August 1935. Two of Ford's players later served in the Senate: William Proxmire and Robert Taft Jr. Proxmire recalled, "Coach Ford was very, very conscientious. . . . They [the players] saw in Ford not only diligence, but a good mind, a first-rate mind." Taft echoed his teammate's sentiments adding, "Some coaches were always shouting but Coach Ford was very calm and spoke to your intelligence."[7]

The following summer, Ford worked for the National Park Service at Yellowstone National Park helping with traffic and feeding the bears at Canyon Station. En route, he visited with his father and stepmother, but they had little to discuss, and probably both parties were relieved when he continued on his journey to Yellowstone the next day. When Gerald told his mother about the meeting with King, she asked him to find a lawyer in New Haven who would sue for the back child support ordered after King's millionaire father had died. The case went to trial, and over a year later, Mrs. Dorothy Ford was awarded $6,303, but King's attorney immediately insisted his client was broke and wanted to settle for one thousand dollars. Dorothy refused, so negotiations seesawed back and forth, with their son in the middle. Eventually, a four thousand dollar settlement was paid, less attorney's fees. The Fords never heard from Leslie King again.

When Ford returned to Yale, he received a hefty raise. The team had won the Ivy League title with a record of seven and one, but he still longed to attend law school. Ford took a couple of classes at Ann Arbor in the summer, and showed his B grades to his boss and the deans of the law school, who allowed him to take two classes in the spring. Upon successfully completing these courses, he was admitted to Yale school as a full-time student while still retaining his coaching job.

During this time, Ford fell head over heels in love with a gorgeous blonde from Maine—Phyllis Brown. She had money and a flair for living; her beauty gained her modeling contracts. For one shoot, *Look* magazine told her to bring a boyfriend for a skiing weekend in Vermont; her boyfriend in the March 12, 1940, layout was Gerald Ford. The attractive couple frequented New York City's nightspots and took in its many attractions, but once he decided he wanted to establish a legal career in Michigan, their affair was over.

In January 1941, Gerald completed his legal training, then returned to Michigan to prepare for the bar exam and plan his career. Another friend, Phil Buchen, was finishing law school at Ann Arbor, and the two men decided to form a law firm. After successfully passing the bar, they worked together, and slowly business grew. Then everything changed on Sunday, December 7, 1941, with the attack on Pearl Harbor.

NAVAL CAREER

Ford joined the US Navy as an ensign and was soon sent for training at the Naval Academy. He

NATIONAL EVENTS				
JUN 26: Two FBI agents and one other die in shoot out at the Pine Ridge Indian Reservation in South Dakota	**JUL 31:** Jimmy Hoffa goes missing	**SEP 5:** Lynette Fromme, a follower of Charles Manson, attempts to assassinate President Ford, but is stopped by Secret Service	**SEP 14:** Elizabeth Seton, first American saint is canonized	**SEP 18:** Patty Hearst is captured in San Francisco

WORLD EVENTS				
APR 17: Pol Pot declares Democratic Republic of Kampuchea in Cambodia and becomes prime minister	**APR 30:** Fall of Saigon; Vietnam War ends	**MAY 28:** Treaty of Lagos signed by 15 West African countries, creating the Economic Community of West African States	**JUN 5:** Suez Canal reopens for the first time after the Six-Day War	**JUN 25:** Emergency declared by Indira Gandhi in India, suspending civil liberties and elections

then went to V-5 pre-flight school at Chapel Hill, North Carolina, as physical fitness instructor. Teaching calisthenics was not exactly what Gerald had in mind as a way to serve his country, and he endeavored to find a way to gain sea duty. Finally in the spring of 1943, Lieutenant Ford received orders to report to the USS *Monterey*, a light aircraft carrier soon to be commissioned out of the Philadelphia Navy Yard. Sailors aboard the *Monterey* liked the young officer. Seaman Second Class Ronald Smith related, "He was the sort of officer who looked out for his men. Nothing ever seemed to rattle him."[8] There would be plenty of action in the coming months to test everyone's nerves.

By November, the *Monterey* was in the Pacific, assigned to the USS *Enterprise* carrier task group, where Ford had double duty—gunnery division officer and athletic director for the ship. He saw action in the Gilbert Islands and then requested transfer of duties and became the assistant navigation officer. From the bridge he watched the task force participate in the "Great Marianas Turkey Shoot," where Japan's carrier-based aircraft were shot down in record numbers. Near Taiwan, they came under attack from Japanese planes, whose torpedoes smashed into the cruisers near the *Monterey*. Other ships towed the two damaged cruisers out of the battle zone, but the entire task force had to slow for this, which made them easy targets for more Japanese air attacks.

Then on December 18, 1943, a violent typhoon bore down and managed to capsize three destroyers. The next day Ford's ship rolled badly in the violent seas, causing one of the planes to break free of its cables, allowing it to smash repeatedly into the other planes and causing gas tanks to puncture. Fires soon started, and since the ship was a converted cruiser lacking the proper ventilation of the larger carriers, the decision was made by the Third Fleet's commander, Admiral William F. Halsey, to abandon ship. The *Monterey*'s commander, Captain Stuart Ingersoll, disagreed and insisted they could take care of the situation if allowed more time. It took seven hours, but fires were finally put out, and the ship was on its way home to Saipan.

Soon afterwards, Ford was granted a short leave, so he returned home, then had to report to Naval Reserve Training Command in Glenview, Illinois. He and other officers, including Rear Admiral O.B. Hardison, decided to time an inspection tour of southern bases with the upcoming football game of Navy against North Carolina at Chapel Hill. The night they flew to North Carolina was rainy, and the pilot landed on a shorter runway than he anticipated, causing them to slide off the tarmac and down an embankment, only stopping when they crashed into trees. Fortunately all managed to escape from the plane before flames engulfed it.

Ford ended his naval career in February 1946, and then returned to Michigan. His earlier law firm had dissolved when his partner joined another one in Ann Arbor, so Ford followed him there. Although busy practicing law, he found community service organizations more satisfying, and he joined many of them, including helping the American Red Cross, the American Legion, the Veterans of Foreign Wars, and the local chapter of the National Association for the Advancement of Colored People (NAACP).

Friends worried about his perpetual bachelor status and encouraged him to meet recent divorcée Betty Warren, who was a fashion coordinator for a local department store and had trained with the Martha Graham dancers. They dated for over a year before marrying on October 15, 1948, in

SUPREME COURT APPOINTMENTS

★★★★★★★★★★

John Paul Stevens, 1975

SEP 22: President Ford survives another attempted assassination

OCT 21: Boston Red Sox beat Cincinnati Reds in sixth game of the World Series

JAN 19: Jimmy Carter wins Iowa Democratic Caucus

MAR 27: Washington, D.C., Metro subway system opens

MAR 31: In right to die debate, New Jersey Supreme Court rules coma patient Karen Ann Quinlan can be taken off her ventilator

APR 1: Apple Computer Company formed

1976

AUG 15: President of Bangladesh is killed in a coup

NOV 22: Juan Carlos becomes king of Spain after death of dictator Francisco Franco

FEB 4: Innsbruck, Austria hosts the Winter Olympics

MAR 24: President Isabel Peron deposed by military in Argentina

MAR 26: Queen Elizabeth II sends first royal email

US POPULATION IN 1974
203,302,031

NATIONAL DEBT IN 1977
$718,943,000,000

Grand Rapids, as Ford managed to squeeze in his wedding amidst campaigning for his first political office—US congressman from the Fifth District.

Attempting to win the primary was no easy task since a local millionaire who ran the Republican Party in the area, Frank McKay, deplored anyone with ideas different from his own. Gerald and his friends decided to challenge McKay and formed a group called the Home Front just before World War II began. In 1948 the Home Front decided to oppose McKay's man, "Barney" Jonkman, for his seat. While Jonkman was in Washington for a special session called by Truman, Ford campaigned aggressively and won over Democrats as well as Republicans who disliked Jonkman's isolationist stance. When Ford asked for a debate with Jonkman, the congressman refused, and began alienating many of his Michigan constituents, including the United Auto Workers and the Grand Rapids Press. Ford won the primary easily, which all but ensured his victory in November's general election in this Republican stronghold; in fact, he won 61 percent of the vote on November 2.

CONGRESSMAN FORD

Six weeks after marrying, the Fords were in Washington finding an apartment, and he learned of his first committee assignment—the Committee on Public Works. Serendipitously, he managed to gain an appointment to the powerful Appropriations committee the following year, and was assigned other subcommittees, as well.

Ford recalls, in his autobiography:

"Very early in my Congressional career, a senior member took me aside and said that as a representative, I could choose one of two alternatives. I could spend most of my time in my office attending to the problems of constituents and providing service to the district, or I could spend my time on the floor of the House listening to the debate, mastering parliamentary procedures, and getting to know the other members personally. I could not do both. . . . I decided to spend time on the floor."[9]

Ford's mentor on the floor of the House was California congressman Richard Nixon, who had been elected to his first term in 1946. Ford admired Nixon's logical approach to debate and decided to invite him to the annual Lincoln Day banquet in Grand Rapids in 1951, which provided the two men with more opportunity to talk and compare views on the nation's political situation. By now Nixon was senator, and would become the vice presidential candidate the following year when Dwight D. Eisenhower became the Republican presidential nominee.

Another member of the 1946 class of freshman congressmen was Jack Kennedy. Both his and Ford's offices were near each other in the far hinterlands of the Old Capitol Office building. This gave the two men plenty of time to chat as they walked to and from the House chamber. Ford said, "I didn't agree with a lot of his liberal philosophy, but I found him a smart, attractive, decent, and honorable man. I liked Jack from the start."[10]

With the election of Republican Dwight D. Eisenhower to the presidency in 1952 came a Republican Congress. Now with his party in the majority, Ford began experiencing the heady tonic known as power. John Taber, senior Republican on the Appropriations committee, called him in to discuss putting him on the defense subcommittee. Taber explained there were three groups—Army, Navy, and Air Force. Since Ford had Navy experience, he seemed a logical candidate for the Army. When the confused congressman questioned this rationale, Taber answered, "You've got too many

NATIONAL EVENTS

APR 1: Conrail formed by US government to control 13 Northeast railroads that had filed bankruptcy protection

MAY 11: President Ford signs Federal Election Campaign Act

MAY 25: President Ford defeats Ronald Reagan in Republican presidential primaries

JUL 3: US Supreme Court rules in *Gregg v. Georgia* that the death penalty is a constitutionally acceptable form of punishment

JUL 4: US bicentennial celebrated across America

JUL 6: First class of women inducted into US Naval Academy

WORLD EVENTS

APR 4: Prince Norodom Sihanouk resigns as leader of Cambodia

JUN 16: Soweto riots in South Africa

JUN 20: Hundreds of Western tourists moved from Beirut to Syria by US military after the murder of the US ambassador

JUN 27: Palestinian extremists hijack an Air France plane from Greece to Uganda

JUL 2: Socialist Republic of Vietnam, a Communist country, created by the unification of North and South Vietnam

friends in the Navy. All those damn admirals will be after you, and you won't resist them. But if you're with the Army, you will tell the generals to go to hell."[11] Ford would take careful notes, and the following year, when the same military commanders were being questioned by the committee, he would pull out his notes, read what they had said a year before, and ask what progress they had made since then. His diligence impressed his colleagues and undoubtedly surprised a few witnesses.

Deciding to see where defense dollars went, Ford volunteered to go on a fact-finding mission to Asia. He visited troops in South Korea (he supported Truman's decision to fight and then switched to Eisenhower's position to end the war) in 1953. Then he flew to Saigon, where he was less than impressed by the French war effort against the Communist-led insurgency. He recorded his impressions in his diary: "Speeches. Pictures. Bally-hoo."[12] Show but no substance. He moved on to Taiwan, where he met General and Mrs. Chiang Kai-shek, and then flew to Tokyo for briefings.

Ford's hard work again impressed his colleagues, who sent him on a foreign trip in 1955, this time to Europe. The Democrats admired Ford and rewarded him with a seat on the ultra-secretive Intelligence Subcommittee on Appropriations, where hearings were held without staff, no transcripts were made, and no records kept. The CIA sent people to brief the group on their activities, of which there were many in the midst of the Cold War.

Betty Ford had become involved in the various congressional wives' organizations and attended teas in between caring for their growing family: Mike was born in 1950, Jack two years later, and after Steve's birth in 1956, Betty rebelled. Raising three children in a two-bedroom apartment was driving her to distraction, and she finally confronted her husband. Oblivious to his wife's predicament but quickly sensing he needed to act, they built a four-bedroom house in Alexandria, and just in time for the addition of daughter Susan, born in 1957. Meanwhile the stress of being a single parent took its toll on Betty, and she began finding solace in alcohol, which, totally unbeknownst to her husband, gradually increased in quantity.

In 1957, Sputnik crossed the sky, and the US government decided it needed a new federal agency to combat the Soviet space threat. A congressional joint committee was formed, and Ford was assigned to serve along with Texas senator Lyndon B. Johnson, who Ford said, "elected himself chairman." The master politician wielded power in impressive style, and no one then was surprised that the headquarters for the new National Aeronautics and Space Administration (NASA) would be in Texas.

For the 1960 presidential election, Ford did not hesitate to support his old friend Richard Nixon. Nixon, too, looked to Ford as a possible running mate, and many of his advisors agreed; however, Eisenhower decreed that Henry Cabot Lodge would be a better choice, so Ford's name was dropped. He still campaigned for the ticket and shared in the disappointment when Nixon lost to Kennedy.

The American Political Science Association bestowed the Congressional Distinguished Service Award on Gerald Ford in 1961: "A moderate conservative who is highly respected by his colleagues of both parties, he symbolizes the hard-working, competent legislator who eschews the more colorful, publicity seeking roles in favor of a solid record of achievement in the real work of the House: Committee work."[13]

JUL 15: Jimmy Carter nominated for president at Democratic National Convention in NYC

JUL 29: First "Son of Sam" killing in NYC; city will be terrorized for next year

AUG 4: First outbreak of Legionnaires' disease in Philadelphia

AUG 19: President Ford defeats Ronald Reagan for the Republican Party nomination

NOV 2: Jimmy Carter defeats incumbent Ford

JUL 4: Israeli commandos rescue hostages of Palestinian hijackers of the Air France plane in Uganda in Entebbe Raid

JUL 10: Mercenaries, one American and three British, are killed by firing squad in Angola

AUG 26: First known outbreak of Ebola virus in Zaire

SEP 9: People's Republic of China chairman Mao Zedong dies

DEC 1: Angola joins the United Nations

DID YOU KNOW?

In his college days, Ford was offered the opportunity to try out for both the Green Bay Packers and the Chicago Bears football teams.

Republicans were smarting over their lackluster performance in the 1962 congressional elections, where they had gained only one seat in the House. Believing that this was partly due to the Republican leadership of the House Republican Conference, some of the younger members encouraged Ford to challenge its leader, Charles Hoeven. Ford agreed and won.

Two days after President Kennedy's assassination, his successor, Lyndon B. Johnson, called Ford. He explained that a commission was being created to study the circumstances surrounding Kennedy's death, and he wanted Ford to be on it. Immediately the congressman thought of his other congressional commitments and attempted to decline, but LBJ's booming voice replied, "Congressman, this is your national duty. You must do it."[14] So Ford became the only Republican on the Warren Commission (named for its chairman, Chief Justice Earl Warren) and worked for the next several months examining evidence, hearing witnesses, and visiting Dallas before drafting their final report. Content with its findings that the committee "found no evidence of a conspiracy," Ford insisted "There was no complicity on the part of the CIA, FBI, Secret Service, Dallas police, or any other state or federal agency. So far as foreign conspiracy is concerned, nothing I have learned in the years since then would prompt me to change any of the major conclusions we reached."[15]

Back at home, Ford attempted to balance the demands of his House career with being a husband and father, but the family usually suffered. Oldest son Mike, who later became a minister said, "He provided very well, but we did miss his presence."[16] When the family took their vacations, such as skiing in Vail, the kids had their father's full attention. Betty, however, still bore the lion's share of parenting and grew to resent it. Her problems escalated when one afternoon in 1964 she was raising a stuck window and by the next day was in excruciating pain. Doctors put her in traction, but felt uncomfortable operating on the problem nerve since it was perilously close to her spinal cord; instead, they gave her painkillers, which she would steadfastly take for many years.

The 1964 presidential election went badly for the Republicans although many, including Ford, were disappointed that the convention chose Barry Goldwater as its candidate; moreover, in Johnson's election victory, he carried with him the majority of both houses of Congress, so now Republicans possessed thirty-six fewer seats in the House. Furious, many Republicans, including Melvin Laird and Donald Rumsfeld, demanded change, and asked Ford to challenge Charlie Halleck for minority leader. A close vote followed, but as of January 1965, Gerald Ford was minority leader of the House.

HOUSE MINORITY LEADER

Ford's first task was to "rebuild the party and bring younger Republicans into the House."[17] He knew that Congress would be inundated by Johnson's Great Society program proposals, and Republicans needed alternatives rather than to just say "no." He formulated a group called Constructive Republican Alternative Proposals, but quickly determined another name might be needed once they realized the acronym would be CRAP. Though Ford and his party's proposals were often defeated, their efforts did point up solutions other than the administration's. In one instance, for example, when LBJ wanted to fight civil rights abuses in certain southern states where black citizens were being denied the right to vote, Republicans countered with their own plan to combat the problem throughout the country. Although the administration's plan passed, Ford refused to give up. His actions, however, raised the ire of the president, who responded with personal attacks, among them that Ford had played too much football without a helmet. Then at the 1968 Gridiron Club's annual dinner, Ford turned this into a joke when he attempted to pull on his old 1935 helmet but the flaps just would not pull down. "Heads tend to swell in Washington,"[18] he quipped and the audience laughed heartily.

Ford presented a weekly televised conference called the "Ev and Jerry" show with Senator Everett Dirksen, the Senate minority leader. Ford felt humbled by Dirksen's finely honed oratorical skills; still, the senator referred to Ford as the "sword" and himself as the "oil can." Ford insisted that no one "could calm troubled waters faster than Ev Dirksen."[19] The two men agreed on most issues with the exception of the Vietnam War. Dirksen had served alongside Johnson for many years, so he supported the president, while Ford was critical of the war's management. At home, the minority leader also incurred criticism from his two teenage sons, who were opposed to the war.

Feeling increasingly isolated and embittered by the ongoing war, President Johnson decided not to run for reelection in 1968. His opponent would be a former colleague of Ford's—Richard Nixon, who asked the minority leader if he would be interested in becoming Nixon's running mate. Ford declined with the hope that he might win Speaker of the House if the Republicans were to win a majority. He then was shocked by Nixon's choice of Maryland governor Spiro Agnew, who had only served two years of a governorship—not much experience for someone only a heartbeat away from the nation's highest office. Nixon and Agnew won, and after the election, Ford was summoned to the White House. There he and LBJ met for an hour discussing the election and its ramifications. The Texan told Ford, "Jerry, you and I have had a lot of head-to-head confrontations, but I never doubted your integrity. When I leave here, I want you to know that we are friends and we always will be, and if I can ever help you, I want you to let me know."[20]

With Nixon's election came more responsibility to push the president's agenda in Congress, but Ford met with resistance not from his colleagues but rather from members of the president's staff, namely the head of the Domestic Council, John Ehrlichman. Ehrlichman continually refused to work with congressional leaders, and at meetings, Ford wrote, "he never said a word; he sat there in the corner, his disdainful expression revealing that he thought he was wasting his time. I was so mad at him that it was hard for me to contain my anger."[21] As the Nixon presidency advanced, Ford and his fellow Republicans worked to ensure that Nixon's plans would be implemented as laws. One such involved revenue sharing of income taxes with the state governments. Its successful passage was owing to a great deal of work by Ford, who headed a coalition of members from both sides of the aisle to pass it in 1971. Not every proposal was successful, however. A welfare program that encompassed job training for its recipients won House approval but was voted down twice by Senate Democrats.

TWENTY-FIFTH AMENDMENT (1967) ★ The Twenty-fifth Amendment provides for presidential succession and explains the procedure should the chief executive become unable to discharge the duties of the office. "Whenever there is a vacancy in the office of the Vice President, the President shall nominate a Vice President who shall take office upon confirmation by a majority vote of both Houses of Congress," states Section 2, and so after vice president Agnew resigned, President Nixon appointed Gerald Ford, who was confirmed by Congress. Then Section 1 was utilized upon Nixon's resignation to allow Ford to take the presidential oath of office: "In case of the removal of the President from office or of his death or resignation, the Vice President shall become President."

WATERGATE

On June 17, 1972, Gerald Ford heard the news that a group of burglars had been captured in an unsuccessful attempt to break into the Democratic headquarters of the Watergate complex in Washington, D.C. His reaction was that of the typical American: how could anybody be so stupid?

Two days later, Ford asked former congressman John Marsh if he thought the burglary was connected to anyone in the White House. Marsh replied that one of the burglars, James McCord, was closely connected to the head of the Committee to Reelect the President, John Mitchell. When Ford later met with Mitchell to discuss the other Republican campaigns, Ford also asked if he or anyone on the committee had a part in the burglary. Mitchell denied any involvement, and for the moment, the minority leader left satisfied, but a few weeks later, John Mitchell resigned from his chairmanship. The dominoes were beginning to fall.

Soon thereafter Nixon won his reelection with a landslide victory, but the coattail effect was missing as the House gained only thirteen seats, and the Senate lost two. With no hope of becoming Speaker for at least two years, Ford began assessing his options. He had now served in the House for a quarter century and earned a comfortable living. The family had their home in Alexandria; the home in Michigan was rented; and now they also owned a condo in Vail, Colorado, for skiing vacations. Retirement beckoned, but he decided he would run one last time in 1974, and then leave Congress in 1977.

Talk of who might be the Republican nominee in 1976 was already percolating, and Ford met with one of the top candidates, former governor (and Democrat) John Connally. Meanwhile, more rats were fleeing the ship of state, with Haldeman and Ehrlichman out, as well as White House counsel John Dean. Ford kept in contact with the White House proceedings via former defense secretary Melvin Laird, who began working on domestic policy in June 1973.

During this time, the minority leader noticed the vice president was becoming increasingly chummy and wanted to play golf with him. By autumn, rumors of Agnew's participation in kickbacks and possible bribery while in office were buzzing everywhere, and he asked Ford to arrange a meeting with House Democrats. The vice president wanted the judiciary committee to begin impeaching him so he could plead his case rather than face resignation. On October 10, 1973, President Nixon summoned Ford, and told him in specific detail the case against Agnew. Nixon explained that the vice president was not being honest with everyone and the attorneys were attempting to figure out a solution. Shortly after the meeting, Agnew's resignation was announced.

Later that evening, Melvin Laird called and asked Ford if he would be willing to serve as vice president. After he and Betty discussed what the change would mean to their family, Gerald called Laird and told him he would accept. Ford doubted he would get the job, figuring his power in the House was not something a Republican president would want to lose; better to pick someone such as John Connally or Ronald Reagan. But on October 12, Chief of Staff Alexander Haig invited Ford to the Oval Office, and there President Nixon offered him the position of vice president. Ford reiterated what he had told Laird of his plans to retire and that he would not be interested in running for president in 1976; Nixon agreed and said Connally should be the Republican nominee anyway. The president then seemed satisfied that Ford would be content in the vice presidential role.

With that settled, Ford was to keep the news to himself and proceed with his normal daily routine. He was to wait until seven that night for the official phone call. As the time ticked toward that hour, Betty was on the family's line downstairs when their private line rang and sixteen-year-old daughter Susan answered. "Dad, the White House is calling," she yelled to her father. He quickly grabbed the phone and heard the news from the president that Ford would be the official nominee for vice president.

Later that evening, Nixon stood in the East Room introducing his nominee to the world. Ford recalled the experience later as resembling a political convention as it was "oddly exuberant."[22] One of the first to call and congratulate him was Spiro Agnew. Ford's name was submitted for confirmation on October 13, and all believed it would receive swift action.

Meanwhile the president was increasingly under fire and confronting a subpoena by federal judge John Sirica to surrender the tapes made of conversations in the Oval Office. Faced with demands by Special Prosecutor Archibald Cox to give up the tapes, Nixon demanded Cox's firing, leading to the "Saturday Night Massacre" in the Justice Department, which ended the federal employment of three of its top attorneys. The news fed the fever of Congress and the people to impeach the president. Ford appealed to Nixon as well, telling him to release the documents, but to no avail.

The confirmation hearings were now beginning for Gerald Ford. No other nominee had withstood such intense scrutiny, as the members of the panel questioned Ford, examined his tax records, and

Two weeks after the Tulane speech, word of another crisis reached the Oval Office. On May 12, the American merchant ship *Mayaguez* was seized by the Khmer Rouge, who insisted it was traveling in Cambodian waters. Determined to appear strong, Ford and his advisors agreed to respond with force, and Marines were sent to attack nearby Koh Tang Island, where the American crew was believed to be held. At the same time, air strikes were launched on two patrol boats, but when the pilot saw Caucasians in the bow of one vessel, he was told to disable but not sink the boat. The Cambodians initiated heavy fire on the Marines, but ultimately the crew was released, much to the relief of their president.

In July, Ford flew to Helsinki to participate in the Conference on Security and Cooperation in Europe, specifically to meet once more with Premier Brezhnev. This time their encounter was not friendly, with much of their disagreement focused on Middle Eastern policy. Nothing positive came from these talks; in fact, many Republicans dismissed Ford's attempt to deal with the Soviets as a "sellout."

Among the world leaders who were willing to work with the United States toward peace in the Middle East was Egyptian president Anwar Sadat, who was also disgruntled with the Soviets. Ford and Sadat began working toward a peace accord that could then be presented to Israel. Kissinger practiced his famed shuttle diplomacy again and emerged with the Second Sinai Accord in September, which provided for Israeli use of the Suez Canal in return for strategic passes on the Sinai Peninsula and certain oil fields returned to Egypt.

September also saw President Ford become the first president to survive two very close brushes with death, just weeks apart. The first occurred on September 7 in Sacramento when the Secret Service disarmed Charlie Manson follower Lynne "Squeaky" Fromme before she could fire a .45-caliber pistol at the president. Two weeks later in San Francisco, middle-aged Sara Jane Moore succeeded in firing a shot, but a bystander managed to deflect it from the president. Both would-be female assassins were sentenced to life imprisonment.

> ***"In all my public and private acts as your president, I expect to follow my instincts of openness and candor with full confidence that honesty is always the best policy in the end."***
>
> —*Gerald R. Ford*

In November 1975, the president decided to make some changes in his cabinet: Secretary of Defense James Schlesinger was replaced by Donald Rumsfeld, and Central Intelligence Agency director William Colby was replaced by US ambassador to China, George Bush. Rumsfeld's assistant Dick Cheney took over his boss's job. Brent Scowcraft replaced Henry Kissinger as head of the National Security Council, but Kissinger remained as secretary of state. Even with these changes, Ford continued to hear a steady stream of criticism from fellow Republican Ronald Reagan, who was positioning himself to capture the 1976 presidential nomination.

As the presidential election year dawned, Ford's staff redoubled efforts to show him as a strong leader. In early 1976, a very public evacuation of Americans from Lebanon was undertaken by US forces. Lebanon was being torn apart by civil war, and many believed that the military operation was overly publicized to make the president appear strong. In July, images of the president attending the various Bicentennial events, including hosting a White House dinner for Queen Elizabeth II and Prince Philip, also worked to improve his image as chief of state within weeks of the Republican convention.

DID YOU KNOW?

In college, Ford worked as a park ranger at Yellowstone.

SAIGON AIRLIFT ★ Buoyed by easy conquests in South Vietnam, North Vietnamese troops escalated their attacks in March and April 1975, causing hundreds of thousands of refugees to flee literally for their lives. Many were gunned down by soldiers while they attempted to leave by any means possible. Americans in Saigon began evacuation procedures. The first was Operation Babylift to send Vietnamese children to America for adoption; one of the thirty flights crashed soon after takeoff, killing over half on board. Then American personnel and South Vietnamese who had been helpful to the Americans departed—more than 120,000, some by air and some by sea. Then Operation Frequent Wind occurred on April 29 and 30, as over 6,000 more were evacuated by helicopters from the American embassy. More than 660 helicopter missions were flown, but not all of the South Vietnamese were rescued; some 300 were left to their fates.

1976 ELECTION

Ford captured the New Hampshire primary and won support in the Northeast and upper Midwest, whereas Ronald Reagan captured the south and western blocs. Still when the Republicans met in Kansas City, they nominated Gerald Ford to be their candidate, but Kansas senator Bob Dole replaced Nelson Rockefeller as his running mate. (Receiving pressure from conservatives, Ford asked Rockefeller to withdraw his name from consideration and, fed up with the ongoing lack of presidential backing, Rockefeller agreed.) The Republican nominees now took aim against the chosen Democrat, Georgia governor, and relative unknown, Jimmy Carter, whom Ford had challenged to a debate in his acceptance speech.

There were actually three debates. The first concentrated on domestic concerns, and Ford was declared the winner. In the second debate, he took a serious misstep, however, by insisting that Eastern Europe was not under Soviet control—an unpardonable gaffe by the American president. He was then unable to regain his footing for the third debate. The political race took the inevitable detours into the many avenues of the media. *Saturday Night Live* star Chevy Chase entertained viewers repeatedly with pratfalls imitating the president stumbling down the steps of Air Force One and nearly landing at Anwar Sadat's feet, quipping, "I thought I'd just drop in."[34]

The weeks before the election, the Commerce Department announced that economic figures showed a decline for the second straight month. When Americans went to the polls, they arrived in the fewest numbers since 1948, and elected Jimmy Carter to the presidency by a small margin: Carter won 49.9 percent of the popular vote to Ford's 47.9 percent, and in the electoral college, Carter took 297 votes to Ford's 241. Without a doubt, the presidential pardon had cast a shadow on Ford's election bid.

RETIREMENT

After attending the swearing in of President Jimmy Carter, the Fords left Washington and headed west to California, where they had bought property at Rancho Mirage. There he played golf and worked on his memoirs, *A Time to Heal,* published in 1979, and maintained an active speaking schedule for many years, as well as serving on the boards of a variety of organizations and corporations.

Ford's busy schedule did not help his wife Betty adjust to post–White House life, and she turned increasingly to her pain pills and alcohol, prompting her family to stage an intervention in 1978. Her subsequent treatment and rehabilitation led her to found the Betty Ford Center to treat addictions. Her openness about her chemical dependency was only another example of the frank talk she had become famous for as First Lady. Following Betty Ford's example, many thousands of people have been treated for some of the most damaging and painful disorders that can afflict a family, and her courageous honesty continues to give hope and support to all those who suffer with addiction.

In 1980, the former president briefly considered another run for office as Ronald Reagan's running mate, but Ford's vision of a co-presidency was not shared by the California governor. The following year the former president proudly opened the Gerald R. Ford Library in Ann Arbor, Michigan. He also began to develop an unlikely friendship with Jimmy Carter, with whom he traveled that same year, along with Richard Nixon, to attend the state funeral of Anwar Sadat. Carter and Ford became friends, and the Fords and the Carters would often spend time together in the coming years.

By the 2000 Republican convention, the former president's health was precarious, as he had suffered two minor strokes, from which he quickly recovered. Six years later, heart problems and a bout of pneumonia resulted in a noticeable decline. Ford passed a milestone, however, in November 2006, when he became the oldest former president in history at the age of ninety-three, surpassing Ronald Reagan and John Adams. He and Betty were also the longest-lived First Couple. But on December 26, 2006, Gerald Ford died at their home in Rancho Mirage, California. After memorial services in Washington, his body was flown to Michigan, and he was buried at his presidential library in Ann Arbor.

In 1988, Gerald Ford was asked by a biographer how he wished to be remembered. He replied: "I want to be remembered as a . . . nice person, who worked at the job, and who left the White House in better shape than when I took it over."[35]

ENDNOTES

1 James Cannon, *Time and Chance, Gerald Ford's Appointment with History*, New York: Harper Collins, 1994, p. 5.

2 Ibid, p. 9.

3 Ibid, p. 15.

4 Ibid, p. 16.

5 Ibid, p. 20.

6 Gerald Ford, *A Time to Heal, The Autobiography of Gerald Ford*, New York: Harper & Row, 1979, p. 50.

7 Cannon, p. 23.

8 Ibid, p. 35.

9 Ford, p. 68.

10 Cannon, p. 53.

11 Ibid, p. 61.

12 Ibid, p. 63.

13 Ibid, p. 71.

14 Ibid, p. 76.

15 Ford, p. 76.

16 Cannon, p. 79.

17 Ibid, p. 85.

18 Ford, p. 84.

19 Ibid, p. 82.

20 Ibid, pp. 87-88.

21 Ibid, pp. 88-89.

22 Ibid, p. 107.

23 Ibid, p. 110.

24 Ibid, p. 112.

25 Ibid, p. 122.

26 Cannon, p. 293.

27 Ibid.

28 Ibid, p. 307.

29 Ibid, p. 313.

30 Ford, p. 203.

31 John Robert Greene, *The Presidency of Gerald Ford*, Lawrence, KS: University of Kansas Press, 1995, p. 77.

32 *Time*, December 8, 1975.

33 Greene, pp. 140-141.

34 Robert T. Hartmann, *Palace Politics, An Inside Account of the Ford Years*, New York: McGraw-Hill, 1980, p. 411.

35 Greene, p. 193.

Jimmy Carter

★ ★ ★ THIRTY-NINTH PRESIDENT ★ ★ ★

LIFE SPAN

- Born: October 1, 1924, in Plains, Georgia

FAMILY

- Father: **(James) Earl Carter Sr.** (1894–1953)
- Mother: **(Bessie) Lillian Gordy Carter** (1898–1983)
- Wife: **(Eleanor) Rosalynn Smith Carter** (1927–); wed on July 7, 1946, in Plains, Georgia
- Children: **John William "Jack"** (1947–); **James Earl III "Chip"** (1950–); **Donnel Jeffrey "Jeff"** (1952–); **Amy Lynn** (1967–)

RELIGION

- Baptist

HIGHER EDUCATION

- Georgia Southwestern College, 1941–1942; Georgia Institute of Technology, 1942–1943; United States Naval Academy, 1943–1946 (class of 1947); Union College, 1952–1953

PROFESSION

- Naval officer, farmer

MILITARY SERVICE

- Served in US Navy (1946–1953); began as ensign and discharged as lieutenant senior grade; served on early nuclear submarines in early 1950s

POLITICAL LIFE

- Georgia state senator (1963–1967)
- Georgia governor (1971–1975)

PRESIDENCY

- One term: January 20, 1977–January 20, 1981
- Democrat
- Reason for leaving office: lost 1980 election to **Ronald Reagan**
- Vice president: **Walter F. Mondale** (1977–1981)

ELECTION OF 1976

- Electoral vote:
  Carter 297;
  Gerald R. Ford 240;
  Ronald Reagan 1

CABINET

SECRETARY OF STATE
Cyrus R. Vance (1977–1980)
Edmund S. Muskie (1980–1981)

SECRETARY OF THE TREASURY
W. Michael Blumenthal (1977–1979)
G. William Miller (1979–1981)

SECRETARY OF DEFENSE
Harold Brown (1977–1981)

ATTORNEY GENERAL
Griffin B. Bell (1977–1979)
Benjamin R. Civiletti (1979–1981)

SECRETARY OF THE INTERIOR
Cecil D. Andrus (1977–1981)

SECRETARY OF AGRICULTURE
Robert S. Bergland (1977–1981)

SECRETARY OF COMMERCE
Juanita M. Kreps (1977–1979)
Philip M. Klutznick (1980–1981)

SECRETARY OF LABOR
F. Ray Marshall (1977–1981)

Jimmy Carter arrived on the national political scene at an opportune time for a Washington outsider. The country had endured two years of the Watergate scandal during the Nixon administration and then, disgruntled with the presidential pardon of Nixon by Gerald Ford, the American electorate retaliated by denying his election and voting for the peanut farmer from Plains, Georgia.

EARLY LIFE

James Earl Carter (known as Earl) had lived in Plains since childhood and operated his own small grocery store in town. Lillian Gordy was studying nursing with the owner of the town's hospital, Dr. Sam Wise, who told his nurse that she should date the young man. Soon a courtship developed, and in September 1923, the couple married at a local minister's home. They moved into rented rooms in the middle of town. On October 1, 1924, she gave birth to James Earl Carter Jr. at Wise Hospital, and over the next thirteen years, Jimmy would be joined by three siblings—two sisters, Gloria and Ruth, and a younger brother, Billy.

When Jimmy was four years old, his family moved to a farm near Archery, Georgia, a town whose population was entirely black except for the Carters and one other white family. Their new home lacked both electricity and running water for the first years, but Earl Carter's income rose steadily as he acquired more lands and more than two hundred black tenants for his farm, which eventually included four thousand acres of cotton and peanut crops. Daughter Gloria later recalled: "Daddy never worked in the fields. He said that one time he worked a half-day and that was it. But he oversaw everything that was done—everything."[1]

Lillian was a trained nurse and frequently away from the home, so she left notes for her children telling them what chores they needed to do in her absence, although nannies and cooks also tended to the family's household needs. Lillian instilled in her children her belief in racial equality and frequently helped the black tenant families of the area who required medical assistance but lacked money. Unlike typical white households of the day, Jimmy's black childhood friends were allowed to come inside and play and eat in the Carter home. Earl, however, disagreed with his wife's views, and when he built a tennis court on the farm, Jimmy was not allowed to invite his African American friends.

Earl Carter expected his son to work hard, do his chores, and tell the truth. If Jimmy crossed his father, he was whipped with a switch cut from a peach tree. Jimmy later remembered, "He was a stern disciplinarian and punished me severely when I misbehaved." But although admitting he resented his father's behavior toward him at times, the future president insisted that "he was always my best friend."[2]

Working was a main component of the young Carters' lives, and that usually entailed working with their major crop—cotton. Jimmy described his dangerous and rather "sticky" duty: "Beginning as a small child just able to carry a gallon bucket, I had a continuing job during the growing season of mixing arsenic, molasses, and water in a large barrel and then helping to apply it by hand to the central buds of every cotton plant in Daddy's fields." They had to be mopped every five days and the molasses mixture soon coated his legs, and once it set up as hard sugar, "so that at night my pants wouldn't fold, but would stand erect in a corner"; and since poison was on them, they were washed separately but not daily, so "it was particularly disgusting to put them back on in the morning."[3]

NATIONAL EVENTS

JAN 17: First execution after reintroduction of death penalty in US, in Utah, by firing squad

JAN 19: Snow falls in Miami, Florida

JAN 20: Jimmy Carter succeeds Gerald Ford as the 39th president

JAN 21: President Carter pardons Vietnam War draft evaders

MAR 9: A dozen armed Muslims take over three buildings in Washington, D.C., holding more than 130 hostage for three days

1977

WORLD EVENTS

JUN 6–9: Celebrations in London for the Queen's 25-year reign

JUN 15: Spain holds first democratic elections after 41 years of Franco's regime

JUL 5: First elected prime minister of Pakistan overthrown

JUL 22: Deng Xiaoping restored to power in Communist China

SEP 10: Last guillotine execution in France

The highlight of the cotton season was picking it, and young Jimmy diligently applied himself alongside the others in this backbreaking toil under the unforgiving sun and stifling humidity of summer. He later proudly recorded, "During my years on the farm I increased from [picking] 50 to a maximum of 150 pounds a day, which was in the range of most adults."[4]

At a young age, Jimmy began growing his own peanuts, then boiling and selling them in Plains. When he was nine years old, Jimmy purchased five bales of cotton at five cents a pound and held them for four years before selling them at a profit of thirteen cents per pound. He used this money to purchase five tenant houses and collected rent for additional income. When he later went away to the US Naval Academy, Earl became his rent collector, but quickly tired of the duty and sold the houses, receiving a 300 percent profit on them for his son.

The Carter children attended school in Plains, and there Jimmy developed a passion for reading, largely owing to the strong influence of Julia Coleman, his seventh grade teacher, who encouraged him to continue his interest through the summer months and compiled a reading list for him that included *War and Peace*. Reading was a useful pursuit in the Carter household since they had an unusual rule—no talking at mealtimes; instead, family members were to bring a book to read or sit and eat silently.

In high school, Jimmy participated in sports, including track and the basketball team (where, as the shortest man on the team, he was nicknamed "Peewee"). Although Carter preferred baseball, helping on the farm came first, and spring planting prevented spring sports. He also liked woodworking and continued that interest into his adult life. Jimmy joined the debate society and was one of three eligible for becoming valedictorian of Plains High School's class of 1941, but he lost to one of his former girlfriends. The class traveled to Florida for its graduation trip, and was later invited to the Carter home for a barbecue.

For college, Jimmy had long ago determined that he wanted to attend the US Naval Academy at Annapolis. His uncle Tom Watson Gordy was in the Navy, and frequently sent letters telling of his duties as a radio man aboard the ships he served. Jimmy was entranced by the life at sea and decided he would go to the Academy. He was not allowed to attend immediately, however, because their local congressman was nominating another candidate for the fall 1941 class, so Jimmy had to content himself with attending nearby Georgia Southwestern College. Congressman Steven Price promised Earl Carter, "I'll give Jimmy an appointment next year, and he won't have to take the full entrance examination if he can make good grades in college,"[5] and he was true to his word. Carter spent a year attending Georgia Tech in Atlanta, taking engineering classes and serving in the naval ROTC. Although he found the coursework challenging, he excelled. Living in Atlanta also opened his eyes to life in the big city.

Then in June 1943, after spending a two-week vacation at home, Carter and another Georgian journeyed by train to Annapolis and their initiation. Hazing was a huge part of the plebes' life, and Jimmy's experience was no exception. He was forced to learn the lyrics to "Marching through Georgia" and was ordered to sing it numerous times. He also had to learn not to smile so much and try to blend in rather than stand out and be a target.

Jimmy also found time to meet and then conduct a long-distance courtship with a friend of

CABINET

(continued)

SECRETARY OF HEALTH, EDUCATION, AND WELFARE (CHANGED IN 1979 TO HEALTH AND HUMAN SERVICES)
Joseph A. Califano Jr. (1977–1979)

Patricia Roberts Harris (1979–1981)

SECRETARY OF HOUSING AND URBAN DEVELOPMENT
Patricia R. Harris (1977–1979)

Moon Landrieu (1979–1981)

SECRETARY OF TRANSPORTATION
Brock Adams (1977–1979)

Neil E. Goldschmidt (1979–1981)

SECRETARY OF ENERGY
James R. Schlesinger (1977–1979)

Charles W. Duncan (1979–1981)

SECRETARY OF EDUCATION
Shirley M. Hufstedler (1979–1981)

JUL 13: New York City blackout of 1977 lasts for 25 hours

AUG 4: US Senate holds hearings on alleged CIA mind-control research program (MKULTRA)

AUG 4: President Carter signs legislation creating US Department of Energy

AUG 10: David Berkowitz, Son of Sam serial killer, captured

AUG 16: Elvis Presley dies

SEP 7: US and Panama sign treaties agreeing the US will transfer control of the canal to Panama at the end of the twentieth century

SEP 12: South African anti-apartheid activist Steve Biko dies in police custody

SEP 21: Nuclear non-proliferation pact signed by 15 countries, including the US and USSR

NOV 19: Egyptian president Anwar Sadat becomes first Arab leader to officially visit Israel

DEC 4: President of the Central African Republic crowns himself emperor

ROSALYNN CARTER (b. 1927) ★ Not since Eleanor Roosevelt had a First Lady become so active in the political activities of the presidency. Her husband wanted her briefed on various domestic and foreign issues so he could discuss them with her and gain her advice. Some in the media began calling her "Mrs. President." Hoping to gain congressional support for her ongoing campaign against mental illness, Mrs. Carter testified before a hearing on Capitol Hill. On other occasions, she was sent as a representative for the president. Just as they had shown the world on inauguration day, walking hand in hand down Pennsylvania Avenue, the two Carters were truly a team.

his sister Ruth. Rosalynn Smith was seventeen years old when she met the naval cadet three years her senior in the summer of 1945. After their first date, he announced to his family that he would marry her. His parents had hoped for him to make a more advantageous match instead of the local girl of modest means, but Jimmy would not listen. When he graduated from the Naval Academy in 1946, following the tradition of the female relatives pinning the shoulder boards on the new officers' uniforms, Rosalynn pinned one and Lillian the other.

A few weeks later, Jimmy and Rosalynn married at the Plains Methodist Church, and after a week-long honeymoon at Chimney Rock, North Carolina, they drove to Norfolk, Virginia, where Jimmy would board the USS *Wyoming* for his first tour.

NAVAL CAREER

Carter later described his time on the *Wyoming* as a "terrible duty"[6] since it was aboard a battleship well past its heyday and now serving as a testing vessel for guns and communication and navigation equipment. Still he and Rosalynn found life in Norfolk pleasant, and in July 1947, they became parents to John (Jack) William Carter. The following year, the nearly forty-year-old battleship was sent to become scrap, and Carter was transferred to the USS *Mississippi*. His tenure here was no more adventuresome than what he had just left; in fact, neither ship ever left Chesapeake Bay, and Ensign Carter longed for more. He later admitted that he considered leaving the service since "the postwar navy was in bad shape. It was a time of great discouragement because we were undermanned, the nation was relaxing after a long and difficult war, and funds allocated for naval operations were meager."[7]

Carter applied for a Rhodes scholarship but was unsuccessful. Looking for a fresh opportunity, he applied to attend submarine school, where he was accepted, so he and his family packed and moved to New London, Connecticut. He graduated third in his class and was assigned to the submarine USS *Pomfret* in Hawaii as its electronics officer. When the sub sailed for Asia, it encountered a ferocious storm, which left him seasick for days, although he refused to yield to it as an excuse from duty. Another night when the boat surfaced to recharge its batteries, he was washed overboard when a gigantic wave broke him away from his station on the bridge. Fortunately he was able to swim through the wave and return to the sub. Life aboard a submarine means close quarters for all, and the officers would play poker nightly in the wardroom—except for Carter. One of his fellow officers remarked, "Jimmy was not one of the guys. We didn't criticize him . . . because he was an incredibly determined and responsible officer. But he was always apart . . . he never really got close to anybody."[8]

NATIONAL EVENTS

JAN 1: Copyright Act of 1976 takes effect

JAN 14–15: Body of former vice president Hubert Humphrey lies in state in the Capitol Rotunda

FEB 8: Senate proceedings broadcast on the radio for the first time

FEB 15: Serial killer Ted Bundy captured

FEB 16: The first computer bulletin board system is created in Chicago

1978

WORLD EVENTS

JAN 23: Sweden becomes first nation to ban aerosol sprays

FEB 21: Ruins of the Great Pyramid of Tenochtitlan discovered in Mexico City

MAR 3: Rhodesia attacks Zambia

MAR 14: Israeli forces invade Lebanon

MAR 18: Prime minister of Pakistan sentenced to death by hanging for ordering the assassination of a political opponent

APR 27: Afghanistan president is killed in a military coup; Democratic Republic of Afghanistan declared on April 30

During this time, the Korean War broke out, and the *Pomfret* was transferred to San Diego, so the Carter family (now including James Earl III, "Chip") moved there briefly before he was transferred back to New London to work aboard a new antisubmarine sub, K-1, which was yet to be commissioned. When it was launched, he was the engineering officer; Lieutenant Commander Frank Andrews recalled him as "all business; no fooling around; professional; organized; smart as hell."[9] While in Connecticut, Rosalynn gave birth to their third son, Donnel Jeffrey (Jeff), in August 1952.

Carter also earned his submarine commander qualification and had been promoted to full lieutenant in June 1952. He decided to try something different and applied for the nuclear submarine program. Captain Hyman Rickover oversaw the program and personally interviewed the applicants. Carter was accepted and assigned to be senior officer on the *Sea Wolf*, which was still being built. Carter transferred to Schenectady, New York, in November 1952, where he and other officers took courses in nuclear physics and worked at the General Electric plant in a nuclear sub mockup. During this time, he was sent on a team to Canada to disassemble a nuclear reactor that had suffered meltdown.

Early in 1953, Jimmy received a fateful phone call from his mother saying that his father was suffering from pancreatic cancer and was not expected to live long. He immediately left for Plains, where Lillian insisted that her eldest son needed to leave the Navy and return home to run his father's business interests, which included over five thousand acres and warehouses. While he understood his need to return, Rosalynn did not. She enjoyed the places they lived and the lifestyle of a naval officer's wife and insisted he stay in the Navy. The couple argued, and later Jimmy said, "She almost quit me,"[10] but the marriage stayed intact, and the five Carters moved to Plains in October 1953.

LIFE IN PLAINS

Now in charge of his father's estate and lands, Jimmy quickly found that money was in short supply. Drought for the past two years had left devastated crops, and the credit extended by his father could not be paid by farmers who had nothing to sell. Believing he could improve his farming yield, he began poring over books and attending classes at the agricultural extension center. His studying gradually paid off, as did his many backbreaking hours working alone at the peanut warehouse. Then in 1955, Rosalynn began working as a bookkeeper and found she thoroughly enjoyed helping in the office.

Jimmy was also interested in bettering the welfare of the people of Plains. He sought and won a state grant to pave its streets; he convinced others in town to combine their resources to build a swimming pool for the town (although it was whites only); he worked in the Lions Club and the Boy Scouts, while Rosalynn was a den mother for Cub Scouts. Carter expanded his business over the years as their income steadily rose; they also bought a former plantation house on the outskirts of town.

The south of the 1950s was one of upheaval and turmoil, especially following the Supreme Court's ruling in 1954 outlawing segregation. When a White Citizens Council was formed in Plains to fight school integration, they invited Jimmy to pay his five-dollar dues, but he refused. They grew more upset when he reiterated his position after being told he would be the only white citizen in Plains not to join. A short boycott of the Carter business followed, as well as expulsion from the

SUPREME COURT APPOINTMENTS
★★★★★★★★★★

None

APR 7: President Carter postpones production of the neutron bomb

MAY 25: First Unabomber attack (mail bomb to Northwestern University)

JUN 28: Supreme Court bars quota systems in college admissions, but allows advantages for minorities

SEP 5: Historic meeting begins at Camp David with Egyptian President Anwar Sadat, Israeli Prime Minister Menachem Begin, and US President Jimmy Carter

JUN 24: President of Yemen Arab Republic is killed

JUN 30: Ethiopia begins massive offensive in Eritrea

AUG 12: Japan and People's Republic of China sign Treaty of Peace and Friendship

OCT 1: Vietnam attacks Cambodia

OCT 27: Israeli prime minister Menachem Begin and Egyptian president Anwar Sadat win Nobel Peace Prize

STATE OF THE UNION

US POPULATION IN 1977
226,542,199

NATIONAL DEBT IN 1981
$1,028,729,000,000

local country club. Then in 1961, as chairman of the local school board, Carter backed a plan to consolidate three local high schools into one large school to provide more educational opportunities for all—including blacks. The issue was voted on as a referendum and soundly defeated. When the Carters drove by their office, a sign now hung that said: "Coons and Carters Go Together."[11]

In 1962, Carter decided to enter the political arena, and after talking to Rosalynn, he submitted his name for the state senate two weeks before the primary election. Once more, just as with the family business, the couple pooled together their talents and effort for a victory, but the crooked politics of Georgia would not permit this. In one county, voters were ordered to scratch out Carter's name. Carter decided to challenge the election, and soon made headlines in the *Atlanta Journal*. Quitman County had been the scene of voter fraud for years, and now it was public knowledge. Hearings were conducted and eventually the election result was overturned; Jimmy was deemed the winner just in time for the general election in November, and he won that as well. He took his seat at the 1963 Georgia General Assembly.

STATE SENATOR

Carter took his position seriously as state senator and studied speed-reading as a means to help him wade through the pile of bills awaiting the legislators. He usually supported the position of the Democratic Party, but would sometimes differ regarding special interests that were being pushed by lobbyists. Jimmy tried to watch out for the poor, whose voice was often not heard in the state capitol.

In the summer of 1963, Georgia was caught up in the storm of racial protest gripping the South including the "freedom riders," who were interracial groups riding buses to protest the discrimination still practiced at bus stations. Violence also occurred in nearby Americus, where a white man was beaten for attempting to escort a black woman to the courthouse so she could register to vote. The Carters supported President Kennedy and his brother, Attorney General Robert Kennedy, for their efforts to break through the segregationist barriers of the South. They were shocked and deeply saddened to learn of the president's assassination. Son Chip was in high school when the news was announced, and the teacher said, "That's good!"[12] prompting the class to applaud. Outraged by such a reaction, Chip picked up his desk and hurled it at the teacher, for which he received a three-day suspension, but his father did not punish him.

Carter won reelection to the state senate in 1964 and began thinking of running for a US congressional seat in 1966. By that time, he had earned a seat on the appropriations committee, and his work on the education committee had proven valuable, including making Georgia Southwestern into a four-year college, and reporters on the state capitol beat listed him as one of the top thirty-five legislators in the nation.

Although wanting to run for the Third Congressional District, events worked against Carter, and Democratic Party leaders implored him to run for governor instead. Jimmy and Rosalynn worked their hardest, traveling across the state meeting people, but it was not enough to win him the Democratic primary. He was now out of office and the Carters' savings account was depleted.

BACK TO PLAINS

Returning to his family and the business, life resumed at the leisurely Plains pace with one

NATIONAL EVENTS

SEP 17: Camp David Accords signed by Israel and Egypt

1979

JAN 1: US and People's Republic of China establish full diplomatic relations

FEB 1: President Carter commutes Patty Hearst's prison sentence

MAR 4: Voyager I photos show Jupiter's rings

MAY 25: First use of the electric chair since the reintroduction of the death penalty in 1976

WORLD EVENTS

DEC 11: Two million demonstrate against the Shah in Iran

1979

One Child Policy implemented in China as it becomes the first nation to register over one billion people

JAN 7: Fall of Phnom Penh and Pol Pot regime

JAN 16: Shah of Iran flees his country, relocates to Egypt

FEB 1: Ayatollah Khomeini returns to Iran after 15 years of exile

exception—their fourth child, Amy Lynn, was born in October 1967, completing the family. Son Jack joined the Navy at the height of the Vietnam War. After experiencing a spiritual renewal and avowing himself as a "born-again Christian," Carter began working on his next campaign, which would result in his successful election to the governorship of Georgia in 1970. His speeches concentrated on attacking the power apparatus of former governor and opponent Carl Sanders and insisted that the governor's office had been improperly used to make Sanders rich; however, Carter was unable to prove his allegations, thus undermining his credibility. Making headlines did work to Jimmy's favor, though, and soon contributions from Coca-Cola, Delta Airlines, and the Cox Broadcasting Company were pouring in. Candidate Carter often promised things to certain groups such as getting rid of a highway commissioner he said had been there too long, but when that commissioner endorsed him, Carter agreed to keep him. Jimmy won the primary, beating Sanders soundly and then easily won the general election.

GOVERNOR CARTER

The new governor announced to his audience in his inaugural speech in January 1971, "that the time for racial discrimination is over." He ordered Martin Luther King Jr.'s portrait hung in the state capitol and worked to end the skewed educational financing of the state, which allowed disproportionate monies be spent for white districts, with black ones receiving scarcely anything. He also appointed blacks to various state agencies and boards and increased the number of African American state employees by 40 percent. Carter, along with other southern governors, including George Wallace, disagreed with forced busing. He did, however, support Atlanta's voluntary busing program.

Another effort in his governorship was the reorganization of the state bureaucracy, and he proclaimed that he would save at least fifty million dollars annually by consolidating agencies and reducing them from 300 to twenty-two. He worked to revamp the state's penal system and improve prison conditions.

While pursuing his course, Carter surrounded himself with fellow Georgians whom he had found helpful in the campaign, including Jody Powell, who became his press secretary; Hamilton Jordan, his executive assistant; and Bert Lance, the state's highway commissioner. Governor Carter experienced major headaches, however, in dealing with his lieutenant governor, Lester Maddox, who attempted to short circuit Carter's reorganization plan, but failed. One of the governor's opponents, Ben Fortson, testified before the Senate's Economy, Reorganization, and Efficiency in Government Committee about the way Carter worked: "Don't pay any attention to that smile. That don't mean a thing. That man is made of steel, determination, and stubbornness. Carter reminds me of a South Georgia turtle. He doesn't go around a log. He just sticks his head in the middle and pushes and pushes until the log gives way."[13]

Carter read and studied the minutest details of legislation and issues, making him quite conversant on any of them. After reading an article about the zero-based budgeting approach being implemented at Texas Instruments, he inaugurated the same for the department heads of the state government. Carter disliked staff meetings and usually would go to the specific person instead, yet continued to be considered aloof by many and not one to practice the personal aspect of politics.

DID YOU KNOW?

Carter is one of three presidents to graduate from the US Naval Academy.

JUN 18: President Carter signs SALT II

JUL 3: President Carter approves secret aid to opponents of the pro-Soviet regime in Afghanistan

SEP 1: Pioneer 11 becomes the first spacecraft to visit Saturn

NOV 3: Greensboro Massacre: group of Ku Klux Klan members shoot and kill five Communist Workers Party members marching in "death to the Klan" rally in North Carolina

FEB 7: Pluto moves inside Neptune's orbit, the first such occurrence since the discovery of both planets

FEB 14: US ambassador to Afghanistan is kidnapped and later killed in Kabul

FEB 17: Start of Sino-Vietnamese War when People's Republic of China invades northern Vietnam

FEB 22: Saint Lucia gains its independence from the United Kingdom

APR 1: Iran becomes an Islamic republic by a 98 percent vote, officially overthrowing the Shah

DID YOU KNOW?

Carter is a self-made millionaire.

In fact, he would invite people to lunch with him, and then charge them for the meal. The governor and first lady soon learned that entertaining was expected of them at the mansion.

Rosalynn decided to publicize mental health issues and volunteered one day a week at a nearby mental hospital. She herself grew depressed in the early days of her husband's governorship, but through meditation and prayer was able to recover.

Carter began rising in southern political circles and hosted the Southern Governors Council. Then they, in turn, appointed him to a variety of regional boards and commissions. He attempted to gain more widespread support for Washington senator Henry "Scoop" Jackson as the Democratic Party's presidential nominee rather than frontrunner George McGovern, whom Carter predicted would never carry the South, and he was proven correct. Afterward, he and his staff decided that he knew just as much as anyone running for the presidency, so Carter began secretly planning his campaign for the presidential nomination in four years. He began writing his autobiography and contacting Democratic Party leaders and others who could offer advice and help.

David Rockefeller appointed Carter to the Trilateral Commission, whose purpose was to bring leaders from the business, political, and academic worlds together biannually to discuss problems common to North America, Western Europe, and Japan. Carter's participation here increased his name recognition elsewhere in the world.

In 1974, he served as the Democratic Party's chairman for the midterm elections. Carter elicited responses from candidates to find what they needed and then provided it. He also campaigned in more than sixty congressional races. Since this was the era of Watergate, Democrats expected to clean up on the majority of races, and they were not disappointed.

Carter made local headlines when he vetoed the Army Corps of Engineers' proposed Spruell Bluff dam project, insisting that it was not necessary, and environmentalists nationwide applauded his stance. He also made a policy speech in Washington about energy conservation. Then in late 1974, presidential hopefuls Ted Kennedy and Walter Mondale announced they were no longer considering running, leaving the field open for a now-former governor of Georgia.

RUNNING FOR PRESIDENT

Carter used the mini-convention of the Democratic Party Organization and Policy in Kansas City, Missouri, in December 1974, to recruit more supporters nationwide, and announced his candidacy for the presidency a few days after it ended. He began making speeches demanding change in government—from the need to select ambassadorial personnel more attuned to the country they were sent, to delineating the demand for more efficient governmental procedures.

Later, Carter wrote about how his grassroots campaign evolved. He traveled the country extensively, introducing himself and working "to recruit supporters and to raise campaign funds; and to obtain maximum news coverage for myself and my stand on the many local and national issues. The most important purpose of all was for me to learn the nation—what it is, and what it ought to be."[14] As the election season dawned, he and his family blanketed Iowa, whose caucuses initiated the process, and there he won nearly 28 percent, the biggest bloc for a candidate that year, and was cast as the "clear winner"[15] by CBS news. He rode the tide for the New Hampshire primary,

NATIONAL EVENTS

NOV 12: President Carter orders an oil embargo in response to the Iran hostage crisis

JAN 4: President Carter implements grain embargo against USSR

MAR 21: President Carter announces US will boycott Summer Olympics in Moscow

APR 7: US severs diplomatic relations with Iran and imposes economic sanctions

1980

WORLD EVENTS

JUN 20: ABC newsman and interpreter are killed by a Nicaraguan National Guard solider; killings captured on tape

NOV 4: Iran hostage crisis begins

DEC 24: Soviet Union invades Afghanistan

JAN 26: Egypt and Israel establish diplomatic relations

APR: Robert Mugabe elected as Zimbabwe's prime minister

MAY 4: Yugoslav president Tito dies

MAY 26: Military government forces and pro-democracy protesters clash in South Korea

where *Newsweek* proclaimed him as "the unqualified winner."[16] His usual stump speech resounded among the voters when he introduced himself as an outsider to Washington and reminded all that he was *not* a lawyer. His words were music to the ears of a country longing to awake from the nightmare of Watergate.

Carter promised honesty, but reporters and critics began pointing to evidence of the candidate saying one thing but having done another. For instance, he insisted he had helped advance Atlanta's busing program, but no one there recalled his attending any meetings or helping in any way. Later when *Harper's* ran a critical piece on him, *Time* responded with its own article: "He has been accused of fudging the issues. He has been charged with telling little white lies—and indeed he has occasionally exaggerated past accomplishments—along with some big ones."[17] His nemesis Lester Maddox also campaigned in New Hampshire, telling the voters that Carter was "two-faced, he's the biggest phony I've ever known, and I just hope to God the American people find out before it's too late."[18]

Aiding in her brother's campaign was sister Ruth Carter Stapleton, who years before had become a Christian evangelist. She now sent out a form letter to prospective voters who want "our nation to be under His blessings and guidance—please pray for Jimmy."[19] Younger brother Billy also provided plenty of sound bites for the newshounds. Jimmy related his favorite:

> *"When one of the reporters remarked that Billy was a little strange, he replied, 'Look, My mama was a seventy-year-old Peace Corps volunteer in India; one of my sisters goes all over the world as a holy-roller preacher; my oldest sister spends half her time on a Harley-Davidson motorcycle; and my brother thinks he is going to be president of the United States. Which one of our family do you think is normal?'"*[20]

While he did not win primaries in all states (losing Massachusetts and Virginia), he still won the majority, giving him momentum that carried to the Democratic national convention in New York City in July 1976.

On the first ballot, Jimmy Carter captured the Democratic presidential nomination, edging out top competitors Morris Udall of Arizona and Governor Jerry Brown of California. For his running mate he chose Minnesota senator Walter Mondale. Their opponents were incumbent president Gerald Ford with Senator Robert Dole of Kansas as his vice president.

Running against Watergate and the Washington establishment was a key point of the Carter strategy. The Nixon pardon was Ford's main drawback, and nothing the president said or did could prevent Americans from considering it and wondering if it had been the correct action. Then Carter provided more fodder for the media when *Playboy* published an interview with him, which quoted the former governor as saying he had lusted after many women and "committed adultery in my heart many times."[21] His language had sometimes been coarse, and worse for Democrats, he had combined Nixon and Johnson in the same breath as being lying presidents. The story caused a maelstrom of protests and titillation.

Then with weeks to go before the election, the first debate was held. Carter insisted on calling his opponent "Mister Ford" rather than "Mister President," so Ford would not have an undue

APR 24–25: Operation Eagle Claw fails to rescue Iran hostages; eight US troops are killed

JUN 23–SEP 6: Record-breaking high temperatures and drought across the US caused thousands of deaths and billions in damages

JUN 27: 19- and 20-year-old males are required to register for a peacetime military draft

NOV 4: Reagan defeats incumbent Carter in presidential election

JUL 27: Deposed Shah of Iran dies in Egypt

AUG 7–14: Lech Walesa leads strikers at the Gdansk shipyard in Poland, first of many such strikes

SEP 17: Solidarity trade union established in Poland

SEP 22: Iraq initiates Iran-Iraq War

DEC 8: Former Beatle John Lennon dies, shot by a deranged fan, in New York City

advantage. He also tried to have the stage altered so that Ford's four-inch height superiority would not be shown on television, but when the cameras rolled, Ford did look presidential and Carter appeared nervous and unsure of himself as he attacked "Mister Ford." Round one went to the president, but he lost the advantage in the next debate on foreign policy when announcing that the Soviets did not dominate Eastern Europe. Carter won the third debate as well; this time he referred to Ford as "Mister President."

Apparently disillusioned by the entire political process, the American people came to the polls in low numbers and voted for Jimmy Carter, who captured 50 percent of the vote, with Ford winning 48 percent. Carter took 297 electoral votes to Ford's 240. Soon after the election, Carter's pollster, Pat Caddell, wrote an analysis of the voting for his boss focusing on perceived weaknesses, including his obvious inexperience and status as an unknown, as well as the perception that he frequently flip-flopped on issues.[22] Now the nation waited to see how a Washington outsider, the first president elected from the Deep South since Zachary Taylor in 1848, would do.

PRESIDENT CARTER

On January 20, 1977, the thirty-ninth president took the oath of office and asked the nation to "create together a new national spirit of unity and trust." Then he and Rosalynn eschewed the traditional limousine ride and instead walked hand in hand the 1.2 miles from the Capitol to the White House. Once in the residence, Carter naturally wanted to head to the Oval Office, but had no idea how to find it, so he told the Secret Service where he planned to go and followed them there. That night he recorded in his diary: "I have a feeling of almost unreality about my being President, but also a feeling of both adequacy and determination that I might live up to the historical standards established by my predecessors."[23]

The next day he signed his first executive order, which granted amnesty to the draft evaders; he immediately heard thunderous protests from thousands, especially the Veterans of Foreign Wars. Barry Goldwater called the president's action "the most disgraceful thing a president has ever done."[24]

More changes were soon announced by the new president. He antagonized longtime staff members when he announced that the White House was reducing costs by requiring all of its staff to take a 10 percent pay cut (which did *not* include the president's salary); he also sold the presidential yacht, and insisted on carrying his own baggage (explaining he would not want to lose his bag). Like Nixon, Carter preferred not to have cabinet meetings for decision-making but insisted that the cabinet meet weekly for each member to present his/her weekly report. Since all received the reports, attendees found the meetings redundant and a waste of time.

Being a Washington outsider made working with Congress a rather prickly situation, and Speaker "Tip" O'Neill attempted to explain this to Carter, but the president was not interested in O'Neill's advice. Although Democrats controlled both houses, they felt no particular loyalty to the head of their party and refused to enact his legislation.

Carter greatly admired Truman and wanted to succeed where his mentor had failed—passing national health care legislation. He blamed the failure on fellow Democrat, Massachusetts senator Edward Kennedy, who also wanted national health care but insisted it be *his* health care plan. Kennedy criticized Carter's plan, and in his memoirs, the former president wrote: "It was a tragedy that his unwillingness to cooperate helped spell the doom of any far-reaching reforms of the health-care system."[25]

Economically, the country had suffered greatly from the dual problems of inflation and unemployment; even though the Ford administration had successfully cut inflation to 6 percent, unemployment still lingered at nearly 8 percent. The House approved the president's proposal to grant a fifty dollar rebate to all taxpayers in hopes that it would stimulate the economy. But when the Senate balked, Carter withdrew the plan, antagonizing many congressional leaders who felt betrayed by his lack of support. Others shared their sense of betrayal when it became clear that Carter would not become a "spending" president, as was Johnson. Civil rights leaders, the heads of unions, and mayors of cities all complained that the president's reality was not measuring up to his campaign promises. Carter was more intent on balancing the budget—no easy task since he had inherited a deficit of over sixty-six billion dollars from the Ford administration— but he believed it was possible to achieve by the end of four years. He did allay some criticism when he signed legislation in 1977 for increased food stamps. Two years later he won praise for breaking the Department of Education away from Health and Welfare by creating its own cabinet post.

This was also the era of deregulation in the hopes that more competition would result in lower prices and better products. Telephone's "Ma" Bell was broken apart to spawn a family of "baby Bells," and the airlines were deregulated, as was the trucking industry. Some of these changes would result in the decline and bankruptcy of numerous businesses.

Developing an energy program was high on the president's list, and he explained that it was significantly tied to the country's security. America had to find alternative resources rather than remain dependent on the whims of foreign nations and the geo-political game of oil. Wearing a sweater in a "fireside chat" for television, Carter explained his program, asking all to do their share by conserving energy, and promised to send a bill to Congress within the next three months. Eventually an energy bill passed both houses that called for deregulation of oil prices and tax credits for energy conservation as well as the creation of a cabinet post—secretary of energy; James Schlesinger was appointed to be the first energy czar. One of the administration's accomplishments was the passage of a windfall-profits tax for the oil companies.

Pollster Pat Cadell advised the new president to present himself as close to the people, an image diametrically opposed to that of Nixon, whose shadow still hung over American politics. The president borrowed from FDR and implemented his own televised "fireside chats" showing Carter, sitting relaxed by a fire wearing his sweater and explaining various policy decisions to Americans at home. The president also visited several town meetings early in his term and met with ordinary Americans to hear their concerns; sometimes he also stayed overnight in their homes. After a few months, these occasions ceased, partly out of impracticality (especially from a Secret Service standpoint), and they no longer seemed needed to introduce the president to his constituents.

In 1977, President Carter finalized an agreement that had been thirteen years in the making—a treaty with Panama that would grant that nation the right to control the Panama Canal and surrounding Canal Zone as of December 31, 1999. Military leaders as well as conservatives, including California governor Ronald Reagan, decried it as nearly treason to give away something built by the United States, and many voiced concerns about region's security once it slipped from American hands. Carter received support from both party leaders in the Senate—Majority Leader Harry Byrd of West Virginia and Minority Leader Howard Baker of Tennessee as well as former president Gerald Ford and his secretary of state, Henry Kissinger, who successfully lobbied Republican senators. Still many Democrats lacked enthusiasm for the handover. Ultimately, the Senate approved the treaty, and in 1979, a twenty-year process began that ultimately ended with Panama taking control over the canal. Although Panamanian leader General Omar Torrijos was pleased by the news, he had an alternate plan should the treaties fail passage: sending in troops to destroy the canal with explosives.

While the president expressed hope to the Soviets that the spirit of détente could be renewed, he also voiced criticism for human rights violations within the Soviet Union and their satellites. Both sides tentatively moved toward further arms reductions, and in 1979, Carter and Soviet premier Leonid Brezhnev signed the Strategic Arms Limitation Talks II (SALT II) pact promising that the US and USSR would limit themselves to 2,250 strategic weapons each. Some in the Senate

DID YOU KNOW?

★★★★★★★★★★

Carter was the first president born in a hospital.

DID YOU KNOW?

Carter was the first president to send his mother on a diplomatic mission.

believed that Carter had not been tough enough, especially after it was learned that without monitoring stations in Iran, compliance by the Soviet Union would be extremely difficult to verify. The Senate refused to ratify the SALT II treaty, but both nations still voluntarily abided by its terms. Other foreign matters soon weighed in.

Carter's insistence on pushing human rights resulted in over a hundred thousand Jews being allowed to flee the USSR; moreover, numerous groups began sprouting in Eastern Europe, including Solidarity in Poland. Others would later credit his actions with providing the foundation that his successor, Ronald Reagan, would use to crush the Soviet power structure. Carter pushed to build up NATO forces and add more American troops to their number. The president also saw military increases in weapons and spending as essential to ensuring the Soviet presence at the bargaining table; however, he did emphatically oppose construction of the B-1 bomber and blocked its funding.

American-Soviet relations deteriorated further with the Soviets' invasion of Afghanistan in 1979, to prop up its Marxist regime. Carter led opposition to this aggression and the following year won support of the UN General Assembly to call for a withdrawal of foreign troops from that nation. When that failed to prod the Soviets into leaving, the United States again led the way as more than sixty nations boycotted the Olympic summer games in Moscow. Embargoes against grain and technological sales were also enacted by the US government against the Soviets. In his State of the Union speech in January 1980, President Carter announced the Carter Doctrine, which said the "attempt by any outside force to gain control of the Persian Gulf region will be regarded as an assault on the vital interests of the United States." Its result could end in military action.

Desirous of continuing Nixon's efforts to improve relations with China, Carter and his diplomatic staff redoubled efforts to expedite the process by inviting Deputy Minister Deng Xiaoping to the United States. While many in the world applauded efforts to have two of its superpowers meet, not all in the US, or particularly Taiwan, were pleased by the announcement on December 15, 1978, that as of January 1, 1979, the US would recognize the People's Republic of China. (Taiwan was assured that previous agreements would be met, including arms sales for the next year.) The Soviet Union also feared improved Sino-American relations and temporarily established a few more roadblocks to the SALT II pact. The Carters were captivated by Xiaoping when he arrived in January 1979 to a round of diplomatic talks (the Middle East and Korean situations were frequently discussed) and cultural events around Washington. The visit went well, and the main objective of improving America's relations with China had been achieved.

President Carter's greatest efforts in foreign policy involved relations with Egyptian president Anwar Sadat and Israeli prime minister Menachem Begin. At Camp David, the three leaders met together, and separately, as they attempted to turn back historical differences in the elusive search for peace. Carter wrote that when he and Begin conferred, the president reminded the prime minister of "the consequences of failure, and the fact that the present influence in the Middle East of both Israel and the United States if we demonstrated to the world that we could not find peace." Carter maintained that neighboring countries including Iran, Saudi Arabia, and of course Egypt, could be drawn into a regional war: "All of them were needed to provide a stabilizing effect on the region in the face of building radical pressures."[26] The leaders argued, visited, and dined together. Much of Carter's frustration dealt with a reality voiced by Sadat: "Some things in the Middle East are not logical or reasonable."[27] The president's patient negotiations paid off, and after nearly two weeks of negotiations in September 1978, the three leaders met and produced the Camp David Accords proclaiming their intention:

> *"After four wars during 30 years, despite intensive human efforts, the Middle East, which is the cradle of civilization and the birthplace of three great religions, does not enjoy the blessings of peace. The people of the Middle East yearn for peace so that the vast*

human and natural resources of the region can be turned to the pursuits of peace and so that this area can become a model for coexistence and cooperation among nations."

This Framework for Peace in the Middle East, and more importantly, the Framework for the Conclusion of a Peace Treaty, became the basis for a formal peace treaty signed in March 1979, which effectively ended hostilities between Egypt and Israel. Other countries in the region would be less inclined to agree to its provisions, however.

MALAISE SPEECH ★ On July 15, 1979, President Carter addressed the nation about a "crisis of spirit" that seemed to permeate the country. (This soon was dubbed the "malaise" speech.) Some of his advisors had told him that he needed to be seen as exercising more leadership, and he told his cabinet that he did not deserve to be reelected the next year if he could not do a better job. Hoping to change directions, he then accepted the resignations of five cabinet members.

IRAN

While peace appeared to be gaining a foothold in one area, it seemed impossible elsewhere. In November 1977, Shah Reza Pahlavi of Iran visited the United States and when asked what problems he feared the most, he replied, "growing terrorism."[28] The shah was caught between two worlds—one embracing traditional Muslim customs, and a modern democratized society. In the fall of 1978, Carter recorded in his diary: "The Shah has moved very rapidly and has alienated a lot of powerful groups, particularly the right-wing religious leaders who don't want any changes made in the old ways of doing things."[29] A year later, one of those dissident religious leaders, the Ayatollah Khomeini, and his militant followers took action against the shah's democratization of society by seizing a group of more than sixty Americans at the US Embassy in Teheran. In return for the hostages, their captors demanded that the United States detain the shah, who had traveled to New York City for medical treatment, and send him back to Iran. These Iranian militants blamed him and the United States for all of the country's ills; however, their leader, Ayatollah Khomeini, ordered his soldiers to release all women and blacks but keep the remaining fifty-two captives. Soon the sight of blindfolded hostages being paraded in front of cameras on the nightly news seemed to mock the president and the power of his office. Was the United States capable of freeing its citizens, or was it merely a nation being held hostage by Islamic radicals?

Hoping to exert substantial diplomatic pressure, the president won support from the UN Security Council, which ordered Iran's release of the hostages, but nothing happened. All Iranian diplomats were expelled; travel to Iran by Americans was forbidden; and Iranian assets were seized by the US government, but still the hostages remained in captivity.

Finally, the president decided to take military action and ordered a rescue in April 1980, but this soon turned into a fiasco, with helicopters malfunctioning while deep in Iran. Then two of them collided at a secret refueling point codenamed Desert I, killing eight. The United States appeared to the world inept and unable to defend its interests. Previous to the hostage crisis, former British prime minister Howard McMillan had proclaimed this presidency as "the weakest American Administration in my lifetime."[30] Now many others concurred in his assessment, and with the presidential election only a few months away, Carter was especially mindful of the growing criticism. He later wrote of the Desert I fiasco, "I am still haunted by memories of that day."[31]

After the botched rescue, the hostages were relocated into smaller groups in various locations. Hopes for their return with the shah's death in July soon evaporated, and Khomeini demanded the late leader's assets be turned over, as well as those that had been frozen. But soon Iran had its own problems when its neighbor Iraq attacked, hoping to seize oilfields near the border. In an effort to support any entity that wished to suppress Iran, the United States was soon sending aid to the leader of Iraq, Saddam Hussein.

DID YOU KNOW?

Carter is a speed-reader and can read over 2,000 words a minute.

Closer to home, Americans grew dismayed in April 1980 by the arrival of tens of thousands of Cuban refugees in what was called the Mariel boatlift. (Earlier Castro had uncharacteristically announced that anyone who wanted to leave Cuba could do so, and soon the Cuban port of Mariel was mobbed by thousands of people eager to leave their island for the US and its freedom.) Their arrival put a strain on the federal government as well as the state of Florida, which received the majority of the new immigrants, many of whom were mentally ill or former prisoners—or both. Angry American taxpayers blamed the president for allowing the surge of immigrants to be allowed into the country, thus creating a burden on the nation's resources.

> ***It is difficult for the common good to prevail against the intense concentration of those who have a special interest, especially if the decisions are made behind locked doors.***
>
> —*Jimmy Carter*

ELECTION OF 1980

The president attempted to curb rising inflation as he geared up for his reelection campaign. Interest rates declined, and a recession developed from a severe drop in consumer spending. Carter still wanted a balanced budget, but members of Congress from both sides of the aisle disagreed. Some backed Republican governor Ronald Reagan's call for tax cuts, while others supported Senator Edward Kennedy's pleas for increased domestic spending. More and more disgusted by the lack of action, Carter fumed: "There is no discipline and growing fragmentation in Congress. . . . They are running out of time, and I am running out of patience. This is a new low in performance for the Congress since I've been in office."[32]

Fed up by Carter's definite conservative bent and refusal to promote liberal programs, Senator Edward Kennedy decided to launch a strong opposition and gain the Democratic nomination for himself. The two men battled through the primaries, with Carter winning all but ten states, but still Kennedy had the popularity of the convention's delegates when he addressed them in New York in August 1980. Carter was nominated once more, as was his vice president, Walter Mondale, following Kennedy's weak show of party solidarity. Their Republican challenger would be the former governor of California, Ronald Reagan.

The two presidential candidates disagreed on nearly every issue, and the Iranian hostage crisis cast a huge shadow over Carter's presidency that he could not escape. Moreover, allegations of his younger brother Billy improperly accepting Libyan funds for airplane sales cast more aspersions on the Carter name. At the end of their debate on October 28, Reagan told the voters to ask themselves if they were better off now than they were four years earlier. Resoundingly, Americans decided they were not—inflation was higher, gasoline was in shorter supply, and of course, Iran had become a hotbed of controversy. Jimmy Carter won forty-nine electoral votes to Reagan's 489 (third-party candidate John Anderson received none).

As he prepared to leave office, Carter was puzzled by the incoming staff's unwillingness to be briefed on Iran—Secretary of State Designate Alexander Haig refused and Caspar Weinberger, Secretary of Defense Designate, likewise declined. With Algerian officials acting as intermediaries, final negotiations were made to free the eight billion dollars in Iranian assets in return for the American hostages. As a final slap to Carter, the Iranians waited until Ronald Reagan had been sworn in as the fortieth president before releasing the fifty-two Americans. The next day, President Reagan asked Carter to fly to Germany to greet the freed Americans.

RETIREMENT

Upon returning to Georgia, the former president threw himself into the planning and creation of the Jimmy Carter Presidential Center and Library in Atlanta, and it opened in stages beginning in January 1987. He also began writing his memoirs, including *Keeping Faith: Memoirs of a President* in 1982, followed by *Everything to Gain: Making the Most of the Rest of Your Life* (with Rosalynn Carter) in 1987. Since then he has produced nineteen other books on a variety of topics.

Carter has also traveled the world extensively, sometimes officially, sometimes for personal reasons. When, in 1981, he was sent with former presidents Nixon and Ford to Anwar Sadat's funeral, he struck up a friendship with Gerald Ford that the two men enjoyed until Ford's death in December 2006. During President Clinton's administration, Carter went to North and South Korea to discuss nuclear disarmament. Frequently the former president has been an official observer in nations where fear of voting fraud was a legitimate concern, including in Panama, Nicaragua, Haiti, Zambia, and Palestine.

Foremost on his agenda of causes is targeting human rights abuses, and he is willing to go anywhere in the world to put his message into action. In 1978, Carter became the first president to visit sub-Saharan Africa, but his interest in that continent did not diminish once he left office. He supported the end of apartheid in South Africa and urged its president, Pieter Botha, to free Nelson Mandela. Also in 1985, Carter created Global 2000, the purpose of which was to alter Africa's projected path of starvation by developing productive farmland via scientific agriculture. He also championed the start of majority rule in Zimbabwe. According to the former president, work in Africa "gives me the most satisfaction of all my endeavors."[33]

Carter's globetrotting was not always viewed favorably by sitting presidents. He attempted to negotiate with China and Vietnam without the Reagan administration's approval, and worked for twenty years to win recognition for the Palestinian Liberation Organization (PLO) and the right for that group to have its own homeland. He raised more eyebrows when the *New York Times* printed an op-ed piece by him regarding his objections to Iranian author Salman Rushdie's book, *The Satanic Verses*, calling it "a direct insult" to Islam and stating that any Western leaders protecting Rushdie are endorsing his beliefs against "our Moslem friends."[34]

In 1988, former presidents Ford and Carter joined forces to develop the American Agenda, whose purpose was to investigate issues and develop position papers that would benefit whoever became the next president. The two men targeted the need for a balanced budget by 1993 and recommended reducing military spending, as well as taxing items, including gasoline, alcohol, and tobacco, to raise additional monies. They presented their report to president-elect George W. Bush in late November, but it did not have the effect they had hoped. Ford later lamented, "Bush praised our report, then never implemented any of our recommendations."[35]

When Democratic president Bill Clinton took office in 1991, he and Carter did not get along, partly owing to an episode during Clinton's governorship when Cuban refugees had been ordered by the Carter administration to be locked up at Fort Chaffee in Arkansas. When some of them broke out, Governor Clinton had to call in National Guard troops, after which he demanded reassurance from the president that no more Cubans would be placed at the fort. President Carter agreed, and then went back on his word. The incident became one of the main

HABITAT FOR HUMANITY ★ A nonprofit Christian organization building housing for those in need around the world, Habitat for Humanity was founded in 1976 by Millard and Linda Fuller, who approached Jimmy Carter to serve on their board of directors. Later, Carter took a more active role and worked on construction projects. Habitat for Humanity has built more than 200,000 homes for low-income families, thanks to the efforts of its volunteers.

BOOKS BY JIMMY CARTER ★ *Why Not the Best?* (1977); *Keeping Faith: Memories of a President* (1982); *Negotiation: The Alternative to Hostility* (1984); *The Blood of Abraham: Insights into the Middle East* (1985; reprinted with additional material, 1993); *Everything to Gain: Making the Most of the Rest of Your Life* (with Rosalynn Carter, 1987); *An Outdoor Journal: Adventures and Reflections* (1988; 1994); *Turning Point: A Candidate, A State and a Nation Come of Age* (1992); *Talking Peace: A Vision for the Next Generation* (1993); *Always a Reckoning, and Other Poems* (1995); *A Government as Good as Its People* (1996); *Little Baby Snoogle-Fleejer* (1996); *Living Faith* (1996); *Sources of Strength: Meditations on Scripture for a Living Faith* (1997); *The Virtues of Aging* (1998); *An Hour Before Daylight: Memories of a Rural Boyhood* (2000); *Christmas in Plains: Memories* (2001); *The Nobel Prize Peace Lecture* (2002); *The Personal Beliefs of Jimmy Carter* (2002); *The Hornet's Nest: A Novel of the Revolutionary War* (2003); *Sharing Good Times* (2004); *Our Endangered Values: America's Moral Crisis* (2005); *Palestine: Peace Not Apartheid* (2006); *Lessons from Life: Personal Reflections with Jimmy Carter* (2012).

campaign issues. Clinton blamed his gubernatorial defeat at the polls on Carter's broken promise, and now the new president barely mentioned Carter's name when talking about influential Democrats. At the inauguration festivities, the Carters were ignored, causing Rosalynn Carter to remark that the Clinton treatment of them was "rude beyond belief. Not even Reagan would have done a thing like that."[36]

The relationship grew even more strained when Carter took it upon himself to visit North Korea in the hope of negotiating a treaty that would prevent the country from developing nuclear weapons. He was not acting at the behest of the White House or State Department, nor did he keep them informed. They learned of the substance of his talks by watching interviews on CNN. President Clinton became so upset he refused to meet Carter for a debriefing in Washington, and various columnists and Republicans assailed Carter for his presumptuousness and naiveté.

During George W. Bush's presidency, Carter often spoke out against the Republican policies, especially when he was campaigning for his son Jack's unsuccessful bid for Nevada congressman. Carter stated that under Bush's guidance, the country had launched "an ill-advised invasion of Iraq based on false premises, false statements, and this has been the major international debacle that our country has brought on Americans." He also criticized Bush for making the "country more sharply divided than it has ever been," and went on to say that, "the American government stand[s] convicted around the world as one of the greatest abusers of civil rights."[37]

Mrs. Carter maintains her passionate crusade, begun when her husband was governor and continued while she was First Lady, to raise awareness of mental health issues. She also developed the Rosalynn Carter Institute for Human Development in 1987 to study the issue of caregiving.

Both the former president and first lady frequently contribute their time and energies to Habitat for Humanity projects throughout the country. Starting in 1984, Carter amazed all when he avoided the political turmoil of an election year to work on rehabbing a six-story New York City apartment building. Those thinking this was merely a publicity stunt or an attempt to rehabilitate his own image were mistaken. Every year, the former president and first lady donate a week to working on a Habitat for Humanity project somewhere in the world (sites have included South Africa, India, and within the US). When President George H.W. Bush talked of volunteerism and his "Thousand Points of Light," many believed Jimmy Carter exemplified that ideal.

Besides his construction projects, the former president continued to make headlines. In 2002,

Carter became the recipient of the Nobel Peace Prize in recognition of his efforts to bring peace to the Middle East when president. (Carter was the second president to receive the honor; Theodore Roosevelt received his in 1906 for helping to negotiate the end of the Russo-Japanese War.)

One accolade near and dear to Carter's heart is the tribute by Anwar Sadat related by Sadat's widow when Jimmy and Rosalynn visited in 1983: "Jimmy Carter is my very best friend on earth. He is the most honorable man I know. Brilliant and deeply religious, he has all the marvelous attributes that made him inept in dealing with the scoundrels who run the world."[38]

ENDNOTES

1 Peter G. Bourne, *Jimmy Carter*, New York: Scribner, 1997, p. 23.

2 Ibid, p. 27.

3 Jimmy Carter, *An Hour Before Daylight*, New York: Simon & Schuster, pp. 180-181.

4 Ibid, p. 181.

5 Ibid, p. 256.

6 Ibid, p. 62.

7 Jimmy Carter, *Why Not the Best?,* Nashville, TN: Broadman Press, 1975, p. 48.

8 *Washington Post*, November 27, 1976.

9 Ibid.

10 Bourne, p. 81.

11 Rosalynn S. Carter, *First Lady from Plains*, New York: Ballantine Books, 1984, p. 46.

12 Bourne, p. 140.

13 *Atlanta Constitution*, December 14, 1971.

14 Bill Adler, *The Wit and Wisdom of Jimmy Carter*, Secaucus, NJ: Citadel Press, 1977, p. 89.

15 Victor Lasky, *Jimmy Carter: The Man and the Myth*, New York: Richard Marek Publishers, 1979, p. 189.

16 Ibid, p. 194.

17 *Time*, March 8, 1976.

18 Lasky, p. 191.

19 Ibid, pp. 210-211.

20 Carter, *An Hour*, p. 266.

21 Robert Scheer, "Playboy Interview: Jimmy Carter," *Playboy*, November 1976.

22 Patrick H. Caddell, "Initial Working Paper on Political Strategy," December 10, 1976.

23 Jimmy Carter, *Keeping Faith*, New York: Bantam Books, 1982, p. 23.

24 Bourne, p. 366.

25 Carter, *Keeping*, p. 87.

26 Ibid, p. 335.

27 Ibid, p. 379.

28 Ibid, p. 435.

29 Ibid, p. 438.

30 William Safire, *The New York Times*, January 4, 1979.

31 Carter, *Keeping*, p. 518.

32 Ibid, p. 529.

33 Douglas Brinkley, *The Unfinished Presidency*, New York: Viking Press, 1998, p. 197.

34 Jimmy Carter, "Rushdie's Book Is an Insult," *New York Times*, March 5, 1989.

35 Brinkley, p. 251.

36 Ibid, pp. 370-371.

37 Speech, September 28, 2006, at Reno, Nevada, by Jimmy Carter.

38 Ibid, p. 106.

Ronald Reagan

★ ★ ★ FORTIETH PRESIDENT ★ ★ ★

LIFE SPAN
- Born: February 6, 1911, in Tampico, Illinois
- Died: June 5, 2004, in Simi Valley, California

NICKNAMES
- Dutch, the Gipper, Ronnie, The Great Communicator

RELIGION
- Disciples of Christ

HIGHER EDUCATION
- Eureka College, 1932

PROFESSION
- Actor

MILITARY SERVICE
- Second lieutenant in US Army Reserve; after December 7, 1941, called up for active service; served in US Army (April 1942–July 1945) and was promoted to captain

FAMILY
- Father: **John "Jack" Edward Reagan** (1883–1941)
- Mother: **Nelle Wilson Reagan** (1885–1962)
- First wife: **Jane Wyman** (1914–2007); wed on January 26, 1940, near Hollywood, California
- Children: **Maureen Elizabeth** (1941–2001); **Michael** (1945–); **Christine** (1947)
- Second wife: **Nancy Davis Reagan** (1923–); wed on March 4, 1952, in San Fernando Valley, California
- Children: **Patricia Ann "Patti" Davis** (1952–); **Ronald Prescott** (1958–)

POLITICAL LIFE
- Governor of California (1967–1975)

PRESIDENCY
- Two terms: January 20, 1981–January 20, 1989
- Republican
- Reason for leaving office: completion of term
- Vice president: **George H.W. Bush** (1981–1989)

ELECTION OF 1980
- Electoral vote: **Reagan** 489; **Jimmy Carter** 49
- Popular vote: **Reagan** 43,899,248; **Carter** 35,481,435

ELECTION OF 1984
- Electoral vote: **Reagan** 525; **Walter Mondale** 13 (Reagan won highest number of electoral votes of any president)
- Popular vote: **Reagan** 54,281,858; **Mondale** 37,457,215

CABINET

SECRETARY OF STATE
Alexander M. Haig Jr. (1981–1982)
George P. Shultz (1982–1989)

SECRETARY OF THE TREASURY
Donald T. Regan (1981–1985)
James A. Baker (1985–1988)
Nicholas F. Brady (1988–1989)

SECRETARY OF DEFENSE
Caspar W. Weinberger (1981–1987)
Frank C. Carlucci (1987–1989)

ATTORNEY GENERAL
William French Smith (1981–1985)
Edwin Meese (1985–1988)
Richard Thornburgh (1988–1989)

SECRETARY OF THE INTERIOR
James G. Watt (1981–1983)
William P. Clark (1983–1985)
Donald P. Hodel (1985–1989)

SECRETARY OF AGRICULTURE
John R. Block (1981–1986)
Richard E. Lyng (1986–1989)

SECRETARY OF COMMERCE
Malcolm Baldridge (1981–1987)
William Verity Jr. (1987–1989)

By 1980, Americans were in desperate need of a positive message. People remained weary from the turbulent '60s and the strife of the Vietnam War. They had been angered by the seeming betrayal by President Nixon during Watergate and in the late 1970s, humiliated by Iranian militants who had held fellow Americans hostage for a year while the world's most powerful nation appeared woefully impotent. Then a tall grandfatherly looking man reminded them of the nation's greatness and promised that there would be a "new day in America." He preached that America not only was good but could still do better. Heartened by his message, voters resoundingly elected Ronald Reagan president. The country's makeover had just begun.

EARLY LIFE

In 1904, Nelle Wilson married Jack Reagan, who sold shoes in a variety of stores and towns around Illinois. They had two sons: Neil (nicknamed "Moon") in 1909, and two years later, Ronald was born in an apartment above a bakery in Tampico, Illinois, on the sixth of February. Taking one look at his ten-pound newborn son, Jack joked, "He looks like a fat little Dutchman."[1] "Dutch" Reagan would be his name until he reached Hollywood.

After a series of stops in small towns and a brief stint on Chicago's South Side, the Reagan family moved to Dixon in 1920, and there they stayed. Dutch loved the small town nestled in the Illinois Rock River valley and home to ten thousand inhabitants, providing enough people to host plenty of activities but small enough for people to get to know each other. Reagan enjoyed hiking cliffs towering over the river that also offered its own recreation—skating in winter and swimming in the summer.

The Reagan family never boasted of wealth; in fact, Neil was sent to the butcher's on Saturdays to ask for liver for their cat. They never owned a cat; the liver was their Sunday dinner. Nelle used oatmeal as a breakfast item as well as mixing it with hamburger for their noonday meal; bones were used to make a week's worth of soup. In later years, Reagan frequently remarked that he never realized his family's poverty when he was young. "I never thought of our family as disadvantaged. Only later did the government decide that it had to tell people they were poor."[2] The family's secret was Jack's drinking, which could send him on long binges and occasionally force Nelle to wrap up her sons and take them to a relative's home. Christmas was the worst time, Dutch recalled, because it was likely Jack would resume his drinking, and that threat cast a pall upon the joy of the coming holiday for the Reagan family.

Every night Nelle read to her sons, and Dutch acquired the skill by following his mother's finger across the words on the page. When he was five years old, his father caught him looking at the newspaper and was amazed that he was actually reading it. Jack Reagan ran to the neighbors to brag about his son and invited them to come and hear him read to them.

Dutch excelled in school; he wanted to do well in sports, but found himself handicapped by small stature and limited athletic skills. He did not realize that most of his problem was due to poor eyesight. Once the problem was determined and new eyeglasses made, Dutch developed more self-confidence. His short height prevented him from playing football in his first years of high school, but once he experienced a growth spurt his junior year and reached nearly five feet eleven, he played right guard—a position that did not

NATIONAL EVENTS

AIDS epidemic begins to be recognized

JAN 20: Ronald Reagan sworn in as 40th president and 52 American captives in Iran are released

MAR 6: Walter Cronkite signs off for the last time after 19 years hosting the CBS *Evening News*

MAR 19: Three workers killed during a test of space shuttle Columbia

MAR 30: Outside a Washington hotel, President Reagan is shot by John Hinckley, who also shoots

1981

WORLD EVENTS

JAN 1: Greece joins the European Community, later the European Union (EU)

JAN 19: Agreement reached between US and Iran to release American hostages held for over a year

JAN 21: The first De Lorean, a stainless steel sports car with gull-wing doors, rolls off the production line in Northern Ireland

JAN 22: The sole terrorist survivor of the Iranian Embassy siege in London pleads guilty and is jailed for life

FEB 13: Rupert Murdoch buys *The Times* and *The Sunday Times* for £12 million

require that he wear glasses. Reagan later described why he "loved playing on the line: for me, it was probably a marriage made in heaven. It's as fundamental as anything in life—a collision between two bodies, one determined to advance, the other determined to resist."[3]

During the summers, Reagan put his strong swimming skills to work as a lifeguard at the Rock River beach. During the seven summers he worked there, he rescued seventy-seven people from drowning. He saved his earnings of fifteen dollars a week for college.

In high school, Dutch developed a talent his mother Nelle also enjoyed—acting. She participated in local theatricals and encouraged her two sons to join, as well. In high school, a new English and drama teacher increased the number of plays produced in the school year, and young Reagan eagerly auditioned and participated in all that he could. He also joined the band as a drum major. The self-confidence he lacked a few years before had been acquired thanks to sports and acting, plus winning election as class president. All indicators pointed to success, and Dutch decided to attend college.

Reagan picked nearby Eureka College, a private school operated by the Disciples of Christ. Part of his reason to attend there was his desire to be close to his girlfriend, Margaret Cleaver, who would also be a freshman. His major hindrance was its cost. His four hundred dollars in savings would not cover all tuition and living expenses, so he was awarded a needy student scholarship and worked at his fraternity house serving meals and doing dishes. Besides being a member of the Tau Kappa Epsilon fraternity, Reagan also worked to land a spot on the football team, but spent his freshman year watching from the bench.

During his first year, Reagan did experience another type of thrill, becoming politically active. To combat growing economic woes, the new college president proposed major cutbacks that would jeopardize graduation for the upperclassmen, and some professors would lose their jobs. Reagan spoke to a crowd of students and professors about the harm of the board's decision and the need to take action by striking. The audience rallied to Reagan's words and he found himself enthralled by the power he wielded. The student strike won the changes they desired, and the new president resigned.

Academics were less important to him than his sports activities, including swimming and track, and Reagan finally earned the right to play football by impressing his coach during practice. He also participated in student government, the yearbook, booster club, and was seriously dating Margaret Cleaver, who now wore his fraternity pin. Dutch also performed in the variety of plays staged at Eureka, and when they participated in a contest at Northwestern University against the drama departments of the eastern Ivy League schools, Eureka placed second, and Reagan captured one of three individual acting awards. The head of Northwestern's speech department urged Reagan to consider an acting career.

RADIO CAREER

Although he graduated in June 1932 with a degree in economics, radio was where Reagan wanted to begin his career. He hitchhiked to Chicago and began knocking on doors of radio stations, only to have them slammed in his face for his lack of experience. Heeding the advice of a station manager who told Dutch that he needed to start somewhere smaller, and then work his

CABINET

★★★★★★★★★★

(continued)

SECRETARY OF LABOR

Raymond J. Donovan (1981–1985)

William E. Brock (1985–1987)

Ann Dore McLaughlin (1987–1989)

SECRETARY OF HEALTH AND HUMAN SERVICES

Richard S. Schweiker (1981–1983)

Margaret M. Heckler (1983–1985)

Otis R. Bowen (1985–1989)

SECRETARY OF HOUSING AND URBAN DEVELOPMENT

Samuel R. Pierce Jr.

SECRETARY OF TRANSPORTATION

Andrew "Drew" Lewis (1981–1983)

Elizabeth H. Dole (1983–1987)

James H. Burnley (1987–1989)

SECRETARY OF ENERGY

James B. Edwards (1981–1982)

Donald P. Hodel (1982–1985)

John S. Herrington (1985–1989)

SECRETARY OF EDUCATION

Terrel H. Bell (1981–1985)

William J. Bennett (1985–1988)

Lauro F. Cavzos (1988–1989)

press secretary James Brady, a Secret Service agent, and a police officer

APR 12–14: First space shuttle (Columbia) flight successfully completed

MAY 6: Maya Lin's design for the Vietnam Veterans Memorial unanimously wins competition

JUN 12: Major league baseball players strike for over one-third of the season

AUG 1: MTV debuts

FEB 23: A coup d'état fails in Spain.

MAR 11: Chilean President Augusto Pinochet is sworn in for another 8-year term

APR 1: Daylight saving time introduced to Soviet Union

MAY 13: Assassination attempt on Pope John Paul II at St. Peter's Square by a Turkish gunman; Pope survives his wound

MAY 21: French Socialist François Mitterand elected president

MAY 25: Gulf Cooperation Council formed in Riyadh between Bahrain, Kuwait, Oman, Qatar, Saudi Arabia, and the United Arab Emirates

BOOK/MOVIE CREDITS ★ While most presidents can boast a book or two (and Ronald Reagan wrote two: *Where's the Rest of Me? The Ronald Reagan Story* [with Richard G. Hubler], 1965, and *An American Life: The Autobiography*, 1990), no other president can claim movie credits. During his acting career, Reagan made 53 movies, including *Love is in the Air* (his first film, 1937); *Hell's Kitchen* (1939); *Knute Rockne—All American* (Reagan's personal favorite, 1940); *King's Row* (1942); *This is the Army* (1943); *Night Unto Night* (1949); *Bedtime for Bonzo* (1951); *Hellcats of the Navy* (co-starring his wife, Nancy Davis, 1957); and *The Killers* (final film, 1964). He was also one of the first actors to transition to the new medium of television. There he hosted *GE Theater* (1954–1962) and *Death Valley Days* (1964–1966) before he decided to enter politics and run for governor.

way up to the large Chicago market, he traveled to Davenport, Iowa, home of station WOC. Dutch auditioned by giving a play-by-play of an imaginary football game that was so convincing he won the job of sports announcer. After a few months of post-season unemployment, Reagan then became a staff member of WOC and a disc jockey, and although his first months of talking on the air were rather wooden, he worked to improve his delivery. It paid off. When WOC closed, the parent company moved Reagan to Des Moines and gave him the sports announcer position at WHO, a station with one of the most powerful transmission signals in the country. Reagan was ecstatic and thrilled that, in the midst of the Depression, he was earning seventy-five dollars a week.

Meanwhile Jack Reagan, a lifelong Democrat, was rewarded for party faithfulness by being named head of the local relief programs. Dixon residents soon came looking for help to feed their families and ensure they did not lose their homes. He found jobs for them, which were appreciated at first, but soon refused because they would no longer be provided handouts if they were working. When Jack was appointed the head of the local Works Progress Administration office, he faced the same problem when relief officials warned workers from accepting jobs since they already received money for *not* working. His son wrote the lesson learned: "The first rule of a bureaucracy is to protect the bureaucracy."[4] Years later, he, too, would encounter its harsh truth.

Dutch enjoyed his four years in Des Moines, but received a letter from Margaret Cleaver, who returned his fraternity pin and engagement ring, saying she had fallen in love with someone else. Heartbroken by the news, Reagan began looking for a new challenge and an escape from Iowa's long cold winters. He worked out a deal to cover both the Chicago Cubs and the Chicago White Sox in spring training in California.

CALIFORNIA AND A CAREER CHANGE

While in southern California, Reagan looked up a singer he knew from WHO, Joy Hodges, who was performing at a nightclub at the Biltmore Hotel. The two enjoyed dinner, and he told her of his dream to become an actor. Joy told him to lose the glasses and then referred him to an agent.

The next day, he visited agent Bill Meiklejohn, who called Warner Brothers studios telling them he had "another Robert Taylor." Immediately Reagan was sent to the studio for a screen test. Dutch returned to the Cubs' training camp and

NATIONAL EVENTS

AUG 3: Professional Air Traffic Controllers Organization (PATCO) strike

AUG 5: All striking PATCO employees are fired by President Reagan for refusing to return to work as he had earlier ordered; US air service reduced

AUG 9: Baseball season resumes after strike ends

AUG 12: IBM markets its first personal computer

WORLD EVENTS

MAY 30: Bangladesh president assassinated

JUN 6: Bihar train disaster in India: 800 killed when 7 coaches of an overcrowded train fall off the tracks into the river

JUN 13: At Trooping the Colour ceremony in London, teenager fires blank shots at Queen Elizabeth II; she is not injured, but he is arrested

JUL 17: Israeli bombers destroy PLO headquarters in Beirut

JUL 29: Wedding of Prince Charles and Lady Diana Spencer at St. Paul's Cathedral

told Warner that he could not wait for the decision by studio head Jack Warner, but needed to return to Iowa. Once in Des Moines, Reagan received a telegram offering him a seven-year contract at two hundred dollars a week. Without hesitation, he sent Meiklejohn his reply: "SIGN BEFORE THEY CHANGE THEIR MINDS DUTCH REAGAN."[5]

In June 1937, Reagan was reinvented, from his hair to his name—"Dutch" had to go. The studio agreed to let him keep his given name, Ronald. He was quickly assigned small parts in B movies, and soon received a raise. He invited his parents to move to California, and Jack began working as an assistant, answering his son's mail. Dutch enjoyed the easygoing lifestyle of the west coast, learned how to surf, and spent many free hours horseback riding. He hoped to move up the studio ladder and in 1940, he finally managed that feat by starring in the movie he long wished to make, *Knute Rockne—All American*, where he portrayed George Gipp, better know as "the Gipper." With accolades from this role, he then starred as Custer opposite Errol Flynn in *Santa Fe Trail*.

During this time, Reagan was also settling down to family life—he married actress Jane Wyman in January 1940. The two had met during filming of *Brother Rat* in 1938 and continued their relationship when they starred in the sequel. Gossip columnist Louella Parsons offered her mansion as the site for the nuptials; afterward the couple moved to a home in Beverly Hills. The following year, they welcomed daughter Maureen. Then in 1945, they adopted a son, whom they named Michael. Another daughter was born prematurely in 1947 but lived only a day. As often happens in Hollywood with acting couples, they grew apart as her career escalated and his seemed stalled. Wyman insisted that much of the reason for their breakup was due to Reagan's growing participation in the Screen Actors Guild. The final divorce was granted in July 1959, leaving her with the children. Reagan was depressed by the divorce, and many friends agree it was his lowest point emotionally.

During World War II, Reagan was ordered to duty at Fort Mason, California. In 1937, he had joined the Army Reserve and was a second lieutenant at the time he was called up. His extremely poor vision prevented him from going overseas, so he was sent to Army Air Force Intelligence in Los Angeles, where he made recruiting and training films. Another duty included screening film footage and making classified films to be sent to the military chiefs in Washington. Reagan and his crew watched in horrified silence as scenes from Nazi concentration camps flickered on the screen. He decided to keep one of the films just in case it might be needed in the future, and years later, he pulled it out when a producer questioned the stories of the Holocaust. Reagan left the service in July 1945 with the rank of captain.

When he returned to his acting career, Reagan became increasingly involved with different organizations, and started speaking out against the potential dangers of communism. He also found himself in the midst of a labor dispute as a director of the Screen Actors Guild, which dragged on for months. During this time, Reagan received a late-night visit from FBI agents asking for his help in informing on activities and persons associated with the Communist Party and the movie industry. Reagan agreed to keep his eyes and ears open. One group that Reagan had joined as a member of its board was the Hollywood Independent Citizens Committee of the Arts, Sciences, and Professions (HICCASP); however, he soon discovered that it was a front for the Communist Party and quickly resigned.

SUPREME COURT APPOINTMENTS

Sandra Day O'Connor, 1981

William H. Rehnquist, Chief Justice, 1986

Antonin Scalia, 1986

Anthony M. Kennedy, 1988

AUG 13: President Reagan signs into law country's largest tax cuts and federal budget cuts in history

AUG 19: Sandra Day O'Connor is first female appointed to US Supreme Court

AUG 24: Mark David Chapman sentenced to 20 years to life for the murder of John Lennon

NOV 23: President Reagan authorizes CIA to recruit Contra rebels in Nicaragua

DEC 28: In Virginia, the first test-tube baby is born

AUG 19: Gulf of Sidra incident: American fighter jets destroy Libyan fighter jets

OCT 6: Egyptian President Anwar Sadat assassinated by members of Egyptian Islamic Jihad organization who opposed Egypt's negotiations with Israel for peace

NOV 30–DEC 17: Arms talks in Geneva between representatives of US and USSR

DEC 13: Martial law declared in Poland due to growing unrest and resistance to communism

STATE OF THE UNION

US POPULATION IN 1981
226,542,199

NATIONAL DEBT IN 1989
$2,857,430,960,187

Alarmed by this incident, Reagan decided that he needed to fight the attempts by the Communists to take over the movie industry, so in 1947, he ran for and won the presidency of the Screen Actors Guild. He then testified before the House Un-American Activities Committee; he urged fellow actors to do the same to ensure their names were clear of any Communist connections.

Finding his career going nowhere, Reagan voiced his frustrations in an interview with Bob Thomas in the *Los Angeles Mirror* in January 1950. He said, "I'm going to pick my own pictures. I have come to the conclusion that I could do as good a job of picking as the studio has done. . . . At least I could do no worse. . . . With the parts I've had, I could telephone my lines in and it wouldn't make a difference." Such talk greatly angered Jack Warner, who fired a letter back to his actor: "If you are not satisfied with the roles you have portrayed in the past, and undoubtedly you will have the same attitude with respect to future roles, I would greatly appreciate your sending me a letter canceling our mutual contractual obligation."[6]

As SAG president, Reagan was called upon to help a young actress, Nancy Davis, who shared the same name as another actress who was a known Communist. Reagan tried to reassure her and continued his attempts over dinner. They soon were dating and on March 4, 1952, they wed at the Little Brown Church, with William Holden and his wife Ardis serving as best man and matron of honor.

The elder Reagan children attended boarding school and now hoped to move in with their father and new stepmother. Life with Jane Wyman for Michael sometimes meant being struck ten times on the leg by a riding crop for misbehavior. He longed to spend more time with his father and fondly remembered the occasional hunting they did together. Later Michael stated, "Dad could give his heart to the country but he just found it difficult to hug his own children."[7] Maureen also found it easier to confide in Nancy than her mother, but they continued their exile to boarding schools and were ordered by their mother to convert to the Catholic faith.

Meanwhile the other Reagan family expanded with the birth of daughter Patricia Ann Davis in October 1952. With Ronald receiving few acting roles, they needed money, so Nancy took one last movie role and costarred in *Donovan's Brain,* and then retired from acting.

Her husband was not retired, but he was not acting much either, thanks to the demise of the studio system. No longer were actors contracted by a single studio; they were now all freelancers. While that provided them more freedom in their roles, they no longer were guaranteed work. One venue that did offer employment was the new medium of television. Reagan was offered the position of host of *General Electric Theater*, and acted occasionally, as well. General Electric's chairman, Ralph Cordiner, also asked Reagan to tour various GE plants and simply chat with the workers and answer questions as a means of extending the company's goodwill to its multiple assembly plants.

His talks became so popular that he frequently was invited to address local service organizations, and he was soon being asked to speak before even larger gatherings. Besides talking about Hollywood, he tried to tie his remarks to the workers' lives. They came to him offering their personal stories and asking questions, and this dialogue became a training ground for the future politician. Espousing his views against the growth of big government and the encroachment of individual

NATIONAL EVENTS

Voicemail patented by Texas Instruments

MAY 2: The Weather Channel airs for the first time

MAY 5: A Unabomber bomb explodes at Vanderbilt University

MAY 9: President Reagan responds to Brezhnev's announcement of arms reduction with his own proposal

JUN 1: US Supreme Court rules that police may search vehicles (including any closed containers) without a warrant if they have "probable cause"

1982

WORLD EVENTS

MAR 10: US initiates embargo against Libyan oil, in retaliation for Libya backing terrorists

MAR 16: Soviet leader Brezhnev announces his country will halt deploying more nuclear weapons in Europe

APR 1: Panama Canal Zone now policed by Panama

APR 2–JUN 14: Falklands War: Argentina invades Falkland Islands; British ultimately retake islands

APR 17: Queen Elizabeth II grants Canada its full independence from the United Kingdom

liberties became the focus of Reagan's remarks rather than a pat speech on the wonders of being a Hollywood actor.

The Reagans enjoyed a comfortable lifestyle thanks to General Electric, who built them a house perched above the Pacific Ocean and packed it with GE appliances and gadgets that could be used as advertising on the show. The Reagans also bought a ranch in the Santa Monica Mountains where they could spend hours riding horses. In 1958, they welcomed a son whom they named Ronald Prescott. Life seemed tranquil, and two years later, Reagan decided after leading an actors' strike to resign from his leadership of the Screen Actors Guild to become a producer.

By the election of 1960, Reagan had decided to take an active part in campaigning. Although he considered himself a Democrat, he grew disenchanted with the growing tendency by many to focus on social programs that increased taxes and promoted dependency—"a welfare state of mind." Reagan was convinced that even Franklin Roosevelt's New Deal programs were never intended to be permanent. Although he had spoken against Richard Nixon when he ran for the Senate in 1948, he decided to support him in 1960 for the presidency. Joe Kennedy attempted to convince Reagan that he should not switch sides (especially against his son John), but Reagan insisted he was going to support Nixon, although he waited two more years to officially change his party affiliation.

After General Electric changed management and instructed Reagan they wanted him to become more of a salesman, he refused, so they canceled the show. Then in 1964, he made his final movie, *The Killers*, in which he played a villain for the first and only time in his career. Apparently moviegoers were not impressed and the movie did poorly at the box office. Reagan, however, was soon back at work on another television series—*Death Valley Days*. He played host for the western and bragged that often he filmed his part still wearing his ranch clothes.

JELLY BEANS ★ When Reagan quit smoking in the 1960s, he substituted jelly beans for his nicotine cravings and always had a candy dish sitting on his desk. He offered them to visitors during his governorship in California and continued the practice as president. For his first inauguration, 40 million jelly beans were consumed by partygoers. During his two terms, the sales of jelly beans climbed.

POLITICS BECKONS

When Barry Goldwater became the Republican presidential candidate in 1964, Reagan happily volunteered to campaign for him since their views on the role of government were nearly identical. He served as co-chairman of the California campaign and frequently appeared at fundraising gatherings. Impressed by one of his typical speeches berating the growth of government and its wastefulness while people were watching their own rights decrease, a group of Republicans decided to buy air time on NBC for Reagan to deliver his speech nationally. So a week before the election, Reagan looked into the camera and told the American people why he had changed parties. He criticized Lyndon B. Johnson's Great Society program and Johnson's comment that "we must accept a 'greater government activity in the affairs of the people.'"[8] The speech was a success, raising eight million dollars for the Goldwater campaign and boosting Reagan's credentials as a Republican Party

JUN 12: 750,000 rally in Central Park against nuclear weapons

JUN 30: Proposed Equal Rights Amendment (ERA) fails ratification by its deadline

JUL 8: Coke introduces Diet Coke

JUL 16: The Reverend Sun Myung Moon is sentenced to 18 months in jail and fined $25,000 for tax fraud

AUG 25: US Marines are deployed to Beirut to oversee the PLO withdrawal from Lebanon

APR 25: Israel withdraws from Sinai Peninsula

JUN 6: Lebanon War starts when Israeli forces move into southern Lebanon to combat Palestinian terrorists who use Lebanon as a sanctuary

JUN 8: President Reagan becomes first American president to address a joint session of British Parliament

JUL 9: Intruder breaks into Queen Elizabeth's bedroom at Buckingham Palace; she is not harmed

AUG 12: Mexico unable to pay its foreign debt, prompting economic crisis that spreads into other Latin American nations

DID YOU KNOW?

Reagan was the first president to have been divorced.

Reagan was the first president who had also been the president of a labor union.

spokesman. After the Republican loss in the election and the lack of support by moderate Republicans, Reagan told a group of Los Angeles County Young Republicans, "We don't intend to turn the Republican Party over to the traitors in the battle just ended. The conservative philosophy was not repudiated," he argued. "We will have no more of those candidates who are pledged to the same socialist philosophy of our opposition."[9]

By now, Republican power players in California began working to convince Ronald that he should contemplate running for governor of California. Maureen had already broached the subject with her father, but while he began to like the idea, Nancy was not so keen about embarking on the campaign trail. Soon a group calling themselves Friends of Ronald Reagan started the drive to draft him, and in January 1966, he announced his candidacy.

Running for governor with no political experience was a handicap that he faced both in the primary and in the general election against Democratic incumbent Edmund (Pat) Brown, who reminded voters, "I'm running against an actor, and you know who killed Abe Lincoln, don't you?"[10] The Hollywood community was divided over supporting and opposing Reagan. Some were close friends but disagreed with his political stance. Richard Nixon wrote letters of support from his law office in New York City. Meanwhile Governor Brown reminded voters that he was "entitled to be reelected. It is ludicrous that the Republican Party would nominate a man without experience," and reminded Californians that he was, after all, "the greatest governor"[11] they had ever had.

To help cover more territory, Nancy also campaigned, although she acknowledged she was hesitant to do so because of a fear of public speaking. Reagan's staffers, however, managed to convince her that appearances across the state would help her husband, so Nancy consented and gradually began liking the experience. One facet of Reagan's life that the party wanted to ignore for fear it would torpedo the campaign was his divorce from Jane Wyman and the two children from that marriage. At one appearance, Maureen Reagan was to speak but was given prepared remarks that totally ignored her and Michael and talked about the two children of Ronald Reagan—Patti and Ron. Dispensing with the canned speech, Maureen related a personal anecdote about herself and Michael with their father. Brown reminded Californians of Reagan's B-movie background by showing clips of *Bedtime for Bonzo*, where Ronald co-starred with a chimp. It did Brown little good, for on November 8, 1966, the voters of California made Reagan their next governor by a nearly million-vote margin.

GOVERNOR REAGAN

Reagan wanted to be sworn in at precisely one minute after midnight on January 1, 1967, the moment when Governor Brown ceased serving. Seven-year-old Ron fell asleep in his grandmother's arms while the rest of the family witnessed his father taking the oath of office underneath the California state capitol rotunda. Then the official swearing in took place publicly a few days later, followed by thousands flocking to the Inaugural Ball, which included some of Hollywood's Republican celebrities.

Nancy hated living in the governor's mansion, which was dilapidated and rundown, with peeling wallpaper and furniture that looked to have been purchased from a second-hand store. She decided the mansion needed major renovations, so the family moved to a more upscale Sacramento home. The Reagans' circle of friends became more affluent as

NATIONAL EVENTS

NOV 13: Vietnam Veterans Memorial dedicated

Cabbage Patch dolls introduced

First cellular phone systems begin in US

MAR 8: President Reagan calls Soviet Union the "evil empire"

MAR 23: President Reagan recommends a strategic defense initiative (SDI) that would destroy enemy missiles in space; program nicknamed "Star Wars" by its detractors

1983

WORLD EVENTS

OCT 1: Sony Corporation releases its first compact disc

FEB 7: Iran invades Iraq

APR 15: First Disney park outside of US opens in Tokyo

APR 18: US embassy in Beirut is bombed and 63 die

SEP 1: Korean airliner shot down over USSR killing all 269 on board

some of them introduced Ron and Nancy to others, including department store heir Alfred Bloomingdale and media magnate Walter Annenberg. Many of these new friends donated furnishings for their new residence.

The California legislature remained in Democratic hands following the 1966 election, and they were in no mood to approve the new governor's plan to trim his predecessor's social programs. Jesse "Big Daddy" Unruh was speaker of the assembly and immediately squared off against Nancy. He attacked the move from the governor's mansion and renting another home filled with new furniture; she replied that they paid the rent, and the new furnishings belonged not to them, but the people of California. She also began to steadily gain a reputation as her husband's most influential aide. Michael Deaver, who worked with Reagan in both Sacramento and Washington, explained that Nancy Reagan did not become involved because of an interest in politics. "Her only agenda was Ronald Reagan, and there was nobody alive who better knew his strengths and weaknesses." Others talked about Nancy's Bureau of Investigations, whom she entrusted to watch for anyone not faithful to her husband. Deaver acknowledged that had it not been for her, "Ronald Reagan would never have become governor of California let alone president of the United States. He knew this better than anyone."[12]

Reagan signed an abortion bill, which he hailed as a victory, since the original one allowed for abortion if the parents thought the baby might have some defect, and he argued it was a short journey from that position to Hitler creating the master race. This bill allowed for abortion if the mother's mental health was in jeopardy or if the pregnancy was caused by rape or incest.

Another major hurdle for the new governor was untangling the financial mess left by the previous administration. The budget had a two hundred million dollar deficit that grew daily, and his appointee as director of finance, Caspar Weinberger, explained that the state's budget had been increasingly in the red, but by making it part of the next fiscal year, they managed to hide it from the public. Within two weeks of his taking office, Reagan was required to provide a balanced budget to the state legislature that would take effect July 1. Drastic cuts were made in projected construction, hiring freezes instituted, and a 10 percent budget cut levied on all state agencies. He had to wage war with the Democrats, and pass a tax increase, but eventually California's budget crisis subsided. Then another dilemma emerged—a budget surplus! When Weinberger asked the governor what to do with the extra money, Reagan immediately suggested giving it back to the taxpayers in the form of a rebate. There would be more to come.

The Vietnam War was the main event of this era, and student protests on college campuses had multiplied and grown more violent. Student leaders from nine University of California campuses asked to meet with the governor. One of their representatives explained, "It's sad, but it's impossible for the members of your generation to understand your own children. . . . You weren't raised in a time of instant communications or satellites and computers. . . . You didn't live in an age of space travel and journeys to the moon." Reagan replied, "You're absolutely right. We didn't have those things when we were your age. We invented them."[13] Then in 1970, when rioting hit the UC campus at Santa Barbara, he deployed the National Guard to bring order to the university and announced, "If it takes a bloodbath, let's get it over with."[14]

APR 26: "Nation at Risk" report on America's schools released

JUN 18: Sally Ride becomes first American woman astronaut in space

AUG 30: Guion Bluford becomes first African American astronaut to travel in space

SEP 17: Vanessa Williams is first African American woman to win Miss America title

OCT: First Lady Nancy Reagan introduces "Just Say No" anti-drug campaign

SEP 6: Soviet Union says it did not realize Korean airliner was a passenger plane when it violated Soviet airspace

OCT 13: Island of Grenada has a coup d'état

OCT 23: Suicide truck bombings in Beirut killing more than 300 people, mostly Americans

OCT 25: US invades Grenada

NOV 11: Reagan is first American president to address Japanese Diet (legislature)

Reagan agreed to run for reelection and easily won a second term in 1970. Welfare reform was now targeted, since its rolls were rapidly growing and threatened to absorb any surplus gained by the governor's fiscal actions. Reagan took his case to the people and explained the problem. He wanted the needy and handicapped to continue to receive their checks, but those who were able-bodied and fraudulently working the system needed to be removed. Californians agreed and buried their legislators under mountains of mail. Reagan won his reform.

Content that the state was now in better shape thanks to his efforts, he approved a fourth rebate to the taxpayers, prompting a top Democrat to exclaim, "Giving that money back to the people is an unnecessary expenditure of public funds." Reagan later bragged about his record, claiming that he and his team "had made the state government less costly, smaller, and more businesslike . . . we made the bureaucracy more responsive to the public; and we began to return some of the power and taxing authority usurped by the state from local communities back to where it belonged, at the local level."[15]

Happy to leave Sacramento, the Reagans left for what they believed would be a brief respite before he ran for the presidency.

BRIEF RESPITE

The original Reagan ranch had been sold soon after his taking office, but they had acquired another property near Santa Barbara that they named Rancho del Cielo, "Ranch in the Sky." They remodeled the small house there, and the couple loved every minute at their hideaway. Early in his governorship, Reagan had developed an ulcer, which had since healed, but this quiet interlude allowed the sixty-five-year-old to grow more robust. He also contemplated his future and the pleas by friends and fellow Republicans that he should make a run for the presidential nomination in 1976. The idea grew in its appeal over the coming months.

The main opposition to Reagan's candidacy was incumbent Gerald Ford and his vice president, Nelson Rockefeller. Many conservatives feared that the liberal-spending New Yorker would win the White House, and they desperately needed someone to counter his influence. They chose Ronald Reagan, who briefly flirted with the idea of creating a third party.

Reagan spent 1975 traveling the lecture circuit and writing columns, both of which proved quite lucrative for the former governor. He attacked the president indirectly by reminding his audience that the mandate of 1972 was in danger of being ignored. Ford did not take Reagan's threatened opposition seriously and twice offered him cabinet posts (Transportation and Commerce), which were turned down. Some Republicans genuinely feared a Reagan run for the nomination as extremely divisive for the party that was still reeling from the Watergate debacle.

In September 1975, Reagan gave a speech to the Executive Club in Chicago and stated his basic theory of the need for government decentralism. He decried the federal government's poor record solving society's problems and argued that a "transfer of authority" would save "more than $90 billion. . . . With such a savings, it would be possible to balance the federal budget, make an initial $5 billion payment on the national debt, and cut the federal personal income tax burden of every American by an average of 23 percent."[16] Ford's campaign team immediately jumped on this and

NATIONAL EVENTS

NOV 2: Martin Luther King Day proclaimed as a national holiday for third Monday every January

Crack cocaine first appears in Los Angeles

JAN 1: AT&T breaks into 22 Bell companies

JAN 24: First Apple Macintosh computers on sale

MAY 8: Longest major league baseball game in history played between Milwaukee Brewers and

1984

WORLD EVENTS

DEC 27: Pope visits and forgives his would-be assassin

Ethiopia suffers multi-year famine

FEB 26: US Marines leave Beirut

MAR 5: Iran accuses Iraq of using chemical weapons

MAR 5: India Prime Minister Indira Gandhi orders attack on Sikh holy place of Harimandir Sahib

decision "convinced people who might have thought otherwise that I meant what I said."[28]

At the same time as the showdown with PATCO, the president was deciding whom he wanted to place in nomination to fill a vacancy on the Supreme Court upon the retirement of Justice Potter Stewart. His attorney general, William French Smith, drew up a list of potential candidates, and after interviewing his first choice, he decided to nominate Sandra Day O'Connor from the Arizona Court of Appeals as the first woman on the US Supreme Court. The Senate voted 99 to 0 for her confirmation.

Early in his presidency, Reagan spoke of the need to wage ideological war against the Soviet Union in the western hemisphere. He addressed Congress in April 1983, reminding them of the proximity of Central America and that their "problems do directly affect the security and well-being of our own people." He asked what would happen to our own prestige abroad if Central American nations fell to communism: "If the United States cannot respond to a threat near our own borders, why should Europeans or Asians believe that we're seriously concerned about threats to them?"[29] Reagan called for free and open elections in Latin America, as well as the end to their own arms race. Although some greeted the president's speech with a yawn, Congress responded by granting millions of dollars in aid.

In 1986, Reagan had another historic opportunity to change the Supreme Court when Chief Justice Warren Burger retired, so the president appointed the most conservative member, William Rehnquist, to the position and nominated Antonin Scalia as his replacement, who also breezed through the confirmation. The next would not prove to be so easy. In 1987, Justice Lewis Powell resigned, and Reagan chose Robert Bork as his replacement. Senate liberals tore his opinions apart and told Americans that Bork was totally against civil rights. The Senate rejected Bork by a vote of fifty-eight to forty-two. Ultimately Anthony Kennedy of the Ninth Circuit Court of Appeals in California was confirmed as Powell's replacement.

The economy began to improve, and the tax cuts proved a mixed blessing. They did drive down the inflation rate, which was at 13 percent when Reagan entered office but only about 5 percent when he left office eight years later. Unemployment also declined considerably after initially increasing to a record high of nearly 11 percent, making it the worst rate since the Great Depression. The rate was half of that by the end of Reagan's administration. While gains were made in those two areas, the national debt rose astronomically. In October 1981, it hit the trillion-dollar mark, and continued to rise, with yearly deficits totaling over one hundred billion dollars. The campaign promise of achieving a balanced budget fell victim to ballooning budgets in certain areas, particularly defense. Here the United States engaged in an arms war with the Soviet Union that ultimately led to that nation's dissolution.

In February 1983, the president used the term "evil empire" to describe the Soviet Union; for many this was perceived as shockingly inflammatory rhetoric. In fact, the state department attempted to remove the phrase from his speech, but Reagan insisted on keeping it. That same speech urged the West to realize that the Soviets "are the focus of evil in the modern world," and Reagan stated that the Cold War was a clear example of the "struggle between right and wrong, good and evil."[30] Later that year, tensions worsened with the shooting down of a South Korean airliner when the plane

FEB 27: US Senate approves televising its activities on a trial basis

SEP 26: William Rehnquist becomes chief justice of Supreme Court following Warren Burger's retirement

OCT 28: Centennial celebration of the Statue of Liberty

NOV 4: Midterm elections result in Democrats regaining control of the Senate

NOV 25: Attorney General Edwin Meese admits that US had diverted funds from selling arms to Iran to use to aid Contra rebels in Nicaragua

FEB 25: Ferdinand Marcos leaves Philippines, where he has ruled for 20 years, and goes into exile in Hawaii

APR 5: Libya is blamed for bombing of a West Berlin discotheque popular among US servicemen that kills three and injures 200 more

APR 15: US planes bomb targets in Libya including Muammar al-Qaddafi's headquarters, killing 15 (some are Qaddafi's children)

APR 26: Largest nuclear disaster at Chernobyl plant in the Ukraine kills 31, many more are harmed, and vast areas declared uninhabitable

OCT 11: Reagan and Gorbachev meet at Reykjavik, Iceland, to discuss disarmament, but talks break down

DID YOU KNOW?

When he was president, Reagan bought a hearing aid, and soon sales for those also rose.

flew into Soviet airspace. All 269 crew and passengers were killed, including a Georgia congressman.

Reagan had steadfastly maintained that Soviets lied a great deal, so negotiating with them was a waste of time. Added to this stance was his insistence that America's military be upgraded and enlarged to turn around the cutback trend of the Carter years. New programs were instituted, including the Stealth bomber and Trident submarines; the B-1 bomber was resumed, while the MX missile program continued with modifications for their placement. More than five hundred missiles were to be placed in Europe in the early 1980s to deter any Soviet action in that quarter. Angered by this show of force, the Soviets attempted to break the will of the Europeans and some Americans by orchestrating a "nuclear freeze" in Western Europe. Celebrities, former diplomats, and current politicians on all levels joined these protests, but the president would not be swayed from his course and commented that he saw no peace demonstrations in Moscow. Reagan firmly believed that the Soviets would not win this contest of wills; supporting him in this were two strong allies—Prime Minister Margaret Thatcher of Great Britain (whose kindred spirit made her a good friend of the president's) and Chancellor Helmut Kohl of West Germany.

Reagan proposed a nuclear arms reduction for both the United States and the Soviet Union as the basis for Strategic Arms Reduction Talks (START). The goal was for the Soviets to withdraw their intermediate range missiles already targeting Western Europe, and in exchange, the Americans would not deploy their new missiles. When asked by negotiator Paul Nitze what to tell the Soviets if they balked at giving up their weapons for ones not even in the field yet, the president said, "Well, Paul, you just tell them that you're working for one tough son of a bitch."[31] Negotiators were told not to fret if the Soviets walked out of their meetings; Reagan reassured them that they would return. Then in 1985, a new leader emerged in Moscow who was more willing to talk with the American president about the future of their respective countries, and Reagan would spend much of his second term working with Mikhail Gorbachev.

The western hemisphere would also keep the new administration extremely busy attempting to quash various fires before they spread. The first occurred only days into his first term when Reagan decided to end aid to Nicaragua as punishment for its providing arms to the El Salvadoran leftist guerrillas, the Sandinistas. The administration did, however, provide aid to the Contra guerrillas in their quest to seize control of Nicaragua from the Communist regime. Congress determined that such action was unlawful and forbid it in 1984 under the Borland Amendment. National Security Advisor John Poindexter and his aide, Lieutenant Colonel Oliver North, covertly continued sending help to the Contras by using money collected from selling arms to Iran, which was engaged in a bloody struggle against its neighbor Iraq under Saddam Hussein.

Throughout this period, Americans were being kidnapped on a regular basis in Lebanon. Targeting Libya as one of the key terrorist-supported nations, Reagan announced in 1981 that all Libyan diplomats were to leave the United States. Problems still continued for Americans in the Middle East, especially in unstable Lebanon, where in 1983, sixteen were killed at the US Embassy in Beirut. There, six months later, trucks laden with explosives were driven into the Marine barracks, killing 241 servicemen. The age of terrorism had begun.

NATIONAL EVENTS

NOV 26: President Reagan announces formation of Tower Commission to investigate Iran-Contra allegations

MAR 4: President Reagan admits that aid to Iran had been used to help rescue hostages

MAR 17: New law requires appliance manufacturers to make their products energy efficient

MAY: In Washington state, first undisturbed Clovis (first people in Americas, dating more than 11,000 years ago) site found

MAY 11: First heart-lung transplant

1987

WORLD EVENTS

JAN 16: Ecuador's president Leon Cordero kidnapped

JAN 20: Archbishop of Canterbury's envoy to Beirut, Terry Waite, is kidnapped

FEB 22: Syrian troops move in and occupy West Beirut

FEB 23: Supernova first observed by astronomers

APR 13: Portugal agrees to return Macau to China in 1999

On the same day as the bombing of the Marines in Beirut, the president received an anguished message from Eugenia Charles, prime minister of Dominica, requesting assistance in Grenada. Pro-Communist activists had slain the Marxist leader, Maurice Bishop; moreover, thousands of Cubans resided there whose purpose Charles believed was to assist in the takeover. The presence of more than a thousand American medical students on Grenada studying at St. George's Medical College posed the disturbing possibility that a second hostage situation was in the making, and the president discussed their fate with his advisors. Once the military agreed that they could go in and extricate the students, Reagan gave the green light.

> ***"Democracy is worth dying for, because it's the most deeply honorable form of government ever devised by man."***
>
> —*Ronald Reagan*

For three days in late October 1983, US troops, combined with those of several Caribbean nations, fought Communist-led forces, including the Cubans, who were well supplied with Soviet weapons. Nineteen Americans died during the fighting, but the students were rescued, and order was restored to the island nation. This was the first effective military action since the days of Vietnam, and although some congressional leaders denounced the invasion and a few even called for the president's impeachment, all was forgotten when the cameras showed the first American student running off the plane and kissing the ground of the South Carolina airbase. For the first time in many years, the American people had pride in their country.

In 1983, the president mentioned his plans for the Strategic Defense Initiative (SDI) as a means for the United States to combat nuclear missile attacks from the Soviets by having ballistic missiles or lasers target incoming nuclear warheads and destroy them above the earth's atmosphere; in short, the war would occur in space rather than in the United States. Criticism was heaped upon Reagan for his belief that such a fanciful idea could work, and soon SDI was dubbed "Star Wars" by its most vociferous critic, Senator Ted Kennedy of Massachusetts. The president, however, did not mind the comparison, since those movies were precisely what he was warning about—the clash of good versus evil.

Even his arms control advisor, Kenneth Adelman, received the news with skepticism; he later admitted that the president's strength was that he was not a "'hidden hand' president who played his cards under the table. His true genius was that he put all his cards on the table and still managed to win most of the time."[32] Reagan's concern about America's lack of defense dated to his pre-campaign days of 1979 when he visited NORAD at Cheyenne Mountain, Colorado, and learned there was no means to prevent a missile attack; we only had monitoring capabilities. Moving ahead to research if such a program was feasible would do no harm, the president insisted over the objections of those clamoring that it would violate the terms of the Anti-Ballistic Missile Treaty of 1972. Arguing that the treaty would not cover this program, the administration pushed ahead with SDI while the Soviet Union fearfully observed and began programs in an attempt to counteract it.

AUG 4: Fairness Doctrine (required television and radio stations to present controversial points of view fairly) is rescinded by FCC

SEP 17: 200th anniversary of the Constitution is celebrated

NOV 18: Congressional panels charge that President Reagan is ultimately responsible for any wrongdoing in Iran-Contra scandal

MAY 17: USS *Stark* in Persian Gulf is hit by Iraqi missiles; more than 50 American sailors killed or injured

JUN 12: President Reagan visits Berlin and issues a challenge for Gorbachev to "tear down this wall!"

DEC 1: Construction on English Channel tunnel begins

DEC 8: Reagan and Gorbachev sign Intermediate-Range Nuclear Forces Treaty in Washington, D.C., that eliminates medium-range intermediate nuclear missiles

DID YOU KNOW?

Reagan was the only president to have been wounded during an assassination attempt and survive.

1984 CAMPAIGN

When the Republicans met in August 1984, there was no speculation about who the nominees for president and vice president would be. Veering from tradition, both Reagan and Bush were nominated and affirmed together in a single roll-call vote. Although some of the moderates worried that Reagan's conservative tone would isolate them, the party pushed forward his agenda, including balancing the budget amendment and the absolute refusal for any tax increase.

Democrats nominated Senator Walter Mondale of Minnesota and made history by making Congresswoman Geraldine Ferraro of New York his running mate. They opposed the various arms programs and demanded higher taxes for the wealthier citizens, as well as corporations.

Reagan and Mondale debated twice, and the president performed poorly in the first debate, stumbling over his words and faltering for answers. Immediately the public and the press speculated that his age was a prime concern—perhaps he was in no shape to run for office, let alone remain in that office another term. Nancy Reagan was indignant, blamed her husband's staff for his poor showing, and demanded that they revamp the way they prepped him for debates. This they did, and it was a much more confident and typical Reagan who countered the charge that age was a problem when asked by Henry Trewhitt of *The Baltimore Sun*. "Not at all, Mr. Trewhitt," Reagan replied. "I want you to know that also I will not make age an issue of this campaign. I am not going to exploit, for political purposes, my opponent's youth and inexperience." Typical Reagan humor had just disarmed the key concern of the campaign.

A week later, Reagan won reelection by a landslide victory, taking 59 percent of the popular vote to Mondale's 41 percent. In the electoral college, the numbers were even more lopsided—Reagan captured 525 votes to Mondale's thirteen (his home state of Minnesota and the District of Columbia). The electoral total was the highest won by any candidate in history.

SECOND TERM

Foreign policy matters would continue to take center stage for his second term. Soviet leader Mikhail Gorbachev met with Reagan for the first time in Geneva, Switzerland, in November 1985 and then again at Reykjavik, Iceland, in February 1986. Immediately the men found each other affable and approachable. Although nothing was decided at Geneva, they talked both formally and informally numerous times and agreed to meet in each other's countries in the future. When they shook hands, Reagan said, "I bet the hard-liners in both our countries are bleeding when they see us shaking hands."[33] Gorbachev smiled and nodded in agreement.

The meeting at Reykjavik did not go well. By now, Reagan had announced his intention to no longer abide by the terms of the Strategic Arms Limitation Talks (SALT) II as agreed to by his predecessor Jimmy Carter. He believed the Soviets had already violated its content, so why remain true to it ourselves, he asked. At Reykjavik, talks seemed to be progressing nicely with Gorbachev until he mentioned that all hinged on the United States giving up SDI. Reagan exploded and reminded the Soviet leader that SDI was not on the bargaining table. He attempted to convince Gorbachev that the technology was not to be feared; in fact, he had learned that the Soviets were developing their own SDI program. Nothing would change Gorbachev's mind. Realizing that SDI was the true target of the

NATIONAL EVENTS

FEB 3: US House of Representatives rejects president's request to send over $36 million to Nicaragua to help Contras

MAR 16: Lt. Col. Oliver North and Vice Admiral John Poindexter are indicted on charges of conspiracy to defraud the United States

JUN 29: US Supreme Court allows special prosecutors to investigate suspected crimes by officials of executive branch

JUL 20: Democratic National Convention nominates Michael Dukakis as its presidential candidate and Lloyd Bentsen as vice president

AUG 18: Republicans nominate Vice President George H.W. Bush and Dan Quayle

1988

WORLD EVENTS

JAN 1: Soviet leader Gorbachev initiates economic reforms (perestroika)

FEB 5: Gen. Manuel Noriega, dictator of Panama, is indicted in Florida for accepting bribes from drug traffickers

MAY 15: Soviet troops begin withdrawing from Afghanistan after being there more than eight years

AUG 20: Iran-Iraq War ends

DEC 7: Earthquake in Armenia kills nearly 25,000 and leaves thousands more injured and homeless

negotiations only made the president more upset. He looked to Secretary of State George Schultz and told him they were leaving, and so Reagan walked out of the summit.

The following month, Reagan ordered that covert operations against Soviet forces in Afghanistan be escalated. Up to this point, mujahadeen guerrillas had received enough technical material and aid to encourage their continued resistance, but increased Soviet support for revolutionary groups in Central America was now matched—and surpassed—by US efforts on the Soviets' own doorstep. This US aid, and especially the transfer of satellite imagery and Stinger shoulder-fired missiles to defend against Soviet helicopter gunships, helped turn the tide in the guerrillas' favor.

Also in the spring of 1986, Reagan took action against the head of Libya, Colonel Mu'ammar Qadhafi, who had ordered earlier attacks on Americans, including the bombing of a West Berlin disco popular with American servicemen. One serviceman was killed and fifty other Americans were wounded (along with 230 others who were hurt in the blast, including a Turkish woman who was killed). With irrefutable evidence that Qadhafi was behind the attack, the president ordered F-111s to bomb Qadhafi's presidential palace in Tripoli. Reagan assured Americans and the world that after attempting "quiet diplomacy, public condemnation, economic sanctions, and demonstrations of military force," he decided to take action. After the bombing, Libya withdrew from overtly practicing terrorism.

A year later, President Reagan appeared on national television and said, "A few months ago I told the American people I did not trade arms for hostages. My heart and my best intentions still tell me that's true, but the facts and the evidence tell me it is not." He went on to discuss the Tower Report, which reviewed activities and blew the whistle on the Iran-Contra dealings of NSA chief John Poindexter and Lieutenant Colonel Oliver North. Reagan admitted that he took "full responsibility for my own actions and for those of my administration. As angry as I may be about activities undertaken without my knowledge, I am still accountable for those activities. As disappointed as I may be in some who served me, I'm still the one who must answer to the American people for this behavior."[34] The

REAGANOMICS ★ "Reaganomics" was a term coined by radio broadcaster Paul Harvey to describe Reagan's plans to stimulate the economy through widespread tax cuts, decreased domestic spending, increased defense spending, and higher interest rates to better control monetary growth. Inflation dropped significantly in the 1980s, from over 13 percent when he took office to around 5 percent at the end of his term. Unemployment also dropped, and by the time Reagan left office, more Americans were employed than ever before; during his presidency over 20 million new jobs had been created, perhaps showing that his belief in trickle-down economics (freeing money for corporations to invest and expand will reach the workers and consumers) had worked. There were downsides, however, to Reaganomics: namely, the national debt soared to over two trillion dollars by the time he left, and the United States went from being a creditor nation to the largest debtor nation in the world. The prosperity of the 1980s would continue for two more presidents and be the longest period of expansion since World War II.

SEP 29: Space shuttle flights resume with launch of Discovery

NOV 8: George H.W. Bush defeats Michael Dukakis in presidential election

NOV 18: President Reagan signs a new law allowing death penalty for drug trafficking

DEC 21: Terrorists blow up Pan Am Flight 103 over Lockerbie, Scotland, killing all 270 on board

DID YOU KNOW?

Reagan was the oldest person to serve as president; he left office when he was 77 years old.

controversy would follow his successor as further investigation continued in the coming years.

The president traveled to Europe in June 1987. Standing before the Brandenburg Gate in West Berlin, still angered by the events at the Reykjavik summit, Reagan gave one of his most important speeches: "General Secretary Gorbachev, if you seek peace, if you seek prosperity for the Soviet Union and Eastern Europe, if you seek liberalization: Come here to this gate! Mr. Gorbachev, open this gate! Mr. Gorbachev, tear down this wall!"[35]

> ***"Freedom is never more than one generation away from extinction. We didn't pass it to our children in the bloodstream. It must be fought for, protected, and handed on for them to do the same."***
>
> *—Ronald Reagan*

Mr. and Mrs. Gorbachev arrived in Washington in December 1987, and the city came down with a case of "Gorby Fever." People flocked to the Soviet leader to shake his hand while traffic in the capital city came to a standstill. Meetings with Reagan started shakily for the president, but he gained confidence and ultimately the men agreed to the terms of the Intermediate-range Nuclear Forces (INF) Treaty, which provided for the destruction of hundreds of various-ranged missiles by both sides as well as allowing independent inspections to ensure this occurred.

The Senate ratified the INF Treaty two days before Reagan traveled to Moscow for yet another summit with Gorbachev. A key topic was the Soviet presence in Afghanistan, which the United States strongly opposed. Human rights were also on Reagan's agenda as he pressed for better treatment for Russian Jews. Just as Gorbachev had been warmly received by Americans, Reagan found the same when he traveled to Moscow. He was deeply touched by the affection shown by the people, and upset when the KGB grabbed and shoved people away. One citizen remarked, "I'm not religious, but I was delighted to hear him end his speeches by saying 'God bless you.' We never heard it before on television."[36] The two men agreed to more minor arms reductions before Reagan headed home.

In January 1986, the country watched another launch of the space shuttle when the Challenger lifted off from Cape Canaveral carrying seven people on board, including two women, one of whom, Christa MacAuliffe, was a New Hampshire teacher. A few seconds into the flight, the shuttle turned into a fireball and plunged back to earth a flaming torch headed into the ocean. A few days later, President Reagan addressed the families of the crew as well as the nation in a memorial service. He pledged, "Man will continue his conquest of space. To reach out for new goals and ever greater achievements—that is the way we shall commemorate our seven Challenger heroes."[37] The economy took a tumble in October 1987 when the stock market suffered a huge decline, and while Wall Street observers quivered in fear, the president was worried about his wife. Nancy had gone to Bethesda Naval Hospital to have a lump removed from her left breast; once it was found to be malignant, a mastectomy was performed. She became the second First Lady, echoing the words of Betty Ford, to remind all women of the need for breast self-exams and annual mammograms. Soon Nancy was back to work, traveling the country in her "Just Say No" campaign against drug abuse.

Representatives from both superpowers continued meeting in arms reduction talks. A few weeks before the end of his term, the president met Gorbachev in New York City. They bid farewell, and Reagan told the Soviet leader that he had full confidence that his successor George Bush would carry on the work they had started.

On the morning of Bush's inauguration, National Security Advisor Colin Powell delivered his final briefing to President Reagan: "The world is quiet today."[38]

RETIREMENT

After watching the inauguration of George Bush, the Reagans returned to California, where they spent much of their time at their beloved ranch. In 1990, he published his autobiography, *An American Life*. Then in November 1994, a letter from the former president announced that he was a victim of Alzheimer's, the same disease that had struck his mother many years before. "I now begin a journey that will lead me to the sunset of my life," he wrote as he bid farewell to the American people as his memory faded away. Visitors were kept from seeing him because Nancy insisted that he would want people to remember him as he was. Then on June 5, 2004, Reagan died from pneumonia. Presidents Ford, Carter, Bush (#41), Clinton, and Bush (#43) attended a memorial service for their colleague at the Ronald Reagan Presidential Library in Simi Valley, California, where he was laid to rest.

Perhaps he would want to be remembered for a line from his farewell address in January 1989: "We meant to change a nation, and instead we changed a world."

ENDNOTES

1 Ronald Reagan, *An American Life*, New York: Simon & Schuster, 1990, p. 21.

2 Ibid, p. 28.

3 Ibid, pp. 40-41.

4 Ibid, p. 69.

5 Ibid, p. 81.

6 Joe Cannon, *Reagan*, New York: G.P. Putnam and Sons, 1982, p. 66.

7 Michael Reagan and Joe Hyams, *On the Outside Looking In*, New York: Zebra Books, 1988, p. 243.

8 R. Reagan, p. 142.

9 Bill Boyarsky, *Ronald Reagan*, New York: Random House, 1981, p. 81.

10 Anne Edwards, *The Reagans*, New York: St. Martin's Press, 2003, p. 88.

11 Ibid, p. 91.

12 Ibid, p. 111.

13 R. Reagan, p. 179.

14 Boyarsky, p. 148.

15 R. Reagan, p. 191.

16 Cannon, p. 203.

17 Ibid, p. 217.

18 Ibid, p. 215.

19 Ibid, p. 226.

20 R. Reagan, p. 209.

21 Ibid, p. 213.

22 William A. DeGregorio, *The Complete Book of US Presidents*, New York: Gramercy Books, 2005, p. 644.

23 Ibid, p. 647.

24 R. Reagan, p. 232.

25 Cannon, p. 403.

26 R. Reagan, p. 260.

27 Donald Mervin, *Ronald Reagan and the American Presidency*, New York: Longman Group, 1990, p. 109.

28 R. Reagan, p. 283.

29 Stephen F. Knott & Jeffrey L. Chidester, *Presidential Profiles: The Reagan Years*, New York: Checkmark Books, 2005, pp. 405-406.

30 Ronald Reagan, Remarks at the Annual Convention of the National Association of Evangelicals, Orlando, Florida, March 8, 1983.

31 Jay Winik, *On the Brink*, New York: Simon & Schuster, 1996, p. 203.

32 Dinesh D'Souza, *Ronald Reagan, How an Ordinary Man Became an Extraordinary Leader*, New York: Free Press, 1997, p. 178.

33 Lou Cannon, *President Reagan, The Role of a Lifetime*, New York: Simon & Schuster, 1991, p. 754.

34 Knott & Chidester, pp. 465-466.

35 R. Reagan, p. 683.

36 Cannon, *President Reagan*, p. 784.

37 Houston *Chronicle*, February 1, 1986.

38 R. Reagan, p. 722.

George H.W. Bush

★ ★ ★ FORTY-FIRST PRESIDENT ★ ★ ★

LIFE SPAN

- Born: June 12, 1924, in Milton, Massachusetts

NICKNAME

- Poppy

FAMILY

- Father: **Prescott Sheldon Bush** (1895–1972)
- Mother: **Dorothy Walker Bush** (1901–1992)
- Wife: **Barbara Pierce Bush** (1925–); wed on January 6, 1945, in Rye, New York
- Children: **George W.** (1946–); **Robin** (1949–1953); **John Ellis "Jeb"** (1953–); **Neil** (1955–); **Marvin** (1956–); **Dorothy** (1959–)

RELIGION

- Episcopalian

HIGHER EDUCATION

- Yale University, 1948

PROFESSION

- Businessman, public official

MILITARY SERVICE

- World War II: Bush enlisted on his 18th birthday in 1942 as a seaman second class in the US Navy; in June 1943 he was commissioned as an ensign and became the navy's youngest pilot. He served in the Pacific, flying 58 bombing missions before returning home in December 1944. He was discharged in September 1945 as a lieutenant (junior grade)

POLITICAL LIFE

- US representative (1967–1971)
- US ambassador to the United Nations (1971–1973)
- Chairman of Republican National Committee (1973–1974)
- Chief US liaison in China (1974–1975)
- Director of Central Intelligence Agency (1976–1977)
- Vice president (1981–1989)

PRESIDENCY

- One term: January 20, 1989–January 20, 1993
- Republican
- Reason for leaving office: defeated in 1992 election by **Bill Clinton**
- Vice president: **James Danforth "Dan" Quayle** (1989–1993)

ELECTION OF 198

- Electoral vote:
  Bush 426;
  Michael Dukakis 111;
  Lloyd Bentsen 1
- Popular vote:
  Bush 47,946,422;
  Dukakis 41,016,429

CABINET

SECRETARY OF STATE
James A. Baker (1989–1992)
Lawrence S. Eagleburger (1992–1993)

SECRETARY OF THE TREASURY
Nicholas F. Brady (1989–1993)

SECRETARY OF DEFENSE
Richard "Dick" Cheney (1989–1993)

ATTORNEY GENERAL
Richard Thornburgh (1988–1991)
William P. Barr (1991–1993)

SECRETARY OF THE INTERIOR
Manuel Lujan (1989–1993)

SECRETARY OF AGRICULTURE
Clayton Yeutter (1989–1991)
Edward Madigan (1991–1993)

SECRETARY OF COMMERCE
Robert Mosbacher (1989–1992)
Barbara H. Franklin (1992–1993)

SECRETARY OF LABOR
Elizabeth Dole (1989–1990)
Lynn Martin (1990–1993)

SECRETARY OF HEALTH AND HUMAN SERVICES
Louis Sullivan (1989–1993)

When George H.W. Bush ran for public office, first for the House of Representatives, and later as vice president and president, much attention was given to his continuing the Bush family legacy of public service from his father, Prescott Bush. Little did anyone realize that the family legacy would extend to the highest office in the land, with George H.W. Bush serving as president only to be followed eight years later by his own son, George W. Bush.

EARLY LIFE

The Bush family lived in America for two centuries before Prescott Bush married Dorothy Walker on August 6, 1921. Prescott served briefly in World War I, graduated from Yale, and became a salesman for Simmons Hardware Company of St. Louis. From there he worked in a variety of positions that took him to Columbus, Ohio; Braintree, Massachusetts; and New York City. In New York he partnered with Averell Harriman in the investment firm of Brown Brothers Harriman & Co. Bush prospered, and the family made its home in Greenwich, Connecticut. By this time, he and wife Dorothy had five children: Prescott, George, Nancy, Jonathan, and William.

Their second son, George Herbert Walker Bush, was born on June 12, 1924, while the couple lived in Massachusetts. George and his siblings were taken care of by a nanny and chauffeur, but pushed by their mother to excel. Dorothy was a fine athlete and encouraged her children to become athletic, as well—family legend has it that she was playing a softball game while in labor with Prescott, and only after hitting a home run did she agree to go inside for the baby's delivery.

The wealthy citizens of Greenwich, among them William Avery Rockefeller, decided to establish their own school to properly educate their young. George attended Greenwich Country Day School until he was thirteen before transferring to Andover preparatory school. His academic prowess was nothing extraordinary; George's teachers later recalled that they never expected he would become president. On the athletic fields, however, he excelled in soccer and baseball, and was elected baseball team captain. He served as senior class president, edited the school newspaper, and helped with school functions such as charity drives. One of his instructors recalled that the teenager "just stood out. . . . Everybody liked the kid. He just had so much enthusiasm."[1] Small wonder George was voted third most popular of his graduating class in 1942.

Although Bush intended to make his next stop Yale, following in his father's footsteps, World War II intervened, and against his parents' wishes, he enlisted in the Navy as a seaman second class on his eighteenth birthday. Like so many young American men after the bombing of Pearl Harbor, Bush longed to join the fight, which he did soon after his graduation from Andover.

NAVY PILOT

George trained as a pilot, and in June 1943, he became an ensign, earned his wings, and the notoriety of becoming the Navy's youngest pilot. His preflight training in Virginia was not without mishap, however. On one occasion when the circus was in a nearby town, the young pilot-in-training could not resist buzzing the fairgrounds, prompting the elephant to bolt from its trainers. Soon after this, a more serious problem presented itself when one of the wheels on his TBF Avenger bomber collapsed, forcing him to crash-land the plane. Bush was not injured, but the plane was so badly damaged that it had to be junked.

NATIONAL EVENTS

JAN 20: Inauguration of George Bush as 41st president

JAN 24: Execution in Florida of convicted serial killer Ted Bundy

FEB 7: The sale or possession of semiautomatic weapons are banned by the Los Angeles City Council

FEB 10: Ron Brown elected to head Democratic National Committee, first African American to lead a major political party

FEB 11: Barbara Clementine Harris becomes first female bishop in the Episcopal Church

1989

WORLD EVENTS

JAN 7: Japanese emperor Hirohito dies, ending Showa era; he is succeeded by Akihito

JAN 18: Communist Party legalizes Solidarity

FEB 14: Union Carbide agrees to pay over $470 million in damages to government of India for Bhopal disaster of 1984

MAR 27: First free elections held in USSR, and Communist Party does poorly

MAY 2: Barbed wire cut down opening border between Hungary and Western Europe

While based in Virginia, Bush also learned how to conduct aerial reconnaissance photography and instructed others how to take photographs during aerial combat. He named his plane *Barbara* in honor of his girlfriend Barbara Pierce. She was a descendant of President Franklin Pierce, and her father was the publisher for two major magazines, *Redbook* and *McCall's*. Barbara attended female preparatory schools and was only sixteen years old when she first met George Bush at a local country club's Christmas party in December 1941. They immediately took a liking to each other and spent that evening talking, as well as the next evening, at another gathering. After returning to their respective schools, their correspondence continued. George and Barbara became engaged at the Walker home in Kennebunkport, Maine, before he left for Virginia—the news came as no surprise to anyone. Barbara left home to attend Smith College in Massachusetts, while George shipped out to the Pacific.

Bush reported to duty at Pearl Harbor in the spring of 1944, and soon learned to fly off the deck of an aircraft carrier. He found the experience exhilarating and later recalled, "There's something about the isolation, the ocean, the tiny carrier below that gets the adrenaline flowing."[2] In eleven months, he successfully landed his plane 116 times on the deck of the *San Jacinto*, no easy feat.

In the spring of 1944, young Bush was kept busy flying two types of missions in the Pacific—photo reconnaissance and bombing, most frequently around the Mariana Islands as American forces were preparing to invade Saipan. Bush's squadron had already bombed Wake Island; now they targeted key Japanese defense points, as well as the radio tower and airstrip on the island of Guam.

On June 19, 1944, fighter planes were ordered to launch against the Japanese in what would become known as the "Great Marianas Turkey Shoot." Young aviator George Bush was hardly in the air before he took a hit. His engine went out, and he radioed his crew, "Oil lines have sucked up shrapnel."[3] The flurry of activity aboard the flight deck of the *San Jacinto* eliminated any possibility of landing there, so he put down in the water. The three men aboard the *Barbara* successfully escaped from the plane and boarded the liferaft, which was soon retrieved by a destroyer, the *C.K. Bronson*.

Once the flight crew returned to the *San Jacinto* two days after the Battle of the Philippine Sea, they were assigned a new plane, which was enlisted as part of Operation Snapshot, a photographic mission ordered by Admiral Chester Nimitz to obtain pictures of Peleliu Island for use in planning a September invasion. Orders were also dispensed to destroy the radio tower on another nearby island, Chichi Jima, which had been extensively fortified by the Japanese and used as a listening post to monitor the American fleet's radio transmissions. The first attempt on Chichi Jima was unsuccessful, so planes were launched the next day to finish the job. Lieutenant Bush piloted his Avenger with his radioman/photographer John Delaney; a substitute, Lieutenant William "Ted" White, filled in as gunner because he wanted to monitor the plane's weapons systems.

Bush's plane was catapulted from the flight deck and was airborne at about 7:15 a.m., and flew toward the target at Chichi Jima; he and his task force of twenty-six F6F Hellcat fighters and nine TBM Avenger bombers came over the island in a V-formation and were quickly under antiaircraft fire. Bush pushed toward his target when he suddenly felt the plane jolt. "Smoke poured into the cockpit, and I could see flames ripping across the crease of the wing, edging towards the fuel

CABINET

★★★★★★★★★★

(continued)

SECRETARY OF HOUSING AND URBAN DEVELOPMENT
Jack Kemp (1989–1993)

SECRETARY OF TRANSPORTATION
Samuel Skinner (1989–1991)

Andrew W. Card (1992–1993)

SECRETARY OF ENERGY
James Watkins (1989–1993)

SECRETARY OF EDUCATION
Lauro F. Cavazos (1988–1990)

Lamar Alexander (1991–1993)

SECRETARY OF VETERANS AFFAIRS
Edward Derwinski (1989–1992), first appointee of this new post

FEB 14: First GPS satellite launched into space

MAR 4: Time, Inc. and Warner Communications announce merger to become Time Warner

MAR 24: Exxon *Valdez* oil tanker runs aground and spills over 11 million gallons into Alaska's Prince William Sound

APR 16: Dilbert comic goes syndicated

MAY 1: Disney-MGM Studios opens in Florida

MAY 20: Chinese government proclaims martial law in Beijing due to growing protests and demonstrators in its Tiananmen Square

MAY 30: Protesters unveil 33-foot-high statue, *Goddess of Democracy*, at Tiananmen Square

JUN 4: Chinese troops and tanks move into Tiananmen Square killing unknown number of civilians (estimates range from several hundred to a few thousand); many others are arrested

JUN 4: Solidarity wins in Poland's first parliamentary elections

tanks,"[4] he recalled. Although the instrument panel was engulfed in smoke, Bush continued his dive toward the target and dropped his bombs, then flew toward the Pacific with flames sweeping down his wings. He yelled for the crew to parachute out but no one responded. He exited the aircraft and jumped, but his altitude was too low to jump clear, and he slammed his head against the horizontal stabilizer. Knowing that he was fighting time before the Japanese would locate him, he "swam like hell"[5] toward his emergency sea pack and quickly inflated his life raft. Bush was in excruciating pain from his gashed forehead and grew nauseous from constantly bobbing up and down in the sea. His fellow pilots shot at the enemy boats attempting to capture him. He was rescued by the US submarine *Finback,* but neither of his crewmembers survived. Later Bush learned that the Japanese reported seeing two parachutes drop from the sky, which meant one of the other men did eject, but no bodies were ever found.

Bush had enough combat time to be rotated back to the States, but he preferred to remain with his squadron, and flew several more missions. He received a letter from the radioman Delaney's sister telling him to stop blaming himself for her brother's fate and told him that Jack had said Bush was "the best pilot in the squadron."[6]

Back home, Bush's parents received word of their son's brush with death and shared the news with Barbara. All were frantic with worry until they heard from him that he would be returning home for the wedding; as it turned out, he did not arrive in time for the original wedding date, but did manage to trek back to Connecticut to wed Barbara on January 6, 1945.

After a short honeymoon at a resort hotel in Georgia, the couple began married life in Virginia, but soon were transferred to Michigan, then Maine, and finally back to Virginia for Bush to receive additional training before being sent back to the Pacific. While in Virginia, Lieutenant Bush heard the joyous news of the Japanese surrender. He would not be needed for the planned invasion of Japan, and on September 18, Bush was discharged from the Navy, having completed fifty-eight missions.

YALE

George had always planned to attend Yale as soon as his military service was completed, so the newlyweds moved to New Haven, Connecticut. On July 6, 1946, George Walker Bush was born. Although busy with his family, Bush still managed to find time to study and was elected to Phi Beta Kappa. Yale's baseball team benefited from his skillful playing at first base and later they chose him as their captain. He was also tapped to join the ultra-secretive Skull and Bones Society, from whose membership would come many of his future campaign contributors.

OIL BUSINESS

After graduation in June 1948, Bush decided to take his new degree in business and economics and head to Odessa, Texas, where he would work for a family friend, Neil Mallon, whose newly acquired company, International Derrick & Equipment Company (Ideco), was part of the burgeoning oil industry of west Texas.

Even though it was difficult at times being in a new place so far from home and family, the young couple thrived on their independence, and George preferred to establish his own name rather than "ride on our father's coattails."[7] Their son kept them amused, as George wrote to a friend, "Whenever

NATIONAL EVENTS

JUN 21: US Supreme Court rules that burning the American flag is a freedom protected by the First Amendment; President Bush calls for a constitutional amendment outlawing flag burning, but it fails to pass Congress

JUL 26: First person indicted for willfully releasing a computer virus

AUG 24: Longtime Cincinnati Reds player and manager Pete Rose agrees to a lifetime ban from baseball because of charges of illegal gambling

AUG 25: Voyager 2 passes by Neptune relaying pictures of it and its moon Triton

WORLD EVENTS

JUL 14: France celebrates its 200th anniversary of the French Revolution

AUG 19: Poland has first non-Communist prime minister in over 40 years

AUG 23: Human chain formed among peoples of Estonia, Latvia, and Lithuania, demanding their independence from the Soviet Union

AUG 23: Hungary opens its border to Austria

SEPT 10: Hungary opens its border to East Germany

OCT 23: Hungary declares itself Hungarian Republic

NOV 7: East Germany's Communist government resigns

I come home he greets me and talks a blue streak, sentences disjointed of course but enthusiasm and spirit boundless," adding, "He tries to say everything and the results are often hilarious."[8]

Neil Mallon wanted George to learn more facets of the business, so in 1949 the family moved to California, where they were transferred to five different towns within one year while Bush worked as a salesman. This meant even more separation from "Bar" and little George. In 1949, a daughter, Pauline Robinson, was born. They called her Robin, and soon the family of four was moving back to Texas. This time, however, they decided to live in Midland and George commuted the twenty miles daily to Odessa.

The family soon made themselves at home in Midland, taking part in various community organizations; the couple taught Sunday school at the First Presbyterian Church and they enjoyed barbecues and gatherings with friends and neighbors. Part of each summer was spent visiting family in Maine and escaping the Texas heat.

In 1953, another member joined the family when John Ellis "Jeb" was born. During this time, little Robin seemed unwell, so her mother took her to the doctor. After running blood tests, the doctor told Barbara the gut-wrenching news: Robin had leukemia, and there was no cure. The heartbroken couple could not accept the pronouncement of a death sentence for their three-year-old daughter and took her to New York City's Memorial Sloan-Kettering Hospital, where George had an uncle on staff. Although medications were tried and blood transfusions administered, there was no way to prevent the inevitable, and in October 1953, Robin slipped into a coma and died. The tragedy drew the couple together, but also made its mark on young George, who now felt responsible for helping his grieving mother. Two years later another son arrived, Neil Mallon (named after George's employer and friend), followed by Marvin in 1956.

By this time, the Bush family had made its first foray into the world of politics. Prescott Bush had won a Senate seat in 1952, at which time George was helping the Republican Party in Midland by managing a reception for Vice President Richard Nixon, who was campaigning for Texas Republicans. When protesters displayed signs and tried to create a ruckus, Bush grabbed the signs, tore them up, and ordered the protesters to disperse.

The oil business provided plenty of opportunity for expansion, and by 1950, George decided he wanted to strike out on his own. He told Mallon of his plans, and the next year, he partnered with John Overbey, who was an expert at discovering untapped sites. Bush provided the financial wizardry, making and maintaining key contacts with backers who had deep pockets. In March 1953, the two joined forces with lawyer-brothers Hugh and William Liedtke and created a new business they named Zapata Petroleum Corporation.

Zapata struck oil repeatedly in the coming years, making all of its officers very wealthy men. They also moved into the riskier business of offshore drilling and invested in a new type of rig that could withstand hurricane-force winds. These rigs proved successful and were later built around the world. Once the oil boom slackened in the late 1950s, Bush decided to whittle down the company's expenses, including its personnel. He took no pleasure in pink-slipping employees, as well as friends, but managed to do this painful task in such a way that he preserved those friendships. Later the business split, and Bush kept the off-shore company with Herbert Walker while Liedtke retained control of Zapata Petroleum,

SUPREME COURT APPOINTMENTS

★★★★★★★★★★

David H. Souter, 1990

Clarence Thomas, 1991

SEP 5: First televised address by President Bush; in it he declares his "war on drugs"

OCT 17: Earthquake hits Oakland-San Francisco region killing more than 60

NOV 7: Country's first elected African American governor is Virginian Douglas Wilder

NOV 20: President Bush signs bill allowing reparation payments of $20,000 to Japanese-Americans interned during World War II

JAN 13: First African American governor, Douglas Wilder, takes office in Richmond, Virginia

1990

End of civil war in Lebanon

JAN 3: Former Panamanian dictator Manuel Noriega surrenders to the US

NOV 9: Checkpoints along Berlin Wall are opened so people may freely pass between both sections of Berlin

NOV 10: End of Communist rule in Bulgaria

NOV 17: "Velvet Revolution" begins in Czechoslovakia

DEC 3: President Bush and Soviet leader Mikhail Gorbachev meet and issue a joint statement that the end of the Cold War is near

DEC 20: US troops invade Panama to seize ousted dictator Manuel Noriega

STATE OF THE UNION

US POPULATION IN 1989
248,718,301

NATIONAL DEBT IN 1993
$4,411,488,883,139

which later merged with Penn Oil Company and became Pennzoil.

In 1959, the family welcomed their last baby, Dorothy, nicknamed "Doro." Bush decided to move the company's headquarters and his family to Houston.

HOUSTON

George continued as president and chairman of the board for Zapata Off-Shore Company and controlled 15 percent of the company's stocks. Zapata's offshore drilling platforms were well-made and used worldwide. The company was humming along, and George was worth a million dollars, but catastrophe struck when Hurricane Betsy blew along the Gulf coast in 1964, destroying their largest drilling barge. Bush decided to chart a different course, so he sold his share of the business in 1966 for $1.1 million and began planning his political future.

By the mid-1960s, Bush was already experienced heading Republican Party organizations on the local level—during the Eisenhower presidency in Midland and then in Houston, where he became the party's chairman for Harris County in 1963. He was an energetic presence around the county and succeeded in raising ninety thousand dollars for the Grand Old Party (GOP). Republicans were facing a major and divisive problem in trying to keep the ultra-conservative John Birch Society supporters from taking over the party. George urged his fellow Party members to continue to allow the JBS to participate rather than run the risk of dividing the Party to such a degree that its position in national government would be in jeopardy; he reminded party leaders that they all shared the common goal of unseating Democrats in the coming elections.

Bush attended the 1964 presidential convention supporting Goldwater, and later that year entered his first political race for the Senate, running against incumbent Democrat Ralph Yarborough. Bush countered the accusation that he was a Yankee carpetbagger by stating that he "was a Texan by choice, not by chance."[9] Yarborough successfully reminded voters of the Birchers' connection with Bush and swept the state on the coattails of fellow Texan Lyndon B. Johnson, winning reelection to the Senate. Although defeated, Bush had succeeded in winning more than a million votes, the biggest Republican tally ever in Texas; moreover, he had won the support of many influential—and wealthy—Texans who would back him in future campaigns. His loss, he later admitted, was partly owing to voters' perception that he would say anything to win their favor: "I took some of the far right positions to get elected. I hope I never do it again. I regret it."[10]

Two years later, Bush ran again, but this time for the newly formed 7th Congressional District. This area included the more affluent part of Houston, which was also mainly Republican. George campaigned throughout the district, knocking on doors and introducing himself. People liked him and found his affable personality extremely approachable. Integration was making its first inroads at this time, and Bush helped advance the process by sponsoring an African American girls' softball team (the George Bush All-Stars) and ensuring that they were allowed to play in the city's tournament. This seemed rather incongruous to those who recalled that he had opposed the Civil Rights Act of 1964. But in November 1966, the family gathered for election results with young George W. posting updates. After all votes were counted, Bush had won the election with a respectable showing from

NATIONAL EVENTS

JAN 18: Washington, D.C. Mayor Marion Barry arrested for drug possession

MAR 18: Two robbers posing as policemen steal twelve paintings from Isabella Stewart Gardner Museum in Boston

APR 24: Hubble space telescope put into orbit by crew of space shuttle Discovery

JUN 26: President Bush announces economy requires a tax increase, thus breaking his campaign pledge of "No new taxes"

JUL 26: Americans with Disabilities Act signed into law by President Bush

WORLD EVENTS

JAN 31: First McDonalds in Moscow opens

FEB 11: South African president F.W. DeKlerk releases Nelson Mandela from prison

FEB 26: USSR promises to withdraw its troops from Czechoslovakia by July 1991

MAY 22: Republic of Yemen formed from the two countries of Yemen Arab Republic and People's Democratic Republic of Yemen

JUL 25: Serbs declare their sovereignty from Croatia

AUG 2: Iraq invades Kuwait

both black and Hispanic minorities, and George Bush was on his way to Washington.

CONGRESSMAN

George Bush's personality won him friends in Congress, and he was chosen as the president of the freshman class. His father, while no longer a senator, was still influential and successfully lobbied the chairman of the powerful Ways and Means Committee, Arkansas representative Wilbur Mills, to find a place for his son. Although Mills did not believe in allowing freshmen on Ways and Means, he invited young Bush aboard.

The Texas congressman fought for the interests of the oil industry during his tenure in Congress, including when it opposed Republican president Richard Nixon. He wrote to a Nixon aide, "I was also appreciative of your telling them how I bled and died for the oil industry. That might kill me off in the *Washington Post* but it darn sure helps in Houston."[11]

In 1967, Bush went to see the Vietnam War for himself. He paid for his own trip and spent two weeks in the region talking with the troops, helicoptering in and out of "hot" landing zones, and witnessing combat for the first time since his own experiences in World War II. What most upset him was the distorted reporting of an incident he witnessed while in Da Nang. The base was bombed in an attack so minor that Bush himself slept through it; the event was reported as a major assault and became a headline story splashed across the front pages of the US press. No one had been killed in the bombing, and the airfield had been closed only briefly. The credibility gap between the event and its reporting was alarming, and Bush was struck by the degree to which media coverage can influence people's perception of reality.

Bush also became aware, during this visit, of the disproportionately large number of servicemen who were black. The next year he decided it was time to move forward on civil rights and voted in favor of the Civil Rights Act of 1968. He was especially interested in its provisions for open housing. His constituents were quick to respond—with venom and hate, and some death threats—the young congressman writing to a friend that he received more mail as a result of his action on civil rights than on any other issue. He knew he would confront the opposition on his next visit home, where he addressed a group at Memorial High School. He explained his position and the injustice of housing being denied to people based on their race or "Latin-American accent." He won the crowd over with his heartfelt belief that open housing provided "a ray of hope for blacks and other minorities locked out by habit and discrimination."[12] With minorities now jumping on the Bush bandwagon, Democrats decided George Bush was unbeatable, so in 1968 he ran unopposed for reelection. Richard Nixon briefly considered asking Bush to be his running mate in 1968, but soon decided that the representative from Texas had too little political experience.

Bush's active involvement with improving people's lives did not stop at the Texas border; he was also deeply concerned with the global overpopulation. He was a firm believer in birth control and family planning as essential in guiding foreign policy and solving the world hunger problem, and was so vocal on the topic that Rep. Wilbur Mills began to refer to him as "Rubbers." Bush also publicly stated his pro-choice position on abortion. Nixon agreed with Bush's goals regarding foreign policy reform, and signed the Family Planning Services and Population Research Act of 1970.

AUG 27: Guitarist Stevie Ray Vaughan dies in a helicopter crash in East Troy, WI

SEP: *Good Defeats Evil* by sculptor Zurab Tsereteli is placed outside the United Nations building in New York City

SEP 11: President Bush announces in a televised address the possibility that US troops will be sent to aid Kuwait against Iraq

SEP 29: Construction is completed (after 80 years) on Washington, D.C.'s National Cathedral

NOV 13: First known World Wide Web (www) page is written

AUG 6: UN Security Council orders trade embargo against Iraq

OCT 3: Reunification of East and West Germany

NOV 12: Enthroning of Akihito as Japan's 125th emperor

NOV 19: Treaty signed by members of NATO and Warsaw Pact nations to reduce weapons in Europe

NOV 29: UN Security Council passes resolution calling for military action against Iraq if it does not leave Kuwait and free foreign hostages by January 15, 1991

DID YOU KNOW?

President Bush made broccoli farmers upset when he announced he did not now nor had he ever liked broccoli. (Undoubtedly some children told their parents they did not need to eat the vegetable if the president had publicly denounced it!)

Looking ahead to the next congressional election, Bush wondered if this would be the time to switch to the Senate. He traveled to former President Johnson's ranch seeking advice. The earthy Texan urged him to do so, explaining, "The difference between being a member of the Senate and a member of the House is the difference between chicken *salad* and chicken *shit*."[13] Bush soon began making plans to defeat his nemesis Ralph Yarborough, but his efforts were soon thwarted when Yarborough was upset in the primaries by Lloyd Bentsen. Bush now seemed unable to formulate an effective strategy against his new opponent, and the Nixon administration failed to provide much assistance, save for a last-minute campaign stop by the president. The race was another defeat for Bush, losing 53–47 percent.

AMBASSADOR TO THE UNITED NATIONS

Prior to Bush's run for the Senate, President Nixon had told him that should he lose the election, he would be provided some type of political appointment. Various positions were considered, but when Bush met with the president on December 9, 1970, he had only one in his mind—that of United States ambassador to the United Nations. Bush offered compelling reasons why he could better represent the administration and its interests than his Democratic predecessor, Charles Yost, not only at the United Nations but also among the New York community. The president was convinced and though he said nothing to Bush at the time, after the meeting he told his aide H.R. Haldeman that the Texas congressman should receive the appointment.

Announcement of Bush's appointment angered many who questioned his expertise in foreign policy. With virtually no experience in international affairs, Bush was perceived as an ambitious politician using the position as a mere stepping-stone. Years later, Nixon confirmed that Bush's inexperience was a consideration, but the president believed that serving at the United Nations would greatly advance Bush's future political career. Bush took his new assignment seriously and eagerly met the challenge of working with representatives from around the globe.

The Bushes perceived their role as ambassadors of America to the world's representatives at the United Nations, and they threw themselves wholeheartedly into the role. They hosted parties at their residence in the Waldorf Towers in New York City, as well as at their country home in Greenwich, Connecticut. On one occasion, they entertained a gathering of the Economic and Social Council at Shea Stadium. Their brand of Texas hospitality was well received by their guests and the press. Although many fellow ambassadors disagreed with continuing American involvement in Vietnam, they warmed to the personal charm of its ambassador to the UN.

The representation of Taiwan, and the exclusion of the People's Republic of China, as members of the United Nations provoked numerous hotly contested debates, which ultimately resulted in a key vote by the General Assembly not to unseat Taiwan in favor of China. While Bush attempted to line up votes in favor of Taiwan, President Nixon and his National Security advisor Henry Kissinger were negotiating behind the scenes to begin diplomatic relations with China; in fact, unbeknownst to Bush, Kissinger was in Beijing just before the UN vote. The ambassador never complained that he was being undercut by his own administration, and the General Assembly cast ballots against Taiwan and Bush, 76–35.

NATIONAL EVENTS

NOV 29: Immigration law passed raising ceiling of legal immigrants to 675,000 annually

Amtrak leaves New York City's Grand Central, making the terminal strictly for commuter transportation

Engineers begin work on Boston's Central Artery Project, the largest public-works project ever undertaken in the United States

JAN 12: Congress approves a bill to use force to liberate Kuwait

1991

WORLD EVENTS

DEC 2: First free German elections held since before World War II; Helmut Kohl becomes chancellor

DEC 6: Iraq releases Western hostages

JAN 13: Bloodshed in Lithuania as Soviet troops move against Lithuanians demanding independence

JAN 16: Operation Desert Storm begins (7:00 p.m. EST) as US launches air strikes against Iraq

JAN 17: Iraq fires Scud missiles into Israel

JAN 23: Cholera epidemic hits South America

One of the key issues facing the United Nations during this period was the Israelis' refusal to yield any of the territory they had won during the 1967 Six Day War. The turmoil in the Middle East turned increasingly global, and even stretched to New York City. There, Jewish radicals rebelled against those demanding the return of Jerusalem and other Arab lands. Their leader, Rabbi Meir Kahane, challenged Bush when he tried to enter the UN building. The rabbi wanted to further publicize the confrontation by appearing on on Dick Cavett's TV talk show, but Bush refused. A terrorist group within the Palestine Liberation Organization (PLO) called "Black September" then made news by seizing Israeli athletes at the Munich Olympic Games in September 1972, killing eleven of the hostages. The United Nations was proving powerless to stop or even slow the dissension as Third World countries eagerly manipulated events by playing the Americans and Soviets against each other in issue after issue. The world was changing, and being US ambassador to the United Nations was no longer the post of power that it had once been.

In October 1972, Prescott Bush died of cancer, and the next month, George was summoned to the White House. Nixon had first considered designating Bush as assistant secretary of the treasury, but after the election, the president decided he wanted someone to replace Bob Dole as the head of the Republican National Committee (RNC). Nixon commented that he wanted Bush for his "loyalty" and that he would be "a total Nixon man—first."[14] So Dole was out and Bush was in.

CHAIRMAN OF THE RNC

When George Bush assumed control of the RNC, stories about the break-in of the Democratic headquarters at the Watergate building were appearing regularly in the press. Bush's main job was to reiterate what President Nixon and his staff steadfastly maintained: they had nothing to do with the burglary. At the same time, he was doing his best to keep the spirits of the party-faithful strong, no easy feat with a growing number of Nixon staffers resigning, and daily revelations making headlines during the Senate Watergate hearings in the summer of 1973. Eventually even the vice president, Spiro Agnew, was forced to resign (owing to charges unrelated to Watergate). Though he would have preferred to be tapped for the vice presidency himself, Bush supported the president's choice of House Minority Leader Gerald Ford, whom Bush knew from his earlier congressional days.

Being chairman of the RNC at this critical time was endlessly frustrating with Watergate on everyone's mind. Bush, though, braved a smile and continued to publicly support Nixon, but found both attendance and contributions at Republican fundraisers to be in shorter supply. Privately Bush pled with the president to release the much-discussed White House tapes as a sure way to win his case. Once he read the transcript and saw for himself that Nixon was not innocent, Bush felt angered by the betrayal. Later he admitted that he was tempted "to blast the president, blast the lie."[15] At the final cabinet meeting, Bush attempted to remind the president of the Republican Party, but Nixon was not willing to listen. Bush then sent a letter to Nixon telling him that the Republican leadership throughout the country thought it best if he resigned.

George and Barbara were on hand to wave farewell to the Nixons as they boarded the helicopter spiriting them away from the White House. Now Bush met with newly sworn-in president Gerald

JAN 16: Serial killer Aileen Wuornos confesses to the murder of six men

JAN 18: Cash-strapped Eastern Airlines ceases operation after 62 years in business

FEB 5: Dr. Jack Kevorkian is barred by a Michigan court from assisting in suicides

MAR 3: A home video records the beating of Rodney King at the hands of Los Angeles police officers

APR 17: For the first time ever, the Dow Jones Industrial Average closes above 3,000 at 3,004.46

FEB 7: Haiti's first democratically elected president, Jean-Bertrand Aristide, takes office

FEB 23: Ground troops move into Kuwait from Saudi Arabia

FEB 26: Iraqi President Saddam Hussein announces his troops will withdraw from Kuwait; they set oilfields ablaze as they depart

APR 3: UN passes a cease-fire resolution in Iraq War and orders that nation to disarm and remove all chemical and biological weapons as well as rid itself of long-range ballistic missiles

Ford, whose first priority was finding himself a vice president. For many within the party, George Bush seemed the perfect candidate—he was younger (late forties), had New England heritage but Texas connections, and was well-heeled among key circles. His easy-going personality was also a plus, but after a *Newsweek* story appeared criticizing Bush for not reporting a forty thousand dollar contribution to his Senate campaign in 1970 as required by law, his hopes were dashed, and New York governor Nelson Rockefeller was named as the vice president-designate. Bush was disappointed, and Ford hoped to satisfy him with a new diplomatic assignment and summoned him to the White House. Three positions were offered: ambassadorships to Great Britain, France, or a new position as liaison to China. It took Bush less than an hour to make his decision, and Barbara enthusiastically supported his choice of going to China.

AMBASSADOR TO CHINA

The Bushes arrived in Beijing in September 1974 and quickly settled into a far different lifestyle. They found themselves treated kindly by the Chinese while officially, the US government was derided on a frequent basis by Chairman Mao's Communist regime. They delighted in cycling through the city and countryside, as well as walking their dog C. Fred around Beijing. They took Chinese language lessons together and spent much of that time, Barbara later recalled, "laughing at each other's terrible accents and mistakes."[16] Although the Bush children were growing up in the States, they still visited their parents frequently, and sixteen-year-old Doro was baptized in the Bible Society Building, making her the first American person baptized in Communist China since 1949.

While they were delighting in immersing themselves in the Chinese culture and landscape, they also played diplomatic hosts for Secretary of State Henry Kissinger. The visits went well, but Kissinger continued to keep Bush out of the loop regarding diplomatic affairs, including when Saigon fell in April 1975. They watched as China incorporated this victory into their May Day celebrations complete with fireworks, singing, and North Vietnam's flags flying everywhere. Then in November, Kissinger sent word to Bush that he should return home to head the Central Intelligence Agency (CIA). Looking back on his time in China, Bush said, "My purpose wasn't to win popularity contests . . . but to get to know the Chinese—and to get them to know Americans—at a personal level."[17] And from all accounts, the ambassador succeeded. Still, he held no illusions about his next post, which he considered a political graveyard.

CIA CHIEF

Greasing the way for Bush's confirmation, Ford announced that he would not be choosing Bush as a vice presidential running mate when he ran for the presidency in 1976. The Senate approved the nominee, and Bush would serve a year heading the intelligence-gathering organization. Much of his time was spent testifying before various congressional committees; in fact, he appeared fifty-one times during his short one-year tenure. Those within the agency were gratified that they had a director determined to restore credibility and pride among its people as he updated its technology, increased its budget, and overhauled the organization's hierarchy by creating two deputy administrators for Intelligence and Administration. Bush attempted to keep the focus positive while others were

NATIONAL EVENTS

MAY 16: Queen Elizabeth II addresses Congress

JUN 12: Chicago Bulls win their first NBA championship, they defeated the Los Angeles Lakers 4–1

JUN 17: Body of former president Zachary Taylor is exhumed to determine if he had been poisoned; no evidence of arsenic is found

JUL 22: Serial killer Jeffrey Dahmer is arrested

AUG 13: Super Nintendo released

WORLD EVENTS

APR 6: Iraq agrees to UN demands

JUN 23–28: UN inspections teams prevented from intercepting Iraqi vehicles carrying nuclear-related equipment

JUN 25: Croatia and Slovenia declare independence from Yugoslavia

AUG: Latvia, Ukraine, Moldova, Kyrgyzstan, and Uzbekistan declare their independence from the USSR

AUG 19: Attempted coup against Gorbachev, and he is placed under house arrest, but coup fails within 72 hours

pointing to possible civil rights abuses by Ford and his administration on the heels of Watergate.

Another group was formed to oversee the CIA and report independently; it was known as Team B. Late in 1976, it published its findings regarding the Soviet weapons threat, which, it was determined, was still very real; détente, the report insisted, was merely a ploy. Bush and his colleagues testified before the newly formed Senate Select Committee on Intelligence that the Soviets were developing laser beams to blast missiles out of the sky; Bush called it "a 'Buck Rogers' kind of thing."[18] This testimony would eventually lead to an arms race that would result in the fall of the USSR.

Both before and after the presidential election, Bush provided president-elect Carter with intelligence briefings, and during the last one, he offered to remain at his post until a replacement was found. Carter declined, so on January 20, 1977, George Bush found himself unemployed. He and Barbara headed back to Houston to buy a house and determine what lay ahead in their future.

RESPITE

Back in Texas, Bush watched as son George embarked on his first political campaign—to win the seat of the 19th congressional district. The senior Bush, however, seemed at a loss, knowing he would have to bide his time until the next presidential election. "He's been in [government] so long, he's getting a bit nervous," one friend admitted to a reporter. "There's nothing available in Texas."[19] Now he would turn to business and try to earn more income than he had during his years of public service. Texas billionaire Ross Perot offered him a job heading a Houston oil company, but Bush declined, which, to Perot, made him an enemy. He did, though, find serving on the boards of directors for a variety of Texas companies appealing and also joined the Trilateral Commission, composed of politicians and businessmen representing interests in Europe, Asia, and the United States. Friends, including long-time associate James Baker, began raising funds for his upcoming campaign.

Another job he took and enjoyed was being adjunct professor at Rice University teaching a course on Organization in Theory and Practice with Dr. Joseph Cooper. The students admired their instructor, whom they found very approachable and open "without any airs, no pretensions."[20] Nothing, though, stopped his onward march toward the 1980 election, and on May 1, 1979, George H.W. Bush announced his candidacy.

Although he was considered one of the top frontrunners, Ronald Reagan had the most name recognition and probability of winning the primaries. Bush tried to tout himself as a moderate rather than conservative like Reagan. He was advised not to attack Reagan through the primaries but keep himself as the alternative to the California governor whose advanced age concerned many. Many of Bush's supporters were from the CIA, but the Bush team wanted to distance themselves from the "spooks." He also gained many former Ford supporters.

Bush wanted a decisive win in the Iowa primary and successfully developed grassroots support by actively campaigning throughout the state. He claimed victory and eyed the next contest in New Hampshire with satisfaction, believing his Yankee heritage would help him there. He and Reagan debated in Manchester, with both men handling themselves well. Bush needed to defeat the "great communicator" in the second debate held in Nashua, but here he was sandbagged by the Reagan team. Bush discovered just prior to the start of the

DID YOU KNOW?

Millie, dog of the First Family, published her own book: ***Millie's Book as Dictated to Barbara Bush***, which described life in the White House.

SEP 22: Dead Sea Scrolls displayed for the first time at California's Huntington Library

OCT 2: Arkansas Governor Bill Clinton announces his candidacy for the presidency in 1992

OCT 11–13: Confirmation hearings for Supreme Court nominee Clarence Thomas, who is accused of sexually harassing Anita Hill

NOV 4: Opening of Ronald Reagan's presidential library

NOV 7: Basketball star Magic Johnson announces that he has HIV

OCT 11: After another standoff between UN inspectors and Iraqi officials regarding weapons, UN passes a resolution that Iraq must unconditionally accept these inspections; Iraq refuses

OCT 27: Turkmenistan declares independence

NOV 6: KGB ceases operations

NOV 18: Hostages Terry Waite (held since 1987) and Thomas Sutherland (held since 1985) are freed by their Muslim kidnappers in Lebanon

NOV 27: UN agrees to begin peacekeeping in Yugoslavia

debate that the other four candidates—Bob Dole, John Anderson, Howard Baker, and Phil Crane—would also participate. This was not what he had agreed to, and Jim Baker hotly protested. Ultimately all were on stage, but Bush did not acquit himself with any skill, and he lost the primary. Still he battled on, and in Pennsylvania, derided Reagan's proposal of utilizing supply-side economics as "voodoo economics." But the Reagan steamroller moved over him and the other candidates, causing them to exit the race one by one. By Memorial Day, it was clear to Baker and others that the best course was to drop out, but Bush resisted. Ultimately he agreed to stop active campaigning on assurance from the Reagan camp that he would not be shut out of the convention.

At the 1980 Republican convention in Detroit, the staffs of Reagan and former president Ford met to see if they could hammer out differences to make a Reagan-Ford ticket. What became clear was the desire by Ford to be a co-president rather than a vice president, and Reagan was uncomfortable with that situation, so the idea was quickly discarded. Although Bush was apparently second choice behind Ford for the vice presidency, he may have been lower on the candidate's list. Reagan confided to a friend, "I have strong reservations about George Bush,"[21] but faced with the reality that Bush was the popular favorite, Reagan decided to ask him. To support Reagan, Bush would now have to withdraw his support on two hot topics—the Equal Rights Amendment (ERA) and abortion. He did this, which provoked criticism from Democrats and moderate Republicans who questioned what type of a leader quickly dismisses positions he has held for years. But Americans were tired of double-digit inflation and the inability of President Carter to free the sixty hostages in Iran, so they voted for Reagan and Bush with a majority of 51 percent.

VICE PRESIDENT

Thanks to the practice of his predecessor, George Bush was granted more authority and access to the president, just as Walter Mondale had enjoyed with Jimmy Carter. Every Thursday, the top two men of the executive branch enjoyed lunch together, with no topic off-limits and what was said stayed in the Oval Office. Of course, Bush continued the tradition of representing the country at various state funerals and functions; he sat on committees, and traveled the country on administration business. He was doing just that in Fort Worth when he was informed of the assassination attempt on Reagan. After Air Force Two landed in Washington, he was told to take the helicopter to the White House and preside over a National Security meeting rather than travel by car. Since by now he knew that Reagan was resting after his emergency surgery, Bush saw no need to rush. After all, "Only the President lands on the South Lawn,"[22] he said, and he traveled by the normal route.

Reagan was grateful to Bush when he realized the lengths the vice president had gone to not usurp any authority. The efforts were rewarded by Bush being asked to remain on the ticket when Reagan ran for reelection in 1984. This time he was opposed by Walter Mondale and Congresswoman Geraldine Ferraro of New York. When Mondale tried to paint Bush as an elitist, Barbara bristled because Ferraro was known to be worth four million dollars. And soon after, Barbara told reporters aboard Air Force Two, "That rich . . . —well, it rhymes with rich—could buy George Bush any day."[23] Barbara was stunned to learn the press had immediately reported it, so she called Ferraro to

NATIONAL EVENTS

DEC 12: Bush signs Soviet Threat Reduction Act to ensure former Soviet stockpiles of weaponry are reduced

US Department of Agriculture announces the creation of a Food Pyramid to replace four basic food groups

MAR 18: Texas billionaire Ross Perot announces he will run as an independent candidate for president

1992

WORLD EVENTS

DEC 8: Agreement by representatives of Russia, Belarus, and Ukraine to end Soviet Union and form Commonwealth of Independent States (CIS); eight more republics join Dec. 21

DEC 25: Mikhail Gorbachev resigns as Soviet president; Supreme Soviet agrees to dissolve the Soviet Union as of DEC 31

JAN 15: Slovenia and Croatia gain independence from Yugoslavia

JAN 16: El Salvador ends its 12-year civil war

FEB 7: European Union founded

offer an apology. She also apologized to George, since she had no intention to sabotage the campaign. Regardless, Reagan and Bush won the election, taking a landslide victory.

Bush logged thousands of miles traveling the world during his vice presidency. He was in Russia for the funeral of Brezhnev; returned to China to assure them of America's interest; journeyed to Beirut after the bombing of the Marine Barracks in 1983; and made several missions to Latin America and Europe. He broke tied votes in the Senate on behalf of the president regarding production of defense weapons, including resuming nerve gas and going forward with his Strategic Defense Initiative (SDI).

The black spot on Bush's vice presidency involved the Iran-Contra affair. When Reagan had taken office, he had resolved to back the Contra rebels of Honduras in their fight against the Marxist Sandinista regime in Nicaragua. When Congress decided to cut off aid to the Contras, members of the administration decided to make up for the loss through private funding. Meanwhile, Reagan had announced there would be no negotiations with terrorists, including those in Iran holding seven Americans they had captured in Lebanon. Through Israeli intermediaries, the United States learned that a weapons deal could lead to the release of the hostages. Then Admiral John Poindexter of the National Security Council and his aide Lieutenant Colonel Oliver North reasoned that monies collected could be funneled to the Contras. After much of this had been arranged, the topic was discussed at various high-level meetings with both Reagan and Bush in attendance, but both would later plead ignorance.

Bush did in fact travel to Jerusalem and met the Israel counterterrorist expert, Amiran Nir, who delivered the possible deal—all hostages released in return for two shipments of military supplies. Bush took the information and soon agreed to send a few spare parts for use on Iran's aging fleet of American-made jets so they could continue to be used in the ongoing war against Iraq, but by now, Bush knew that at least one hostage had been executed. He then traveled to Egypt and Jordan, telling their leaders to send word to Iraqi president Saddam Hussein that America would support him in his fight against Iran. Hussein would gain by becoming America's beneficiary of technology to win his war against his neighbor. In November 1986, Reagan assured everyone, "We did not—repeat, did not—trade weapons or anything else for hostages,"[24] but less than a week later, the president had to admit that money from weapons sales had been channeled to the Contras.

The Iran-Contra mess followed Bush into the political campaign for the Republican nomination in 1988. Then in an interview with Dan Rather for the *CBS Evening News*, Bush was caught off guard by the correspondent's attack on his involvement in Iran-Contra. Again, Bush denied any wrongdoing and resented Rather's accusations of hiding information that the public should know. Bush referred him to the congressional investigations, which had found nothing untoward about his and Reagan's involvement. But he did say, "I went along with it—because you know why, Dan . . . When I saw Mr. Buckley [the slain hostage], when I heard about Mr. Buckley being tortured to death, later admitted as a CIA chief. So if I erred, I erred on the side of trying to get those hostages out of there."[25]

APR 29: LAPD officers found "not guilty" of beating of African American Rodney King, although it was videotaped; verdict results in days of riots

MAY 5: Twenty-seventh Amendment ratified, which prevents Congress from granting itself a retroactive or midterm raise

JUL 16: Bill Clinton and Al Gore become Democratic nominees for president and vice president

JUL 16: Ross Perot withdraws from presidential race

FEB 25–26: Massacre of more than 600 Azerbaijani citizens reportedly by Armenian troops

APR 6: Serbian troops besiege city of Sarajevo after Bosnia and Herzegovina (without Serbian delegates) decide to declare independence from Yugoslavia

APR 28: Republic of Serbia and Republic of Montenegro form their own country, Federal Republic of Yugoslavia

JUN 22: Skeletons of Czar Nicholas II and Czarina Alexandra are found in northern Russia

1988 PRESIDENTIAL CAMPAIGN

Bush knew his main competition to take the Republican presidential nomination was Kansas senator Bob Dole. The two vied with each other in primary after primary. At this time, Reagan was attempting to work out a deal to remove Panamanian dictator Manuel Noriega from power when it was revealed that in the 1970s, Noriega had worked for the CIA as an informant during Bush's watch. This revelation did not help his poll numbers, and Bush lost Iowa. His defeat was only temporary, however, because he took the lead in New Hampshire and captured the primaries of "Super Tuesday." Dole soon had enough, and by winning Pennsylvania, George Bush had the necessary votes to clinch the nomination.

When he learned of the administration's plan to buy off Noriega with the promise of removing sanctions against Panama and indictments against the dictator, Bush became angry and argued with the president in front of staff members. Reagan remained unmoved and announced he would go forward with the plan, but to the vice president's relief, it soon fell through. Noriega remained in charge of both a nation and a major drug smuggling operation.

Bush hoped to campaign with a boost from Reagan, but the president offered half-hearted support. Only at the Republican convention in New Orleans did Reagan seem enthused about Bush's candidacy when he told the loyal party crowd: "George, just one personal request: Go out there and win one for the Gipper!"[26]

When it came time for Bush's acceptance speech, he looked out to the convention's audience and to those watching on television and derided his rival Massachusetts governor Michael Dukakis for not speaking out against taxes. Then Bush proclaimed words that would come back to haunt him: "The Congress will push me to raise taxes and I'll say, 'no.' And they'll push, and I'll say 'no.' And they'll push again, and I'll say to them: Read my lips: no new taxes!'" Bush wanted America to become a "kinder, gentler nation" aided by the help of volunteers, or as speechwriter Peggy Noonan called them, "a thousand points of light."

Bush charged after his opponent, touting the governor's record on crime as being soft by allowing weekend furloughs to felons. A television ad depicted convicted murderer Willie Horton, a black man, who raped a white woman while on his pass. Republicans hammered Dukakis for Boston harbor's pollution, his veto of a proposal to make the Pledge of Allegiance mandatory in school, as well as his opposition to school prayer. Some Republicans, however, were dismayed by Bush's extremely negative campaign and the focus on the periphery issues rather than the major topics. Dukakis, likewise, targeted Bush and his part (or nominal role) in the Reagan administration, as well as his choice of vice president—junior senator Dan Quayle of Indiana, who seemed ill-prepared for the glare of the national spotlight, let alone for the office only a heartbeat away from the presidency. Still, Bush captured 54 percent of the popular vote to Dukakis's 46 percent; Bush won 426 electoral votes to 111 for Dukakis. For the first time since Martin Van Buren, a sitting vice president had won the White House, although Republicans nationwide lost ground in governorships as well as congressional seats, so Bush would have to contend with a Democratic Senate and House.

PRESIDENT BUSH

Most expected the transition from the Reagan to the Bush presidency to proceed smoothly, and it

NATIONAL EVENTS	**AUG:** Mall of America, world's largest shopping mall, opens in Bloomington, Minnesota	**AUG:** AT&T begins marketing first videophones (over $1,000)	**AUG 21:** Republican Party nominates George Bush and Dan Quayle	**OCT 1:** Perot supporters ignore his announcement that he is exiting the race	and make sure he is on ballot in all 50 states, so he reenters the race
WORLD EVENTS	**JUL 6–29:** UN inspectors refused access to Iraqi Ministry of Agriculture stage a sit-in, but eventually leave without conducting inspection	**JUL 10:** Former Panamanian dictator Manuel Noriega found guilty on drug and racketeering charges, sentenced to 40 years	**OCT 31:** Pope John Paul II declares the Catholic Church made a mistake when it condemned Galileo as a heretic in 1633	**NOV 11:** Church of England allows women to become priests	**NOV 25:** Czechoslovakia General Assembly votes to divide into two—Czech Republic and Slovakia as of January 1, 1993

did—up to a point. In his inaugural address, the new president said, "A new breeze is blowing." The world was changing, with the Eastern Bloc near crumbling and the Soviet Union on the brink of collapse. Bush admitted that the country had accumulated a troubling national debt that required action and pledged to bring it down. No doubt many in the audience wondered how that would happen with "no new taxes."

The new president now looked ahead to having his cabinet confirmed by the Senate, and immediately one of his selections was in trouble. Senator John Tower of Texas was Bush's first choice for defense secretary, but the Democrats demanded retribution for the nastiness of the campaign, and Tower became the payback. Charges of alcohol abuse, womanizing (including one instance of enjoying the company of a KGB agent), and his ties with defense contractors made him suspect to charges of conflict of interest. Bush stubbornly refused to withdraw the nomination, and for the first time since 1959, the Congress voted down a cabinet nominee.

Next in line for the position was House minority whip, Richard Cheney of Wyoming, who easily won confirmation. He was well-liked by his House colleagues on both sides of the aisle and had served the executive branch once before as President Ford's chief of staff.

Although he had to deal with a Democratic Congress, the president retained the power of the veto, which he used forty-four times in four years and was overridden only once. Usually he attempted to work out differences before legislation reached a critical stage, but sometimes that was not possible. When Congress passed a minimum wage increase from $3.35 to $4.55 an hour, he vetoed the bill and insisted he would do it again to any raise over $4.25. Eventually, the two sides negotiated a compromise with an increase to $3.80 in 1990 and $4.25 the following year.

Bush was outraged in 1989 by the Supreme Court decision *Texas v. Johnson*, which allowed flag burning as protected by the First Amendment. This so upset him that he sent a proposed constitutional amendment banning flag burning to Congress, but both houses voted it down.

Economically, outward signs seemed to indicate positive factors, including an inflation rate of only 3 percent and decreasing interest rates. The growing national debt, however, created a drain and with fewer jobs being created, a recession set in and unemployment grew. October 1989 saw the stock market tumble. By 1990, it seemed the only way to combat the increased demands on the treasury was to do the unthinkable and raise taxes on the middle and upper income brackets.

Earlier in the 1980s, savings and loan institutions (S&Ls) had used deposits to invest in the real estate market; when it boomed, so did they. But by the mid-1980s, the market began slumping, and some S&Ls began folding. Then new legislation was passed deregulating these financial institutions in the hope that would create incentive for them to be more cautious in their investments, but some unscrupulous managers continued to invest in riskier schemes that gobbled up customers' deposits. One director caught in the mess was thirty-three-year-old Neil Bush, son to the president, who had been courted by the directors of Silverado Savings, Banking, & Loan Association in Colorado. He then began an oil exploration firm with two partners, but that dissolved just prior to his father's election. By that time, Silverado had gone bankrupt and left its investors with nothing.

In 1989, the Financial Institutions Reform,

DID YOU KNOW?

Both George and Barbara Bush are related to former president Franklin Pierce.

NOV 3: Bill Clinton wins presidential election

DEC 24: President Bush pardons former secretary of defense Caspar Weinberger and five other Reagan administration officials indicted for lying about Iran-Contra

DEC 3: UN votes to send peacekeeping force with humanitarian aid to Somalia (famine killed more than 300,000)

DEC 9: American troops arrive in Somalia

DEC 9: Prime Minister John Major announces that Prince Charles and his wife Diana, the Princess of Wales, have separated

Recovery, and Enforcement Act was passed to bail out the multitude of savings and loans that had overextended themselves and left their depositors empty-handed. After this, the Treasury Department took a more active role overseeing the industry and its deposits would now be insured by the Federal Deposit Insurance Corporation, as were banks. The bail-out was estimated to cost taxpayers more than five hundred billion dollars over forty years.

Posturing himself as the "education president," Bush vowed to implement higher standards for America's schools and pledged to support reforms that recognized excellence. With a budget that he wanted to cut rather than add, education received no extra funding to support the reforms; instead, they were to be paid for by the states and local communities. When those lacked the resources, reforms failed to occur. The president attempted to take his case to the states by hosting an education summit for governors at the University of Virginia (founded by Thomas Jefferson). This was only the third time in American history that a president had summoned governors to meet for a common problem. (The first had been Theodore Roosevelt for conservation, and thirty years later his cousin Franklin hosted one to discuss ways to help people during the Great Depression.)

The president was also concerned by America's ongoing drug problem, which showed no signs of decreasing, so he appointed Reagan's secretary of education, William Bennett, to become director of the Office of National Drug Control Policy, but he was quickly dubbed the "drug czar." Most attention was toward the enforcement of anti-drug laws, and frustrating attempts to curtail shipments into the country from Latin America.

Within the country, two pieces of far-sweeping legislation were welcomed by the president. The Americans with Disabilities Act was already on its path in Congress when Bush took office, but he voiced support from the time of his inauguration and proudly signed it into law on July 26, 1990. This prevented discrimination by employers toward hiring people with disabilities. Better access for handicapped individuals was also mandated regarding transportation and ease of accessibility for customers.

The Environmental Protection Agency (EPA) became more active and worked to eliminate the use of asbestos. In 1990, the Bush White House claimed victory with congressional passage of amendments to the Clean Air Act of 1970. These new laws restricted car emissions and required cleaner-burning fuels. It set National Air Quality Standards for cities which were to be staggered into force over the coming decade. Helped in the timing of this legislation was the disastrous oil spill in Alaska caused by the oil tanker the Exxon *Valdez* in March 1989. This ecological nightmare took six months to clean up and pointed to the fragile balance between man and the environment.

Bush also believed in conservation and created more than ninety wildlife refuges and set aside nearly two million acres of wetlands. Thankful for the efforts by the White House, John Turner, president of the Conservation Fund, said "No president since Teddy Roosevelt has done more to protect the wild heritage of America than George Bush."[27]

FOREIGN AFFAIRS

Soon after taking office, the president and First Lady traveled to China on a state visit. They welcomed the chance to see once more the country they had adored during their brief tenure in the 1970s. During the interim, Bush had met several times with China's leader, Deng Xiaoping. The China they saw in March 1989 was radically different than the one they had experienced fifteen years before. Student dissidents were becoming more outspoken against the Communist regime. A month after the president's visit, thousands of Chinese students occupied Tiananmen Square, and Deng Xiaoping denounced their activities. Soon another international visit by Soviet leader Mikhail Gorbachev only incited more protests against communism and praise for Gorbachev and perestroika.

Once Gorbachev left, martial law was declared, and on June 4, tanks moved onto the square and machine guns shot anyone who refused to move. Three thousand were killed and another ten thousand wounded in the bloodbath (although People's Republic of China official figures are much lower). The world watched spellbound while a single student stood before a column of four tanks, halting their advance until people pulled him away. The crackdown continued in the following days as the government rounded up and arrested more dissidents and banned the foreign press.

Events in China frustrated Bush's hopes to continue building a better relationship with that vital nation. He deplored the Communist's iron fist but also disagreed with those who advocated cutting off all ties. Many in Congress wanted to revoke everything including its recently approved "Most Favored Nation" status for trade. Sanctions were imposed and loans delayed while NSA advisor Brent Scowcroft visited China to explain the president's position. His assistant Lawrence Eagleburger reported to Secretary of State James Baker, "I think the smarter ones absorbed the message that we can do a lot more for them when they aren't killing their own people."[28]

With the reforms implemented by Mikhail Gorbachev earlier in the 1980s, the path was cleared for the Soviet Union to begin breaking from its Communist leanings. Prior to his taking office, Bush had met with Gorbachev and Reagan in New York. There he and the Soviet leader took part in a heated exchange prompted by Bush's remark: "What assurance can you give me that perestroika and glasnost will succeed?" Gorbachev testily replied, "Not even Jesus Christ knows the answer to that question!" Then the Soviet leader added, "You'll see soon enough that I'm not doing this for show. . . . I'm engaged in real politics. . . . It's going to be a revolution nonetheless."[29]

Once in office, Bush decided he needed to stop and thoughtfully consider what Gorbachev as the leader of the USSR and Eastern Europe was really doing. He asked the National Security Council to draft the speech, and most of it was crafted by the head of the Soviet and Eastern Central Europe departments, Condoleezza Rice. The speech was delivered at Texas A&M's commencement in May 1989: "No generation can escape history. We are approaching the conclusion of an historic postwar struggle between two visions: one of tyranny and conflict and one of democracy and freedom." Bush reached back to the Eisenhower era when he said, "Containment worked. And now it is time to move beyond containment to a new policy for the 1990s."[30] A new initiative was introduced called "open skies," which provided open access for both the United States and the USSR to fly over each other's nations, particularly their weapons defense areas.

BERLIN WALL FALLS ★ East German citizens began gaining access to the West in the summer of 1989 when Hungary and later Czechoslovakia opened their borders and allowed them to pass through. Once the new East German government announced they would open the border, at midnight on November 9, 1989, thousands enthusiastically swarmed the 28-mile-long Berlin Wall. Many climbed on top and began chipping away at the symbol, erected nearly four decades before, that had long separated one people.

Soon after his speech, Bush attended a NATO summit in Brussels. There he discussed his hope that the Soviets would negotiate with NATO to limit conventional forces and weapons in Europe. "If the Soviet Union accepts this fair offer, the results would dramatically increase stability on the continent and transform the military map of Europe."[31] When the president traveled to West Germany, he again made headlines by announcing, "The cold war began with the division of Europe. It can only end when Europe is whole." Bush strongly believed that reunification of Germany was key to changing the face of Europe. He added in his speech in Mainz, "Unity and strength are the catalyst and prerequisite to arms control."[32] Newspaper editorials on both sides of the Atlantic lauded the president's visit as a triumph.

During the coming months, the Eastern Bloc of nations tore themselves away from communism and began their first steps toward independence. In Poland, Czechoslovakia, Bulgaria, and Hungary,

AMERICANS WITH DISABILITIES ACT OF 1990 ★ The ADA prohibited discrimination against Americans who have "physical or mental impairment that substantially limits a major life activity." Businesses and those providing public accommodations as well as public transportation were required to make their facilities accessible to wheelchairs. Employers were also prohibited from discriminating against anyone because of a person's disability.

democratic elections took place. On November 9, 1989, the Berlin Wall fell and its people on both sides freely mingled, and less than a year later, the two Germanys became one.

In 1990, Bush and Gorbachev held a summit meeting in Washington where they agreed to reduce their weapons (arms and chemical) stockpiles. Then in November 1990, they and other leaders signed a mutual non-aggression pact between the nations of NATO and those of the Warsaw Pact (whose membership dissolved their alliance six months later). By spring 1991, weapons and troops were removed from Europe. Then in July 1991, the two world leaders signed the Strategic Arms Reduction Treaty (START) II, which would dismantle the nuclear arsenals of both nations over the coming years.

Within the Soviet Union, change was gathering momentum like a snowball rolling down a mountainside, and their first free elections were held in March 1989. In August 1991, a coup d'état was attempted against Gorbachev, but it failed, and he was freed from house arrest. Earlier Bush had warned the Soviet leader of this threat, but Gorbachev had downplayed any danger. Soon Soviet satellite republics began splitting from Moscow's orbit to establish their own nations, and Gorbachev resigned as president of the dissolving union on December 25, 1991. What Ronald Reagan had called "the evil empire" was no more.

Difficulties with neighbors closer to home also plagued Bush during the early portion of his term. For years, Manuel Noriega had troubled the American government with his contribution to the ongoing drug problem within the United States. Now the president wanted the Panamanian dictator's reign to end. Former president Carter had witnessed the widespread fraud of elections there in 1989. A coup failed in October of that year and its leader executed, and then Noriega's forces captured two Americans, killing one and torturing the other. These actions convinced Bush to take military action.

On December 20, 1989, Operation Just Cause was launched with fourteen thousand American troops landing in Panama, joined by thirteen thousand who were already stationed in the Canal Zone. They bombarded and quickly seized key military installations to neutralize Noriega's paramilitary thugs and the country's Panama Defense Force. Capturing the leader was a top priority, but it took weeks before he was tracked down and taken into custody. A Florida grand jury had indicted Noriega the year before on various drug charges, so he was delivered to Miami, where he stood trial and was found guilty on eight federal charges of drug smuggling, money laundering, and racketeering. He was sentenced to forty years in prison without parole, but later that term was cut by ten years. Noriega is currently serving his time in Miami.

Many in the world community objected to the military invasion of Panama and the seizing of its leader, although most Panamanians supported the drastic action by the United States which returned democracy to that nation. Twenty-three Americans died in the invasion and about five hundred Panamanian soldiers and civilians were killed.

Meanwhile, with the decline of the Soviet Union in the late 1980s and its ultimate dissolution in 1991, outside support for Communist efforts in Central America waned and eventually dried up altogether, forcing revolutionary elements to moderate their positions and engage in the democratic process. The ruling Sandinista regime in Nicaragua agreed to hold free multi-party elections in 1990, while in El Salvador, the Marxist guerrillas were faring badly in battles against US-backed government forces. Seeing the writing on the wall, they entered into negotiations, which led first to a ceasefire, then an agreement to lay down their arms.

START (STRATEGIC ARMS REDUCTION TREATY) I ★ START I was signed by the Soviet Union and the United States on July 31, 1991, but within two months, the USSR had dissolved, leaving nuclear warheads in four of its republics: Russia, Belarus, Ukraine, and Kazakhstan. The Lisbon Protocol was signed among those four nations and the United States in May 1992, reiterating the terms of the START I treaty. Among its terms: limits of 1,600 ICBMs (intercontinental ballistic missiles) per side and no more than 6,000 accountable nuclear warheads to be extant seven years after the treaty went into effect.

PERSIAN GULF WAR

During Reagan's second term, the United States lent assistance to Iraqi dictator Saddam Hussein in his war against neighboring Iran. When Iran appeared on the brink of winning after several years of extremely bloody fighting, America aided the Soviet-equipped Iraqi Army by supplying military intelligence, loans, and encouraging third-country arms sales in order to ensure that it had the materials it needed to continue the fight. While not particularly caring for either antagonist, the United States had long-standing distrust of Iran stemming from its 1979 seizing of Americans from the embassy. Both the Reagan and Bush administrations felt Iran was more likely to push itself into countries in the region, prompting disruptions of oil. Once the war ended, the Iraqi dictator decided to sell the food sent by the United States and other countries, and used the profit to purchase weapons, which he then turned on his own people. Elements within the Bush administration urged patience in dealing with Hussein while Congress demanded sanctions against him, but Bush remained opposed, fearing that the sanctions could cause destabilization of the region.

Iraq and Iran had fired barrages of Soviet- and Chinese-made Scud missiles at each other's capital cities of Baghdad and Teheran during the war, and Saddam Hussein ordered that modifications be made to the missile to lengthen its range enough to reach Israel. Angered by this and his other antagonistic moves, President Bush refused another loan to Iraq. Although thwarted, Hussein looked about and found an easy target—the oil fields of Kuwait. That country had earlier frustrated his attempt to raise OPEC's oil prices by refusing to obey the cartel's directive to reduce production. He also owed that government over ten billion dollars in loans from his war with Iran, so he calculated that seizing the small nation would also wipe out the debt. By mid-July 1990, unmistakable evidence of thousands of Iraq Republican Guard troops massing on their border with Kuwait was picked up by US intelligence. When they reached the point ten miles from the border, Colin Powell, chairman of the Joint Chiefs of Staff, ordered General Norman Schwarzkopf, military commander of the Persian Gulf region, to ready his troops for war.

Just after midnight on August 2, Iraqi soldiers and tanks rolled across the desert into Kuwait. Worried that Iraq's real objective was to attack Saudi Arabia, Bush consulted with National Security advisor Brent Scowcroft, General Colin Powell, Secretary of Defense Dick Cheney, and General Norman Schwarzkopf. The leaders agreed that American forces could be mobilized not only to defend Saudi Arabia but also to push Hussein's troops from Kuwait, but they needed time to prepare. Meanwhile the president consulted British prime minister Margaret Thatcher and Saudi king Fahd regarding the situation. Bush told Fahd that "the security of Saudi Arabia was vital—basically fundamental—to US interests and really to the interests of the Western world."[33] Fahd was soon enlisting the support of other Arab nations in the region to join a coalition being formed by the Americans and British, which soon included the Soviets, as well.

The United Nations echoed the sentiments of the world's people in condemning Hussein and demanded that his troops withdraw from Kuwait. Meanwhile President Bush was working the phones, speaking to world leaders and explaining why they wanted to be on the same team as the United States. He received unparalleled support not only from European and Asian leaders but from those in the Middle East, as well, who disliked their bullying neighbor. One who was specifically courted by both sides was the Soviet Union. Secretary of State James Baker met with Soviet foreign minister Eduard Shevardnadze, whose country often provided weapons to Iraq. They issued a joint statement calling for "an international cutoff of all arms supplies to Iraq."[34] The Soviets felt bound to support the Americans in this effort because of the ongoing aid that was being funneled into the USSR from the United States to help prop up their shaky economy.

Beyond the arms embargo, though, Bush and most of his advisors wanted military action, but Baker argued against it, claiming the Soviets would oppose any aggressive moves. Gorbachev ultimately agreed to a UN resolution allowing for military force if necessary, to ensure the embargo was followed. British prime minister Margaret Thatcher reminded the president of her nation's support and reminded him that even though there were difficulties working with the coalition, "This is no time to go wobbly."[35]

On August 7, the 82d Airborne and two squadrons of F-15 fighters arrived in Saudi Arabia, followed by A-10 "tank busting" fighter bombers. Although their numbers were no match for the 140,000 Iraqi troops, their presence was to provide "a line in the sand," as Bush told the American people in an address he made to the nation on the night of August 8. He explained the purpose was to defend Kuwait, Saudi Arabia, and "other friends in the Persian Gulf" while demanding the immediate withdrawal of Iraqi forces from Kuwait. By the end of the month, for the first time since the Tet Offensive in 1968, reservists were called up for duty.

More troops arrived in Saudi Arabia in the coming months as part of the defensive force known as Desert Shield. They came from other countries, but the United States supplied the most and readied itself for war. Some nations, including Germany, Japan, and Korea, provided monetary support, but the majority of the bill for Desert Storm was paid for by Saudi Arabia, Kuwait, and the United Arab Emirates. On January 9, 1991, Congress granted the president permission to take military action against Iraq if all other alternatives had failed.

A week later, after numerous warnings and ultimatums by the United Nations had been repeatedly ignored, Operation Desert Storm roared into action with air attacks against Baghdad and Iraqi forces in Kuwait. Iraq responded by launching seven Scud missiles against Israel, who wanted to retaliate but was strongly requested by Bush not to play into Hussein's hand of desiring to turn the fighting into a "holy war" and force the Arabs out of the coalition. Future Scud attacks were lessened by the arrival of American Patriot air-defense missiles and the targeting of Saddam's mobile- and fixed-launch sites by air and special operations forces.

Night after night, US and coalition aircraft flew strikes against targets in Iraq and Kuwait and encountered great success. After one attack, Hussein insisted a baby formula plant had been hit, but later it was found to produce chemical weapons. Frustrated, his country under fire, Hussein then ordered Scud missiles be launched against Saudi Arabia, as well as Israel. On January 28, President Bush stated, "The war in the gulf is not a Christian war, a Jewish war, or a Muslim war—it is a just war. . . . Our cause could not be more noble."[36] In February, the Iraqi ambassador to the UN demanded that the bombing end or his country would begin using weapons of mass destruction.

To complete the job, the coalition forces launched their ground attack at 4:00 a.m. on February 24. "Shock and awe" overwhelmed Iraqi soldiers, who often surrendered to coalition troops rather than fight to the death, while many "elite" Republican Guard formations succeeded in escaping from the two-pronged coalition attack. Finding resistance not as difficult as planned, Kuwait was quickly liberated from its invader. When word reached Bush, he met with his cabinet about the next step. Was the war over now that Kuwait was liberated? Should troops move farther into Iraq to topple Hussein? While some wanted the latter, they had to understand that it was never the objective and more importantly, it was not what the coalition had agreed to help do. Kuwait was to be freed, nothing more, nothing less. Bush asked, "Why not end it today?" His chief of staff John Sununu suggested halting it and calling it the "100 Hour War." The group unenthusiastically agreed and Colin Powell phoned Schwarzkopf with the message, which was not welcomed by many military leaders who saw some of their strategic objectives unmet. But the decision was made, and the public was told on the night of February 27 that hostilities had ceased. Troops came home to a hero's welcome, and Bush's approval rating shot to 90 percent, the highest of any president in polling history. He seemed an easy shoe-in for reelection.

"READ MY LIPS: NO NEW TAXES!" ★ The main phrase associated with President George H.W. Bush and uttered during his appearance before the Republican convention in 1988. A growing deficit and a shaky economy with a slumping stock market made him commit to raising taxes for the 1991 budget. Feeling betrayed by the president, many voters then turned to a third party candidate, Ross Perot, in 1992, which helped cause Bush's defeat at the polls.

REELECTION CAMPAIGN

Going into the election season, Bush seemed less than enthusiastic about campaigning, let alone winning another term. One factor was the loss of good friend and political consultant Lee Atwater. Another problem was the president's listlessness, which was found to be caused by Graves' Disease, a disorder of the thyroid that also attacks the immune system—an affliction shared by his wife. Conflicts among staff members also concerned the president, who dreaded the upcoming fundraising and campaigning required by a candidate.

During this time, the economy continued slipping toward a recession, with more on the unemployment rolls each month. When many wanted to see increased unemployment benefits, the president refused, arguing that such action would break the budget. In the summer of 1991, the people watched as the president's nominee for the Supreme Court, Clarence Thomas, defended himself against charges of sexual harassment by Anita Hill, a former colleague when he taught at Oral Roberts University. Thomas received the Senate's confirmation, but many wondered aloud if he was the best candidate for the position.

As the campaign kicked off early in 1992, Bush suffered from a staff that lacked experience and knowledge of how to run an effective campaign. He soon was pitted against the youthful governor of Arkansas, Bill Clinton, who was coached by Democratic consultant James Carville to keep his message on point, namely, "It's the economy, stupid." Then to add to the mix, Texan Ross Perot decided to throw his Stetson into the ring and possibly settle an old score against Bush. His candidacy thrilled some voters who liked his non-political background to head a third party, but he withdrew from the race in July, only to reenter it in October.

The Republican convention was held in Houston in August, and there the party platform sounded more conservative than their candidate; in fact, it denounced Bush's tax increases. The Democrats chose Bill Clinton, and the two men and Ross Perot debated three times. During one debate, the camera caught Bush looking at his watch as though he wished it would all be over; this brief glimpse was replayed numerous times on the evening news. Although he tried to criticize Clinton for not serving in the Vietnam War and called his economic plan "Elvis economics," the president did not have much to counter Clinton's and Perot's hits at his handling of the economy. To the American voter, Clinton appeared to be a breath of fresh air, and he was elected by 43 percent of the popular vote, while Bush lost with 37 percent, and undoubtedly Perot took much of the electorate that would have supported the president with his 19 percent.

RETIREMENT

After watching the inauguration of his successor, George and Barbara Bush bade farewell to Washington and flew to their home in Houston.

WORLD WIDE WEB ★ Personal computers had appeared in the early to mid-1980s, but the Internet was just beginning to gain in popularity. In 1990, the World Wide Web was created by Tim Berners-Lee. Two years later, Jean A. Polly coined the term "surfing the Internet." By the end of 1993, Web use had grown by over 341,000 percent. And it was only the beginning . . .

There they began to lead a quiet lifestyle. Multiple international trips filled much of their retirement; in fact, they visited more than fifty countries. A planned assassination attempt by Iraqi agents during their visit to Kuwait was discovered and thwarted in 1993.

Bush's autobiography, *Looking Forward,* with Victor Gold, was published in 1988, followed the next year by *Man of Integrity,* with Doug Wead. He also co-authored *A World Transformed* with General Brent Scowcroft in 1998. His letters and personal thoughts were published in two books: *All the Best* and *Heartbeat.* Barbara joined her husband, writing her memoirs, as well as a couple of children's books about their dogs, *C. Fred's Story* and *Millie's Book.*

In 1991, the George Bush Presidential Foundation was created as the basis for a library and museum to be built on the grounds of Texas A&M University in College Station, Texas, which opened to the public in the fall of 1997. Bush also joined the boards of various charitable organizations, while Barbara continued her longtime interest in literacy (partly due to their son Neil's problem with dyslexia). In 1989 she had founded the Barbara Bush Foundation for Family Literacy and continues as its honorary chairwoman and helps with its annual fundraiser.

Two of the Bush sons soon followed their father's footsteps into the political arena, and the proud parents enjoyed seeing son George become the governor of Texas and son Jeb the governor of Florida. Then the former first couple campaigned and addressed the Republican convention in 2000, which nominated son George as the presidential candidate, and a few months later, he and his father became the second such team to have served in the presidency.

After the enormous devastation experienced by people of the Gulf coast following Hurricanes Katrina and Rita, former presidents Bush and Clinton forged an unlikely partnership and began making public appearances and commercials asking for donations to help the hurricane victims. Their common plea was quite effective, raising over $130 billion in a little more than a year. The two men seemed to genuinely like each other and Clinton laughingly referred to himself as "George Bush's straight man."[37] Unlike the months when the two were campaigning and debating each other, Bush seemed more relaxed, a "kinder, gentler" man than the embattled president of before.

In December 1992, riding his final time aboard Air Force One from the family retreat at Kennebunkport, Maine, Bush took some time to reflect. He wrote a note that is now exhibited at his presidential library: "I hope history will show I did some things right."[38]

ENDNOTES

1 Herbert S. Parmet, *George Bush, The Life of a Lone Star Yankee*, New York: Scribners, 1997, p. 40.

2 Joe Hyams, *Flight of the Avenger: George Bush at War*, New York: Berkeley Books, 1992, p. 72.

3 Parmet, p. 53.

4 George Bush, with Victor Gold, *Looking Forward: An Autobiography*, New York: Bantam Books, 1988, p. 36.

5 Parmet, p. 57.

6 Hyams, p. 193.

7 Parmet, p. 67.

8 Peter Schweizer and Rochelle Schweizer, *The Bushes: Portrait of a Dynasty*, New York: Doubleday, 2004, p. 98.

9 Parmet, p. 102.

10 Fitzhugh Green, *George Bush: An Intimate Portrait*, New York: Hippocrene Press, 1991, p. 91.

11 David Yergin, *The Prize*, New York: Simon & Schuster, 1991, p. 754.

12 Bush, p. 101.

13 Ibid.

14 Parmet, p. 157.

15 Ibid, p. 165.

16 Barbara Bush, *A Memoir*, New York: Charles Scribner's Sons, 1994, p. 112.

17 Tom Wicker, *George Herbert Walker Bush*, New York: Penguin Books, 2004, p. 41.

18 Parmet, p. 200.

19 *The Texas Observer*, October 7, 1977.

20 Parmet, p. 211.

21 Ibid, p. 245.

22 G. Bush, p. 222.

23 B. Bush, p. 195.

24 Parmet, p. 315.

25 *CBS Evening News*, January 25, 1988.

26 Richard Reeves, *President Reagan: The Triumph of Imagination*, New York: Simon & Schuster, 2005, p. 477.

27 John Robert Greene, *The Presidency of George Bush*, Lawrence: University Press of Kansas, 2000, p. 75.

28 James A. Baker III, *The Politics of Diplomacy: Revolution, War, and Peace*, New York: G.P. Putnam's Sons, 1995, p. 110.

29 Michael Beschloss and Strobe Talbot, *At the Highest Levels: The Inside Story of the End of the Cold War*, Boston: Little, Brown, 1993, pp. 10-11.

30 George Bush, Commencement speech, Texas A&M University, May 12, 1989.

31 Parmet, p. 389.

32 Ibid, p. 390.

33 Greene, p. 150.

34 Ibid, p. 114.

35 Ibid, p. 119.

36 *Military Review*, "The Gulf War," September 1991, p. 73.

37 Associated Press, November 13, 2006.

38 Greene, p. 181.

William J. Clinton

★ ★ ★ FORTY-SECOND PRESIDENT ★ ★ ★

LIFE SPAN
- Born: August 19, 1946, in Hope, Arkansas

NICKNAMES
- Bill, Comeback Kid, Slick Willie

RELIGION
- Baptist

HIGHER EDUCATION
- Georgetown University, 1968
- Oxford University, 1968–1970
- Yale Law School, 1973

PROFESSION
- Professor, lawyer

MILITARY SERVICE
- None

FAMILY
- Father: **William Jefferson Blythe III** (1918–1946)
- Stepfather: **Roger Clinton** (died 1967)
- Mother: **Virginia Cassidy Blythe Clinton Dwire Kelley** (1923–1994)
- Wife: **Hillary Rodham Clinton** (1947–); wed on October 11, 1975, in Fayetteville, Arkansas
- Children: **Chelsea Victoria** (1980–)

POLITICAL LIFE
- Attorney General of Arkansas (1977–1979)
- Governor of Arkansas (1979–1981, 1983–1992)

PRESIDENCY
- Two terms: January 20, 1993–January 20, 2001
- Democrat
- Reason for leaving office: completion of term
- Vice president: **Albert Gore Jr.** (1993–2001)

ELECTION OF 1992
- Electoral vote: **Clinton** 370; **George H.W. Bush** 168; **Ross Perot** 0
- Popular vote: **Clinton** 44,908,233; **Bush** 39,102,282; **Perot** 19,741,048

ELECTION OF 1996
- Electoral vote: **Clinton** 379; **Bob Dole** 159; **Perot** 0
- Popular vote: **Clinton** 47,402,357; **Dole** 39,198,755; **Perot** 8,085,402

CABINET

SECRETARY OF STATE
Warren Christopher (1993–1997)
Madeline Korbel Albright (1997–2001)

SECRETARY OF THE TREASURY
Lloyd M. Bentsen (1993–1994)
Robert E. Rubin (1995–1999)
Lawrence H. Summers (1999–2001)

SECRETARY OF DEFENSE
Les Aspin Jr. (1993–1994)
William J. Perry (1994–1997)
William S. "Bill" Cohen (1997–2001)

ATTORNEY GENERAL
Janet Reno (1993–2001)

SECRETARY OF THE INTERIOR
Bruce Babbitt (1993–2001)

SECRETARY OF AGRICULTURE
Mike Espy (1993–1994)
Dan Glickman (1995–2001)

SECRETARY OF COMMERCE
Ronald H. Brown (1993–1996)
Mickey Kantor (1996–1997)
William Daley (1997–2001)

When winning his two political offices—governor of Arkansas and president of the United States—Bill Clinton presented a youthful exuberance that strongly appealed to the electorate. Others would point to his relative youth as the reason for some of his mistakes in judgment that would ultimately lead him to becoming only the second president in history to experience an impeachment trial.

EARLY LIFE

Part of the post–World War II baby boom, William Jefferson Blythe III was born on August 19, 1946, at Julia Chester Hospital in Hope, Arkansas. His mother, Virginia Cassidy, was working as a nurse in a Shreveport, Louisiana, hospital when she met William J. Blythe. They were instantly captivated by each other, even though he had brought in his date, who was suffering an appendicitis attack. After he left the hospital, Blythe and Virginia dated and continued seeing each other. She had no idea he had been married four times previously, and they married on September 3, 1943, in Texarkana, Arkansas. Since he had been drafted a few months before meeting her, Virginia knew he would soon be going to war, and within a few weeks he shipped out for duty in Africa and Europe.

After Blythe's return in December 1945, he found work in Chicago and brought Virginia there. She soon discovered she was pregnant and by spring was living with her parents back in Hope. William was on his way there in May when his car skidded out of control near Sikeston, Missouri, and he was thrown from the car. Landing unconscious in a ditch, he drowned in three feet of water, never knowing his son.

Virginia left Hope soon after her husband's death to study anesthesiology for a year in New Orleans and left her son with her parents. When she returned, she worked as a nurse in the local hospital and began dating again. One of her boyfriends was Roger Clinton, a car salesman who also enjoyed drinking and gambling—"pretty wild and woolly,"[1] according to a family friend. He moved from Hot Springs to Hope, where he was opening a Buick dealership, and the two saw each other regularly, which caused no shortage of whispers since he was still married at the time. Eventually he divorced his wife, and he and Virginia wed on June 19, 1950, in a chapel near the Hot Springs racetrack. Since her family disapproved of the match, none of them—including her four-year-old son—attended the nuptials.

During his early years, young Billy, as he was called, was raised by his grandparents. His grandmother Edith worked to instill in her grandson the importance of education, and he later recalled her drilling him in numbers and the alphabet at an early age: "I was reading little books when I was three."[2] His grandfather Eldridge took him to his small store and allowed the boy to mingle with the customers, both black and white, a small island of integration in a segregated southern world. Playing with other children, Billy found himself bigger than them and clumsier. One day in kindergarten, he tripped while jump roping and broke his leg in three places.

When he was seven years old, Billy said goodbye to his grandparents and friends in Hope and moved with his mother and stepfather to Hot Springs, where Roger had bought a farm, hoping to turn his luck around after losing the dealership. Billy's half-brother, Roger Jr., joined the family in 1956.

Billy enrolled in St. John's School, which was a Catholic elementary school with an all-white student population. The boy excelled in his subjects,

NATIONAL EVENTS

JAN 7: EPA releases report citing hazards posed by second-hand smoke

JAN 18: First observance of Martin Luther King Day in all 50 states

JAN 20: Bill Clinton inaugurated as nation's 42nd president

FEB 5: President Clinton signs Family and Medical Leave Act

FEB 26: Bombing of World Trade Center by a van parked under North Tower

1993

WORLD EVENTS

JAN 1: Official dissolution of Czechoslovakia into Czech Republic and Slovakia

JAN 3: President George H.W. Bush and Russian President Boris Yeltsin sign Strategic Arms Limitation Treaty (START II)

JAN 19: Iraq refuses UN inspectors and starts military operations along Iraq-Kuwait DMZ; US Tomahawk missiles hit military targets and end the threat

MAR 12: North Korea announces it will no longer abide by the Nuclear Nonbut the nuns complained that he always insisted on answering the questions posed in class. He soon gained a reputation as a peacemaker among the children and wanted everyone to like him, which may have been in response to the ongoing bickering and fighting he endured at home that had only heightened with his stepfather's increased drinking.

Meanwhile, Roger Clinton was attempting to become a farmer, but with no more success than he had at running a car dealership. While at the farm, Billy experienced a fright—he was butted repeatedly by a ram, giving the child "the awful lest [sic] beating I ever took,"[3] and received injuries that required stitches.

Never adept at sports, Billy found his niche in other areas, particularly music. He loved listening to the radio and he and his mother became fans of Elvis Presley. He played the saxophone skillfully and won a state competition. He joined the Mason's organization for instilling leadership qualities in young men, the DeMolay, and rose to their highest rank. Billy continued earning exceptional marks in his subjects, and while he enjoyed talking politics and economics, he also liked hanging out with girls.

A critical event occurred in the Clinton family when Bill was fourteen. His stepfather had been drinking excessively and proceeded to beat Virginia behind their closed bedroom door. Hearing the frightening sounds of punches and screams, scared little Roger began crying hysterically, prompting his older brother to take action. Bill broke down the door, shuffled his mother to safety, then confronted his stepfather and ordered him to never touch his mother again. No one in Bill's school had any idea of the emotional turmoil occurring in his home. Later Clinton said these experiences actually helped: living through "a lot of adversity in our life when I was growing up . . . gave me a high pain threshold, which, I think, is a very important thing to have in public life. You have to be able to take a lot of criticism—suffer defeats and get up tomorrow and fight again."[4]

The couple divorced in May 1962, but Roger soon pleaded that he had reformed and begged Virginia to forgive him and try again. She consented, and they remarried in August 1962. During the interim, Bill did something that surprised everyone, the reason for which he never fully explained. He went to court to change his name to William Jefferson Clinton, stunning his mother by taking the name of the man whom she had just divorced.

In the summer of his junior year, Bill participated in Boys State (a leadership organization for high school students). Before attending, he had already determined he would run for senator rather than governor because that would put him on track to get elected to its national organization, Boys Nation. This met in Washington, D.C., and included a meeting with the president of the United States. Clinton won and spent the week of July 19, 1963, meeting other boys from across the nation, as well as lawmakers. The young men role-played various government positions, but the highlight came on Wednesday, July 24, when they met President Kennedy in the White House Rose Garden. Bill situated himself toward the front of the line to be sure he would be able to shake the president's hand. This he did, and cameras caught the moment of one president welcoming a future president. Clinton returned to Arkansas bubbling with enthusiasm for politics.

He spent his senior year busy with band, his studies, DeMolay, and socializing with friends, but the tragic news of President Kennedy's assassination shocked him, as it did the rest of the nation.

CABINET

★★★★★★★★★★

(continued)

SECRETARY OF LABOR
Robert B. Reich (1993–1997)

Alexis Herman (1997–2001)

SECRETARY OF HEALTH AND HUMAN SERVICES
Donna E. Shalala (1993–2001)

SECRETARY OF HOUSING AND URBAN DEVELOPMENT
Henry G. Cisneros (1993–1997)

Andrew M. Cuomo (1997–2001)

SECRETARY OF TRANSPORTATION
Federico R. Pena (1993–1997)

Rodney E. Slater (1997–2001)

SECRETARY OF ENERGY
Hazel R. O'Leary (1993–1997)

Federicko F. Pena (1997–1998)

Bill Richardson (1998–2001)

SECRETARY OF EDUCATION
Richard W. Riley (1993–2001)

SECRETARY OF VETERANS AFFAIRS
Jesse Brown (1993–1997)

Togo D. West Jr. (1998–2001)

FEB 28: Raid of Branch Davidian compound near Waco, Texas, to serve warrants for federal firearms violations to its leader David Koresh results in deaths of four FBI agents and five Davidians; 51-day standoff begins

MAR 11: Janet Reno confirmed by Senate and becomes America's first female attorney general

APR 19: Fire at Branch Davidian compound kills 76 of its members and ends standoff

APR 22: Holocaust Memorial Museum dedicated in Washington, D.C.

proliferation Treaty and no longer allow inspections to nuclear sites

MAR 27: Jiang Zemin becomes new leader of People's Republic of China

APR: Kuwait government announces it uncovered plot to assassinate former President Bush while he was visiting Iraq

JUN 27: President Clinton orders cruise missile attack on Iraq Intelligence headquarters in Baghdad in retaliation for assassination plot against former President Bush

DID YOU KNOW?

As a delegate of Boys Nation, Clinton visited the White House and met President Kennedy in 1963.

As graduation drew nearer, he decided that he wanted to attend the relatively new School of Foreign Service at Georgetown University. His choice was based on the location because Clinton yearned to return to Washington. Once accepted, he worried about the cost, knowing his family had very limited finances, but they told him to go anyway, figuring something could be arranged once he arrived.

COLLEGE

Graduating fourth in his high school class of 327 in May 1964, Clinton was selected to give the benediction. "Make us care so that we will never know the misery and muddle of life without purpose," he prayed, "and so that when we die, others will still have the opportunity to live in a free land."[5] Following an uneventful summer, including working at Boys State as a counselor, Bill and his mother traveled east for some sightseeing and freshman orientation. Although at first glance, both students and faculty wondered what the rural fellow from Arkansas was doing among the conservative well-to-do young men of the east, within a short time, Clinton felt at ease at the Jesuit school, meeting and interacting with young people from very different backgrounds, including President Johnson's daughter Luci.

Bill wasted no time cranking up his political machine to win election as the freshman class president. He did not spend much time in other activities, however, as class work kept him busy since now he truly had to work to maintain good grades in his rigorous course of study. He later recalled with fondness one professor who preached to his students, "The future can be better than the past, and each individual has a personal, moral obligation to make it so."[6]

He returned to Arkansas for the summer and there he helped family friend Judge Roy Holt with his campaign for the Democratic nomination for governor. Clinton played chauffer to Mrs. Holt and her two daughters. They traversed the state visiting large and small towns, where the Georgetown sophomore payed special attention to segregation. He wrote to his current girlfriend, "We are campaigning in the heart of cotton country, south and east Arkansas where Negroes are still niggers—and I couldn't believe my eyes when I saw restrooms and waiting rooms still marked in Colored and White. It made me so sick to my stomach."[7] Holt lost the election, but Clinton gained valuable experience of how campaigns were run. He also asked Judge Holt to contact Senator William Fulbright regarding an internship at the capitol.

Bill returned to Georgetown, where he won his second election and became the sophomore class president. He also began working two part-time internships on Capitol Hill, in addition to his full slate of classes, where he continued to maintain an A average. Working for Senator Fulbright as an intern opened Clinton's mind to ideas he had not entertained before, and he viewed the Vietnam War through the eyes of Fulbright and his staff. The young man had generally accepted the need to defend South Vietnam because President Johnson said it was the right thing to do. But the senators on the Foreign Affairs committee with Fulbright tended to disagree, and soon their views were adopted by the intern.

In his senior year, Bill suffered an election upset for class president because the student body did not believe his platform was progressive enough in providing them more freedom of choice and opportunities in their classes. Clinton decided his loss was due to lack of communication with the

NATIONAL EVENTS	**JUL:** Mississippi and Missouri Rivers flood several midwestern states	**JUL 19:** President Clinton announces "Don't ask, don't tell" policy for gays in military	**AUG 10:** President Clinton signs Revenue Reconciliation Act into law to levy tax increases to fight federal deficit	**NOV 30:** President Clinton signs Brady Bill requiring five-day waiting period before purchasing a gun	**DEC 8:** President Clinton signs North American Free Trade Agreement (NAFTA) to end tariff barriers between US and its neighbors
WORLD EVENTS	**SEP 13:** President Clinton presides over public handshaking by Israeli prime minister Yitzhak Rabin and PLO leader Yasser Arafat	**SEP 21:** Beginning of constitutional crisis in Russia when its president Boris Yeltsin dissolves its legislature	**SEP 29:** Earthquake kills more than 10,000 in India **OCT 2:** Russia on brink of civil war but security and military leaders back Yeltsin	**OCT 3:** Battle in Mogadishu, Somalia, between local militias and American troops results in 19 Americans and 500 Somalis killed	**OCT 5:** Resistance against Yeltsin crushed **NOV 1:** European Union officially begins

electorate and pledged in the future he would not make the same mistake.

In November 1967, Clinton experienced a loss and a blessing simultaneously with the passing of his stepfather from cancer. Later that month, young Clinton appeared before a regional selection board that awarded the prestigious Rhodes scholarships for students to study abroad. Impressing the judges with his knowledge and charisma, Bill scored another triumph.

Clinton graduated from Georgetown with a degree in international affairs in June 1968, then in October left by ship for England, where he studied for the next two years at Oxford University. Before departing, his step-uncle talked to some friends on the draft board who agreed to defer his induction so he could attend Oxford. However, the draft notice arrived in late April 1969, causing Clinton no small amount of anxiety about what he should do. Young men were allowed to finish their current school term before reporting, so he did just that and returned to Arkansas.

As soon as he arrived home, he began calling friends and contacts to see how he could avoid actually becoming a "grunt." Ultimately, an acquaintance from Oxford who had returned home earlier, Cliff Jackson, managed to pull some strings as head of the Republican Party in Arkansas. A deal was formulated that Clinton would join the ROTC at the University of Arkansas (UA); he would enter their law school in the fall of 1969 and begin the ROTC in the spring of 1970, which would make him a commissioned officer three years later. This arrangement killed the draft notice, so he would not have that hanging over his head. Relieved, Clinton agreed to the plan, and all was set to go into action. Then he had second thoughts and decided that while he did want to attend law school, he deemed UA's to be inferior, so now with his draft deferment granted, he saw his way open to return to Oxford. The process of deciding what to do apparently made him a nervous wreck for weeks and he wrote to one friend that the deliberation had "ravaged my own image of myself."[8] Reneging on the deal upset a great many people, including Cliff Jackson, who later angrily recalled how he had made arrangements to allow Clinton the ROTC slot because the young man had promised, "I want to serve my country. I will go into the ROTC, the army reserve, whatever—I just don't want to go as a draftee."[9]

After returning to England, Bill began looking the part of a hippie, growing out his hair and beard, wearing sandals and looking rather unkempt. He also helped organize a protest against the Vietnam War in London. Clinton took time to write a long letter to Colonel Eugene Holmes, who oversaw UA's ROTC program, and explained why he had left Arkansas rather than fulfill his commitment. He insisted that he had anguished over the choice but "I didn't see, in the end, how my going in the army and maybe going to Vietnam would achieve anything except a feeling that I had punished myself and gotten what I had deserved."[10] Consequently he decided it best for him to return to England for his second year.

Besides taking courses in philosophy, economics, and political science, Bill found time for sightseeing, including an excursion to the home of one of his favorite poets—Dylan Thomas. He also toured Eastern Europe and part of the Soviet Union during his winter break at the end of December 1969 into January 1970. Then that spring, he decided to return and study law at Yale, which had awarded him a scholarship.

SUPREME COURT APPOINTMENTS

★★★★★★★★★★

Ruth Bader Ginsberg, 1993

Stephen G. Breyer, 1994

JAN 20: The Citadel admits its first female student on orders from Supreme Court, but she soon drops out

FEB 5: Conviction of Byron De La Beckwith for killing civil rights leader Medgar Evers in 1963

FEB 11: Paula Jones alleges Clinton had made sexual advances towards her three years earlier; he denies the charges

MAR 4: Four al-Qaeda terrorists convicted of World Trade Center bombing

APR 22: Death of former President Richard Nixon in New York City

1994

JAN 14: President Clinton and Russian leader Yeltsin sign Kremlin Accords to continue nuclear disarmament; specifically targets cutting nuclear arsenal in Ukraine

FEB 3: President Clinton ends nearly 20-year trade embargo between US and Vietnam

FEB 6: Nearly 70 civilians killed by Bosnian Serb Army bomb lobbed into Sarajevo market square

FEB 28: US jets shoot down four Serbian fighter jets for violating no-fly zone over Bosnia-Herzegovina

STATE OF THE UNION
★★★★★★★★★★

US POPULATION IN 1993
281,421,906

NATIONAL DEBT IN 2000
$5,674,178,209,886.86

PRESIDENT'S SALARY
$200,000/year

Once he was back in the States, Bill decided to stay clear of Arkansas and went first to Washington, D.C., then on to New Haven, Connecticut. He soon became part of a campaign team for Joe Duffey, a liberal Yale professor running for the Senate, and experienced the heartbreak of defeat when Duffey lost at the polls.

Later Clinton said he "went to Yale Law School to learn more about policy. And in case my political aspirations didn't work out, I wanted a profession from which I could never be forced to retire."[11] There he learned from professors at both ends of the political spectrum; in fact, his two classes on Constitutional law provided the two extremes—conservative Robert Bork, who later became President Reagan's unsuccessful nominee to the US Supreme Court, and another class taught by fellow Rhodes scholar and liberal Charles Reich.

While legal studies kept Clinton somewhat occupied, he also found time to campaign for local Democratic candidates, as well as date a young lady from the Chicago area, Hillary Rodham. Bill and Hillary found that they agreed on politics and desired to change the world. Soon they were inseparable and lived together during their second year at Yale, where, besides taking a full load of classes, Bill also worked two jobs—helping a local attorney and teaching an undergraduate criminal law class at the University of New Haven. Any spare time was spent campaigning for the Democratic Party and its 1972 presidential candidate, George McGovern.

LEGAL CAREER

Bill and Hillary finished law school and now looked to the future. Clinton was planning to return to Arkansas and begin practicing law until one of his professors mentioned a last-minute vacancy at the University of Arkansas Law School at Fayetteville. He applied and, despite his inexperience, was offered a position to begin that fall. Bill invited Hillary to join him, but she went to work for Marian Edelman and the Children's Defense League in Cambridge, Massachusetts. She did, however, visit him and took the Arkansas bar exam.

As the House Judiciary Committee began preparing its possible impeachment charges against President Nixon, its chief counsel asked Clinton to join the team. He deferred but recommended Hillary. While Bill might have been interested, he was now considering running for Congress in the 3rd Congressional District. Keeping up a hectic schedule, he continued teaching his classes and campaigned for Congress. Unfortunately one sometimes got in the way of the other, and when he took his students' exams to grade while on the campaign trail, he lost five of them. One belonged to Susan Webber, who later was the judge of a famous case against her former teacher; Clinton said, "I don't think she ever forgave me."[12]

During that summer of 1974, the president resigned and Bill's second stepfather, beauty salon owner Jeff Dwire, died from diabetes. Virginia understood that her son could only take a short break from his campaigning and urged him to resume after the funeral. Still he was unable to beat incumbent John Paul Hammerschmidt, who was one of the few Republicans to win in the first election since Nixon's resignation.

Clinton returned to his teaching and was happier now that Hillary had taken a position at UA as well and was keeping active running the school's legal aid clinic. He surprised her by buying a charming house they had seen for sale, and then on October 11, 1975, the couple was married in its living room.

NATIONAL EVENTS

AUG 12: Major league baseball players strike, so season ends early without a World Series

SEP 12: Cessna flown into South Lawn of White House about 1:49 a.m.; its pilot killed in the crash

SEP 13: President Clinton signs into law Assault Weapons Ban

OCT 29: Francisco M. Duran goes to the White House and fires 29 rounds from his semi-automatic weapon before Secret Service agents subdue him; he is sentenced to 40 years imprisonment for attempting to assassinate the president

WORLD EVENTS

MAR 15: US troops withdraw from Somalia

APR 6: Plane carrying presidents of African nations of Berundi and Rwanda shot down by a missile

APR 7: Rwandan Genocide begins resulting in more than 500,000 murders of Tutsis by rival Hutu militias

MAY 6: Opening of Channel Tunnel connecting England and France

MAY 9: Inauguration of Nelson Mandela as first black South African president

ATTORNEY GENERAL

Still itching to enter the political arena, Clinton decided to run for state attorney general in 1976. He was cast against two other Democrats—the secretary of state and assistant attorney general; the Republicans, however, had no candidate for the position, so all Clinton had to do was win the primary. Although he failed to win the approval of the labor element when he refused to sign a petition to rid the state of its right-to-work law, his active campaigning across the state swept him to victory in the primary with nearly 56 percent of the votes. Since he did not need to worry about his own election, he concentrated on heading the Carter campaign for president in Arkansas.

Now that he was an office-holding Democrat on the state level, he and Hillary were sometimes invited to the Carter White House. As attorney general, he used utility rates as his focus and created an energy division and opposed the telephone companies when they wanted to raise pay-phone rates to a quarter. Energized by life on the political scene, he shared his life's philosophy with a friend who was feeling rather miserable: "If you're not having fun, it just becomes work, and it's time to move on to something else."[13]

By the end of 1977, Clinton had decided to embark on his next campaign—the governorship. There were four others running in the primary, but none had much chance. Hillary became their target because she was an attorney at the city's most prestigious law firm. Another criticism was over the continued use of her maiden name. Her husband argued that she was really "old-fashioned" but also "witty and sharp without being a stick in the mud. She's just great."[14] Clinton won the primary and easily took the election. At the age of thirty-two, he would become the leader of the state of Arkansas and the youngest governor in the country.

GOVERNOR

The crowd listening to their youthful governor deliver his inaugural address heard promise and optimism as Clinton told them, "For as long as I can remember, I have believed passionately in the cause of equal opportunity, and I will do what I can to advance it. For as long as I can remember, I have deplored the arbitrary and abusive exercise of power by those in authority, and I will do what I can to prevent it."[15] His budget proposal was onerously thick and too long to engage the interests of the lawmakers. Although wanting to go in all directions simultaneously, the new governor decided to make his mark by improving the roads of his state. To do this he needed money, so it was announced that truck and car license fees would increase. This was immediately attacked by the trucking industry and their main users—the poultry businesses of the state. Clinton backed off and shifted the burden to the private sector and amended the bill so fees were to be based on weight, so those with older cars and trucks paid more than those who owned newer models.

The governor also angered people by the way he did business. He would often be late, sometimes hours behind in arriving to meetings. Clinton had his staff overbook his schedule, trying to squeeze in everyone he wanted to see, but when there wasn't enough time, he would fly into a rage over the handling of his schedule. Two of his top staffers left before his two-year term was over.

Clinton found being governor was no easy job. Concerned that the timber industry was acting recklessly using clear-cutting in the Ouachita Mountains, he established a timber management

DID YOU KNOW?

Clinton is the first president to have been a Rhodes scholar.

NOV 5: Former president Reagan announces in a letter that he has been diagnosed with Alzheimer's

NOV 8: Republicans win control of both houses of Congress in midterm elections

NOV 8: George W. Bush defeats incumbent Ann Richards to become governor of Texas

DEC 19: Investigation begins into Whitewater scandal

AUG 11: Fidel Castro will no longer impose emigration restrictions on his people; President Clinton, fearful of an onslaught of immigrants, orders they will receive no special status

AUG 31: At midnight, IRA agrees to halt its violent opposition and begin peace talks about future of Northern Ireland

SEP 3: Russia and China agree not to target nuclear weapons at each other

task force to study the problem. They held hearings and soon the timber companies and people with timber rights for their lands made their views known to the governor. Although Clinton insisted he had expressed no position, he did ask for voluntary restrictions, but no longer considered any mandatory action against the lumber industry.

In 1980, the governor faced a crisis of safety and a showdown with the Carter White House. Fort Chaffee was the detention site for eighteen thousand illegal Cuban refugees from the Mariel boatlift who were then being processed, but on May 26, some two hundred broke out of the camp. Clinton ordered the military to tighten controls and ordered National Guard and state troopers to stake out positions in the Fort Smith vicinity as a safeguard. A riot erupted on June 1, with the military guards standing aside while Cubans burst through the fence and moved toward a nearby town. Clinton met with the local citizens to calm their fears—and their tempers—to prevent any vigilante violence. He was promised by a White House official that no more refugees would be sent, but two months later that assurance was broken when refugees were moved from other resettlement camps to Fort Chaffee. Clinton went into a rage, ranting obscenities at the official at the White House, reminding him how hard he had worked for Carter, saying actions like this would hurt both of their chances in their upcoming reelection campaigns. Clinton's words fell on deaf ears, but he still fought for the president as Carter and Edward Kennedy vied for the Democratic nomination.

Earlier that year, the Clintons had added a new member to the family—Chelsea Victoria (named for Judy Collins's song "Chelsea Morning") was born on February 27, 1980. Bill proudly showed his new daughter throughout the halls of the hospital. Now he and Hillary worked on his reelection campaign, but the mood of his state and country were different this time around, and his Republican opponent Frank White defeated him with a margin of 52 percent to 48 percent. The loss stunned Clinton, who angrily maintained that Carter was partly to blame for the upset. Determined not to fail again, he immediately began working on his strategy to retake the governorship in 1982.

INTERIM

Once the Clintons found a new home in Little Rock, Bill went to work for a law firm and Hillary continued her career at the Rose Law Firm. When friends visited the couple, they noticed that Hillary seemed perfectly content in her career while he was totally miserable in his. Political consultant Dick Morris, who had helped him to win the election to the governorship, said Clinton would ask: "'Gee, do you think I can come back? Do you think I've had it?'" Morris found his former client now "like a patient afflicted with cancer wondering if he had any chance of survival."[16]

After long consideration and reflection upon his last campaign, Clinton decided it had been lost by not hitting Frank White hard when he launched inflammatory commercials against the governor and the mess at Fort Chaffee. When he attended a Democratic meeting in Des Moines, Clinton told his audience, "When someone is beating you over the head with a hammer, don't sit there and take it. Take out a meat cleaver and cut off their hand."[17]

In February 1982, Clinton embarked on his next campaign by airing a television ad in which he admitted his earlier mistakes and asked the voters to give him a second chance. Hillary also decided to make a break with the past and announced

NATIONAL EVENTS

APR 19: Oklahoma City bombing: Timothy McVeigh leaves a bomb in a rented van in front of Alfred P. Murrah Federal Building; bomb kills 168, including 19 children in its daycare facility

1995

WORLD EVENTS

SEP 19: American troops invade Haiti to restore its elected leader Jean-Bertrand Aristide to power

SEP–OCT: Iraq refuses to cooperate with UN inspectors and begins placing troops along Kuwait border; US deploys troops within Kuwait

OCT 15: Iraq backs down after receiving warning from UN; troops withdraw from Kuwait border

JAN 1: World Trade Organization replaces GATT

JAN 31: President Clinton grants emergency loan of $25 billion to Mexico to save it from economic disaster

she would be campaigning as "Mrs. Bill Clinton" rather than Hillary Rodham to appease the electorate. At first the TV ad appeared to hurt Clinton, so he went on the attack against the other Democratic candidates. This seemed to be more effective, and in June he won the primary. A rematch was in the offing between Clinton, the former governor, and current governor Frank White. This time, Clinton knew his political future was over if he failed.

Redoubling his efforts and with a staff equally pledged to the task, the Clintons stumped the state and won the election, beating the incumbent 55 percent to 45 percent and making Clinton the first Arkansas governor to lose an election but later retake the office.

GOVERNOR—AGAIN

Clinton knew he needed to concentrate on one issue for this term, and he chose education reform. In May 1983, the state supreme court declared that the state's funding of education was unconstitutionally inequitable. Ranked forty-ninth in money spent on education, one area that needed serious restructuring was funding. Knowing the people would not stand for a significant tax increase, Clinton decided (after Morris conducted a poll) that raising the state sales tax would be the best method. Hillary then was assigned to head the Education Standards Committee to investigate the state of education in Arkansas. They held hearings throughout the state and discovered that, along with the poor teacher pay (which was so low that many received food stamps), some instructors were not fit to be in the profession. This discovery prompted lawmakers to push for competency testing.

Governor Clinton called a special session of the legislature to pass his education package, and he insisted that testing must remain, or forget the whole thing. Teachers, including their union, the Arkansas Education Association (AEA), vigorously campaigned in their local districts as well as at the state capitol to vote down the tests; some feared minority teachers would do poorly because of cultural bias on the exams. Meanwhile, one of the AFL-CIO leaders, Bill Becker, convinced Clinton to add a rebate for low-income families for the sales tax on food. Although he originally agreed to this, Clinton soon changed his mind when it started hitting opposition in the state senate. Becker cried "foul," and did not soon forget the governor's double dealing.

Once the education reforms were enacted, some improvement was noted, including more class offerings in subjects such as foreign language, as well as higher level math and science courses. More seniors went to college; however, test scores for the state remained low.

In the summer of 1984, Bill was shocked to learn of the drug problems of his brother Roger, who took and dealt cocaine on a regular basis, then boasted he had nothing to fear since he was the governor's brother. The state police initiated a sting operation and caught Roger on camera, and he was convicted and received a two-year prison sentence. Virginia and her two sons entered family counseling, where they discussed the longtime woes and addictions of Roger Clinton Sr., and how it had scarred and affected all three members long after he was dead.

Roger's arrest was front-page news in Arkansas, and although some worried that it might hurt Bill's chances at reelection, it did not. Clinton again swept to victory, this time with a 63 percent to 37 percent landslide in the same election that Ronald Reagan defeated Walter Mondale for the presidency.

DID YOU KNOW?

Clinton plays the saxophone and sometimes played it on television and at campaign events.

JUN: US Supreme Court strikes down laws supporting using race as a determinant for federal programs or redrawing congressional district boundaries

JUL: Record heat wave hits much of the US

JUL 27: Korean War Memorial dedicated in Washington, D.C.

SEP 1: Rock and Roll Hall of Fame opens in Cleveland

MAR 3: UN peacekeeping mission ends in Somalia

MAR 20: Japanese religious cult releases poisonous gas Sarin into Tokyo trains

MAR 22: Russian cosmonaut sets space duration record of 438 days before returning to earth

JUL 1: Iraq admits it had biological weapons

JUL 11: Bosnian Muslims (Bosniaks) slain as part of a genocide campaign conducted by Bosnian Serbs in Srebrenica; over 8,000 die

During his next term as governor, Clinton concentrated on improving the economy by cutting unemployment, and traveled to other states, where he attempted to lure businesses to Arkansas, but these efforts yielded mixed results. He worked to keep the current factories and plants working and made deals when they were looking to close. Sometimes he used Wal-Mart as his ace in the hole to bolster failing businesses. When Sanyo threatened to pull out, he convinced them to stay if he could persuade Wal-Mart to sell their televisions. It worked. He negotiated a similar deal with Van Heusen shirts to keep that plant open.

Clinton advocated giving more authority to the state's housing agency to grant bonds, require at least 5 percent of the state pension funds to be invested within Arkansas, and not to dump recently foreclosed farms on a market that was already real-estate heavy. The legislature agreed to his package, and he signed their bill banning late-term abortions. He did veto an increase in gas taxes to fund a new road program because he had made a campaign pledge against new taxes, so he felt duty bound to honor that promise. They overrode that veto—the only one overturned in his dozen years as governor.

During 1985, Clinton edged closer to the national spotlight. He delivered the Democratic response to President Reagan's State of the Union message in January. He also became active in the Democratic Leadership Council. Wanting to run again in 1986, he began his campaign to become the second longest-serving governor of the state since Reconstruction. This time in the primary, Clinton faced off against two former governors—Frank White and Orval Faubus, who was best known for attempting to prevent the integration of Central High School in Little Rock in 1957. Again Clinton claimed victory, this time winning 64 percent of the vote. The nation's governors elected him as their leader and the chairman of the Education Commission of the States, which would serve as a clearinghouse of ideas to improve education.

For his next term, the governor continued his efforts to develop the state's economy and improve its education, and then added welfare reform (which he later referred to as "a way station on the road to independence"[18]) to his list. For this Clinton traveled to Washington and testified before a congressional committee with other governors, asking them for the means to keep people from having to turn to welfare in the first place by attacking societal problems such as teen pregnancy, illiteracy, and drug abuse.

Clinton found himself being invited to speak in various states, increasing speculation about whether he would be a candidate for the presidential nomination in 1988. Although ambition stirred, he believed his duty as governor required him to remain on the job to ensure his reforms were enacted, so he decided he would pass on this election; after all, he was only forty-one years old and had plenty of opportunity ahead.

He was invited by fellow governor Michael Dukakis of Massachusetts to deliver the nominating speech at the Democratic convention in Atlanta. Unfortunately, Clinton's speech proved too long for the audience, who talked and milled about the convention hall rather than listen attentively. This was all too obvious to the audience watching at home, who figured whatever the governor of Arkansas was saying must not have been important. An Arkansas friend and Hollywood producer, Harry Thomason, suggested Clinton get back in the saddle by appearing on Johnny Carson's *Tonight Show*. A more

NATIONAL EVENTS

- **OCT 3:** Jury finds O.J. Simpson not guilty in murdering his ex-wife Nicole Brown Simpson and Ronald Goldman
- **NOV 14:** Party politics in Congress create a standoff in agreeing to a budget, so federal government runs with reduced staff
- **NOV 28:** End of 55 mph highway limits signed into law by President Clinton
- **APR:** PalmPilot introduced
- **APR 3:** Commerce Secretary Ron Brown killed in a plane crash over Croatia

1996

WORLD EVENTS

- **AUG 4:** Croatian forces fight back against Serbian troops and begin advancing into Bosnia, completing "ethnic cleansing"
- **AUG 30:** NATO forces bomb Serbian positions in Bosnia
- **OCT 30:** Referendum for Quebec's independence
- **NOV 4:** Israeli Prime Minister Yitzhak Rabin assassinated
- **FEB 9:** End of cease-fire with IRA when bomb explodes in East London
- **MAR 1:** UN inspectors denied access to Iraq, but are allowed to enter sites several days later

relaxed side revealed itself to the nationwide audience and people enjoyed watching the youthful governor swapping quips with Carson and then playing his saxophone with Doc Severinsen.

In 1989, Clinton pushed ahead with more reforms, including extension of the preschool HIPPY program, required "grade cards" of schools, comparison of schools' performance, and the goal of ridding adult illiteracy. These programs and others demanded more funding, which required higher taxes. He appointed Dr. Jocelyn Elders to head the Department of Health with a primary objective of lowering the teen pregnancy rate and starting health clinics in schools.

After pondering the question of whether to run for yet another term, Clinton finally decided to do so, but first asked his wife if she was interested in running for governor. Hillary insisted that he needed to make his decision first. More competition met him in the primary, and he faced a harder match in the election, but again he was victorious (57 percent to 43 percent).

He embarked on his next term with more reforms and cajoled lawmakers into voting with him, but he also found time to continue his extensive speaking engagements throughout the nation. Now Clinton was mixing with the Hollywood elite and wealthy power players of the Democratic Party, many of whom looked upon him as their best hope for the upcoming presidential campaign. He even received a phone call from a White House aide to President Bush, asking if he planned to run and telling him that if he did, they would destroy him personally.

In the summer of 1991, the first "Clinton for President" signs popped up in Arkansas, and the next month, he hired his treasurer for the campaign. Reporters began hitting him with questions regarding his personal life, including whether he had smoked marijuana. He replied that he had not violated American drug laws (sidestepping the issue since he had used it while in England). Possible womanizing was also raised, to which he replied all marriages had their problems, and his was no different. Then on October 3, he officially announced his candidacy for president.

1992 CAMPAIGN

Knowing he had to have a good showing in the New Hampshire primary, Clinton recruited men and women to staff an office in Manchester while he began making numerous campaign appearances. He found several parallels between this state and Arkansas and felt quite comfortable getting out and meeting its people. The liberal wing of the Democratic Party decided that Clinton was too centrist, so they pushed other candidates, including Tom Harkin of Iowa, Bob Kerrey of Nebraska, and Paul Tsongas of Massachusetts, all with extensive congressional experience. Undaunted by the competition, Clinton pushed his agenda by emphasizing reforms achieved in Arkansas—welfare, education, environment, and increased law enforcement—to a national audience. His staff also grew with the additions of James Carville and Madeline Albright.

In late January 1992, a story broke that had been briefly reported earlier regarding Gennifer Flowers, a woman who claimed to have had a longtime affair with Clinton. She originally denied the story, and then retracted her statement, and reporters pressed the governor for his account. Deciding the best offense was a good defense, Bill and Hillary appeared on the CBS program *60 Minutes*, where he denied Flowers's charges but admitted that he had been involved in extramarital

APR 3: Suspected "Unabomber" Theodore Kaczynski arrested in Montana (accused of series of mail bombings that killed three and injured more than 20 others)

APR 4: Freedom to Farm Act signed into law ending government subsidies and regulations of what can be planted

JUL 19: President Clinton opens Summer Olympic Games in Atlanta

JUL 27: Bomb explodes at Centennial Olympic Park in Atlanta during Olympics killing one and injuring 111

MAR 19: Bosniaks take over all of Sarajevo

APR 18: Returning fire by Hezbollah from Lebanon, Israel shells UN compound at Qana, leaving more than 100 Lebanese civilians dead

MAY: UN officials oversee destruction of Iraqi biological warfare production

JUN 25: Khobar Towers in Saudi Arabia bombed and 19 American servicemen killed

JUL 5: First mammal to be cloned (Dolly the sheep) is born in Scotland

affairs. Both denied that their marriage was any type of "arrangement," insisting they were in love and committed to each other.

Another bombshell hit a few days later with a story about Clinton dodging the draft during the Vietnam War. At first he said he had not received preferential treatment, but later admitted there had been a deferment. Then, Colonel Holmes's account was made public about the deal arranged with ROTC only to have Clinton renege and return to Oxford. Holmes also published Clinton's letter. The double-barrel effects of both stories devastated the Clinton camp, but they decided to push forward since the New Hampshire primary was only a little over a week away. Although his poll numbers had dropped, he rebounded on election day to come in second to Paul Tsongas. Despite losing other February New England races, Clinton won the southern primaries and caucuses, as well as those in Hawaii and Missouri, then moved on to take Illinois and Michigan.

More criticism of Hillary's work with her law firm as a conflict of interest hit the campaign, and as attention moved to New York's primary, she again became the focus regarding a real estate investment years earlier when the couple had invested with friends Jim and Susan McDougal in property along the White River in the Ozarks, hoping it would become extremely profitable. When that failed to materialize, the McDougals paid the Clintons their share of the down payment, and Jim McDougal entered the savings and loan business. This, too, proved unprofitable, and he retained Hillary as his attorney, a relationship that was painted as unscrupulous during the campaign and later.

The marijuana question was raised again during a debate with Democratic nominee and California governor Jerry Brown. Clinton responded that he had tried it while in Oxford "but did not inhale."[19] His response was ridiculed soundly by the media, and he later lamented that it only added to the growing list of questions about his character.

Still, Clinton won the primaries of New York, as well as Pennsylvania, California, and a slate of others throughout the nation, providing him with enough delegates to win the nomination. He appeared on television programs, gaining national exposure as the unofficial Democratic presidential nominee, and three days before leaving for the party's convention in New York, he chose Senator Al Gore of Tennessee as his running mate. Then as soon as the convention ended, the Clintons and Gores boarded a bus to begin a tour of the north from New Jersey to Illinois, with plenty of stops along the way.

The Republicans hammered at Clinton and Hillary as opposing family values at their convention, where they nominated George Bush for a second term. Ross Perot entered the race as a third party candidate, and the trio debated three times in the final month before the election. Clinton did well in each, defending his record and his character against Bush's assault on the draft question. By the third debate, Clinton announced his support of the North American Free Trade Agreement recently negotiated by the Bush administration with Canada and Mexico to maximize free trade opportunities for all concerned.

Prior to the election, newspapers across the country endorsed Clinton, including some who usually supported Republican candidates. Some Republicans also backed him publicly, including Connecticut governor and former US senator Lowell Weicker and Sarah and James Brady (Reagan's communications director,

NATIONAL EVENTS	**AUG 15:** Republicans nominate Kansas senator Bob Dole for president	**AUG 22:** Welfare reform enacted, which shifts burden to states to provide aid to needy families	**AUG 29:** Democrats renominate Bill Clinton and Al Gore	**SEP:** President Clinton signs Comprehensive Test Ban Treaty to ban nuclear testing	**SEP 21:** Defense of Marriage Act signed into law by President Clinton refusing to recognize same-sex marriages
WORLD EVENTS	**AUG 23:** al-Qaeda leader Osama bin Laden calls for war against the US	**AUG 28:** Prince and Princess of Wales are divorced **AUG 31:** Iraq violates its No-Fly Zone in the north and captures a town in Kurdistan	**SEP 3:** US leads retaliation against Iraq (Operation Desert Strike) **SEP 27:** Taliban capture Afghanistan's capital, Kabul	**NOV:** Again UN inspectors find banned missile components in Iraq and are prevented from taking evidence	**NOV:** Arab broadcasting station al-Jazeera begins broadcasting via satellite from Qatar

wounded during an assassination attempt on the president). The gap that had widened earlier was closing as the election approached, but Bush was unable to overcome Clinton's lead. On election day, the polls saw an increase of 10 percent, perhaps some of this attributable to Ross Perot's involvement in a three-way race. Once the votes were counted, Clinton won 43 percent of the popular vote, Bush won 37 percent, and Perot 19 percent. In the electoral college, Clinton took 370 votes, Bush 168, with Perot carrying none. Bush, who earlier seemed invincible due to his popularity during the Persian Gulf War, now faced the fact that he was one of only four incumbent presidents who was not reelected. That job now belonged to the forty-six-year-old governor of Arkansas.

BRADY HANDGUN VIOLENCE PREVENTION ACT ★ Signed into law by President Bill Clinton on November 30, 1993, and enacted February 28, 1994, the Brady Handgun Violence Prevention Act had been debated in Congress for six years before being passed. Named for President Reagan's press secretary, James Brady, who was shot during the assassination attempt on the president's life in 1981, the bill's main purpose was to establish a five-day waiting period to allow a background check to be done before a citizen could purchase a gun. This was changed in 1998 when the FBI-run NICS (National Instant Criminal Check Background System) went online and expedited background checks.

PRESIDENT CLINTON

After taking his oath of office, the forty-second president of the United States pledged to make changes: "We must invest more in our own people—in their jobs and in their future—and at the same time cut our massive debt. . . . It will not be easy. It will require sacrifice. But it can be done and done fairly."

The Clinton family soon settled into their new life at the White House, and the staff adapted to having a youngster again, the first since Amy Carter in the 1970s. Hillary had already been asked by her husband to head a commission on healthcare; meanwhile, she recruited a staff and settled in an office in the East Wing of the White House.

During her time as the first lady of Arkansas, Hillary had headed a task force on rural healthcare, as well as the one on education standards, so she assumed the job of chairing one looking into national healthcare would be similar. She was mistaken. The group encompassed cabinet members and other staffers of the White House, as well as a plethora of officials from government agencies, Congress, healthcare representatives, economists, etc.—some six hundred members, which proved far too unwieldy to run effectively, and many quit believing the President's Task Force would accomplish nothing. The group officially disbanded in May 1993. Both Democrats and Republicans in Congress disagreed among themselves about what healthcare reform should entail, so the outpouring of support that the president and Mrs. Clinton had expected never materialized.

The first legislation signed by the new president was the Family and Medical Leave Act, which provided workers time off when a family member was ill or a new child was born. Although healthcare was stymied, Congress did approve his economic stimulus package including deficit reduction by raising taxes on the upper income bracket and

NOV 5: Bill Clinton wins presidential reelection

DEC 29: Guatemala ends its 36-year civil war

1997

JAN 22: Madeleine Albright confirmed as first female secretary of state

JAN 19: Israel turns over its last city on West Bank to Palestinians

FEB 13: Allegations made that Chinese Embassy funneled contributions to Democratic campaigns in 1996

FEB 23: Fire breaks out on Russian Mir space station

MAR 4: President Clinton refuses to fund any research for human cloning

JUL 1: United Kingdom relinquishes sovereignty over Hong Kong to China

MAY 25: Strom Thurmond becomes longest serving member of US Senate at just under 42 years

AUG 31: Diana, former Princess of Wales, dies early in the morning after a car crash in Paris

corporations. The campaign pledge to grant tax cuts to the middle class was quietly discarded.

Another of Clinton's campaign promises had been to lift the ban on homosexuals serving in the military. This, however, ran into ferocious opposition from some members of the military establishment, as well as congressional leaders. Soon the new policy became "Don't ask, don't tell," which disappointed gay and lesbian groups who hoped the new president would bring a more open attitude to the Armed Forces.

Upon learning of an Iraqi plot to assassinate former president George Bush on a visit to Kuwait, Clinton decided that the United States needed to take retaliatory action, and General Colin Powell, chairman of the Joint Chiefs of Staff, recommended a strike on Iraq's intelligence headquarters in Baghdad using Tomahawk missiles. The president ordered his first military action. Prior to the attack, Clinton phoned Bush to tell him of the plot and his plan. Presidential aide George Stephanopoulos listened rather incredulously to his boss tell Bush, "We completed our investigation. Both the CIA and FBI did an excellent job. It's clear it was directed against you. I've ordered a cruise-missile attack."[20] Most of the twenty-three missiles hit their target, but unfortunately, three overshot and killed eight citizens of Baghdad.

At home, terrorism shook the country with a bomb exploding at New York City's World Trade Center, which killed six people and injured over a thousand. Soon five suspects with ties to a radical Middle Eastern group were convicted for the crime.

Two days after the New York bombing, on February 28, 1993, violence erupted near Waco Texas when FBI agents from the ATF (Bureau of Alcohol, Tobacco, and Firearms) attempted to penetrate the Branch Davidian compound where sect leader David Koresh had gathered his flock. Four agents were killed and more were wounded during the confrontation. For the next two months, the cult and law enforcement engaged in a standoff that was not broken until Attorney General Janet Reno went to the president and asked permission for a raid, saying that the FBI had informed her they could not continue keeping their resources tied down in Waco. Clinton gave the green light, and the raid proceeded, but it went badly, with the majority of Branch Davidians killed, including twenty-five children who died in a fire started by Koresh's people after the FBI launched tear gas into their building. Criticism immediately fell on the administration and its handling of the affair, with Reno publicly taking responsibility.

In May, headlines announced the firing of the White House Travel Office staff, in an episode nicknamed "Travelgate." The seven who worked there were holdovers from previous administrations and immediately replaced by Clinton people, including one of the president's cousins. Those fired retaliated by filing protests, and all but one were quickly reassigned other positions within the government. Billy Dale, the travel director, however, was not so fortunate. He was charged with financial malfeasance and ultimately put on trial. The jury took less than two hours to acquit him, and in recognition of his thirty years of service, the Senate agreed to pay his legal fees.

Eventually his case became the focus of a House probe into whether the Clinton staff had acted appropriately by demanding Dale's FBI files and prosecuting him. When the House asked for records, they were at first refused, then sent only a small fraction. This led to a larger investigation of what became known as "Filegate," which revealed

NATIONAL EVENTS

JUN 2: Timothy McVeigh convicted of 15 counts of murder and conspiracy for Oklahoma City bombing of the Alfred P. Murrah Federal Building in 1995 and next day sentenced to death

JUL 4: Pathfinder space probe lands on Mars

JUL 21: USS *Constitution*, US Navy's oldest commissioned ship, celebrates its 200th birthday by sailing a short distance

AUG 1: Merger between MacDonnell-Douglas and Boeing completed

WORLD EVENTS

SEP: Several attempts by Iraqi officials to divert inspectors or destroy records/data regarding their weapons programs

SEP 6: Diana's funeral at Westminster Abbey is watched by one billion people worldwide

NOV 17: Islamic militants gun down 62 tourists outside tomb of Hatshepsut's Temple in Egypt

DEC 3: More than 120 countries sign a treaty banning land mines, but US, Russia, and China do not sign

DEC 30: Worst massacre in Algerian uprising kills more than 400 in four villages

staffers within the Clinton White House had improperly obtained and kept hundreds of FBI files on people from previous administrations (mainly Republican) for months. Their purpose in doing so was never fully explained and Attorney General Reno appointed Kenneth Starr as special prosecutor to investigate. He was replaced by Robert Ray, whose report in 2000 stated that there was nothing linking people in the White House to the acquisition of the confidential files.

Later in 1993, the president signed the Brady Bill, which provided gun control and required background checks and waiting periods of up to five days to purchase handguns. Another piece of legislation signed by the president, with his predecessors—Ford, Carter, and Bush—beside him, was NAFTA, created to allow more open trading opportunities between the United States and its neighbors to the north and south.

On the foreign front, Clinton learned that foreign affairs demanded a great deal of a president's attention. He attempted to win support of the British and French to do more in Bosnia, where intense fighting between Serbs and Bosnians was turning the former nation of Yugoslavia into a bloodied land. The president argued for NATO air strikes and removing the arms embargo, so that weapons could be sent to the Bosnian Muslims for defense.

Soon after burying his beloved mother Virginia, in January 1994, the president traveled to Russia to meet with its leader, Boris Yeltsin. Then in June, Clinton represented the United States in France for the fiftieth anniversary ceremony of D-Day.

North Korea grabbed the world's attention when it prevented inspectors from the International Atomic Energy Agency (IAEA) to visit nuclear sites in mid-March 1994. Clinton countered by ordering Patriot missiles to South Korea, as well as recommending economic sanctions be imposed by the United Nations. Former president Jimmy Carter volunteered to mediate the crisis with North Korea and meet with President Kim Il-sung. Clinton agreed, and based on their talks, inspectors could remain, provided that the United States backed away from sanctions. This agreement was soon declared null and void by Sung's son Kim Jong-il and heir when the Korean leader died on July 8, 1994.

In September 1993, Israeli prime minister Yitzhak Rabin and PLO leader Yasser Arafat came to the White House to sign a historic pledge including Israeli recognition of the Palestinian Authority and assurance to grant part of its lands in Gaza and the West Bank. Behind the scenes, Clinton and his staff worked to ensure the two leaders could meet cordially for the historic occasion. Rabin was not sure he wanted to shake Arafat's hand and mentioned

INDEPENDENT COUNSEL ★ In the aftermath of Watergate, Congress attempted to prevent any future abuse of power, so in 1978, it created the post of independent counsel (originally named special prosecutor), which would function separately from the Attorney General, but could be dismissed by that cabinet member. Over the years, multiple independent counsels have been ordered to investigate members of the executive branch, but none has received more publicity than Kenneth Starr. He investigated allegations about President Clinton's business dealings, the suicide of Vince Foster (deputy White House counsel), and the Monica Lewinsky affair, which led to the Starr Report and the filing of impeachment charges by the US House of Representatives.

JAN 22: Unabomber Theodore Kaczynski sentenced to life without parole

JAN 26: President Clinton appears on national television denying he had ever had sexual relations with White House intern Monica Lewinsky

JAN 27: First Lady Hillary Clinton says her husband's attackers are part of a "vast right-wing conspiracy"

JAN 28: Ford Motor Company announces it is buying Volvo Corporation

FEB 6: Washington National Airport renamed Ronald Reagan Washington National Airport

1998

FEB 3: US military pilot accidentally kills 20 people in Italy when he flies too low, cutting the cable of their cable-car

FEB 20: Saddam Hussein negotiates with UN to allow inspectors in Iraq to prevent military action by US and Britain

FEB 23: Osama bin Laden declares a jihad against Jews and crusaders

APR 6: Pakistan tests medium-range missiles capable of hitting targets in India

APR 10: Good Friday Agreement signed by Irish Catholics and British officials to end fighting in Northern Ireland

NAFTA ★ The North American Free Trade Agreement was originally created by President George H.W. Bush, Canadian prime minister Brian Mulroney, and Mexican president Carlos Salinas de Gortari in 1992. President Clinton continued his predecessor's work and pushed it through Congress, signing NAFTA in 1993; it went into effect January 1, 1994. Although critics voiced concern from all three countries that it would ruin them economically, that has not proven true. Trade and employment have increased, but disagreements still occur among the three nations regarding agricultural exports. After 9/11, concerns have also greatly increased about the "open border" policy between the United States and its neighbors.

this to Clinton, who told him, "The whole world will be watching, and the handshake is what they will be looking for." Rabin very reluctantly agreed, saying, "I suppose one does not make peace with one's friends."[21] All went fairly well in another tentative step toward Middle East peace.

As a result of civil war disrupting life in the east African nation of Somalia, the United Nations voted to send food to the famine-struck country. In October, American Delta Force and Ranger troops were sent to capture Somali warlord Mohammed Aidid, who was responsible for violence in and around the capital city of Mogadishu. Black Hawk helicopters delivered the Americans in broad daylight and mayhem quickly ensued. Two were shot down, and the pilot of one was caught under the wreckage. Refusing to leave behind one of their own, the Rangers formed a defensive perimeter and fought an onslaught of hundreds of Somalis. Later rapid reaction forces joined with the Rangers and two Delta members were killed at the crash site while attempting to protect the injured pilot. The fighting wore on through the rest of the day and night of October 3. Once the conflict ended, there were eighteen dead Americans and nearly eighty more were wounded, as well as more than three hundred dead Somalis. Immediately congressional leaders demanded withdrawal, especially after viewing the grim footage of two of the dead Americans being dragged through the streets of Mogadishu.

As the president wrapped up his first year in office, another scandal was brewing. This was the resurrection of the story from the campaign regarding the investment he and Hillary had made years before. The Resolution Trust Corporation announced that they were starting an investigation into Jim McDougal's Madison Guaranty; this had at least partly been precipitated by the suicide of Hillary's former law partner and later deputy White House counsel Vince Foster. The press heard someone was seen removing files from his office, and the bloodhounds were on the scent. At first the White House refused access to the Whitewater files, but eventually the staff convinced the First Lady and her husband that disclosure would be the best route. Clinton later acknowledged that handing over the records immediately would have allowed the matter to move off the front pages more quickly.

In August 1994, the president asked for an independent counsel to be assigned to investigate Whitewater. Special Prosecutor Kenneth Starr, a former appeals court judge and Bush appointee, took charge. Clinton would regret his request and later wrote that allowing a special prosecutor was "the worst presidential decision I ever made, wrong on the facts, wrong on the law, wrong on the politics, wrong for the presidency and the

NATIONAL EVENTS

MAR 4: US Supreme Court rules that sexual harassment laws also apply to same-sex incidents

MAR 5: Lt. Col. Eileen Collins becomes first woman named to command a Space Shuttle mission

MAY 18: Suit filed in federal court against Microsoft by US and 20 states

MAY 22: Secret Service agents may be compelled to testify rules a federal judge

JUN 25: US Supreme Court rules that line-item veto is unconstitutional

WORLD EVENTS

MAY 11: India conducts underground nuclear tests

MAY 28: Pakistan conducts more nuclear testing; US and Japan impose economic sanctions on it and India for their nuclear testing

JUL 3: Japan launches its first space probe

JUL 17: 100 nations decide to create International Criminal Court to try those accused of war crimes, genocide, etc.

JUL 17: Remains of Czar Nicholas II and family are interred at St. Catherine's Chapel in St. Petersburg

Constitution. . . . What I should have done is release the records, resist the prosecutor, give an extensive briefing to all the Democrats who wanted it, and ask for their support."[22] Mrs. Clinton's main concern was the publicity regarding their tax returns of 1978 and 1979, which revealed her taking a one thousand dollar investment and soon after, making one hundred thousand dollars in profit. While this scandal went into the next year, a new one began percolating.

Paula Jones had met Clinton when he was governor, and now that he was president, began publicizing details of his alleged misconduct. At a speech to the Conservative Political Action Committee convention, she levied her charges against the president, and soon they were national news. Jones then filed a lawsuit demanding compensation for sexual harassment. Attorneys of both sides wrangled through court from Arkansas District Court where the case was heard by Clinton's former student, Susan Webber Wright, who allowed the case to be postponed until after his 1996 election; afterward, she dismissed the case. Jones then appealed, and the case went to the US Supreme Court, allowing that she had the right to sue a president and he could not claim immunity. Although she insisted that a condition of settlement was an admission and demanded an apology from Clinton, she received neither, but was awarded $850,000 in an out-of-court settlement in November 1998.

In September 1994, the White House was under fire again when two of the president's cabinet members—Secretary of Agriculture Mike Espy and Secretary of Housing and Urban Development Henry Cisneros—resigned amid talk of possible illegal bribery by Espy and payments to a mistress of Cisneros.

During this time, the president was also dodging criticism over taking military action in Haiti. The island nation's military had deposed the elected leader Jean-Bertrand Aristide, and the United States had attempted to put him back in power the year before, but the effort failed. With twenty thousand American troops at his side, Aristide was reinstated as Haiti's leader.

Democrats worried they would lose ground during the mid-year elections since Clinton's popularity had decreased due to the various scandals and problems of his first two years. Their concerns were well-founded as Republicans gained significantly in both houses and, for the first time since Eisenhower's presidency, they commanded the majority in both. Some Democrats started defecting from their party and joining the Republicans.

Early in 1995, the president learned of a pending economic crisis in Mexico because of the steep drop in the peso's value. This hurt Mexico's borrowing capabilities, and it needed a loan to pay off its debts that were coming due. Most Americans disliked the idea of bailing out their neighbor; however, Clinton approved loaning twenty-five billion dollars, all of which was paid with interest within the next two years. He later reflected, "Helping Mexico was the right thing for America."[23]

Another terrorist shock, this one homegrown, came on April 19, 1995, with a truck bombing outside of the federal building in Oklahoma City. This was not a foreign plot by religious fanatics; instead, it was the work of Timothy McVeigh, a disgruntled American who felt betrayed by the government and its attack on the Branch Davidians at Waco two years earlier. Some 168 innocent people were killed, including nineteen children, most of them in the building's daycare center. On May 5, Clinton led

JUL 24: Two security guards killed and a tourist wounded by lone gunman at the Capitol

AUG 19: President Clinton admits to improper relationship with Monica Lewinsky and says he misled the American people

SEP 11: Special Prosecutor Kenneth Starr delivers 445-page report to Congress detailing his investigation into the president's private life

SEP 29: Congress passes "Iraq Liberation Act" stating the US wants to depose Saddam Hussein and institute a democratic government

OCT 29: John Glenn, original Mercury astronaut, now becomes oldest person in space at age 77

AUG 5: Iraq refuses to cooperate with UN inspectors

AUG 7: Yangtze River floods in China and kills 12,000

AUG 7: US embassies in Tanzania and Kenya are bombed by al-Qaeda; 224 are killed and 4,500 injured

AUG 19: Russian economic crisis—ruble devalued; banks close; millions lose their savings

NOV 13: President Clinton orders air strikes on Iraq but cancels it after Iraq promises cooperation with UN

NOV 26: Iraq refuses to cooperate with UN inspectors

DID YOU KNOW?

Clinton made a record number of foreign trips as president—133.

the memorial service for the victims, and his words were directed at others of McVeigh's ilk: "I say to you, all of you . . . there is nothing patriotic about hating your country, or pretending that you can love your country but despise your government."[24] Soon, barriers were erected and Pennsylvania Avenue was blocked from traffic in front of the White House.

In southeastern Europe an ongoing war escalated among the three main groups of what had been Yugoslavia—the Serbs, Croats, and Bosnians. Clinton urged NATO to act against the violence, and after some hesitation, it was agreed to lift the arms embargo on the antagonists. A team was sent by the president to meet with the leaders of the different factions, but some were killed when their armored personnel carrier ran off a mountainous road and burst into flames. In April, a plane carrying Secretary of Commerce Ron Brown and a trade delegation that were to discuss ways to improve the economy in the Balkans, crashed in Croatia.

With the end of the year approaching, Congress and the president still were at loggerheads regarding the 1996 budget. Clinton wanted to push for a balanced budget that he believed could be achieved by 2004. The Republican majority in Congress wanted reductions in domestic programs, including Medicare and education to offset the president's proposed tax cuts. With no agreement, the federal government shut down, with each side blaming the other. Early in 1996, they came to an agreement and the budget was signed. Welfare reform was another matter. Clinton wanted to see it change to follow the policy he had established in Arkansas—take people off the welfare rolls and put them into jobs.

In the summer of 1996, the president signed bills helping Americans in a variety of ways: the Food Quality Protection Act; the Safe Drinking Water Act; a raise in the minimum wage by ninety cents; the Kennedy-Kassebaum bill to prevent people from losing insurance coverage when changing jobs; welfare reform that granted many benefits Clinton had wanted, including guaranteed medical care and food aid; and a raise in the level of childcare assistance. Some opposed the latter initiative because it placed a five-year limit on benefits and omitted legal immigrants from receiving food stamps.

Meanwhile, Iraqi leader Saddam Hussein bullied his way past the UN restrictions imposed on him following the Gulf War and began waging war against people within his own country. The president responded by ordering an air attack on Iraqi forces in September 1996, ending Iraqi combat operations against the Kurds in northern Iraq.

1996 CAMPAIGN

Delegates had little to debate at their convention in Chicago as they overwhelmingly chose Clinton and Gore as the Democratic ticket. Coming into the convention, Clinton had easily won his party's primaries. In his book *My Life*, he states: "My acceptance speech was easy to give because of the record: the lowest combined rate of unemployment and inflation in twenty-eight years; 10 million new jobs; 10 million people getting the minimum wage increase."[25]

Republicans meeting in San Diego chose longtime Republican congressional leader, Senator Bob Dole of Kansas, who was the Senate majority leader and earlier had been Ford's running mate in the unsuccessful campaign of 1976. Now twenty years later, he headed the ticket with former NFL quarterback and New York congressman Jack Kemp. Ross Perot ran again for the Reform Party.

During his first term, Clinton had steadily moved toward the center, so on many issues he and

NATIONAL EVENTS

NOV 19: US House of Representatives Judiciary Committee begins impeachment proceedings against President Clinton

FEB 12: President Clinton acquitted in his impeachment trial of all charges

MAR 21: Bertrand Piccard and Brian Jones become first Americans to successfully circumnavigate the globe in a hot air balloon

1999

WORLD EVENTS

DEC 16: American and British air strikes against Iraqi targets begin

DEC 21: Three UN Security Council members (France, Germany, and Russia) want economic sanctions lifted against Iraq and end inspections

DEC 26: Iraq promises to shoot down any British or American planes flying over its "no-fly zones"

JAN 1: Introduction of Euro currency

MAR 12: Czech Republic, Hungary, and Poland join

MAR 24: NATO launches air strikes against Yugoslavia (first time NATO attacked a nation)

Dole did not differ significantly. Their personalities were what set them apart. Although Dole was known for his wit, he seemed wooden in his campaign appearances. This starkly contrasted with the president's easygoing manner, which appealed more to the voters. Polls showed that although people had reservations about Clinton's character, they still liked him as president. On November 5, 1996, over 49 percent of the American people voted for Bill Clinton to serve a second term; 41 percent voted for Dole; and 8 percent for Perot. Clinton won 379 electoral votes to Dole's 159; Perot claimed none.

SECOND TERM

For his second inaugural address, Clinton built on the theme that his presidency would take the country into the twenty-first century: "Government is not the problem, and government is not the solution. We—the American people—we are the solution. . . . As times change, so government must change." He reminded his audience of recent historic events: "And for the very first time in all of history, more people on this planet live under democracy than dictatorship." A few weeks later in his State of the Union address, he asked Congress to join him in declaring that their common goal was upgrading education by developing national tests to measure standards, creating better schools, demanding more certified teachers, and setting the goal of having all classrooms connected to the Internet in three years.

Daughter Chelsea graduated from high school that spring and after visiting and applying to a variety of universities, she chose Stanford. In September, her parents joined with others at freshmen orientation and helped move Chelsea into her dorm room. Younger Secret Service agents were selected who were better able to blend into the campus atmosphere.

The president visited Helsinki in March 1997, where he and Boris Yeltsin attempted to come to an agreement regarding weapons reduction, which the Soviets worried would put them at a disadvantage according to the START II terms. A START III was discussed, but the Russian Duma was not interested. Meanwhile, attempts to calm tension in the Middle East by hosting King Hussein of Jordan, Prime Minister Netanyahu of Israel, and Yasser Arafat at different times met with mixed results. Chinese president Jiang Zemin arrived in October 1997 for the first US-China summit in eight years. Although the two parties did not reach any major agreement, their meeting kept the leaders of the world's superpowers in a dialogue that the world vitally needed to maintain.

In December, Vice President Al Gore, a longtime spokesman for environmental issues, attended the Kyoto conference and signed the protocol. The document calling for reducing harmful emissions of greenhouse gases has never been submitted to the Senate for approval. It was deemed unfair, since no limits or timetables were placed on developing countries, whose emissions were already radically increasing and would continue to do so in the future.

In his memoirs, Clinton states: "When 1998 began, I had no idea it would be the strangest year of my presidency. . . . Because everything happened at once, I was compelled as never before to live parallel lives, except that this time the darkest part of my inner life was in full view."[26] As the Paula Jones case moved forward, her attorneys subpoenaed a White House intern, Monica Lewinsky, to ask about an alleged affair. She denied any romantic involvement with the president. Soon rumors started surfacing claiming the opposite was true.

APR 20: Columbine High School in Littleton, Colorado, becomes a killing zone when two of its students, Eric Harris and Dylan Klebold, gun down 12 students and a teacher before killing themselves

APR 21: Last American billboards for cigarettes taken down

JUN 12: Texas governor George W. Bush announces he is a candidate for Republican presidential nomination

JUL 16: John F. Kennedy Jr., his wife, and her sister die when the plane Kennedy is piloting goes down off coast of Martha's Vineyard

MAY 7: NATO forces accidentally target Chinese embassy in Belgrade and kill three workers

JUN 9: Federal Republic of Yugoslavia and NATO sign a peace treaty

NOV 6: Australians vote to preserve monarch as their head of state

DEC 17: New UN inspection team created to work with Iraq but that nation refuses to cooperate

DEC 20: Portugal hands over sovereignty of Macau to People's Republic of China

The president responded with a public statement insisting that he had "never had sexual relations with that woman."[27]

Hillary appeared on the *Today Show* defending her husband. She told host Matt Lauer that the Clintons were engaged in a battle against a "vast right-wing conspiracy that has been conspiring against my husband since the day he announced for President."[28] Independent counsel Kenneth Starr continued his probing, newspapers printed rumors, and the president attempted to pretend nothing was bothering him. All three Clintons traveled to Africa and China before returning home to bad news.

On August 7, bombs planted by the Islamic terrorist organization al Qaeda ripped through the American embassies in Kenya and Tanzania. More than two hundred were killed, including twelve Americans. A few days later while on vacation in Martha's Vineyard, the president ordered an attack on al Qaeda training camps in Afghanistan and two Sudanese targets—a tannery and chemical plant—that were either owned or used by the terrorist leader Osama bin Laden. The cruise missiles hit their targets, but bin Laden was not in the camp. Clinton issued executive orders for economic sanctions against bin Laden and al Qaeda. He also granted the CIA authority to use "lethal force to apprehend bin Laden."[29] Some critics maintained that his actions were merely a ploy to move the public's attention from the ongoing scandal with Monica Lewinsky.

IMPEACHMENT

On August 17, 1998, the president made a brief televised message admitting that he and Ms. Lewinsky had been involved in an "inappropriate relationship," which resulted from a "lapse in judgment" and a "personal failure"[30] by him. He made the announcement following his testimony before a grand jury. This admittance of guilt followed on the heels of Lewinsky providing a dress to Starr which she claimed had the president's DNA; tests confirmed this.

Kenneth Starr delivered his report to the House Judiciary Committee, which was considering filing impeachment charges against the president. Between the Lewinsky scandal and the threat of impeachment, Democrats worried that their chances at winning mid-term elections would be greatly diminished. To the surprise of the pundits, Democrats not only held their own in the Senate, but gained five seats in the House, although Republicans continued to hold majorities in both houses. Shortly after the election, Senator Patrick Moynihan, longtime senator of New York, announced he would not run again, and Congressman Charlie Rangel called the First Lady to suggest she run for Moynihan's seat. She told him, "I'm honored you would think of me, but I'm not interested, and besides, we have a few other outstanding matters to resolve right now."[31]

The primary "outstanding matter" was the question of impeachment. In October, when Starr delivered his mega report, he also recommended to the committee that there were eleven grounds for impeachment. By doing so, Starr's actions went further than independent counsel did in the Watergate era. At that time, they collected evidence and turned it over to the House, leaving its members to fulfill their constitutional duty of determining whether to impeach. In December, the House of Representatives approved two articles of impeachment: perjury (during grand jury testimony) and obstruction of justice (covering up the truth in the Paula Jones case). President Clinton immediately

NATIONAL EVENTS

DEC 14: Customs officials discover trunkload of explosives driven by an Algerian-national coming to US from Canada; he was trained in an al-Qaeda camp

APR 3: Federal judge rules Microsoft violated monopoly laws and the Sherman Antitrust Act

JUL 31–AUG 3: Republican National convention nominates Governor George W. Bush and Dick Cheney as their ticket

AUG 8: Confederate submarine *H.L. Hunley* raised to the surface; it sank in 1864

2000

WORLD EVENTS

DEC 31: Panama Canal officially handed over to its government by the US

DEC 31: Computer operators worry about Y2K with arrival of year 2000

JAN 1: World celebrates new millennium (although does not actually begin for another year)

MAY 23: Israeli troops withdraw from southern Lebanon

JUL 25: Concorde Air France flight crashes just after take-off in Paris, other Concordes are grounded pending investigation

issued a statement denouncing the partisan motivation for the actions by the House.

On January 7, 1999, Chief Justice William Rehnquist took his position as the presiding officer of the proceedings as outlined in the Constitution, and William Jefferson Clinton became only the second president in history to face possible removal from office. After hearing testimony for over a month, the Senate voted on impeachment. Needing a two-thirds majority to convict, the president was acquitted on both charges with votes of fifty-five to forty-five on Article I (perjury) and fifty to fifty on Article II (obstruction of justice). Released from the gripping impeachment drama, the president could now devote his full time and energies to the work at hand, of which there was plenty.

MID-TERM ELECTIONS ★ In 1994, the president lost the Democratic Congress, and for the first time since the 1950s, both houses were in the hands of the Republican Party. Many Americans supported the Republican-backed "Contract with America," crafted by soon-to-be Speaker of the House Newt Gingrich. Among the terms of the contract were pledges to make congressional reforms, improve governmental fiscal responsibility, anticrime legislation, welfare reform, strengthen national security, and limit punitive damages in lawsuits.

COMPLETING HIS TERM

The country's economy was strong, and Clinton announced that for the first time in decades, the nation not only had a balanced budget, but a projected surplus, as well. News from the foreign front was less positive. Monitoring the efforts by Saddam Hussein to avoid the UN weapons inspections sometimes required tough talk, and at other times, military action. Previously when Hussein denied access to the inspectors, the United States complained to the United Nations, which then passed resolutions ordering him to comply. All were ignored as Saddam continued to obstruct weapons inspectors and fired on British and American aircraft patrolling the UN's "No Fly" Zone. In December 1998, Clinton and British prime minister Tony Blair ordered Operation Desert Fox to bomb Iraq's supply of "substantial amounts of biological and chemical materials," as well as "some [unaccounted] missile warheads." Said future Speaker of the House Nancy Pelosi: "Saddam Hussein has been engaged in the development of weapons of mass destruction technology which is a threat to countries in the region and he has made a mockery of the weapons inspection process."[32] The bombing lasted four days, but the administration admitted that it "had no way to know how much of the proscribed material had been destroyed."[33]

The Balkans region continued to prove volatile, with ongoing fighting between Serbs and Kosovar Albanians prompting the United States to push for and obtain NATO agreement to launch air strikes on Yugoslavia. The attacks, which continued for over two months, finally ended when Yugoslav president Slobodan Milosevic signed a pledge to remove his troops from Kosovo. Unfortunately, one of the NATO strikes hit the Chinese embassy in Belgrade and killed three (the bombing was due to using an old map of the area with the building identified as a military installation). Although Clinton attempted to call and apologize to Jiang Zemin, the Chinese leader at first refused to accept the call, and the Chinese launched multi-day protests against the United States. But relations improved later in the year when the administration

AUG 14–17: Democrats nominate Vice President Al Gore and Connecticut senator Joe Liebermann for their party's ticket

NOV 7: Presidential election, but results uncertain due to disputed results in Florida, which take months and several trips to court to decide

NOV 7: Hillary Clinton wins election to US Senate, the first for a First Lady

DEC 12: US Supreme Court rules in *Bush v. Gore* to halt recounts of certain Florida counties; Bush is declared the winner

OCT 12: Two suicide bombers explode in small boat anchored next to USS *Cole*, destroyer docked in Aden, Yemen; 17 US sailors die and 40 are wounded

NOV: Saddam Hussein reiterates his stance against UN inspectors

NOV 16: President Clinton becomes first sitting US president to visit Vietnam

DID YOU KNOW?

Clinton was the first Democratic president to win reelection since Franklin D. Roosevelt.

successfully negotiated a trade agreement, which allowed more American products in China with lower tariffs, as well as its membership in the World Trade Organization.

Early in 2000, rumors that the First Lady might run for the New York Senate seat seemed to be true. On January 4, she purchased a home in Chappaqua, New York, and a month later announced her candidacy. Some critics assailed her as being a "carpetbagger," while others saw her as a "curiosity."[34] Throughout the coming months, Mrs. Clinton balanced her duties of First Lady with those of candidate and spent the bulk of her time campaigning through New York state. Her hard work paid off, and in November 2000, she was elected as their new US senator.

During this time, the president was attempting to make inroads in several areas, including the Middle East. He hosted a summit with the leaders of Israel and Palestine, Ehud Barak and Yasser Arafat, in an attempt to bring peace to the region, but two weeks of negotiations failed to resolve the ongoing conflicts. Within months, they would be fighting again.

In October, violence crept closer to the United States when the USS *Cole*, an American destroyer anchored at Yemen's port of Aden, was struck by a terrorist bomb linked to al Qaeda and Osama bin Laden. Seventeen Americans were killed, but no retaliation was ordered by the White House. By now, bin Laden and his organization had been linked to numerous plots, as well as actual bombings, including the Khobar Towers (which housed American soldiers) in Saudi Arabia in 1996, and the bombings of the American embassies in Tanzania and Kenya in 1998. Bin Laden was increasing the frequency of his attacks and, less than a year after the bombing of the *Cole*, his terrorist followers would strike within the United States itself.

Completing his presidency with a nod toward environmentalists and his vice president Al Gore, Clinton ordered the creation of national monuments in western states, thus protecting millions of wilderness acres. He also halted the construction of roads and logging in many national forests and furthered restrictions of public lands with limits on mining and grazing.

When Gore ran for the presidency in 2000, he kept considerable distance between himself and Clinton until very late in the campaign. Then, with the election results up in the air because of problems in the Florida balloting, the president remained mum until after the Supreme Court decision ordering an end to a series of recounts. The decision, which Clinton called "appalling," put an end to Vice President Gore's presidential hopes.

In his final weeks in office, Clinton became the first president to visit Vietnam. In January, he met with president-elect George W. Bush and told him his greatest threats would be "Osama bin Laden and al Qaeda; the absence of peace in the Middle East; the standoff between nuclear powers India and Pakistan; and the ties of the Pakistanis to the Taliban and al Qaeda; North Korea and then Iraq." The president then admitted to Bush his "biggest disappointment was not getting Osama bin Laden; that we might still achieve an agreement in the Middle East, and that we had almost tied up a deal with North Korea to end its missile program."[35] Only time would tell if Clinton's predictions would come true.

By now Whitewater was history, and the independent counsel acknowledged that there was not enough evidence to convict either of the Clintons with fraud or any other crime. The president did, nevertheless, pardon friend Susan McDougal, who had sat in jail rather than testify against him in the Whitewater case. On his last day in office, he also pardoned billionaire Marc Rich under indictment for aiding the enemy (Iran) and evading millions of dollars in taxes. Rich had denounced his US citizenship and moved to Israel, where Ehud Barak called the president asking him to grant Rich a pardon. Rich's ex-wife Denise had also pled his case. She was a major contributor to both the Democratic Party and the new Clinton Library in Little Rock. News of this pardon struck many, including Democrats, as being wrong, but Clinton insisted that he made his decision "based on the merits."[36]

On January 3, the First Lady made history when she was sworn in by Vice President Al Gore as a US senator. On January 17, President Clinton addressed the nation in a farewell message, reminding Americans of the progress made improving the economy but warned about the continued threats from terrorism. He then addressed the challenge of America's diversity: "We must remember that America cannot lead in the world unless here at home we weave the threads of our coat of many colors into the fabric of one America. As we become ever more diverse, we must work harder to unite around our common values and our common humanity."[37]

RETIREMENT

After the Clintons moved to their new home in New York, the former president pleased African American leaders by opening an office in Harlem. The year 2004 was a significant year for Clinton as his autobiography *My Life* was published and the Clinton Presidential Library and Museum opened in Little Rock. During his retirement, the former president has made a considerable income on the lecture circuit, and more recently, has made numerous appearances with former president George H.W. Bush on behalf of the Hurricane Katrina and Asian Tsunami relief efforts.

ENDNOTES

1 Nigel Hamilton, *Bill Clinton: An American Journey, Great Expectations*, New York: Random House, 2003, p. 38.

2 Ibid, p. 44.

3 *Arkansas Democrat-Gazette*, April 15, 1990.

4 David Gallen, *Bill Clinton: As They Know Him: An Oral Biography*, New York: Gallen Publishing Group, 1994, pp. 25-26.

5 Bill Clinton, *My Life*, New York: Alfred A. Knopf, 2004, p. 67.

6 Ibid, p. 78.

7 David Maraniss, *First in His Class: A Biography of Bill Clinton*, New York: Simon & Schuster, 1995, p. 79.

8 Ibid, p. 179.

9 Hamilton, p. 200.

10 Maraniss, p. 203.

11 Clinton, p. 178.

12 Ibid, p. 221.

13 Maraniss, p. 352.

14 Rex Nelson, *The Hillary Factor*, New York: Gallen Publishing Group, 1993, p. 209.

15 Governor Bill Clinton's Inaugural Address, January 9, 1979.

16 Maraniss, pp. 392-393.

17 Ibid, p. 396.

18 Clinton, p. 326.

19 Ibid, p. 405.

20 George Stephanopoulos, *All Too Human*, Boston: Little, Brown, 1999, p. 162.

21 Ibid, p. 543.

22 Ibid, p. 574.

23 Ibid, p. 645.

24 Joe Klein, *The Natural: The Misunderstood Presidency of Bill Clinton*, New York: Broadway Press, 2002, p. 143.

25 Clinton, p. 723.

26 Ibid, p. 771.

27 William A. DeGregorio, *The Complete Book of US Presidents*, New York: Gramercy Books, 2005, p. 738.

28 Hillary Rodham Clinton, *Living History*, New York: Simon & Schuster, 2003, p. 455.

29 B. Clinton, p. 804.

30 Ibid, p. 802.

31 H. Clinton, p. 483.

32 http://www.house.gov/pelosi/, Congresswoman Nancy Pelosi, California, 8th District, Statement on US Military Strike Against Iraq, December 16, 1998.

33 B. Clinton, pp. 833-834.

34 H. Clinton, p. 511.

35 B. Clinton, p. 935.

36 Ibid, p. 941.

37 Bill Clinton, Farewell Address, January 18, 2001.

George W. Bush

★ ★ ★ FORTY-THIRD PRESIDENT ★ ★ ★

LIFESPAN
- Born: July 6, 1946, in New Haven, Connecticut

NICKNAMES
- Dubya, Shrub

RELIGION
- Methodist

HIGHER EDUCATION
- Yale, 1968
- Harvard MBA, 1975

PROFESSION
- Businessman

MILITARY SERVICE
- Enlisted as an airman in Texas National Guard in 1968; became a pilot, then commissioned a second lieutenant; discharged in 1973

FAMILY
- Father: **George Herbert Walker Bush** (1924–)
- Mother: **Barbara Pierce Bush** (1925–)
- Wife: **Laura Welch Bush** (1946–); wed on November 5, 1977, in Midland, Texas
- Children (twins): **Barbara Pierce** (1981–); **Jenna Welch** (1981–)

POLITICAL LIFE
- Governor of Texas (1995–2000)

PRESIDENCY
- Two terms: January 20, 2001–January 20, 2009
- Republican
- Reason for leaving office: completion of term
- Vice president: **Richard "Dick" Cheney** (2001–2009)

ELECTION OF 2000
- Electoral vote: **Bush** 271; **Albert Gore Jr.** 266; **Abstention** 1
- Popular vote: **Bush** 50,460,110; **Gore** 51,003,926; **Ralph Nader** 2,883,105; **Patrick Buchanan** 449,225

ELECTION OF 2004
- Electoral vote: **Bush** 286; **John Kerry** 252; **Ralph Nader** 0
- Popular vote: **Bush** 62,040,610; **Kerry** 59,028,111; **Nader** 463,653

CABINET

★★★★★★★★★★

SECRETARY OF STATE
Colin Powell (2001–2005)
Condoleezza Rice (2005–2009)

SECRETARY OF THE TREASURY
Paul O'Neill (2001–2003)
John W. Snow (2003–2006)
Henry M. Paulson Jr. (2006–2009)

SECRETARY OF DEFENSE
Donald H. Rumsfeld (2001–2006)
Robert M. Gates (2006–2009)

ATTORNEY GENERAL
John Ashcroft (2001–2005)
Alberto Gonzales (2005–2007)
Michael B. Mukasey (2007–2009)

SECRETARY OF THE INTERIOR
Gale Norton (2001–2005)
Dick Kempthorne (2006–2009)

SECRETARY OF AGRICULTURE
Ann M. Venman (2001–2005)
Mike Johanns (2005–2007)
Edward T. Schafer (2008–2009)

SECRETARY OF COMMERCE
Don Evans (2001–2005)
Carlos M. Gutierrez (2005–2009)

George W. Bush entered office under a cloud of doubt, with Democrats crying "Foul!" following the month-long drama of recounting ballots in Florida, and court battles there and in the Supreme Court. But on January 20, 2001, Bush took the oath of office and ignored the criticism while he settled himself into the job. His legitimacy continued to be questioned, but the objections became moot when planes flew into the World Trade Center and the Pentagon on September 11, 2001.

EARLY LIFE

Both George H.W. Bush and his wife Barbara Pierce came from well-to-do eastern families. The two had met while teenagers at a country club dance near their Connecticut homes, and they continued corresponding once they returned to their private schools. After the attack on Pearl Harbor, Bush enlisted as soon as he graduated from Andover and turned eighteen. He trained as a bomber pilot and flew missions in the Pacific theater before returning home and marrying Barbara. Bush decided to attend Yale and it was in New Haven, Connecticut, that they welcomed their firstborn and named him George Walker Bush on July 6, 1946.

Following graduation, the Bush family packed their bags and moved to Odessa, Texas, where George wanted to start a career in the burgeoning oil industry. The young couple decided that nearby Midland would be a better town to raise their growing family, which now included Pauline Robinson, known as "Robin," born in 1950, and John "Jeb," born three years later.

Young George could usually be found outside playing with other children all day and into the evening. Baseball was his favorite game, just as it had been for his father, a star player at Yale. Later the younger Bush described a proud moment in his life when his dad told him, "Son, you've arrived. I can throw it to you as hard as I want to."[1] Describing the town of Midland as having a "frontier" atmosphere, with tumbleweeds blowing into their yard and blinding dust storms, his father admitted the environment had rubbed off on his young son. He wrote of his son who was not quite five: "Georgie has grown to be a near-man, talks dirty once in a while and occasionally swears. He lives in his cowboy clothes."[2]

George attended Sam Houston Elementary and San Jacinto Junior High in Midland. He continued his interest in athletics, joined the football team in junior high, and always had plenty of friends. Many of his schoolmates also had fathers involved in the oil industry, which required them to be gone for long periods of time, and mother Barbara was the law of the Bush household. She was not afraid to mete out punishment whenever required, as when he repeated a racial slur he had heard—she promptly took him aside and washed out his mouth with soap.

For the entertainment of his class, one day Georgie decided to take a marker and draw long sideburns and a beard on his face. His teacher did not find his artistic skills amusing and took him to the principal's office where the principal used the "board of education" to paddle the boy three times. When Barbara complained about the use of corporal punishment, the principal explained that part of the reason was the boy's demeanor—he had "swaggered in as though he had done the most wonderful thing in the world." Barbara then switched her support to the principal. Times like this flustered George's father, who wrote, "Georgie aggravates the hell out of me at times (I am sure I do the same to him), but then at times I am so proud of him I could die."[3]

NATIONAL EVENTS

JAN 16: President Clinton awards former president T. Roosevelt posthumous Medal of Honor for his service during the Spanish-American War

JAN 20: Inauguration of George W. Bush as 43rd president

JUN 5: Jim Jeffords, Vermont senator, switches allegiance from Republican to Democratic Party, thus altering balance of parties in the Senate

JUN 7: Tax cut bill signed into law by President Bush

JUN 11: Timothy McVeigh executed for the Oklahoma City bombing

2001

WORLD EVENTS

JAN 17–20: Upheaval in Philippine government with threat of impeachment for President Joseph Estrada; Philippine military backs a new government; Gloria Macapagal-Arroyo becomes the new president

JAN 26: Earthquake kills more than 20,000 in India

JAN 31: One Libyan terrorist convicted for participating in blowing up Pan Am Flight 103 over Lockerbie, Scotland, in 1988

FEB: Bombing by British and American planes over Iraq

In 1953, George saw little of his parents or his sister Robin, who had just been diagnosed with leukemia. He and Jeb remained in Texas while his parents and Robin traveled to New York City for treatment, but she lost her fight in October. George later described the day he looked up to see his family had arrived at his elementary school, and he ran out to greet his parents and sister, only to be told she had died. He described the moment of learning the truth as "the starkest memory of my childhood, a sharp pain in the midst of an otherwise happy blur."[4] When he attended a football game with his father and friends, young George said that he wished he were Robin. Immediate silence fell over the group. His father asked him why. "I bet she can see the game better from up there than we can down here,"[5] he answered.

The boy obviously thought a lot about his sister, but he also was concerned that his mother was not herself. She mourned her loss and clung to Georgie and Jebby when they were home. Barbara, however, did not realize how her behavior was affecting her older son until she heard him tell a neighbor child that he could not play because he "couldn't leave his mother. She needed him." Barbara decided to start resuming a normal life because "I realized I was too much of a burden for a little seven-year-old boy to carry."[6]

After his seventh grade year (which included winning his first political office and becoming class president), George transferred to the private Kinkaid School in Houston when his family moved there in 1959. By this time, he had two more brothers, Neil and Marvin, as well as a sister, Dorothy, known as Doro. At Kinkaid, he continued his interest in sports, especially football, and quickly made a new group of friends. This would provide a good foundation for Bush's next stop—the prestigious preparatory school Phillips Academy in Andover, Massachusetts, which both his father and grandfather, Senator Prescott Bush, had attended.

Although the campus reveled in the autumn glory for which New England is famous, young George found the school "cold and distant and difficult"[7] when he arrived in 1961. Discovering that he was behind academically, George knew he had to apply himself, and would often sit on the floor after "lights out" to continue his studying in the light from under the door. He struggled, but managed to earn decent grades. His athletic prowess also failed to measure up to Andover standards, and he did not get much gametime on their football or baseball teams, and was a second-string player on the basketball team. All of this was in marked contrast to the pictures of his father leading the school to glory on the baseball team.

Deciding to combine his love of sports with his natural affability, George introduced stickball competition to the student body his senior year. He organized a league, with himself in charge as "high commissioner," and continued a lifelong practice of giving everyone a nickname; he called himself "Tweeds Bush" in honor of Boss Tweed of New York's Tammany Hall. The dorms then fronted teams for a tournament. Bush recalled, "Stickball was a way of spreading joy, sharing humor, and lightening up what was otherwise a serious and studious environment."[8]

Bush had made a name for himself by befriending the other students. Although never a star athlete at Andover, he became a top cheerleader, and he threw himself wholeheartedly into the task, developing skits and more nicknames for the players. When the dean considered ending George's cheering career, fearing that the cheerleaders were drawing

CABINET

★★★★★★★★★★

(continued)

SECRETARY OF LABOR
Elaine Chao (2001–2009)

SECRETARY OF HEALTH AND HUMAN SERVICES
Tommy G. Thompson (2001–2005)

Michael O. Leavitt (2005–2009)

SECRETARY OF HOUSING AND URBAN DEVELOPMENT
Melquiades Martinez (2001–2003)

Alphonso Jackson (2004–2008)

Steve Preston (2008–2009)

SECRETARY OF TRANSPORTATION
Norman Y. Mineta (2001–2006)

Mary E. Peters (2006–2009)

SECRETARY OF ENERGY
Spencer Abraham (2001–2005)

Samuel W. Bodman (2005–2009)

SECRETARY OF EDUCATION
Rod Paige (2001–2005)

Margaret Spellings (2005–2009)

SECRETARY OF VETERANS AFFAIRS
Anthony Principi (2001–2005)

R. James Nicholson (2005–2007)

AUG 6: Briefing for President Bush on (Osama) "Bin Laden Determined to Strike in US"

SEP 6: US drops its lawsuit against Microsoft

SEP 11: al Qaeda terrorists succeed in hijacking four airplanes in eastern US cities—two hit World Trade Center, one hits Pentagon, and one crashes in Pennsylvania after passengers attempt to seize control from hijackers; nearly 3,000 people die

SEP 18: Anthrax attacks via mail to various targets including TV networks and newspaper publishers

FEB 20: Foot and mouth disease breaks out in Great Britain

APR 1: US spy plane collides with Chinese plane, forcing it to land in China; American crew detained for ten days

APR 1: Slobodan Milosevic, former president of Federal Republic of Yugoslavia, surrenders and will be tried for war crimes

APR 1: Netherlands becomes first nation in the world to allow same-sex marriages

APR 28: American Dennis Tito becomes first space tourist when he travels onboard Russian spacecraft Soyuz TM-32

CABINET
★★★★★★★★★★

(continued)

James B. Peake (2007– 2009)

SECRETARY OF HOMELAND SECURITY

Tom Ridge (2003–2005), first to serve in this new post

Michael Chertoff (2005–2009)

attention from the team, the student newspaper published an editorial in Bush's defense. As head cheerleader, he did a masterful job of warming up the crowd for the biggest game of the year, the annual match against Exeter. Bush worked the fans for an hour, spinning yarns and telling anecdotes about each player. His classmates later recalled that this was when he learned valuable skills necessary for a political career such as "how to work a crowd, how to exploit a captive audience, how to come off wholesome and energetic and winning."[9] He did not, though, attempt to win any political office during his time there, but he was appointed to the respected position of proctor of a sophomore dorm during his senior year, and at the end of the year was voted second as "Big Man on Campus," a distinction normally won by the top athlete.

The Bush family expected George to follow in his family's footsteps when it came time to select a college. So Bush applied to Yale, but considered the University of Texas as his backup should he not be accepted. He need not have worried; Yale accepted the young Texan, and so he was off to Connecticut for the fall of 1964.

Andover's high academic standards stood George in good stead when he began to matriculate at Yale. There he decided to major in one of his favorite subjects, history, and worked on the side. In his sophomore year, he pledged Delta Kappa Epsilon fraternity, which was known for its raucous parties. He was president of DKE his junior year and impressed his frat brothers when he could name all fifty pledges.

He was a pitcher on the freshman baseball team, but the competition was too keen for him to be on varsity, so he switched to rugby and managed to be on the top team by his senior year. Although not a cheerleader, he did enjoy throwing himself into the competitive atmosphere, but one time it got him into trouble. After Yale defeated rival Princeton in a football game, George was among the revelers attempting to take down the goal post when the police intervened and ordered them to leave town. As a junior, Bush was invited to join the "ultra-secret" society Skull and Bones, another legacy shared with his father.

The spring of 1968 brought many changes to the country, with unrest breaking out throughout the nation, especially following the assassination of civil rights leader Dr. Martin Luther King Jr. Protests against the Vietnam War now took center stage, and for Bush and his classmates, it was time for them to make a decision: stay and enlist or escape to Canada. Rather than enlisting in the Army, Bush decided to once more follow in his dad's footsteps and become a pilot.

Bush chose the Texas Air National Guard, serving in the 147th Fighter Interceptor Group, based in Houston. After his Yale graduation, he began basic training in the summer of 1968, followed by pilot training later that fall. The student pilots started on small aircraft, including the T-41, then the T-37, the T-38, and finally the F-102 Delta Dagger. He graduated in December 1969, and his father proudly pinned the second lieutenant wings on his son.

Although politicians would later try to discredit Bush's Guard service as a way to avoid going to Vietnam, at the time he enlisted, pilots from his air group were performing combat missions in Vietnam. He inquired about volunteering for active duty flying the F-102 in Vietnam after completing his combat training in June 1970, but the Air Force was phasing that aircraft out of Vietnam service. By the time Bush left the National Guard in 1973, he had flown more than six hundred hours with nearly half of his time in either the F-102 or its trainer.

NATIONAL EVENTS

OCT 5: Tom Ridge becomes first Homeland Security Advisor

OCT 9: Two US senators receive anthrax letters

OCT 26: Patriot Act passed

NOV 13: President Bush signs executive order allowing military tribunals for foreigners suspected of terrorism against the US

DEC 2: Enron becomes biggest bankruptcy declared in US history

WORLD EVENTS

MAY 7: Bosnia-Herzegovina is site of Serbian nationalists attacking group of elderly Bosnian Muslims; 300 killed

JUN 7: Tony Blair and his Labour Party win elections

JUN 19: US missile hits northern Iraq soccer field and kills 23

NOV 1: US begins bombing Taliban targets in Afghanistan

NOV 10: People's Republic of China joins World Trade Organization (WTO)

ADRIFT

After he finished his pilot training and returned to Texas in 1970, Bush began a period of drifting; he simply did not know how he wanted to spend his time. George tried a variety of jobs and spent a great deal of his time simply enjoying life in Houston.

In 1972, Bush transferred for a while to the Alabama National Guard, where he helped on a senate campaign. His National Guard attendance would later become a point of dispute, but he still accumulated a little more than the minimum required to keep him active in the Guard as the Air Force and other armed services engaged in deep personnel cuts in the wake of America's pullout from Vietnam.

Great-uncle Herb Walker gave him a job at his new agricultural company, Stratford, and soon George was traveling to Central America and Florida on the lookout for possible businesses to purchase. Within a short time, he learned that digesting business reports and visiting plants did not interest him, so he soon left the job. His father was not pleased by George's action, and one day called him to discuss it. "In our family and in life, you fulfill your commitments," his father told him. "You've disappointed me."[10]

The words hit George with great force. When he related the encounter to a friend, he said, "Those were the sternest words to me, even though he said them in a very calm way. He wasn't screaming, and he wasn't angry, but he was disappointed."[11] His father could not understand why his oldest son kept drifting without any sense of purpose to his life. In 1972 when the family was enjoying their Christmas vacation together, another episode occurred underlining the tension between the two generations. Fifteen-year-old Marvin was having a tough time at Andover, so George invited him to go along on a visit to a friend's house. They were gone for hours, and spent much of the time drinking. On their return, George knocked over a neighbor's trashcan with his car, creating an awful racket.

As far as the elder Bush was concerned, the noise was nothing compared to seeing his underage son drunk, so he told Jeb to bring "Junior" to him. The swagger that had cost Bush a paddling in fourth grade now carried him into the study. "I hear you're looking for me. You wanna go *mano a mano* right here?" Immediately Jeb stepped in and quickly diffused the situation by telling their father some big news: George had been accepted to Harvard Business School. When asked why this had not been mentioned sooner, George replied, "Oh, I'm not going. I just wanted to let you know I could get into it."[12]

George would attend Harvard the following year, but during the interim he joined Professionals United for Leadership (PULL), which was a charity-run organization managed by two former pro football players who had asked Congressman George H.W. Bush about creating a mentoring program for the underprivileged in Houston. This was a cause both George Bushes could support. George threw himself into the work and loved helping the kids. One of the founders, Ernie Ladd, later said, "He was the first real white boy that all of the kids really loved."[13]

But in the fall, Bush was on his way to Harvard. He studied hard, and with a sense of maturity, earned higher grades than he had at Yale. However, according to classmates, Bush did not exactly look the part of a Harvard MBA candidate. He attended class wearing his National Guard bomber jacket and cowboy boots, and kept a paper cup by his desk to spit his tobacco juice.

SUPREME COURT APPOINTMENTS

★★★★★★★★★★

John Roberts, Chief Justice, 2005

Samuel Alito, 2006

DEC 11: Zacarias Moussaoui (French citizen of Moroccan descent) indicted by US government for aiding in planning 9/11 attacks

DEC 13: US announces withdrawal from 1972 Anti-Ballistic Missile Treaty

JAN 8: President Bush signs into law bipartisan bill No Child Left Behind to improve American public education, but critics assail its heavy emphasis on testing and lack of funding for needed improvements

JAN 22: Kmart becomes largest retailer in American history to file for Chapter 11 bankruptcy protection

2002

NOV 14: Northern Alliance troops take Kabul as Taliban forces flee

DEC 27: People's Republic of China obtains permanent trade status with US

JAN 16: UN places arms embargo on Osama bin Laden, Taliban, al Qaeda

FEB 9: Britain's Princess Margaret dies of complications from a stroke

FEB 12: Slobodan Milosevic begins his war crimes trial

MAR 1: US and allies invade eastern Afghanistan

STATE OF THE UNION

US POPULATION IN 2001
281,421,906

NATIONAL DEBT IN 2006
$8,506,973,899,215.23

PRESIDENT'S SALARY
$400,000/year

TEXAS SUCCESS

Bush completed his degree and decided his future lay in Midland, Texas, so he moved to his long-ago hometown. Texas oil was making many men millionaires, and its lure was hard to resist for the twenty-nine-year-old. George used fifteen thousand dollars from a trust fund to start investing in oil leases throughout the southwest. Eventually he started his own business, which he called Arbusto (Bush in Spanish), and in 1977, thanks to investments from family members and their wealthy friends, George's Arbusto Energy company began drilling for oil. His first well was dry, but he plugged along and enjoyed better luck with later wells.

That same year, Bush decided to follow the family's political tradition and ran for the congressional seat for his district. Soon after he declared his candidacy, friends invited George to their home for a barbecue. They also invited another friend, elementary school teacher Laura Welch. The two immediately connected, and after a whirlwind five-week romance, they announced their engagement. The Bush family wholeheartedly approved of the quiet young lady who had captured their son's heart. George and Laura wed at the United Methodist Church in Midland on November 6, 1977.

Their first task together was to continue his fight for the congressional seat. They aggressively campaigned throughout the west Texas district, putting hundreds of miles on their car as they crisscrossed the arid plains. Although Bush won the hard-fought primary, he lost the general election. Being portrayed by the Democrats as a carpetbagger from a wealthy Connecticut family who attended eastern schools undoubtedly was partly to blame for his loss. The voters simply did not believe him to be a true Texan. George was shaken by the defeat and felt ashamed for having failed the Bush family name.

Returning full time to Arbusto, George threw himself into his work. The oil market was booming, and his business followed. He expanded the company and renamed it Bush Exploration, which merged in 1983 with Spectrum 7, an investment company. The boom lasted a few more years, but then with lower overseas oil prices, domestic oil was less attractive, so Bush decided to sell his company. He traded its assets for stock in Harken Energy and joined the company as its chief operating officer. The experience of the past decade had been invaluable in learning how to run a business, manage materials, and work with the most valuable resource—people.

During this time, Bush underwent a personal battle with alcohol. Increasingly, he turned to drinking to lessen his load, and the family worried that at the rate he was going, it would destroy him. He was ecstatic when, on November 25, 1981, he and Laura became the parents of fraternal twins who were named for their two grandmothers—Barbara and Jenna. Fed up with her husband's drinking and not wanting their daughters to grow up with an alcoholic father, Laura let him know it had to stop. Helping in the process was longtime family friend Reverend Billy Graham, who met with George at Kennebunkport and talked to him numerous times on the phone. George also joined his church's men's Bible study group, but still used humor to help ease his personal pain. When someone talked about the problems growing up as a "PK—preacher's kid," Bush laughed and replied, "You think that's tough? Try being a VPK [vice president's kid]."[14]

NATIONAL EVENTS

JAN 29: President Bush uses term "Axis of Evil" to describe Iraq, Iran, and North Korean terrorist activities

MAY 21: US Department of State names seven nations that sponsor terrorism: North Korea, Iraq, Iran, Cuba, Libya, Sudan, and Syria

MAY 22: Former KKK member Bobby Frank Cherry convicted for 1963 bombing deaths of four girls at 16th Street Baptist Church in Birmingham

JUN 27: US Supreme Court approves use of school vouchers

WORLD EVENTS

MAR 19: Afghanistan invasion ends

MAR 30: The Queen Mother dies at age 101

MAY 12: Former President Jimmy Carter becomes first to visit Fidel Castro

JUN 3: Queen Elizabeth II celebrates her Golden Jubilee

JUL 5: Iraq refuses to cooperate with UN inspectors

JUL 15: American member of the Taliban, John Walker Lindh, convicted of aiding the enemy and sentenced to prison

SEP 10: Switzerland joins the UN

When his father began developing a national campaign to win the Republican nomination, he asked George to help, and the family moved temporarily to Washington while he worked as a special assistant for his dad. He was the one required to make decisions and oversee strategy, as well as act as intermediary between the organization and the "Silver Fox,"[15] a.k.a. Barbara Bush. He was not consulted, however, when his father chose a running mate; in fact, George attempted to change his dad's mind when it was announced that Dan Quayle was his pick because he believed his father needed someone with more credibility and credentials to help the ticket.

But it was a proud son who had the honor as head of the Texas delegation at the 1988 Republican Convention in New Orleans to announce that its votes went to George Bush, which were enough to put him over the top. George W. told the crowd, "For a man we respect and a man we love, for her favorite son and the best father in America . . . the man who made me proud every single day of my life and a man who will make America proud, the next President of the United States."[16] Meanwhile, Texas Governor Ann Richards was ridiculing the vice president at the Democratic convention, where she told the audience, "Poor George, he can't help it . . . he was born with a silver foot in his mouth."[17] George W. would not forget nor forgive that remark.

After watching his father's inauguration and enjoying the comforts of being guests at the White House, George and his family moved back to Texas. Now the question was, what next? Deciding to take his lifelong love and passion for baseball and turn it into a profitable business, he convinced a group of investors to take the plunge, and in April 1989, they bought 86 percent of the Texas Rangers. To help pay off his $500,000 loan for most of his share, Bush sold his stock in Harken for $850,000. Although the price temporarily dropped soon afterward, it later was worth twice as much.

Bush loved attending the Rangers' games, sitting in his seat by the dugout and chatting with other fans. He took his job seriously, though, and fired people as needed, including the manager. Thinking that a new stadium would attract bigger crowds, Bush successfully lobbied for the people to pay a half-cent higher sales tax for its construction, with the team kicking in the rest of the money. In 1994, the Rangers moved to their new ballpark, Ameriquest Field in Arlington, and attendance nearly doubled. Two years after its opening, Bush and his group of investors sold their shares in the team for $250 million; his part was $14.9 million—a tidy profit from his $606,000 investment of only seven years earlier.

POLITICS

By the time the Rangers moved into their new home, George was attempting to relocate as well—to the governor's mansion in Austin. Brother Jeb was running for governor of Florida in 1998; in fact, his candidacy had started much earlier than George, who announced he was opposing Ann Richards a year before the election. Both brothers wanted their father to help in both campaigning and drumming up financial support.

Laura Bush was not terribly excited about her husband's political ambitions because the family was now financially secure and living in a nice north Dallas home, the girls had friends, and it seemed very doubtful that anyone could topple the popular Governor Richards. George moved forward anyway, and recruited a longtime member of his father's campaign staff, Karl Rove. He

OCT 2: Congress passes joint resolution granting president power to take military action as necessary against Iraq

OCT 2: Beltway Sniper begins rampage with five shootings in Maryland

OCT 16: President Bush signs Iraq War Resolution

OCT 24: Two Beltway snipers apprehended

NOV 5: Republican Party wins control of both houses of Congress in midterm elections

NOV 25: President Bush signs Homeland Security Act into law, creates new cabinet position

OCT 12: Bombing in two Bali nightclubs kills more than 200

OCT 26: US, South Korea, and Japan order North Korea to dismantle its nuclear weapons program

NOV: First reported cases of SARS (severe acute respiratory syndrome) in China

NOV 8: UN Security Council passes Resolution 1441 ordering Saddam Hussein to disarm or face "serious consequences;" Iraq agrees to comply

DID YOU KNOW?

In 1998, George and Jeb Bush became the first brothers since the 1960s to win governorships of two states on the same day. Earlier the Rockefellers had won (Nelson in New York and Winthrop in Arkansas).

also enlisted the aid of former Texas Republican Party director Karen Hughes.

George and Barbara Bush worried that their son was making a huge mistake taking on the popular Texas governor. But he told them that he did not need to "erode [Richards's] likeability" but rather her "electability."[18] He was eager to campaign against the woman who had ridiculed his father and then started referring to "Junior" as "shrub." Rather than wage a battle of personalities, Bush decided to offer four issues as his platform: education, stiffening penalties against juvenile offenders, welfare reform, and reforming the amounts of damages allowed in civil cases. Many Texas newspapers applauded his platform and his unwillingness to indulge in a vindictive campaign. Apparently the people of Texas also liked his ideas—they chose him to be their next governor. He won 53 percent of the vote to Richards's 46 percent.

GOVERNOR

Winning the governorship of Texas was rather bittersweet for George because, while he won, younger brother Jeb had lost his bid for the same post in Florida. Still, the Bush family came together in Austin for George's inauguration in January 1999. All understood that George would not have an easy time pushing his agenda through the Texas legislature, which was dominated by Democrats and headed by Lieutenant Governor Bob Bullock.

Bush's top priority was reforming education; he was appalled to learn of the astounding number of Texas youth who were unable to read. He worked with experts to develop ways to attack the problem, including granting more autonomy to the local school districts; raising standards and eliminating social promotion; transferring emphasis from teaching whole language to a return to phonics; and using tests to hold schools accountable for their results. Bush worked with educational professionals and business and industry leaders, and pled for parents to do their part in encouraging their children to read. Within his first term, the results were encouraging, with improved test scores across the board, including for minority students.

One of the problems for Texas education, according to its governor, was the inequity of its tax system. So halfway through his first term, he decided to overhaul the entire tax structure. Funding by the state was low, so that needed to be rectified since this forced local districts to raise their property taxes. Bush decided that taxes needed to be lowered. Businesses were paying taxes at varying levels, which he insisted needed to be made into a flat tax system. In November 1996, the governor announced he was seizing the billion-dollar surplus and freezing it from being used as the down payment for a tax cut. Bush's plan was rejected by the legislature; however, voters approved the tax cut as a referendum.

Tort reform made its way to the legislature first, and lawyers actively lobbied legislators to block any attempts by the governor to impose punitive damage limits. Bush thought excessive damages were costly for all concerned and opposed them. He wanted a limit of less than a million dollars, which was opposed by the Democrats and Lieutenant Governor Bullock. The lieutenant governor appointed a committee to work on the problem, and Bush sent a representative, as well. Bullock referred to the governor as "too stubborn and bullheaded for his own good," but the two sides still managed to agree to a compromise of $750,000. Once the deal was made, Bullock called Bush "the greatest Governor ever."[19]

NATIONAL EVENTS

JAN 10: 62,000 additional troops sent to Persian Gulf

JAN 24: Official beginning of Department of Homeland Security operations

FEB 1: Space shuttle Columbia disintegrates on reentry, killing all seven astronauts

APR 10: Congress approves National Amber Alert law

MAY 1: End of formal combat in Afghanistan

MAY 4–10: Historic tornado week in US—393 rip through 19 states

2003

WORLD EVENTS

JAN 10: North Korea announces withdrawal from Nonproliferation Nuclear Treaty

FEB 5: Secretary of State Colin Powell presents America's case for invading Iraq to UN Security Council

MAR: Three Middle Eastern nations ask Saddam Hussein to resign rather than bring war to the region

MAR 1: Pakistan arrests the mastermind of 9/11 attacks, Khalid Shaikh Mohammed

MAR 17: President Bush gives Saddam Hussein ultimatum to relinquish control and leave Iraq, along with his sons, or face war

Prior to the mid-1990s, juvenile justice in Texas meant sending kids to a "boot camp," where they loafed and did nothing constructive all day. Bush's appointee to the Texas Youth Commission, Steve Robinson, soon changed that. Young people wore uniforms and lived a strictly regimented life defined by discipline and constructive use of their time—a radical departure from the concept of "easy jail time." Juvenile offenders were photographed and finger printed to help in tracking gang members. The state also lowered the age to fourteen for offenders of violent crimes to be tried as adults and put into adult prisons. Weapons-free zones were established near schools. "Tough love" became the motto for rehabilitating youthful offenders. They were no longer treated as victims, but rather people who had chosen the wrong path and now had to suffer the consequences for their decisions. Learning how to make better choices in the future became part of their rehabilitation.

Faith-based initiatives also became a priority, especially after Bush became aware that a successful program, Teen Challenge of South Texas, was about to be closed by the state because it did not meet its guidelines for a drug and alcohol rehabilitation program, but was dispensing prayer rather than medication. This program yielded results, Bush argued, and should be kept open, and it was. He ordered a task force to study the possibility of expanding ways for the religious institutions of Texas "to help people in need without violating the important principle of separation of church and state."[20] That report then provided the foundation for faith-based initiatives to be passed in the coming years, including partnering these groups with state agencies as part of his welfare reform.

Bush had campaigned for changes to the welfare system. He proposed time limits on receiving benefits, as well as requiring those who were able-bodied to either work or train to work (including attending school). Also, he wanted recipients to sign a pledge promising to be drug-free and ensure that their children were immunized and attended school.

Unable to enact all of his reforms in one term, Bush decided to run for reelection. He wanted to continue his educational reforms, including the end of social promotions, and argued that students should be tested every few years. If they failed to attain a score of 70 on the Texas Basic Skills test, remediation should address whatever deficiency they had. Critics of the plan were skeptical and insisted that by holding students to this higher accountability level, the number failing would skyrocket.

The governor's other campaign issue was granting Texans a tax cut from their state's surplus. Bush proposed returning $2.6 billion to the taxpayer while still providing greater state aid to education. The people decided they liked what they had seen in the previous four years, and for the first time in Texas history, a governor won a second consecutive term. Bush won in a landslide against Democratic land commissioner Garry Mauro, with an advantage of 69 percent to 31 percent.

2000 CAMPAIGN

Even before the gubernatorial election, Bush started hearing questions about whether or not he was running for the Republican presidential nomination. Finally, deciding that all of the speculation was a distraction from his work and the future gubernatorial campaign, Bush called a press conference in 1997 to announce he did not know whether he would run for president. When asked why he was making such a statement in the midst

DID YOU KNOW?

Bush and his father (George H.W. Bush) are the second father-son team to serve in the presidency. John and John Quincy Adams were the first.

MAY 29: Microsoft agrees to pay AOL $750 million as settlement in antitrust lawsuit

JUN 27: FTC announces No-Call Registry to prevent telemarketers from calling to begin in October

JUL 24: Congressional report on 9/11 faults FBI and CIA for not taking terrorist threats seriously

OCT 7: Californians recall governor Gray Davis and vote in movie star Arnold Schwarzenegger in his place

DEC 10: Supreme Court upholds McCain-Feingold Act reforming campaign finance and banning soft money to political campaigns

MAR 19: US begins bombing Iraq

MAR 20: Land troops of US, United Kingdom, Poland, and

APR 9: Baghdad freed of Hussein's control

JUL 22: Two of Saddam Hussein's sons are killed by

AUG: Paris heat wave kills 3,000

AUG 11: NATO takes over peacekeeping mission in

OCT 15: China launches its first manned space mission

OCT 24: Last flight of a Concorde airplane

DEC 12: US forces capture Saddam Hussein near Tikrit, Iraq

PRESIDENTIAL ELECTIONS WHEN THE POPULAR VOTE WINNER LOST THE ELECTORAL VOTE—AND THE ELECTION ★ 1824: No one emerged from the electoral vote with a majority, although Andrew Jackson won the popular vote. The House of Representatives, however, declared John Quincy Adams the winner.

1876: A product of Reconstruction-era politics, three states turned in two sets of electoral results—one each for Samuel J. Tilden and Rutherford B. Hayes. With disputed results, no one was the clear winner. Congress decided Hayes was the winner by a vote of a specially created committee.

1888: Benjamin Harrison won the electoral vote and the presidency, but Grover Cleveland won the popular vote.

2000: Neither candidate—Bush or Gore—had the majority of the Electoral College. Certain ballots of Florida became the focus of a legal dispute and, after a US Supreme Court decision, recounts were halted, and Florida's electoral votes went to George W. Bush, as did the presidency.

of an election, Bush said that the people had the right to know that it was a possibility when they cast their vote to keep him as governor. Apparently it made little difference in the election.

At this time, former president Bush wrote a letter to Hugh Sidey, longtime journalist for *Time*, as well as a good friend, describing the pride he felt toward his two sons running for governor in their respective states. Calling George "good" but admitting that his oldest son was "uptight at times, feisty at other times," he continued his description:

> *He includes people. He has no sharp edges on issues. He is no ideologue, no divider. He brings people together and he knows how to get things done. He has principles to which he adheres but he knows how to give a little to get a lot. He doesn't hog the credit. He's low on ego, high on drive. All the talk about his wild youth days is pure nuts. His character will pass muster with flying colors.*[21]

Bush was a key figure at the meeting of Republican Governors, and speculation of a possible presidential bid grew. When a British reporter pressed for the Texan's philosophy, Bush replied, "I'm a conservative with heart."[22] That would be taken by his speechwriter and changed to become "compassionate conservative."

To prepare himself for becoming a candidate, Bush hosted fifteen policy conferences in Austin, meeting with experts in their particular fields, from health care and social security to defense and economics. One thing he learned was that the prospering '90s were about to run out, and economic experts recommended a tax cut to lessen the taxpayers' burden. A lesson he had learned from his father's campaign: no promises of "no new taxes." Once he made his decision to run for the Republican nomination, his father and family quickly acted to mobilize financial and political support from friends who had been cultivated over the years, leaving the field of other potential candidates little access to cash.

With over a year to go before the Republican convention, Bush had already garnered the endorsements of 117 congressmen and ten senators; moreover, over thirty-six million dollars was raised during the first part of 1999. Once the campaign season began, Bush won in Iowa, but lost to Arizona

NATIONAL EVENTS

DEC 24: Washington state admits some of its livestock has "mad cow" disease

JAN: Critics charge that President Bush exaggerated threat of WMD (weapons of mass destruction) to garner support for Iraq war

JAN 7: President Bush proposes amnesty program for illegal immigrants

FEB 3: CIA states no imminent danger by Iraq prior to US invasion in 2003

MAR 2: NASA announces that its Mars rover has found evidence that its landing area once had water

2004

WORLD EVENTS

DEC 19: Libyan leader Moammar al-Qadhafi admits to developing weapons of mass destruction, but now promises to dismantle the program

MAR 19: Investigation begins over Iraq's Oil for Food program and possible corrupt ties to UN officials

MAR 29: Seven former Soviet republics/bloc nations join NATO

APR 28: Allegations that abuse of prisoners by American soldiers at Abu Ghraib prison become public

JUN 28: Iraqi interim government takes political control from coalition

senator John McCain in the New Hampshire primary. He came back to win most of the key primaries, and after losing on Super Tuesday, McCain dropped out of the race.

In July, the Republican convention in Philadelphia named George W. Bush as the nominee. Earlier in the campaign, he had asked longtime family friend and politician Dick Cheney to head a committee to determine the best running mate for the Bush ticket. After interviews and discussions, Bush decided he wanted a man with more than a quarter century of experience in government, from the time of the Nixon and Ford administrations. Cheney was asked to be the vice presidential candidate, and he accepted the party's nomination. His long-time experience, including a stint in Congress and as secretary of defense under Bush Sr., was beneficial to the ticket.

Many anticipated a fairly lopsided race because Democratic nominee Al Gore was following in the footsteps of Bill Clinton, who remained a popular president despite having weathered impeachment proceeedings. The economy, while slowing down, was still good, and indications pointed to Gore coasting to victory. Polls, however, consistently showed Bush and Gore running neck and neck throughout the campaign. Bush continued pushing an agenda similar to what he had run on in Texas—improving education and granting tax cuts to taxpayers. He also insisted that there needed to be reforms in Social Security, welfare, and Medicare.

The two candidates debated three times, but these debates did little to significantly affect their ratings. Barbara Bush warned there would likely be an "October surprise," which turned out to be the old news of George's drinking and driving resurfacing. More allegations of drug use years before dogged Bush, but none were substantiated. The seesawing in the polls continued; both camps knew the race would be close, but neither imagined it would end as it did.

Once the polls closed on November 7, 2000, on the East Coast, news outlets began projecting winners for those states. No significant problem emerged until some began calling Bush the winner in Florida based on exit polling data, and later, Gore called to concede. As the night wore on and more actual numbers came in, the networks changed their predictions and now said Gore won Florida. Gore made another phone call to retract his earlier concession. When Bush questioned him and argued that his brother had received assurances from state election officials that Bush had indeed won Florida, Gore countered, "Let me explain something. Your younger brother is not the ultimate authority on this."[23]

When the Florida votes were tallied, Bush had won, but by a slim margin of less than two thousand votes, which under state law meant all counties using machine tabulations had to be recounted. Once this was done, Bush had a victory margin of just over three hundred votes. Democrats then pushed for an additional hand recount in four heavily Democratic counties, and Bush sued in federal court to halt the hand recount, thus beginning the war of the lawsuits. Both Gore and Bush spent weeks alternately suing in state and federal courts to start/stop recounts of certain Florida ballots. Debates regarding certification and deadlines ensued. Republican Secretary of State Katherine Harris said she would not accept the hand recounts, but the state Supreme Court, all appointed by Democratic governors, ordered the recounts to continue. The country watched the unfolding drama of election officials holding ballots up to the light trying to determine whether

MAY 29: National World War II Memorial dedicated in Washington, D.C.

JUN 5: Former President Ronald Reagan dies at his California home

JUL 21: First release of 9/11 Commission's report

JUL 26–29: Democratic National Convention meets and nominates Massachusetts senator John Kerry and South Carolina senator John Edwards for their party's ticket

SEP 1: More than 1,000 schoolchildren and adults taken hostage by Chechen terrorists

SEP 2: UN demands all foreign troops leave Lebanon

SEP 3: Russians storm Chechen-held school and kill 335 (some terrorists and some hostages), with hundreds more wounded

DEC 26: Catastrophe hits Asia as earthquake of 9.3 magnitude creates gigantic tsunami waves that crash ashore on islands and mainland Asia; more than 186,000 are known dead, with tens of thousands more missing

DID YOU KNOW?

George W. Bush was a part-owner of the Texas Rangers baseball team.

the chad (the small piece of paper removed for desired candidates on punch-card ballots) was punched through, and the term "hanging chad" (those only partially punched) entered the national dialogue.

After multiple trips to the state courts and two to the US Supreme Court, the Supreme Court ruled in *Bush v. Gore* that the recounts in Florida should end, and the state should certify its winner in time for the December 12 electoral election deadline. Moreover, the Court insisted that this decision was not a precedent for future elections but "limited to the present circumstances."[24]

The state's Republican legislature then certified the party's electors who, in turn, voted for George W. Bush. This tipped the electoral college to 271 for Bush, giving him one more vote than required to win the presidency. Gore then conceded the election for a second time, with the knowledge that had he carried his home state of Tennessee, the entire issue of Florida would be moot, and Gore would have become the forty-third president. Although this was only the fourth time in history that the popular and electoral vote tallies split, many Democrats insisted that they had been robbed of the presidency, and some called for reforms in the electoral process.

PRESIDENT BUSH

Continuing with his theme of volunteerism hand-in-hand with "compassionate conservatism," Bush asked the American people in his inauguration speech "to defend needed reforms against easy attacks, to serve your nation, beginning with your neighbor. I ask you to be citizens. Citizens, not spectators. Citizens, not subjects. Responsible citizens, building communities of service and a nation of character."

The Bushes attended every one of the eight inaugural balls thrown in their honor. The next morning, there was an emotional meeting in the Oval Office between the past president Bush and his son. "Mr. President," said George Sr. "Mr. President," returned the current president, and then both men wept.[25]

The Oval Office was a symbol of the presidency, and its new occupant believed it should be respected as such. He forbade anyone, including himself, from entering it without adhering to a strict dress code—suits for women, coats and ties for men. His father proudly talked of how "honor and dignity"[26] were being restored to the White House.

One of the first measures that Bush lobbied to win bipartisan congressional support for was his tax cut of $1.3 trillion, passed in May 2001. Hoping to curb the recession that was beginning to erode the economy, the president touted tax cuts advocated by his predecessors Reagan and Kennedy as a beneficial means to stimulate growth. Amid dire predictions of catastrophe by opponents, the tax cuts helped move the economy upward, but at a stiff price—a ballooning deficit.

Prior to taking office, Bush had sought the aid of Senator Ted Kennedy, who understood the power of a family and its dynasty, and they pledged to work together to enact educational reform. Other Democrats, however, were unwilling to join forces with the Republican president. Still, Bush was successful in gaining enough bipartisan cooperation to pass "No Child Left Behind" (NCLB) legislation to improve test scores of the nation's youth, increase funding for schools, and, originally, to grant private vouchers to parents if their school had a history of underperformance. This latter portion was removed, and complaints would

NATIONAL EVENTS

AUG 30–SEP 2: Republicans renominate George W. Bush and Dick Cheney

NOV 2: Bush wins reelection and Republicans gain more congressional seats

2005

JAN 20: Second inauguration for President George W. Bush

MAR 1: US Supreme Court rules death penalty unconstitutional for anyone under age of 18

JUL 26: First Space Shuttle mission in 2½ years begins when Discovery blasts off

WORLD EVENTS

JAN 30: Iraq has its first free elections in nearly 50 years

FEB 10: North Korea admits to having nuclear weapons

FEB 16: Kyoto Protocol on global warming takes effect but US and Australia do not participate

soon pour in that NCLB was another example of a government mandate that was left to the states and local districts to scrounge for funding.

In August 2001, the president announced funding of stem-cell research, but federal monies could only be spent on utilizing existing stem-cell lines. In a televised address, Bush explained that he wanted the research to go forward in the hopes that it could find cures to such diseases as diabetes and Parkinson's. He did, however, object to harvesting frozen embryos, and ordered a presidential council appointed to monitor stem-cell research.

Increasingly during the first months of his administration, Bush was perceived as an isolationist. For example, like his Democratic predecessor, he was skeptical of the Kyoto Protocol calling for the curbing of carbon dioxide emissions to fight air pollution, and the United States officially announced it would not adhere to the treaty. The president maintained that the treaty's exemption of China and India and other underdeveloped nations was wrong and its "compliance would cause serious harm to the US economy."[27] Although arguing that his administration would work to fight pollution and help the environment, there was little evidence that he could call up that supported his claim that the environment was a priority. Millions of acreage hitherto considered safe from development was released for logging, drilling, and mining. Clean air and water standards were also lowered.

In the spring of 2001, Bush faced his first foreign policy crisis when a Chinese fighter jet collided with a US Navy surveillance aircraft, forcing the American plane to land in China, and soon its crew was being held by the Chinese army. After receiving an apology, the crew was released, and later President Jiang Zemin visited Bush in Crawford, Texas.

9/11

On Tuesday morning, September 11, 2001, the president arrived at Emma E. Booker Elementary School in Sarasota, Florida, to meet with a class of second graders. Just before entering, he was told that a plane had crashed into the World Trade Center. He took his seat at the front of the class, and as different children read to the president, Chief of Staff Andy Card whispered into his ear, "A second plane hit the tower. America is under attack."[28] Bush gave a curt nod, pursed his lips, and attempted to at least appear like he was still listening to the class. He complimented the children on their reading but quickly told the reporters covering the story that they would move elsewhere to talk.

After hearing updates from Cheney and others in Washington and confirming that his wife and daughters were safe, Bush announced he wanted to return to the White House, but Cheney advised against it, arguing that they did not know if more terrorists were waiting to attack. Another airliner soon crashed into the Pentagon, and a fourth plunged into a Pennsylvania field following its passengers' efforts to ensure it did not reach its destination somewhere in Washington, D.C.

The president flew to airbases in Louisiana and then Nebraska for briefings and short news conferences, but by the afternoon, with all air flights grounded, and military jets patrolling the skies, Bush ordered Air Force One back to Washington. From there he addressed the American people that night: "Today, our fellow citizens, our way of life, our very freedom came under attack in a series of deliberate and deadly terrorist acts." Telling the people that America was strong, and reassuring them that the country's government was fully functional, the president reminded his audience

DID YOU KNOW?

George W. Bush is the only president to have graduated from Harvard with an MBA.

AUG 29: Hurricane Katrina hits Gulf coast, hitting New Orleans especially hard

SEP 24: Hurricane Rita visits Gulf coast, causing worse damage in areas earlier hit by Katrina

SEP 29: John Roberts sworn in as chief justice after death of William Rehnquist

JAN 31: Samuel Alito sworn in as new assistant justice to Supreme Court

FEB 11: Vice President Cheney accidentally wounds friend while quail hunting

2006

MAY 10: Assassination attempt on President Bush while visiting Tbilisi, Georgia, but hand grenade

AUG 18: China and Russia hold their first joint military exercise

SEP 12: Hong Kong Disneyland opens

OCT 15: Iraq holds referendum on its

JAN 1: During a pricing dispute with Russia, the country cuts off the supply of natural gas to Ukraine

JAN 4: After Israeli Prime Minster Ariel Sharon suffers a stroke, the powers of the office are transfer to Vice Prime Minister Ehud Olmert

EVENTS OF SEPTEMBER 11, 2001

7:58 A.M. ★ United Flight #175 departs Boston for Los Angeles. Fifty-six passengers, two pilots, and seven flight attendants are on board. It is hijacked soon after takeoff and heads for New York.

7:59 A.M. ★ American Flight #11 also departs Boston for Los Angeles with eighty-one passengers, two pilots, and nine flight attendants. It, too, is hijacked and diverted to New York.

8:01 A.M. ★ United Flight #93 departs Newark, New Jersey, for San Francisco carrying thirty-eight passengers, two pilots, and five flight attendants.

8:10 A.M. ★ American Flight #77 leaves Washington Dulles for Los Angeles with seventy-eight passengers on board and a crew of two pilots and four flight attendants. It is hijacked soon after takeoff.

8:46 A.M. ★ American #11 flies into the North Tower of the World Trade Center.

9:03 A.M. ★ United #175 flies into the South Tower of the World Trade Center. Soon after, the FAA closes all New York City area airports.

9:25 A.M. ★ FAA grounds all domestic flights.

9:45 A.M. ★ American #77 crashes into the Pentagon.

10:05 A.M. ★ South Tower collapses.

10:10 A.M. ★ United #93 crashes into rural Somerset County, Pennsylvania. It was later discovered that passengers bravely attempted to wrestle control of aircraft from hijackers to prevent tragedy in Washington, D.C.

10:28 A.M. ★ North Tower collapses.

TOTAL NUMBER OF FATALITIES ★ 2,973 fatalities (not including the 19 hijackers); 2,602 of the victims were from the Twin Towers; all on board the four hijacked airplanes died; 125 at the Pentagon, and more than 400 rescue workers in New York City.

Zacarias Moussaoui, a French citizen of Moroccan descent, was the only person to face criminal charges for the events of September 11. At times he claimed guilt for aiding in the planning of 9/11 with fellow al Qaeda members, and at other times denied knowledge of their terrorist plot, but in May 2006, he was found guilty of six felony charges, including terrorism, and was sentenced to life imprisonment.

NATIONAL EVENTS

MAR 9: President Bush signs a renewal of Patriot Act

MAR 31: Baseball commissioner Bud Selig asks for investigation into possible steroid use by players

APR 25: Record tax receipts—$36.4 billion received

MAY 3: Major cola manufacturers agree to remove sweetened carbonated drinks from school vending machines by 2009

JUN 16: Congress rejects setting arbitrary deadlines for pullout of troops from Iraq

WORLD EVENTS

JAN 25: Militant organization Hamas wins majority of seats in Palestinian Legislative Council election

JAN 27: Year of Mozart—250th anniversary celebration of the birth of Wolfgang Amadeus Mozart

FEB 7: Egyptian passenger ferry sinks in the Red Sea with 1,400 people onboard

FEB 22: Terrorists bomb and damage the Al Askari Mosque, Shiite holy site in Samarra, Iraq

MAR 11: Michelle Bachelet becomes first female president of Chile

that the country had "stood down enemies before and we will do so again this time."[29] The country had embarked on its "war on terror."

On September 14, the president addressed the congregation assembled in Washington's National Cathedral, as well as those watching on television. "We are here in the middle hour of our grief," the president opened. He reminded all that "our responsibility to history is already clear: to answer these attacks and rid the world of evil." While most of his speech was what one expected to hear on such a somber occasion, he did insert comments to remind all that America was at war. "This conflict was begun on the timing and terms of others. It will end in a way, and at an hour, of our choosing."[30]

When the president arrived at the site of Ground Zero in downtown New York City, he found destruction beyond anything he had imagined. Toiling amidst the rubble were people wanting revenge, and one worker yelled as he walked by, "Don't let me down!" Those words and the man's intense look bore directly into the soul of the commander in chief. A few minutes later, the president climbed aboard the wreckage of a fire truck and, harkening back to his cheerleading days at Yale, put a bullhorn to his mouth and began reciting his prepared remarks when someone shouted, "I can't hear you," and others echoed the same sentiment. Bush smiled and replied, "I can hear you. The rest of the world hears you. And the people who knocked these buildings down will hear all of us soon!"[31] The crowd whooped in response and the president beamed.

The first major action was the creation of a new cabinet position, the Department of Homeland Security, to improve both the protection of America and the communication among various law enforcement agencies, so information about potential threats would be shared between them.

On October 8, the president told the American people: "On my orders the United States military has begun strikes against al Qaeda terrorist training camps and military installations of the Taliban regime in Afghanistan." This action was only being taken, Bush reminded his audience, after the refusal of the Taliban to cooperate. Their military camps were where Osama bin Laden and his partners-in-terror trained recruits, including those involved in the hijackings of September 11. Soon eleven thousand American troops were deployed to Afghanistan, and with the support of some of its Afghan allies, the United States managed to overthrow the strict Islamist Taliban regime and replace it with a more moderate government. Osama bin Laden, however, proved an elusive quarry, hiding in the towering mountains along Afghanistan's border with Pakistan. But many al Qaeda leaders were successfully caught, and they provided vital information about future terrorist attacks that were consequently quashed.

The State of the Union address in January 2002 unveiled what became known as the Bush Doctrine, which decreed that the world was now one of sovereign nations and terrorist states. To keep America secure, it now claimed the right and authority to preemptively strike any country that aided international terrorists, and Bush pointedly talked of the "axis of evil"—Iraq, Iran, and North Korea; all were labeled potential threats to world peace.

Within six months of the attacks, Congress passed the Patriot Act, granting the federal government sweeping powers to fight terrorism, such as using wiretaps, collecting personal information, including health and medical records, as well as

JUN 29: Supreme Court rules that prisoners at Guantanamo Bay are subject to Geneva Convention and cannot be tried by military courts unless approved by Congress

JUL 10: Concrete slabs fall from top of Boston traffic tunnel (part of "Big Dig" project), killing a woman

JUL 19: President Bush vetoes Stem Cell bill, which would have allowed expansion of embryonic stem cell lines; it is the president's first veto

MAR 11: Slobodan Milosevic found dead in his prison cell, cause believed to be heart attack, but some believe he was murdered

APR: Zacarias Moussaoui sentenced to life imprisonment for aiding in 9/11 attacks

JUN 5: Division and independence of Montenegro and Serbia

JUN 29: Women first participate in electoral process in Kuwait

AUG 14: UN cease-fire takes effect in Israel-Palestine conflict

DID YOU KNOW?

Laura Bush, former school librarian, has long been an advocate of reading and started the Texas Book Festival when her husband was governor. As First Lady, she established the National Book Festival held annually at the Library of Congress.

collecting records from libraries and universities. Many organizations objected to what was perceived as attacks on civil liberties, and some successfully won in court. In March 2006, however, the Patriot Act was renewed with most of its provisions becoming permanent.

IRAQ

A great deal of Bush's second year in office was spent in the preliminaries of war against Iraq. First, there was the ongoing issue of UN inspections teams, which had been mandated following the Persian Gulf War. Those inspections had been allowed to cease, and after wrangling in negotiations for two months and with the threat of US action, Iraqi officials agreed to allow inspectors back into their country in November. At first the country appeared to cooperate, but officials were evasive in answering inspectors' questions about their weapons. Earlier American intelligence had convinced the Clinton administration that Saddam Hussein had stockpiles of weapons of mass destruction (WMDs); moreover, the British had corroborating information.

Secretary of State Colin Powell addressed the UN Security Council early in February 2003 and insisted that Iraq was not complying with previous UN resolutions. France and Russia, who were allies of Iraq, refused to take any action beyond the inspections. Without UN-sanctioned support, the United States and Great Britain decide to take joint military action. UN inspectors left Iraq on March 18, and the following day, the invasion of Iraq began.

IRAQ WAR

Dubbed "Iraqi Freedom," the mission of the coalition forces was to end the reign of Saddam Hussein and capture the weapons of mass destruction. Launched on March 19, the beginning of the campaign consisted of aerial bombardment designed to weaken the leadership of Iraq and its capabilities to wage war by removing communications. Ground troops began moving into southern Iraq from Kuwait. More aerial bombardment in Baghdad over prime targets heralded the "shock and awe" phase, to emphasize the overwhelming nature of the coalition's attack. Tough fighting ensued against the Iraqi Republican Guard near Basra and other locations as the troops moved toward Baghdad, and a question began to be asked that would be repeated in the days, months, and years ahead: does America have enough troops in Iraq? Secretary of Defense Donald Rumsfeld maintained throughout that yes, the United States had enough "boots on the ground." Others remained skeptical.

As the invasion continued, specially trained units hunted for signs of WMDs, and as time marched on and no stockpiles were found, more criticism was heard. Some believed that the UN inspectors should have been granted more time to carry out their mission before any military action was taken; others charged that Bush and British prime minister Tony Blair had lied to the world by saying that there were WMDs when the leaders knew there were none in order to give them a convenient cover for an illegal invasion. The controversy raged for years afterward.

By April 9, 2003, Baghdad was in coalition hands, and soon other Iraqi strongholds fell.

On May 1, the Pentagon announced that major combat operations were over. The next day, Bush arrived on the aircraft carrier *Abraham Lincoln* in a military jet. Under a huge banner requested by the ship's crew, Bush praised the work of the military and reiterated the Pentagon's announcement. He

NATIONAL EVENTS

AUG 15: Census Bureau reports growth of immigrants in US households increased by 16 percent since 2000

SEP 30: US deficit drops to $247.7 billion, lowest in four years

NOV 7: Democrats win midterm elections and majority in both houses of Congress

NOV 12: Gerald Ford becomes longest-lived president in history

DEC 26: Gerald Ford dies at his home in Rancho Mirage, California

WORLD EVENTS

AUG 24: International Astronomical Union announces Pluto no longer considered a planet

SEP 19: Royal Thai Army stages coup d'état

OCT 9: North Korea claims to have conducted its first nuclear test

NOV 5: Saddam Hussein sentenced to death by Iraqi tribunal

NOV 20: Iran and Syria recognize Iraq

DEC 30: Saddam Hussein executed

was criticized for the banner and for his attire—the flight suit he wore during the trip was similar to those worn during his National Guard days. In the coming months, the president received more criticism as the fighting continued, and many wondered if the focus on Iraq had diverted Bush's attention from finding Osama bin Laden.

There was good news on December 13 when American troops found Saddam Hussein in an underground hideaway near Tikrit. He was taken into custody and later tried for his crimes against his own people, found guilty in an Iraqi court, and executed in December 2006.

Meanwhile, the new Iraqi interim government began taking its first shaky steps in leading the fragile nation. Problems soon developed between the two Muslim sects of Shiites and Sunnis in establishing their roles in their country's future.

Two reports in 2004 contained news that faulty intelligence led the administration to believe there were WMDs when, in fact, there were none. More people launched allegations that the invasion of Iraq was merely a ploy to gain access to its profitable oil fields, and all were reminded of the oil connections of both President Bush and Vice President Cheney. Around the time of these damaging reports, photographs were released showing American soldiers abusing Iraqi prisoners at the Abu Ghraib detention facility. During these last months of 2003, support for the war began to decrease.

All of these criticisms were hurled at Bush during the 2004 reelection campaign; he and Cheney were opposed by Massachusetts senator John Kerry and his running mate, John Edwards of North Carolina. Both candidates were reminded of their Vietnam-era history—Kerry's fighting record and medals were called into question by a group called Swift Boat Veterans for Truth, who ran damaging television ads against him. Footage of Kerry's anti-Vietnam War protests and testimony before Congress were replayed many times. The president's National Guard service was also scrutinized and ridiculed as being far from the front and the fighting. The two men disagreed on most major issues, and Bush continually reminded the American people that they would be safer with him in the White House than with his opponent, who originally voted for the war but then voted against funding it. Bush supporters decried Kerry's history of "flip-flopping" on issues as making him unsuited for the job of commander in chief.

On domestic issues, the two candidates disagreed regarding abortion—Bush opposed; Kerry supported. On gay marriage, Bush opposed, and while Kerry said he did, too, he also believed that gay civil unions should be legal.

The three presidential debates between Bush and Kerry were inconclusive. Despite numerous endorsements for John Kerry by Hollywood celebrities and newspapers, the American people reelected George W. Bush. He won with 51 percent of the popular vote, Kerry receiving 48 percent, and Independent candidate Ralph Nader garnering 1 percent. In the electoral college, Bush won 286 votes to Kerry's 252.

SECOND TERM

Before the president's second inaugural, the majority of his cabinet announced their resignation, including Secretary of State Colin Powell and Attorney General John Ashcroft. Two historic appointments were made in their places—Condoleezza Rice became the first African American woman heading the State Department, and Alberto Gonzales was the first Latino in charge of the Justice Department.

JAN 3: Former president Gerald Ford buried in Grand Rapids, Michigan

JAN 4: Nancy Pelosi becomes first woman speaker of US House of Representatives

JAN 10: President Bush announces additional 21,500 troops to Iraq

FEB 10: US senator Barack Obama of Illinois announces presidential bid

APR 16: Virginia Tech massacre

2007

JAN 1: Bulgaria and Romania join the European Union

JAN 1: Slovenia adopts the euro

JAN 1: Angola joins OPEC

JAN 1: South Korean Ban Ki-moon replaces Kofi Annan as Secretary-General of the

JAN 11: Vietnam joins the World Trade Organization as 150th member

FEB 27: Suicide attack at Bagram Air Base while VP Dick Cheney is visiting kills 23, but Cheney is not injured; Taliban claims responsibility

FEB 11: Portugal legalizes abortion

The main topic on Bush's domestic agenda for 2005 was the privatization of Social Security. This program had long been considered a political hot potato. Although he had campaigned on the premise and believed it was one of the mandates of the election, Bush had to concede defeat when Congress refused to support such a radical change in Social Security. The president did, however, have a quiet victory on the healthcare front with the enactment of a 2003 law granting more choice to Medicare recipients for their prescription medicines. Although critics proclaimed it was too confusing and ultimately too costly, the program went into effect in 2006 with minimal problems.

Domestically, the Bush administration took a major hit in August 2005, when Hurricane Katrina wrecked havoc along the Gulf coast, destroying towns in Mississippi, Alabama, and Louisiana, including much of the greater New Orleans area, and leaving more than 1,800 people dead. Decrying the government's actions as being "too little too late," critics insisted that Bush should have sent more help in sooner and provided more aid throughout the disaster.

The president could point to some success in Iraq with the election of the Iraqi Assembly in December 2005, but as time went on, the patience of the American people for the continuing war in Iraq wore thin. Their dissatisfaction revealed itself in the midterm elections of 2006. For the first time in more than a decade, Democrats took control of both houses of Congress, winning a thirty-seat majority in the House of Representatives, but only a slim one in the Senate—51–49. The next day, President Bush remarked, "I'm obviously disappointed with the outcome of the election and, as the head of the Republican Party, I share a large part of the responsibility."[32]

With the war in Iraq continuing to drain the public's confidence and patience, Bush pledged to the new Democratic leadership in Congress, House Speaker Nancy Pelosi and Senate Majority Leader Harry Reid, that "I'm open to any idea or suggestion that will help us achieve our goals of defeating the terrorists and ensuring that Iraq's democratic government succeeds."[33]

THE "SURGE" AND THE WAR ON TERROR

Reacting to growing criticism of his handling of the war in Iraq, President Bush made two major announcements early in January 2007: first, he would change leadership there and place Lt. General David Petraeus, who had formerly commanded a combat division in the country, in charge of operations. Second, 21,000 more troops would be sent to Iraq to provide security in Baghdad, as well as in al-Anbar Province, where much of the region was under the control of insurgents. Bush maintained that the additional military strength would quell the growing sectarian violence and provide the time and conditions conducive to reconciliation among political and ethnic factions. This move pleased many Republicans, including Arizona Senator John McCain who had been pushing for a "surge" in American military power.

In May 2007, President Bush vetoed a $124 billion bill for funding the wars in Afghanistan and Iraq because it included a timetable for troop withdrawal. Bush said, "Setting a deadline for withdrawal is setting a date for failure, and that would be irresponsible."[34] Opponents, including Senate Majority Leader Harry Reid, had pronounced the month before that "the war is lost"[35] and argued that "the surge should not go forward,"[36] but could not gain enough support to overcome the president's stand. Later in the summer, General

NATIONAL EVENTS

MAY 3-9: Queen Elizabeth II visits US

JUN 2: Four people charged with terror plot to blow up JFK International Airport in New York

APR 25: A congressman introduces articles to impeach Vice President Dick Cheney

MAY 12: Virginia commemorates 400th anniversary of Jamestown

JUL 24: Minimum wage increases for first time in 10 years; raised from $5.15 to $5.85/hour

WORLD EVENTS

APR 17: The Pound Sterling hits a 15-year high against the US dollar

APR 21: Presidential elections are held in Nigeria

MAY 6: Nicholas Sarkozy elected president of French Republic

JUL 7: Live Earth Concerts are held in cities around the world

JUL 19: Prathiba Patil is elected as the first female president of India

Petraeus testified to Congress that the American military needed to remain in Iraq longer to meet its goals, but predicted that by July 2008 a withdrawal of some of the "surge" troops might be possible. As a follow-up to the commander's testimony, Bush stated that he agreed with his field commander and voiced his confidence that troop strength could drop from the current 169,000 to 130,000. During this time, the President also signed an executive order prohibiting cruel and unusual punishment to be administered to terrorist suspects. Critics argued that it did not go far enough in outlining what could be considered torture.

On the war's fifth anniversary in March 2008, President Bush spoke about the fight in Iraq: "Five years into this battle, there is an understandable debate about whether the war was worth fighting, whether the war was worth winning, and whether we can win it. The answers are clear to me. Removing Saddam Hussein from power was the right decision, and this is a fight that America can and must win."[37] A few days later, a roadside bomb killed four American soldiers, bringing the death total to 4,000. Yet, the month of June saw the lowest American casualties thus far in the war—nineteen deaths.

Another reason for the surge's success was the shift in how the war was conducted. Previous to the influx of soldiers, the U.S. military had cleared neighborhoods of terrorists, but then lacked enough men to keep those areas secure. With increased troops, they made their presence permanent, and trust developed between them and local Iraqis, who no longer had to fear that they would be at the mercy of insurgents when the Americans left. More tips on where to find enemy hideouts and roadside bombs were received by the U.S. and Iraqi militaries. Tribal sheiks also took more leadership, and the people, who had grown weary of the constant upheaval caused by violence, followed their lead. Once the areas were secured, day-to-day activities resumed. On November 27, 2008, less than two years after President Bush announced the surge, the Iraqi parliament approved the Status of Forces Agreement stating that U.S. troops would be withdrawn from the populated areas by June 2009, and that all others would be removed by the end of 2011. Henceforth, any American presence in Iraq would be in accordance with agreements negotiated between the two governments as is done wherever there are U.S. bases or training personnel.

Not everyone approved of the surge, and when Bush made his final presidential appearance in Iraq in December 2008, an Iraqi journalist threw his shoes at the American leader in a gesture of extreme disrespect. Bush ducked being hit with the shoes and made light of the incident, but the video played around the world and provided his last image in Iraq.

Meanwhile, violence in Afghanistan had increased in June 2008, when forty-five American, NATO, and Afghani troops were killed, the highest number since the invasion of 2001. The situation had been growing steadily worse ever since 2006, when the Pakistani government cut a deal with the Taliban insurgents that effectively granted them a sanctuary in a "tribal area" bordering Afghanistan. U.S. forces, already heavily committed to Iraq, responded by conducting targeted air attacks on insurgent leaders in Pakistan. Though these attacks were very effective, it was clear to Bush and his new Defense Secretary, Robert Gates, that such measures could only delay, not prevent, Taliban inroads into southern Afghanistan. Based on the broad consensus among Democrats and Republicans in Congress that American combat

AUG 1: Mississippi River bridge in Minneapolis, Minnesota, collapses during rush hour and kills 13

AUG 30: US Air Force B-52 flies from Minot AFB in North Dakota to Barksdale AFB in Louisiana, carrying 6 nuclear warheads

SEP 13: President Bush tells nation that he plans to lower troop strength in Iraq from 169,000 to 130,000 by July 2008

OCT 12: Former Vice President Albert Gore and the United Nations' Intergovernmental Panel on Climate Change share the Nobel Prize for their work to bring attention to climate change

AUG 1: Boy Scouts celebrates its 100th birthday worldwide

OCT 6: Pakistan President Pervez Musharraf easily wins a third term, but his party is the only one on the ballot

OCT 28: Argentina's First Lady, Cristina Fernández de Kirchner, wins the presidential election

NOV 28: Pakistan President Musharraf relinquishes control of the military, which significantly reduces his power as president

DEC 2: United Russia, President Vladimir Putin's party, wins easy victory in the election, among complaints that the election was rigged

strength in Afghanistan must be increased, Bush and Gates pledged to the Afghani government and NATO that the United States would raise its troop levels in 2009.

Insisting that intelligence officials should have "all available tools"[38] for interrogating terrorist suspects, the president vetoed an absolute ban on "waterboarding," even though use of the technique had been suspended several years earlier. Then in July 2008, Congress passed the Foreign Intelligence Surveillance Act granting the government additional powers to use wiretaps on those suspected of being terrorists both in the United States and elsewhere in the world.

ECONOMY

After coming to office with a recession, which was then exacerbated by the attacks of September 11, 2001, the country saw nearly six years of growth under Bush. By 2007, signs began pointing to possible problems. The first was the housing industry. As adjustable interest rates began to rise, some Americans found themselves unable to pay their mortgage. Foreclosures climbed, and on December 6, 2007, Bush announced an agreement with mortgage firms to freeze interest rates for five years, hoping to blunt the crisis. A slowing economy in January 2008 forced the president to announce an economic stimulus plan of $145 billion, which allowed rebates to lower- and middle-income taxpayers. His plan received bipartisan support and easily passed.

On February 1, the Bureau of Labor Statistics announced that for the first time in fifty-two months jobs had decreased. This announcement fueled fears of a possible recession. The Federal Reserve system moved in March to loan $200 million to banks to spur them to release more credit. Fannie Mae and Freddie Mac, the two largest American mortgage companies, were next to receive bailout monies in hopes that refinanced mortgages would prevent more foreclosures. This failed to solve the problem, so in September, Treasury Secretary Henry Paulsen announced that the U.S. government would be taking over both companies. Within a week, Wall Street was rocked by news of the failures of Merrill Lynch and Lehman Brothers. The Dow Jones average dropped over 500 points, the worst decline since September 11. Observers feared it could drop more if action was not taken. President Bush and Treasury Secretary Paulsen asked Congress to pass legislation to ease the crisis. The House of Representatives refused the $700 billion bailout, prompting a 700-point drop on Wall Street. A few days later, a somewhat modified bailout bill passed.

Over the summer, gas prices compounded the public's economic woes when prices soared to over $4 a gallon. Hoping to ease this situation, Bush lifted a ban on offshore drilling. Many opposed this move, saying its effect would not be felt for decades (the congressional moratorium on offshore drilling remained).

By this time, stock prices were dropping around the world. Soon the administration decided to use $250 billion to recapitalize nine of the leading banks in hopes of stabilizing the economy. October ended with more bad news when it was announced that the GDP (gross domestic product) had dropped for the first time in seventeen years, and that the Consumer Price Index dropped a full percentage point, the largest decrease ever in its sixty-one-year history. In November, the Treasury department and Federal Reserve announced an $800 billion plan to help with lending by government underwriters for various types of loans, including mortgage, credit card, and student. All

NATIONAL EVENTS

OCT 20–NOV 9: Wildfires in southern California rage out of control, causing a million people to evacuate

NOV 5–FEB 12: Writers Guild of America strikes

JAN 22: Federal Reserve makes its largest single-day cut in interest rates when it lowers the rate by 0.75 percent

FEB 5–6: Worst tornado outbreak in over 20 years kills more than 50 people in southern US

FEB 12: General Motors announces a loss of $722 million in the fourth quarter of 2007, making the entire loss for 2007 $38.7 billion

2008

WORLD EVENTS

DEC 16: Britain turns over control of the province of Basra to Iraqi government

DEC 27: Former Pakistan President Benazir Bhutto is killed in a campaign rally

JAN 2: For first time in history, oil prices hit $100 a barrel

JAN 25: China experiences worst snowstorm in 50 years and 133 die

FEB 24: Raul Castro elected unanimously by Cuba's National Assembly to succeed his brother as president

of this affected American automobile manufacturers and falling automobile sales prompted General Motors and Chrysler to ask for bailout money. The two auto giants subsequently received over $17 billion in loans from the government. Again, hoping to ease tightened credit, the Federal Reserve dropped its interest rate to 0.25 and later 0 percent.

More bad news came in November as the Labor Department issued a statement that job losses for the month were the worst since 1974, and the National Bureau of Economic Research announced that the country had been in recession since December 2007. Moreover, manufacturing had dropped to its lowest point in twenty-six years. Fearing future layoffs, consumers kept their money in their pockets, and retailers reported dismal Christmas sales. Consumer spending in December 2008 dropped by nearly 1 percent, and would have been far worse had not the sales of existing homes shot up by 6.5 percent, with advances continuing into January due to a combination of special lending programs and capital injections into the banks. The *Wall Street Journal* dryly noted that "Credit spreads have narrowed from their horrific range of last autumn, a sign that the government's decision to prevent a collapse of the financial system has done some good."[39]

Other signs of a recovering economy began to emerge as the president's time in office drew to a close. Lower interest rates prompted increased applications for both new mortgages and the refinancing of existing ones. In terms of income, real hourly earnings rose 3.5 percent in November and 3.3 percent in December, with January seeing a steep jump of 1 percent in consumer spending—the first monthly rise since June. Corporate bond markets also began to thaw as some $127 billion was issued in January, more than any month since May. The economy was still a long way from being a picture of health, but its resilience and ability to heal itself was beginning to be felt, and the public watched carefully to see if the worst was over.

LOOKING TO RETIREMENT

By this time, Barack Obama had been elected as the next president, and Bush ordered his staff to work closely with the incoming administration to prepare as smooth a transition as possible. Too many precarious factors demanded that the new president be informed and ready to take charge on Inauguration Day.

During his final days in office, Bush reviewed his past two terms before the press and gave a farewell address to the nation. He reminded his audience that he would be spending much of his retirement working on his presidential library at Southern Methodist University, where he also wanted to establish a policy center. He admitted he had made mistakes, but as he told the nation on January 16, 2009, "I've always acted with the best interests of our country in mind. I have followed my conscience and done what I thought was right. You may not agree with some tough decisions I have made, but I hope you can agree that I was willing to make the tough decisions."[40]

MAR 23: 4,000th American death in Iraq

MAY 14: Polar bear designated as "threatened" and eligible for protection under Endangered Species Act

MAY 25: NASA's Phoenix spacecraft is the first to land on the northern polar region of Mars

JUN 19: US announces lowest fatality rate in Iraq since war began in 2003 with only 19 deaths in May

JUN 27: Bill Gates, founder and CEO of Microsoft, steps down as its leader so he can devote more time to philanthropy

MAR 2: Palestinian Prime Minister Mahmoud Abbas suspends peace talks with Israel as fighting continues between Israel and Hamas

MAR 10: 400 Buddhist monks participate in a protest march in Tibet to commemorate the failed uprising of 1959 that resulted in the Dalai Lama fleeing to India

MAY 1: US missile kills top Islamic militant leader in

MAY 21: For the first time in eight years, Israel and Syria try to negotiate a peace deal

MAY 28: The newly elected Nepal Constituent Assembly votes to dissolve the 239-year-old monarchy and form a republic

> *"There have been disappointments. Abu Ghraib, obviously, was a huge disappointment, during the presidency. You know, not having weapons of mass destruction was a significant disappointment. I don't know if you want to call those mistakes or not, but they were…things didn't go according to plan, let's put it that way. And, anyway, I think historians will look back and they'll be able to have a better look at mistakes, after some time has passed. … There is no such thing as short-term history. I don't think you can possibly get the full breadth of an administration until time has passed. You know…did a president's decisions have the impact that he thought they would…over time? Or how did this president compare to future presidents, given a set of circumstances that may be similar or not similar? I mean, it's just impossible to do and I'm comfortable with that."*
>
> —*George W. Bush, 2009*

NATIONAL EVENTS				
AUG 17: Michael Phelps makes Olympic history upon winning his 8th gold medal at the Beijing Summer Games	**AUG 27:** Barack Obama becomes the Democratic Party's candidate for the presidency; Senator Joseph Biden of Delaware is his running mate	**SEP 4:** John McCain becomes the Republican Party's presidential nominee; he chooses Alaskan Governor Sarah Palin as his running mate	**SEP 7:** US government assumes control of nation's largest lenders, Fannie Mae and Freddie Mac	**SEP 16:** US government agrees to an $85 billion rescue of American Insurance Group (AIG), an insurer of financial institutions

WORLD EVENTS				
JUN 19: Egypt brokers a cease-fire between Israel and Hamas	**JUL 2:** After being held for nearly six years in Colombia by rebels, 15 hostages are freed by commandos	**AUG 8:** Georgia attacks South Ossetia, a separatist region within Georgia; the following day, Russian troops move against Georgia	**AUG 8–24:** Summer Olympic Games held in Beijing, China	**AUG 18:** Pervez Musharraf resigns as Pakistan's president

ENDNOTES

1 George W. Bush, *A Charge to Keep*, New York: Harper Collins, 2001, p. 16.

2 William A. DeGregorio, *The Complete Book of U.S Presidents*, New York: Gramercy Books, 2005, p. 756.

3 Peter Schweizer and Rochelle Schweizer, *The Bushes: Portrait of a Dynasty*, New York: Doubleday, 2004, p. 134.

4 Bush, p. 14.

5 Barbara Bush, *A Memoir*, New York: Charles Scribner's Sons, 1994, pp. 46-47.

6 Ibid.

7 G. Bush, p. 19.

8 Ibid, p. 21.

9 Schweizer, p. 152.

10 *Newsweek*, August 7, 2000, p. 32.

11 Ronald Kessler, *A Matter of Character: Inside the White House of George W. Bush*, New York: Sentinel, 2004, p. 34.

12 Schweizer, p. 220.

13 Ibid, p. 221.

14 Ibid, p. 335.

15 Ibid, p. 338.

16 Ibid, p. 364.

17 Ibid.

18 Ibid, p. 421.

19 G. Bush, pp. 117-118.

20 Ibid, p. 214.

21 George Bush, *All the Best, George Bush*, New York: Scribner, 1999, p. 618.

22 Karen Hughes, *Ten Minutes from Normal*, New York: Viking, 2004, p. 110.

23 Schweizer, p. 489.

24 *Bush v. Gore*, December 12, 2000, Supreme Court ruling.

25 Schweizer, p. 500.

26 Ibid, p. 502.

27 George W. Bush letter to Senators Hagel, Helms, Craig, and Roberts, March 21, 2001.

28 Schweizer, p. 513.

29 George W. Bush speech, September 11, 2001.

30 Bob Woodward, *Bush at War*, New York: Simon & Schuster, 2002, p. 67.

31 Ibid, p. 70.

32 George W. Bush press conference, November 8, 2006.

33 George W. Bush cabinet meeting, November 9, 2006.

34 cbsnews.com.

35 Ibid.

36 Ibid.

37 cnn.com.

38 infoplease.com.

39 "A Capital Strike," *Wall Street Journal*, January 31, 2009.

40 cnn.com.

SEP 29: Dow Jones experiences its steepest drop in history (778 points) amid reports that the House had rejected a $700 billion bailout plan; they reverse their vote a few days later and the Emergency Economic Stabilization Act is signed into law

NOV 4: Barack Obama is elected as America's 44th president

NOV 19: Consumer Price Index shows one percentage point drop in October, the most in its 47-year history; this news prompts Dow Jones to drop 427.47 points and for first time in 5 years, the average declines below 8,000 points

AUG 26: Russia recognizes independence of breakaway Georgian republics of South Ossetia and Abkhazia

SEP 27: China's first spacewalk occurs when Zhai Zhigang goes outside the Shenzhou VII spacecraft

NOV 9: China announces a stimulus package of more than $586 billion to be spent on infrastructure projects

NOV 26: Terrorists attack multiple targets in Mumbai, India, killing 170 and wounding more than 300

DEC 5: Human remains found 17 years earlier now officially announced to be those of Czar Nicholas II of Russia

BARACK H. OBAMA

★ ★ ★ FORTY-FOURTH PRESIDENT ★ ★ ★

LIFESPAN
- Born: August 4, 1961, in Honolulu, Hawaii

NICKNAMES
- Barry

RELIGION
- Christian

HIGHER EDUCATION
- Occidental College, Columbia University, 1983
- Harvard Law School, 1991

PROFESSION
- Lawyer, community organizer

MILITARY SERVICE
- None

FAMILY
- Father: **Barack Obama Sr.** (1936–1982)
- Stepfather: **Lolo Soetoro** (ca. 1935–1987)
- Mother: **Ann Dunham** (1942–1995)
- Wife: **Michelle Robinson Obama** (1964–); wed on October 18, 1992, in Chicago, Illinois
- Children: **Malia Ann** (1998–); **Natasha**, known as **Sasha** (2001–)

POLITICAL LIFE
- State Senator of Illinois (1997–2004)
- US senator (2005–2008)

PRESIDENCY
- January 20, 2009–
- Democrat
- Vice President: **Joseph Biden** (2009–)

ELECTION OF 2008
- Electoral vote: **Obama** 365; **John McCain** 173
- Popular vote: **Obama** 69,456,897; **McCain** 59,934,786

ELECTION OF 2012
- Electoral vote: **Obama** 332; **Mitt Romney** 206
- Popular vote: **Obama** 65,398,038; **Romney** 60,732,794

CABINET
★★★★★★★★★★

SECRETARY OF STATE
Hillary Rodham Clinton
(2009–)

SECRETARY OF THE TREASURY
Timothy F. Geithner
(2009–)

SECRETARY OF DEFENSE
Robert M. Gates
(2009–2011)

Leon E. Panetta
(2011–)

ATTORNEY GENERAL
Eric H. Holder Jr.
(2009–)

SECRETARY OF THE INTERIOR
Kenneth L. Salazar
(2009–)

SECRETARY OF AGRICULTURE
Thomas J. Vilsack
(2009–)

SECRETARY OF COMMERCE
Gary F. Locke
(2009–2011)

John E. Bryson
(2011–2012)

Rebecca M. Blank
(2012–)

SECRETARY OF LABOR
Hilda L. Solis
(2009–)

SECRETARY OF HEALTH AND HUMAN SERVICES
Kathleen Sebelius
(2009–)

BARACK H. OBAMA

The United States economy was in precarious shape and the American people had grown weary of war. So when the Democratic candidate campaigned repeatedly for "Hope and change," the people listened. On November 4, 2008, Barack Obama became the first African American elected to the presidency, and the nation anxiously waited to see how this relatively young man would handle the serious issues before him.

CHILDHOOD

Barack Obama's background was decidedly unique for a president.

His mother Ann Dunham had grown up in a middle-class home, the daughter of Stanley and Madelyn Dunham of Kansas. The couple had eloped just before the bombing of Pearl Harbor, and after Stanley's war service, they returned to Kansas but later moved to Texas, California, and Seattle where Stanley worked in the furniture business. Following Ann's graduation in Seattle, Stanley learned of a new furniture store opening in Hawaii, and the thought of going there on the eve of its statehood greatly appealed to him. So the three made the move.

Once in Hawaii, Ann began attending the University of Hawaii where the shy eighteen-year-old soon made a friend in the school's first African student, Barack Obama. The Dunhams had long considered themselves liberal in their attitude towards race. In fact, their grandson later speculated that was their prime reason for leaving Texas, where Ann had been harassed by children for playing with a black girl. Now her parents encouraged Ann to bring home this young man so that they could meet him.

Barack Obama, Sr. was a native of Kenya. Madelyn Dunham later said that one of his attributes had been a "voice like black velvet . . . with a British accent."[1] Obama was a member of the Luo tribe and had grown up on his family's farm. His academic prowess brought him recognition and opportunity. After attending a school in Nairobi and studying in London, he traveled to the University of Hawaii in 1959 to study econometrics. By this time, he was married and had a wife and child who remained in Kenya. He told Ann of his other family but assured her they were divorced. She later found this to be untrue.

Late in 1960, the couple was married. Then on August 4, 1961, Barack Hussein Obama, Jr. was born. Soon afterward, Barack Sr. received news of a Harvard scholarship. Even though the financial arrangement did not include taking his new family, that didn't stop Barack Sr. from leaving Hawaii, Ann, and his son behind. Once it became clear that this situation was not temporary, Ann divorced Barack Sr., who ultimately moved to his native Kenya with another American wife who bore him two children.

Ann's next husband was another foreign student, Lolo Soetoro of Indonesia. In 1967, Lolo, Ann, and her six-year-old son began their life together in his homeland. Barack embraced his new free life of running and playing with other children, but at school there were rules, and misbehavior meant feeling the sting of the teacher's bamboo stick. He later wrote of his new diet that included dog, snake, and grasshoppers. He also recalled the poverty of the people and the sight of his mother attempting to give money to beggars, only to see that there were always more than she had money. Lolo taught the boy some boxing, but mainly Barack remembered his stepfather's life lessons: "Men take advantage of weakness in other men . . . . Better to be strong. If you can't be

NATIONAL EVENTS

JAN 15: US Airways Flight 1549 crashes into the Hudson River shortly after take-off from LaGuardia. All survive with only minor injuries and hypothermia. A flock of geese are blamed

FEB 27: President Obama announces that US troops will leave Iraq by Aug 31, 2010

APR 2: Former Illinois Governor Rod Blagojevich is indicted on 19 charges for attempting to sell Obama's former Senate seat

APR 12: US Navy saves American ship captain Richard Phillips and kills 3 pirates

2009

WORLD EVENTS

JAN 17: Israel declares cease-fire to its nearly month-long Gaza War

JAN 26: Iceland's government and banking system collapse prompting resignation of its prime minister

First trial begins for the International Criminal Court. Defendant is Thomas Lubanga, rebel leader from the Democratic Republic of

FEB 7: Worst bushfires in Australian history killing over 170 people. Melbourne records highest temperature ever—115°F

APRIL 1: Albania and Croatia admitted to NATO

strong, be clever and make peace with someone who's strong. But always better to be strong yourself. Always."[2]

A sister, Maya, was born to the family, but by this time, tension began to grow between Ann and Lolo. Obama attended an Islamic school in Indonesia while having daily English lessons with his mother. She also reminded the boy of his African American heritage and shared inspirational stories of Dr. Martin Luther King, Jr. and Thurgood Marshall. Ann grew increasingly worried, however that her son's future would be seriously impaired the longer he remained away from the United States. By 1971, preparations were made for Barack to return to Hawaii and live with his grandparents. It was time he went home.

HAWAII

In Hawaii, Barack's grandparents, whom he called "Gramps" and "Toots," became his surrogate parents. He moved into their apartment and soon found himself enrolled in the prestigious Punahou Academy. Barry, his nickname used by friends and family, at first stood out among the other fifth graders who wore stylish clothes and lived in nice homes. Obama could boast neither. His grandfather struggled to earn a living as an insurance agent while his grandmother had steadily worked her way up the ladder at a local bank from secretary to vice president, the first woman to do so in Honolulu.

Although the ten-year-old Barack was not familiar with American sports like football, he soon learned and made friends. That Christmas, two visitors stayed for a month—his mother from Indonesia and his father from Africa. Years later, Barack admitted that he did not vividly recall what they said during their time together, just a collection of images remained in his memory. Barack Sr., however, did criticize the grandparents and Ann for not pushing Barry harder and making him study more. It was only near the end of the visit when the two generations of Obama men took time to bridge their gap. Barack Sr. turned on African music and taught his son some tribal dances. It was the only time during Barry's life that he felt any real connection to his father and it was over all too soon. In an interview decades later, Obama admitted that his personal drive originated from his father, a man who he barely knew but spent years trying to measure up to: "Every man is trying to live up to his father's expectations or make up for his mistakes. In my case, both things might be true."[3]

By the time Barack was in high school, his mother had separated from his stepfather Lolo and returned to Hawaii with her daughter Maya. Ann re-enrolled at the University of Hawaii to pursue postgraduate studies in anthropology, and her now teenage son joined them. Barry made satisfactory grades and also enjoyed just lounging on the beach or surfing. He also found himself drawn to basketball, and spent hours at the courts near his grandparents' apartment or at school. He later admitted that his passion exceeded his skill, yet he spent hours playing. When Ann decided to return to Indonesia to do her fieldwork, she wanted both of her children to accompany her. Obama, however, balked at leaving his free and fun lifestyle behind, so she relented and agreed that he could resume living with his grandparents.

Obama later wrote of his angst in his adolescence growing up biracial and without a father. He began making attempts to come to terms with his racial heritage. He immersed himself in black literature: W.E.B. Dubois, Langston Hughes, and James Baldwin became his nightly companions, rather than the homework that sat unfinished.

CABINET
★★★★★★★★★★

(continued)

SECRETARY OF HOUSING AND URBAN DEVELOPMENT
Shaun L.S. Donovan (2009–)

SECRETARY OF TRANSPORTATION
Raymond L. LaHood (2009–)

SECRETARY OF ENERGY
Steven Chu (2009–)

SECRETARY OF EDUCATION
Arne Duncan (2009–)

SECRETARY OF VETERANS AFFAIRS
Eric K. Shinseki (2009–)

JUNE 1: General Motors files for Chapter 11 bankruptcy (4th largest in US history)

JUN 12: All American televisions switch from analog to digital

JUN 22: Deadliest crash in Washington DC metro history involving two subway trains, kills 9 and wounds over 70 others

JUN 25: Death of Michael Jackson, American pop singer

JUL 3: Alaska Governor Sarah Palin announces her resignation effective July 26

APR 21: UNESCO launches the World Digital Library

MAY 25: North Korea successfully conducts its second nuclear test (first was in 2006)

MAY 31: Milvina Dean, last survivor of the *Titanic* dies. She had been its youngest passenger (2 months old)

JUN 12: Protests erupt across Iran regarding its presidential election.

JUL 22: Parts of Asia enjoy the world's longest solar eclipse of the 21st century—lasts over 6 minutes

DID YOU KNOW?

Obama may have a dog now, but as a child in Indonesia his pet was a monkey named Tata.

The work that Barack found the most comfort in was *The Autobiography of Malcolm X*. Obama later wrote that "[Malcolm's] repeated acts of self-creation spoke to me; the blunt poetry of his words, his unadorned insistence on respect, promised a new and uncompromising order, martial in its discipline, forged through sheer force of will."[4]

COLLEGE

By his senior year, Ann had returned and found her son floundering. His grades had dropped, he was experimenting with drugs, drinking and smoking, and showed no interest in college or a future. Ann pushed her son to apply to colleges, and ultimately he received a full scholarship to Occidental College in Pasadena, California.

Obama's freewheeling lifestyle continued in California, and there he met more people with the same interests. He later wrote that he carefully chose his friends and joined leftist political groups in order to avoid being mistaken as a "sellout." Obama became known for his activism. He pushed to have representatives of the African National Congress visit Occidental and was the first speaker at a rally to protest Occidental's refusal to oppose South African apartheid. Here, Obama experienced his first thrill giving a political speech.

In 1981, Barack decided to transfer to Columbia University to study political science and international relations. Switching colleges was a transition but the change to the milieu of New York City was amazing to the twenty-year-old. Still, the young man chose to resist much of the allure of the city that never sleeps and instead attended classes and read ravenously. He referred to this period as leading a monk-like existence and initiated a daily fitness routine, which included running several miles. This new emphasis continued, and friends could see a difference in his temperament if he missed a workout.

Obama graduated in 1983 and promptly landed a job with Business International Corporation as a research assistant. His job writing articles for this firm with global connections to American businesses paid the bills and provided him with an opportunity to see his future as an international businessman. The image troubled him, and he continued to tell others of his dream to be a community organizer. He later admitted he was not sure what one did when he left to become one.

The jobs he had as a community organizer in Brooklyn and Harlem were part-time positions and did not pay enough to meet his expenses. Obama's life changed when he heard from Jerry Kellman, a Chicago community organizer who needed workers to help the city's extremely poor black population on the South Side. Kellman headed the Developing Communities Project and convinced the young man that he could make a difference. Within a week of his meeting with Kellman, Obama packed and moved to Chicago.

COMMUNITY ORGANIZING IN CHICAGO

For three years Barack Obama worked tirelessly with the people of Chicago's South Side, with community leaders, and interdenominational church groups, trying to find ways to bring jobs, stability, money, and power to those who felt most disenfranchised. Little victories happened along the way but were soon wiped out by bigger disappointments. The Altgeld Gardens housing project became Obama's first assignment. Located near a landfill, factory, and sewage plant, this decrepit housing complex was home to nearly two thousand residents. Obama succeeded in having the Chicago Housing Authority make improvements to the project's appalling conditions.

NATIONAL EVENTS	**JUL 4:** Statue of Liberty crown reopens for first time in 8 years following its closure after 9/11 attacks	**JUL 13:** Confirmation hearings begin for US Supreme Court nominee Sonya Sotomayor. She is the first Hispanic justice	**OCT 19:** US announces it will no longer prosecute use of medical marijuana	**NOV 5:** Shooting at Fort Hood, Texas, leaves 13 dead and 32 wounded. Major Nidal Hasan, army psychiatrist is arrested for the crime.	**NOV 13:** NASA scientists announce they have found water in one of the moon's craters
WORLD EVENTS	**AUG 3:** Bolivia becomes first South American country to declare that indigenous people have the right to govern themselves	**AUG 4:** North Korea releases two American journalists after former President Bill Clinton meets with Kim Jong-il	**SEP 29:** 8.1 earthquake triggers a tsunami that hits Samoa and American Samoa, killing nearly 200	**SEP 30:** Another earthquake kills 1,000 in Indonesia	**OCT 1:** Paleontologists claim that fossils found in Ethiopia in 1992 are the oldest in human ancestry

Kellman pushed Obama to connect with the people he was there to help. Conducting daily interviews, sitting around a kitchen table and hearing someone's life story aided the young man understand people in a way he had never known before. Still, major blocks remained to his efforts to help people of the South Side. Schools were deteriorating, and although no one argued otherwise, few were willing to fight it. Obama and others wanted to start a mentoring network for youth. A common theme of fatherless black youth hit a responsive chord with Obama. He tried to help some of the young men he met along the way.

One of Obama's major disillusions came when he realized that the ministers were unwilling to cooperate because they competed against each other. One of them, Reverend Jeremiah A. Wright of the Trinity United Church of Christ, cautioned him, "You are not going to organize us. That's not going to happen."[5] Although his hopes of winning support of the various churches did not materialize, Obama found that he and the Rev. Wright had much in common. After bouncing around church to church without finding one he particularly liked, Obama found a spiritual home at Trinity.

With the death of Harold Washington, Chicago's first black mayor, in November 1987, Obama's enthusiasm for community organization waned. He now looked to do something else and believed further work required a law degree. Before heading to law school, though, he decided to take a trip to Kenya and attempt to connect with his African roots.

> ***"It was the call of workers who organized; women who reached for the ballot; a president who chose the moon as our new frontier; and a King who took us to the mountaintop and pointed the way to the Promised Land. Yes we can, to justice and quality. Yes we can, to opportunity and prosperity. Yes we can heal this nation. Yes we can repair this world."***
>
> *—Barack Obama, 2008*

AFRICA

Barack Obama, Sr. had passed away while his son was at Columbia University. Afterwards, Barack was visited by his half-sister, Auma, and encouraged by friends in Chicago to make the pilgrimage to meet his father's family. For several weeks, Barack met relatives and attempted to learn bits of the Luo (his father's tribal language). Spending time in Nairobi and traveling to a small village in Kenya where he met more relatives, he encountered a variety of experiences and gained a keener understanding of both his father and himself. On his first day in Africa, his Auntie Zeituni told his half-sister Auma to make sure he did not get lost again. Unsure what this meant, Barack asked Auma, and she explained that it was an expression used for either a person

SUPREME COURT APPOINTMENTS

★★★★★★★★★★

Sonia Sotomayor, 2009

Elena Kagan, 2010

DEC 1: President Obama announces a surge of 30,000 additional troops will be sent to Afghanistan

DEC 15: Boeing 787 Dreamliner makes its maiden flight from Everett, Washington

DEC 21: New US regulation introduced a three-hour limit for airlines waiting on the tarmac without feeding passengers or letting them de-plane

JAN 21: US Supreme Court rules that corporations cannot be limited on contributions to political campaigns

2010

OCT 10: Armenia and Turkey normalized relations for the first time since the Armenian genocide

DEC 16: Astronomers announce they have discovered water on an exoplanet

JAN 4: The Burj Khalifa opens in Dubai. It is the world's tallest building.

STATE OF THE UNION
★★★★★★★★★★

US POPULATION IN 2012
313,847,465

NATIONAL DEBT IN 2012
$16,203,845,445,635.71

PRESIDENT'S SALARY
$400,000/year

who had not been around for a while or one who left and eventually forgot his family and roots. Its meaning for him remained ambiguous.

HARVARD

Now with some questions answered, Obama returned to the United States to begin his studies at Harvard Law School. For the next three years, Barack dedicated himself to the study of law. He stood out among the incoming first-year students since he was twenty-seven years old and had already toiled as a community organizer for the past three years. His life experiences provided him with a grounding and maturity which aided him. One classmate, Cassandra Butts, later remarked about how "he came to discussions with much more life experience than most of the students."[6]

Although he did indeed spend many an hour studying in the library, Obama also found time to make friends and liaisons. He joined the Black Law Students Association and served on its board of directors as well as spoke at various functions. Obama often wove in the theme of using their exceptional education to give back to their communities. This belief came to the forefront when he participated in a debate among the African-American population of Harvard's professional schools. What should they call themselves: black or African American? After hearing the different opinions, Obama cut through the rhetoric: "You know, whether we're called black or African Americans doesn't make a whole heck of a lot of difference to the lives of people who are working hard, you know, living day to day, in Chicago, in New York. That's not what's going to make a difference in their lives. It's how we use our education in these next three years to make their lives better. You know, that's what's going to have an impact on making the US a more just place to live, and that's what's going to have an impact on their lives."[7]

Obama's grades, writing, and popularity among staff and students won him a place on the staff of the prestigious *Harvard Law Review*. Serving on this staff adds quite a cachet to any resume but to become its president is akin to being handed the keys to the kingdom. The president is elected from the *Review*'s staff of students, and at first Obama expressed that he would not run. While most staffers planned to acquire a clerkship with a federal judge or become a member of a law school faculty, he knew that his future did not rest on winning this post. Helping Chicago's South Side population did not require this, but after friends urged him to reconsider, Obama ran. Voting all day, the staff gradually weeded out the field to two. One was Obama. After assurances that no position would be kept from the *Review*'s pages, conservative students threw in their support, and Barack Obama became the first black editor in the *Review*'s 103-year history.

Obama's election immediately made headlines. Obama explained his feelings to a reporter for the *Los Angeles Times* in March 1990: "For every one of me, there are thousands of young black kids with the same energies, enthusiasm and talent that I have who have not gotten the opportunity because of crime, drugs and poverty. I think my election does symbolize progress but I don't want people to forget that there is still a lot of work to be done."[8]

Not all were pleased. Some black students complained that Obama did not fill as many staff slots as he could have with minorities. Race relations were particularly strained at Harvard during this time, because its only tenured African American professor, Derek Bell, took a leave-without-pay to

NATIONAL EVENTS

FEB 22: President Obama announces his health-care reform plan

MAR 11: Agreement reached on claims by rescue and health workers at Ground Zero. Over 657 million awarded to 10,000 plaintiffs

APR 20: BP Deepwater Horizon, oil rig explodes, kills 11 people and creates a massive oil leak into the Gulf of Mexico. Resulting oil leaks continued for months afterward.

APR 23: America's strictest immigration law goes into effect in Arizona

WORLD EVENTS

JAN 12: 7.0 earthquake hits Haiti, killing 230,000 and nearly destroying Port-au-Prince

JAN 27: Apple launches the iPad

JAN 28: Toyota recalls 2.4 million cars on 3 continents due to gas pedal problems

FEB 8: Toyota recall reaches over 8 million

FEB 12–28: Winter Olympics take place in Vancouver, Canada

protest the unwillingness of administration to hire other black professors. Some more left-leaning staff members also expressed concerns about the number of students from the conservative Federalist Society whom Obama gave positions to.

Treading through this minefield, Obama showed a willingness to work with everyone. People later noted that because he could so easily converse with both sides, one often had no idea what his true feelings were. One of his professors, Charles J. Ogletree Jr., said, "He can enter your space and organize your thoughts without necessarily revealing his own concerns and conflicts."[9] Obama's editorship might not have been as rigorous as some would have preferred, so the next year, the staff chose "a tougher editor" and "someone who would be a more rigorous blue-penciler."[10]

Obama's time spent coordinating quarreling factions at the *Review* provided him with an experience that proved beneficial in his later political career. But for now, he looked to returning to his community involvement in Chicago as well as resuming his courtship of attorney Michelle Robinson.

MARRIAGE

Obama had met Michelle in the summer of 1989 after his first year at Harvard. He was an intern at the corporate law firm of Sidley Austin, where Michelle was an attorney assigned to be his mentor. Many tried to talk him up to her, but she later stated that she had misgivings about "this good-looking, smooth-talking guy," since he was her trainee and she worried that it would "look pretty tacky"[11] to date the only other black on the staff. Barack, however, refused to be deterred.

Michelle was born in 1964 to a middle-class family from Chicago's South Side. She had excelled in sports and academics, later attending Princeton University and Harvard Law School. Once the couple was engaged, Michelle decided to alter her career path and joined Mayor Richard Daley's staff. After finishing at Harvard, Obama put his legal career on hold while he directed Illinois Project Vote, an effort to register Chicago's black population for the 1992 presidential election. His efforts helped ensure victory in Illinois for President Bill Clinton, as well as the historic election of Carol Moseley Braun, the first black woman senator. Obama also had the task of writing his memoir. In between everything else, Barack and Michelle married on October 18, 1992, at Rev. Wright's Trinity United Church of Christ.

The following year, Michelle joined with AmeriCorps to start Chicago's office of Public Allies. Here she worked tirelessly for three years to establish a firm foundation for this agency devoted to putting unemployed young people to work. Her tenure was hailed as a tremendous success. She followed this with a stint at the University of Chicago as associate dean of student services and later as director of community affairs for the University of Chicago Hospitals.

After getting married, the Obamas settled into the Hyde Park neighborhood. In 1998, they welcomed their first daughter, Malia; three years later, their second daughter Sasha was born. By this time, Obama's political career was starting, and Michelle had a new role—political wife.

LAUNCH OF POLITICAL CAREER

Following the 1992 election, Obama began a two-pronged legal career—teaching constitutional law part-time at the University of Chicago and taking a job with the Chicago civil rights firm of Miner, Barnhill & Galland. Although he never

DID YOU KNOW?

During World War II, Madelyn Dunham, Obama's grandmother, worked at the Boeing plant in Wichita, Kansas.

MAY 2: Bomb found in car parked at New York's Times Square. Faisal Shahzad, a Pakistani who recently became a US naturalized citizen, is later arrested.

MAY 10: President Obama nominates Elena Kagan, Solicitor General and former Harvard Law School Dean, to US Supreme Court

MAY 25: President Obama announces 1,200 US National Guard troops to be sent to US-Mexico border

JUN 23: General Stanley McChrystal fired as commander of war in Afghanistan following critical remarks in a magazine article

FEB 27: 8.8 earthquake strikes Chile and triggers tsunami in the Pacific. At least 500 are killed in one of the most powerful earthquakes in recorded history

APR 14: Volcanic ash from ice caps under Iceland causes major disruptions in air traffic across northern and western Europe

MAY 15: 16-year-old Jessica Watson of Australia became youngest person to sail around the world unassisted

DID YOU KNOW?

Obama is left-handed. Other left-handed presidents include James A. Garfield, Herbert Hoover, Harry S. Truman, Gerald Ford, Ronald Reagan, George H.W. Bush, and Bill Clinton.

tried a case himself, he assisted other attorneys who represented a variety of clients with discrimination suits. One of these suits was against the state of Illinois, charging it with failure to follow federal laws in allowing voter registration of the poor. Obama also represented black voters of Chicago who successfully sued that they had been discriminated against when new ward boundaries for the city had been drawn after the 1990 census. Through his work at the firm and close association with Judson Miner, who had been counsel in Mayor Washington's administration, Obama gained key political contacts that would assist him when he decided to make the dive into that arena. After a few years of practicing law, Obama decided that working for change through the courts was entirely too slow of a process; instead, he determined the best way to seek reform was through running for office.

> *"Today I say to you that the challenges we face are real. They are serious and they are many. They will not be met easily or in a short span of time. But know this, America—they will be met."*
>
> *—Barack H. Obama, 2009*

Obama saw his first opportunity to enter politics when State Senator Alice Palmer announced she was running for Congress and made clear that he had her blessing to campaign for her seat. Obama filed for candidacy in August 1995, just one month after his memoir, *Dreams from My Father*, was published. Palmer, in fact, had selected him as her successor and revealed this at a meeting of another Hyde Park resident, William Ayers, professor and well-known radical of the 1960s. The two candidates' friendship grew cold, however, when Palmer's Congressional campaign slumped, and she told Obama that she wanted to resume running for her state senate seat. By now, Obama had a strong organization helping him and believed he had a good chance to win, so he refused to relinquish his candidacy. In a move that showed the idealistic candidate's grasp of hardball politics, Obama challenged Palmer's candidacy on technical grounds, saying that she hadn't garnered enough signatures in the right amount of time. Palmer was blocked from running and the other Democratic challengers also quit, so Barack Obama ran as the sole candidate for his party in the primary. In such an overwhelmingly Democratic district, this equated to an easy victory in November 1996. The thirty-four-year old had successfully begun his political career.

STATE POLITICS

After arriving in Springfield, Obama found himself an outsider looking in. First, the Republican Party had the majority in the state senate. Second, other black senators did not provide a warm welcome for the freshman senator. Bad feelings remained about his unwillingness to drop from the race and allow fellow African American Alice Palmer to be reelected; nor did the press find him particularly ingratiating. Knowing he would need

NATIONAL EVENTS

JUN 28: US Supreme Court rules that state and local gun laws cannot limit citizens' rights to bear arms as protected in the 2nd Amendment

JUL 25: 1st appearance on Wikileaks of 90,000 American confidential leaked documents related to the war in Afghanistan

AUG 31: Operation Iraqi Freedom ends

SEP 16: US poverty rate hits a 15-year high (14.3% of Americans living at/under poverty level)

SEP 17: Soap opera *As the World Turns* ends a 54-year run

WORLD EVENTS

MAY 19: Major world powers including US, Russia, and China, impose a 4th set of sanctions against Iran to force it to stop its nuclear-enrichment program

JUN 13: US announces it has found over $1 trillion in untapped mineral resources in Afghanistan

JUN 24: American John Isner and Nicolas Mahut of France complete the longest championship tennis match in history—11 hours in a match that lasted over three days at Wimbledon. (Isner wins)

some help to understand the world of state politics, Obama began working with aide Dan Shomon, a Springfield veteran who proved a useful sounding board. Shomon took Obama on an illustrative road trip through southern Illinois to show him how to connect with conservative rural voters who were traditionally suspicious of Chicago politicians. It was the kind of bridge-building exercise that would be essential if Obama ever hoped to run for higher office.

At first, Obama failed to make much headway. Realizing that he had to would have to switch gears in order to be successful as a lawmaker, the mild-mannered, intellectual Obama changed, learning golf and joining in a weekly poker game with fellow legislators.

Emil Jones, Jr., the senate's Democratic leader, also from the South Side, chose the freshman Obama to push through campaign reform legislation. This was Obama's first major task, and he scored a major win with a 52–4 vote. Other bills that Obama co-sponsored during his first years included compensation of crime victims for property losses, working to help hospitals deal with sexual assault cases, investigation into nursing home abuses, and increasing funding for after-school programs. He became known for working with Republicans to pass legislation. Obama described his willingness to "bring all sides of an issue to the table and you make them feel they are being listened to."[12]

Aching to make a difference on the national level, in 1999, Obama decided to run against the popular incumbent and former Black Panther Bobby Rush in the Democratic primary for US Congress. Again, Obama was criticized for trying to unseat another black politician. Then some began questioning his "blackness," pointing to his biracial heritage, Hawaii upbringing, and attending predominantly white colleges. It was an easy victory for Rush. Obama later wrote of his difficulty continuing with the campaign after realizing halfway through that he was going to lose. He explained, "The politician's loss is on public display. . . . it's impossible not to feel . . . as if you have been repudiated by the entire community, that you don't have what it takes, and that everywhere you go the word 'loser' is flashing through people's minds."[13]

Returning to Springfield, Obama resumed his legislative work and attempted to gain more political support from his Democratic colleagues. He chaired the committee on Health and Human Services and served on others including Education and Welfare. He championed abortion rights and supported stem cell research. In other legislation, he backed unions and favored imposing a use tax for natural gas and restoring the estate tax to Illinois.

Still, Obama felt frustrated. He sought office on a higher level. Looking ahead to 2004, he spied an opportunity in the US Senate seat of Republican incumbent Peter Fitzgerald. Although many pledged support, they also cautioned him not to run, warning that he would likely lose and put a great strain on his family in the process. Nevertheless, Obama viewed this as his final opportunity and seized it. Friends began making inquiries, and slowly a financial base of support in Chicago made a Senate run viable.

In the fall of 2002, before formally announcing his Senate candidacy, Obama spoke to an antiwar rally in Chicago. He told them he was not totally opposed to war but was opposed to the impending invasion of Iraq, calling it "a dumb war" that was "based not on reason but on passion, not on principle but on politics."[14] He later admitted that although "it was a hard speech to give,"[15] it was also the speech he was proudest of.

NOV 4: Republicans win a majority of seats in the US House but Democrats keep control of Senate in mid-term elections

DEC 22: President Obama repeals the military's "Don't Ask, Don't Tell" policy that had forbidden military personnel from openly admitting homosexuality

JUL 8: First 24-hour flight completed by a solar-powered aircraft

AUG 5: Russian President Vladimir Putin bans grain exports as production drops due to the worst heat-wave in Russia in 130 years

AUG 14: First ever Youth Olympics held at Singapore

OCT 13: 33 Chilean miners rescued after being trapped 69 days

OCT 29: President Obama announces that explosive material was found in packages en route to the US from Yemen

DID YOU KNOW?

The Secret Service gave Obama the code name "Renegade."

Emil Jones, Jr., now president of the Illinois Senate, agreed to help Obama strengthen his legislative credentials. Legislation was given him to guide through the senate that would help his profile; likewise, Jones kept Obama's campaign schedule in mind to ensure that key votes did not occur while he was gone. (Obama's voting record in the Illinois senate would later be questioned when it was learned that he voted "present" 130 times, when he did not wish to be on the record voting for/against a controversial issue such as abortion, which could trouble voters in later campaigns.)[16]

When the primary campaign began, the front-runner was at first Don Hynes, whose father had a history in Chicago politics and who also originally had strong union backing. However, once Obama's pro-labor state legislation demonstrated an active willingness to work for their cause, unions such as the Service Employees Union International endorsed the relatively unknown candidate. Other unions soon followed. Opponent Gery Chico excelled at providing the pithy sound bites that audiences tended to prefer to the longer speeches that Obama was prone to give. In fact, Obama worked to improve his public speaking skills by studying African American ministers and imitating their cadence and rhythm. David Axelrod, Obama's media consultant, devised a campaign theme of "Yes, we can," with commercials pledging change in Washington if Barack Obama was elected. The voters believed, and he handily won the primary with 53 percent of the vote. Now it remained to be seen if he could win a general election against the Republican incumbent Jack Ryan.

Ryan had served in the Illinois legislature with Obama, and he, too, had the good looks to help his candidacy. But not long before the general election, Ryan found himself awash in scandal. In the summer of 2004, newspapers successfully sued to open Ryan's sealed divorce records. The resulting revelations about Ryan's aberrant sex practices (which included pushing his then-wife, actress Jeri Ryan, to accompany him to sex clubs) caused him to drop out of the race. While the Republican Party frantically cast about for a replacement, an increasingly popular Barack Obama was selected as the keynote speaker at the 2004 Democratic convention.

Few senatorial candidates are provided as rich an opportunity as awaited Barack Obama on July 27, 2004, when he addressed the crowd at Boston's Fleet Center arena and the millions watching at home. In a speech that called for an end to the electorate's increasing polarization, he told the audience, "there's not a liberal America and a conservative America; there's the United States of America. There's not a black America and white America and Latino America and Asian America; there's the United States of America." He went on to quote from Dr. Martin Luther King, Jr., saying that his belief in "the audacity of hope" also included "the hope of a skinny kid with a funny name who believes that America has a place for him, too."[17] His speech received rave reviews and pushed Obama into another strata of political achievement.

Now, candidate Obama drew huge crowds wherever he went. Sometimes all of the adulation and attention became overwhelming for both he and Michelle. By August, Republicans had drafted black conservative (and non-Illinois resident) Alan Keyes to oppose Obama. The tidal wave of popularity was too much for the last-minute rival to fight. Obama won the senate seat by a historic margin of 70 to 29 percent.

NATIONAL EVENTS

JAN 8: US Congresswoman Gabrielle Giffords of Arizona is wounded in an assassination attempt. Six are killed and 13 wounded

FEB 15: Public employees and union supporters begin protest in Madison, Wisconsin, against government regulations. His actions will spur the Arab Spring movement

2011

WORLD EVENTS

NOV 28: Over 250,000 confidential cables released on Wikileaks

DEC 8: SpaceX becomes the first private firm to successfully launch and recover a spacecraft

DEC 11: Two bombings in Stockholm, Sweden, are traced to a Muslim terrorist

JAN 4: Tunisian street seller dies from burns received a month earlier when he set himself on fire in protest of

SENATOR

On January 4, 2005, Michelle and daughters Sasha and Malia watched proudly as Barack was sworn in as a US senator. Afterwards the family posed for pictures and six-year-old Malia asked, "Daddy, are you going to be president?"[18] Others were asking the same question, and the next day, Obama told reporters that he was not planning to run for president in 2008. Instead, he found his life quite full as he learned to negotiate the turns and pitfalls of life in the capital city.

Obama gained a seat on the Foreign Relations committee and within the year traveled to Europe, Russia, and the Middle East. He and Republican Richard Lugar co-sponsored legislation to lessen the threat of unsecured conventional weapons throughout the world and traveled to Russia and the Ukraine to discuss their ideas. Obama supported building a fence between the US and Mexico as a means to halt growing illegal immigration. He continued his push to fight global warming and supported a bill to significantly reduce the emission of greenhouse gases by 2050. He upset liberals by certifying George W. Bush's reelection despite objections regarding Ohio ballots and then confirming the appointment of Condoleezza Rice as Secretary of State. His advisors recommended that he continue to pursue this middle of the road course should he later want to attain higher office.

Obama went home on weekends and held forty town hall meetings in Illinois during his first year in the Senate. He reminded constituents not to expect much from the first term of a junior senator and kept a generally low media profile. Though refusing most interview requests, he did make an exception and appeared on a Sunday talk show to discuss the aftermath of Hurricane Katrina. Outraged African American leaders such as Rev. Jesse Jackson denounced the Bush administration and the slow response by the emergency agencies to help the people of New Orleans who were predominantly black. When Obama was asked about this, his tone was more measured, "I think that the important thing for us now is to recognize that we have situations in America in which race continues to play a part, that class continues to play a part, that people are not availing themselves of the same opportunities, of the same schools, of the same jobs, and because they're not, when disaster strikes, it tears the curtain away from the festering problems that we have beneath them . . . ."[19]

In August 2006, Senator Obama and his family and extended entourage of staff and reporters left for a trip to Africa. It was considered a congressional delegate excursion which also included visiting his father's homeland again. The journey began in South Africa where Obama visited the jail cell that had housed Nelson Mandela for eighteen years. While in that country, Obama also spoke out against South African president Thabo Mbeki who refused to take action against the AIDS crisis plaguing his nation. To Obama's disappointment, Mbeki refused to meet him during his stay.

The next stop was Kenya, where Obama was mobbed by a nation who claimed him as their own. After visiting Nairobi, the group moved farther inland and visited his grandmother's village of Kisumu. There in the town's hospital, the Obamas had blood samples drawn for AIDS testing to demonstrate to Africans that the test was safe and would not give a person the disease. They traveled to his father's farm compound and visited with family members. After a safari and a quick

DID YOU KNOW?

Obama was a lecturer of constitutional law at the University of Chicago from 1993 until his election to the US Senate in 2004.

Governor Scott Walker's plan to limit collective bargaining for public workers

FEB 23: Obama administration announces it will no longer prosecute cases for Defense of Marriage Act of 1996

MAR 25: National Football League shuts down, and owners lock out the players

MAY 5: Major flooding along Ohio and Mississippi Rivers prompts evacuation in several states

JAN 14: Tunisian government falls

FEB 11: Egyptian President Hosni Mubarak resigns

FEB 22–MAR 14: World's oil prices skyrocket 20 percent due to uncertainty over Libya and its oil output

MAR 11: 9.0 earthquake hits Japan, triggering a tsunami. Over 15,000 are killed and emergencies are declared at four Japanese nuclear power plants

DID YOU KNOW?

Republican Senator John McCain co-sponsored the Secure America and Orderly Immigration Act with Obama in 2005.

detour to Chad to meet refugees from Darfur, Obama left Africa, and he hoped that his visit had given people there hope and the willingness to work towards improving their homeland.

CAMPAIGN FOR THE PRESIDENCY

Following his successful Africa trip, the talk increased of Senator Obama running for president. Others insisted that he was more interested in the governorship of Illinois. His popularity had been bolstered by appearances throughout the country to sell his second book, *The Audacity of Hope*, for which he won a Grammy award for his audio version. Obama's youthful looks and optimistic tone appealed to many. It became increasingly difficult to dismiss the growing push for him to run for the Democratic nomination. Michelle was initially was opposed, but soon became convinced that it was the right thing to do.

On February 10, 2007, on the steps of the Illinois statehouse in Springfield, Barack Obama officially announced his candidacy for the Democratic presidential nomination. At this time, Senator Hillary Clinton of New York was considered to be the frontrunner. However, both candidates quickly gained donors and each had $20 million in their campaign coffers. Popular television host Oprah Winfrey announced her support of Obama and made a campaign tour on his behalf that many believed added tens of thousands of votes for him.

The first balloting in Iowa in January 2008 went to Obama, but the primary in New Hampshire was a close vote with Clinton winning. The two candidates see-sawed during the coming months, with Obama winning most of the southern primaries and the two splitting New England, but Clinton pulled a major win in California. Clinton had more political experience and was better known to voters. But the Obama campaign's canny use of the Internet and bloggers kept donations pouring in and increased voter interest, making him a surprisingly tough foe for Clinton to defeat.

Still, Obama's campaign hit a few missteps. Questions about his true beliefs surfaced when film footage was released of Rev. Wright's sermons in which, among other things, he blamed the 9/11 attacks on the United States and made anti-white statements. Since Wright's church had been the place of worship for Senator Obama and his family for twenty years, concerns were immediately raised that Wright's hate speech must be affirmed by the Obamas or else they would have left his church. After attempts to distance himself from Rev. Wright, Obama ultimately announced that his family no longer attended Trinity United Church of Christ, and an announcement of Wright's retirement soon followed.

Then the candidate himself made a serious gaffe when talking at a private fundraiser in San Francisco. Obama told the donors that they needed to understand why he was lagging in the polls in Pennsylvania and the Midwest was because of their broken-down economies. Then he said, "And it's not surprising then they get bitter, they cling to guns or religion or antipathy to people who aren't like them or anti-immigrant sentiment or anti-trade sentiment, as a way to explain their frustrations."[20] Immediately critics pounced on this remark as proof that Obama was not as he professed. He was the elite Harvard graduate and candidate for the rich and famous. Both of his two main rivals, Senator Clinton and Republican Senator John McCain derided Obama for being out of touch. He fired back that he had a better understanding of the typical voter than either. Senator

NATIONAL EVENTS

MAY 15: Mississippi River floods to 56.3 feet, over 13 feet above flood stage at Vicksburg, Mississippi. This beats the earlier record set in 1927.

MAY 22: Deadly tornado hits Joplin, Missouri, killing over 140

JUN 2: Former Massachusetts governor Mitt Romney officially announces he is a candidate for the 2012 presidential election

JUN 24: New York becomes the largest state to legalize same-sex marriage

WORLD EVENTS

MAR 19: UN authorizes reconnaissance flights to begin over Libya due to civil war unrest in the country

MAR 25: Syrian military cracks down on pro-democracy demonstrators. A few days later the entire cabinet of President Bashar Assad resigns

APR 11: France bans full-face veils in public in efforts to protect its French identity and separatist actions by Muslims

APR 29: Prince William, second in line to the British throne, weds Catherine "Kate" Middleton at

Clinton went on to win the Pennsylvania primary, but by the end of May, Obama had secured the majority of pledged Democratic delegates for the convention.

Meeting in Denver, the Democratic national convention officially nominated Barack Obama to be their candidate for the presidency. He, in turn, nominated Senator Joseph Biden of Delaware to be his running mate. The two would oppose Republican candidate Senator McCain of Arizona and his vice presidential nominee Governor Sarah Palin of Alaska. Obama delivered his acceptance speech on August 28 and talked of his plans for the future and the change he hoped to bring:

> *"Our government should work for us, not against us. It should help us, not hurt us. It should ensure opportunity not just for those with the most money and influence, but for every American who's willing to work.*
>
> *"That's the promise of America, the idea that we are responsible for ourselves, but that we also rise or fall as one nation, the fundamental belief that I am my brother's keeper, I am my sister's keeper.*
>
> *"That's the promise we need to keep. That's the change we need right now."*[21]

For the next two months, Obama and McCain toured the country. Repeatedly, McCain charged Obama with lack of experience—a claim that Clinton had also used against him. His voting record in the Illinois Senate of 130 "present" votes and a lackluster record in the US Senate were touted as proof that he did not take his legislative role seriously. Voters, however, continued to swell rallies for Obama and openly admitted that they preferred his freshness and lack of experience to someone like McCain whose twenty-five years in Congress made him too much of an insider.

As Election Day drew nearer, the American economy went into a downturn, causing President Bush's popularity to drop more, and due to party association, Senator McCain's as well. McCain's statement that he believed "that the fundamentals of our economy were strong" was derided, especially when it came on the heels of his uncertainty regarding how many homes he and his wife owned. Obama hit McCain with being out of touch with America, and images of the youthful forty-seven-year old candidate versus the white-haired seventy-two year old veteran underscored Obama's recurring mantra of "Change!"

When November 4, 2008, arrived, the American people went to the polls in record numbers, and with the declining economy on many minds, they cast their vote for change. Barack Obama easily won both the popular and electoral votes, becoming the nation's first African American president.

TRANSITION TO THE WHITE HOUSE

Within the week, the Obamas arrived at the White House to meet with President and Mrs. Bush. Bush had already promised a smooth transition, citing the nation's critical issues required that the next president be ready to serve as of January 20. As President-Elect Obama selected staff members, they arrived in Washington and began working with their Bush counterparts to ensure this transition was seamless. Meanwhile, Obama considered a variety of potential appointees to his cabinet, some of them surprising. He tapped his former rival Senator Clinton to be Secretary of State and decided to keep Bush appointee Robert

JUL 5: Casey Anthony is found not guilty of murdering her little girl Caylee. The case had captured attention from the disappearance of Caylee who was nearly three.

JUL 21: Space Shuttle *Atlantis* lands at Cape Canaveral, and ends America's space shuttle program

AUG 5: Standard & Poor lowers US bond rating from the top AAA to AA+. This is first time it had declined.

SEP 17: Occupy Wall Street protests begin

Westminister Abbey. Three billion watch the wedding around the world

MAY 1: President Obama announces the death of Osama bin Laden in Pakistan

MAY 4: Rival Palestinian factions Fatah and Hamas sign a peace accord

MAY 16: European Union (EU) agrees to a €78 billion bailout for Portugal

JUN 4: Chilean volcanic eruption causes air traffic disruption for South America, Australia, and New Zealand. Over 3,000 evacuated

Gates as Defense Secretary. To head the Treasury Department, Obama selected Timothy Geithner, president of the Federal Reserve Board of New York. In total, the Obama cabinet would reflect America's diversity, with women, blacks, Hispanics, and Asians well represented.

The president-elect forwarded his stimulus plan to Congress, and his team hoped for its passage by inauguration day. This, however, was not possible due to its enormous scope and price tag. Although much of its money would be provided to states, some of the governors worried about the "strings attached" that would force the permanent addition of programs to their budgets after the stimulus monies ran out in two years.

Obama's inauguration was centered around a celebration of the 300th birthday of another president from Illinois—Abraham Lincoln—and used his phrase "A new birth of freedom" from the Gettysburg Address as the theme. A major celebration occurred on the eve of the inauguration at the Lincoln Memorial.

The twentieth of January 2009, dawned as a perfect winter's day. The Obamas met with President and Mrs. Bush at the White House before the motorcade to the capitol. There Joseph Biden was sworn in as Vice President and then Chief Justice John Roberts swore in Barack Hussein Obama as America's forty-fourth president. Millions watched around the world and witnessed this historic moment. (There was a miscue in the swearing-in when Roberts put the word "faithfully" at the wrong place in the oath, so Obama repeated it. To ensure there was no problem, another swearing in occurred the following evening when the oath was said correctly.)

In his inauguration speech, the new president told the nation,

"And yet at this moment, a moment that will define a generation, it is precisely this spirit that must inhabit us all. For as much as government can do, and must do, it is ultimately the faith and determination of the American people upon which this nation relies." President Obama continued: "Our challenges may be new. The instruments with which we meet them may be new. But those values upon which our success depends — honesty and hard work, courage and fair play, tolerance and curiosity, loyalty and patriotism — these things are old. These things are true. They have been the quiet force of progress throughout our history.

"What is demanded, then, is a return to these truths. What is required of us now is a new era of responsibility — a recognition on the part of every American that we have duties to ourselves, our nation and the world; duties that we do not grudgingly accept, but rather seize gladly, firm in the knowledge that there is nothing so satisfying to the spirit, so defining of our character than giving our all to a difficult task."[22]

FIRST TERM: SETTING AN AGENDA

Shortly after entering office, President Obama enjoyed a wave of popularity and was even awarded a Nobel Peace Prize. The luxury of working with a Democratic majority in both houses of Congress also allowed him to initiate an ambitious agenda for his first 100 days. Some priorities, however, took a back seat due to the deteriorating economic situation. As he explained in a presidential news conference held in March 2009 on his 100th day in office: ". . . [W]hen I first started this race, Iraq was a central issue, but the economy appeared on

NATIONAL EVENTS

OCT 5: Steve Jobs, founder of Apple, dies of pancreatic cancer

NOV 5: Penn State defensive coordinator Jerry Sandusky arrested on 40 charges of sexual abuse that lasted over a 15-year period

DEC 15: US declares formal end to Iraq War

WORLD EVENTS

JULY 9: South Sudan secedes from Sudan

JUL 11: Britain's *The News of the World* ends publication following a series of scandals

JUL 22: Norwegian Anders Behring Breivik kills 77 in twin terrorist attacks in Norway

SEP 5: India and Bangladesh put in motion a plan to end 40-year dispute over their border

SEP 23: Palestine requests UN membership

the surface to still be relatively strong. There were underlying problems that I was seeing with health care for families and our education system and college affordability and so forth, but obviously, I didn't anticipate the worst economic crisis since the Great Depression."[23] He and the country would watch as the economy continued its freefall.

With unemployment figures rising as more Americans received pink slips, Congress and the president worked together to create a stimulus package of $787 billion titled "The American Recovery and Reinvestment Act of 2009". The bill's main provisions extended unemployment benefits, funded public works through "shovel-ready projects,"[26] and provided some health-care benefits. The vote revealed a strong partisan divide. House minority leader John Boehner, who with the rest of the House Republicans, voted against the stimulus package, said it was only about "spending, spending, and more spending" rather than "Jobs. Jobs. Jobs."[27] More partisan showdowns would loom in the future.

Despite the stimulus, unemployment rates continued to rise, as did criticism for the $787 billion price tag, and the president later said that "shovel-ready was not as shovel-ready as we expected." By October, unemployment topped 10 percent, something the country had not seen for over a quarter of a century. Another incentive was also created in the languishing housing market: first-time home buyers were offered an $8,000 tax credit. Still, the economy refused to improve.

Meanwhile, two major American automakers, General Motors and Chrysler, fought to stay afloat financially. Before Obama took office, the Bush administration had approved a $17.4 billion government bailout loan, but the financial situations of both companies remained dire. During the first six months of 2009, $5 billion in loans was pumped into them from both United States and Canada to prevent their collapse, but ultimately both GM and Chrysler were taken over by the US government and underwent managed bankruptcies.

NOBEL PEACE PRIZE-WINNING PRESIDENTS

In 1866, Swedish scientist Alfred Nobel invented dynamite and also developed over 350 patents in a variety of areas, including rubber and synthetic silk. Although Nobel's most famous invention revolutionized weapons of the late nineteenth century, he desired for his legacy to be one of peace. To that end, Nobel provided in his will for those who helped humanity in the areas of physics, chemistry, literature, medicine, and peace to be honored with the Nobel Peace Prize. The first was granted in 1901. Among those receiving this prize have been four American presidents:

1906 – Theodore Roosevelt for his work to end the Russo-Japanese War.

1919 – Woodrow Wilson for his efforts to start the League of Nations following World War I.

2002 – Former President Jimmy Carter for his efforts to resolve conflicts throughout the world and provide humanitarian aid.

2009 – Barack Obama for "his extraordinary efforts to strengthen international diplomacy and cooperation between peoples."[24]

One former vice president has also won the honor, Albert Gore, Jr., in 2007, for "efforts to build up and disseminate greater knowledge about man-made climate change."[25]

JAN 5: President Obama announces plans for defense cuts to create a leaner, more effective military

FEB 11: American pop star Whitney Houston dies at age 48

2012

SEP 25: Saudi Arabia grants women's suffrage

OCT 20: Libyan civil war ends when its leader Mu'ammar Qadhafi is killed in Sirte

DEC 29: Pacific islands of Samoa and Tokelau transfer from east to west across international date line to be in line with major trading

JAN 4: EU agrees to impose oil embargo against Iran

FEB 1: Soccer fans erupt into a deadly brawl in Egypt that kills over 70

Ultimately the Italian automaker Fiat purchased Chrysler and, three years later, President Obama announced that "Chrysler has repaid every dime and more of what it owes the American taxpayer from the investment we made during my watch."[28] The administration, however, did forgive much of the loan provided in the last days of the Bush presidency (over $1 billion).

GM continued to hemorrhage money, and by the summer of 2009 had absorbed $19.4 billion in additional cash infusions from American taxpayers. Its bankruptcy required a major restructuring as well as the sale of many of its assets, and by the end of the summer, the United States was officially the major stockholder of GM. An additional attempt to prop up the automobile industry was introduced in the summer of 2009. "Cash for Clunkers" offered economic incentives to encourage Americans to trade in their old cars for newer, more efficient models. This popular program quickly ran out of steam when funds became exhausted within weeks.

Campaigning in 2012, Obama would herald the rescue of US automakers: "I believe in American workers. I believe in this American industry. And now the American auto industry has come roaring back."[29] While some Americans agreed with the president's assessment, GM dealers who had been ordered to close their doors and the 211,000 auto industry workers who lost their jobs during 2008–2009 (52,800 were regained by the end of 2012) might argue over the wisdom of the government's restructuring plan. Others look at the bailout for GM as another example of government helping an American company but at the great cost of adding billions to the deficit. Critics, upset with the government's takeover, would later point to the $25 billion shortfall on the government's return on its investment of GM. By the time of Obama's reelection campaign, the government still held more than 30 percent of GM stock.

Economists agreed that the initial bailout of the American auto industry was the right thing to do at the time. If either or both companies had completely collapsed, the economy's slide could have proved even more disastrous, causing higher unemployment and endangering pension plans. Whether or not the taxpayer-funded $80 billion bailout and government restructuring of GM and Chrysler was a wiser move than allowing the kind of bankruptcy proceedings commonly seen in the airline industry was a question that would continue into the 2012 election campaign.

HEALTH CARE OVERHAUL

Previous Democratic presidents had attempted to create a national health-care system but their efforts had fallen short. The most recent attempt, by President Bill Clinton and his wife Hillary, had collapsed on itself early in his first term. Now using valuable political capital gained with his historic election, President Obama intended to succeed where others had tried and failed.

On February 24, 2009, in his first State of the Union address, President Obama stated that the country needed to address health-care reform. He stated:

> *"This is a cost that now causes a bankruptcy in America every thirty seconds. By the end of the year, it could cause 1.5 million Americans to lose their homes. In the last eight years, premiums have grown four times faster than wages. And in each of these years, one million more Americans have lost their health insurance. It is one of the major*

NATIONAL EVENTS

MAY 2: $120 million paid for *The Scream* in New York City making it the highest price paid on art at auction

MAY 9: President Obama declares his support for gay marriage; a major change in his stance

MAY 17: For the first time in US history; non-whites are the majority of births in the 12-month period ending July 2011

MAY 18: Mark Zuckerberg, founder and CEO of Facebook, oversees its first public offering on the New York Stock Exchange. Its price quickly plummets

WORLD EVENTS

FEB 6: Diamond Jubilee begins for Britain's Queen Elizabeth II who celebrates her 60th year of rule

FEB 12: Proposed government austerity measures lead to over 80,000 Greeks taking to the streets in protest

MAR 4: Vladimir Putin wins presidential election. Russian people and other governments declare fraud. Police arrest protesters

MAR 11: US soldier goes on shooting spree, killing 16 Afghan civilians

MAR 13: *Encyclopaedia Britannica* announces it will cease its print edition for the first time in its 244-year history

reasons why small businesses close their doors and corporations ship jobs overseas. And it's one of the largest and fastest growing parts of our budget. Given these facts, we can no longer afford to put health-care reform on hold. We can't afford to do it."[30]

Obama went on to explain that all Americans were entitled to "quality, affordable health care" and promised it would be "paid for in part by efficiencies in our system." He went on to say that he was about to begin bringing together Democrats and Republicans to start working on this issue.[31]

The "healthcare summit" opened the following week, and while some of the participants wrangled over what should or should not be included, lawmakers began creating legislation. Although the Democrats held majorities in both houses of Congress, not all favored the same ideas. Some preferred a "public option" (government-supplied health care); others disagreed. When politicians headed back home in the summer of 2009 to hold town hall meetings to address concerns, angry constituents were ready with questions and comments.

By now the Tea (Taxed Enough Already) Party, which had coalesced earlier in the year around economic issues, was kicking into full gear. Not an actual political party, but a loose network of small-government conservative activists, the Tea Party objected to the legislation's cost and government interference, and scared many with their talk of possible "death panels" of unelected bureaucrats. Some town-hall meetings were cancelled by nervous legislators amid worries that health-care reform could be stopped before it reached the White House. President Obama attempted to soothe the naysayers and promised that he would not be "pulling the plug on Granny."[32]

In a surprise upset in Massachusetts, Republican Scott Brown won a special election taking Senator Ted Kennedy's longtime Democratic seat (Kennedy had died six months earlier from brain cancer). Now without their supermajority, Senate Democrats would not be able to break a possible Republican filibuster. The health-care bill was successfully pushed forward just before the Christmas recess, however, through an internal process called "reconciliation," normally meant only for budget legislation. House Democrats secured enough votes to pass the Senate's version in March 2010 and promised to make adjustments later. On March 23, 2010, President Obama signed the bill into law. Technically named the Patient Protection and Affordable Care Act, it was already popularly known as simply "Obamacare."

The next challenge for the president's health-care reform was the courts. States immediately launched challenges and many wondered how an individual mandate could be constitutional. Since lower courts had reached conflicting opinions, the US Supreme Court stepped in to serve as final arbiter, hearing arguments in March 2012. Their decision was handed down by Chief Justice John Roberts in June.

The Court stunned many—Democrats and Republicans alike—when Roberts announced in the 5–4 decision that the individual mandate was a tax and as such, was permitted by law. On the other hand, the court also ruled that states would not have to take on the burden of additional Medicaid enrollees, as this provision of Obamacare was deemed outside of the jurisdiction of Congress. Said Roberts: "Members of this court are vested with the authority to interpret the law; we possess neither the expertise nor the prerogative to make policy judgments. Those decisions are entrusted to our nation's elected leaders, who can be thrown

JUN 5: Wisconsin Republican Governor Scott Walker wins his recall election

JUN 25: US Supreme Court rules on Arizona immigration law and upholds checking immigration status when law enforcement make arrests

JUN 28: US Supreme Court upholds individual mandate in Affordable Health Care Act but rules that states have no obligation to set up the needed framework

MAY 1: President Obama and Afghan President Karzai sign agreement that US will continue to provide development assistance in Afghanistan for 10 years after American troops withdraw in 2014

MAY 12–AUG 12: 2012 World Expo held at Yeosu, South Korea

JUN 2: Former Egyptian President Hosni Mubarak sentenced to life imprisonment for having protesters killed

JUN 8: UN declares civil war in Syria

THE CITIZENS UNITED DECISION

One of the most contentious issues to arise during Obama's first term over which he would have little or no control was the case of *Citizens United v. Federal Election Commission.* A conservative nonprofit organization, Citizens United had run afoul of campaign guidelines when it tried to distribute a documentary titled *Hilary: The Movie* via video-on-demand using corporate money instead of funds from its related political action committee. Their challenge to the FEC's ruling made it to the Supreme Court. The court's dramatic 5–4 January 2010 decision decisively changed the nation's campaign financing landscape, stating in effect that political spending (not direct contributions to candidates, which was still limited) by groups like corporations and labor unions was protected as free speech and in essence, unlimited. Obama, a former lecturer on constitutional law at the University of Chicago, was unvarnished in his criticism during his State of the Union speech later in the month, saying "I don't think American elections should be bankrolled by America's most powerful interests." Supreme Court Justice Samuel Alito, who voted with the majority, was visibly uncomfortable during that part of Obama's speech and was seen shaking his head in disagreement.

out of office if the people disagree with them. It is not our job to protect the people from the consequences of their political choices."[33]

Plans proceeded for the gradual implementation of the law through 2020, with most major provisions in place by 2014.

2010 MIDTERM ELECTION

With the economy still in the doldrums and the war in Afghanistan continuing to drag along, Americans headed into the midterm elections. Since these elections are often viewed as a referendum on the president, many watched them in keen anticipation. Concern about the newly passed Patient Protection and Affordable Health Care Act was a major factor, as was the rapid proliferation of regulations from different government agencies such as the Environmental Protection Agency (EPA), which had been largely lasseiz-faire during the previous administration, and increasingly strict banking guidelines that alarmed Wall Street and the business communities.

Illegal immigration rose to the forefront as the country debated Arizona Senate Bill 1070. Frustrated by the federal government's refusal to enforce laws regarding illegal immigration, the Arizona legislature had taken action. The resulting bill required immigrants to carry documentation in an effort to stem the tide of illegal immigrants flooding Arizona borders. The firestorm of controversy around the constitutionality and morality of this bill, which Obama was publicly critical of, made immigration into one of the most contentious issues of the new president's first term. Although deportations increased and illegal immigration dropped during Obama's

NATIONAL EVENTS

JUL 20: A dozen people slain in an Aurora, Colorado, theater watching the premiere of the new Batman movie. James Holmes is arrested and charged with 142 counts

AUG 4: American swimmer Michael Phelps concluded the Olympic Games with his 18th career gold medal and a total of 22 medals

AUG 28: Hurricane Isaac delays the opening day of Republican National Convention in Tampa, Florida

SEP 15: National Hockey League is locked out by owners. Possible cancellation of entire season

WORLD EVENTS

JUN 24: First Chinese spacecraft to perform docking maneuver in space

Mohamed Morsi of the Muslim Brotherhood wins Egypt's first competitive presidential election

JUL 27–AUG 12: Olympic Games held in London

JUL 30–31: India experiences world's worst power outage leaving 620 million without power

AUG 17: Russian all-female punk band arrested for hooliganism and sentenced to 2 years in a penal colony

first term, both as a result of increased enforcement and the slackened economy (which reduced demand in businesses that hired large numbers of illegal immigrants), the president's critics used his opposition to the Arizona bill as a sign that he was weak on the issue. (In June 2012, the US Supreme Court upheld the key provision of the Arizona law saying that law enforcement officials had "to make a reasonable attempt to determine the immigration status of a person stopped, detained or arrested if there's reasonable suspicion that person is in the country illegally."[34] This provision was considered the most controversial of the law and the only part upheld by the highest court in a 5–3 decision.)

This issue, along with the others, brought even more attention to the insurgent Tea Party movement, which supported a broad slate of far-right Republican candidates. Their efforts paid off. While Tea Party-backed candidates lost as many seats as they won in the Senate, Republicans took a decisive majority in the House of Representatives, gaining more than sixty seats. This marked the largest gain for a political party in the House since 1948. John Boehner became the new Speaker of the House. Now the country awaited the next chapter: Would there be bipartisanship as both sides proposed, or would gridlock take hold?

AFGHANISTAN AND IRAQ

It came as no surprise to the US military that President Obama would continue the drawdown of forces from Iraq begun by the previous administration. The new commander in chief quickly reaffirmed the timetable for disengagement hammered out in the 2008 Status of Forces Agreement between the Iraqi and US governments. On February 27, 2009, the president arrived at Marine Camp Lejeune, North Carolina, to pledge that all combat units would be out of Iraq by the summer of 2010 and all others gone by the end of 2011. Obama stated that the Iraqis would have to continue the job and said, "We cannot sustain indefinitely a commitment that has put a strain on our military, and will cost the American people nearly a trillion dollars."[35] What remained unsaid was the need for many of the American troops in Iraq to be dispatched to Afghanistan.

A month later, President Obama posed the question asked by some as to why America was still in Afghanistan. He answered, "I want the American people to understand that we have a clear and focused goal: to disrupt, dismantle and defeat al Qaeda in Pakistan and Afghanistan, and to prevent their return to either country in the future. That's the goal that must be achieved. That is a cause that could not be more just."[36] He explained that 17,000 more troops would be sent to Afghanistan. Additional training would be done with Afghan units—both military and civilian—so they could take over more responsibility.

Not all were pleased by the president's speech, which echoed many of the same goals set forth by his predecessor, George W. Bush. Some Democrats (already displeased by Obama's failure to follow up on his campaign promise to close the prison at Guantanamo Bay) wanted American troops to leave immediately and would grow even more critical when it became apparent that Obama was ramping up Bush's policy of using unmanned Predator drones to attack insurgent leaders hiding across the border in neighboring Pakistan. More concerns surfaced in the fall of 2009 when General Stanley McChrystal, who had been appointed by Obama to head American troops in Afghanistan, issued a lengthy assessment arguing that current troop strengths were insufficient to attain US victory.

OCT 22: American cyclist Lance Armstrong is stripped of his 7 Tour de France titles amid multiple charges of doping. He is banned from the sport for life.

OCT 23: Apple launches iPad Mini

OCT 24–30: Hurricane Sandy hits the northeast coast of the US creating massive power outages and widespread destruction

for singing an anti-Putin song at a cathedral. Human rights advocates worldwide decry the decision

AUG 21: American deaths reach 2000 in Afghanistan

AUG 22: Russia joins the World Trade Organization

SEP 11–27: Terrorists attack various targets in Egypt, Yemen, Germany, and other countries over protests of

SEP 11: Terrorists linked to al Qaeda attack US consulate at Benghazi, Libya, killing the American

McChrystal stated, "Failure to gain the initiative and reverse insurgent momentum in the near term (next 12 months)—while Afghan security capacity matures—risks an outcome where defeating the insurgency is no longer possible."[37] Two months later, President Obama deliberated on possible actions to take to turn the tide in Afghanistan.

Although Vice President Biden and other Democratic leaders, including Speaker of the House Nancy Pelosi, desired to draw down troops, Obama wanted to see success in the war-torn nation. Leaning on his regional commander, General David Petraeus, for guidance in conducting a surge similar to the one many believed had helped stave off defeat in Iraq, the president announced that 30,000 more troops would be dispatched to Afghanistan as soon as possible (mid-2010), but then exit no later than July 2011. The strategy was to go into the country, overwhelm the Taliban, al Qaeda, and other insurgent elements, then leave. The president had no intention of allowing Afghanistan to turn into his Vietnam.

Disagreement on the administration's handling of Afghanistan resurfaced in June 2010 when an interview with General McChrystal appeared in *Rolling Stone* magazine. In the article, the general and his aides described their skirmishes with the president and others in his administration, including Vice President Biden. Only Secretary of State Hillary Clinton seemed to escape unscathed, because she supported McChrystal and had said, "If Stan wants it, give him whatever he needs."[38] Upset by his military commander's public comments, President Obama relieved him of his duties and replaced him with General Petraeus in June 2010.

Taking over counter-insurgency efforts in Afghanistan, Petraeus decided to continue emphasizing the human factor. Increased effort was made to cite atrocities committed by the Taliban on the Afghan people with the hope that they would take a more active role in ridding themselves of the terrorists among them. This technique was also intended to remind NATO allies of the destructive capabilities of the enemy and its multiple human rights violations, thus prompting the allies to give second thoughts to any ideas of withdrawal. This tactic was not without risks, however, since the Afghan people might find these reminders of the Taliban's violence frightening. As one military official explained, "No matter how much [an Afghani] may want you to win, if he thinks your adversary is going to win he's going to remain aloof, and he's going to withhold his support."[39]

HUNT FOR OSAMA BIN LADEN

Ever since the infamous 9/11 attacks on the World Trade Center and Pentagon in 2001, the American people and their government had sought the leader who masterminded this attack on innocent civilians. Osama bin Laden's name became familiar around the globe; his picture appeared on television and websites. The hunt was on and a $25 million reward was offered for him, dead or alive.

President Bush left office without capturing this elusive quarry, so the Obama administration continued the search. Occasional messages, some videotaped, others only on audio, purported to be bin Laden. Some scoffed and argued that he had most likely died years before in the many attacks on Taliban strongholds in the mountains along the Afghanistan-Pakistan border. Still, doubts lingered.

After nearly a decade of intelligence-gathering, CIA director Leon Panetta went to the president in the summer of 2010 with the Agency's assessment that bin Laden was hiding inside a walled com-

NATIONAL EVENTS

NOV 6: President Barack Obama is reelected. Republicans maintain control of the US House of Representatives while Democrats keep majority of Senate seats

NOV 9: CIA Director David Petraeus resigns as news of an FBI investigation, an extramarital affair, and possible security problems surface

NOV 21: Hostess Brand ceases business, declaring bankruptcy

WORLD EVENTS

OCT 9: Taliban shoots 14-year-old girl in Pakistan who had openly defied them in wanting an education. She was taken to England for treatment of her head and neck wounds

NOV 14: Israel launches attacks against Hamas in Palestine and kill one of Hamas's main military commanders

DEC 21: Many around the world believe Mayan calendar shows this to be the day that the world ends. If you are reading this, the believers were wrong.

pound in a wealthy area of Abbottabad, Pakistan. Various assault options were offered and debated. Blasting the compound to the ground, killing all inside as well as some in neighboring houses, was unthinkable. Another option was to drop bombs with a smaller blast radius that would not kill the neighbors. The problem remained, though: How would one be sure that Osama bin Laden had died? A third option was to send a Special Operations team in by helicopter to take the compound along with its inhabitants. Targeting bin Laden could be done, although whether or not he should be taken as prisoner offered thorny legal issues. President Obama ordered to move forward with the ground attack plan.

On the night of May 2, 2011, members of Seal Team Six—codenamed Red Squadron—entered the compound. President Obama, Vice President Biden, and Secretary of State Clinton anxiously watched the events unfold at the White House. None of them could be sure that the mission would not turn into another disaster like President Carter's *Desert One* hostage rescue mission in 1980. Moving swiftly, Seal Team Six wasted no time in gaining access to and killing Osama bin Laden. The next day, Obama announced the death of the terrorist leader. Internationally, tension mounted between the US and Pakistan as many believed that Pakistani officials must have been aware that bin Laden was living in their country.

IRAN'S GREEN REVOLUTION AND THE ARAB SPRING

In June 2009, the Iranian people went to the polls and voted. The votes were counted, and to the people's shock, the dictator Mahmoud Ahmadinejad claimed victory. Mir Hossein Mousavi, a former Iranian prime minister, had supposedly lost, but the Iranian people refused to accept defeat in an election widely believed to have been stolen. Utilizing the Internet and social media, massive protests were organized. In Tehran, three million people asked, "Where is my vote?" Others wondered why the rest of the world, especially the United States, was not interceding on their behalf. On November 4, the anniversary of the takeover of the American embassy in 1979, the protest was not openly anti-American. Instead, the protesters objected to the nuclear weaponization of their country. They also demanded of Obama: "You are either with us—or with them."[40] The American government remained silent and inactive. Students in universities, and people throughout the country in the hundreds of thousands demanded a voice. Their government expressed its own through sheer force of arms. Protesters were captured, imprisoned, and often tortured. Many were executed. Televised trials, during which some of the leaders confessed their "crimes," signaled that for the time being, the totalitarian regime had won. When no word emanated from the Obama administration, some pondered if the president hesitated because he did not want to endanger any possible future nuclear disarmament talks with Ahmadinejad. Another argument against the administration publicly supporting the protestors (one also advanced by some of Ahmadinejad's Iranian critics) was that it would have given Ahmadinejad's allies an excuse to portray the protesters as Western dupes, but this was cold comfort to those pleading for help via the Internet from deep inside Iran.

The administration's silence on Iran would be a source of criticism by Republicans vying for their party's nomination in 2012, but the turmoil in the Middle East was only just getting started as a pro-democracy movement began inauspiciously in the

NOV 23: Larry Hagman, *Dallas*' J.R. Ewing dies at the age 81

DEC 5: Eight-day walkout by port workers in Los Angeles and Long Beach ends

Arab world in January 2011. The previous month, Tunisian fruit vendor Mohamed Bouazizi became outraged when police demanded he stop selling without a permit. In protest, Bouazizi set himself on fire, prompting his countrymen to take to the streets shouting opposition to their government. Within a month, the Tunisian dictator had fled the country, and the flame of discontent was already spreading across other Arab states.

Egypt felt the sting of opposition next. In February 2011, after weeks of nonstop protests, Hosni Mubarak, Egypt's authoritarian president for the previous three decades, also stepped down from power. The United States, one of Egypt's staunchest allies, stood by, surprising both Mubarak's government and his military. Mubarak would later go on trial for corruption and the killing of protestors. The Muslim Brotherhood, despite being driven underground in 1948, was nevertheless the most well-organized political group in Egypt. The Brotherhood insisted that it only wanted to be one part of a new democratic regime. It wasn't long, though, before pro-democracy activists would find themselves fighting attempts by the Brotherhood to create a theocratic regime even less democratic than the one they had just toppled.

A civil war soon erupted in Libya, and air support provided by France, Britain, and the United States ultimately turned the tide in the rebels' favor. Unable to escape, longtime Libyan dictator Moammar Gadhafi was found in hiding and killed by a mob. The government of Yemen also toppled in 2011, while Bahrain's King Hamad Al Khalifa kept tenuous control only through the military intervention of Saudi Arabia and the United Arab Emirates. Meanwhile, President Bashar Assad of Syria became embroiled in a civil war and brutally turned his large air force on civilian targets in rebel-held areas despite protests from the world community.

What these upheavals of change meant for the United States remained to be seen. Desirous of spreading democracy, American leaders hailed the people's revolt but it was feared that the cost could be considerable. Some of the ousted leaders, especially Mubarak, were key allies to the United States. Loss of influence in a war-prone area of the world could easily prove problematic. The Obama administration initiated meetings with the new Egyptian government. While some felt uneasy allying themselves with the Muslim Brotherhood, others believed there was not much choice. According to Shadi Hamid of the Brookings Center in Doha, Qatar, the situation had changed as far as the Arab world was concerned. "I think there is a growing perception in the Arab world that the US is a power in decline and that it doesn't have as much influence and leverage as it used to. And for that reason, they don't have to listen to the US; they can defy the US."[41]

Using the backdrop of the Arab Spring, President Obama pledged to grant financial support to Arab countries that chose democracy. Speaking at the US State Department on May 19, 2011, the President praised those who worked for democracy, chided anti-democratic rulers who tenaciously clung to power, and told Syrian President Bashar Assad that he had a choice: "he [could] lead that transition or get out of the way." President Obama also took the opportunity to state his preference for Israel to return to the 1967 border with Palestine.[42] Israeli Prime Minister Benjamin Netanyahu quickly dismissed Obama's proposal, claiming it to be "unrealistic" and "indefensible."[43] The division between the American president and Israel, who had never had a very cordial relationship, appeared to some as a major rift in the friendship of two longtime allies.

THE ECONOMY AND THE 2012 ELECTION

With the economy demonstrating virtually no improvement, economists espoused theories for why it continued to be sluggish. A few Canadians working for a satirical magazine decided that the downturn was just the vehicle for launching a grassroots effort to draw attention to Wall Street. Using the Twitter hashtag #OCCUPYWALLSTREET, a new movement was born. The first protest started on September 17, 2011, in New York City's financial district. Proclaiming themselves to be the "99 Percent," (as opposed to the one percent who held most of the nation's wealth), the Wall Street protesters inspired other similar efforts across the nation. Violence sometimes accompanied the movement, and some communities such as Oakland, California, demanded an end to the protests. Due to evictions, a lack of clear objectives, and the onset of cold weather, the activists melted away, but their sentiment remained. Economic inequality became a favorite topic for the 2012 election. President Obama took up the cause as he confronted his most likely Republican opponent, Mitt Romney, a millionaire who many considered the embodiment of the one-percenters.

While Republican candidates vied for their party's votes through an exhausting series of primaries and debates, Obama was unopposed and continued his work as president. Looking towards his own reelection, though, he changed course on gay marriage. Earlier in his political career, he had supported gay marriage and opposed the Defense of Marriage Act. Then in 2008, he announced that he believed marriage was a between a man and a woman, but he approved of civil unions. In May 2012, citing his "evolving" views (and likely pushed on the issue by Vice President Biden's off-the-cuff remarks about it), he declared that he was in favor of gay marriage. This marked a strong counterpoint to the traditional Republican position of opposing same-sex marriage.

The following month, Obama decided to alter the nation's immigration course. The Dream Act, legislation with bi-partisan sponsorship, had failed to become law after several attempts. Its main objective was to create a path for citizenship for youth brought to the United States illegally. President Obama announced in June that American policy would no longer include deporting young illegal immigrants who were brought to the country as children. The president stated that this policy would be "more fair, more efficient and more just." He insisted that it was not to be construed as amnesty. Still, Republicans believed that was exactly its purpose. Many were angered that Obama used an executive order to bypass legislation, but the president derided the cry that the move was politically motivated and insisted that it was "the right thing to do."[44]

Winning the majority of Republican primaries was former Massachusetts governor Mitt Romney, a multi-millionaire who had been the co-founder and chief executive officer of Bain Capital, a private equity investment firm. His Wall Street credentials proved to be a favorite target of Democrats. Romney's image as an economic elitist was hammered in by pro-Obama campaign ads and further underscored by a taping of the candidate himself telling a group of supporters that "[t]here are 47 percent of the people who will vote for the president no matter what. All right, there are 47 percent who are with him, who are dependent upon government . . . . [M]y job is not to worry about those people. I'll never convince them they should take personal responsibility and care for their lives."[45] Romney apologized for the remark, but the harm was done, and his image remained that of the wealthy white man who cared nothing for those with less.

Romney chose Wisconsin senator Paul Ryan as his running mate. This move was not without risks, as Ryan had upset many with his budget plan calling for significant reductions in federal entitlements as necessary for decreasing the federal deficit over time. Democrats again pointed to the Republicans as the unfeeling party. Though Obama presided over a country with the worst economy since the Great Depression, he was still viewed as the candidate who cared. After a first debate in which Obama seemed ill-prepared and disinterested next to the crisp and debate-ready Romney, the two following debates were considered narrow wins for the president. In the days leading up to the election, the country seemed equally divided. Democrats believed that Romney had been forced so far to the right in the early debates that later attempts to moderate his positions wouldn't hold water with centrist voters. Republicans were reassured by historical precedent which indicated that no incumbent president with such a poor-performing economy and low approval numbers could ever win reelection. Polls indicated the race was too close to call.

Then, in late October, Hurricane Sandy hit the northeast coast with a wallop. Not wanting to follow in the footsteps of Bush after Hurricane

Katrina, President Obama and his spokesmen immediately reminded Americans that the state and local authorities take the lead in natural disasters but offered assurances that federal aid would be available soon. Although seeing New Jersey's Republican governor, and staunch Romney surrogate Chris Christie, hugging Obama and praising the president's leadership offered a picture of bipartisanship at a time when many wavering voters wondered about his ability to lead, most voters had made up their minds long before. Distrust of Wall Street and the business community, as well as a slowly improving economy and an ugly primary season, propelled the president's reelection.

The forecasted close election failed to materialize. While Obama garnered nearly 6.9 million fewer votes than in 2008, he nevertheless bested Romney by some 3.5 million votes. Although he won fewer states than in 2008, Obama still maintained a sizeable majority of 332–206 in the Electoral College.

LOOKING TO A SECOND TERM

Two interconnected scandals broke around the time of the election. The first erupted on September 11, 2012, when American ambassador Chris Stevens and three other US government employees were killed in Benghazi, Libya. Administration officials, including Secretary of State Hillary Clinton, UN Ambassador Susan Rice, and the president himself cited an inflammatory anti-Muslim YouTube video, which had been sparking riots across the Middle East, as being the cause for an impromptu demonstration that turned violent. It soon became clear, however, that the video had nothing to do with the attack. Instead, it was a planned, deliberate assault by an al Qaeda affiliate conducted just days after the organization was declared to have been rendered ineffective by the Obama administration's efforts. Worse yet, Ambassador Stevens had personally requested additional security for the US mission in Libya but saw it reduced instead. Questions also arose over why so little support was provided during the seven-hour assault on the beleaguered Americans.

Little, though, was reported by most media outlets until three days a fter the election when David Petraeus, who had become the CIA Director upon leaving the army, resigned, due to his engagement in an extramarital affair.

The resignation came just days before Petraeus was scheduled to appear a second time before a congressional committee investigating the events of Benghazi. During his initial testimony as CIA Director, he supported the video story. After a week's delay and more details became public, Petraeus, now a private citizen, testified that the CIA had known right from the beginning that the well-organized attack had not evolved from a demonstration that had gotten out of control.

Worries about the economy also moved to the forefront at this time. Negotiations from earlier in Obama's first term had set a deadline at the end of 2012 for an agreement to reduce the deficit by a specific amount. If no agreement was reached, the country faced the possibility of the so-called "fiscal cliff," with deep, automatic budget cuts and tax hikes coming into effect in January 2013. Seeing the possibility of more government gridlock as the House of Representatives remained in Republican hands and the Senate still firmly Democratic, the country waited to see who would make the first move. House Speaker John Boehner said that if Obama received a mandate by being reelected, so had the Republicans who had campaigned against raising "job killing" taxes.

The number of Americans with full-time employment had declined by 5.9 million between September 2007 and November 2012 and the Bureau of Labor Statistics reported that while the unemployment rate had edged down to 7.9 percent, it was 14.6 percent when accounting for "involuntary part-time workers" such as a computer programmer working in a fast-food restaurant while waiting for the job market to improve. Though some aspects of the country's economy were in better shape than when Barack Obama took the reins of office, few of its citizens would have said that things had come all the way back.

Said *Washington Post* associate editor Bob Woodward:

"No matter who is president, [he] is the chief strategist. Presidents set the tone. They say this is how we're going to do things and fix things. In the case of Obama and the first term, and the economic issues, he didn't fix them. And he didn't find a way to work his will. And you see Lincoln and Jefferson and Eisenhower did. Now, we're catching Obama midstream. He still has another four years. The interesting question is going to be, how he takes victory."[46]

As Obama's first term wound down, decisions made in his first four years but "backloaded" for implementation until after 2012 if he should win reelection—the Affordable Health Care Act, payroll and income tax increases, as well as an expanded regulatory structure—would create the foundation for his second term.

> *"Democracy in a nation of 300 million can be noisy and messy and complicated. We have our own opinions. Each of us has deeply held beliefs. And when we go through tough times, when we make big decisions as a country, it necessarily stirs passions, stirs up controversy. That won't change after tonight, and it shouldn't. These arguments we have are a mark of our liberty. We can never forget that as we speak people in distant nations are risking their lives right now just for a chance to argue about the issues that matter, the chance to cast their ballots like we did today."*
>
> —*Barack Obama, Election Night, 2012*

ENDNOTES

1 David Mendell, *Obama, From Promise to Power,* New York: HarperCollins, 2007, p. 29.

2 Barack Obama, *Dreams from My Father,* New York: Three Rivers Press, 2004, p. 41.

3 Mendell, p. 40.

4 Obama, p. 86.

5 Mendell, p. 69.

6 Obama, p. 86.

7 Ibid., p. 87.

8 Tammerlin Drummond, *Los Angeles Times,* March 19, 1990.

9 Jodi Kantor, *New York Times,* January 28, 2007.

10 Eleanor Kerlow, *Poisoned Ivy: How Egos, Ideology, and Power Politics Almost Ruined Harvard Law School,* NY: St. Martin's Press, 1994, p. 11.

11 Mendell, p. 94.

12 Ibid., p. 128.

13 Barack Obama, *The Audacity of Hope,* New York: First Vintage Books, 2007, p. 128.

14 Mendell, p. 175.

15 Ibid, p. 176.

16 *New York Times,* December 20, 2007.

17 Barack Obama, 2004 Democratic Keynote Address, July 27, 2004.

18 Mendell, p. 303.

19 *This Week with George Stephanopoulos,* September 11, 2005.

20 *Chicago Sun-Times,* April 12, 2008.

21 American rhetoric.com

22 Barack H. Obama, inauguration speech, January 20, 2009.

23 Reuters, "Obama: Didn't Foresee Severity of Economic Crisis," April 29, 2009.

24 "The Nobel Peace Prize 2009," accessed November 23, 2012, http://www.nobelprize.org/nobel_prizes/peace/laureates/2009/press.html.

25 "The Nobel Peace Prize 2007," accessed November 23, 2012, http://www.nobelprize.org/nobel_prizes/peace/laureates/2007.

26 David Jackson, "Obama Jokes About 'Shovel-Ready Projects,'" *USA Today,* June 13, 2011.

27 David M. Herszenhorn, "Recovery Bill Gets Final Approval," *New York Times,* February 14, 2009.

28 David Jackson, "Obama and Chrysler Repayment—What He Really Said," *USA Today,* June 6, 2011.

29 Zachary A. Goldfarb, "Auto Bailout Was Not Unmitigated Success," *Washington Post,* September 6, 2012.

30 "Address Before a Joint Session of Congress, February 24, 2009," American Presidency Project, University of California at Santa Barbara, accessed November, 23, 2012, http://www.presidency.ucsb.edu/ws/index.php?pid=85753.

31 Ibid.

32 Julie Rovner, "Kill Grandma? Debunking A Health Bill Scare Tactic," Minnesota Public Radio, August 12, 2009, http://minnesota.publicradio.org/features/npr.php?id=111729363.

33 Abner Greene "Roberts Shuffles the Deck with Health Care Decision," *The National Law Journal,* June 28, 2012, http://law.fordham.edu/27026.htm.

34 Alia Beard Rau, "Arizona Immigration Law: Supreme Court Upholds Key Portion of Senate Bill 1070," *The Arizona Republic,* June 25, 2012, http://www.azcentral.com/news/politics/20120603arizona-immigration-law-supreme-court-opinion.html.

35 Ewen MacAskill, "Six years after Iraq invasion, Obama sets out his exit plan," *The Guardian,* February 27, 2009.

36 "Remarks by the President on a New Strategy for Afghanistan and Pakistan," The White House, March 27, 2009, http://www.whitehouse.gov/the_press_office/Remarks-by-the-President-on-a-New-Strategy-for-Afghanistan-and-Pakistan.

37 Eric Schmitt and Thom Shanker, "General Calls for More US Troops to Avoid Afghan Failure," *New York Times,* September 21, 2009.

38 Michael Hastings, "The Runaway General," *Rolling Stone,* July 8–22 2012, web: June 25, 2012, http://www.rollingstone.com/politics/news/the-runaway-general-20100622.

39 Anna Mulrine, "How Petraeus Has Changed the Afghanistan War," *Christian Science Monitor,* December 31, 2010.

40 Abbas Milani, "The Green Movement," The Iran Primer, United States Institute of Peace, http://iranprimer.usip.org/resource/green-movement.

41 Deborah Amos, "Is The Arab Spring Good Or Bad For The US?" NPR, January 9, 2012, http://m.npr.org/news/front/144799401?singlePage=false.

42 Lara Setrakian, "US on Arab Spring: Inching Forward, Slapping Wrists, Nudging Dictators," ABC News, June 16, 2011, http://abcnews.go.com/blogs/headlines/2011/06/us-on-arab-spring-inching-forward-slapping-wrists-nudging-dictators.

43 Peter Beaumont, "Netanyahu's Rejection of Obama's 1967 Border Deal Leaves Peace Talks in Tatters," *The Guardian*, May 21, 2011.

44 Tom Cohen, "Obama Administration to Stop Deporting Some Young Illegal Immigrants," CNN.com, June 16, 2012, http://www.cnn.com/2012/06/15/politics/immigration/index.html.

45 "Romney to Campaign Donors: Obama Voters 'Dependent,' See Selves as 'victims,'" CBS News, September 17, 2012, http://www.cbsnews.com/8301-503544_162-57514609-503544/romney-to-campaign-donors-obama-voters-dependent-see-selves-as-victims/.

46 *Face the Nation with Bob Schieffer*, November 25, 2012, http://www.cbsnews.com/video/watch/?id=50135800n.

INDEX

Please note: battles and treaties are listed under their locations, e.g., "Versailles, Treaty of." Illustrations are indicated by *italicized* page numbers.

A

B

C

D

G

H

N

O

P

Q

R

S

T

U

V